Be

D0013204

CRUISING
& CRUISE SHIPS

2020

BY DOUGLAS WARD
THE WORLD'S FOREMOST AUTHORITY ON CRUISING

◉ Walking Eye App

Your Berlitz Cruising and Cruise Ships guide now includes a free app and eBook version of the book, all included for the same great price as before. They are available to download from the free Insight Guides Walking Eye app, found in the App Store and Google Play. Simply download the Walking Eye container app to access the eBook and app.

Multiple eBooks & apps available

Now that you've bought this book you can download the accompanying app and eBook for free. Inside the Walking Eye container app, you'll also find the whole range of other Insight Guides destination apps and eBooks, all available for purchase.

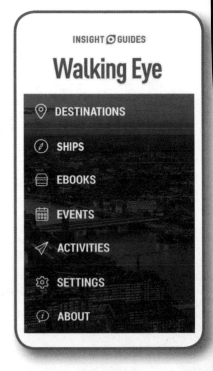

Events & activities

Free access to information on a range of local guided tours, sightseeing activities and local events in any destination, with the option to book.

ecutives, cruise travel agents, and crew members alike.

To date, I have taken over 1,120 cruises and 159 transatlantic crossings, plus countless Panama Canal transits, shipyard visits, numerous ship-naming ceremonies, overnights, and maiden voyages.

This book is a tribute to everyone who has made my seafaring experiences possible, especially my mother and father, and I thank the cruise lines for their assistance during the complex scheduling, sailing, inspection, evaluation, and rating processes.

How to use this book

This book is divided into two sections. The first helps you to define what you are looking for in a cruise vacation and advises on how to find it; it provides a wealth of information. Specialist cruises are discussed, too, culminating with that ultimate travel experience: the world cruise.

The book's main section profiles 310 ocean-going cruise and expedition ships. From large to small, from unabashed luxury and exclusivity to ships for the budget-minded, they are all here.

The ratings and evaluations are a painstaking documentation of my personal work. I travel throughout the world, and I sail for up to 150 days each year and take around 50 flights to do so. All evaluations are made objectively, without bias, partiality or prejudice.

My intention has always been to make this the most informative and useful guidebook possible, and to help you to make informed decisions about the ship(s) you choose for your next cruise(s).

Although price indicators are given for some things such as alternative restaurants, spa treatments, and other items, prices may have changed since this book went to press. Do check all prices with your respective cruise line.

Most of the statistical information contained in the ship profiles has been supplied by the cruise companies. You are welcome to send details of any errors or updates to me at: shipratings@hotmail.com.

My constant travel and ship inspection schedule means I am frequently at sea, and I no longer answer mailed letters.

Enjoying the view from a cabin balcony.

New to Cruising?

Are you all at sea about cruises, when it seems like everyone around you has taken one, but you haven't? Here's what you'll need to know before you first step aboard.

Over 70 companies operate around 350 ocean-going cruise ships and provided cruise vacations to more than 27 million passengers in 2018, and so the choice is huge.

It's an obstacle course, like trying to choose between different models of car; you start with a base price, then choose all the optional extras before getting the model you want. In other words, it's *not* the inclusive vacation that you thought you were buying, but an 'unbundled' product that requires you to make decisions.

The good news is that an ocean cruise can be a memorable vacation, but after your first cruise, be prepared for the feeling of addiction that so often hits.

The trick? Find the right ship and cruise to suit your needs – whether you are a solo traveler, a couple, a family with children, or simply well-traveled.

What exactly is a cruise?

A cruise is a change from everyday life on land. It is a (mostly) pre-paid, hassle-free vacation. You sleep in the same bed each night, the ship takes you from destination to destination, and only one currency is used on board.

Everything's close at hand and there are always polite people to help you. It facilitates multi-generational togetherness, solo adventuring, and total escapism. And, some of the world's most beautiful places are best seen from a cruise ship.

Why take a cruise?

Value for money. A cruise represents excellent value for money, considering everything that is provided. As it's mostly pre-paid, there are few financial decisions to make once on board.

Convenience. You may be able to drive to your port of embarkation (doorstep cruising). If not, the cruise line or your booking agent can make all the arrangements, including flights, baggage handling, and transfers to and from the ship. Once on board, you simply unpack once!

Comfort. A cabin or suite is your home away from home. It can be as small as a cubicle (at about 60 sq ft/6 sq m), as large as a villa (at over 4,000 sq ft/372 sq m), or anything in between.

Good food. Dining is one of the pleasures of a cruise, and all your meals are included from breakfast through to late-night snacks; most ships can accommodate specific dietary needs.

Family togetherness. A cruise offers a safe, family-friendly environment, and many ships have good children's facilities and supervised activities.

Learning experience. Most ships have guest speakers/lecturers, so you can learn while you cruise.

Adventure. A cruise can be an adventure. It can take you to places that are impossible to reach by almost any other means, such as the Antarctic Peninsula, the Arctic, or to remote islands with no access by air.

Staying healthy. You can pamper yourself in a spa, although body-pampering treatments are at extra cost. With all the available food, simply pace yourself to stay healthy.

Entertainment. Cruise ships provide a wide range of professional entertainment, from colorful large-cast productions and acrobatic shows to intimate classical instrumental recitals and small jazz combos, while during the day, there are activities galore – enough to keep even the most active occupied.

Will I need a passport?

Yes, plus any appropriate authorizations and visas. If you already have a valid passport, ensure that it has at least six months left on it at the *end* of the

The words say it all!

Celebrity Silhouette, Labadee Island.

cruise. In some ports (such as Venice, Italy, and all ports in Russia) you are required to carry your passport when ashore.

10 steps to a good first cruise experience

1. Find a cruise-booking specialist. Although the Internet is a popular research tool, it pays to find a specialist (note: some Internet-only 'agencies' with slick websites can disappear without trace – with your money).

Describe your preferences (relaxation, visiting destinations, adventure, activities, entertainment, etc.), so that your agent can find a cruise and ship that is right for you, for the right reasons, and at the right price.

They can guide you through all the important details, such as choice of cabin and dining arrangements. They may also have insider tips, knowledge about available upgrades, and pre- and post-cruise programs.

2. Where to? Choose your preferred area: Alaska, Australia/New Zealand, the Bahamas, the Baltic, Bermuda, the Caribbean, Hawaii, Indian Ocean, the Mediterranean, Northern Europe, South Africa, South America, South Pacific, Southeast Asia, the US East Coast, etc. When you want to cruise: Alaska, for example, is not available during the winter; the Caribbean may be too hot for you in summer; Northern Europe is best in the summer, while South America and Southeast Asia are best in the winter. If you are interested in a special theme, such as Carnival in Rio or Formula One

racing in Monte Carlo, this will determine the date of your cruise.

3. How long? Decide on the length of cruise you want. Allow traveling time to get to and from your ship, particularly if it is in an area far from home, or during winter. A standard Caribbean cruise length, for example, is seven days, although you could try a three- or four-day short-break Bahamas or Mexican Riviera cruise. In Northern Europe 12–14 days are more typical, while for an around-South America cruise, you'll need 30 days or more. For visiting the Antarctic Peninsula, allow 14–21 days, while an around-the-world cruise takes 90–120 days.

4. Choose the right ship. Size matters! Choose the right size ship for your needs. Do you want to be with 100, 500, 1,000, or 5,000-plus others on your vacation? Generally speaking, the larger the ship, the greater the focus on it as the destination.

ONLINE CHECK IN

Most cruise companies now expect you to check in online. Paper cruise tickets and other documents formerly used are now collectors' items.

There are usually three steps before you can print your boarding pass.

Step 1: Your details.

Step 2: Cruise ticket contract (do read the small print).

Step 3: Print your boarding pass and baggage tags.

Or perhaps you would like to experience cruising under sail; or with specialist lecturers; or an adventure/expedition cruise; or a coastal/an inland waterways cruise.

5. Choose the right accommodation. For a first cruise, choose an outside-view cabin. In an interior ('no-view') cabin you won't know how to dress when you wake up, because you can't see the weather outside. However, interior no-view cabins are good if you like to sleep in a dark room. If you are concerned about motion sickness (it's not common, but it can happen), choose a cabin in the ship's center.

The average cabin size aboard a large resort ship is 180–200 sq ft (17–18.5 sq m); anything less and you'll feel cramped. The more space you want, the more it will cost. Cabins with a balcony cost more than non-balcony cabins.

6. Dining. If there are two seatings for dinner, it could be wise to choose the later seating (typically at 8:30pm), so that you have enough time ashore in port without having to rush back to shower and change for the first seating (typically at 6:30pm).

Many ships have several dining venues, and you go where and when and with whom you like, though some venues cost extra.

7. Health and fitness. If you like body-pampering treatments, check that your ship has the right facilities. Book spa treatments early, as appointment slots go quickly. Some cruise companies allow you to book online, but this means planning your time in advance. Most ships have exercise classes.

8. Families. Choose a family-friendly ship. Most large resort ships have good facilities for youngsters; mid-size and small ships have more limited facilities, and some ships have none. Children usually love cruising, finding it educational, fun, sociable, and safe.

For those who don't want children around, there are several child-free ships from which to choose.

9. Dress code. The dress code is mostly casual aboard the large resort ships. In general, no formal attire is needed, although there are exceptions, such as on a transatlantic crossing aboard Cunard's *Queen Mary 2*, where formality is part of the evening tradition. It sounds obvious, but ships move, so flat or low-heeled shoes are strongly recommended for women.

10. Extra expenses. Budget for extra-cost items such as shore excursions, drinks (unless they are included), and drink 'packages,' meals in extra-cost dining venues, spa treatments, casino gaming, and other personal items. Allow extra money, too, for souvenirs and gifts. Finally, make sure you have full insurance cover for your vacation.

Sunrise in the southern Atlantic Ocean.

Relaxing on a day at sea aboard a large resort ship.

Digital details

Today, most people use cell phones, tablets, or laptops and expect to be able to use them at any time.

You can use your device aboard ship, but once you leave port your cell phone will automatically lock into a ship's digital marine network, incurring a charge. At sea, your cell is out of range with land-based carriers and will be slower than normal. Note that some ships have notices outside their restaurants prohibiting the use of cell phones (for social etiquette).

What to expect

Stepping aboard for the first time? Here is what you need to know about a typical embarkation.

You've arrived at the airport closest to your ship's embarkation point, and retrieved your luggage. A cruise company representative will be holding a sign displaying the cruise line's name. Your luggage – make sure it has your cabin number displayed clearly on it – is placed together with that of other passengers. The next time you see your bags should be in your cabin.

The check-in desks are in the passenger terminal. If you have suite-grade accommodation, there will be a separate check-in desk. (Note: don't buy liquor to take on board – it will be confiscated.)

Getting aboard

You'll go through security screening, just as at airports. Then it's a few paces to the gangway. You will probably be greeted by the snap-happy photographers, ready to take your portrait, bedraggled as

THE BRIDGE

A ship's navigation bridge is manned at all times, both at sea and in port. Besides the captain, who is master of the vessel, other senior officers take 'watch' turns for four- or eight-hour periods. In addition, junior officers are continually honing their skills as experienced navigators, waiting for the day when they will be promoted to master.

The captain is always in command at times of high risk, such as when the ship is entering or leaving a port, when the density of traffic is particularly high, or when visibility is severely restricted by poor weather.

Navigation has come a long way since the days of the ancient mariners, who used only the sun and the stars to calculate their course across the oceans. The space-age development of sophisticated navigation devices (using satellites) has enabled us to eliminate the guesswork of early navigation (the first global mobile satellite system was introduced in 1979).

A ship's navigator today uses a variety of sophisticated instruments to pinpoint the ship's position at any time and establish its course.

you may appear after having traveled for hours. Just say no (firmly) if you don't want your photograph taken.

At the ship end of the gangway, staff will welcome you aboard.

Things to check

Once in your cabin, check that it's clean and tidy? Are the beds properly made? Is there ice in the ice container? Check the bathroom; make sure there are towels and soap. If there are problems, tell your cabin steward.

Memorize the telephone number for medical emergencies, so you know how to call for help.

Your luggage probably will not have arrived yet – particularly if it is a large resort ship – but don't wait in the cabin ...take a walk. If you're hungry, head to the self-serve buffet.

Familiarize yourself with the ship's layout. Learn which way is forward and aft, and how to reach your cabin from the main stairways. This is also a good time to learn how to get from your cabin to the outside decks in an emergency.

Control that thirst

Picture this: you're thirsty when you arrive in your cabin. You see a bottle of water with a tab around its neck. Read the notice on the tab: 'This bottle is provided for your convenience. If you open it, your account will be charged $4.50.'

On deck, you are greeted by a smiling waiter offering you a colorful drink. But, put your fingers on the glass as he hands it to you and he'll also ask for your cruise card. There, you've just paid $7.95 for a drink full of ice worth 5¢.

The cost of drinks soon adds up. Note that aboard some ships mixers such as tonic for gin may be charged separately.

The safety drill

A Passenger Safety Drill must take place before a ship sails from the embarkation port (this was introduced following the *Costa Concordia* tragedy in 2012.) It is mandatory that you attend the drill, and pay attention – it could save your life. Directions to your assembly station are posted on the back of the cabin door. By now, your luggage probably will have arrived.

Titanic-style stairway aboard *Insignia*.

HIGHLIGHTS
ENTERTAINMENT

Suggested dress tonight: Smart Casual

THEATER SHOW: FLY
Who doesn't love a Broadway show? Enjoy this toe-tapping, finger-snapping spectacular, filled with singing and dancing to the memorable music of great American composers.
7:00pm, 8:15pm & 9:30pm, Metropolitan Theater, decks 6 & 7 (Fwd)

THEATRE SHOW: CLASICOS LATINOS
10:30pm, Metropolitan Theater, decks 6 & 7 (Fwd)
No reservation required

THEATER COMEDY SHOW: BEERPROV
Adults Only. R Rated
Unscripted Comedy at Sea.
Brand new jokes each and every night, find out yourself why BeerProv has been called " the funniest live comedy show you'll ever see"
11:15pm, Metropolitan Theater, decks 6 & 7 (Fwd)
No reservation required

SIMULCAST BINGO

Any bingo lovers on board? Fantastic. We just wanted to give you the heads up for the big heads down. One game, two locations to play!
11:00am, Metropolitan Theater, decks 6 & 7, Fwd & Miami Beach Pool, deck 16, aft

MSCINEMA AL FRESCO:
Pirates Of The Caribbean - Dead Men Tell No Tales
Starring: Johnny Depp & Geoffrey Rush
Rated: PG 13
Duration: 2h 9min
6:45pm & 11:00pm, Miami Beach Pool, deck 16 Aft

COUNTRY & WESTERN GAME SHOW
Join your Cruise Staff for this funny challenge in country style!
9:00pm, Haven Lounge, deck 7, Aft

COUNTRY & WESTERN PARTY
Join your Cruise Staff and fellow Guests for an evening of dancing!
10:30pm, Haven Lounge, deck 7, Aft

FOOD & BEVERAGE

TEPPANYAKI BY ROY YAMAGUCHI
The modern East-West cooking style of Japanese cuisine will come to life via four teppanyaki grills. With a modern twist on Asian cuisine, guests can sit at the cooking stations to watch their delicious Japanese dishes come to life in front of their eyes. Expert chefs will cook with flare on an open grill - a visual spectacle and feast for the senses with flames and sizzling ingredients all coming together to form flavorful dishes.
ASIAN FUSION BY ROY YAMAGUCHI
The à la carte restaurant will serve gourmet Asian creations in a stylish venue with incredible sea views.
SUSHI BY ROY YAMAGUCHI
The Sushi Bar will serve the freshest sushi, sashimi and tempura.

Important to know

USING THE GYM
The gym welcomes guests aged 14 years and over, from 6:00am to 10:00pm each day. Please wear appropriate sportswear, including sneakers. During peak time, please limit your workout to 20 minutes

A SMALL DONATION CAN CHANGE PEOPLE'S LIVES
MSC is supporting the Andrea Bocelli Foundation, bringing hope to children in Haiti. Use the donation form in your cabin to donate $2 and help us to change a life!
For further info, please contact Reception - Guest Service.

SAFETY THROUGHOUT THE SHIP
Please avoid running around the ship. This is especially important in and around the pool areas. Always use the hand-rails, and keep fingers away from open doors.

24/7 ONBOARD LIBRARY SERVICE
Take advantage of our wide range of titles available 24/7 in the Library on (deck 7 Aft) and simply return any borrowed books by 12:00 on the day before you disembark.

This is an example of a full day at sea aboard *MSC Seaview*. So, there really is plenty of life on a day at sea and absolutely no time to become bored.

Today's Timetable

Morning

TIME	ACTIVITY	VENUE (DECK)
07:30	Keep CALM and Yoga Video by Denise Keller (For Early Risers)	Zouk Beach Club (17 AFT)
08:30 - 09:15	Bring the Heat Walk a Mile Challenge with Friends	Jogging Track (17 MID)
09:00 - 12:00	Registration for Marathon at Sea	Box Office (6 FWD)
09:00 - 12:00	Reach For The Stars Registration and Audition from 5-16 years old	Box Office (6 FWD)
09:00 - 12:00	Registration for Private Ballroom Dance Class (minimal charges apply)	Box Office (6 FWD)
09:00 - 12:00	Ropes Course and Rock Climbing Wall **	Open Deck (18 AFT)
09:00 - 18:00	Shuffleboard **	Open Deck (17 AFT)
09:00 - 19:00	Water Slides **	Water Slide Park (20 AFT)
09:00 - 00:00	Arcade * (minimal charges apply)	Arcade (16 MID)
09:00 - 01:00	Open Play (Mini Golf, Ping-Pong and Giant Chess)**	SportsPlex (19 AFT)
09:30	Abdominal class (Chargeable)	Fitness Center (15 FWD)
09:30	Designer Watch Sale	The Dream Boutiques (7 AFT)
09:30	Citizen Watch Sale, 35% OFF	The Dream Boutiques (7 AFT)
09:30 - 10:15	Bachata Dance Class	Main Pool Deck (16 MID)
09:45	BVLGARI sale event	The Dream Boutiques (7 AFT)
10:00	Beauty Sale	The Dream Boutiques (7 AFT)
10:00 - 12:00	Airbrush Tattoo Session by Tania	Palm Court (19 FWD) /Portside
10:30 - 11:30	Thomas Kinkade- Painter of Light Seminar	Lobby (6 FWD)
10:30 - 12:30	Omega & Longines 15% off Sale	The Dream Boutiques (7 AFT)
11:00 - 11:45	Masquerade Mask Painting	Zouk (17 AFT)
11:00 - 11:45	Dance Class with your Professional Dancers (free)	Main Pool Deck (16 MID)
11:15	Jewelry Try on Event & Sale	The Dream Boutiques (7 AFT)

Evening

TIME	ACTIVITY	VENUE (DECK)
18:00	Cinema at Sea - Teen Beach Movie	Lobby (6 FWD)
19:00 - 19:45	The Voyage of a Lover's Dream	Zodiac Theatre (7 FWD)
19:00 - 19:45	Pre - Selling of Bingo Tickets	Lobby (6 FWD)
20:00	Lancôme Seminar & Sale	The Dream Boutiques (7 AFT)
20:00 - 20:45	Jackpot Bingo Game with Jackpot Prize of HKD 128,888	Lobby (6 FWD)
21:00 - 21:45	The Voyage of a Lover's Dream	Zodiac Theatre (7 FWD)
21:00 - 22:00	Celebrity Head with Cruise Staff	Lobby (6 FWD)
21:00	Cinema at Sea - The 5th Wave	Zouk Beach Club (17 AFT)
21:15	Guess the Carat Weight	The Dream Boutiques (7 AFT)
22:00 - 22:45	Masquerade Theme Night Party with Endless Summer Band	Tributes (8 FWD)
22:45 - 23:30	Rhythm Divine: Latin Ballroom Dance Show	Zodiac Theatre (7 FWD)
23:00	Cinema at Sea - Steve Jobs	Lobby (6 FWD)

* Denotes a charge for these activities
** Weather and natural light conditions permitting

"Dream Moments"

Throughout your cruise, our film team will be capturing your treasured experiences during our main events and activities onboard. Tune into Channel 5 of your stateroom television and watch your movie unfold! Your 'Dream Moments' will also be shown daily in the Lobby, Deck 6 FWD.

Afternoon

TIME	ACTIVITY	VENUE (DECK)
12:15 - 12:45	Pre - Selling of Bingo Tickets	Lobby (6 FWD)
13:00 - 13:45	Jackpot Bingo Game with Jackpot Prize of HKD 118,888	Lobby (6 FWD)
13:00 - 17:00	Registration for Private Ballroom Dance Class (minimal charges apply)	Box Office (6 FWD)
14:00	BootCamp (Chargeable)	Fitness Center (15 FWD)
14:00 - 15:00	Summer Beauty Event	Lobby (6 FWD)
14:00 - 16:00	Reach For The Stars - REHEARSALS	Zodiac Theatre (7 FWD)
14:00 - 19:00	Ropes Course and Rock Climbing Wall **	Open Deck (18 AFT)
14:00 - 01:00	Glow Bowling *	Zouk (17 AFT)
14:30 - 15:30	Activity for Teens: Ropes Course **	Open Deck (18 AFT)
15:00	Dream Boutiques Fashion Show	Bar 360 (6 MID)
15:00 - 16:00	Ballroom Dance Class with our Professional Ballroom Dancers (free)	Palm Court (19 FWD)/Portside
15:00 - 16:45	Marathon At Sea: (Basketball, Safety Archery, Bubble Football & Golf Competition)	SportsPlex (19 AFT)
15:15	TRX (Chargeable)	Fitness Center (15 FWD)
15:30	Diamond & Gemstone Sale	The Dream Boutiques (7 AFT)
15:30	Michael Kors 25% off Sale	The Dream Boutiques (7 AFT)
16:15	Stretch & Relax (Chargeable)	Fitness Center (15 FWD)
16:30	Lost in Space OMEGA Event	Lobby (6 FWD)
17:00 - 17:45	Dream Theme Night Colour My World Dance Class	Main Pool Deck (16 MID)
17:45	Photo Session with Captain	Lobby (6 FWD)

Photo Corner (6 FWD) 08:30- 22:30
Capture the special connections between loved ones and the stories you share. Book a once-in-a-lifetime photoshoot with our professional photographers today!

Pop-up Market (6 MID) 09:00-23:00
Come and visit our magical retail corner (next to Bar 360) and check out our exclusive Dream Cruises souvenir range. From T-shirts, adapters to power banks, there's something for everyone.

Souvenir Market (7 MID) 09:00-23:00
Come and visit our souvenir market. We offer different types of exclusive Dream Cruises souvenir range. You can even find snacks like dried fruits, nuts and milk powder here!

Live Art Auction Palm Court (19 FWD) 13:00-14:30
Join us for one of the most exciting live event this cruise-Live Art Auction! Complimentary raffle, champagne and complimentary work of art just for attending.

Tour Counter Tributes (8 FWD) 09:00-17:00
There will always be a destination waiting for you to discover. Join our tours to explore and make your dreams come true.

Nansha Disembarkation Transfer Arrangement

For guests disembarking Friday - Nansha, transportation from Nansha Terminal to:
-Da Sha Tou Terminal at HKD 56 per person (adult & child)
-Guangzhou South Railway Station at HKD 56 per person (adult & child)
-Guangzhou airport at HKD 56 per person (adult & child)
-Jin Zhou MTR at HKD 56 per person (adult & child)
-Shenzhen airport at HKD 73 per person (adult & child)
-Shenzhen City at HKD 73 per person (adult & child)
Tickets available 09:00 - 17:00 on Tributes (8 FWD) .

This is an example of a full day at sea aboard *Genting Dream*.

Cruising Uncovered

Many cruise line websites and brochures are hype over reality. We answer the questions most frequently asked by those new to this type of vacation and by experienced passengers.

Cruises are packaged vacations, offering overall good value for money, with accommodation, meals, and entertainment included. But look out for the little hidden extras that are not made clear in the brochures. For example, some ships have 'drinks-inclusive' fares, while others let you choose from one of several 'beverage packages' available.

Here are some of the most commonly asked questions, covering those items the brochures often gloss over.

Is cruising good value?

Yes, thanks in part to the economic downturn that forced the cruise lines to offer more incentives – such as onboard credit, cabin upgrades, and other perks – in an effort to keep their companies afloat, their ships full, and their crews fully employed.

Your cruise price is protected by advance pricing, so you know before you go that your major outgoings have already been set. A fuel surcharge is the only additional cost that may change at the last minute.

Allure of the Seas in Haiti.

Isn't cruising expensive?

Compare what it would cost on land to have all your meals and entertainment provided, plus transportation to different destinations, fitness and sports facilities, leisure activities, educational talks, cocktail parties, and other social functions, and you'll see the good value of a cruise.

What you pay determines your accommodation size, location, and style. The choice ranges from basic to luxury, so give yourself a budget, and ask your professional travel supplier how to make the best use of it.

Is the brochure price firm?

Cruise brochure prices are set by cruise line sales and marketing departments. It's the price they would like to achieve to cover themselves against currency fluctuations, international bonding schemes, and the like. But discounts and incentives attract business, and so there is always some leeway. Travel agents receive a commission, so, as a consumer, always ask for the 'best price,' watch for special offers in newspapers and magazines, and talk to your travel agent.

How do I get the best discount?

Book ahead for the best discounts, as they normally decrease closer to the cruise date. The first cabins to sell out are usually those at minimum and maximum prices (top suites). Premium rates usually apply to Christmas/New Year cruises. Make sure that all port charges and government fees are included in the quote.

Although bargains do exist, always check the cabin location and what's included. Highly discounted fares may apply only to certain dates and itineraries; for example, the eastern Caribbean instead of the more popular western Caribbean.

A bargain price may be subject to a booking deadline or may be 'cruise only,' so you must arrange your own transportation. If air transportation *is* included, changes or deviations may not be possible. And don't even think about those online adverts that shout 'Only $49 per day, per person.' What you get is basic, basic, basic, and, once aboard, you'll need to spend money at every turn.

Your accommodation choice and location may not be available. You could be limited to first seating for dinner aboard a two-seating ship (less convenient if you are busy with activities or excursions during the day). Finally, highly discounted fares may not apply to children, and port charges, handling fees, fuel surcharges, or other taxes may be extra.

Should I book online or through a travel agent?

You've found an ideal cruise online – fine. But, if a cruise line suddenly offers special discounts for your sailing, or cabin upgrades, or if things go wrong with your booking, your Internet booking service may prove difficult to access for post-purchase questions. Your travel agent, however, can probably make special discounts work for you and perhaps even provide upgrades.

The Internet may be a useful resource tool, but I would not recommend it as the place to book your cruise, unless you know exactly what you want, and can plan ahead – and it doesn't work for groups. You can't ask questions, and much of the information provided is marketing hype. Most websites providing cruise ship reviews have paid advertising, or something to sell, and the sound-bite information can be misleading. Be aware that many Internet booking agents are unlicensed and unregulated, and some add a 'booking fee.'

If you book with an Internet-based cruise agency, you should confirm with the cruise line that the booking is confirmed and that any payments have been received. Large travel agency groups and consortiums often reserve blocks of cabins; smaller independent agencies may be able to access discounts unavailable online. Cruise lines consider travel agents as their preferred distribution system and provide special discounts and value-added items not available online.

Do travel agents charge for their services?

Travel agents do not charge for their services, but they earn a commission from cruise lines. Consider a travel agent as your business advisor, not just a ticket agent. They will handle all matters relevant to your booking including the latest information on itinerary changes, fuel surcharges, discounts, and travel and cancellation insurance.

Your travel agent should find exactly the right ship for your needs and lifestyle. Some sell only a limited number of cruise lines (known as 'preferred suppliers'), because they receive 'overrides' on top of their normal commission. (They may know their limited number of ships well, however.)

Note that some travel agents may charge for booking airline tickets.

How do I get my cruise documents?

Most cruise lines have changed to online bookings and check-in. You'll need to print your own boarding passes, travel documents, and luggage tags. If you go through a cruise-travel agent, they can do this for you.

Your documents will allow you to pass through the port's security to get to your ship. Only the more upscale cruise lines, expedition companies, and sail-cruise ship lines provide wallets for documents, cruise tickets, luggage tags, and colorful destination booklets – cruise lines operating large resort ships have all abandoned such niceties.

Queen Mary 2 has 24 kennels on board.

Should I purchase cancellation insurance?

Yes, if it is not included, as cruises (and air transportation to/from them) must be paid in full before your documents are issued. If you cancel at the last minute – even for medical reasons – you could lose the whole fare. Pay by credit card, if you have one – you're more likely to get your money back if your booking agency goes bust.

Cruise lines may accept cancellations more than 30 days before sailing, but all charge full fare if you don't turn up on embarkation day. Many lines do not return port taxes, which are not part of the cruise fare.

Travel insurance

Cruise lines and travel agents routinely sell travel cover policies that, on close inspection, appear to wriggle out of payment due to a litany of exclusion clauses. Examples include pre-existing medical conditions (ignoring this little gem could cost you dearly) and valuables left unattended on a tour bus, even if the guide says it is safe and that the driver will lock the door.

7 QUESTIONS TO ASK A TRAVEL AGENT

1. Is air transportation included in the cabin rate quoted? If not, how much will it be? What other costs will be added – these can include port charges, insurance, gratuities, shore excursions, laundry, and drinks?
2. What is the cruise line's cancellation policy?
3. If I want to make changes to my flight, routing, dates, and so on, are there any extra charges?
4. Do you have preferred suppliers, or do you book any cruise on any cruise ship?
5. Is your agency bonded and insured? If so, by whom?
6. Have you sailed aboard the ship I want to book or that you are recommending?
7. Is insurance included if I book the shore excursions offered by the cruise line?

Which are the major cruise lines?

There are nine major cruise lines (defined by me as those with 10 ships or more): AIDA Cruises, Carnival Cruise Line, Celebrity Cruises, Costa Cruises, Holland America Line, MSC Cruises, Norwegian Cruise Line, Princess Cruises, and Royal Caribbean International.

Won't I get bored?

No chance! Whether you want to lie back and be pampered or be active nonstop, you can do it on a cruise. And, in case you think you may feel cut off without contact, almost all large resort ships (those carrying over 2,501 passengers) have ship-wide Wi-Fi, Internet access, movies, and digital music libraries.

Why is it so expensive for solo travelers?

Almost all cruise lines base their rates on double occupancy, so when you travel alone the cabin portion of your fare reflects an additional supplement. Although most new ships are built with cabins for double occupancy, some companies may find a cabin companion for you to share with, if you wish, although you would lose your personal privacy. Some companies sell two-bed cabins at a special single rate.

How about holiday season cruises?

Celebrating the festive lifestyle is even more special aboard ship, where decorations add to the sense of occasion. However, the large resort ships are usually full during the main holiday periods. (Don't travel at these busy times, if you want to have the facilities of a large resort ship but want to be able to relax.)

What about 'Spring Break' cruises?

If you take a cruise aboard one of the large resort ships (the most popular brands for these are Carnival Cruise Lines, Norwegian Cruise Line, and Royal Caribbean International) during the annual Spring Break (usually in March) expect to find hordes of students causing mayhem.

Can I cruise to Antarctica aboard a large resort ship?

Some large resort ships claim to include Antarctica on their itineraries, but you may be very disappointed. Ships carrying over 500 participants are not allowed to land passengers and are restricted to 'scenic' cruising, so the likelihood of zooming in on penguin colonies is slim. Choose one of the specialist expedition ships that carry only about 200 passengers to experience this vast frozen continent properly.

What are shore excursions?

At each port of call you can go ashore and explore the surrounding areas on a guided tour (a good way to see the main sights and highlights), or independently. In most cases, shore excursions cost extra, although some cruise lines (the more upscale ones) may include one shore excursion in each port.

Do ships have bathtubs?

Sadly, bathtubs are on their way out, except for in the higher-priced suites on the large resort ships, or aboard the smaller, more luxe cruise ships. Once standard, bathtubs have now largely been replaced by spacious shower enclosures.

Do cruise lines have loyalty programs?

Many companies have loyalty clubs or programs which offer discounts, credits, and onboard benefits unavailable to non-members. Programs are based either on the number of cruises taken, or, more fairly, on the number of nights sailed. There's no charge to join, but many benefits to gain if you keep cruising with the same line.

Cunard's three Queens dance in the river Mersey on May 26, 2015 in Liverpool.

Some companies allow you to transfer point levels to a sister brand. There are usually several levels (a maximum of six at present), such as Silver, Gold, Platinum, Diamond, Titanium, etc., depending on the cruise line. Reaching the higher levels requires more effort because the cruise companies are overwhelmed by the sheer number of passengers in their respective clubs/programs.

What do the letters in front of a ship name mean?

There are four key ship prefixes: MS = Motor Ship; MV = Motor Vessel; RMS = Royal Mail Ship (there's only one – Queen Mary 2); SS = Steam Ship.

How do I book multiple cabins close to each other?

Cruise lines (and cruise travel agents) like to book multiple cabins at the same time and are usually accommodating. Book early for the best chance of getting adjacent cabins, and do avoid guaranteed cabins.

Is there enough to keep kids busy?

Most cruises provide families with more quality time than any other type of vacation, and family cruising is the industry's largest growth segment, with activities tailored to various age groups (see the Family Cruising chapter).

Do we need to take towels and soap?

No. Both of these are provided by the cruise ship. Some ships have individual soaps, and some fit liquid soap and shampoo in wall-mounted dispensers. Towels for the pool deck are provided either in your cabin or by the pool.

Do cruise ship pools have lifeguards?

In general, no, except for Disney Cruise Line, Norwegian Cruise Line and Royal Caribbean International.

Do youth programs operate on port days?

Most cruise lines also operate programs on port days, although they won't be as extensive as on days at sea.

A birthday aboard a Carnival Cruise Line ship.

Are there adults-only ships?

Companies that operate small and mid-size adults-only ships include Cruise & Maritime Voyages (Columbus, Magellan, Marco Polo), P&O Cruises (Arcadia, Aurora), Saga Cruises (Saga Discovery, Saga Sapphire) and Virgin Voyages (Scarlet Lady). The minimum age may be different depending on the company, so do check for the latest information.

Do ships provide a daily program for each day at the beginning of the cruise, so I can plan my days ahead?

Apart from minor changes that may need to be made each day (due to weather conditions, or substitutions), there's no reason why this can't be done.

How can I celebrate a birthday or anniversary?

If you have a birthday or anniversary or other special occasion to celebrate during your cruise, let the cruise line know in advance. They should be able to arrange a cake for you, or a special 'Champagne breakfast' in bed. Some cruise lines offer anniversary packages – for a fee – or a meal in an alternative restaurant, where available.

7 TIPS TO GET THE BEST TRAVEL INSURANCE

1. Shop around. Don't accept the first travel insurance policy you are offered.
2. If you purchase travel cover online, check the credentials of the company underwriting the scheme. Deal with well-established names instead of looking for the cheapest deal.
3. Read the policy details carefully and make sure you know exactly what you are covered for.
4. Beware the 'box ticking' approach to travel cover, which is often done quickly in lieu of providing proper advice. Insurers should not be allowed to apply exclusions that have not been

clearly pointed out to you.
5. Ask for a detailed explanation of all exclusions (including those for 'hazardous' sports like horseback riding, cycling, kayaking, jet-skiing, or ziplining), excesses, and limitations.
6. If you purchase your own air transportation, check whether your insurance policy covers you if the airline fails, or if bad weather prevents you from joining your ship on time.
7. Check the procedure you need to follow if you are the victim of a crime, such as your wallet or camera being stolen while on a shore excursion.

Do cruises suit honeymooners?

Absolutely. A cruise is the ideal setting for romance, for shipboard weddings aboard ships with the right registry (they can also be arranged in some ports, depending on local regulations), receptions, and honeymoons. And for those on a second honeymoon, many ships can perform a 'renewal of vows' ceremony; some will make a charge for this service.

Do some people really live on board?

Yes! There are several 'live aboard' passengers who simply love traveling the world continuously – and why not? They sell their house, put possessions into storage, step on board, and disembark only when the ship has to go into dry dock for refits.

Is a repositioning cruise cheaper?

When ships move from one cruise region to another, it is termed 'repositioning.' For instance, when ships move between the Caribbean and Europe, typically in April/May, or between Europe and the Caribbean (typically in October/November), cruise fares are often discounted. The ships rarely sail full, so the value for money is excellent. Some cruise lines use this time to do essential maintenance work, so always check before you book to make sure that all facilities will be available.

How inclusive is all-inclusive?

All cruise lines have different interpretations of the word 'inclusive.' It usually means that transportation, accommodation, food, and entertainment are wrapped up in one neat package. If drinks are included, it's mostly a limited range of low-quality brands (standard spirits) chosen by the cruise line, and bartenders tend to be overgenerous with ice for cocktails. 'Mostly inclusive' might be a better term to use.

Outdoor breakfast aboard *Seven Seas Voyager*.

Tell me more about extra costs

While cruise lines offer appealingly low fares, most try hard to maintain revenues by increasing the cost of onboard choices (particularly for restaurants not included in the cruise fare), including beverages. Expect to spend at least $25 a day per person on extras, plus $10–15 a day per person in gratuities (unless they are included). Here are the approximate prices per person for a typical seven-day cruise aboard a well-rated mid-size or large resort ship, based on an outside-view two-bed cabin:

Cruise fare: $1,000
Port charges: $100 (if not included)
Gratuities: $50
Total cost per person: $1,150

This is less than $165 per person per day, which seems reasonable when you consider all it covers.

However, your seven-day cruise costs can easily increase when you start adding on extras such as excursions, cappuccinos, drinks (unless they are included), mineral water, Internet access, gratuities, and other items. Allowing about $1,000 extra per person may be a good idea.

More examples of extra-cost items are provided only as guidelines; these may have changed since this book was completed, so always check with the cruise line, onboard concession, or your travel provider for the latest prices) include:

Aqua Spa use: $30–50 per day
Babysitting (per hour): $10
Bottled water: $2.50–7 (per bottle)
Cappuccino/espresso: $2.50–4.50
Cartoon character bedtime 'tuck-in' service: $20–25
Dry-clean dress: $10
Dry-clean jacket: $10
Golf simulator: $25 (30 minutes)
Group cycling class: $12–20
Hair wash/set: $40–75
Haircut (men): $30–50

7 MONEY-SAVING TIPS

1. Research online, but book through a specialist cruise-travel agency.
2. Cut through the sales hype and get to the bottom line, and make sure that all taxes and fees are included.
3. Book early – the most desirable itineraries and cabins go first. If air travel is involved, remember that air fares tend to rise in peak seasons.
4. Book a cabin on a lower deck – the higher the deck, the more expensive it will be.
5. An interior (no view) cabin is cheaper, if you can live without natural light.
6. Be flexible with your dates – go off-season, when fares will be lower.
7. Purchase travel cancellation insurance – your cruise is an investment, after all.

The Haven Courtyard relaxation area aboard *Norwegian Jade*.

Ice cream: $2.50–4
In-cabin (on-demand) movies: $6.95–12.95
Internet connection: $0.50–0.95 per minute
Laundry: wash one shirt: $3–4
Laundry soap: $1–1.50
Massage: $3-plus a minute (plus tip)
Shuttle bus in ports of call: $5–10
Sodas (soft fizzy drinks): $2–4
Specialty dining (cover charge): $15–100 each
Wine/cheese tasting: $25–50
Wine with dinner: $7–500
Yoga or Pilates class: $12–20

What are port charges?

These are levied by various ports visited, rather like city taxes imposed on hotel guests. They help pay for the infrastructure required to provide facilities including docks, linesmen, security and operations personnel, and porters at embarkation and disembarkation ports.

Should I take a back-to-back cruise?

If you're considering two seven-day back-to-back cruises, for example eastern Caribbean and western Caribbean, bear in mind that many aspects of the cruise – the seven-day menu cycle, one or more ports, all shows and cabaret entertainment, even the cruise director's jokes and spiel – may be duplicated.

Do ships have different classes?

Gone are official class distinctions. Differences are now found mainly in the type and size of accommodation chosen, its location, and whether or not you have butler service or drinks included.

Hotels have presidential suites, executive floors, and so forth, while airlines have First Class, Busi-

ness Class, and Economy Class (some airlines now have different levels and prices in economy, such as premium economy, 'no-frills' and hand-luggage-only economy). In other words: Pay More, Get More.

Some cruise lines have a 'concierge lounge' for use only by occupants of accommodation designated as suites, thus reviving the two-class system.

'Private Enclaves' (exclusive areas) have been created by Celebrity Cruises (*Celebrity Edge* only), Dream Cruises (Dream Palace), MSC Cruises (Yacht Club, with drinks included), and Norwegian Cruise Line (The Haven) for occupants of the most expensive suites, in an effort to insulate their occupants from the masses. The result is a 'ship within a ship' (private enclave with key-card access).

Most companies have, in essence, created two classes: (1) Suite-grade accommodation; (2) Standard cabins (either exterior view or interior – no view).

Cunard has always had several classes for transatlantic travel (just like scheduled airlines), but this is designated by restaurant (Queens Grill, Princess Grill, or Britannia Restaurant), assigned according to the accommodation grade chosen.

Do ship's decks have names or numbers?

Ships can have both names and/or numbers. Historically, ships used to have only deck names (example: Promenade Deck, 'A' Deck, 'B' Deck, 'C' Deck, Restaurant Deck, and so on). As ships became larger, numbers started appearing (copying ferry deck markings).

However, some ships don't have a Deck 13; examples include the ships of AIDA Cruises, Carnival Cruise Line, Celebrity Cruises, Costa Cruises, P&O Cruises Australia (*Pacific Dawn* and *Pacific Explorer* only), and Princess Cruises, or any cabin with the number ending in 13 in it. Dream Cruises ships don't have a Deck 4 or Deck 14 (considered unlucky for Chinese passengers – Dream Cruises' main clientele), while the ships of MSC Cruises don't have a Deck 17 – considered unlucky by Italians.

Can I eat when I want to?

Most major cruise lines offer 'flexible dining', so you can choose (with some limitations) when you want to eat, and with whom you dine, during your cruise – or a choice of several restaurants. As with places to eat ashore, reservations may be required, you may also have to wait in line at busy periods, and occupants of the top suites get priority.

Aboard large resort ships (2,501-plus passengers) the big entertainment shows are typically staged twice each evening, so you end up with the equivalent of two-seating dining anyway.

What is specialty dining?

Mass-market dining isn't to everyone's taste, so many ships have dining venues other than the main restaurant. These usually cost extra, but the food quality, preparation, and presentation are decidedly better. You may need to make a reservation for dinner.

What's the minimum age for drinking alcohol?

Aboard most ships based in the US and Canada, the minimum drinking age is 21. However, for ships based throughout the rest of the world, it is generally 18. But you should always check with your chosen cruise line.

Are drinks packages good value?

Yes, if you like to drink a lot. They can vary hugely between cruise ships, and some also add a mandatory gratuity. Also, the choice may not include your favorite brands ('premium' brands come at an extra cost). However, on port-intensive itineraries when you are off the ship almost every day, think about the number of drinks you actually need; it may better to 'drink as you go.'

What does a typical drinks package cost?

Typically, about $50 per day, per person, plus a 15 percent gratuity, if you book ahead of your cruise; all persons in the same cabin must purchase the package. However, if you purchase the same package once you are on board, it could rise to $60 (plus gratuity). Note that on some European cruises, you may also be charged VAT (Value Added Tax).

Can I bring my own booze on board?

No, at least not aboard most cruise lines, as it will be confiscated. Some smaller lines might, however, turn a blind eye if you bring your favorite wine or spirit on board for in-cabin consumption.

How about service standards?

To estimate the standard of service, look at the crew-to-passenger ratio – provided in each ship profile in this book. The best service levels are aboard ships with a ratio of one crew member to every two passengers, or higher. The best ships, from the point of view of crew living and working conditions, also tend to be the most expensive ones – the adage 'you get what you pay for' tends to be all too true.

Do ships have room service?

While most cruise ships provide free 24-hour room service, some ships charge a delivery fee for items such as food and beverages, including tea and coffee (particularly late at night). A room service menu will be in your cabin. Aboard sail-cruise ships such as those of Sea Cloud Cruises or Star Clippers, there's no room service. If you occupy suite-grade accommodation, you may get additional services such as afternoon tea-trolley service and evening canapés, at no extra cost. Some ships may offer room service specialties, for example a Champagne breakfast, at extra cost (Princess Cruises, for example).

FIVE RIP-OFFS TO WATCH OUT FOR

1. Internet charges. Cruise lines often overcharge for use of the Internet (connections are by satellite).

2. Currency conversion. If you use a foreign credit card to pay your account, you could incur unseen currency conversion charges, known in the trade as dynamic currency conversion (DCC). When you pay your bill, the price quoted is recalculated into a 'guaranteed' price, often higher than the rate quoted by banks or credit card companies.

3. Double gratuities. Some cruise lines typically imprint an additional gratuity line on signable receipts for such things as spa treatments, extra-cost coffees, and other bar charges, despite a 15 percent gratuity having already been added.

Example: for an espresso coffee costing $2.80, a 15 percent tip of 42 cents is added, thus making the total cost $3.22. You sign the receipt, but one line above the signature line says 'Additional Gratuity' – thus inviting you to pay a double gratuity.

4. Transfer buses. The cost of airport transfer buses in some ports, such as Athens and Civitavecchia (the port for Rome). A cheaper option is to take the train instead.

5. Mineral water. The cost of bottled mineral water for shore excursions. Example: one cruise line charges $4.50, but then adds another 15 percent service charge or gratuity 'for your convenience,' even though you open it yourself! Budget accordingly.

Should I tip for room service?

No. It's part of the normal onboard duties that the hotel staff are paid to carry out. Watch out for staff aboard the large resort ships saying that they don't always get the tips that are 'automatically added' to onboard accounts – it's a ploy to get you to tip them more in cash.

Do any special food events take place?

In addition to birthdays, anniversaries and other celebrations, special events, or special celebration dinners, or 'foodertainment' event may be featured once each cruise. Examples of this include a Champagne Waterfall (Princess Cruises) and Rijsttafel (pronounced 'rice-taffle'), rice-based Indonesian food to which small items of meat, seafood, and vegetables are added (Holland America Line).

Some cruise lines feature a British Pub Lunch (featuring fish and chips, or sausages and mash) or late-morning 'Frühschoppen' (German sausages, pretzels, and beer). Others still offer an old standby, the Baked Alaska Parade, also known as 'Flaming Bombé Alaska.' This usually happens on the night before the last night of a typical cruise (also known as 'Comment Form Night'), although some companies have replaced this with a Chef's Parade. Traditionally, February 1 is the official Baked Alaska Day.

Do ships still serve bouillon on sea days?

Some ships carry on the tradition of serving or making bouillon available at 11am each sea day. Examples include the ships of Cunard, Fred. Olsen Cruise Lines, Hapag-Lloyd Cruises, Hebridean Island Cruises, P&O Cruises, Phoenix Reisen, and Saga Cruises.

Do ships still use plastic straws for drinks?

Several cruise companies have totally replaced plastic straws with paper or bamboo straws, including Crystal Cruises, Hapag-Lloyd, and Lindblad.

Do all ships have USB sockets in the cabins?

Many new ships (those under five years old) do, but most do not. The best advice is to take a USB charger plug with you.

Do all ships have self-service launderettes?

Some cruise lines do (AIDA Cruises, Carnival Cruise Line, Cunard, Holland America Line, Princess Cruises, for example), and some don't (Celebrity Cruises, Costa Cruises, MSC Cruises, Norwegian Cruise Line, Royal Caribbean International). Companies that don't have them may offer 'family bundles' at a special price. Many ships do have a retractable clothesline in the bathroom, however, which is good for those small items.

Do ships have proper dance floors?

No. For social dancing, a properly 'sprung' wood floor is the best for social (ballroom) dancing. Ships

A spot of social dancing aboard *Queen Elizabeth*.

with good, large wooden dance floors include *Asuka II*, *Aurora*, *Britannia*, *Queen Elizabeth*, *Queen Mary 2*, and *Queen Victoria*.

Do all ships have swimming pools?

The largest is the half Olympic size (82ft/25m in length) pool aboard Celebrity Apex, Celebrity Edge, *Mein Schiff 1*, *Mein Schiff 2*, *Mein Schiff 3*, *Mein Schiff 4*, *Mein Schiff 5*, and *Mein Schiff 6*. Most, however, are a maximum of just over 56ft (17m) long. They are usually located on one of the uppermost decks.

Many large resort ships have aqua parks or multi-pool deck complexes that include long waterslides (examples: *Carnival Sunshine*, *Norwegian Bliss*, *Symphony of the Seas*). Some ships have 'infinity' pools on an aft deck, so, when you are in the pool it looks like you're at one with the sea (examples include *MSC Preziosa* and *Viking Sun*).

Some ships have completely separate adult-only, family pools, and toddler pools, such as *Disney Dream*, *Disney Fantasy*, *Disney Magic*, and *Disney Wonder*. The family-friendly large resort ships usually have separate pools and tubs for children in different age groups located within children-only zones, or aqua parks. Some ships have pools that can be covered by retractable glass domes – useful in case of inclement weather; others only have open-air pools, yet trade in cold weather areas in winter. A few ships have heated pools – examples include *Independence of the Seas* and *Spirit of Discovery*.

Poolside movie screens adorn large resort ships, including *Carnival Destiny*.

While most pools are outside, some ships also have indoor pools located low down, so that the water doesn't move about when sea conditions are unkind. Examples include *Astor, Deutschland,* and *Spirit of Discovery.*

Some smaller ships have only a 'dip' pool – just big enough to cool off in on hot days, while others may have hot tubs only (no pool).

Note that when there is inclement weather, the pools are emptied to avoid the water sloshing around.

Do all ships have freshwater pools?

All the ships of Disney Cruise Line and most of the large resort ships (such as *Allure of the Seas*) have freshwater pools. Some ships, however, do have saltwater pools, with the water for the pools being drawn from the sea, and filtered.

How are swimming pools kept clean?

All shipboard swimming pools have chlorine – a member of the residual halogen group – added (a minimum of 1.0–3.0 ppm in recirculated swimming pools), while some have chemically treated saltwater pools. Pools are regularly checked for water-flow rates, pH balance, alkalinity, and clarity – all entered into a daily log.

Do any ships have walk-in pools (instead of steps)?

Not many, because of space considerations, although they can often be useful for older passengers. Some ships do, however (examples include *Aurora, Crystal Serenity,* and *Crystal Symphony.*)

What's the difference between an outside and an interior cabin?

An 'outside' (or 'exterior') cabin has a window (or porthole) with a view of the outside, or there is a private balcony for you to step on to be outside. An 'interior' (or 'inside') cabin means that it doesn't have a view of the outside, although it may have a 'virtual' window or balcony.

Some balcony cabins appear rather cheap. Is there a catch?

It may be cheaper because it has an obstructed view – often because it's in front of a lifeboat. Always check the deck plan, because it may be that it's only partially obstructed.

Can I visit the bridge?

Usually not – for insurance and security reasons – and never when the ship is manoeuvring into and out of port. However, some companies run extra-cost 'Behind the Scenes' tours. The cost varies, but it can be as much as $150 per person.

Are there any female captains?

Yes, there are. Some examples (in the year order they became captain):

2007: Karin Stahre-Jansen, Sweden (Royal Caribbean International)

2010: Inger Klein Olsen, Faroe Islands (Cunard)

2010: Sarah Breton, UK (P&O Cruises)

2011: Lis Lauritzen, Denmark (Royal Caribbean International)

2013: Margrith Ettlin, Sweden (Silversea Cruises)
2016: Belinda Bennet, UK (Windstar Cruises)
2016: Kate McCue, USA (Celebrity Cruises)
2016: Serena Melani, Italy (Regent Seven Seas Cruises)
2018: Nicole Lagosch, Switzerland (AIDA Cruises)
2019: Kathryn Whittaker (Sea Cloud Cruises)
Serena Melani will become the first female captain to launch a new ship, the *Seven Seas Splendor*, in 2020. There will be many more in future, as the role of women in a once male-dominated cruise industry increases, setting an example for the hospitality world.

Can I bring golf clubs?

Yes, you can. Although cruise lines do not charge for carrying them, some airlines (especially budget ones) do. Some ships cater for golfers with mini-golf courses on deck and electronically monitored practice areas.

Golf-themed cruises are popular, with 'all-in' packages allowing participants to play on some of the world's most desirable courses. Hapag-Lloyd Cruises and Silversea Cruises, for example, operate a number of golf-themed sailings.

Do cell (mobile) phones work on board?

Most cruise lines have contracts with maritime phone service companies. Cell (mobile) phone signals piggyback off systems that transmit Internet data via satellite. When your ship is in port, the ship's network may be switched off, and you will pay the going local (country-specific) rate for mobile calls if you can manage to access a local network.

Are there any ships without in-cabin WLAN wiring? I am allergic to it.

The 94-passenger *Sea Cloud II* comes to mind, as well as some of the older ships that have not been retro-fitted with WLAN cabling.

Where can I watch movies?

Some ships have real movie theaters, but most don't. Many large resort ships have large show lounges that are also equipped for screening movies (mainly in the afternoons), or have huge open-air movie sceens on the pool deck.

Some ships have small-capacity screening rooms, typically for 100–200 passengers, where movies may be shown several times daily, and special rooms for showing 3D and 4D movies (these often include fast-paced adventure movies, surround sound, and moving seats). Carnival's 4,000-passenger *Carnival Vista* was fitted with the first IMAX theater at sea; *Carnival Horizon* now has one, too.

Movies are provided by a licensed film distribution or leasing service. Many newer ships have replaced or supplemented movie theaters with in-cabin infotainment systems (with pay-on-demand movies).

Are there any ships without televisions?

Yes – the 64-passenger sailing ship *Sea Cloud*.

Can I take an iron to use in my cabin?

No. However, some ships have self-service launderettes (see page 23), which include an ironing area. Check with your cruise line.

What is expedition cruising?

Expedition cruises are operated by specialists such as Hapag-Lloyd Expedition Cruises and Quark Expe-

Europa provides free bicycles for passengers.

---

15 THINGS NOT INCLUDED IN 'ALL-INCLUSIVE'

1. Dining in extra-cost restaurants
2. Premium (vintage) wines
3. Specialty ice creams
4. Specialty teas and coffees
5. Wine/spirit tastings/seminars
6. Internet and Wi-Fi access
7. Spa treatments
8. Some fitness classes
9. Personal training instruction
10. Use of steam room/saunas
11. Laundry, pressing (ironing), and dry-cleaning
12. Personal shopping
13. Professional souvenir photographs
14. Casino gaming
15. Medical services

MS Astor passing through the Pedro Miguel Locks on the Panama Canal.

ditions, using small ships that have ice-strengthened hulls or specially constructed ice-breakers that enable them to reach areas totally inaccessible to standard cruise ships. These vessels have a relaxed, casual atmosphere, with multiple expert lecturers and expedition leaders accompanying every voyage.

What is a Panamax ship?

This is one that conforms to the maximum dimensions possible for passage through the Panama Canal – useful particularly for around-the-world voyages. The 50-mile (80-km) canal transit takes from eight to nine hours.

Is there a cruise that skips ports?

Yes, but it isn't really a cruise. It's a transatlantic crossing, from New York to Southampton, England (or vice versa), aboard *Queen Mary 2*.

Can I shop in ports of call?

Many passengers embrace retail therapy when visiting ports of call such as Dubai, Hong Kong, St. Maarten, St. Thomas, and Singapore, among many others. However, it's prudent to exercise self-control. Remember that you'll have to carry those purchases home at the end of your cruise.

Do I have to go ashore in each port?

Absolutely not! In fact, many passengers enjoy being aboard 'their' ships when there are virtually no other passengers aboard – the ship becoming the destination. Also, if you book a spa treatment, it could be less expensive during this period than when the ship is at sea. Many ships have price differentials for sea days and port days.

Can I bring my pet?

No, with one exception: the regular transatlantic crossings aboard Cunard's ocean liner *Queen Mary 2*, which has carried more than 500 pet animals since its debut in 2004 (the one-way cost is $800–1,000 for a single kennel; cats are required to have two kennels – one as a litter tray – at a cost of $1,600). It has 22 air-conditioned kennels for dogs and cats (no birds) and dedicated kennel attendants. Pets must have the required certification and vaccination against rabies.

Can I fly in the day before or stay an extra day after the cruise?

Cruise lines often offer pre- and post-cruise stay packages – either included or at additional cost. The advantage is that you don't have to do anything else – all will be taken care of. If you book a hotel on your own, however, you may have to pay an 'air deviation' fee if you don't take the cruise line's air arrangements, or you want to change them.

What are the downsides to cruising?

Much-anticipated ports of call can be aborted or changed due to poor weather or other conditions. Some popular ports (particularly in the Caribbean) can become extremely crowded – there can be up to 12 ships at the same time in Barcelona or St. Thomas, disgorging 20,000-plus people.

Many common irritations could be fixed if the cruise lines really tried. Entertainment, for instance, whether production shows or cabaret acts, is typically linked to dinner times, which can be inconvenient.

What legal rights do I have?

It would seem almost none! After reading the Passenger Ticket Contract, you'll see why. A 189-word sentence in one contract begins 'The Carrier shall not be liable for ...' and goes on to cover the legal waterfront. Check all your documentation very carefully before you travel.

Where did all the money go?

Apart from the cruise fare itself, incidentals could include government taxes, port charges, air ticket tax, and fuel surcharges. On board, extra costs may include drinks, mini-bar items, specialty coffees, shore excursions (especially those involving flightseeing tours), Internet access, beauty treatments, casino gaming, photographs, laundry and dry-cleaning, babysitting services, wine tasting, bottled water placed in your cabin, and medical services.

A cruise aboard a ship belonging to a major cruise line could be compared to buying a car, whereby motor manufacturers offer a basic model and price, and then tempt you with optional extras to inflate the cost. Cruise lines say income generated on board helps to keep the basic cost of a cruise reasonable. In the end, it's up to you to exercise self-restraint to keep those little extras from mounting up to a very large sum.

Does a ship's registry (flag state) matter?

Not really. Some years ago, cruise ships used to be registered in their country of operation, so Italian Line ships (with all-Italian crews) would be registered only in Italy, and Greek ships (with all-Greek crews) would be registered only in Greece, etc. To avoid prohibition, some American-owned ships were re-registered to Panama. Thus was born the flag of convenience, now called the 'Flag State.'

Today's ships no longer have single-nationality crews, however, so where a ship is registered is not of such great importance. Cunard and P&O Cruises ships, for example, are now registered in Bermuda, so that weddings can be performed on board.

Today, the most popular flag registries are (in alphabetical order): the Bahamas, Bermuda, Italy, Japan, Malta, the Marshall Islands, Panama, and The Netherlands. This fragmented authority means that all cruise ships come under the IMO (International Maritime Organization, within the United Nations) when operating in international waters – 12 nautical miles from shore. A country only has authority over the ship when it is either in one of its own ports or within 12 nautical miles offshore.

How are ships weighed?

They aren't. They are measured. Gross tonnage is a measurement of the enclosed space within a ship's hull and superstructure (1 gross ton = 100 cubic ft).

Is anyone building a cruise ship powered by liquefied natural gas (LNG)?

Yes, the following companies have LNG ships on order: AIDA Cruises, Carnival Cruise Lines, Costa Cruises, MSC Cruises, P&O Cruises. While the main challenge is space to store the fuel, several LNG-powered ships are on order. Meanwhile, AIDA Cruises has dual fuel capability, including LNG. There's also one nuclear-powered cruise vessel: the Russian Arctic expedition ship *50 Years of Victory*, which debuted in 2008.

Why is a coin laid under the mast of ships as they are built?

According to a 2,000-year old shipbuilding tradition, the coin brings good luck, and also protects the ship's keel.

How long do cruise ships last?

In general, a very long time. For example, during the *QE2*'s almost-40-year service for Cunard, the ship sailed more than 5.5 million nautical miles, carried 2.5 million passengers, completed 25 full world cruises, and crossed the Atlantic more than 800 times. But the *QE2* was built with a very thick hull, whereas today's thin-hulled cruise ships probably won't last as long. Even so, the life expectancy is typically a healthy 30 years.

Staring at the horizon helps with seasickness.

Helping to stop norovirus.

Where do old cruise ships go when they're scrapped?

They go to the beach. Actually, they are driven at speed onto a not very nice beach at Alang in India, or to Chittagong in Bangladesh, or to Pan Yo in China – the main shipbreaking places. Greenpeace has claimed that workers, including children, at some sites have to work under primitive conditions without adequate equipment to protect them against the toxic materials that can be released into the environment. In 2009, a new IMO guideline – the International Convention for the Safe and Environmentally Sound Recycling of Ships – was adopted.

Will I get seasick?

Today's ships have stabilizers – large underwater 'fins' on each side of the hull – to counteract any rolling motion, and most cruises are in warm, calm waters. As a result, fewer than 3 percent of passengers become seasick. Yet it's possible to develop some symptoms – anything from slight nausea to vomiting.

Both old-time sailors and modern physicians have their own remedies, and you can take your choice or try them all, as follows:

When you notice the first movement of a ship, walk back and forth on the deck. You will find that your knees will start to get their feel of balance and counteraction.

Find a place where the sea breeze will blow into your face (fresh air is arguably the best antidote to seasickness), and, if you are nauseous, suck an orange or a lemon.

Eat lightly. Don't make the mistake of thinking a heavy meal will keep your stomach anchored. It won't.

When on deck, focus on a steady point, such as the horizon.

Dramamine (dimenhydrinate, an antihistamine and sedative introduced just after World War II) will be available aboard in tablet (chewable) form. A stronger version (Meclizine) is available on prescription (brand names for this include Antivert, Antizine, Bonine, and Meni-D). Ciba-Geigy's Scopoderm (or Transderm Scop), known as 'The Patch,' contains scopolamine and has proven effective, but possible side effects include dry mouth, blurred vision, drowsiness, and problems with urinating.

If you are really distressed, the ship's doctor can give you, at extra cost, an injection to alleviate discomfort. Note that this may make you drowsy.

A natural preventive for seasickness, said to settle any stomach for up to eight hours, is ginger in powder form. Mix half a teaspoon in a glass of warm water or milk, and drink it before sailing.

'Sea Bands' are a drug-free method of controlling motion sickness. Usually elasticated and available in different colors, they are slim bands that slip onto the wrist. They have a circular 'button' that presses against the acupressure point Pericardium 6, or P6 (Nei Guan) on the mid-forearm. Attach them a few minutes before you step aboard and wear on both wrists throughout the cruise.

Another drug-free remedy is Reletex, a watch-like device worn on the wrist. First used for patients undergoing chemotherapy, it emits a small neuro-modulating current that stops peristaltic waves in the stomach causing nausea and vomiting.

RULES OF THE ROAD

Ships, the largest moving objects made by man, are subject to stringent international regulations. They must keep to the right in shipping lanes, and pass on the right (with certain exceptions). When circumstances raise some doubt, or shipping lanes are crowded, ships use their whistles in the same way that an automobile driver uses directional signals to show which way he will turn. When one ship passes another and gives a single blast on its whistle, this means it is turning to starboard (right). Two blasts mean a turn to port (left).

The other ship acknowledges by repeating the same signal. Ships switch on navigational running lights at night – green for starboard, red for port, plus two white lights on the masts, with the forward one lower than the aft one.

A ship's funnel (smokestack) is one other means of identification, each line having its own design and color scheme. The size, height, and number of funnels were all points worth advertising at the start of the 20th century. Most ocean liners of the time had four funnels and were called 'four-stackers.'

Is having hay fever a problem?

People who suffer from hay fever and pollen allergies may benefit greatly from a cruise. Almost all sufferers I have met say that their symptoms simply disappear on a ship – particularly when it is at sea.

Are hygiene standards high enough?

News reports often focus on hygiene and sanitation aboard cruise ships. In the 1980s, the North American cruise industry agreed with the Centers for Disease Control (CDC) that hygiene and sanitation inspections should be carried out once or twice yearly aboard all cruise ships carrying American passengers, and the Vessel Sanitation Program (VSP) was born. The original intention of the VSP was to achieve and maintain a level of sanitation that would lower the risk of gastro-intestinal disease outbreaks and assist the cruise industry to provide a healthy environment for passengers and crew.

It is a voluntary inspection, and cruise lines pay handsomely for each one. For a ship the size of *Queen Mary 2*, for example, the cost would be $17,940; for a ship the size of *Azamara Journey*, it would be about $8,970. However, the inspection points are well accepted by the international cruise industry. Inspections cover two main areas: 1) water sanitation, including free chlorine residuals in the potable water system, swimming pool, and hot tub filters; and 2) food sanitation: food storage, preparation, and serving areas, including bars and passenger service pantries.

The ships score extremely well – those that undergo inspections, that is. Some ships that don't regularly call on US ports would possibly not pass the inspections every time. Older ships with outdated galley equipment and poor food-storage facilities would have a harder time complying with the United States Public Health (USPH) inspection standards. Some other countries also have strict health inspection standards. However, if the same USPH inspection standards were applied to restaurants and hotels ashore in the US, it is estimated that at least 95 percent or more would fail.

What about the norovirus?

This temporary but highly contagious condition occurs worldwide. Humans are the only known hosts, and only the common cold is reported more frequently than viral gastroenteritis as a cause of illness in the US. About 23 million Americans each year are diagnosed with the effects of the Norwalk-like virus (NLV gastroenteritis, sometimes known as winter vomiting virus or norovirus). It is more prevalent in adults and older children than in the very young.

Norovirus is part of the 'calicivirus' family. The condition itself is self-limiting, mild, and characterized by nausea, vomiting, diarrhea, and abdominal pain. Although it can be transmitted by person-to-person contact, it is more likely to arrive via contaminated foods and water. Shellfish (most notably clams and oysters), salad ingredients (particular salad dressings), and fruits are the most often implicated in noroviral outbreaks.

A mild and brief illness typically occurs 24 to 48 hours after consuming contaminated food or water, and lasts for 24 to 72 hours. If you board a ship after norovirus has struck, bread and bread rolls, butter, and salt and pepper shakers may not be placed on tables, but will be available on request during meals.

When an outbreak occurs, the ship will immediately be sanitized, and affected passengers may be

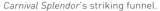

Carnival Splendor's striking funnel.

confined to their cabins to stop the condition spreading. Crew members and their livelihoods can also be affected, so they will want any outbreak contained as quickly as possible.

Are incidents on the rise? Yes, but so is the number of cruise ships. Should cruise lines pay compensation? I don't think so. In my experience, almost all outbreaks have occurred because someone has brought the condition with them from ashore.

How can you avoid the bug? Don't drink from aircraft water dispensers on the way to join your cruise – they are seldom cleaned thoroughly. Always wash your hands thoroughly before eating (particularly when going to the self-serve buffet) and after using the toilet, both on the plane and the ship.

Most ships provide liquid gel dispensers as a preventative – at the gangway and outside the dining venues (especially the self-serve buffets). Ships constructed after October 2011 must provide washbasins in self-serve buffets (one per 100 seats) under the United States Public Health's Vessel Sanitation Program. Several cruise lines now show a 'Wash Your Hands' video at muster stations following the passenger emergency drill.

What do ships do about garbage?

The newest ships are models of recycling and efficient waste handling. Cooking oil, for example, is turned into biodiesel. Garbage is sorted into dry and wet bins, and the dry garbage is burned on board or compacted for offloading in selected ports. Aluminum cans are offloaded for recycling. As for sewage, ships must be three nautical miles from land before they can dump treated sewage and 12 miles for sewage and food waste.

Collins cigar smokers' lounge aboard *Europa 2*.

Where is smoking allowed?

Smoking is generally allowed only in designated areas on open decks. Almost no cruise companies allow smoking in cabins or on balconies. Some lines place a notice in each cabin advising you that a hefty cleaning fee will be added to your onboard account if evidence of smoking in your cabin is found.

Almost all cruise lines prohibit smoking in restaurants and food service areas. Most ships now allow smoking only in designated areas of open decks.

What about cigars?

Cigar-smoking lounges are found aboard many ships, but some are now being converted into private lounges for high-rollers (that's gaming, not cigars). These are among the best: *Asuka II, Crystal Serenity, Crystal Symphony, Europa, Europa 2, Seven Seas Explorer, Seven Seas Mariner,* and *Seven Seas Voyager.* The biggest humidors and the largest selection of cigars can be found aboard *Europa* and *Europa 2*.

Note that the air purification system in a ship's cigar lounge will often not be effective enough if someone comes in to smoke a cigarette, and you may suffer the consequences of inhaling second-hand cigarette smoke.

How about freighter travel?

Slow freighter voyages appeal to independent travelers (about 3,000 passengers annually travel aboard them) who don't require constant entertainment but want comfortable accommodation and the joy of days at sea. For more information, contact the specialists:
www.cruisepeople.co.uk/freighters.htm
www.freightertravel.co.nz
www.freightervoyages.eu
www.travltips.com

Cruising's Growth

When the first jet aircraft made most former passenger liners redundant, some were scrapped, but others gave birth to the modern cruise industry.

Although Bahamas/Caribbean cruises from Miami resurfaced in the 1950s with a ship named *Nuevo Dominicano* (ex-*New Northland*), it was not until the 1960s that cruising was updated and re-packaged for a society that had an increasing amount of leisure time on its hands.

Some 35 years ago, the first edition of this same-author book listed 120 ships, some of which are still operating in one form or another. Today, that number has grown to over 400, including the small ships operating coastal and inland waterways cruises. But many well-known cruise lines have also gone to the deep blue seabed. Indeed, since 1990 more than 70 cruise companies have either merged, or been taken over, or simply gone out of business, including such well-liked firms as Chandris Cruises, Epirotiki, Renaissance Cruises, Royal Cruise Lines, Royal Viking Line, and Sun Line Cruises.

Some start-up lines, using older ships and aimed at specific markets, also came and went – companies such as American Family Cruises, Festival Cruises, Fiesta Marina Cruises, Premier Cruise Lines, and Regency Cruises. In came new shiny tonnage, complete with vanity logos and adornments painted on all-white hulls – the attributes of the industry's emerging giants. Fresh thinking transformed the design of accommodation, the use of public spaces, and the growing number of food and entertainment venues.

Yield management, a term purloined from the airline industry, was introduced. These days, company executives think of little else, because running a cruise company is all about economics.

Modern cruising is born

In the early 1960s, passenger-shipping directories listed over 100 passenger lines. At that time it was cheaper to cross the Atlantic by ship than by plane, but the introduction of the jet aircraft changed that rapidly, particularly with the appearance of the Boeing 747 in the early 1970s. In 1962, more than 1 million people crossed the North Atlantic by ship; in 1970, that number was down to 250,000.

The success of the jumbo jet created a fleet of unprofitable and out-of-work passenger liners that appeared doomed for the scrapyard. Even the famous big 'Queens,' noted for their regular weekly transatlantic service, were at risk. Cunard White Star Line's *Queen Mary* (81,237 gross tonnage) was withdrawn in September 1967. Cunard tried to fight back with Cunard-Eagle Airways but then formed a short-lived BOAC-Cunard joint venture with the British Overseas Aircraft Corporation, flying 707s and Super VC10s.

Cunard's *Queen Elizabeth,* at 83,673 gross tonnage the largest-ever passenger liner (until 1996), made its final crossing in November 1968.

Ships were sold for a fraction of their value. Many lines went out of business. Those that survived attempted to mix transatlantic crossings with voyages south to the sun. The Caribbean (including the Bahamas) became appealing, cruising became an alternative, and an entire new industry was born, with new lines being formed exclusively for cruising.

Then smaller, more specialized ships arrived, capable of accessing the tiny ports of developing Caribbean islands; there were no commercial airlines taking vacationers to the Caribbean then, and few hotels. Companies established their headquarters in Florida. Cruising was reborn. California became the base for cruises to the Mexican Riviera, while Vancouver was the focus for summer cruises to Alaska.

Flying passengers to embarkation ports was the next logical step, and soon a working relationship emerged between the cruise lines and the airlines. Air/sea and 'sail and stay' packages thrived – joint cruise and hotel vacations with inclusive pricing. Some old liners came out of mothballs, purchased

Cunard linked up with BOAC in the early 1960s.

Disney Dream features AquaDuck, the first-ever shipboard water coaster.

by emerging cruise lines and refurbished for warm-weather cruising operations with their interiors redesigned and refitted. During the late 1970s, the modern cruise industry grew at a rapid rate.

Cruising today

Today's cruise concept hasn't changed much from that of earlier days, although it has been improved, refined, expanded, and packaged for ease of consumption. Cruising today attracts people of all ages, socio-economic backgrounds, and tastes. It's no longer the shipping business, but the hospitality industry.

When I first started sailing in 1965, ships had almost no air conditioning (only forced air ventilation), the voltage was direct current (not alternating current, as now), bell boys attended elevators, there were no show lounges, computers, or fresh water pools (or showers), or vacuum toilets. Although ships have long been devoted to eating relaxation and traveling in comfort, they now offer a huge range of activities, and more learning and life-enriching experiences. For the same prices as a quarter of a century ago, you can cruise aboard the latest large resort ships with fine restaurants that offer varied cuisines, luxurious spas, and high-quality shows. And there are so many more places to visit than ever, from Acapulco to Antarctica, Bergen to Bermuda, Dakar to Dominica, and St Thomas to Shanghai.

The 'small is beautiful' concept has really taken hold in the cruising world, particularly with the more upscale/exclusive brands. Those with high-quality, low-capacity ships provide a highly personalized range of services and top-level hospitality. This means better-trained, more-experienced staff serving fewer passengers and higher-quality food, with more meals cooked to order. Small ships can also visit less crowded ports.

Some cruise companies have expanded by 'stretching' their ships – accomplished by cutting a ship in half

and inserting a newly constructed midsection (ranging from approximately 65-130 ft/20m-40m, thus instantly providing space for more accommodation and public rooms, while maintaining the same draft.

'Stretched' ships (with year of 'stretch') include: *Albatros* (1983), *Balmoral* (2007), *Berlin* (1986), *Black Watch* (1981), *Boudicca* (1982), *Braemar* (2008), *Enchantment of the Seas* (2005), *MSC Armonia* (2014), *MSC Lirica* (2015), *MSC Opera* (2015), *MSC Sinfonia* (2015), *Silver Spirit* (2018), *SuperStar Aquarius* (1998), *SuperStar Gemini* (1998), and *Marella Dream* (1990).

Exclusivity

Exclusive communities at sea are proliferating. These 'gated' areas are for those paying extra to live in a larger suite and gain access to 'private' facilities, concierge lounges, and private sunbathing areas. Ships that have them: *Celebrity Edge*, *Explorer Dream*, *Genting Dream*, *MSC Divina*, *MSC Fantasia*, *MSC Meraviglia*, *MSC Preziosa*, *MSC Seaside*, *MSC Seaview*, *MSC Splendida*, *Norwegian Bliss*, *Norwegian Breakaway*, *Norwegian Epic*, *Norwegian Escape*, *Norwegian Gem*, *Norwegian Getaway*, *Norwegian Jade*, *Norwegian Jewel*, *Norwegian Pearl* and *World Dream*. Two-class cruising – in some cases, three-class cruising – is in vogue.

PIER PRESSURE

Large resort ships can mean overcrowded ports. The most congested ports – where several ships carrying thousands of passengers may be in port at the same time – include the following:
Caribbean/Bahamas: Antigua, Barbados, Grand Cayman, Nassau, St. Maarten, St. Thomas.
Europe/Mediterranean: Barcelona, Civitavecchia (the port for Rome), Venice.
Other ports: Cabo San Lucas, Juneau, Ketchikan, Sydney.

What's Ahead

A record number of new ships is on order, as cruise companies battle it out to provide facilities to woo newcomers to cruising.

Between 2020 and 2027, more than 100 new ships of various sizes will debut, with some stunning facilities, smart technology, the latest in propulsion (including fuel made from liquefied natural gas, or LNG), and emissions controls. The creative juices have also been flowing from the interior designers, to provide more gimmicks to attract passengers and increase comfort levels.

In 2019 the new ships delivered varied in size, from Aurora Expeditions' 100-passenger *Greg Mortimer* to Costa Cruises' 5,200-passenger, dual-fuel-powered *Costa Smeralda*. Given the economics of scale and shipbuilding costs, the new 'optimum' size for large resort ships is now about 150,000 tons, with a capacity of 3,500–4,500 passengers.

Demand for innovation and the latest facilities is propelling new ship orders, and companies are investing billions of dollars in order to compete and update their hardware. Meanwhile, experienced passengers expect better-quality food and dining experiences, and simplified cruise pricing. Today, you pay only for what you want – I call it the 'pay-more, get-more' principle.

As for ship design, this is evolving, too, with more streamlining of the shape and bows. The large resort ships are also now assigning more space for outdoor promenades, al fresco indoor-outdoor eateries, and beach-style facilities for warm-weather itineraries.

Interior design

Designers acknowledge that ship lounges need to be used for many things in a single day, from morning bingo through to evening cocktail parties, and need to be flexible. Progressive spaces is the latest buzzword to describe multi-use public rooms; many incorporate mood lighting to create day-to-night lounges. With more fire-retardant materials (fabrics and soft furnishings) now certified for marine use, designers have a greater variety from which to choose.

Tech: The future is already here

Smart tech is allowing for faster embarkation/disembarkation – a most welcome development. Aboard some of the newest ships, you can use your smartphone (or a coin-sized medallion) to not only open your cabin door, but also to access your account, provide interactive directions, have beverages delivered to your cabin, make reservations,

buy drinks at the bar, and participate in trivia challenges. More tech-rich features have already been introduced, such as facial recognition for embarkation/disembarkation (Dream Cruises), personal digital assistants, and voice activation and recognition technology (MSC Cruises). Looking further ahead, cabins may become self-cleaning and robots could handle your laundry, serve your meals, and maybe even wash your hair!

What challenges lie ahead?

The main challenges ahead include sourcing qualified crew members and hotel service staff (particularly waiters with a passion for service) with the right language skills, improving infrastructure in ports of call, and scheduling destination calls.

What's the cost of a new cruise ship?

A small ship such as the 604-passenger *Seabourn Ovation* would cost about $250 million; the 930-pas-

A Royal Caribbean International *Oasis*-class ship.

The Royal iQ app helps to manage the cruise.

Caribbean International started a three-year program of revitalizing its ships, adding more commonality in features and eateries, as well as focussing on its 'private' island day attractions.

Cruise companies often add more cabins during refurbishment, increasing occupancy levels and more revenue possibilities but reducing the amount of space per passenger (passenger space ratio). Usually, there's no corresponding increase in the number of crew so the crew to passenger ratio decreases. Also, because no new elevators are added, there is greater congestion and increased waiting time.

Companies with older ships tend to sell them off to smaller or new operators. Some, such as AIDA Cruises' *AIDAcara*, would be hard to sell on given the low number of crew cabins.

Stretch marks

Stretching' older ships may also make sense in light of the cost of a new ship and the typical two-year time frame needed for completion and delivery. Even so, refits are expensive, at around $2 million a day, with that figure being pushed up by material, equipment, and labor costs. Silversea Cruises, for example, 'stretched' its *Silver Spirit* in 2018 by adding a new 49ft (15m) mid-section in 'cut-and-insert' operations at Fincantieri's shipyard in Palermo, Italy. While a 'chop-and-stretch' operation adds more cabins, frustratingly, additional elevators are rarely installed to help with the increased number of passengers.

senger *Viking Jupiter* would cost around $400 million; the 4,200-passenger *Norwegian Bliss* would cost about $700 million; the 5,496-passenger *Symphony of the Seas* would cost approximately $1.3 billion.

Nonstop refurbishment

Ships no longer in the first flush of youth need cosmetic surgery and regular makeovers in order to keep up their appearance. Items such as balcony doorframes need replacing, suites/cabins need updating, and navigational, safety, and technical machinery needs updating. For example, in 2019 Royal

New ships to debut			
Cruise line	Ship name	Gross tonnage	No. of lower beds
2021			
AIDA Cruises	TBA	183,900	5,200
Celebrity Cruises	Celebrity Beyond	117,000	2,900
Costa Cruises	TBA	183,900	5,200
Crystal Yacht Expedition Cruises	TBA	20,000	200
Disney Cruise Line	TBA	140,00	2,500
Dream Cruises	TBA	204,000	5,000
Hapag-Lloyd Expedition Cruises	HANSEATIC spirit	16,100	240
Holland America Line	Ryndam	99,500	2,650
Lindblad Expeditions	TBA	12,300	126
MSC Cruises	MSC Seashore	154,000	5,300
Mystic Cruises	World Navigator	9,300	176
Ponant	Le Commandant Charcot	30,000	270
Royal Caribbean International	Melody of the Seas	227,000	5,400
Scenic	TBA	17,085	228
Seabourn	Seabourn Venture	23,000	264
Silversea Cruises	Silver Dawn	40,700	596
Vantage Cruise Line	Ocean Explorer	8,000	180
Viking Cruises	Viking Venus	47,800	930
Virgin Voyages	TBA	110,000	2,860

Choose Where to Cruise

Cruise lines visit around 2,000 destinations, from the Caribbean to Antarctica, from the Mediterranean to the Baltic, and from Northern Europe to the South Pacific.

Where can I go on a cruise? As the saying goes: the world is your oyster. There are more than 30,000 different cruises to choose from each year, and about 2,000 cruise destinations. A cruise can also take you to places inaccessible by almost any other means, such as Antarctica, the North Cape, or the South Sea islands.

Itineraries vary widely, so different companies may offer the same or similar ones simply because these have been tried and tested. Narrow the choice by noting the time spent at each destination call (a few ships may stay overnight in port) and whether the ship docks in port or lies at anchor – it can take time to get ashore by the tender.

Caribbean

There are more than 7,000 islands in the Caribbean Sea, although many are uninhabited. Caribbean cruises are usually destination-intensive, with three, four or more ports in one week, depending on whether you sail from a Florida port or from a Caribbean port such as Barbados or San Juan. This means you could be visiting at least one port a day, with little time at sea for relaxation, so by the end of the cruise you might need another week to unwind. Saying that, you'd otherwise need a private jet to accomplish a destination a day, so a cruise is far better value.

June 10 to November 30 is the official Caribbean Atlantic hurricane season (this includes Bermuda, the Bahamas, and Florida). Cruise ships can change course quickly to avoid weather problems, which can also mean a change of itinerary. When that happens, cruise lines will generally not offer compensation, nor will travel insurance providers.

Geographically, the Caribbean region is large enough to be split into sections: eastern, western, and southern.

Eastern Caribbean. Cruises sail to the Leeward and Windward islands, and might include calls at Antigua, Barbados, Dominica, Martinique, Puerto Rico, St. Croix, St. Kitts, St. Maarten, St. Lucia, and St. Thomas.

Western Caribbean. Cruises sail to the Cayman Islands, Mexico, and Jamaica, and might call at Calica, Cozumel, Grand Cayman, Grand Turk, Playa del Carmen, Ocho Rios, and the island of Roatán.

Southern Caribbean. Cruises might call at Antigua, the Netherlands Antilles (Aruba, Bonaire, Curaçao), Barbados, La Guaira (Venezuela), Tortola, and San Juan.

Cuba, the Caribbean's largest island, which has nine World Heritage sites, holds a fascination for many. Several cruise lines have called there during the past 25 years with no US passengers on board.

'Private' island beach days

Several cruise lines with Bahamas/Caribbean itineraries feature a 'private island' day. NCL pioneered the trend when it bought a former military outpost in 1977. So far, it has spent millions upgrading its facilities.

These islands, or secure protected beaches, usually leased from the owning governments, have all that's needed for an all-day beach party. There are no reservations to make, no tickets to buy, no hassles with taxis. But you may be sharing your 'private' island with more than 5,000 others from a single large resort ship.

Such beach days are not all-inclusive, however, and command premium prices for items such as snorkel gear and mandatory swim vests, rental pleasure craft, 'banana' boat fun rides, floating beach mats, private waterfront cabanas for the day, sunfish sailboat rental, floating foam mattresses, and hammock rental.

Renting an air-conditioned cabana with private deck and sunbeds for the day will set you back

Perfect Day at CocoCay, Royal Caribbean's private island in the Bahamas.

around $500 (there are just 11 at Harvest Caye, an island base for exploring Belize).

One bonus is that such an island will not be cluttered with hawkers and hustlers, as are so many Caribbean beaches. And, because they are 'private,' there is security, and no fear of being mugged.

The new Thrill waterpark at Royal Caribbean International's CocoCay includes an over-the-water zip line, 13 waterslides, and a wave pool, at extra cost. The most dramatic island experience, however, has more to do with nature than the beaches. It's MSC Cruises' newly introduced Ocean Cay marine reserve island (on a 100-year lease), developed jointly with the Bahamas government and designed by ecologists at a cost of $200 million, open November 2019. One highlight is that the cruise ships stay late in Ocean Cay, so evening events can take place. It's all the more unusual for another, smaller private island nearby, available for up to 40 persons to rent.

Alaska

Alaska is popular (well over 1 million people traveled by cruise ship in 2018) because it is still a vast, relatively unexplored region, and cruise ships offer the best way to see the state's magnificent shoreline and glaciers. The wide range of shore excursions includes floatplane and helicopter tours, mostly to glaciers and salmon fisheries. Other excursions include 'dome car' rail journeys to Denali National Park to see North America's highest peak, Mt. McKinley.

Crown Princess in Glacier Bay, Alaska.

Pre- and post-cruise journeys to Banff and Jasper National Parks can be made from Vancouver.

There are two popular cruise routes: **The Inside Passage Route**, a 1,000-mile (1,600-km) stretch of protected waterways carved by Ice Age glaciers. This usually includes visits to tidewater glaciers, such as those in Glacier Bay's Hubbard Glacier or Tracy Arm – just two of the 15 active glaciers along the bay's 60-mile (100-km) coastline. Glacier Bay was established in 1986 as a biosphere reserve, and in 1992 the 3.3-million-acre (1.3-million-hectare) park became a World Heritage Site. Typical ports might include Juneau, Ketchikan, Skagway, and Haines. **The Glacier Route** usually includes the Gulf of Alaska during a one-way cruise between Vancouver and Anchorage. Typical ports might include Seward, Sitka, and Valdez.

Holland America Line and Princess Cruises own many facilities in Alaska (hotels, tour buses, even trains), and between them have invested hundreds of millions of dollars; in fact, Holland America Line is Alaska's largest private employer. Both companies take in excess of 250,000 passengers to Alaska each year. Other lines depend on what's left of the local transportation for their land tours. In ports with limited docking space, some ships anchor rather than dock.

With around one million cruise passengers a year visiting Alaska, and several large resort ships likely to be in port on any given day, there's so much congestion in port that avoiding crowded streets can be difficult. Even nature is retreating; with more people around, wildlife is harder to spot. And many of the same shops found in the Caribbean are now found in Alaska.

The more adventurous might consider one of the more unusual Alaska cruises to the far north, around the Pribilof Islands (superb for bird-watching) and into the Bering Sea.

Alaska can be wet and windy, and excursions may be canceled or changed. Even if it's sunny in port, glaciers have their own weather systems and helicopter flightseeing excursions are vulnerable. Take an Alaska cruise in May or August, when it gets darker earlier, for the best chance of seeing the Northern Lights.

Greenland

The world's largest island, the inappropriately named Greenland (Kalaallit Nunaat), in the Arctic Circle, is around 82 percent covered with ice – actually compressed snow – up to 11,000ft (3,350m) thick. Its rocks are among the world's oldest, yet its ecosystem is one of the newest.

The glacier at Jacobshavn, also known as Ilulissat, is the world's fastest moving, creating a new iceberg every five minutes. Gunnbjorn Fjeld, the island's highest mountain at 3,700 meters (12,000 feet), is also the highest mountain north of the Arctic Circle. Greenland, which was granted home rule by Denmark in 1978, makes a living from fishing. The island is said to have more dogs than people – its population is 68,400 – and dogs are an important means of transport. If your expedition voyage begins in Greenland, you'll probably fly to Kangerlussuaq to join the ship.

Iceland

Cruising around Iceland, located just south of the Arctic Circle, and her fjords is akin to tracing Viking legends across the land of fire and ice. Geysers, lava fields, ice sheets, hot springs, fjords, inlets, remote coastal stretches, waterfalls, snow-clad peaks, and the towering icebergs of Jökulsárlón can all be part of an Icelandic adventure cruise, as can seeking out the elusive Northern Lights (Aurea Borealis) at night. Cruises typically visit the capital, Reykjavík, and Akureyri, the largest town in the north.

Canada/New England

These 10- to 14-day cruises travel between New York or Boston and Montreal (northbound and southbound). Ports may include Boston; Québec City, Québec; Charlottetown, Prince Edward Island; Sydney and Halifax, Nova Scotia; Bar Harbor, Maine; and Saguenay, Québec.

The ideal time to sail is during the fall, when the leaves dramatically change color. Shorter five-to-seven-day cruises – usually from New York or Boston – go north to take in the fall foliage.

Europe and the Mediterranean

Traveling within Europe (including the Aegean, Baltic, Black Sea, Mediterranean, and Norwegian fjord areas) by cruise ship makes economic sense. Although no single cruise covers every port, cruise ships do offer a comfortable way of exploring a rich mix of destinations, cultures, history, architecture, lifestyles, and cuisines – without you having to pack and unpack each day.

European cruises have become increasingly popular because so many of Europe's major cities – Amsterdam, Athens, Barcelona, Copenhagen, Dubrovnik, Genoa, Helsinki, Lisbon, London, Monte Carlo, Nice, Oslo, St. Petersburg, Stockholm, and Venice – are on the water. It is far less expensive to take a cruise than to fly and stay in decent hotels, paying extra for food and transport. You will not have to try to speak or understand different languages when you are aboard ship (unless you prefer to), as you would ashore – if you choose the right ship. Aboard ship you use a single currency – typically US dollars, British pounds, or euros. A wide variety of shore excursions are offered. Lecture programs provide insights into a culture before you step ashore.

Small ships are arguably better than large resort ships, as they can obtain berthing space – the large resort ships may have to anchor in more of the smaller ports, so it can take time to get to and from shore, and you'll probably have to wait for shore-

A Viking Ocean Cruises ship in Venice.

tender tickets. Many Greek islands are accessible only by shore tender. Some companies allow more time ashore than others, so compare itineraries in the brochures; it's probably best to choose a regional cruise line (such as Celestyal Cruises) for these destination-intensive cruises, for example.

A Baltic and Northern capitals cruise is an excellent way to see several countries in a week or so, and enjoy different architecture, cultures, cuisines, history, and stunning scenery. The season for most cruises to this region runs from May to September, when the weather really is at its best. These cruises typically start from Bergen or Copenhagen, and usually include Stockholm (the gateway to the archipelago is awash with islands and country cottages), Helsinki, Tallinn, and an overnight stay in the treasure chest city of St. Petersburg – for many, the highlight of the cruise – with its sumptuous architecture, palaces, and Hermitage Museum. Most ships include at least one overnight stay, so that you can also take in a ballet or circus performance.

Norwegian fjords

These cruises usually include a visit to Bergen and a tram ride to the peak of Mt. Floyen, with stunning views over the city and harbor on a good-weather day. A highlight could be a visit to Troldhaugen in Bergen – the stunning home (and now a museum) of Edvard Grieg, Norway's most famous composer.

However, it's the sheer scenic beauty of cruising through fjords such as Eidfjord, Geirangerfjord, Hardangerfjord, and Sognefjord that inspires travelers. Typical visits will include Bergen, Flåm, Olden, Ålesund, and Oslo.

Around the British Isles

Traveling around the British Isles' more than 7,455 miles (12,000km) of coastline by cruise ship provides a unique perspective. The major sights – and some unexpected gems – of England, Scotland, Wales, the Republic of Ireland, and Northern Ireland can be covered in a single cruise that typically lasts 10–14 days. Because the British Isles are compact – Great Britain actually consists of thousands of islands – the actual sea time is short. But the range of experiences is vast: the turquoise waters off the Scilly Isles and the coast of Cornwall in England's southwest; the northern highlights in Scotland's more remote, nature-rich islands; the laid-back lifestyle of Ireland; the charm and distinctive voices of Wales; and then there are towering castles, incredible gardens, the England of Shakespeare, and, of course, the coastline itself.

Canary Islands

The sun-kissed Islas Canarias, a Spanish archipelago and the outermost region of the European Union, are located just off the northwest coast of mainland Africa – they are actually closer to Africa than Europe. With a year-round temperature of 70 degrees Fahrenheit (21 degrees Celsius) the islands provide a fine setting for a winter escape.

The islands of Gran Canaria, Tenerife, La Gomera, Lanzarote, Fuerteventura, La Palma, and Hierro make up the itinerary of some cruises to the region.

A Canary Islands cruise usually includes a call at Funchal on the Portuguese island of Madeira. Another attraction here is Ponta de São Lourenço, which offers some of the island's most stunning views.

Greek islands
Cruises that start or end in Athens (Piraeus is its port) may include visits to some of the most popular Greek islands and destinations such as Hydra, Poros,

Pride of America sails past the Na Pali coast, Kauai.

Mykonos, Santorini, Patmos, Katakolon, Delos, Itea, and Zakynthos.

Small ships sometimes sail through the slender Corinth Canal, which connects the Gulf of Corinth with the Saronic Gulf in the Aegean Sea. The canal, which is 6.4km (4 miles) in length and just 21.4 meters (70ft) wide at its base, separates the Peloponnese from the Greek mainland, thus making the peninsula an island.

Middle East

The Middle East cruise region includes the Arab countries bordering the Arabian and Red seas, and the southeastern Mediterranean. Countries with cruise facilities and places of historic interest are: Bahrain, Egypt, Iran (one of the author's favorite shore excursions was to the ancient site of Persepolis, near Shiraz), Jordan, Oman, Qatar, and the seven sheikdoms – the governing bodies of the United Arab Emirates (UAE). You will need to carry your passport with you in almost all these countries – it will be available at the ship's reception desk. It is advisable to check current government advice on how safe it is to travel to specific countries in the Middle East – check https://travel.state.gov and www.gov.uk/foreign-travel-advice for further details. Travel warnings can have an impact on your insurance coverage, so it's worth checking. Cruise companies, however, will adjust their itineraries as needed to avoid this being a problem.

Abu Dhabi and Dubai are the main Middle Eastern cruise bases, although cruise terminal and handling facilities are still limited. If you visit Dubai, note that public displays of affection such as hand-holding or kissing are not permitted, and you cannot drink alcohol in a public place. If you fly into Dubai with prescription medicines, make sure you have the appropriate, signed prescription. The best time to go is November to April.

South Africa and Indian Ocean

Attractions include cosmopolitan cities, wine tours, wildlife safaris, unspoiled landscapes, and uninhabited beaches. Itineraries include sailings starting or finishing in Cape Town, along the western side of Africa, with possible calls at Walvis Bay, the Cape Verde archipelago, and the Canary Islands, or cruising to East African ports such as Port Elizabeth, Richards Bay, Durban, Zanzibar, and Mombasa (Kenya). Some cruise lines focus on sailings from Cape Town to the eastern islands in the Indian Ocean, such as Madagascar, Mauritius, Reunion, the Seychelles and Maldives.

The Mexican Riviera

These cruises typically sail from Los Angeles or San Diego, along Mexico's west coast, calling at ports such as Cabo San Lucas, Mazatlán, Puerto Vallarta, Ixtapa/Zihuatanejo, Manzanillo, and Acapulco. They

Cruise lines: private islands			
Cruise line	Name of island	Location	First used
Carnival Cruise Line	Amber Cove	Dominican Republic	2015
Celebrity Cruises	Catalina Island	Dominican Republic	1995
Costa Cruises	Serena Cay	Dominican Republic	1996
Disney Cruise Line	Castaway Cay	Bahamas	1998
Holland America Line	Half Moon Cay	Bahamas	1997
MSC Cruises	Ocean Cay Marine Reserve	Bahamas	2019
Norwegian Cruise Line	Great Stirrup Cay	Bahamas	1977
Norwegian Cruise Line	Harvest Caye	Belize	2015
Princess Cruises	Princess Cays	Eleuthera, Bahamas	1992
Royal Caribbean Int.	CocoCay	Bahamas	1990
Royal Caribbean Int.	Labadee	Haiti	1986
Virgin Voyages	Bimini	Bahamas	2020

may include a call in the Baja Peninsula, Mexico's northernmost state. Be aware that there has been a considerable amount of crime even in the most visited ports (Puerto Vallarta and Manzanillo) in the past few years. Also, a number of cruise tourists have been caught out by rip tides and rogue waves when swimming in Cabo San Lucas.

Panama Canal

Some cruises take you through the Panama Canal, constructed by the US after the failure of a French effort begun in 1882 with a labor force of over 10,000 but plagued by disease and financial problems – more than 22,000 people died. The US took over the building effort in 1904, and the waterway opened on August 15, 1914, shaving more than 7,900 nautical miles off the distance between New York and San Francisco. The canal runs from *northwest* to *southeast* (not west to east), covering 51 miles (82km) of locks and gates and dams. Control of the canal passed from the US to Panama in 2000.

PANAMA CANAL LOCKS

While the existing Panama Canal locks measure 963x106ft (293.5x32m), with 39.5ft (12m) maximum draft, the new ones are 1,200x160ft (366x49m), with 49.9ft (15m) maximum draft. They allow almost all cruise ships, including Royal Caribbean International's *Oasis of the Seas*-class and Cunard's *Queen Mary 2*, to pass through (*Disney Wonder* was the first cruise ship to go through the new locks, in April 2017), although there is still the problem of a bridge at Panama City not being high enough for some ships to pass underneath. These ships need more than 200ft (61m) of air draft – the height from the waterline to the topmost part of the ship – but the present limit of the Panama Canal is 190ft (58m).

Between the Caribbean and the Pacific, a ship is lifted 85ft (26m) in a continuous flight of three steps at Gatun Locks to Gatun Lake, through which it travels to Gaillard Cut, where the canal slices through the Continental Divide. It is lowered at Pedro Miguel Locks 31ft (9.4m) in one step to Miraflores Lake, then the remaining two steps to sea level at Miraflores Locks before passing into the Pacific.

Ships move through the locks under their own power, guided by towing locomotives. The 50-mile (80-km) trip takes eight to nine hours. All this effort isn't cheap; cruise ships over 30,000 tons pay a fee of $134 per occupied bed. So, a ship with 3,000 passengers would pay a one-way transit fee of $402,000!

Most Panama Canal cruises depart from Fort Lauderdale or San Juan, calling at islands such as Aruba or Curaçao before entering the canal and ending in Acapulco, Los Angeles, or San Francisco. In 2008, the Inter-American Development Bank approved a $400 million loan to help finance the historic Panama Canal Expansion Program. The new three-step locks feature 16 rolling instead of mitre gates, each weighing around 3,300 tons. The visitor center may be included in tours from the port of Colon.

Hawaii and its islands

The islands of Hawaii, America's 50th state, are a tropical feast. Although relatively close together, they have many differences. For example, the lush, Garden-of-Eden-like Kauai is a world away from Oahu, with its urban metropolis of ever-busy Honolulu. The two parts of the Big Island, Kona and Hilo, are really opposites.

Although several cruise lines feature Hawaii once or twice a year, usually on Circle Pacific or special Hawaii sailings, only one ship is allowed to cruise in the state year-round: Norwegian Cruise Line's US-flagged *Pride of America*. Note that anything purchased aboard, including drinks, is subject to Hawaii sales tax, although this doesn't apply to ships registered outside the US.

South America

Cruises around Cape Horn between Santiago or Valparaíso in Chile and Buenos Aires in Argentina (with Patagonia and the magnificent Chilean fjords in between) are increasingly popular. The optimum season is November to March, and most cruises last 14 days. However, operating costs are high, because several countries are involved. Pilotage charges, for example, are among the highest in the world. Chile and Peru require compulsory tugs (extra cost). Steep charges for provisioning and supplies, visa complexities, and infrastructure issues all push up the cost.

Sailing southbound, ports might include Puerto Montt (Chile), Punta Arenas (Chile), and Ushuaia (Argentina), the world's southernmost city and the starting point for many expedition cruises to the Antarctic Peninsula.

Coming up the continent's east coast, ports may include Puerto Madryn (Argentina) and Montevideo (Uruguay). Slightly longer itineraries might include a call at Port Stanley in the Falkland Islands.

A few cruise lines also operate seven-day cruises from Rio de Janeiro, Brazil, mainly for Brazilians – who typically love to dance the night away and don't rise until nearly afternoon. Called 'eat late, sleep late' cruises, these are generally aboard large resort ships chartered to local companies.

Amazon River

The Amazon River is long – around 4,080 miles (6,566km) from close to its source in the Peruvian Andes, to Belém on South America's Atlantic coast – and contains one-fifth of the earth's water supply. Home to a tenth of the planet's animal species and plant life, it has approximately 1,100 tributaries, and is often so wide you can't see the riverbank on the opposite side. Between 400 and 500 indigenous communities live among the Amazon rainforest – the world's largest tropical rainforest, at 5.5 million sq km.

Cruises usually start in the Caribbean from ports such as Barbados and end up in Manaus (or vice versa), although starting in Manaus, with its muddy red-brown water, and ending up in the clear blue waters of the Caribbean may be the more appealing option. Calls along the way may be made in Parintins, Alter do Chão, Santarém, and Belém. Only the real expedition ships, such as Hapag-Lloyd Cruises' *HANSEATIC nature* or *HANSEATIC inspiration* can venture farther upriver from Manaus (Brazil) to as far as Iquitos, Peru, close to the source.

Manaus, located around 1,000 miles (1,600km) from the ocean, was built by barons of the rubber industry. Today, it really is a gaudy metropolis (home to over 1.7 million), but its opera house, built in 1896, remains a much-visited icon and still stages concerts.

One must-do shore excursion is a rainforest walk with a knowledgeable Brazilian guide to give you an insight into the richest variety of life on the planet. But make sure you have plenty of insect re-

THE OCEANS ON WHICH WE SAIL...

Oceans – large bodies of saline water – form 71 percent of the surface of the earth and are a major component of its hydrosphere. Some 86 percent of the water we drink comes from oceans, and they absorb 48 percent of the carbon that we humans launch into the atmosphere. The world's oceans form an incredible natural recycling organ.

In addition, there are many seas (smaller branches of an ocean). These are often partly enclosed by land, the largest being the South China Sea, the Caribbean Sea, and the Mediterranean Sea.

In size order, the world's five oceans are:
Pacific Ocean. The planet's largest ocean, the Pacific measures a colossal 60,060,700 sq miles (155,557,000 sq km). That equates to some 28 percent of the earth and means it is equal in size to all of the land area of the earth. It is located between the Southern Ocean, Asia, Australia, and the Western Hemisphere.

Atlantic Ocean. The world's second-largest ocean measures 29,637,900 sq miles (76,762,000 sq km) – a relative puddle compared with the Pacific.

Located between Africa, Europe, the Southern Ocean, and the Western Hemisphere, it includes the Baltic Sea, Black Sea, Caribbean Sea, the Gulf of Mexico, the Mediterranean Sea, and the North Sea.

Indian Ocean. Next, at No. 3, is the Indian Ocean, which is just slightly smaller than the Atlantic, at 26,469,900 sq miles (68,566,000 sq km). It is located between Africa, the Southern Ocean, Asia, and Australia.

Southern Ocean. Quite a drop down in size is the world's fourth-largest, and also its newest, ocean, measuring 7,848,000 sq miles (20,320 000 sq km). The Southern Ocean extends from the coast of Antarctica to 60 degrees south latitude.

Arctic Ocean. Finally, there's the Arctic Ocean, which measures some 5,427,000 sq miles (14,056,000 sq km) – a mere baby compared with its big brothers. What it lacks in size (in ocean terms, that is), it makes up for in terms of outreach, extending between Europe, Asia, and North America. Most of its waters are north of the Arctic Circle.

pellent – more than 200 varieties of mosquito inhabit the Amazon Basin.

Galápagos Islands

These islands, 600 miles (966km) west of Ecuador in the Pacific Ocean, are a microcosm of our planet. Some 13 major and 7 minor islands plus scores of islets make up the Galápagos, which are fed by the nutrient-rich Cromwell and Humboldt currents. The fertile waters can be cold, even on the equator.

The Ecuadorians jealously guard their islands and prohibit the movement of almost all non-Ecuador-registered cruise vessels within its boundaries. The best way to follow in the footsteps of Charles Darwin, who visited the islands in 1835 aboard the *Beagle*, is to fly to Quito and cruise aboard an Ecuadorian-registered vessel.

The government of Ecuador set aside most of the islands as a wildlife sanctuary in 1934, while uninhabited areas were declared national parks in 1959. The national park includes approximately 97 percent of the islands' landmass, together with 20,000 sq miles (52,000 sq km) of ocean. The Charles Darwin Research Station was established in 1964, and the government created the Galápagos Marine Resources Reserve in 1986.

The Galápagos National Park tax is $100 (children ages 2 to 12 pay $50), plus $10 for an Immigration Control Card, which must be obtained before you travel. Smoking is prohibited on the islands, and no more than 50,000 visitors a year are admitted. In 2012 new rules stopped ships from visiting most islands more than once in a 14-day period. Some cruise lines require vaccinations for cruises that include Ecuador, although the World Health Organization does not. In 2019, the 100-passenger *Celebrity Flora* – a new ship specially designed and built for the Galápagos experience debuted.

Australia and New Zealand

Australia and New Zealand offer a wealth of cruising possibilities, with a growing number of port cities attracting cruise ships. Apart from the major destinations, such as Sydney, Melbourne, Brisbane, and Perth (Australia), and Auckland, Christchurch, and Wellington (New Zealand), there are numerous smaller destinations, such as Adelaide, Cairns, and the Great Barrier Reef.

Then there's Tasmania's Hobart and the stunning former penal colony of Port Arthur – Tasmania's official top tourist attraction, renowned for its beautiful grounds. Scenic cruising along Tasmania's coastline is glorious, particularly in the area such as Wineglass Bay and Great Oyster Bay. The best time to go is November to March, i.e. summer in Australasia.

The extraordinarily beautiful Kimberley region, in Australia's Northwest Territories, essentially in the area between Broome and Darwin, is a must for chasing waterfalls (particularly the King Cascades

Passengers encounter a giant tortoise in the Galápagos Islands.

Waterfall on the Prince Regent River), and coral reefs. The best time to go is in April or May, after the rainy season, for the best waterfall action (as well as fishing and mud crabbing). Landings are by Zodiac inflatable rubber craft or by helicopter for a visit to the sandstone formation of the 350-million years old Bungle Bungle Range.

Asia

With such a rich tapestry of different countries, cultures, traditions, food, and sights to see, Asia should be high on the list of places to visit for the inquisitive traveler, and what better way to do this than by cruise ship. China, Japan, Indonesia, Malaysia, Singapore, Thailand, and Vietnam can all be visited by cruise ship. Indeed, 'marquee' ports such as Singapore, Hong Kong, Yokohama, and Bangkok are all good points from which to join your cruise. The region has so much to offer that it's worth taking a cruise of 14 days or longer to discover many of the fascinating destinations that await. Avoid September and October, however, because this is typhoon (hurricane) season.

South Pacific

The region is large, and so are the distances between island groups. Still, the area has inspired many people to travel to them to discover the unique lifestyle of its indigenous peoples. The region encompasses Tahiti and her islands in French Polynesia, the Marquesas, Trobriand, Pitcairn, and Cook island groups, among others – like string of pearls. Some magical names come to mind – Bora Bora, Moorea, Easter Island, Fiji, and Tonga.

Ship as a Destination

While a cruise is mainly about visiting incredible places, large resort ships are enticing people to stay on board by creating floating mini-cities packed with entertainment and dining venues.

'Meet a ship so revolutionary, it is the destination' – Celebrity Cruises, of new ship *Celebrity Edge* in late 2018. How true this is, because like all large resort ships (those carrying between 2,500 and 7,000 passengers) it has some really impressive features and facilities. Large resort ships are, in effect, mini-cities packed with entertainment and activity centers for families with children (for ages up to 17 years), stunning water parks with towering waterslides, multi-level atriums, multiple dining choices, spas and fitness facilities, and a huge range of accommodation. In fact, there is so much choice, there's hardly any time left to go ashore.

Suggestion: skip a port and stay on board and you can avoid long lines and irritating tender ticket operations when going ashore, for shore excursions, and for security screening when coming back on board. Voila; a more relaxing (a relative term aboard a large resort ship) cruise experience – and finally time to sit and read a good book or two. Naturally, this option may be best for regular passengers who have 'been there, done that'.

Symphony of the Seas' Central Park.

Large resort ships could also be a good choice for those with impaired mobility who want to travel but have comfort-factor surroundings, dining choices, and entertainment options, along with medical facilities close at hand. However, some ships have somewhat disjointed layouts, so always check the deck plan carefully, or speak to your specialist booking agent or cruise line directly.

Large resort ships typically have a number of restaurants, eateries, and casual food venues. These provide a chance to try a range of cuisines, although some of these may incur extra charges or have items with individual pricing. The ships will typically have a steakhouse or *churrascaria* (for steaks and grilled seafood), an Italian restaurant, and an Asian venue. Other restaurants may specialize in Chinese, Indian, or Japanese-style (sushi bar and teppanyaki grill) food, while some ships feature delis and fast-food outlets, including burger bars, pizzerias, and cake shops. One recent trend is for extra-cost fish and seafood venues, with fishmonger-style displays of fish and seafood on crushed ice. There may also be supper clubs, usually with entertainment such as dinner and a show.

It was Royal Caribbean International who, in 2009, introduced the then-revolutionary *Oasis of the Seas*, the largest cruise ship in the world at the time and the first to measure over 200,000 tons, carrying around 5,408 vacationers at double occupancy. Why revolutionary? Well, because the ship's beam (width) was increased to 65 meters (213ft), which allowed for a split, V-shaped aft superstructure. It also meant that the ship could be taller, increasing the amount of usable space. Designers were then able to create seven different 'neighborhoods' in the ship, with a large indoor Royal Promenade as the central focal point. It was, in effect, a 'mobile resort vacation' for families. And so the large resort ship became the destination.

The boast

The large resort ship companies constantly try to generate media interest through boasts of ships with the 'largest day bed at sea,' 'the longest waterslide at sea,' 'the only ice rink at sea,' or 'the longest indoor promenade.' This may be true (at least for a few months), but it merely invites competition to see who can add more gizmos, develop more tech, and create more media hype in the tabloid newspapers and weekend sections.

A recent trend is to build in an open promenade deck; many cruise ships built before 2010 considered them an unnecessary waste of space and a throwback to the ocean liner era and transatlantic crossings. However, the whole wraparound deck is not always dedicated solely to walking because it often also acts as an extension of the indoor-outdoor dining theme. While this is good in fine weather conditions – and a welcome relief to to the busyness and noise of the pool deck – it is not so practical when cruising in cooler climates such as Alaska. A few sunloungers may also be strewn around the promenade deck.

Floating cities

A typical 5,000-passenger ship may include the following facilities:

Pool deck

Almost all large resort ships have them: huge waterparks on one of the upper outer (pool) decks, with super-long twisting water slides, drenching water buckets, and unexpected aqua sprays. Active pursuits span jungle-style, rope-walking courses high atop the decks, surf-riding, rock-climbing, and abseiling walls, or even SkyRide 'bicycles' suspended in the air (Carnival Cruise Line), dodgem cars, and go-karts (Norwegian Cruise Line). It really is all the fun of the seaside, with some fairground bling thrown in.

Some of the most extensive waterpark/pool deck innovations can be found aboard the ships of Carnival Cruise Line, Dream Cruises, MSC Cruises, Norwegian Cruise Line, and Royal Caribbean International.

The result is an invasion of formerly quiet sunbathing areas and swimming pools (some ships have pools that are 25m/82ft long), with little remaining space for lounging near a pool. This is particularly true aboard ships that feature a pay-extra 'retreat' (or 'sanctuary') for adults, usually hidden at the front of the ship, with its own pool(s), hot tubs, bar, eatery, and open and shaded lounge areas.

Libraries

One common feature of destination ships is an onboard library – in fact, the library is the most popular room for passengers aboard Cunard's *Queen Mary 2*. Some large resort ships have libraries and comfortable chairs for reading, but others don't because, for most cruise companies, a library is a non-revenue area. These companies have libraries (or 'lifestyle lounges' that include a coffee shop): Holland America Line, MSC Cruises, Norwegian Cruise Line (although not *Norwegian Bliss*, *Norwegian Breakaway*, *Norwegian Getaway*, or *Norwegian Joy*), Princess Cruises, and Royal Caribbean International.

Artwork uncovered

Large resort ships often have whimsical, eclectic pieces of art as decorative elements, fea-

The London-inspired Royal Promenade on *Voyager of the Seas*.

Pride of America's Washington Library.

tures, photo opportunities, and talking points, created specifically for each ship. Some sculptures have beautifully rounded shapes and graceful lines, while moving kinetic sculptures or decorative lighting can transform an otherwise sterile atrium (lobby) space. A striking artwork installation often becomes the central focal point, particularly aboard the ships with multi-deck atriums.

One fine example would be the classic car. Indeed, there appears to be a constant connection between Royal Caribbean International and cars. It started with the race-red 1964 Morgan convertible sportster (formerly owned by the chairman of Royal Caribbean Cruise Ltd) that appeared on the Royal Promenade of Royal Caribbean International's *Voyager of the Seas*. The trend took off, and replicas of similar Morgan cars from the 1960s (each in a different color) were also installed aboard *Voyager*-class ships – *Freedom of the Seas* (black), *Independence of the Seas* (iridescent blue), and *Liberty of the Seas* (orange). Replicas then appeared on the Royal Promenade of the Oasis-class ships: a red 1936 Mercedes-Benz 540K on *Allure of the Seas*; a black Jaguar XK 120 Roadster on *Harmony of the Seas*; a black 1936 Auburn Bobtail Speedster on *Oasis of the Seas*; a rolled-up red VW Beetle aboard *Symphony of the Seas*.

Ships may also house artwork collections from established or up-and-coming artists. You can even take a step-by-step tour of the artwork and decorative installations in some ships, like you would in a gallery. *MSC Grandiosa*, for example, features the first professionally curated fine-art museum at sea.

Some ships have self-guided art tours – ideal when in port and most passengers are off discovering. This is one of the cultural benefits of cruising aboard a large resort ship.

Note that there are also invasive art auctions (normally not on port days), but these are not items from the interior decor of the ship. Also, the 'art' sold is an eclectic mix of items, usually by a specialist concession, and is of questionable value.

Entertainment

Entire 'book' shows feature Broadway/West End musicals such as *Cats*, *Grease*, *Hairspray*, *Mamma Mia*, *Priscilla Queen of the Desert*, and *Saturday Night Fever* (aboard Royal Caribbean International), while aboard the ships of Disney Cruise Line you could expect to see *Beauty and the Beast*, and *Toy Story* among others.

Large-scale original production shows featuring 16–20 singers and dancers (including male and female lead vocalists) and stunning backdrops are often better than the shows you might see on New York's Broadway or in London's West End. Some ships also have stunning aerobatic and acrobatic performances to take your breath away.

Aboard most Royal Caribbean International ships, a large ice rink hosts superb ice-skating shows, and the ice rink can often be used by passengers for daytime skating experiences and lessons.

Some ships also have comedy clubs, typically for smutty late-night, adult-only 'comedy.' Casinos are also considered as entertainment, but aboard most ships, the casino would be closed when docked, as would the shops, depending on the region and port (although it is a requirement in most ports, there is no actual global regulation).

Spas

An increasing amount of space is dedicated to spa and fitness centers, with a wide range of facilities and services, including saunas and steam rooms,

---

SEVEN REASONS TO STAY ON BOARD

1. Experience the ship and all it has to offer – without the crowds.
2. Enjoy a leisurely start to the day and indulge in a late breakfast (perhaps in bed), because it's your vacation. Try something different: one of the areas, facilities, or activities that you haven't been able to experience yet.
3. Make the most of a quieter spa experience – have a body-pampering treatment, often at a discount.
4. Go to the library and read a book (assuming that your ship has a library), and relax – without even looking at a digital device.
5. Try one of the sports-related activities at a more relaxed pace.
6. Take an uninterrupted self-guided tour of all the artwork that you can't see well when the ship is busy.
7. Take the opportunity to snap photos of the public rooms and other spaces without others getting in the way.

hairdresser's and barber's, facials, massages, and other body-pampering treatments (including couples' rooms), acupuncture, salt baths, etc. Many ships now have accommodation with private spa access, and spa-themed amenities and decor.

Sports facilities

Although it depends on which large resort ship you choose, you may be able to try sky-diving on an iFly simulator, go ice-skating, or take a spin in go-carts or dodgem cars. There may be the chance to try your hand on the climbing walls, rope walks, surf-riders, or virtual reality sports (F1 driving in a simulator, for instance).

You may be able to, with a few others, play basketball, go bowling, tee off on the mini-golf courses, or try one of the three that were always found aboard the ocean liners of yesteryear – shuffleboard, ring toss, and table tennis. For something gentler there's walking on an open promenade deck that encircles the ship. Afterwards, you could head to a sports bar to watch a good game.

Shops

Shopping at sea is a favorite sport for many; the attraction being the marketing gimmick 'duty free,' which is cruise-ship speak for goods sold in a foreign country that have entered that country without the imposition of local import taxes. The idea is that anything purchased would be at a lower price than in your home country.

You'll usually find shops clustered in a group, typically in a boulevard-like setting, or arranged around the atrium lobby decks. Brand names are always popular with shoppers looking for something special or a 'bargain' in jewelry and wrist-watch stores. During each cruise, 'special' sales are held – ideal for finding that inexpensive gift for someone, in relative comfort. The shops are not open when the ship is in port, however, due to international regulations.

Families with children

Kids have a whale of a time aboard the large resort ships, and some companies have tie-ins with well-known brand names, including characters from the Walt Disney stable aboard the Disney Cruise Line ships; Dr. Seuss, aboard the Carnival Cruise Line ships; and Lego (think bricks and play walls galore) and Chicco aboard the ships of MSC Cruises. On a port day, there may be fewer activities, but there will still be plenty for the young ones to do, and that leaves parents with more me-time.

Port days

If you decide not to go ashore on a port day (the 'great escape' for most passengers), you'll find you have much of the ship to yourself. Waiting times for popular sports activities will vanish. Selected spa treatments will often offered at a discount. Lines will disappear from the reception desk, the spa, at the self-serve buffet or burger bar. Intrusive revenue announcements will be silenced. The casino and shops will be closed, but you're unlikely to miss them for a day.

If you want a little peace and quiet on the pool deck, however, it might be prudent to ask a pool deck supervisor to turn down the volume of the music. Another benefit: you'll get better, faster service should you need anything, and if you want to book another cruise, the sales desk will be easier to get to.

The colorful pool on board *Navigator of the Seas*.

Choose the Right Ship

What's the difference between large and small ships? Are new ships better than older ones? Here is the low-down to make sure you select the right ship on which to sail away.

There's something to suit virtually all tastes when it comes to which ship to choose. Ships are measured (not weighed) in gross tonnage (GT) and come in four principal sizes (based on lower bed capacity):

Large resort ships: 2,501–6,500 passengers (measure 101,001–230,000 gross tonnage).
Think: double-decker bus (with some seats better than others).

Mid-size ships: 751–2,500 passengers (50,001–101,000 gross tonnage).
Think: long-distance coach (comfortable seats).

Small ships: 251–750 passengers (5,001–50,000 gross tonnage).
Think: mini-van (some are executive types; some are more mainstream).

Boutique ships: 50–250 passengers (1,000–5,000 gross tonnage).
Think: private car (luxury, mid-range, or compact).

Good signage aboard *Celebrity Reflection*.

Space

For an idea of the amount of the personal space around you, check the 'Passenger Space Ratio' given for each ship in the listings section (gross tonnage divided by the number of passengers, based on lower bed capacity.

Passenger space ratio:
51 and above: excellent
31 to 50: very spacious
21 to 30: not very spacious
20 and under: very cramped

Large resort ships (2,501–6,500 passengers)

These ships provide a well-packaged vacation (I call it 'Crowd Cruising'), usually in a seven-day cruise.

However, if you meet someone on the first day and want to meet them again, make it a specific place and time; remember that your new acquaintance may always be at a different meal seating.

It is the standard of service, entertainment, lecture programs, level of communication, and finesse in dining services that can move these ships a few points into higher rating categories. Choose a higher-priced suite and the service improves. In other words: Pay More, Get More (PMGM).

Large resort ships are like supermarket sausages – incredibly homogenous. They are highly programmed. It is difficult, for example, to go for a swim at night – pools are usually netted over by 6pm and sunloungers are stacked and secured, so having Champagne delivered to outdoor hot tubs for a romantic late-night celebration is impossible. The flexibility for which cruise ships were once known has gone – victims of company 'policy,' centralised control, and reliance on interactive digital devices. Welcome to 'conveyor-belt' cruising, with few cultural offerings. Also, because there's 'music' everywhere, take some noise cancelling headphones if you want to read a book in a 'quiet' place.

Mid-size ships (751–2,500 passengers)

These ships suit the smaller ports and are more maneuverable than the large resort ships. Several operate around-the-world cruises and other long-distance itineraries to destinations not really feasible aboard many small ships or large resort ships. It's much easier to find your way around, so less walking is involved, and lines seldom form.

There is a big difference in the amount of space available. Accommodation varies from large 'pent-

Royal Caribbean's mega ship *Harmony of the Seas*.

Advantages and disadvantages of large resort ships	
Advantages	**Disadvantages**
They have the widest range of public rooms facilities and features, often a walk-around promenade deck outdoors, and more space (but more passengers).	Finding your way around the ship can be frustrating, and signage can be confusing.
They generally have more dining options.	The itineraries are limited by ship size, and there may be tender ports where you need to take a number, sit in a lounge, and wait... and wait.
The newest ships have state-of-the-art electronic interactive entertainment facilities.	They are floating hotels – with many announcements – and many cost-extra items. They are like retail parks surrounded by cabins.
You can expect abundant entertainment, including lavish Broadway musicals and Las Vegas-style production shows.	Finding quiet spaces to read a book will be challenging, except in a pay-extra retreat.
There are more facilities and activities for people of all ages, particularly for families with children.	There will be a lack of available elevators at peak times.
Children of all ages will have a whale of a time.	Room-service breakfast is not generally available on the day of disembarkation.
They generally sail well in open seas in bad weather.	You may have to use a sign-up sheet to use fitness equipment like treadmills or exercise bikes.
Announcements could be in several languages.	The restaurant service staff is trained to provide fast service, so it's almost impossible to dine at leisure.
The large choice of cabins means a wide range of price points.	Food is prepared on a large scale – cooking for 5,000 is not quite the same as cooking for a dinner party of eight.
There will be a huge variety of passengers on board – good for socializing.	Telephoning room service can be frustrating due to automatic telephone-answering systems.
Floating malls offer shopping opportunities for clothing, watches, and jewelry.	Expect lines for embarkation, reception, buffet meals, shore excursions, security checkpoints, and disembarkation.
The newest ships have large spas and extensive body-pampering facilities.	Each evening, deckchairs are taken away, or strapped up, so they can't be used.
There are more outdoor aqua park facilities – popular with families.	In-cabin music is typically supplied through the infotainment system; it may be impossible to turn off the picture while listening.
There are large casino gaming facilities.	Some large resort ships have only two main passenger stairways.

Advantages and disadvantages of mid-size ships	
Advantages	**Disadvantages**
They are neither too large, nor too small; their size and facilities often strike a happy balance.	Few mid-size ships have large showlounges for large-scale production shows, so entertainment tends to be more of the cabaret variety.
It is easy to find one's way around.	They don't offer as wide a range of public rooms and facilities as the large resort ships.
They generally sail well in bad weather, being neither high-sided like the large resort ships, nor too shallow draft like some of the small ships.	Most activities will be geared to couples, and solo travelers might feel left out.
Lines seldom form, except on ships approaching 1,600 passengers.	Aboard some ships, bathrooms may be small and cramped.
They appear more like traditional ships than most of the larger vessels, which tend to be more 'boxy' in shape and profile.	There are fewer opportunities for social gatherings.

house suites' with butler service to small interior cabins with no view. These ships will generally be more stable at sea than 'small ships,' due to their increased size and draft. They provide more facilities, more entertainment, and more dining options than smaller ships, although they are principally geared to couples. There is some entertainment but the showlounges are smaller – better for cabaret and small group performances. There are more structured activities than aboard small ships, but less than aboard large resort ships.

Small ships (251–750 passengers) and boutique ships (50–250 passengers)

Choose a small or boutique ship for an intimate cruise experience and fewer fellow passengers.

These are more like small inns than mega-resorts.

Some of the world's most exclusive cruise ships belong in this group – but so do most of the coastal vessels with basic, unpretentious amenities, sail-cruise ships, and the expedition-style cruise vessels that take passengers to see natural wonders and off-the-beaten-track places.

Select this size of ship if you don't need much in the way of entertainment gambling casinos, several restaurants, fitness classes and sports facilities, or waiting in lines for anything. If you want to swim early morning or late evening, or have Champagne in the hot tub at midnight, it's easier aboard boutique or small ships than aboard larger ships, where more rigid programs lead to inflexible, passenger-unfriendly thinking.

Pool deck aboard *Independence of the Seas*.

An illustrated nature talk aboard *National Geographic Explorer*.

Advantages and disadvantages of small ships/boutique ships	
Advantages	**Disadvantages**
Most provide 'open seating' in the dining room; this means that you can sit with whomever you wish, whenever you wish, for all meals.	They don't have the bulk, length, or beam to sail well in open seas in inclement weather conditions.
They provide a totally unstructured lifestyle, offering a level of service not found aboard most of the larger ships, and no – or almost no – announcements.	They don't have the range of public rooms or open spaces that the large resort ships can provide.
They are at their best in warm-weather areas.	Options for entertainment are more limited than on larger ships.
They are capable of offering true culinary excellence, with fresh foods cooked to order.	The cost – this is the upper end of the market, and doesn't come cheap.
They're more like small inns than mega-resorts.	The size of cabin bathrooms (particularly the shower enclosures) is often disappointing.
It's easy to find your way around, and signage is usually clear and concise.	The choice of shore excursion opportunities is more limited.
They provide an 'open bridge' policy, allowing passengers to visit the navigation bridge when it is safe to do so.	Swimming pools will be very small; in fact, they are more like 'dip' pools.
Some small ships have a hydraulic marina water-sports platform at the stern and carry equipment such as jet skis and scuba/snorkeling gear.	Many of the smaller ships do not have balcony cabins because the accommodation decks are too close to the waterline.
They can visit the more off-beat ports of call that larger ships can't.	
When the ship is at anchor, going ashore is easy and speedy, with a continuous tender service and no lines. Access to these less-crowded ports means more exclusivity.	

A game of quoits aboard *Boudicca*.

Most have 'open seating' for dining, so you can sit with whomever you wish, whenever you wish, for meals. Small ships are capable of offering true culinary excellence, with fresh foods cooked to order.

Of course, the smaller the ship, the fewer the facilities and public rooms, and they may not sail as well in open sea conditions; except for the specialist expedition ships, they are best in warm-weather areas. Pools will be small, but some ships carry watersports equipment, launched from an aft platform.

What about age?

A ship's condition depends on the level of maintenance it has received, and whether it has operated on short or longer cruises – short cruises cause more wear and tear. Many passengers like older ships, as they tend to have fewer synthetic materials in their interior decor. It's inevitable that most older ships won't match the latest high-tech hardware, but today's ships aren't built with the same loving care as in the past.

The biggest of the big: ships over 150,000 gross tonnage				
Ship name	**Cruise line**	**Gross tonnage**	**Passengers**	**Year built**
Symphony of the Seas	Royal Caribbean International	228,081	5,488	2018
Harmony of the Seas	Royal Caribbean International	226,963	5,496	2016
Allure of the Seas	Royal Caribbean International	225,282	5,400	2010
Oasis of the Seas	Royal Caribbean International	225,282	5,400	2009
AIDAnova	Aida Cruises	183,900	5,000	2018
Costa Nova	Costa Cruises	183,900	5,200	2019
MSC Grandiosa	MSC Cruises	181,000	4,888	2019
MSC Meraviglia	MSC Cruises	171,598	4,500	2017
MSC Bellissima	MSC Cruises	171,598	4,888	2019
Anthem of the Seas	Royal Caribbean International	168,666	4,180	2015
Odyssey of the Seas	Royal Caribbean	168,666	4,180	2020
Ovation of the Seas	Royal Caribbean	168,666	4,180	2016
Quantum of the Seas	Royal Caribbean International	168,666	4,180	2014
Spectrum of the Seas	Royal Caribbean International	168,666	4,180	2019
Norwegian Bliss	Norwegian Cruise Line	167,800	4,200	2018
Norwegian Escape	Norwegian Cruise Line	165,157	4,266	2015
Norwegian Joy	Norwegian Cruise Line	165,157	3,900	2017
Norwegian Epic	Norwegian Cruise Line	155,873	4,200	2010
Freedom of the Seas	Royal Caribbean International	154,407	3,634	2006
Independence of the Seas	Royal Caribbean International	154,407	3,634	2008
Liberty of the Seas	Royal Caribbean International	154,407	3,634	2007
MSC Seaside	MSC Cruises	153,516	4,134	2017
MSC Seaview	MSC Cruises	153,516	4,134	2018
Genting Dream	Dream Cruises	151,300	3,360	2016
World Dream	Dream Cruises	151,300	3,360	2017

Choose Your Accommodation

From interior cupboard-size cabins to huge suites you can get lost in, there are shipboard living spaces for all wallets, but there's more to it than price tag.

Ideally, you should feel at home when at sea, so it is important to choose the right accommodation, even if most of your time in it is spent with your eyes shut. Choose wisely (dependent on your budget, of course), for if you find that your cabin (incorrectly called a 'stateroom' by some companies) is too small when you get to the ship, it may be impossible to change it, as the ship could be full.

Cruise lines designate cabins only when deposits have been received – they may, however, guarantee the grade and rate requested. If this isn't done, or if you find a disclaimer such as 'All cabin assignments are confirmed upon embarkation of the vessel,' get a guarantee in writing that your cabin will *not* be changed.

There are four principal types of accommodation (although there are many variations on each type, such as those that cater for passengers with mobility issues): interior (no-view or virtual-view) cabins, outside-view cabins with a window, outside-view cabins with a balcony (or virtual balcony), and suites.

Cabin sizes

Cabins provide more or less the same facilities as hotel rooms, except space. Most cruise companies favor providing large public rooms over large cabins.

Today's ships have more standardized cabin sizes, because they are made in modular form. I consider 180 sq ft (16.7 sq m) to be the absolute *minimum* acceptable size for a 'standard' cabin today.

Cabin location

I recommend an 'outside-view' cabin for your first cruise; an 'interior' (no view) cabin has no portholes or windows, making it more difficult to get oriented or to gauge the weather.

Cabins in the ship's center are more stable and tend to be quieter and vibration-free. Ships powered by diesel engines can transmit vibrations at the stern.

Take into account personal habits and needs when choosing your accommodation location. If you like to go to bed early, avoid a cabin close to the disco. If you have mobility issues, choose a cabin close to the elevator.

Generally, the higher the deck, the higher the cabin price, and the better the service (a leftover from transoceanic times, when upper-deck cabins and suites were superior).

Cabins at the front of a ship may be slightly crescent-shaped (outer walls may follow the curvature of the ship's hull).

The suite life

Suites are the most luxurious and spacious of all shipboard accommodation, and typically come with butler service. A suite (in the sense of a 'suite of rooms') should comprise a lounge or sitting room that is separated from a bedroom by a solid door (not just a curtain or half-height room divider), a bedroom with a large bed, one or more bathrooms, and an abundance of walk-in closet, drawer, and other storage space. The best suites are in the most desirable position and are private, have good views, and the highest-quality bed linen and pillow choice. Some cruise lines inaccurately describe their accommodation as suites, but beware, many are nothing more than large cabins with curtains dividing sitting and sleeping areas.

'Private Enclaves' (exclusive areas) have been created by Celebrity Cruises (Celebrity Apex and *Celebrity Edge* only), Dream Cruises (Dream Palace), MSC Cruises (Yacht Club), and Norwegian Cruise Line (The Haven) for occupants of the most expensive suites in an effort to insulate their occupants from

Premium cabin aboard *Marella Discovery*.

STATEROOM VS CABIN EXPLAINED

In the 1830s, the steamer *George Washington* had 26 cabins, and, since there were then 26 states in the United States union, each room was given the name of a state. Since that time, US-based companies have called their cabins 'staterooms.' In most other countries, 'stateroom' means 'rooms of state.'

Seven Seas Explorer suite balcony.

the masses. The result is a 'ship within a ship' (private enclave with key-card access).

However, occupants have to share the rest of the ship with those in lower-priced accommodation, and their luggage will still be lumped with everyone else's.

'Spa suite' accommodation

Spa suites – not to be confused with the 'thermal spa suites' (comprising sauna, steam room, and herbal showers), which are found in the on-board spa – are usually located adjacent to or near the ship's spa. They often have 'spa-added' features such as a bathroom with window into the sleeping area, bathtub, and mood lighting, and perhaps special health teas or herbal infusions. Some cruise lines may even include a spa treatment such as a massage or facial, in the 'spa suite' package, plus unlimited access to the actual spa.

Examples of ships with spa suites include *Celebrity Reflection, Costa Deliziosa, Costa Fascinosa, Costa Favolosa, Costa Luminosa, Costa Pacifica, Costa Serena, Europa, Europa 2, MSC Divina, MSC Fantasia, MSC Preziosa,* and *MSC Splendida*. Some ships also have a spa-food-menu-only restaurant.

10 THINGS A BUTLER CAN DO

1. Assist with unpacking your suitcase
2. Bring you board games or a pack of cards
3. Bring you menus for dining venues and serve course-by-course meals in your suite
4. Arrange a private cocktail party
5. Arrange for laundry/cleaning items
6. Make dining reservations
7. Provide afternoon tea or canapés
8. Book shore excursions
9. Make your spa reservations
10. Shine your shoes

Are balconies worth it?

Romeo and Juliet thought so. And they're addictive, too. A private balcony (or veranda, terrace, or lanai), for which you pay a premium, is just that. It is a mini-terrace adjoining your cabin, where you can sit, enjoy the private view, smell the sea, dine, or have a massage.

Some private balconies aren't so private, though. Balconies not separated by full floor-to-ceiling partitions don't quite cut it (examples include *Carnival Sunshine, Oriana, Pacific Aria, Queen Mary 2, Seven Seas Mariner, Seven Seas Voyager,* and *Veendam*). You could be disturbed by noise from your neighbor.

Many large resort ships have balconies that are too small to accommodate even two reclining chairs; they may have plastic matting or plain painted-steel decking instead of traditional (expensive) hardwood. The average size of a cabin balcony aboard a large resort ship is about 9 by 6ft (2.7x1.8m) or about 55 sq ft (5.1 sq m), but they can measure as much as 30 times that.

Suites with forward-facing private balconies may not be so good, as the wind speed can make them all but unusable. Ships with balconies of this kind include *Silver Cloud, Silver Muse, Silver Shadow, Silver Spirit, Silver Whisper, Silver Wind, Star Legend, Star Pride,* and *Star Spirit*. And when the ship drops anchor in ports of call, the noise pollution can be extremely irritating – as on *Silver Cloud* and *Silver Wind*, for example.

For the best in privacy, a balcony suite aft is hard to beat, and some of the largest afloat can be found there – sheltered from the wind, such as aboard *Marina* and *Riviera* (Oceania Cruises).

Note that having a balcony means that space is often taken away from either the cabin or the bathroom, which is why today's bathrooms are smaller and almost none have bathtubs.

One of the most novel balcony additions can be found aboard the expedition cruise ships *HANSEATIC inspiration* and *HANSEATIC nature*, where two suites have extendable balconies with a solid glass floor so occupants get the sensation of sitting just above the water (and more importantly, space is not taken away from the interior).

All private balconies have railings to lean on, but some have solid steel plates between the railing and deck, so you can't look out to sea when seated (*Costa neoRomantica, Dawn Princess, Grand Classica, Oceana, Sea Princess* and *Sun Princess* are examples). Better are ships with clear-glass balconies (*Aurora, Brilliance of the Seas, Mein Schiff 1, Mein Schiff 3, Mein Schiff 4, Mein Schiff 5, Mein Schiff 6,* and *Radiance of the Seas,* for example) or ones with horizontal bars.

Balcony doors can be heavy and difficult to open. Many ships have doors that slide open (examples: *Crystal Serenity, Grand Princess,* and *Norwegian Gem*); a few have doors that open inward (examples: *Silver Cloud, Silver Wind, Star Breeze, Star Legend,* and *Star Pride*); some have doors that open outward (examples: *Nieuw Amsterdam, Legend of the Seas, Marella Discovery 2, Queen Elizabeth,* and *Queen Victoria*).

Balcony-less balconies

A 'new' type of balcony emerged in 2018, aboard *Celebrity Edge* (but lacking a mosquito screen, so those pesky insects can come and visit you whenever they want!). Copied from riverships in Europe, it consists of floor-to-ceiling windows in two parts, with the upper section lowered by electric touch button. This creates a 'balcony' like space, but it's actually just a large opening window. The advantage is that it doesn't take space away from the cabin and allows the fresh air in. However, it doesn't work for sunbathers, or for anyone wanting to sit on a (real) balcony and have food, or drinks. In other words, they are 'pretend balconies' that just don't work well for ocean-going cruise ships.

French balconies

A 'French' balcony (also called a 'Juliet' or 'Juliette' balcony) is neither French, nor a balcony as such. It is a full floor-to-ceiling sliding door with a tiny ledge that allows you to stick out your toes and smell the fresh air, and with railings for safety.

Interior-view balconies

These are the least expensive balcony options on cruise ships and can be found aboard Royal Caribbean International's *Allure of the Seas, Harmony of the Seas, Oasis of the Seas* and *Symphony of the Seas*. These 'interior' balcony cabins overlook one of two 'neighborhoods': Central Park, with its trees and plants, or The Boardwalk, at the stern of the ship. However, they really are classed as outside balcony cabins – if it rains, your balcony *can* get wet. Also, people scream as they career along the Zipline above the Boardwalk balconies (except on *Harmony of the Seas*), so they can be really noisy

by day. Although, when no one is zipping, you may have a view of the sea (and perhaps the acrobatic AquaShow) at the ship's stern.

Balconies that lack privacy

If you choose a Riviera Deck (Deck 14) balcony cabin aboard *Azura* or *Ventura*, for example, you can oversee many balconies on the decks below yours – particularly those on C Deck and D Deck – because they are built out to the ship's sides. If you have such a cabin, it would be unwise to sunbathe or sit naked on your balcony. Not only that, but almost *all* balcony cabins can be seen from the navigation bridge, where the staff members are equipped with binoculars (for lookout purposes).

Interior 'virtual' balconies

For the latest in interior design, there's the 'virtual' balcony. Royal Caribbean International's *Anthem of the Seas, Ovation of the Seas,* and *Quantum of the Seas* have them, and so do many interior cabins retrofitted on *Navigator of the Seas*. They give the cabins an 'outside' feel, and feature 6ft 7in (2m) 'screens' with a live video feed from cameras mounted on the front and aft of the ship fed through the ship's computer server and fibre-optic cables. With curtains on either side of the (almost) floor-to-ceiling wall 'screen' (which you can turn off), the 'balcony' is positioned on a forward- or aft-facing cabin wall. Naturally, these cabins command a premium price.

Upstairs and downstairs

Allure of the Seas, Anthem of the Seas, Aurora, Celebrity Edge, Harmony of the Seas, Oasis of the Seas, Ovation of the Seas, Quantum of the Seas, Queen Mary 2, and *Symphony of the Seas* have 'loft'-style or 'duplex' accommodation, with a living room downstairs and bedroom upstairs.

Family cabins

Although a small number of large resort ships have suites/cabins that can sleep up to 14, the

10 CABIN LOCATIONS TO AVOID

Avoid booking a cabin in one of the following locations aboard the large resort ships:
1. Cabins under the pool deck (noise is created by people dragging deck chairs, pool party games, and loud music).
2. Cabins under the exterior promenade deck (noise and thumping from people jogging and walking, or moving sun loungers).
3. Cabins under or above late-night venues such as discos and lounges or bars with music.
4. Cabins adjacent to a self-service launderette (due to noise from machines and people).
5. Cabins looking into a central atrium (they won't be very private) and will be subject to

noise from parades, entertainment, and loud music.
6. Cabins with 'obstructed views' (these are often heavily discounted or offered at the last minute and can be noisy).
7. Cabins on a lower deck aft, due to noise from the engines and/or generators.
8. Cabins forward on a lower deck, due to noise from bow thrusters or arrival in tender ports when the anchors are lowered.
9. Cabins with interconnecting doors, due to noise from your neighbors and thin walls.
10. Cabins adjacent to crew or service doorways as these often slam shut.

majority of 'Family' cabins accommodate between 3 and 10, with 3 or 4 being the most common (typically these cabins tend to have twin- or queen-sized beds for the adults, and a pull-out sofa bed for the youngsters). In busy school vacation periods, however, these tend to be sold quickly, so try to plan ahead and book early.

An alternative would be to look for cabins with interconnecting doors – good for parents with teenagers, for example; the door can be locked from both sides.

Solo traveler cabins

Solo travelers have long been considered an afterthought by most cruise lines, although some firms are now beginning to appreciate how useful cabins specifically designed for solo travelers can be. Instead of turning away business, companies such as Cunard have retrofitted their ships with several cabins for solos. Interestingly, the now-retired *Queen Elizabeth 2* (or *QE2*, as she was known) had 132 cabins for solo travelers.

Norwegian Cruise Line has approximately 100 well-designed but small 'studio' cabins for solo travelers aboard *Norwegian Bliss*, *Norwegian Breakaway*, *Norwegian Epic*, *Norwegian Escape*, *Norwegian Getaway*, and *Norwegian Joy*. SAGA is another company known for its numerous solo traveler cabins. Some cruise lines offer their double-occupancy cabins for solo travelers, at a special price or at an added percentage.

If you are traveling with friends and in a party of three or more and don't mind sharing a cabin, you'll save money, so you may be able to afford a higher-grade cabin.

How much?

Accommodation cost is related to size, location, facilities, and services. Each line implements its own system according to ship size, age, construction, and

profit potential. It may be better to book a low-grade cabin on a good ship than a high-grade cabin on a poor ship, depending on your budget.

Cabin numbers

Nautical tradition aboard ocean-going ships dictates that even-numbered cabins should be on the port side (left when looking forward; the same as the lifeboats), and most companies follow this rule.

Some companies – including Celebrity Cruises, MSC Cruises, SAGA Cruises, and TUI Cruises – have odd-numbered cabins on the port side. Strangely, *Costa neoRiviera*, *Costa neoRomantica*, and *Costa Victoria* also have odd-numbered cabins on the port side, although all other Costa ships follow nautical tradition. Meanwhile, aboard Royal Caribbean International's *Freedom of the Seas*, *Independence of the Seas*, and *Liberty of the Seas*, outside cabins have even numbers, and interior cabins have odd numbers. But AIDA Cruises places both even- and odd-numbered cabins on the same side, whether port or starboard side. The admiralty would never approve!

And, so to bed

Aboard ship, the bed frames are usually made of steel or tubular aluminum for fire-protection purposes, although some older ships may have (flame-retardant) wood frames. Some have rounded edges, while others have square edges (watch your legs on these), particularly when the mattress is contained within the bed frame.

Some beds have space underneath for your luggage, while others have drawers fitted for additional storage space, so your luggage has to be stored elsewhere in the cabin.

Mattresses

These can be hard, semi-hard, or soft. If your mattress is not to your liking, ask your cabin steward if it can be changed – most ships have spares. Bed boards are also usually available to make the bed firmer.

Some cruise lines provide simple foam mattresses, while others place more emphasis on providing extra comfort. Regent Seven Seas Cruises, for example, provides a custom-designed 'Suite Slumber Bed' – a plush euro-top mattress capped with a double layer of memory foam and dressed in the finest linens to assure a refreshing sleep.

Ultra-expensive Tempur-Pedic memory mattresses can be found aboard Un-Cruise Adventures (*Safari Endeavor*, *Safari Explorer*, *Safari Legacy*, and *Safari Quest*).

There are differences between mattress sizes in the UK, US, and Europe, depending on which supplier a cruise line specifies when a ship is outfitted or when bed frames and mattresses are replaced.

10 REASONS WHY PEOPLE LIKE BALCONIES

1. You can access fresh air.
2. You can see the sea.
3. You get the maximum amount of natural light.
4. You can have tea/coffee or breakfast outside.
5. You can see what the weather is like, to decide how to dress.
6. You may see the stars (and shooting stars) at night.
7. You can sunbathe in private – assuming that the ship is in the right position and your balcony isn't overlooked.
8. You can escape from the noise of the entertainment areas.
9. You can take pictures of the sea from within your cabin.
10. You can boast about it to your friends.

Duvets

Down duvets, fine bed linens, and plush mattresses are what superior sleeping environments are all about. Duvets are usually goose down or cotton filled, and range from 3.5 togs (thin) to 13.5 togs (thick), the tog rating being the warmth measurement. Anyone with allergies should try a spun down duvet, which is filled with non-allergenic polyester microfiber.

Duvet covers can be for single, double, queen-, or king-size mattresses. If you request a queen-size bed configuration when you book your cruise, request an overlay, otherwise there will be a crack between the beds. Not all ships have these, but the luxury/premium grade ships, and ships with suite-grade accommodation, should do so.

Duvet covers and sheets of 100 percent cotton (up to 400 thread count) are best, but may be more difficult for a ship's laundry to handle. But they do provide those wonderful moments when you slip into bed.

Pillows

Many ships have a 'pillow menu' in suite-grade accommodation. This gives you a choice of several different pillow types, including hop-filled or hypoallergenic, goose down, Hungarian goose down (considered the best), silk-filled, body pillow (as long as an adult body, providing full support at to the head and neck at the top and, lower down, to legs and knees), Tempur-Pedic, isotonic or copy-cat memory foam.

Facilities

The standard is a small private bathroom with shower, washbasin, and toilet. Higher-grade cabins and suites may have full-size bathtubs. Some have a whirlpool bath and/or bidet, a hairdryer, and more space. Most cabins come with the following: flat-screen television 'infotainment' system or regular television (regular satellite channels or closed circuit); two beds (possibly, another one or two upper berths), or a double, queen- or king-size bed (some twin beds can be pushed together to form a double/queen). Depending on cabin size, they should also have: a chair, or chair and table, or sofa and table, or, in higher grades, even a separate lounge/sitting area; telephone (for inter-cabin or ship-to-shore calls); refrigerator/wet bar (higher grades); electrical outlets for personal appliances, usually 110 and/or 220 volts; vanity/desk unit with chair or stool; personal safe; closet space, drawer space, plus under-bed storage for suitcases; bedside night stand/table unit.

Some older ships may have upper and lower berths. A 'berth' is a nautical term for a bed held in a wooden or metal frame. A 'Pullman berth' tucks away out of sight during the day, usually into the bulkhead or ceiling. You climb up a short ladder at night to get into an upper berth.

Spa suite bathroom aboard *Europa*.

Lego Experience on an MSC cruise.

Cruising for Families

Cruising is a great vacation for families, but be sure to choose the right cruise line and ship for your needs.

Well over two *million* under-18s went on a cruise in 2018 – proving just how well cruising suits families with children. Ships provide a virtually crime-free, safe, contained environment, and, for younger kids, there are so many fun things to keep them entertained (particularly on the latest ships); for older children and teens, there's plenty to do, giving them a certain level of independence, which always goes down well. Meanwhile, parents can enjoy vacationing together as a family, and have some well-earned 'me' time. With dining, entertainment, sporting and active outdoor areas, wellness facilities, and more available, it makes it easier to combine with parenting. But planning family vacations can be complicated, with so many things to think about. Here's what you need to know.

Family-friendly ships

It goes without saying that you need to choose the right ship. The newest large resort ships have excellent facilities for children of all ages, plus water parks with adrenaline-pumping waterslides, rope-climbing courses, and other neat things.

Carnival Cruise Line, Disney Cruise Line, Dream Cruises, MSC Cruises, Norwegian Cruise Line, Princess Cruises, and Royal Caribbean International employ teams of trained counselors, with special programs off-limits to adults. Other cruise lines may only have token programs in major holidays only, with limited activities and only a few general staff allocated to look after children. Check whether the cruise line offers the right facilities for your needs at other times. Many ships have full programs for children during days at sea, but these may be limited when the ship is in port. If the ship has a playroom, ask if it is open and supervised on every day of the cruise. All programs are included in the cost of your cruise.

Carnival Cruise Line, Disney Cruise Line, MSC Cruises, Norwegian Cruise Line, Princess Cruises, and Royal Caribbean International provide pagers (or wrist bands) for parents; others provide them only for special-needs children. In-cabin telephones aboard some ships can be set to 'in-cabin listening,' allowing parents to call their cabin from any of the ships' telephones and eavesdrop.

Most cruise lines give children colored bracelets, to be worn at all times. These identify which muster station they belong to in the event of an emergency, as well as showing which children are enrolled in which activity programs.

Some youth programs allow older children to sign themselves out of youth centers, if authorized to do so by a parent. This makes it easy for children to meet family members somewhere – by the pool or restaurant, for example – or the cabin. If authorization isn't granted, only designated adults can sign them out of programs, typically by showing some ID or by providing a password created at the beginning of the cruise.

Disney Cruise Line, Norwegian Cruise Line and Royal Caribbean International provide trained lifeguards during pool open hours. Other cruise lines expect parents to watch their children when using a ship's swimming pools – in 2015, an eight-year-old boy drowned in the pool aboard *Liberty of the Seas*.

Note that a ship's medical department isn't set up for pediatric services (cruise ship doctors are generalists).

Aboard one of the ships catering to more international passengers, such as Costa Cruises, Dream Cruises, MSC Cruises, or Star Cruises, your youngsters may find themselves surrounded by children

The Epic Plunge waterslide on board *Norwegian Epic*.

speaking other languages. This might be a little confusing to them at first, but in most cases, it will prove to be an adventure in learning and communication that adds immensely to their vacation.

Age groups

Cruise lines generally divide young cruisers into distinct age groups. As an example: infants (3 months–up to 3 years); children (3–10); pre-teens (11–12); and teens (13–17).

Cruising with babies and infants

Many new or recent parents want to take their babies with them when they cruise. Check the minimum age requirements for your chosen cruise line and itinerary; they vary according to the cruise, length, and region. By choosing the right ship, a cruise with baby should hopefully be much more enjoyable than most package holidays on land. The biggest attractions include only having to pack and unpack the baby things once, plus the convenience of having everything (food, entertainment, activities, etc.) absolutely on hand. There may also be a crèche/nursery (see below), plus there's always room service, if you prefer to dine in your cabin.

Bottle warmers are available for babies, as are bottle sterilizers – upon request – so there's no need to bring your own. Highchairs are also available upon request for meal times. For babies already on solids, menu items can be pureed and blended for them.

Check the ship's itinerary to see whether the vessel docks alongside in each port. This is easier than being at anchor, when shore tenders must be used; these may require you to go down a rigged ladder to a small boat waiting to take you ashore, which is not easy with an infant in tow.

Check with the cruise line or your booking agent before you book as to what equipment is available, and whether any of it needs to be pre-booked (a refrigerator for milk, for example). Some cruise ships will lend you cribs, strollers (some charge a rental fee), bouncy seats, books, toys, cots, bed guards, and other items.

An inexpensive umbrella-type stroller is invaluable in airports, aboard ship (Carnival Cruise Line offers them for rent aboard ship), and ashore. Small is better because it takes up less space in cabins, elevators, and self-serve buffet areas. It will be easier to maneuver at the cruise terminal, and for negotiating open deck areas.

Consider taking a car seat for flights, buses, and taxis, and a sling-style baby carrier for hands-free baby carrying when negotiating stairways, and for shore outings.

Request a crib as soon as possible and book as early (ships carry only a limited number). However, while it's fine to order cribs and camp beds, you'll soon find there's little room to move about, so book as large a cabin as your budget allows. If you have a non-walker, consider a balcony cabin to give you more breathing space – you can relax on the balcony, while your infant naps in the cabin.

Disposable diapers (nappies), wipes, and sterilizing fluid can be purchased aboard most family-friendly ships, but they are expensive, so it's wise to bring your own supplies. If you book a Disney Cruise Line ship, you can order diapers and other products

SUGGESTED PACKING LISTS FOR INFANTS

Traveling by plane? Suggested items for your carry-on bag:
Diapers (or pull-ups) and changing pad.
Antibacterial wipes (take plenty).
Snacks.
Drinks (small).
Small toys and books to keep your infant happy.
Pacifiers and bibs (if your child uses them).
A camera (or smartphone).

Suggested items for your checked luggage:
Diapers/pull-ups, deodorized disposal bags, and wipes, if your child is not potty-trained.
Any toiletries your infant may need, including special baby soap and shampoo (these are not provided by cruise lines), lotions, sunscreen, toothbrush, and toothpaste.
Outlet plugs for childproofing.
Clothes.
Bibs.
Pacifiers.
First-aid kit and any medication such as pain relievers, fever reducers, and the name and contact

details of your infant's pediatrician (for comfort).
Plastic bags for any snacks for shore excursions.
Ziplock bags – useful for soiled clothing.
Portable potty seat (if your infant is potty-trained).
Swim diapers.
Swim vest: make sure it's of an approved type.
Sunglasses and sun hat (if your cruise is in or to a warm weather area).
Bottles and sip cups: cruise lines don't provide these. They can be washed in your cabin, so a little dish detergent and bottle brush could be useful.
Formula: ready-to-feed variety is convenient but bulky. Alternatively, bring powder and buy bottled mineral water from the ship's bar (a more expensive option).
Utensils.
Inflatable toys such as beach balls and zoo animals are inexpensive and easy to pack (you won't be able to borrow toys from the ship's playroom).
Picture books to keep baby amused.

online at www.babiestravellite.com. These will be delivered to your cabin.

As for laundry, it's best to use the self-service launderette, if your ship has one – not all do, so check before booking. Pack all-detergent sheets (they are easier to transport than liquid detergent). Many ships offer laundry 'bundles' (either a set number of items, or all-you-can-bundle into a provided laundry sack), depending on the cruise line, for a set price.

You'll need to look after your child the whole time unless you choose a ship with a proper nursery and qualified staff to look after infants. Ships with a nursery for ages six months to 36 months include: *Allure of the Seas, Anthem of the Seas, Disney Dream, Disney Fantasy, Disney Magic, Disney Wonder, Harmony of the Seas, Oasis of the Seas, Quantum of the Seas, Spectrum of the Seas, and Symphony of the Seas*. Ships with a free night nursery include: *Azura, Britannia, Iona, Oceana, Queen Elizabeth, Queen Mary 2, Queen Victoria,* and *Ventura*.

Children under three years old need to be potty-trained to take part in any group activities. Check with the cruise line whether babies and infants are allowed in paddling and swimming pools, and whether they must wear swim diapers.

Note that you may have to bathe infants/small children in a cabin with a small shower enclosure, possibly with a fixed-head shower; choosing a cabin with a bathtub makes it easier to do bathtime. Some ships (e.g. those of Costa Cruises) have baby baths available. Make sure you have adequate medical insurance, and take your infant's medical information in case of an emergency.

Minimum age accepted

It's important to check the minimum age requirements for your chosen cruise line and itinerary, because they can vary according to the cruise, length, and region. Here's our list of 12 principal cruise lines and the minimum age allowed for sailing, which was correct at time of going to press.

Carnival Cruise Line
Minimum sailing age: 6 months (12 months on transatlantic, Hawaii, and South America cruises).

Celebrity Cruises
Minimum sailing age: 6 months (12 months for transatlantic and transpacific, and some South America cruises).

Costa Cruises
Minimum sailing age: 6 months.

Cunard
Minimum sailing age: 6 months (some sailings); 12 months for transatlantic and transpacific crossings, world cruise segments, and Hawaii cruises.

Disney Cruise Line
Minimum sailing age: 3 months.

Dream Cruises

In the It's A Small World Nursery aboard *Disney Dream*.

Minimum sailing age: 6 months (note: any child whose travel document is attached to the parent's passport must travel with the accompanying parent).

Holland America Line
Minimum sailing age: 12 months.

MSC Cruises
Minimum sailing age: 3 months.

Norwegian Cruise Line
Minimum sailing age: 6 months.

P&O Cruises
Minimum sailing age: 6 months (12 months for transatlantic cruises) aboard the family-friendly ships *Azura, Britannia, Oceania,* and *Ventura*.

Princess Cruises
Minimum sailing age: 6 months.

Royal Caribbean International
Minimum sailing age: 6 months for many itineraries; 12 months for any cruises with three or more sea days, and for all transatlantic, transpacific, Hawaii, and South Pacific cruises.

Babysitting

If you take baby (or babies) along, and you want some time to yourself, you'll need the services of a babysitter. Some, but not all, ships have babysitting services; some have restricted hours (meaning you'll need to be back by midnight like a grown-up Cinderella); and some have group babysitting, not in-cabin care. In some ships, stewards, stewardesses, and other staff may be available as private babysitters for an hourly charge. For example, *Queen Mary 2* has children's nurses and English nannies. *Azura, Oceana,* and *Ventura* have a 'night nursery' for two- to five-year-olds.

Feeding infants under three

Selected baby foods are stocked by ships catering to infants, but ask your booking agent to get confirmation in writing that they'll be provided. Some cruise lines may even mash food up for your child, if you ask. If you need a special brand of baby food, advise your booking agent well in advance, or bring your own. Parents providing organic baby foods, such as those obtained from health-food stores, should be aware that cruise lines buy their supplies from general food suppliers and not from the smaller specialized food houses. You may need to check in advance whether the ship has whole or soy milk available, for example.

Cruising with children ages 3–10

Assuming that they don't get seasick, children of this age should love cruising. They love to get involved right from the planning stages, learning how big the ship is, what facilities it has on board, etc. All very exciting!

One thing to note – if your budget allows, and you think your young children will be happy at sea for this long – is that it's best to avoid cruises of fewer than seven days, because they tend to attract the party-going types out for a good time.

Once on board, go to the children's clubs and sign in your youngsters – you need to give their name, cabin number, and details of allergies to any foods or materials (this typically applies up to an age according to cruise line). You'll probably be given a pager in case you need instant contact. Children's activities are mostly about team participation events, so they may seem highly programmed to some youngsters used to getting their own way.

In addition to the clubs, there are plenty of other facilities on deck that will appeal to children of this age, from aqua parks to chill-out rooms to sports activities such as rope courses. Most large resort ships close their pools at 6pm, although MSC Cruises are exceptions to this – aboard *MSC Preziosa*, for example, a large, covered family pool is open until 9pm.

Disney goes cruising

In 1998, Disney Cruise Line introduced the first of two large resort ships for families with children, with cruises of three, four, and seven days. *Disney Magic* and *Disney Wonder* were joined by *Disney Dream* in 2011 and by *Disney Fantasy* in 2012. The casino-free ships have ambitious entertainment programs, all centered around Disney and its stable of famous characters. Disney has its own Art Deco passenger terminal at Port Canaveral, Florida, plus a fleet of special motorcoaches.

Each ship carries over 40 children's and youth counselors, plus lifeguards at the family pool. Families preparing to sail with toddlers under three can access an online service to order baby supplies in advance of their cruise and have them delivered to their cabin. The service, exclusive to Disney Cruise Line, is provided by Babies Travel Lite (www.babiestravellite.com), an online retailer with more than 1,000 brand-name baby products including diapers, baby food, infant formula, and specialty travel items. The ships sail in the Caribbean, the Bahamas, Alaska, the Mediterranean, and the Baltic. Disney calls at its own 1,000-acre (405-hectare) private island on Bahamas

Rock-climbing is a popular onboard activity for teenage travelers.

and Caribbean cruises – about 50 miles (80km) north of Nassau in the Bahamas, Castaway Cay has its own ship-docking pier. Locals say it had been a military landing strip that was once used by drug runners. Beaches are divided into family-friendly and adults-only 'quiet' sections.

Barbie is aboard

Royal Caribbean International and Mattel have free Barbie-related activities in the Adventure Ocean youth club, plus an additional cost 'Barbie Premium Experience,' with pink cabin decorations, a Barbie doll blanket, tote bag and toothbrush, special tea with pink cupcakes and dainty dishes, and a mermaid dance class featuring dances from the movie *Barbie in a Mermaid Tale 2*, among other perks.

Dr. Seuss is aboard too

Not to be outdone, Carnival Cruise Line's 'Seuss at Sea' program has an array of immersive youth, family, dining, and entertainment experiences featuring the amazing world and words of Dr. Seuss. Main dining rooms aboard each ship feature 'The Green Eggs and Ham Breakfast' with the Cat in the Hat and Friends. Children (parents can go too) can eat playful foods from Dr. Seuss's imagination, notably green eggs and ham, moose juice, goose juice, fruit and pancake stacks, funky French toast, and more. (Note that traditional breakfast favorites are also available.) Dining room staff members wear Dr. Seuss-inspired uniforms, and characters such as the

Basketball fun aboard a Carnival ship.

Cat in the Hat, Thing One and Thing Two, and Sam join families at their tables for interaction and photo opportunities. This takes place on the first sea day of each cruise (cost: $5 per person).

Also, there are Dr. Seuss-themed toys, games, and arts and crafts activities. Some ships have a Dr. Seuss Bookville Seuss-themed play space with iconic decor, colors, shapes, and funky furniture, where families can relax. And movies such as *The Cat in the Hat* and Dr. Seuss's *How the Grinch Stole Christmas* are shown outdoors on Lido Deck Seaside Theater screens.

Carnival also introduced 'Seuss-a-Palooza Story Time,' an interactive reading event that brings the characters of Dr. Seuss to life. It usually takes place inside a tent on the main showlounge stage on a sea day. There may also be a Character Parade with Dr. Seuss characters along the Promenade, and themed retail items are also for sale.

Cruising with older children (pre-teens 11–12)

Some cruise lines provide extra attention for the 'Tweens.' Supervised group activities and activity/play centers mean that parents won't have to be concerned, and will be able to enjoy themselves, knowing that their children are in good hands, enrolled in special programs. Activities typically include make-up and cookery classes, arts and crafts projects, group games, interactive computer programs, character parades and scavenger hunts, and watching movies and video wall programming. Then there are the outdoor activities such as waterslides, miniature golf, and swimming and other sports events for the pre-teens.

Cruising with teenagers (13–17)

Teens love cruising, too, and many large resort ships have dedicated 'no adults allowed' zones and chill-out rooms. Teens-only activities include deck parties, pool parties, sports tournaments, poolside games, karaoke, discos, dances, computer games,

---

SAFETY TIPS AT SEA

In case children get lost or separated from their parents, most cruise lines provide them with colored wristbands, which must be worn at all times. Disney Cruise Line has 'Mickey Bands' – magic bracelets that use radio tracking to locate the exact whereabouts of children at any time.

Young children love to climb, so don't ever leave them on a balcony alone. On the open decks, ships have railings – these are either horizontal bars through which children cannot get their heads, or they are covered in glass/plexiglass under a thick wooden top rail.

It's a good idea to walk your children between your cabin and the playroom/activity center, so that all of you are familiar with the route.

Discuss safety issues with your kids, and, with youngsters who are old enough to read, warn them not to walk into 'Crew Only' areas at any time.

Children's lifejackets are available aboard most cruise ships that carry children. However, check your cabin as soon as you embark. If no child's or infant's life vests are provided, see your steward right away.

Junior chefs of Princess Cruises.

video arcades, activity clubs, and talent shows. Some ships provide musical instruments for jam sessions (Royal Caribbean International, for example). Sports activities include rock-climbing, rollerblading, basketball, and riding the wave surfer.

With some cruise lines the fun can extend ashore, with beach barbecues, 'chill out' and sports events. There's usually almost unlimited food, too, although some of it may not be very nutritious.

Choosing the right cabin

Cruise lines know that 'families who play together want to stay together.' Although connecting cabins and Pullman beds are nothing new on family-friendly ships, brands such as Disney Cruise Line, Norwegian Cruise Lines, and Royal Caribbean International have taken group-friendly accommodations more seriously than some others.

Families cruising together often find that sharing a confined space causes distress. It's best to choose the largest accommodation option you can afford. Before booking, check the size of the cabin and pace it out at home, remembering that the size quoted on ship deck plans includes the bathroom. If you have a large or extended family, cabins with interconnecting doors may be the most practical option.

Certain ships may work best for certain age groups. For example, multigenerational groups might consider large resort ships such as Royal Caribbean International's *Allure of the Seas, Harmony of the Seas, Oasis of the Seas* or *Symphony of the Seas*, or Disney Cruise Line ships thanks to their wide range of facilities and eateries.

If you are a large or extended family, some ships (such as those of Norwegian Cruise Line) have family cabins and suites that can sleep up to 14. Larger cabins or suites simply have more space than standard cabins and may include sofa beds.

If you are traveling with teens, consider booking them an adjoining cabin or one across the hallway from yours. You get your own space, your teens will have their own bathroom and privacy, and you give them freedom, but at arm's length. If your children are younger, a cabin with an interconnecting door is a good option, if the budget allows. Many ships have cabins with two lower beds and one or two upper berths. In some cabins, the two lower beds can't be pushed together to form a queen-size bed for parents. This means mom and dad and one or two children all have separate beds. Some ships, such as *Disney Dream, Disney Fantasy, Disney Magic, Disney Wonder, Europa 2, Norwegian Bliss, Norwegian Breakaway, Norwegian Epic, Norwegian Escape, Norwegian Getaway,* and *Norwegian Joy* have cabins with two bathrooms, and a privacy curtain to screen off your youngsters.

Dependent on how young your children are (and how safe you feel this would be), you might like to opt for a cabin with a balcony. An interior (no-view) cabin may be adequate for a short cruise, but could be claustrophobic on a longer one. To get access to fresh air without a balcony, you'd have to keep trudging up to the open deck, carrying towels and other paraphernalia. However, if you don't anticipate spending much time in your cabin, an interior (no-view) cabin is cheaper, although the storage space limitations may prove frustrating.

Children's fares

Children under two travel free with many cruise lines and airlines. Most cruise lines offer special rates for children sharing their parents' cabin. The cost is often lower than third and fourth person share rates.

Although many adult cruise rates include airfare, most children's rates don't. Also, although some lines say children sail 'free,' they must pay port taxes as well as airfare.

Dining with children

Flexibility is the key. Coaxing children out of a pool and getting them dressed and ready to sit quietly through a four-course dinner every night can be tough. Work out a compromise by eating dinner together occasionally at the buffet. Most ships offer a tempting menu of children's favorites as well as special mealtimes for children.

Children with special needs

If a child has special needs, advise the cruise line before you book. Children needing one-to-one care or assistance must be accompanied by a parent or guardian when in the children's play center.

Practical matters: passports

Note that separate passports are required for all children traveling internationally. If you have an *adopted* child, you may also need Adoption Placement Papers, as well as the child's Birth Certificate.

Confirming a guardian's identity

A Parent and Guardian Consent Form (PGCSA) will be needed at or before embarkation, if you are a parent, grandparent, or guardian with a passport surname different from that of any child traveling with you. Without this form, which includes passport information of the child's legal parent, you will be denied boarding. Check with your cruise provider if you are unclear.

Single parents

A few cruise lines have introduced their versions of the 'Single Parent Plan' (e.g., Disney Cruise Line, P&O Cruises). This offers an economical way for single parents to take their children on a cruise, with a parent and one child sharing a two-berth cabin, or a parent with more children sharing a three- or four-berth cabin.

As a single parent with just one child, you may have to pay for two adults (double occupancy), so it's important to check the pricing policy of each cruise line you're interested in. It may also be better to take an adult friend and share the cost (in some cases, your child could travel free).

Family reunions and birthdays

A cruise can provide the ideal place for a family get-together, with or without children, and, because it's an almost all-inclusive vacation, you won't have to haggle about who pays for the extras.

With pricing that includes accommodation, meals, entertainment, use of most of the ship's recreational facilities, and travel to various destinations, a cruise represents very good value for money. Cruise lines

also make special offers to groups. Let your travel agent make the arrangements, and ask for a group discount if there are more than 15 of you.

Family groups may have the option to ensure even greater value by purchasing everything in advance, from cruise fares to shore excursions, drinks packages, spa packages, and pre-paid gratuities. Additional savings can be realized through reduced fares for third and fourth passengers in each cabin, and some cruise lines offer 'kids sail free' programs.

Formal nights

Some ships have nights when traditional 'formal attire' is the suggested dress code. If you don't want your children to dress formally (although some children really enjoy getting dressed up – it's a bit like going to a birthday party or prom night), you can opt out of the festivities, and simply head for one of the casual dining options instead. Or your kids may prefer to opt out and go to the children's clubs or teen rooms and hang out while you go to the captain's cocktail party.

Tips for cruising with children

Take wet wipes for those inevitable clothes stains, and anti-bacterial hand wipes and face wipes to keep you cool when it's hot outside.

Take a highlighter pen – good for marking the daily program and shore excursion literature, so you can focus on what's important to you and the children.

Take an extension cord or power strip (although note that not all cruise lines allow them), because there will be plenty of things to plug in (chargers for games consoles, cell (mobile) phone, and iPod/iPad, etc.). Most cabins provide only one electrical outlet.

SHIPS THAT CATER WELL FOR CHILDREN

These ships have been selected for the quality of their children's programs and facilities:
Aida Cruises: *AIDAnova, AIDAperla, AIDAprima*
Carnival Cruise Line: *Carnival Breeze, Carnival Dream, Carnival Freedom, Carnival Horizon, Carnival Magic, Carnival Splendor, Carnival Vista*
Celebrity Cruises: *Celebrity Apex, Celebrity Eclipse, Celebrity Edge, Celebrity Equinox, Celebrity Reflection, Celebrity Solstice*
Costa Cruises: *Costa Deliziosa, Costa Diadema, Costa Fascinosa, Costa Favolosa, Costa Fortuna, Costa Luminosa, Costa Magica, Costa Pacifica, Costa Serena*
Cunard: *Queen Mary 2*
Disney Cruise Line: *Disney Dream, Disney Fantasy, Disney Magic, Disney Wonder*
Dream Cruises: *Genting Dream, Explorer Dream, World Dream*
MSC Cruises: *MSC Bellissima, MSC Divina, MSC*

Fantasia, MSC Preziosa, MSC Meraviglia, MSC Seaside, MSC Seaview, MSC Splendida
Norwegian Cruise Line: *Norwegian Bliss, Norwegian Breakaway, Norwegian Epic, Norwegian Encore, Norwegian Escape, Norwegian Getaway, Norwegian Joy*
P&O Cruises: *Azura, Britannia, Iona, Ventura*
Princess Cruises: *Majestic Princess, Regal Princess, Royal Princess, Sky Princess*
Royal Caribbean International: *Adventure of the Seas, Allure of the Seas, Anthem of the Seas, Explorer of the Seas, Freedom of the Seas, Harmony of the Seas, Independence of the Seas, Liberty of the Seas, Mariner of the Seas, Navigator of the Seas, Oasis of the Seas, Ovation of the Seas, Quantum of the Seas, Spectrum of the Seas, Symphony of the Seas, Voyager of the Seas*
TUI Cruises: *Mein Schiff 1, Mein Schiff 2, Mein Schiff 3, Mein Schiff 4, Mein Schiff 5, Mein Schiff 6*

Ropes course aboard *Norwegian Breakaway*.

A pop-up laundry basket could prove useful for keeping everyone's dirty laundry separate from clean items (really useful in small cabins).

Refillable water bottles (empty until you are on board ship) are useful for shore excursions, beach days, and other outings.

Take lots of high-factor sunscreen (SPF50 or above).

A set of walkie-talkie radios can prove useful for keeping track of everyone's whereabouts – if everyone remembers to turn them on!

Glow sticks – kids love them – for use as night lights (they are cheap and come in different colors – one for each night).

Shore excursions

Note that shore excursions in the Caribbean and Alaska are expensive for children – in fact, almost the same prices as for adults. Many cruise ships in the Caribbean visit a 'private' island for a day. Lifeguards will be on duty at assigned swimming locations. Operators take advantage of the captive market, so rental of beach and water-sports items can be expensive.

It's best not to book a long shore excursion if you have an infant, unless you know that they (and you!) can handle it. Diaper-changing facilities are likely to be limited (and non-existent on buses).

Can you cruise when pregnant?

In 2010, a 30-year-old woman on a four-night Baja cruise aboard *Carnival Paradise* gave birth on board to a premature baby. In 2016, a woman who gave birth three weeks early, one day before the ship berthed in Brooklyn, called her baby Benjamin Brooklyn.

It can happen. If your pregnancy is routine and healthy, there's no reason not to go on a cruise. Indeed, a cruise could be a great getaway before you deal with the things associated with an upcoming childbirth. First, ask about any restrictions imposed by your chosen cruise line. Some cruise lines may let you sail even in your 27th week of pregnancy (as in the second case above), but most will not accept you from your 24th week onwards. You may be required to produce a doctor's note. (It is advisable to check with your doctor or midwife that you are safe to travel, prior to sailing, anyway.)

Be sure to purchase travel insurance that will cover you for last-minute cancellation and medical treatment due to pregnancy complications, both on board and in ports of call.

How grandparents can bridge the generation gap

Many children love to go cruising with grandparents, perhaps because they anticipate fewer restrictions than they have at home. And busy parents like the idea, too, particularly if the grandparents make a contribution to the cost and offer the possibility of a rest.

Having enrolled their grandchildren in age-related groups for daytime activities aboard ship (note the limitations on activities for children under three, as mentioned above), grandparents will be able to enjoy the adults-only facilities, such as the wellness and spa treatments. Not surprisingly, it's the large resort ships that provide the widest choice of facilities for both age groups. For those not averse to ubiquitous cartoon characters, Disney Cruise Line provides some facilities for adults and children in separate areas, but also allows them to mix in others.

Before you leave home

Grandparents should remember that, in addition to their grandchildren's passports, they should also bring along a letter signed by the parent authorizing any necessary medical attention. A Parent and

SHIPS THAT CATER BEST TO INFANTS

Disney Cruise Line: *Disney Dream, Disney Fantasy, Disney Magic, Disney Wonder*
MSC Cruises: *MSC Bellissima, MSC Divina, MSC Fantasia, MSC Grandiosa, MSC Meraviglia, MSC Preziosa, MSC Seaside, MSC Seaview, MSC Splendida*
P&O Cruises: *Azura, Britannia, Iona, Ventura*
Royal Caribbean International: *Allure of the Seas, Harmony of the Seas, Oasis of the Seas, Ovation of the Seas, Quantum of the Seas, Spectrum of the Seas, Symphony of the Seas*

A family goes snorkeling in the Caribbean.

Guardian Consent Form (PGCSA) will be needed at or before embarkation, if you are a grandparent (or parent or guardian) with a passport surname different from that of any child traveling with you. Check with your cruise provider about this.

Ground rules should be established with a child's parent(s) present to avoid potential problems. An important issue is whether a child will be allowed to roam the ship unsupervised, given that some cruise lines allow children as young as eight to sign themselves out of supervised programs. Walkie-talkies are a good solution to this issue. They work well aboard ships, and allow adults and children to stay in constant touch.

On board

Most cruise lines offer scheduled activities from 9am to noon, 2–5pm, and 7–10pm. This means you can drop your grandchild off after breakfast, relax by the pool, go to a lecture, or take part in other activities, and pick them up for lunch. After a couple of hours together, they can rejoin their friends, while you enjoy an afternoon movie or siesta.

Shore excursions

Consider your grandchild's interests before booking expensive shore excursions (example: flightseeing in Alaska). It's also best to avoid long bus rides, shopping trips, and scenic tours, and better to choose excursions that feature water and/or animals. Exam-

ples include snorkeling, aquariums, or nature walks. Remember to pack snacks. In some ports, it may be better to explore on your own. If your grandchildren are really young, full-day shore excursions are a probably bad idea.

5 GREAT SPLASH-TASTIC WATERSLIDES

Waterslides are always a highlight for youngsters, who can't wait to go for a ride once they are on board.
Aquaduck (Disney Cruise Line)
This waterslide is four decks high and extends over the edge of the ship – scary. You'll find it on *Disney Dream* and *Disney Fantasy*.
Epic Plunge (Norwegian Cruise Line)
This waterslide will have your youngsters doing the loop-de-loop down a long slide that ends in – surprise, surprise – a nice big splash.
Kaleid-O-Slide (Carnival Cruise Line)
This waterslide ends in a giant funnel that swirls you around and spits you out with a splash! You'll find it on Carnival's newest ship and *Carnival Vista*.
Caesar's Slide (Dream Cruises)
The half-million-dollar stainless steel waterslide aboard *Explorer Dream* starts 34.5ft (10.5m) above the deck and swirls and swoops through over 328ft (100m) before emptying out into a water break.

Cruising for Solo Travelers

Cruise prices are geared toward couples. Yet about one in four cruise passengers travels alone or as a single parent. How do they fare?

Cruising, in general, is designed for couples. Many solo passengers feel that cruising penalizes them, because most lines charge them a solo-occupancy supplement. The reason is that the most precious commodity aboard any ship is space. Since a solo-occupancy cabin is often as large as a double and is just as expensive to build, cruise lines feel the premium price is justified. What's more, because solo-occupancy cabins are at a premium, they are less likely to be discounted.

Solo supplements

If you are not sharing a cabin, you'll be asked to pay either a flat rate or a solo 'supplement' to occupy a double-occupancy cabin by yourself. Some lines charge a fixed amount as a supplement, regardless of the cabin category, ship, itinerary, or length of cruise. Since there are so few solo-occupancy cabins, it's best to book as far ahead as you can. One notable exception is Norwegian Cruise Line, whose *Norwegian Bliss*, *Norwegian Breakaway*, *Norwegian Epic*, *Norwegian Escape*, *Norwegian Getaway* and Norwegian Joy all have a pleasant

Cunard provides social dance hosts.

section with Studio cabins – small, but popular for solo cruisers.

Some cruise lines charge low solo supplements on selected voyages. Saga Cruises has no additional supplements for solo travelers on any cruise, but offers special fares. Look out for sneaky cruise lines that may try to charge you *twice* for port charges and government taxes by including that non-existent second person in the cabin you occupy as a solo traveler – check your final invoice carefully.

Guaranteed solo traveler rates

Some lines offer solo travelers a set price for a double cabin but reserve the right to choose the cabin. This means that you could end up with a rotten cabin in a poor location or a wonderful cabin that happened to be unallocated.

Guaranteed share programs

These allow you to pay what it would cost each half of a couple for a double-occupancy cabin, but the cruise line will find another passenger of the same gender (and with preferences such as smoking or non-smoking) to share it with you. If the line doesn't find a cabin-mate, a solo traveler may have the cabin to themselves at no extra charge. Some cruise lines don't advertise a guaranteed share program in their brochures but they will often try to accommodate such bookings at times when demand for space is comparatively light.

Solo dining

A common irritation concerns dining arrangements. Before your cruise, make sure that you request a table assignment based on your personal preferences; table sizes are typically for two, four, six, or eight. Do you want to sit with other solo travelers? Or do you like to sit with couples? Or is a mixture of both ok? And are you happy to sit with passengers who might not speak your language?

When on board, make sure you are comfortable with the dining arrangements, particularly in ships with fixed table assignments, or request a move to a different table. Aboard ships with open seating or other dining venues, you can choose which venue you want to eat in, and when.

Cruising for women traveling solo

A cruise ship is as safe for women as any major vacation destination. It may not, of course, be entirely hassle-free, but it should not be a 'meat market' that keeps you under constant observation.

If you enjoy meeting other solo travelers the easiest way is to participate in scheduled activities. However, beware of embarking on an affair with a ship's officer or crew member, as you may not be the only one to have done so.

Gentlemen cruise hosts

The female-to-male passenger ratio is typically high, especially among older people, so some cruise lines provide male social hosts. They may host a table in the dining room, appear as dance partners at cocktail parties and dance classes, join bridge games, and accompany women on shore excursions.

These men, usually over 55 and retired, are outgoing, mingle easily, and are well groomed. First introduced aboard Cunard's *QE2* in the mid-1970s, gentlemen dance hosts are now employed by a number of cruise lines, including Crystal Cruises, Cunard, Holland America Line, Regent Seven Seas Cruises, and Silversea Cruises.

If you think you'd like such a job, do remember that you'll have to dance for several hours most nights, and be proficient in just about every kind of dance.

A DJ keeps youthful late-night clubbers dancing.

OPTIONS FOR LGBTQ TRAVELERS

Several US companies specialize in ship charters or large group bookings for gay and lesbian passengers. These include the California-based Atlantis (www.atlantisevents. com), San Francisco's lesbian specialist Olivia (www.olivia.com), or New York's Pied Piper Travel (www.piedpipertravel.com).

In 2018, an LGBT Getaways Cruise took place aboard *Celebrity Silhouette*, organized by Cruises Inc., CruiseOne, and Dream Vacations (US companies). One drawback of LGBTQ whole-ship charters is that they're as much as 20 percent more expensive than the equivalent general cruise. Another is that they have been greeted with hostility by religious objectors on some Caribbean islands such as Grand Cayman, Jamaica, and Bermuda. One Atlantis cruise was even denied the right to dock. But their advantage is that they provide an accepting environment and LGBTQ-oriented entertainment, with some big-name comedians and singers.

Another idea is to join a LGBTQ affinity group on a regular cruise at normal prices; these groups may be offered amenities such as private dining rooms and separate shore excursions.

If you are concerned that on a mainstream cruise you might be seated for dinner with unsympathetic companions, opt for a cruise line offering 'open-choice seating' (where you sit where you want, when you want at dinner, and you can change time you dine), for example Carnival Cruise Line, Celebrity Cruises, Holland America Line, Norwegian Cruise Line, Princess Cruises, and Royal Caribbean International (request this option when you book). That doesn't mean that any of the major cruise companies are not LGBTQ-friendly – many have regular 'Friends of Dorothy' gatherings, sometimes scheduled and sometimes on request – though it would be prudent to realize that Disney Cruise Line, for example, will not really offer the ideal entertainment and ambience. Among the smaller companies, Windstar's ships have a reputation for being LGBTQ-friendly.

Gay families are catered to by R Family Vacations (www.rfamilyvacations.com), although it's not essential to bring children. Events may include seminars on adoption and discussion groups for teenagers in gay families.

Transgender passengers may encounter some problems, such as the passport name being of one gender, while appearance and dress reflect another. Ships sometimes encounter problems in some ports when passenger ID cards do not match the gender on the ship's manifest.

Cruising for Romantics

No need to worry about getting to the church on time – you can be married at sea, get engaged, renew your vows, or enjoy a honeymoon.

Two classic TV shows, *The Love Boat* (US) and *Traumschiff* (Germany), boosted the concept of cruising as a romantic vacation, the natural culmination of which would be getting married at sea – the ultimate 'mobile wedding.' Such ceremonies have become such big money-earners that, after 171 years, Cunard changed the registry of its three ships in 2011 from its traditional home port of Southampton to Hamilton, Bermuda, partly because its British registry didn't allow for weddings at sea. As a result, couples can now say 'I do' aboard *Queen Mary 2* in the middle of the North Atlantic; the first such wedding was in May 2012.

Saying 'I do' aboard ship

This popular option includes a honeymoon conveniently in the same location and a 'wedding planner,' who can sort out all the nitty-gritty details such as arranging flights, hotels, transportation, and inclusive packages. For the bride, spa and beauty services are immediately on hand, and you literally can sail into the sunset after the reception.

Check first in your country of domicile whether such a marriage is legal, and ascertain what paperwork and blood tests are needed. It is up to you to prove the validity of such a marriage. The captain could be held legally responsible if he has married a couple not entitled to wed.

It's relatively easy to get married aboard almost any cruise ship when it's alongside in port, and

several cruise lines offer special wedding packages. These include the services of a minister to marry you, wedding cake, Champagne, bridal bouquet and matching boutonnière for the bridal party, a band or musician to perform at the ceremony, and an album of wedding pictures. Note that US citizens and 'green card' residents may need to pay sales tax on wedding packages.

Asuka Cruise, Azamara, Celebrity Cruises, Cunard, Dream Cruises, P&O Cruises, Princess Cruises, Royal Caribbean International, and Sea Cloud Cruises – among others – offer weddings aboard their ships. The ceremonies can be performed by the captain, who is certified as a notary, when the ships' registry – Bermuda, Japan, or Malta, for example – recognizes such unions. Japanese citizens can also be married at sea aboard one of the Japan-registered cruise ships such as *Asuka II*.

Expect to pay about $3,000 plus about $500 for licensing fees. Harbor-side or shore-side packages vary according to the port.

Even if you don't get married aboard ship, you could have your wedding reception on one. Contact the director of hotel services at the cruise line. The cruise line will go out of its way to help, especially if you follow the reception with a honeymoon cruise – and a cruise, of course, also makes a fine, worry-free honeymoon.

Sunset aboard Cunard's *Queen Mary 2.*

UK-based passengers should know that P&O Cruises hosts a series of cruises called the 'Red-Letter Anniversary Collection' for those celebrating 10, 15, 20, 25, 30, 35, 40, 45, 50, 55, or 60 years of marriage. The cruise comes with a complimentary gift, such as a leather photograph album, or – less romantic, but very useful – free car parking at Southampton.

Getting married ashore

Another option is to have a marriage ceremony in an exotic destination with your reception and honeymoon aboard ship afterwards. For example, you could get married on the beach in Barbados or Hawaii; on a glacier in Juneau, Alaska; in a villa in Rome or Venice; in an authentic Tahitian village; in Central Park, New York; or on Disney's Castaway Cay in the Bahamas, with Mickey and Minnie at hand. Note that your marriage license must be from the jurisdiction in which you will be married. If you set your heart on a Bermuda beach wedding, for example, the license to marry must be obtained in Bermuda, no matter what your nationality is.

Getting engaged aboard ship

For those not quite ready to tie the knot, Princess Cruises has a special 'Engagement Under the Stars' package that allows you to propose to your loved one in a personal video that is screened just before an evening movie at a large poolside screen aboard some of the company's ships.

Renewal of vows

Many cruise lines perform 'renewal of vows' ceremonies. A cruise is a wonderful setting for reaffirming to one's partner the strength of commitment. A handful of ships have a small chapel where this ceremony can take place; otherwise, it can be anywhere aboard ship – a most romantic time is at sunrise or

A honeymoon couple enjoy being pampered aboard an MSC Cruises ship.

sunset on the open deck. The renewal of vows ceremony is conducted by the ship's captain, using a non-denominational text.

Some companies have complete packages for purchase, which include music, Champagne, hors d'oeuvres, certificate, corsages for the women, and so on.

Cruising for honeymooners

There are many advantages in honeymooning at sea: it is a hassle-free and safe environment; and you get special attention if you want it. It is easy to budget in advance, as one price often includes airfare, cruise, food, entertainment, several destinations, shore excursions, and pre- and post-cruise hotel stays. Also, some cruise lines offer discounts if you book a future cruise to celebrate an anniversary.

Although no ship provides real bridal suites, many have suites with king-size beds. Some also provide tables for two in the dining room, should you wish to dine together without having to make friends with others. A variety of honeymoon packages are available; these might include Champagne and caviar for breakfast, flowers in your suite/cabin, complimentary cake, and a private captain's cocktail party.

Some cruise ships have Sunday departures, so couples can plan a Saturday wedding and reception before traveling. Pre- and post-cruise hotel accommodation can also be arranged.

Most large resort ships accommodate honeymoon couples well. However, couples averse to crowds might try one of the smaller cruise ships such as those of Hapag-Lloyd Cruises, Regent Seven Seas Cruises, Sea Cloud Cruises, Seabourn, Silversea Cruises, or Windstar Cruises.

And for quiet moments? The deck to the forward part of a ship, near the bridge, is the most dimly lit part and the quietest – except perhaps for some wind noise.

PRACTICAL TIPS FOR HONEYMOONERS

Remember to take a copy of your marriage license or certificate, for immigration (or marriage) purposes, as your passports will not yet have been amended. Since you may well wish to share a large bed with your partner, check with your travel agent and cruise line to make sure the cabin you have booked has such a bed. Better still, book a suite, if the budget allows. It's important to check and double-check to avoid disappointment.

If you plan to combine your honeymoon with getting married along the way – in Hawaii or Bermuda, for example – and need to take your wedding gown aboard, there's usually space to hang it in the dressing room next to the stage in the main showlounge, especially aboard the large resort ships.

Cruising for Seniors

People everywhere are living longer and healthier lives, and cruise lines are keen to cater to their particular needs.

Although cruise lines have been striving, with some success, to embrace all age groups, the over-60s remain an important segment of the market. Group cruising for seniors, in fact, is growing in popularity and is a good way for like-minded people to vacation together. Nowhere is this more evident than in Japan's 'Golden Week,' a collection of four national holidays within seven days in late April/early May, when seniors clamor for available cabins.

One trend for seniors is toward longer cruises – even round-the-world cruises, if they can afford them. Some opt for an adults-only ship such as *Magellan* (CMV), *Aurora, Arcadia,* or *Oriana* (P&O Cruises), or *Saga Discovery, Saga Sapphire* (Saga Cruises), for example. There are bargains to be had, too. Organizations for seniors such as AARP (American Association of Retired Persons) in the US and Saga in the UK often offer discount fares and upgrades.

Some seniors who may have had major surgery or have mobility problems cannot fly, or don't wish to,

Making new friends aboard *Oasis of the Seas*.

are helped by the 'Homeland Cruising' trend, which enables them to embark at and disembark from a nearby port in their home country. In the US, the number of homeland ports increased dramatically following the terrorist attacks of September 2001. In the UK, some cruise ships sail from ports in both the north and south of the country. The same is true elsewhere, as language-specific cruise lines and ships proliferate.

But all is far from perfect. Some cruise lines have yet to recognize that, with seniors as with other groups, one size does *not* fit all. Only a few, for example, take the trouble to provide the kind of items that millions of seniors need, such as large-print editions of daily programs, menus, and other printed matter.

Special diets

While the wide range of cuisine aboard many ships is a big attraction, cruise lines understand that many passengers are on special diets. Lighter menu options are available aboard most ships, as well as vegetarian and vegan choices. Options include low-sodium, low-fat, low-cholesterol, and sugar-free entrées (main courses) and desserts. A booking agent will ensure that special dietary needs are recorded.

Healthier eating

You don't have to put on weight during a cruise. Many health-conscious seniors prefer smaller portions of food with good taste and nutritional value rather than overflowing plates.

Heart-healthy diets are in demand, as are low-fat, low-carbohydrate, salt-free, or low-salt foods. Denture wearers often request food that includes softer items.

Those seeking lighter fare should be aware that most cruise lines have an 'always available' section of heart-healthy items that can be cooked plainly, such as grilled or steamed salmon, skinless chicken breast, lean sirloin steak, or baked potatoes.

Gentlemen hosts

Because more female than male seniors cruise, cruise lines have developed 'gentlemen host' programs. These are gentlemen, typically over 55 years of age, selected for their social skills and competence as dance partners, for dining table conversation, and for accompanying passengers on shore excursions.

Cruise lines with gentlemen hosts include: Celebrity Cruises, Crystal Cruises, Cunard, Holland America Line, P&O Cruises, Princess Cruises, Regent Seven Seas Cruises, Seabourn, Silversea Cruises.

Enrichment programs

Many seniors want to learn about a destination's history and culture rather than be told which shops to visit ashore. Lecturers of academic quality are found aboard some smaller ships such as *Spirit of Discovery* (Saga Cruises). Some lines, like Crystal Cruises, have special-interest lecturers on topics such as archaeology, food and wine, ornithology, and military history.

Tips for seniors

If you're traveling solo, it's important to check the price of any single supplements.

If you take medication, make sure you have enough with you. Some ships have a dress-up code, while most are casual. Choose a ship according to your own lifestyle and tastes.

If you have mobility difficulties, choose one of the newer ships that have public rooms with an 'open-flow' style of interior design. Examples include *Arcadia, Balmoral, Eurodam, Magellan, Nieuw Statendam, Queen Elizabeth, Queen Mary 2,* and *Queen Victoria.* Older ships, such as *Marco Polo,* have 'lips' or doors between public rooms.

Enrichment lecture aboard a small ship.

Best facilities

Among the cruise lines that provide the facilities and onboard environment that seniors tend to enjoy most are: American Cruise Lines, Azamara, Blount Small Ship Adventures, Crystal Cruises, Fred. Olsen Cruise Lines, Hebridean Island Cruises, Holland America Line, Noble Caledonia, Oceania Cruises, P&O Cruises, Pearl Seas Cruises, Regent Seven Seas Cruises, Saga Cruises, Sea Cloud Cruises, Seabourn, and Silversea Cruises.

WHY SENIORS LIKE CRUISING – BUT CAN OFTEN FIND IT FRUSTRATING

Thumbs up
A cruise is an excellent choice for those who like to be independent while having the chance to meet other like-minded people.

Cruising is stress-free and relaxing. You don't have to keep packing and unpacking as you do on a land-based tour.

It's safe. You travel and dine in comfort and safety, while your floating hotel takes you to a choice of around 2,000 destinations all over the world.

Lecturers and lessons in everything from golf to computing provide a chance to learn something new.

There's plenty of entertainment – shows, cinema, casinos, games, and dances.

All main and self-serve buffet meals are included in the fare, and those passengers on special diets can be easily accommodated.

Senior singles, in particular, find it easy to meet others in a non-threatening environment. Some ships provide male dance hosts, screened and subject to a strict code of ethics, who can also act as escorts on shore excursions.

Most ships have 24-hour room service and a 24-hour reception desk.

Passengers with disabilities can find ships that cater to their needs.

Ships carry a medical doctor and one or more trained nurses. In an emergency, treatment can

be arranged.

Thumbs down
Online check-in procedures, and hard-to-read Passenger Ticket Conditions and Contracts only provided online.

Credit card-size electronic key cards to cabins – it is often unclear which end of these to insert, and difficult for those with poor eyesight.

Booking events and meals via the in-cabin 'interactive' television/keypad system; it is user-unfriendly for many seniors. All services should be readily accessible via the telephone.

Poor, difficult-to-read signage such as 'You are here' deck plans unreadable from farther away than an inch (2.5cm).

Menus with small, hard-to-read typefaces (and non-black ink), and daily programs that require a magnifying glass to be legible.

Buffets with plates only, requiring several visits, and cutlery too heavy to hold comfortably.

Anything that requires a signature – for example: bar, shore excursions, spa bills with small print.

Libraries with few books, if any, in large-print format – notably recent novels.

The absence of a 'concierge' for seniors.

Public toilets not clearly marked.

The lack of music-free lounges and bars for conversation and drinks.

Cruising to Suit Special Needs

Cruising for those with physical disabilities offers one of the most hassle-free vacations possible. But it's important to choose the right ship and to prepare in advance.

If you have a mobility issue or any other kind of physical disability (this includes visual or hearing impairments), a large resort ship really is a destination in itself, and provides a very comfortable way to travel in style, with accommodation, meals, entertainment, public rooms and open-air facilities in a hotel-style environment, plus abundant staff to help you have an enjoyable time. On-site medical facilities also add to the comfort factor. It's a very therapeutic environment. However, do tell the cruise line (or your travel agent) at the time you book about your physical disability; otherwise, you may legally be denied boarding by the cruise line.

Wheelchair-users considering a cruise may be nervous at the thought of getting around. However, you'll find that crew members aboard most ships are extremely helpful. Ships built in the past five to 10 years have the most up-to-date suites, cabins, and accessible shipboard facilities for those with disabilities. Many new ships also have text telephones and listening device kits for the hearing-impaired (including in showlounges aboard some ships). Special dietary needs can often be met, and many cabins

Many cruise ships offer an ideal environment for people with disabilities.

have refrigerators – useful for those with diabetes who need to keep insulin supplies cool.

Special haemodialysis cruises cater for dialysis patients. For the very best in dialysis care and travel arrangements, contact Dr. Peter Rittich at: www.diacare. ch. Other providers include www.dialysisatsea.com. Typically, a renal care specialist team consisting of a nephrologist, dialysis nurses, and certified technicians will be provided. Some ships (examples include *Astor*, *Europa*, and *Europa 2*) have first-class dialysis equipment (such as the Fresenius 4008 B) permanently installed in a special dialysis room in the medical center.

If you use a wheelchair, take it with you – ships carry a limited number for emergency hospital use only. An alternative is to rent an electric wheelchair, which can be delivered to the ship on your sailing date.

Arguably the weakest point of cruising for people with limited mobility is any ship-to-shore tender operation. Ships' tenders simply aren't designed for wheelchair-users – and neither are landing platforms (exceptions include Celebrity Apex and Celebrity Edge).

Little problems to consider

Unless cabins and bathrooms are specifically designed, problem areas include the entrance, furniture configuration, closet hanging rails, beds, grab bars, the height of toiletries cabinet, and the wheel-in shower stall. The elevators may present the biggest obstacle, and you may get frustrated at the wait time involved. In older ships, controls often can't be reached from a wheelchair. Narrow hallways can be a problem when trying to pass housekeeping carts.

Some ships have access-help hoists installed at swimming pools. Examples include *Celebrity Eclipse*, *Celebrity Equinox, Celebrity Reflection,* and *Celebrity Silhouette,* the pool in 'The Haven' aboard *Norwegian Breakaway, Norwegian Epic, Norwegian Escape, Norwegian Getaway, Norwegian Gem,* and P&O Cruises' *Aurora, Britannia,* and *Iona*.

It can be difficult to access areas including self-serve buffets, and many large resort ships provide only oval plates (no trays) in their casual eateries. So, you may need to ask for help.

Some insurance companies may prohibit smaller ships from accepting passengers with severe disabilities. Some cruise lines will send you a form requesting the dimensions and weight of your wheelchair, stating that it has to fold to be taken inside the cabin.

Note that wheelchairs, mobility scooters, and walking aids must be stored in your cabin – they *cannot* be left in the hallway outside your cabin.

Only five cruise ships have direct wheelchair-access ramps to lifeboats: *Amadea*, *Asuka II*, *Crystal Serenity*, *Crystal Symphony*, and *Europa*.

Avoid pitfalls

Start by planning an itinerary and date (as far in advance as possible), and find a cruise specialist agency suited to your needs. You should also follow up on all aspects of a booking yourself to avoid slip-ups; many cruise lines have a department or person to handle requests from disabled passengers.

Choose a cruise line that lets you select a specific cabin, not just a price category.

If the ship doesn't have any specially equipped cabins, book the best outside cabin in your price range, or choose another ship.

Check whether your wheelchair will fit through your cabin's bathroom door or into the shower area and whether there is a 'lip' at the door. Don't accept 'I think so' as an answer. Get specific measurements.

Choose a cabin close to an elevator. Not all elevators go to all decks, so check the deck plan. Smaller and older vessels may not even have elevators, making access to even the dining room difficult.

Avoid, at all costs, a cabin down a little alleyway shared by several other cabins, even if the price is attractive. It's hard to access a cabin in a wheelchair from such an alleyway. Midships cabins are less affected by vessel motion – good if you are concerned about possible rough seas. The larger – and therefore more expensive – the cabin, the more room for maneuvering.

Hanging rails in the closets on most ships are positioned too high for wheelchair-users to reach – even the latest ships seem to repeat this basic error. Many cruise ships, however, have cabins to suit people with limited mobility. They are typically fitted with roll-in closets and have a pull-down facility to bring your clothes down to any height you want.

Meals in some ships may be served in your cabin, on special request, but few ships have enough space in the cabin for dining tables. If you opt for a dining room with two fixed-time seatings for meals, the second is more leisurely. Alert the restaurant

Douglas Ward tests accessibility around a ship.

manager in advance that you would like a table that leaves plenty of room for your wheelchair.

Make sure that the contract specifically states that if, for any reason, the cabin is not available, that you will get a full refund and transportation back home as well as a refund on any hotel bills incurred.

Advise the cruise line of the need for proper transfer facilities such as buses or vans with wheelchair ramps or hydraulic lifts.

If you live near the port of embarkation, arrange to visit the ship to check its suitability – most cruise lines will be accommodating.

Hand-carry your medical information. Once on board, tell the reception desk help may be needed in an emergency.

Coping with embarkation

The boarding process can pose problems. If you embark at ground level, the gangway may be level or inclined. It will depend on the embarkation deck of the ship, availability of a terminal-to-ship flybridge, and/or the tide in the port.

DOORS CAN PRESENT A CHALLENGE FOR WHEELCHAIR-USERS

The design of cruise ships has traditionally worked against people with limited mobility. To keep water out or to prevent water escaping from a flooded area, raised edges (lips) – unfriendly to wheelchairs – are often placed in doorways and across exit pathways. Also, cabin doorways, at a standard 24in (60cm) wide, are not big enough for wheelchairs, for which about 30in (76cm) is needed.

Bathroom doors, whether they open outward or inward, similarly hinder maneuverability (an electrically operated sliding door would be better). Bathrooms in some older ships are small and

full of plumbing fixtures, often at odd angles – awkward for wheelchair movement. Those aboard new ships are much better, but plumbing may be located beneath the complete prefabricated module, making the floor higher than that in the cabin, so a ramp is needed. Some cruise lines will, if given advance notice, remove a bathroom door and hang a fabric curtain in its place, and provide a ramp for the doorway if needed.

Access to outside decks may be through doors that must be opened manually rather than via automatic electric-eye doors.

A cabin number in Braille aboard *Costa Serena*.

You may need to embark from an upper terminal level, so the gangway could be of the floating loading-bridge type, like those used at major airports. Some have flat floors; others may have raised lips at regular intervals.

Ship-to-shore tenders

Cruise lines should – but don't always – provide an anchor emblem in brochures for ports of call where a ship will be at anchor instead of alongside. If the ship is at anchor, the crew will lower you and your wheelchair into a waiting tender and then, after a short boat ride, lift you out again onto a rigged gangway or integral platform. If the sea is calm, this maneuver proceeds uneventfully; if the sea is choppy, it could vary from exciting to somewhat harrowing.

Holland America Line is one of the few companies to make shore tenders accessible to disabled people, with a special boarding ramp and scissor lift so that wheelchair passengers can see out of the shore tender's windows. Celebrity Cruises' *Celebrity Beyond*

QUESTIONS TO ASK BEFORE YOU BOOK

Are any public rooms or public decks inaccessible to wheelchairs?
Will special transportation be provided for the transfer from airport to ship?
Will you need to sign a medical release?
If you need a collapsible wheelchair, can this be provided by the cruise line?
Can the ship supply a raised toilet seat?
Will crew members be on hand to help?
Will you be guaranteed a good viewing place in the showlounge if seated in a wheelchair?
How do you get from your cabin to lifeboats in an emergency, if the elevators are out of action?
Does the cruise line's travel insurance (with a cancellation or trip interruption) cover you for any injuries while you are aboard?
Most disabled cabins have twin beds or one queen-size bed. Anyone with a child with disabilities should ask whether a suitable portable bed can be installed.

---

and *Celebrity Edge* provide the best solution, with a large platform (Rising Edge) for direct tender loading, and an adjacent elevator.

Help for the hearing-impaired

Difficulties for such passengers include hearing announcements on the public address system, using the telephone, and poor acoustics in key areas such as where shore tenders are boarded.

Some cruise lines have special 'alert kits.' These include 'visual-tactile' devices for those unable to hear a knock on the door, a telephone ringing, or the sound of an alarm clock. Crystal Cruises' *Crystal Serenity* and *Crystal Symphony*, and TUI Cruises' *Mein Schiff 1*, *Mein Schiff 2*, *Mein Schiff 3*, *Mein Schiff 4*, *Mein Schiff 5*, and *Mein Schiff 6* have movie theaters fitted with special headsets for those with hearing difficulties.

Finally, when going ashore, particularly on organized excursions, be aware that some destinations are simply not equipped to handle people with hearing impairment.

Cruising for the blind and sight-impaired

Any blind or partially sighted persons must be accompanied by a non-disabled person, occupying the same cabin. A few cruise lines will allow seeing-eye dogs (guide dogs).

All elevators and cabins have Braille text. Some large resort ships (examples include *Celebrity Reflection*, *Celebrity Silhouette*, *MSC Divina*, *MSC Fantasia*, *MSC Meraviglia*, *MSC Preziosa*, *MSC Seaside*, and *MSC Splendida*) have Braille pads subtly hidden under each lower section of handrail in the main foyers, which is user-friendly, and welcome.

Recent improvements

Many new ships now provide mobility-limited cabin bathrooms with collapsible shower stools mounted on shower walls, and bathroom toilets have collapsible arm guards and lower washbasins. Other cabin equipment may include a vibrating alarm clock, door beacon (with a light that flashes when someone knocks on the door), television with closed-caption decoders, and a flashing light as fire alarm. Other features to look out for include:
Kits for the hearing-impaired, available on request.
Induction systems for the hearing-impaired.
Dedicated wheelchair positions in the showlounge or cinema.
Electrical hoists to access pools and hot tubs.

Although public rooms do not have special seating areas, most showlounges do – almost always at the back, adjacent to the elevators – for wheelchair-users.

Wheelchair accessibility

Each cruise ship reviewed in this book is rated in its data listing for wheelchair accessibility. Accommodation for wheelchair-users has extra-wide doors. If you take an electric scooter, you will need to store it in the cabin (it cannot be left outside in the hallway).

Cruising to a Theme

A whole world of special-interest, hobby and lifestyle theme cruises awaits your participation.

What's your interest? Think of it and you'll probably find a cruise dedicated to it. These are the special cruises that don't really fit into the normal range of offerings, although they usually follow the same itinerary.

Theme cruises are primarily 'regular' cruises, but with additional programs, linked to personalities and subject specialists. With seminars and hands-on learning sessions, music, dances or concerts, sports, activities, and leisure on the menu, the possibilities are endless. Also, you travel with people who have the same interests, or passions, or to increase your knowledge of a particular subject. You could also be close to your favorite celebrity and get to talk to them in person.

If you are cruising as a regular passenger and not part of the theme cruise group (assuming that the ship is not a full theme cruise charter), be aware that some public rooms may be blocked off for one or more days for special activities and functions – or even the whole cruise. Whole dining rooms may also be part of the theme charter and may be out of commission for regular passengers.

Music on the high seas

Music has always been a popular feature of shipboard entertainment, and special-interest music festivals, celebrations, and even competitions at sea have been part of the modern-day cruise scene since the 1960s. It's like having a special backstage pass to be up-close-and-personal with world-class musical talent.

Solo instruments are an unusual item for a theme cruise, but in 1986 the first Accordion Festival at Sea – with over 600 accordionists on board competing for financial and other prizes – took place aboard Chandris Fantasy Cruises' *Galileo*. It was not a full ship charter, so the other passengers were fascinated by the richness of performances of this versatile instrument.

Even before that, however, starting in 1976, a Classical Music Festival At Sea took place annually aboard the Paquet French Cruises' 650-passenger *Mermoz* until the early 1990s (and wine, all other drinks, and shore excursions were included in the fare). The artistic director André Borocz organized the whole event, including booking about 70 musicians who sailed on each of these special cruises (either in the Mediterranean or Caribbean). World-class artists such as James Galway, Barbara Hendricks, Jean-Pierre Rampal, Maurice André,

Mstislav Rostropovich, Yo-Yo Ma, Emmanuel Ax, Schlomo Mintz, Bobby McFerrin, and the English Chamber Orchestra sailed aboard the ship, with music concerts performed ashore – usually in the evening – in Caribbean venues such as Papa Doc's Citadelle in Haiti, La Popa Monastery in Cartagena, or, in Europe, the ancient Greek theatre at Epidaurus, the Teatro Mercadante in Naples, or the ancient open-air theatre at Xanthos, Turkey.

What was unusual, and fun, was to watch these world-famous artistes rehearsing in the daytime – often in their bathrobes – with passengers (also in bathrobes or casual clothing) attending; then, at around 6pm, everyone donned tuxedos for the evening. The close contact and the interaction between performers and the music-loving passengers were wonderful. Suffice it to say that this was indeed a very special theme cruise.

In 1993 Paquet French Cruises was purchased by Costa Cruises, which was itself purchased by the Carnival Corporation in 1996. In 1999 Paquet

Néstor Torres performs as part of The Grammy Experience aboard *Norwegian Getaway*.

Cruises was dismantled, and the *Mermoz* ship was scrapped in 2008.

Today, several cruise lines have taken up the Classical Music Festival at Sea theme, with Hapag-Lloyd's annual Ocean Sun Festival the most prestigious and sought-after event.

The company also hosts the Stella Maris International Vocal Competition (opera, song, and oratorio) in cooperation with renowned opera houses throughout the world. Up-and-coming opera singers from around the world compete aboard *Europa* to win €15,000 and a recording contract with the German classical music record label, Deutsche Grammophon.

Celebrity singers

In the early 1990s, Celebrity Cruises had Connie Francis, Liza Minelli, and Gladys Knight and the Pips as headline acts in a special series of high-profile headline names to perform aboard the company's (then new) *Horizon* on the ship's popular New York to Bermuda cruises.

Cool jazz

Staying on the music theme, Big Band theme cruises have also always been popular, with bands such as the Glenn Miller Orchestra, Tommy Dorsey Orchestra, Count Basie Orchestra, and the Duke Ellington Orchestra all having been part of the music on the high seas theme. In October 2015, Cunard hosted the first-ever Blue Note-themed crossing aboard *Queen Mary 2* showcasing Blue Note's 75th anniversary All Star Band. It featured keyboardist Robert Glasper, trumpeter Keyon Harrold, tenor saxophonist Marcus Strickland, guitarist Lionel Loueke, bassist Derrick Hodge, and drummer Kendrick Scott. Herbie Hancock was the headline act on one of two more special Blue Note-themed crossings in 2016, as was jazz vocalist Gregory Porter.

Jazz greats such as Dizzy Gillespie and Clark Terry (trumpet), Woody Herman (clarinet), Benny Carter, Buddy Tate, Gerry Mulligan (saxophone), Junior Mance, Mel Powell, and Paul Broadnax (piano), Howard Alden (guitar), Keter Betts, Major Holley, Milt Hinton, and Kiyoshi Kitagawa (double bass), Chuck Riggs and Louis Bellson (drums), Mel Tormé (voice), the Harlem Blues and Jazz Band, and Joe Williams and the Festival Jazzers have all sailed and played on Norwegian Cruise Line's 'Floating Jazz Festival' cruises aboard the now-scrapped *Norway* and other ships in the fleet (organized by Hank O'Neal).

Today, the Smooth Jazz Cruise (also known as 'The Greatest Party At Sea') has been attracting well-known names such as the jazz violinist Ken Ford, guitarist-vocalist George Benson, bassist Marcus Miller, guitarist Earl Klugh, saxophonists David Sanborn, Mindi Abair, Paul Taylor, and Richard Elliott, and jazz fans – principally aboard Holland America Line ships.

Off your rocker

Today, rock 'n' roll stars and fans have also taken to cruising, with music-themed charters of ships becoming more prevalent.

The Moody Blues with Peter Dalton, Roger Daltrey, The Zombies, Carl Palmer and The Orchestra with ELO, Starship, Little River Band, and Yes have all featured on cruises. Not to be left out, grown-up 'boy bands,' including the Backstreet Boys and New Kids on the Block, have also been cruising.

In 2020, *Independence of the Seas* operates on a four-night cruise with around 20 bands and rock artists, from Miami, under the brand name Rock Legends Cruise (rocklegendscruise.com). Expect more of the same, as rock 'n' roll and blues bands go cruising to replace the loss of land-based venues and revenue (merchandising aboard a cruise ship with a captive audience is a massive incentive).

Although classical music and jazz cruises tend to last 7 to 14 days, most other music themes, such as rock 'n' roll, or heavy metal ones, tend to be shorter (and less expensive).

Soul train

Usually a full-ship charter, a re-creation of the popular music show *Soul Train* includes artists such as Gladys Knight and Earth, Wind and Fire, together with numerous artists that have been part of the television show, created and hosted by Don Cornelius. The artists, dancers, and fans have a blast, and enjoy the close interaction with each other (www.soultraincruise.com). In 2016, Smokey Robinson performed aboard Celebrity Constellation.

Going up country

Country and Western and Gospel music theme cruises also pop up occasionally. In 2019, *Carnival Valor* sailed on a four-night ShipRocked cruise (its 19th) from Galveston (Texas) for a real 'Hootenanny at Sea.' Stars who have sailed in the past few years include the band Alabama, Trace Adkins, Montgomery Gentry, Wynonna, Neal McCoy, Love and Theft, Craig Morgan, Lonestar, Kenny Rogers, Vince Gill, Larry Gatlin and the Gatlin Brothers, The Oak Ridge Boys, Mel Tillis, and Kathy Mattea. There are also songwriter workshops and karaoke (judged by the professionals), late-night dance parties, and a little unscheduled jammin' along the way.

Strictly Come Dancing with the stars

Fans of TV's *Strictly Come Dancing* ballroom dancing shows will find special theme cruises with P&O Cruises (www.pocruises.com).

Family themes

Aboard the ships of Disney Cruise Line, *everything* is Disney – every song heard, every game played, every participation event, race, or party – it's the complete Disney at sea package.

Royal Caribbean International has its own star themes at sea, including characters from the DreamWorks Experience such as Alex from *Madagascar*, Fiona and Puss in Boots from *Shrek*, and Po from *Kung Fu Panda*.

Culinary theme cruises

Food and wine cruises have always attracted interest, although some are better than others. Most have tended to be more like presentation lectures at cooking stations set on a large stage, and always seem to leave audiences wanting to ask questions one-on-one rather than as part of a general audience.

Wine-themed cruises are especially popular with oenophiles (wine lovers), who get to meet owners and specialists from various world-famous vineyards with wine talks and tasting sessions as part of the pleasure of these special voyages.

Star Wars

In 2016, Disney Cruise Line designated eight sailings aboard *Disney Fantasy* as *Star Wars* cruises. *Star Wars* films were shown, and Darth Vader, Stormtroopers, Chewbacca, Boba Fett, and other characters from across the *Star Wars* galaxy were aboard for meet-and-greet sessions.

A shipboard version of the Jedi Training Academy invited young Jedi hopefuls to learn lightsaber moves from a Jedi master.

Families participated in *Star Wars* trivia games, while themed arts and crafts, games, and activities were featured daily.

In 2019 there were nine *Star Wars* sailings aboard *Disney Fantasy*. May the Force be with you!

Not your regular theme cruise

Other unusual theme cruises include naturist vacations – clothing-free vacations. Bare Necessities has been doing it since 1990, although participants do dress to go to the dining room. The Big Nude Boat Cruise 2016 took place aboard *Celebrity Constellation*. Then there's Dream Pleasure Tours (http://dreampleasuretours.com), founded in 2007 for sensual indulgence. This company charters ships for hedonistic lifestyle cruises, including for the LGBTQ and swinger communities. A swingers' (adventurous couples) cruise took place in 2016 aboard *MSC Divina*, with a Bliss Cruise (for couples) aboard *Celebrity Silhouette*.

The Harley-Davidson Motorcycle Rally At Sea has been happening for around 10 years aboard Celebrity Cruises. Dress code: biker attire. There's a belly smacker contest; a treasured chest (women); best beard (men); and a contest for the best tattoo.

Some cruises are just magical adventures in themselves. In 2013, everyone's favorite wizard, the venerable Harry Potter, took to the seas with his own theme cruise.

Other themed cruises include Wellness, Fitness, 'Mind, Body and Spirit,' and 'Life Modification' cruises (the first Holistic Health Cruise at sea was aboard *Cunard Countess* in 1976 and included Ida Rolf – the esteemed creator of the extreme massage technique known as Rolfing – on board). Then there's the Quilting and Girlfriends cruise – for girls who cruise to quilt (https://stitchinheaven.com); castles and gardens cruises (www.hebridean.co.uk); and scrapbooking cruises (www.cruiseandcrop.com).

A complimentary music class aboard *Crystal Serenity*.

Several cruise lines also have golf-themed cruises, but perhaps the best packages are put together by companies including Crystal Cruises, Hapag-Lloyd Cruises, Regent Seven Seas Cruises, and SeaDream Yacht Club, all of which operate smaller-size ships for a more personal experience.

Corporate cruising

Corporate incentive organizations and seagoing conferences need to have such elements as accommodation, food, or entertainment for delegates organized as one contract. Cruise companies have specialized departments to deal with all the details. Helpfully, many larger ships have almost identical cabin sizes and configurations.

Once a corporate contract is signed, no refund is possible, so insurance is essential. Although you may need only 70 percent of a ship's capacity for your purposes, you will have to pay for the whole ship if you want an *exclusive* charter.

Although you can contact cruise lines directly, I strongly recommend contacting the Miami-based ship charter specialists Landry & Kling (http://landrykling.com), who can arrange whole-ship charters for theme cruises.

Maiden and inaugural voyages

It can be fun to take part in the maiden voyage of a new cruise ship. Or you could join an inaugural voyage aboard a refurbished, reconstructed, or stretched ship after a refit or drydock. However, you'll need a degree of tolerance – and be prepared for some inconveniences, such as slow or non-existent service in dining venues. Indeed, new restaurants – or reconfigured ones following a refit – may not even be operable.

One thing is certain: any maiden voyage is a collector's item, but Murphy's Law – 'If anything can go wrong, it will' – can prevail. If it's a new ship, for instance, the crew may not be familiar with the layout, and some equipment may not be working properly (or may even be completely missing). Service aboard new or significantly refurbished ships (or a new cruise line) is likely to be uncertain and can easily end up a disaster. An existing cruise line may use experienced crew from its other vessels to help 'bring out' a new ship, but they may have problems training new staff.

Plumbing and electrical items tend to cause the most problems, particularly aboard reconstructed and refurbished vessels. Examples: toilets that don't flush or don't stop flushing; faucets incorrectly marked, where 'hot' really means 'cold'; and 'automatic' telephones that refuse to function.

In the entertainment department, items such as spare spotlight bulbs may not be in stock. Or what if the pianos arrive damaged, or audio-visual materials for the lecturers haven't been delivered? Or the manuals for high-tech sound and lighting equipment may be in a foreign language

Items such as menus, postcards, writing paper, infotainment system remote control units, door keys, towels, pillowcases, glassware, and even toilet paper may be lost in the bowels of the ship (no pun intended), or simply not ordered.

If you feel any of these mishaps might spoil your cruise, I would advise you to wait until the ship has been in service for at least three months, by which time a ship will have 'bedded down.'

The author taking part in a culinary class aboard *Britannia*.

Expedition Cruising Uncovered

There has been an explosion in the 'go wild' nature discovery segment of cruising due to the upsurge of interest in the planet, helping you to discover some of the world's most remote places.

Like sport-utility vehicles, the newest expedition ships now offer a comfortable lifestyle as a base to experience nature safely – no more being squeezed into telephone-box-sized cabins.

Expedition voyages (they are not really cruises, per se) are poles apart from other types of cruising. There is, however, some confusion between expedition cruises and discovery/exploration cruises, which are more about nature and off-the-map destinations, with a sense of pioneering and adventure thrown in. Participants joining real (polar) expedition voyages need to be pretty self-reliant and more interested in doing or learning than in being entertained as they'll find themselves an active participant in almost every aspect of the voyage.

Naturalists, historians, and lecturers are aboard each ship to provide background information and observations about wildlife.

Collectible expedition/exploration experiences

Get some northern exposure by venturing all the way to the North Pole, or by walking on pack ice in the Arctic Circle or watching orcas and visiting penguin rookeries in Antarctica, the Falkland Islands, and South Georgia (the only place to see king penguins). Or, you could go 'birding' in the Aleutian Pribilof Islands, search for 'lost' peoples in Papua New Guinea, explore the Amazon basin, view the Bradshaw rock art in the Kimberley, or watch real dragons on Komodo island.

Exploring in comfort

Briefings and lectures bring cultural and intellectual elements to expedition voyages, which are all about being immersed in nature. An expedition leader has a team and works closely with the ship's captain and marine operations department. The ships are designed and equipped to sail in ice-laden waters, yet they have a shallow-enough draft to glide over coral reefs without damage.

Without traditional cruise ports, the ships must be totally self-sufficient, capable of long-range cruising, and totally environmentally friendly. There's no professional entertainment. Instead, recaps of the day's experiences take place each evening, and board games and library books are always available. Note: the 'library' is typically a few bookshelves filled with polar and nature-related reference books, usually part of the multimedia/observation lounge. Some ships have a separate lecture and multimedia room, while aboard the smallest ships, the observation lounge usually doubles up as the lecture room.

The expedition experience itself really comes alive by the use 'Zodiacs' – inflatable but rigid (open) craft that can seat up to a dozen participants (note that landings on icy terrain can be demanding and very challenging when there are no landing stages). The feel of sea spray and wind on your face gives you a thrill, and the sense of exhilaration that this really is something different from any cruising you may have done previously.

What's included

Experienced expedition leaders
Specialist lectures
All meals (breakfast, lunch, dinner)
Coffee, tea, hot chocolate, around the clock
All shore landings (as per the daily program)
All Zodiac cruising (as per the daily program)
An expedition parka (for you to take home – so remember to allow extra space when you are packing)
Waterproof boots (on loan) for shore landings

How expedition cruising developed

Lars-Eric Lindblad pioneered expedition cruising in 1966. The Swedish-American turned travel into adventure by going to parts of the world tourists had not visited. After chartering several vessels for voy-

A Polar-Code compliant expedition ship nudging through ice.

Zodiacs on a 'soft' expedition in Papua New Guinea.

ages to Antarctica, he organized the construction of a small ship capable of going almost anywhere in comfort and safety. In 1969, *Lindblad Explorer* was launched; it soon earned an enviable reputation in adventure travel. Others followed.

To put together expedition voyages, companies turn to specialist advisers. Scientific institutions are consulted; experienced world explorers and naturalists provide up-to-date reports on wildlife sightings, migrations, and other natural phenomena. Sea days are spent preparing, and participants are kept physically and mentally active. Avoid such an adventure voyage if you are not completely mobile, because getting into and out of Zodiacs (inflatable shore landing craft) can be tricky, even in good weather conditions.

Expedition companies provide parkas and waterproof boots, but you will need to take waterproof trousers (and plenty of warm clothing) for Antarctica and the Arctic.

What's ahead

Many of the present 'expedition' ships over 10 years old have already passed their sell-by date and don't comply with the new Polar Code (1) PC6 requirements. PC6 covers technical, crew and procedural requirements for vessels operating in the polar regions of the world, which came into force in January 2017. The vessels must be able to break 90cm of first-year ice. The safety section of the code applies to all passenger ships (ships constructed prior to 2017 must comply with the code by the first or immediate or renewal survey). Hence the orders for so many new state-of-the-art ships.

In 2019, a number of new highly specialized expedition ships debuted for the first time for many years. *Crystal Endeavor* (2020) and *Scenic Eclipse* (2019) both carry submersible mini-vessels, including SEABOB underwater scooters. However, the per-person cost to participate is fairly prohibitive (plus you'll need to be covered by highly specialized insurance), due to the use of one or two helicopters and other specialist equipment. Perhaps more useful are the land-

ing craft aboard Hapag-Lloyd's new specialist ships *HANSEATIC nature* and *HANSEATIC inspiration.* These include environmentally friendly, electric-powered Zodiacs but no helicopters or submersibles – considered to be high-maintenance with operational and logistics liabilities. The new expedition ships incorporate a dynamic positioning system – vital in polar ice conditions (most expedition ships over five years old don't have them).

Expedition leaders

The best expedition voyages are not only about the latest ships and technical equipment, but about the expedition leaders themselves, and their experience and professionalism. Also, perhaps the most experienced (and environmentally conscientious) company, Hapag-Lloyd Expedition Cruises does not add extra charges for such things as kayaking, snow-shoeing, or paddle-boarding in ice-laden waters, or for other side excursions, whereas companies like Hurtigruten, Oceanwide Expeditions, Poseidon Expeditions, Quark Expeditions, and several others, do.

A day in the life

Be prepared, after the first day, as you get used to your new surroundings, have collected your appropriately-sized parka and boots and attended safety and Zodiac landing briefings, expedition voyages always include several early morning calls, nature sightings, and sheer physical endurance. But the result is worth all the effort, because the memories you will collect, and the experiences you will have, cannot be learned from books or television or by armchair travel – this is total immersion, and you need to be a participant – not simply a passive passenger!

To get the most out of a polar expedition cruise, be prepared to be flexible. Expedition ships don't always run to a time schedule, because there are so many variables when dealing with weather, ice conditions, and other operational issues.

Antarctica

Think of Vangelis' Antarctica. See the 'Frozen Planet' for yourself. While Arctic ice is only a few feet thick, the ice of Antarctica is thousands of feet thick, and of many, many different colors. The continent was first sighted in 1820 by the American sealer Nathaniel Palmer, British naval officer Edward Bransfield, and Russian captain Fabian Bellingshausen (the second man to cross the Antarctic Circle).

For most, it is just a windswept frozen wasteland – the ice mass contains almost 90 percent of the world's snow and ice (and 70 percent of the world's water), while its treeless land mass is nearly twice the size of Australia. For others, it represents the last pristine place on earth, with an abundance of marine and bird life.

Around 45,000 people a year visit Antarctica, mostly by expedition cruise ships. The British research station

Port Lockroy, located on Goudier Island in the Palmer Archipelago and established in 1944, is the most visited site in the Antarctic Peninsula, with about 20,000 expedition cruise visitors annually during the five-month austral summer. It is also the site for nesting Gentoo penguins. There is 24-hour sunshine during the austral summer, but not a single native inhabitant (volunteer staff at the station have a six-month contract). Its ice is as much as 2 miles (3km) thick, and its total land mass equals more than all the rivers and lakes on earth and exceeds the land mass of China and India combined. Icebergs can easily be the size of Belgium. The region has a raw beauty, vivid colors, and can overload the senses. Research stations set up by various nations are dotted about the Antarctic Peninsula, and because they are staffed mainly by scientists, they welcome expedition cruise visitors – particularly after being holed up for the harsh Antarctic winters, when going outside is next to impossible.

There are two ways to reach the cold continent by sea.

From Ushuaia in Argentina, Punta Arenas, or Puerto Williams in Chile, across the Drake Passage, to the Antarctic Peninsula (the most popular route). The peninsula is visited (sometimes together with South Georgia) by the 'soft' expedition cruise ships and even normal-size cruise ships with ice-hardened hulls. From Ushuaia or Punta Arenas, it takes two days to reach the Antarctic Peninsula (about 560 nautical miles from Cape Horn), to see the pristine Antarctic ice and observe the wildlife. The best time is mid-November, when penguins come ashore for courtship and nesting. South Georgia is famous, because the explorer Ernest Shackleton is buried in Grytviken – a former Norwegian whaling station.

From Hobart (Australia) or Auckland (New Zealand) to the Ross Ice Shelf, it takes about seven days to reach the eastern side of the continent in the Ross Sea (hence it is more expensive than leaving from Argentina or Chile). On the way from Australia, Tasmania or New Zealand, adventure voyages might call at Balleny Islands, just below latitude 70o (the islands are named after English whaling captain John Balleny, who discovered the archipelago during an expedition to the high southern latitudes in search of sealskins and whale oil in 1837). Onwards to the more remote 'far side' – the Oates and Scott coasts, McMurdo Sound, and the famous Ross Ice Shelf – which can be visited only by genuine icebreakers, as the katabatic winds can easily reach more than 100mph (160kph). However, a highlight will be a visit to Robert Falcon Scott's well-preserved Discovery Hut (built between 1902 and 1904) at Cape Evans on Ross Island – surrounded by McMurdo Station and its ice wharf. It has been frozen in time since 1912 (with over 8,000 items – including many tins of food). You can also visit Shackleton's hut from the Nimrod expedition (1907–09) at Cape Royds on Ross Island (it contains over 5,000 items), and Mawson's huts at Cape Denison in the eastern sector (a replica of one of Mawson's huts (built by the Mawson's Huts Foundation) opened in December 2013; it sits on the dockside in Hobart, Australia. Approximately halfway between Australia and Antarctica is Macquarie Island, home to virtually the entire world population of royal penguins.

The first ship carrying participants on a complete circumnavigation of Antarctica was the 114-passenger *Kapitan Khlebnikov*, operated by Quark Expeditions, in 1996–97.

Only 100 participants *per ship* are allowed ashore at any given time (so aboard the smaller ships, two landings per day are normal). If you cruise aboard one of the larger ships that claim to include Antarctica on their itineraries, it will only be to view the scenery from the ship. Moreover, the chances of rescue in the event of dangerous pack ice crushing a normal cruise ship hull are virtually nil.

Most large ship operators thankfully exited Antarctica due to a ban on carrying or burning heavy fuel oil below 60 degrees south latitude (and marketing people haven't got a clue about the dangers

PROTECTING SENSITIVE ENVIRONMENTS

Only ships capable of meeting new 'zero discharge' standards will be allowed to cross environmentally sensitive areas. Expedition cruise companies are concerned about the environment, and they spend a great deal of time and money in educating their crews and participants about safe procedures.

They observe the 'Antarctic Traveler's Code,' based on the 1978 Antarctic Conservation Act, designed to protect the region's ecosystem, flora, and fauna.

The Antarctic Treaty Meeting in Kyoto in 1994 made it unlawful, unless authorized by permit, to enter certain special protected areas (SPAs), or discharge or dispose of pollutants. The original Antarctic Treaty, signed in 1959 by 12 nations

active in the region, defined Antarctica as all of the land and ice shelves south of 60 degrees South latitude. The signatories: Argentina, Australia, Belgium, Chile, France, Japan, New Zealand, Norway, South Africa, the Soviet Union, the UK, and the US.

Ships carrying over 500 participants are not allowed to land and are restricted to 'scenic' cruising, so the likelihood of a large resort ship zooming in on penguins is low. It would not be possible to rescue so many passengers (plus crew) in the event of an emergency. Also, large resort ships burn heavy oil (now banned in the Antarctic region) rather than the lighter oil used by the specialist expedition ships, which also have ice-strengthened hulls.

New expedition ships: 2020–2021 (in company order)					
Company	Ship name	Size (gross tons)	Passengers	Length (m)	Length (ft)
2020					
Crystal Yacht Expedition Cruises	Crystal Endeavor	19,800	200	164.2	538.7
Hurtigruten	Fridtjof Nansen	20,000	530	140	459.3
Lindblad Expeditions	National Geographic Endurance	12,300	126	124.4	418.1
Mystic Cruises	World Voyager	9,300	176	126.0	413.3
Scenic	TBA	16,500	228	165.7	543.6
Victory Cruise Lines	Ocean Victory	8,000	160	126.0	413.3
2021					
Crystal Yacht Expedition Cruises	TBA	25,000	200	183.0	600.3
Hapag-Lloyd Cruises	HANSEATIC spirit	16,100	230	138	452.7
Hurtigruten	TBA	20,000	530	140	459.3
Lindblad Expeditions	TBA	12,300	126	124.4	418.1
Mystic Cruises	World Discoverer	9,400	176	126.0	413.3
Ponant	Le Commandant Charcot	30,000	270	150.0	492.1
Seabourn	Seabourn Venture	23,000	264	170.0	557.7
Vantage Cruise Line	TBA	8,000	186	104.0	341.2

of ice and erratic weather conditions), leaving travel to the region mainly in the hands of the specialist expedition ship operators. 'Antarctic' fuel (lighter-grade distillate fuel) is the world's highest cost fuel for ship use. However, some large and mid-size ships also carry the special fuel, which allows them to continue traveling to Antarctica – although these are for cruising only, not passenger landings.

For real expedition cruising, choose a ship that includes a flotilla of Zodiacs, proper boot-washing and disinfection stations, expedition equipment, experienced expedition leaders, ice captains, and no extra charges for items like kayaking or hiking. Companies with the most experience that stand out from the crowd are Hapag-Lloyd Expedition Cruises, Quark Expeditions, and Poseidon Expeditions.

As I was completing this edition of the book, I looked at a video on the website of an adventure travel company advertising expedition cruises to 'Falklands, South Georgia and Antarctica.' However, along with footage of icebergs, penguins and seals, there was footage of polar bears – but there are no polar bears in Antarctica – they are found only in the northern (Arctic) hemisphere! This shows how amateurish some companies are in trying to attract customers to their discounted offers.

Wildlife you may see or come into contact with includes orcas, dolphins, six species of Antarctic seals, penguins, and various species of lichen and flora, depending on the area visited.

Bioscientific concerns

There is a growing concern among the bioscientific community that humans are introducing pathogens to the continent (reverse zoonosis). Although the established research stations appear to be the biggest part of the problem, it is likely that the number of expedition cruise visitors will be controlled and restricted further in the near future to protect the wildlife – particularly birds (including penguins, of course). The general rule is, take only drinking water (no food, seeds, nuts, etc.), and leave nothing behind. When you return from a Zodiac 'wet' landing in icy waters, you'll go through a decontamination process, whereby everything (boots, walking poles, bags, etc.) is washed thoroughly.

Timing

From November to March is the Antarctic summer. The peak season of December and January provides the best chance for a calm Drake Passage crossing, and it's when the penguin chicks hatch (in November and December, female seals nurture their pups). In November, abundant sea ice may mean it's not possible to land – particularly on the eastern side of the peninsula. February and March are late in the season, but it's the best time to see whales and fur seals in the peninsula, and when penguin chicks are moulting.

Tip: Choose Ushuaia or Puerto Montt as your starting point (ships that start in Buenos Aires or Montevideo take much longer to get to the Antarctic Peninsula so you actually spend very little time there).

Tip: Choose a ship that carries less than 250 passengers for the best Antarctica expedition experience.

Tip: If you have a special diet, advise the cruise operator as early as possible, so that any necessary or unusual food items can be obtained.

Tip: Above all, be flexible – the weather can be extremely unpredictable, and proposed itineraries may have to be changed at short notice.

Typical temperatures in the region range from -10C to +10C. Expedition cruises to Antarctica go only in the Antarctic summer when the average is about 0C (taking into account the wind chill factor).

Packing for Antarctica

Head: A woollen hat that covers your ears as well as your head; a neck gaiter that can cover your face; polarized sunglasses to protect your eyes from the intensity of the sun's glare (and the intensified reflection of the sun on the ice and icebergs).

Body: Wear layers. Start with thermal underwear, tops and long johns made from hydrophobic fabrics rather than cotton), then fleece sweaters (parkas will be provided on board).

Hands: Waterproof gloves (one size larger than normal so that you can wear a thinner pair of lined gloves next to your skin).

Legs: Waterproof trousers (essential for Zodiac landings and exploration rides).

Feet: Wellington boots will be supplied on board but remember to take plenty of socks.

On Board: Everyday clothes (a welcome change from all the layers and waterproof clothing needed for venturing ashore).

Camera: Take clear waterproof bags (find a plastic alternative) to cover your camera, so that condensation forms inside the bag and not on your camera when returning from the cold to the warmth of your ship. Make sure you know how to operate your camera with gloves on – frostbite is a real danger. Pack extra batteries (the cold air quickly reduces battery life) and a battery charger.

The High Arctic

This is an ocean surrounded by continents, whereas Antarctica is an ice-covered continent surrounded by ocean. The Arctic Ocean itself is an immense, deep basin of polar water. The Arctic Circle itself is located at 66 degrees, 33 minutes, 3 seconds North, although this really designates where 24-hour days and nights begin. The Polar Zone includes the waters around the eastern coast of Greenland and the Canadian Arctic Islands, and the Arctic Basin. The High Arctic is best defined as that region north of which no trees grow, and where water is the primary feature of the landscape.

Poseidon Expeditions and Quark Expeditions are the Arctic expedition cruise specialists, and operate under the strict guidelines of the Association of Arctic Expedition Cruise Operators (AECO), the body committed to minimizing the impact of visit to the Far North. These highly specialized expeditions to the Top of the World (the North Pole, at 90 degrees North) are undertaken only at the height of the Arctic summer, in June and July, usually aboard the world's most powerful icebreaker – the Russian nuclear-powered *50 Years of Victory* – which can crush ice up to 10ft (3m) thick (the ship can only operate in cold water conditions so

CRACKING THE NORTHWEST PASSAGE

In 1984, Salen Lindblad Cruising (today known as Quark Expeditions) made maritime history with the pocket-sized *Lindblad Explorer* by negotiating a westbound voyage through the Northwest Passage, a 41-day epic that started from St. John's, in Newfoundland, Canada, and ended at Yokohama, Japan. The search for a Northwest Passage to the Orient – finding a sea route connecting the Pacific and Atlantic oceans through the treacherous Canadian Arctic Archipelago – had attracted brave explorers for more than four centuries, and, despite numerous attempts and loss of life including the English explorer Henry Hudson in 1610, a 'white passage' to the East remained an elusive dream. The Norwegian explorer Roald Amundsen's 47-ton ship *Gjoa* eventually navigated the route in 1906, taking three years to do so. It was not until 1943 that a Canadian ship, St. Roch, became the first vessel in history to make the passage in a single season. *Lindblad Explorer* became the 34th vessel, and the first cruise passenger ship to complete the Northwest Passage.

Photographing penguins in Antarctica.

that the water can cool the pressurized water reactors). An onboard helicopter whisks you between the ship and the North Pole, if the ship is unable to reach the exact geographic center (this would be verified by GPS and Inmarsat satellite coordinates) because of dense fog or other prevailing conditions.

This really is a once-in-a-lifetime adventure. Only 250 participants managed to visit the North Pole in 2016. Because you will be flying to Murmansk to join the ship (after a briefing about safety and security), an individual Russian visa will be needed.

The Northwest Passage

Long sought after, it was only in 1911 that the very dangerous Northwest Passage linking the Atlantic and Pacific oceans was first found and navigated. Passenger ships that have navigated it include *Lindblad Explorer* (1984), *World Discoverer* (1985), *Society Explorer* (1988), *Frontier Spirit* (1992), *Kapitan Khlebnikov* (1994, 1995, 1998, 2006, 2007, 2008), *Hanseatic* (1995, 1996, 1997, 1999, 2010, 2012), and *Bremen* (2009, 2010). In 2013, 2015, and 2017 unusual double crossings took place; *Hanseatic* went east to west, while *Bremen* went west to east. In 2016 and 2017, the much larger Crystal Serenity made a crossing escorted by a Canadian icebreaker when the ice cover was very thin, but in 2018, Ponant's *Le Boréal* and *Le Soléal* were forced to abandon their scheduled crossing because of heavy ice, under the advice of the Canadian Coast Guard. In 2021, the new Crystal Endeavor is scheduled to negotiate the passage. The only time to go is August to September.

Other expedition areas

While this chapter covers the most sought-after expedition cruise areas, there are other 'soft' expedition cruises that take you to some of the less visited or accessible areas of the world, such as the Amazon River, the Galápagos islands, Greenland, the Kimberleys (Australia) and Papua New Guinea, among others. These are more about discovering places and areas seldom seen and not part of large resort ship cruising, but where the use of Zodiacs is an essential part of the experience; these small ships don't need an ice-hardened hull and all the equipment associated with ice-laden regions. These regions are covered in the 'Choose Your Destination' chapter.

All existing ships certified to SOLAS (Safety of Life at Sea) and sailing in polar waters, are expected to carry the Polar Code ship certificate. In the Antarctic, the Polar Code is in force in all waters south of latitude 60 'S; in the Arctic in all waters north of 60 'N (with deviations to include southern Greenland and Svalbaard but excluding Iceland and Norway).

THE EXPEDITION COMPANIES

Albatros Expeditions

A relative newcomer, the Denmark-based company, founded by Soren Rasmussen, started as a tour operator in the 1980s, but year-round expedition-style cruising became a reality in 2018 (with ships operated under charter). The company's expedition employees are enthusiastic, but given the operating conditions in Antarctica, whether they have the experience when in challenging operating conditions remains to be seen. Albatros Expeditions has chartered two small expedition ships from SunStone, the first (*Ocean Victory*) to debut in 2020, with a second (*Ocean Albatros*) set to debut in 2022.

Antarctica21

This small company, based in Punta Arenas, is chartering a brand new 100-passenger small expedition ship (Magellan Explorer) for use on its Antarctica fly-cruise program, starting in 2019. The ship was built by ASENAV, in Chile. The company also operates a 71-seat aircraft for (two-hour) flights from Punta Arenas to King George Island, where the ship is based for the whole season. It provides a way to experience an Antarctic expedition cruise without having to sail through the Drake Passage (which takes about 36 hours).

Antarpply Expeditions

Based in Ushuaia, Argentina, this company specializes in (comparatively) inexpensive Antarctic expedition cruises including the Falkland Isles, the Weddell Sea and South Shetland Isles, plus South Georgia, during the austral summer. It has 'soft' expedition ship, the basic and very dated *Ushuaia*, but the quality of its voyages and operation is nowhere near as good as the more experienced specialist international companies. Gratuities are not included.

Aurora Expeditions

This small Australian company was founded in 1993 by Australian Mount Everest veteran and geologist Greg Mortimer, and adventure travel specialist Margaret Werner. Until now the company has chartered various small ships. In the latter half of 2019 however, a new expedition vessel, *Greg Mortimer*, debuted. Gratuities are not included.

Coral Expeditions

This small company, based in Queensland in northern Australia, was founded by a fisherman-entrepreneur, Captain Tony Briggs, but is now owned by Capital Holdings. The company (formerly Coral Princess Cruises) specializes in cruises of the Kimberley region in north-western Australia, the Great Barrier Reef, and other remote tropical areas in the Asia-Pacific region with boutique-size ships. The company's newest ship, the 120-passenger *Coral Adventurer* debuted in 2019.

G Adventures

This Canadian company, based in Toronto, was founded in 1990 as GAP Adventures by Bruce Poon Tip, using funds from his own personal credit cards only. The company has a grassroots approach to travel and operates its own ship – the now-outdated 140-passenger MS *Expedition* – on polar expedition cruises.

Hapag-Lloyd Expedition Cruises

The company started expedition cruises in 1990 with the 164-passenger *Bremen*, for its German-speaking passengers. As expedition cruising grew in popularity, the company took over Hanseatic from Hanseatic Tours. Both ships have now been withdrawn from the fleet (replaced by new ships). The company is known for operating its ships in the most environmentally friendly manner, accompanied by the very best expedition leaders in the business.

The company publishes its own excellent handbooks (in both English and German) on expedition regions such as the Arctic, Antarctica, Amazonia, and the South Sea Islands, as well as exclusive maps. Gratuities are not included.

Two new expedition cruise ships (*HANSEATIC inspiration* and *HANSEATIC nature*) entered service in 2019, with *HANSEATIC spirit* to follow in 2021.

Heritage Expeditions

This youth-minded adventure travel company, based in Christchurch, New Zealand, focuses on expedition-style cruising for small groups, specifically to Antarctica, the Sub-Antarctic and Russian Far East. The company was founded in 1985 by biologist Rodney Russ who worked for the New Zealand Wildlife Service for many years. It has a single ship, the very small (really basic; no frills) Russian oceanographic research vessel *Shokalskiy*.

Hurtigruten

The company is an amalgamation of two coastal ferry shipping companies (OVDS and TVDS, formerly known as Norwegian Coastal Voyages). The company has dabbled in 'soft' expedition-style cruises, albeit aboard the Fram (think utilitarian, with very modest décor), built for polar and Greenland cruising. The high passenger capacity hybrid coastal and expedition-style ship, the much-delayed *Roald Amundsen* was delivered in 2019; with *Fridtjof Nansen* following in 2020. However, the vessels are too large for true expedition cruising in Antarctica. Some activities (such as sea kayaking and stand-up paddle-boarding excursions) are at extra cost. Gratuities are not included.

Lindblad Expeditions

Lars-Eric Lindblad started the whole concept of expedition cruising with a single ship, the *Lindblad Explorer*, in 1969, taking adventurous travelers to remote regions of the world. Sven-Olof Lindblad (son of Lars-Eric) runs the company.

In partnership with the National Geographic Society, the company operates small, really basic vessels for coastal cruises in the USA. National Geographic photographers take part in all cruises.

The National Geographic Society celebrated its 125th anniversary in 2013, when the company purchased Orion Expedition Cruises, based in Australia. The ship was renamed *National Geographic Orion*, when it was transferred to the Lindblad fleet in March 2014. A new specialist expedition ship (*National Geographic Endurance*) debuted in 2019. Gratuities are not included.

Mystic Cruises

Mystic Invest is the parent company of Mystic Cruises, and is owned by Portuguese entrepreneur Mário Ferreira. The company has multiple brands that specialize in tourism and travel. It owns and operates a fleet of riverships on Portugal's Douro River, and charters several vessels to other operators. It also owns well-known Nicko Cruises, which caters mainly to German-speaking passengers. The company is building a fleet of three expedition-style ships: the first, *World Explorer*, debuted in 2019, and is chartered to Nicko Cruises during the summer season and Quark Expeditions during the winter season. A second ship, *World Discoverer*, is due in 2020, with a third, *World Navigator*, due in 2021.

Oceanwide Expeditions

Founded in 1961 as the Dutch 'Plancius Foundation' to operate cruises around Spitzbergen (Norway), the company changed its name in 1996 to Oceanwide Expeditions in order to offer adventures farther afield. It specializes in small group polar-expedition voyages and active shore visits rather than employing

National Geographic Explorer off Antarctica.

experienced lecturers. It operates two (very basic) expedition ships, *Ortelius* and *Plancius*.

OneOcean Expeditions
Based in Toronto, Canada, this small company was founded by Andrew Prossin. It doesn't own any expedition ships itself but charters them from the pool of specialist Russian vessels. Environmental responsibility is a key ingredient for its staff, who are all personable and very customer-oriented. The company charters *Resolute* (formerly *Hanseatic*) under charter from its German owner.

Poseidon Expeditions
Poseidon Expeditions is an Arctic expedition cruise specialist (founded and owned by Nikolay Saveliev in 2003). Expeditions to the North Pole (90 degrees North) are operated at the height of the Arctic summer, in June and July, aboard the Russian nuclear-powered *50 Years of Victory*. Only 10,741 people had ever been to the North Pole when I went in July 2016.

The company also operates the smaller *Sea Spirit* – the only non-Russian foreign-flag ship permitted to operate in the territorial waters of Franz Joseph Land (Russia's most northernmost territory, 550 miles/900km from the North Pole and 1,900 miles/3,000km from Moscow) in the Arctic Circle from Svalbard without first calling at a mainland Russian port. *Sea Spirit* also goes to the Antarctic Peninsula. Some activities (such as sea kayaking, stand-up paddle-boarding, and paddling excursions) are at extra cost. Gratuities are not included.

The author and his wife at the true North Pole.

Quark Expeditions
The company was founded in 1991 by Lars Wikander, Mike McDowell, and silent partners the Salen family (formerly of Salen-Lindblad Cruises). It specializes in providing up-close-and-personal Arctic and Antarctic expedition cruises. In 2007, it merged with Peregrine Shipping, and was then bought by German travel company TUI Travel.

Quark Expeditions is an associate member of IAATO (International Association of Antarctica Tour Operators) and has specialized in chartering powerful Russian icebreakers to provide participants with memorable experiences (adventure cruising for toughies). In 2019, a custom-designed expedition ship was chartered from Mystic Invest for the polar seasons, and Nicko Cruises operates the vessel during the summer season. In 2020 the now Seattle-based company debuts its very own newbuild; some activities (such as sea kayaking, stand-up paddle-boarding, and paddling excursions) are at extra cost. Gratuities are not included.

Scenic
The company was founded in Newcastle, Australia, in 1986 by Glen Moroney, as Scenic Tours. It owns and operates several riverships in Europe, under two brands: Scenic and Emerald Waterways. The company has now entered expedition/discovery cruising with its own, custom-designed ship (complete with helicopter and submersible). The first – the much-delayed *Scenic Eclipse* – was delivered in 2019. The cruises are fully inclusive of gratuities and drinks, with a few select, cost-extra premium brands.

Silversea Cruises
Silversea Cruises started as a mostly privately owned cruise line. It was founded in 1992 by the Lefebvre d'Ovidio family from Rome (previously co-owners of Sitmar Cruises) and is based in Monaco. The company is now majority-owned by the Royal Caribbean corporation. It has two specialist ships for 'soft' expedition cruising (*Silver Explorer* and *Silver Discoverer*), with another (*Silver Galapagos*) for year-round Galápagos cruises, plus the larger *Silver Cloud* and *Silver Wind*, adapted for 'soft' expedition-style cruises. Gratuities are included as part of the company's 'all-inclusive' culture.

Vantage Cruise Line
Vantage Cruise Line is an offshoot of Boston-based Vantage Deluxe World Travel. It was founded in 1983 by Gordon Lewis, whose son, Henry, is the present president (his brother Alan Lewis is president of competitor Grand Circle Cruise Lines). River cruises started in 1999. The company sells direct, via e-brochures instead of travel agents. It caters exclusively to North Americans and specializes in trips for solo travelers. The chartered expedition-style ship (set to debut in 2021) is the company's first venture into this market.

Coastal Cruises

Being all at sea doesn't appeal? You can stay close to dry land by journeying round the coasts of Australia, Europe, and North and South America.

The marine wonderland of the Great Barrier Reef, a World Heritage Site off the northeast coast of Australia, is the earth's largest living coral reef – it actually consists of more than 2,800 individual coral reefs. It is visited by around 70 local Australian boutique-size ship operators, who mostly offer one- to four-night cruises to the reefs and Whitsunday Islands. The area is excellent for scuba diving and snorkeling.

June through September is humpback whale-watching season; the Reef shelters the young whales, while the adults nurture them in the shallow waters. Note that the Australian government levies an environmental charge of A\$6.50 per day (A\$3.25 for those spending less than three hours in the Marine Park) on everyone over four years of age visiting the Great Barrier Reef and its environs.

Norway

An alternative to traditional cruise ships can be found in the year-round coastal cruising along the shores of Norway to the Land of the Midnight Sun aboard the ships of the Hurtigruten Group. The fleet consists of small, comfortable, working express coastal vessels and contemporary cruise vessels that deliver mail, small packaged goods, and foodstuffs, and take passengers to the communities spread on the shoreline.

Invariably dubbed 'the world's most beautiful voyage,' this is a 1,250-mile (2,012-km) journey from Bergen in Norway to Kirkenes, close to the Russian border (half of which is north of the Arctic Circle) and takes 12 days. The service started in 1893 to provide connection to communities when there were no roads, and the name Hurtigruten – meaning 'fast route' – reflects the fact that this coastal express was once the most reliable communication link between southern Norway and its remote north. Today the company carries more than 300,000 passengers a year. It's a good way to meet Norwegians, who treat the service like a bus.

You can join it at any of the 34 ports of call and stay as long as you wish because the vessels sail every day of the year (some port calls are of only one hour or so – enough to get off and on and unload freight). Most ports are repeated on the return journey, but stop at different times, so you may get a different feeling for a place, even if you've also visited it.

Note that double beds are available only in suite-grade accommodation (other cabins are dimensionally challenged, with sparse decor, furnishings, and minimal luggage storage space); many of the beds are fixed in an L-shape, or in a bed and sofa/bed combination. Most of the ships do not have stabilizers, and there is no doctor on board, nor indeed any medical facilities, but gratuities are included in the fare.

At the height of summer, north of the Arctic Circle, there are almost 24 hours of daylight (there is no sunset between April 19 and August 23). Between November and February, the northern lights – if the atmospheric conditions are right – create spectacular arcs across the sky. Some specialist voyages are aimed at wildlife, birdwatchers, astronomy, and others, while onboard concerts and lectures celebrate the work of Norwegian composer Edvard Grieg.

The ships can accommodate between 144 and 652 passengers. The newest ships have an elevator that can accommodate a wheelchair passenger, but, otherwise, they are plain, basic, simply practical vessels, with food that is more canteen-style than restaurant. A 24-hour restaurant provides items at extra cost. Note that the price of alcoholic drinks is extremely high (you can take your own on board), as it is throughout Norway, and that the currency is the Norwegian krone.

Archipelago-hopping can be done along Sweden's eastern coast, too, by sailing in the daytime and staying overnight in one of the many small hotels en route. One vessel sails from Norrtälje, north of Stockholm, to Oskarshamn, near the Baltic island of Öland, right through the spectacular Swedish archipelago.

The Hurtigruten Group also operates utilitarian ships for expeditions to the Arctic, Antarctic, and Greenland.

Scotland

The fishing town of Oban, two hours west of Glasgow by road, is the base for one of the world's finest cruise experiences. *Hebridean Princess* is a real gem, with Laura Ashley-style interiors – posh enough to

A Hurtigruten ship on Norway's Arctic coast.

Hebridean Princess in the Scottish islands.

have been chartered by Queen Elizabeth II for a fam-ily-only celebration of her 80th birthday in 2006. The food is excellent, and includes locally sourced Scot-tish beef, local seafood, and seasonal vegetables. There's fine personal service.

This ship, owned by Hebridean Island Cruises, car-ries up to 50 passengers around some of Scotland's most magnificent coastline and islands. If you cruise from Oban, you can be met at Glasgow airport or rail-way station and taken to the ship by motor coach. Take lots of warm clothing, however (layers are best), as the weather can be changeable and often inclement.

Hurtigruten ships			
Ship	Tonnage	Built	Berths
Finnmarken	15,000	2002	638
Fram *	12,700	2007	328
Fridtjof Nansen *	20,000	2019	530
Kong Harald	11,200	1993	490
Lofoten	2,621	1964	147
Midnatsol **	16,053	2003	652
Nordkapp	11,386	1996	464
Nordlys	11,200	1994	482
Nordnorge	11,386	1997	455
Nordstjernen **	2,621	1956	114
Polarlys	12,000	1996	479
Richard With	11,205	1993	483
Roald Amundsen *	20,000	2019	530
Spitsbergen	7,025	2009	200
Trollfjord	15,000	2002	648
Vesterålen	6,261	1983	316
* for expedition voyages only			
** for 'soft' expedition-style cruises			

North America

Coastal cruise ships flying the American flag offer a complete change of style from the large resort cruise ships. They are American-owned and Ameri-can-crewed, and very informal. Being US-registered, they can start from and return to a US port without being required to call at a foreign port along the way – which a foreign-flagged cruise ship must do.

Accommodating up to 200 passengers, the ships are rarely out of sight of land. These cruises are low-key, low-pace, and not really for active types. Their operators seek out lesser-known areas, offering in-depth visits to destinations inaccessible to larger ships, along both the eastern and western seaboards of the US, including Alaska.

Most passengers are seniors. Many prefer not to fly, and wherever possible drive or take a train to join their ship. During the summer, you might see a cou-ple of children on board, but in general small kids are not allowed. There are no facilities for them, and no staff to look after them.

Destinations. Eastern US and Canadian sea-board cruises include the St. Lawrence River, Atlan-tic Coastal Waterways, New England (good for fall cruises), Cape Cod and the Islands – and Cape Cod Canal, the Deep South, and Florida waterways.

Inland, cruises can be found in the Great Lakes (typically including calls at Windsor/Detroit, Sault Ste. Marie, Thunder Bay, Duluth, and Mackinac Is-land) – and the Welland Canal. Western seaboard cruises cover Alaska, the Pacific Northwest, Califor-nia Wine Country, and Baja California/Sea of Cortez. Cruises focus on historically relevant destinations, nature and wildlife spotting, and coastal viewing. On some cruises, these boutique-size ships can dock adjacent to a town, allowing easy access on foot.

The ships. These pocket-sized 'D-class' vessels (USA classification) ships are under 2,500 gross ton-nage and are subject neither to bureaucratic regula-tions nor to union rules. They are restricted to cruis-ing no more than 20 miles (32km) offshore. Public room facilities are limited. Because the vessels are

COASTAL CRUISE LINES IN NORTH AMERICA

The cruise companies are: Alaskan Dream Cruises, American Cruise Lines, Blount Small Ship Adventures, Lindblad Expeditions/National Geographic, Pearl Seas Cruises, UnCruise Adventures, and Victory Cruise Lines (owned by American Queen Steamboat Company).

What differentiates them? American Cruise Lines, Pearl Seas Cruises, and UnCruise Adventures provide better food and service than the others. American Cruise Lines' and Pearl Seas Cruises' (ocean-going) ships have larger cabins, and more public rooms. Drinks are included aboard the ships of American Cruise Lines and Victory Cruise Lines.

USA coastal ships					
Company	Ship name	Entered service	Passengers (lower beds)	Crew	Passengers/ crew ratio
Alaska Dream Cruises	Admiralty Dream	1979	54	21	2.5/1
	Alaskan Dream	1986	40	18	2.2/1
	Baranof Dream	1980	50	19	2.6/1
	Chichagof Dream	1984	74	30	2.4/1
American Cruise Lines	American Star	2007	94	27	3.4/1
	Constellation	2017	161	41	3.9/1
	Constitution	2018	161	41	3.9/1
	Independence	2010	97	27	3.5/1
Blount Small Ship Adventures	Grande Caribe	1997	83	17	4.8/1
	Grande Mariner	1998	83	17	4.8/1
Lindblad Expeditions/National Geographic	National Geographic Quest	2017	100	35	2.8/1
	National Geographic Sea Bird	1981	70	22	3.1/1
	National Geographic Sea Lion	1982	72	22	3.1/1
	National Geographic Venture	2018	100	35	2.8/1
UnCruise Adventures	Wilderness Adventurer	1983	60	25	2.4/1
	Wilderness Discoverer	1992	76	26	2.9/1
	Wilderness Explorer	1976	76	26	2.9/1
Victory Cruise Lines	Victory I	2001	220	77	2.8
	Victory II	2001	220	77	2.8

US-registered, there is no casino. They really are casual, no-frills ships with basic facilities, no swimming pools, little artwork, no glitz in terms of the interior decor, and their diesel engines and generators are noisy. They usually have three or four decks and, except for the ships of American Cruise Lines, sister company Pearl Seas Cruises, Lindblad Expeditions/ National Geographic, and Victory Cruise Lines, there is no elevator. Stairs can be steep and are not recommended for anyone with walking difficulties. Because of this, some have an electric chair-lift.

Accommodation is in outside-view cabins, some opening directly onto a walking deck, which is inconvenient when it rains. Each has a picture window and tiny bathroom. They are basic, with little closet space – often just a curtain across a space with a hanging rod for clothes. Many don't have a television set or telephone. There's no room service, and you may have to turn your own bed down. Cabins are closer to the engines and generators than aboard larger ships, so the noise of the generator humming can be disturbing. The quietest cabins are at the bows – although there could be noise from the bow thruster. Most cruising is, however, done in the early morning, so that passengers can sleep better at night.

Tall passengers should note that the bed length rarely exceeds 6ft (1.8m). Although soap is provided, it's best to bring your own shampoo, conditioner, and other toiletries. Blount Small Ship Adventures ships do not have cabin keys. Hot and cold-water lines may run close to each other in your bathroom, delivering neither really hot nor really cold water, and sound insulation is quite poor.

Activities. The main evening event is dinner in the dining room, with one seating. This can be a family-style affair, with passengers at long tables and the food passed around.

The cuisine is decidedly American, with fresh local specialties. Menus aboard the ships of Alaskan Dream Cruises and Blount Small Ship Adventures are limited; those aboard the ships of American Cruise Lines and Lindblad Expeditions/National Geographic offer slightly more variety. You'll probably be asked in the morning to choose which of two main courses you'd like for dinner.

Evening entertainment is after-dinner conversation. Most vessels are in port during the time, so you can easily go ashore for the local nightlife, although most passengers simply go to bed early.

The cost. These cruises are expensive, with an average daily rate of $400–800 a person, plus gratui-

Cruising Under Sail

Want to be free as the wind? Think about cruising under sail, with towering masts, the creak of the deck, and gleaming white sails to power the ship along.

There's simply nothing that beats the thrill of being aboard a multi-mast tall ship, sailing under thousands of square feet of canvas through waters that mariners have sailed for centuries. This is cruising in the traditional manner of seafaring, aboard authentic sailing ships, contemporary copies of clipper ships, or high-tech cruise-sail ships, which provides a genuine sailing experience, while keeping creature comforts.

Mealtimes apart, there are no rigid schedules, so life aboard can be liberatingly unstructured. Weather conditions may often dictate whether a scheduled port visit will be made or not, but passengers sailing on these vessels are usually unconcerned. They would rather savor the feeling of being at one with nature, albeit in a comfortable, civilized setting, and without having to do the work themselves. The more luxurious sailing ships are

The *Sea Cloud* crew goes up the rigging.

the closest most people will get to owning their own mega-yacht.

Real sail-cruise ships

While we have all been dreaming of adventure, a pocketful of designers and yachtsmen committed pen to paper, hand in pocket and rigging to mast, and came up with a potpourri of stunning vessels to delight the eye and refresh the spirit. Examples include *Flying Clipper* (new in 2019, and the world's largest passenger sailing ship), *Royal Clipper, Sea Cloud, Sea Cloud II, Sea Cloud Spirit* (scheduled to debut in 2020), *Star Clipper,* and *Star Flyer* – all of which have beautiful retro decor to convey the feeling of yesteryear and a slower pace of life.

Of these, *Sea Cloud,* built in 1931, restored in 1979, and adapted to comply with the latest safety regulations of the International Convention for the Safety of Life at Sea (SOLAS), is the most exhilarating and romantic sailing ship afloat. It operates under charter for part of the year, and sails in both the Caribbean and the Mediterranean.

The activities are few, so relaxation is the key, in a stylish but unpretentious setting. The food and service are extremely good, as is the interaction between the 69 passengers and 60 crew members, many of whom have worked aboard the ship for many years. One bonus is the fact that a doctor is available on board at no charge for emergencies or seasickness medication.

A modern interpretation of the original *Sea Cloud,* a second ship, named *Sea Cloud II,* was built and introduced in 2001.

Contemporary sail-cruise ships

To combine sailing with push-button automation, try *Club Med 2* (Club Mediterranée) or *Wind Surf* (Windstar Cruises) – with five tall aluminum masts, they are the world's largest sail-cruise ships – and *Wind Spirit* and *Wind Star* (Windstar Cruises), with four masts. Not a hand touches the sails; they are computer-controlled from the navigation bridge.

The traditional sense of sailing is almost absent in these ocean-going robots, because the computer keeps the ship on an even keel. Also, some people find it hard to get used to the whine of the vessels' generators, which run the lighting and air-conditioning systems 24 hours a day.

From a yachtsman's viewpoint, the sail-to-power ratio is poor. That's why these cruise ships with sails have engine power to get them into and out of port.

The beautiful *Sea Cloud* under full sail.

The *Sea Cloud* and *Star Clipper* ships do it by sail alone, except when there is no wind, which doesn't happen all that often.

On some itineraries, when there's little wind, you could be motor-powered for most of the cruise, with only a few hours under sail. The three Windstar Cruises vessels and one Club Med ship are typically under sail for about 40 percent of the time.

The Windstar ships carry mainly North American passengers, while the Club Med vessel caters mainly to French speakers.

Another slightly smaller vessel is the chic *Le Ponant.* This three-mast ship caters to just 64 French-speaking passengers in elegant, yet casual, high-tech surroundings, advancing the technology of the original Windstar concept. The ship made news in 2008, when its crew was held to ransom by pirates off the Somali coast; no passengers were on board at the time.

When the engine cuts in

So, do you get to cruise under sail most of the time? Not really. Aboard the ships of Sea Cloud Cruises and Star Clippers, because they are real sailing ships, you could be under sail for most of the night when the ships are under way, as long as there is wind, of course, and on the days or part days at sea.

The ship's small engine is used for maneuvering in and out of port. In the Caribbean, for example, the trade winds are good for most of the year, but in the Mediterranean the winds are not so potent.

Aboard the ships of Windstar Cruises, however, the itineraries are so port-intensive that the computer-controlled sails are hardly ever used today – so the experience can be disappointing.

HOW TO MEASURE WIND SPEEDS

Understanding wind patterns is important to sailing ships, but the numbering system for wind velocity can confuse. There are 12 velocities, known as 'force' on the Beaufort scale, devised in 1805 by Sir Francis Beaufort, an Irish-born hydrographer and officer in Britain's Royal Navy. It was adopted internationally in 1874 as the official means of recording wind velocity. They are as follows, with descriptions of the ocean surface:

Force 0 (0–1mph): Calm; glassy (like a mirror).
Force 1 (1–3mph): Light wind; rippled surface.
Force 2 (4–7mph): Light breeze; small wavelets.
Force 3 (8–12mph): Gentle breeze; large wavelets, scattered whitecaps.
Force 4 (13–18mph): Moderate breeze; small waves, frequent whitecaps.
Force 5 (19–24mph): Fresh breeze; moderate waves, numerous whitecaps.
Force 6 (25–31mph): Strong breeze; large waves, white foam crests.
Force 7 (32–38mph): Moderate gale; streaky white foam.
Force 8 (39–46mph): Fresh gale; moderate waves.
Force 9 (47–54mph): Strong gale; high waves.
Force 10 (55–63mph): Whole gale; very high waves, curling crests.
Force 11 (64–72mph): Violent storm; extremely high waves, froth and foam, poor visibility.
Force 12 (73+mph): Hurricane; huge waves, thundering white spray, visibility nil.

Transatlantic Crossings

You may be facing some unpredictable weather, but there's something romantic and adventurous about this classic ocean voyage.

This should be one of life's essential travel experiences. Crossing the 3,000 miles (4,830km) of the North Atlantic by ship is a great way to avoid the hassles of airports. I have done it 158 times and always enjoy it immensely – and unlike flying, there's no jet lag. Yet the days when ships were built specifically for crossings are almost gone. The only one offering a regularly scheduled service is Cunard's *Queen Mary 2 (QM2)*, built with a thick hull designed to survive the worst weather the North Atlantic has to offer.

Step aboard and it's like stepping back in time. It's a leisurely seven-day voyage (just being at sea provides an intoxicating sense of freedom that few destinations can offer), on five of which the clocks will be advanced (eastbound) or put back (westbound) by one hour. You can take as many bags as you want, and even your pets – *QM2*'s 24 kennels are overseen by a full-time kennel master, and there is an outdoor walking area. Book well in advance if you want to travel with your dog, however, as numbers are strictly limited.

The 2,691 passenger *QM2* is the largest ocean liner ever built, and a destination on its own. New in 2004, it measures 148,528 gross tons. It has a wide walk-around promenade deck outdoors, and its forward section is under cover from the weather or wind (three times around is 6,102 ft/1,860 m, or 1.1 miles/1.8km).

By comparison, *QM2*'s smaller half-sisters *Queen Elizabeth* and *Queen Victoria* both measure about 90,000 gross tons. The *QE2*, which was retired in 2008, measured 70,327 gross tons – the ill-fated *Titanic* measured a mere 46,328 gross tons. The difference is that *QM2* is a thick-hulled ocean liner, designed to withstand the pressures of the North Atlantic and its unpredictable weather.

The North Atlantic can be as smooth as glass or as rough as old boots, although in my experience it's rare for the weather to be bad for an entire crossing. But when it *is* a bit choppy, its heavy beauty really is mesmerizing – never, ever boring. However, make sure you always use the handrails when you move around, and use the elevators rather than the stairs.

When the ship is under way at speed (above 25 knots – about 30 land miles per hour) on a windy day, a cabin balcony is pretty useless, and the promenade deck is a challenging place to be – if you can even get outside, that is! It can be bitterly cold on deck in winter in the open seas of the Atlantic, so you may never open your balcony door. If you do book a balcony cabin, choose the port side on westbound crossings and the starboard side on eastbound crossings – if the weather is kind and the sun is shining, you'll get the sun. Sometimes, visibility is low (think pea-soup fog), and you'll hear the ship's horn – a powerful, haunting sound – bellowing every two minutes.

Tip: If you have any dental concerns, take a dental repair kit (there is no dentist on board).

Queen Mary 2 leaving New York City.

During the crossing

Once *Queen Mary 2* has left port, and settled down at sea on the second day, the natural rhythm of life slows down, and you begin to understand that time spent at sea, with few distractions, is special indeed, and completely different from any 'normal' cruise. It allows you some well-earned 'me' time – to pamper yourself in the spa, to attend a lecture by a well-known author or other personality, or simply to relax and read a book from the wonderful library on board. Cunard has a list of '101 Things To Do On A *Queen Mary 2* Transatlantic Crossing' – just in case you really do want to be active. But, best of all, you can turn off your mobile phone – and have a digital detox.

Apart from distinguished guest speakers, *QM2* has a wide variety of leisure facilities, including a superb planetarium (several different shows, for which you'll need to make a reservation) and a 1,000-seat theatre for evening shows. There are acting classes, bridge (the card-playing kind) groups, big-band-style dance sessions, movies, exercise, cooking, and computer classes, so you'll never be bored in mid-ocean. There are usually three formal (tuxedo) nights and four informal nights during a 7-night crossing, when an outbreak of elegance prevails, and gentlemen dance hosts are always kept busy by the number of solo female passengers who love to go dancing.

One of the ship's most used facilities is its outstanding library and bookshop – it offers around 10,000 books (of which 8,400 are in English and 800 in German, with the rest in Japanese, Spanish, Italian and French) in cabinets that have to be locked by hand – central locking was never part of the ocean liner setup. Shame that it's no longer run by Ocean Books, which always provided real librarians who knew their books, but now by a shopping concession instead.

There's always a cozy chair to curl up on to read, or just admire the sea, and, if the weather's decent, you can even swim outside; this, however, tends to be rare –except in the height of summer – because of the ship's speed and wind speed.

One of the classic things to do is to enjoy the typically British afternoon teatime, complete with cakes, scones, pastries, and finger sandwiches – all served by a rather hurried white-gloved staff – together with tea, and accompanied by live, light classical music.

The problem is that you'll find there simply isn't enough time to do everything, and there's no way you'll ever get bored aboard this ship.

You can also get married in mid-Atlantic during a crossing. Cunard started its its now popular 'Weddings At Sea' program in 2012. The first couple to be married by the ship's captain was Dr. William DeLuca (from the US) and Kelly Lewis (from the UK). They couldn't decide whether to marry in the UK or the US, so they chose halfway between the two (it was their first crossing, and, indeed, their first-ever vacation at sea). The couple chose Cunard because of the company's 'distinguished history of transatlantic crossings.' Note that only one wedding per day can be arranged, with a time of 11am or 3.30pm. Ceremonies take place only on days at sea, and every detail is planned by an onboard wedding coordinator. The cost starts at $2,500.

A memorable arrival

The day before you arrive in New York, Southampton, or (occasionally) in Hamburg, Germany, the disembarkation procedures will arrive in your suite or cabin. If you are in a hurry to disembark, you can opt to carry your own bags by registering for 'Express Disembarkation.'

Arriving in New York is one of cruising's iconic experiences, but you'll need to be up early. You'll see the lights of Long Island on your starboard side at about 4:30am, while the Verrazzano–Narrows suspension bridge, at the entrance to New York harbor, will be dead ahead. *QM2* usually passes the State of Liberty at about 6am – when a cabin with a balcony on the port side will give you the best views – and then makes a right turn opposite the statue towards the Brooklyn Cruise Terminal. On the occasions when the ship berths at Pier 90 in Manhattan at the Passenger Terminal, it will turn left towards the Hudson River – you'll get the best views of the Manhattan skyline at this point from a cabin with balcony on the starboard side. Arrival always creates a sense of anticipation of what lies ahead, and the feeling that, after a week of being cosseted, you will be thrust back into the fast lane with full force.

Leaving New York/arriving in Southampton

If you sail from Red Hook Point in Brooklyn, the last thing you'll notice before entering the ship is the overhead banner that declares: 'Leaving Brooklyn? Fuhgeddaboudit!' And that, dear reader, is *precisely* what a transatlantic crossing will have you do.

For arrival in Southampton, *QM2* will usually round the Isle of Wight at about 4:30am, and be berthed alongside in Southampton by around 6:30am. Immigration is upon arrival in either New York or Southampton.

Repositioning crossings

Other cruise ships crossing the Atlantic are really little more than repositioning cruises – a way of moving ships that cruise the Mediterranean in summer to the Caribbean in winter, and vice versa, usually in spring and fall. Most of these ships cross the Atlantic using the sunny southern route, departing from southern ports such as Fort Lauderdale, San Juan, or Barbados, and ending the journey in Lisbon, Genoa, or Copenhagen via the Azores or the Canary Islands, off the coast of northern Africa.

These repositioning trips take longer – between eight and 12 days – but they do offer an alternative way of experiencing the romance and adventure of a crossing – with a number of sea days for total relaxation. Note that when the weather is not so good, the outdoor swimming pools will probably be out of use on repositioning crossings.

World Cruises

Taking an around-the-world cruise is a great way to travel without having to pack and unpack constantly. But choose carefully: some ships spend very little time in ports.

Since Cunard operated its first world cruise aboard the *Laconia* in 1922, this has become the ultimate classic journey – more a voyage of discovery than a cruise. It is defined as the complete circumnavigation of the earth in a continuous one-way voyage, typically including both the Panama and Suez canals. Ports of call are carefully planned for their interest and diversity, and the entire voyage can last six months or longer.

Galas, themed balls (for example, Cunard's Black & White Ball and Royal Ascot Ball), special social events, top entertainers, and, typically, well-known lecturers are all part of the package. It's a great way of exchanging the northern winter for the southern sun in a grand voyage that is over 32,000 nautical miles long, following in the wake of Ferdinand Magellan, who led his round-the-world voyage in 1519–22, although he himself was killed en route.

Around-the-world cruises generally pursue the sun in a westbound direction, which gives the added bonus of gaining an hour each time a ship goes into the next time zone. Travel in an eastbound direction – between, for example, Europe and Australia – and you lose an hour each time. A few ships that include an around-South America voyage will generally travel in a southbound, then westbound, direction.

Aurora transiting the scenic Panama Canal.

A world cruise means letting time stand still, enjoying stabilized, air-conditioned comfort in luxury cabins, combined with extraordinary sightseeing and excursions on shore and overland. It is all about exchanging familiar environments with new ones, glamorous evening soirées, special social parties, themed balls, and entertainment that ranges from intimate recitals to large-scale shows and headline cabaret specialty acts. Best of all: you need pack and unpack just once during a three-month circumnavigation.

It generally appeals to retirees, anyone who simply wants to escape the winter, and those who delight in roaming the world in search of new experiences, sights, sounds, cultures, and aromas. However, two young children, Henrique D'Amore Nogeuira (age 6) and Lorenna D'Amore Nogeuira (age 4) made history when they took a 180-day world cruise with parents Diego and Drielle D'Amore Nogeuira aboard Oceania Cruises' *Insignia* in 2018.

There are four aspects to a good world cruise: itinerary, ship, price, and the cruise line's experience. Some of the most ambitious itineraries are those operated by cruise lines such as Hapag-Lloyd Cruises and Phoenix Reisen (whose itineraries usually feature more than 60 ports of call, compared to the average 35). Staying overnight in several ports of call means that you can plan to meet friends, go out for dinner, and enjoy nights out on the town. But check cruise line websites and brochures and itineraries carefully, because some ships spend surprisingly little time in port. There'll be lots of sea days, during which your suite or cabin can be a private refuge, so it's worth choosing the best you can afford.

World cruise segments

If you want to experience all the extra things that around-the-world cruises provide but don't have the three months needed, most lines offer the cruise in several 'segments.' This way you can try the ship and service levels before investing the time and money needed for a full circumnavigation. The most popular length for a segment is 20–30 days.

'Segmenters,' as they are known, will typically add on a stay pre- or post-cruise in a destination combining a cruise 'n' stay vacation. In this way, they can visit exotic destinations such as China, the South Pacific, the Indian Ocean, or South America, while also enjoying the elegance, comfort, splendid food, and good company of their cruise ship.

Bear in mind that you get what you pay for. Ships that we have rated at four stars or more will probably include shuttle buses from your ship to town centers; ships rated three stars or less will not.

Ships that roam worldwide during the year offer the most experienced world cruises or segments. In August 2016, for example, *Europa 2* operated a world voyage lasting 337 days, divided into three routes and more than 20 segments.

In 2020, Oceania Cruises' *Insignia* will sail 44,000 miles (71,000km) on its 180-day world cruise, cross the equator 4 times, cross 27 time zones, visit 95 ports in 38 countries, have 17 overnight stays, 24 islands, cross 18 seas, and have a choice of 70 shore excursions.

What's the cost?

Prices for a full world cruise vary depending on the cruise line, ship, number of days, and accommodation chosen. The following examples are taken from 2020 world cruise brochures, with per person prices based on two per cabin.

Arcadia (P&O Cruises): from £12,269 (100 days, from Southampton)
Boudicca (Fred. Olsen Cruise Lines): from £14,999 (168 days, from Dover)
Insignia (Oceania Cruises): from $41,999 (134 days, from Miami)
MSC Magnifica (MSC Cruises): from £11,249 (117 days, from Genoa)
Seven Seas Mariner (Regent Seven Seas Cruises): from £53,629 (132 days, from San Francisco)
Silver Whisper (Silversea Cruises): from $62,000 (140 days, from Fort Lauderdale)

One of the more unusual ships to operate an around-the-world cruise in 2020 is the Japanese ship *Asuka II* (ex-*Crystal Harmony*) from Yokohama.

Substantial discounts and special incentives are offered if you book early. The lowest-grade cabins tend to sell out fastest, so book as soon as you can to secure one of these. Some cruise lines quote only a 'from' price as a lead-in rate and provide the price for the largest suites upon application.

Passengers booking a full world cruise may enjoy a pre-cruise five-star hotel stay and an extravagant dinner with the cruise line's top executives, plus other special events during the cruise (not available to 'the segmenters'), and onboard credits. Generally, excursions are not included (exception: Regent Seven Seas Cruises).

Some cruise lines reserve the right to add a surcharge if the NYMEX (New York Mercantile Exchange Index) oil price exceeds $70 a barrel – read the fine print in the brochure. Also, the lowest prices may not include the airfare, if required.

Some ships include alcoholic drinks and wine in their cruise fares (such as *Crystal Serenity*, *Seabourn Ovation*, *Seven Seas Mariner*, and *Silver Spirit*), but many do not. There will inevitably be the question of gratuities to staff, if not included in the fare, factor in about $20 per person, per day to your budget.

Europa 2 anchored in Bora Bora.

Shore excursions

Part of the excitement of an around-the-world voyage is the anticipation of seeing new destinations and planning how best to use your time. This is where the expertise of a cruise line's shore-excursion departments and concierges can prove worthwhile.

Aboard some ships, tailor-made excursions are available, as are extras such as arranging private cars with a driver and guide for a few hours or a whole day.

Overland tours lasting from one to five days are sometimes featured. Here, you leave the ship in one port and re-join in another a few days later – for example, leave the ship in Mumbai, fly to Agra to experience the Taj Mahal, and perhaps ride aboard the

PLANNING

For passengers, one of the most important decisions to make will be about what clothes to pack for different climates and conditions. What's good is that once you are aboard, you will only need to unpack once. Also, you can take as much luggage as you wish. (However, note that many of the smaller ships have very limited luggage storage space, and drawer space for clothes may also be minimal.) If you need to fly to join the cruise, you can send your luggage on ahead with a courier service. Although all ships have laundries, some also have self-service launderettes (the place to go for all the inside gossip), so you can clean small items that you need to reuse quickly. Tip: take a dental repair kit, because there is no dentist on board.

For an operator, planning a world cruise involves daunting organization. For example, more than 700,000 main meals are prepared during a typical world cruise aboard *Queen Mary 2*. A ship of its size needs two major crew changes during a three-month-long voyage. Hundreds of professional entertainers, lecturers, bands, and musicians must be booked a year in advance.

Queen Mary 2 in Sydney during a world cruise.

Maharajas' Express train, then fly to another port to re-join the ship. Depending on the 'overland' country, you may need to apply for a visa before your voyage.

One frustration for independent passengers not wishing to join organized excursions is the lack of port information. The answer is to do the research yourself. Books in the ship's library should help if you haven't done your homework before embarking, as, of course, will information available over the Internet.

Celebrations at sea

On around-the-world cruises, special dates for English-speaking passengers are usually observed with decorations, dinners, dances, teas, and menus that reflect the occasion. Examples include: Burns Night, Valentine's Day, Australia Day, April Fool's Day, May Day, etc.

FLAGS AND PENNANTS

Looking at the mast of a cruise ship, you will see several different flags and pennants being used. If you know your flags, then you can read the mast like a book. A ship always flies its own 'house' flag proudly on the mast. When a vessel pulls into port, the national flag of the country being visited is flown in courteous recognition of the host country. Should the ship's captain request a local pilot to assist with maneuvering in and out of channels or ports where a local expert is required to take charge, a blue-and-yellow flag with vertical stripes is flown. A half-red, half-white flag divided vertically shows passengers (and other vessels) that a pilot is on board.

Jan 25: Robert Burns Night (Burns Dinner).
Jan 26: Australia's National Constitution Day.
Feb 6: New Zealand (Waitangi) Day.
Feb 14: St. Valentine's Day.
Mar 1: St. David's Day (patron saint of Wales).
Feb/Mar (Tue before Lent): Shrove Tuesday (pancakes galore)
Mar 17: St. Patrick's Day (patron saint of Ireland – think green beer).
Apr 1: April Fool's Day (a morning of jokes and tricks).
Apr 23: St. George's Day (patron saint of England).
May 1: May Day (traditional Morris dancing).

Two special ceremonies form part of the passenger participation events on a traditional around-the-world cruise:

Crossing the Equator, when King Neptune (Neptunus Rex, the old man of the sea), his wife Amphitrite, and the Royal Court initiate those crossing the line for the first time (called pollywogs). An old naval tradition, it is usually conducted at the poolside – with inevitable results.

Crossing the International Date Line, where you gain or lose a day, depending on whether you're traveling eastbound or westbound. The imaginary line, at approximately 180 degrees longitude, isn't straight but zigzags to avoid splitting countries apart. Although it was established with international agreement, there are no formal treaties or conventions. It has confused explorers, navigators, and travelers ever since man began circumnavigating the globe 500 years ago. In Jules Verne's *Around the World in 80 Days* Phileas Fogg and his crew returned to London one day late (or so they thought), but it was the extra day gained by crossing the International Date Line that enabled them to win their wager.

35 Wonderful Cruise Experiences

During the 35-year lifespan of this book, I have been privileged to enjoy some wonderful experiences aboard cruise ships. Here, in no particular order, are 35 wonderful cruise experiences.

Fingal's Cave
Passing within an arm's distance of Fingal's Cave on the uninhabited island of Staffa (one of Scotland's Inner Hebridean Islands), as Felix Mendelssohn's *Hebrides Overture* (inspired by the real molten lava rock cavern) was played on the open back deck of the pocket-sized *Hebridean Princess*. At the time – late one chilly morning in spring – I was sitting wrapped in a tartan blanket under a grey, foreboding sky, enjoying a single malt whisky.

Slice of ice
Watching from the observation deck above the bridge of *Hanseatic*, as the ship sliced slowly through the pack-ice in the incredibly scenic, steep-sided Lemaire Channel in the Antarctic Peninsula.

'Europa's Best'
Tasting some beautiful artisan cuisine prepared by chefs whose restaurants had three Michelin three stars aboard Europa for the annual Europa's Best event in Antwerp. Some of the finest cheese and wine producers from Austria, France, Germany, and Switzerland displayed their wares, too. This culinary heaven can be enjoyed by anyone with a ticket.

Bite of Apple
Gliding past the Statue of Liberty in the early-morning mist and then approaching the New York skyline, from the outside deck aboard *Queen Mary 2*. Anyone can experience this, whether aboard *Queen Mary 2* or any cruise ship sailing into New York.

The Royal Box
Having breakfast in a 'Royal Box' on deck aboard the boutique ships *SeaDream I* or *SeaDream II* while at sea in a warm weather area.

Culinary tour de force
Enjoying freshly sliced tuna and yellowtail sashimi at Nobu Matsuhisa's Silk Road Sushi Bar aboard *Crystal Serenity*. Not only was this a culinary tour de force, but watching the Japanese chefs was entertaining, too.

Amalfi magic
Sitting on the corner balcony of a Club Suite aboard *Azamara Quest*, admiring the beautiful scenery of Sorrento, Italy, with the ship at anchor off the famed coastline and a Limoncello to hand.

Candles in the wind
Dining by candlelight at the aft terrace café of *Aegean Odyssey* while watching the mesmerizing patterns created on the water by a full, seemingly orange moon in Southeast Asia.

Noodles in Alaska
Sitting on my balcony, breathing in the fresh air and enjoying room-service steaming hot udon noodles, while transiting Alaska's Inside Passage aboard *Nippon Maru*.

Sydney sights
Being outside on deck watching as *Queen Mary 2* turned majestically in Sydney Harbour and sidled up to Circular Quay, close to the Sydney Harbour Bridge and Opera House. All this with hundreds of spectators.

Blue lagoon nights
Lying down in the padded 'Blue Lagoon' seating area at the stern of the *Sea Cloud*, watching the sails directing this wonderful tall ship and seeing a shooting star pass quickly overhead – a most serene experience.

Shackleton's grave
One Christmas Day, paying homage in Grytviken – the former Norwegian whaling station in South Georgia – with passengers from the expedition ships *Bremen*

Douglas Ward at Shackleton's grave, South Georgia.

and *Hanseatic*. We toasted the explorer Sir Ernest Shackleton with Aquavit at his grave.

The green flash
Cruising aboard a *Hurtigruten* ship, near Hammerfest or Honningsvag on the northern coast of Norway in October, and seeing the 'green flash' of the northern lights appear on the horizon, as the sun dipped and disappeared.

Under the stars
Standing on deck at the front of the ship, just before bedtime, in one of the wonderfully comfortable cotton sleep suits provided aboard *SeaDream I* and *SeaDream II*. The rhythm of the ship was lulling me to sleep as it sailed to its next destination.

Spiderman
Sitting in the netting hanging at the bowsprit (front) of the sail-cruise ship (tall ship) *Star Flyer* – an exhilarating experience. On this occasion, the ship was gliding gracefully through the water on a perfect, sun-filled day in the azure blue Caribbean Sea.

Misty morning
Standing on the foredeck of a cruise ship entering Ha Long Bay, a Unesco-protected World Heritage site in the Gulf of Tonkin in Quang Ninh Province in north-eastern Vietnam. Go in the early morning, when the mist is heavy, for an ethereal feeling of calmness. The dramatic limestone karsts (stone islands) surrounding the ship loom up from the sea-level cloud of heavy air.

Queen and country
Taking a bath in Cabin 1066 of the *Queen Elizabeth 2* one evening during a transatlantic crossing, listening to Elgar's *Pomp and Circumstance* on the in-cabin broadcast system and thinking: how incredibly British.

Canal move
Watching as steel-wired electric mules (each costing over $2 million) pull your cruise ship into position in one of the lock chambers at Miraflores Locks, in the Panama Canal.

Bird's-eye view
Being aboard a cruise ship sailing into or out of Venice, gliding past St Mark's Square. It's a view of Venice you only get from the deck (or balcony – if yours is on the correct side) of a waterborne vessel.

Steps away
Being aboard a small cruise ship moored alongside the State Hermitage Museum in St. Petersburg, Russia. This takes you literally just a few steps away from the iconic building – one of the largest and oldest museums in the world, with over 3 million items in its collection, including some stunning Fabergé eggs.

Titanic pose
Standing with outstretched arms, just like Kate Winslet in the movie *Titanic*, at the front of *Braemar*, as the ship glided slowly through the Swedish archipelago towards Stockholm.

On top of the world
Standing at 90 degrees north – the geographic North Pole (it's actually an ice flow) – literally looking down the world (the first human set foot there in 1948). I reached the North Pole in 2016 aboard

The Blue Lagoon thermal hot spring, Iceland.

the stunning Russian nuclear-powered icebreaker *50 Years of Victory*.

Bathtub cruising

Staring at the horizon while lying in the bathtub in the 'wet room' (with heated floor) in one of the two Deck 10 Crystal Penthouse suites aboard *Crystal Symphony*, as the ship glided through open water.

Grand spa

Sitting in the hot bath of the grand spa aboard Asuka II late at night – looking out over the city lights in Naha, the port for Okinawa, Japan.

Paw power

Being pulled by a team of huskies in Juneau, Alaska, as we sped past glaciers and ice peaks (taken in combination with a flight to Mendenhall Glacier).

Slipping away

Sitting on the deck of a pocket-sized cruise ship in Glacier Bay, Alaska, watching the blue glacial ice calving, making you rock and roll as it slipped, slid, and crashed into the water within inches of your body.

Melting away

Sitting in a pool of silica- and sulphur-rich geo-thermal water in Iceland's Blue Lagoon – a man-made outlet, close to the Svartsengi Power Station and part of the lava field located on the Reykjanes Peninsula. This is offered as part of a tour from your cruise ship.

Surprise, surprise

Meeting someone you never expected to, or thought possible to meet. On cruises over the years, I have been fortunate enough to meet, talk to, and have a drink with some well-known film stars and other famous personalities including Elizabeth Taylor and Richard Burton, Tippi Hedren, Dame Margot Fonteyn, and the great conductor Leopold Stokowski.

Photo opportunity

Being aboard a photo tender arranged by the cruise line (in my case, this was aboard a tall ship) and taking photographs as the tall ship was under full sail and not slowing down. An exhilarating experience that you can still enjoy.

Passing the lava

Being aboard a cruise ship off the north coast of Sicily, where you pass close to Stromboli in action. The almost constantly erupting volcano bursts into life and emits incandescent lava.

Natural wonders

I was on deck aboard an expedition cruise ship in Antarctic waters when a number of killer whales (or-

cas) began splashing in the water just off the starboard side aft, making the ship roll. They were so close that I could have touched one of their dorsal fins. A spectacular show of nature.

New Year's Eve pyrotechnics

Being aboard ship supping Champagne while enjoying the magnificently colorful New Year's Eve fireworks display in Funchal, Madeira. A cruise ship offers the very best vantage point for this fantastic display.

Zip-a-dee-doo-dah

Careening along the zipline strung between rows of cabins high above the deck of *Allure of the Seas, Harmony of the Seas* or *Oasis of the Seas*. Quite a surprise to the occupants of some of the interior promenade balcony cabins!

Maiden cruise

Enjoying the anticipation and excitement of a maiden voyage aboard a brand new ship is an experience highly prized among cruise collectors. Just be prepared for the fact that it might not all be smooth sailing, and there might be teething troubles.

Three-Michelin-starred chef Kevin Fehling aboard *Europa*.

Happy ever after

Looking for a partner? I met my wife aboard a Japanese cruise ship many years ago. You too, could meet the person of your dreams aboard a cruise ship – it happens all the time.

35 WAYS TO UPGRADE YOUR CRUISE EXPERIENCE

There are many ways to enhance your cruise and vacation – some of which will add little or no cost, and some may cost more, but add value and comfort. Your cruise booking agent may also be able to obtain additional 'perks' at no additional cost to you. Here are 35 suggestions for you to consider.

1. Take a digital detox cruise – turn off your mobile phone for a whole cruise, or at least a few days.

2. Go farther afield – take a cruise to an area of the world you haven't yet been to.

3. If you need to fly to get to your ship, consider upgrading from Economy (Coach) Class to Business or First Class.

4. Upgrade your accommodation (if the ship is not full) by paying extra when on board.

5. Be the first to sleep in a brand new bed by booking a maiden voyage aboard a brand new ship.

6. Upgrade your accommodation, if the budget allows. Consider upgrading from an interior (no-view) cabin to one with a window, or a 'virtual' balcony.

7. Consider upgrading from a 'standard' cabin with a window to one with a balcony.

8. If possible, upgrade from a balcony cabin to a suite, as you'll get more 'perks' and better service.

9. Consider upgrading from a 'suite' with just a shower enclosure to a suite, with both a bathtub and a separate shower enclosure.

10. And think about upgrading from standard suite to a grand suite, a penthouse suite, or an 'owner's suite' for even more recognition and more 'perks.'

11. For a more intimate dining experience, reserve a table in one of the extra-cost (à la carte) restaurants.

12. Upgrade your fitness level – have a 'no elevator' day (or two, or more).

13. Upgrade your health by eating lighter, 'heart-healthy' options.

14. If you are a meat eater, have a meat-free day (numerous non-meat choices are available aboard any cruise ship).

15. For a special day, have breakfast in bed – with Champagne.

16. Try a higher-quality wine or Champagne on a special day (birthday, anniversary, or other celebration).

17. Book a culinary lesson aboard a ship with built-in cooking stations, so you can experience 'hands-on' with a professional.

18. Upgrade your drinks package from 'standard' to 'premium' and taste better brands, drinks, and wines.

19. Take a look at your ship at arm's length in a 'glass capsule' aboard *Anthem of the Seas*, *Ovation of the Seas*, *Quantum of the Seas*, or *Spectrum of the Seas*.

20. Try a new activity – sign-up for something you'd never considered doing before.

21. Learn something new: for example, how to play a keyboard instrument. You can take part in free hands-on classes aboard *Crystal Serenity* or *Crystal Symphony*.

22. Book a session or two with a personal trainer.

23. If you've never had one, try a body-pampering treatment (suggestions: a full body massage, a facial, or, if you are traveling with a partner, a couples massage).

24. Book a private (extra-cost) deck night aboard *Azamara Journey*, *Azamara Pursuit*, or *Azamara Quest*. The experience involves drinks, a hot tub, and sleeping on deck.

25. If you're married, why not think about renewing your commitment in a Renewal of Vows ceremony?

26. Take a social dance lesson – learn how to do the waltz, foxtrot, quickstep, samba, or tango.

27. Reserve a 'Royal Box' (Champagne and chocolates included) in the Royal Court Theater for the show aboard Cunard's *Queen Elizabeth* or *Queen Victoria*.

28. Take a transatlantic crossing aboard a real ocean liner. Queen Mary 2 is the only ship built for all weather conditions in the North Atlantic. It's one of the best ways to arrive in a different continent without jet lag.

29. If you are traveling with a baby, take advantage of a night nursery (free aboard Cunard and P&O Cruises ships, but at extra cost aboard most others), so you can have some 'me-time' in the evening – and some decent sleep.

30. When you come back from a morning excursion, instead of heading to the self-serve buffet, have a calm room-service lunch.

31. Get real insight into a place you want to visit by booking a private tour with a local guide.

32. Book a post-cruise stay, so disembarkation day becomes less frenetic and gives you time to adjust to 'normality.'

33. Take a cooking class aboard a ship that has a dedicated built-in culinary center.

34. Leave the kids at home (with grandparents) and choose an adults-only ship.

35. Close up the house and take an around-the-world cruise.

Life Aboard

This A to Z survey covers the astonishing range of facilities that modern cruise ships offer and tells you how to make the most of them.

Air conditioning

Cabin temperature is regulated by an individually controlled thermostat, so you can adjust it to suit yourself. However, aboard some ships, the cabin air conditioning can't be turned off.

Art auctions

Aboard many large resort ships, art auctions provide cruise line revenue. They are participation events – though 'free Champagne' given to entice customers is usually sparkling wine and not authentic Champagne, while most of the art is rubbish.

Art 'appraisal prices' are done by the art provider, a company that pays a cruise line to be on board. Watch out for 'retail replacement value,' a misleading term used by the art salespeople. Listen for phrases such as 'signed in the stone' – it means that the artists did not sign the work – or *'pochoire'* (a stencil print less valuable than an original etching or lithograph). If the auctioneer tries to sell a piece of art (particularly a 'block' print or woodcut/engraving) with an 'authenticated signature,' don't buy it – when it's delivered to your home and you have it appraised, you'll probably find it's not genuine.

Cashless cruising

An imprint of your credit card is taken at embarkation or when you register online, permitting you to sign for everything if it's not automatically charged to your cabin key card. Before the end of the cruise, a detailed statement is delivered to your cabin. You simply settle your account with one payment (by cash or credit card) before your final disembarkation.

However, it's easy to overspend, so budget wisely and watch your spending.

Some cruise lines irritatingly discontinue their 'cashless' system for the last day before disembarkation. Some may add a 'currency conversion service charge' to your credit card account if it is not in the cruise line's currency.

Comment cards

On the last (or penultimate) day of the cruise you will be asked to fill out a 'comment card.' Some lines offer 'incentives' such as a bottle of Champagne. Be truthful, as the form serves as a means of communication between you and the cruise line (as in many chain hotels). Pressure from staff to write 'excellent' for everything is rampant, but, unless you highlight problems you have encountered, things won't improve.

Disembarkation

This can be the most trying end to any cruise. The cruise director gives an informal talk on customs, immigration, and disembarkation procedures. The night before the ship reaches its disembarkation destination, you may receive a customs form to complete. Save any receipts from any 'duty-free' items you may have purchased in case a customs officer asks for them.

The night before arrival at your cruise's final destination, place your main baggage outside your cabin on retiring (the cruise line will give its time deadline). It will be collected and offloaded on arrival. Leave out fragile items and the clothes you intend to wear for disembarkation and onward travel – it is amazing just how many people pack absolutely everything. Anything left in your cabin will be considered hand luggage.

'Me-time' beauty treatment.

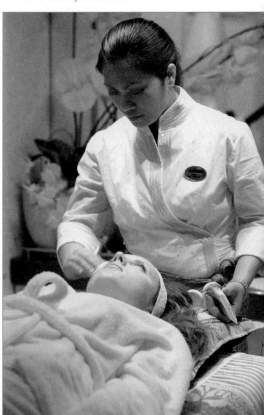

Disembarking from large resort ships can be tedious.

Before disembarking, remember to empty your personal safe. You cannot go ashore until all baggage has been offloaded and customs and/or immigration inspections or pre-inspections have been carried out. In most ports, this takes two to three hours after arrival.

On disembarkation day, breakfast will probably be early (it might be better to miss breakfast and sleep later). Even worse than early breakfast is the fact that aboard many ships you will be required to leave your cabin early, only to wait in crowded public rooms until your color-coded disembarkation grouping is called.

Once off the ship, you identify your baggage on the pier before going through customs inspection. Porters may be there to assist you.

Duty-free liquor

If you buy any 'duty-free' liquor along the way, it will be taken from you at the gangway as you board and given back to you the day before you disembark. This is because cruise lines want you to buy your alcohol on board.

Engine room

For insurance and security reasons, visits to the engine room are seldom allowed. Some ships have a technical information leaflet or a behind-the-scenes video on the cabin infotainment system. Some ships offer extra-cost 'Behind-the-Scenes' tours, which include the Engine Control Room (but not the engine room).

Etiquette

Two points that are sometimes overlooked:

1) International copyright laws prohibit you from recording the professional entertainment shows.
2) It is fine to dress in a casual manner onboard ship, but disrespectful to staff if you enter a ship's dining room in just a bathing suit, or with bare feet.

Gratuities/tips

Aboard many large resort ships, tipping seems to be mandatory rather than voluntary. Gratuities, typically of around $14 per person ($17 or so for occupants of suite-grade or butler-service accommodation), per day, are added automatically to your shipboard account. These may need to be converted to your credit card currency at the prevailing rate.

As an example, aboard most ships of Norwegian Cruise Line, the standard per person per day gratuity (at the time of going to press) is $14.50 ($17.50 for suite-grade occupants. That amounts to: $101.50 or $122.50 per person for a 7-day cruise.

Be aware that cabin stewards have been known to scroll through passengers' accounts on the in-cabin infotainment system, and can tell if you have opted out of the automatic gratuity charge!

Gratuities are included in the cruise fare aboard some ships, but even so, extra gratuities are often expected by the staff. Aboard some ships, strong suggestions are made regarding tips by tacky cruise directors.

Tips are normally given on the last evening of a cruise of up to 14 days' duration. For longer cruises, give half the tip halfway through and the rest on your last evening.

Aboard many ships, a gratuity (typically of 15 percent) is automatically added to your bar check, whether you get good service or not, and a gratuity (of 15–20 percent) may be added for spa treatments.

Internet access and cell (mobile) phones

Smartphone/cell phone use aboard ships is common, and most have ship-wide Wi-Fi (at a price). Before you cruise, check with your phone operator for the international roaming rates applicable to your tariff. Calls (at sea) are handled by a marine telecommunications network, which passes on international roaming charges to your phone operator.

Signal strength can vary substantially from hour to hour. The farther north you get, the closer the telecommunications satellite is to the horizon, so signals tend to fade in and out, and waiting for web pages to appear on your computer screen can be frustrating.

Turn off Data Roaming to save charges and Location Services to prevent apps from constantly trying to update your location. Turn off the 'Push' option relating to your e-mail, because some accounts, including Gmail, push the data to your smartphone, incurring charges even if you don't open any e-mails. Turn off the option to synchronize data between devices, because it consumes bandwidth trying to keep your accounts up to date. Better still – have a digital detox and turn your mobile phone off completely.

Launch (shore tender) services

Enclosed or open motor launches ('tenders') are used when your cruise ship is unable to berth at a port or island. In such cases, a regular launch service is operated between ship and shore for the port call. Aboard the large resort ships, you'll need to obtain a tender ticket, usually given out in one of the lounges, unless you are on an organized excursion, which take priority. The procedure can be lengthy.

When stepping on or off a tender, extend 'forearm' to forearm' to the person who is assisting you. Do not grip their hands because this has the unintentional effect of immobilizing the helper.

Laundry and dry cleaning

Most ships offer a full laundry and pressing (ironing) service. Some ships may also offer dry-cleaning facilities. A detailed list of services, and prices, will be in your cabin. Your steward will collect and deliver your clothes. Some ships have self-service launderettes, well equipped with washers, dryers, and ironing facilities. There may be a charge for washing powder and for the use of the machines.

Library

Some ships have a library offering a selection of books, reference material, and periodicals. Aboard the smaller ships, the library is open 24/7. Aboard the large resort ships, the library may be open only for a few hours a day and lack a real librarian with whom passengers can discuss books and authors. *Queen Mary 2, Queen Elizabeth,* and *Queen Victoria* have the largest libraries. Unfortunately, many

Tenders transport passengers when a ship can't dock, as seen here aboard *Regatta*.

ships state that they have a library, but it may be nothing more than a few shelves, with paperback books in no particular order. These ships often lack reference books such as a world atlas, Scrabble and crossword dictionaries, rules for board games, or a thesaurus.

Aboard specialist expedition ships, the library is one of the most important – and most used – facilities, and high-quality reference books on all aspects of nature, marine life, and polar exploration are provided.

Lido

Aboard the larger ships, this deck is for waterparks, pools, hot tubs, and other active and recreation facilities, often with intrusive 'background' music. Aboard most cruise ships, it also includes an adjacent self-serve buffet.

Lost property

Contact the reception desk immediately if you lose or find something.

Mail

You may be able to buy stamps and mail letters at the reception desk. Some ships use the postal privileges and stamps of their flag of registration; oth-

ers buy local stamps at ports of call. Mail is usually taken ashore by the ship's port agent just before the ship sails.

Medical care

Doctors aboard most cruise ships work as a concession. They are required to have current medical licensing, three years of post-medical school clinical practice, certification in emergency medicine, family practice, or internal medicine or experience as a GP or Emergency Ward doctor. So, if you have a serious health issue that predates your cruise, or a permanent disability, you need to be upfront about it (and any treatment) with your travel agent or the cruise line's reservationist before you book. They may be able to advise you on a ship that best meets your needs.

Anyone with long-term health issues should get prescriptions made up for the whole period of the cruise, because many places will not process prescriptions from other countries. Aboard some ships, you may be charged for filling a prescription as well as for the cost of prescribed drugs. Take out a travel insurance policy that reimburses you for visits to the onboard medical service, but check the small print. Insurance companies often refuse to pay out if you had a condition you didn't mention

Splashaway Bay aboard *Liberty of the Seas*.

No bathing suits in the casual eatery, please!

when you purchased the policy. Most medical care on cruise ships is perfectly adequate. In case it isn't, the cruise lines have a clause that says they are not responsible for the malpractice of their doctors.

Photographs

Professional photographers on board take digital pictures of you at embarkation and throughout the cruise. They cover all the main events and social functions, such as a captain's cocktail party. Photographs can be viewed without any obligation to buy.

Pre-paid drinks

Most large resort ships offer drinks packages in an effort to 'add value.' However, although these booze-cruise packages mean that you don't need to sign each time you order a drink, they really are a temptation to drink more. Some packages include wine, but it's the cruise line's choice – not yours.

Reception desk

Also known as the purser's office, guest relations, or information desk, it will be centrally located. It is the nerve center of the ship for information and problems.

Religious services

Interdenominational services are conducted on board many ships – usually by the captain or staff captain. All Costa Cruises' ships have a small private chapel. Denominational services may also be held by clergy traveling as passengers.

Room service

Beverages and snacks are available at most times. Liquor is normally limited to the opening hours of the ship's bars. Some ships charge for room service.

Sailing time

In each port, sailing and all-aboard times are posted at the gangway. The all-aboard time is usually half an hour before sailing. If you miss the ship, it's entirely your responsibility to get to the next port of call to rejoin the vessel.

Swimming pools

Most ships have swimming pools outdoors; some have pools that can be covered by glass domes in case of inclement weather, while a handful of ships have indoor pools located on a low deck. Pools may be closed in port owing to local health regulations. Diving is not allowed (pools are shallow).

Some ships use excessive chlorine or water-treatment agents, which might cause bathing suits to fade.

Telephone calls

Most ships have direct-dial satellite telephones, so you can call anywhere in the world. Ships have an internationally recognized radio call sign, a combination of letters and digits, for example: C6SE7.

A wine tower aboard *Celebrity Eclipse*.

To reach a ship from land, dial the International Direct Dial (IDD) code for the country you are calling from, followed by the ship's telephone number.

Anyone without a direct-dial telephone should call the High Seas Operator. The operator will need the name of the ship, together with the ocean code: At-lantic East is 871; Pacific is 872; Indian Ocean is 873; Atlantic West/Caribbean/US is 874.

Television

Programming is obtained from a mixture of paid satellite feeds and onboard videos. Some ships lock on to live international news programs such as CNN or BBC World, or to text-only news services. Satellite television reception can sometimes be poor because ships constantly move out of the satellite's narrow beam.

Valuables

Most cabins have a small personal safe, but items of high value should be kept in a safety deposit box at the reception desk.

Water sports

Some small ships have a water sports platform aft. These ships usually carry windsurfers, water-ski boats, jet skis, water skis, and scuba and snorkel equipment, usually at no extra charge – except for scuba equipment. Make sure you are covered by your travel insurance if you want to partake in water sports.

Wine and liquor

The cost of drinks on board is generally lower than on land since ships have access to duty-free liquor. Drinks may be ordered in the dining room, at the ship's bars, or from room service.

Some ships sell duty-free wine and liquor to drink in your cabin. You can't normally bring these into the dining room or public rooms, nor any duty-free wine or liquor bought in port. These rules protect bar sales, a substantial source of onboard revenue.

DID YOU KNOW...?

...that *Splendour of the Seas* (now *TUI Discovery*) was the first ship to include an iPad in every cabin? It was in 2011.

...that bingo game numbers aboard most ships only use numbers up to 75? On some UK-based cruise lines, however, the bingo numbers go to 99.

...that there is no Deck 13 aboard any ships of Princess Cruises? Good for the superstitious.

...that Royal Caribbean International's *Legend of the Seas* (presently Marella Cruises' *Marella Discovery 2*) was named with the world's largest bottle of Champagne? It had to be specially made and was a 'Sovereign-size' bottle (the equivalent of 34 bottles) of Moët & Chandon Champagne.

...that the first vessel built exclusively for cruising was Hamburg-America Line's two-funnel *Princessin Victoria Luise*? This luxury yacht even included a private suite for the German Kaiser.

...that the United States Line's *Manhattan* of 1931 was the first ship to have a cocktail named after it?

...that when sailing from England to the Caribbean in 'the old days' a rule of thumb was to sail south until the butter melts, then proceed west?

...that the longest bar aboard any cruise ship can be found aboard *AIDAcara*? It is 195ft (59.5m) long.

...that someone forgot to score the Champagne bottle when Dame Judi Dench named *Carnival Legend* in Harwich, England, on August 21, 2002? On the first two tries, the bottle didn't break. Then Dame Judi took the bottle in her hands and smashed it against the side of the ship. When it broke, the Champagne went all over her, and she was dubbed Dame Judi Drench.

...that from January 2000 until the ship was retired in 2008 octogenarian American Beatrice Muller made Cunard Line's *Queen Elizabeth 2* her permanent home at sea? She preferred life aboard to the daily drudgery of household chores and bills back home and paid a set amount to reside in Cabin 4068.

Cuisine

Anyone determined to eat around the clock could do so aboard many ships, but the health-conscious should exercise restraint, especially at self-service buffets.

Dining rooms and restaurants aboard any cruise ship are the collective lifeblood of the entire ship and hospitality experience. Except for the facilities and destinations, it's the food that most people remember and talk about.

Cruise lines love to boast about their food – and often with their celebrity TV chefs – who only sail occasionally for a bit of show. The reality is that most meals aboard most ships are not gourmet affairs. How could they be, when a kitchen has to turn out hundreds of meals at the same time? Most ships simply can't deliver the 'Wow' factor the brochure promises.

From morning until night, food is offered to the point of overkill, even aboard the most modest cruise ship. Aboard large resort ships, pizzas, burgers, hot dogs, ice cream, and frozen yogurt are almost always available. If you're still hungry, there's 24-hour room service, which, aboard some large resort ships, may cost extra. Some ships have extra-charge bistros, cafés, and patisseries.

As in most restaurants on land, you get what you pay for. High-quality ingredients cost money, so it's unrealistic to expect low-cost cruises to offer anything other than low-cost, pre-cooked food (with an overabundance of carbohydrate-rich components such as potato, rice, pasta, and bread).

Most cruise ship cuisine compares favorably with 'banquet' hotel food. You can expect a selection of palatable and complete meals served properly in comfortable surroundings. Menus are typically displayed outside the dining room each day, while they may also be delivered to suite occupants. Depending on the ship and dining venue, some menus (and wine lists) are larger than newspapers, while others are dinky, with little choice.

Major cruise lines bulk-purchase food items, which means low-quality ingredients and cheaper cuts of meat, often 'enhanced' with preservatives. That said, cruise lines do sometimes upgrade food

items – Carnival Cruise Line and Royal Caribbean International, for example, introduced free-range eggs aboard their ships back in 2011. The trend now is for several 'alternative' (extra-cost) restaurants.

Food Tip: If you order an omelet, ask for it to be made (in front of you) with real eggs – many companies use the more convenient, 'liquid egg' mix.

What's new?

Lighter meals are more sought after by passengers concerned about their health and weight, so 'bistro'-style cuisine is being introduced by more cruise lines (particularly the smaller companies, such as Oceania Cruises.

Where's the (USDA) beef?

Menus, particularly in extra-cost venues, often state that their steaks are made with prime USDA (United States Department of Agriculture) beef. It's wise to ask which grade, as there are three main ones: USDA Prime (produced from young, well-fed beef

Chef Cornelius Gallagher puts the finishing touches to a Celebrity dessert.

BARBECUES AND HOT ROCK GRILLS

Some ships feature hot rocks grills. This is for steaks, grilled meats, and seafood presented on a platter that includes a scorching hot rock base – so you can cook however little or well you want it done yourself. It makes for a pleasant change, in a casual pool deck environment. Seabourn and Silversea Cruises pioneered this option.

Exquisite selection of sweet treats on a Celebrity cruise.

cattle; this provides the best-quality meat, with more marbling, meaning more moisture and better flavor); USDA Choice (some marbling – good for decent-quality steak); and USDA Select (leaner, with a rougher texture, and no marbling – adequate for BBQ). Other grades are: Standard, Commercial, Utility, Cutter, and Canner. Several cruise ships are introducing onboard maturation cellars, or cabinets, for drying meat. While the term 'dry-aged' beef confuses many, it comes from the British tradition of conserving beef by 'natural drying.' Some cuts are particularly good for grilling, and some breeds are preferred over others, due to their individual specificity. Meat specialists talk about the depth of quality, mostly depending on the length of maturation (it generally takes between 30 and 45 days).

CELEBRITY CHEFS

Several cruise lines have partnered with well-known chefs to devise menus for their cost-extra dining venues. Celebrity Cruises, for example, worked with three-star Michelin chef Michel Roux from 1989 until 2007 (even before that, the long-defunct Royal Viking Line worked with Paul Bocuse, with his own restaurant aboard *Royal Viking Sun*). It's worth paying extra because the price is less than it would be in the celebrity chef's land-based restaurants.

Most celebrity chefs sail only one or two cruises a year, but Germany's three-star Michelin chef Dieter Müller set a new benchmark when he sailed for up to half a year to run his eponymous restaurant aboard Hapag-Lloyd Cruises' highly-rated *Europa*. He's now been replaced by Hamburg's three-star Michelin chef Kevin Fehling, whose land-based restaurant is 'The Table').

Fresh versus frozen

Aboard low-priced cruises, you will typically be served portion-controlled frozen food that has been reheated. Fresh fish and the best cuts of meats cost more, and this is reflected in the cruise price. Aboard some ships, the 'fresh' fish – often described as 'catch of the day' – has clearly had no contact with the sea for some time.

Also, note that many items of 'fresh' fruit may have been treated with 1-MCP (methylcyclopropene) to make them last longer – apples, for example, may be up to a year old.

Sushi bars are a fashionable addition today. However, as the galley (kitchen) facilities on ships are generally inadequate to turn out food something as super-fresh as sushi, the only ships with authentic sushi bars and authentic sushi/sashimi are *Asuka II*, *Crystal Serenity*, *MSC Musica*, *MSC Poesia*, and *Nippon Maru*, and *Pacific Venus*.

Bread and pastry items

While there are exceptions, much of the bread baked aboard cruise ships is unappealing, because, with little time for fermentation of natural yeast, it is made instead with instant dough that contains dried yeast from packets. Many baked goods and pastry items are made mostly from refined flours and sugars.

Self-serve buffets

Most ships have self-serve buffets for breakfast and lunch (some also for dinner), and many seem to be called Marketplace (or Market Place), trying to get you to believe that the food is 'farm-to-table' fresh. But while buffets look fine at first, they don't after a few minutes of attack by passengers. Self-serve buffets have become more user-friendly by including more 'active cooking' stations and food islands, which help to break up lines created by typical straight-line buffet counters (which always remind me of school lunches.). Sadly, the buffet 'food' aboard most cruise ships has been blessed by the same magic wand of tastelessness. Dare to ask for something that's not on the display, however, and any form of human communication ceases and supervisors become invisible. For example: trying to get a freshly cooked four-minute soft-boiled egg at a breakfast buffet is a challenge. I am always met with: 'We've only got the ones in the bowl (or dish), sir.' But the 'eight-minute' eggs in the bowl have been sitting there since they were boiled at 4.30am before the buffet opened, and they're still under the infrared heat lamp at 9.30am! Plus, there are typically no eggcups – or small spoons to eat them with!

Nor can you expect to find the following at the large resort ships' breakfast and lunch buffets: warm plates (for 'hot' food items), fish knives, a smoked salmon omelet, soy milk, brown rice, fresh herbs, loose tea, or freshly grated nutmeg for oatmeal or cream of wheat. If you have food allergies, self-serve buffets will present a challenge, but, always, always, ask for help with regard to what's in what.

How buffets evolved

Lido deck buffets became popular because passengers relaxing at the poolside didn't want to dress to go to the dining room for lunch. So, self-serve buffets evolved from sunshine and the casual clothing concept.

Cruise ship self-serve buffets really started in 1969 with the introduction of Norwegian Caribbean Line's mv Sunward – an ex-Baltic cruise ferry – operating Miami to Bahamas "sunshine" cruises.

Almost all cruise ships have self-serve buffets. They are popular because they are casual, simplistic, and you can take as much or as little as you want (or need). Thankfully, the "all you can eat" type is going out of style. Now, more discerning passengers (including real 'foodies') are looking for healthier choices.

The 'Line System' consists of trays moved along rails in front of the buffet counters. The 'Island System' usually features 'active' stations (manned by cooks), with items (omelets, or pasta, for example) cooked individually in front of you

Trays are usually used for the Line System. The plates are usually oval-shaped and made from melamine because they withstand the high dishwasher temperatures.

Cold food displays are usually in white ceramic dishes, while hot food is usually displayed in stainless steel 'bain marie' units.

Deli-style (take-away) food

Take-away deli-style food can be found in outlets aboard some ships, for those times when you may want to sit somewhere quietly but still have a little pre-wrapped casual snack (think: small ready-made sandwiches, wraps, burritos, salad 'pots' with quinoa or bulgur wheat, for example). This started with the so-called 'café culture' found in coffee and sandwich shops at home.

Examples of companies with small, no extra-cost deli-style outlets for take-away food include P&O Cruises (aboard *Britannia*); Royal Caribbean International (Park Café aboard *Allure of the Seas*, *Harmony of the Seas*, *Oasis of the Seas*, and *Symphony of the Seas*).

Poolside grills

Poolside grills are popular, but usually attract long lines. Burgers and hot dogs may sound attractive, but are often disappointing. Aboard most large resort ships, it's not really possible to grill burgers individually. Aboard the smaller ships, however, they can be ordered and individually cooked.

Burgers are typically presented in a display tray for you to collect and then install your favorite

The captain giving a toast.

toppings (usually tomato slices, onions, and an iceberg lettuce leaf), with mustard and tomato ketchup in packets or pump bottles. However, the burgers may have been steamed, not grilled, before being placed in the display tray, because steaming them keeps them moist. If you like yours grilled, say so.

As for hot dogs, these may be either grilled or steamed. Commercially supplied dogs will be pre-cooked and only need warming and serving in a white bread roll. In case you don't eat certain types of meat, you may need to ask whether they are made of beef, pork, chicken, or a combination of these or other meat.

DID YOU KNOW?

The 'menu' (French) or 'bill of fare' (English) was originally never presented at the table. Meals consisted of two main courses, each with a variety of dishes – anything from 10 to 40. The first dishes were usually placed on the table before diners entered (thus the word *entrée*). When these had been consumed, they were removed or relieved by another set of dishes, known as the *relevé*, from the French 'to relieve' (a term no longer used in modern dining).

It was in 1541 that Duke Henry of Brunswick was seen to refer to a long slip of paper, which provided the order of the dishes. By referring to the list he could see what was coming next, and this enabled him to reserve his appetite accordingly. It is presumed that the menu was thus derived from this (or a similar) event.

It was common custom then to present a large bill of fare at the end of the table for patrons to read. Only later did the menu become smaller in size. It follows that a number of copies were then made, allowing each diner to have his/her own copy of the menu.

Sushi may be one of the healthier casual eatery options available.

For anyone on a special diet, alternatives may be available, including vegetarian and vegan, fish, lobster or shrimp burgers.

Alternative restaurants

Most new cruise ships have a number of specialty restaurants and dining venues that provide alternatives to the large main dining rooms. Extra-cost specialty restaurants were pioneered in 1936 by RMS *Queen Mary* (Verandah Grill, for first-class passengers only (who paid just over £1), and introduced in modern times by Norwegian Cruise Line in 1988 (The Bistro – an à la carte, extra-cost French dining spot). But it was Star Cruises that introduced *multiple* venues – seven of them – aboard *Star Aquarius* in 1993; some were included in the cruise price, others cost extra. Thus, was born 'Freestyle Cruising' – or dine where you want, when you want, and with whom you wish.

These specialist restaurants are smaller, à la carte venues, for which you make a reservation. In return, you get better food, wine selection, service, and ambience. Celebrity chefs may add to the mix and are asked to establish their own 'at sea' dining venues, or collaborate on menus for shipboard eateries, although they seldom appear on board. Usually, the menu remains the same throughout the cruise (hence the chefs can concentrate on getting it absolutely right), and also to give as many passengers as possible the chance to book and enjoy the venue.

Some specialty restaurants can also be entertaining, such as the Teppanyaki Grill aboard *Genting Dream*, *MSC Seaside*, and *Norwegian Bliss*, among others. Watch while the chefs chop, slice, and flip the food as they cook on an iron griddle next to the seating area. Twiddling and spinning utensils is part of the show!

Chef's Table

Pay-extra Chef's Tables, typically limited to a maximum 12 participants, are now found aboard many ships; they feature multiple fine-dining courses, with wine pairings for each course. The food is presented by the executive chef – hence the name Chef's Table.

Cooking classes

Speaking of chefs, culinary (cooking) classes and food-preparation demonstrations are hot today (no pun intended) aboard a handful of ships, sometimes given by visiting celebrity chefs and pâtissiers. Some ships have built-in cooking equipment – whole kitchens with induction cooktops workstations and stainless-steel washbasins within self-contained fire zones – stuffed with the latest equipment for hands-on participants.

AIDA Cruises' *AIDAnova*, Oceania Cruises' *Marina*, *Riviera*, Hapag-Lloyd Cruises *Europa 2*, and Regent Seven Seas Cruises' *Seven Seas Explorer* all have a fully equipped studio kitchen (each work station has an induction hob, washbasin, and preparation counter), for hands-on cooking classes. P&O Cruises'

Britannia also has one – called the 'Cooking Club' – created by TV chef James Martin. *Europa 2* has state-of-the-art Miele equipment in its Miele Culinary Arts School, with the same heat level controls as found in the company's domestic kitchen equipment, while most built-in cruise ship cooking studios have industrial equipment, with different heat levels to those you would find on equipment for home use. There are between 12 and 24 cooking stations (for example, *Europa 2* has 12; *Seven Seas Explorer* has 18; *Britannia* has 24), so classes are limited in size accordingly.

The classes, typically on sea days, are part of the entertainment program and are fun and educational. Most classes incur a charge towards the ingredients, which will be pre-weighed and portioned. You'll also be provided with an apron and a hat, given tips about food preparation, and you'll probably eat what you have learned to make (it may include a glass of wine or Champagne – or two), which makes it a well-rounded, enjoyable experience. Typically, you will be asked to wear enclosed flat shoes, long trousers, and a long-sleeve top (mainly for safety reasons).

Classes usually start with some background information, some food history, followed by a description of the ingredients you will use and what you will learn to cook, as well as kitchen and equipment safety information. They typically last about 45 minutes to one hour.

Some cruise lines have associations with various cooking schools or food magazines. Examples include Holland America Line and America's *Food & Wine* magazine; Oceania Cruises and *bon appétit* magazine; Regent Seven Seas Cruises and the legendary Le Cordon Bleu culinary arts school (founded in Paris, France in 1895; today the educational organization has schools in most major cities around the world).

Pop-up kitchens can appear in showlounges or theaters aboard some ships that don't have a separate purpose-built culinary studio installed (Holland America Line started this trend). They can also be used aboard ships that promote specially themed food and wine cruises.

Culinary demonstrations are part of onboard programming, and often themed according to the region and itinerary.

Some cruise lines, like Azamara, offer excursions that include a cooking course in a culinary school in a port such as Honfleur, France; Royal Caribbean International sometimes offers a tour of the Martelli pasta making factory in Tuscany together with a lesson in how to make your own pasta.

Cruise lines with large resort ships, such as Carnival Cruise Line, Costa Cruises, MSC Cruises, Norwegian Cruise Line, Princess Cruises, and Royal Caribbean International – may have shore excursions that include culinary demonstrations (or even a little hands-on experience, such as pretzel making), but don't have built-in cooking facilities for passengers.

Viking Ocean Cruises has a well-organized extra cost excursion with the executive chef, to the local market, followed by a meal later the same day using the chosen ingredients, in The Kitchen – a venue within a venue (The Chef's Table).

Cooking classes for children, in various age groups, are also popular, entertaining and educational. MSC Cruises has them, as do P&O Cruises aboard its *Britannia*, and Princess Cruises. Kids learn how to make cookies and pizza dough, among other things.

MSC Cruises, in conjunction with Endemol Shine Group, hosts a MasterChef Juniors at Sea cooling competition aboard all its ships for kids aged 5–12 years. Specifically designed to encourage an interest in cooking and healthy eating, the recipes were devised by Rukmini Iyer – 2013 MasterChef winner and author of two cookbooks, including *The Green Roasting Tin: Vegan and Vegetarian One Dish Dinners*.

Special diets

Cruise lines cater most to general tastes, and cruise ship food tends to be liberally sprinkled with salt, with vegetables often cooked with sauces containing dairy products, salt, and sugar. If you are allergic to ingredients such as nuts or shellfish, want lactose-free, salt-free, low-cholesterol, low-fat or fat-free, gluten-free, or semi-fluid food, or have any other dietary restrictions, let the cruise line know in writing well ahead of time and ask them to confirm that the ship can meet your needs. Once on board, check again with the restaurant manager.

FEEL-GOOD EATING TIPS

While a ship's self-serve buffet allows you to choose what and how much, there is a tendency for many passengers to overdo it. It's easy to consume more calories than you actually need, so pace yourself. Here are some tips on how to cut down on calories:

Remember that you don't have to order – or eat – every course.

Ask for half-size portions, or children's portions.

Eat some items from the 'heart-healthy,' lighter options, or 'spa' menu, if available.

Eat more fruits and vegetables – some ships have juicers, for freshly squeezed or fresh-pressed items (possibly as part of the spa menu); depending on the ship, there may be an extra cost for this.

It's best not to go to the restaurant when you are 'starving.' Instead, try eating a healthy snack before any heavy meal.

Try not to eat too late in the evening – or too many late-night bites.

Limit your alcohol intake.

Not all cruise ships cope well with those on vegan or macrobiotic diets who regularly need freshly squeezed juices; many large resort ships use commercially canned or bottled juices containing preservatives and may not be able to provide really fresh juices.

Feel-good food

You can gain weight when cruising, but it's not inevitable. In fact, taking a cruise could be a good reason to get serious about your wellbeing. Weight- and health-conscious passengers should exercise self-restraint, particularly at self-service buffets.

Many ships' menus include 'heart-healthy' or 'lean and light' options, with calorie-filled sauces replaced by so-called 'spa' cuisine. It may also be wise to choose grilled or poached fish – salmon or sea bass, for example – rather than heavy meat dishes or fried food items.

Quality and variety are directly linked to the per-passenger budget set by each cruise line and are dictated by suppliers, regions, and seasons. Companies operating large resort ships buy fruit at the lowest price, which can translate to unripe bananas, tasteless grapes, and hard-as-nails plums. The smaller, more upscale ships usually carry better-quality ripe fruits as well as the more expensive varieties such as dragon fruit, carambola (starfruit), cherimoya, cactus pear, guava, kumquat, loquat, passion fruit, physalis (Cape gooseberry), rambutan, and sharon fruit.

Even some of the world's largest resort ships have 'calorie-control' eats, where nothing is more than 500 calories. Carnival Cruise Line has a Mongolian barbecue section on their buffets, and tofu is a regular feature. Crystal Cruises features more grains and fresh fruits on its buffets than is standard, and you'll find Ayervedic breakfast items in *Europa 2*'s Yacht Club.

Plant-based cuisine

In 2011, SeaDream Yacht Club introduced 'raw food' dishes. The company tapped into the Hippocrates Health Institute's Life Transformation Program and introduced a complete additional menu. 'Raw' means that ingredients are raw, organic, enzyme-rich, and vegan: no meat, fish, eggs, or dairy items, and nothing heated above 118 degrees Fahrenheit (48 degrees Celsius), to retain as many micronutrients as possible.

Items include fresh sprout and vegetable juices, plant-based protein foods, and pasta made from spinach leaves and coconut meat. Desserts are often created from cashews, almond milk, and coconut butter.

The oatmeal factor

One factor that I have found to be quite consistent across most ships is what I call the 'oatmeal factor':
how various cruise ships provide a basic item such as a bowl of oatmeal.

Standard. Hot oatmeal (supermarket brand oats) mixed with water, with little or no chance of obtaining tahini (sesame seed paste) to add taste to the oatmeal. You get it from a soup tureen at the buffet, and put it into a plastic or inexpensive bowl yourself (or it may be served in the dining room); it is eaten with plastic or basic canteen cutlery.

Premium. Hot oatmeal, water, salt, and a little olive oil; served in a higher-quality bowl, by a waiter or waitress, with hotel-quality (or better) cutlery. It's possible that the ship will have tahini, to add taste and creaminess. It's also possible that the waiter/waitress will ask if you'd like hot or cold milk with your oatmeal. There may even be a doily between the oatmeal bowl and base plate.

Luxury. Hot oatmeal (medium or large flakes), water, salt, tahini, a little (extra virgin) olive oil, and nutmeg, with a dash of blended Scotch (whisky); served in a high-quality brand-name bowl (Versace), with base plate and doily, and Hepp- or Robbe & Berking-quality silverware. The waiter/waitress will ask if you'd like hot or cold milk with your oatmeal.

Incomparable. Hot Scottish (large flakes, hand-ground) oatmeal, water, sea salt, tahini, and nutmeg (grated at the table), high-quality cold-pressed olive oil, and a layer of rare single-malt Scotch; served in small-production hand-made china, with base plate and doily, and sterling silver cutlery. The waiter/waitress will ask if you'd like hot or cold milk (or anything else) with your oatmeal.

Service

Aboard many ships, passengers are often in a hurry (to get to a show or shore excursion) and want service to be fast. They also don't like seeing empty plates in front of them, and so service speeds up because waiters need to clear the empty plates away as soon as someone has finished eating a particular course ('American Service'). In what is termed 'European Service', however, there should *always* be a pause between courses, not only for conversation, but to let the appetite and digestive tract recover, and to anticipate the arrival of the next course.

WHERE TO FIND REAL ALE

Most major cruise lines offer mainly branded canned lagers. The best beer from the barrel and bottled beers are stocked by UK-based cruise lines such as Cunard and Fred. Olsen Cruise Lines, P&O Cruises, and Saga Cruises, although many real ales do not travel well. However, AIDA Cruises and Carnival Cruise Lines have a micro-brewery aboard some ships, and sells so you can take home a four-pack (or two).

Mouth-watering premium-quality Wagyu beef.

Plate service versus silver service

Plate service. When the food is presented as a complete dish (now the normal presentation), as the chef wants it to look. It works well and means that people seated at a table will be served at the same time and can eat together.

Silver service. When the component parts are brought to the table separately, so that the diner, not the chef, can choose what goes on the plate and in what proportion (best when there is plenty of time, but this is rare aboard today's ships). What some cruise lines class as silver service is actually silver service of vegetables only, with the main item, whether it is fish, fowl, or other meat, already plated.

Note that few large resort ships provide proper fish knives or the correct soup spoons – oval for thin bouillon-style soups and round for creamy soups.

National differences

Different nationalities tend to eat at different times. North Americans and Japanese, for example, tend to dine early (6–7pm), while many Europeans and South Americans prefer to eat much later (at least 8–11pm). Brazilians traditionally like dinner at midnight. During Ramadan, Muslims cannot eat during the daytime, but typically order room-service meals during the night.

Beef, lamb, and pork cuts are different on both sides of the Atlantic, so what you ordered may not be the cut, shape, or size you expected. For example, there are 15 British cuts of beef, 17 American cuts, and 24 French cuts. There are six American cuts of lamb, eight British cuts, and nine French cuts. There are eight American cuts of pork, 10 British cuts, and 17 French cuts.

Seating

Depending on the size of the ship, it may have single, two, or open seatings:

Open seating. You can sit with whomever you wish at any available table, at any time the restaurant is open.

Single seating. This doesn't mean seating for single passengers. It means you can choose when you wish to eat (within dining room hours), but you will have the same table assigned for the whole cruise.

Two seatings. You are assigned (or choose) one of two seating times: early or late.

Some ships operate two seatings for all meals, and some do so only for dinner. Some ships operate a mix of open seating or fixed dining times,

Remy, a more upscale, top-deck restaurant aboard *Disney Dream*.

for greater flexibility. Dinner hours may vary when the ship is in port to allow for the timing of shore excursions. Ships that operate in Europe and the Mediterranean or in South America may have later meal times to suit their clientele.

The captain's and senior officers' tables

The captain usually occupies a large table in or near the center of the dining room on 'formal' nights, with senior officers such as the chief engineer and hotel manager hosting adjacent tables. However, the tradition is disappearing, as ship dress codes are now ultra-casual. The table usually seats eight to 12 people picked from the passenger or 'commend' list by the hotel manager. If you are invited to the captain's table (or any senior officer's table), it is gracious to accept.

Dining room and galley staff

Although celebrity chefs make the headlines, it's the ship's executive chef who plans the menus, orders the food, organizes and supervises staff, and arranges all the meals.

The restaurant manager, also known as the maître d'hôtel (not to be confused with the ship's hotel manager), is an experienced host, with shrewd perceptions about compatibility. It is his or her responsibility to seat you with suitable companions.

The best waiters are those trained in hotels or catering schools. They provide fine service and quickly learn your likes and dislikes. They normally work aboard the best ships, where dignified professionalism is expected, and living conditions, salary and benefits are good.

Some lines contract the running and staffing of dining rooms to a specialist maritime catering organization. Ships that cruise far from their home country find that professional caterers, such as the Miami-based Apollo Group or Hamburg-based Sea Chefs, do an outstanding job.

Hygiene standards

Galley equipment is in almost constant use, and regular inspections and maintenance help detect potential problems. There is continual cleaning of equipment, utensils, bulkheads, floors, and hands.

Cruise ships sailing from or visiting US ports are subject to in-port sanitation inspections. These are voluntary, not mandatory inspections, carried out by the United States Public Health (USPH) Department of Health and Human Services, under the auspices of the Centers for Disease Control (CDC). Cruise lines pay thousands of dollars for each inspection.

A tour of the galley proves to be a highlight for some passengers, when a ship's insurance company permits.

In accordance with international standards, all potable water brought on board, or produced by distillation aboard cruise ships, should contain a free chlorine or bromine residual equal to or greater than 0.2ppm (parts per million). This is why drinking water served in dining rooms may taste of chlorine.

Entertainment

The bigger the ship, the bigger the show, with tired old song-and-dance routines now replaced by full-scale Broadway hits and Disney musicals.

Cruise lines with large resort ships have upped the ante lately, competing to attract attention by staging super-lavish, high-tech productions that are licensed versions of Broadway shows, with cruise lines signing partnership deals with musical producers, composers, and songwriters.

Lavish productions: what's playing

Cats
Grease
Hairspray
Mamma Mia
Priscilla Queen of the Desert
Saturday Night Fever

These big theater shows (aboard some Norwegian Cruise Line and Royal Caribbean International ships), with impressively large casts, are versions specially adapted to fit a large resort ship's main stage, typically last about 90 minutes. They are modified slightly and fine-tuned in order to fit in with the ship's operational schedule – not to mention dinner. The performing standards, energy, and enthusiasm of these big musicals are outstanding – definitely giving the land versions a run for their money.

Other big shows

Disney Cruise Line has fine stage shows, including *Aladdin: A Musical Spectacular (Disney Fantasy)*, taken from the Disney stable, plus *Believe*, developed specifically for *Disney Dream*. A proven family favorite is *Toy Story – The Musical*. Disney has separate entertainment shows for adults, too.

The good news is you don't pay extra to see the show, except if it's part of a supper club (including dinner). There are also few bad seats in the house, you don't have to find a parking place, or find a restaurant to eat in before or after the show – and there's always a handy bar nearby.

Royal Caribbean International's *Allure of the Seas*, *Harmony of the Seas*, *Oasis of the Seas*, and *Symphony of the Seas* each have an outdoor 'AquaTheater' (with a part-watery stage), where high-dive aquabatics and comedy provide entertainment spectaculars not to be missed.

Showlounges and shows

Large resort ship showlounges are high-tech auditoriums that would blow many theaters out of the water. They house million-dollar arrays of light and sound technology, floor-to-ceiling LED screens for backdrops and special effects, hydraulic stages that can move in multiple directions, and fittings for aerial acts.

Colorful, 'one-size-fits-all' Las Vegas-style production shows have evolved enormously aboard the large resort ships, as have stages, technical equipment, and facilities. Although they still can't match the budgets of Las Vegas, they can certainly beat many shore-side venues. Most production shows have two things in common: little or no audience contact, and intense volume. With few exceptions, the equation 'volume = ambience' is thoroughly entrenched in the minds of many young audio-visual technicians.

Overall, there's little elegance in most production shows, and all are too long. The after-dinner attention span of most cruise passengers seems to be about 35 minutes, but most production shows run for about 35 to 45 minutes.

The majority of show 'dancing' today consists of stepping in place, while pre-recorded backing tracks are often synthetic and grossly imbalanced.

Some cruise lines have a live showband to back the large-scale shows. The band plays along with a pre-recorded backing track to create an 'enhanced' or larger sound. Some companies, such as Disney Cruise Line, use only a pre-recorded track. This has little 'feel' to it, unlike a live showband that can generate empathy

A performance of *Grease* aboard *Harmony of the Seas*.

Priscilla Queen of the Desert aboard *Norwegian Epic.*

and variation – and provide work for real musicians. Although live music may contain minor imperfections, which some might regard as 'characterful', most passengers would prefer it to canned music.

Great expectations

Many passengers, despite having paid comparatively little for their cruise, expect top-notch entertainment and the most dazzling shows with slick special effects, just as one would find in the best venues in Las Vegas, London, or Paris (at a price). There are many reasons why the reality is different. Cruise brochures tend to over-hype entertainment. International star acts invariably have an entourage that accompanies them to any venue: their personal manager, their musical director (often a pianist or conductor), a rhythm section with bass player and drummer, and a hairdresser. On land, one-night shows are possible, but aboard ship, an artist can seldom disembark after just one night, especially when it involves moving equipment, costumes, stage props, and baggage. This makes the deal logistically and financially unattractive for all but the largest ships on fixed itineraries, where a marquee-name act would be a draw.

Most entertainers don't like to be away from their 'home base' for long periods, as they rely on reliable phone and Internet access for managing their careers. Nor do they like the long contracts that most ships must offer in order to amortize the high costs.

THE COST OF STAGING A SHOW

Staging a lavish production show can easily cost $1 million, plus performers' pay, costume cleaning and repair, royalties, and so on. To justify that cost, shows must remain aboard for 18 to 24 months.

Some smaller operators see entertainment as an area for cost-cutting, so you could find yourself entertained by low-budget singers and bands.

Entertaining but predictable

So many acts from one cruise ship to the next are interchangeable with each other. Ever wonder why? It relates to the limited appeal of a cruise ship gig. Entertainers aboard ships have to live with their audiences for several days and perhaps weeks – something unheard of on land – as well as work on stages aboard older ships that were not designed for live performances.

Entertainment aboard large resort ships is directed toward family cruising. This is predominantly a family audience, so entertainment must appeal to a broad age range. That partly accounts for the frequency of formulaic Cirque du Soleil-style acrobatic routines and rope climbing. The only *real* Cirque du Soleil show (with specially designed showroom) can be found aboard MSC Cruises' *Meraviglia*.

A cruise line with several ships has an entertainment director and several assistants, and has at their disposal entertainment agencies that specialize in entertainment for cruise ships. As a result, regular passengers are likely to see the same acts time after time on various ships.

Mistakes do happen, however. It is no use, for example, booking a juggler who needs a floor-to-ceiling height of 12ft (3.7m) but finds that the ship has a showlounge with a height of just 7ft (2m) – although I did overhear one cruise director ask if the act 'could juggle sideways'; or a concert pianist when the ship only has an upright honky-tonk piano.

Trying to please everyone

The toughest audience is one of mixed nationalities, each of which will expect entertainers to cater exclusively to their particular linguistic group. Given that cruise lines are now marketing to more international audiences in order to fill ever-larger ships, the problem of finding the right entertainment is far more acute – which is why *Queen Mary 2* is to be envied for the visual appeal of its 20-minute-long *Illuminations* planetarium shows.

Cruise lines operating small ships offer more classical music, guest lecturers, and top authors than seven-day package cruises heading for the sun.

These performers – and ship entertainers generally – need to enjoy socializing. Successful shipboard acts tend to be good mixers, are presentable when in public, do not take drugs or drink excess alcohol, are not late for rehearsals, and must cooperate with the cruise director.

Part of the entertainment experience aboard large resort ships is the glamorous 'production show,' the kind of show you would expect to see in a Las Vegas show palace – think flesh and feathers – with male and female lead singers and Madonna or Marilyn Monroe look-alike dancers, a production manager, lavish backdrops, extravagant sets, grand lighting, special effects, and stunning custom-designed costumes. Many cruise company executives know little about entertainment, and still favor plumes and huge feather boas paraded by showgirls who *step*, but don't *dance*.

Book back-to-back seven-day cruises (on alternating eastern and western Caribbean itineraries, for example), and you'll probably find the same two or three production shows and the same acts on the second week of your cruise. The way to avoid seeing everything twice is to pace yourself.

Other entertainment

Most ships organize acts that, while not nationally known 'names,' can provide two or three different shows during a seven-day cruise. These will be singers, illusionists, puppeteers, reality TV show wannabes, hypnotists, and even circus acts, with wide age-range appeal. Also, comedians who perform 'clean' material can find employment year-round on the cruise ship circuit. These popular comics enjoy good accommodation, are mini-stars while on board, and may go from ship to ship on a standard rotation every few days. There are raunchy, late-night 'adults only' comedy acts in some of the ships with younger audiences, but few have enough material for several shows. In general, the larger a ship, the broader the entertainment program will be.

Movies on deck

Showing movies on the open deck has been part of the cruise scene since the 1970s, when they were often classic black-and-white films shown at midnight. In those days, the screens were small, roll-down affairs, and the projectors were set up on makeshift pedestals. The result was often images that vibrated, and sound that quivered.

Speed forward into the 21st century. Most large resort ships now have huge outdoor poolside LED movie screens that cost around $1 million each. The screens are complemented by 50,000- to 80,000-watt sound systems for a complete 'surround the deck' experience.

Princess Cruises started the trend (at this author's suggestion, no less) in 2004 aboard *Grand Princess* with its 'Movies Under the Stars' program, but now all companies with large resort ships have them. The experience is reminiscent of the old drive-in movies, the difference being that cruise lines often supply blankets and even popcorn free of charge.

Movies and other presentations are shown day and night, and may include special films for junior cruisers, as well as major sporting events such as the Super Bowl or World Cup soccer are also presented.

Smaller cruise ships, expedition cruise ships, and sail-cruise ships typically have little or no entertainment. Aboard those ships, after-dinner conversation, reading, and relaxation become the entertainment of choice.

What's on

Entertainment is listed in the 'daily program' – a mini-newspaper for the day ahead that is delivered to your suite/cabin each night when your bed is turned down.

FAMOUS CRUISING MOVIES (IN DATE ORDER)

One Way Passage (1932). Bittersweet story about a shipboard romance between a man (William Powell) condemned to be executed and a terminally ill woman (Kay Francis).

The French Line (1954). Life aboard the French Line's *Liberté*, depicted as being frivolous, promiscuous and romantic. Stars Jane Russell, Gilbert Roland, and Arthur Hunnicutt.

An Affair to Remember (1957). Two movie greats (Cary Grant and Deborah Kerr) meet aboard a passenger ship, although most of the movie is actually about the Empire State Building in New York.

A Night to Remember (1958). Another movie about the last night aboard *Titanic*, this movie is dramatically realistic and quite terrifying in parts, and it makes you realize that oceans and seas can be treacherous. The cast includes Kenneth More, Anthony Bushell, Robert Ayres, and Honor Blackman.

The Last Voyage (1960). A movie about (what else) a sinking ship. Instead of effects, a real ship (*Ile de France*) was used in this gripping movie. Robert Stack and Dorothy Malone star.

Carry on Cruising (1962). A classic British comedy about a group of individuals (played by *Carry on* icons Kenneth Williams, Sidney James, and Kenneth Connor), who go cruising, with a heavy emphasis on innuendo and slapstick.

Ship of Fools (1965). A fine cast, including Vivian Leigh, Simone Signoret, and Lee Marvin, find themselves aboard the same pre-war passenger ship. A splendid example of character study.

The Poseidon Adventure (1972). There are some fine scenes of life upside down aboard a ship on this adventure movie starring Gene Hackman, Ernest Borgnine, Shelley Winters, and Roddy McDowell.

Titanic (1996). Although you already know the ending, the story and dramatic effects of this movie starring Leonardo DiCaprio and Kate Winslet make it compelling to watch, especially considering its length.

Out to Sea (1997). Starring Jack Lemmon and Walter Matthau this is a playful movie about two 'gentlemen hosts,' who join the cruise staff of a cruise ship in the Caribbean (it's not *quite* like this in real life). The ships used in the movie were Holland America Line's *Westerdam* and *Queen Mary* (the original, now a museum ship and hotel, located in Long Beach, California).

Speed 2: Cruise Control (1997). A madman hijacker takes control of a cruise ship (based on *Seabourn Legend*, whose real captain, Erik Anderssen, and other onboard staff, appeared in the film). The ending is dramatic (shot on the Caribbean island of St. Martin), but the plot is not. The engine room must be enormous, if the film is to be taken seriously! Sandra Bullock, Jason Patric, and Willem Dafoe star.

Casinos

Place your bets. Glitzy onboard casinos flash their lights to attract your patronage, and bring Las Vegas-style gaming to open waters. But, watch out, Lady Luck can also bite your wallet.

Shipboard casinos

The word casino comes from the Italian for 'little house,' which referred to a small part of a larger villa used for music, dancing, and socializing. Water-borne gambling started in the mid-1800s aboard Mark Twain-era steamboats on the USA's Mississippi River – when it quickly became a profession – with an estimated 600 to 800 of them plying their trade on the river during the Gold Rush days. Today's ocean-going cruise ships have really taken over (the first recorded casino was aboard the 1906 French ocean liner *La Provence*). So, whether you are a serious gamer or simply want to try your luck on the slot machines, shipboard casinos are now considered a major part of the entertainment, particularly aboard the large resort ships.

Games and rules

The most popular table games include a variety of poker (or video poker) games (Caribbean Stud, Let it Ride, Texas Hold'em, Three Card, etc.). Other table games include blackjack, single-deck blackjack, craps, and roulette. A few ships also have baccarat (including baccarat banque, chemin de fer, and punto banco – the most widely played).

Ships must follow the gaming rules established by the Nevada Gaming Control Board, or other licensed

Norwegian Breakaway casino.

jurisdiction – usually the flag state of the ship. House rules typically include the following provisions:

Only adults are allowed to play the slots or the tables.

Cruise lines must post at every gaming table the minimum and maximum betting limits for each game.

Nothing personal is permitted on the tables.

Opening hours

Unlike casinos on land, most shipboard casinos are not open 24/7. They are always closed in port, with the exceptions of Bermuda, where they are open from 9pm–5am, and Nassau, in the Bahamas, where they stay open from 7pm–3am. Shipboard casinos are typically open once a ship leaves port, but not until it leaves territorial waters – 12 nautical miles away from the coastline (in Alaska it's 3 nautical miles). When a ship passes 24 miles, it is, according to international maritime law, in international waters.

Open all hours

Mobile gaming and wagering was introduced in 2013 by Celebrity Cruises (and in 2015 aboard some of the Carnival Corporation brands), enabling you to play almost anywhere on board – for example when lounging by the pool. You simply download the app prior to cruising (from the App Store for iOS devices, or from Google Play for Android devices).

Payment

Payment for casino credit and chips/tokens can be made in several ways, including by credit card or a pre-loaded 'virtual wallet.' A few ships have cash-only machines, but most operate by touch cards (your cabin card) or tokens. Note that some cruise lines impose a 'service fee' if you charge cash or casino tokens to your cabin charge card (Carnival Cruise Line, for example). Some cruise lines don't allow you to use onboard credit to purchase casino play currency.

Some cruise lines have an app that can be downloaded to your smartphone and then used for playing at the casino once you have loaded and validated your 'virtual wallet' with the casino cashier.

Winnings

Any winnings (and left-over casino chips) must be cashed in on board.

VIP Players Clubs

Some cruise lines reach out to 'high rollers' – those who might play in private clubs or VIP rooms on land, for high stakes. Cruise lines have their own versions of VIP clubs and attract players by giving perks (onboard credit, discounts on future cruises, etc.) and loyalty cards (these are different to a cruise line's loyalty club), just like casinos on land. Examples include Carnival Cruise Line (Ocean Players Club); Celebrity Cruises (Blue Chip Club); Dream Cruises (Resorts World Premium Club), Norwegian Cruise Line (Casinos at Sea Players Club); and Royal Caribbean International (Club Royale). Typically, a minimum of $5,000 casino credit is required, with a maximum of $100,000. There may also be a separate check-in line for VIP club players. High rollers may be invited by a cruise line to travel free or at reduced cost, provided that they participate in various (high-priced) tournaments.

Slots

Slot machines (invented in the 1890s by Charles Fey) bring in more than half of a casino's profits. If you like to play the slots, it may be better to sign up to a cruise line card club. This brings rewards, depending on how much you play. More play equals bigger rewards (including invitations to special events, discounted drinks, etc.). Sometimes, cruise lines offer double or even treble points after midnight. Winnings can be transferred to your card, so you can change machines.

The most popular slot machines are those of the 'reel' type, consisting of a number of spinning wheels that display fixed symbols, but video-display machines are increasing in popularity. Some are of the hybrid type – a mix of reel and video.

Many ships have penny slots, but this could turn out to be much more expensive than the 'lead-in' price (note that penny slot machines typically pay out based on the amount of money that is being bet, and not on the number of times the machine is used).

Tournaments

Shipboard casino and slot tournaments are programmed regularly, with blackjack and slots the most common. You participate by paying a certain amount, and then no more money is spent during the tournament. Some ships provide free (or reduced cost) drinks as an added incentive.

Smoking

Smoking is allowed in some shipboard casinos, depending on the cruise line. There is no smoking in casinos aboard the ships of Celebrity Cruises, Crystal Cruises, Cunard, Oceania Cruises, Regent Seven Seas Cruises, Seabourn, Silversea Cruises, and Windstar Cruises. Some companies, such as Carnival Cruise Line and Royal Caribbean International, have no-smoking sections within the casino, but in health terms this is as effective as having smokers at one end of an aircraft and nonsmokers at the other.

Slot machines ready aboard *Genting Dream*.

Design

Cruise ship casinos have evolved dramatically in terms of design, flow, and noise control. Most ships are designed so that passengers (including children) need to walk through them to reach either the restaurant or showlounge (although they won't be allowed to play the slots). However, aboard ships with multiple passenger room decks this may not be the case – which means it's easier to keep children away from the slot machines.

Both Norwegian Cruise Lines' *Norwegian Spirit* and Dream Cruises' *Explorer Dream*, for example, have casino facilities at one end of a main public room deck, behind closed doors, so children cannot walk through – much better.

Which cruise lines don't have casinos?

Examples include Disney Cruise Line, Hapag-Lloyd Cruises, Phoenix Reisen, Saga Cruises, Sea Cloud Cruises, and Viking Ocean Cruises, plus many of the small-ship and expedition cruise lines. Also, Japanese cruise ships cannot pay in cash if you win, so soft toys ('gifts') are awarded instead, as prizes.

A little warning

Casinos are a major source of revenue for many cruise lines. So, if you plan to play, only do so with what you can afford to lose.

The odds

Unlike land-based casinos, shipboard casinos don't need to compete with the casino next door, so don't expect the odds to be good. Note that some ships have blackjack tables with a card-shuffle machine to mix the cards, but this increases the odds in favor of the house.

Excursions Ashore

Escorted tours in ports of call cost extra, but they are often the best way to get a nutshell view of a destination and make the most efficient use of your limited time ashore.

Shore excursions used to be limited to cheesy city tours, but today's excursions are extraordinarily varied, from crocodile-spotting in the Amazon to kayaking in Alaska, and from elephant riding in Thailand, to dogsledding in Greenland. Most offer good value, but it's easy to spend more on excursions than on buying the cruise.

Shore excursions are offered by cruise lines in order to enhance a destination visit. Booking with a cruise line avoids the hassle of arranging your own excursions, and you'll be covered by the cruise line's insurance just in case things do go wrong. General city tours are designed to give you an overview and show you the highlights in a limited time period – typically about three hours. Other excursions provide a mind-boggling array of possibilities, including some that may be exclusive to a particular cruise line – even overland tours are part of the excursions available on longer cruises.

Not all tours are by bus. Some may be by bicycle, boat, car, or mini-van. Some cruise lines also offer private, tailor-made excursions to suit you, a family,

Playing with the stingrays in Nassau.

or small group. A private car, with a tour guide who speaks your language, for example, may be a good way for a family to get to know a foreign destination.

To get the most out of your shore visits, doing a little research – particularly if you are visiting foreign countries – will pay dividends. Once on board, attend the shore-excursion lectures, or watch destination and shore-excursion videos on the television in your cabin.

Once your ship reaches a destination, it must be cleared by local officials before you are free to go ashore. In most ports, this is accomplished speedily. Meanwhile, you may be asked to assemble for your organized tours in one of the ship's public rooms. You'll need to carry the ship's identification card with you, to be checked at the gangway, and for when you re-board. Remember to take the ship's telephone number with you, in case of emergencies.

How tiring are excursions?

Most tours will involve some walking; some require extensive walking. Most cruise lines grade their excursions with visual symbols to indicate the level of difficulty, for example in terms of fitness required.

How expensive are they?

For an average three-hour city sightseeing tour, expect to pay $40–100, and for whole-day excursions with lunch, $100–250. Flightseeing or seaplane sightseeing tours will cost $250–400, depending on the location, what is included, and time involved – the flightseeing itself typically lasts about 30–45 minutes.

What should I take with me?

Only what's necessary; leave any valuables aboard ship, together with any money and credit cards you do not plan to use. Groups of people are often targets for pickpockets in some destinations. Also, beware of excursion guides who give you a colored disk to wear for 'identification' – they may be marking you

A TICKET TO RIDE

Many companies with large resort ships charge extra for shuttle buses to take you from the port or other docking area to a local city or town center. The port with the highest charge is Venice, Italy, where the transport is by motorboat between the cruise terminals and St. Mark's Square.

as a 'rich' tourist for local shopkeepers. It's always prudent to wear comfortable rubber-soled shoes, particularly in older ports, where there may be cobblestones or other uneven surfaces.

How can I make a booking?
Several cruise lines allow you to book shore excursions online before you cruise, which means that some popular excursions may sell out before you even get to your ship.

If you need to cancel a shore excursion, you usually need to do so at least 24 hours before its advertised departure time. Refunds are at the discretion of the cruise line, and refunds of pre-paid tickets booked online can take a long time to make and can incur currency-exchange losses.

How to tell which excursions are good?
If it's your first cruise, try to attend the shore-excursion briefing (or watch the in-cabin infotainment system). Read the excursion literature before you book.

Most excursions are designed for general interest. If you want to see something that isn't described in the excursion literature, skip it. Go on your own or with friends.

Brochure descriptions of shore excursions, often written by personnel who haven't visited the ports of call, can be imprecise. All cruise lines should adopt the following definitions in their descriptive literature, lectures, and presentations: the term 'visit' should mean actually entering the place or building concerned; the term 'see' should mean viewing from the outside – as from a bus, for example.

35 DESTINATION EXCURSIONS TO EXPERIENCE

1. **Icy Straight Point, Alaska:** Take a trip on the world's longest zipline. With a 1,320ft (402m) vertical drop, the ZipRider transports participants from mountain peak to harbor-side beach at 60mph (97kph).
2. **Juneau, Alaska:** A flightseeing trip to Mendenhall Glacier, plus an Alaska salmon bake.
3. **Skagway, Alaska:** The historic White Pass & Yukon Route Railroad train tour.
4. **Grand Cayman, The Caribbean:** Snorkeling with the stingrays at Stingray City.
5. **Jamaica, The Caribbean:** Horseback riding on the beach at Montego Bay or Ocho Rios.
6. **St. Maarten, The Caribbean:** Join the America's Cup Regatta adventure tour and compete in an actual yacht race.
7. **Cozumel, Mexico:** Go snorkeling around Columbia Reef and Palancar Reef, just two of Cozumel's famous reefs.
8. **Dublin, Ireland:** Visit the original Guinness brewery.
9. **Edinburgh, Scotland:** Take a whisky distillery tour.
10. **London, England:** Join the London by Night tour. This includes a West End musical or play.
11. **Naples, Italy:** Take the boat tour to the island of Capri to visit the famous Blue Grotto cave.
12. **Nice, France:** Enjoy this elegant city, plus the Corniche and the medieval hilltop village of Eze.
13. **Palma de Mallorca:** Tour the former Carthusian monastery of Valldemossa. Frédéric Chopin and George Sand lived here in 1838.
14. **Rome, Italy:** Visit the Vatican's Sistine Chapel.
15. **Sorrento, Italy:** Visit to the ruins of Pompeii, plus the Amalfi Coast and Sorrento.
16. **Venice, Italy:** Take a romantic trip on a gondola.
17. **Reykjavík, Iceland:** Take the Ring of Fire tour of the warm geothermal waters of the Blue Lagoon and visit an active volcano.
18. **St. Petersburg, Russia:** Sign up for a guided walking tour through the Hermitage Museum, or an excursion to the Catherine Palace, summer residence of the tsars.
19. **La Coruña, Spain:** Pay homage in the city of Santiago de Compostela, home to the shrine of St. James.
20. **Aqaba, Jordan:** Tour to the 'Rose-Red City' of Petra.
21. **Dubai, United Arab Emirates:** Take a 4x4 Dune Drive Safari Tour.
22. **Mumbai, India:** Go on a Buddhist Trail tour to the Kanheri Caves.
23. **Hilo, Hawaii:** Marvel at the Kilauea Volcano tour in Volcanoes National Park.
24. **Key West, USA:** Take the Conch Train Tour in Ernest Hemingway's favorite town.
25. **Hamilton Island, Australia:** Cruise/tour the Great Barrier Reef.
26. **Melbourne, Australia:** Brave the shark diving in the aquarium tour on the banks of the Yarra River.
27. **Singapore:** Take the Night Safari tour.
28. **Kuala Lumpur, Malaysia:** Visit the Petronas Twin Towers and the city's vibrant night markets.
29. **Buenos Aires:** Take the Steak and Tango night tour.
30. **Ushuaia, Argentina:** Ride the world's southernmost train.
31. **Cape Town, South Africa:** Tour of Cape Town and Table Top Mountain by vintage car.
32. **Mombasa, Kenya:** Tour of Tsavo National Park, one of Kenya's oldest game parks.
33. **Chiang Mai, Thailand:** Take an excursion to Bhubing Palace to see the royal gardens and serene surroundings.
34. **Bergen:** Enjoy a short concert at Edvard Grieg's house, museum, and delightful gardens.
35. **Ha Long Bay:** Tour in a junk boat through the misty waters and limestone islands.

City excursions are basically superficial. To get to know a city intimately, go alone or with a small group. Go by taxi or bus, or explore on foot.

If you don't want to miss the main sightseeing attractions in each port, organized shore excursions provide a good solution. They also allow you to meet fellow passengers with similar interests.

In the Caribbean, many sightseeing tours cover the same ground, regardless of the cruise line you sail with. Choose one and then do something different in the next port. The same is true of the history and archaeology excursions in the Greek islands, where the same ancient gods put in frequent appearances.

What if I lose my ticket?

Report lost or misplaced tickets to the shore excursion manager. Aboard most ships, excursion tickets, once sold, become the sole responsibility of the buyer, and the cruise line isn't generally able to issue replacements.

Are there private excursions?

Most cruise line-organized excursions work on the 'one-size-fits-all' principle. However, a more personalized alternative exists for anyone looking for privately guided tours and land experiences. Tailor-made 'build-your-own' excursions, arranged by a 'travel concierge,' provide private tours of a destination and its environs. These could include lunch or dinner in a hard-to-book top-class restaurant, a visit to a private museum, or other bespoke requirements for small groups.

The right transportation and private guide will be arranged, and all arrangements taken care of – at a cost, of course. A cruise line destination 'expert' will plan an excursion, arrange the right transportation, and attend to all the other details that make the experience more personal. It's all about exclusivity – at a price.

Going ashore independently – and safely

The main advantage of going independently is that you do so at your own pace and see the sights you want to see. If you hire a taxi for sightseeing, negotiate the price in advance, and don't pay until you get back to the ship or to your destination. If you are with friends, hiring a taxi for a full- or half-day sightseeing trip can often work out far cheaper than renting a car – and it's probably safer and more relaxing. Try to find a driver who speaks your language.

Exploring independently is straightforward in the major cruise ports of the Aegean, Alaska, the Bahamas, Bermuda, the Caribbean, the Mexican Riviera, the Canary Islands, the Mediterranean, and the South Pacific's islands. If you don't speak the local language, carry some identification (but not your actual passport, unless required – keep a photocopy with you instead), the name of your ship (and its telephone number, for emergencies), and the area in which it is docked. If the ship is anchored, and you take a launch tender ashore, observe landmarks near the landing place, and write down the location – or take a photo. This will help if you get lost and need to take a taxi back to the launch.

Shopping on a shore excursion with Norwegian Cruise Line.

White-water rafting in Costa Rica.

Remember that ships have schedules – and sometimes tides – to meet, and they won't wait for you if you return late. If you are in a launch port and severe weather approaches, the ship's captain could make a decision to depart early to avoid being hemmed in by an approaching storm. Although this is rare, it has happened, especially in the Caribbean. If it does, in the port, locate the ship's agent, who will try to get you back on board.

Planning on going to a quiet, secluded beach to swim? First check with the shore excursion manager – some beaches may be considered off-limits because of a dangerous undertow, drug pushers, or persistent hawkers. And don't even think of going diving alone – even if you know the area well.

If you explore independently and need medical help, you could risk missing the ship when it sails. Unless the destination is a familiar one, first-time cruisers are probably safer booking excursions organized by the ship and vetted by the cruise line. Also, if you have a problem during a tour, the cruise line should be able to sort it out on the spot.

The main downside of going it alone is the possibility of delay. If there is a problem with your chosen mode of transport, you could miss the ship as a result. In such a case, you are responsible for getting to the ship. This may not be easy if the next port of call is in another country, and you don't have your passport. Also, be aware that cruise lines do change itineraries occasionally, due to weather, political or other factors. If you book your own tours, and it's a tender port where the ship has to remain at anchor offshore, you may need to wait until passengers on the ship's organized tours have been offloaded. This can take two or more hours aboard some of the large resort ships.

10 DESTINATION NIGGLES

These destinations are lovely places, but watch out for the following nuisances.

1. Cagliari, Italy. Poor beaches and staggeringly overpriced shops.

2. Grenada. Intrusive hawkers on Grand Anse and other beaches.

3. Gibraltar. The rock's fine, but that's it – there's nothing else other than duty-free liquor, and some Barbary apes.

4. Naples, Italy. Trying to cross the road from the cruise terminals to town can be a nail-biting experience.

5. Cannes, France. There can be dog muck all over the sidewalks, so tread warily!

6. Portofino, Italy. Several ships disgorging passengers onto the skinniest strip of land in summer.

7. St. Maarten. When six large resort ships are docked at the same time.

8. Ensenada, Mexico. Pickpocketing and begging in the area surrounding the cruise ship docking area, which is unsafe at night.

9. Ocho Rios, Jamaica. Constant hustling to get you to buy something, and the general unsafe feeling.

10. Juneau, Alaska. The tacky souvenir shops are simply overwhelming.

Above all, make sure your chosen travel insurance covers you fully.

Shopping aboard

Many ships have designer brands (clothing items, cosmetics, perfume, watches) on board at duty-free prices, so you don't need to spend time shopping ashore. Some ships have private rooms where you can view expensive jewelry or watches in private. Onboard shops are closed while the ship is in port, however, due to international customs regulations. Good discounts are often offered on the last day of the cruise.

Shopping ashore

Aboard ship, a 'shopping lecturer' will give a presentation about shopping in the various ports of call. Many cruise lines operating in Alaska, the Bahamas, the Caribbean, and the Mexican Riviera engage an outside company that provides the services of a shopping lecturer. Most talks are about designer jewelry and watches – high-ticket items that boost commissions to cruise lines. The shopping lecturers' heavily promote selected shops, goods, and services, authorized by the cruise line, which receives a commission. Shopping maps, with selected stores highlighted, are usually placed in your cabin, and sometimes include a guarantee of satisfaction valid for 30 days.

During organized shore excursions, be wary of stores recommended by tour guides – they may be receiving commissions from the merchants. Shop around before you purchase. When buying local handicrafts, make sure they have indeed been made locally. Be wary of 'bargain-priced' name brands, as they may be counterfeit. For watches, check the guarantee.

Some of the world's shopping havens put serious temptation in the way of visitors. Top of the list are Hong Kong, Singapore, and Dubai (especially in the Mall of the Emirates – a shopping resort rather than a mall – and the Dubai Mall, with over 1,200 shops, including the only Bloomingdale's outside the US).

Shopping tips

Know in advance just what you are looking for, especially if your time is limited; when time is no problem, browsing can be fun.

When shopping time is included in an excursion, be wary of stores repeatedly recommended by tour guides, as they may be receiving commissions from the merchants.

When shopping for local handicrafts, make sure they have indeed been made locally. It can happen that a so-called local product has in fact been made in Taiwan, Hong Kong, or another Far Eastern country. It pays to check.

Be wary of 'bargain-priced' name brands such as Gucci bags and Rolex or Omega watches – they are probably counterfeit. Check the serial numbers to see whether they are genuine or not. For watches, check the guarantee.

Shopping in the center of Fort de France, Martinique.

Spas and Wellness Facilities

The 'feel-good factor' is alive and well aboard the latest cruise ships, which offer a growing array of beauty salons and body-pampering treatments.

Land-based health spas have long provided an array of body pampering treatments for those who want to counter the stressful effects of everyday life. Responding to the rise in 'wellness' awareness, today's ships now have elaborate spas to rival those on land, where whole days of almost-continuous treatments are on offer, at a price. Once the domain of women, spas now cater almost as equally for men.

Anyone unaccustomed to spas may find some of the terminology daunting: aromatherapy, hydrotherapy, ionithermie, rasul, thalassotherapy. Spa staff will help you choose the treatment that best suits you and your needs. Do visit the spa on embarkation day, when staff will be on hand to show you around and answer questions. Some cruise lines let you prebook spa treatments online before your cruise.

Avoid booking massage treatments when the ship is about to leave port (usually in the late afternoon/early evening), because there may be interruptive announcements, plus noise and vibration from the propulsion machinery.

Facilities

Large resort ships have facilities that may include saunas, steam rooms, rasul chamber, several body treatment rooms, thalassotherapy (saltwater) pool, relaxation area, changing/locker rooms, and a beauty salon. Some ships have acupuncture treatment clinics, and some have a built-in juice bar. Some offer a couples' experience, complete with spa suites for rent by the day or half-day. Note that saunas and steam rooms may be mixed gender, or separate, depending on the cruise line.

Thermal suites

Thermal suites provide a combination of various warm scented rain showers, saunas, steam rooms, and thalassotherapy pools, and the promise of ultimate relaxation. Although most ships don't charge for use of the sauna or steam room, some do. A number of ships even add a gratuity to a spa day pass, while some ships limit the number of passes available – aboard Cunard's *Queen Elizabeth* and *Queen Victoria,* for example, the limit is 40 persons per day.

Personal spa suites

Each spa suite consists of a large room with floor-to-ceiling windows, a heated floor, abundant relaxation space, towels, and bathrobes. They may also include a sauna, steam room, shower enclosure, tiled and

heated relaxation loungers, hydraulic massage tables, and a choice of massage oils.

They will also have herbal tea-making facilities and are usually bookable for a couple of hours, a half-day, or a full day.

Pampering treatments

Stress-reducing and relaxation treatments are offered, combined with the use of seawater, which contains minerals, micronutrients, and vitamins. Massages might include Swedish remedial massage, shiatsu, and aromatherapy oils. You can even get a massage on your private balcony aboard some ships.

Having body-pampering treatments aboard a cruise ship can be wonderful, as the ship can provide a serene environment; when enhanced by a massage or facial, the benefits can be even more therapeutic. So, before you actually book your relaxing massage, find out whether the treatment rooms are quiet enough.

Treatments are usually available only until about 8pm, whereas some passengers would welcome

Taking a salt bath aboard *Norwegian Breakaway.*

having a massage late at night before retiring to bed – the challenge being that most shipboard spas are run by concessions, with wellbeing treated as a daytime-only activity.

Some ships also offer 'Spa Days' with a whole day of body-pampering treatments, often termed 'wellness packages.' Expect to pay up to $500 a day *in addition to* the basic cruise fare.

Berlitz Tip: Check the daily program for 'port day specials' and packages that make the prices more palatable.

Fitness centers

Virtual-reality exercise machines are found in the techno-gyms aboard many ships, with state-of-the-art muscle-pumping and body-strengthening equipment, universal stations, treadmills, bicycles, rowing machines, and free weights.

Most fitness centers are open only until early evening, although one exception is Norwegian Cruise Line, whose gyms are open 24 hours a day. And if you've forgotten your workout clothes, you can probably purchase new items on board.

Typical exercise classes include high-intensity/low-impact aerobics, aquacise (pool-based) classes, interval training, stretch and relax, super body sculpting, fabdominals, sit and be fit, and walk-a-mile.

Group exercycling, kick-boxing, Pilates and yoga classes, body-composition analysis, and personal trainer sessions cost extra.

Massage

Having a massage aboard ship can be a good stress-busting experience, although if it's not right it can prove frustrating, and expensive. A whole range of

treatments and styles has evolved from the standard Swedish Remedial Massage.

Here are some favorite massage moments (always taken in the late afternoon or early evening, preferably just before sundown):

Aboard *Celebrity Constellation, Celebrity Infinity, Celebrity Millennium,* or *Celebrity Summit,* on the balcony of a Sky Suite.

Aboard *Royal Clipper,* in a private massage hut on an outside deck.

Aboard *Genting Dream,* on the floor of a junior suite bedroom.

Inside a beach cabana ashore on Castaway Cay or Half Moon Cay in the Bahamas, or as part of a private beach day (*SeaDream I* and *II*) in the British Virgin Islands.

Make appointments for a massage as soon as possible to get the time and day of your choice. On some ships, massage may be available in your cabin (or on your private balcony), if it's large enough to accommodate a portable massage table.

A gratuity is often added automatically to spa treatments. Elixirs of youth, lotions and potions, creams, and scrubs – all are sold by therapists, typically at the end of your treatment, for you to use when you get home. But beware, these are expensive items, so don't fall for the sales talk.

Treatments

Although massage is the most popular shipboard spa treatment, most ships also offer facials, manicures, pedicures, teeth whitening, and acupuncture. Most are based on holistic Asian therapies. Some examples include: *mandi lulur,* a scrub made from herbs, essential oils, and rice to soften the skin; and

A gym with a view on a Celebrity cruise.

A romantic couples' massage in the Senses Spa & Salon aboard *Disney Magic*.

boreh, a warm Balinese herb, rice, spice, galangal water, and oil body wrap for detoxification.

The spa will provide towels, robes, and slippers, but it's best to store valuables safely in your cabin prior to your appointment. Some spas offer disposable underwear for body treatments such as a Body Salt Glow or Seaweed Wrap.

Acupuncture. Used to prevent and remedy many maladies, this works by inserting super-fine needles into special points on the skin.

Halotherapy. This detox treatment uses a Himalayan crystal salt bed for deep relaxation and body detoxing. It involves lying on a bed of 290lbs (131.5kg) of Himalayan salt crystals heated from 90 to 104 degrees Fahrenheit (32–40 degrees Celsius), and breathing in the salt-infused air. The salt contains 84 essential minerals as fine particles.

Moxibustion. This is a treatment that involves the insertion of hair-thin needles, dipped into mugwort (*Artemisa capillaris),* into one of the body's many acupuncture points.

Body scrub

This treatment cleanses and softens the skin, and draws out impurities using aromatic oils, creams, lotions, and perhaps sea salt, together with exfoliation (removal of dead skin cells).

Body wrap

Often called a body mask, this treatment typically includes the use of algae and seaweeds applied to the whole body. The body is then covered in aluminum foil and blankets. There are many variations on this theme, using mud from the Dead Sea or the Mediterranean, or sea salt and ginger, or cooling cucumber and aloe, or combinations of herbs and oils that leave you with a warm glow. The aim is to detoxify, firm, and tone the skin, and reduce cellulite.

Facials

Aromatherapy facial. This treatment typically uses aromatic oils such as lavender, sandalwood, and geranium, plus a rejuvenating mask and accompanying creams and essences to 'lift' the skin and facial muscles.

Rejuvenation facial. This is typically a classic French facial, which utilizes the latest skin care products enriched with essential plant and vitamin-rich oils. This facial aims to reduce lines and wrinkles.

Other popular treatments include eye lifting, volcanic mud masks, and manicures.

Rasul chamber

This is a steam chamber (Hammam) that is typically fully tiled, with a domed roof and Moorish decor. You paste yourself or your partner, if you are traveling as a couple, with three types of mud and sit down while gentle steam surrounds you. The various types of mud become heated, and then you're in a mud bath, after which you rub yourself (or perhaps each other) with large crystals of rock salt.

Reflexology

The body's energy meridians exist as reflex points on the soles of the feet. The therapist uses thumb pressure to stimulate these points to improve circulation and restore energy flow throughout the body.

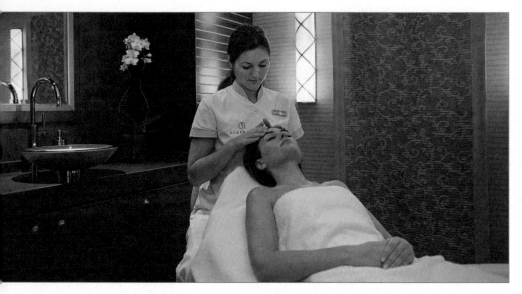

About Face – 'me-time' for your face.

WHO RUNS THE SPAS?

Aboard most ships, the spa and fitness areas are operated by a specialist concession, although each cruise line may have a separate name for the spa, such as AquaSpa (Celebrity Cruises), The Greenhouse Spa (Holland America Line), Lotus Spa (Princess Cruises), etc.

Aboard the large resort ships, spa staff tends to be young, enthusiastic 'therapists,' who will try hard to sell you own-brand beauty products, for a commission.

Steiner Leisure is the largest concession, operating spas aboard more than 100 ships. The company, founded in London in 1901 by Henry Steiner, began its ambitious growth in 1926, when Herman Steiner got involved in the family beauty salon on his father's death. He opened salons throughout England, became official cosmetician to the late Queen Elizabeth the Queen Mother, and won his first cruise ship contract in 1956. The company closed its land-based salons in the 1990s, as its cruise ship business burgeoned. It bought Elemis, a lifestyle range of plant-based beauty products, and acquired Mandara Spas, developed in the US alongside its Elemis Spas. In 2010 it bought The Onboard Spa Company.

Other spa concessions include: Blue Ocean (MSC Cruises); Canyon Ranch At Sea (Celebrity Cruises, Cunard, Oceania Cruises, and Regent Seven Seas Cruises); Carita (Ponant); LivNordic (Viking Ocean Cruises); and Ocean Spa (Hapag-Lloyd, TUI Cruises).

Teeth whitening

This treatment uses one of several methods, including bleaching strips, pen, gel, and laser bleaching. Carbamide peroxide, when mixed with water, forms hydrogen peroxide – the substance most used in teeth-whitening procedures. Power bleaching uses light energy to accelerate the process.

Thalassotherapy

The use of seawater to promote wellbeing and healing dates back to ancient Greece. Today, shipboard spas have whole bath rituals involving water and flower petals, herbs, or mineral salts.

Spa cuisine

Originally designed as low-fat, low-calorie meals for weight loss using grains, greens, and sprouts, spa cuisine now includes whole grains, seasonal fruits and vegetables, and lean proteins – ingredients low in saturated fats and cholesterol, low-fat dairy products, and reduced salt. These foods provide the basis for balanced nutrition and portion sizes, while maintaining some flavor, texture, and taste; foods are typically grilled rather than baked or fried.

Sports facilities

Sports facilities might include basketball, paddle tennis (a sort of downsized tennis court), and electronic golf simulators. Some boutique/small-size 'luxury' ships offer kayaking, water-skiing, jet skiing, and wake boarding for no extra charge. In reality, however, the water sports equipment is typically only used on one or two days (or part days) during a seven-day cruise.

Top of the Range

Of the 70-plus ocean-going cruise lines operating internationally, only a handful provides the kind of stylish ships aboard which the word 'no' is virtually unheard.

One person's luxury is another person's standard. Luxury (elegant, sumptuous) should be a flawless combination of ship, facilities, understated decor, culinary excellence, impeccable service – and arriving in style. Unfortunately, the words luxury, luxe, and premium – all used interchangeably – have been degraded through constant overuse by marketeers and advertisers.

Brochure vs reality

The brochure shows a photo of Champagne at embarkation. The reality: it's sparkling wine. The brochure shows a photo of a couple having a romantic white tablecloth-dressed dinner at a table for two outdoors on deck (with not a hint of a breeze). The reality: very few ships can deliver this. The brochure (or video) shows a large resort ship free from crowds or lines. The reality: near-impossible, particularly at embarkation and disembarkation.

Little and large

Size is important. Boutique and Small Ships (characterized by Berlitz as having 50–250 and 251–750 passengers, respectively) can get into ports that larger ships can't. They can also get closer to the center of large cities. For example, in St. Petersburg, Russia, large and mid-size ships (such as those of Crystal Cruises and Regent Seven Seas Cruises) dock about one hour from the center, while boutique/small ships, such as those of Hapag-Lloyd Cruises, Ponant, Seabourn, or Silversea Cruises, can dock right next to the Hermitage Museum in the heart of the city.

One area where 'luxury' ships differ least from large resort ships is in shore excursions, particularly in the Caribbean and Alaska, where almost all cruise operators are obliged to use the same local tour operators, and local tour operators treat all cruise passengers the same – as if they are children visiting for the first time.

Large resort ships (for 2,501–7,000 passengers) have some ultra-large penthouse suites or 'villas' with massive amounts of space, but, once you leave your accommodation, you face the same food as everyone else on board. Also, these ships simply cannot provide the kind of personal service and attention to detail that the boutique/small ships can. There are, of course, exceptions – to some degree. For example, in the exclusive Dream Palace aboard Dream Cruises ships, the Yacht Club of MSC Cruises and The Haven aboard Norwegian Cruise Line ships are examples of the good levels of personal service that can be provided aboard the large resort ships. However, once you leave your 'private living space,' you mix with everyone else, particularly if you want to see a show, have a coffee in the café, disembark at ports of call, or go on organized shore excursions. That's when you appreciate the fact that smaller is better: the small ships cater to fewer passengers and are more relaxed..

These are ships suited to those not seeking the active, family-friendly, and entertainment-driven cruise experiences that large resort ships offer, and they provide facilities and service levels hard to find elsewhere. While they boast about being the best, or boast the awards they receive annually from various bodies (often invited or coerced responses), few provide a fine luxury experience.

What are the differences?

Luxury varies by degrees. Although the differences are immediately noticeable when you sail aboard and compare them all, some of the variations in style, service, and – especially – staff training are far more subtle. One thing is certain: the word 'no' should be virtually unheard.

Some ships have more public space per passenger. Some definitely have more highly trained service personnel rather than technical staff per passenger. Some have better food and service. Some have entertainment; some don't. Some have more fresh flowers in public areas than others – they're very evident aboard the ships of Hapag-Lloyd Cruises but not aboard Silversea Cruises' ships, for instance (where

Butler service aboard Silversea Cruises.

Penthouse suite, aboard *Seven Seas Mariner*.

Prosecco – not Champagne – is provided on embarkation).

Crystal Cruises, for example, has an excellent program of cultural lecturers, professional bridge (the card game, not the navigation bridge) instructors, together with its Yamaha 'Passport to Music' program on each cruise, whereas others (Regent, Seabourn, SeaDream, and Silversea) don't. Hapag-Lloyd has excellent lecturers, and a PGA golf professional aboard every cruise.

The following facilities, services, and approaches are found and experienced aboard the ships of Hapag-Lloyd Cruises, Seabourn, and SeaDream Yacht Club, but not aboard the ships of Crystal Cruises, Regent Seven Seas Cruises, or Silversea Cruises:

Anticipation – more widely practiced by better-trained staff, who are also more adept at passenger recognition (remembering your name and preferences).

Waiters/waitresses escort guests to the dining table and to the dining room exit after meals.

Relaxed embarkation/disembarkation at your leisure.

Cabin stewardesses leave handwritten notes.

There are no announcements, and no background music plays in public rooms, accommodation hallways, or elevators.

The chef invites passengers to accompany him/her on visits to local food markets.

More space, better service

These ships have an excellent amount of open deck and lounging space, and a high passenger space ratio when compared to large resort ships (which are typically under 35 gross tonnage per passenger); the two SeaDream ships being the exception, due to their small size.

In warm-weather areas, the ships of Seabourn and SeaDream Yacht Club all of which have fold-down aft platforms, with jet skis, kayaks, snorkeling gear, windsurfers, etc. at no extra cost, typically for one day each cruise (the others do not).

Hapag-Lloyd's *Europa* (space ratio: 70.4) and *Europa 2* (space ratio: 83.0) both have a fleet of rigid inflatable craft for in-depth exploration and shore adventures, plus an ice-hardened hull and crew members who understand the *culture* of their passengers. They also have mattresses that are 7ft (2.1m) long.

A good night's sleep

These ships feature premium-quality mattresses and bed linen (all of 100 percent cotton, with a thread count of 300 or more). There's always a little brand-consciousness going on, and some may be better than others.

Crystal Cruises, for example, features Bellora, from Milan (made in India using Egyptian cotton). Silversea Cruises features Egyptian cotton sheets, pillowcases, and duvet covers by Pratesi (founded in 1860), whose custom-made linens come from Tuscany, Italy – the company is known for supplying the Italian and other European aristocracy.

Good pillows are also important for a good night's sleep. You may be able to choose one of several different shapes and fillings. Crystal Cruises' pillow menu, for example, offers a choice of seven, including a Side Sleeper Pillow (down or down alternative); Back Sleeper Pillow (down or down alternative); Stomach Sleeper Pillow (down or down alternative); and Body Pillow (down alternative).

Depending on the cruise line, other choices might include hypoallergenic, hop-filled, or lavender-scented pillows.

15 THINGS TO EXPECT

1. Flawless (well, close to) personal service and attention to detail.
2. Genuine Champagne at embarkation (not sparkling wine).
3. Personalized stationery.
4. A crew that anticipates your needs, responds quickly to your requests, and doesn't say 'no' or 'impossible.'
5. No announcements (except for emergencies).
6. No background music in public rooms, hallways, and elevators.
7. High passenger space ratio (35 to 83 gross tons per passenger).

8. High crew to passenger ratio (1.5 to 1.0 or better).
9. The finest-quality bed linens, duvets, towels, and bathrobes.
10. A pillow menu.
11. High-quality toiletries (Aveda, Bulgari, for example).
12. No charge for on-demand movies or music.
13. More overnight or extended port stays.
14. Separate gangway for passengers and crew (where possible).
15. Shoeshine service.

A good night's sleep – outside

For something quite different, SeaDream Yacht Club has indulgent 'Balinese Dream Beds' for sleeping under the stars (in a secluded area at the front of the ship on the uppermost open deck), a delightful idea for honeymooners or anyone celebrating a special occasion Custom-made pyjamas are supplied, and you can take them home with you.

Creative cuisine

Fine dining is the highlight of ships in this category and is more of an entertainment feature than these ships' entertainment shows – if there are any. Good company and conversation are crucial. You can expect to find plenty of tables for two, a calm and refined dining atmosphere, open or one-seating dining, by candlelight (when permitted), with high-quality china and silverware, large wine glasses, fresh flowers, a fine wine list, and sommeliers who can discuss fine wines. Service should be unhurried (not like the two-seating ships, where meals tend to be served as speed trials by waiters), well-paced, and unobtrusive.

It's really about non-repetitive, creative cuisine, high-quality ingredients, moderate portions, and attractive presentation, with fresh local fish and other items provided (when available) and cooked to order (not in batches), and meat of the highest grade. Caviar, foie gras, black/white truffles and other exotic foods, and fresh vegetables (instead of frozen or canned vegetables) are among the products that feature. Caviar aboard Europa and Europa 2 is typically from farmed sturgeon, and is excellent, while caviar aboard most other ships in this category is from the American farmed hackleback variety of sturgeon, or paddlefish 'caviar' (calling it 'caviar' is really stretch-

ing it). The caviar (from Uruguay) aboard the Seabourn ships is decent, however.

Some ships provide silver covers for entrées (main courses), creating extra 'wow' effect. Passengers may also be invited to visit local markets with the chef aboard the ships of Hapag-Lloyd Cruises, Seabourn, and SeaDream Yacht Club.

Some luxury ships provide even more special touches. Europa and Europa 2, for example, make their own breakfast preserves and ice cream, as well as fresh-pressed or freshly squeezed or pressed juices (most others provide pasteurized juices from concentrate) on board. Mint tea is made with fresh mint leaves and not from a teabag, for example, and it is properly served in a teapot. All (except Hapag-Lloyd Cruises) provide 'free' bottled mineral water.

Lunch and dinner menus may be provided in your suite/cabin in advance, and special orders are often possible. Room-service menus are extensive, and meals can be served in your suite/cabin (either on the balcony or inside on portable or fixed tables). It is also possible to have a private dinner setup on deck – wonderful in the right location.

Not Luxury

A prime example of luxury not being delivered can be seen aboard the ships of SeaDream Yacht Club, Seabourn, and Silver Cruises where, on buffets, cheese is pre-diced or sliced – not exactly gourmet dining where diners want to choose the amount themselves.

Drinks: included or not?

Crystal Cruises, Regent Seven Seas Cruises, Seabourn, SeaDream Yacht Club, and Silversea Cruises provide wine with dinner (Crystal Cruises, Seabourn, and Silversea also include wine with lunch), although the wines are typically young, and not from first-class houses. Windstar Cruises includes soft drinks and bottled water only (alcoholic beverages cost extra). Real premium brands and classic vintage wines cost extra.

Hapag-Lloyd Cruises charges for alcoholic beverages (although beer and soft drinks are provided in all cabins/suites). Crystal Cruises and Regent Seven Seas Cruise Line provide an all-inclusive product, including gratuities (although passengers always seem to add more). Crystal, Ponant, Regent, Seabourn, SeaDream, and Silversea include all drinks, but only the most standard brands and a limited choice of wines that may not be to your taste. Hapag-Lloyd Cruises doesn't include alcoholic drinks because those favored by its discerning passengers tend to be of a superior standard to those brands carried by the other companies mentioned here (as an example, Hapag-Lloyd Cruises carries over 45 types of premium gin aboard Europa and Europa 2, whereas Ponant's 'explorer' ships stock only the most basic brand of gin). In addition, this gets around the problem of passengers who don't drink alcohol not wishing to subsidize those that do.

TOP OF THE RANGE`

These 22 ships (listed alphabetically, by company) belong to 7 cruise lines and are the cream of the cruise industry in terms of style, finesse, staff training, cuisine, service, hospitality, and finesse. The ships are fully reviewed in the ratings section of this book, with Berlitz scores awarded for accommodation, food, service, entertainment, and the overall cruise experience.

Crystal Cruises: Crystal Serenity, Crystal Symphony
Hapag-Lloyd Cruises: Europa, Europa 2
Regent Seven Seas Cruises: Seven Seas Explorer, Seven Seas Mariner, Seven Seas Voyager
Seabourn: Seabourn Encore, Seabourn Odyssey, Seabourn Ovation, Seabourn Quest, Seabourn Sojourn
SeaDream Yacht Club: SeaDream I, SeaDream II
Silversea Cruises: Silver Muse, Silver Shadow, Silver Spirit, Silver Whisper, Silver Wind
Windstar: Star Breeze, Star Legend, Star Pride.

Comparing luxury ships

Ship name	Company (in alphabetical order)	Size	Passenger space ratio	Crew to passenger ratio	Water sports toys	Hand-held showers	Personal bathroom products
Crystal Serenity	Crystal Cruises	Mid-size	62.6	1.7	No	Yes	Etro
Crystal Symphony	Crystal Cruises	Mid-size	53.1	1.7	No	Yes	Etro
Europa	Hapag-Lloyd Cruises	Small	70.4	1.4	No	Yes	Own brand
Europa 2	Hapag-Lloyd Cruises	Small	83.0	1.3	No	Yes	Own brand
Seven Seas Explorer	Regent Seven Seas Cruises	Small	74.6	1.3	No	Yes	Guerlain
Seven Seas Mariner	Regent Seven Seas Cruises	Small	67.9	1.6	No	Yes	Canyon Ranch
Seven Seas Voyager	Regent Seven Seas Cruises	Small	59.8	1.6	No	Yes	Canyon Ranch
Seabourn Encore	Seabourn	Small	67.2	1.3	Yes	Yes	Therapies (Molton Brown)
Seabourn Odyssey	Seabourn	Small	71.1	1.3	Yes	Yes	Therapies (Molton Brown)
Seabourn Ovation	Seabourn	Small	67.2	1.3	Yes	Yes	Therapies (Molton Brown)
Seabourn Quest	Seabourn	Small	71.8	1.3	Yes	Yes	Therapies (Molton Brown)
Seabourn Sojourn	Seabourn	Small	71.8	1.3	Yes	Yes	Therapies (Molton Brown)
SeaDream I	SeaDream Yacht Club	Boutique	37.9	1.1	Yes	Yes	Bulgari
SeaDream II	SeaDream Yacht Club	Boutique	37.9	1.1	Yes	Yes	Bulgari
Silver Muse	Silversea Cruises	Small	78.8	1.4	Yes	Yes	Bulgari
Silver Shadow	Silversea Cruises	Small	72.8	1.4	No	No	Bulgari and Ferragamo
Silver Spirit	Silversea Cruises	Small	64.9	1.5	No	No	Bulgari and Ferragamo
Silver Whisper	Silversea Cruises	Small	72.8	1.4	No	No	Bulgari and Ferragamo
Silver Wind	Silversea Cruises	Small	57.6	1.3	No	No	Bulgari and Ferragamo
Star Breeze	Windstar Cruises	Boutique	47.0	1.7	Yes	Yes	Therapies (Molton Brown)
Star Legend	Windstar Cruises	Boutique	46.9	1.7	Yes	Yes	Therapies (Molton Brown)
Star Pride	Windstar Cruises	Boutique	47.0	1.7	Yes	Yes	L'Occitane

The Major Cruise Lines

We compare what the major cruise companies (reviewed in alphabetical order) have to offer when it comes to facilities, service, and ambience.

The major cruise lines

There are nine major cruise lines (those with 10 ships or more). They are: AIDA Cruises, Carnival Cruise Line, Celebrity Cruises, Costa Cruises, Holland America Line, MSC Cruises, Norwegian Cruise Line, Princess Cruises, and Royal Caribbean International.

What they have in common

All offer one thing: a well-packaged cruise vacation, generally of seven days, typically with a mix of days at sea and port days, plenty of food, friendly service, large-scale shows and trendy cabaret acts, large casinos, shopping malls, and extensive spa and fitness facilities.

The ships have a lot in common, too. All have art auctions, bingo, horse racing, shopping talks, facilities and programs for children and teens, wedding vows/renewal programs, and Wi-Fi or Internet connect centers. All are dedicated to generating higher revenue returns.

Standing in line for embarkation, disembarkation (and shore tenders, shore excursions, and shuttle buses in ports of call), and for self-serve buffets is inevitable. But the ships differ in their characters, facilities, maintenance, space, crew-to-passenger ratio, food and service, and crew training. You'll be escorted to your cabin only if you book Yacht Club-grade accommodation aboard the ships of MSC Cruises. Aboard other lines, staff at the ship-side of the gangway simply point you in the right direction.

What makes them different

Ships belonging to the major companies may look similar, but they differ not only in their layout, decor, and passenger flow but also in small details. Even towel sizes and the number of days between bed-linen changes can vary widely.

AIDA CRUISES

Ships

AIDAaura (2003), *AIDAbella* (2008), *AIDAblu* (2010), *AIDAcara* (1996), *AIDAdiva* (2007), *AIDAluna* (2009), *AIDAmar* (2012), AIDAmira (1999/2019), AIDAnova

Germany-based AIDA Cruises is one of the Carnival brands.

(2019), *AIDAperla* (2017), *AIDAprima* (2016), *AIDAsol* (2011), *AIDAstella* (2013), *AIDAvita* (2002)

About the company

The former East German shipping company Deutsche Seereederei (DSR) and its marketing arm Seetours (Deutsche Seetouristik) were assigned the traditional cruise ship *Arkona* as part of the 1985 East–West integration, including a contract with the Treuhandanstalt (the agency that privatized East German enterprises) to build a new ship. It did this in 1996 with *Aida*, designed to appeal to young, active German-speaking families, which created a seagoing version of the popular Robinson Clubs – a sort of German Club Med copy. When *Aida* first debuted the company struggled at first.

In 1998 it was purchased by Norwegian Cruise Line, which re-sold it to its original Rostock-based owners. P&O acquired it in 1999; it is now a successful multi-ship sub-brand of Carnival Corporation,

WHICH CRUISE LINE DOES WHAT BEST

 AIDA Cruises is for youthful German-speaking families who like lively surroundings and bright colors in a club-like resort package. The ships have good entertainment and take care of kids and teens well. The dress code is ultra-casual, and food is more about quantity than quality – unless you pay extra for dining in a 'specialty' restaurant.

 Carnival Cruise Line is for all-round fun, activities, and casinos for the lively, no-sleep-needed youth market. Carnival doesn't sell itself as a 'luxury' or 'premium' cruise line, which it certainly isn't. It delivers exactly the well-packaged cruise vacation its brochures promise. Its ships have good entertainment facilities and features, and some include extra-cost dining spots for the more discerning passenger.

 Celebrity Cruises is a 'premium' line offering 'modern luxury.' However, some aspects are not premium – for example, recorded 'music' blaring over pool decks 24 hours a day is not relaxing. Celebrity Cruises is more akin to Royal Caribbean International, but with a more upmarket wrapper and contemporary design features.

Costa Cruises is all about quasi-Italian style and lively ambience for families. Swimming pools are full of children in peak holiday periods. Costa provides first-time cruise passengers with a packaged holiday that is a mix of contemporary surroundings and basic fare, accompanied by loud everything. Most passengers are Italian.

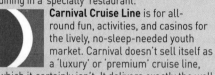

Holland America Line has the right touches for seniors and retirees: lots of flowers, yesteryear traditions, cooking demonstrations, and specialty grill venues. The ships are best suited to older couples and solo travelers who like an unhurried setting, with good-quality surroundings. There's plenty of eclectic antique artwork, decent – though not gourmet – food, and service from a smiling crew (many of whom are Indonesian/Filipino), who lack the finesse many expect from a so-called 'premium' product.

 MSC Cruises – a family-owned, Swiss-based company with an Italian heritage (its name is Mediterranean Shipping Company). The company displays fine pan-European flair, with a high level of service and hospitality training from a friendly, multilingual crew. It has evolved quickly as the 'new kid on the block.' Of all the major cruise lines, it's also very clean. Bed linen and towels are changed every third day, and bathrobes in suites daily, unlike most other brands.

 Norwegian Cruise Line is a really good choice for a first cruise for families with children, with a wide choice of eateries, great entertainment, and friendly service staff. Its ships are best suited to first-time, youthful solo passengers, couples, families with children, and teenagers who want upbeat, color-rich surroundings, plenty of entertainment lounges and bars, and high-tech sophistication – in one programmed, well-packaged vacation.

 Princess Cruises offers consistent product delivery and somewhat restrained decor. Choose Princess Cruises if you enjoy being with families and fellow passengers of mid-50s and upwards, who want a well-organized cruise experience with unpretentious middle-of-the-road cuisine, a good range of entertainment, and an excellent shore excursion program – arguably the best run of any of the major cruise lines. On the down side, several of its ships do now seem somewhat dated.

 Royal Caribbean International is really known for its Caribbean itineraries, for first-time cruisers and families. The newest ships are stunning, and filled with high-tech gismos, plus entertainment including slightly scaled-down versions of well-known Broadway shows. The ships are for active, young-minded cruisers of all ages who enjoy mingling in a large ship setting with plenty of life. The food is more about quantity than quality – unless you pay extra for dining in a 'specialty' restaurant.

under the control of its Costa Cruises division. AIDA Cruises is known for its large self-serve buffet eateries instead of traditional waiter service.

What is it really like?

The ships have become more sophisticated entertainment venues, and Club Teams (entertainment staff) interact with passengers. The company has its own training schools in several countries, plus a recognized training academy in Rostock, Germany.

The decibel levels are high – it is impossible to escape the noise and loud music, and 'background' music played in cabin hallways and elevators 24/7.

There are three pricing levels – AIDA Premium, AIDA Vario, and Just AIDA – depending on what you want to be included. Opt for the basic, price-driven 'Just Aida' package and the cruise line chooses the ship, itinerary, and accommodation for you – sort of a pot-luck cruise, based on or close to the dates you choose.

CARNIVAL CRUISE LINE

Ships

Carnival Breeze (2012), *Carnival Conquest* (2002), *Carnival Dream* (2009), *Carnival Ecstasy* (1991), *Carnival Elation* (1998), *Carnival Fantasy* (1990), *Carnival Fascination* (1994), *Carnival Freedom* (2007), *Carnival Glory* (2003), *Carnival Horizon* (2018), *Carnival Imagination* (1995), *Carnival Inspiration* (1996), *Carnival Legend* (2002), *Carnival Liberty* (2005), *Carnival Magic* (2011), *Carnival Miracle* (2004), *Carnival Panorama (2019)*, *Carnival Paradise* (1998), *Carnival Pride* (2002), *Carnival Sensation* (1993), *Carnival Spirit* (2001), *Carnival Splendor* (2008), *Carnival Sunrise* (1999), *Carnival Sunshine* (1996), *Carnival Valor* (2004), *Carnival Victory* (2000), *Carnival Vista* (2016)

About the company

Israel-born Ted Arison (born Theodore Arisohn), whose ambition was to be a concert pianist, founded Carnival Cruise Line, the world's largest and most successful single cruise line, in 1972, with one ship, *Mardi Gras* (formerly *Empress of Canada*). Carnival wanted to be different, and developed its 'fun ship' concept. It worked, appealing to people of all ages and backgrounds.

Its first new ship, *Tropicale*, debuted in 1982. In 1984 Carnival started advertising on television, introducing a wider public to the idea of cruising. It introduced the first cruise ship measuring over 100,000 gross tons – *Carnival Destiny* (now named *Carnival Sunshine*) – in 1996.

Today, the Carnival Corporation, parent company of Carnival Cruise Line, is run by Micky Arison, who also owns the NBA's Miami Heat basketball team. Over 20 new ships have been introduced since the line was founded in 1972, several of which are now tired and outdated.

Enjoying the splash park aboard a Carnival Cruise Line ship.

What is it really like?

Carnival's fleet of ships is among the oldest of the major cruise companies. The ships are well suited to multi-generational groups, and for family reunions.

The dress code is ultra-casual – indeed, the waiters are better dressed than most passengers. Carnival is all about 'happy' and 'fun' – cruise directors tell passengers to 'make some noise' – and towels shaped like animals, scheduled participation activities, yelling and screaming. But it's an impersonal cruise experience, and solo travelers can get lost in the crowds of couples. Repeat customers carry a Gold or Platinum card for better recognition from 'service' staff.

The ships are clean – if you don't look too closely. Open deck space may look adequate when you board, but on sea days you can expect your plastic deck chair (if you can find one that's free) kissing its neighbor (it's probably tied to it). There are no cushioned pads, so sunloungers are uncomfortable to sit on for any length of time.

TV movies – only for pay-per-view movies. The ship's daily program is mostly devoted to persuading you to spend money.

For children

Carnival is family-friendly and carries over 700,000 children a year. 'Camp Carnival,' the line's child/youth program, is well organized. There are five age groups: Toddlers (ages two to five), Juniors (six to eight), Intermediate (nine to 11), Tweens (12–14, Circle C), and Late Teens (15–17, with Club 02). Even the under-twos can be catered to. Soft-drinks packages can be bought for children (adults, too). Note that a babysitting service is not generally available after 10pm.

In 2014 Carnival partnered with children's specialist Dr. Seuss and introduced 'Seuss at Sea,' with immersive family dining (think 'green eggs and ham' for breakfast, served by waiters in Dr. Seuss-inspired uniforms). Characters such as the Cat in the Hat, Thing One and Thing Two, and Sam are in attendance, and there are also special showings of movies such as *The Cat in the Hat* and *How the Grinch Stole Christmas*.

CELEBRITY CRUISES

Ships

Celebrity Apex (2020), Constellation (2002), Celebrity Eclipse (2010), Celebrity Edge (2018), Celebrity Equinox (2009), Celebrity Flora (2019), Celebrity Infinity (2001), Celebrity Millennium (2000), Celebrity Reflection (2012), Celebrity Silhouette (2011), Celebrity Solstice (2008), Celebrity Summit (2001), Celebrity Xpedition (2001)

Carnival Liberty calls at Roatán in Honduras Bay.

The decibel level is high: it is impossible to escape the loud music, and 'background' music is played in hallways, elevators and pool decks 24/7.

Passenger niggles: Intrusive photographers are everywhere. There's no listing of the free in-cabin

THE BIG PLAYERS: WHO OWNS WHOM

Carnival Corporation
- AIDA Cruises
- Carnival Cruise Line
- Costa Cruises
- Cunard
- Holland America Line
- P&O Cruises
  - P&O Cruises (Australia)
- Princess Cruises
- Seabourn

Norwegian Cruise Line Holdings
- Norwegian Cruise Line
- Oceania Cruises
- Regent Seven Seas Cruises

Genting Hong Kong
- Crystal Cruises
- Dream Cruises
- Star Cruises

Royal Caribbean Cruises
- Azamara
- Celebrity Cruises
- Pullmantur Cruises
  - TUI Cruises (50%)
- Royal Caribbean International

About the company

Celebrity Cruises was the brainchild of Harry H. Haralambopoulos, and brothers John and Michael Chandris, London-based Greek cargo ship owners and operators of the former Chandris Lines and Chandris Cruises. In 1989, as the cruise industry was gaining momentum, they were determined to create a newer, better cruise line, with new ships, larger, more standard cabins, and greater focus on food, and service in the European tradition.

Its image as a 'premium' line is justified because the product delivery on board is superior to (and the price is higher than) that of its parent company, Royal Caribbean International, which bought it in 1997 for $1.3 billion. 'Premium' line Celebrity Cruises is now more akin to Royal Caribbean International, but with a more upmarket wrapper.

The ships are recognizable by a large 'X' on the funnel, denoting the third letter from the end of the Greek alphabet, the Greek 'chi' or 'Ch' in English, for Chandris, the founding family.

In 2007 Celebrity Cruises created the sub-brand Azamara Cruises (now simply known as Azamara), with three ships (of around 700 passengers): *Azamara Journey* (2000) *Azamara Pursuit* (2018), and *Azamara Quest* (2000).

What is it really like?

The ships are clean and well maintained. There are always flowers and flower displays.

Celebrity Equinox leaves Istanbul.

Celebrity Cruises delivers a well-defined North American cruise experience at a modest price. If the budget allows, book a suite-category cabin for the extra benefits it brings – it's worth it. Strong points include a higher standard of service and a 'zero announcement policy.' Such touches differentiate Celebrity Cruises from its competitors. Celebrity Cruises also has some eclectic sculptures and original artwork, from Picasso to Warhol, found at sea.

The ships have more staff than other ships of comparable size and capacity, especially in the housekeeping and food and beverage departments. However, the company has seen fit to remove items, such as personalized stationery, from some accommodation grades, it has substituted cloth napkins with paper ones, and has reduced the amount and quality of fresh flower displays (although there are still some).

Sadly, intrusive music is played almost everywhere, and any lounge designated as 'music-free' is typically full of activities and participation events, so it's hard to find a quiet corner to sit and read.

For children

Junior passengers are divided into Shipmates (three to five years), Celebrity Cadets (six to eight years), Ensigns (nine to 11 years), Admiral T's (12–14 years), and Teens (13–17).

On sea days the program is crammed with things to do, with an emphasis on revenue-enhancing activities such as art auctions, bingo, and horse racing.

COSTA CRUISES

Ships

Costa Atlantica (2000), *Costa Deliziosa* (2010), *Costa Diadema* (2014), *Costa Fascinosa* (2012), *Costa Favolosa* (2010), *Costa Fortuna* (2003), *Costa Luminosa* (2009), *Costa Magica* (2004), *Costa Mediterranea* (2003), *Costa neoRomantica* (1993), *Costa Pacifica* (2009), *Costa Serena* (2007), *Costa Smerelda* (2019), *Costa Venezia* (2019), *Costa Victoria* (1996)

About the company

Costa Cruises traces its history back to 1860, when Giacomo Costa started an olive oil business. The first ship, in 1924, transported that oil. After he died in 1924, his sons, Federico, Eugenio, and Enrico, inherited the business. First they bought *Ravenna*, a cargo ship, to cut transport costs for their olive oil empire. In 1948, Costa's first passenger ship, the *Anna 'C'*, carried passengers in style from Genoa to South America. In 1997, Costa Cruises was bought by the US's Carnival Corpora-

Making an entrance down the Grand Foyer aboard a *Celebrity Millennium*-class ship.

tion and UK's Airtours plc. Three years later Carnival took full control.

Costa specializes in cruises for Europeans or passengers with European tastes – particularly Italians – during the summer. It has initiated an aggressive newbuild policy in recent years, in order to modernize the company's aging fleet of different-size ships. The ships operate in three main markets: the Mediterranean, the Caribbean, and South America.

Most ships are well maintained, although there are inconsistencies throughout the fleet. The same is true of cleanliness – some ships are very clean, while others are a little dusty around the edges, as are its shore tenders. The company's safety procedures came under scrutiny when *Costa Concordia* struck rocks and capsized off the Italian island of Giglio in January 2012.

What is it really like?

Costa is noted for its lively 'Italian' ambience. There are few Italian crew members, however, although many officers are Italian. The dress code is casual, even on formal nights. This is a cruise company for those who like to party. If you want quiet, take earplugs – good ones. On European and Mediterranean cruises, most passengers speak Italian, Spanish, French, and German. On Caribbean itineraries, a high percentage of passengers speak Spanish, as the ships carry passengers from Latin American countries in addition to passengers from North America.

Costa ships are best suited to young couples, singles, and families with children who enjoy big-city life, a multicultural social mix, outdoor cafés, constant activity, eating late, and loud entertainment, and are happy with food more notable for quantity than quality. All printed materials (room service folio, menus, etc.) are in six languages: Italian, English, French, German, Portuguese, and Spanish. Announcements are made in at least four languages.

Expect lots of children of all ages if you book for peak holiday period cruises; note that in Europe at certain times (such as Easter) schoolchildren have long vacations. On some European itineraries, passengers embark and disembark in almost

---

CELEBRITY'S CLASSY APPROACH

There are several 'classes' of accommodation, but choose a suite grade and you get many more perks such as priority embarkation, disembarkation and tender tickets, specialty dining and spa reservations, double-bed overlay (no more falling 'between the cracks' for couples). It also offers a pillow menu, throw pillows on sofas, fruit baskets, binoculars, and larger beach towels. Balconies may feature better-quality furniture.

Best foot forward beside a Costa funnel.

every port, which makes for a disjointed cruise experience, with almost no start or end to the cruise. There is little information for passengers who want to be independent in ports of call and not take the organized excursions.

There is extensive smoking on board. No-smoking zones and signs are often ignored to the frustration of non-smokers, and ashtrays are moved at whim; many of the officers and crew also smoke, even when moving through public rooms, so they don't enforce the no-smoking zones.

Cabins tend to be small, but the decor is fresh, and the bathrooms are very practical. Some ships have cabin bathrooms with sliding doors – an excellent alternative to inward-openers that use up space.

Costa neoRiviera, *Costa neoRomantica*, and *Costa Victoria* have a dated European feel. They are lively without being too much, or pastel-toned without being boring, while all the other newer ships have an in-your-face brashness similar to Carnival's ships, with grainy and unflattering digital artwork on walls and panels, and in elevators.

For children

Junior passengers are in three groups: Kids Club (ages three to six); Junior Club (seven to 12); and Teen Club (13–17). Programs vary by ship, itinerary, and season. Group babysitting is available 6.30–11pm. During port days, babysitting is available generally 8.30am–12.30pm and 2.30–6.30pm.

HOLLAND AMERICA LINE

Ships

Amsterdam (2000), *Eurodam* (2008), *Koningsdam* (2016), *Maasdam* (1993), *Nieuw Amsterdam* (2010), *Nieuw Statendam* (2018), *Noordam* (2006), *Oosterdam* (2003), *Rotterdam* (1997), *Veendam* (1996), *Volendam* (1999), *Westerdam* (2004), *Zaandam* (2000), *Zuiderdam* (2002)

About the company

Holland America Line (HAL) was founded in 1873 as the Netherlands-America Steamship Company, shipping immigrants to the New World from Rotterdam. It moved its headquarters to New York in 1971. It bought into Alaskan hotels and transportation when it acquired Westours in 1983 and is one of the state's biggest employers. In 1989, it was acquired by Carnival Corporation, but retained its Seattle-based headquarters.

HAL carries both traditional cruise passengers (senior citizens, alumni groups) and multi-generational families. It tries hard to keep its Dutch connections, with antique artefacts and traditional decor, as well as Indonesian stewards. It rents a private island, Half Moon Cay, in the Bahamas.

What is it really like?

The brand encompasses basically two types of ship. Younger families with children and grandchildren are best suited to *Eurodam*, *Nieuw Amsterdam*, *Nieuw*

Statendam, Noordam, Oosterdam, Westerdam, and *Zuiderdam,* whereas those of senior years – HAL's traditional audience of repeat passengers – are best suited to the smaller, less glitzy *Amsterdam, Maasdam, Rotterdam, Veendam,* and *Zaandam.* All ships have teakwood outdoor promenade decks, while most rivals have artificial grass or some other form of indoor-outdoor covering. Lifestyle lounge-like Explorations Cafés have been built into its ships.

Holland America Line has a training school in Jakarta, Indonesia, and pre-trains crew members who have never been to sea before. Many crew members have been promoted to supervisory positions due to new ship introductions, but few have the formal training, professional, communication or management skills required.

The company operates many theme-related cruises and has a good program of life-enrichment lecturers, and its 'Culinary Arts' program includes celebrity guest chefs and interactive cooking demos.

Lighter-option meals are available for the nutrition- and weight-conscious, as are Kosher (pre-prepared) meals.

A two-deck dining room is typical aboard Holland America Line ships.

Regular coffee is half-decent, but weak. Extra-cost espresso/cappuccino coffees (Dutch) are better, served in proper china, but not quite up to the standard of Celebrity or Costa.

For children
Club HAL: Junior passengers are divided into three age groups: three to eight, nine to 12, and teens. Programming is based on the number of children booked on any given sailing, with children's counselors provided as needed (at least one per 30 children).

MSC CRUISES

Ships
MSC Armonia (2001), *MSC Bellissima* (2019), *MSC Divina* (2012), *MSC Fantasia* (2008), *MSC Grandiosa* (2019), *MSC Lirica* (2003), *MSC Magnifica* (2010), *MSC Meraviglia* (2017), *MSC Musica* (2006), *MSC Opera* (2004), *MSC Orchestra* (2007), *MSC Poesia* (2008), *MSC Preziosa* (2013), *MSC Seaside* (2017), *MSC Seaview* (2018), *MSC Sinfonia* (2005), *MSC Splendida* (2009)

About the company
The HQ of the world's largest privately owned cruise line is in Geneva, Switzerland, but was actually founded in Belgium in 1970. It's also home to parent company Mediterranean Shipping Company, the world's second-biggest container shipping company. It started in the cruise business by acquiring Italian company Star Lauro in 1995, with two older ships, *Monterey* and *Rhapsody*. It then purchased *Melody*, followed by two almost new ships from bankrupt Festival Cruises.

MSC Cruises has grown incredibly fast and is, unusually, owned by a shipping-based family, not a faceless corporation. In 2014, the company 'chopped and stretched' four ships to update them and accommodate more passengers (*MSC Armonia, MSC Lirica, MSC Opera,* and *MSC Sinfonia*). Then, 2017 saw the addition of *MSC Meraviglia* and *MSC Seaside* – stunning, very different ships with an array of facilities and family-friendly attractions. With the new ships came a brand rollout that prepared the company for future growth and innovation, and for partnerships with leading brands such as Chicco, Cirque du Soleil, Lego, TechnoGym, Harmon and Samsung.

What is it really like?
MSC Cruises' ships are suited to families with children, and good for those who enjoy big-city life, a multinational and multicultural atmosphere, outdoor cafés, and constant activity accompanied by plenty of live music and late nights.

MSC Cruises has four distinct price categories, each including different things, so it's important to choose the right package for your needs and cruise experiences. They are Bella (for a basic, price-driven

MSC Fantasia's Topsail Lounge.

experience), Fantastica (for greater comfort and flex-ibility), Wellness (aimed at health and fitness), and Aurea (for more inclusions).

The largest ships (*MSC Bellissima, MSC Grandiosa, MSC Meraviglia, MSC Seaside, MSC Seaview*) have an exclusive lounge and restaurant for Yacht Club-grade passengers, and *MSC Divina, MSC Bellissima, MSC Meraviglia, MSC Preziosa* and *MSC Seaside* each have a separate dining room for Yacht Club occu-pants, with open-seating, a private sun deck oasis pool, bar, café and sunbathing areas, private access to the Aurea Spa, priority embarkation, a concierge, and butler service.

Why is the company so successful? It's the soft-ware (crew), its multi-national abilities, and attention to the finer details.

The ships typically operate in English, with some announcements also in French, German, Italian, and Spanish. During the cruise, there are few announce-ments. Given this multilingual emphasis, production shows and other major entertainment displays are more visual than verbal. For the same reason, the ships don't generally carry lecturers.

Cigar lovers will find a selection of real Cuban smokes in the cigar lounges.

The decor is decidedly European/Mediter-ranean (except for the ships dedicated to North America), with understated elegance and really high-quality soft furnishings and other materi-als such as Italian marble, and Swarovski crystal glass stairways.

For children

Children are divided into three age groups, with facilities to match: Mini Club (ages three to nine); Junior Club (10–13); and Teenagers Club (over 14, a pre-paid Teen Card is available). While the fa-cilities and play areas aren't as extensive as those aboard some other major lines, a 'baby parking' service is useful when parents want to go ashore on excursions. MSC Cruises' mascot is Do-Re-Mi – the von Trapp family of *The Sound of Music* fame would no doubt be delighted.

NORWEGIAN CRUISE LINE

Ships

Norwegian Bliss (2018), *Norwegian Breakaway* (2013), *Norwegian Dawn* (2002), *Norwegian Epic* (2010), *Norwegian Encore (2019)*, *Norwegian Es-cape* (2015), *Norwegian Gem* (2007), *Norwegian Getaway* (2014), *Norwegian Jade* (2006), *Norwegian Jewel* (2005), *Norwegian Joy* (2017), *Norwegian Pearl* (2006), *Norwegian Spirit* (1998), *Norwegian Star* (2002), *Norwegian Sun* (2001), *Norwegian Sky* (1999), *Pride of America* (2005)

About the company

Norwegian Cruise Line, the originator of contemporary cruising, was founded in 1966 by three Norwegian shipping companies as Klosters Sunward Ferries and was renamed Norwegian Caribbean Line in 1967. It was bought by Star Cruises in 2000, and has been replacing its older, smaller ships with brand new, larger vessels. NCL also operates one ship with a mostly American crew and a base in Hawaii.

Freestyle Cruising is how NCL describes its operation – although it's hard to detect style in the onboard product (I call it American Bistro-style). Its fleet is diverse, so the cruise experience can vary, although this makes for interesting character variation between the various ship categories. There is more standardization aboard the larger, newer ships. The senior officers are the only thing that's Norwegian.

Most standard cabins are extremely small, though they are laid out in a practical manner.

What is it really like?

If this is your first cruise, you should enjoy a good overall vacation in a lively, upbeat setting. The lifestyle is contemporary, fresh, creative, and sporty, with a casualness typical of youthful city dwellers, and with its 'eat when you want' philosophy, the shipboard ambience is ultra-casual. The dress code is, too – indeed, the waiters are probably better dressed than many passengers. The staff members are generally congenial, and you'll find a high percentage of women in cabin and restau-

rant service departments – more than most major cruise lines.

There's plenty of lively music, constant activity, entertainment, and food that's mainstream and acceptable, but nothing more, unless you pay extra to eat in the specialty dining spots. All this is delivered by a smiling, very friendly service staff, who can lack polish, but are obliging. In the latest wheeze to extract revenue, NCL is offering extra-cost 'Backstage Tours.'

For children

Splash Academy and Entourage programs divide children into several age groups: Guppies (ages 6 months to three years); Junior sailors (three to five); First Mates (six to eight); Navigators (nine to 12); and two Teens groups (13–14 and 15–17). The kids and teens clubs were developed in conjunction with UK-based King's Foundation and Camps, a charity that provides quality sports and activity programs. Group babysitting services are also available, at an extra charge. Special price packages are available for soft drinks.

PRINCESS CRUISES

Ships

Caribbean Princess (2004), Coral Princess (2002), Crown Princess (2006), Diamond Princess (2004), Emerald Princess (2007), Golden Princess (2001), Grand Princess (1998), Island Princess (2003), Majestic Princess (2017), Pacific Princess (1999), Regal Princess (2014), Royal Princess (2013), Ruby Prin-

The Ocean Place complex aboard Norwegian Getaway.

THE MA.

THE CRUISE

144

cruising, foo
creasing e
be subje
desig
P
fa

Playing air hockey in a Princess Cruises teen centre.

cess (2008), *Sapphire Princess* (2005), *Sea Princess* (1998), Sky Princess (2019), *Star Princess* (2002), *Sun Princess* (1995)

About the company

Princess Cruises was founded by Stanley McDonald in 1965 with one ship, the chartered former passenger ferry *Princess Patricia,* for cruises along the Mexican Riviera. In 1974, the company was bought by the UK's Peninsular and Oriental Steam Navigation Company (P&O), and in 1988 P&O/Princess Cruises merged with the Italian line Sitmar Cruises. In 2000, Carnival Corporation and Royal Caribbean Cruises fought a protracted battle to buy Princess Cruises. Carnival won.

The company provides comfortable mainstream cruising aboard a fleet of mainly large resort ships (plus one small ship), and its routes cover the world. The ships have a higher-than-average passenger space ratio than competitors Carnival or Royal Caribbean International, and the service is friendly without being showy. In 2010 the company converted to fully digital travel documents (no more ticket document wallets).

What is it really like?

The ships are clean and well maintained, and the open promenade decks of some ships have teak deck lounge chairs, while others are plastic. Only *Coral Princess* and *Island Princess* have full walk-

around open promenade decks; aboard the other ships you can't walk completely around the ship without negotiating steps. There is a nice balance of officers, staff, and crew members. Note that there is no Deck 13, which is good news for superstitious passengers.

There are proper cinemas aboard most ships, as well as outdoor poolside mega-screens for showing evening 'movies under the skies.'

Lines form at peak times at the information office, and for open-seating breakfast and lunch in the main dining rooms. Passengers receive turndown service and a pillow chocolate each night, bathrobes (on request), and toiletry kits (larger ones for suite/mini-suite occupants). All cabins have a hairdryer, which is sensibly located at a vanity desk unit in the lounge area. In 2012, smoking was prohibited in cabins and on cabin balconies.

The ships have an adults-only area called 'The Sanctuary,' an extra-cost retreat forward of the mast. It has thickly padded sunloungers both in the sun and in the shade, a swim-against-the-current pool, and two outdoor cabanas for massages. I recommend The Sanctuary as a retreat from the bustle of the rest of the ship. It's worth the extra cost.

Princess's food and entertainment is geared to the North American market, but British and other European nationalities should feel at ease, safe in the knowledge that this is highly organized, packaged

, and service. There is, however, an in-
phasis on onboard revenue, so expect to
ted to daily advertising of art auctions and
er' watches.

ncess Cruises' ships are best suited to couples,
ilies with young children and teenagers, and ma-
ure solo travelers who like to mingle in a large ship
setting with sophisticated surroundings and decent
entertainment.

Shipboard hospitals have live SeaMed tele-med-
icine link-ups with specialists at the Cedars-Sinai
Medical Center in Los Angeles for emergency help
– useful mainly for passengers who reside in the US.

Princess Cays is the company's own 'private island' in the Caribbean. It's all yours (along with a
couple of thousand other passengers) for a day. However, it's a tender ride away from the ship and getting
to it takes time.

If Carnival's ships have the brightest decor im-
aginable, the decor aboard Princess Cruises' ships
is the opposite – bland in places, with much use of
neutral tones, calm colors, and pastels.

For children

Children are divided into three age groups: The Tree-
house (ages three to seven); The Lodge (eight to 12);
and The Beach House (13–17). Princess Cruises has
good children's counselors and supervised activities.

Some balconies can be overlooked from above, as
aboard *Ruby Princess*.

ROYAL CARIBBEAN INTERNATIONAL

Ships

Adventure of the Seas (2001), *Allure of the Seas* (2010),
Anthem of the Seas (2015), *Brilliance of the Seas* (2002),
Empress of the Seas (1990), *Enchantment of the Seas*
(1997), *Explorer of the Seas* (2000), *Freedom of the
Seas* (2006), *Grandeur of the Seas* (1996), *Harmony of
the Seas* (2016), *Independence of the Seas* (2008), *Jewel
of the Seas* (2004), *Liberty of the Seas* (2007), Majesty of
the Seas (1992), *Mariner of the Seas* (2004), *Navigator
of the Seas* (2003), *Oasis of the Seas* (2009), *Ovation of
the Seas* (2016), *Quantum of the Seas* (2014), *Radiance
of the Seas* (2001), *Rhapsody of the Seas* (1997), *Serenade of the Seas* (2003), *Spectrum of the Seas* (2019),
Symphony of the Seas (2018), *Vision of the Seas* (1998)

About the company

Royal Caribbean Cruise Line was founded by three
Norwegian shipping company dynasties in 1969: Arne
Wilhelmsen, I.M. Skaugen, and Gotaas-Larsen (who
was more of a sleeping partner). Its first ship, *Song of
Norway*, debuted in 1970, followed by *Nordic Prince* and
Sun Viking. Royal Caribbean was different from Carnival and Norwegian Cruise Line in that it had brand new
ships; the others had only old, pre-owned tonnage. In
1978, *Song of Norway* was transformed in the cruise
industry's first 'chop-and-stretch' operation, while
1988 saw the debut of the first 'extra-large' cruise
ship, *Sovereign of the Seas (no longer under RCI)*.

In 1997, Royal Caribbean International (RCI)
bought Celebrity Cruises for $1.3 billion. Ten years
later, the company created sister company Azamara
Club Cruises with three ships (in essence operated
by Celebrity Cruises).

What is it really like?

RCI, which has carried over 50 million passengers
since its founding in 1970, provides a well-integrat-
ed, fine-tuned, and comfortable cruise experience,
but there's nothing royal about it except the name.
The product is consistent but homogeneous. This
is cruising for mainstream America. The ships are
innovative, and all have some have public rooms,
lounges, bars, and fun gimmicks for active types.

In 2019, RCI started a three-year program of revitalizing its ships, adding more commonality in features
and eateries, as well as focussing on its 'private' island day attractions.

Its largest ships (*Oasis*-class, *Freedom*-class,
Quantum-class, and *Voyager*-class) differ from its
other ships, mainly in the internal layout, by having
a large mall-like high street – a social focal point
– with several lounges and bars. Indeed, they are
rather like malls with ships built around them. Also,
in placing much emphasis on 'active' outdoors areas,
space is taken away from pool areas, leaving little
room just to sit and relax or sunbathe.

Oasis of the Seas' Central Park.

The ships in the next group *(Brilliance of the Seas, Jewel of the Seas, Radiance of the Seas, and Serenade of the Seas)* have many balcony cabins. *Enchantment of the Seas, Grandeur of the Seas, Rhapsody of the Seas,* and *Vision of the Seas* also have lots of glass in the public areas, but fewer balcony cabins. *Freedom of the Seas* pioneered a concierge lounge for suite-grade occupants.

All ships have a multitrack rock-climbing wall. You'll need to plan what you want to take part in wisely, as almost everything requires you to sign up in advance.

Almost everywhere has intrusive background music, even in the elevators and passenger hallways. There are many unwelcome announcements for activities that bring revenue, such as art auctions and bingo.

Standing in line for embarkation, the reception desk, disembarkation, for port visits, shore tenders, and for the self-serve buffet stations is inevitable. It's hard to escape the ship's photographers – they're everywhere. Service personnel are friendly. The elevators talk to you, though 'going up/going down' is informative but monotonous. The signage and illuminated picture displays of decks are all good, particularly aboard the Oasis-class ships. However, there are no cushioned pads for the deck lounge chairs.

'Suite-Class' occupants get a personal butler/concierge who can arrange everything for you.

Interior decor has strong Scandinavian design influences, with some eclectic sculpture and artwork. 'Wayfarer' signage and deck plans are excellent. In 2017, the company reduced the number of cabin categories, and standardized them across all its ships. Well done!

For children

RCI's youth programs include 'My Family Time' dining and extra-cost packages such as a supervised 'Lunch and Play' option. An extra-cost in-cabin babysitting service is available as are soda and juice packages for the under 17s.

Children and teens are divided into seven age-appropriate groups: Royal Babies (six to 18 months); Royal Tots (18–36 months); Aquanauts (three to five years); Explorers (six to eight years); Voyagers (nine to 12 years); Navigators (12–14 years); and Teens (15–17 years).

HOW TO GET HITCHED AT SEA

Princess Cruises has the most extensive wedding program of any of the major lines, with its 'Tie the Knot' wedding packages. The captain can legally marry American couples at sea aboard its Bermuda-registered ships. This is by special dispensation and should be verified when in the planning stage, since it may vary according to where you reside.

Wedding at sea packages include a personal wedding coordinator. Live music, a candlelit celebration officiated by the captain, Champagne, fresh floral arrangements, a bridal bouquet, boutonnière, a photographer, and a wedding cake can all be laid on, depending on the cruise line and package.

You'll also get keepsake Champagne flutes, and a wedding certificate. Tuxedo rental is available. Harborside or shoreside packages vary according to the port. For the latest rates, see Princess Cruises' website or your travel agent.

e Smaller Cruise Lines

While the major cruise lines dominate the mass market, dozens of smaller companies cater for more specialist tastes and small port experiences.

The international cruise industry comprises over 70 companies. While most major cruise lines are owned and operated by large corporations (except MSC Cruises, a family firm), there are many smaller cruise lines. Some don't actually own their own ships, but charter them from ship-owning and ship-management companies for year-round or seasonal operation (Marella Cruises, for example).

The smaller companies are listed in alphabetical order. For information on expedition cruise companies, see page 79.

Alaskan Dream Cruises

Allen Marine Tours is family-owned by members of the Kaagwaantaan Clans of the Tlingit people and operate only in Alaska. It formed a new micro-cruise company, Alaskan Dream Cruises, in 2010, after buying two Cruise West 78-passenger vessels when Cruise West declared insolvency and ceased operations. *Spirit of Columbia* and *Spirit of Alaska* became *Admiralty Dream* and *Baranhof Dream* in 2011. Another ship, *Chichagof Dream*, (ex-*Nantucket Clipper*), was added in 2016.

American Cruise Lines

ACL was originally formed in 1974, at the beginning of American coastal passenger shipping, but it went bankrupt in 1989, the ships were sold off, and the

company lay dormant. The original owner, Charles Robertson, a renowned yachtsman who used to race 39-ft (12-m) America's Cup yachts, resurrected it in 2000, and built its own ships in its own small shipyard in Salisbury, Maryland, on the Chesapeake Bay.

ACL's ships (*American Constellation, American Constitution, American Glory, American Spirit, American Star, Independence*) ply the inter-coastal waterways and rivers of North America's coastal regions. They provide an up-close, intimate experience for passengers who don't need luxury, or much in the way of entertainment or pampering but enjoy American history and culture, and service from an all-American college-age staff, who go through the company's extensive in-house training programs. The 'D-class' vessels are less than 2,500 gross tonnage, and are subject neither to bureaucratic regulations nor to union rules.

In 2011, the company also started operating diesel-powered stern paddle-wheelers (replica steamboats) on the Mississippi River, and the Columbia and Snake rivers in the US Pacific Northwest. Port charges are extra. The company's sister brand is Pearl Seas Cruises.

Asuka Cruise

Nippon Yusen Kaisha, the world's largest shipping company, owned the well-known, US-based upscale

Azamara Journey cruising the Norwegian fjords.

brand Crystal Cruises. It created its own NYK Cruise division – today branded as Asuka Cruise – in 1989 with one Mitsubishi-built ship, *Asuka*, for Japanese-speaking passengers. In 2006, *Asuka* was sold to Germany's Phoenix Reisen, and the former *Crystal Harmony* was transferred from Crystal Cruises to become *Asuka II*. The ship, known for its excellent Japanese and western food, operates an annual around-the-world or long Grand Pacific cruise, plus a wide array of both short and long cruises in the Asia-Pacific region. Coffee- and tea-making facilities are provided in each cabin, as is a large selection of personal toiletries. Gratuities are included in the cruise fare.

Australis

This company, based in Santiago, Chile, operates cruises to the Chilean fjords, Patagonia, and Tierra del Fuego – some of the world's most fascinating but hostile environments. It caters increasingly to an international clientele, with Spanish as the official onboard language (English is also spoken). Don't expect high standards on board, but the service is friendly, and the organization and operations are good. The cruises are 'all-inclusive,' with an open bar for beverages, including wine and gratuities. In 2013 the company shortened its name from Cruceros Australis to Australis.

Azamara

Founded in 2007 this company (formerly Azamara Cruises) is an offshoot of Celebrity Cruises. Having started with little direction, the company was revitalized in 2009–10 by new president Larry Pimentel. It operates three 700-passenger ships, taking passengers to smaller and less visited ports that the large resort ships can't get into.

Azamara specializes in providing high-quality dining, and the ships offer a floating 'country club' experience. This line is in direct competition with the ships of Oceania Cruises – except that Oceania doesn't charge extra to dine in its specialty restaurants. However, Azamara has longer port stays and more overnight port stays.

The onboard experience is a notch above that aboard the ships of parent company Celebrity Cruises, modified to suit those wanting a more sophisticated cruise experience aboard smaller ships. Its strengths are the food and European-style service; each ship has two extra-charge restaurants in addition to the main dining venues. Included are gratuities to dining and housekeeping staff, coffee and tea 24 hours a day, and shuttle buses in ports of call, where needed. Complimentary standard spirits, wines, and international beers during bar opening hours were introduced in March 2013. One area where Azamara tries to differentiate itself is by providing long-stay port days – including several overnight stays – as well as 'AzAmazing Evenings' cultural excursions within its immersive destination programs. The company's

three ships (*Azamara Journey*, *Azamara Pursuit*, and *Azamara Quest*) underwent an extensive refurbishment program in 2016/17, and look refreshed, with lighter, brighter decor.

Blount Small Ship Adventures

This company was founded in 1966 by the late Luther H. Blount, an engineer and inventor of the American steam trawler, who built his cruise vessels in his own shipyard in Warren, Rhode Island. The firm was established as a family-run venture, and today, as the oldest US-flag cruise line still operating, it is run by Luther's daughter, Nancy Blount.

Cruises are operated like private family outings, using two unpretentious ships that have been specially constructed to operate in close-in coastal areas and inland waterways of the eastern US seaboard, with forays to the Bahamas and Caribbean during the winter. The onboard experience is strictly no-frills cruising in really basic, down-to-earth surroundings that have a 1950s feel.

Its early-to-bed passengers – average age 72 years – are typical of those who don't like glitz or all things trendy. Blount Small Ship Adventures introduced select beers and house wines with lunch and dinner on cruises in 2013.

Celestyal Cruises

Established in 2014, Celestyal Cruises is a sub-brand of Louis Cruises. It has three all-white ships: the 966-passenger *Celestyal Crystal*, the 800-passenger *Celestyal Nefeli*, and the 1,450-passenger *Celestyal Olympia*. The ships are dedicated to cruises in the Greek isles, Croatia, and Turkey – destinations with which the company's Cyprus-based parent company (Louis Cruises) has many years of experience, particularly with group travel.

Club Med Cruises

Club Med became renowned for providing hassle-free family vacations. The first Club Med village was started in 1950 on the Spanish island of Mallorca, but the concept became so popular it grew to more than 100 vacation villages throughout the world.

Club Med Cruises, an offshoot, introduced its first oceangoing cruise vessel in 1990, the computer-controlled sail-cruise ship *Club Med II* (extensively refurbished in 2008). Aboard the all-inclusive ship, the so-called *gentils organisateurs* serve as super-cruise staff and 'rah-rah' cheerleaders, carrying out entertainment and activity programs, for the mainly French-speaking passengers. *Club Med II* has a sister ship, Windstar Cruises' *Wind Surf*, which provides a relaxed onboard experience. Gratuities are included.

CMV (Cruise and Maritime Voyages)

This UK-based company (with 50 percent owned by Greece's Maritime Group) existed for many years as a sales and marketing organization representing several small cruise lines. It now charters and operates three ships owned by other companies. The firm, some of whose owners originally worked for long-defunct CTC Cruises, specializes in adults-only (16 and over) cruises from regional UK ports, and provides traditional cruise features such as mid-morning bouillon, and captain's welcome and farewell dinners. The onboard product, particularly the food, is at the lower end of the market. *Magellan* and *Marco Polo* are ships operated for ex-UK cruises, while Vasco da Gama operates under the Transocean Cruises name mainly for the German-speaking market.

Crystal Cruises

Crystal Cruises was founded in 1988 by Nippon Yusen Kaisha (NYK), the world's largest cargo ship and transportation company, with a fleet of more than 700 ships. The American-managed company is based in Century City, Los Angeles. *Crystal Harmony,* the company's first ship, was built in Japan, and debuted in New York in May 1990 to great acclaim. Meanwhile, Crystal Cruises introduced two new ships, *Crystal Symphony* in 1995, and *Crystal Serenity* in 2000, the first built in Finland, the second in France. In 2006 *Crystal Harmony* was transferred to parent company NYK as *Asuka II* for its Asuka Cruise division, for Japanese speakers.

The ships operate worldwide itineraries with flair. Both ships are superbly maintained, and passengers who seek fine food and excellent service in a sophisticated setting should be delighted with their choice of ship and company. There is even an excellent Nobu sushi/sashimi bar aboard *Crystal Serenity*.

Open-seating dining was introduced in January 2011 for the first time, but passengers can still opt for fixed-time dining. In spring 2012 Crystal Cruises

adopted all-inclusive pricing, with drinks, wines, and gratuities included. In 2015 the company was acquired by Genting Hong Kong (owner of Genting Cruise Lines, the parent company of Dream Cruises and Star Cruises and a minor shareholder of Norwegian Cruise Line Holdings Ltd). It introduced Crystal Yacht Cruises (rebranded in 2016 as Crystal Yacht Expedition Cruises) with the introduction of the refurbished *Crystal Esprit*. The company's ambitious expansion plans have since been scaled back somewhat, but there are still three 'Executive-class' ships due for introduction in 2022, plus an expedition-style ship (*Crystal Endeavor*), to debut in 2020.

Cunard

Cunard was established in 1839, as the British and North American Royal Mail Steam Packet Company, to carry the Royal Mail and passengers from the Old World to the New. Its first ship, *Britannia,* sailed on its maiden voyage on American Independence Day in 1840. The author Charles Dickens crossed the Atlantic aboard the ship in 1842 together with 62 other passengers, 93 crew members, one cow, and, most important, Her Majesty's mails and dispatches. Since 1840, Cunard has always had ships built to sail across the North Atlantic. From 1850 until the arrival of *QE2* in 1969, all of the line's ships and those of White Star Line (with which Cunard merged in 1934) had several classes. Your luggage label, therefore, declared not only your name but also what you could afford. Today, there's no class distinction, other than by accommodation grade.

Cunard celebrated its 175th anniversary in 2015. One is still reminded of the company's illustrious history. For example, Cunard was the first company to

Crystal Serenity alongside in Malta.

Queen Elizabeth and *Queen Mary 2* rendezvous in Sydney.

take passengers on regularly scheduled transatlantic crossings. It introduced the first passenger ship to be lit by electricity (*Servia*, 1881) and the first steam turbine engines in an ocean liner (*Carmania*, 1905). The line was the first to have an indoor swimming pool aboard a ship (*Aquitania*, 1914), and it pioneered the around-the-world cruise (*Laconia*, 1922). Cunard long held the record for the largest passenger ship ever built (*Queen Elizabeth*, between 1940 and 1996).

The ships incorporate a lot of maritime history and the grand traditions of ocean liners – as opposed to the other ships, with their tendency toward tacky high-street trappings. Cunard is also the *only* cruise line that lets you take your dog or cat with you (*Queen Mary 2* transatlantic crossings only).

While Samuel Cunard was from Halifax, Nova Scotia, he established the company in Liverpool. Today, the company is owned by the American Carnival Corporation. The three *Queens* were built in France and Italy, registered in Hamilton, Bermuda, with a home port of Southampton, England. The onboard currency is the US dollar.

Cunard has four distinct accommodation grades, each linked to a specific restaurant: Queens Grill, Princess Grill, Britannia Club, and Britannia.

Cunard has one real ocean liner (*Queen Mary 2*). It provides a regular transatlantic crossing service from April to December, while the company's two other two ships are more about regular cruising, albeit in ocean-liner style. All three (a fourth is scheduled to debut in 2022) are best suited to a wide range of seasoned and well-traveled couples and solo travelers who enjoy the cosmopolitan setting of an ocean liner. Dressing more formally for dinner is encouraged, although – with the exception of the grill rooms – the cuisine is largely of mass-market quality, with many traditional British and French dishes.

Disney Cruise Line

Disney Cruise Line is the most family-centric of all cruise lines. It was Lawrence (Larry) P. Murphy, executive vice-president of the Walt Disney Company, who was the guiding light in the early 1990s behind the expansion of the company into the cruise business. Previously, Disney had flirted with cruising by participating in a licensing agreement with a Florida-based cruise line, the now-defunct Premier Cruise Lines, with three vintage ships based in Port Canaveral. Murphy and other Disney executives explored the possibility of creating their own ships when the licensing agreement ran out. They concluded that pairing with an established cruise line wouldn't work because of Disney's policy of generous spending on the guest experience.

The solution: create a new cruise line, wholly owned and controlled by Disney, to be known as Disney Cruise Line. The company committed an astonishing $1 billion to the project.

Two mid-size ships, *Disney Magic* (1998) and *Disney Wonder* (1999) were the first cruise ships since the 1950s to be built with two funnels. Everything aboard the ships is Disney – every song, every piece of artwork, every movie and production show – and Mickey's ears adorn the ships' funnels. There's no casino and no library. However, its 'rotation dining'

Disney takes its brand to Alaska.

concept proved to be completely Disneylogical; you move, together with your waiter, to each of three identically sized restaurants – each with different decor – in turn.

One new, larger ship, *Disney Dream,* joined the fleet in 2011; sister ship *Disney Fantasy* arrived in 2012.

You can buy a package combining a short stay at a Disney resort and a cruise. Gratuities are not included in the cruise fare. Disney has its own cruise terminal at Port Canaveral, Florida, its design being an imaginative but close copy of the Ocean Terminal in Southampton, UK, frequented by yesteryear's ocean liners but little used today. The terminal and pier were extended in 2010 and connected to a new parking garage. Two new (slightly larger) ships are on order for delivery in 2022 and 2023.

Dream Cruises

Owned by Genting Cruise Lines, this brand is a sister company to Star Cruises. Dream Cruises has three ships. The stunning *Genting Dream* started sailing in November 2016, joined by sister ship *World Dream* in 2017, and followed by the slightly smaller *Explorer Dream* (ex-*SuperStar Virgo*). The company is a much more upscale and advanced version of Star Cruises, and it is aimed specifically at the Asian (and particularly, mainland Chinese) market, with an abundance of bright decor and some very upbeat, colorful razzle-dazzle shows.

For part of the year, the assigned ship offers embarkation in multiple countries, including its home port of Hong Kong, Two, new 204,000-ton large resort ships are scheduled to debut in 2020 and 2021. Gratuities are included.

Fred. Olsen Cruise Lines

This Norwegian family-owned and family-run company was founded in Hvitsten, a town on Oslofjord, Norway, in 1848. Today, a fifth-generation Olsen, Anette, owns and runs the company from its headquarters in Suffolk, England. The group also has interests in hotels, aviation, shipbuilding, ferries, and offshore industries. The company specializes in cruises for adults, who are usually retired and of senior years – typically over 65.

Aboard the ships, interior design reflects traditional design features, and dressing for dinner is expected on four nights during a two-week cruise. Many theme cruises, such as gardening and horticulture, and Scottish country dancing, hosted by recognized television celebrities, are regular features. The company welcomes solo passengers as well as couples and delivers a quintessentially 'British' cruise experience, albeit by a mainly Filipino hotel service staff.

The first ship dedicated exclusively to cruising debuted in 1987, and now ships cruise year-round out of UK ports, including Dover, Southampton, Liverpool, Newcastle, Greenock, Leith, Belfast, and Dublin (good for UK-based no-fly passengers). Some ships operate fly-cruises from Canary Island ports, or Caribbean ports such as Barbados in winter. The company operates a fleet of pre-owned ships, two of which are seriously old, but comfortable and really well-maintained. However, the company's strengths are in its extremely friendly and helpful crew, the homely small ship environment, and the variety of its food, with everything geared to British tastes, including coffee-/tea-making facilities in all cabins.

Gratuities are not included in the cruise fare, but are automatically charged to your onboard account. Drink prices are extremely reasonable aboard the ships, where the social scene is courteous, friendly, and warm, and gentlemen hosts are aboard each cruise as dancing partners for unaccompanied women.

The company has long supported the efforts of the UK's Royal National Lifeboat Institution (RNLI), and organizes fund-raising to purchase new lifeboats for the charity.

FTI Cruises

This company, part of the Munich-based FTI Touristik (founded in 1983), bought its only ship from Saga Cruises in 2011 and started its cruise operations in May 2012 for the German-speaking market. The ship, *Berlin,* is known in Germany for low-cost, good-value, well-organized cruising for passengers not expecting luxury or premium.

Hapag-Lloyd Cruises

Germany's two most famous ocean-liner companies, the Bremen-based Norddeutscher Lloyd (founded in 1847) and the Hamburg-based Hamburg America Line (founded in the same year), merged in 1970 to become Hapag-Lloyd. The company no longer operates regularly scheduled transatlantic crossings but promotes instead ships in two different market segments (*Bremen* is operated by Hapag-Lloyd Expedition Cruises); the 400-passenger *Europa* and the informal 516-passenger *Europa 2* (for international travelers and families with children) are in the luxury market, for destination-intensive cruises. The staff on board makes all its own breads, soups, pâtés, jams, and preserves from scratch.

Hapag-Lloyd Cruises hosts the annual Stella Maris International Vocal Competition, which attracts top-notch up-and-coming operatic singers from around the world. A top prize of €15,000 is offered, as well as a Deutsche Grammophon recording contract. The company also sponsors an annual Ocean Sun Festival – for classical/chamber music devotees (concerts are often held ashore as part of the program). Gratuities are included.

Hapag-Lloyd Expedition Cruises

(see Expedition Cruises chapter)

Hebridean Island Cruises

The company (formerly Hebridean International Cruises) was set up in 1989 under the Thatcher government's British Enterprise Scheme, and has its headquarters in Skipton, Yorkshire. It is independently owned and operates one all-inclusive boutique ship, *Hebridean Princess,* which conveys the atmosphere of English country-house life – and specializes in cruises for mature adults. Gratuities and all port taxes are included, as are most excursions. The ship offers cruises around the Scottish islands, with occasional sailings to

English ports, the Channel Islands, and Norway. Each cabin has coffee- and tea-making facilities. The Queen granted Hebridean Island Cruises a royal warrant in her jubilee year. Gratuities are included.

Hurtigruten

The company is an amalgamation of two shipping companies (OVDS and TVDS) and provides year-round service along the Norwegian coast, calling at 34 ports in 11 days. Hurtigruten, formerly known as the Norwegian Coastal Voyage, has also recently developed expedition-style cruises, albeit aboard ships that have been converted for the purpose, rather than specifically built for expedition cruises. So, as long as you think utilitarian and modest decor, you'll get the idea of life aboard one of the Hurtigruten ships, which are practical rather than beautiful. Even aboard the newest ships, the food and service are fairly basic – there's a lack of green vegetables, for example – but the ships provide a way to see many, many ports along the coast of Norway in a modestly comfortable, laid-back manner.

Jalesh Cruises

Jalesh Cruises, a brand name under the direction of Zen Cruises, is part of parent company Essel Group, a major powerhouse in India, with holdings in news, media, entertainment, and more. The company started operations from Mumbai with one ship, *Karnika* (ex-*Pacific Jewel, Ocean Village Two, AIDAblu, Arosa Blu, Crown Princess*), on short cruises in the Indian Ocean.

Lindblad Expeditions

Lars-Eric Lindblad (see also page 83) started the whole concept of expedition cruising with a single ship, *Lindblad Explorer,* in 1969, taking adventurous travelers to remote regions of the world. Today, his son, Sven-Olof

Hapag-Lloyd's *Bremen* in the Corinth Canal, Greece.

Lindblad, runs the company, but with an array of really small ships. It's all about nature, wilderness, wildlife, off-the-beaten-path adventures, and learning, with ships that provide basic levels of comfort, food, and service. In 2020, a more expedition-style ship (*National Geographic Endurance*) is scheduled to debut.

Marella Cruises

In 1973 Thomson Cruises (the former name of Marella Cruises) ventures into the cruise industry when it chartered two ships, *Calypso* and *Ithaca,* from the Greek-owned Ulysses Line. It was a disaster, and the company withdrew from cruising two years later (Ulysses Line became known as Useless Line).

The company started again in 2002 (as Thomson Cruises) after seeing rival tour operator Airtours run ships successfully. Marella Cruises charters its ships, preferring instead to leave ship operations, management, and catering to specialist maritime companies. In 2017 the company changed its name to Marella Cruises (in Celtic it means 'Shining Sea'). The company features cruises for the whole family aboard *Marella Dream, Marella Discovery,* and *Marella Discovery 2* – catering principally to the British market. However, in 2019 the company added one ship for adults-only cruising (*Marella Explorer 2*), but all ships feature all-inclusive cruising (including basic gratuities).

MOPAS

Osaka Shosen Kaisha was founded in 1884 in Osaka, Japan. In 1964 it merged with Mitsui Steamship, to become Mitsui OSK Passenger Line (MOPAS). It is now one of the oldest and largest shipping companies in the world.

It entered cruise shipping in 1989 with *Fuji Maru*, the first cruise ship in the Japanese-speaking domestic market (now no longer in service). The company specialized in incentive meetings and groups at sea rather than cruising for individuals, but this steadily changed into more cruises for individuals. The firm operates a single ship, the very comfortable *Nippon Maru* (extensively refurbished in 2010), based in Japan for Japanese-speaking passengers. Gratuities are included in the cruise fare.

Mystic Cruises

Mystic Cruises is now a Portugal-based cruise company that owns and operates riverships on the Douro river in Portugal. It also own Germany-based Nicko Cruises. The company's first ocean-going ship is an expedition-style vessel that complies with Polar Code 6. It charters the 176-passenger ship (*World Explorer*) to Quark Expeditions and Nicko Cruises, which each operate it for part of each year. Two more identical ships (*World Voyager* and *World Navigator*) are scheduled for introduction in 2020 and 2021, respectively.

Nicko Cruises

Germany-based Nicko Cruises took delivery of its 176-passenger *World Explorer* from owner Mystic Cruises (see above) in the summer of 2019. The company is new to the expedition-cruise segment and will need to learn fast in order to catch up with other, more established operators in this highly specialized field, where operating costs are high.

Noble Caledonia

London-based Noble Caledonia, established in 1991, operates three boutique-size sister ships, *Caledonian Sky, Hebridean Sky,* and *Island Sky,* each carrying around 100 passengers. It also sells cruises aboard a wide range of small-ship and expedi-

Aboard *Hebridean Princess*, cruising around Scotland and its islands.

The horseshoe staircase aboard Oceania's *Marina*.

tion cruise companies as well as river cruises. It markets to British passengers of mature years, and operates cruises, generally in sheltered water areas, with cultural-interest themes, and so is not recommended for children.

The company, whose financial partners include Sweden's Salen family, who had been very involved with expedition cruising in the past, has an excellent reputation for well-organized cruises and tours, accompanied by good lecturers. It specializes in itineraries that would be impossible to operate aboard larger ships. A Commodore Club gives repeat passengers advance information about new voyages and special offers. Gratuities are included.

Oceania Cruises

The company's ships provide English-style charm in a country-club atmosphere ideal for middle-aged and older couples seeking relaxation. Cruises are usually 10–14 days. Its trademarks are comfortable cabins, warm and attentive service, and fine dining combining French culinary expertise and top-quality ingredients. Breads and other baked goods, such as Poilâne-quality croissants, are excellent.

In 2006, Oceania Cruises was bought by Apollo Management, a private equity company that owns Regent Seven Seas Cruises and 50 percent of Norwegian Cruise Line (NCL), now under the umbrella of Prestige Cruise Holdings. There are six ships – *Insignia, Marina, Nautica, Regatta, Riviera*, and *Sirena* – catering to between 684 and 1,250 passengers. Two new 1,200-passenger ships (similar to Marina

and Riviera) are on order, scheduled for delivery in 2022 and 2025.

With multiple-choice dining at no extra cost, these ships suit anyone who prefers small and mid-size ships to large resort vessels. Bottled mineral water, soft drinks, and beer are included in the price.

P&O Cruises

P&O's full name is the Peninsular and Oriental Steam Navigation Company, though none of its ships is powered by steam turbines. Based in Southampton, England, it was founded in 1837, just before Samuel Cunard established his company, and was awarded a UK government contract in 1840 to carry the mail from Gibraltar to Alexandria.

P&O Cruises acquired Princess Cruises in 1974, Swan Hellenic in 1982, and Sitmar Cruises in 1988. In 2000 it demerged from its parent to establish itself as P&O Princess plc. It was bought by the Carnival Corporation in 2003, and celebrated its 175th anniversary on July 3, 2012, when all seven ships (at the time) assembled in Southampton.

P&O Cruises has always been a traditional British cruise company, never quite matching the quality aboard the Cunard ships, which have more international passengers. With P&O having mainly British captains and navigation officers and Indian/Goanese service staff, the British traditions of unobtrusive service are preserved. British food favorites provide the comfort factor in a single-language setting that provides a home-from-home on ships for families with children, or on adults-only ships.

Aboard the maiden voyage of P&O Cruises' *Britannia*.

The company has British passengers who want to sail from a UK port – except for winter Caribbean cruises from Barbados. It also operates adults-only ships, (Aurora and Arcadia), so the two products differ widely in their communal spaces. P&O also operates theme cruises – on antiques, art appreciation, classical music, comedy, cricket, gardening and horticulture, jazz, Scottish dancing, etc. The ships usually carry ballroom-dance instructors. Bed linen is changed twice a week – not as often as, for example, on MSC Cruises, where it is changed every two days. The decor is a mix of British traditional (think comfy, somewhat dated, non-glitzy armchairs, and wood paneling) and bland. British artists are featured aboard all ships – *Ventura*, for example, displays works by more than 40 of them. Its newest ship, Iona is dual-fuel-powered (including LNG) and debuts in 2020.

P&O Cruises Australia

Founded in 1932, the Australian division of P&O Cruises provides fun entertainment for the beer-and-bikini brigade and their families, and specializes in cruises in the Pacific and to New Zealand. The line is maturing, though, and is now a mainstream operator – particularly so with its latest ships, which are larger, more contemporary hand-me-down vessels (*Pacific Dawn, Pacific Pearl* from P&O Cruises and Princess Cruises; and *Pacific Aria* from Holland America Line), from companies that are part of the Carnival Corporation (Princess Cruises' *Golden Princess* is scheduled to become Pacific Adventure in October 2020). The ships have open-seating dining and

specialty restaurants such as Australian celebrity chef Luke Mangan's 'Salt Grill.' Cruise pricing is in three levels, depending on what you want included.

Paradise Cruise Line

This two-ship company is owned by Celebration Cruise Holdings, which also owned the now-defunct Imperial Majesty Cruise Line, whose reputation suffered from high-pressure telemarketing campaigns. Its ships, *Grand Celebration* (originally built for Carnival Cruise Line in 1987) and *Grand Classica* (formerly operated by Costa Cruises) operate two-night cruises from the Port of Palm Beach, in Florida, to the Bahamas.

The ships provide a highly programmed but absolutely basic party getaway cruise with bog-standard food, and much pressure for revenue from its dining, casino, and expensive shore-excursions.

Paul Gauguin Cruise Line

Created by the Boston-based tour operator Grand Circle Travel, Paul Gauguin Cruises (now named Paul Gauguin Cruise Line) took over the marketing and operation of *Paul Gauguin* in 2009 from Regent Seven Seas Cruises, which had operated the ship since its inception. Also in 2009, the ship was bought by the Tahiti-based investor Richard Bailey and his company Pacific Beachcomber, which owns Polynesian resort hotels (including four InterContinental Hotels).

Pearl Seas Cruises

Founded in 2007 by Charles Robertson, Pearl Seas Cruises is now a sister company to American Cruise

Lines. It has a single ship (a second ship order was canceled), *Pearl Mist*, which was the subject of poor shipbuilding and contract arguments in its early days. *Pearl Mist* was rejected as not fit for purpose by the owner, but she was finally completed and debuted in 2014. The ship's loyalty club is the Oyster Society.

Phoenix Reisen

Based in Bonn, Germany, the company for many years operated low-budget, tour-operator-style destination-intensive cruises for German speakers. It now has a loyal, widespread audience and more contemporary ships, with better food and service, particularly aboard *the* newly acquired *Amera (ex-Prinsendam)*, *Amadea*, and *Artania*.

To keep costs down, Phoenix charters its ships for long periods. It is consistently praised for its extremely good itineraries, particularly on world cruises, its pre- and post-cruise programs, and its excellent value for money. The wonderfully comprehensive Phoenix brochure provides photographs of its captains and cruise director, as well as bar lists and drink prices – a refreshing change from the brochures provided by most cruise companies. Single-seating dining is standard, as are low drink prices, and there is no constant pushing for onboard revenue – again different from most rivals.

Phoenix acquired *Artania* (formerly P&O Cruises' *Artemis* and originally *Royal Princess*, named by Princess Diana) in 2011, and also operates the lower-priced *Albatros* (originally *Royal Viking Sea*). Gratuities are included.

Plantours Cruises

This company, based in Bremen, Germany, provides low-budget cruises for German speakers aboard its single small, chartered cruise ship, *Hamburg*, which was formerly Hapag-Lloyd Cruises' *Columbus*. The company also sells cruises on the rivers of Europe and Russia, with riverships operated by various companies.

Ponant

The company was founded in 1988 by Philippe Videau and Jean-Emmanuel Sauvé. It started life as La Compagnie des Iles du Ponant, and was a subsidiary of the state-owned CMA CGM (Compagnie Maritime d'Affrètement/Compagnie Générale Maritime), until its acquisition by Bridgepoint Capital, a private equity company, in 2012. In 2015, Ponant was acquired by Artemis, the holding company of French billionaire François Pinault and his family.

The head office is in Marseille, France, and it operates one boutique-size, high-tech sail-cruise ship, *Le Ponant*. In 2004, the company purchased the Paris-based tour operator Tapis Rouge International (specializing in premium travel). Four small ships were introduced between 2010 and 2015. Four more ships have been ordered, for delivery in 2018 and 2019. Ponant teams with French partners such as Veuve Clicquot, Hermès (bathroom products), Ladurée (macarons), and Alain Ducasse (Ducasse Conseil), one of the world's most highly decorated chefs.

Ponant increasingly markets cruises in both English and French to international passengers and onboard announcements are made in both languages, but the onboard product is decidedly French in style.

Poseidon Expeditions

Poseidon Expeditions is the Arctic expedition cruise specialist (founded and owned by Nikolay Saveliev in 2003). The company (see page 86) operates under the

Waterslides on the top deck of *Pacific Dawn*, a P&O Australia ship.

The softly lit Horizon Lounge Deck aboard *Seven Seas Voyager*.

strict guidelines of the Association of Arctic Expedition Cruise Operators (AECO), the body committed to minimizing the impact of visits to the Far North. Expeditions to the North Pole (90 degrees North) are operated only at the height of the Arctic summer, in June and July, aboard the world's most powerful icebreaker – the Russian nuclear-powered *50 Years of Victory* (it can crush ice up to 10ft/3m thick).

This really is a once-in-a-lifetime adventure. Only 10,741 people had visited the North Pole when I was fortunate enough to go in July 2016.

The company also operates the smaller Sea Spirit – the only non-Russian foreign-flag ship permitted to operate in the territorial waters of Franz Joseph Land in the Arctic Circle from Svalbard without first calling at a mainland Russian port. In 2004 the company achieved the inaugural Northeast Passage via the North Pole.

Pullmantur Cruises

The cruise division was set up as part of Pullmantur, the Spain-based holiday tour operator founded in 1971. Its cruising division was established in 2000 when it bought *Oceanic* (then known as the Big Red Boat) from the defunct Florida operator Premier Cruise Lines. In 2006, Pullmantur Cruises was bought by Royal Caribbean Cruises; in 2015 it was sold to private equity company Springwater Capital. The company mainly serves the Spanish-speaking market, operating all-inclusive cruises for families with children to the Caribbean and Europe. Gratuities are included in the cruise fare. Pullmantur Cruises

has a fleet of four ships (*Horizon, Monarch, Sovereign,* and *Zenith*), all emblazoned with Pullmantur Cruises painted in red on their white hulls.

Regent Seven Seas Cruises

This company has a complicated history. It was born out of Seven Seas Cruises, which was originally based in San Francisco to market the cruise ship *Song of Flower* (belonging to 'K'-Line, a cargo operator based in New Jersey), as well as expedition cruises aboard the chartered *Hanseatic* (then belonging to Hanseatic Tours). The lyre, logo of that ship, became RSSC's logo.

For many years, the company was part of the Carlson group, and operated as Radisson Seven Seas Cruises. Carlson Hospitality Worldwide ventured into cruising via its Radisson Hotels International division – hence, Radisson Diamond Cruises (when Radisson Diamond joined in 1992). In 1994 Radisson Diamond Cruises and Seven Seas Cruise Line merged to become Radisson Seven Seas Cruises, and in 2007 it became Regent Seven Seas Cruises.

In 2007 the company was bought by US-based investment group Apollo Management, and, together with Oceania Cruises, was placed under the umbrella of its Prestige Cruise Holdings. The company spent $40 million to refurbish its then fleet of three ships in 2009–10.

It operates worldwide itineraries and strives to pay close attention to detail and provide high-quality service aboard its small cruise ships, of which there are four: *Seven Seas Explorer* (debuted in 2016), *Seven Seas Mariner, Seven Seas Navigator,* and *Seven Seas*

Voyager. A fifth ship (*Seven Seas Splendor*) is on order and scheduled to debut in 2020.

It provides drinks-inclusive cruising, which means that beverages and gratuities are included, as are shore excursions – even delicious *illy* coffees are included. Passengers pay extra only for laundry services, beauty services, casino, and other personal items.

Saga Cruises

Saga, based in Folkestone, England, was created by Sidney De Haan as a company offering financial services and holidays to the over-60s. As the company's success grew, it reduced this limitation in 1995 to the over-50s and allowed companions older than 40. Its travel division flourished because it became known for providing personal attention from a caring staff. Instead of sending passengers to ships operated by other companies, it decided to buy its own ships and market its own product under the Saga Holidays brand.

Saga Shipping (Saga Cruises), the cruising division of Saga Holidays, was set up in 1997 when it purchased *Saga Rose* (formerly *Sagafjord*), followed soon after by *Saga Ruby* (formerly *Vistafjord*), and, in 2010, *Saga Pearl II* (formerly *Astoria*). *Saga Sapphire* (ex-*Europa*) arrived in 2012.

Another brand, Spirit of Adventure, was added in 2006, and in 2007 Saga merged with Britain's Automobile Association. The 'Adventure' cruise brand ended in November 2013, when *Quest for Adventure* became *Saga Pearl II* again.

Saga emphasizes British seamanship and training, and its fleet manages to retain the feel of traditional, elegant, adults-only cruising. It offers open-seating dining, and attentive service from a mainly Filipino hotel service crew aboard ships with many solo-occupancy cabins. It takes care of some of the little details that other lines have long forgotten.

All gratuities, and door-to-door transfers, are included. The company has two new ships on order: *Spirit of Discovery*, which debuted in 2019, and *Spirit of Adventure*, which follows in 2020.

Scenic

The company (see also page xxx) was founded in Newcastle, Australia, in 1986 by Glen Moroney, as Scenic Tours, and it began by operating coach tours throughout Australia. In 2008, it began river cruise operations in Europe (mainly for Australasian passengers). It now owns and operates several riverships in Europe, under two brands: Scenic, and Emerald Waterways. The company, which is still Australian owned, changed its name to Scenic in 2015. It operates two small 'discovery' ships, the first of which debuted in 2019. Gratuities are included.

Sea Cloud Cruises

This company was founded in 1979 by a consortium of ship-owners and investors known as the Hansa Treuhand (active in commercial vessel management, engineering, and construction), with headquarters in Hamburg, Germany. It owns and operates two genuine tall ships (cruise-sail vessels), the legendary *Sea Cloud* (built in 1931 for the cereal heiress Marjorie Merriweather Post), and the 1990-built *Sea Cloud II*. A third sail-cruise ship, *Sea Cloud Spirit, is* set to debut in 2020.

The company has many corporate clients who charter the two sail-cruise ships, while a number

Paul Gauguin was built specifically to operate in French Polynesia.

of luxury cruise and travel specialist companies sell cruises to individuals. The onboard style and product delivery are something special, with elegant retro decor and fine food and service.

Seabourn

Originally founded in 1986 as Signet Cruise Line, the company, then owned by Norwegian industrialist Atle Brynestad, had to change its name in 1988 as a result of a lawsuit brought by a Texas ferry company that had already registered the name Signet Cruise Lines (no ships were ever built for cruising, however).

In 1998, a consortium, which included the Carnival Corporation and Norwegian investors, bought Seabourn Cruise Line and merged its operations into Cunard, which was acquired from Kvaerner. The fleet then included three ships plus *Seabourn Goddess I* and *Seabourn Goddess II* (bought by SeaDream Yacht Cruises in 2002 and named *SeaDream I* and *SeaDream II*) and *Seabourn Sun* (now Holland America Line's *Prinsendam*). The Carnival Corporation acquired 100 percent of Seabourn Cruise Line in 1999.

Three new, larger ships joined the company between 2009 and 2011. All three have an aft water-sports platform, as well as a wider number of dining and spa options, and a greater amount of space, for more passengers. Seabourn Cruise Line was briefly rebranded as The Yachts of Seabourn in 2009–10, but then became simply Seabourn. The company is managed from the headquarters of Carnival-owned Holland America Line in Seattle, USA. Gratuities are included.

Seabourn Odyssey's water-sports platform.

In February 2013, the three smaller ships were sold to Xanterra Parks & Resorts, parent company of Windstar Cruises. *Seabourn Pride* was delivered in mid-2014; *Seabourn Legend* and *Seabourn Spirit* were delivered in 2015. Seabourn Encore in 2016, and *Seabourn Ovation* in 2018.

Note that quality has been reduced substantially since the management has been taken over by Holland America Line, with various cutbacks reflecting the downgrade – Prosecco is served rather than Champagne, for example; poor canapés and disappointing cheese and meat selections are provided in place of the better offerings of yesteryear, and reduced dining hours and fixed disembarkation by 8am are now standard. Overall, it's a less upmarket product than previously.

SeaDream Yacht Club

Larry Pimentel, an American, and his Norwegian business partner Atle Brynestad, founder of Seabourn Cruise Line (now called, simply, Seabourn), jointly created the company by buying the former Sea Goddess Cruises' ships. They introduced them in 2002 to an audience anxious for exclusivity, personal pampering, and cuisine prepared to order.

Its two ships, *SeaDream I* and *SeaDream II*, have been refreshed several times – although *SeaDream I* is in a better shape than *SeaDream II* – and are often chartered by companies or private individuals who appreciate the refined, elegant, but casual atmosphere on board. The 112-passenger ships operate year-round in the Caribbean and Mediterranean, and provide all-inclusive beverages and open-seating

Relaxed lifestyle aboard *SeaDream I*.

dining at all times, and a high degree of personalized service, all in a cozy, club-like atmosphere, with great attention to detail and personal idiosyncrasies. The company has a new ship on order, scheduled to debut in 2021. Brynestad is the company's chairman and sole owner. Gratuities are included.

Serenissima Cruises

Vladimir Esakov, the Russian owner/operator of the rivership *Volga Dream*, purchased the former *MS Andrea* (a Hurtigruten vessel) in 2012, renamed it *Serenissima* and formed Serenissima Cruises to market the ship. The company has a long-standing association with the UK's Noble Caledonia.

Silversea Cruises

Silversea Cruises is a mostly privately owned cruise line. It was founded in 1992 by the Lefebvre d'Ovidio family from Rome (previously co-owners of Sitmar Cruises), and is based in Monaco.

Antonio Lefebvre d'Ovidio was a maritime lawyer and professor of maritime law before acquiring and operating cargo ships and ferries in the Adriatic. He took his family into partnership with Boris Vlasov's Vlasov Group (V-Ships) to co-own Sitmar Cruises, until that company merged with Princess Cruises in 1988.

Silversea Cruises has generated tremendous loyalty from its frequent passengers, who view the ships as their own upscale home from home. All Silversea ships have teak verandas, all-inclusive beverages, and open-seating dining. The company (see also page 86) is known for its partnership with the hospitality organization Relais & Châteaux. A new, 540-passenger all-suite ship, *Silver Spirit,* debuted at the end of 2009 (it underwent a 'chop and stretch' operation in 2019). *Silver Muse* debuted in 2017, with more than a design nod to Hapag-Lloyd's *Europa 2*, but the ship still has the look and feel of a Silversea Cruises product. More new ships are on order.

Star Clippers

Swedish-born yachtsman Mikael Krafft founded Star Clippers in 1991 with *Star Flyer* and then *Star Clipper,* both true tall ships. The company went on to build the largest tall ship presently sailing, the five-mast *Royal Clipper*, a truly stunning ship when under sail. Friendly service in an extremely laid-back setting, under the romance of sail (when there is enough wind) is what Star Clippers is all about, and the food variety, creativity, and quality are all extremely good. The company's new five-mast ship (*Flying Clipper*) is expected to debut in 2019/2020.

These real tall (sail-cruise) ships sail in the Caribbean, Baltic, Mediterranean, and South-east Asia.

Star Cruises

The company was incorporated in 1993 as a subsidiary of Malaysia's Genting Berhad, set up in 1965 by the late Tan Sri (Dr) Lim Goh Tong as a multinational Asian corporation. Today, Star Cruises comes under the umbrella of Genting Cruise Lines – itself part of

Sea lion with *Silver Galapagos* in the distance.

Genting Hong Kong. The group's various businesses include palm oil production, power generation, property development, biotechnology, oil and gas production, plus leisure activities including resort hotels and casino/entertainment complexes in several countries, plus cruise ships. Almost single-handedly, Star Cruises opened up the Asia-Pacific cruise region (except for Japan).

Genting Hong Kong operates ships dedicated to specific markets. Its brands include Crystal Cruises, Dream Cruises (which started operations in 2016), and Star Cruises. Gratuities are included.

Transocean Cruises

Founded in 1954, Transocean Cruises (formerly Transocean Tours) is based in Bremen, Germany. In 1991, the Black Sea Shipping Company's Delfin Caravelle (presently Silversea Cruises' Silver Explorer) was chartered to Transocean Tours. Declared insolvent in 2009, the company was absorbed into the UK's Cruise & Maritime Voyages (CMV), together with the Transocean-chartered Astor cruise ship.

The company now specializes in selling low-cost but high-value cruises aboard several ships owned by parent company CMV: Astor, Columbus, Magellan, Marco Polo, Vasco da Gama, mainly for its German-speaking clientele. Gratuities are included.

TUI Cruises

The Germany-based TUI Group has several divisions but started its own cruise line in 2009 with *Mein Schiff 1*, a mid-size ship (formerly *Celebrity Galaxy*) that underwent a huge reconstruction program. *Mein Schiff 2* (formerly *Celebrity Mercury*) was added in 2011. Further new ships followed: *Mein Schiff 3* debuted in 2014, *Mein Schiff 4* in 2015, *Mein Schiff 5* in 2016, and

Mein Schiff 6 in 2017. Two more ships are under construction, to debut in 2018 and 2019 as the new *Mein Schiff 1* and *Mein Schiff 2*, respectively.

Aboard all TUI Cruises ships, all cabins have an espresso machine, and a wide choice of dining venues and food styles, with an emphasis on healthy eating and high-quality ingredients. Much attention is placed on the extensive wellness facilities aboard the ships, which are geared extensively to family cruising. Gratuities are included in the 'all-inclusive' fare, and the company provides many things that other cruise lines don't, making this a very good value-for-money, high-quality cruise line.

UnCruise Adventures

This micro-cruise line was founded in 1997 as American Safari Cruises. It was bought in 2008 by InnerSea Discoveries, owned by the former chief executive officer of American Safari Cruises, Dan Blanchard. It purchased the website and database files of now-defunct Cruise West in order to expand its reach to small-ship enthusiasts, and has a fleet of very small motor yacht-type vessels for six to 86 passengers for expensive cruises in Alaska and the Pacific Northwest. While the vessels are decent, there are few facilities, and the one-seat dining experience is very casual. The advantage of these intimate vessels is that they can take you up close to fascinating parts of Alaska that larger ships can't reach. InnerSea Discoveries changed its name to UnCruise Adventures in 2013.

Venus Cruise

Founded in 1988, Venus Cruise, which was first known as Japan Cruise Line, is owned by four ferry companies: Shin Nihonkai Ferry, Kyowa Shoji, Hankyu Ferry, and Kanko Kisen. Its headquarters are in Osaka, Japan. As Japan Cruise Line, the company at first operated company and incentive charter cruises before branching out into cruises for individuals. The company caters exclusively to Japanese speakers and has a single ship, *Pacific Venus,* which offers cruises in the Asia-Pacific region as well domestic cruises in Japan. Gratuities are included in the cruise fare.

Viking Ocean Cruises

A sister to the long-established Viking River Cruises, this company aims to provide both ocean-going and river cruises to the same passengers and market segment – a unique approach in the cruise industry. The product is aimed squarely at adults who want comfort and some elements of luxe, but no glitz, and at a price that includes many items other cruise lines charge extra for (such as ship-wide Wi-Fi). This has proved to be a great success. Its chairman is Torstein Hagen, originally a major shareholder owner of the long-defunct but much-respected Royal Viking Line.

Staying away from large resort ships, the company ordered mid-size ships for 930 passengers. For the ships' size, they offer an impressive array of public rooms and dining options, and modern, uncluttered Scandinavian design. Itineraries are designed so that they stay longer in ports and include overnight stays at some ports, so that passengers can take in the nightlife and cultural attractions of some destinations. Its first ship, *Viking Star*, debuted in spring 2015. The company has established a fine onboard product that is well placed to grow further in the coming years.

Virgin Voyages

This new rock-star cruise line was established by Virgin Group founder Richard Branson, together with Bain Capital (the majority shareholder). The goal: to 'be different' to all other cruise lines. Branson has put families to bed by creating adults-only party ships, with overflowing hip hype and marketing aimed at younger passengers. The Florida-based company promises a twist on the classic Virgin brand – passengers are called 'sailors' and there are no dress codes or gratuities. The company's first ship is named, appropriately, *Scarlet Lady*, and debuts in 2020.

Voyages to Antiquity

Founded in 2007 by Gerry Herrod, who previously formerly created the now-defunct Ocean Cruise Lines, the company has just one ship, *Aegean Odyssey*, painstakingly converted into a comfortable small cruise ship with a fairly decent profile. The cruises are for British and American passengers who seek longer cruises and educational experiences. Gratuities to dining and housekeeping staff are included, as are most shore excursions, plus wines with lunch and dinner.

Windstar Cruises

Founded by New York-based Karl Andren in 1984 as Windstar Sail Cruises, the company built high-class sail-cruise ships with computer-controlled sails, outfitting them in a contemporary decor designed by Marc Held. The first ship, *Wind Star*, debuted in 1986 to great acclaim, and was followed by *Wind Spirit* (1988) and *Wind Surf* (1990).

Windstar Cruises was sold to Holland America Line in 1988. The company, with headquarters in Seattle, US, was sold in 2007 to the Ambassadors Cruise Group, wholly owned by Ambassadors International. It was purchased again in 2011 by Xanterra Parks & Resorts.

In 2014, Windstar took delivery of the former *Seabourn Pride*, renamed *Star Pride,* and, in mid-2015, two more Seabourn ships – *Seabourn Legend* (now *Star Legend*), and *Seabourn Spirit* (now *Star Breeze*).

In 2019, the three ships underwent a 'chop-and-stretch' operation which added a mid-section of about 25 meters (82ft) and increased the passenger capacity from 212 to 312.

The style is casual and unregimented, but smart, with service by Indonesian and Filipino crew members. Itineraries include some off-the-beaten-track ports not frequented by large resort ships. The onboard product is decidedly American ultra-casual, with unfussy bistro-style cuisine, and service that lacks the finesse and the small details that could make it a much better experience overall.

The main pool on *Viking Star* when the roof is closed.

What To Do If ...

Here are 18 practical tips for a good cruise experience, and advice on what to do if you have a problem.

1. Your luggage does not arrive at the ship

If you booked as part of the cruise line's air/sea package, the airline is responsible for locating your luggage and delivering it to the next port. If you arranged your own air transportation, it is wholly *your* problem. Always have easy-to-read name and address tags *inside* as well as *outside* your luggage. Keep track of claim documents, and give the airline an itinerary and list of port agents.

2. You miss the ship

If you miss the ship's departure at the port of embarkation, and you are traveling on an air/sea package, the airline will arrange to get you to the ship, possibly at the next port of call. If you are traveling 'cruise-only,' however, then you are responsible for flights, hotel stays, and transfers.

It is up to you to get back to the ship before the appointed sailing time. Miss the ship and you'll need

One answer to lack of storage space aboard *Queen Elizabeth*.

to get to its next port at your own cost. *Always* take a copy of your passport with you, just in case.

Ships have also been known to leave port early because of impending inclement weather conditions or natural disasters. If this happens, the ship's port agent will be there to assist you. Always take the port agent's name and telephone contact details with you.

3. Your cabin has no air conditioning, it is noisy, or there are plumbing problems

If there is anything wrong in your cabin or bathroom, tell your cabin steward or go to the reception desk immediately. Some cabins are located above the ship's laundry, generator, or galley; others may be above the disco. If the ship is full, it will be difficult to change.

4. You have noisy cabin neighbors

First, politely tell your neighbors that you can hear them brushing their hair as the cabin walls are so thin, and would they please not slam the drawers shut at 2am! If that does not work, complain to the hotel manager (via the reception desk).

5. You have a problem with a crew member

Go to the reception desk and explain the problem. Insist on a full written report of the incident, which must be entered into the ship's daily log by the staff captain (deputy captain).

6. You don't like your dining room seating

Many ships operate two seatings for dinner. When you book your cruise, you choose whether you want the first or second seating. The line and the restaurant manager will make every attempt to please you. If you want second seating and are given first seating, there may be little the restaurant manager can do if the ship is full.

7. You want a table for two and are put at a table for eight

Explain why you are not satisfied to the restaurant manager, who should be able to resolve the situation.

8. You cannot communicate with your waiter

Dining room waiters might be of a nationality and language completely foreign to yours, with limited fluency in your language. This could prove frustrat-

Larger restaurants, such as *Carnival Conquest*'s Renoir, seat hundreds of diners.

ing for a whole cruise. See the restaurant manager, and ask if there is a waiter with whom you can communicate.

10. The food is not the gourmet cuisine portrayed in the brochure

If the food is not as described (for example, whole lobster is shown in the brochure, but only cold lobster salad is provided once during the cruise, or the 'fresh squeezed' orange juice on the breakfast menu is anything but), inform the restaurant manager.

11. A large group has taken over the ship

Sometimes, large groups have pre-booked public rooms for meetings. Make your displeasure known to the hotel department immediately. If nothing is resolved, tell your booking agent, and write a follow-up letter to the line when you get home.

12. A port of call is deleted from the itinerary

Read the fine print in the brochure *before* you book. A cruise line is under no obligation to perform the stated itinerary. For whatever reason – political unrest, weather, mechanical problems, safety, etc. – the ship's captain has the ultimate say.

13. You leave personal belongings on a tour bus

If you find you've left something on a tour bus, tell the shore excursion staff. The tour operator will then be contacted to see whether any items have been handed in.

14. You are unwell aboard ship

There will be a qualified doctor (who generally operates as a concession). Medical facilities usually include a small pharmacy. Although there are charges for medical services, almost all cruise lines offer insurance packages that include medical coverage for most eventualities. It is wise to take out this insurance when you book.

15. The ship's laundry ruins your clothes

If any of your clothing is ruined or discolored by the ship's laundry, tell your cabin steward(ess) and register a complaint at the reception desk. Obtain a copy of the complaint, so you can follow up. Unfortunately, you will probably find a disclaimer on the laundry list stating that liability is limited to about $1 per item.

16. You have extra charges on your bill

Check your itemized bill carefully, then go to the reception and ask to be shown the charge slips. Make sure you get a copy of your bill *after* any modifications have been made.

17. You fly internationally to join your cruise

If your cruise begins a long way from your home, it makes sense to fly to your cruise departure point and stay overnight *before* your cruise. You will start the cruise refreshed and adjust better to any time changes.

18. You are unhappy with your cruise experience

If your ship delivers less well than the brochure promises, then let your booking agent and the cruise line know immediately.

Cruising and the Environment

The good: traveling by sea produces an estimated 36 times less carbon dioxide than flying. The bad: that's still not good enough.

Although marine vessels are responsible for almost 3 percent of the world's greenhouse gases, the world's fleet of oceangoing cruise ships produces just 0.1 percent of those emissions.

Eco diligence

Today's newest ships are ultra-smart – engines and generators are the cleanest ever, and much more fuel-efficient than even five years ago.

Cruise companies are trying harder to achieve an integrated approach to reduce pollution and noxious air emissions, and retrofit older ships with more efficient equipment. New ships benefit from improved hydrodynamic hull design. Advanced hull coatings also improve efficiency, while careful handling of solid and liquid waste helps lower fuel consumption and CO2 emissions. Flue gas from shipboard incinerators is recycled and wastewater is treated according to tough eco-friendly standards. Energy recovery

(waste-heat recovery) is also incorporated into new ships.

The result is a generous reduction in NOx – the term for a group of highly reactive gases containing nitrogen and oxygen in varying amounts. High-efficiency emissions-control technology such as selective catalytic converters further reduces NOx, and allows greater monitoring and computer control.

Europa 2 is the first cruise ship to be equipped with an SCR-catalytic converter, reducing nitrogen oxides (including nitrogen dioxide) by almost 95 percent.

Scrubber technology

In 2013, *Norwegian Breakaway* became the first cruise ship to recover and re-use the HFO fraction of waste oil as fuel for the diesel engines – to meet the low sulfur emission requirements that came into effect in January 2015. The ship's waste oil separator system has only two moving parts and leaves only

Solar panels aboard *Celebrity Solstice*.

non-pumpable 'super-dry' solids for landing as dry waste. The separated water, with an oil content of less than 1,000ppm, is pumped to the bilge-water tank as part of the waste oil and bilge-water handling system.

Some ship hulls are treated with 'foul-release' paint containing fluoropolymers or glass-flake vinyl ester resins – non-toxic substances that help reduce CO_2 emissions by using less fuel. However, ships that have switched from heavy-fuel oil to low-sulfur fuels have experienced greater fuel-pump wear, increasing maintenance, operational, and replacement costs.

Other measures

Other eco-friendly measures include the use of LED lighting rather than fuel-guzzling halogen lighting, and cabin lights that function only when a cabin key card is inserted into a device inside the cabin. Motion-activated lighting in closets is now common, as is the replacement of single-use plastic cups by melamine and/or porcelain, the use of permanent dispensers instead of plastic single-use soap/shampoo bottles/packs, and the replacement of plastic laundry bags with re-washable cotton bags.

Using darkness-activated sensors that switch on the ship's external lights at dusk and chilled river rocks that retain low temperatures for buffet items, rather than ice, also helps. Then there are heat-deflecting window coatings and the latest wastewater treatment technology.

Emissions Control Areas

In 2009 the British Isles introduced the first Emissions Control Areas (ECA) around its shores, including the English Channel, followed by 10 countries in the Baltic and North Sea region. The International Maritime Organization (IMO) formally established a North American Emission Control Area in August 2012, an area ringing the US/Canada (including Alaska) coast with a 200-mile (320-km) exclusion zone. The IMO's global air emissions standards called for a progressive reduction of SOx (sulfur dioxide) emissions from 3.5 percent in January 2012, to 0.5 percent by January 2020.

The aim of ECAs is to improve the air quality of coastal cities and inland ports by reducing the emission of ship-generated air pollutants such as sulfur oxides, nitrogen oxides and particulate matter.

LNG

Cruise ships are being built to use LNG (liquefied natural gas) fuel to avoid running the diesel generators in port; *AIDAnova*, which debuted in 2018, is the first LNG-powered cruise ship. (It's worth noting, however, that LNG storage tanks require 3.5 times the space of conventional fuel tanks, so retrofitting existing ships is impractical.) An LNG-based power barge can generate and supply electricity while in port, reducing CO_2 emissions considerably, with almost no SOx, NOx, or particle emissions. This may be a better solution than 'bridge' (interim solution) technology cold ironing, in which power is simply generated on land in the normal way and made available in port, allowing a cruise ship to turn off its generators to reduce emissions.

WHAT IS MARPOL?

Short for 'Marine Pollution,' the International Convention for the Prevention of Pollution from Ships (MARPOL 73/78 – the dates refer to its adoption) is the convention to which all member countries of the UN agency the International Maritime Organization (IMO) subscribe. It was designed to minimize pollution of the oceans and seas, including dumping, and pollution by oil and exhaust gases, whether by operational or accidental causes. The original MARPOL Convention was signed on February 17, 1973 modified in 1978, and came into force in October 1983. Presently, some 146 countries, representing 99 percent of the world's shipping tonnage, are signatories to the Convention. Ships flagged under these countries are subject to its requirements, regardless of where they sail.

---

9 WAYS CRUISE LINES REDUCE THEIR WASTE

Cruise lines reduce the solid waste they generate by bulk-buying. Other examples include:
1. Advanced purification systems to treat wastewater.
2. Ships eliminating, or severely reducing the use of, plastic drink straws.
3. Ships actively recycling glass, metals, wood, cardboard, and paper.
4. Excess heat generated in engine boilers being rerouted to power evaporators used in the process of turning seawater into potable water.
5. Special high-tech compacters processing garbage (the one aboard *Queen Mary 2*, for example, is four decks high).
6. Dry-cleaning machines using non-hazardous detergents formulated with soy, banana, and orange extracts.
7. Materials printed on board being produced using soy-based inks.
8. The only solid waste discharged to sea being food waste (considered safe because either sea creatures consume it or natural elements break it down in the water). Some cruise lines use only seafood farmed from sustainable sources.
9. Ships offloading used cooking oil for recycling to bio-diesel.

Cruising and Safety

How likely is an accident at sea? What if there's a fire? Can you fall overboard? How good are medical facilities aboard? Here's a practical guide to onboard safety.

When Costa Cruises' 3,800-passenger *Costa Concordia* capsized off the coast of Tuscany in January 2012 with the loss of 32 lives, questions of safety at sea inevitably arose. But this tragedy was avoidable: if *Costa Concordia*'s captain hadn't deviated from his computer-set course to sail close to the island of Giglio, it could have been just another uneventful Mediterranean cruise. The company was so fortunate with its crew, who did a wonderful job of evacuating more than 3,000 passengers from the stricken ship, in what were rather chaotic circumstances.

Other losses over the past 25 years include *Jupiter* in 1988 and *Royal Pacific* in 1992, both following collisions; *Explorer*, which struck an iceberg

Cabins are checked during a passenger emergency drill.

near Antarctica in 2007; and *Sea Diamond*, which foundered on a reef off the Greek island of Santorini in 2007. Given that over 27 million people take a cruise every year, the number of serious incidents is extremely low. After more than 50 years of sea travel, during which I have experienced fires and groundings, I know that cruising remains one of the safest forms of transportation.

Safety measures

All cruise ships built after 2010 with a length of 394ft (120m) or greater, or with three or more main vertical zones, must have two engine rooms, so that if one is flooded or rendered unusable, a ship can safely return to port without requiring evacuation. This requirement came about because of the increasing size of today's cruise ships, and the fact that several ship fires and loss of propulsion/steering have occurred.

Other safety measures include muster drills, bridge procedures, life-jacket availability and location, lifeboat loading drills, recording of passenger nationalities for on-shore emergency-services personnel, and the securing of heavy objects.

International regulations require all crew to undergo basic safety training *before* being allowed to work aboard any cruise ship (on-the-job training is no longer enough). All safety regulations are governed by the international SOLAS Convention, introduced in 1914 in the aftermath of *Titanic*'s sinking in 1912. A mandatory passenger muster drill prior to departure from the port of embarkation is part of the SOLAS Convention. Passengers who don't attend may be disembarked prior to sailing.

All cruise ships built since 1986 must have either totally or partially enclosed lifeboats with diesel engines that can operate even if the lifeboat is inverted.

Since October 1997, cruise ships have had: all stairways enclosed as self-contained fire zones; smoke detectors and smoke alarms fitted in all passenger cabins and public spaces; low-level lighting showing routes of escape; all fire doors controllable from the ship's navigation bridge; all fire doors that can be opened from a remote location; and emergency alarms audible in all cabins.

Since 2002, all ocean-going cruise ships on international voyages carry voyage data recorders (VDRs), similar to black boxes aboard aircraft, and, since October 2010, SOLAS regulations have prohibited the use of combustible materials in all new cruise ships.

Crew members attend frequent emergency drills, lifeboat equipment is regularly tested, and fire-detecting devices and alarm and fire-fighting systems are regularly checked. I have strongly recommended that all ships fit rechargeable flashlights under each passenger bed – advice that was forwarded to the IMO. In the meantime, take a small flashlight in case an emergency arises during a blackout or during the night.

What to do in ultra-rough sea conditions

Bring a hat and wear it in rough sea conditions, to avoid injuries from flying objects in any of the public rooms. Always carry medication with you so you're prepared in the event of a possible evacuation emergency, as happened in the case of *Viking Sky* in 2019, when the ship was drifting rather close to the shore due to loss of propulsion.

Is security good enough?

Cruise lines are subject to stringent international security regulations. Passengers and crew can embark or disembark only by passing through a security checkpoint. Cruise ships maintain zero tolerance for crime or offenses against the person, and trained security professionals are employed aboard all cruise ships.

It is recommended that you keep your cabin locked at all times when you are not there. Cruise lines do not accept responsibility for any money or valuables left in cabins and suggest that you store them in your in-cabin safe.

You will be issued with a personal boarding pass when you embark. This includes your photo, muster or lifeboat station, restaurant seating, and other pertinent information, and must be shown at the gangway each time you board. You will be asked for a government-issued photo ID, such as a passport.

Passenger lifeboat drill

A passenger lifeboat drill, announced publicly by the captain, must be held for embarking passengers *before* the ship departs the port of embarkation.

Attendance is compulsory. Learn your boat station or assembly point and how to get there in an

Listening to information on safety during a passenger emergency drill.

emergency. Note your exit and escape pathways and how to put on a lifejacket correctly. The drill takes no more than 20 minutes and is potentially life-saving (the 600-passenger *Royal Pacific* took fewer than 20 minutes to sink after its collision in 1992).

Can you accidentally fall overboard?

All cruise ships have railings at least 3ft 7in (1.1m) high to protect you and your children, so rest assured that instances of passengers falling overboard are extremely rare. However, it does occasionally happen, as reports in the press testify – usually the tragic result of reckless behavior.

Shipboard injury

Slipping, tripping, and falling are the major sources of shipboard injury. Here are some things you can do to minimize the chance of injury.

Aboard many ships, raised thresholds separate a cabin's bathroom from the sleeping area. Mind your step to avoid a stubbed toe or banged head.

Don't hang anything from the fire sprinkler heads on cabin ceilings.

Walk with caution when the outer decks are wet. This applies especially to solid steel decks – falling on them can be painful.

Don't throw a lighted cigarette or cigar butt, or knock out your pipe, over the ship's side. These can easily be sucked into an opening in the ship's side or onto an aft open deck area and cause a fire.

Surviving a shipboard fire

Shipboard fires can generate an incredible amount of heat, smoke, and often panic. In the unlikely event that you are in one, try to remain calm and think logically and clearly.

When you first get to your cabin, check the way to the nearest emergency exits. Count the number of cabin doorways and other distinguishing features to the exits in case you have to escape without the benefit of lighting. All ships provide low location lighting systems.

Fire drill aboard *Hanseatic*.

Testing lifeboats on *Voyager of the Seas*.

Exit signs are normally located just above your head – this is virtually useless, as smoke and flames rise. Note the location of the nearest fire alarm and know how to use it in case of dense smoke.

If you are in your cabin, and there is fire in the passageway outside, put on your lifejacket. If the cabin's door handle is hot, soak a towel in water and use it to turn the handle. If a fire is raging in the passageway, cover yourself in wet towels if you decide to go through the flames.

Check the passageway. If there are no flames, walk to the nearest emergency exit or stairway. If there is smoke in the passageway, crawl to the nearest exit. If the exit is blocked, go to an alternate one. It may take considerable effort to open a heavy fire door to the exit. Don't use the elevators.

If there's a fire in your cabin or on the balcony, report it immediately by telephone. Then leave your cabin, close the door behind you, sound the alarm, and alert your neighbors.

SAFETY MEASURES

Fire control
If the fire alarm is sounded, a siren is automatically set off on the bridge. A red panel light will be illuminated on a large plan, indicating the section of the ship that must be checked, so that the crew can take immediate action.

Ships are sectioned into several zones, each of which can be isolated. In addition, almost all ships have a water-fed sprinkler system that can be activated at the touch of a button, or automatically activated when sprinkler vials are broken by fire-generated heat.

Emergency ventilation control
This automatic fire-damper system also has a manual switch that can stop or control the flow of air to all areas; in this way reducing the fanning effect on flame and smoke via air-conditioning and fan systems.

Watertight doors
Throughout the ship watertight doors can be closed off, in order to contain the movement of water flooding the vessel. All watertight doors can be operated electrically and manually, which means that nobody can be trapped in a watertight compartment.

Britannia Restaurant aboard *Queen Elizabeth*.

How We Evaluate the Ships

Ships and their facilities count, but just as important are the standards relating to food, service, staff training, and hospitality. This section explains how the Berlitz points system works.

I have been evaluating and rating cruise ships and the onboard product professionally since 1980. I also receive reports from my small team of trained assessors. The Berlitz ratings are conducted with *total objectivity*, from a set of predetermined criteria, using a modus operandi designed to work across the entire spectrum of oceangoing cruise ships, in all segments of the business.

There really is no 'best cruise line in the world' or 'best cruise ship' – only the ship and cruise that is right for you. After all, it's the overall enjoyment of a cruise as a vacation that's important. Therefore, different criteria are applied to ships of different sizes, styles, and market segments throughout the world (vacationers of different nationalities look for different things).

The evaluation and rating of cruise ships is about as contrary to soccer as you can get. In soccer, the goalposts are always in the same place. But with cruise ships, they keep changing, as the industry evolves.

This section includes 300 oceangoing cruise ships in service (or due to enter service) and chosen by the author for inclusion when this book was completed. The ships have been carefully evaluated, taking into account up to 400 separate items based on personal cruises, visits, and revisits to ships. In the scoring room, these are channeled into 20 major areas, each with a possible 100 points. The maximum possible score for any ship is therefore 2,000 points.

For user-friendliness and reasons of space on the printed page, scores are further divided into five main sections: Ship, Accommodation, Food, Service, and Cruise Experience.

Cruise lines, ship owners, and operators should note that ratings may be adjusted annually as a result of increased competition, the introduction of newer ships with better facilities, and other market- or passenger-driven factors.

The ratings more reflect the standards of the cruise product (the software: the dining experience, the service, and the hospitality aspects of the cruise), and less the physical plant (the hardware). Thus, although a ship may be the latest, most stunning vessel in the world in terms of design and decor, if the 'software' and actual product delivery are not so good, the scores and ratings will reflect these aspects more clearly.

The stars beside the name of the ship at the top of each page indicate the 'Overall Rating.' The highest number of stars awarded is five stars (★★★★★+),

and the lowest is one star. This system has been universally recognized throughout the global hospitality industry for over 30 years. A plus (+) indicates that a ship deserves just that little bit more than the number of stars attained. However, it is the *number of points achieved* rather than the number of stars attained that perhaps is more meaningful when comparing ships.

The star system

★★★★★+ 1,851–2,000 points
★★★★★ 1,701–1,850 points
★★★★+ 1,551–1,700 points
★★★★ 1,401–1,550 points
★★★+ 1,251–1,400 points
★★★ 1,101–1,250 points
★★+ 951–1,100 points
★★ 801–950 points
★+ 651–800 points
★ 501–650 points

Douglas Ward at work.

A touch of real caviar on *SeaDream*.

WHAT THE RATINGS MEAN

1,851–2,000 points ★★★★★+

You can expect an outstanding, top-class cruise experience – it doesn't get any better than this. It should be truly memorable, and with the highest attention to detail, finesse, and personal service – how important you are made to feel is critical. The decor must be elegant and tasteful, measured by restraint and not flashiness, with fresh flowers and other decorative touches in abundance. The layout of the public rooms may well follow *feng shui* principles.

Any ship with this rating must be just about unsurpassable in the cruise industry, and it has to be very, very special, with service and hospitality levels to match. There must be the highest-quality surroundings, comfort, and service levels, the finest and freshest quality foods, including all breads and rolls baked on board. Highly creative menus, regional cuisine, and dining alternatives should provide maximum choice and variety, and special orders will be part of the dining ritual.

Meals (particularly dinners) are expected to be memorable affairs, correctly served on the finest china, with a choice of wines of suitable character and vintage available, and served in the correct-sized sommelier glasses of the highest quality (Riedel or Schott).

The service staff will take pleasure in providing you with the ultimate personal, yet unobtrusive, attention with the utmost of finesse, and the word 'no' should not be in their vocabulary. This is the very best of the best in terms of refined living at sea, but it is seriously expensive.

1,701–1,850 points ★★★★★

You can expect a truly excellent, memorable cruise experience, with the finesse and attention to detail commensurate with the amount of money paid. The service and hospitality levels will be extremely high from all levels of officers and staff, with strong emphasis on fine hospitality training – all service personnel members must make you feel important.

The food will be at the high level expected from what is virtually the best possible at sea, with service that should be very attentive yet unobtrusive. The cuisine should be memorable, with ample taste. Special orders should never be a problem. There must be a varied selection of wines, which should be served in glasses of the correct size.

Entertainment is expected to be of prime quality and variety. Again, the word 'no' should not be in the vocabulary of any member of staff aboard a ship with this rating. Few things will cost extra on board, and brochures should be more 'truthful' than those for ships with a lower rating.

1,551–1,700 points ★★★★+

You can expect to have a high-quality cruise experience that will be memorable, and just a little short of being excellent in all aspects. Perhaps the personal service and attention to detail could be slightly better, but, nonetheless, this should prove to be a fine all-round cruise experience, in a setting that is extremely clean and comfortable, with few lines (queues) anywhere, a caring attitude from service personnel, and a good standard of entertainment that appeals to a mainstream market.

The cuisine and service must be carefully balanced, with mostly fresh ingredients and varied menus that should appeal to almost anyone, all served on high-quality china.

This should prove to be an extremely well-rounded cruise experience, probably in a ship that is new or almost new. There will be fewer 'extra-cost' items than ships with a slightly lower rating.

1,401–1,550 points ★★★★

You can expect to have a very good-quality all-round cruise experience, most probably aboard a modern, highly comfortable ship that will provide a good range of facilities and services. The food and service will be quite decent overall, although decidedly not as 'gourmet' and fanciful as the brochures with the always-smiling faces might have you believe.

The service on board will be well organized, if a little robotic and impersonal at times, and only as good as the cruise line's training program allows. You may notice a lot of things cost extra once you are on board, although the typically vague brochure tells you that these things are 'available' or are an 'option.' However, you should have a good time, and your bank account will be only moderately damaged.

1,251–1,400 points ★★★+

You can expect to have a decent-quality cruise experience, aboard a ship where the service levels should be good, but perhaps without the finesse that could be expected from a more upscale environment. The crew aboard any ship achieving this score should reflect a positive attitude towards hospitality, and a willingness to accommodate your needs, up to a point. Staff training will probably be in need of more attention to detail and flexibility.

Food and service levels in the dining venues should be reasonably good, although special or unusual orders might prove more difficult to accommodate. There will probably be a number of extra-cost items you thought were included in the price of your cruise – although the brochure typically is vague and states that the things are 'available' or are an 'option.'

1,101–1,250 points ★★★

You can expect a reasonably decent, middle-of-the-road cruise experience, with a moderate amount of space and quality in furnishings, fixtures, and fittings. The cabins are likely to be a little on the small side. The food and service levels will be quite acceptable, although not at all memorable, and somewhat inflexible with regard to special orders, as almost everything is standardized.

The level of hospitality will be moderate but little more, and the entertainment will probably be weak. This is a good option, however, for those looking for the reasonable comforts of home without pretentious attitudes, and comparatively little damage to their bank statement.

951–1,100 points ★★+

You can expect an average cruise experience in terms of accommodation (typically with cabins that are dimensionally challenged), the quality of the ship's facilities, food, wine list, service, and hospitality levels, in surroundings that are unpretentious. In particular, the food and its service might be disappointing.

There will be little flexibility in the levels of service, hospitality, and staff training and supervision, which will be no better than poor in comparison with that of ships of a higher rating. Thus, the overall experience will be commensurate with the comparatively small amount of money you paid for the cruise.

801–950 points ★★

You can expect to have a cruise experience of modest quality aboard a ship that is probably in need of more attention to maintenance and service levels, not to mention hospitality. The food may be quite lacking in taste, homogenized, and of low quality, and service is likely to be mediocre at best. Staff training is likely to be minimal, and staff turnover may be high. The 'end-of-pier' entertainment could well leave you wanting to read a good book.

651–800 points ★+

You can expect to have only the most basic cruise experience, with little or no attention to detail, from a minimally trained staff that is probably paid low wages and to whom you are just another body. The ship will, in many cases, probably be in need of much maintenance and upgrading, and will probably have few facilities. Dismal entertainment is also likely. On the other hand, the price of a cruise of this rating will probably be alluringly low.

501–650 points ★

You can expect to have a cruise experience that is the bottom of the barrel, with little in terms of hospitality or finesse. Forget about attention to detail – there won't be any. This would equal a stay in the most basic motel on land, with few facilities, a poorly trained, seemingly uncaring staff, and a ship that needs better maintenance.

The low cost of a cruise aboard a ship with this rating should provide a strong clue to the complete absence of any quality, particularly for food, service, and entertainment. You might remember this cruise, but for all the wrong reasons.

Distribution of points

These are the percentage of the total points available that are allocated to each of the main areas evaluated:

The ship: 25 percent
Accommodation: 10 percent
Food: 20 percent
Service: 20 percent
Entertainment: 5 percent
The cruise experience: 20 percent

The categories 'Entertainment' (including lecturers and expedition staff) and 'The cruise experience' may be combined for boutique ships, tall ships, and expedition ships, and adjusted accordingly.

CRITERIA

The ship

Hardware/maintenance/safety. This score reflects the general profile and condition of the ship, its age, exterior paint, decking and caulking; swimming pool and surrounds; deck furniture; shore tenders; and lifeboats and other safety items. It also reflects interior cleanliness (public restrooms, elevators, floor and wall coverings, stairways, passageways, and doorways); food-preparation areas and refrigerators; and garbage handling, compacting, incineration, and waste-disposal facilities.

Outdoor facilities/space. This score reflects the overall open deck space; swimming pools/hot tubs and their surrounds; congestion; type of deck lounge chairs (with or without cushioned pads) and other deck furniture; sports facilities; shower enclosures; changing facilities; towels; and quiet areas.

Interior facilities/space/flow. This score reflects the use of public spaces; flow and congestion; ceiling height; lobby, stairways, and hallways; elevators; public restrooms and facilities; signage, lighting, air conditioning, and ventilation.

Decor/furnishings/artwork. This score reflects the overall interior decor and soft furnishings; carpeting (color, pattern, and practicality); chairs (comfort); ceilings and treatments; artwork (paintings, sculptures, and atrium centerpieces); and lighting.

Spa/fitness facilities. This score reflects the spa, wellness, and fitness facilities, including location, accessibility, lighting and flooring materials. Also: fitness machines and fitness programs; sports facilities and equipment; indoor pools; hot tubs; grand baths; hydrotherapy pools; saunas; steam rooms; treatment rooms; changing facilities; jogging and walking tracks; and open promenades.

Accommodation

Cabins: suites and cabins. This score reflects the design, layout, balconies and partitions (whether full

Balcony cabins at the aft (back) of *Costa Serena*.

floor-to-ceiling partition or part partitions), beds/ berths, cabinetry, and other fittings; closet and drawer space, bedside tables and reading lights; vanity unit, bathroom facilities, cabinets and storage for toiletries; lighting, air conditioning, and ventilation; audio-visual facilities; artwork; insulation, noise, and vibration. Suites should not be so designated unless the bedroom is completely separated from the living area.

Also covers cabin service directory of services, interactive TV; paper and personalized stationery; telephone information; laundry lists; tea- and coffee-making equipment; flowers; fruit; bathroom personal amenities kits, bathrobes, slippers, and the size and quality of towels.

Cuisine

Cruise lines put maximum emphasis on how good their food is, often to the point of overstatement. There are, of course, at least as many different tastes as there are passengers. As in any good restaurant, you generally get what you pay for.

Dining venues/cuisine. This score reflects the physical structure of dining rooms, layout, seating, and waiter stations; lighting and ambience; table setups; linen, china, and cutlery quality and condition. Also: menus, food quality, creativity, appeal, taste, texture, presentation (garnishes and decorations); tableside cooking (if any); wine list; price range; and service. Alternative dining venues are also checked for menu variety, food and service, ambience, decor, seating, noise levels, china, cutlery, and glassware.

Casual eateries/buffets. This score reflects hot and cold display units and sneeze guards, 'active' stations, tongs and other serving utensils; food displays; temperatures; labeling; deck buffets; decorative elements; and staff communication.

Quality of ingredients. This score reflects taste, consistency, and portion size; grades of meat, fish, and fowl; and the price paid by the cruise line for food per passenger per day.

Tea/coffee/bar snacks. This score reflects the quality and variety of teas and coffees, including afternoon tea/coffee and presentation; whether mugs or cups and saucers are used; whether milk is served in the correct containers or in sealed packets; whether self-service or served. It also reflects the quality of cakes, scones, and pastries, bar/lounge snacks, hot and cold canapés, and hors d'oeuvres.

Service

Dining rooms. This score reflects staff professionalism: the maître d'hôtel (restaurant manager), section headwaiters, waiters and assistants (busboys), sommeliers and wine waiters; place settings, cutlery, and glasses; and proper service (serving, taking from the correct side), communication skills, attitude, flair, uniform, appearance, and finesse. Waiters should note whether passengers are right- or left-handed and, when tables are assigned, make sure that cutlery and glasses are placed on the side of preference.

Bars. This score reflects lighting and ambience; seating; noise levels; attitude and communication skills, personality, and service.

Cabins. This score reflects the cleaning and housekeeping staff, butlers (for suite occupants), supervisory staff, bedding/bathrobe changes, language and communication skills.

Open decks. This score reflects the service for beverages and food items; placement and replacement of towels on deck lounge chairs, and tidiness of any associated deck equipment.

Entertainment

The score reflects the overall entertainment program and its appeal, showlounge (stage/bandstand); technical support, lighting, sound systems; production shows (story, plot, cohesion, costumes, quality, choreography, and vocal content); cabaret acts, bands and solo musicians.

Aboard specialist ships such as those offering expedition cruises, or sail-cruise ships such as *Sea Cloud*, where entertainment is not a feature, the score relates to the lecture program, library, movies on demand, videos, and use of water-sports items such as jet skis, windsurfers, kayaks, and snorkeling gear, etc.

The cruise experience

Activities program. This score reflects social activities and events; cruise director and staff (visibility, professionalism, and communication); special-interest programs; port, shopping, and enrichment lecturers; water-sports equipment, instruction, marina or retractable water-sports platforms, and any enclosed swimming area.

Movies/television program. This score reflects movies picture and sound quality; in-cabin infotainment system and audio channels.

Hospitality factor. This score reflects the hospitality and professionalism of officers, middle management, cruise staff, and crew; appearance; and communication skills.

Overall product delivery. This score reflects the quality of the overall cruise as a vacation – what the brochure states and promises, and what is delivered.

Notes on the rating results

Ship evaluations and ratings have become ever more complex. Although a ship may be the newest, with all the latest facilities, it is the food and service that often disappoint, plus security lines/checks and issues relating to signing up for activities.

Cruise companies state that food quality is a trade-off against lower prices, but this implies a downward spiral that affects quality and service.

Finally, it is the little things that add to points lost on the great scorecard.

What the Descriptions Mean

Each of the following ship reviews is preceded by a panel providing basic data on the ship's size and facilities. Here we explain how to interpret the categories.

Ship size (based on lower bed capacity)
Large resort ship: 2,501–6,500 passengers
Mid-size ship: 751–2,500 passengers
Small ship: 251–750 passengers
Boutique ship: 50–250 passengers

Cruise line
The cruise and the operator may be different if the company that owns the ship does not routinely market and operate it. Tour operators often charter ships for their exclusive use (for example Thomson Cruises).

Entered service
Where two dates are given, the first is for the ship's maiden (paid) passenger voyage, and the second is the date it began service for the current operator.

Propulsion
The type of propulsion is given (gas turbine, diesel, diesel-electric, or nuclear). The second half denotes the number of propellers or fixed or azimuthing pods.

The favored drivers are eco-friendly diesel-electric or diesel-mechanical propulsion systems that propel ships at speeds of up to 28 knots (32mph). Only Cunard's *Queen Mary 2*, with a top speed of more than 30 knots (34.5mph), is faster. LNG (liquified natural gas)-powered ships made their debut in 2018.

Royal Caribbean International's *Harmony of the Seas*, *Allure of the Seas*, and *Oasis of the Seas* off Port Everglades, Florida.

Passenger space is an important factor in the enjoyment of a cruise.

More than 80 cruise ships are now fitted with the pod propulsion system, first introduced in 1990. Resembling a huge outboard motor fitted below the waterline, it replaces the long-used conventional rudder, shaft, and propeller mechanisms, saves valuable machinery space, and makes stern thrusters redundant.

Pods are compact, self-contained units powered by internal electric propulsion motors. They are turned by the hydraulic motors of the steering gear, and can turn through 360 degrees (azimuthing). This allows even the largest ships to maneuver into tight spaces without help from tugs.

Most ships have two pods; some have three (*Allure of the Seas*, *Harmony of the Seas*, *Oasis of the Seas*, *Symphony of the Seas*) or even four units (*Queen Mary 2*). Each pod weighs about 170 tons, but the four pods attached to *Queen Mary 2* weigh 250 tons each – more than an empty Boeing 747 jumbo jet; two are fixed, two are azimuthing. Ships with pod propulsion systems have no noticeable vibration or engine noise aft, unlike ships with conventional propulsion systems.

Some older ships have 'Becker' rudders, where the main body has a hinged, second part. This second, or aft, section can be pointed in a different direction from the main body; the result is more control over the waterflow.

Passenger capacity

This is based on two lower beds per cabin, including cabins for solo occupancy.

Passenger space ratio (gross tonnage per passenger)

Achieved by dividing the gross tonnage by the number of passengers (lower bed capacity including solo-occupancy cabins).

Passenger to crew ratio

Achieved by dividing the number of (lower-bed) passengers by the number of crew.

Cabin size range

From the smallest cabin to the largest suite (including 'private' balconies), in square feet and square meters and rounded up to the nearest whole number.

Wheelchair-accessible ratings

Cabins designed to accommodate wheelchair-users. There are four accessibility ratings:

Best. This ship is recommended as most suitable for wheelchair-users.

Good. Reasonably accessible.

Fair. Just about accessible.

None. This ship is not suitable.

About prices

Any price examples given in the ship reviews are provided *only* as a guideline and may have changed since publication. Always check with the cruise company or your cruise booking agent for the latest prices.

The Star Performers

Having reviewed the following 300-plus cruise ships, Berlitz names the top-rated ships in their size categories for 2020.

Despite constant claims by cruise companies that their ship has been named 'Best Cruise Line' or 'Best Cruise Ship' by this or that magazine or online readers' poll, there really is no such thing – there is only the ship that is right for you. Few operators can really deliver a ship, product, and crew worthy of the highest Berlitz star rating – it's all about excellence, and passion.

For this 2020 edition, only two ships have again achieved the standard and score required for them to be awarded membership in the most exclusive 'five-stars-plus' category:

1 *Europa 2*

Hapag-Lloyd Cruises

1864 points ★★★★★+

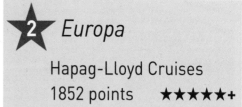

2 *Europa*

Hapag-Lloyd Cruises

1852 points ★★★★★+

These are both beautiful, but slightly different, ships to cruise aboard, with a fine amount of space per passenger, hallways with high ceilings, a fine range of dining venues and types of cuisine, and attentive, friendly, yet unobtrusive personal service.

However, *Europa* and *Europa 2* really are exclusive, high-priced ships, so we have also included a selection of best cruise ships (sister ships, in some cases, where they are close to identical) denoted by the star category and listed in order of points scored overall, with the highest-scoring ships first. Entries are listed according to their Berlitz score, where applicable, or else in alphabetical order by cruise line or ship's name.

Europa 2's layout.

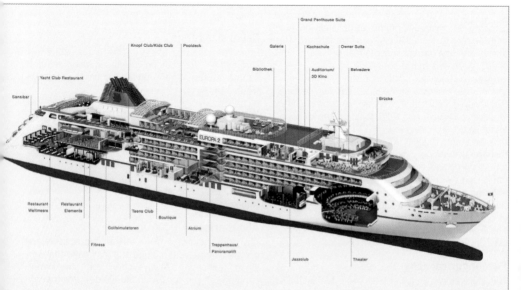

AND THE WINNER IS...

THE TOP 20 LARGE RESORT SHIPS
(2,501–6,500 passengers)

Queen Mary 2. Part transatlantic ocean liner, part cruise ship, this iconic vessel has something for all ages.

Queen Mary 2	1681 out of 2000	★★★★+
Mein Schiff 1	1654 out of 2000	★★★★+
Mein Schiff 2	1654 out of 2000	★★★★+
Mein Schiff 6	1626 out of 2000	★★★★+
Mein Schiff 5	1625 out of 2000	★★★★+
Mein Schiff 3	1614 out of 2000	★★★★+
Mein Schiff 4	1614 out of 2000	★★★★+
Genting Dream	1569 out of 2000	★★★★+
World Dream	1569 out of 2000	★★★★+
MSC Seaview	1558 out of 2000	★★★★+
MSC Bellissima	1555 out of 2000	★★★★+
MSC Seaside	1554 out of 2000	★★★★+
MSC Meraviglia	1551 out of 2000	★★★★+
MSC Divina	1539 out of 2000	★★★★
MSC Fantasia	1532 out of 2000	★★★★
MSC Preziosa	1532 out of 2000	★★★★
MSC Splendida	1526 out of 2000	★★★★
Celebrity Edge	1512 out of 2000	★★★★
Anthem of the Seas	1494 out of 2000	★★★★
Quantum of the Seas	1476 out of 2000	★★★★

AND THE WINNER IS...

THE TOP 20 MID-SIZE SHIPS
(751–2,500 passengers)

Sissel Kyrkjebø, Godmother for the *Viking Jupiter*, posing for a picture during the Float Out Ceremony.

Viking Jupiter	1691 out of 2000	★★★★+
Viking Orion	1690 out of 2000	★★★★+
Viking Sea	1689 out of 2000	★★★★+
Viking Sky	1689 out of 2000	★★★★+
Viking Sun	1689 out of 2000	★★★★+
Viking Star	1688 out of 2000	★★★★+
Crystal Serenity	1687 out of 2000	★★★★+
Crystal Symphony	1678 out of 2000	★★★★+
Riviera	1599 out of 2000	★★★★+
Marina	1594 out of 2000	★★★★+
Asuka II	1586 out of 2000	★★★★+
Queen Elizabeth	1562 out of 2000	★★★★+
Queen Victoria	1558 out of 2000	★★★★+
Artania	1431 out of 2000	★★★★
Disney Fantasy	1423 out of 2000	★★★★
Disney Dream	1419 out of 2000	★★★★
Explorer Dream	1405 out of 2000	★★★★
MSC Opera	1399 out of 2000	★★★+
MSC Lyrica	1389 out of 2000	★★★+
Celebrity Millennium	1381 out of 2000	★★★+

AND THE WINNER IS...

THE TOP 20 SMALL SHIPS
(251–750 passengers)

Europa 2. The world's highest scoring ship overflows with contemporary interior design, style, and finesse in food and service for sophisticated international travelers.

Europa 2	1864 out of 2000	★★★★★+
Europa	1852 out of 2000	★★★★★+
Silver Muse	1660 out of 2000	★★★★+
Silver Spirit	1633 out of 2000	★★★★+
Seabourn Encore	1628 out of 2000	★★★★+
Seabourn Ovation	1628 out of 2000	★★★★+
Seabourn Odyssey	1624 out of 2000	★★★★+
Seabourn Sojourn	1618 out of 2000	★★★★+
Seven Seas Explorer	1618 out of 2000	★★★★+
Silver Shadow	1597 out of 2000	★★★★+
Silver Whisper	1597 out of 2000	★★★★+
Seven Seas Voyager	1568 out of 2000	★★★★+
Seven Seas Mariner	1545 out of 2000	★★★★
Seabourn Quest	1529 out of 2000	★★★★
Deutschland	1507 out of 2000	★★★★
Amadea	1486 out of 2000	★★★★
Nippon Maru	1485 out of 2000	★★★★
Azamara Pursuit	1483 out of 2000	★★★★
Le Soleal	1483 out of 2000	★★★★
Le Boreal	1478 out of 2000	★★★★

AND THE WINNER IS...

THE TOP 20 BOUTIQUE SHIPS
(50–250 passengers)

HANSEATIC nature – an outstanding, intimate expedition ship with excellent food and hospitality.

HANSEATIC nature	1791 out of 2000	★★★★★
Sea Cloud	1702 out of 2000	★★★★★
Sea Cloud II	1701 out of 2000	★★★★★
SeaDream I	1679 out of 2000	★★★★+
SeaDream II	1679 out of 2000	★★★★+
Royal Clipper	1512 out of 2000	★★★★
Le Bougainville	1505 out of 2000	★★★★
Le Dumont d'Urville	1505 out of 2000	★★★★
Le Champlain	1504 out of 2000	★★★★
Resolute	1504 out of 2000	★★★★
Le Lapérouse	1503 out of 2000	★★★★
Le Lyrial	1498 out of 2000	★★★★
Star Legend	1473 out of 2000	★★★★
Hebridean Princess	1472 out of 2000	★★★★
Caledonian Sky	1468 out of 2000	★★★★
National Geographic Orion	1467 out of 2000	★★★★
Island Sky	1466 out of 2000	★★★★
Star Pride	1464 out of 2000	★★★★
Star Breeze	1463 out of 2000	★★★★
Silver Explorer	1453 out of 2000	★★★★

ADVENTURE OF THE SEAS
★★★+

A LARGE SHIP THAT'S BIG ON THINGS TO DO FOR THE WHOLE FAMILY

Size:	Large Resort Ship
Tonnage:	137,276
Cruise Line:	Royal Caribbean International
Former Names:	none
Builder:	Kvaerner Masa-Yards (Finland)
Entered Service:	Nov 2001
Length (ft/m):	1,020.6/311.1
Propulsion/Propellers:	diesel-electric (75,600kW)/3 pods (2 azimuthing, 1 fixed)
Total Crew:	1,185
Passengers (lower beds):	3,319
Passenger Space Ratio (lower beds):	41.4
Passenger/Crew Ratio (lower beds):	2.7
Cabins (total):	1,262
Size Range (sq ft/m):	151.0–1,356.2/14.0–126.1
Cabins (for one person):	5
Cabins with balcony:	765
Cabins (wheelchair accessible):	26
Wheelchair accessibility:	Best
Elevators:	14
Casino (gaming tables):	Yes
Self-Service Launderette:	No
Onboard currency:	US$

THE SHIP. *Adventure of the Seas* (a Voyager-class ship) is a large, floating leisure resort with a host of facilities. The ship offers a healthy amount of space per passenger and excellent entertainment for the whole family. Outdoor decks are full of fun water park features, plus there's a rock-climbing wall, so there's little time left to sit and relax or sunbathe. This is consistent, homogeneous mainstream cruising for young-minded cruisers of all ages who enjoy mingling on a large, lively ship with constant activity.

Standout features include a four-deck-high Royal Promenade (long atrium), the main interior social and focal point. The length of two American football fields, it rises through 11 decks at both ends, and has cafés, shops, bars and interior 'promenade view' bay window cabins that look onto it. Comedy art includes a trompe l'oeil painter climbing up the walls. Arched across the promenade is a captain's balcony. A stairway connects with the deck below, with a Schooner Bar (a piano lounge common to all Royal Caribbean International ships) and a flashy, large Casino Royale.

Other standouts include a regulation-size ice-skating rink (Studio B), with real ice, with 'bleacher' seating for up to 900 and broadcast facilities.

Overall, this is a fine all-round ship for all age groups but be aware of the extra cost for many optional items (including drinks, drink packages, and excursions).

BERLITZ'S RATINGS

	Possible	Achieved
Ship	500	354
Accommodation	200	132
Food	400	220
Service	400	255
Entertainment	100	66
Cruise Experience	400	248

OVERALL SCORE 1275 points out of 2000

In late 2017, the ship underwent an extensive $61-million refurbishment, with new cabins added (but no extra elevators), plus dual racer waterslides (Cyclone and Typhoon), a FlowRider surf simulator, Splashaway Bay (children's aqua park), and Chops Grille.

It's wise to plan what you want to do wisely – almost everything requires you to make reservations/sign up in advance. There is no escape from recorded rap-rich background 'music' everywhere – even in the elevators, passenger hallways, and saunas. Live music is on the volume-heavy side, and there are unwelcome (and unnecessary) announcements for activities that bring revenue, such as art auctions and bingo.

There are many cost extra items in the various optional dining venues, drink packages, and excursions, but overall the ship delivers a well-orchestrated cruise vacation at a decent price.

Expect lines for the reception desk, shore excursions, shore tenders, and in the self-serve buffet stations. Niggles include intrusive photographers, few quiet places to sit and read, no cushioned pads for deck sunloungers, small cabin 'bath' towels, noisy (vacuum) toilets, and frosted drinks in 'souvenir' glasses pushed to the hilt. Do budget extra for additional cost items and expect to be subjected to flyers and advertising promotions.

Service personnel are friendly and the digital 'Wayfarer' system is informative, although the speaking 'elevator going up/going down' quickly becomes boring.

ACCOMMODATION. There is a wide range of cabin price grades, including: interior (no-view) cabins, balcony cabins, and suites (the largest is the Royal Suite). Many cabins are of a similar size, which is good for incentives and large groups, and 300 have interconnecting doors (good for families).

Some 138 interior cabins have bay windows views into the interior Royal Promenade horizontal atrium – a cruise industry first when the ship originally debuted. Occupy a cabin with a connecting door to another cabin and you may be able to hear your neighbors.

DINING. The main dining room seats 1,919, on three levels, each named after a famous composer: Mozart, Strauss, and Vivaldi. All have the same menu. A dramatic staircase connects all three levels, and huge support pillars obstruct sight lines from many seats. Two small wings, La Cetra and La Notte. Place settings, china, and cutlery are of good quality.

Main dining room cuisine is all about standardized banquet catering and batch cooking. Menu descriptions sound tempting, but the food, although prepared well enough, is just so-so. Items like lobster or premium steaks come at extra cost, but they will be cooked individually to your liking. Green vegetables are scarce – provided basically for decoration – but salad items are plentiful, and desserts are pretty good. Bread and pastry items are so-so (these are thawed and then baked from frozen 'starter' dough), and croissants lack any hint of butter. Vegetarian and children's menus are also available. Note that there are no wine waiters.

Extra cost, reservations required eateries include: Chops Grille (added in 2017) for premium-quality steaks and seafood in a bistro-style setting; Giovanni's Table (open for dinner only) for Euro-Italian cuisine; Johnny Rockets, a retro 1950s all-day, all-night diner has hamburgers, extra-cost malt shakes, and jukebox hits, with both indoor and outdoor seating.

For casual (free) eats: Windjammer Café, a large venue for casual buffet-style, self-help breakfast (the busiest time), lunch, and light dinners; it's often difficult to find a table, and, by the time you do, your food could be cold.

Island Grill (inside the Windjammer Café) is for casual dinners (no reservations needed), with a grill and open kitchen.

Promenade Café: for Continental breakfast, all-day pizzas, ice cream, yogurt, pastries, and specialty coffees (in paper cups).

ENTERTAINMENT. The 1,350-seat Lyric Theater is a stunning showlounge located forward. It has Art Nouveau-themed decor and spans five decks, with only a few slim pillars and almost no disruption of sight lines. Excellent production shows are presented here by a large cast and live band.

SPA/FITNESS. The ShipShape health spa includes an aerobics room, fitness center with muscle-training equipment, treatment rooms, and men's and women's sauna/steam rooms, plus a Solarium (with sliding glass-dome roof).

Aft of the funnel is a rock-climbing wall, with five climbing tracks. Other sports facilities include Flow-Rider surf simulator, The Perfect Storm (dual water-slides), a full-size basketball court, and Adventure Dunes – a nine-hole, par 26 golf 'course'.

AEGEAN ODYSSEY
★★★

CULTURAL EXPLORATION AND LEARNING ARE THE BIG DRAW FOR THIS SHIP

Size: .... Small Ship	Passenger/Crew Ratio (lower beds): 1.8
Tonnage: 12,094	Cabins (total): 216
Cruise Line: .... Voyages to Antiquity	Size Range (sq ft/m): 130.0–550.0/12.0–51.0
Former Names: ... *Aegean I, Aegean Dolphin, Dolphin,*	Cabins (for one person): 26
Alkyon, Narcis	Cabins with balcony: 42
Builder: .... Santierul N. Galatz (Romania)	Cabins (wheelchair accessible): 2
Entered Service: 1972	Wheelchair accessibility: .... Fair
Length (ft/m): 460.9/140.5	Elevators: 2
Propulsion/Propellers: .... diesel (10,296kW)/2	Casino (gaming tables): .... No
Total Crew: 200	Self-Service Launderette: .... No
Passengers (lower beds): 408	Onboard currency: .... US$
Passenger Space Ratio (lower beds): 29.6	

THE SHIP. This small and somewhat dated ship was tastefully converted and provides a comfortable environment. Its profile includes a well-shaped funnel that balances an angular stern – the result of a 'chop-and-stretch' operation many years ago. Originally built to carry munitions, the ship's hull is strong, and the open deck space, covered in teak, is good for a small ship.

The Promenade Deck houses most public rooms. A forward observation lounge, The Charleston Lounge has a large dance floor and bar, and classy black and red decor. The ship also has a good-size library. Some public room fittings are held together by the 'patch-and-fix' method, but pleasing, warm color combinations help create a spacious, open feel. Despite the shakes and rattles of the interior fittings when at full speed, it's the character of the ship, its generous open deck space (and gorgeous, highly polished thick wood handrails), and an excellent lecture and enrichment program that all help to nudge the final score higher than one would normally expect for a 1970s ship. It will appeal to mature-age couples and solo travelers looking for an enriching experience on a smart yet traditional ship. Gratuities are included, as are selected wines with dinner (or beer/soft drinks), most shore excursions, and bottled mineral water. Note that the ship will be chartered for three years to non-profit, US-based Road Scholar (operated by Voyages to Antiquity) from April 2020.

ACCOMMODATION. There are many different price grades (six of which are for solo-occupancy cabins), with

BERLITZ'S RATINGS	Possible	Achieved
Ship	500	278
Accommodation	200	118
Food	400	227
Service	400	243
Entertainment	100	50
Cruise Experience	400	215

OVERALL SCORE 1131 points out of 2000

about half designated as Balcony Class. The numbering is nautically incorrect, however, with even-numbered cabins on the starboard side instead of on the port side of the ship, but lifeboat numbering is correct. Most cabins have an outside view, with similar sizes and configuration. All have a small refrigerator. Closet, drawer, and luggage storage space is limited in the lower-grades; most bathrooms are partly tiled, with storage space for toiletries.

DINING. The Marco Polo Restaurant is located on the lowest passenger deck and has a high ceiling. Seating is mostly at large tables (there are no tables for two) in an open-seating (dine when and with whom you want). Portholes, not windows, are set high, and allow natural light in during the day. The cuisine is Continental, but the selection of breads, cheeses, and fruit is limited. Meats, fish, and poultry items are not of a high quality. For casual meals, self-serve breakfast and lunch buffets are available at the Terrace Café, with indoor-outdoor seating that includes a 'Tapas on the Terrace' each evening, and daily grilled specialties.

ENTERTAINMENT. The Ambassador Lounge is a single-level lounge/bar with tub chairs or banquette seating. Sight lines from many seats are obstructed due to several support pillars.

SPA/FITNESS. The pleasant Wellness Center has a men's dry sauna, women's wet sauna (steam 'pods'), two treatment rooms, a beauty salon, and a fitness area.

AIDAAURA
★★★+

THIS UPBEAT, FAMILY-FRIENDLY SHIP IS FOR CASUAL, NO-FRILLS CRUISING

Size: .... Mid-size Ship	Passenger/Crew Ratio (lower beds): 3.0
Tonnage: 42,289	Cabins (total): 633
Cruise Line: .... AIDA Cruises	Size Range (sq ft/m): 145.3–344.4/13.5–32.0
Former Names: .... none	Cabins (for one person): 0
Builder: .... Aker MTW (Germany)	Cabins with balcony: 60
Entered Service: ....Apr 2003	Cabins (wheelchair accessible): 4
Length (ft/m): 665.5/202.8	Wheelchair accessibility: .... Good
Propulsion/Propellers: diesel-electric (27,150kW)/2	Elevators: 6
Total Crew: 389	Casino (gaming tables): .... No
Passengers (lower beds): 1,266	Self-Service Launderette: .... Yes
Passenger Space Ratio (lower beds): 33.4	Onboard currency: .... Euros

THE SHIP. *AIDAaura* has quite a modern profile, with a swept-back funnel and wedge-shaped stern. The bows show the red lips/ and blue eyes of *Aïda* (from Verdi's opera, written in 1871). Open deck space is reasonable. Dip pools, hot tubs, and tiered seating provide a 'beach-like' environment.

AIDA Bar, the main social gathering place common to all AIDA ships, has a star-shaped bar and tables for standing drinkers. Other facilities include a shore-excursion counter, library, seminar rooms, duty-free shop, several bars and lounges, and eateries.

There are children's and youth programs (in five age groupings), and Club Team members are dedicated to making sure that all have a good time.

This is über-casual cruising for youthful German-speaking urbanite families, with tablecloth-free eating, and little contact with the few staff. The dress code is simple: casual (no ties) at all times.

ACCOMMODATION. There are several grades, from (more) spacious suites to interior (no-view) cabins. Contrary to maritime tradition (even-numbered cabins on the port side, odd-numbered cabins on the starboard side), cabin numbers progress numerically (example: 8201–8276 on the port side; 8101–8176 on the starboard side). All have two beds convertible to queen-size. Some

BERLITZ'S RATINGS		
	Possible	Achieved
Ship	500	331
Accommodation	200	129
Food	400	232
Service	400	256
Entertainment	100	71
Cruise Experience	400	259

OVERALL SCORE 1278 points out of 2000

also have extra beds/berths for kids; some have interconnecting doors.

The decor is bright and whimsical, with multi-patterned fabric accents, and wood-trimmed round-edged cabinetry. Beds have duvets and a colorful, Arabian-style overhead fabric canopy; windows have full pull-down blackout blinds. Lifeboats may obstruct views in some central cabins. Bathrooms are compact, with shower enclosure, washbasin, toilet and wall-mounted wash/shampoo dispenser (take your own toiletries if you require other items), and two towels. Cotton bathrobes are provided for suite-grade occupants. Night-time turndown service is not provided.

Balcony cabins have easy-open sliding doors; those on the lowest deck can be overlooked from the decks above.

Suite-grade accommodation has more space, better-quality furniture and furnishings, and a slightly larger bathroom with tub/shower.

DINING. Two self-serve eateries (for main meals) are included in the cruise fare: the Markt and Karibik, with open seating at tables of four to eight. Cutlery hangs in a rack (there are no soup spoons, only dessert spoons). It is often challenging to find a seat or a clean table.

The standard of food ranges from adequate to moderately good, with creative displays and presentation, and many food islands – always with a good selection of breads, cheeses, cold cuts, fruits, and make-your-own coffee and multiple-choice teas/tisanes.

Beer is at the push of a button or a pull of the tap, and table 'wine' is in carafes. Beverage stations open only during restaurant opening hours unless you go to the extra-cost coffee bar (Café Mare). Vending machines dispense out-of-hours snacks.

The (reservations required, extra cost) Rossini Restaurant (open for dinner) offers reasonably sound food and service.

ENTERTAINMENT. The Theater spans two decks, with a raised stage and bench seating with back rests. Sight lines are good from most seats, except some balcony sections with interruption from thick safety rails.

SPA/FITNESS. Body and Soul Spa has two saunas (one dry, one wet, with glass walls), body-pampering treatment rooms, relaxation area, showers, and ice walls. Outside (forward) is a bi-level 'FKK' (Freikoerperkultur – naked) sunbathing deck. A beauty/hair salon is located behind the showlounge.

AIDABELLA
★★★+

THIS UPBEAT, FAMILY-FRIENDLY SHIP IS GOOD FOR NO-FRILLS CRUISING

Size:	Mid-size Ship	Passenger/Crew Ratio (lower beds):	3.1
Tonnage:	69,203	Cabins (total):	1,025
Cruise Line:	AIDA Cruises	Size Range (sq ft/m):	145.3–473.2/13.5–44
Former Names:	none	Cabins (for one person):	0
Builder:	Meyer Werft (Germany)	Cabins with balcony:	480
Entered Service:	Apr 2008	Cabins (wheelchair accessible):	11
Length (ft/m):	826.7/252.0	Wheelchair accessibility:	Good
Propulsion/Propellers:	diesel-electric (36,000 kW)/2	Elevators:	10
Total Crew:	646	Casino (gaming tables):	Yes
Passengers (lower beds):	2,050	Self-Service Launderette:	Yes
Passenger Space Ratio (lower beds):	33.7	Onboard currency:	Euros

THE SHIP. *AIDAbella* is a smart sea-going urban theme park for young-at-heart German-speaking families, and kids will have fun with all the activities run by the Club Team. The ship has a swept-back funnel, wedge-shaped stern, and many bold colors. The bows show the red lips and blue eyes of *Aïda* (from Verdi's 1871 opera). AIDA Cruises (Germany's largest cruise line), is part of Costa Cruises, which itself is owned by Carnival Corporation.

Dip pools, hot tubs, splash and play areas, and tiered seating areas occupy the pool deck. There is no wrap-around outdoor promenade deck, although you can walk around the funnel area.

Several decks of public rooms and facilities sit above the accommodation decks. Most public room names are shared aboard the company's ships: AIDA Bar, for example, is the main social gathering place, with a star-shaped bar (one of the longest at sea), with many standing tables. There are other bars and lounges, and a small casino, observation lounge and 'art' gallery. In the shore tender embarkation area is a street scene, with bar/coffee counter and lookout 'balcony.' It's ultra-casual and all printed material is in German. Eating is more about quantity than quality, in self-serve (tablecloth-free) buffet eateries, unless you pay extra for eating in a 'specialty' restaurant, as on land. You get lots of high-energy entertainment,

BERLITZ'S RATINGS		
	Possible	Achieved
Ship	500	360
Accommodation	200	130
Food	400	234
Service	400	259
Entertainment	100	72
Cruise Experience	400	262

OVERALL SCORE 1317 points out of 2000

fun activities, and self-serve buffet restaurants – although the number of staff is small. Decibel levels are high – it's impossible to escape the rap-rich 'music' in the cabin hallways and elevators 24/7.

ACCOMMODATION. Accommodation grades range from deluxe suites to interior (no-view) cabins.

Contrary to maritime tradition (even-numbered cabins on the port side, odd-numbered cabins on the starboard side – like the lifeboats), cabin numbers progress numerically (example: 8201–8276 on the port side; 8101–8176 on the starboard side). All have two beds (convertible to queen-size). Some cabins also have two extra beds/berths, and some have interconnecting doors – good for families.

The decor is bright and minimalist. Cabins have multi-patterned fabrics, wood-trimmed, round-edge cabinetry, and rattan/wood-look furniture. Beds have duvets and overhead fabric canopy; windows have full pull-down blackout blinds (useful in destinations with long daylight hours). Note that the night-time turndown service (standard aboard most ships) is not provided.

Bathrooms are compact, with shower enclosure, small washbasin and toilet. Only a wall-mounted body wash/shampoo dispenser is provided, so take any other toiletries you may need.

Cabins with balconies have an easy-to-open sliding door, small drinks table and chairs, and a hammock (for one slim person). Note: balconies on the lowest deck can be overlooked by anyone on the decks above. Some cabins (5103, 5104, 5105, 5106, 5203, 5204, 5206 – forward on Deck 5) have an obstructed outside view.

DINING. Three self-serve eateries: Markt (Market), Bella Vista (for Italian cuisine), and Weite Welt (Wide World) restaurants have open seating at tables of four to eight. Cutlery is in a rack (not really hygienic), and there are no soup spoons (only dessert spoons). Food islands and active stations host a selection of breads, cheeses, cold cuts, fruits, coffee and teas. The fish section also has its own fish-smoking unit.

Push-button beer and table wine carafes for lunch and dinner are standard. The beverage stations open only during restaurant opening hours, except for an extra-cost coffee bar, while vending machines dispense out-of-hours snacks.

Reservations required, extra cost venues include Buffalo Steakhouse (for good steaks); Rossini Restaurant – with waiter service and à la carte cuisine. Casual eateries include a Sushi Bar, and Pizzeria Mare.

ENTERTAINMENT. The Theatrium has a raised stage, and is open to the central foyer on three levels (decks 9, 10, and 11), and topped by a glass dome.

SPA/FITNESS. Body and Soul wellness/oasis area spans two decks (with stairway connection), with saunas, steam rooms, and body treatment rooms (most named after places associated with the design theme), plus a fitness room with high-tech equipment, neat showers, funky changing rooms, plus a tropical garden with waxed palm trees and loungers. Sport enthusiasts can play billiards, volleyball or squash. An open-air wellness 'FKK' deck for relaxation/nude sunbathing is forward of the ship's mast.

AIDABLU
★★★+

THIS IS AN UPBEAT, FAMILY-FRIENDLY SHIP FOR NO-FRILLS FAMILY CRUISING

Size:	Mid-size Ship	Passenger/Crew Ratio (lower beds):	3.1
Tonnage:	71,100	Cabins (total):	1,096
Cruise Line:	AIDA Cruises	Size Range (sq ft/m):	145.3–473.2/13.5–44
Former Names:	none	Cabins (for one person):	0
Builder:	Meyer Werft (Germany)	Cabins with balcony:	491
Entered Service:	Apr 2010	Cabins (wheelchair accessible):	11
Length (ft/m):	831.1/253.3	Wheelchair accessibility:	Good
Propulsion/Propellers:	diesel-electric (36,000 kW)/2	Elevators:	10
Total Crew:	646	Casino (gaming tables):	Yes
Passengers (lower beds):	2,194	Self-Service Launderette:	Yes
Passenger Space Ratio (lower beds):	34.4	Onboard currency:	Euros

THE SHIP. The ship has a modernish profile, with swept-back funnel and wedge-shaped stern (back), while the bows display the red lips and blue eyes of *Aïda* (from Verdi's 1871 opera). AIDA Cruises, Germany's largest cruise line, is part of Costa Cruises, which is itself part of Carnival Corporation.

Open deck space is limited but does include some quiet space above the navigation bridge. Dip pools and hot tubs, plus seating areas, are in a cascading setting on the pool deck, with splash and play areas. There is no stroll-around promenade deck, although you can walk outdoors around the funnel area.

Most public rooms and facilities are above the accommodation decks, and *AIDAblu* has the same names for its public room as all ships in the fleet: AIDA Bar, for example, the main social gathering place, where the principal feature is a star-shaped bar (it's among the longest at sea), with many tables for standing drinkers.

A small casino has gaming tables and slot machines. There is also a separate aft sports deck, an observation lounge, and an 'art' gallery. The embarkation entryway has a bar and a lookout 'balcony,' cheerfully painted to look like a street scene in a city like Copenhagen.

A cruise aboard *AIDAblu* is all about cruising for youthful, laid-back German-speaking families with a diverse selection of children's and youth programs

BERLITZ'S RATINGS		
	Possible	Achieved
Ship	500	358
Accommodation	200	129
Food	400	234
Service	400	262
Entertainment	100	72
Cruise Experience	400	263

OVERALL SCORE 1318 points out of 2000

(and Club Team members dedicated to making sure that everyone has a good time). An AIDA cruise isn't cheap, but includes high-tech entertainment, fun activities, self-serve buffet restaurant food, and casual, tablecloth-free eating, but few staff. Port taxes and gratuities are included.

ACCOMMODATION. There are several price grades, from suites to interior (no-view) cabins, so cabin choice is simple.

Contrary to maritime traditions (even-numbered cabins on the port side, odd-numbered cabins on the starboard side), cabin numbers progress numerically (example: 8201–8276 on the port side; 8101–8176 on the starboard side). All suites and cabins have two beds (convertible to queen-size bed). Some cabins also have two extra beds/berths for children; some cabins have interconnecting doors.

The decor is bright, youthful, rather minimalist, and slightly whimsical. All cabins are accented with multi-patterned fabrics, wood-trimmed cabinetry, and rattan or wood-look furniture. Beds have duvets and a colorful overhead canopy. The windows have full pull-down blackout blinds (useful in destinations with long daylight hours).

Bathrooms are compact, practical units, with shower enclosure, small washbasin and toilet. Only a wall-mounted body wash/shampoo dispenser is provided, so take your own toiletries if you require more than this.

Thick cotton bathrobes are provided, as are face and small 'bath' towels, in different colors. A hairdryer is located in the vanity unit in the cabin. There is no night-time turndown service.

Balcony cabins have an easy-open sliding door, a small drinks table, and two small chairs. Some cabins (forward on Deck 5 – Nos 5103, 5104, 5105, 5106, 5203, 5204, 5206) have a balcony with an outside 'view' (more like outside light), but are obstructed by steel bulkheads.

Suite-grade accommodation offers more drawer and storage space, better-quality furniture and furnishings, a larger lounge area, a bathroom with a tub, and a larger balcony (those at the front and stern are the most desirable).

DINING. There are three self-serve eateries: Markt (Market), Bella Vista (for Italian cuisine), and East restaurants. Additionally, there's a Buffalo Steakhouse (which serves excellent steaks), an à la carte Rossini Restaurant with waiter and sommelier service, a Sushi Bar, a Pizzeria Mare, and Café Mare. These venues are open at set times (there are no 24-hour-a-day outlets, because there is little demand), although the Pizzeria typically is open until late.

In the three self-serve restaurants, meals are taken when you want them, with open seating at tables of four to eight. Cutlery hangs in a rack, and there are no soup spoons, only dessert spoons.

Multiple food islands and active stations cut down on the waiting time for food. There is always a big selection of breads, cheeses, cold cuts, fruits, and make-your-own coffee and teas – with a choice of more than 30 types of loose-leaf regular and herbal teas. There are 1,200 items of food, and the fish section has its own fish-smoking unit.

Beer is available at the push of a button or a pull of the tap, and table wine is provided in carafes on each table for lunch and dinner. Beverage stations open only during restaurant opening hours, but there is an extra-cost coffee bar (Café Mare). For something to nibble on, vending machines dispense out-of-hours snacks.

Other dining options. Rossini Restaurant, with mostly high-back seats, is small and intimate. Open for dinner only, it has a set menu, plus daily 'specials,' à la carte pricing, and reservations are required. Tablecloths are provided, the food is good, and service is acceptable.

Buffalo Steakhouse has an open 'display' kitchen, and offers various steak cuts, plus roast lamb rack. Wine or any other drinks cost extra.

A 12-seater sushi counter is for Japanese-style sushi and sashimi dishes, at extra cost.

A wine bar, Vinotheque, located in front of the Weide Welt (Wide World) Restaurant, offers premium wines, and Davidoff cigars (although you can't smoke them at the bar – or anywhere inside the ship). Worth mentioning is a Brauhaus microbrewery with good beer at a reasonable price and table-service food in a beer garden setting.

ENTERTAINMENT. The central, tri-level Theatrium (showlounge) is open to the main foyer and other public areas, and topped by a glass dome. Amphitheater-style seating is on three decks (the bench seating on the two upper levels – but not on the lower level – has back supports), plus standing tables, although sight lines to the raised thrust stage area are less than good from many of the seats.

SPA/FITNESS. The extensive Body and Soul wellness/oasis area is located on two decks (connected by a stairway). There is also an open-air wellness 'FKK' deck for relaxation/nude sunbathing forward of the ship's mast.

AIDACARA
★★★

THIS IS A BUSY, FAMILY-FRIENDLY SHIP FOR FRUGAL CRUISEGOERS

Size:	Mid-size Ship	Passenger/Crew Ratio (lower beds):	3.1
Tonnage:	38,557	Cabins (total):	590
Cruise Line:	AIDA Cruises	Size Range (sq ft/m):	145.3–376.7/13.5–35.0
Former Names:	Aida, Das Clubschiff	Cabins (for one person):	0
Builder:	Kvaerner Masa-Yards (Finland)	Cabins with balcony:	48
Entered Service:	Jun 1996	Cabins (wheelchair accessible):	6
Length (ft/m):	634.1/193.3	Wheelchair accessibility:	Good
Propulsion/Propellers:	diesel(21,720kw)/2	Elevators:	5
Total Crew:	370	Casino (gaming tables):	No
Passengers (lower beds):	1,180	Self-Service Launderette:	Yes
Passenger Space Ratio (lower beds):	32.6	Onboard currency:	Euros

THE SHIP. AIDAcara has a modernish profile with a swept-back funnel and wedge-shaped stern. The bows feature the red lips/and blue eyes of Aïda (from Verdi's 1871 opera) Open deck space is reasonable while dip pools, hot tubs, and seating areas are in a tiered setting with a 'beach-like' theme.

AIDA Bar, the social gathering place common to all AIDA ships, has a star-shaped bar and tables for standing drinkers. Other facilities include a shore-excursion counter, library, seminar rooms, duty-free shop, several bars and lounges, and eateries.

There are children's and youth programs (in five age groupings), and Club Team members are dedicated to making sure that all have a good time.

This is über-casual cruising for youthful German-speaking families, with tablecloth-free eating, and few staff. The dress code is simple: casual (no ties) at all times.

ACCOMMODATION. There are several grades, from larger suites to interior (no-view) cabins. Cabin numbers progress numerically (example: 8201–8276 on the port side; 8101–8176 on the starboard side). All have two beds convertible to queen-size. Some also have extra beds/berths for kids; some have interconnecting doors.

The decor is bright and whimsical, with multi-patterned fabric accents, and wood-trimmed

BERLITZ'S RATINGS		
	Possible	Achieved
Ship	500	305
Accommodation	200	110
Food	400	222
Service	400	239
Entertainment	100	66
Cruise Experience	400	240

OVERALL SCORE 1182 points out of 2000

round-edged cabinetry. Beds have duvets and a colorful, Arabian-style fabric canopy overhead; windows have full pull-down blackout blinds. Lifeboats obstruct views in some central cabins. Bathrooms are compact, with a shower enclosure, washbasin, toilet and wall-mounted wash/shampoo dispenser, two towels (face towel and small 'bath' towel). Bathrobes are provided for suite-grade occupants. Night-time turndown service is not provided.

Balcony cabins have easy-open sliding doors, but those on the lowest deck can be overlooked from those on the decks above.

Suite-grade accommodation has more space, better-quality furniture and furnishings, and a slightly larger bathroom with tub/shower.

DINING. Two self-serve eateries (for main meals) are included in the cruise fare: the Markt and Karibik, with open seating at tables of four to eight. Cutlery hangs in a rack (there are no soup spoons, only dessert spoons). It is often challenging to find a seat or a clean table.

The standard of food ranges from adequate to moderately good, with creative displays and presentation and many food islands – with a selection of breads, cheeses, cold cuts, fruits, and make-your-own coffee and multiple-choice teas/tisanes.

Beer is at the push of a button or a pull of the tap, and table 'wine' is in carafes. Beverage stations open only during restaurant opening hours, except for extra-cost Café Mare. Vending machines dispense out-of-hours snacks.

The (reservations required, extra cost) Rossini Restaurant (open for dinner) has reasonably sound food and service and tablecloths.

ENTERTAINMENT. The bi-level Theater has a raised stage and bench seating with back rests.

Sight lines are good from most seats, except some balcony sections with interruption from thick safety rails.

SPA/FITNESS. Body and Soul Spa has two saunas (one dry, one wet, with glass walls), body-pampering treatment rooms, relaxation area, showers, and ice walls. Outside (forward) is a bi-level 'FKK' (Freikoerperkultur – naked) sunbathing deck. A beauty/hair salon is located behind the showlounge.

AIDADIVA
★★★+

TRY THIS MID-SIZE FAMILY-FRIENDLY SHIP FOR A GOOD-TIME CASUAL CRUISE EXPERIENCE

Size:	Mid-size Ship	Passenger/Crew Ratio (lower beds):	3.1
Tonnage:	69,203	Cabins (total):	1,025
Cruise Line:	AIDA Cruises	Size Range (sq ft/m):	145.3–473.2/13.5–44
Former Names:	none	Cabins (for one person):	0
Builder:	Meyer Werft (Germany)	Cabins with balcony:	480
Entered Service:	Apr 2007	Cabins (wheelchair accessible):	11
Length (ft/m):	830.0/253.3	Wheelchair accessibility:	Good
Propulsion/Propellers:	diesel-electric (36,000 kW)/2	Elevators:	10
Total Crew:	646	Casino (gaming tables):	Yes
Passengers (lower beds):	2,050	Self-Service Launderette:	Yes
Passenger Space Ratio (lower beds):	33.7	Onboard currency:	Euros

THE SHIP. *AIDAdiva* is a smart choice for young-at-heart German-speaking families (the Club Team members take good care of kids and teens). In fact, it's a Robinson Club-like floating resort, with a contemporary profile, swept-back funnel, wedge-shaped stern, and many bold colors. The bows have the telltale red lips and blue eyes of *Aïda* (from Verdi's 1871 opera). AIDA Cruises (Germany's largest cruise line), is part of Costa Cruises, itself owned by Carnival Corporation.

Dip pools, hot tubs, and seating areas are in a tiered pool-deck setting, with splash and play areas. There is no walk-around outdoor promenade deck, although you can walk around the funnel area, and around part of Deck 5.

Several decks of public rooms and facilities are above the accommodation decks, with most public room names shared by all the company's ships: AIDA Bar, for example, is the main social gathering place, with a star-shaped bar and many tables for standing drinkers. There is a small casino, an observation lounge, and 'art' gallery. In the tender embarkation entryway (it looks like a street scene) a bar/coffee counter and lookout 'balcony' provides a nice welcome.

It's all ultra-casual, and printed material is in German only. Eating is more about quantity than quality, in self-serve (tablecloth-free) buffet eat-

BERLITZ'S RATINGS		
	Possible	Achieved
Ship	500	351
Accommodation	200	129
Food	400	231
Service	400	261
Entertainment	100	70
Cruise Experience	400	262

OVERALL SCORE 1304 points out of 2000

eries, unless you pay extra for eating in a 'specialty' restaurant. There are lots of high-energy entertainment, fun activities, and self-serve buffet restaurants, but few staff. Decibel levels are high – it's impossible to escape the rap-rich 'music' in the cabin hallways and elevators 24/7.

ACCOMMODATION. There are several accommodation grades, from deluxe suites to interior (no-view) cabins.

Contrary to maritime tradition (even-numbered cabins on the port side, odd-numbered cabins on the starboard side – like the lifeboats), cabin numbers progress numerically (example: 8201–8276 on the port side; 8101–8176 on the starboard side). All have two beds (convertible to a queen-size bed). Some cabins have two extra beds/berths; some have interconnecting doors – good for families.

The decor is bright, minimalist, and slightly whimsical, with multi-patterned fabrics, wood-trimmed, round-edge cabinetry, and rattan/wood-look furniture. Beds have duvets and fabric canopy overhead; windows have full pull-down blackout blinds (useful in destinations with long daylight hours); a hairdryer is in the vanity unit. Note that the night-time turndown service (standard aboard almost all ships) is not provided.

Bathrooms are compact but practical, with shower enclosure and wall-mounted body wash/shampoo dispenser, small washbasin and toilet.

Cabins with balconies have an easy-open sliding door, small drinks table and chairs, plus a hammock (for one person). Balconies on the lowest deck can be overlooked by anyone on the decks above. Some cabins (5103, 5104, 5105, 5106, 5203, 5204, 5206 – forward on Deck 5) have an obstructed outside view.

DINING. Three self-serve eateries: Markt (Market), Bella Vista (for Italian cuisine), and Weite Welt (Wide World) restaurants have open seating at tables of four to eight. Cutlery is in a rack (not really hygienic); there are no soup spoons (only dessert spoons). Food islands and active stations cut down on the waiting time. There is always a selection of breads, cheeses, cold cuts, fruits, coffee and teas. The fish section also has its own fish-smoking unit.

Push-button beer is available, and table wine carafes are on each table for lunch and dinner. The beverage stations open only during restaurant opening hours, except for the extra-cost coffee bar (Café Mare). Vending machines dispense out-of-hours snacks.

Reservations required, extra cost venues include Buffalo Steakhouse (for good steaks); Rossini Restaurant – with waiter service and à la carte cuisine. Casual eateries include a Sushi Bar, and Pizzeria Mare.

ENTERTAINMENT. The tri-level Theatrium is open to the central foyer, and topped by a glass dome. There is bench-seating, with back supports on the two upper levels, plus standing tables, but sight lines to the raised stage are not all good.

SPA/FITNESS. Body and Soul wellness/oasis area spans two decks (with stairway connection), with saunas, steam rooms, and body treatment rooms (most named after places associated with the design theme), plus a fitness room with high-tech equipment, neat showers, funky changing rooms, and a tropical garden with waxed palm trees and loungers. Sport enthusiasts can play billiards, volleyball or squash. An open-air wellness 'FKK' deck for relaxation/nude sunbathing is forward of the ship's mast.

AIDALUNA
★★★+

AN UPBEAT, FAMILY-FRIENDLY, AND CHEERFUL SHIP, BUT IT LACKS ANY FINESSE

Size:	Mid-size Ship	Passenger/Crew Ratio (lower beds):	3.1
Tonnage:	69,203	Cabins (total):	1,025
Cruise Line:	AIDA Cruises	Size Range (sq ft/m):	145.3–473.2/13.5–44
Former Names:	none	Cabins (for one person):	0
Builder:	Meyer Werft (Germany)	Cabins with balcony:	480
Entered Service:	Apr 2009	Cabins (wheelchair accessible):	11
Length (ft/m):	831.1/253.3	Wheelchair accessibility:	Good
Propulsion/Propellers:	diesel-electric (36,000 kW)/2	Elevators:	10
Total Crew:	646	Casino (gaming tables):	Yes
Passengers (lower beds):	2,050	Self-Service Launderette:	Yes
Passenger Space Ratio (lower beds):	33.7	Onboard currency:	Euros

THE SHIP. *AIDAluna* caters well to German-speaking families. It's rather like a floating Robinson Club, with a contemporary profile, swept-back funnel, and wedge-shaped aft. The bows show the red lips and blue eyes of *Aïda* (from Verdi's 1871 opera). AIDA Cruises (Germany's largest cruise line), is part of Costa Cruises, which itself is owned by Carnival Corporation.

Dip pools, hot tubs, and tiered seating areas on the pool deck inspire a 'beach-like' environment, with splash and play areas. There is no wraparound outdoor promenade deck, although you can walk around the funnel area. .

Several decks of public rooms and facilities are above the accommodation decks, with most public room names shared aboard all the company's ships: AIDA Bar, for example, is the social gathering place; it features a star-shaped bar (with a combined length among the longest at sea), with many tables for standing drinkers. There are multiple bars and lounges, a small casino, an observation lounge, and 'art' gallery. The tender embarkation area looks like a street scene, and a bar/coffee counter and lookout 'balcony' provides a nice welcome.

The dress code is ultra-casual and all printed material is in German only. Eating is more about quantity than quality, in self-serve (tablecloth-free) buffet eateries, unless you pay extra for

BERLITZ'S RATINGS		
	Possible	Achieved
Ship	500	351
Accommodation	200	129
Food	400	232
Service	400	262
Entertainment	100	72
Cruise Experience	400	263

OVERALL SCORE 1309 points out of 2000

eating in a 'specialty' restaurant, as on land. There is high-energy entertainment, fun activities, and self-serve buffet restaurants. The number of staff is small, but the decibel levels are high – it's impossible to escape rap-rich 'music' in cabin hallways and elevators 24/7.

ACCOMMODATION. There are several accommodation grades, from deluxe suites to interior (no-view) cabins.

Contrary to maritime tradition (even-numbered cabins on the port side, odd-numbered cabins on the starboard side – like the lifeboats), cabin numbers progress numerically (example: 8201–8276 on the port side; 8101–8176 on the starboard side). All have two beds (convertible to a queen-size bed). Some cabins also have two extra beds/berths, and some have interconnecting doors – good for families.

The decor is bright, minimalist, and slightly whimsical. Cabins have wood-trimmed, round-edge cabinetry, and rattan/wood-look furniture. Beds have duvets and fabric overhead canopy; windows have full pull-down blackout blinds (useful in destinations with long daylight hours); a hairdryer is in the vanity unit. Note that night-time turndown service (standard aboard most ships) is not provided.

Bathrooms are compact but practical, with shower enclosure, small washbasin and toilet. Only a wall-mounted body wash/shampoo dispenser is provided, so take any other toiletries you may need.

Cabins with balconies have an easy-to-open sliding door, small drinks table and chairs, plus a hammock (for one slim person). Note: balconies on the lowest deck can be overlooked from the decks above. Some cabins (5103, 5104, 5105, 5106, 5203, 5204, 5206 – forward on Deck 5) have an obstructed outside view.

DINING. Three self-serve eateries: Markt (Market), Bella Vista (for Italian cuisine), and Weite Welt (Wide World) restaurants have open seating at tables of four to eight. Cutlery is in a rack (not really hygienic); there are no soup spoons (only dessert spoons). Food islands and active stations cut down on waiting time. There is always a selection of breads, cheeses, cold cuts, fruits, coffee and teas. The fish section also has its own fish-smoking unit.

Beer and table wine is provided for lunch and dinner. Note that beverage stations open only during restaurant opening hours, except for an extra-cost coffee bar (Café Mare). Vending machines dispense out-of-hours snacks.

Other venues (some at extra cost) include Buffalo Steakhouse (for good steaks); Rossini Restaurant – with waiter service and à la carte cuisine. Casual eateries include a Sushi Bar, Almhütte ('alpine hut', a Bavaria-inspired eatery), and Pizzeria Mare.

ENTERTAINMENT. The Theatrium is open to the central foyer on three levels, and topped by a glass dome. There is bench-seating, with back supports on the two upper levels, plus standing tables, but sight lines to the raised stage are not all good.

SPA/FITNESS. Body and Soul wellness/oasis area is spread over two decks (with stairway connection), with saunas, steam rooms, and body treatment rooms (most named after places associated with the design theme), plus a fitness room with high-tech equipment, neat showers, funky changing rooms, plus a tropical garden with waxed palm trees and loungers. Sport enthusiasts can play billiards, volleyball or squash. An open-air wellness 'FKK' deck for relaxation/nude sunbathing is forward of the ship's mast.

AIDAMAR
★★★+

THIS MID-SIZE SHIP IS A PLAYGROUND FOR FAMILY-FRIENDLY, CASUAL CRUISING

Size:	Mid-size Ship	Passenger/Crew Ratio (lower beds):	3.1
Tonnage:	71,304	Cabins (total):	1,097
Cruise Line:	AIDA Cruises	Size Range (sq ft/m):	145.3–473.2/13.5–44
Former Names:	none	Cabins (for one person):	0
Builder:	Meyer Werft (Germany)	Cabins with balcony:	491
Entered Service:	Apr 2012	Cabins (wheelchair accessible):	11
Length (ft/m):	831.1/253.3	Wheelchair accessibility:	Good
Propulsion/Propellers:	diesel-electric (36,000 kW)/2	Elevators:	10
Total Crew:	646	Casino (gaming tables):	Yes
Passengers (lower beds):	2,194	Self-Service Launderette:	Yes
Passenger Space Ratio (lower beds):	34.6	Onboard currency:	Euros

THE SHIP. *AIDAmar* is for German-speaking families (Club Team members take good care of kids and teens). It's a Robinson Club-like floating resort, with a contemporary profile, swept-back funnel, wedge-shaped stern, and many bold colors. The bows show the red lips and blue eyes of *Aïda* (from Verdi's 1871 opera). AIDA Cruises (Germany's largest cruise line), is part of Costa Cruises, which itself is owned by Carnival Corporation.

Dip pools, hot tubs, and seating areas are in a tiered setting on the pool deck – a 'beach-like' environment, with splash and play areas. There is no wrap-around outdoor promenade deck, although you can walk around the funnel area, and around part of Deck 5.

Several decks of public rooms and facilities are above the accommodation decks, with most public room names shared aboard all the company's ships: AIDA Bar, for example, is the social gathering place; it features a star-shaped bar (with a combined length among the longest at sea), with many tables for standing drinkers. There are several other bars and lounges, small casino, an observation lounge, and 'art' gallery. In the embarkation entryway (it looks like a street scene) a bar/coffee counter and lookout 'balcony' provides a nice welcome.

The dress code is ultra-casual and all printed material is in German only. Eating is more about

BERLITZ'S RATINGS		
	Possible	Achieved
Ship	500	351
Accommodation	200	129
Food	400	232
Service	400	261
Entertainment	100	72
Cruise Experience	400	262

OVERALL SCORE 1307 points out of 2000

quantity than quality, in self-serve (tablecloth-free) buffet eateries, unless you pay extra for eating in a 'specialty' restaurant, as on land. You get lots of high-energy entertainment, fun activities, and self-serve buffet restaurants – although the number of staff is small. Decibel levels are high – it's impossible to escape rap-rich 'music' in the cabin hallways and elevators 24/7.

ACCOMMODATION. There are several accommodation grades, from deluxe suites to interior (no-view) cabins.

Contrary to maritime tradition (even-numbered cabins on the port side, odd-numbered cabins on the starboard side – like the lifeboats), cabin numbers progress numerically (example: 8201–8276 on the port side; 8101–8176 on the starboard side). All have two beds (convertible to a queen-size bed). Some cabins also have two extra beds/berths, and some have interconnecting doors – good for families.

The decor is bright, minimalist, and slightly whimsical, with multi-patterned fabrics, wood-trimmed, round-edge cabinetry, and rattan/wood-look furniture. Beds have duvets and fabric headboard canopy; windows have full pull-down blackout blinds (useful in destinations with long daylight hours); a hairdryer is in the vanity unit. Note that the night-time turndown service (standard aboard almost all ships) is not provided, and there is no cabin service after 3pm.

Bathrooms are compact but practical, with shower enclosure, small washbasin and toilet. Only a wall-mounted body wash/shampoo dispenser is provided, so take any other toiletries you may need.

Cabins with balconies; these have an easy-to-open sliding door, small drinks table and chairs, plus a hammock (for one slim person). Note: balconies on the lowest deck can be overlooked by anyone on the decks above. Some cabins (5103, 5104, 5105, 5106, 5203, 5204, 5206 – forward on Deck 5) have an obstructed outside view.

DINING. Three self-serve eateries: Markt (Market), Bella Vista (for Italian cuisine), and Weite Welt (Wide World) restaurants have open seating at tables of four to eight. Cutlery is in a rack (not really hygienic); there are no soup spoons (only dessert spoons). Food islands and active stations cut down on the waiting time. There is always a selection of breads, cheeses, cold cuts, fruits, coffee and teas. The fish section also has its own fish-smoking unit.

Push-button beer is provided, and wine carafes are on each table for lunch and dinner. The beverage stations open only during restaurant opening hours, except for the extra-cost coffee bar (Café Mare). Vending machines dispense out-of-hours snacks.

Reservations required, extra cost venues include Buffalo Steakhouse (for good steaks); Rossini Restaurant – with waiter service and à la carte cuisine. Casual eateries include a Sushi Bar, and Pizzeria Mare.

ENTERTAINMENT. The Theatrium is open to the central foyer on three levels, and topped by a glass dome. There is bench-seating, with back supports only on the two upper levels, plus standing tables, but sight lines to the raised stage are not all good.

SPA/FITNESS. Body and Soul wellness/oasis area is spread over two decks (with stairway connection), with saunas, steam rooms, and body treatment rooms (most named after places associated with the design theme), plus a fitness room with high-tech equipment, neat showers, funky changing rooms, plus a tropical garden with waxed palm trees and loungers. Sport enthusiasts can play billiards, volleyball or squash. An open-air wellness 'FKK' deck for relaxation/nude sunbathing is forward of the ship's mast.

AIDANOVA
★★★+

THIS TECHNOLOGICALLY ADVANCED SHIP HAS NUMEROUS FEATURES FOR THE ACTIVE

Size:	Large Resort Ship	Passenger/Crew Ratio (lower beds):	3.4
Tonnage:	183,900	Cabins (total):	2,500
Cruise Line:	AIDA Cruises	Size Range (sq ft/m):	139.9–785.0/713.0–73.0
Former Names:	None	Cabins (for one person):	0
Builder:	Meyer Werft (Germany)	Cabins with balcony:	1,655
Entered Service:	December 2018	Cabins (wheelchair accessible):	
Length (ft/m):	1,105.6/337.0	Wheelchair accessibility:	Good
Propulsion/Propellers:	LNG/diesel/2 azimuthing pods	Elevators:	22
Total Crew:	1,500	Casino (gaming tables):	Yes
Passengers (lower beds):	5,000	Self-Service Launderette:	No
Passenger Space Ratio (lower beds):	36.7	Onboard currency:	Euros

THE SHIP. This is the first large, stunning resort-style cruise ship (think: *AIDAprima* on steroids) that can operate using only LNG to power its four, main dual-fuel engines. Much larger than all other AIDA ships, there is more open deck space, more public bars, lounges, and eating venues – and, naturally, it accommodates many more passengers. Also, in a complete change of direction – it's the first ship in the fleet with a high (proper) crew complement to provide the service levels required in the many multiple dining venues and to staff the various facilities (in other words, it's a regular cruise ship).

Outdoor facilities include a Four Elements water park with two large waterslides, rock climbing walls, and pools, splash pools, hot tubs, and poolside mega-screen; a complete walk-around open promenade deck; AIDA Beach Club (a relaxation zone by day that morphs into a party zone at night); and various open deck sunbathing spots.

Inside, you'll meet Pepper, a 4-ft- (1.2-m-) tall white humanoid robot, who is seaworthy and speaks English, German, and Italian, although he won't take your carry-on luggage. You'll see several Pepper clones around the ship, acting as information helpers.

There are 17 restaurants and eateries, 23 bars and drinking places (including a two-deck high AIDA plaza lounge), numerous lounges, a large fitness center, and a small casino. The ship produces its own (lager) beer in its Brauhaus.

BERLITZ'S RATINGS		
	Possible	Achieved
Ship	500	400
Accommodation	200	135
Food	400	232
Service	400	261
Entertainment	100	77
Cruise Experience	400	267
OVERALL SCORE 1372 points out of 2000		

AIDAnova is all about cruising for youthful, laid-back, German-speaking families with a diverse selection of children's and youth programs and a horde of enthusiastic Club Team members dedicated to making sure that everyone has a good time – all in a carefree beach club-like setting that makes tattoos welcome. An AIDA cruise isn't cheap, but there is constant high-tech entertainment, fun activities, and plenty of food in the self-serve (tablecloth-free) buffet restaurants. Port taxes and basic gratuities are included. The dress code is simple: casual (no ties) at all times.

Whether you'll have time to try everything the ship has to offer is debatable. You will certainly need to plan well in order to manage your time successfully (and you may need a vacation afterwards – to recover!). There are three pricing levels – AIDA Premium, AIDA Vario, and Just AIDA – depending on what you want to be included.

ACCOMMODATION. There are numerous accommodation grades. The price you pay depends on the size, location, and grade you choose, from the smallest interior (no view) cabin (140 sq ft/13 sq m) to the largest penthouse suite (785 sq ft/73 sq m), including 24 cabins (12 with balcony, 12 interior no view) for solo travelers (a first for AIDA Cruises), and family cabins that sleep up to five. However, most are of the basic, no frills type (think Ikea-style fittings lacking rounded edges and minimalist decor). Suite grades get a Segafredo coffee machine.

DINING. The feeding of the 5,000-plus includes large serve-yourself buffet venues Markt Restaurant, Weite Welt Restaurant, and Bella Donna (Italian). Family venues include Fuego Restaurant, Sharfe Ecke, and East West Restaurant. All are included in the cruise fare.

Cost-extra venues include The Oceans (for seafood), Time Machine Restaurant (think: waiters with magic wands), Rossini (high-quality cuisine), Buffalo Steakhouse (American fare), Brasserie French Kiss (classic French cuisine), Brauhause Restaurant, Ristorante Casa Nova (Mediterranean cuisine), a Churrascaria Steakhouse, a Sushi Bar and Teppanyaki Asia Grill, and Street Food Mile.

Extra cost Starbucks coffees can be found in Café Mare, while a cooking studio provides hands-on (cost-extra) cooking classes.

ENTERTAINMENT. A large Theatricum spans three decks and is for the big shows (AIDA Cruises is known for its contemporary entertainment with attitude). Look for artists' entry through 'The Tunnel.'

SPA/FITNESS. The Body and Soul Organic Spa spans two decks, and includes five (co-ed) saunas, steam rooms, high-tech fitness center, a relaxation zone with hot tubs, and numerous body treatment rooms. Sports facilities include a basketball/volleyball court, golf simulator, golf cage, putting green, a high rope-walk course, rock climbing, and a jogging track.

AIDAPERLA
★★★★

THIS COLORFUL ULTRA-CASUAL CRUISE SHIP IS FOR YOUTHFUL GERMAN-SPEAKING FAMILIES

Size:	Large Resort Ship	Passenger/Crew Ratio (lower beds):	3.6
Tonnage:	124,100	Cabins (total):	1,643
Cruise Line:	AIDA Cruises	Size Range (sq ft/m):	139.9-914.9/13.0-85.0
Former Names:	none	Cabins (for one person):	0
Builder:	Mitsubishi Heavy Industries (Japan)	Cabins with balcony:	1,133
Entered Service:	Jul 2017	Cabins (wheelchair accessible):	29
Length (ft/m):	984.2/300.0	Wheelchair accessibility:	Good
Propulsion/Propellers:	diesel-electric/2 azimuthing pods	Elevators:	18
		Casino (gaming tables):	Yes
Total Crew:	900	Self-Service Launderette:	Yes
Passengers (lower beds):	3,286	Onboard currency:	Euros
Passenger Space Ratio (lower beds):	37.7		

THE SHIP. When you first step aboard, you may be greeted by Pepper, a 4-ft- (1.2-m-) tall white humanoid robot, who is seaworthy and speaks English, German, and Italian, although he won't take your carry-on luggage. You'll see Pepper(s) around the ship during the cruise, too, as information helpers.

AIDAperla has an unmistakably stark upright bow – a throwback to the early 20th-century ocean liners. It provides more of a 'cutting-edge' slicing effect through the water, giving greater speed. The cruise line's iconic pursed red lips adorn the bow. The ship has a dual-fuel propulsion system, which includes the possibility to switch to LNG fuel, when available.

The outdoor pools, located on Lanai Deck, can be used during the warmer summer season, when the waterslide (which starts at the funnel and courses through the colorful Beach Club) and a rock-climbing wall can be used.

A private 'Patio-Bereich' is an adults-only retreat with its own pool, lounge areas, and bar – the first aboard an AIDA ship.

Below the apartment blocks of balcony cabins, but above the safety (lifeboat) deck, alfresco eateries and hot tubs provide the outdoor lifestyle enjoyed by many. The eateries are not well protected from wind and rain, however, so they may prove to be underused during cool weather conditions.

Inside is the two-decks-high AIDA Beach Club, aft of the almost mid-ship-placed funnel; this can be

BERLITZ'S RATINGS		
	Possible	Achieved
Ship	500	402
Accommodation	200	143
Food	400	241
Service	400	270
Entertainment	100	77
Cruise Experience	400	283

OVERALL SCORE 1416 points out of 2000

covered by a large glass roof, which helps bring the outside inside during winter cruises in cold weather regions, reducing the open deck space.

Other features include glass panoramic elevators and a skywalk. The all-white Champagne Bar is cool. One bar has an ultra-Batman feel to it. There are numerous other bars (both indoors and outdoors, including a Brauhaus, for onboard-brewed beer), a cooking studio, library, biking station, shops, and an art gallery. The bar to try is at the bow – the Splash Bar!

AIDAperla is for youthful, laid-back, German-speaking families, with a diverse selection of children's and youth programs and enthusiastic Club Team members to make sure that everyone has a good time. An AIDA cruise isn't cheap, but you do get lots of high-tech entertainment, fun activities, and plenty of food at the self-serve buffet restaurants (with tablecloth-free eating), although not much contact with the relatively small number of staff. Port taxes and gratuities are included. The dress code is simple: casual (no ties) at all times.

ACCOMMODATION. Modern and minimalist but cheerful, it ranges from small interior (no-view) cabins to large two-bedroom suites, and one owner's suite.

Suites range from 344.4–914.9 sq ft (32–85 sq m), but most cabins are much more compact, starting at

139.9 sq ft (13 sq m). Suites have more drawer and storage space, better-quality furniture and furnishings, a larger lounge area, and a slightly larger bathroom with a tub (and larger balcony). Those at the front and stern are the most desirable.

Balcony cabins have beds adjacent to a floor-to ceiling door that slides open.

Thick cotton bathrobes are provided, as are two towels (a face towel and a 'bath' towel), in two different colors.

DINING. There are 13 dining and eatery choices (some with waiter service, some at extra cost; some include drinks such as beer and wine) in the company's self-serve Markt (Market) and Weite Welt (World Wide) restaurants. Here the chairs don't have armrests – they are uncomfortable, so you won't want to stay a long time – like shopping mall food court eateries ashore. The decor is, however, pleasingly bright. The food displays are attractive, and beer is available at the push of a button or a pull of the tap; table wine is provided in carafes on each table for lunch and dinner.

There's also Bella Donna Restaurant, and East Restaurant.

French Kiss is a casual French-style brasserie (the first of its type aboard an AIDA Cruises ship), with red/black chairs and the red lips of *Aïda* as the decor theme; there's also a Chef's Kitchen (part of the Cooking School), and even a Scharfe Ecke for popular Currywurst.

Restaurant Casa Nova is an elegant (extra-cost) Venetian-inspired venue with elegant surroundings, offering a white tablecloth setting for dinners (although the chairs are not comfortable and lack armrests).

Buffalo Steakhouse has an open 'display' kitchen, and features various prime steak cuts and sizes – Delmonico, New York Strip Loin, Porterhouse, and Filet, plus bison steaks – and roast lamb rack.

Reservations are required in Buffalo Steakhouse, Casa Nova Restaurant, Brasserie French Kiss, and Rossini-Gourmet Restaurant. Drinks are included in: Bella Donna, East Restaurant, French Kiss, Fuego Family Restaurant, Markt Restaurant, Scharfe Ecke, and the Weite Welt Restaurant. Worth a mention is a Brauhaus micro-brewery, with beer at reasonable prices.

ENTERTAINMENT. The tri-level Theatrium acts (no pun intended) as the showlounge; it is in the ship's center. It has an LED stage backdrop, but no bandstand. Shows are produced by AIDA Cruises' in-house department in a joint venture with SeeLive (Hamburg's Schmidt's Tivoli Theater).

SPA/FITNESS. The ship has an expansive Body and Soul Organic Spa, with multiple body-pampering treatment rooms, extra-cost saunas, steam rooms, thalassotherapy bath, changing rooms, and a beauty salon, plus manicure and pedicure salons. Extra-cost private couples 'wellness suites' are bookable.

Body and Soul sports activities include indoor cycling. Electric bicycles and extra-cost Segways are also available at the Biking Station, and there's a 2,152 sq ft (200 sq m) floating ice-rink on the Sports Deck (winter season only).

AIDAPRIMA
★★★★

FINE FAMILY-FRIENDLY SHIP FOR YEAR-ROUND CASUAL BUT ACTIVE CRUISES

Size:	Large Resort Ship	Passenger/Crew Ratio (lower beds):	3.6/1
Tonnage:	124,100	Cabins (total):	1,643
Cruise Line:	AIDA Cruises	Size Range (sq ft/m):	139.9–914.9/13.0–85.0
Former Names:	none	Cabins (for one person):	0
Builder:	Mitsubishi Heavy Industries (Japan)	Cabins with balcony:	1,133
Entered Service:	May 2016	Cabins (wheelchair accessible):	29
Length (ft/m):	984.2/300.0	Wheelchair accessibility:	Good
Propulsion/Propellers:	diesel-electric/2 azimuthing pods	Elevators:	18
Total Crew:	900	Casino (gaming tables):	Yes
Passengers (lower beds):	3,286	Self-Service Launderette:	Yes
Passenger Space Ratio (lower beds):	37.7	Onboard currency:	Euros

THE SHIP. *AIDAprima* has a stark upright bow (unusual for a cruise ship), a throwback to the early 20th-century ocean liners. It provides more of a 'cutting-edge' slicing effect through the water, giving greater speed. The cruise line's iconic pursed red lips adorn the bows. This is the first ship in the cruise industry to be fitted with a dual-fuel propulsion system, which includes the possibility to switch to LNG fuel, when available. When you first step aboard, you may be greeted by Pepper, a 4-ft- (1.2-m-) tall white humanoid robot, who is seaworthy and speaks English, German, and Italian, although he won't take your carry-on luggage. You'll see Pepper(s) around the ship during the cruise, too, as information helpers.

The outdoor pools, located on Lanai Deck, can be used during the warmer summer season, when the waterslide (which starts at the funnel and courses through the colorful Beach Club) and a rock-climbing wall can be used.

A private 'Patio-Bereich' is an adults-only retreat with its own pool, lounge areas, and bar – the first aboard an AIDA ship.

Below the apartment blocks of balcony cabins, but above the safety (lifeboat) deck, alfresco eateries and hot tubs provide the setting for the outdoor lifestyle enjoyed by many. The eateries are not well protected from wind and rain, however.

Inside, there's the two-decks-high AIDA Beach Club, located aft, which can be covered by a large

BERLITZ'S RATINGS		
	Possible	Achieved
Ship	500	401
Accommodation	200	143
Food	400	241
Service	400	267
Entertainment	100	77
Cruise Experience	400	283

OVERALL SCORE 1412 points out of 2000

glass dome, helping to bring the outside inside during the winter cruises in the cold weather regions of Europe.

Other features include glass panoramic elevators and a skywalk. The all-white Champagne Bar is cool. One bar has an ultra-Batman feel to it. There are 17 other bars (both indoor and outdoor, including a Brauhaus, for onboard-brewed beer), a cooking studio, library, biking station, shops, and an art gallery. The bar to try is at the bow – the Splash Bar!

AIDArima is all about cruising for youthful, laid-back, German-speaking families with a diverse selection of children's and youth programs and enthusiastic Club Team members dedicated to making sure that everyone has a good time. An AIDA cruise isn't cheap, but you do get lots of high-tech entertainment, fun activities, and plenty of food at the self-serve buffet restaurants (tablecloth-free eating), although there's little contact with the relatively small number of staff. Port taxes and gratuities are included. The dress code is simple: casual (no ties) at all times.

ACCOMMODATION. Modern and minimalist but cheerful, it ranges from small interior (no-view) cabins to large two-bedroom suites, and one owner's suite.

Suites range from 344.4–914.9 sq ft (32–85 sq m), but most cabins are much more compact, starting at 139.9

sq ft (13 sq m). Suites have more drawer and storage space, better-quality furniture and furnishings, a larger lounge area, and a slightly larger bathroom with a tub (and a larger balcony) than standard cabins. Those at the front and aft are the most desirable.

Balcony cabins feature beds adjacent to the floor-to ceiling door that slides open. Thick cotton bathrobes are provided for everyone, as are two towels (a face towel and a 'bath' towel), in two different colors. Note: there is no turndown service in the evening.

DINING. There are 13 dining and eatery choices (some with waiter service, some at extra cost). In the self-serve Markt (Market) and Weite Welt (World Wide) restaurants, the chairs don't have armrests – they are uncomfortable, so you won't want to stay a long time – like shopping mall food court eateries. The decor is, however, pleasingly bright – yellows and oranges to stimulate the senses (plus a little cream to calm them), with Moroccan-style lampshades hanging from a plain ceiling over tables. Food displays are attractive, and beer is available at the push of a button or a pull of the tap, and table wine is provided in carafes on each table for lunch and dinner.

Other eateries include Bella Donna Restaurant, and East Restaurant, while French Kiss is a casual French-style brasserie (the first of its type aboard an AIDA Cruises ship), with red/black chairs and the red lips of *Aïda* as the decor theme; there's also a Chef's Kitchen (part of the Cooking School), and even a Scharfe Ecke for popular Currywurst.

Restaurant Casa Nova is an elegant (extra-cost) Venetian-inspired venue, with a white tablecloth setting for dinner (although the chairs are uncomfortable and lack armrests).

Buffalo Steakhouse has an open 'display' kitchen, and features various prime steak cuts and sizes – Delmonico, New York Strip Loin, Porterhouse, and Filet, plus bison steaks – and roast lamb rack.

Reservations are required in Buffalo Steakhouse, Casa Nova Restaurant, Brasserie French Kiss, and Rossini-Gourmet Restaurant. Drinks are included in: Bella Donna, East Restaurant, French Kiss, Fuego Family Restaurant, Markt Restaurant, Scharfe Ecke, and the Weite Welt Restaurant. Worth a mention is a Brauhaus micro-brewery, with good beer at reasonable prices.

ENTERTAINMENT. The Theatrium acts (no pun intended) as the showlounge; it is located in the ship's center and spans three levels; it has an LED stage backdrop, but no bandstand. Shows are produced by AIDA Cruises' in-house department in a joint venture with SeeLive (Hamburg's Schmidt's Tivoli Theater).

SPA/FITNESS. The Body and Soul Organic Spa is expansive, with multiple body-pampering treatment rooms, extra-cost saunas, steam rooms, thalassotherapy bath, changing rooms, beauty salon, and manicure and pedicure salons. Extra-cost private couples 'wellness suites' are bookable. Sports activities include indoor cycling. Electric bicycles and extra-cost Segways are also available at the Biking Station, and there's a 2,152 sq ft (200 sq m) floating ice-rink on the Sports Deck (winter season only).

AIDASOL
★★★+

THIS CONTEMPORARY, CASUAL, NO-FRILLS CRUISING IS FOR MULTI-GENERATIONAL FAMILIES

Size:	Mid-size Ship	Passenger/Crew Ratio (lower beds):	3.1
Tonnage:	71,304	Cabins (total):	1,097
Cruise Line:	AIDA Cruises	Size Range (sq ft/m):	145.3–473.2/13.5–44
Former Names:	none	Cabins (for one person):	0
Builder:	Meyer Werft (Germany)	Cabins with balcony:	491
Entered Service:	Apr 2011	Cabins (wheelchair accessible):	11
Length (ft/m):	831.1/253.3	Wheelchair accessibility:	Good
Propulsion/Propellers:	diesel-electric (36,000 kW)/2	Elevators:	10
Total Crew:	646	Casino (gaming tables):	Yes
Passengers (lower beds):	2,194	Self-Service Launderette:	Yes
Passenger Space Ratio (lower beds):	34.6	Onboard currency:	Euros

THE SHIP. *AIDAsol* is a smart sea-going adventure park, ideal for young-at-heart German-speaking families. In fact, it's another sister ship in the AIDA fleet, with the signature contemporary profile, swept-back funnel, wedge-shaped stern, and many bold colors. The bows show the red lips and blue eyes of *Aïda* (from Verdi's 1871 opera). AIDA Cruises (Germany's largest cruise line), is part of Costa Cruises, which itself is owned by Carnival Corporation.

Dip pools, hot tubs, and seating areas are in a tiered setting on the pool deck – a 'beach-like' environment, with splash and play areas. There is no wrap-around outdoor promenade deck, although you can walk around the funnel area and around part of Deck 5.

Several decks of public rooms and facilities are above the accommodation decks, with most public room names shared aboard all the company's ships: AIDA Bar, for example, is the main social gathering place; it features a star-shaped bar (with a combined length among the longest at sea), with many tables for standing drinkers. There are several other bars and lounges, and a small casino, an observation lounge, and 'art' gallery. In the embarkation entryway (which looks like a street scene), a bar/coffee counter and lookout 'balcony' provide a nice welcome.

The dress code is ultra-casual, and all printed material is in German only. Eating is more about

BERLITZ'S RATINGS		
	Possible	Achieved
Ship	500	352
Accommodation	200	130
Food	400	232
Service	400	260
Entertainment	100	72
Cruise Experience	400	263

OVERALL SCORE 1309 points out of 2000

quantity than quality, in self-serve (tablecloth-free) buffet eateries, unless you pay extra for eating in a 'specialty' restaurant, as on land. You get lots of high-energy entertainment, fun activities, and self-serve buffet restaurants – although the number of staff is small. Decibel levels are high – it's impossible to escape the rap-rich 'music' in the cabin hallways and elevators 24/7. There are three pricing levels – AIDA Premium, AIDA Vario, and Just AIDA – depending on what's included. So, pay more, get more!

ACCOMMODATION. There are several accommodation grades, from deluxe suites to interior (no-view) cabins.

Contrary to maritime tradition (even-numbered cabins on the port side, odd-numbered cabins on the starboard side – like the lifeboats), cabin numbers progress numerically (example: 8201–8276 on the port side; 8101–8176 on the starboard side). All have two beds (convertible to a queen-size bed). Some cabins also have two extra beds/berths, and some have interconnecting doors – good for families.

The decor is bright, minimalist, and slightly whimsical, with multi-patterned fabrics, wood-trimmed, round-edge cabinetry, and rattan/wood-look furniture. Beds have duvets and fabric headboard canopy; windows have full pull-down blackout blinds (useful in destinations with long daylight hours); a hairdryer is in the vanity unit. Note that the night-time turn-down service (standard aboard almost all ships) is not provided, and there is no cabin service after 3pm.

Bathrooms are compact but practical, with shower enclosure, small washbasin and toilet. Only a wall-mounted body wash/shampoo dispenser is provided, so take any other toiletries you may need.

Cabins with balconies; these have an easy-to-open sliding door, small drinks table and chairs, plus a hammock (for one slim person). Note: balconies on the lowest deck can be overlooked by anyone on the decks above. Some cabins (5103, 5104, 5105, 5106, 5203, 5204, 5206 – forward on Deck 5) have an obstructed outside view.

DINING. Three self-serve eateries: Markt (Market), Bella Vista (for Italian cuisine), and Weite Welt (Wide World) restaurants have open seating at tables of four to eight. Cutlery is in a rack (not really hygienic); there are no soup spoons (only dessert spoons). Food islands and active stations cut down on the waiting time. There is always a selection of breads, cheeses, cold cuts, fruits, coffee and teas. The fish section also has its own fish-smoking unit.

Push-button beer is available, and table wine carafes are on each table for lunch and dinner. The beverage stations open only during restaurant opening hours, except for the extra-cost coffee bar (Café Mare). Vending machines dispense out-of-hours snacks.

Reservations are required at extra-cost venues, including Buffalo Steakhouse (for good steaks) and Rossini Restaurant – with waiter service and à la carte cuisine. Casual eateries include a Sushi Bar and Pizzeria Mare.

ENTERTAINMENT. The Theatrium is open to the central foyer on three levels (decks 9, 10, and 11), and topped by a glass dome. There is bench-seating, with back supports only on the two upper levels, plus standing tables, but sight lines to the raised stage are not all good.

SPA/FITNESS. Body and Soul wellness/oasis area is spread over two decks (with stairway connection), with saunas, steam rooms, and body treatment rooms (most named after places associated with the design theme), plus a fitness room with high-tech equipment, neat showers, funky changing rooms, and a tropical garden with waxed palm trees and loungers. Sport enthusiasts can play billiards, volleyball or squash. An open-air wellness 'FKK' deck for relaxation/nude sunbathing is forward of the ship's mast.

AIDASTELLA
★★★+

THIS MID-SIZE FAMILY-FRIENDLY RESORT SHIP IS FOR BASIC BUT FUN CRUISING

Size:	Mid-size Ship	Passenger/Crew Ratio (lower beds):	3.1
Tonnage:	71,304	Cabins (total):	1,097
Cruise Line:	AIDA Cruises	Size Range (sq ft/m):	145.3–473.2/13.5–44
Former Names:	none	Cabins (for one person):	0
Builder:	Meyer Werft (Germany)	Cabins with balcony:	722
Entered Service:	Mar 2013	Cabins (wheelchair accessible):	11
Length (ft/m):	831.1/253.3	Wheelchair accessibility:	Good
Propulsion/Propellers:	diesel-electric (36,000 kW)/2	Elevators:	10
Total Crew:	646	Casino (gaming tables):	Yes
Passengers (lower beds):	2,194	Self-Service Launderette:	Yes
Passenger Space Ratio (lower beds):	34.6	Onboard currency:	Euros

THE SHIP. *AIDAstella* is easily recognizable thanks to the red lips and blue eyes of *Aïda* (from Verdi's 1871 opera) on the bows and its swept-back funnel, wedge-shaped stern, and bold color scheme. AIDA Cruises (Germany's largest cruise line), is part of Costa Cruises, which itself is owned by Carnival Corporation. The ship is a floating resort for young-at-heart German-speaking families.

Dip pools, hot tubs, and seating areas are in a tiered setting on the pool deck – a 'beach-like' environment, with splash and play areas. There is no wrap-around outdoor promenade deck, although you can walk around the funnel area, and around part of Deck 5.

Several decks of public rooms and facilities are above accommodation decks, with most public room names shared aboard all the company's ships: AIDA Bar, for example, is the main social gathering place; it features a star-shaped bar (with a combined length among the longest at sea), with many standing tables. There are several other bars and lounges, a small casino, an observation lounge, and 'art' gallery. In the embarkation entryway (it looks like a street scene), a bar/coffee counter and lookout 'balcony' provide a nice welcome.

The dress code is ultra-casual, and all printed material is in German only. Eating is more about quantity than quality, in self-serve (tablecloth-free) buffet eateries, unless you pay extra for eating in a 'specialty' restaurant, as on land. You get lots of high-energy

BERLITZ'S RATINGS		
	Possible	Achieved
Ship	500	352
Accommodation	200	130
Food	400	232
Service	400	261
Entertainment	100	72
Cruise Experience	400	264
OVERALL SCORE 1311 points out of 2000		

entertainment, fun activities, and self-serve buffet restaurants – although staff numbers are low. Decibel levels are high (it's impossible to escape rap-rich 'music' in cabin hallways and elevators 24/7). There are three pricing levels – AIDA Premium, AIDA Vario, and Just AIDA – depending on what's included. So, pay more, get more!

ACCOMMODATION. There are several accommodation grades, from deluxe suites to interior (no-view) cabins.

Contrary to maritime tradition (even-numbered cabins on the port side, odd-numbered cabins on the starboard side – like the lifeboats), cabin numbers progress numerically (example: 8201–8276 on the port side; 8101–8176 on the starboard side). All have two beds (convertible to a queen-size bed). Some cabins also have two extra beds/berths, and some have interconnecting doors – good for families.

The decor is bright, minimalist, and whimsical, with multi-patterned fabrics, wood-trimmed, round-edge cabinetry, and rattan/wood-look furniture. Beds have duvets and fabric headboard canopy; windows have full pull-down blackout blinds (useful in destinations with long daylight hours); a hairdryer is in the vanity unit. Note that the night-time turndown service (standard aboard almost all ships) is not provided, and there is no cabin service after 3pm.

Bathrooms are compact but practical, with shower enclosure, small washbasin and toilet. Only a wall-mounted body wash/shampoo dispenser is provided, so take any other toiletries you may need.

Cabins with balconies have an easy-to-open sliding door, small drinks table and chairs, and a one-person hammock. Note: balconies on the lowest deck can be overlooked by anyone on the decks above. Some cabins (5103, 5104, 5105, 5106, 5203, 5204, 5206 – forward on Deck 5) have an obstructed outside view.

DINING. Three self-serve eateries: Markt (Market), Bella Vista (for Italian cuisine), and Weite Welt (Wide World) restaurants have open seating at tables of four to eight. Cutlery is in a rack (not really hygienic); there are no soup spoons (only dessert spoons). Food islands and active stations cut down on the waiting time. There is always a selection of breads, cheeses, cold cuts, fruits, coffee and teas. The fish section also has its own fish-smoking unit.

Push-button beer is available, and table wine carafes are on each table for lunch and dinner. The beverage stations open only during restaurant opening hours, except for the extra-cost coffee bar (Café Mare). Vending machines dispense out-of-hours snacks.

Reservations required at extra-cost venues, including Buffalo Steakhouse (for good steaks and grilled food) and Rossini Restaurant – with waiter service and à la carte cuisine. Casual eateries include a Sushi Bar and Pizzeria Mare.

ENTERTAINMENT. The Theatrium is open to the central foyer on three levels (decks 9, 10, and 11), and topped by a glass dome. There is bench-seating, with back supports only on the two upper levels, plus standing tables, but sight lines to the raised stage are not all good.

SPA/FITNESS. Body and Soul wellness/oasis area is spread over two decks (with stairway connection), with saunas, steam rooms, and body treatment rooms (most named after places associated with the design theme), plus a fitness room with high-tech equipment, neat showers, funky changing rooms, and a tropical garden with waxed palm trees and loungers. Sport enthusiasts can play billiards, volleyball or squash. An open-air wellness 'FKK' deck for relaxation/nude sunbathing is forward of the ship's mast.

AIDAVITA
★★★+

AN UPBEAT, FAMILY-FRIENDLY SHIP FOR VIBRANT, BUSY, CASUAL CRUISING

Size:	Mid-size Ship
Tonnage:	42,289
Cruise Line:	AIDA Cruises
Former Names:	none
Builder:	Aker MTW (Germany)
Entered Service:	Apr 2002
Length (ft/m):	666.5/202.8
Propulsion/Propellers:	diesel-electric/2
Total Crew:	389
Passengers (lower beds):	1,266
Passenger Space Ratio (lower beds):	33.4
Passenger/Crew Ratio (lower beds):	3.0
Cabins (total):	633
Size Range (sq ft/m):	145.3–344.4/13.5–32.0
Cabins (for one person):	0
Cabins with balcony:	60
Cabins (wheelchair accessible):	4
Wheelchair accessibility:	Good
Elevators:	6
Casino (gaming tables):	No
Self-Service Launderette:	Yes
Onboard currency:	Euros

THE SHIP. *AIDAvita* has a swept-back funnel and wedge-shaped stern, while the bows feature the red lips and blue eyes of *Aïda* (from Verdi's1871 opera). The open deck space is reasonable, with its 'beach-life' theme – think tiered dip pools, hot tubs, and seating areas.

AIDA Bar, the main social gathering place common to all AIDA ships, has a star-shaped bar and tables for standing drinkers. Other facilities include a shore-excursion counter, library, seminar rooms, duty-free shop, several bars and lounges, and eateries.

There are children's and youth programs (in five age groupings), and Club Team members are dedicated to making sure that everyone has a good time.

This is über-casual cruising for youthful German-speaking urbanite families, with tablecloth-free eating, and little contact with the few staff. The dress code is simple: casual (no ties) at all times.

ACCOMMODATION. There are several grades, from (more) spacious suites to interior (no-view) cabins. Contrary to maritime tradition (even-numbered cabins on the port side, odd-numbered cabins on the starboard side), cabin numbers progress numerically (example: 8201–8276 on the port side; 8101–8176 on the starboard side).

BERLITZ'S RATINGS		
	Possible	Achieved
Ship	500	330
Accommodation	200	129
Food	400	231
Service	400	255
Entertainment	100	70
Cruise Experience	400	259
OVERALL SCORE 1274 points out of 2000		

All have two beds convertible to queen-size. Some also have extra beds/berths for kids; some have interconnecting doors.

The decor is bright and whimsical, with multi-patterned fabric accents and wood-trimmed, round-edged cabinetry. Beds have duvets and colorful, Arabian-style headboard-to-ceiling fabric canopy; windows have full pull-down blackout blinds. Lifeboats may obstruct views in some central cabins. Bathrooms are compact, with a shower enclosure, washbasin, toilet, wall-mounted wash/shampoo dispenser (take your own toiletries if you require other items), and two towels (a face towel and a small 'bath' towel). Cotton bathrobes are provided for suite-grade occupants. Night-time turndown service is not provided.

Balcony cabins have easy-open sliding doors, but those on the lowest deck can be overlooked from those on the decks above.

Suite-grade accommodation has more space, better-quality furniture and furnishings, and a slightly larger bathroom with tub/shower.

DINING. Two self-serve eateries (for main meals) are included in the cruise fare: the Markt and Karibik, with open seating at tables of four to eight. Cutlery hangs in a rack (there are no soup spoons, only dessert spoons). It is often challenging to find a seat or a clean table.

The standard of food ranges from adequate to moderately good, with creative displays and presentation, and many food islands – always with a good selection of breads, cheeses, cold cuts, fruits, and make-your-own coffee and multiple-choice teas/tisanes.

Beer is at the push of a button or a pull of the tap, and table 'wine' is in carafes. Beverage stations open only during restaurant opening hours unless you go to the extra-cost coffee bar (Café Mare). Vending machines dispense out-of-hours snacks.

The extra-cost Rossini Restaurant (open for dinner) features a tablecloth setting and reasonably sound food and service; reservations required.

ENTERTAINMENT. The Theater (showlounge) is two decks high, with a raised stage and bench seating. Sight lines are good from most seats, except some balcony sections with interruption from thick safety rails.

SPA/FITNESS. Body and Soul Spa has two saunas (one dry, one wet, with glass walls), body-pampering treatment rooms, relaxation area, showers, and ice walls. Outside (forward) is a bi-level 'FKK' (Freikoerperkultur – naked) sunbathing deck. A beauty/hair salon is located behind the showlounge.

ALBATROS
★★★

THIS SHIP IS GOOD FOR LOW-PRICE, NO-FRILLS LONGER CRUISES FOR GERMAN SPEAKERS

Size:	Mid-size Ship	Passenger/Crew Ratio (lower beds):	2.5
Tonnage:	28,078	Cabins (total):	449
Cruise Line:	Phoenix Reisen	Size Range (sq ft/m):	123.7–679.2/11.8–63.1
Former Names:	Crown, Norwegian Star I, Royal	Cabins (for one person):	12
	Odyssey, Royal Viking Sea	Cabins with balcony:	15
Builder:	Wartsila (Finland)	Cabins (wheelchair accessible):	0
Entered Service:	Nov 1973/Apr 2004	Wheelchair accessibility:	Fair
Length (ft/m):	674.2/205.5	Elevators:	5
Propulsion/Propellers:	diesel (15,840 kW)/2	Casino (gaming tables):	No
Total Crew:	340	Self-Service Launderette:	Yes
Passengers (lower beds):	862	Onboard currency:	Euros
Passenger Space Ratio (lower beds):	32.5		

THE SHIP. *Albatros*, originally built for long-distance cruising for the long-defunct Royal Viking Line, has been through many refurbishments. There is ample open deck and sunbathing space, although the popular aft pool area is always busy.

The ship (now over 45 years old) has a good array of public rooms, including several lounges and bars, most of which are elegant in an old-school way, with high, indented ceilings. The Observation Lounge is particularly pleasant. Wide stairways and foyers boost the sense of space, even when the ship is full. The atmosphere is very casual, as is the dress code. A gratuity is added to bar accounts, but drink prices are very reasonable.

The Phoenix cruise staff is always bright, friendly, and helpful, and the shore excursion team is knowledgeable.

The ship best suits mature German-speaking adults and families seeking a low-budget, good-value vacation in a comfortable ship with character and multiple intimate public rooms.

ACCOMMODATION. There are many price grades, from expansive suites with private balcony to standard outside-view cabins and small interior (no view) cabins. A Captain's Suite is located at the front, below the navigation bridge, with forward-facing views. Nine other Penthouse Suites have a

BERLITZ'S RATINGS

	Possible	Achieved
Ship	500	296
Accommodation	200	124
Food	400	215
Service	400	237
Entertainment	100	60
Cruise Experience	400	247

OVERALL SCORE 1179 points out of 2000

separate bedroom and living area, and private balcony. Most other cabins have an outside view and are quite well appointed, with a generous amount of storage space; however, some bathrooms in the lower categories have awkward access. All cabins have a TV, bathrobe, and personal safe. Suites and 'comfort cabins' also have a minibar.

DINING. The two dining rooms (Mowe and Pelikan) both have high ceilings, and feel quite spacious. Dining is in one seating at assigned tables for two to eight. Breakfast and lunch can be taken in the dining rooms or outdoors at a self-service buffet. Mid-morning bouillon is a Phoenix seagoing tradition, as is a Captain's Dinner (formal night), and a Buffet Magnifique.

The service is friendly and attentive, and the food itself is quite acceptable. Decent table wines are included for lunch and dinner, and better-quality wines can also be purchased.

ENTERTAINMENT. The Pacific Lounge (show-lounge) seats about 500, but several pillars obstruct sight lines from some places. Small-scale shows are presented by a small team of resident singers/dancers.

SPA/FITNESS. There is a gymnasium, sauna, two steam rooms, body-treatment rooms, and a beauty salon.

ALLURE OF THE SEAS
★★★★

A FINE MEGA-LARGE, FAMILY-FRIENDLY, MULTI-CHOICE SHIP FOR CASUAL CRUISING

Size:	Large Resort Ship
Tonnage:	225,282
Cruise Line:	Royal Caribbean International
Former Names:	none
Builder:	Aker Yards (Finland)
Entered Service:	Dec 2010
Length (ft/m):	1,181.1/360.0
Propulsion/Propellers:	diesel-electric (97,200kW)/3 pods (2 azimuthing, 1 fixed)
Total Crew:	2,164
Passengers (lower beds):	5,408
Passenger Space Ratio (lower beds):	41.6
Passenger/Crew Ratio (lower beds):	2.4
Cabins (total):	2,704
Size Range (sq ft/m):	150.6–1,523.1/14.0–141.5
Cabins (for one person):	0
Cabins with balcony:	1,956
Cabins (wheelchair accessible):	46
Wheelchair accessibility:	Good
Elevators:	24
Casino (gaming tables):	Yes
Self-Service Launderette:	No
Onboard currency:	US$

THE SHIP. When it debuted in 2010, *Allure of the Seas* became the world's largest cruise ship – 2ins (5cm) longer than sister *Oasis of the Seas*, the world's first cruise ship measuring over 200,000 tons, which debuted in 2009. The 227,700-ton *Harmony of the Seas* held the title of world's largest cruise ship until it was superceded in late 2018 by the 228,081-ton *Symphony of the Sea*.

This is a real 'Moveable Leisure Resort Vacation' for families, and a credit to Royal Caribbean International's design team, packed with innovative design elements.

Much outdoor and indoor/outdoor space is devoted to aqua parks and sports facilities, leaving little space for sunbathing (sunloungers are so tightly packed together that there's little space to put your belongings!). An adults-only open-air solarium and rentable cabanas are part of the outdoor scene.

There are many bars and places to eat/snack, so public spaces are arranged as seven 'neighborhoods': Central Park, the Coney Island-style Boardwalk, the Royal Promenade, the Pool and Sports Zone, Vitality at Sea Spa/Fitness Center, Entertainment Place, and Youth Zone.

The Royal Promenade is a shopping mall, with casual eateries (including Starbucks), shops, video screens, changing color lights at every step, and parades. Interior-view cabins have balconies with Central Park views. A hydraulic, oval-shaped Rising Tide Bar moves slowly through three decks

BERLITZ'S RATINGS

	Possible	Achieved
Ship	500	397
Accommodation	200	136
Food	400	225
Service	400	284
Entertainment	100	87
Cruise Experience	400	285

OVERALL SCORE 1414 points out of 2000

to link the Royal Promenade with Central Park.

The Boardwalk (think: Coney Island) has shops, several eateries, and a superb carousel. Central Park has real vegetation (trees and a living plant wall).

It's best to plan what you want to do to get the most out of your cruise vacation, and almost everything requires you to make reservations/sign up in advance. Do budget extra for additional cost items and promotions.

Niggles include lines at the reception desk, for shore tenders and excursions, self-serve buffet stations, intrusive photographers, few quiet places to sit and read, no cushioned pads for sunloungers, small cabin 'bath' towels, noisy (vacuum) toilets, unwelcome announcements for revenue activities, fibreglass – not wood - railings, expensive ice-laden frosted drinks in 'souvenir' glasses, the speaking 'elevator going up/going down. rap-rich recorded 'music' everywhere (even in elevators, hallways and saunas), while live music is volume-heavy. Also, if you have an interconnecting door cabin, you may hear your neighbors.

Service personnel are friendly, however, and the digital 'Wayfarer' system is informative. Do budget extra for additional cost items and expect flyers and advertising promotions. Overall, this is a fine all-round ship for all age groups but be aware of the extra cost for many optional items (including drinks, drink packages, and excursions.

ACCOMMODATION. There are many, many accommodation price grades, reflecting the choice of location and size, from interior (no view or virtual view cabin to bi-level loft suites, family suites and ultra-large owner's suites. Suite occupants have access to a concierge lounge and associated services. The cabin-numbering system is confusing and there are no solo-occupancy cabins. The doors open outwards (towards you), as in many European hotels, and in many lower-grade rooms, closet access is awkward.

In many balcony and non-balcony cabins, electrical sockets are inconveniently located below the vanity desk; also, it's challenging to watch the infotainment screen from the bed.

Wash basins in non-suite grade cabins are low, at just 30.5ins (77.5cm) above the floor, and tiny. Warning – it's easy to hit your head on the mirror above. Small soap bars are provided; shampoo is in a dispenser in the shower enclosures, which have wall-fixed shower heads. Although there is no soap dish or indentation in the washbasin surround, one useful touch is a blue ceiling bathroom nightlight.

Boardwalk cabins are exposed to noise and whatever is happening on the Boardwalk, including rehearsals, bells from the carousel forward (its 18 sculptured wooden animal figures took six weeks to carve), late-night revelers, plus screaming daytime zipliners and loud music from poolside bands. Those close to the aft Aqua Theater can use their balconies for a great view of any shows. The lowest deck of Boardwalk-view cabins has windows but no balcony (actually the view is mainly of the top of things such as the carousel). The best Boardwalk balcony cabins are on decks 8 to 12. For more privacy, try a sea-facing balcony cabin, not one overlooking the Boardwalk.

Crown Accessible Loft Suite has its own elevator for the mobility-challenged.

DINING. Opus, the huge main dining room spans three decks and has two seating times (early or late) for dinner, although you can also choose 'My Time Dining' and eat at your preferred time.

The cuisine is all about standardized banquet catering and batch cooking. Menu descriptions sound tempting, but the food, although prepared well enough, is just so-so. Green vegetables are scarce – they're provided basically for decoration – but salad items are plentiful, and desserts are pretty good. Rice is often used as a source of carbohydrates. Breads and pastry items are so-so (these are thawed and then baked from frozen 'starter' dough), and items such as croissants lack any hint of butter.

For a change to the main dining room, try one of the alternative dining venues. These are:

150 Central Park: the most exclusive restaurant (extra cost), combines haute-cuisine with nifty design. A kitchen observation window allows you to watch the chefs in action.

Chef's Table: An extra cost venue (six-course meal with wine), hosted by the executive chef, but, with just 14 seats, getting a reservation can be difficult.

Giovanni's Table: a rustic Italian-style venue for toasted herb breads, pizzas, salads, pastas, sandwiches, braised meat dishes, and stews.

Izumi Hibachi & Sushi has Japanese-style cuisine, including a Teppanyaki menu.

Sabor Taquería & Tequila Bar is for modern Mexican eats, while Wonderland Imaginative Cuisine features novel, quirky creations.

Vintage (wine bar) has a decent wines, cheese and tapas (with a per item charge).

Central Park Café, a casual deli-style indoor/outdoor food market and eatery, for freshly prepared salads, made-to-order sandwiches, panini, crêpes, and soups.

Other Boardwalk snacking spots: Donut Shop (for hot dogs, wieners, bratwurst, and other sausages), and an Ice Cream Parlor.

Elsewhere, eateries include Sorrento's Pizzeria; Park Café (for salads and light bites); and a Wipe Out Café.

ENTERTAINMENT. The 1,380-seat Amber Theater spans three decks and stages the musical *Mamma Mia!* – a 90-minute-long production (performed four times each cruise). Also, *Frozen in Time* is a must-see ice show.

A 750-seat AquaTheater, outside (aft) has a 6,000-sq-ft (560-sq-m) stage, and is a combination show theatre, sound stage, and event space. Try the viewing places high in the aft wings on both sides.

SPA/FITNESS. The Vitality at Sea Spa includes a Vitality Café for extra-cost health drinks and snacks. Facilities include almost 160 cardio and resistance machines; an extra-cost thermal suite has saunas, steam rooms, and heated tiled loungers (to use it you must buy a spa pass).

It's not large. Don't book a massage when the ship is due to arrive or leave an anchor port – some treatment rooms experience immense vibration when the anchor is raised.

Sports facilities include two Flow-Rider surfboard pools, golf putting course, ziplining (screaming mandatory), and an ice-skating rink (amazingly popular with kids) and a large jogging track.

AMADEA
★★★★

A STYLISH, SPACIOUS SHIP WITH FINE FOOD AND SERVICE, FOR GERMAN SPEAKERS

Size:	Small Ship	Passenger/Crew Ratio (lower beds):	2.0
Tonnage:	28,856	Cabins (total):	297
Cruise Line:	Phoenix Reisen	Size Range (sq ft/m):	182.9–649.0/17.0–60.3
Former Names:	*Asuka*	Cabins (for one person):	0
Builder:	Mitsubishi Heavy Industries (Japan)	Cabins with balcony:	122
Entered Service:	Dec 1991/Mar 2006	Cabins (wheelchair accessible):	2
Length (ft/m):	632.5/192.8	Wheelchair accessibility:	Fair
Propulsion/Propellers:	diesel (17,300kW)/2	Elevators:	5
Total Crew:	292	Casino (gaming tables):	No
Passengers (lower beds):	594	Self-Service Launderette:	Yes
Passenger Space Ratio (lower beds):	48.5	Onboard currency:	Euros

THE SHIP. When introduced in 1991 as *Asuka*, this was the first all-new ship specially designed and built in Japan for its domestic market. It was sold to Phoenix Reisen and, as *Amadea*, started cruising for German-speaking passengers in 2006.

More upscale than other ships in the fleet, the ship has pleasing exterior styling and profile, with a large, squat funnel. There is ample open deck and sunbathing space, plus a wide walk-around teakwood promenade deck outdoors, good for strolling.

The 'cake-layer' stacking of the public rooms hampers passenger flow and makes it rather disjointed because public rooms are separated from accommodation. The interior decor is understated, with pleasing color combinations, quality fabrics, and fine soft furnishings. There's some fascinating Japanese artwork, including Noriko Tamura's *Song of the Seasons*, a four-deck-high mural on the wall of the main foyer staircase – in many shades of pink and red. The relaxing Vista Lounge (an observation lounge and bar) is also used for afternoon tea.

Harry's Bar, a lounge/bar (think: contemporary gentleman's club), has wood-paneled walls, burgundy leather chairs, and a light, airy feel. Located in a quiet area is the library, with deeply comfortable armchairs, and a fireplace with electric fire. Cigar smokers will find the Havanna Club a cozy little hideaway.

BERLITZ'S RATINGS

	Possible	Achieved
Ship	500	363
Accommodation	200	156
Food	400	304
Service	400	303
Entertainment	100	74
Cruise Experience	400	286

OVERALL SCORE 1486 points out of 2000

The dress code is a mix of formal and informal; during the day it's casual. There is a self-service launderette with eight washing machines – useful for long cruises. Overall, the ship provides an extremely comfortable and serene cruising environment. Because it absorbs people well, there is rarely a feeling of crowding. All gratuities are included.

ACCOMMODATION. There are several price categories, but just five types of suites and cabins. Three decks (8, 9, and 10) have suites and cabins with a private balcony (but no outside light fitting).

All grades have ocean views, but some are slightly obstructed by the gangway when in the raised (stowed) position. All have delightful cherry wood cabinetry, with rounded edges. Cabin soundproofing is excellent, and there is a good amount of closet and drawer space (including lockable drawers), refrigerator, and personal safe.

Most grades have bathrooms with bathtubs (and cabins available with shower), and all have a tiled floor and bath/shower area. While the suite bathrooms are generously proportioned, the 'standard' bathrooms are practical but small.

Two suites provide the largest accommodation. Each has a separate bedroom, walk-in closet with luggage deck, and twin beds that convert to a queen-size bed. The marble-clad bathroom is large and has a whirlpool tub set alongside large ocean-view windows overlooking the private balcony, and twin washbasins in a marble surround. There is a living room and separate guest bathroom. The private balcony is quite large and features a tropical plant set in a glass display enclosure.

Many cabins have a private balcony with full floor-to-ceiling partition with sliding door (and awkward door handles) and green synthetic turf floor.

DINING. The two main restaurants have open seating for meals. The Four Seasons has two sections. The Amadea Restaurant is located on a higher deck. The cuisine is the same in both venues. For casual breakfasts and lunches, there's an informal self-serve Lido Café with plenty of outdoor seating, adjacent to a small pool and hot tub. With this ship, Phoenix Reisen has taken its

cuisine and service to a high level by spending more money per passenger per day (reflected in the cruise fare).

ENTERTAINMENT. The Atlantic Lounge hosts most entertainment events, including shows, social functions, and lectures. It spans two decks, with seating on both levels, and an extra-large wooden dance floor for social dancing.

SPA/FITNESS. The spacious wellness center has large ocean-view windows, two baths, one hot tub, two saunas, steam room with wooden floor, several shower enclosures, a changing area with vanity counter, gymnasium, body-pampering treatment rooms, plus a relaxation area. Sports facilities include a golf court, driving cage, and putting green.

AMERA
★★★+

A REIMAGINED PREMIUM SHIP OFFERING GOOD-VALUE COMFORT TO GERMAN SPEAKERS

Size:	Mid-size Ship	Passenger/Crew Ratio (lower beds):	1.8
Tonnage:	38,848	Cabins (total):	419
Cruise Line:	Phoenix Reisen	Size Range (sq ft/m):	137.7–723.3/12.8–67.2
Former Names:	*Royal Viking Sun*	Cabins (for one person):	3
Builder:	Wartsila (Finland)	Cabins with balcony:	166
Entered Service:	Dec 1988/May 2019	Cabins (wheelchair accessible):	10
Length (ft/m):	674.2/205.5	Wheelchair accessibility:	Good
Propulsion/Propellers:	diesel /2	Elevators:	4
Total Crew:	443	Casino (gaming tables):	Yes
Passengers (lower beds):	835	Self-Service Launderette:	Yes
Passenger Space Ratio (lower beds):	46.5	Onboard currency:	Euros

THE SHIP. This is a well-designed ship with sleek lines, a sharply raked bow, and a well-rounded profile with a dark blue hull and white superstructure; it has a wide teakwood outdoor walk-around promenade deck. It is a good complement to Phoenix Reisen's existing fleet of ships, and well suited to older German-speaking couples and solo travelers who enjoy mingling in unhurried surroundings. While the main swimming pool is quite small, there is plenty of open deck space and numerous sunloungers.

The interior layout is spacious, with impressive public rooms (some with high ceilings) and tasteful decor. Wood and chromed-steel handrails are on all stairways, which are wide. The Panorama Lounge (observation lounge) is elegant and popular. Other facilities include self-service launderettes (useful on long voyages), a guest lecture program, an excellent spa, teakwood decks, and a high degree of comfort. *Amera* offers a fine cruise experience in spacious, contemporary surroundings, at a decent price, with gratuities included.

ACCOMMODATION. There are several grades, ranging from sizeable suites (each named after a destination) to interior (no view) cabins. Most cabins are of generous proportions and nicely equipped; many have a small balcony. All have walk-in closets, lockable drawers, full-length mirrors, hairdryers, cotton towels, and flat-screen infotainment systems. Some cabins have third berths, and some have interconnecting doors –

BERLITZ'S RATINGS		
	Possible	Achieved
Ship	500	341
Accommodation	200	138
Food	400	268
Service	400	275
Entertainment	100	66
Cruise Experience	400	274
OVERALL SCORE 1362 points out of 2000		

good for couples who want his and hers bathrooms and more space, or for families with children. Four well-equipped, L-shaped cabins for disabled passengers are well designed, fairly large, and have wheel-in bathrooms with shower facilities and specially equipped clothes closets.

DINING. Ocean Restaurant is the main dining room, with 300 seats. It has extensive ocean-view windows, and there is good space around the tables (with two to eight seats), in an open seating arrangement. A second, smaller venue, the Amera Restaurant has around 100 seats. A more intimate fine-dining venue, Pichler's Restaurant, has 60 seats and ocean views. High-quality steaks and seafood are among items on the menu, and reservations are required. There is a well-chosen, high-end wine list, with modest pricing.

Lido Restaurant offers casual, self-serve buffet-style eats for breakfast, lunch, and dinner; it has seating for 300 indoors and 200 outdoors.

ENTERTAINMENT. The Atlantic Showlounge hosts production shows and cabaret in an amphitheater-style room, with banquette and individual seating.

SPA/FITNESS. Ocean Spa has treatment rooms with showers, a Rasul chamber (for mud and gentle steam heat), a gymnasium with aft views, sauna, and steam room. Golfers can play in an electronic golf simulator room, which has its own bar.

AMSTERDAM
★★★+

DUTCH-STYLE DÉCOR, TRADITIONS, AND FRIENDLY SERVICE AWAIT MATURE CRUISERS

Size:	Mid-size Ship
Tonnage:	62,735
Cruise Line:	Holland America Line
Former Names:	none
Builder:	Fincantieri (Italy)
Entered Service:	Oct 2000
Length (ft/m):	780.8/238.0
Propulsion/Propellers:	diesel-electric (37,500kW)/2 azimuthing pods
Total Crew:	650
Passengers (lower beds):	1,380
Passenger Space Ratio (lower beds):	45.4
Passenger/Crew Ratio (lower beds):	2.1
Cabins (total):	690
Size Range (sq ft/m):	184.0–1,124.8/17.1–104.5
Cabins (for one person):	0
Cabins with balcony:	172
Cabins (wheelchair accessible):	20
Wheelchair accessibility:	Good
Elevators:	12
Casino (gaming tables):	Yes
Self-Service Launderette:	Yes
Onboard currency:	US$

THE SHIP. *Amsterdam*, a close sister to *Rotterdam*, has a nicely raked bow and familiar interior flow and design style. It is the first ship in the HAL fleet to feature an azimuthing pod propulsion system, with pods powered by a diesel-electric system, so there's almost no vibration. There is a glass-covered pool on the Lido Deck between the mast and the twin funnels, watched over by a sculpture of a brown bear catching salmon.

BERLITZ'S RATINGS		
	Possible	Achieved
Ship	500	377
Accommodation	200	142
Food	400	220
Service	400	268
Entertainment	100	73
Cruise Experience	400	276

OVERALL SCORE 1356 points out of 2000

The interior decor retains much of the traditional ocean liner detailing enjoyed by frequent passengers, with some use of medium and dark wood paneling. However, some color combinations – particularly for the chairs and soft furnishings – are eclectic. Much of the artwork reflects the line's past, including items depicting the city of Amsterdam's history.

The interior focal point is a three-deck-high atrium, in an oval shape; a whimsical 'Astrolabe' in its center. Clustered in the lobby are the reception desk, shore-excursion desk, photo shop, and photo gallery.

There are three principal passenger stairways. The casino, in the middle of a major passenger flow on one of the entertainment decks, has gaming tables and slot machines.

HAL provides free ice cream at certain times, plus canapés in all bars, but the charge to use the washing machines and dryers in the self-service launderette is irritating.

Perhaps the ship's best asset is its personable Filipino and Indonesian crew, although communication (in English) can be frustrating at times, particularly in the dining room and buffet areas.

Amsterdam is extremely comfortable, with some elegant decorative features. On the negative side, the quality of food and service is poor, and there's a lack of understanding of what it really takes to make a 'luxury' cruise experience, despite what is touted in Holland America Line's (HAL's) brochures.

ACCOMMODATION. This is spread over five decks (some cabins have full or partially obstructed views), in many grades. With one deck of suites and a dedicated, private Concierge Lounge, it's a two-class ship. No cabin is more than 130ft (40m) from a stairway, so it very easy to find your way. Although 81 percent of cabins have outside views, only 25 percent of those have balconies.

The 'standard' interior and outside-view cabins are tastefully furnished and have twin beds convertible to a queen-size bed – but space is tight for walking between beds and vanity unit. There is decent closet and drawer space for short cruises. The tiled bathrooms are disappointingly small, the shower 'tubs' are tiny, and storage for toiletries is poor.

The Verandah Suites and four Penthouse Suites on Navigation Deck share a private Concierge Lounge (for making dining arrangements, booking shore excursions, and for other requests).

Four Penthouse Suites each have a separate steward's entrance, separate bedroom, wet bar, and large bathroom.

DINING. La Fontaine Dining Room seats 747, spans two decks, and has a stained-glass ceiling measuring almost 1,500 sq ft (140 sq m), with a floral motif and fiber-optic lighting. There are tables for two to eight, but few are for two. Both open seating and fixed (assigned tables and times) seating are available, while breakfast and lunch are open seating (you'll be seated by restaurant staff when you enter). Tablecloths, Rosenthal china, and good cutlery are provided.

With a few exceptions, the cuisine is unmemorable, and lacks passion and taste, because it's all about batch cooking. There's a distinct lack of variety of green vegetables, much use of rice, canned fruit, and already sliced and diced cheese. Still, you get friendly service from smiling Indonesian and Filipino stewards, and the plates are attractive.

The 88-seat, extra-cost Pinnacle Grill has better food and presentation than the main dining room. It's open for lunch and dinner, and reservations are required. Its whimsically surreal artwork features scenic landscapes. Pacific Northwest steaks and seafood is featured, with small portions and few vegetables.

Lido Buffet Restaurant is open for casual dinners on all except the last night of each cruise, in an open-seating arrangement. Tables are set with crisp linens, flatware, and standard stemware.

For casual breakfasts and lunches, the Lido Market has old-style, stand-in-line, serve-yourself canteen food – adequate for anyone used to TV dinners, but definitely not lavish as the brochures claim. Although the salad items appear adequate when displayed, they are too cold and lack taste. The constant supply of iceberg lettuce doesn't seem to go away, and there is little choice of other, more suitable, lettuces, and greens. Each evening, a section opens as Canaletto, featuring popular Italian-style dishes.

Also, a poolside 'Dive-In at the Terrace Grill' features signature burgers (Dive-In sauce), hot dogs, and fries.

The room service menu is very limited, as is food delivery.

ENTERTAINMENT. The 577-seat Queen's Lounge is for all production shows, cabaret acts, and other entertainment. It spans two decks, with main and balcony level seating. The stage has hydraulic lifts and three video screens, and closed-loop system for the hearing-impaired.

While HAL is not known for its fine entertainment, the line offers a consistently good, tried-and-tested array of cabaret acts. The production shows, while decent enough, fall short on storyline, but have colorful costuming and lighting.

Lincoln Center Stage is a music and performance venue. The Crow's Nest (atop the navigation bridge) has a dance floor, and there's and serenading string music in the Explorer's Lounge, among other venues.

SPA/FITNESS. Ocean Spa is one deck above the navigation bridge at the very forward part of the ship. It has a gym with exercise machines, treadmills, and forward views over the ship's bows. There's an aerobics exercise area, a beauty salon, several treatment rooms, men's and women's saunas, steam rooms, and changing areas. Few fitness classes are free.

For the sports-minded, two paddle-tennis courts are located aft on Sports Deck.

ANTHEM OF THE SEAS
★★★★

A HIGH-TECH, HIGH-ENERGY, GIZMO-FILLED FAMILY-FRIENDLY FLOATING RESORT

Size:	Large Resort Ship	Passenger/Crew Ratio (lower beds):	3.2
Tonnage:	168,666	Cabins (total):	2,090
Cruise Line:	Royal Caribbean International	Size Range (sq ft/m):	101.1–799.7/9.4–74.3
Former Names:	none	Cabins (for one person):	34
Builder:	Meyer Werft (Germany)	Cabins with balcony:	1,571
Entered Service:	Mar 2015	Cabins (wheelchair accessible):	34
Length (ft/m):	1,112.2/339.0	Wheelchair accessibility:	Good
Propulsion/Propellers:	diesel-electric (41,000kW)/2 azimuthing pods	Elevators:	16
		Casino (gaming tables):	Yes
Total Crew:	1,300	Self-Service Launderette:	No
Passengers (lower beds):	4,180	Onboard currency:	US$
Passenger Space Ratio (lower beds):	40.3		

THE SHIP. *Anthem of the Seas* is sister to *Ovation of the Seas (2016)*, *Quantum of the Seas (2014)*, and *Spectrum of the Seas (2019)*, and incorporates the latest in tech-intensive bling and entertainment features, and then some. The exterior design employs the latest in hydrodynamics, hull shape, and low emissions. The stern slopes nicely – it looks like it could be the front!

There are many standout features on this ship. Aft is Two70 – a multi-level venue that is a casual living area by day and a high-energy entertainment venue by night, with dynamic robotic screens complementing its huge video wall.

One novel feature is North Star. Quite the engineering marvel, it is a 14-person (including the operator) glass pod that lifts you from above the pool deck for a moving, bird's-eye view, like a posh giant 'cherry picker,' and, with an outreach of almost 135ft (41m), is quite a ride! Located just aft of the mast, it is complimentary (and wheelchair-accessible), but only operates on sea days.

RipCord by iFly is a simulated skydiving experience in a two-storey vertical wind tunnel that lets you experience the thrill of skydiving in a safe, controlled environment. The unit uses a powerful air flow to keep you up – like a giant hairdryer underneath you! It is aft of the funnel housing and accommodates 13 persons for each class, including two 'hovering in the air' experiences, instruction, and gear. Both attractions are bookable at the interactive digital kiosks

BERLITZ'S RATINGS

	Possible	Achieved
Ship	500	407
Accommodation	200	135
Food	400	295
Service	400	279
Entertainment	100	88
Cruise Experience	400	290

OVERALL SCORE 1494 points out of 2000

(adjacent to elevators) and tablets in public areas.

The SeaPlex complex features adrenalin-boosting bumper-car rides, and alternates as a roller-skating rink and basketball court. There's also a rock-climbing wall, and a FlowRider surfing simulator.

Inside, the decor is contemporary, rainbow colorful, and jazzy. The interior focal point is the three-storey-high Royal Esplanade, which includes Michael's Genuine Pub, Sorrento's (pizza outlet), a Bionic Bar (no creative mixology – just ice, standard drinks, and no conversation – but it's novel). Music Hall (a two-deck-high entertainment room), plus several shops, the Schooner Bar, Boleros (Latin bar), Chops Grille (for steaks and grilled seafood), Izumi (for Japanese-style cuisine), and Wonderland.

This ship provides a fine cruise experience for the whole family, but, be warned: you'll need forward planning and to make reservations – for the best cruise experience. Look out for 'Gigi' the pink giraffe outside on the starboard side of Deck 15 – you can't miss it – it's 33ft (10m) high.

What this fine resort ship does superbly well is entertain you, and I highly recommend it for a first cruise, because of the excellent range of activities, the entertainment, and some good dining and eatery experiences.

Niggles include the high cost for fast Wi-Fi connectivity, and the double-bed day 'cabanas' atop the pool deck.

ACCOMMODATION. There are many different accommodation price grades and categories, with price dependent on size and location. Every cabin has a view, whether real or virtual. 'Virtual' balconies – first introduced aboard *Navigator of the Seas* in 2013 – are good for the interior cabins; they can provide real-time ocean views, but you *can* turn them off. Optional wristbands (with RFID technology) provide access to your cabin and act as your charge card (you have to take them off in order to give them to the bartender); unfortunately, they are uncomfortable to wear.

Several new accommodation categories and types have been introduced aboard this ship. Standard cabins are about 9 percent larger than those aboard the *Oasis*-class ships. Note that suite-grade accommodation occupants can take all their meals in the exclusive Coastal Kitchen.

Loft cabins (including a 975 sq ft/90.5 sq m Owner's Loft) vary in size, but measure about 502 sq ft (46.6 sq m) and are located at the ship's stern.

Inter-connecting family cabins are great for multi-generational groups. The 15 units consist of a junior suite, balcony cabin, and interior studio connected through a shared vestibule. Together they can create 575.8 sq ft (53.5 sq m) of living space with three bedrooms, three bathrooms, and a 216-sq-ft (20-sq-m) balcony.

There are 34 'studio' cabins (12 have real balconies; all have wall beds) for solo occupancy, a first for RCI. As there's no supplement for solo travelers, they have their own price category.

Even the smallest bathroom is well designed, with touches such as a night light, and shower and vanity hooks, while cabins have bedside power outlets, ample storage space, and a USB socket.

Negatives: the tablet-based infotainment systems don't answer questions, and the room service menu for breakfast is poor.

DINING. There are 18 restaurant and eatery choices (there's no single main dining room as such – it's divided into four sections: The Grande, Chic, American Icon Grill, and Silk). There are two seatings for dinner (first and second), or you can opt for 'My Time Dining' for more flexibility.

Main dining room cuisine is all about standardized banquet catering and batch cooking. Menu descriptions sound tempting, but the food, although prepared well enough, is just so-so. However, you can have items such as lobster or filet mignon (steak) at an extra cost – and they will be cooked individually for you. Green vegetables are scarce – provided basically for decoration – but salad items are plentiful, and desserts are pretty good. Rice is often used as a source of carbohydrates. Breads and pastry items are so-so (these are thawed and then baked from frozen 'starter' dough), although items such as croissants lack any hint of butter.

Some extra-cost restaurants require reservations, which can prove frustrating; the menus are the same each night, and service can be slow (there are no assistant waiters).

The following are complimentary (with tablecloths for dinner):

The Grande: with 432 seats, the ship's most elegant restaurant (think Southern mansion hospitality) features classic dishes reminiscent of the days of grand ocean liners.

Chic: this 434-seat restaurant features 'contemporary' cuisine and sauces made from scratch.

Silk: this 434-seat restaurant offers pan-Asian cuisine.

American Icon Grill: this 430-seat restaurant serves many of America's favorite 'comfort-food' dishes.'

Extra-cost venues:

Wonderland: based on Fire, Ice, Water, Earth, and Dreams, this surreal 62-seat *Alice in Wonderland*-inspired venue offers food with a quirky touch, including several dishes using liquid nitrogen for smoke-infused specialties (worth the extra cost).

Jamie's Italian: it's a 132-seat, reservations-required tablecloth-free Euro-Italian bistro – and was British celebrity chef Jamie Oliver's first restaurant at sea.

Chops Grille: for premium-quality steaks and grilled seafood.

Chef's Table: this exclusive 16-seat venue (located within Chops Grille) is good for private parties, with wine-and-food pairing.

Izumi: a 44-seat Japanese-Asian fusion cuisine venue including hot-rock tableside cooking, sashimi, sushi, and sake.

Johnny Rockets: a retro 1950s all-day, all-night diner-style eatery for hamburgers, extra-cost malt shakes, and jukebox hits (all tables feature a mini-jukebox). A-la-carte pricing applies.

For serve-yourself meals at no extra cost, there's the 860-seat Windjammer Marketplace buffet. Other casual spots at no extra cost include: The Café at Two70°; SeaPlex Dog House, Sorrento's – for pizza slices and calzones – and Café Promenade.

ENTERTAINMENT. The Royal Theater spans three decks and is the place for 'book' shows and large-scale production shows by a resident troupe of singers and dancers (reservations advised).

There's also entertainment by night at Two70° and in the Music Hall (DJs and theme nights).

SPA/FITNESS. Vitality at Sea Spa facilities include a thermal suite (definitely not worth the extra cost), beauty salon, barber shop, and gymnasium with Technogym equipment. Massage and other body-pampering therapies take place in 19 treatment rooms.

ARCADIA
★★★+

THIS IS A VERY BRITISH, CONTEMPORARY AND STYLISH ADULTS-ONLY SHIP

Size:	Mid-size Ship	Passenger/Crew Ratio (lower beds):	2.3
Tonnage:	84,342	Cabins (total):	1,000
Cruise Line:	P&O Cruises	Size Range (sq ft/m):	170–516.6/15.7–48
Former Names:	none	Cabins (for one person):	6
Builder:	Fincantieri (Italy)	Cabins with balcony:	684
Entered Service:	Apr 2005	Cabins (wheelchair accessible):	30
Length (ft/m):	936.0/285.3	Wheelchair accessibility:	Good
Propulsion/Propellers:	diesel-electric (34,000kW)/ 2 azimuthing pods	Elevators:	14
		Casino (gaming tables):	Yes
Total Crew:	886	Self-Service Launderette:	Yes
Passengers (lower beds):	1,994	Onboard currency:	UK£
Passenger Space Ratio (lower beds):	42.2		

THE SHIP. *Arcadia*, originally intended to be a Holland America Line ship, then Cunard Line's *Queen Victoria*, was transferred instead to P&O Cruises (all three are owned by Carnival Corporation).

Outdoors facilities include a walk-around promenade deck (the ship's forward section is covered), with plenty of sunloungers and cushioned pads. A Lido Deck pool has a moveable glass-domed cover – useful in poor weather. Panoramic exterior glass-wall elevators in the central foyer travel between all 10 passenger decks. Pod propulsion is provided, so there's no vibration.

The layout provides a decent horizontal flow, with most public rooms, shops, bars, and lounges set open-plan style on two decks, and the signage is practical, so finding your way around is quite easy, except that the upper public room deck layout is disjointed. The interior decor is geared towards the contemporary. It is restrained and lacks the traditional features for which P&O Cruises is known. There are 3,000 works of art, costing $4 million, by British artists.

Facilities include a forward-facing Crow's Nest observation lounge, a florist, a shopping arcade, small Monte Carlo casino library (with leather armchairs), a 30-seat boutique screening room, and The Retreat (a good place to chill out). Standout bars include the Spinnaker Bar (with a display of ship models), a 'traditional' English pub (The Rising

BERLITZ'S RATINGS		
	Possible	Achieved
Ship	500	340
Accommodation	200	131
Food	400	241
Service	400	264
Entertainment	100	68
Cruise Experience	400	258

OVERALL SCORE 1302 points out of 2000

Sun, with Boddingtons draught beer), plus a bar overlooking a modest three-deck-high lobby. *Arcadia* blends time-honored British cruising with contemporary facilities, but is quite different from other ships in the fleet. It is registered in Bermuda, so UK and US passport holders can be legally married by the ship's captain (always check for the latest requirements). You can also renew your vows in an extra-cost ceremony. The ship underwent a refurbishment program in 2013, in which one new suite and 23 new cabins were added (including 6 for solo travelers) in a new structure aft of the Crow's Nest, plus a cost-extra Sindhu Restaurant (for British-Indian fusion cuisine), which replaced the former Orchid Restaurant.

Many extra onboard revenue centers have appeared aboard P&O Cruises' ships.

Passenger niggles: there is no room for card games such as bridge; there's pitiful dance floor space; and the embarkation system keeps people waiting in a lounge after check-in and security until boarding card letters are called. The small public toilets are missing touches such as flowers; there are no poolside towels (you must take them from your cabin); and the pre-dinner announcements are robotic. The noisy air conditioning cannot be turned off in cabins or bathrooms.

Arcadia is for couples and solo travelers seeking a mid-size, adults-only ship, with entertainment geared to British tastes, an informal setting, and plenty of public rooms.

ACCOMMODATION. There are numerous price grades, including suites, mini-suites, cabins with private balcony, and twin-bedded cabins either with or without a window.

Cabin doors and elevators also have numbers in Braille. Cabins have duvets, flat-screen infotainment system (the audio channels are also on the television, but you can't turn the picture off), tea/coffee-making sets with Tetley teabags and long-life milk, small refrigerator, vanity/writing desk, personal safe, and a hairdryer; bathrooms have half-size tubs/showers/washbasins, and toilets. Personal toiletries are provided, with larger bottles and more choice for suite occupants.

Also standard are stylish bed runners, Slumberland 8ins (20cm) sprung mattresses, duvets, Egyptian cotton towels and robes, plus in-cabin toning and fitness facilities for passengers who would prefer to exercise in private.

Niggles include the space-hogging tea/coffee-making set on the small vanity desk in basic cabin grades; closets with hanging space too narrow for the width of a jacket; lack of drawer space; poor-quality plastic hangers; and no hooks for belts.

In twin-bed cabin grades, when the beds are pushed together, there's little room to maneuver.

Accommodation designated as suites and mini-suites have more space (some are really just the size of two cabins), including larger bathrooms. So-called 'butler' service is provided, but, unlike most lines with these kinds of grades, bottled water costs extra, as do soft drinks.

DINING. The Meridian Restaurant, aft, is on two decks, and connected by a spiral staircase. It features 11 fine glass fiber-optic ceiling chandeliers created by Neil Wilkin. A podium with grand piano graces the upper level (for Freedom Dining). There are two seatings (Club Dining) in the lower level, and tables seat two to eight. The wine list is 'ho-hum' average, but good value, although the wine glasses are small.

Other dining options. Ocean Grill, by Marco Pierre White (for prime steaks and seafood – with lots of taste). East Restaurant has fine panoramic views, Asian-fusion spice-heavy cuisine created by Michelin-starred chef Atul Kochhar, and its own bar. Reservations are required in both venues, and a cover charge applies.

For casual meals and snacks, there's a self-serve 24-hour eatery The Belvedere, a section of which becomes another venue at night, serving Indian cuisine. There's also an open-deck Neptune Grill and Caffè Vivo (indoors, adjacent to the library).

ENTERTAINMENT. The Palladium showlounge has three seating tiers (in both banquette-style and uncomfortable individual tub chairs), and high-tech staging, lighting, and sound systems. Sight lines to the stage are generally good.

Late-night party types can dance and scream in The Globe. Professional dance hosts and teachers are usually on board, but ballroom-dance aficionados should note that there are few wood dance floors.

SPA/FITNESS. Ocean Spa has a fitness area with forward ocean views, 10 body-pampering treatment rooms, a thermal suite with a hydrotherapy pool, sauna and steam room, and two small unisex saunas at no charge, but in a location that discourages their use (the extra-cost thermal suite is better). While the tiny sauna is free, there's a charge to use the Aqua Pool. To get from the changing room to the sauna you must walk across a carpeted foyer.

Additionally, The Retreat is a cost-extra relaxation space, and for calming tai chi and yoga classes. Sports facilities include a sports court for racquet or football games, a golf driving range, and the traditional shuffleboard and ring toss.

ARTANIA
★★★★

A COMFORTABLE, SPACIOUS SHIP FOR MATURE-AGE GERMAN-SPEAKING CRUISERS

Size:	Mid-size Ship	Passenger/Crew Ratio (lower beds):	2.2
Tonnage:	44,348	Cabins (total):	588
Cruise Line:	Phoenix Reisen	Size Range (sq ft/m):	182.9–1,124.8/17.0–104.5
Former Names:	Artemis, Royal Princess	Cabins (for one person):	0
Builder:	Wartsila (Finland)	Cabins with balcony:	273
Entered Service:	Nov 1984/Apr 2011	Cabins (wheelchair accessible):	4
Length (ft/m):	754.5/230.0	Wheelchair accessibility:	Good
Propulsion/Propellers:	diesel (29,160kW)/2	Elevators:	6
Total Crew:	520	Casino (gaming tables):	No
Passengers (lower beds):	1,176	Self-Service Launderette:	Yes
Passenger Space Ratio (lower beds):	37.7	Onboard currency:	Euros

THE SHIP. *Artania* has a traditional walk-around teak deck, extensive outdoor deck and sunbathing space, and a wave-action swimming pool.

The interior decor reflects the feeling of space, openness, and light. There are several nicely appointed public rooms, bars, and lounges, plus wide passageways and three spacious stairways.

A Pacific Lounge, set around the funnel base, has fine views and a peaceful environment during the day; each evening it becomes a lively nightclub. Around the central stairway foyer, is the popular Harry's Bar; there's also a Bodega (tavern) for food and drinks.

Artania should provide a fine experience in spacious, reserved contemporary surroundings, at a decent price. It is best suited to German-speaking couples and solo travelers seeking to cruise in a modern, but unpretentious, mid-size ship.

ACCOMMODATION. All of the cabins have outside views; 270 have private balconies. There are just four accommodation types (including suites), although there are 21 price categories. All of the cabins (most of which have twin beds convertible into a queen-size bed) are comfortable and well appointed.

All cabins have a large shower enclosure, color TV, hairdryer, personal safe, and European two-pin sockets. Also standard are high-quality sprung mattresses, European duvets, and cotton towels. L'Occitane toiletries are supplied, as are chocolates

BERLITZ'S RATINGS		
	Possible	Achieved
Ship	500	343
Accommodation	200	133
Food	400	293
Service	400	303
Entertainment	100	74
Cruise Experience	400	285

OVERALL SCORE 1431 points out of 2000

on your pillow each night. Prompt, attentive room service is provided 24 hours a day.

Some cabins on both Apollo Deck and Orion Deck have full or partial lifeboat- and safety equipment-obstructed views, but some have extra sofa beds fitted, which is good for families during the busy school-holiday periods.

The 12 largest suites are attractive, but, with the exception of the Royal Suite, they are not large, and the balconies are small, although all have teak decking. Suite occupants get an expanded range of toiletries and complimentary mineral water.

DINING. Vier Jahreszeiten (Four Seasons) restaurant is conveniently adjacent to the lobby, while one deck above is Artania Restaurant, with its own adjacent bar. Casual meals can be taken in the indoor-outdoor Lido Restaurant.

ENTERTAINMENT. The Atlantik Showlounge hosts shows, drama, and cabaret acts, and it's good to note that volume is normally kept to an acceptable level.

SPA/FITNESS. Artania Spa contains a gym with muscle-toning equipment, saunas and changing rooms. There's also a steam bath, ice-fountain, and salon, plus facilities for table tennis, table soccer, shuffleboard, and darts.

ASTOR
★★★

THE TRADITIONAL STYLE AND RESTFUL DÉCOR IS COMFORTABLE FOR MATURE-AGE CRUISERS

Size: .... Small Ship	Passenger/Crew Ratio (lower beds): 1.9
Tonnage: 20,606	Cabins (total): 295
Cruise Line: ...... Cruise and Maritime Voyages (CMV)	Size Range (sq ft/m): 140.0–280.0/13.0–26.0
Former Names: .... *Fedor Dostoyevskiy, Astor (II)*	Cabins (for one person): 0
Builder: ... Howaldtswerke Deutsche Werft (Germany)	Cabins with balcony: 0
Entered Service: .... Feb 1987/Apr 1997	Cabins (wheelchair accessible): 0
Length (ft/m): 579.0/176.5	Wheelchair accessibility: .... Fair
Propulsion/Propellers: .... diesel (15,400kW)/2	Elevators: 3
Total Crew: 300	Casino (gaming tables): .... Yes
Passengers (lower beds): 590	Self-Service Launderette: .... No (ironing room only)
Passenger Space Ratio (lower beds): 34.9	Onboard currency: .... Euros

THE SHIP. *Astor* is a fairly attractive all-white ship with a raked bow, a large square funnel, and a balanced profile. It has been well maintained and refurbished over the years. *Astor* was its original name, the larger of two vessels bearing the same name in the 1980s, built for long-defunct Astor Cruises. It has much traditional styling, teakwood decking, and polished wood railings and interior fittings. There is good open deck and sunbathing space, with cushioned pads for sunloungers.

Public rooms are comfortable and most have high ceilings, and include a showlounge, Captain's Club lounge, library, card room, and two shops, while an intimate, wood-paneled Hanse Bar (for draft beers), has an outdoor area, and is a late-night hangout. There is no crowding anywhere and no annoying background music in hallways or elevators.

The mainly European hotel staff is friendly but not obtrusive. Port taxes, insurance, and gratuities are included, and drinks prices are reasonable.

Astor is operated by Cruise & Maritime Voyages, and cruises in Australasian waters during southern-hemisphere summers. It is a comfortable ship, for couples and solo travelers of mature years. It is a good-value-for-money vacation, with appealing itineraries and destinations, adequate but uninspiring food, and friendly service.

BERLITZ'S RATINGS

	Possible	Achieved
Ship	500	267
Accommodation	200	115
Food	400	205
Service	400	247
Entertainment	100	58
Cruise Experience	400	225

OVERALL SCORE 1117 points out of 2000

ACCOMMODATION. Accommodation (suites and cabins), with numerous price categories, is spread over three decks, with rosewood cabinetry, plain beige walls, and blackout blinds (good for midnight sun cruises).

Note that Suite 105 faces the piano in the conference room opposite (and is subject to music rehearsal sounds).

All grades have a minibar, personal safe, duvets, cotton towels, bathrobe, soap, shampoo, shower cap, sewing kit, and fruit basket, but bathroom towels are small. In some cabins, day sofas convert to beds. The room service menu is limited, and sandwiches cost extra (little else is available).

DINING. The Waldorf Dining Room has two seatings. Service is friendly and unpretentious.

Food quality and presentation are basic, and lack 'wow' factor. In addition to the regular entrées/main courses (typically three for dinner), there may also be a pasta dish and a vegetarian specialty dish. The wine list offers (young) wines from several regions (all at inexpensive to moderate price levels), but wine glasses are small.

Two small specialty dining spots (one for Italian cuisine, the other for a 'romantic dinner') are reservations-only, extra-cost venues (with larger wine glasses).

Casual breakfast and lunch buffets are repetitive, with limited choice.

ENTERTAINMENT. The single-level Show-lounge is for cabaret and mini-concerts, but 14 pillars obstruct the sight lines. The stage is also the dance floor, and can't be raised for shows.

SPA/FITNESS. The Wellness Oasis, on a low deck, has a sauna, steam room, solarium, indoor pool, beauty salon, treatment rooms, and changing areas. A separate fitness center, with techno-machinery and exercycles, is on Bridge Deck. Sports facilities include a basketball court, shuffleboard courts, and a large (aft) deck-chess game.

ASTORIA
★★+

THIS RATHER ELDERLY SMALL SHIP HAS CHARACTER NOT SEEN ABOARD TODAY'S LARGER SHIPS

Size:	Small Ship	Passenger/Crew Ratio (lower beds):	2.0/1
Tonnage:	16,144	Cabins (total):	277
Cruise Line:	Cruise and Maritime Voyages (CMV)	Size Range (sq ft/m):	129.2-376.7/12.0-35.0
Former Names:	Athena, Caribe, Valtur Prima	Cabins (for one person):	2
Builder:	Varco Chiapella (Italy)	Cabins with balcony:	8
Entered Service:	Feb 1948/Mar 2015	Cabins (wheelchair accessible):	0
Length (ft/m):	525.2/160.1	Wheelchair accessibility:	None
Propulsion/Propellers:	diesel/2	Elevators:	2
Total Crew:	280	Casino (gaming tables):	Yes
Passengers (lower beds):	550	Self-Service Launderette:	No
Passenger Space Ratio (lower beds):	28.0	Onboard currency:	UK£

THE SHIP. Although it's very dated and has had many incarnations, operators and names, this lovingly maintained classic ship, with its dark, strong, riveted hull, funnel placed amidships, and a 'sheer' (longitudinal curvature of the main deck) not seen aboard today's section-built ships, holds a special charm for those not seeking the newest floating resorts. It was a transatlantic liner before being converted into a cruise ship in 1994. It has a large sponson (duck tail-like) stern apron, added to aid stability. The ship is for adults only, who can expect a comparatively inexpensive cruise in traditional surroundings, with limited facilities and food, and simple entertainment.

However, this *is* a high-density ship, leaving little space to move around in, and its fixed gangway may be steep, depending on port and tidal conditions. Outdoors is a walk-around teakwood promenade deck; many real wood sunloungers are provided, although open deck sunbathing space is minimal, and the mall swimming pool is really just a dip/plunge pool.

Astoria has non-glitzy but surprisingly modern interiors that are charming in their own way. Most public rooms are located on one deck (Calypso Deck); these include a library, card room, casino (with gaming tables and slot machines), several bars, and a chapel. The ship is operated by CMV under charter from her Lisbon-based owner.

BERLITZ'S RATINGS

	Possible	Achieved
Ship	500	265
Accommodation	200	116
Food	400	209
Service	400	234
Entertainment	100	50
Cruise Experience	400	206

OVERALL SCORE 1080 points out of 2000

ACCOMMODATION. There are numerous accommodation price grades, and the price you pay depends on the size, location, and grade you choose.

All cabins have a mini-bar, TV, and safe. Bathrooms have a combination tub/shower and a good amount of indented space for toiletries. Eight suites each have a small private balcony, and a separate lounge/living area with table and chairs; bathrooms have whirlpool bathtubs with showers, toilet, washbasin, and bidet.

Some cabins (on Promenade Deck) have lifeboat-obstructed views, and some on Mediterranean Deck may pick up noise from the public rooms on the deck above. The largest accommodation is one rather nice Owner's Suite.

DINING. The Olissipo Restaurant has two sections. It is quite attractive, and tables are for two to eight persons. The food quality is in line with the low cost of the cruise.

For basic casual meals, the Lotus Lounge is a self-serve buffet venue.

ENTERTAINMENT. Calypso Show Lounge is the main show lounge, but the views to the stage area are obstructed from many seats. There is a sizeable bar at the back of the room.

SPA/FITNESS. There's a workout room, sauna, steam room, body therapy rooms, and beauty salon.

ASUKA II
★★★★+

AN ELEGANT, SPACIOUS, BUT DATED SHIP WITH FINE FOOD, FOR JAPANESE-SPEAKING CRUISERS

Size:	Mid-size Ship	Passenger/Crew Ratio (lower beds):	1.7
Tonnage:	50,142	Cabins (total):	462
Cruise Line:	Asuka Cruise	Size Range (sq ft/m):	198.1–949.4/18.4–88.2
Former Names:	*Crystal Harmony*	Cabins (for one person):	0
Builder:	Mitsubishi Heavy Industries (Japan)	Cabins with balcony:	260
Entered Service:	Jul 1990/May 2006	Cabins (wheelchair accessible):	4
Length (ft/m):	790.5/240.9	Wheelchair accessibility:	Good
Propulsion/Propellers:	diesel-electric (32,800kW)/2	Elevators:	8
Total Crew:	470	Casino (gaming tables):	Yes
Passengers (lower beds):	800	Self-Service Launderette:	Yes
Passenger Space Ratio (lower beds):	52.0	Onboard currency:	Japanese Yen

THE SHIP. Although now over 25 years old, *Asuka II* (formerly *Crystal Harmony*), is a handsome, well-balanced ship with raked clipper bow, sleek lines, and Nippon Yusen Kaisha (NYK) Line's double red band on the funnel. There is almost no sense of crowding anywhere, and the fact that form follows function means that comfort is built in. There is a wide wrap-around teakwood deck for walking, and an abundance of open deck space.

Inside, the layout is completely different from the first *Asuka* in that there is a horizontal flow through the public rooms, which better suits the age range of NYK's typical passengers. The design combines some large ship facilities with the intimacy of rooms found aboard many smaller ships. There is a wide assortment of public entertainment lounges and small intimate rooms. Fine-quality fabrics and soft furnishings, china, flatware, and silver are used.

Outstanding are the Vista (observation) Lounge and tranquil, elegant Palm Court, while adjacent are an Internet room and a Chashitsu (Japanese 12-tatami mat room). Other public spaces and facilities include the Mariner's Club Lounge (piano bar/lounge), Cigar Bar, Bistro Café, Casino Corner, Mahjong Room with eight tables, Compass Room (meeting and activities room), a book/video library, and the Stars karaoke bar. The theater is a dedicated room with high-definition video projection. There is a self-

BERLITZ'S RATINGS		
	Possible	Achieved
Ship	500	392
Accommodation	200	154
Food	400	336
Service	400	306
Entertainment	100	81
Cruise Experience	400	317

OVERALL SCORE 1586 points out of 2000

service launderette on each deck – practical for long cruises.

Asuka II is a relaxing, grand hotel afloat – offering the equivalent standard as Tokyo's top hotels – and provides abundant choices and flexibility. It has most things that the discerning traveler needs, space, and the comfort and the facilities of a mid-size vessel capable of long voyages. The company pays attention to its repeat passengers, particularly those in Deck 10 penthouses and suites.

Unfortunately, dining is in two seatings, which makes its timing highly structured – there are two shows, because the showlounge can't seat everyone at once. While this works well in the Japanese market; overall, the arrangement detracts from the otherwise fine setting of the ship and the professionalism of its staff. All gratuities are included.

Asuka II is best suited to Japanese-speaking travelers (typically over 60) seeking a sophisticated ship with high-quality fittings and furnishings, a wide range of public rooms and facilities, and excellent food and service ('omotenashi' hospitality) from a well-trained staff. It is the attention to detail that makes this ship so pleasant.

in 2020, the ship will undergo an extensive refurbishment.

ACCOMMODATION. There are five categories of suites and cabins (including four Royal Suites with private balcony; Asuka Suites with balcony; suites with balcony; cabins with balcony; cabins without balcony). Regardless of the category, duvets and down pillows are provided, as are other niceties. All cabins have a color TV, mini-refrigerator, personal safe, small couch and coffee table, excellent sound-proofing, a refrigerator and minibar, full tea-making set, satellite-linked telephone, hairdryer, and slippers. A full range of toiletries (including shampoo, hair rinse, shower cap, soap, cotton pads, razor set, hairbrush, and more) is provided, and cotton towels are plentiful.

Deck 10 penthouses. Four Royal Suites, whose entrance doorway has a door phone and camera, have fine ocean-view Japanese-style bathrooms, with quality German fittings including a large overhead shower, jet bathtub, two washbasins, and abundant storage space for toiletries (L'Occitane products are provided).

Other Deck 10 suites. All Deck 10 suites/cabins are attended by social officers, and complimentary in-room dining service is offered.

Deck 9/8/7/5 cabins. Many cabins have a private balcony (in fact, half of all cabins have private balconies, with outside lights) and are very comfortable. But they are a little tight for space, with one-way traffic past the bed. Some cabins have lifeboat-obstructed views, so do check the deck plan carefully.

Although well appointed, the bathrooms (except for those in Deck 10 accommodation) are compact, but all have electric 'washlet' high-cleanse toilets.

DINING. The Four Seasons Dining Room is the pleasant main dining room and has a raised central section. It has ample space around each table (for two to eight).

Dinner is in two seatings, with no set table assignments.

Umihiko is a Japanese extra-charge restaurant, with its own authentic sushi bar and live fish tanks for absolutely fresh sashimi. It provides a refined, intimate dining experience with fine ocean views. Reservations are required.

Prego, with 40 seats and ocean views to starboard and aft, is for occupants of the Royal Suites and Asuka Suites. The menu is the same as the main dining room, but in a more intimate setting.

For casual meals, beverages, and ice cream, the Lido Café has a good self-serve buffet area; it is located high in the ship and has ocean views from large picture windows. There is also a Lido Garden Grill, a large area with wooden tables and chairs, and bar.

Additionally, The Bistro, located on the upper level of the two-deck-high lobby, is a casual spot for coffees and pastries; it has the atmosphere of a European street café.

ENTERTAINMENT. The Galaxy Lounge (show-lounge) is a large room on one level, with a sloping floor. The sight lines are good from most seats, although a few pillars obstruct the view from some. Both banquette-style and individual seating is provided.

SPA/FITNESS. The Grand Spa includes a large Grand Bath/cleansing center (one for men, one for women), with integral sauna (for men) and steam room (for ladies). Other facilities include five treatment rooms (longevity, water, wind, prosperity, harmony) including one for couples. There's a separate sauna, steam rooms, changing rooms for men and women, a beauty salon, and a relaxation area. Another part of the spa houses a gymnasium, with ocean-view windows on one side.

The Asuka Aveda Salon and Spa offers a wide range of body-pampering treatments using Aveda brand products. The spa also offers a kimono dressing service, which costs ¥8,000-¥10,000 (about $115).

There is an excellent amount of open deck space, with a long swimming pool. Sports facilities include a full-size paddle tennis court, putting green, and golf driving range.

AURORA
★★★+

A TRADITIONAL, BRITISH-STYLE ADULTS-ONLY SHIP WITH GOOD FACILITIES

Size:	Mid-size Ship	Passenger/Crew Ratio (lower beds):	2.2
Tonnage:	76,152	Cabins (total):	934
Cruise Line:	P&O Cruises	Size Range (sq ft/m):	150.6–953.0/14.0–88.5
Former Names:	none	Cabins (for one person):	4
Builder:	Meyer Werft (Germany)	Cabins with balcony:	406
Entered Service:	May 2000	Cabins (wheelchair accessible):	22
Length (ft/m):	885.8/270.0	Wheelchair accessibility:	Good
Propulsion/Propellers:	diesel-electric (40,000kW)/2	Elevators:	10
Total Crew:	816	Casino (gaming tables):	Yes
Passengers (lower beds):	1,864	Self-Service Launderette:	Yes
Passenger Space Ratio (lower beds):	40.7	Onboard currency:	UK£

THE SHIP. *Aurora* (now 20 years old) was built specifically for Britain's more traditional cruise passengers. The ship has larger cabins and suites and more dining options. Following an extensive make-over, it is now an adults-only ship.

It has a large, glass-domed indoor/outdoor swimming pool – good in all weather conditions. The aft is nicely rounded, with several tiers overlooking the open decks and pool. There is good sunbathing space and an extra-wide walk-around outdoor promenade deck, with plenty of plastic sunloungers (cushioned pads are available).

Aurora's interior focal point is a four-decks-high atrium lobby with a 35-ft- (10.6-m-) high, Lalique-style fiberglass sculpture of two mythical figures behind a veil of water.

Among the 12 lounges/bars, the nicest are Anderson's, with fireplace and mahogany paneling, and Crow's Nest, with a one-sided model of former P&O liner *Strathnaver* of 1931 (scrapped in Hong Kong in 1962). A cinema also doubles as a concert and lecture hall.

Aurora is a mid-size ship that is for UK-UK cruises (good for anyone not wanting to fly). The ship has the facilities of a small resort, with food and service that come with a sense of Britishness, although the decor is rather bland.

ACCOMMODATION. There are numerous cabin-size and price categories, including two bi-level

BERLITZ'S RATINGS		
	Possible	Achieved
Ship	500	320
Accommodation	200	128
Food	400	244
Service	400	268
Entertainment	100	67
Cruise Experience	400	263
OVERALL SCORE 1290 points out of 2000		

penthouses, suites with balconies, mini-suites with balconies, cabins with balconies, standard outside-view cabins, and interior (no-view) cabins.

All grades have polished cherry wood laminate cabinetry, full-length mirror, personal safe, mini-fridge, infotainment screen, individually controlled air conditioning, twin beds convertible to a queen-size/ double bed, stylish bed runners, Slumberland sprung mattresses, duvets, Egyptian cotton towels, sofa, coffee table, and tea/coffee-making facilities (long-life milk is provided). Cabins with balconies have sliding glass floor-to-ceiling doors that are easy to open; the partitions are almost full-length also, so they really are quite private and can't be overlooked from above.

Cabin insulation could be better, however, and the magnetic catches in drawers and on closet doors are noisy. Although most doorways are 26ins (66cm) wide, the actual access is 2ins (5cm) less because of the doorframe; however, some doorways are only 21.5ins (55cm) wide. Most cabins have two lower beds that convert to a queen-size bed; there is closet space, but few drawers.

The largest are two Penthouse Suites. The There are 22 well-outfitted, wheelchair-accessible cabins; most are located close to an elevator. However, D165 on Deck 8 is between forward and mid-ships stairways, from where it is difficult to access the public rooms on Deck 8 without first going to the deck below, due to several steps and tight corners. Eight wheelchair-accessible cabins have a balcony.

DINING. The two main dining rooms (each seats about 525) have tables for two to 10. The midships Medina has a vaguely Moorish theme, and 'Freedom dining' (open seating for dinner) with Marco Pierre White dishes on gala evenings, while Alexandria, with windows on three sides, has an Egyptian theme and two dinner seatings ('Club dining'). The china is Wedgwood; the silverware Elkington.

The cuisine is straightforward, no-nonsense British food, reasonably well presented on nice china. However, it tends to be rather bland and uninspiring. It is typical of mass-banquet catering with standard fare comparable to that found in a family hotel in a classic English seaside town. The wine list is 'ho-hum' average, but good value, although the red and white wine glasses are small.

You can also dine in The Glasshouse restaurant/ wine bar (selected by Olly Smith); or Sindhu (on the upper deck of the atrium lobby), for an Indian-fusion menu designed by Atul Kochhar. Both are extra-cost venues, for which reservations are required.

Casual, self-serve breakfasts and lunches can be taken from the self-serve buffet in The Orangery, which has ocean views. Other casual dining spots include the Sidewalk Café (for fast-food items poolside), The Beach House (for lava-rock sizzle food), a Champagne bar, and Raffles coffee and chocolate bar (minus the ceiling fans).

ENTERTAINMENT. There is a wide variety of mainly British entertainment, from production shows and cabaret acts.

SPA/FITNESS. The Oasis Spa is amidships on Lido Deck, just forward of the Crystal swimming pool. Facilities include a workout room, sauna and steam room (both unisex, so take a bathing suit), a beauty salon, a spiral staircase, and a relaxation area overlooking the Riviera pool.

AZAMARA JOURNEY
★★★★

THIS IS AN INFORMAL SHIP WITH COUNTRY-HOUSE DECOR AND FINE FOOD CHOICES

Size:	Small Ship
Tonnage:	30,277
Cruise Line:	Azamara
Former Names:	Blue Star, Blue Dream, R6
Builder:	Chantiers de l'Atlantique (France)
Entered Service:	Feb 2000/May 2007
Length (ft/m):	591.8/180.4
Propulsion/Propellers:	diesel (18,600kW)/2
Total Crew:	400
Passengers (lower beds):	680
Passenger Space Ratio (lower beds):	42.7
Passenger/Crew Ratio (lower beds):	1.6
Cabins (total):	340
Size Range (sq ft/m):	151.0–818.0/14.0–76.0
Cabins (for one person):	0
Cabins with balcony:	249
Cabins (wheelchair accessible):	6
Wheelchair accessibility:	Fair
Elevators:	4
Casino (gaming tables):	Yes
Self-Service Launderette:	Yes
Onboard currency:	US$

THE SHIP. The ship has a deep blue hull and white superstructure topped by a large, square blue funnel. A lido deck has a small swimming pool flanked by two hot tubs, good sunbathing space, and comfortable sunloungers. Although there is no outdoor walk-around promenade deck, a short jogging track encircles the pool deck (one deck above it). The uppermost outdoors deck includes a golf driving net and shuffleboard court. There are no wooden decks outdoors – the floor is covered instead by a sand-colored rubberized material. Smoking is permitted only in designated spots on the open decks. The interior decor is in good taste, and full of light, contemporary colors.

Public rooms are spread over three decks, and getting around is easy. The reception hall has a staircase with intricate wrought-iron railings. A large observation lounge (The Living Room) is forward on an upper deck. It has a long bar with forward views – for the barmen, that is, as anyone seated at the bar faces aft. There's a bar in each restaurant entrance, plus a Martini Bar. There's also a Mosaic Café, a Luxe Casino, and a shop (Boutique C).

The Drawing Room (the ship's library) is a delightful restful room, designed in the Regency style, with a fireplace, a high, indented trompe l'oeil ceiling, and a good selection of books, plus comfortable wingback chairs with footstools, and sofas.

BERLITZ'S RATINGS		
	Possible	Achieved
Ship	500	379
Accommodation	200	134
Food	400	279
Service	400	311
Entertainment	100	76
Cruise Experience	400	290

OVERALL SCORE 1469 points out of 2000

Standard drinks and wines are included (premium brands cost extra). Gratuities to housekeeping and dining staff are included in the fare. Shuttle buses are provided free when needed in ports of call.

Azamara Journey, virtually identical to *Azamara Quest* in features and fittings, best suits mature couples seeking to get away from the crowds aboard a small, contemporary ship with a wide range of bars and lounges, at a slightly lower cost than the luxury lines. The ship is large enough to offer a little entertainment and several dining venues, but small enough to be able to choose uncrowded ports, making for a comfortable, club-like ambiance and enjoyable overall experience.

ACCOMMODATION. There are several suite and cabin price grades. The price you pay reflects the size and location of your chosen accommodation. All have butler service (but it's more a case of better-dressed cabin stewards). The lowest four grades of interior and outside-view cabins are extremely compact units. *Azamara Journey* calls them staterooms, but they are just cabins – and rather tight for two persons, particularly for cruises of over seven days. The bathrooms are postage-stamp sized, and you'll be fighting with the shower curtain, as well as storage space for toiletries. The standard cabins cannot, in any sense, be considered luxury, and even premium is stretching it a bit.

All cabins have two lower beds convertible to a queen-sized bed, good under-bed storage areas, flat-screen TV, good closet space, thermostat-controlled air- conditioning, hairdryer, telephone and voicemail, and 100 percent cotton towels. Most cabins also have a personal safe, and refrigerator with mini bar.

For the extra cost, it's wise to choose a suite or cabin with a balcony. Some cabins have interconnecting doors, while 18 cabins on Deck 6 have lifeboat-obstructed views.

DINING. Discoveries (main dining room) has around 340 seats, a raised central section (conversation at these tables may be difficult, due to its low ceiling height), and open-seating dining. There are large ocean-view windows on three sides, several prime tables overlooking the stern, and a small bandstand for live dinner music. Menus change daily for lunch and dinner, and wine is included. Adjacent to the restaurant is a Martini Bar, with a cozy fireplace.

Aqualina Restaurant is aft on the port side of Deck 10; it has 96 seats and windows along two sides, and features Italian/Mediterranean cuisine. A Tasting Menu, including wine pairing, is available.

Next door is Prime C, which features premium-quality steaks and grilled seafood items. It has 98 seats, windows on two sides, and a set menu, but no tablecloths.

Both Aqualina and Prime C incur a cover charge (included for occupants of top-grade suites).

Windows Café has indoor and outdoor seating (combined, for just over 150, not really enough when cruising in cold areas). It is open for breakfast, lunch, and casual dinners, and incorporates a small Sushi Café.

All dining venues have open-seating dining, although reservations are needed in the Aqualina Restaurant and Prime C, where there are mostly tables for four or six (there are few tables for two). All cappuccino and espresso coffees cost extra.

Mosaic Café features extra-cost Italian coffees, teas, and pastries. Also, a Poolside Grill provides fast-food items (some grilled to order). A self-serve soft ice cream machine is located adjacent to its beverage station. Coffee and tea are free 24 hours a day.

ENTERTAINMENT. Cabaret, located forward, is the venue for most entertainment events.

SPA/FITNESS. The Sanctum spa has a fitness room with high-tech cardiovascular equipment, an extra-cost thalassotherapy pool, steam room, and several body-treatment rooms. An 'Acupuncture at Sea' clinic provides treatments that are operated independently of the spa (as a concession).

AZAMARA PURSUIT
★★★★

THIS SMALL SHIP IS FOR ADULT-ONLY CRUISING AND IS SUITED TO AMERICAN TASTES

Size:	Small Ship	Passenger/Crew Ratio (lower beds):	1.8
Tonnage:	30,277	Cabins (total):	355
Cruise Line:	Azamara	Size Range (sq ft/m):	145.3–968.7/13.5–90.0
Former Names:	Adonia, Royal Princess, Minerva II, R8	Cabins (for one person):	0
Builder:	Chantiers de l'Atlantique (France)	Cabins with balcony:	258
Entered Service:	February 2001/June 2018	Cabins (wheelchair accessible):	4
Length (ft/m):	592.0/180.4	Wheelchair accessibility:	Good
Propulsion/Propellers:	diesel/2	Elevators:	4
Total Crew:	300	Casino (gaming tables):	Yes
Passengers (lower beds):	710	Self-Service Launderette:	Yes
Passenger Space Ratio (lower beds):	42.6	Onboard currency:	UK£

THE SHIP. The ship has an all-white hull and superstructure. The lido (pool) deck has reasonable sunbathing space.

There may not be marble bathroom fittings or other expensive niceties, but *Azamara Pursuit* is a pleasant ship, best suited to mature couples.

Last in a series of eight almost identical ships originally built for the long-defunct Renaissance Cruises in 2001, it is well proportioned, and has the feel of an informal country hotel. The interior decor, designed by Scotsman John McNeece, is a throwback to the heavy hardwood style of the ocean liners of the 1920s and 1930s, and includes detailed ceiling cornices, real and faux wrought-iron staircase railings, wood- and leather-paneled walls, and trompe l'oeil ceilings.

Public rooms are spread over three decks. The reception hall has a staircase with intricate, real wrought-iron railings (a copy of the staircase aboard SS *Titanic*), but these are cleverly painted on plexiglas panels on the stairways on other decks.

Anderson's, the social hub of the ship, is a rather delightful, wood-paneled lounge with a fireplace, a long bar with bar stools, and the feel of a traditional country club.

The Regency-style drawing Room library is a delightful, restful room, with a fireplace, a high, indented trompe l'oeil ceiling, books, comfortable wingback chairs with footstools, and sofas to fall asleep on.

BERLITZ'S RATINGS		
	Possible	Achieved
Ship	500	382
Accommodation	200	135
Food	400	279
Service	400	319
Entertainment	100	76
Cruise Experience	400	292
OVERALL SCORE 1483 points out of 2000		

The Living Room has great views through floor-to-ceiling windows, and comfortable seating. A long bar faces forward, so the bartenders have the best view. There is a small central bandstand and wooden dance floor forward of the bar.

Sadly, there are no wooden decks outdoors; they are covered by a sand-colored rubberized material instead. There's no walk-around promenade deck, although you can stroll on open decks on the port and starboard sides.

The ship is large enough to offer a little entertainment and several dining choices, but small enough to be able to choose uncrowded ports, making for a very comfortable, club-like ambiance and enjoyable overall experience.

ACCOMMODATION. There are six basic cabin size categories, in many price categories. Some cabins have interconnecting doors, and some cabins on Deck 6 have lifeboat-obstructed views. There are two interior accommodation passageways.

Standard outside-view and interior cabins are compact units, and tight for two. They have twin or queen-size beds, with good under-bed storage, personal safe, a vanity desk with large mirror, and reasonable closet and drawer storage in rich, dark woods.

Balcony cabins have sliding glass doors. Some 14 cabins on Deck 6 have lifeboat-obstructed views. The tiled-floor, plain wall bathrooms are compact, but include a shower stall with a removable hand-held shower unit, wall-mounted hair-dryer, cotton towels, toiletries storage shelves, and retractable clothesline.

Six Owner's Suites and four Master Suites provide abundant space and are worth the extra cost. They are located in the forward and aft positions. Particularly nice are those overlooking the stern, on decks 6, 7, and 8. They have extensive balconies that cannot be overlooked. There is an entrance foyer, living room, bedroom (the bed faces the sea), audio unit, bathroom with Jacuzzi tub, and small guest bathroom.

DINING. There are three restaurants, plus a casual self-serve buffet-style venue and an outdoor grill: Discoveries Restaurant, aft, has a raised central section, large ocean-view windows on three sides, and several prime tables overlook the stern. Dining is at assigned tables, in two seatings. The noise level can be high, the result of a single-deck-height ceiling and noisy waiter stations. Adjacent to the restaurant entrance (it forms part of it) is the Discoveries Bar – a cozy, open lounge and bar, with a fireplace.

All dining venues have open-seating dining, although reservations are needed in Aqualina Restaurant, and Prime C, where there are mostly tables for four or six (there are few tables for two). Suite-grade occupants get unlimited access. All cappuccino and espresso coffees cost extra.

The Mosaic Café serves Italian coffees, as well as teas and pastries (no extra cost). Additionally, a Poolside Grill provides fast-food items (some items are grilled to order). A self-serve soft ice cream machine is located adjacent to its beverage station. Coffee and tea are free 24 hours a day.

Windows Café, with indoor and outdoor seating, is a self-serve eatery, while the Poolside Grill is for casual fast food and grilled food items.

ENTERTAINMENT. The Cabaret Lounge is a single-level room, with a large bar at the back (the bartender probably has the best views of the stage).

SPA/FITNESS. The Sanctum has a fitness room with some muscle-toning equipment, a large hot tub, steam rooms for men and women (but no saunas), treatment rooms, and a beauty salon. A spa concession provides beauty and wellness treatments and exercise classes – some of which may cost extra. On deck are a small swimming pool, two hot tubs, a jogging track, a golf practice net, and shuffleboard courts.

AZAMARA QUEST
★★★★

THIS SMALL SHIP IS REMINISCENT OF A COMFORTABLE COUNTRY CLUB

Size:	Small Ship	Passenger/Crew Ratio (lower beds):	2.3
Tonnage:	30,277	Cabins (total):	358
Cruise Line:	Azamara	Size Range (sq ft/m):	156.0–484.3/14.5–45.0
Former Names:	Blue Moon, Delphin Renaissance, R7	Cabins (for one person):	0
Builder:	Chantiers de l'Atlantique (France)	Cabins with balcony:	232
Entered Service:	Oct 2000/Oct 2007	Cabins (wheelchair accessible):	4
Length (ft/m):	591.8/180.4	Wheelchair accessibility:	Fair
Propulsion/Propellers:	diesel (18,600kW)/2	Elevators:	4
Total Crew:	306	Casino (gaming tables):	Yes
Passengers (lower beds):	716	Self-Service Launderette:	Yes
Passenger Space Ratio (lower beds):	42.2	Onboard currency:	US$

THE SHIP. *Azamara Quest* was originally one of a series of eight almost identical ships in the long-defunct Renaissance Cruises fleet (when it was in operation, between 1998 and 2001, it was the cruise industry's only totally no-smoking cruise line). In 2007 it joined Azamara Cruises (now known simply as Azamara), and underwent an almost $20-million make-over. The hull is deep blue, while the super-structure is white.

An outdoors lido deck has a swimming pool flanked by two hot tubs and good sunbathing space with wooden sunloungers; one of the aft decks has a thalassotherapy pool. The exterior decks are covered by a rubber and sand-like surface. The uppermost outdoors deck includes a golf driving net and shuffleboard court. The interior decor is elegant, in the style of ocean liner decor of the 1920s.

The ship is large enough to offer a little entertainment and several dining options, but small enough to be able to choose uncrowded ports, making for a very comfortable, club-like ambiance and enjoyable overall experience. Standard drinks and wines are included (premium brands cost extra). In 2016, the ship underwent a major refurbishment program that refreshed all accommodation and public areas, with lighter decor that has brightened the interiors.

ACCOMMODATION. There are several suite and cabin price grades. The price reflects the size and

BERLITZ'S RATINGS		
	Possible	Achieved
Ship	500	380
Accommodation	200	134
Food	400	279
Service	400	312
Entertainment	100	76
Cruise Experience	400	290

OVERALL SCORE 1471 points out of 2000

location of your chosen accommodation. All have so-called butler service, although they are simply better-dressed cabin stewards. The standard interior and outside-view cabins (the lowest four grades) are extremely compact units. *Azamara Quest* calls them staterooms, but they are simply cabins – and rather tight for two persons, particularly for cruises longer than seven days. The bathrooms are postage-stamp-sized, and you'll be fighting with the shower curtain and frustrated by the limited storage space for toiletries. The standard cabins cannot, in any sense, be considered luxury, and even premium is stretching it a bit.

All cabins have two lower beds convertible to a (sleep-together) queen-sized bed, good under-bed storage areas, flat-screen TV, good closet space, thermostat-controlled air conditioning, hairdryer, telephone and voicemail, and 100 percent cotton towels. Most cabins also have a personal safe, and refrigerator with minibar.

For the extra cost, it's wise to choose a suite or cabin with a balcony. Some cabins have interconnecting doors while 18 cabins on Deck 6 have lifeboat-obstructed views.

Accommodation grades are as follows: Club ocean-view cabins with balcony; Club Deluxe Veranda cabins; Club Continent Suites and superior exterior-view cabins with veranda; Club Spa Suites; Club Ocean Suites (Decks 6, 7); and Club World Owner's

Suites with balcony (much in demand are those over-looking the stern, on decks 6, 7, and 8).

Suite-grade occupants get priority boarding, tender service, and other perks including free espressos/cappuccinos, bottled water, and silk-wrapped hangers. Note that suites/cabins located at the stern can suffer from vibration when the ship is at or close to full speed, or maneuvering in port.

DINING. Discoveries, the main dining room, has around 340 seats, a raised central section (conversation may be difficult, due to its low ceiling height), and open-seating dining. There are large ocean-view windows on three sides, some with prime tables overlooking the stern. The menu changes daily for lunch and dinner, and wine is included. Adjacent to the restaurant is a Martini Bar, with a cozy fireplace.

Aqualina Restaurant is at the aft of the ship on the port side of Deck 10; it has 96 seats, windows along two sides, and serves Mediterranean cuisine. A Tasting Menu includes wine.

Prime C is located at the aft of the ship on the starboard side of Deck 10, and features premium-quality steaks and grilled seafood items. It has 98 seats, windows along two sides, and a set menu.

Both Aqualina and Prime C incur a cover charge (free for occupants of top-grade suites).

Windows Café has indoor and outdoor seating (combined, for just over 150, not really enough when cruising in cold areas or in the winter months). It is open for breakfast, lunch, and casual dinners, and incorporates a small Sushi Café.

All dining venues have open-seating dining, although reservations are needed in the Aqualina Restaurant and Prime C, where there are mostly tables for four or six (there are few tables for two). Suite-grade occupants get unlimited access. All cappuccino and espresso coffees cost extra.

The Mosaic Café serves Italian coffees, as well as teas and pastries (no extra cost). Additionally, a Poolside Grill provides fast-food items (some items are grilled to order). A self-serve soft ice cream machine is located adjacent to its beverage station. Coffee and tea are free 24 hours a day.

ENTERTAINMENT. Celebrity Cabaret, located forward, is the venue for all main entertainment events, which include a mix of classical concerts, revues, comedy, and drama.

SPA/FITNESS. The Sanctum spa has a gymnasium with high-tech muscle-toning equipment, an extra-cost thalassotherapy pool (outside, forward on deck), and several treatment rooms. An 'Acupuncture at Sea' clinic provides treatments that are operated independently of the spa (but also as a concession).

AZURA
★★★+

THIS LARGE RESORT SHIP WITH SEDATE DECOR IS PERFECT FOR BRITISH STYLE AND TASTES

Size:	Large Resort Ship	Passenger/Crew Ratio (lower beds):	2.4
Tonnage:	115,055	Cabins (total):	1,557
Cruise Line:	P&O Cruises	Size Range (sq ft/m):	134.5–534.0/12.5–49.6
Former Names:	none	Cabins (for one person):	18
Builder:	Fincantieri (Italy)	Cabins with balcony:	910
Entered Service:	Apr 2010	Cabins (wheelchair accessible):	25
Length (ft/m):	951.4/290.0	Wheelchair accessibility:	Good
Propulsion/Propellers:	diesel-electric (42,000kW)/2	Elevators:	12
Total Crew:	1,239	Casino (gaming tables):	Yes
Passengers (lower beds):	3,096	Self-Service Launderette:	Yes
Passenger Space Ratio (lower beds):	37.2	Onboard currency:	UK£

THE SHIP. *Azura* (like close sister ship *Ventura*) has a flat, upright stern; it looks like a giant hatchback, although its side profile is softer and more balanced. There is an outdoor promenade walkaround deck (if you include the steps in the forward section); it's also narrow in some places, with sunloungers in the way.

There are three main swimming pools: two on the pool deck, one aft. There's not a lot of outdoor deck space – unless you pay extra to use The Retreat – a covered, adults-only zone above the spa. It has a faux-grass floor, private cabanas, and steward service; it is much quieter, and may be worth it. A large open-air movie screen (SeaScreen) sits forward of the funnel.

Inside, a three-deck atrium, with integral dance floor, is the focal point (town center). Four large, three-deck-high black granite archways provide 'gateways' to the center. It's the place to see and be seen – as are the specialty dining venues. Also, in the atrium is a small open-plan library (but it's poor for reading when atrium events are staged), with computers. There's also a Java Café for extra-cost coffees, teas, cakes, pastries, and snacks.

Other rooms, bars, and lounges include a casino (The Exchange); an urban 'warehouse' bar; Blue Bar, the ship's social hub; Brodie's, a 'traditional' British pub (named after Brodie McGhie Willcox, P&O's co-founder); and the Planet Bar, high in the ship, with a video wall.

BERLITZ'S RATINGS

	Possible	Achieved
Ship	500	372
Accommodation	200	144
Food	400	246
Service	400	284
Entertainment	100	75
Cruise Experience	400	269

OVERALL SCORE 1390 points out of 2000

The upper-deck public room layout means you can't easily go from one end of the ship to the other without first going down, along, and up (frustrating for anyone who has limited mobility).

Azura suits families with children and adult couples who are seeking a big-ship environment with comfortable, unstuffy surroundings, lots of options, and a distinctly British flavor. However, the ship tends to over-promise, and under-deliver.

ACCOMMODATION. There are many price grades, but just six types of accommodation: suite with balcony; family suite with balcony; outside-view twin/queen with balcony; outside-view twin/queen; interior cabin, and solo traveler cabin. Although there are more balconies than aboard *Ventura*, more than a third of all cabins don't have an outside view. Some have extra third/fourth berths that fold down from the ceiling.

There are the 18 solo-occupancy cabins (a first for P&O Cruises), in a small port side section, plus 'spa' cabins, with added amenities and direct access to the ship's spa, and two large suites for large groups.

While the suites are very small when compared to those of lines such as Celebrity Cruises or Norwegian Cruise Line, they are intelligently laid out, and feel spacious.

Standard in all cabins: bed runners, duvets, Slumberland 8ins (20cm) sprung mattresses, and Egyptian cotton towels. Tea/coffee-making facilities are adequate, but with UHT, not fresh, milk. Bathrobes are provided only for certain grades. There are UK three-pin sockets, plus US-style 110-volt sockets for electrical devices.

Open closets provide good access, but the 'no trust' attached hangers can bang against the wall when the ship is 'moving'. Balcony cabins have wood railings atop glass dividers, plastic floors, a couple of small chairs and drinks table, and an outside light. Most cabin bathrooms are small, as are the shower enclosures; amenities are by The White Company.

Wheelchair-accessible cabins, which have a large, user-friendly shower enclosure, are mostly located in the front section of the ship, but one of the main restaurants is aft. So be prepared for lots of wheeling time, and waiting time at the elevators.

There is no room service breakfast on disembarkation day, when you must vacate your cabin early.

DINING. The marketing blurb claims that there are 10 restaurants. Rubbish! There are five genuine restaurants (Peninsular, Oriental, Meridian, Sindhu, and Epicurian); the others are bistro-style eateries or fast-food venues.

The Peninsular, Oriental, and Meridian restaurants share the same menus. Oriental offers fixed (Club) seating dining at assigned tables. In the Meridian and Peninsular restaurants, you can dine when you want, with whomever you want, when open – P&O calls it 'Freedom Dining,' although at peak times there can be a bit of a wait; it's not open for breakfast or lunch. Occasionally, special dinners are served in the main dining rooms, one of which is a Chaîne des Rôtisseurs event.

Wheelchair users should note that to take breakfast in the self-serve casual eatery, you may need to wheel across the decks with the forward and midship pools and a sea of deck chairs – not easy. Alternatively, you can order room service breakfast, but for cold items only.

The cuisine is straightforward, no-nonsense British food, reasonably well presented on nice Wedgwood china. But it tends to be rather bland and uninspiring. It is typical of mass-banquet catering with standard fare comparable to that found in a family

hotel in a classic English seaside town. The wine list is 'ho-hum' average, but good value, although both red and white wine glasses are small.

Specialty (extra cost, reservation required) dining venues include Indian-themed Sindhu is overseen by Michelin-star chef Atul Kochhar (think British-Indian fusion cuisine), and cooked to order. Seating includes several alcove-style areas – so it's impossible for waiters to serve correctly without reaching across others at the table. Epicurian is a reservations-only, extra-charge restaurant in a quiet setting, with ample space around tables for decent service, and an outdoor terrace.

For the Glass House, TV wine expert Olly Smith helped create a 'Select Dining' restaurant/wine bar, featuring seafood and grilled items paired with wines chosen by Smith (it's strange that there are no decanters). You can also have a glass of wine, without food.

Venezia is a large, casual, self-serve buffet eatery/food hall, open almost around the clock, with large indoor-outdoor seating areas. However, the layout is confined and can get horribly congested. The Beach House (a special closed-off section of Venezia) is a cost-extra casual evening eatery, with waiter service. On the same deck, adjacent to the forward pool, are a poolside grill and pizzeria. Additionally, 24-hour room service is available in cabins.

ENTERTAINMENT. The 800-seat Playhouse showlounge spans two decks at the front of the ship, with two large video screens on either side of the stage; the sight lines are good from all seats.

Manhattan Lounge, a multi-function venue, hosts family shows and cabaret acts, plus late-night disco, while Malabar has decor based on the hotels on Marine Drive, Mumbai. Cabaret, live bands, and dancing are featured here. Meanwhile, the Planet Bar is an activities room by day and a club by night.

SPA/FITNESS. The Oasis Spa – located forward, almost atop the ship – has a gymnasium, aerobics room, beauty salon, separate men's and ladies' sauna and steam rooms (no charge), and 11 treatment rooms. An internal stairway connects to the deck below, which hosts an extra-charge Thermal Suite.

BALMORAL
★★★+

A WELL-DESIGNED SHIP WITH A VERY BRITISH AMBIENCE FOR MATURE-AGE TRAVELERS

Size:	Mid-size Ship	Passenger/Crew Ratio (lower beds):	3.0
Tonnage:	43,537	Cabins (total):	828
Cruise Line:	Fred. Olsen Cruise Lines	Size Range (sq ft/m):	153.9–613.5/14.3–57.0
Former Names:	Norwegian Crown, Crown Odyssey	Cabins (for one person):	91
Builder:	Meyer Werft (Germany)	Cabins with balcony:	121
Entered Service:	Jun 1988/Jan 2008	Cabins (wheelchair accessible):	9
Length (ft/m):	715.2/218.1	Wheelchair accessibility:	Good
Propulsion/Propellers:	diesel (21,330kW)/2	Elevators:	4
Total Crew:	471	Casino (gaming tables):	Yes
Passengers (lower beds):	1,747	Self-Service Launderette:	Yes
Passenger Space Ratio (lower beds):	24.9	Onboard currency:	UK£

THE SHIP. *Balmoral*, formerly *Norwegian Crown*, is a well-designed and built ship, originally constructed for the long defunct Royal Cruise Line. Norwegian Cruise Line then operated the ship for many years, before it was transferred to Orient Lines in 2000, and then back to Norwegian Cruise Line in September 2003.

Fred. Olsen Cruise Lines bought the ship in 2007 and refurbished it, including a 'chop and stretch' operation with the addition of a 99ft (30.2m) midsection. The company's logo includes the Norwegian flag, but the ship is registered in the Bahamas.

It has a relatively handsome, nicely balanced exterior profile, and one standout feature is its full, walk-around teak promenade deck outdoors, although it gets a little narrow in the forward section. There are well-polished wood railings on balconies and open decks, plus a jogging track on the uppermost deck. Atop the ship is the Observatory Lounge, with fine ocean views, central dance floor, and bar. Out on deck, there is a heated salt-water pool, but little shade, and no glass cover for inclement weather.

The main public rooms are on Lounge Deck. At the front is the Neptune Lounge (showlounge), with an integral bar at the back; a raised stage and wood dance floor are surrounded by amphitheater-style seating in banquettes with small drinks tables. To its aft are shops, while a curved staircase connects this deck with the reception lobby on the deck below.

BERLITZ'S RATINGS		
	Possible	Achieved
Ship	500	348
Accommodation	200	140
Food	400	258
Service	400	263
Entertainment	100	64
Cruise Experience	400	269
OVERALL SCORE 1342 points out of 2000		

Next is the Braemar Lounge, including an Internet center with good privacy separation, plus a library and separate card room. Aft of Braemar is the Morning Light Pub (named after the very first Fred. Olsen ship, *Morning Light*). It is more a lounge than a real pub, but it does have draft beer. Aft is the Palms Café, a casual self-service, buffet-style café.

The high lobby has a large gold sculpture in the shape of a globe of the world by the famous Italian sculptor Arnaldo Pomodoro (called *Microcosm, Macrocosm*); it used to revolve.

Balmoral offers a wide range of itineraries, which keeps people coming back to this very comfortable ship; passengers also receive a log of each cruise to take home. Niggles include an inflexible bed layout in some cabins, and dated decor in some older cabins.

Drinks prices are very reasonable, but laundry/dry-cleaning prices are high.

Balmoral is best suited to British couples and solo travelers wanting destination-intensive cruising in a ship with European style and character, a sense of space, comfortable surroundings, decent facilities, and realistic pricing. The crew is warm and friendly, and should help make your cruise enjoyable.

ACCOMMODATION. There are several price categories; typically, the higher the deck, the higher the price. Most cabins are of the same size and layout, have blond wood cabinetry and accents, an abundance of mirrors, and closet and drawer space, and are very well equipped. All accommodation grades have a color TV, a hairdryer, music console (plus a button that can be used to turn announcements on or off), personal safe, and private bathroom with shower (many upper-grade cabins have a good-size tub).

All towels are 100 percent cotton, and quite large; a soap and shampoo dispenser is wall-mounted, and a shower cap is provided. Duvets (single) are standard, but blankets and bed linen are available on request, as are double-bed-size duvets. Extra-cost, on-demand movies are available from the in-cabin Infotainment System.

Soundproofing is generally good. Some cabins have interconnecting doors to make a two-room suite – useful for families.

The largest cabins are the suites on Highland Deck 10. They are quite spacious and provide a sleeping area and separate living room, with nicely finished wood cabinetry and a large amount of closet and drawer space, together with a large, white marble-clad bathroom with a full-size tub and integral shower. There is a large private balcony, although some balconies can be overlooked from the deck above.

Nine wheelchair-accessible cabins provide plenty of space to maneuver, and all have a bathroom with roll-in shower. But wheelchair accessibility in some ports on the various itineraries operated by this ship – particularly in Europe – may prove frustrating, and wheelchair-accessible transportation may be limited.

Cabins in the added midsection have attractive, light, airy, contemporary decor. Some on the upper decks (decks 8 and 9) have bathrooms with a vertical window with a direct view from the large shower enclosure through the sleeping space to the outside, providing an enhanced feeling of spaciousness. Bathrooms have shower enclosures rather than tub/shower combinations (some have two washbasins), and enough storage space for toiletries.

DINING. The Ballindalloch Restaurant, aft, has ocean-view windows on the sides, and operates two seatings. It has comfortable seating at tables for two to eight. However, the waiter stations are exposed and noisy; indeed, trying to hold a conversation can be frustrating.

Other dining options. The Avon Restaurant and Spey Restaurant, both named after rivers, are aft on Highland Deck 10 – the deck with the higher-priced suites. Floor-to-ceiling windows provide abundant light. The decor is contemporary and minimalist, and the noise level is low – good for comfortable conversation. These venues also operate two seatings.

Palms Café has about 70 seats and is an alternative, more intimate venue for casual self-serve buffet meals.

All eateries have open seating for breakfast and lunch.

ENTERTAINMENT. Neptune Lounge is the entertainment venue for shows, cabaret acts, lectures, and some social functions. It is a single-level room with tiered seating levels. Sight lines are generally good, but they could be better.

Revue-style production shows are staged by a resident troupe of singers and dancers.

SPA/FITNESS. There is a reasonably decent – but small – indoor wellness facility, with a fitness room with great ocean views, plenty of gym equipment, and several body-treatment rooms.

BERLIN
★★+

THIS IS A SMALL, MODESTLY COMFORTABLE SHIP FOR BASIC 'DESTINATION-A-DAY' CRUISING

Size:	Small Ship
Tonnage:	9,570
Cruise Line:	FTI Cruises
Former Names:	*FTI Berlin, Spirit of Adventure, Berlin, Princess Mahsuri, Berlin*
Builder:	... Howaldtswerke Deutsche Werft (Germany)
Entered Service:	Jun 1980/May 2012
Length (ft/m):	457.0/139.3
Propulsion/Propellers:	diesel (7,060kW)/2
Total Crew:	168
Passengers (lower beds):	412
Passenger Space Ratio (lower beds):	23.2

Passenger/Crew Ratio (lower beds):	2.4
Cabins (total):	206
Size Range (sq ft/m):	92.5–191.6/8.6–17.8
Cabins (for one person):	0
Cabins with balcony:	0
Cabins (wheelchair accessible):	2
Wheelchair accessibility:	None
Elevators:	1
Casino (gaming tables):	No
Self-Service Launderette:	Yes
Onboard currency:	Euros

THE SHIP. *Berlin* (formerly *FTI Berlin*), an angular ship, has an all-white ice-strengthened hull and a profile made more balanced by a thin blue line. It starred for many years in the long-running German TV show *Traumschiff* (Dream Ship, which predated Love Boat). FTI Cruises bought the ship from previous owners Saga Cruises in 2011.

The interiors are crisp, contemporary, and well appointed, with tasteful European decor and furnishings. The The swimming pool, aft, is just a 'dip' pool. The surrounding open-deck and sunbathing space is tight, (it's in the same area as the outdoor seating of the Verandah Restaurant). There is only one elevator and it doesn't go to the two topmost decks or Spa Aquarius on the lowermost deck. The accommodation hallways are rather narrow.

This ship is best suited to German-speaking couples and solo travelers seeking a vacation in a ship that is unpretentious and provides a reasonable standard.

ACCOMMODATION. There are four types: Superior Suite, Junior Suite, standard outside-view, and standard interior cabins, in several price categories. Most cabins are small, but comfortable enough for short cruises. There are no balcony cabins. While most cabins have fixed twin beds, more than 60 cabins have double beds. Bathrooms have showers (no tubs), and storage space for toiletries is limited. All cabins have

BERLITZ'S RATINGS		
	Possible	Achieved
Ship	500	277
Accommodation	200	110
Food	400	189
Service	400	222
Entertainment	100	41
Cruise Experience	400	195
OVERALL SCORE 1034 points out of 2000		

a refrigerator and TV/DVD player. Cabins nearest the engine room suffer from more noise. Contrary to maritime tradition, odd-numbered cabins are on the port side (while odd-numbered lifeboats are on the starboard side).

The largest: two Owner's Suites (Rhapsody and Sonata); both have a double bed, lounge area, extra closet and drawer space, larger bathroom, binoculars, and shoe horn/clothes brush.

DINING. The 280-seat restaurant has large, ocean-view picture windows, and dark wood accents. There are tables for four or six, and dining is in one seating.

Casual breakfasts, lunches and dinners can be taken in the Verandah Restaurant, a self-serve buffet-style venue with indoor and outdoor seating areas. A variety of well-prepared, attractively presented items is the norm, with of cold cuts, cheeses, bread, and pastry items.

ENTERTAINMENT. The 250-seat Main Lounge is a single-level venue for cabaret, but used mainly for concerts and lectures. The Yacht Club Lounge/Bar is the evening/late-night gathering place.

SPA/FITNESS. Spa Aquarius. This indoor health spa includes a shallow swimming pool, small fitness area, massage room, sauna, and relaxation room. A beauty salon is adjacent to the Library.

BLACK WATCH
★★★

THIS SHIP PROVIDES REALLY GOOD VALUE FOR MATURE-AGE CRUISERS

Size:	Mid-size Ship	Passenger/Crew Ratio (lower beds):	2.2
Tonnage:	28,613	Cabins (total):	421
Cruise Line:	Fred. Olsen Cruise Lines	Size Range (sq ft/m):	135.6–819.1/12.6–76.1
Former Names:	Star Odyssey, Westward, Royal Viking Star	Cabins (for one person):	38
		Cabins with balcony:	70
Builder:	Wartsila (Finland)	Cabins (wheelchair accessible):	4
Entered Service:	Jun 1972/Nov 1996	Wheelchair accessibility:	Fair
Length (ft/m):	674.1/205.4	Elevators:	4
Propulsion/Propellers:	diesel (13,400kW)/2	Casino (gaming tables):	Yes
Total Crew:	350	Self-Service Launderette:	Yes
Passengers (lower beds):	804	Onboard currency:	UK£
Passenger Space Ratio (lower beds):	35.5		

THE SHIP. Its name is taken from the famous Scottish Black Watch regiment. There is a good amount of open deck space, and a wide walk-around teakwood promenade deck

The interior decor is restful, with wide stairways and foyers, soft lighting and no glitz, though the artwork is uninspiring. In general, good materials, fabrics (including the Black Watch tartan), and soft furnishings provide a comfortable feeling in public rooms (most are spacious, with high ceilings and located in a user-friendly horizontal layout.

There is a good range of public rooms, bars and lounges, including a library/internet-connect area, cinema with a steeply tiered floor (few ships today have a dedicated cinema) so it rarely feels crowded; The Observatory displays nautical memorabilia, while the Morning Light Pub tends to be the social gathering space and has a self-help beverage corner for coffees and teas and comfortable chairs.

Although well maintained, this ship is now over 40 years old, so little problems such as gurgling plumbing, creaking joints, and other idiosyncrasies can occur, and air conditioning may not work well in some cabins. However, after a 2016 refurbishment it still looks good.

Black Watch is best suited to mature-age travelers looking for a British environment that is comfortable but unstuffy. The friendly Filipino staff provide a good (although not faultless) service. Passenger niggles include: butter, margarine and preserves in

BERLITZ'S RATINGS		
	Possible	Achieved
Ship	500	295
Accommodation	200	119
Food	400	241
Service	400	247
Entertainment	100	60
Cruise Experience	400	254

OVERALL SCORE 1216 points out of 2000

packets; poor coffee; lines at the cramped buffet; poor wine service; and too few staff for the increase in passengers after the addition of more cabins. *The* cruises are well organized, with free shuttle buses in many ports of call.

ACCOMMODATION. There are many price grades (and one unlisted Owner's Suite), including four for solo travelers, from small, no-view cabins to spacious suites with separate bedrooms. Most cabins are for two, but some can sleep up to five.

All have hairdryers, duvets, cotton towels, personal safe, mini-fridge, and wall-mounted soap and shampoo dispensers in the bathrooms. Suite-grades also get bathrobes, cold canapés each evening, and priority restaurant seating.

A number of cabins in the aft section of decks 3, 4, and 5 can suffer generator noise, and some bathrooms have awkward access.

DINING. The 340-seat Glentanar Dining Room has a high ceiling, a white sail-like focal point, chairs with armrests and ample table space. The Orchid Room is a small offshoot for intimate dining. Brigadoon (54 seats), is a small, intimate venue. Breakfast and lunch are open-seating but dinner is in two seating times.

The cuisine is attractively presented, with a good selection of cheeses and vegetarian options. There is a decent range of wines, at modest prices, but few knowledgeable stewards.

A poolside Grill Restaurant costs extra (for dinner) but is very pleasant.

ENTERTAINMENT. The 400-seat Neptune Lounge (some pillars obstruct sight lines) features small-scale shows presented by resident singers/ dancers, cabaret acts, live music in several lounges, and British singalongs.

SPA/FITNESS. Facilities (not wheelchair-accessible) include a gymnasium, steam rooms, saunas, and changing rooms. Most fitness classes cost extra. There is a large paddle tennis court, golf practice nets, shuffleboard, and ring toss.

BOUDICCA
★★★

AN OLDER-STYLE SHIP WITH TRADITIONAL BRITISH DECOR AND AMBIENCE

Size:	Mid-size Ship	Passenger Space Ratio (lower beds):	33.8
Tonnage:	28,388	Passenger/Crew Ratio (lower beds):	2.3
Cruise Line:	Fred. Olsen Cruise Lines	Cabins (total):	437
Former Names: *Grand Latino, SuperStar Capricorn, Hyun-*		Size Range (sq ft/m):	135.6–579.1/12.6–53.8
dai Keumgang, SuperStar, Capricorn, Golden Princess, New		Cabins (for one person):	35
Sunward, Birka Queen, Sunward, Royal Viking Sky		Cabins with balcony:	92
Builder:	Wartsila (Finland)	Cabins (wheelchair accessible):	4
Entered Service:	Jun 1973/Feb 2006	Wheelchair accessibility:	Fair
Length (ft/m):	674.1/205.4	Elevators:	5
Propulsion/Propellers:	diesel (13,400kW)/2	Casino (gaming tables):	Yes
Total Crew:	320	Self-Service Launderette:	Yes
Passengers (lower beds):	839	Onboard currency:	UK£

THE SHIP. Acquired by Fred. Olsen Cruise Lines in 2005, this well-proportioned ship, originally built for long-distance cruising for the now-defunct Royal Viking Line, has a sharply raked, sleek bow and appearance. It was 'stretched' in 1982 with the addition of a 91ft (28m) midsection. The single funnel bears the company's starfish logo and balances the profile of this ship. The name *Boudicca* comes from the Queen of the Iceni tribe that occupied England's East Anglia, who led a dramatic revolt against the Romans in AD 61; her body is supposedly buried under Platform 10 in London's King's Cross Station.

There is a good amount of open deck and sunbathing space and a complete walk-around teak promenade deck outdoors; in fact, there is plenty of space everywhere and few pinch points because the ship absorbs people well.

The interior decor is restful, with a mix of English and Nordic styles (particularly the artwork), wide stairways and foyers, soft lighting, and no glitz. Most public rooms have high ceilings.

There are several (small) public rooms, bars, and lounges, unlike on the newer (larger) ships built today; a fine observation lounge, a small casino, card room, large library, and a Secret Garden Lounge. *Boudicca* is an extremely comfortable ship in which to cruise, with a moderate standard of food and service from a friendly, mostly Filipino staff, Expect very good-value cruises in a relaxed environment with

BERLITZ'S RATINGS

	Possible	Achieved
Ship	500	300
Accommodation	200	119
Food	400	241
Service	400	247
Entertainment	100	60
Cruise Experience	400	254

OVERALL SCORE 1221 points out of 2000

many home comforts, British food, and entertainment.

Although the ship has benefited from an extensive refit and refurbishment, it is now over 40 years old, so little problems such as gurgling plumbing, creaking joints, and other idiosyncrasies can occur, and the air conditioning may not be all that it should be. Port taxes are included for UK passengers. Gratuities are not included.

Niggles include: packets of butter, margarine, and preserves (instead of jars); lack of sugar choice; poor coffee; lines at the cramped buffet; and few wine waiters.

ACCOMMODATION. There is something for every taste and wallet, from spacious family suites to small interior cabins. While most cabins are for two people, some can accommodate a third, fourth, or even a fifth person. There are 20 price categories of cabins and one Owner's Suite (the price of which isn't in the brochure), including four grades of cabin for solo occupancy – spread across most cabin decks (not just the lower decks, as is the case with some cruise lines) and three have a private balcony. Most cabins have bathtubs, but some lower grades have a shower enclosure only.

All grades have duvets, large cotton bathroom towels, hairdryer, and a shower wall-mounted soap and shampoo dispenser. Suite-grade occupants also get a cotton bathrobe, cold canapés each evening, and priority seating in the restaurants.

The room service menu is limited, but an abundance of food is available at most times. All cabins had a facelift in 2017. Only a few suites have private balconies.

DINING. The main dining room has three sections: Indian Ocean, Tintagel, and Four Seasons; each with a high ceiling and ample space at each table. The decor is reserved, the chairs, which have armrests, are comfortable.

Breakfast and lunch are in an open-seating arrangement, with two seating times for dinner. Self-service displays cold food items for breakfast and lunch.

The cuisine is attractively presented, and a wide selection of cheeses suits most British tastes; vegetarian options are available. You'll also find pub favorites such as bangers and mash, toad in the hole, and spotted dick. Breakfast buffets tend to be repetitious, although they appear to satisfy most passengers. There is a reasonably decent range of wines at unpretentious prices.

Coffee and tea are available in the Secret Garden Café (part of the Secret Garden Lounge), but, sadly, not round-the-clock.

A casual self-serve deck buffet is in the Poolside Café, while an 80-seat poolside Grill Restaurant costs extra for dinner, but menu items include premium steaks and lobster and the surroundings are pleasant.

ENTERTAINMENT. The Neptune Lounge is for shows, cabaret acts, and lectures. It seats about 400, although some pillars obstruct sight lines from some seats. The entertainment consists of small-scale shows presented by a small team of resident singers/dancers, and cabaret acts.

There is plenty of live music for social dancing (many of the musicians are Filipino) and listening in several lounges, and good British singalongs are a feature.

SPA/FITNESS. A decent amount of ocean-view space is given to providing health and fitness facilities, including sauna/steam rooms, gymnasium/aerobics room, and changing rooms, while a beauty salon is located in a window-less area. Some fitness classes are free, and some cost extra.

Sports facilities include golf practice nets, shuffleboard, and ring toss.

BRAEMAR
★★★

A SMART-LOOKING SHIP WITH DECOR SUITED TO CASUAL BRITISH CRUISERS

Size:	Mid-size Ship
Tonnage:	24,344
Cruise Line:	Fred. Olsen Cruise Lines
Former Names:	Norwegian Dynasty, Crown Majesty, Cunard Dynasty, Crown Dynasty
Builder:	Union Navale de Levante (Spain)
Entered Service:	Jul 1993/Aug 2001
Length (ft/m):	639.7/195.0
Propulsion/Propellers:	diesel (13,200kW)/2
Total Crew:	371
Passengers (lower beds):	930
Passenger Space Ratio (lower beds):	25.9
Passenger/Crew Ratio (lower beds):	2.3
Cabins (total):	484
Size Range (sq ft/m):	139.9–349.8/13.0–32.5
Cabins (for one person):	38
Cabins with balcony:	79
Cabins (wheelchair accessible):	4
Wheelchair accessibility:	Fair
Elevators:	5
Casino (gaming tables):	Yes
Self-Service Launderette:	Yes
Onboard currency:	UK£

THE SHIP. *Braemar* has attractive exterior styling, and a lot of glass space. There is a good amount of open deck and sunbathing space for its size, and this includes two outdoor bars – one aft and one midships adjacent to the two swimming pools and paddling pool – that have Boddingtons and Stella Artois keg beers. Four open decks, located aft, provide a decent space for reading.

The teak promenade is a wrap-around deck for walking. You can also go right to the ship's bow – good for Titanic pose photographs. Faux teak floor covering is on the pool deck itself, which has two pools; it looks tacky, but works well in warm-weather areas.

Inside, there is a pleasant five-deck-high, glass-walled atrium on the starboard side. Off-center stairways add a sense of spaciousness to a clever design that floods interiors with light. The decor is warm and inviting, with contemporary, but not brash, Art Deco color combinations. Artwork is colorful and pleasant, in the Nordic manner.

The Morning Light Club is an open-plan lounge and bar, split by a walkway leading to the show-lounge (forward), lifestyle lounge (incorporating the library, Internet center, and Café Venus), a card room/arts and crafts center, and boutique (midships). Despite being open, it has cozy seating areas and is very comfortable, with a tartan carpet. A model of the first Fred. Olsen ship named *Braemar* (4,775 gross tonnage) is displayed in the center

BERLITZ'S RATINGS		
	Possible	Achieved
Ship	500	287
Accommodation	200	117
Food	400	231
Service	400	238
Entertainment	100	56
Cruise Experience	400	246
OVERALL SCORE 1175 points out of 2000		

of the room, as is a large carved wood plaque bearing the name of the Scottish Braemar Castle.

The staff is attentive, and the hospitality factor is good. The company really does offer extremely good-value cruises in a relaxed, welcoming, and laid-back environment.

In 2008, a 102ft (31m) midsection extension was inserted, providing additional cabins and balcony 'suites.' Facilities added or changed include a second swimming pool and more sunbathing space, an observatory lounge, a new restaurant, and a pub-style bar.

There can be a bit of a wait for shore tenders and for the few elevators aboard this ship. British passengers should note that no suites or cabins have bathtubs.

Passenger niggles include: lines at the cramped self-service buffet; poor wine service (few wine waiters); the use of packets of butter, margarine, and preserves; the lack of choice of sugar; weak coffee; and badly worn bathroom fittings. There is a self-service launderette (£2 for wash and dry) – and the company may charge for shuttle buses in some ports of call.

This smart-looking mid-size ship suits middle-aged and older passengers seeking a casual, un-stuffy environment in a ship with British food and entertainment. It's a refreshing change for those who don't enjoy larger, warehouse-size ships. But it does roll somewhat, probably because of its shallow draft design, meant for warm-weather cruise areas.

ACCOMMODATION. There are several cabin price categories; the higher the deck, the higher the price. All grades have a television and hairdryer (some are awkward to retract from their wall-mount holders), European-style duvets, and cotton bathroom towels (bathrobes are available upon request in suite-grade cabins). There is no separate audio system in the cabin, but music is on one of the TV channels, although you'll have to leave the picture on. Suites, however, do have a CD music system.

When Fred. Olsen Cruise Lines bought the ship, it converted a number of cabins from double-occupancy units to solo traveler cabins.

Some cabins suffer from poor soundproofing; passengers in cabins on Deck 4 in particular are disturbed by anyone running or jogging on the promenade deck above. Cabins on the lowest deck (Deck 2) in the ship's center are subject to noise from the adjacent engine room.

DINING. The restaurants (Thistle and Grampian) are assigned according to your accommodation grade. The Thistle Restaurant is in a pleasing, attractive room, with large ocean-view windows on three sides; its focal point is a large oil painting on a wall behind a buffet food counter. However, space is tight, and tables are extremely close together, making proper service difficult. There are tables for two to eight, and Porsgrund china with a Venus pattern.

There are two seatings for dinner, and an open seating for breakfast and lunch. The menu is varied. Salad items are basic, with little variety, although there is a decent choice of dessert items. For breakfast and lunch the dual food counters are functional, but the layout is not ideal and at peak times creates congestion. The Grampian Restaurant is located aft at the top of the ship, with fine aft views. Service is attentive (if hurried) in both venues.

Casual breakfasts and luncheons can also be taken in the self-service buffet in the Palms Café, although these tend to be repetitive. There is indoor and outdoor seating. Although it is the casual dining spot, tablecloths are provided. The indoor flooring is wood, making it a noisy room; some tables adjacent to the galley entrance should be avoided at all costs.

Out on the pool deck, there is a barbecue grill for casual eating – welcome when the ship is in warm-weather areas.

ENTERTAINMENT. The Neptune Showlounge sits longitudinally along one side, with tiered amphitheater-style seating, but its layout is less than ideal for shows or cocktail parties. There is often congestion between first- and second-seating passengers at the entrance.

Unfortunately, 15 pillars obstruct sight lines to the stage, and the banquet and individual tub chair seating arrangement is quite poor.

The entertainment mainly consists of small-scale production shows and mini-musicals presented by a small troupe of resident singers/dancers, and cabaret acts. They are rather amateurish, but enjoyable.

SPA/FITNESS. The health spa facilities are limited. The 'spa' includes a combined gymnasium/aerobics room, and a separate room for women and men with sauna, steam room, and tiny changing area. Most fitness classes cost extra.

BREMEN
★★★★

A FINE, STRONG EXPEDITION SHIP FOR IN-DEPTH DISCOVERY CRUISES

Size:	Boutique Ship	Passenger/Crew Ratio (lower beds):	1.7
Tonnage:	6,752	Cabins (total):	82
Cruise Line:	Hapag-Lloyd Expedition Cruises	Size Range (sq ft/m):	174.3–322.9/16.2–30.0
Former Names:	*Frontier Spirit*	Cabins (for one person):	0
Builder:	Mitsubishi Heavy Industries (Japan)	Cabins with balcony:	18
Entered Service:	Nov 1990/Nov 1993	Cabins (wheelchair accessible):	2
Length (ft/m):	365.8/111.5	Wheelchair accessibility:	None
Propulsion/Propellers:	diesel (4,855kW)/2	Elevators:	2
Total Crew:	94	Casino (gaming tables):	No
Passengers (lower beds):	164	Self-Service Launderette:	No
Passenger Space Ratio (lower beds):	41.1	Onboard currency:	Euros

THE SHIP. This aging, but strong and well-maintained, purpose-built all-white expedition vessel has a modern profile and excellent equipment. It is equipped with 12 Zodiac inflatable craft and has a handsome, wide squat for good stability. The ship's long cruising range and ice-hardened hull allow it to access even the most remote destinations. The ship carries the highest ice classification for passenger vessels.

Zero-discharge of waste matter is fiercely practiced; this means that absolutely nothing is discharged into the ocean that does not meet with the international conventions on ocean pollution (MARPOL). Equipment for in-depth marine excursions is provided, including a 'boot bathroom' – a washing station with three water hoses and boot-cleaning brushes.

There is almost a walk-around deck – if you go up and down steps at the front of the deck, while an open deck behind the mast provides a good viewing platform that's also useful for sunbathing on warm-weather cruises.

The ship has a decent number of public rooms for its size, including a forward-facing observation lounge/lecture room, and a main lounge (The Club) with a high ceiling, bandstand, dance floor and large bar, and an adjacent library with 12 bookcases (most books are in German).

Bremen has a very loyal following and is a highly practical expedition cruise ship, which can provide

BERLITZ'S RATINGS		
	Possible	Achieved
Ship	500	308
Accommodation	200	130
Food	400	306
Service	400	310
Entertainment	100	68
Cruise Experience	400	294
OVERALL SCORE 1416 points out of 2000		

you with a fine educational experience. All shore landings and tours are included, as is seasickness medication. There are always expert lecturers, and a friendly crew. It has two microscopes, and a plankton-collection net for in-depth studies.

The ambience is completely casual and unstuffy (no dressy clothes needed). Also, there is no music in hallways or on open decks.

On Arctic/Antarctic cruises, parkas (waterproof outdoor jackets) and tough 'snow-grip' boots are supplied, but you should take strong waterproof trousers and thick socks, plus thermal underwear. Each of the fleet of 12 Zodiacs (rubber-inflatable landing craft) is named after a place or ethnic group: Amazon, Antarctic, Asmat, Bora Bora, Cape Horn, Deception, Jan Mayen, Luzon, Pitcairn, San Blas, Spitzbergen, and Ushuaia. On Arctic and Antarctic cruises, it is simply delightful to go to the bridge wings late at night to stargaze under pollution-free skies – watch officers are always pleased to explain star formations.

Insurance, port taxes, and all staff gratuities are included, and a logbook is provided at the end of each expedition cruise for all participants – a reminder of what's been seen and done during the course of the adventure.

There's no 'bulbous bow,' which means that the ship can pitch in some more challenging sea conditions; however, it does have stabilizers. The pool is small, as is the open deck space around it, although there are both shaded and open areas. In-cabin announcements cannot be turned off (on cruises in the Arctic and Antarctic regions, announcements are often made at or before 7am on days when shore landings are permitted). Sadly, the ship, despite aging well, was not built with good cabin soundproofing.

Hapag-Lloyd publishes its own excellent handbooks, in both English and German, on expedition regions such as the Arctic, Antarctica, Amazonia, and the South Sea Islands, as well as exclusive maps. Note that Bremen was sold to Scylla (operator of many European riverships), and will be handed over in May 2021.

ACCOMMODATION. There are just four different configurations. All cabins have an outside view – those on the lowest deck have portholes, while the others have picture windows. All are well equipped for the size of the vessel. Each has wood accenting, infotainment system, telephone, refrigerator (soft drinks are provided free and replenished daily), vanity desk with 220-volt European-style sockets, and a lounge area with small drinks table.

Cabins have either twin beds (convertible to a queen-size bed, but with individual European cotton duvets) or double bed, according to location, plus bedside reading lights and alarm clock. There is a small indented area for outerwear and rubber boots, and a small drawer above the refrigerator unit provides warmth when needed for such things as wet socks and gloves.

Each cabin has a private bathroom (totally replaced in 2010) with a tiled floor, shower enclosure with curtain, toiletries shelf, washbasin and low-height toilet (vacuum type), a decent amount of under-basin storage space, and an electrical socket for shavers. Large towels and cotton bathrobes are provided, as is a range of Crabtree & Evelyn toiletries (shampoo, body lotion, shower gel, soap, and shower cap).

Each cabin has some illuminated closet space (large enough for two weeks for two), although the drawer space is limited – suitcases can be stored under the beds. Some Sun Deck and Bridge Deck cabins also have a small balcony (*Bremen* was the first expedition cruise vessel to have these) with a wood handrail, but no exterior light. Balconies have two teak chairs and a small drinks table, but are small

and narrow, doors that open outwards onto the balcony, taking up space.

Two Sun Deck suites have a separate lounge area with sofa and coffee table, bedroom with wall clock, large walk-in closet, and marble bathroom with tub and basin.

DINING. The dining room has open seating when operating for mixed German and international passenger cruises, and open seating for breakfast and lunch, with one sitting for dinner (assigned seats) when operated solely as a German-speaking cruise. It is fairly attractive, with pleasing decor and pastel colors; it has big picture windows and 12 pillars in inconvenient positions – the result of old shipbuilding techniques.

The food, made with high-quality ingredients, is extremely good. Although the portions are small, the presentation is appealing to the eye – and you can always ask for more. There is an excellent choice of freshly made breads and pastries, and a good selection of cheeses and fruits.

Dinner typically includes a choice of two appetizers, two soups, an in-between course, two entrées (mains), and two or three desserts, plus a cheese board (note: Continental Europeans typically have cheese before dessert). There is always a vegetarian specialty, as well as a healthy-eating option. The service is good, with smartly dressed, bilingual (German- and English-speaking) waiters and waitresses.

As an alternative, breakfast and luncheon buffets are available in The Club, or outside on the Lido Deck (weather permitting), where the Starboard Bar/Grill features grilled food.

ENTERTAINMENT. The Club is the social focus point for gatherings after meals and before expedition landings ashore. There is no formal entertainment as such. At the end of each cruise, the ship's chart is auctioned off one evening to the highest bidder, with profits donated to charity.

SPA/FITNESS. There is a small fitness room, a large sauna, and beauty salon with integral massage table. Out on the open deck is a small swimming pool, which is heated when the ship is sailing in cold-weather regions such as the Arctic or Antarctica.

BRILLIANCE OF THE SEAS
★★★+

THIS SHIP HAS CONTEMPORARY, STYLISH DECOR FOR YOUTHFUL ACTIVE FAMILIES

Size:	Mid-size Ship	Passenger/Crew Ratio (lower beds):	2.5
Tonnage:	90,090	Cabins (total):	1,056
Cruise Line:	Royal Caribbean International	Size Range (sq ft/m):	165.8–1,216.3/15.4–113.0
Former Names:	none	Cabins (for one person):	0
Builder:	Meyer Werft (Germany)	Cabins with balcony:	577
Entered Service:	Jul 2002	Cabins (wheelchair accessible):	24
Length (ft/m):	961.9/293.2	Wheelchair accessibility:	Good
Propulsion/Propellers:	gas turbine/2 azimuthing pods	Elevators:	9
Total Crew:	869	Casino (gaming tables):	Yes
Passengers (lower beds):	2,112	Self-Service Launderette:	No
Passenger Space Ratio (lower beds):	42.6	Onboard currency:	US$

THE SHIP. Along the port side of *Brilliance of the Seas*, a central glass wall provides great views (balcony cabins occupy the space on the starboard side). A gently rounded stern presents a nicely tiered appearance, giving the ship a well-balanced look, and one of two swimming pools can be covered by a glass dome for use in all-weather conditions. A nine-deck-high atrium lobby (Centrum) is the focal and social meeting point. On its various levels, it houses the R Bar (for creative cocktails), several passenger service counters, an art gallery, and Café Latte-tudes (for extra-cost coffee). Close by is the decidedly flashy Casino Royale (for table gaming and slot machines) and other public bars and lounges, and a library.

At the top of the ship a Viking Crown Lounge is set around the ship's funnel; this functions as an observation lounge during the day, and in the evening it's a high-energy dance club.

ACCOMMODATION. A wide range of suites/outside-view and interior (no-view) cabins come in several categories and price groups. Except for the six largest suites (called Owner's Suites), which have king-size beds, almost all other cabins have twin beds that convert to queen-size beds. There are 14 wheelchair-accessible cabins, 8 with a private balcony.

BERLITZ'S RATINGS

	Possible	Achieved
Ship	500	336
Accommodation	200	134
Food	400	220
Service	400	278
Entertainment	100	70
Cruise Experience	400	250

OVERALL SCORE 1288 points out of 2000

All cabins have rich (faux) wood cabinetry, including a vanity desk (with hairdryer), faux silent-close wood drawers, infotainment system, a personal safe, and three-sided bathroom mirrors. Some cabins have ceiling-recessed, pull-down berths for third and fourth persons – although closet and drawer space would be extremely tight for four – and some have interconnecting doors.

Most bathrooms have tiled accenting and a terrazzo-style tiled floor, and a small half-moon shower enclosure, cotton towels, a small cabinet for toiletries, and a shelf.

Occupants of cabins designated as suites get to use a private Concierge Lounge, where priority dining-room reservations, shore excursion bookings, and beauty salon/ spa appointments can be made.

Many 'private' balcony cabins are not particularly private and can be overlooked from the Solarium's port and starboard wings, and from other locations.

DINING. Minstrel, the main dining room, spans two decks; the upper deck level has floor-to-ceiling windows, while the lower deck level has windows. It seats 1,104, and has music of the Middle Ages as its decorative theme. There are tables for two to 10. Adjacent are two small private dining rooms (Zephyr, with 94 seats, and Lute, with 30 seats).

Choose either one of two seatings or 'My Time Dining' (eat when you want during dining room hours) when you book. Minstrel is closed for lunch on most days, which means scrambling for food and seating in the Windjammer Café – an awful prospect after returning from morning excursions.

Menu descriptions sound tempting, but the food is just so-so. However, you can have items like lobster or filet mignon (steak) at an extra cost, cooked to order. Green vegetables are minimal – provided mainly for decoration – but salad items are plentiful, and desserts are pretty good. Rice is often used as a source of carbohydrates. A vegetarian menu is available. Breads and pastry items are so-so (these are thawed and then baked from frozen 'starter' dough), although items such as croissants lack any hint of butter. This is banquet catering, with food comparable to that found in American family-style restaurants ashore – mostly disappointing and without much taste.

Other dining and eatery options (some cost extra) include:

Chops Grille Steakhouse (on Deck G) has 95 seats and an open (show) kitchen; it features premium veal chops and steaks (New York Striploin Steak, Filet Mignon, Prime Rib of Beef). Elsewhere, there's Giovanni's Table (an Italian trattoria), Izumi (for Asian cuisine), Rita's Cantina (for Mexican-style cuisine), a Chef's Table (for food-and-wine-pairing dinners), and Park Café (a deli-style venue).

Casual meals (for breakfast, lunch, and dinner) can be taken in the self-serve, buffet-style Windjammer Café, accessed directly from the pool deck. It is impossible to get a hot plate for hot food because the plates are plastic, so things go cold quickly.

ENTERTAINMENT. The Pacifica Theatre (showlounge) is three decks high, has 874 seats, including 24 stations for wheelchairs, and good sight lines from most seats.

The entertainment is always upbeat. There is even background music in all corridors and elevators, and constant music outdoors on the pool deck.

SPA/FITNESS. Vitality at Sea Spa and Fitness Center includes a solarium with whirlpool and counter-current swimming under a retractable glass roof, gymnasium with cardiovascular machines, aerobics room, men's and women's sauna and steam rooms, and treatment rooms. All are on two of the uppermost decks.

Sports facilities include a 30ft (9m) rock-climbing wall, golf course, jogging track, basketball court, nine-hole miniature golf course with novel decorative ornaments (Fairways of Brilliance), indoor/outdoor country club with golf simulator, and an exterior jogging track.

BRITANNIA
★★★★

THIS FLOATING 'SMALL BRITAIN' HAS ALL THE RIGHT FAMILY-FRIENDLY TRIMMINGS

Size:	Large Resort Ship	Passenger/Crew Ratio (lower beds):	2.6
Tonnage:	143,730	Cabins (total):	1,837
Cruise Line:	P&O Cruises	Size Range (sq ft/m):	174.0-387.5/15.0-36.0
Former Names:	none	Cabins (for one person):	18
Builder:	Fincantieri (Italy)	Cabins with balcony:	1,313
Entered Service:	Mar 2015	Cabins (wheelchair accessible):	37
Length (ft/m):	1,082.6/330.0	Wheelchair accessibility:	Best
Propulsion/Propellers:	diesel-electric (62,400kW/2	Elevators:	12
Total Crew:	1,400	Casino (gaming tables):	Yes
Passengers (lower beds):	3,737	Self-Service Launderette:	Yes
Passenger Space Ratio (lower beds):	38.4	Onboard currency:	UK£

THE SHIP. Modeled on the *Royal Princess* platform, *Britannia* – named by Queen Elizabeth II and bearing the same sterling name as her former, slightly smaller Royal Yacht Britannia – is a thoroughly British ship. It incorporates the classic features of ships such as *Aurora* into a design that is contemporary but not brash. The stern is nicely tiered – reminiscent of the back of an American Airstream trailer (caravan), but the bow (the front) is extremely short. Sadly, there is no open walk-around promenade deck; there's no Deck 13 either. *Britannia* has a rising sun logo on its two funnels (it's presently the only P&O Cruises ship with two funnels), while along the side of the hull there's no mistaking the Union Jack – at 308.4ft (94m) long, it's a big, bold statement.

On the open (family-friendly) deck are two main swimming pools (Lido and Riviera) and several hot tubs (close by is a Pizzeria, Lido Grill, and Grab & Go). Some nights may feature sound-and-light shows performed by the ship's resident dance and vocal troupe (Headliners). To escape the general noise and hubbub of the family-friendly pools and water-splash features, it's worth paying extra to use the adults-only Retreat (just forward of the mast on Deck 17), with its own serenity pool and two hot tubs.

Unusually for P&O Cruises, this ship's interiors were created by a single designer; the result is restrained, tasteful modern design throughout. The interior focal point – and social hub – is a charm-

BERLITZ'S RATINGS

	Possible	Achieved
Ship	500	400
Accommodation	200	151
Food	400	260
Service	400	286
Entertainment	100	73
Cruise Experience	400	278

OVERALL SCORE 1448 points out of 2000

ing three-deck-high atrium lobby, with curved staircases and four panoramic elevators. Intended to be a ship for all types of passenger, specific areas are designed for different age groups and lifestyles.

On the lower level of the atrium (Deck 5) is Market Café, for delightful (extra-cost) patisserie items by British-based (French-born) celebrity chef Eric Lanlard as well as coffees, cakes, and pastries, a gelateria, and the Blue Bar. Also close by is The Limelight Club (a supper club-style dining venue). Other levels host a range of shops and a café.

On the middle level (Deck 6) is Brodies (another comfortable place for lounging and drinking – named after Brodie Willcox, co-founder of the Peninsular & Oriental Steam Navigation Company), a fairly small casino with gaming tables and slot machines, and several shops. On the upper level (Deck 7) is the comfortable Java Café, for extra-cost Costa coffees, and The Glass House extra-cost restaurant.

There are 13 restaurants and eateries and 13 bars to choose from (a favorite is the Blue Bar in the atrium lobby). Atop the ship is the Crow's Nest Bar – a feature aboard P&O ships. Like a large London club, with panoramic views, it's a good meeting place for pre-dinner cocktails and after-dinner lounging, serving a selection of British artisan gins (and more than 70 bottled beers and ales). Adjacent are two meeting rooms, the Marlow Suite (named after a former P&O Cruises managing director) and the Ivory Suite; both are on the port side, while a small library is located on the starboard side.

A constant complaint is the fact that although there are elevators in the center of the ship, there are no stairs between decks 7 and 16 (only at the forward and aft stairways), and waiting for elevators can be very frustrating. The score, therefore, reflects this serious design fault.

ACCOMMODATION. There are five categories: suites; deluxe balcony cabins; outside and balcony cabins; interior (no-view) cabins; single interior cabins and (pleasant) single cabins with balcony; and wheelchair-accessible cabins (roll-in shower only – no bathtubs). All of the outside suites and cabins have private balconies (the best are those on the port and starboard side corners aft – with numbers A726, A727, B725, B726, C736, C737, D738, D739, E742, E743, F730, F731, G732, and G733). The decor is restrained (think chocolate, beige, and cream). All shower enclosures are glazed. Suite-grade occupants get bathrobes, 'butler' service, and chic bathroom toiletries, but note that many suite-grade balconies are disappointingly small and narrow.

All accommodation features a large flat-screen TV for films on demand, as well as products from The White Company, and tea/coffee-making facilities with specialty teas (long-life milk is provided, so if you want fresh milk, ask your room steward). Balcony cabins have rubberized (not wood) decking, sliding glass doors, and low-grade chairs. Note that balcony cabins with a sofa are more comfortable than those without, since they provide seating for a couple together. Cabins for passengers with disabilities are fitted with roll-in showers.

DINING. The three main dining rooms are Meridian, Oriental, and Peninsular. Most chairs lack armrests. While Oriental features fixed dining times for dinner, Meridian and Peninsular are for 'Freedom Dining,' so you choose the seating time to suit (early one evening, late the next, for example). Celebrity chef Marco Pierre White has created special dishes to be featured in the main dining rooms on gala evenings. The wine list is 'ho-hum' average, but good value, although both red and white wine glasses are small.

Epicurean Restaurant (adjacent to Reception on Deck 5) is quite elegant and has arguably the best cuisine on board (especially the cheese selection). White individual chairs, however, have uncomfortable curved half armrests.

The Glass House offers trendy light cuisine, with wine and food pairings by TV wine expert Olly Smith – but there's not a decanter in sight.

Sindhu features British-Indian fusion cuisine, with menus designed by Michelin-starred Atul Kochhar (his other sea-going restaurants are aboard *Azura* and *Ventura*).

The Limelight Club is a dinner and (small) show supper club.

Horizon Restaurant is the main self-serve buffet-style eatery (open 24/7); it has several 'active' stations (for pancakes, omelets, quiches, noodles) plus 'grab and go' sandwiches, filled rolls, and deli-style eats – most of which lacks taste, because almost nothing is made to order. There's also a grill for fast-food items such as hamburgers and hot dogs, and pizzas at poolside grill stations.

In case you want to hone your culinary skills, a 24-station culinary kitchen – part of the James Martin Cookery Club – can be found aft on Deck 17. Various celebrity chefs (including 'Food Heroes' James Martin, Marco Pierre White, and Atul Kochhar) and other invited chefs may take part and host master-classes throughout the year.

ENTERTAINMENT. The 936-seat Headliners Theatre is for colorful large-scale productions and top cabaret entertainment by the Headliners troupe of singers and dancers. It has gently tiered seating (with good stage views from almost all seats); an LED stage backdrop provides great sets and lighting effects.

Live Lounge is for live music, cabaret acts, and comedy, but late at night it morphs into a disco/late-night spot, with bar.

The Crystal Room has a large traditional wooden dance floor, grand piano, and dance hosts to help you dance better or teach you something new.

The Studio is a multi-function venue for talks, films, cooking and other demonstrations, recitals, game shows, and conferences.

SPA/FITNESS. The Oasis Spa, located forward on the lowest deck (Deck 5) close to the atrium lobby, includes a thermal suite, thalassotherapy pool, treatment rooms, beauty salon, and a rentable 'private spa villa' for couples, plus a spa shop.

Sports facilities include a 'short' tennis court, and an Arena Sports area that includes a combined football/basketball/cricket court, and other deck games, plus a gymnasium and aerobics room (on Deck 17).

CALEDONIAN SKY
★★★★

THIS DELIGHTFUL COUNTRY INN AFLOAT IS FOR FOR WELL-SEASONED TRAVELERS

Size:	Boutique Ship	Passenger/Crew Ratio (lower beds):	1.5
Tonnage:	4,200	Cabins (total):	57
Cruise Line:	Noble Caledonia	Size Range (sq ft/m):	215.0–365.9/20.0–34.0
Former Names:	Sunrise, Hebridean Spirit, Sun Viva 2,	Cabins (for one person):	0
	MegaStar Capricorn, Renaissance VI	Cabins with balcony:	23
Builder:	Nuovi Cantieri Apuania (Italy)	Cabins (wheelchair accessible):	0
Entered Service:	Mar 1991/Jul 2012	Wheelchair accessibility:	None
Length (ft/m):	297.2/90.6	Elevators:	1
Propulsion/Propellers:	diesel (5,000kW)/2	Casino (gaming tables):	No
Total Crew:	74	Self-Service Launderette:	No
Passengers (lower beds):	114	Onboard currency:	UK£
Passenger Space Ratio (lower beds):	36.8		

THE SHIP. Caledonian Sky has a modern look, and a traditional single funnel. It was one of a series of eight similar ships built for long-defunct Renaissance Cruises and acquired by Noble Caledonia in 2011, after use as a private yacht for an Abu Dhabi-based individual.

There are (slim) teakwood walking decks outdoors, and ample open deck space. The deck furniture is hardwood, sunloungers have thick cushioned pads, and exterior handrails are of finely polished wood. There is also a teak water sports platform aft, and 10 Zodiac landing craft for up-close-and-personal coastal excursions or 'wet' landings.

The interior design is reminiscent of a small country house hotel; the lounge has the unmistakable feel of a British traditional drawing room with a large, white Bath stone fireplace and is the social point (Inspector Hercule Poirot would be very much at home here).

Although several support pillars are obstructions in some public rooms and hallways, the ambience is warm and quiet (no music in passageways or elevator). Unobtrusive service from a Filipino and East European crew is the hallmark of this ship. Gratuities, transfers, shore excursions, plus house wine, beer, and soft drinks during lunch and dinner, are included.

Overall, this is a delightful boutique (pocket-sized) ship experience – for those who abhor big-ship cruising.

BERLITZ'S RATINGS

	Possible	Achieved
Ship	500	342
Accommodation	200	151
Food	400	317
Service	400	307
Entertainment	100	60
Cruise Experience	400	291

OVERALL SCORE 1468 points out of 2000

ACCOMMODATION. There are several grades of double or twin-bedded cabins and four grades of cabins for solo travelers. Dressing tables have three-sided vanity mirrors, and there is tea/coffee-making equipment, a refrigerator/minibar (stocked with fresh milk and mineral water), direct-dial satellite telephone, personal safe, ironing board, and electric trouser press. However, there is no switch to turn announcements off. Two suites provide lots of extra space.

The marble-clad bathrooms are good but there's a small step between bedroom and bathroom.

DINING. The elegant, wood-paneled Restaurant has ocean-view portholes, with assigned tables in a single seating for dinner, and open-seating for breakfast and lunch. There are tables for two to eight; some chairs have armrests, some don't. Fresh ingredients are often bought locally when possible, and desserts are worth saving space for. Breakfasts and lunches are also available outdoors at the alfresco café.

ENTERTAINMENT. The Club Lounge is for social gatherings and talks (there is no formal entertainment or forced parlor games).

SPA/FITNESS. An Asian-style spa, aft, is peaceful, and contains a hairdressing salon, gymnasium, steam room, shower, and relaxation area.

CARIBBEAN PRINCESS
★★★+

A MULTI-CHOICE LARGE RESORT SHIP FOR CASUAL FAMILY CRUISING IN COMFORT

Size:	Large Resort Ship	Passenger/Crew Ratio (lower beds):	2.6
Tonnage:	112,894	Cabins (total):	1,557
Cruise Line:	Princess Cruises	Size Range (sq ft/m):	163–1,279/15.1–118.8
Former Names:	none	Cabins (for one person):	0
Builder:	Fincantieri (Italy)	Cabins with balcony:	881
Entered Service:	Apr 2004	Cabins (wheelchair accessible):	25
Length (ft/m):	951.4/290.0	Wheelchair accessibility:	Good
Propulsion/Propellers:	diesel-electric (42,000kW)/2	Elevators:	14
Total Crew:	1,163	Casino (gaming tables):	Yes
Passengers (lower beds):	3,114	Self-Service Launderette:	Yes
Passenger Space Ratio (lower beds):	36.2	Onboard currency:	US$

THE SHIP. *Caribbean Princess* carries 500 more passengers than half-sisters *Golden Princess*, *Grand Princess*, and *Star Princess*, due to an extra accommodation deck. Despite the ship's greater capacity, the outdoor deck space remains the same, as do the number of elevators. In 2019, a Reef Family Splash Zone (water playground with water jets and showers) was added, for multi-generational families.

A sheltered faux teak (painted steel) promenade deck almost wraps around the ship (three times around is one mile). 'Movies Under the Skies' and major sporting events are shown on a 300-sq-ft (28-sq-m) poolside movie screen.

Unlike the outside decks, there is ample space inside. Public rooms include a casino with gaming tables and over 260 slot machines, a small library and Internet-connect room, and a wood-paneled Wheelhouse Bar with memorabilia and ship models tracing part of parent company P&O's history. Aft is a ship-wide, glass-walled disco pod with great views from its extreme port and starboard side windows. The passenger flow is generally good, and there is little congestion, except waiting for elevators at peak times.

Passenger niggles include the user-unfriendly automated telephone system, the small cabin towels, several extra-cost items such as ice cream, plus the charge (in coins) for the washers and dryers in self-service launderettes.

BERLITZ'S RATINGS		
	Possible	Achieved
Ship	500	347
Accommodation	200	122
Food	400	246
Service	400	282
Entertainment	100	74
Cruise Experience	400	268

OVERALL SCORE 1339 points out of 2000

Overall, however, Princess Cruises delivers a consistently fine, comfortable, well-packaged product, always with a good degree of style, at a competitive price.

ACCOMMODATION. There are six principal types of cabins and configurations: grand suite, suite, mini-suite, outside-view double cabins with balcony, outside-view double cabins, and interior double cabins, in a bewildering choice of price categories, depending on size and location.

Even top-grade suites are small in comparison to suites aboard many other ships. Cabin attendants have many cabins to look after (typically 20), which does not translate to much personal service.

Most interior (no view) and outside-view cabins are functional, although few drawers are provided, and are quite attractive, with warm, pleasing decor and fine soft furnishing fabrics.

Note that wheelchair-accessible cabins have no mirror for dressing, and no full-length hanging space.

All cabins receive turndown service and pillow chocolates nightly, bathrobes (on request), toiletry kits, and a hairdryer. Bathrooms have tiled floors, and a decent amount of open shelf storage space for toiletries, but the plain walls are, well, just plain.

Most outside-view cabins on Emerald Deck have lifeboat-obstructed views. Some cabins can accommodate a third and fourth person in upper berths; however, the lower beds cannot then be converted into a queen-size bed. Some cabins have interconnecting doors – good for families. There are no cabins for solo travelers.

DINING. The three main dining rooms are Coral, Island, and Palm. Palm has traditional two seating dining; Coral and Island have 'anytime dining' (you may have to wait for a table at peak times). Each has multi-tier sections in a non-symmetrical design that breaks the large spaces into smaller sections for better ambience; each has its own galley. Four elevators go to Fiesta Deck (Coral and Island restaurants), but only two go to Plaza Deck 5 (Palm Restaurant). A gratuity is automatically added to all beverage bills, including wines.

Although portions are generous, the food and its presentation are disappointing (standardized). Fish often has sauces or coatings, the choice of fresh green vegetables is limited, few garnishes are used, and cheese is either pre-sliced or diced. This is banquet catering for large numbers. Pasta dishes are acceptable (though voluminous), typically served by section headwaiters, who may also make 'something special just for you' (for favorable comments and gratuities).

Extra-cost, reservations-necessary Sabatini's and Crown Grill are open for lunch and dinner on sea days. Sabatini's is an Italian eatery with decor depicting Tuscan villas and gardens, named after Trattoria Sabatini, the historic institution in Florence. Crown Grill serves premium steaks, chops, and grilled seafood. Seating is mainly in semi-private alcoves, and there is a show kitchen.

World Fresh Marketplace, with indoor-outdoor seating, is open almost 24 hours a day for casual self-serve buffet meals (on oval plastic plates); it has large ocean-view windows on both sides. At night, two aft, extra-cost sections turn into Planks (for family-style BBQ food) and Steamers (for East Coast-style seafood).

Other casual eateries include a poolside burger bar (Salty Dog Grill), Planks (BBQ) Steamers Seafood, and Slice pizza bar; extra charges apply for items from the coffee bar/patisserie or the caviar/Champagne bar.

International Café, on Deck 5 in The Plaza, offers specialty coffees, pastries, light lunches, and cakes, some at no extra cost.

There's 24-hour room service – but some items are unavailable during early morning.

ENTERTAINMENT. The Princess Theater spans two decks and has comfortable seating on both main and balcony levels. Colorful production shows are the domain of the resident troupe of singers and dancers.

Club Fusion, located aft, features cabaret, lectures, bingo, and horse racing, while Explorers Lounge hosts cabaret acts and dance bands. Princess Cruises employs gentleman dance hosts.

SPA/FITNESS. Lotus Spa, forward on Sun Deck, is home to a sauna, steam room, and changing rooms; common facilities include a relaxation/waiting zone, body-pampering treatment rooms, and a gymnasium with muscle-pump equipment and ocean views.

CARNIVAL BREEZE
★★★+

FUN FOR A FIRST FAMILY-ORIENTED CRUISE, WITH A SPLASH-TASTIC WATER-SLIDE

Size:	Large Resort Ship	Passenger/Crew Ratio (lower beds):	2.6
Tonnage:	128,251	Cabins (total):	1,845
Cruise Line:	Carnival Cruise Line	Size Range (sq ft/m):	185.0–430.5/17.1–40.0
Former Names:	none	Cabins (for one person):	0
Builder:	Fincantieri (Italy)	Cabins with balcony:	905
Entered Service:	Jun 2012	Cabins (wheelchair accessible):	35
Length (ft/m):	1,004.0/306.0	Wheelchair accessibility:	Good
Propulsion/Propellers:	diesel-electric (75.600kW)/2	Elevators:	20
Total Crew:	1,386	Casino (gaming tables):	Yes
Passengers (lower beds):	3,690	Self-Service Launderette:	Yes
Passenger Space Ratio (lower beds):	34.7	Onboard currency:	US$

THE SHIP. The ship's profile is quite well balanced, with a rakish (but short) front and rounded stern. A WaterWorks pool deck has many water amusements – including a long orange multi-deck 'Twister Water Slide' and a catch-you-off-guard 'Power Drencher.' There's a Seaside Theater screen for poolside movies and a laser light show, but the general open deck space is small considering the number of passengers. For a quieter environment, try Serenity, an adults-only, extra-charge retreat, with two large hot tubs.

A full walk-around open promenade deck is lined with deck chairs, and four 'scenic whirlpools' are cantilevered over the water for good views.

On a lower deck, The Ocean Plaza, with around 190 seats, is a comfortable place by day and a lively entertainment venue by night. Its indoor/outdoor café has a bandstand and a large circular dance floor.

The Caribbean-themed interior decor is very bright. Many of the public rooms, lounges, bars, and nightspots are located on two main public room/entertainment decks, which are accessed via an 11-deck-high atrium, whose ground level has a cantilevered bandstand atop a large dance floor.

Public rooms include The Song (Jazz Bar), Ocean Plaza, which is quiet during the day, lively at night, the Jackpot casino, a 232-seat conference room, and a library (with wine bar, but few books).

BERLITZ'S RATINGS

	Possible	Achieved
Ship	500	349
Accommodation	200	129
Food	400	210
Service	400	251
Entertainment	100	68
Cruise Experience	400	245

OVERALL SCORE 1252 points out of 2000

Carnival Breeze is a big floating playground, with almost 5,000 passengers when full. It has lots of facilities for young families with children, who will love the outdoor pool deck and its facilities. However, there's no escape from the incredibly loud rap, rock, and vocal music throughout the ship.

ACCOMMODATION. There are numerous cabin price categories, from interior (no-view) cabins to much larger 'spa' and balcony suites. Whether you go for high end or low end, all include plush mattresses, good-quality duvets, linens, pillows, and tropical decor (the cabin doors have cabana-style slats to get the mood going). Colors are a mix of light browns and nautical blues, but accommodation deck hallways are bright, even at night. Note that cabins on Deck 12 are subject to noise from kids having fun on the deck above – so forget that afternoon nap!

DINING. There are two main dining rooms: Sapphire (midships) and the smaller Blush (aft), each with main and balcony levels (stairways connect them), and two small annexes, for small groups. Note that the two main dining rooms are closed for lunch on port days.

Don't even think about a quiet table for two, or a candlelit dinner on deck. This is all about table mates, social talk, lively meals, fast eating, and fast service. Tables do have tablecloths, silverware, and iced water/iced tea whenever you want it. Choose either fixed time dining (6pm or 8.15pm) or flexible dining (during opening hours).

Except for surprisingly good breakfasts, the food is carbohydrate-rich and non-memorable (this is banquet-style 'batch' production cooking), with simple presentation, few garnishes, and many dishes disguised with gravies and sauces. The selection of fresh green vegetables, bread and bakery items (thawed and then baked from frozen 'starter' dough), cheeses, and fruits is limited, and there is heavy use of rice, canned fruit, and jellied desserts.

'Spa Carnival Fare' provides a healthier food option. Vegetarian and children's menus are also available, but they wouldn't get a generous score for their nutritional content.

Extra-cost Fahrenheit 555 Steakhouse has an à la carte menu, good table settings, china and silverware, leather-bound menus, and premium-quality steaks and grilled seafood items.

Lido Marketplace – a copy of the name used aboard (sister company) AIDA Cruises ships – is a large, self-serve buffet facility, with indoor/outdoor seating (lower level) and indoor-only seating (upper level). Designated areas feature different types of ethnic cuisine. It includes a Mongolian Wok on the upper level, open for tablecloth-free buffet dinners (no candles). Cucina del Capitano is an Italian extra-charge eatery, also on the upper level, with pasta at lunch and 'authentic' Italian specialties at night.

Guy's Burger Joint (for burgers and fries) and BlueIguana Cantina (for Tex-Mex fast-food items including burritos, tacos, and enchiladas) adorn the pool deck. Other eateries include Fat Jimmy's C-Side BBQ (for grilled items like kielbasa/Polish sausage, grilled chicken breast, and pulled pork sandwiches), and Bonsai Sushi (Carnival's first full-service sushi venue), with decor by graffiti artist Erni Vales, and sushi, sashimi, and bento boxes.

Kids have their own restaurant towards the top of the atrium.

ENTERTAINMENT. The 1,964-seat Ovation Showlounge spans three decks, with horseshoe-shaped seating around a large stage. Sight lines are generally good, except from some seats at the back of the lower level. Large-scale production shows, with lots of skimpy costumes and feathers, are typical, together with snappy cabaret acts, all accompanied by a live showband.

The Limelight, aft, seats 425, and has a stage, dance floor, and large bar. For late-night raunchy adult comedy, it becomes the Punchline Comedy Club.

For an active movie experience, check out the Thrill 5D Theater, whose seats really move you.

SPA/FITNESS. The expansive Cloud 9 Spa spans three decks. The uppermost level includes extra-cost indoor/outdoor private spa relaxation areas. A spiral staircase connects two of the decks.

The spa offers a wide range of treatments, and there are 10 rooms for this. An extra-charge Thermal Suite features the sensory-enhanced soothing heated chambers: Laconium, Tepidarium, Aroma, and Oriental steam baths.

CARNIVAL CONQUEST
★★★

THIS IS A VIVID, FUN-FILLED SHIP FOR ULTRA-CASUAL FAMILY CRUISING

Size:	Large Resort Ship	Passenger/Crew Ratio (lower beds):	2.5
Tonnage:	110,239	Cabins (total):	1,487
Cruise Line:	Carnival Cruise Line	Size Range (sq ft/m):	179.7–482.2/16.7–44.8
Former Names:	none	Cabins (for one person):	0
Builder:	Fincantieri (Italy)	Cabins with balcony:	574
Entered Service:	Dec 2002	Cabins (wheelchair accessible):	25
Length (ft/m):	951.4/290.0	Wheelchair accessibility:	Good
Propulsion/Propellers:	diesel-electric (63,400kW)/2	Elevators:	18
Total Crew:	1,160	Casino (gaming tables):	Yes
Passengers (lower beds):	2,974	Self-Service Launderette:	Yes
Passenger Space Ratio (lower beds):	37.0	Onboard currency:	US$

THE SHIP. *Carnival Conquest* has the same well-balanced profile as close sisters *Carnival Sunshine*, *Carnival Freedom*, *Carnival Glory*, *Carnival Liberty*, *Carnival Triumph*, and *Carnival Victory*.

Amidships on the open deck is a long water slide (200ft/60m long), tiered sunbathing decks positioned between two swimming pools, hot tubs, and a poolside movie screen (Seaside Theater). There are three decks full of lounges, bars, and lots of rooms to enjoy, plus two atriums: the largest, the forward, glass-domed Artists Atrium spans nine decks, while an aft atrium rises through three decks.

The ship's interior decor is all about Impressionist painters such as Degas, Toulouse Lautrec, Gauguin, Cézanne, and others. Murano glass flowers on antiqued brass stems are displayed in several public areas.

Tahiti Casino has numerous gaming tables and over 320 slot machines. There are several nightspots for different musical tastes (except for classical music lovers), such as the Degas Lounge, Vincent's Piano Bar, Henri's Dance Club, and Gauguin's Bar.

Overall, it is a floating playground for the young and young-at-heart, and anyone who enjoys constant stimulation and participation events, together with the three 'Gs' – glitz, glamour, and gambling. This is 'fun' cruising Vegas style – and an all-American fun experience.

While the cuisine is just so-so, the real fun begins at sundown when Carnival really excels in sound,

BERLITZ'S RATINGS

	Possible	Achieved
Ship	500	335
Accommodation	200	125
Food	400	208
Service	400	247
Entertainment	100	68
Cruise Experience	400	237

OVERALL SCORE 1220 points out of 2000

lights, and razzle-dazzle shows (think skin and feathers).

Niggles include: a large number of dining room pillars, and utilitarian public toilets. It is impossible to escape from noise and loud music (it's even played in cabin hallways and lifts). You have to carry a credit card to operate the personal safes, which is inconvenient. There may be lines for shore excursions and security control when re-boarding.

The ship was extensively refurbished in 2012. This included the installation of a Guy's Burger Joint (in partnership with Guy Fieri of Food Network); a poolside RedFrog Rum Bar (including ThirstyFrog Red – Carnival's private-label draft brew) and BlueIguana Tequila Bar, and a Sports Bar (an interactive venue with video games and a 24/7 sports ticker). Meanwhile, Cherry on Top is a shop full of bins of candy, and novelty gift items.

ACCOMMODATION. There are numerous cabin-price categories, in seven different grades: suites with private balcony; deluxe outside-view cabins with private balcony; outside-view cabins with private balcony; outside-view cabins with window; cabins with a porthole instead of a window; interior cabins; and interior cabins with upper and lower berths.

Five decks of cabins have private balconies – over 150 more than *Carnival Triumph* or *Carnival Victory*, for example. But many are not so private, and can be overlooked.

There are 18 spa cabins, clustered around and behind Spa Carnival, so you can get out of bed and go straight to the treadmill without having to go through any public room.

Most cabins have all the basics, although the furniture is angular with sharp corners. Three decks of cabins (eight on each deck, each with balcony) overlook the stern. Most cabins have twin beds, convertible to a queen-size bed.

DINING. There are two main dining rooms: the 744-seat Renoir Restaurant, and the larger 1,044-seat Monet Restaurant, both two decks high, and both with a balcony level (larger in the Monet Restaurant). In the Renoir Restaurant, two additional wings (called Cassatt and Pissarro) can accommodate large groups in a private setting.

Don't even think about a quiet table for two, or a candlelit dinner on deck. Dining aboard a Carnival ship is all about table mates, social talk, lively meals, fast eating, and fast service. Tables do have tablecloths, silverware, and iced water/iced tea whenever you want it. Choose either fixed time dining (6pm or 8.15pm) or flexible dining (during opening hours). The main dining rooms are closed for lunch on port days, so you will need to go to the serve-yourself buffet – or order room service.

Except for breakfasts, which can be good, the food is starch-heavy (it's banquet-style, mass-produced cooking, after all), with simple presentation, few garnishes, and many dishes disguised with gravies and sauces. The selection of fresh green vegetables, bread and bakery items (these are thawed and then baked from frozen 'starter' dough), cheeses, and fruits is limited, while rice, canned fruit and jellied desserts are plentiful.

'Spa Carnival Fare' provides a healthier food option. Vegetarian and children's menus are also available, but they wouldn't get a generous score for their nutritional content.

Waiters sing and dance, so think 'foodertainment' rather than food quality. Also, there are no wine waiters, and the wine glasses are small. For something really simple, an 'always available' list of 'Carnival Classics,' includes mahi-mahi (fish), baby back ribs (beef), and grilled chicken.

The Point is a reservations-only, extra-cost dining venue for steaks, seafood and other items. Wall murals are in the style of post-Impressionist painter Georges Seurat's Le Cirque (The Circus).

Cézanne Restaurant is a casual self-serve, food court-style lido deck eatery, with a capacity for over 1,200, and decor like a 19th-century French café.

Other (complimentary) eateries include: Guy's Burger Joint, a poolside venue for hand-made burgers and fresh-cut fries; Blueiguana Cantina Mexican eatery (for snack food such as tacos and burritos).

ENTERTAINMENT. The Toulouse-Lautrec Showlounge is a multi-deck showroom seating 1,400, with a revolving stage, hydraulic orchestra pit, and seating on three levels (the upper levels being tiered through two decks).

SPA/FITNESS. SpaCarnival is a fairly large health and fitness complex, accessed from the forward stairway. Facilities include a gymnasium (packed with muscle machines and exercise equipment), treatment area, sauna and steam rooms for men and women, and a beauty salon.

CARNIVAL DREAM
★★★

FUN FOR A FIRST CRUISE EXPERIENCE, WITH A SPLASH-TASTIC WATER-SLIDE

Size:	Large Resort Ship	Passenger/Crew Ratio (lower beds):	2.6
Tonnage:	128,251	Cabins (total):	1,823
Cruise Line:	Carnival Cruise Line	Size Range (sq ft/m):	185.0–430.5/17.1–40.0
Former Names:	none	Cabins (for one person):	0
Builder:	Fincantieri (Italy)	Cabins with balcony:	887
Entered Service:	Sep 2009	Cabins (wheelchair accessible):	35
Length (ft/m):	1,004.0/306.0	Wheelchair accessibility:	Good
Propulsion/Propellers:	diesel-electric (75,600kW)/2	Elevators:	20
Total Crew:	1,367	Casino (gaming tables):	Yes
Passengers (lower beds):	3,646	Self-Service Launderette:	Yes
Passenger Space Ratio (lower beds):	35.1	Onboard currency:	US$

THE SHIP. *Carnival Dream*'s bows are short, but its profile is balanced, with a rakish front and rounded stern. On-deck attractions include Carnival WaterWorks aqua park, with a long orange multi-deck 'Twister Water Slide' and popular 'Power Drencher' (a big hit with kids), a main pool and the Seaside Theater movie screen. The general open deck space is really poor for the number of passengers carried, so sunbed loungers are packed like sardines.

Meanwhile, Serenity is an adults-only, extra-charge retreat.

Lower down is a full walk-around open promenade deck; it's lined with deck chairs, and it's difficult to navigate through them. Four 'scenic whirlpools,' cantilevered over the water, have sea views. Higher up, Lido Deck 10 offers an open-deck area.

The interior decor is bright (take sunglasses). Most public rooms, lounges, and bars are on Dream Street or Upper Dream Street. The Dream Lobby is the connection point for people and ship functions; take one of the glass-walled elevators for a neat view. There are three main elevator towers: forward, amidships, and aft.

Many lounges, bars, and nightspots – including a dance club with a twist, offering indoor/outdoor access – are accessible via an 11-deck-high atrium, the ground level of which has a neatly cantilevered bandstand atop a large dance floor. The Page Turner (great name) is the library, although there are few

BERLITZ'S RATINGS		
	Possible	Achieved
Ship	500	344
Accommodation	200	129
Food	400	205
Service	400	251
Entertainment	100	68
Cruise Experience	400	239
OVERALL SCORE 1236 points out of 2000		

books. Jackpot is a colorful casino, with gaming tables and slot machines. Other rooms include The Song (Jazz Bar) and Ocean Plaza – a quiet area during the day, and lively at night. Three-dozen Internet terminals are scattered around the ship, but most have no privacy. There's also a 232-capacity conference room, The Chambers.

The indoor/outdoor Ocean Plaza, with around 190 seats, is a comfortable spot for people-watching by day and a trendy entertainment venue by night, with dance floor and bandstand.

The layout is disjointed, and prior to second seating there is much congestion on Upper and Lower Dream streets. Passenger niggles highlight the barely warm food in the two main dining rooms, long lines for self-serve food items in the food court, and annoying announcements.

Gratuities are automatically charged to your onboard account.

ACCOMMODATION. There are several cabin price categories, and six cabin types. The price depends on the grade and location you choose. Whether you go for high end or low end, all accommodation includes Carnival's Comfort Bed with plush mattresses, good-quality duvets, linens, and pillows. Straight accommodation deck hallways create the cell-block look, and they are bright, very bright, even at night. There are also lot of interior (no-view) cabins. The cabins to go for are those at the stern: they are quieter and offer great aft ocean views on decks 6, 7, 8, and 9.

Some cabins can accommodate five persons – useful for families. There is a wide selection of balcony cabins and suites, including 'Cove Balcony' cabins that are the closest to the waterline.

Adjacent to the Serenity Spa are 65 'Cloud 9' spa cabins. They include a number of amenities and privileges (all 20 are situated aft of the lower level, with direct access to it).

DINING. The two main restaurants are the 1,180-seat Crimson (midships) and smaller 828-seat Scarlet (aft). Each has two levels: main and balcony (stairways connect both levels), with the galley on the lower level. Forward of Crimson are two small annexes, used as private dining venues. Choose between fixed-time dining or flexible dining (during opening hours). Note that the main dining rooms are closed for lunch on port days, so you are forced to go to the self-serve buffet. Note also that bakery items are thawed and heated from frozen.

The Gathering Lido Restaurant is a large self-serve buffet facility, with indoor/outdoor seating areas. The venue includes a Mongolian Wok and Pasta Bar on the upper level. Go off-peak and it's better.

No-cost outdoor eateries include Guy's Pig & Anchor Barbeque Smokehouse; Pizzeria del Capitano (with five types of pizza); and BlueIguana (for Mexican-style tacos and burritos).

The extra-cost Chef's Art seats 139 and has great views from its aft location high on Spa Deck 12, and an à la carte menu that focuses on premium-quality steaks and seafood items. On Promenade Deck you'll find Bonsai Sushi, a tribute-to-sushi venue.

ENTERTAINMENT. The 1,964-seat Encore Showlounge spans three decks at the front of the ship, with seating in a horseshoe shape around the stage; the sight lines are generally good, except from some seats at the back of the lowest level. Large-scale production shows, with lots of feathers and skimpy costumes, are staged, accompanied by a live showband.

The 425-seat Burgundy Lounge, aft, has a stage, dance floor, and bar, and is for smutty, no-holds-barred, late-night 'adult comedy.' Caliente, a nightclub, provides ultra-loud Latin dance music.

SPA/FITNESS. The expansive Cloud 9 Spa is set over three decks in the front of the ship. The uppermost deck includes indoor/outdoor private spa relaxation areas, at extra cost. A spiral staircase connects two of the decks.

There are several private rooms for body treatments, including a VIP room, a large massage room for couples, a Rasul mud treatment room, and dry flotation rooms. An extra-charge 'Thermal Suite' has sensory-enhanced soothing herb-scented heated chambers, and Oriental steam baths.

CARNIVAL ECSTASY
★★★

THIS IS A FLOATING FUN PALACE FOR ULTRA-CASUAL FIRST-TIME CRUISERS

Size:	Mid-size Ship	Passenger/Crew Ratio (lower beds):	2.2
Tonnage:	70,526	Cabins (total):	1,026
Cruise Line:	Carnival Cruise Line	Size Range (sq ft/m):	173.2–409.7/16.0–38.0
Former Names:	*Ecstasy*	Cabins (for one person):	0
Builder:	Kvaerner Masa-Yards (Finland)	Cabins with balcony:	52
Entered Service:	Jun 1991	Cabins (wheelchair accessible):	22
Length (ft/m):	855.8/263.6	Wheelchair accessibility:	Fair
Propulsion/Propellers:	diesel-electric (42,240kW)/2	Elevators:	14
Total Crew:	920	Casino (gaming tables):	Yes
Passengers (lower beds):	2,056	Self-Service Launderette:	Yes
Passenger Space Ratio (lower beds):	34.4	Onboard currency:	US$

THE SHIP. *Carnival Ecstasy* (second in a series of eight almost identical ships in Carnival's *Fantasy*-class) is over 25 years old and tired. Although externally angular, and with limited open deck space, this is nonetheless a popular ship for first-timers. The aft decks tend to be less noisy, since most activities are around the main pool. There is no walk-around open promenade deck, but there is a short jogging track. The lifeboats (six double as shore tenders) are positioned high.

The interior spaces are well utilized, and the general passenger flow is good. The interior design – the work of architect Joe Farcus – is clever, functional, and very colorful. The design theme is mythical muses and music.

The ship's interior social and focal point is an 'open' atrium lobby, with a balconied shape recalling some of the world's great opera houses; it spans six decks, and is topped by a large glass dome. The lowest level includes a purser's desk, shore excursion desk, an Atrium Bar and a small sushi bar.

There are public entertainment lounges, bars, and clubs galore, with something for everyone (except quiet space). They are connected by a double-width City Highlights Boulevard, and have a mix of classic and garish design elements. You'll find a Rolls-Royce car (and coffee shop) on this indoor promenade, and the Crystal Palace Casino. There is also a fine-looking library and reading room, but few books,

BERLITZ'S RATINGS

	Possible	Achieved
Ship	500	293
Accommodation	200	121
Food	400	202
Service	400	247
Entertainment	100	62
Cruise Experience	400	232

OVERALL SCORE 1157 points out of 2000

and small conference room. From venues such as the Stripes Dance Club/Disco to the Society Cigar Bar, the interior decor is entertaining.

Carnival Ecstasy is for anyone who enjoys constant stimulation and participation events. Because it's a large resort ship, there will be lines for shore excursions, security control when re-boarding, and disembarkation, plus sign-up sheets for fitness equipment. Loud vocal 'music' is everywhere. Shore excursions are booked via the 'Fun Vision' infotainment system, so obtaining advice and suggestions is not easy, the food is basic, and the Art Gallery 'works' are tacky.

ACCOMMODATION. There are several types, according to facilities, size, and location. Most cabins have plain and unmemorable decor, but they have decent storage space, and practical bathrooms. However, with a queen-bed configuration instead of a twin-bed layout, one person must clamber over the bed – an ungainly exercise.

Book an outside-view suite and you get more space, and eclectic decor and furniture.

Room service is available 24/7, although in most cabins, only cold food is available; suite-grade occupants have more (both hot and cold) choice.

DINING. Wind Star and Wind Song (main dining rooms), are amidships and aft, with ocean-view windows and a low ceiling height (think: noisy). Choose either fixed-time dining or flexible dining (during opening hours).

The food is so-so (although breakfasts are good), presentation is simple, with few garnishes. The selection of fresh green vegetables, bread and rolls (thawed and heated from frozen 'starter' dough), cheeses, and fruits is limited, and there is heavy reliance on rice, canned fruit, and jellied desserts. There are no wine waiters. However, this is standard banquet catering. For something simple, try the 'always available' 'Carnival Classics' such as mahi-mahi, baby back ribs, and grilled chicken. Both dining rooms are closed for lunch on port days.

The Panorama Bar & Grill features casual self-serve buffet fare; it includes a deli counter and pizzeria. At night, it becomes the Seaview Bistro (an alternative to the big dining rooms), for pasta, steaks, salads, and desserts. A patisserie offers extra-cost specialty coffees and sweets.

Other (complimentary) eateries include: Guy's Burger Joint, a poolside venue developed with Food Network personality Guy Fieri (for hand-made burgers and fresh-cut fries) and BlueIguana Cantina Mexican (for Mexican snack food such as tacos and burritos).

ENTERTAINMENT. The 1,010-seat Blue Sapphire Showlounge hosts production shows (with a cast of vocalists and a clutch of dancers) and major cabaret acts – although 20 pillars obstruct some views.

SPA/FITNESS. SpaCarnival is a glass-wrapped complex. It has a gymnasium with ocean-view windows and muscle-pumping equipment, aerobics room, men's and women's sauna and steam rooms, beauty salon, and body treatment rooms. Most fitness classes cost extra. For sports, there's basketball, volleyball, and table tennis, plus a banked jogging track outdoors above the spa, and a mini-golf course.

CARNIVAL ELATION
★★★

THIS FLOATING FUN PALACE IS GOOD FOR AN ULTRA-CASUAL FAMILY CRUISE

Size:	Mid-size Ship	Passenger/Crew Ratio (lower beds):	2.2
Tonnage:	70,390	Cabins (total):	1,026
Cruise Line:	Carnival Cruise Line	Size Range (sq ft/m):	173.2–409.7/16.0–38.0
Former Names:	Elation	Cabins (for one person):	0
Builder:	Kvaerner Masa-Yards (Finland)	Cabins with balcony:	152
Entered Service:	Mar 1998	Cabins (wheelchair accessible):	22
Length (ft/m):	855.8/263.6	Wheelchair accessibility:	Fair
Propulsion/Propellers:	diesel-electric (42,842kW)/2 azimuthing pods	Elevators:	14
		Casino (gaming tables):	Yes
Total Crew:	920	Self-Service Launderette:	Yes
Passengers (lower beds):	2,056	Onboard currency:	US$
Passenger Space Ratio (lower beds):	34.4		

THE SHIP. *Carnival Elation* is an externally angular but popular ship for anyone taking a first cruise, although it is now over 20 years old.

One of two in a series of eight *Fantasy*-class ships (the other is *Carnival Paradise*) with a 'pod' propulsion system, it gives a vibration-free ride.

Open deck space is cramped. The aft is quieter, whereas most activities are around the main swimming pool and hot tubs. There's also Serenity – an adult-only 'quiet' space on Deck 9 aft. There is no walk-around open promenade deck, although there is a short jogging track atop ship. The lifeboats, six of which act as shore tenders, are positioned high up.

The interior spaces are well utilized. The general passenger flow is busy but good; the interior design functional, and colorful. The theme is mythical muses, and composers and their compositions.

The interior social and focal point is an 'open' atrium lobby spanning six decks, topped by a glass dome, with purser's and shore excursion desks, an Atrium Bar, and a small sushi bar on one side.

There are multiple public entertainment lounges, bars, and clubs, connected by a double-width Elation's Way and Promenade, a sort of Main Street, including a good-looking library and reading room, but few books, and a small conference room.

BERLITZ'S RATINGS		
	Possible	Achieved
Ship	500	294
Accommodation	200	121
Food	400	202
Service	400	250
Entertainment	100	62
Cruise Experience	400	233
OVERALL SCORE 1162 points out of 2000		

Carnival Elation is cruising Splash Vegas style – an all-American experience. The real fun begins at sundown when the ship comes alive. On the down side, expect lines for shore excursions, security control when re-boarding, and disembarkation. There is noisy rap and rock music everywhere, too many loud, annoying announcements, and much hustling for drinks.

ACCOMMODATION. There are several grades, priced according to size and location. Cabins have plain decor, but are fairly practical, with decent storage space and simple bathrooms. However, with a queen-bed configuration instead of twin beds, one person has to clamber over the bed – not ideal.

Outside-view suites have more space and are mildly attractive, but small. Room service items are available 24/7, although in most cabins, only cold food is available; occupants of suite-grade accommodation have more (both hot and cold) to choose from.

DINING. There are two main dining rooms, Imagination and Inspiration (assigned according to your cabin), amidships and aft. They have ocean-view windows and are noisy, but the decor is bright and colorful. Choose either fixed-time dining (6pm or 8.15pm) or flexible dining (during opening hours).

The food is so-so (except for the multi-choice breakfasts, which are good), with simple presentation and few garnishes. Bakery items are thawed and heated from frozen. There are no wine waiters, and the wine glasses are small. Waiters sing and dance, and there are parades – more 'foodertainment' than food quality. For something simple, try the 'always available' (during dining rooms' opening hours) list of 'Carnival Classics.' Note that the main dining rooms are closed for lunch on port days.

Tiffany's Lido Restaurant features casual self-serve buffet food, including Guy's Burger Joint and BlueIguana Cantina (for Mexican eats).

ENTERTAINMENT. The Mikado Showlounge presents colourful production shows and cabaret acts – although 20 pillars obstruct some views.

SPA/FITNESS. SpaCarnival is a glass-wrapped complex on the uppermost interior deck. It has a gymnasium with ocean-view windows and muscle-pumping equipment, aerobics room, men's and women's sauna and steam rooms, beauty salon, and body treatment rooms. Most classes incur an extra charge. For sports, there's basketball, volleyball, and table tennis, plus a banked jogging track above the spa, and a mini-golf course.

CARNIVAL FANTASY
★★★

ULTRA-CASUAL CRUISING AND ENTERTAINMENT FOR THE WHOLE FAMILY

Size:	Mid-size Ship	Passenger/Crew Ratio (lower beds):	2.2
Tonnage:	70,367	Cabins (total):	1,026
Cruise Line:	Carnival Cruise Line	Size Range (sq ft/m):	173.2–409.7/16.0–38.0
Former Names:	Fantasy	Cabins (for one person):	0
Builder:	Kvaerner Masa-Yards (Finland)	Cabins with balcony:	152
Entered Service:	Mar 1990	Cabins (wheelchair accessible):	22
Length (ft/m):	855.8/263.6	Wheelchair accessibility:	Fair
Propulsion/Propellers:	diesel-electric (42,240kW)/2	Elevators:	14
Total Crew:	920	Casino (gaming tables):	Yes
Passengers (lower beds):	2,056	Self-Service Launderette:	Yes
Passenger Space Ratio (lower beds):	34.4	Onboard currency:	US$

THE SHIP. *Carnival Fantasy* is the first (in a series of eight almost-identical ships). It has always been a popular ship – good for a first cruise. It is now over 25 years old and the oldest in the fleet, and sports the company's trademark red, white, and blue wing-tipped funnel. The open deck space is inadequate when the ship is full. A Carnival Water-Works – complete with long (about 300ft/90m) and short water slides with water-burst fountains – is a good, active area for children. There's also a Serenity adult-only 'quiet' lounging space outdoors on Deck 9 aft.

There is no walk-around open promenade deck, but there is a short jogging track atop the ship (the lifeboats – six double as shore tenders – are also positioned high up).

The interior spaces are well utilized. The general passenger flow is good, and the interior design is clever and very colorful, inspired by the ancient city of Pompeii.

The interior focal point is a balcony-shaped 'open' atrium lobby. It spans six decks and is topped by a glass-domed roof. The lowest level houses the purser's and shore-excursion desks, a popular Atrium Bar (with live music), and, off to one side, a small sushi bar that is a good meeting place.

The public rooms are connected by the double-width Via Marina Promenade – a sort of shipboard Main Street – and include a nice-looking library and reading room (with few books) and the Club 21 Casino.

BERLITZ'S RATINGS		
	Possible	Achieved
Ship	500	293
Accommodation	200	121
Food	400	202
Service	400	246
Entertainment	100	62
Cruise Experience	400	230

OVERALL SCORE 1154 points out of 2000

Carnival Fantasy is a floating playground for the young and young-at-heart, and perfect if you enjoy constant stimulation and participation events. Because it's a large resort ship, lines form for security control when re-boarding, at the Purser's Desk, for shore excursions, and for disembarkation.

While the cuisine is just so-so, the vibe gets going at sundown when Carnival really excels in volume, lights, and shows. From venues such as the Electricity Dance Club/Disco to the Majestic Cigar Bar, the ship's bars and lounges will certainly entertain you.

However, there are many annoying revenue announcements, a never-ending hustle to get you to buy ice-filled drinks, and no escape from the incredibly high-volume 'music.'

ACCOMMODATION. There are several accommodation price grades; you pay for size and location. Standard outside-view and interior (no-view) cabins have decor that is plain, but they are adequate (most have the same size and appointments), with decent storage space and practical, no-nonsense bathrooms. However, with a queen-bed configuration instead of a standard twin-bed layout, note that one person has to clamber over the bed to get to the far side. Book a suite and you get more space – and more eclectic decor and furniture.

Many cabins feature interconnecting doors – good for families with children.

Room service items are available 24/7, but in standard-grade cabins only cold food is available, while occupants of suite-grade accommodation have a greater range (both hot and cold) of choice.

DINING. Celebration and Jubilee, the large main dining rooms, are located amidships and aft. Both have ocean-view windows and very bright decor, but they are noisy. Choose either fixed-time dining (6pm or 8.15pm) or flexible dining (during opening hours).

Overall, the food is carbohydrate-rich, with simple presentation, few garnishes, and many dishes disguised with gravies and sauces. The selection of green vegetables, breads, cheese, and fruit is limited (bread is thawed, then baked from frozen 'starter' dough), and there is much use of canned fruit and jellied desserts. The waiters sing and dance, so think 'foodertainment' rather than food quality. For something simple, an 'always available' list of 'Carnival Classics' includes mahi-mahi (fish), baby back ribs (beef), and grilled chicken. Note that the two main dining rooms are not open for lunch on port days.

The Paris Lido restaurant features casual self-serve buffet eats. At night, it becomes the Seaview Bistro, an alternative for pasta, steaks, salads, and desserts. Other casual eateries include Guy's Burger Joint (named after TV personality Guy Fieri), Blue Iguana (Mexican cantina-style), and Bonsai Sushi. There is no specialty (extra-charge) restaurant, unlike some of the other ships in the fleet.

ENTERTAINMENT. The Universe Showlounge features colorful production shows and major cabaret acts, although 20 pillars obstruct some views.

SPA/FITNESS. SpaCarnival is a glass-wrapped 'spa' complex on the uppermost interior deck, forward of the ship's mast. It has a gymnasium with ocean-view windows and muscle-pumping equipment, an aerobics room, men's and women's sauna and steam rooms, a beauty salon, and treatment rooms. Some fitness classes incur an extra charge. For sports, there's basketball, volleyball, and table tennis, plus a banked jogging track outdoors above the spa, and a mini-golf course.

CARNIVAL FASCINATION
★★★

A VIBRANT, FLOATING MOVIE SET FOR CASUAL FAMILY CRUISING

Size:	Mid-size Ship	Passenger/Crew Ratio (lower beds):	2.2
Tonnage:	70,538	Cabins (total):	1,026
Cruise Line:	Carnival Cruise Line	Size Range (sq ft/m):	173.2-409.7/16.0-38.0
Former Names:	*Fascination*	Cabins (for one person):	0
Builder:	Kvaerner Masa-Yards (Finland)	Cabins with balcony:	250
Entered Service:	Jul 1994	Cabins (wheelchair accessible):	22
Length (ft/m):	855.8/263.6	Wheelchair accessibility:	Fair
Propulsion/Propellers:	diesel-electric (42,240 kW)/2	Elevators:	14
Total Crew:	920	Casino (gaming tables):	Yes
Passengers (lower beds):	2,056	Self-Service Launderette:	Yes
Passenger Space Ratio (lower beds):	34.4	Onboard currency:	US$

THE SHIP. *Carnival Fascination* – now over 20 years old – is the fourth in a series of eight almost-identical *Fantasy*-class ships. Inside, it is a bright, contemporary playground for the young and young-at-heart families. It has good entertainment facilities and features, and extra-cost dining spots for some different eats. It is well suited to multi-generational groups, and for family reunions.

BERLITZ'S RATINGS		
	Possible	Achieved
Ship	500	294
Accommodation	200	121
Food	400	202
Service	400	250
Entertainment	100	62
Cruise Experience	400	232
OVERALL SCORE 1161 points out of 2000		

With a full ship, the open deck space is really limited, because it's crammed with Carnival WaterWorks, a waterpark that includes a long 'Twister' slide (great for kids) and sunloungers. The aft decks, however, tend to be less noisy, because most activities are focused around the main swimming pool and hot tubs (one with a thatched shade). But, Serenity, an extra-cost, adult-only 'quiet' lounging space on Deck 9 aft, can be a nice escape. While there isn't a walk-around open promenade deck, there is a short jogging track. The lifeboats, six of which double as shore tenders, are positioned high in the ship.

The interior design – the work of architect Joe Farcus – is clever and very colorful, with oodles of neon and glitz. The design theme is Hollywood and the movies.

A six-deck-high atrium lobby is topped by a domed roof. The lowest level houses the purser's desk, shore excursion desk, Atrium Bar (with live music), and, off to one side, a small sushi bar – a good social meeting place.

There are public entertainment lounges, bars, and clubs galore, connected by a double-wide Via Marina Promenade, with a mix of classic and contemporary design elements – something for everyone (except quiet space).

Gamers and slot-players alike can grab a piece of the almost non-stop action in the Club 21 Casino. There is also a library and reading room (but few books), and a small conference room. As for the 'art' in the Art Gallery it's ultra-tacky!

Some 24 life-like beloved movie characters are dotted along the Via Marina Boulevard (think selfies with Marilyn Monroe, James Dean, and Lucille Ball); Clark Gable is in the Tara A Carnival cruise is all about having fun, which begins at sundown with sound, lights, and shows. From venues such as the Diamonds Are Forever Dance Club/Disco to the Beverly Hills Cigar Bar, the ship will certainly entertain you.

On the downside, there are many annoying announcements, a never-ending hustle to get you to buy ice-filled drinks, and relentless super-loud rap and rock music everywhere.

ACCOMMODATION. Several grades of accommodation are priced by size and location. Standard outside-view and interior (no-view) cabins have plain, non-memorable décor, but they are fairly comfortable and spacious enough (most are of the same size and appointments), with adequate storage and practical bathrooms. However, with a queen-bed configuration instead of a standard twin-bed layout, note that one person has to clamber over the bed to get to the far side.

Outside-suite occupants have more space, eclectic décor, and better furniture. These are mildly attractive, but so-so, and they are much smaller than similar suites aboard ships of competing companies.

Room service items are available 24/7, but in standard cabins only cold food is available; suite-grade occupants get a greater choice of both hot and cold items.

DINING. The two large main dining rooms, Sensation (amidships) and Imagination (aft) have ocean-view windows and bright decor, but they are very noisy due to the low ceiling height. Choose either fixed-time dining or flexible dining times (during opening hours).

The food is carbohydrate-heavy; think banquet-style batch production cooking. The choice of fresh green vegetables, breads, cheeses, and fruits is limited, and there is much use of canned fruit and jellied desserts (bread, rolls, and other bakery items are made from frozen 'starter' dough). There are no wine waiters, and the wine glasses are very small. The waiters sing and dance – so 'service' equates to 'foodertainment.'

Tropical Coconut Grove Bar & Grill (lido café) is for self-serve buffet eats; Guy's Burger Joint is for burgers and freshly cut fries; and BlueIguana Cantina is for Mexican snack food such as tacos and burritos. Poolside watering holes include the BlueIguana Tequila Bar and RedFrog Rum Bar.

A patisserie has extra-cost specialty coffees and sweets, and a so-called sushi bar, off to one side of the atrium lobby bar, is open prior to dinner; however, if you know anything about sushi, don't expect authenticity.

There is no specialty (extra-charge) restaurant, as aboard some of the larger ships in the Carnival fleet.

ENTERTAINMENT. The Palace Showlounge is for large-scale production shows and major cabaret acts; note, however, that 20 pillars obstruct sight lines from some seats.

SPA/FITNESS. SpaCarnival is a glass-wrapped 'spa' complex on the uppermost interior deck, forward of the ship's mast. It has a gymnasium with ocean-view windows and muscle-pumping equipment, an aerobics room, men's and women's sauna and steam rooms, a beauty salon, and treatment rooms. Some fitness classes incur an extra charge. For sports, there's basketball, volleyball, and table tennis, plus a banked jogging track outdoors above the spa, and a mini-golf course.

CARNIVAL FREEDOM
★★★

THIS FUN-FILLED, CASUAL CRUISE SHIP REALLY COMES ALIVE AT NIGHT

Size:	Large Resort Ship	Passenger/Crew Ratio (lower beds):	2.5
Tonnage:	110,320	Cabins (total):	1,487
Cruise Line:	Carnival Cruise Line	Size Range (sq ft/m):	179.7–484.2/16.7–44.8
Former Names:	none	Cabins (for one person):	0
Builder:	Fincantieri (Italy)	Cabins with balcony:	574
Entered Service:	Feb 2007	Cabins (wheelchair accessible):	25
Length (ft/m):	951.4/290.0	Wheelchair accessibility:	Good
Propulsion/Propellers:	diesel-electric (63,400kW)/2	Elevators:	20
Total Crew:	1,150	Casino (gaming tables):	Yes
Passengers (lower beds):	2,974	Self-Service Launderette:	Yes
Passenger Space Ratio (lower beds):	37.0	Onboard currency:	US$

THE SHIP. *Carnival Freedom* shares the same generally balanced profile as sisters *Carnival Conquest*, *Carnival Glory*, *Carnival Liberty*, *Carnival Radiance*, *Carnival Sunrise*, *Carnival Sunshine*, and *Carnival Valor.* Immediately recognizable is the trademark swept-back wingtip funnel. In 2019 the ship underwent a refurbishment that added Water-Works AquaTunnel and Twister waterslides, PowerDrencher tipping water bucket and a Splash Zone area for kids.

Carnival's Seaside Theater for movies on an upper outside deck recalls those classic drive-in movie theaters, with seating in tiered rows and the screen in front. Also outside is Serenity, an adult-only quiet spot at the top and front of the ship – a nice escape from all the hubbub on the open decks below.

Inside, the decor is a kaleidoscopic blend of colors (most are a mix of dark and gaudy) to stimulate and excite the senses, and it is dedicated to time and the decades. The deck and public room layout is fairly logical (except for getting from the aft-placed Posh Dining Room to the showlounge, because you have to go up and down a deck or two). Most public rooms are on one deck off a main interior boulevard, above the two main dining rooms (Chic and Posh). They include the Babylon Casino, with gaming tables and over 300 slot machines, the fine Havana Cigar Bar, Monticello *Carnival Freedom* is a large floating playground for the young and young-at-heart, with lots of participation events, together with the three

BERLITZ'S RATINGS

	Possible	Achieved
Ship	500	344
Accommodation	200	125
Food	400	208
Service	400	250
Entertainment	100	66
Cruise Experience	400	237

OVERALL SCORE 1230 points out of 2000

'Gs' – glitz, glamour, and gambling. This is cruising Splash Vegas style – a fun, all-American experience. Because it's a large resort ship, expect lines for shore excursions, security control when re-boarding, and disembarkation.

While the cuisine is just so-so, the fun begins at sundown, with razzle-dazzle shows and late-night reverie.

Niggles include the many pillars that impede passenger flow, particularly in the dining room (it's difficult for the waiters to serve food properly); the non-stop infomercials on the cabin infotainment system (you can, however, turn the system off); the super-loud rap and rock 'music' everywhere; and some rather juvenile cruise directors.

ACCOMMODATION. There are numerous cabin price categories, in several different suite/cabin types, sizes, and grades. These include suites with private balcony; deluxe outside-view cabins with private balcony; outside-view cabins with private balcony; outside-view cabins with window; cabins with a porthole instead of a window; interior cabins; and interior (no-view) cabins with upper and lower berths.

There are five decks of cabins with private balconies. The standard cabins are of modest size, although the furniture is square and angular (no rounded edges). However, there's plenty of drawer space, and space for toiletries in bathrooms. Three decks of cabins (eight on each deck, each with private balcony – they are very pleasant) overlook the stern. Most cabins have twin beds that can be converted to a queen-size bed format.

There is a group of 18 'spa' cabins, directly around and behind SpaCarnival; so fitness devotees can get out of bed and go straight to the treadmill without having to go through any of the public rooms first.

DINING. There are two principal dining rooms (Chic, located midships, seating 744; and Posh, aft, seating 1,122). Both are two decks high and have a balcony level (the balcony level in Posh is larger than the one in Chic). Choose either fixed-time dining (6pm or 8.15pm) or flexible dining (during opening hours). Note that they are not open for lunch on port days.

Overall, the food is quite starchy, with simple presentation, few garnishes, and many dishes disguised with gravies and sauces. The selection of fresh green vegetables, breads, cheeses, and fruits is limited (bread is thawed and then baked from frozen 'starter' dough), and there is heavy use of canned fruit and jellied desserts. The waiters sing and dance, so think 'foodertainment' rather than food quality. There are no wine waiters, and the wine glasses are small. For something simple, try the 'always available' list of 'Carnival Classics,' including mahi-mahi (fish), baby back ribs (beef), and grilled chicken.

There are few tables for two, but among my favorites are a pair of tables for two right at the back of the restaurant, with ocean views aft.

The Sun King Supper Club (reservations required) features prime dry-aged steaks and grilled seafood items. It's worth paying the cover charge to taste what Carnival can deliver in terms of better quality food.

The Freedom Restaurant, a casual self-serve international food court-style lido deck eatery, has two main serving lines. Each night it morphs into Seaview Bistro and provides a dress-down alternative for pasta, steaks, salads, and desserts.

Other casual eateries include Guy's Burger Joint (named after TV's Guy Fieri), Blue Iguana (Mexican cantina-style), and Bonsai Express (for sushi).

ENTERTAINMENT. The Victoriana Main Lounge (named after England's Queen Victoria) is the ship's multi-deck showlounge, seating up to 1,400 and staging colorful Las Vegas-style production shows and major cabaret acts. It has a revolving stage, hydraulic orchestra pit, good (but overly loud) sound, and seating on three levels (the upper levels are tiered through two decks); a proscenium arch acts as a scenery loft. The decor is medieval – drinks tables look like shields, and coats of armor and towers with stained-glass windows flank the stage.

An alternative entertainment venue is the aft lounge, with 425 seats, live music, and late-night cabaret acts including smutty adult comedy.

There's also the 100-seat Scott's Piano Bar.

Body-throbbing music sensations can be found in the disco, which includes a video wall with live projection from the dance floor.

SPA/FITNESS. SpaCarnival is above the navigation bridge. Facilities include a solarium, eight treatment rooms, lecture rooms, sauna and steam rooms for men and women, a beauty parlor, a large gymnasium with floor-to-ceiling, ocean-view windows, and an aerobics room with instructor-led classes (some at extra cost).

CARNIVAL GLORY
★★★

THIS IS AN ULTRA-CASUAL FUN-FILLED SHIP FOR FIRST-TIME CRUISERS

Size:	Large Resort Ship
Tonnage:	110,239
Cruise Line:	Carnival Cruise Line
Former Names:	none
Builder:	Fincantieri (Italy)
Entered Service:	Jul 2003
Length (ft/m):	951.4/290.0
Propulsion/Propellers:	diesel-electric (63,400kW)/2
Total Crew:	1,160
Passengers (lower beds):	2,974
Passenger Space Ratio (lower beds):	37.0
Passenger/Crew Ratio (lower beds):	2.5
Cabins (total):	1,487
Size Range (sq ft/m):	179.7–482.2/16.7–44.8
Cabins (for one person):	0
Cabins with balcony:	590
Cabins (wheelchair accessible):	25
Wheelchair accessibility:	Good
Elevators:	14
Casino (gaming tables):	Yes
Self-Service Launderette:	Yes
Onboard currency:	US$

THE SHIP. There are three decks full of public lounges, bars, and lots of rooms to play in, together with good facilities and programs for children.

A makeover in 2012 added two half-decks at the front of the ship, extended two other decks aft, and added 182 cabins (but no extra elevators), plus several new, and some revamped, eateries, and more. These include an Alchemy Bar – for 'mixologist' (bartender) cocktails; a (music-free) Amidships on the open deck there is a water slide (200ft/60m long), plus tiered sunbathing decks between two swimming pools, several hot tubs, and large poolside movie screen (Seaside Theater). For adults to escape the outdoor activities and noise there is Serenity – an extra-cost adults-only relaxation area, located on two decks at the top, forward-most part of the ship.

The interior decor is a fantasyland of colors, in every hue of the rainbow. Most public rooms are located off the Kaleidoscope Boulevard – the main interior promenade, which is great for strolling and people-watching. The larger of two atriums, Colors Lobby spans nine decks in the forward third of the ship. Check out the interpretative paintings of US flags at the Color Bar. The smaller aft atrium goes through three decks.

Carnival is all about cruising Splash Vegas style – it's a fun, all-American experience. The cuisine is just so-so, but the excitement really begins at

BERLITZ'S RATINGS		
	Possible	Achieved
Ship	500	340
Accommodation	200	125
Food	400	207
Service	400	247
Entertainment	100	64
Cruise Experience	400	234
OVERALL SCORE 1217 points out of 2000		

sundown when Carnival excels in sound, lights, razzle-dazzle shows, and late-night high-volume sounds. There are nightspots and watering holes for just about every musical taste (except classical music), such as the Ivory Club Bar, Ebony Aft Cabaret Lounge, Cinn-a-Bar (Piano Bar), White Heat Dance Club, and Bar Blue.

Niggles: the modifications and additions, while good, have also created a crowded, congested ship. Also, the open deck space is poor considering the large passenger numbers. The pool deck is cluttered, and there are no cushioned pads for the sunloungers. There is constant hustling for drinks. Since it's a large resort ship, expect lines for shore excursions, security control when re-boarding, and disembarkation, along with sign-up sheets for fitness equipment. Also, note that loud rap and rock music is everywhere.

ACCOMMODATION. There are numerous cabin price categories, in seven different grades: suites with private balcony; deluxe outside-view cabins with private balcony; outside-view cabins with private balcony; outside-view cabins with window; cabins with a porthole instead of a window; interior cabins; and interior cabins with upper and lower berths. The price reflects the grade, location, and size.

Several decks of cabins have a private balcony, although many of these are not actually private, as they can be overlooked from various public locations.

During the makeover, a number of Spa-grade cabins were added adjacent to the Carnival Spa and Serenity area; these have all the usual fittings, plus special spa-related extras, and easy access to the spa.

Standard cabins are of an adequate size and are equipped with the basics, although the furniture is angular, and lacks rounded edges. Three decks of cabins (eight on each deck, all with private balcony – these are nice) overlook the stern. Most cabins with twin beds can be converted to a queen-size bed format.

Book one of the Category 11 or 12 suites, and you will get more space and a larger number of perks and privileges.

DINING. The two main dining rooms, Golden and Platinum, are two decks high, with seating on both levels. The decor includes wall coverings featuring a pattern of Japanese bonsai trees. Choose either fixed-time dining (6pm or 8.15pm) or flexible dining (during opening hours).

Overall, the food is quite starchy, with simple presentation, few garnishes, and many dishes disguised with gravies and sauces. The choice of fresh green vegetables, bread and bakery items (these are thawed and then baked from frozen 'starter' dough), cheeses, and fruits is limited, and there is heavy use of canned fruit and jellied desserts. The waiters sing and dance, so think 'foodertainment' rather than food quality. Also, there are no wine waiters, and the wine glasses are small. For something very simple, there's an 'always available' list of 'Carnival Classics' such as mahi-mahi (fish), baby back ribs (beef), and grilled chicken.

Other (complimentary) eateries include: Guy's Burger Joint, a poolside venue developed with Food Network personality Guy Fieri (for handmade burgers and freshly cut fries) and BlueIguana Cantina Mexican eatery (for Mexican snack food such as tacos and burritos). Poolside watering holes include a BlueIguana Tequila Bar, and a RedFrog Rum Bar.

For something different, try the (extra-cost) Emerald Room, which features large premium-quality steaks and grilled seafood, and has lighting fixtures that look like giant emeralds.

The two-level Red Sail Restaurant is for casual self-serve eats; it includes a Mexican counter for burritos and tacos, a deli, and on the upper level, a fish 'n' chip shop (there is seating on both levels).

ENTERTAINMENT. The multi-deck Amber Palace Showlounge seats 1,400. It has a revolving stage, hydraulic orchestra pit, superb sound, and seating on three levels (the upper levels being tiered through two decks). A proscenium arch over the stage acts as a scenery loft.

Jazz lovers could head for the Bar Blue, while the Cinn-A-Bar is a piano bar, with curved aluminum walls – so 'bending' notes should be easy.

SPA/FITNESS. SpaCarnival is a fairly large health, fitness, and spa complex. You'll find it directly above the navigation bridge forward, and accessed from the forward stairway.

Facilities include a gymnasium (packed with muscle machines and exercise equipment), body treatment area, sauna and steam rooms for men and women, and a beauty salon.

CARNIVAL HORIZON
★★★+

A SHIP FOR ACTION-PACKED FAMILY FUN AND CARDIO-ACTIVE OUTDOOR ACTIVITIES

Size:	Large Resort Ship	Passenger/Crew Ratio (lower beds):	2.5
Tonnage:	135,000	Cabins (total):	1,823
Cruise Line:	Carnival Cruise Line	Size Range (sq ft/m):	161.4–344.4/15.0–32.0
Former Names:	none	Cabins (for one person):	0
Builder:	Fincantieri (Italy)	Cabins with balcony:	887
Entered Service:	Mar 2018	Cabins (wheelchair accessible):	35
Length (ft/m):	1,054.7/321.5	Wheelchair accessibility:	Good
Propulsion/Propellers:	diesel-electric (62,370kW)/2 azimuthing pods	Elevators:	16
		Casino (gaming tables):	Yes
Total Crew:	1,450	Self-Service Launderette:	Yes
Passengers (lower beds):	3,954	Onboard currency:	US$
Passenger Space Ratio (lower beds):	34.1		

THE SHIP. *Carnival Horizon* is a sister ship to *Carnival Vista*. The design is itself old – based mostly on *Carnival Destiny* of 1996, with an array of activity-fueled fun for the whole family. This is essentially a ship built around its Dr. Seuss-themed WaterWorks aqua park and the many other bling-filled attractions to keep you occupied. *Carnival Horizon* really is all about the fun of the fair at sea – and at high volume.

So, line up to pedal a bike on the suspended track of Sky Ride – maybe even cycle to the next port! Other attractions include a large Water-Works aqua park, with its 445-ft (136m) Kaleid-O-Slide, a twisting, corkscrew-turning waterslide adventure with kaleidoscopic effects (a favorite with kids).

Considering the number of passengers carried, the swimming pools are really small and crowded, as is the open deck (sunbathing) space, although there are several (relatively) quiet spots on a lower, exterior promenade deck.

An adults-only (extra-cost) Serenity area atop the ship at the front provides an escape from the noisy, family-filled decks below, with hot tubs, massage 'huts,' sunloungers, a bar, and other 'take a break' facilities.

There is a full walk-around open promenade deck – but it's lined with deck chairs and restaurant terraces. Aft, two 'scenic whirlpools' hang over

BERLITZ'S RATINGS		
	Possible	Achieved
Ship	500	373
Accommodation	200	133
Food	400	211
Service	400	251
Entertainment	100	68
Cruise Experience	400	260

OVERALL SCORE 1296 points out of 2000

the water (as part of the Havana Outside area), with sea views.

The interior decor is warmer than that of *Carnival Vista*. Facilities include a small IMAX Theater for movies and documentary content, a large Vista Casino (adjacent to the atrium), a Thrill Theater for a moving 4-D experience, and many other lounges and bars. However, the ship's layout is rather disjointed and the 'smart' elevators are frustrating to use.

The social center of the ship is the central atrium. Counters for guest services and shore excursions are just off the atrium; aft of the lobby is Reflections Dining Room.

Most public rooms, lounges, bars, and nightspots are located on two main public room/entertainment decks.

The myriad bars include a sports bar, the trendy Havana Bar, Alchemy Bar (for 'mixologist' cocktails, and Guy's Pig & Anchor smokehouse (with micro-brewery and Carnival's own brews).

Families with children have lots of hyper-activity sporty areas outdoors, plus play rooms for kids and teens (in multiple locations), and youth counselors in charge, so parents and minders can get some 'me' time, too.

What Carnival does well is provide almost non-stop excitement, fun, and entertainment. While the cuisine is just so-so, the real fun begins at sundown, when the upbeat kicks in.

ACCOMMODATION. The range of cabin sizes, locations, grades and prices includes 'Family Harbor' – family cabins that can sleep up to five. Whether you go for high end or low end, all include plush mattresses, good-quality duvets, bed linen and pillows. The suites are not large, although they are practically laid out, while some of the standard cabins are fine for two but become crowded for three or more.

All cabins have spy-hole doors, twin beds convertible to queen-size beds, individually controlled air conditioning, infotainment screen, and telephone. Some cabins can accommodate a third and fourth person, but have little closet space, and only one personal safe. Some Deck 3 cabins have lifeboat-obstructed views. Among the most desirable suites/cabins are on five aft-facing decks, with private balconies overlooking the stern and ship's wash. There's no vibration – a bonus provided by the pod propulsion system.

DINING. Reflections (1,474 seats) and Meridian (702 seats) are the two main dining rooms for served meals (breakfast, lunch, and dinner) in early or late seating or 'Your Time' dining (note that these restaurants are not always open in port). Meridian Restaurant has some tables with fine aft views (on both main and balcony levels – although the upper level has a low ceiling). You can also order selections from the (extra-cost) steakhouse menu.

Alternative eateries (some at extra cost) include: Lido Marketplace (self-serve buffet venue); Cucina del Capitano (Italian fare – the only venue with tablecloths); Seafood Shack (outdoors); Fahrenheit 555 (an extra-cost steakhouse for premium-quality cuts and seafood; Ji Ji Asian Kitchen; Bonsai Sushi and Bonsai Teppanyaki (a first for Carnival); and Guy's Pig & Anchor Smokehouse. Fat Jimmy's (barbecue) and BlueIguana (Mexican) are poolside.

Families with youngsters might like to indulge in a Green Eggs and Ham breakfast, while Chef's Table (for foodies) includes a little showbusiness from the chef for up to 12 diners (both are at extra cost).

ENTERTAINMENT. The Liquid Lounge (show-lounge) spans two decks and is the venue for Carnival's Vegas-style production shows (think feathers and skin) and cabaret acts.

A second entertainment lounge is the Limelight Lounge (for smutty adult comedy), while the bordello-colored Piano Bar offers lighter fare.

A small IMAX Theater has a three-deck high screen, while adjacent is a multi-dimensional, special-effects experience in the Thrill Theater; both are at extra cost, along with popcorn and movie snacks. Adjacent is a video arcade (The Warehouse).

SPA/FITNESS. Cloud 9 Spa is on two levels, with treatment rooms, men's and women's infrared saunas and hammam (slow steam and mud room – good for couples), relaxation lounger, fitness center, as well as 'pay more' thermal suites, plus a VIP treatment room for Spa Suite occupants.

Activity/sports facilities include an outdoor Sky-Course suspended ropes course (always fun on a moving ship), Sky Gardens mini-golf course, and a Skycourt (for baseball). The Clubhouse at SportS-quare includes mini-bowling, ping-pong, arcade basketball, and video games.

CARNIVAL IMAGINATION
★★★

THIS FUN SHIP COULD BE A GOOD CHOICE FOR HIGH-ENERGY FAMILY CRUISING

Size:	Mid-size Ship	Passenger/Crew Ratio (lower beds):	2.2
Tonnage:	70,367	Cabins (total):	1,028
Cruise Line:	Carnival Cruise Line	Size Range (sq ft/m):	173.2–409.7/16–38
Former Names:	Imagination	Cabins (for one person):	0
Builder:	Kvaerner Masa-Yards (Finland)	Cabins with balcony:	152
Entered Service:	Jul 1995	Cabins (wheelchair accessible):	22
Length (ft/m):	855.0/260.6	Wheelchair accessibility:	Fair
Propulsion/Propellers:	diesel-electric (42,240kW)/2	Elevators:	14
Total Crew:	920	Casino (gaming tables):	Yes
Passengers (lower beds):	2,056	Self-Service Launderette:	Yes
Passenger Space Ratio (lower beds):	34.4	Onboard currency:	US$

THE SHIP. *Carnival Imagination* (now over 20 years old) has a swept-back wing-like funnel above the outdoor pool deck, but the open deck space itself is inadequate when the ship is full. The aft decks used to be less noisy when all the activities were focused around the main swimming pool and hot tubs, but now it has a Carnival WaterWorks – with long (about 300ft/90m) and short waterslides and water-burst fountains – it's a very active area. For quiet, adult-only space, pay extra to go to Serenity, on Deck 9 aft.

There is no walk-around open promenade deck, but there is a short jogging track. The lifeboats, six of which double as shore tenders are positioned high.

The interior spaces are well utilized, but busy. The general passenger flow is good, and the interior design – by Miami-architect Joe Farcus – is clever and bizarrely colorful. The theme is the legendary symbols of antiquity (think winged deities and beings).

A stylish, 'open' balcony-shaped atrium lobby spans six decks, and is topped by a large glass dome. The lowest level houses the purser's desk and shore-excursion desk, the Atrium Bar (with music), and a small sushi bar off to one side.

There are public entertainment lounges, bars, and clubs galore, with something for everyone (except quiet space). The public rooms, connected by a double-width Via Marina Promenade, combine a colorful mix of classic and contemporary design

BERLITZ'S RATINGS

	Possible	Achieved
Ship	500	294
Accommodation	200	121
Food	400	202
Service	400	250
Entertainment	100	62
Cruise Experience	400	229

OVERALL SCORE 1158 points out of 2000

elements. Most public rooms and attractions lead off from this boulevard, which runs between the showlounge (forward) and Xanadu lounge aft. Gamers and slot-players have almost non-stop action in the El Dorado Casino. There is also a nice-looking library and reading room (but few books), plus a 1,200-sq-ft (111-sq-m) conference room.

The *sine qua non* of a Carnival cruise is all about fun, which begins at sundown, when the ship excels in lights, volume, and show. *Carnival Imagination* is a floating playground for the young and young-at-heart, and features constant stimulation and lots of participation events. Since it's a large resort ship, there will be lines for the likes of shore excursions, security control when re-boarding, and disembarkation.

Downsides include many annoying announcements, the never-ending hustling to get you to buy ice-filled drinks, and loud rap and rock music.

ACCOMMODATION. There are several accommodation grades, priced by size, and location. Standard outside-view and interior cabins have clinical, unmemorable decor. They are marginally comfortable (most are the same size and appointments), with good storage space and practical, well-designed no-nonsense bathrooms. With a queen-bed configuration instead of a twin-bed layout, one person has to clamber over the bed.

Suite occupants get more space, quirky furniture, and perks, although the suites are much smaller than those aboard vessels of a similar size of competing companies.

Families have 50 connecting cabins to choose from – good if you want your children close by, but maybe not *that* close.

Room service items are available 24 hours a day, although in standard cabins, only cold food is available (there are more choices for suite-grade accommodation).

DINING. Two large main dining rooms, Pride and Spirit, are amidships and aft. Both have ocean-view windows and bright decor, but they are noisy because the ceilings are low. Choose either fixed-time dining (6pm or 8.15pm) or flexible dining (during opening hours). Note that they are not open for lunch on port days.

Except for breakfasts (which are good), the carbohydrate-rich food is unmemorable, with simple presentation and few garnishes. This is batch cooking production catering. The selection of fresh green vegetables, bread and bakery items (baked from frozen 'starter' dough), cheeses, and fruits is limited, and there is heavy use of canned fruit and jellied desserts. The waiters sing and dance (think 'foodertainment' rather than food quality).

For something simple, a selection of always available (when the dining rooms are open) 'Carnival Classics' includes mahi mahi (fish), baby back ribs (beef), and grilled chicken.

Horizon Bar & Grill is a casual self-serve buffet venue. It includes a deli counter and pizzeria. At night, it becomes Seaview Bistro, for pasta, steaks, salads, and desserts. The food selection, though limited, makes a change from the large, crowded, noisy main dining rooms.

Other (complimentary) eateries include: Guy's Burger Joint, a poolside venue developed with Food Network personality Guy Fieri (for burgers and fresh-cut fries) and BlueIguana Cantina Mexican eatery (for Mexican snack food like tacos and burritos).

ENTERTAINMENT. The Universe Showlounge hosts large-scale production shows and cabaret – although 20 pillars obstruct some views. During a typical cruise, there will be several shows, with lead singers and a clutch of dancers backed by a large live band.

SPA/FITNESS. SpaCarnival is a glass-wrapped complex on the uppermost deck, forward of the ship's mast. It has a gymnasium with ocean-view windows and muscle-pumping equipment, aerobics room, men's and women's sauna and steam rooms, beauty salon, and body treatment rooms. Some fitness classes incur an extra charge. For sports: basketball, volleyball, table tennis, a banked jogging track outdoors above the spa, and a mini-golf course.

CARNIVAL INSPIRATION
★★★

THIS ULTRA-COLORFUL SHIP IS GOOD FOR A FIRST CASUAL CRUISE EXPERIENCE

Size:	Mid-size Ship	Passenger/Crew Ratio (lower beds):	2.2
Tonnage:	70,367	Cabins (total):	1,028
Cruise Line:	Carnival Cruise Line	Size Range (sq ft/m):	173.2–409.7/16–38
Former Names:	*Inspiration*	Cabins (for one person):	0
Builder:	Kvaerner Masa-Yards (Finland)	Cabins with balcony:	152
Entered Service:	Apr 1996	Cabins (wheelchair accessible):	22
Length (ft/m):	855.0/260.6	Wheelchair accessibility:	Fair
Propulsion/Propellers:	diesel-electric (42,240kW)/2	Elevators:	14
Total Crew:	920	Casino (gaming tables):	Yes
Passengers (lower beds):	2,056	Self-Service Launderette:	Yes
Passenger Space Ratio (lower beds):	34.4	Onboard currency:	US$

THE SHIP. *Carnival Inspiration* is the sixth in a series of eight almost identical *Fantasy*-class ships. Although over 20 years old, it is good for anyone taking a first cruise. Pool deck highlights include the aqua park WaterWorks, with a 334ft (101.8m) Twister Waterslide, dual Speedway Splash slides, and water-burst fountains – a splash-tastic area for kids. However, the open deck space for sunbathing is limited when the ship is full. Because most activities happen around the main pool and hot tubs (one has a thatched shade), the aft decks tend to be less noisy. An alternative is Serenity – an adult-only 'quiet' (extra-cost; minimum age 21) lounging space on Deck 9 aft. Sadly, there is no walk-around open promenade deck. The lifeboats, six of which double as shore tenders, are positioned high up.

The interior, designed by Joe Farcus, is clever, functional, and extremely colorful. The decor theme is the arts (in an Art Nouveau style) and literature; it includes a mix of classic and contemporary design elements.

The interior focal point (and social meeting place) is the 'open' atrium lobby, with a balconied shape (including decoration resembling the necks and heads of violins). It spans six decks, has a marble staircase, and is topped by a glass-domed roof. The purser's desk and shore-excursion desk occupy the lowest level.

There are public entertainment lounges, bars, and clubs galore, with something for everyone (except

BERLITZ'S RATINGS

	Possible	Achieved
Ship	500	295
Accommodation	200	121
Food	400	202
Service	400	251
Entertainment	100	62
Cruise Experience	400	232

OVERALL SCORE 1163 points out of 2000

quiet space). The public rooms, connected by a double-width Inspiration Boulevard, feature many contemporary design elements. Most public rooms and attractions lead off from this boulevard – a sort of shipboard Main Street, which runs between the showlounge (forward) and the Candlelight lounge aft. Gamers and slot players alike can enjoy the almost non-stop action in the Monte Carlo Casino.

The Shakespeare What's it like? *Carnival Inspiration* is a floating playground for the young, but there will be lines for shore excursions, security control when re-boarding, and disembarkation, as well as sign-up sheets for fitness equipment.

There are many annoying announcements, a never-ending hustle to get you to buy (ice-laden) drinks, and no escape from the loud rap and rock music.

ACCOMMODATION. There are several accommodation grades, priced according to size and location. Standard outside-view and interior cabins have plain decor; they are marginally comfortable, yet practical (most are of the same size and appointments), with good storage space and, no-nonsense bathrooms. However, with a queen-bed configuration instead of a twin-bed layout, one person needs to clamber over the bed.

Choose a suite and you get more space, plus eclectic decor and furniture. The suites are mildly attractive, but they are much smaller than those aboard ships of a similar size of competing companies. A small gift basket of toiletry samples is provided in all grades.

Room service is available 24 hours a day, although in standard cabins, only cold food is available, while suite-grade occupants get both hot and cold items to choose from.

DINING. Two large main dining rooms, Mardi Gras and Carnivale (the names of Carnival's first two ships), are amidships and aft, respectively. Both have ocean-view windows and bright decor, but are noisy, due to low ceilings. Choose either fixed-time dining (6pm or 8.15pm) or flexible dining (during opening hours). Note that the two main dining rooms may not be open for lunch on port days.

Except for breakfasts (which are good), the food is quite starchy, with simple presentation, few garnishes, and many dishes disguised with gravies and sauces. The selection of fresh green vegetables, breads, cheeses, and fruits is limited (bread and bakery items are baked from frozen 'starter' dough), and there is heavy use of canned fruit and jellied desserts. The waiters sing and dance, so think 'food-ertainment' rather than food quality. For something really simple, an 'always available' list of 'Carnival Classics' includes mahi-mahi (fish), baby back ribs (beef), and grilled chicken.

Brasserie Bar & Grill is a large self-serve buffet, for non-memorable fare; it includes a deli counter and pizzeria.

Other (complimentary) eateries include: Guy's Burger Joint, a poolside venue developed with Food Network personality Guy Fieri (for burgers and fresh-cut fries) and BlueIguana Cantina Mexican (for Mexican-style tacos and burritos).

A patisserie offers specialty coffees and sweets (extra charge), and a sushi bar off to one side of the atrium lobby bar is open prior to dinner only.

ENTERTAINMENT. Paris Main Lounge is the venue for large-scale production shows and major cabaret acts, although 20 pillars obstruct views from some seats. The resident show troupe includes vocalists and a clutch of dancers, backed by a large live band.

Spa/Fitness. SpaCarnival is a glass-wrapped 'spa' complex on the uppermost interior deck, forward of the ship's mast. It has a gymnasium with ocean-view windows and muscle-pumping equipment, aerobics room, men's and women's sauna and steam rooms, beauty salon, and body treatment rooms. Some fitness classes incur an extra charge. For sports, there's basketball, volleyball and table tennis, plus a banked jogging track outdoors above the spa, and a mini-golf course.

CARNIVAL LEGEND
★★★

THIS IS A CONTEMPORARY SHIP FOR A FUN-FILLED ACTIVE FAMILY CRUISE

Size:	Mid-size Ship	Passenger/Crew Ratio (lower beds):	2.2
Tonnage:	85,942	Cabins (total):	1,062
Cruise Line:	Carnival Cruise Line	Size Range (sq ft/m):	185–490/17.1–45.5
Former Names:	none	Cabins (for one person):	0
Builder:	Kvaerner Masa-Yards (Finland)	Cabins with balcony:	750
Entered Service:	Aug 2002	Cabins (wheelchair accessible):	16
Length (ft/m):	959.6/292.5	Wheelchair accessibility:	Good
Propulsion/Propellers:	diesel-electric (62,370kW)/2 azimuthing pods	Elevators:	15
		Casino (gaming tables):	Yes
Total Crew:	1,030	Self-Service Launderette:	Yes
Passengers (lower beds):	2,124	Onboard currency:	US$
Passenger Space Ratio (lower beds):	40.4		

THE SHIP. *Carnival Legend* – sister to *Carnival Miracle*, *Carnival Pride*, and *Carnival Spirit* – shares the same layout and configuration. There's no vibration – a bonus provided by the pod propulsion system. Designed for families with children and for entertainment, it has been modified to suit Australasian tastes.

The open deck and sunbathing space is not extensive, but there are two swimming pools, one of which can be covered by a sliding glass dome in case of inclement weather. A Water Park and Kids Splash Zone has water wheels, spraying jets, water blasters, pull ropes, two Mini Racer slides, and more (watch out for the giant water bucket), but the really big attraction is Green Thunder, a thrill ride that starts 100ft (30m) above sea level. The floor suddenly drops out of the platform, and you plummet in a near-vertical drop at about 23ft (7m) a second. When you hit the water in the fast waterslide, you twist and turn through a transparent tube that extends over the side of the ship. Kids love it. On the negative side, the open deck space is a bit tight when the ship sails to full capacity in warm-weather areas.

For some quiet time, an extra-charge, adults-only area, Sanctuary, which is located aft, has its own bar, pool, hot tub and other facilities.

The interior decor is dedicated to the world's great legends, from the heroes of antiquity to 20th-century jazz masters and athletes – an eclectic mix that somehow works.

BERLITZ'S RATINGS		
	Possible	Achieved
Ship	500	328
Accommodation	200	125
Food	400	207
Service	400	242
Entertainment	100	63
Cruise Experience	400	239
OVERALL SCORE 1204 points out of 2000		

Most bars and lounges are on two entertainment/public room decks; the upper featuring an exterior promenade deck. The Hollywood Boulevard walkway connects many of the public rooms on Atlantic Deck, one deck above Promenade Deck, which hosts a large Club Merlin Casino (you have to walk though it to get to the main level of the showlounge from the restaurant, aft). In a 2014 makeover, RedFrog Pub (featuring Carnival's own Thirsty-Frog Red draft brew), Bonsai Sushi (a sushi venue with Asian-style decor and food items), and Cherry on Top candy store were added.

A colorful atrium lobby spans eight decks, with wall decorations best seen from above the main lobby level, including a mural of the Colossus of Rhodes.

Other facilities include a wedding chapel, a shopping street with boutique stores, a photo gallery, and an observation balcony in the center of the vessel, at the top of the multi-deck atrium.

The real fun begins at sundown, when Carnival turns up the heat with its razzle-dazzle shows, and late-night music.

Niggles include the small reception desk in the atrium lobby, which is often congested. Many pillars obstruct passenger flow – the ones in the dining room, for example, make it difficult for proper food service by the waiters. Books and computers are cohabitants in the ship's Holmes library/Internet center, but anyone wanting a book has to lean over others who may be using a computer, which is an awkward arrangement. Finally, there's no escape from the incredibly high-volume contemporary music blaring out throughout the ship.

ACCOMMODATION. There are numerous cabin categories, priced by grade, location, and size, including suites (with private balcony), outside-view cabins with private balcony, 68 ocean-view cabins with French doors (pseudo balconies that have doors that open, but no balcony to step onto), and a healthy proportion of standard outside-view to interior (no-view) cabins.

All cabins have spy-hole doors, twin beds that can be converted into queen-size beds, individually controlled air conditioning (it can't be switched off), TV, and telephone. A number of cabins on the lowest deck have lifeboat-obstructed views. Some cabins can accommodate a third and fourth person – useful if you have small children – although they have little closet space and only one personal safe.

Among the most desirable suites and cabins are those on five of the aft-facing decks; these have balconies overlooking the stern and ship's wash.

DINING. Truffles Restaurant is the large, two-deck-high, 1,300-seat main dining room, with seating on both upper and main levels. Its expansive ceiling has large murals of a Royal Copenhagen china pattern, and there are wall-mounted glass cases displaying fine china. Small rooms on upper and lower levels can be booked for groups of up to 60. Choose either fixed-time dining (6pm or 8.15pm) or flexible dining (during opening hours). Note that the main dining room is not open for lunch on port days.

The food is starch-heavy (lots of rice and potatoes), with simple presentation, and few garnishes (although breakfasts are surprisingly decent). The selection of fresh green vegetables, bread and bakery items (these are thawed and then baked from frozen 'starter' dough), cheeses, and fruits is limited, and there is much canned fruit and jellied desserts. The waiters sing and dance, so think 'foodertainment' rather than food quality. There are no wine waiters, and wine glasses are small. For something

really simple, an 'always available' list of 'Carnival Classics' includes mahi-mahi (fish), baby back ribs (beef), and grilled chicken.

The Unicorn Café (Lido restaurant) is a self-serve food court-style buffet-style casual eatery (part of it wraps around the upper section of the huge atrium), with indoor and outdoor seating. Movement around the buffet area is slow, however. Each night, it morphs into Seaview Bistro, for serve-yourself dinners. Adjacent to the main pool is a Guy's Burger Joint and Blueiguana Cantina.

Golden Fleece Steakhouse is an extra-cost dining spot atop the ship, with around 150 seats and a show kitchen; it features prime steaks and grilled seafood. Reservations are required. The decor features the Greek legend of Jason and the Argonauts (the bar hosts a large sculpture of the Golden Fleece).

ENTERTAINMENT. The 1920s movie theatre-style, four-deck-high, 1,170-seat Follies Showlounge is the venue for large-scale production shows and cabaret, best seen from the upper three levels. Directly underneath the showlounge is the Firebird lounge and bar.

Almost every lounge/bar, including Billie's Bar (a piano lounge) and Satchmo's Club (a nightclub with bar and dance floor), has live music in the evening. Finally, for the lively, there's a disco, and, for the unreserved, there's always karaoke.

SPA/FITNESS. SpaCarnival spans two decks above the bridge in the forward part of the ship. Lower-level facilities include a solarium, several treatment rooms, sauna and steam rooms for men and women, and a beauty salon. The upper level hosts a gymnasium with floor-to-ceiling ocean-view windows, and an aerobics room.

There are two centrally located swimming pools outdoors: one can be used in inclement weather due to its retractable glass dome. Adjacent are two whirlpool tubs. Another smaller pool is for children. An outdoor jogging track is located around the mast and the forward part of the ship; it doesn't go around the whole ship, but it's long enough for a decent workout.

CARNIVAL LIBERTY
★★★

THIS ULTRA-COLORFUL SHIP SHOULD BE GOOD FOR FIRST-TIME CRUISERS

Size:	Large Resort Ship
Tonnage:	110,320
Cruise Line:	Carnival Cruise Lines
Former Names:	none
Builder:	Fincantieri (Italy)
Entered Service:	Jul 2005
Length (ft/m):	951.4/290.0
Propulsion/Propellers:	diesel-electric (63,400kW)/2
Total Crew:	1,160
Passengers (lower beds):	2,974
Passenger Space Ratio (lower beds):	37.0
Passenger/Crew Ratio (lower beds):	2.5
Cabins (total):	1,487
Size Range (sq ft/m):	179.7–482.2/16.7–44.8
Cabins (for one person):	0
Cabins with balcony:	574
Cabins (wheelchair accessible):	25
Wheelchair accessibility:	Good
Elevators:	18
Casino (gaming tables):	Yes
Self-Service Launderette:	Yes
Onboard currency:	US$

THE SHIP. *Carnival Liberty* has a fairly balanced profile. Amidships on the open deck are a splashy waterslide (200ft/60m long), tiered sunbathing decks and small pool, several hot tubs, and a large Seaside Theater movie screen. An extra-cost Serenity retreat provides quiet sunbathing space and a pool with retractable glass dome, just for adults, aft of the funnel. Inside are three decks full of lounges, 10 bars, and lots of rooms to play in.

The public room decor salutes master trades such as ironwork, masonry, pottery, and painting. The layout is logical, so finding your way around is easy. Most public rooms are located off a main boulevard – an interior promenade that is good for strolling and people-watching – particularly from the Jardin Café or Promenade Bar. Other hangouts and drinking places include The Stage (live music/karaoke lounge), the Flower Bar (main lobby), Gloves Bar (sports bar), Paparazzi (wine bar), and The Cabinet.

Carnival Liberty is a floating playground for the young and young-at-heart, and anyone who enjoys constant stimulation and lots of participation events, together with the three 'Gs' – glitz, glamour, and gambling. It's cruising Splash Vegas style – a fun, all-American experience. Because it's a large resort ship, there will be lines for the likes of shore excursions, security control when re-boarding, and disembarkation, as well as sign-up sheets for fitness equipment.

BERLITZ'S RATINGS		
	Possible	Achieved
Ship	500	330
Accommodation	200	126
Food	400	208
Service	400	241
Entertainment	100	64
Cruise Experience	400	234
OVERALL SCORE 1203 points out of 2000		

While the cuisine is just so-so, the real fun begins at sundown, when it excels in terms of sound, lights, razzle-dazzle shows, and late-night high-volume sounds.

Niggles include the many pillars in the dining room, public toilets that are utilitarian and need cheering up, a lack of flowers, and annoying revenue-generating announcements. It is impossible to escape from noise and loud music (it's even played in cabin hallways and lifts), not to mention smokers.

ACCOMMODATION. There are numerous cabin price categories: suites with balcony; deluxe outside-view cabins with balcony; outside-view cabins with balcony; outside-view cabins with window; cabins with a porthole instead of a window; interior cabins; and interior cabins with upper and lower berths. The price reflects the grade, location, and size. Five decks of cabins have a private balcony, but many are not so private, because they can be overlooked from various public locations.

There are 18 'spa' cabins, clustered around and behind SpaCarnival, so you can get out of bed and head straight to the treadmill without having to go through any public rooms.

Standard cabins are of good size and have all the basics, although the cabinetry is angular (no rounded corners). Eight balcony cabins on each of three decks overlook the stern (desirable). Most cabins with twin beds are convertible to a queen-size bed format.

DINING. There are two main dining rooms, Golden Olympian Restaurant, forward, seating 744, and Silver Olympian Restaurant, aft, seating 1,122. Choose either fixed-time dining (6pm or 8.15pm) or flexible dining (during opening hours). Note that the main dining room is not open for lunch on port days. Two small wings (the Persian Room and Satin Room) can accommodate groups.

The food is carbohydrate-rich and non-memorable (except for breakfast, which is good), with simple presentation and few garnishes. Many dishes are disguised with gravies and sauces. The choice of green vegetables, bread and bakery items (these are thawed and then baked from frozen 'starter' dough), cheeses, and fruits is limited, and there is heavy use of canned fruit and jellied desserts. Also, there are no wine waiters, and the wine glasses are small. For something really simple, go for the 'always available' list of 'Carnival Classics' such as mahi-mahi (fish), baby back ribs (beef), and grilled chicken.

Two-level Emile's is a casual self-serve international food court-style Lido Deck eatery, Guy's Burger Joint (named after TV's Guy Fieri), Blue Iguana (Mexican cantina-style), and Bonsai Sushi. Harry's Steakhouse is a more intimate setting for prime meats and seafood (a cover charge applies).

ENTERTAINMENT. The Venetian Palace Showlounge is a 1,400-seat multi-deck showroom for large-scale Las Vegas-style production shows and major cabaret acts.

The Victoria Lounge is another, smaller venue, located aft; it seats 425 and typically features live music and late-night cabaret acts, including smutty adult comedy.

The Tattooed Lady Dance Club is a discotheque for the hearing-impaired; it includes a video wall with projections live from the dance floor. There's also the 100-seat Piano Man bar, with keyboard-inspired decor.

SPA/FITNESS. SpaCarnival spans two decks (above the navigation bridge), accessible from the forward stairway. Lower level facilities include a solarium, body treatment rooms, lecture rooms, sauna and steam rooms for men and women, and a beauty parlor; the upper level hosts a large gymnasium with expansive ocean view windows, and an aerobics room. Most fitness classes cost extra.

CARNIVAL MAGIC
★★★

THE WHOLE FAMILY SHOULD REALLY ENJOY THIS HIGH-ENERGY FLOATING RESORT

Size:	Large Resort Ship	Passenger/Crew Ratio (lower beds):	2.6
Tonnage:	128,048	Cabins (total):	1,823
Cruise Line:	Carnival Cruise Line	Size Range (sq ft/m):	185.0–430.5/17.1–40.0
Former Names:	none	Cabins (for one person):	0
Builder:	Fincantieri (Italy)	Cabins with balcony:	887
Entered Service:	Jun 2011	Cabins (wheelchair accessible):	35
Length (ft/m):	1,004.0/306.0	Wheelchair accessibility:	Good
Propulsion/Propellers:	Diesel-electric (75,600kW)/2	Elevators:	20
Total Crew:	1,367	Casino (gaming tables):	Yes
Passengers (lower beds):	3,646	Self-Service Launderette:	Yes
Passenger Space Ratio (lower beds):	35.1	Onboard currency:	US$

THE SHIP. *Carnival Magic*, sister to *Carnival Dream*, is 13 percent larger than earlier close sister *Carnival Splendor*. A standout feature is a long (over 312ft/95m) Twister Waterslide, part of WaterWorks on the pool deck – it's lots of fun for kids. However, there simply isn't enough open deck space for the number of passengers the ship carries, so sunbed loungers are tightly packed together. An extra-charge retreat called Serenity is for adults only.

There is a full walk-around open promenade deck, with deck chairs. Four 'scenic hot tubs' are cantilevered over the sea and provide fine views, but they do get crowded, and rowdy. Lido Deck 10 has a good open-deck area, with small pool and a large Seaside Theater LED movie screen and laser light show.

Although the ship's bows are short, its profile is nicely balanced, with a rakish front and a more rounded stern. The ship is based on the original design for *Carnival Sunshine*, and includes some of the design flaws of the *Sunshine*-class, but with a passenger capacity increase of over 1,000. The interior decor is vivid, and the atrium lobby is the connection point for ship functions and for meeting people. Take the glass-walled elevators for a neat view, though you may need sunglasses. It's good to see three main elevator towers: forward, amidships, and aft, unlike larger ships such as *Oasis of the Seas*, which, although it carries many more passengers, has only two such towers.

BERLITZ'S RATINGS		
	Possible	Achieved
Ship	500	332
Accommodation	200	128
Food	400	208
Service	400	244
Entertainment	100	64
Cruise Experience	400	238
OVERALL SCORE 1214 points out of 2000		

The Ocean Plaza is a comfortable area by day and an entertainment venue by night. The indoor/outdoor café and live music venue has a bandstand where a variety of musical genres are showcased, a large circular dance floor, and around 190 seats. A floor-to-ceiling curved glass wall separates the room, dividing indoor and outdoor seating areas. An adjacent bar offers coffees, ice creams, and pastries. The Page Turner (great name) is the ship's library, while Jackpot is – you guessed it – the colorful, large, lively casino, with abundant gaming tables and slot machines.

Other rooms include The Song (Jazz Bar) and Ocean Plaza (a sort of quiet area during the day, but busy at night with live entertainment); Internet-connect computer terminals are scattered throughout the ship, but few have much privacy. There's also a 232-capacity conference room (The Chambers). This was the first Carnival ship to have a pub, the poolside RedFrog Pub, with its own-label beer, ThirstyFrog Red. Also popular is BlueIguana Tequila Bar and the Alchemy Bar, both added in a 2016 refurbishment.

So, what's it like? *Carnival Magic* is a floating playground for the party-loving young. The cuisine is not at all memorable, but there's plenty to do for all the family. Because it's a large resort ship, there will be lines for shore excursions, security control when re-boarding, and disembarkation, as well as sign-up sheets for fitness equipment. There are many annoying and loud announcements, and a never-ending hustle to get you to buy alcoholic drinks full of ice, and other things.

ACCOMMODATION. There are many different cabin price categories, but just six cabin types. All accommodation includes the Carnival Comfort Bed with good-quality duvets, mattresses, linens, and pillows. However, the straight accommodation deck hallways create rather a cell-block look, and they are bright – very bright – even at night. There are also lot of interior cabins (perhaps those to go for are those aft) with great rearward ocean views on decks 6, 7, 8, and 9). There is a wide selection of other balcony cabins and suites, including 'Cove Balcony' cabins (these are the closest to the waterline). Adjacent to the Cloud 9 Spa are 'Cloud 9' spa cabins. They provide a number of 'exclusive' amenities and privileges, and easy access.

DINING. The main restaurants are Northern Lights, a 1,180-seat amidships dining room, and the smaller 828-seat aft dining room, Southern Lights. Each has two levels: main and balcony (the galley is on the lower level). Two small annexes can be reserved as private dining rooms. Expect all-singing, all-dancing waiters to entertain you, while you search for the elusive green vegetables. Choose either fixed-time dining (6pm or 8.15pm) or flexible dining (any time between 5.45 and 9.30pm). Note that these are not open for lunch on port days.

Except for breakfasts (which are very good), the food is starch-heavy and non-memorable, with simple presentation and few garnishes. Many dishes are disguised with gravies and sauces. The selection of fresh green vegetables, bread and bakery items (these are thawed and then baked from frozen 'starter' dough), cheeses, and fruits is limited, and there is much use of canned fruit and jellied desserts. There are no wine waiters, and wine glasses are small. For something simple, an 'always available' list of 'Carnival Classics' includes mahi-mahi (fish), baby back ribs (beef), and grilled chicken.

Lido Marketplace, the ship's large (but not large enough) self-serve buffet facility, has indoor/outdoor seating areas on the lower (main) level and indoor-only seating on the upper level. A number of designated areas provide different types of ethnic cuisine. It gets seriously congested – particularly for breakfast – and the food is pretty basic. The venue includes a Mongolian Wok and Pasta Bar on the upper level.

Forward of the buffet venue is Pizzeria del Capitano (expanded in 2016). Other (complimentary) eateries include: Guy's Burger Joint (think: Food Network personality Guy Fieri), a poolside venue for handmade burgers and fresh-cut fries, and, aft on the same deck, another Fieri-designed eatery called Guy's Pig & Anchor Bar-B-Que Smokehouse (open at lunchtime on sea days only). There's also Bluelguana Cantina for Mexican snack food such as tacos and burritos. Poolside watering holes include Bluelguana Tequila Bar and RedFrog Rum Bar.

The reservations-required Prime seats 139 and features an à la carte menu and nice china and silverware. It's worth paying the cover charge to get a taste of what Carnival can deliver. There's a sushi venue, too, called Sushi and More, on Promenade Deck.

ENTERTAINMENT. The 1,964-seat Showtime Theater spans three decks at the front of the ship, with horseshoe-shaped seating wrapping around a large proscenium-arched stage. The sight lines are generally good, except from some of the seats at the back of the lowest level. Large-scale production shows with lots of feathers and skimpy costumes are staged, together with snappy cabaret acts, all with a live showband.

The 425-seat Spotlight Lounge, aft, has a stage, dance floor, and large bar, and hosts late-night 'adult comedy,' while Caliente is a loud, Latin nightclub.

SPA/FITNESS. The Cloud 9 Spa is a large health and wellness center. The uppermost deck includes indoor/outdoor private spa relaxation areas, at extra cost.

There are 17 treatment rooms, including a VIP room, a large massage room for couples, a Rasul mud treatment room, and two dry flotation rooms. An extra-charge 'Thermal Suite' comes with the typical sensory-enhanced heated chambers: Laconium, Tepidarium, Aroma, and Oriental steam baths. There are two steam rooms, one each for men and women, and a small unisex sauna with a floor-to-ceiling window on its starboard side.

A large contained outdoor SportsSquare for adults is for basketball, football, and volleyball. There's an outdoor weight-training circuit (SkyFitness), and the cutely named Turf on Surf miniature golf course. Perhaps the highlight is SkyCourse – a 230ft (70m)-long outdoor rope course, suspended above the uppermost deck. After all those activities, you'll need a cruise to relax.

CARNIVAL MIRACLE
★★★

THIS FUN-FILLED, FAMILY-FRIENDLY SHIP IS FOR HIGH-ENERGY CRUISING

Size:	Mid-size Ship
Tonnage:	85,942
Cruise Line:	Carnival Cruise Line
Former Names:	none
Builder:	Kvaerner Masa-Yards (Finland)
Entered Service:	Apr 2004
Length (ft/m):	959.6/292.5
Propulsion/Propellers:	diesel-electric (62,370kW)/2 azimuthing pods
Total Crew:	961
Passengers (lower beds):	2,124
Passenger Space Ratio (lower beds):	40.4
Passenger/Crew Ratio (lower beds):	2.2
Cabins (total):	1,062
Size Range (sq ft/m):	185.0–490.0/17.1–45.5
Cabins (for one person):	0
Cabins with balcony:	750
Cabins (wheelchair accessible):	16
Wheelchair accessibility:	Good
Elevators:	15
Casino (gaming tables):	Yes
Self-Service Launderette:	Yes
Onboard currency:	US$

THE SHIP. *Carnival Miracle* is sister to *Carnival Legend, Carnival Pride*, and *Carnival Spirit.* One thing that stands out (apart from Carnival's wing-tipped red, white and blue funnel) is a long Twister Waterslide, part of The WaterWorks on pool deck, which includes multiple water-spray fountains – all good fun for active kids.

Open deck and sunbathing space is not extensive, but there are two small swimming pools (coverable by a sliding glass dome when required). An extra-cost, adults-only area, Sanctuary, has its own bar, pool, hot tub, and other facilities. Located aft on Lido Deck, it is for anyone wanting a quieter space for sunbathing and relaxation.

Inside, the decor is dedicated to 'fictional icons,' including the Phantom of the Opera, Sherlock Holmes, Philip Marlowe, and Captain Ahab. Bronze statues of Orpheus and Ulysses adorn the swimming pools.

There are two main entertainment/public room decks; the upper has an exterior promenade deck. A 'Yellow Brick Road' walkway connects many of the public rooms, including a large Club Merlin Casino with gaming tables and slot machines.

The colorful atrium lobby spans eight decks and has wall decorations best seen from above the main lobby level. Take a drink from the lobby bar and look upwards – the surroundings are visually stunning, or overpowering, depending on your viewpoint.

BERLITZ'S RATINGS	Possible	Achieved
Ship	500	331
Accommodation	200	126
Food	400	208
Service	400	241
Entertainment	100	63
Cruise Experience	400	236

OVERALL SCORE 1205 points out of 2000

Other facilities include a wedding chapel, a shopping street, with boutique stores, a photo gallery, video games room, and an observation balcony in the center of the vessel, at the top of the multi-deck atrium. The large Mr Lucky's Casino invites wishful gamers and slot players.

Niggles include the small reception desk in the atrium lobby, which can become very congested. Many private balconies are not so private and can be overlooked from public locations. You need a credit card to open the personal safe in your cabin – impossible if your credit cards and wallet are inside the safe! In 2015, some facilities were added or changed. These included a RedFrog Pub (it dispenses Carnival's own brew, ThirstyFrog Red), an Alchemy Bar (for vintage pharmacy-inspired cocktails), four new production shows, and *Hasbro, The Game Show* (live versions of favorite games).

Niggles: Many pillars obstruct passenger flow – the ones in the dining room make it difficult for proper food service by the waiters for example. Books and computers cohabit the ship's Holmes library/Internet center, but anyone wanting a book has to lean over others who may be using a computer, which is an awkward arrangement.

ACCOMMODATION. There are many cabin categories, priced by grade, location, and size, including suites with private balcony, outside-view cabins with private balcony, ocean-view cabins with French balconies (pseudo balconies that have opening doors but no balcony to step onto), and a healthy proportion of standard outside-view to interior cabins.

All cabins have spy-hole doors, twin beds that can be converted into a queen-size bed, individually controlled air conditioning, infotainment system, and telephone. A number of cabins on the lowest deck have lifeboat-obstructed views. Some cabins can accommodate a third and fourth person, but have little closet space, and only one personal safe. Audio channels are provided on the infotainment system but you can't turn the picture off, nor can you turn off the air conditioning in cabins or bathrooms.

Among the most desirable suites and cabins are those on five aft-facing decks, with private balconies overlooking the stern. You might think that these would suffer from vibration, but they don't, thanks to the 'pod' propulsion system.

For extra space (finances permitting), it's worth booking one of the larger deluxe balcony suites on Deck 6, with private teakwood balcony.

DINING. The Bacchus Dining Room is the 1,300-seat main restaurant; it spans two decks, with seating on both upper and main levels, with large murals on the ceiling of the upper level. The galley is underneath the restaurant, with escalator access. Tables are for two to eight; small rooms on both upper and lower levels can be booked for groups of up to 60. Choose either fixed-time dining (6pm or 8.15pm) or flexible dining (between 5.45pm and 9.30pm). Note that it is not open for lunch on port days.

The food really is carbohydrate-rich and non-memorable (it's mass catering, after all), with simple presentation and few garnishes. Many dishes are disguised with gravies and sauces. The selection of fresh green vegetables, bread and bakery items (these are thawed and then baked from frozen 'starter' dough), cheeses, and fruits is limited, and there is heavy use of rice, canned fruit and jellied desserts. The waiters sing and dance, so think 'foodertainment' rather than food quality. Also, there are no wine waiters, and the wine glasses are small. For something really simple, an 'always available' list of 'Carnival Classics' includes mahi-mahi (fish), baby back ribs (beef), and grilled chicken.

For casual eats, Horatio's Lido Restaurant is an extensive self-serve buffet-style eatery that forms the aft third of Deck 9 (part of it wraps around the upper section of the atrium). Unicorn murals are everywhere. It includes a central area with a deli sandwich corner, Asian corner, rotisserie, salad bar, international counter, a dessert counter, and a 24-hour pizzeria, and has both indoor and outdoor seating. Movement around the buffet area is in a slow-go line.

Nick & Nora's is an upscale dining spot for premium-quality steaks and grilled seafood, with just 156 seats and a show kitchen. It has good views over the atrium lobby.

ENTERTAINMENT. The 1,170-seat Phantom Showlounge is the venue for large-scale production shows and cabaret shows, and spans three decks. Spiral stairways at the back connect all three levels (the upper levels are best). Directly underneath the showlounge is the Mad Hatter's Ball Lounge and bar.

Almost every lounge/bar, including Sam's Piano Bar, the Jazz Lounge, and Jeeves Lounge, has live music in the evening. Finally, for the very lively, there's a disco; and there's always karaoke.

SPA/FITNESS. SpaCarnival spans two decks (above the navigation bridge), accessible from the forward stairway. Lower level facilities include a solarium, body treatment rooms, lecture rooms, sauna and steam rooms for men and women, and a beauty parlor; the upper level hosts a large gymnasium with expansive ocean view windows, and an aerobics room. Most fitness classes cost extra.

CARNIVAL PANORAMA
★★★+

THIS IS A HIGH-ENERGY, ULTRA-CASUAL SHIP THAT THE WHOLE FAMILY CAN ENJOY

Size:	Large Resort Ship
Tonnage:	135,000
Cruise Line:	Carnival Cruise Line
Former Names:	none
Builder:	Fincantieri (Italy)
Entered Service:	Nov 2019
Length (ft/m):	1,054.7/321.5
Propulsion/Propellers:	diesel-electric/2 azimuthing pods
Total Crew:	1,450
Passengers (lower beds):	3,954
Passenger Space Ratio (lower beds):	34.1
Passenger/Crew Ratio (lower beds):	2.5
Cabins (total):	1,823
Size Range (sq ft/m):	161.4–344.4/15.0–32.0
Cabins (for one person):	0
Cabins with balcony:	887
Cabins (wheelchair accessible):	35
Wheelchair accessibility:	Good
Elevators:	16
Casino (gaming tables):	Yes
Self-Service Launderette:	Yes
Onboard currency:	

THE SHIP. *Carnival Panorama* (sister to *Carnival Horizon* and *Carnival Vista*) is a bright and ultra-lively contemporary playground for the young and young-at-heart families.

An extensive outdoor aqua park features multiple twisting waterslides and splash zones with tipping bucket, alongside the challenging SkyCourse rope course. On sea days, the open deck space will be extremely lively, so expect your sunlounger – if you find one that's free – to be married to its neighbor (plus, there are no cushioned pads, so they're uncomfortable to sit on for any length of time).

There are public entertainment lounges, bars, and clubs galore (including a large casino), with something for everyone (except quiet space), and lots of quirky interior decor.

The dress code is ultra-casual (at least the waiters are well dressed). Carnival Panorama is a 'fun' floating fairground at sea, from towels shaped like animals, to excited passengers taking part in scheduled participation activities. It's best to go with friends; otherwise, it's an impersonal experience. It may not matter too much for first-timers, but repeaters might experience a distinct sense of déjà vu (although a Gold or Platinum card may provide better recognition from 'service' staff). There is a library (and inclusive serve-yourself wine), but few books. The ship has good entertainment facilities and extra-cost dining spots for more eating choices. It is well suited to multi-generational families, and if you enjoy casinos, joining Carnival's Ocean Players

BERLITZ'S RATINGS		
	Possible	Achieved
Ship	500	376
Accommodation	200	133
Food	400	211
Service	400	251
Entertainment	100	68
Cruise Experience	400	263
OVERALL SCORE 1302 points out of 2000		

Club brings benefits, depending on your skill level.

Niggles include intrusive photographers, annoying announcements, ear-splitting music everywhere, and the never-ending hustling to get you to spend money. Expect lines to form for shore excursions, security control when re-boarding, and disembarkation.

ACCOMMODATION. Accommodation prices depend on size, grade, and location. From the smallest interior (no-view) cabin to the largest suite, the accommodation is practical, with bright decor and good design. Expect flexible bedside reading lights, multiple USB sockets, space for digital devices, sliding shoe racks in closets, and ample underbed storage space.

DINING. There are two main dining rooms (forward and aft). Overall, the carbohydrate-rich food comes with simple presentation and few garnishes. This is standardized catering cuisine – batch cooking, if you will. The choice of fresh green vegetables, breads (baked from frozen 'starter' dough), cheeses, and fruits is limited, and there is heavy use of canned fruit and jellied desserts. Waiters sing and dance, so think 'foodertainment' rather than food quality. For something simple, Carnival Classics, such as mahi-mahi (fish), baby back (beef) ribs, and grilled chicken, are always available.

Alternative eateries (some at extra cost) include: Lido Marketplace (self-serve buffet venue); Cucina del Capitano (Italian fare); Seafood Shack; Fahrenheit 555 Steakhouse; Ji Ji Asian Kitchen; Bonsai Sushi and Bonsai Teppanyaki; Guy's Burger Joint (featuring Fieri's signature rubs and spices); Guy's Pig & Anchor Bar-B-Que Smokehouse (barbecue); and BlueIguana (Mexican). Families with youngsters might like to indulge in a Green Eggs and Ham breakfast (extra cost), while Chef's Table (for foodies) includes a little showbusiness from the chef, with wine pairing, for up to 12 diners (extra cost).

ENTERTAINMENT. The 1,400-seat showlounge is a stunning room for large-scale, high-decibel razzle-dazzle productions. A multiplex media entertainment complex includes a small (extra cost) IMAX theatre, poolside mega-screen, and 3D thrill theater.

SPA/FITNESS. The two-level Cloud 9 Spa hosts treatment rooms, men's and women's infrared saunas and hammam (steam and mud – good for couples), relaxation lounger, and fitness center, as well as 'pay more' thermal suites, plus a VIP treatment room for Spa Suite occupants.

Activity/sports facilities include an outdoor Sky-Course rope course (always fun on a moving ship), Sky Gardens mini-golf course, and a Sky Court for baseball. The Clubhouse at SportSquare includes mini-bowling, ping-pong, arcade basketball, and video games.

CARNIVAL PARADISE
★★★

THIS FAMILY-FRIENDLY 'FUN' SHIP IS FINE FOR ULTRA-CASUAL CRUISING

Size:	Mid-size Ship	Passenger/Crew Ratio (lower beds):	2.2
Tonnage:	70,390	Cabins (total):	1,026
Cruise Line:	Carnival Cruise Line	Size Range (sq ft/m):	173.2–409.7/16.0–38.0
Former Names:	*Paradise*	Cabins (for one person):	0
Builder:	Kvaerner Masa-Yards (Finland)	Cabins with balcony:	152
Entered Service:	Nov 1998	Cabins (wheelchair accessible):	22
Length (ft/m):	855.0/260.6	Wheelchair accessibility:	Fair
Propulsion/Propellers:	diesel-electric (42,842kW)/2 azimuthing pods	Elevators:	14
Total Crew:	920	Casino (gaming tables):	Yes
Passengers (lower beds):	2,052	Self-Service Launderette:	Yes
Passenger Space Ratio (lower beds):	34.2	Onboard currency:	US$

THE SHIP. *Carnival Paradise* (the last in a series of eight sister ships) now over 20 years old, provides a vibration-free ride thanks to its pod propulsion system. The lifeboats are positioned high in the ship, not low down, as in today's ships. There is no walk-around open promenade deck.

While the open deck space is inadequate when the ship is full (38 more cabins were added in 2018) and everyone wants to be outside, the aft decks tend to be less busy, because most activities are focused around the main pool, hot tubs, and the WaterWorks Aqua Park. For quieter times, cost-extra Serenity is exclusively for adults – and worth it.

The interior design is by Miami-based architect Joe Farcus; it's clever, functional, and colorful; the theme is yesteryear's ocean liners.

The main social and focal point is the 'open' atrium lobby, with a balconied shape; styled to impress, it spans six decks and is topped by a glass dome. The lowest level houses the purser's desk and shore-excursion desk, Atrium Bar (with live music), and a small sushi bar off to one side.

There are many public entertainment lounges, bars, and clubs, with something for everyone (except quiet space), connected by a double-wide promenade (think 'Main Street') between the showlounge (forward) and the Queen Mary Lounge aft. The Majestic Casino has gaming tables and slot machines. Standout rooms include The Blue Riband library (there are models of ocean liners, but few books) and the

BERLITZ'S RATINGS		
	Possible	Achieved
Ship	500	293
Accommodation	200	122
Food	400	203
Service	400	247
Entertainment	100	61
Cruise Experience	400	234

OVERALL SCORE 1160 points out of 2000

Rock and Roll Discotheque with its guitar-shaped dance floor.

Carnival Paradise is for the young-at-heart. Expect lines for shore excursions, security control when re-boarding, and disembarkation.

Carnival is not known for fine cuisine, but the real fun begins at sundown, when the ship excels in sound, lights, and high decibel shows. Venues from the Rex Dance Club/Disco to the Rotterdam Cigar Bar will certainly keep you occupied.

Niggles include many annoying announcements, high volume music, persistent photographers, and the never-ending hustling to get you to spend money.

ACCOMMODATION. There are numerous accommodation price grades, according to size and location. Standard outside-view and interior cabins have simple, unpretentious decor. They are practical (most are of the same size and appointments), with good storage space and no-nonsense bathrooms. With a queen-bed configuration layout, note that one person has to clamber over the bed to get in, and it's awkward. Suites have a little more space, but they are much smaller than those aboard ships of a similar size of competing companies.

Room service is available 24/7, although in standard cabins only cold food is available. Suite-grade occupants can choose from a greater range of hot and cold items.

DINING. The two large main dining rooms, Elation (amidships) and Destiny (aft) have ocean-view windows and bright decor, but they are noisy (due to the low ceiling height). Choose either fixed-time dining or flexible dining.

Breakfasts are surprisingly good, with ample choice, while dinners are mediocre affairs and unmemorable, with simple presentation and few garnishes. The selection of fresh green vegetables, bread, rolls (baked from frozen 'starter' dough), cheeses, and fruits is limited, and there is heavy use of rice, canned fruit, and jellied desserts. There's a modest wine list, but no wine waiters, and wine glasses are small. The waiters sing and dance (think 'eatertainment' rather than food quality). For something simple, there's an 'always available' list of 'Carnival Classics.' Note that the two main dining rooms are not open for lunch on port days.

Paris Lido Restaurant is for self-serve buffet eats; it includes a deli/salad counter and pizzeria. Guy's Burger Joint, a poolside fast food venue developed with Food Network personality Guy Fieri, and Bluelguana Cantina (for Mexican-style tacos and burritos) were added in 2018.

A patisserie has specialty coffees and sweets (extra charge), and a so-called sushi bar off to one side of the atrium lobby bar (the sushi should not be called authentic).

ENTERTAINMENT. The 1,010-seat Normandie Main Lounge hosts colorful production shows and major cabaret acts – although 20 pillars obstruct views form some seats. A troupe of singers and a clutch of dancers are backed by a live band.

SPA/FITNESS. SpaCarnival is a complex on the uppermost interior deck forward. It has a gymnasium, aerobics room, men's and women's sauna and steam rooms, beauty salon, and body treatment rooms. Some fitness classes cost extra. For sports, there's basketball, volleyball, and table tennis, plus a banked jogging track outdoors above the spa, and a mini-golf course.

CARNIVAL PRIDE
★★★

TRY THIS CASUAL SHIP FOR A FUN-FILLED, CONTEMPORARY FAMILY-FRIENDLY CRUISE

Size:	Mid-size Ship	Passenger/Crew Ratio (lower beds):	2.2
Tonnage:	85,920	Cabins (total):	1,062
Cruise Line:	Carnival Cruise Line	Size Range (sq ft/m):	185.0–490.0/17.1–45.5
Former Names:	none	Cabins (for one person):	0
Builder:	Kvaerner Masa-Yards (Finland)	Cabins with balcony:	750
Entered Service:	Jan 2002	Cabins (wheelchair accessible):	16
Length (ft/m):	959.6/292.5	Wheelchair accessibility:	Good
Propulsion/Propellers:	diesel-electric (62,370kW)/2 azimuthing pods	Elevators:	15
Total Crew:	1,029	Casino (gaming tables):	Yes
Passengers (lower beds):	2,124	Self-Service Launderette:	Yes
Passenger Space Ratio (lower beds):	40.4	Onboard currency:	US$

THE SHIP. *Carnival Pride* is sister to *Carnival Legend*, *Carnival Miracle*, and *Carnival Spirit*, with the same layout and configuration. Designed for families, the ship has plenty of facilities, so kids should have a good time.

While the open deck and sun-bathing space is not extensive, there are two pools: one can be covered by a sliding glass dome when needed, while a smaller pool is for children. An extra-charge, adults-only quiet area, Sanctuary, has its own bar, pool, hot tub, and other facilities.

Inside, the interior decor has an art theme (including nude figures – reproductions from the Renaissance period). Even the elevator doors and interiors contain blown-up, grainy graphic copies of some the great masters like Gauguin, Matisse, and Jacopo Vignali. It's an eclectic mix.

An interior walkway, the Yellow Brick Road, connects many of the public rooms, one deck above Promenade Deck, which also has a number of public rooms aft.

The colorful atrium lobby spans eight decks; its wall decorations are best seen from the viewing areas on any deck above the lobby level, and there's a huge reproduction of Raphael's *Nymph Galatea*.

Other facilities include a shopping street with boutique stores, photo gallery, video games room, and a wedding chapel, plus an observation balcony at the top of the multi-deck atrium and the Winner's Club

BERLITZ'S RATINGS		
	Possible	Achieved
Ship	500	323
Accommodation	200	124
Food	400	207
Service	400	244
Entertainment	100	62
Cruise Experience	400	240
OVERALL SCORE 1200 points out of 2000		

Casino (you have to walk though it to get to the main level of the show-lounge from the restaurant).

Carnival Pride is a floating playground for the young and young-at-heart, and anyone who enjoys lots of participation events plus glitz, glamour, and gambling. This is a fun, all-American experience, but there could be lines for the likes of shore excursions, security control when re-boarding, and disembarkation, as well as sign-up sheets for fitness equipment.

Niggles include annoying announcements and constant hustling to get you to buy drinks, jewelry, and trinkets, while obtaining advice and suggestions for shore excursions is not easy. The small reception desk in the atrium lobby is almost always congested. It's hard to escape from noise and excessively loud 'music' (even in cabin hallways and lifts). Many private balconies can be overlooked from public locations. You need a credit card to open the personal safe, so you can't store all your credit cards inside it!

ACCOMMODATION. There are many cabin categories, priced by grade, location, and size. The range includes suites (with private balcony), outside-view cabins with private balcony, some ocean-view cabins with French doors (pseudo balconies that have doors which open, but no step-out balcony), and a healthy proportion of standard outside-view to interior cabins.

The cabins have spy-hole doors, twin beds convertible into a queen-size bed, television, and telephone; some cabins on the lowest deck have lifeboat-obstructed views. Some can accommodate a third and fourth person, but the closet space is pokey, and there's only one personal safe.

Among the most desirable suites and cabins are those on five aft-facing decks, with private balconies aft.

DINING. The 1,300-seat Normandie Restaurant, the main dining room, has seating on two levels. Choose either fixed-time dining (lower level) or flexible dining (upper level) during restaurant opening hours. Normandie is not open for lunch on port days.

Overall, the food is quite starchy, but acceptable (and the multi-choice breakfasts are good), with simple presentation, few garnishes, and many dishes disguised with gravies and sauces. The choice of fresh green vegetables, bread and bakery items (thawed and then baked from frozen 'starter' dough), cheese, and fruits is limited. There are no wine waiters, and wine glasses are small. For something simple, an 'always available' list of 'Carnival Classics' includes mahi-mahi (fish), baby back ribs (beef), and grilled chicken.

For casual eats: Mermaid's Grill Lido Restaurant (late-night bites are repetitive), Guy's Burger Joint, BlueIguana (Mexican fare), and Bonsai Sushi.

There's also the reservations-required David's Steakhouse, an upscale extra-cost dining venue with 156 seats, a show kitchen, great views over the atrium lobby, and fine table settings, with good china and silverware.

ENTERTAINMENT. The glamorous 1,170-seat Taj Mahal Showlounge is for large-scale Vegas-style (think feathers and skimpy costumes) production shows with eardrum-splitting volume. Spiral stairways at the back connect all three levels.

Almost every lounge/bar has live music in the evening, and for the really lively, there's Beauties Dance Club (a disco), and there's always karaoke.

SPA/FITNESS. SpaCarnival spans two decks. Facilities on the lower level include a solarium, eight treatment rooms, lecture rooms, sauna and steam rooms for men and women, and a beauty parlor. The upper level hosts a large gymnasium with ocean views, and an aerobics room.

An outdoor jogging track is close to a basketball court and mini-golf.

CARNIVAL SENSATION
★★★

TRY THIS ULTRA-COLORFUL, CASUAL SHIP FOR A FIRST CRUISE

Size:	Mid-size Ship	Passenger/Crew Ratio (lower beds):	2.2
Tonnage:	70,536	Cabins (total):	1,020
Cruise Line:	Carnival Cruise Line	Size Range (sq ft/m):	173.2–409.7/16.0–38.0
Former Names:	Sensation	Cabins (for one person):	0
Builder:	Kvaerner Masa-Yards (Finland)	Cabins with balcony:	152
Entered Service:	Nov 1993	Cabins (wheelchair accessible):	20
Length (ft/m):	855.0/260.6	Wheelchair accessibility:	Fair
Propulsion/Propellers:	diesel-electric (42,240kW)/2	Elevators:	14
Total Crew:	920	Casino (gaming tables):	Yes
Passengers (lower beds):	2,040	Self-Service Launderette:	Yes
Passenger Space Ratio (lower beds):	34.4	Onboard currency:	US$

THE SHIP. *Carnival Sensation* is the third in a series of eight *Fantasy*-class sister ships and is now over 25 years old.

It is well liked and good for families and partygoers taking a first cruise, but with a full ship the open deck space is inadequate. The aft decks used to be less noisy when all the activities were focused around the main pool and hot tubs, but now that the WaterWorks – with long and short waterslides and water-burst fountains – has been added, it's the active area for families. Serenity, however, is an extra-charge, quiet, adult-only space on Deck 9 aft.

There is no walk-around open promenade deck, although there is a short jogging track atop ship. The lifeboats, six of which double as shore tenders, are positioned high in the ship.

The interior is well designed, and the general flow is good, with 'entertainment architecture' that is bright and cheerful. The theme is the arts (in a sort of Art Nouveau style) and literature. It includes a colorful mix of classic and contemporary design elements.

The interior social meeting center is an 'open' atrium lobby, with a balconied shape; it spans six decks, and is topped by a glass domed roof. The lowest level houses the purser's and shore-excursion desks, an Atrium Bar (with live music), plus a small sushi bar off to one side.

BERLITZ'S RATINGS		
	Possible	Achieved
Ship	500	293
Accommodation	200	121
Food	400	202
Service	400	245
Entertainment	100	62
Cruise Experience	400	229
OVERALL SCORE 1152 points out of 2000		

There are public entertainment lounges, bars, and clubs galore, with something for everyone (except quiet space). Most public rooms and attractions lead off from Sensation Boulevard – a shipboard Main Street, which runs between the showlounge (forward) and the Plaza Aft lounge, with Joe's Café (for coffees and teas). For gamers and slot-players there's almost non-stop action in the Club Vegas Casino.

The Oak Room is a pleasant reading room, but has few books. Meanwhile, the Kaleidoscope Discotheque, with dozens of video monitors and dance floor, hits you with a dazzling variety of stimulating, electric colors.

This ship is definitely not for anyone seeking a quiet, relaxing cruise. Niggles include annoying announcements and never-ending hustling to incite you to buy drinks, jewelry, and trinkets. Also, shore excursions are booked via the infotainment system, so obtaining advice and suggestions in person is not easy.

ACCOMMODATION. There are many different accommodation price grades, ranked by facilities, size, and location. The standard outside-view and interior cabins have a rather plain decor. They are fairly comfortable, and practical (most are of the same size and appointments), with good storage and no-nonsense bathrooms. However, if you have a queen-bed configuration instead of the standard twin-bed layout, note that one person has to clamber over the bed to get to the far side – a potentially ungainly exercise.

Suite occupants get more space, and more eclectic decor and furniture. Suites are reasonably attractive, but actually quite small. Some 50 cabins have interconnecting doors – good for families with children.

Room service is available 24 hours a day, although in standard cabins, only cold food is available; those in suite-grade accommodation get a greater range of items (both hot and cold) to choose from.

DINING. The two large main dining rooms, Fantasy (amidships) and Ecstasy (aft), both have ocean-view windows and bright decor, and they are noisy. Choose either fixed-time dining (6pm or 8.15pm) or flexible dining (during opening hours).

The food is virtually unmemorable (except for breakfasts, which are very good), with simple presentation and few garnishes. The selection of fresh green vegetables, bread, rolls (baked from frozen 'starter' dough), cheeses, and fruits is limited, and there is heavy use of rice, canned fruit, and jellied desserts. The waiters sing, dance, serve wine, and take part in waiter parades – so it's more about 'eatertainment' than food quality.

This is basic catering – with all its attendant standardization and production cooking, which makes it difficult to obtain anything unusual or 'off-menu.' For something simple, there's an 'always available' list of 'Carnival Classics,' including mahi mahi (fish), baby back ribs (beef), and grilled chicken (when the dining rooms are open). The two main dining rooms are not open for lunch on port days.

Other (complimentary) eateries include a large Seaview Bar & Grill (lido café), for self-serve buffet eats; Guy's Burger Joint, a poolside venue developed with Food Network personality Guy Fieri (for handmade burgers and freshly cut fries); and BlueIguana Cantina eatery (for Mexican-style tacos and burritos). A patisserie offers cost-extra specialty coffees and sweets. There is no specialty (extra-charge) restaurant, as aboard some of the larger ships in the fleet.

ENTERTAINMENT. The Fantasia Main Lounge is for Vegas-style (think feathers and skimpy costumes) production shows and major cabaret acts entertain the crowds. However, some 20 pillars obstruct the views from several seats.

SPA/FITNESS. SpaCarnival is a glass-wrapped 'spa' complex on the uppermost interior deck, forward of the ship's mast. It has a gymnasium with ocean-view windows and muscle-pumping equipment, aerobics room, men's and women's sauna and steam rooms, beauty salon, and body treatment rooms. Some fitness classes incur an extra charge. For sports, there's basketball, volleyball and table tennis, plus a banked jogging track outdoors above the spa, and a mini-golf course.

CARNIVAL SPIRIT
★★★

GOOD FOR A FUN-FILLED FAMILY-FRIENDLY CRUISE IN A CONTEMPORARY SETTING

Size:	Mid-size Ship	Passenger/Crew Ratio (lower beds):	2.2
Tonnage:	85,920	Cabins (total):	1,062
Cruise Line:	Carnival Cruise Line	Size Range (sq ft/m):	185.0–490.0/17.1–45.5
Former Names:	none	Cabins (for one person):	0
Builder:	Kvaerner Masa-Yards	Cabins with balcony:	750
Entered Service:	Apr 2001	Cabins (wheelchair accessible):	16
Length (ft/m):	959.6/292.5	Wheelchair accessibility:	Good
Propulsion/Propellers:	diesel-electric (62,370kW)/2 azimuthing pods	Elevators:	15
		Casino (gaming tables):	Yes
Total Crew:	930	Self-Service Launderette:	Yes
Passengers (lower beds):	2,124	Onboard currency:	US$
Passenger Space Ratio (lower beds):	40.4		

THE SHIP. *Carnival Spirit* is a sister to *Carnival Legend*, *Carnival Miracle*, and *Carnival Pride*, with the same layout and configuration.

This ship is all about active entertainment. Following a 2012 refurbishment before its Australia deployment, much of its outdoor deck space was designated a Water Park and Splash Zone, with water wheels, spraying jets, water blasters, pull ropes, two Mini Racer slides, and more.

Then there's the really big attraction, Green Thunder, a thrill ride that starts 100ft (30m) above sea level. The floor suddenly drops out of the platform, and you plummet in a near-vertical drop at about 23ft (7m) a second. When you hit the water in the fast waterslide, you twist and turn through a transparent tube that extends over the side of the ship. Kids will love it, but need to be 42ins (1.1m) tall to be able to experience it. The open deck space is a bit tight when the ship sails at full capacity in warm-weather areas.

An extra-charge, adults-only area, Sanctuary, has its own bar, pool, hot tub, and other facilities. Located at the aft of the ship on Lido Deck, it is a pleasant area for anyone seeking a quieter space for sunbathing and relaxation – and to escape the many children on board during major holidays.

An interior walkway, named the Fashion Boulevard, connects many of the major public rooms on Atlantic Deck, one deck above Promenade Deck,

BERLITZ'S RATINGS

	Possible	Achieved
Ship	500	330
Accommodation	200	124
Food	400	207
Service	400	252
Entertainment	100	62
Cruise Experience	400	235

OVERALL SCORE 1210 points out of 2000

which is also home to a number of public rooms, including a large Louis XIV Casino.

The colorful atrium lobby, which spans eight decks, has wall decorations best seen from any of the multiple viewing balconies on any deck above the main lobby level.

Perhaps the most dramatic room is the Pharaoh's Palace Showlounge, which spans three decks in the forward section. Directly underneath is the Versailles Lounge, which has a bar in its starboard aft section.

Other facilities include a winding shopping street with boutique stores, photo gallery, video games room, wedding chapel, and an observation balcony in the center of the vessel, at the top of the multi-deck atrium. The large Winner's Club Casino has many gaming tables and slot machines.

While the cuisine is just average, the real fun begins at sundown, when the ship excels in terms of sound, lights, razzle-dazzle shows, and late-night high-volume sounds.

ACCOMMODATION. There are many different cabin categories, priced by grade, location, and size. The range includes suites (with private balcony), outside-view cabins with private balcony, ocean-view cabins with French doors (pseudo balconies that have doors which open, but no balcony to step out onto), and a healthy proportion of standard outside-view to interior cabins.

Among the most desirable suites and cabins are those on five of the aft-facing decks; these have private balconies overlooking the stern and ship's wash. You might think that these units would suffer from vibration, but they don't – a bonus provided by the pod propulsion system. For extra space, book one of the larger deluxe balcony suites on Deck 6, with private teakwood balcony.

DINING. The Empire Restaurant is the large, two-deck-high, 1,250-seat main restaurant. Small rooms on both upper and lower levels can be closed off for groups of up to 60. Choose either fixed-time dining or flexible dining. The restaurant is not open for lunch on port days.

While breakfasts are decent, the carbohydrate-rich dinners are ho-hum affairs (it's mass catering, after all), with simple presentation and few garnishes. Also, many dishes are disguised with gravies and sauces. The selection of fresh green vegetables, bread and bakery items (these are thawed and then baked from frozen 'starter' dough), cheeses, and fruits is limited, and there is heavy use of rice, canned fruit, and jellied desserts. There are no wine waiters, and wine glasses are small. For something really simple, an 'always available' list of 'Carnival Classics' includes mahi-mahi (fish), baby back ribs (beef), and grilled chicken.

La Playa Grille Lido Restaurant is a large casual self-serve food court buffet-style eatery. It includes a deli sandwich corner, an Asian corner, a rotisserie, salad bar, an international (Taste of the Nations) counter, and a 24-hour pizza counter. Both indoor and outdoor seating is available.

Other (complimentary) eateries include: Guy's Burger Joint, a poolside venue developed with Food Network personality Guy Fieri (for burgers and cut fries). Aft on the same deck is Guy's Pig & Anchor Bar-B-Que Smokehouse (sea-day lunchtime only). There's also BlueIguana Cantina for Mexican snack food such as tacos and burritos.

Nouveau Steakhouse is a premium venue with 156 seats and a show kitchen. It is located in the lower, forward section of the funnel housing, with neat views over the colorful atrium lobby (the four-person tables tucked beneath the overhang of the upper level are cozy and have ocean views). Fine table settings, china, and silverware are provided, a cover charge applies, and reservations are needed.

ENTERTAINMENT. The glamorous 1,167-seat Pharaoh's Palace is the venue for large-scale production shows and cabaret, which are best seen from the upper levels. Directly underneath the show-lounge is the Versailles Lounge and bar.

Almost every lounge/bar, including the Shanghai Piano Bar, the Club Cool Jazz Club, and the Artists' Lobby Lounge, has live music in the evening. Finally, for the very lively, there's the Dancin' Dance Club for thumping music; and there's always karaoke.

SPA/FITNESS. SpaCarnival spans two decks; it is located directly above the navigation bridge and has 13,700 sq ft (1,272 sq m) of space. Facilities on the lower level include a solarium, eight treatment rooms, lecture rooms, sauna and steam rooms for men and women, and a beauty parlor. The upper level consists of a large gymnasium with floor-to-ceiling windows on three sides, including forward-facing ocean views, and an aerobics room with instructor-led classes.

There are two centrally located pools outdoors, one with a retractable glass dome cover. An outdoor jogging track is located around the ship's mast: it doesn't go around the whole ship, but it's long enough for a workout.

CARNIVAL SPLENDOR
★★★

THIS FAMILY-FRIENDLY, FUN-FILLED SHIP HAS A GREAT WATER PARK DECK

Size:	Large Resort Ship	Passenger/Crew Ratio (lower beds):	2.5
Tonnage:	113,323	Cabins (total):	1,487
Cruise Line:	Carnival Cruise Line	Size Range (sq ft/m):	179.7–484.2/16.7–44.8
Former Names:	none	Cabins (for one person):	0
Builder:	Fincantieri (Italy)	Cabins with balcony:	574
Entered Service:	Jul 2008	Cabins (wheelchair accessible):	25
Length (ft/m):	951.4/290.0	Wheelchair accessibility:	Good
Propulsion/Propellers:	diesel-electric (63,400kW)/2	Elevators:	18
Total Crew:	1,150	Casino (gaming tables):	Yes
Passengers (lower beds):	2,974	Self-Service Launderette:	Yes
Passenger Space Ratio (lower beds):	37.0	Onboard currency:	US$

THE SHIP. *Carnival Splendor* shares the same profile as sisters *Carnival Conquest*, *Carnival Freedom*, *Carnival Glory*, *Carnival Liberty*, *Carnival Sunshine*, *Carnival Triumph*, *Carnival Valor*, and *Carnival Victory*, although it was originally designated as a ship for Costa Cruises.

The deck and public room layout is fairly logical (although a little disjointed). Most of the public rooms are located on a deck off a main interior boulevard, above a deck that contains the two main dining rooms. The interior decor is basically 50 shades of pink. Public rooms include a large Royal Flush Casino, with gaming tables and over 300 slot machines.

Recalling the drive-in movie theaters of the 1950s, the Seaside Theater shows movies, and sports features on deck, with tiered row seating and a forward-facing screen (and popcorn). Ship-wide Wi-Fi costs extra.

Carnival Splendor is a floating playground for the young and young-at-heart, and anyone who enjoys constant stimulation and lots of participation events, together with the three 'Gs' – glitz, glamor, and gambling. This really is cruising "Splash Vegas" style. Because it's a mid-sized ship, there can be lines for shore excursions, security control when re-boarding, disembarkation, and sign-up sheets for fitness equipment.

The *essence* of a Carnival cruise is all about having fun, which begins at sundown, with sound, lights,

BERLITZ'S RATINGS		
	Possible	Achieved
Ship	500	337
Accommodation	200	127
Food	400	208
Service	400	244
Entertainment	100	62
Cruise Experience	400	235
OVERALL SCORE 1213 points out of 2000		

razzle-dazzle shows, and late-night high-volume sounds.

Minor niggles include the many pillars that obstruct passenger flow, particularly in the dining rooms, making it difficult for the waiters to serve, and the food (particularly the baked goods), which is pretty average.

Note that in December 2019 *Carnival Splendor* will be transferred to P&O Cruises (Australia), and, following refurbishment, will be modified to suit Australasian tastes.

ACCOMMODATION. There are many different cabin price categories. These include suites and 'spa' suites with balcony; deluxe outside-view cabins with private balcony; outside-view cabins with private balcony; outside-view cabins with window; cabins with a porthole instead of a window; interior cabins; and interior cabins with upper and lower berths (good for families with very small children). There are five decks of cabins with private balconies. Cabins on Deck 12 are subject to lots of noise from kids having fun on the deck above – so forget that afternoon nap. Although there is room service, the menu is poor.

DINING. There are two main dining rooms, the 744-seat Black Pearl, amidships, and the 1,122-seat Gold Pearl, aft. Both are two decks high with main and balcony levels. There's a choice of either fixed-time or flexible dining. There are not many tables for two, but my favorites are the ones right at the back of the Gold Pearl restaurant, with aft ocean views. Note that the dining rooms are not open for lunch on port days.

Don't even think about a quiet table for two, or a candlelit dinner on deck. This ship is all about table mates, social talk, lively meals, fast eating, and fast service. Tables do have tablecloths, silverware, and iced water/iced tea whenever you want it.

Breakfasts are pretty decent, with ample choice, but dinners are ho-hum affairs, because the food is carbohydrate-rich, with simple presentation, and few garnishes. The choice of fresh green vegetables, bread and baked goods (thawed and then baked from frozen 'starter' dough), cheeses, and fruits is limited, and there is heavy use of rice, canned fruit and jellied desserts.

'Spa Carnival Fare' provides a healthier food option; vegetarian and children's menus are also available, but they wouldn't get a generous score for their nutritional content.

The extra-cost (reservations-required) Pinnacle Steakhouse has fine table settings, china, and silverware, leather-bound menus, and seats 108. The specialties are USDA dry-aged prime steaks and seafood items, and a cover charge applies.

Lido Restaurant, a casual self-serve international food court-style eatery, includes a New York-style deli, a pizzeria, and a grill for fast food items (think: burgers and hot dogs); the salad bar, however, is poor.

ENTERTAINMENT. The large, multi-deck Spectacular Showlounge seats 1,400, and features colorful Vegas-style production shows (all feathers and skimpy costumes) and major cabaret acts. It has a revolving stage, hydraulic orchestra pit, good sound, and seating on three levels (the upper levels are tiered through two decks).

An alternative venue is El Morocco, a 425-seat lounge (aft). It has live music and late-night cabaret acts including adult comedy. Adjacent is a Grand Piano Lounge/Bar.

SPA/FITNESS. Cloud 9 Spa spans two decks and includes 16 spa suites. Located above the navigation bridge, it is accessed from the forward stairway.

Lower level facilities include a gymnasium, solarium, a thermal suite (with extra cost saunas and steam rooms – some infused with herbal aromas), thalassotherapy pool (check out the huge Chinese dogs), and beauty salon. The upper level houses massage/body treatment rooms, including two VIP suites (one for couples, one for wheelchair users), Rasul chamber (Arabian mud treatment), flotation therapy room, treatment rooms, and outdoor relaxation areas on port and starboard sides with integrated massage cabana.

CARNIVAL SUNRISE
★★★

THIS IS A FLOATING FUN PALACE FOR ULTRA-CASUAL FAMILY CRUISING

Size:	Large Resort Ship	Passenger/Crew Ratio (lower beds):	2.7
Tonnage:	101,509	Cabins (total):	1,494
Cruise Line:	Carnival Cruise Line	Size Range (sq ft/m):	179.7–482.2/16.7–44.8
Former Names:	none	Cabins (for one person):	0
Builder:	Fincantieri (Italy)	Cabins with balcony:	508
Entered Service:	Oct 1999	Cabins (wheelchair accessible):	25
Length (ft/m):	893.0/272.2	Wheelchair accessibility:	Good
Propulsion/Propellers:	diesel-electric (34,000kW)/2 azimuthing pods	Elevators:	18
Total Crew:	1,100	Casino (gaming tables):	Yes
Passengers (lower beds):	2,988	Self-Service Launderette:	Yes
Passenger Space Ratio (lower beds):	33.9	Onboard currency:	US$

THE SHIP. *Carnival Sunrise* (formerly *Carnival Triumph*) is a contemporary ship (extensively transformed and updated in spring 2019) designed specifically for families, with a new WaterWorks aqua park featuring waterslides, a tipping bucket, and SportSquare (with ropes course) – a hit with children.

On the Lido Deck, there is one small pool (with adjacent hot tubs). A long waterslide travels 200ft (60 meters) from just aft of the ship's mast. There are also sunloungers outside (no cushioned pads), plus a large poolside movie screen.

Inside, the decor is relatively tasteful. There are basically three decks full of bars and lounges. The focal point is a nine deck-high (atrium) lobby, topped by a glass-domed roof. The lowest deck features a square-shaped bar, facing forward to glass-walled elevators.

Carnival Sunrise is a floating playground for the young, and anyone who enjoys constant stimulation and participation events, together with the three 'Gs' – glitz, glamour, and gambling. The cuisine is just so-so, but, hey, this is cruising Splash Vegas style – and it's a fun, all-American experience. But, expect lines for shore excursions, security control when re-boarding, and disembarkation; and relentless noise.

ACCOMMODATION. There are numerous price categories, depending on grade, location, and size (over half of all cabins have outside views). They are

BERLITZ'S RATINGS

	Possible	Achieved
Ship	500	332
Accommodation	200	124
Food	400	207
Service	400	242
Entertainment	100	61
Cruise Experience	400	235

OVERALL SCORE 1201 points out of 2000

spread over four decks, with balconies which have glass balustrades. They have all the basics, although the furniture is angular (no rounded edges).

Many cabins have upper and lower bunk beds – good for small children. Interactive 'Fun Vision' technology includes movies on demand, for a fee. Bathrooms, with good-size showers, have good storage space for toiletries. Book a suite, and you get Skipper's Club priority benefits.

DINING. There are two main dining rooms, one forward (with windows on two sides) and the other aft (with windows on three sides). Tables are for two to eight.

Choose either fixed-time dining or flexible dining (during opening times). Note that the two dining rooms are not open for lunch on port days. Although the menu choice looks good, the actual cuisine is simply adequate (except breakfasts, which are good).

Most food is starchy and non-memorable, with simple presentation and few garnishes. The selection of fresh green vegetables, bread and bakery items (thawed and then baked from frozen 'starter' dough), cheeses, and fruit is limited, and there is heavy use of rice, canned fruit, and jellied desserts. Also, there are no wine waiters, and the wine glasses are small. An 'always available' list of simple 'Carnival Classics' includes mahi-mahi (fish), baby back ribs (beef), and grilled chicken.

Fahrenheit 555 Steakhouse (located within one of the two main restaurants) is a reservations-required, extra-cost venue, for premium-quality steaks and grilled seafood.

For ultra-casual eating, the Lido Deck self-serve buffet area has several sections, including a deli and an Asian section (Lucky Bowl). The buffet is often congested, particularly for breakfast (try one of the main dining rooms for a more relaxed breakfast).

Outside on deck are a pizzeria, Guy's Pig & Anchor Bar-B-Que Smokehouse, and Cucina del Capitano for Italian cuisine. Revamped bars include the poolside RedFrog Rum Bar (serving Carnival's own draft brew), BlueIguana Bar for frozen Mexican-style cocktails and tequila, and a sports bar with video games and a 24/7 sports ticker.

ENTERTAINMENT. The two-deck Liquid Lounge is the venue for production shows and main cabaret acts. Added in 2019 was a Limelight Lounge/Punchliner Comedy Club (think late-night smutty comedy).

SPA/FITNESS. SpaCarnival spans two decks, and facilities include a solarium, treatment rooms, men's and women's saunas and steam rooms, a beauty parlor; a large gymnasium with ocean views, and an aerobics room. Most fitness classes cost extra.

CARNIVAL SUNSHINE
★★★

THIS VIBRANT SHIP IS GOOD FOR A FIRST-TIME ACTIVE CRUISE EXPERIENCE

Size:	Large Resort Ship	Passenger/Crew Ratio (lower beds):	2.6
Tonnage:	102,853	Cabins (total):	1,503
Cruise Line:	Carnival Cruise Line	Size Range (sq ft/m):	179.7–482.2/16.7–44.8
Former Names:	Carnival Destiny	Cabins (for one person):	0
Builder:	Fincantieri (Italy)	Cabins with balcony:	418
Entered Service:	Nov 1996	Cabins (wheelchair accessible):	25
Length (ft/m):	892.3/272.0	Wheelchair accessibility:	Good
Propulsion/Propellers:	diesel-electric (63,400kW)/2	Elevators:	18
Total Crew:	1,150	Casino (gaming tables):	Yes
Passengers (lower beds):	3,006	Self-Service Launderette:	Yes
Passenger Space Ratio (lower beds):	34.2	Onboard currency:	US$

THE SHIP. *Carnival Sunshine* (formerly *Carnival Destiny* when the ship debuted in 1999) was the first cruise ship with a gross tonnage that exceeded 100,000. After a lengthy refurbishment, the ship shouts 'Party, party, party!' That said, it's a good ship for families with children.

The ship – now over 20 years old – has short bows and a distinctive, large, swept-back wing-tipped funnel. Tiered sunbathing decks positioned between small swimming pools, several hot tubs, and a large poolside movie screen have transformed the area.

Also, on the open deck and aft of the funnel is WaterWorks, including a 334ft (101.8m) Twister waterslide, and Speedway Splash slide – so you and a competitor race down the Twister to a splashy finish.

The interior decor is a sensory wonderland. There are three decks full of lounges and bars, lots of rooms to play in, and a double-width indoor promenade. A glass-domed rotunda Sunshine Atrium lobby – with bar, two panoramic elevators and dual stairway – is nine decks high. An always-busy Sunshine Casino has ample gaming tables for serious gamers, and over 320 slot machines.

In spring 2013 a much-needed makeover (costing $155 million) lasted almost three months and added two half-decks at the front of the ship, extended two other decks aft, added 182 cabins (but no extra elevators), and several new and other revamped eateries. Public rooms include Piano Bar 88 (named for the

BERLITZ'S RATINGS	Possible	Achieved
Ship	500	327
Accommodation	200	123
Food	400	206
Service	400	247
Entertainment	100	62
Cruise Experience	400	240
OVERALL SCORE 1205 points out of 2000		

88 keys on a grand piano); Alchemy Bar, for 'mixologist' cocktails; a (music-free) What's it like? *Carnival Sunshine* is a floating playground for the young. The cuisine is not at all memorable, but there's plenty to do for all the family. Because it's a large resort ship, there will be lines for shore excursions, security control when re-boarding, and disembarkation, as well as sign-up sheets for fitness equipment. Other downsides include the many annoying announcements and the never-ending hustle to get you to buy alcoholic drinks full of ice and other items.

ACCOMMODATION. There are several accommodation categories (Captain's Suite, Grand Suite, Ocean Suite, Premium Balcony Cabin, Scenic Oceanview Cabin, Oceanview Cabin, Interior Cabin, and Small Interior), and several price grades, depending on size and location. Over half of all cabins have ocean views, and, at 225 sq ft (21 sq m), they are a decent size. Some cabins, spread over four decks, have private balconies with glass rather than steel balustrades for better, unobstructed ocean views; balconies have bright fluorescent lighting. However, there are many interior (no-view) cabins.

During the 2013 refit, 95 Cloud 9 Spa Cabins were added over three decks in the front of the ship, adjacent to the Cloud 9 Spa and Serenity adult-only area; these have all the usual fittings, plus special spa-like extras, and access to the Cloud 9 Spa.

Standard cabins are of an adequate size and come equipped with all the basics, although the furniture is angular (think Ikea flatpack). Three decks of cabins (eight on each deck, each with private balcony) overlook the stern – these are very nice.

Three categories of cabins, both outside and interior, have upper and lower bunk beds, which is useful for families with small children.

Note that the soundproofing between cabins is poor and cabin doors have (non-closable) vents, so any noise from the hallway filters through.

DINING. There are two main restaurants: the Sunrise Forward Dining Room, with windows on two sides; and the Sunrise Aft Dining Room, with windows on three sides). Each is a single deck high and has bright, modern design and decor.

The Sunset dining room has a wall of glass overlooking the stern. There are tables for four, six, and eight and even a few tables for two – nice for honeymooners. Choose either fixed-time dining (6pm or 8.15pm) or flexible dining (during opening hours). Although menu choices look good, the actual cuisine delivered is unmemorable. Still, the waiters try to impress with lots of dancing on tables and other hoopla, telling everyone they're having fun. Note that the two main dining rooms are not open for lunch on port days.

Breakfasts are surprisingly good, with ample choice, while dinners are ho-hum affairs – carbohydrate-rich, with simple presentation and few garnishes. Many dishes are disguised with gravies and sauces. The selection of fresh green vegetables, bread and bakery items (these are thawed and then baked from frozen 'starter' dough), cheeses, and fruit is limited, and there is heavy use of rice, canned fruit, and jellied desserts. The waiters sing and dance, so think 'foodertainment' rather than food quality. Also, there are no wine waiters, and the wine glasses are small. For something really simple, an 'always available' list of 'Carnival Classics' includes mahi-mahi (fish), baby back ribs (beef), and grilled chicken.

Fahrenheit 555 Steakhouse is an extra-cost, reservations-required dining spot for fine steaks (arguably worth the extra money) and grilled seafood dishes. There are many tables for two, although they are close together, as well as larger tables, and the seating is comfortable.

For casual eats, Ocean Plaza (Lido Market Place) is a food court-style self-serve eatery with plenty of food displays (a copy of the self-serve Markt Restaurants aboard AIDA Cruises ships). It includes a 24-hour pizzeria (Pizzeria del Capitano). There's no bar in the venue itself – but there are several on the adjacent pool deck.

A JavaBlue Café with 'comfort' snacks is in the Fun Hub Internet-connect area. A Havana Bar is located within the Market Place, as is a RedFrog Pub, pouring Carnival's own house brew, ThirstyFrog Red. Adjacent, but outside, are: Cucina del Capitano (for Italian cuisine, with made-to-order pasta dishes); the BlueIguana Cantina Mexican-style street eatery (for tacos and burritos); Ji Ji's Asian Kitchen, which features lunchtime stir-fry dishes; a pizzeria; a patisserie (extra charge for pastries); a car-culture-inspired Guy's Burger Joint for fast foods including burgers and hot dogs; and a RedFrog Rum Bar.

For something more unusual, or to celebrate, you can also choose to eat at the Chef's Table (it's reserved for only 12 hungry diners, at $75 each), which includes a look into the galley when it's in full operation, followed by a specially prepared multi-course dinner.

ENTERTAINMENT. The 800-seat two-level Liquid Lounge (showlounge) is the setting for high-energy production legs-and-feathers shows and large-scale cabaret acts – is quite stunning. It has a revolving stage, hydraulic orchestra pit, good sound, and seating on three levels (the upper levels being tiered through two decks). A proscenium arch over the stage acts as a scenery loft.

Other entertainment options include a Hasbro Game Show and the Punchliner Comedy Club presented by George Lopez and, the Liquid Lounge for those high-volume disco sounds.

SPA/FITNESS. Cloud 9 Spa spans two decks. It is located above the navigation bridge, and is accessible via the forward stairway. Lower-level facilities include a solarium, body treatment rooms, sauna and steam rooms for men and women, and a beauty salon; the upper level houses a fitness room with ocean-view windows on three sides, and an aerobics room for instructor-led classes (some at extra cost).

SportSquare is an outdoor recreation area with a suspended ropes course (and some great views).

CARNIVAL VALOR
★★★

THIS CASUAL FLOATING FUN PALACE IS A GOOD CHOICE FOR THE WHOLE FAMILY

Size:	Large Resort Ship	Passenger/Crew Ratio (lower beds):	2.3
Tonnage:	110,239	Cabins (total):	1,487
Cruise Line:	Carnival Cruise Line	Size Range (sq ft/m):	179.7–482.2/16.7–44.8
Former Names:	none	Cabins (for one person):	0
Builder:	Fincantieri (Italy)	Cabins with balcony:	574
Entered Service:	Dec 2004	Cabins (wheelchair accessible):	25
Length (ft/m):	951.4/290.0	Wheelchair accessibility:	Good
Propulsion/Propellers:	diesel-electric (34,000kW)/2	Elevators:	18
Total Crew:	1,160	Casino (gaming tables):	Yes
Passengers (lower beds):	2,974	Self-Service Launderette:	Yes
Passenger Space Ratio (lower beds):	37.0	Onboard currency:	US$

THE SHIP. *Carnival Valor* is one of a series of look-alike ships (the others are *Carnival Conquest*, *Carnival Freedom*, *Carnival Glory*, *Carnival Liberty*, *Carnival Radiance*, *Carnival Splendor*, *Carnival Sunrise*, *Carnival Sunshine*, and *Carnival Valor*).

Amidships on the open deck, a waterslide (200ft/60m) spans two decks and empties onto the pool deck below, which also has a large movie (Seaside Theater) screen. The terraced pool deck is cluttered, particularly when the ship is full, and there are no cushioned pads for the deck chairs. Aft of the funnel an extra-cost Serenity retreat just for adults provides quiet sunbathing space and a pool with retractable glass dome.

Inside are three decks full of lounges, bars, and lots of rooms to play in. Public rooms are given a visual theme, and, on *Carnival Valor*, this is about famous personalities, including the dancer and singer Josephine Baker and the aviator Charles Lindbergh. The layout is fairly logical and easy to navigate.

There is a double-width indoor promenade, and an atrium lobby that spans nine decks, topped by a glass dome. A square-shaped bar sits on the lowest level and faces forward towards panoramic glass-walled elevators. A sports bar has tables displaying sports memorabilia.

The ship is a floating playground for the young-at-heart and anyone who enjoys taking part in the many participation events, together with glitz, glamour, and gambling (the Shogun Casino is large, and has

BERLITZ'S RATINGS

	Possible	Achieved
Ship	500	329
Accommodation	200	124
Food	400	207
Service	400	241
Entertainment	100	61
Cruise Experience	400	236

OVERALL SCORE 1198 points out of 2000

an abundance of gaming tables and slot machines. Among other attractions: the Iliad On the downside, because it's a large resort ship, expect lines for shore excursions, security control when re-boarding, at disembarkation, and sign-up sheets for fitness equipment. Getting away from people and rap 'music' is virtually impossible.

ACCOMMODATION. There are numerous price categories, depending on grade, location and size. Over half of all cabins are outside, and, at 225 sq ft (21 sq m), they are among the largest in the standard market. They are spread over four decks and have private balconies extending from the ship's side; these have glass rather than steel balustrades for unobstructed ocean views, as well as bright fluorescent lighting. The standard cabins are of good size and have all the basics, although the furniture is angular, with no rounded edges. Three decks of cabins – eight per deck, each with private balcony – overlook the stern (back).

There are eight penthouse suites, each with a large balcony. Although decent in their appointments, at only 483 sq ft (44.9 sq m), they are really quite small. In cabins with balconies, the partition between each balcony is open at top and bottom, so you can hear neighbor noise.

There are also cabin categories with upper and lower bunk beds – lower beds are preferable (unless you have kids), but this is how the ship absorbs hundreds of extra passengers over and above the lower bed capacity.

Interactive 'Fun Vision' technology lets you choose movies on demand, for a fee. Note: the room service menu is poor, as is cabin soundproofing.

DINING. The ship has two main dining rooms, one forward (Lincoln) with windows on two sides and 706 seats, and the other (Washington) aft with windows on three sides and 1,090 seats. Each spans two decks and features a dozen domes and chandeliers. Washington has two-deck-high glass walls looking aft. Tables are for two to eight.

Choose either fixed-time dining or flexible dining (during opening hours). The entrances have comfortable drinking areas for pre-dinner cocktails. Note that the two main dining rooms are not open for lunch on port days.

Breakfasts are surprisingly good, with ample choice, while dinners are ho-hum affairs, but otherwise the food is pretty starchy and non-memorable (it's mass catering, after all), with simple presentation and few garnishes. Also, many dishes are disguised with sauces. The selection of fresh green vegetables, bread, and bakery items (these are thawed and then baked from frozen 'starter' dough), cheeses, and fruit is limited, and there is heavy use of rice, canned fruit, and jellied desserts. There are no wine waiters, and the wine glasses are small. For a simple meal, an 'always available' list of 'Carnival Classics' includes mahi-mahi (fish), baby back ribs (beef), and grilled chicken.

Options for more casual dining: a self-serve buffet-style eatery has seating on two levels. Included are a New York-style deli, a Chinese restaurant with wok preparation, and a 24-hour pizzeria, which typically serves an average of more than 800 pizzas every day.

A (complimentary) Guy's Burger Joint was added in a 2016 refurbishment – the free-of-charge poolside venue is in partnership with TV's Food Network personality Guy Fieri for handmade burgers and freshly cut fries.

Scarlett's Steakhouse is a reservations-only, extra-cost venue, for prime USDA steaks and grilled seafood. It has fine table settings, china, and silverware, as well as leather-bound menus, and a design theme set around Scarlett O'Hara, the heroine of Margaret Mitchell's classic novel *Gone With the Wind*. It's worth the extra cost, if you like really good steaks.

ENTERTAINMENT. The tri-level Ivanhoe show-lounge is stunning; it has a revolving stage, hydraulic orchestra pit, and seating on three levels, the upper levels being tiered through two decks. A proscenium arch over the stage is a scenery loft. Aft is a smaller Eagles Lounge, for cabaret and late-night comedy.

SPA/FITNESS. SpaCarnival spans two decks and is accessible from the forward stairway. Lower level facilities include a solarium, body treatment rooms, lecture rooms, sauna and steam rooms for men and women, and a beauty parlor; the upper level hosts a large gymnasium with expansive ocean view windows, and aerobics room. Most fitness classes cost extra.

CARNIVAL VICTORY
★★★

THIS IS A FUN SHIP FOR A FAMILY-FRIENDLY FIRST CRUISE ADVENTURE

Size:	Large Resort Ship
Tonnage:	101,509
Cruise Line:	Carnival Cruise Line
Former Names:	Carnival Victory
Builder:	Fincantieri (Italy)
Entered Service:	Aug 2000
Length (ft/m):	893.0/272.2
Propulsion/Propellers:	diesel-electric (34,000kW)/2 azimuthing pods
Total Crew:	1,100
Passengers (lower beds):	2,758
Passenger Space Ratio (lower beds):	36.8
Passenger/Crew Ratio (lower beds):	2.3
Cabins (total):	1,379
Size Range (sq ft/m):	179.7–482.2/16.7–44.8
Cabins (for one person):	0
Cabins with balcony:	508
Cabins (wheelchair accessible):	25
Wheelchair accessibility:	Good
Elevators:	18
Casino (gaming tables):	Yes
Self-Service Launderette:	Yes
Onboard currency:	US$

THE SHIP. Carnival Victory's sister ships are Carnival Conquest, Carnival Freedom, Carnival Glory, Carnival Liberty, Carnival Sunshine (originally named Carnival Destiny), and Carnival Valor. The ship has extremely short bows (the front), but looks balanced overall.

This is a large, family-friendly resort ship with upper exterior decks full of sports and waterpark attractions (but sunloungers don't have cushioned pads). The layout is logical and fairly easy to navigate. The theme of the interior decor is the oceans of the world, with seahorses, corals, and shells proliferating.

There are three decks full of lounges, 10 bars, and lots of rooms to explore and play in (including an expansive casino, with gaming tables and slot machines). There is a double-width indoor promenade, with statues of Neptune at both ends, and a glass-domed rotunda atrium lobby spans nine decks. On the lowest level is a square-shaped bar, which faces glass-walled panorama elevators.

Niggles include standing in lines for shore excursions, security control when re-boarding, and disembarkation, and well as for filling in sign-up sheets for fitness equipment.

The real fun on this ship begins at sundown when lights, razzle-dazzle shows, and late-night high-volume sounds abound. In April 2020, the ship will undergo an extensive refit and be renamed Carnival Radiance. It will include the following additional venues: 555 Fahrenheit Steakhouse; Bonsai Sushi; Shaq's Big Chicken Eatery, Guy's Pig & Anchor Bar-B-Que Smokehouse; Cucina del Capitano (for Italian-style eats), Chef's Table (for multi-course 'degustation' menu); and a Lido Marketplace.

BERLITZ'S RATINGS	Possible	Achieved
Ship	500	329
Accommodation	200	124
Food	400	208
Service	400	238
Entertainment	100	61
Cruise Experience	400	235
OVERALL SCORE 1195 points out of 2000		

ACCOMMODATION. The price you pay depends on the grade, location, and size you choose. Accommodation ranges from interior (no-view) cabins to larger Captain's Suites.

Standard cabins are of decent size and have all the basics, although the furniture is angular, and the decor is bland; the bathrooms, however, are quite practical. Soundproofing could be better.

Cabins with balconies (those overlooking the stern are really nice) have glass rather than steel balustrades for unobstructed ocean views, and bright lighting. Note that the partition between each balcony is open at top and bottom, so you will hear your neighbors.

DINING. There are two main dining rooms, Atlantic (forward) with windows on two sides and 706 seats, and Pacific (aft) with windows on three sides and 1,090 seats. Each spans two decks, and features a dozen domes and chandeliers. Tables are for four to eight, and even a few tables for two. The dining room entrances have comfortable drinking areas.

Choose either fixed-time dining in one of two seatings or flexible dining (during opening hours). Although the menu choice looks good, the actual cuisine delivered is quite unmemorable. Note that the two main dining rooms may not be open for lunch on port days.

Breakfasts are surprisingly good, with ample choice, while dinners are ho-hum affairs (think carbohydrate-rich mass catering). Presentation is simple (although the dishes look decent, the taste is minimal), few garnishes are used, and many dishes have heavy gravies and sauces. Baked goods are cooked from frozen. The choice of fresh green vegetables, cheeses, and fruit is limited, and there is heavy use of rice, canned fruit, and jellied desserts.

There are no wine waiters, and the wine glasses are small. For a more basic meal, try the 'always available' (during dining rooms opening hours) list of 'Carnival Classics.'

A casual 'international' self-serve buffet-style eatery (the Mediterranean Lido Restaurant) includes a deli (for sandwiches and wraps), a seafood shack and a pizzeria (Pizzeria Arno), which often provides over 800 pizzas every day.

Added in 2018: a poolside BlueIguana Cantina Mexican-style street eatery (for tacos and burritos); a patisserie (extra charge for pastries); a car-culture-inspired poolside Guy's Burger Joint for fast food, including burgers and hot dogs; and a RedFrog Rum Bar.

The one reservations-only, extra-cost dining spot is The Steakhouse. It features prime USDA steaks and grilled seafood items (perhaps worth paying extra for). It has better table settings, china, and silverware, and a design theme set around Scarlett O'Hara, the heroine of Margaret Mitchell's classic novel *Gone With the Wind*.

ENTERTAINMENT. The large tri-level Caribbean Main Lounge (showlounge) has a revolving stage, hydraulic orchestra pit, and seating on three levels, the upper levels being tiered through two decks, and a proscenium arch. Other entertainment spots include the Club Arctic (disco), Punchliner (for smutty adult 'comedy'), and the Irish Sea Piano Bar (good for singalongs).

SPA/FITNESS. SpaCarnival spans two decks (above the navigation bridge), accessible from the forward stairway. Lower level facilities include a solarium, body treatment rooms, lecture rooms, sauna and steam rooms for men and women, and a beauty parlor; the upper level hosts a large gymnasium with expansive ocean view windows, and an aerobics room. Most fitness classes cost extra.

CARNIVAL VISTA
★★★+

A SHIP FOR FAMILY FUN ENTERTAINMENT AND CARDIO-ACTIVE OUTDOOR FACILITIES

Size:	Large Resort Ship	Passenger/Crew Ratio (lower beds):	2.7
Tonnage:	135,000	Cabins (total):	2,000
Cruise Line:	Carnival Cruise Line	Size Range (sq ft/m):	161.4–430.5/15.0–40.0
Former Names:	none	Cabins (for one person):	0
Builder:	Fincantieri (Italy)	Cabins with balcony:	887
Entered Service:	May 2016	Cabins (wheelchair accessible):	35
Length (ft/m):	1,054.7/321.5	Wheelchair accessibility:	Good
Propulsion/Propellers:	diesel-electric/2 azimuthing pods	Elevators:	16
		Casino (gaming tables):	Yes
Total Crew:	1,450	Self-Service Launderette:	Yes
Passengers (lower beds):	4,000	Onboard currency:	US$
Passenger Space Ratio (lower beds):	33.7		

THE SHIP. Although its design is quite old – based mostly on *Carnival Destiny* of 1996 – this (*Carnival Breeze*-plus) ship nevertheless provides an array of activity-fueled fun for the whole family. *Carnival Vista* is all about the fun of the fair at sea.

So, line up to get on your bike to pedal the suspended track of Sky Ride – maybe cycle yourself to the next port! Other attractions include a large WaterWorks aqua park, which features a 445ft (136m) Kaleid-O-Slide, a twisting, corkscrew-turning waterslide adventure with kaleidoscopic effects (a variation on the Sky-Walk rope course aboard *Carnival Magic*), and an excellent place to keep the kids occupied.

Considering the number of passengers carried, the swimming pools are disappointingly small, as is the open deck space, because of all the activity features crammed in. However, there's usually no shortage of available sun loungers.

The ship has a full walk-around open promenade deck, but it's lined with deck chairs. Also at the aft, two 'scenic whirlpools' are cantilevered over the water (as part of the Havana Outside area), with fine sea views.

Inside, facilities include an IMAX Theater (for blockbuster movies and documentary content), a large Vista Casino (adjacent to the atrium), a Thrill Theater (for a 4D moving experience), and many other lounges and bars, although the ship's layout is a little disjointed.

BERLITZ'S RATINGS	Possible	Achieved
Ship	500	369
Accommodation	200	133
Food	400	210
Service	400	251
Entertainment	100	68
Cruise Experience	400	253

OVERALL SCORE 1284 points out of 2000

The main social center of the ship is the atrium, with large LED screens to provide mood-changing backdrops. Counters for guest services and shore excursions are just off the atrium, while aft of the lobby is the Reflections Dining Room.

Many of the public rooms, lounges, bars, and nightspots are located on two main public room/entertainment decks. These can be accessed via an 11-deck-high atrium lobby, with a cantilevered bandstand atop a massive dance floor on the ground level.

The myriad bars include a sports bar, a trendy Havana Bar, Alchemy Bar (for 'mixologist' cocktails, and a RedFrog Pub (with Carnival's own brews: the ThirstyFrog Red; ThirstyFrog Port Hoppin' IPA; ThirstyFrog Caribbean Wheat; and ThirstyFrog Java Stout).

An adults-only (extra-cost) Serenity area atop the ship at the front provides a beach-like escape from the noisy family-filled decks below, with hot tubs, sunloungers, a bar, and other facilities, including massage 'huts.'

Families with children are well catered for, not only with hyper-activity sporty areas outdoors, but also play rooms for kids and teens (in several different locations), and plenty of youth counselors to take charge, so parents and carers can get some 'me' time, too.

What Carnival does well is to provide lots of almost non-stop excitement, and entertainment fun, and this ship provides the right setting for it all. While the cuisine is pretty uninspiring, the real fun begins at sundown, when the entertainment kicks in.

ACCOMMODATION. The range of cabin sizes, locations, grades and prices includes 'Family Harbor' – family cabins that can sleep up to five. Whether you go for high end or low end, all include plush mattresses, and good-quality duvets, bed linen, and pillows. The suites are not large, although they are laid out practically, while some of the standard cabins are fine for two but crowded for three or more (there's only one personal safe).

All cabins have spy-hole doors, twin beds that can convert into queen-size beds, controllable air conditioning, infotainment set, and telephone. Some cabins can accommodate a third and fourth person, but they have limited closet space. A number of cabins on Deck 3 have lifeboat-obstructed views.

Among the most desirable are those on five of the aft-facing decks; these have private balconies overlooking the stern and ship's wash. There's no vibration, a bonus provided by the pod propulsion system.

CUISINE. The two main dining rooms – Horizons and Reflections – are for served meals (breakfast and lunch are open seatng, dinner is in two seatings; note that chairs don't have armrests). Horizons Restaurant has some tables at the stern with fine views (on both main and balcony levels – although the upper level has a low ceiling), plus a bar. You can (at extra cost) also have selections from the steakhouse menu.

Don't even think about a quiet table for two, or a candlelight dinner on deck. This is all about table mates, social talk, lively meals, fast eating, and fast service. Tables do have tablecloths, silverware, and iced water/iced tea whenever you want it. Choose either fixed time dining or flexible dining (during opening hours). Breakfasts are surprisingly good, with ample choice, while dinners are non-memorable (it's mass catering), and simple presentation, few garnishes, and many dishes disguised with gravies and sauces. The selection of green vegetables, bread and bakery items (thawed and then baked from frozen 'starter' dough), cheeses, and fruit is limited, and there is heavy use of canned fruit and jellied desserts.

'Spa Carnival Fare' provides a healthier food option; vegetarian and children's menus are also available, but they wouldn't get a generous score for their nutritional content.

Lido Marketplace is a self-serve, buffet-style casual eatery; close by are other eateries (no extra cost), including Guy's Burger Joint (named after TV foodie Guy Fieri), BlueIguana Cantina (for Mexican snack burritos and tacos), and Pizzeria del Capitano. There's also Fat Jimmy's C-Side BBQ – oh, and you can get some light bites at The Taste Bar, hot dogs at SeaDogs in SportSquare, sandwiches at the Carnival Deli, and frozen yoghurt at Swirls.

Extra-cost dining spots include: Fahrenheit 555 steakhouse (for prime meats and grilled seafood); Bonsai Sushi Restaurant, for Japanese-style cuisine (with indoor and outdoor seating); Seafood Shack, a New England-style indoor-outdoor eatery (for steamed lobster, crab cakes, and fried shrimp); Cucina del Capitano (for Italian-style cuisine), and Ji-Ji Asian Kitchen (for Asian fusion cuisine). Families with youngsters might like to indulge in a Green Eggs and Ham breakfast (extra cost), while Chef's Table (for foodies) includes a little showbusiness from the chef for up to 12 diners (also at extra cost).

ENTERTAINMENT. Liquid Lounge, the showlounge, spans two decks and is the venue for Vegas-style production shows (all feathers and skimpy costumes) and 'A'-list cabaret acts.

A second entertainment lounge is Limelight Lounge (for adult comedy), while a Piano Bar offers a gentler tone.

An IMAX Theater has a three-deck high screen, while adjacent is a multi-dimensional, special-effects experience in the Thrill Theater; both are located on Upper Promenade Deck. Extra-cost popcorn and movie snacks are available, of course, and next door is a video arcade.

SPA/FITNESS. The bi-level Cloud 9 Spa has treatment rooms, men's and women's infrared saunas and hammam (slow steam and mud room – good for couples), relaxation lounger, fitness center, and (cost-extra) thermal suites, plus a VIP treatment room for Spa Suite occupants.

Activity/sports facilities include an outdoor Sky-Course suspended ropes course (always fun on a moving ship), Sky Gardens mini-golf course, and a Skycourt (for baseball). The Clubhouse at SportSquare includes mini-bowling, ping-pong, arcade basketball, and video games.

CELEBRITY CONSTELLATION
★★★+

THIS SHIP'S UNDERSTATED DECOR PROVIDES A STYLISH SETTING FOR FAMILIES

Size:	Mid-size Ship	Passenger/Crew Ratio (lower beds):	2.0
Tonnage:	90,940	Cabins (total):	1,085
Cruise Line:	Celebrity Cruises	Size Range (sq ft/m):	165.1–2,530.0/15.34–235.0
Former Names:	Constellation	Cabins (for one person):	0
Builder:	Chantiers de l'Atlantique (France)	Cabins with balcony:	569
Entered Service:	May 2002	Cabins (wheelchair accessible):	26
Length (ft/m):	964.5/294.0	Wheelchair accessibility:	Best
Propulsion/Propellers:	gas turbine/2 azimuthing pods	Elevators:	12
Total Crew:	999	Casino (gaming tables):	Yes
Passengers (lower beds):	2,170	Self-Service Launderette:	No
Passenger Space Ratio (lower beds):	44.6	Onboard currency:	US$

THE SHIP. *Celebrity Constellation* is sister to *Celebrity Infinity*, *Celebrity Millennium*, and *Celebrity Summit*. Sadly, there is no walk-around outdoor promenade deck.

Inside, the decor is of understated elegance, with high-quality materials, including much wood, glass, and marble.

A four-deck-high atrium, with an enclosed room for shore excursions, houses the reception desk, and financial services. Four glass-walled elevators travel through 10 decks, including the tender stations. Standout bars: a Martini Bar with frosted countertop, and a Cellar-Masters wine bar.

A cruise aboard a mid-sized ship provides a good range of choices. Travel in one of the suites, and you get better service levels.

ACCOMMODATION. There are many price grades from which to choose, depending on your preference for the size and location – and your budget. These range from standard interior (no view) and outside-view cabins (with or without balcony) to spacious suite grades Aqua, Concierge, Royal, Celebrity, and Penthouse, plus wheelchair-accessible cabins (with wheel-in showers), positioned close to the elevators.

If you choose a balcony cabin on one of the upper decks, note that it could be shaded under the pool deck, which extends over the ship's side – and by many balconies (not good for private sunbathing). Some suites have extremely large balconies – check

BERLITZ'S RATINGS		
	Possible	Achieved
Ship	500	354
Accommodation	200	148
Food	400	254
Service	400	278
Entertainment	100	71
Cruise Experience	400	263

OVERALL SCORE 1368 points out of 2000

the deck plan before choosing. Note that a charge for room service applies between 11pm and 6am.

DINING. The 1,198-seat San Marco Restaurant (main dining room) spans two decks, with a connecting stairway and a large aft glass wall (electric blinds provide different backdrops). Dinner is in two seatings, with open seating for breakfast and lunch, at tables for two to 10, with quality linen, china, and glassware.

The cuisine has traditional and modern culinary influences; overall, it's decent but uninspiring; there are too many sauces and too little use of garnishes. For higher-quality food, pay extra to eat in the specialty venues, for better cuts of meat and food cooked to order instead of the standardized batch cooking provided in the main dining room.

The (free) coffee is weak and poor (dining room espresso/cappuccino coffees incur a charge, because they are treated as a bar item). For premium-quality Lavazza coffee, it's worth paying extra in Café al Bacio.

Suite occupants dine in the exclusive Luminae restaurant, with tableside preparation of signature dishes, an eclectic menu, and an extensive wine list.

Blu (port side, upper level entrance to the San Marco dining room), is for occupants of Aqua-class accommodation.

Qsine is an extra-cost, reservations-required, tablecloth-free 'fun-food' venue, with digital food and wine menus and cute video snapshots. Its quirky multi-flavor, multi-color small-bite 'show business' items tease the taste buds, and is presented in unusual ways – even on sticks – like 'lollipop' cuisine.

Tuscan Grill is an extra-cost, reservations-required venue for Italian-style cuisine.

Oceanview Café is a self-serve buffet-style eatery with around 750 seats. Oceanview Café (with around 750 seats) is a casual self-serve buffet area, with various food stations and do-it-yourself options. Pizzas are made on board from pizza dough and do not come ready made for reheating, as with many cruise lines. There's also a Burger Bar outside just aft of the mast.

Café al Bacio & Gelateria, on the uppermost (third) level of the atrium lobby, is for (extra-cost) coffees, pastries, cakes, and ice creams, while Sushi on Five has extra-cost sushi and hot noodle and hot pot dishes.

ENTERTAINMENT. The 900-seat Celebrity Theater (showlounge) features colorful production shows and major cabaret acts. Spanning three decks, it has seating on all three levels.

SPA/FITNESS. Canyon Ranch SpaClub facilities include a large thalassotherapy pool under a glass dome, with 'health' bar for light breakfast and lunch items and freshly squeezed fruit and vegetable juices.

CELEBRITY ECLIPSE
★★★★

THIS LARGE, STYLISH PREMIUM SHIP IS GOOD FOR FAMILY-FRIENDLY CRUISING

Size:	Large Resort Ship	Passenger/Crew Ratio (lower beds):	2.3
Tonnage:	121,878	Cabins (total):	1,426
Cruise Line:	Celebrity Cruises	Size Range (sq ft/m):	182.9–1,668.4/17.0–155.0
Former Names:	none	Cabins (for one person):	0
Builder:	Meyer Werft (Germany)	Cabins with balcony:	1,216
Entered Service:	Jun 2010	Cabins (wheelchair accessible):	30
Length (ft/m):	1,033.4/315.0	Wheelchair accessibility:	Best
Propulsion/Propellers:	diesel (67,200kW)/2 azimuthing pods	Elevators:	12
		Casino (gaming tables):	Yes
Total Crew:	1,210	Self-Service Launderette:	No
Passengers (lower beds):	2,852	Onboard currency:	US$
Passenger Space Ratio (lower beds):	42.7		

THE SHIP. This slimline ship is a sister to *Celebrity Equinox* (2009), *Celebrity Reflection* (2012), *Celebrity Silhouette* (2011), and *Celebrity Solstice* (2008). It has a steeply raked stern, which includes a mega-yacht-style ducktail platform above the ship's propulsion pods; it is attractive, and nicely balances the ship's contemporary profile.

Behind the two smallish funnels is a real grass outdoor area, the Lawn Club. This is the authentic stuff – not green fake turf – and it seems to like the salty air. The club is open to all, so you can putt, play croquet or bocce ball (like bowling or French boules), picnic on the grass, or perhaps sleep on it. Several pool and water-play areas are found on Resort Deck: one in a glass-roofed solarium, a sports pool, a family pool, and a wet zone. The deck space around the two pools, however, isn't large enough for the number of passengers carried.

The interior spaces are well designed, with most of the entertainment rooms forward, and dining venues located aft. There's a wine bar with sommelier; a cocktail lounge reflecting the jazz age of the 1930s and '40s; a bar with the look of an ocean-going yacht; Quasar, a bar with designs from the 1960s and '70s and large screens that create a nightly light show synchronized to music; and an observation lounge with a dance floor.

Celebrity's signature Martini Bar, with its frosted bar and more than 100 varieties of vodka and martinis, has a small alcove called Crush with an ice-filled

BERLITZ'S RATINGS		
	Possible	Achieved
Ship	500	388
Accommodation	200	159
Food	400	259
Service	400	284
Entertainment	100	73
Cruise Experience	400	280
OVERALL SCORE 1443 points out of 2000		

table where you can participate in caviar and vodka tasting. It's noisy and congested.

An innovative Hot Glass Show, housed in an outdoor studio on the open deck as part of the Lawn Club and created in collaboration with Corning Museum of Glass, includes demonstrations and a narrated performance of glass-blowing. Resident glass-blowing artists also host workshops.

An Apple 'iLounge' has Apple MacBook Pro work stations (you can also buy Apple products). Elevator call buttons are located in a floor-stand 'pod' and, when the elevator arrives, a glass panel above it turns from blue to pink. Gratuities are automatically charged to your onboard account.

ACCOMMODATION. This is both practical and comfortable. There are numerous price grades, depending on size and location. Even-numbered cabins are on the starboard side, and odd-numbered cabins are on the port side, contrary to maritime tradition (even numbers on the port side, odd numbers on the starboard side – like the lifeboats).

In non-suite-grade cabins there is little space between bed and wall, but all accommodation includes twin beds convertible to a queen- or king-size bed with premium bedding, sitting area, and vanity desk with hairdryer, but little drawer space. Although closets have good hanging space, other storage space is limited. Bathrooms have a shower enclosure, toilet, and *tiny* washbasin. A charge of $3.95 for room service applies between 11pm and 6am.

Note that cabins 1551–1597 on the port side and 1556–1602 on the starboard side on Penthouse Deck (Deck 11) suffer from 'aircraft carrier' syndrome because they are directly under the overhanging Resort Deck. They have little exposure to sun or light, so sunbathing is out of the question. Many thick supporting struts ruin the view from these cabins, which are otherwise pleasant enough.

Other accommodation grades are: Veranda; Family Veranda; Concierge; Ocean View; and Interior (no-view) cabins. Suite-grade categories are: Aqua; Sky; Celebrity; Royal; and Penthouse. Suites have much more space, larger balconies with good-quality sun-loungers, and more personal amenities.

DINING. Moonlight Sonata is the 1,430-seat two-deck main dining room (included in the cruise price). It has ocean views on the port and starboard sides, and two seating times; anyone choosing 'Celebrity Select Dining' is usually assigned to the upper level. It's contemporary, and, despite its size, very comfortable. A two-deck-high wine tower is a great focal point.

Suite-class occupants can dine in Luminae restaurant, with tableside preparation of signature dishes, an eclectic menu, and a selection of over 400 wines.

Blu is a 130-seat specialty restaurant just for the occupants of Aqua-class cabins. The room has a pleasing, but rather cool, blue decor.

The following dining spots provide an alternative to the main dining room, good for special occasions or just for something different.

Murano is an extra-cost, reservations-required venue offering high-quality traditional dining with a French flair and fine table settings (with tablecloth), including large Riedel wine glasses.

Tuscan Grille is an extra-cost venue for Kobe beef and premium-quality steaks. Its entrance has beautifully curved arches – it's like walking into a high-tech winery. There are fine views from huge aft-view windows.

Qsine is an extra-cost, reservations-required, tablecloth-free 'fun-food' restaurant, with trendy interactive iPad food and wine menus that include cute foodie video snaps. The food consists of multi-flavored, small-bite items to tease your taste buds, and is presented in unusual ways – even on sticks.

For snacks and less ambitious meals, options include: Bistro on Five for extra-cost sushi, noodle and hot pot dishes and Café al Bacio & Gelateria (a coffee lounge for Lavazza Italian coffees). It is on one side of the main lobby, but it's small and lines quickly form at peak times. The seating is mostly in large, very comfortable armchairs.

Oceanview Café and Grill is an expansive, tray-free, casual self-serve buffet. A number of food 'islands' help to prevent lines, and the flow is good; the signage is clear and concise. A wide variety of food items is available, and plates are available at each of the 'islands' and cooking stations (such as 'Eggs and More' for breakfast). However, it *is* challenging to get a warm plate for hot food items.

AquaSpa Café is for lighter options – low-salt dishes, including salad items, plus grilled items like salmon and chicken.

The Mast Bar Grill and Bar is an outside venue offering fast food.

ENTERTAINMENT. The 1,115-seat Eclipse Theater (the main showlounge) stages three circus-themed production shows featuring acrobatics.

Colorful theme nights are held in the Observation Lounge (whose bland daytime decor comes alive at night thanks to mood lighting effects). The 200-seat Celebrity Central hosts stand-up comedy, cooking demonstrations, enrichment lectures, and feature films. Quasar is a high-volume nightclub.

An Entertainment Court showcases street performers, psychics, and caricaturists, and is in the center of the ship. There's also a big-band-era cocktail lounge with live jazz-styled music, set adjacent to the Murano, the specialty restaurant.

SPA/FITNESS. The Canyon Ranch SpaClub is laid out over two decks. A large fitness center includes kinesis (pulleys against gravity) workout equipment, plus all the familiar gym machinery.

An extra-cost, unisex thermal suite features several steam and shower mist rooms and a glacial ice fountain, plus a calming relaxation area with heated tiled beds, and an acupuncture center.

CELEBRITY EDGE
★★★★

THIS SPACIOUS SHIP OOZES SMART-TECH CONTEMPORARY CRUISING FOR STYLE LOVERS

Size:	Large Resort Ship	Passenger/Crew Ratio (lower beds):	2.2
Tonnage:	129,500	Cabins (total):	1,467
Cruise Line:	Celebrity Cruises	Size Range (sq ft/m):	204.5–2,165.7/19.0–243.0
Former Names:	none	Cabins (for one person):	16
Builder:	STX (France)	Cabins with balcony:	0
Entered Service:	Dec 2018	Cabins (wheelchair accessible):	23
Length (ft/m):	1,003.9/306.0	Wheelchair accessibility:	Best
Propulsion/Propellers:	diesel/2 azimuthing pods	Elevators:	12
Total Crew:	1,320	Casino (gaming tables):	Yes
Passengers (lower beds):	2,918	Self-Service Launderette:	No
Passenger Space Ratio (lower beds):	44.3	Onboard currency:	US$

THE SHIP. With its snub-nose and tiered aft decks, *Celebrity Edge* is the result of an enhanced Solstice-class ship and product refinement (and then some), but is slightly shorter and smaller, so it's easier to get into more ports. However, the passenger space ratio is high for this fuel-efficient large resort ship. It's the first Celebrity ship to have a long pool (25m – half the Olympic length), copied from TUI Cruises' Mein Schiff series.

The ship makes an impression with its airy, open design and mood lighting, and is a prime example of the ship as a destination, with an abundance of eclectic artwork. Standouts include a novel 'Magic Carpet' on the exterior starboard side – a bar/lounge/eatery on a 90-seat, 90-ton platform that can move vertically between decks 2 and 16 (with 'open' air conditioning); it is also a tender platform (it can obstruct views from some cabins). Another is the 'Rooftop Garden' and Grill (aft of the funnel), an urban space with live foliage, while the Meeting Place is a 183sq m (1,969 sq ft) space for event meetings. The atrium lobby with integral cafe spans three decks, and its focal point is a seven-ton, color-changing LED chandelier that hangs over the Martini Bar and always-busy adjacent coffee lounge (drinks cost extra).

Because of the demand for exclusivity even in a large resort ship, Celebrity Cruises introduced its own 'Ship within a Ship' concept (as aboard the ships of Dream Cruises, MSC Cruises and Norwegian

BERLITZ'S RATINGS		
	Possible	Achieved
Ship	500	419
Accommodation	200	158
Food	400	264
Service	400	293
Entertainment	100	80
Cruise Experience	400	298

OVERALL SCORE 1512 points out of 2000

Cruise Line) with some 176 suites, while The Retreat is a serene indoor/outdoor adult-only area with a pool, hot tubs, multiple suites, and a private-access lounge, but constant 'background' music. Some 24 rentable cabanas are on the main pool deck, reducing the space for other sunloungers (here, too, there's no escape from the relentless deck music).

With a whole host of bars and lounges and some innovative design elements and features, this ship is a fine all-round resort at sea for all age groups. However, be aware that there are many cost-extra items, such as in the various optional 'dining and eating venues (most lack tablecloths), drink packages, and excursions. Strong points include a good service and hospitality standard (with more staff than other ships of comparable size and capacity, especially in the housekeeping and food and beverage departments), and a minimum announcement policy. What's it like: busy and noisy, in a contemporary setting. This is smartphone cruising with all its implications, and you'll need to be tech-savvy.

ACCOMMODATION. With 10 accommodation decks, the price you pay depends on the size, location, and grade. From the smallest interior (no-view) cabin to the largest of the 176 suites, there are many price grades. Note that even-numbered cabins are on the starboard side, and odd-numbered cabins are on the port side, contrary to maritime tradition (even numbers on the port side, odd numbers on the starboard side – like the lifeboats).

Two 'above the bridge' two-bedroom, two-bathroom (his 'n' hers) Iconic Suites are the largest, with multiple rooms, lounges, and outdoor terraces overlooking the bows. Suite-class occupants get 'butler'-style service, priority embarkation, and other privileges ('pay more, get more').

Ocean-view cabins (about 60 percent of the total) have a large electric window that slides down halfway to give you an open-air 'balcony'-like feel (copied from the European riverships), with two closeable bi-fold doors. It's a neat idea that saves building actual balconies and allows more space to be devoted to the cabin interior – nice, but it's not for private sunbathing like on a real balcony – and there's no mosquito screen. In other words, they are not genuine balconies, but large windows (Celebrity calls them 'infinity' balconies). All cabins have touch-button lighting with four settings (morning, afternoon, evening, and sleep).

DINING. The Main Dining Room spans two decks and operates two restaurants: Cosmopolitan Cyprus for fixed or anytime dining.

Aqua-class occupants dine in Blu. Suite occupants dine in Luminae, a bi-level venue with large windows that open, and menus designed by Michelin-starred chef Cornelius Gallagher (but no tablecloths).

Celebrity Cruises' cuisine is quite creative, trendy, and slightly more health-oriented (i.e. less reliance on salt and food modifiers) than that of many of its competitors.

Other venues (some cost extra): Tuscan Restaurant (for Italian fare); Normandie (for French/Continental cuisine); Fine Cut Steakhouse (for prime steaks and seafood); 'Rooftop Garden' and Grill (aft of the funnels for steaks cooked to your liking); Raw on 5, a raw-bar style seafood eatery (think oysters and Champagne) that connects with the Magic Carpet occasionally for indoor-outdoor drinks and snacks; Le Grand Bistro (a French-style patisserie), with indoor-outdoor seating; Eden, a three-deck high glass-enclosed aft lounge/eatery with supper club entertainment; 'Dining on the Edge' is a novelty-factor, 90-seat lounge/bar/eatery on the Magic Carpet – a platform that moves vertically between decks 2 and 16 (cantilevered over the ship's side).

The self-serve buffet-style Oceanside Restaurant has several sections for different food types, while outdoors is the Mast Bar (for burgers, fries and hot dogs).

ENTERTAINMENT. The expansive, state-of-the-art Oculus Theater has a 'thrust' stage that juts out into the audience and is the venue for colorful and edgy custom-designed production shows, performed by its own troupe of vocalists and dancers.

An interesting, throbbing nightclub is Eden (think: angels, drinking and debauchery, not 'Garden of'), with aerial displays and high-energy DJ sounds. Meanwhile, The Club is a bi-level space for event meetings, clubby entertainment, and smutty adult-only 'comedy'.

SPA/FITNESS. The Spa includes a large fitness center with familiar muscle-pumping machinery (you need to sign-up for fitness classes). Facilities include a Spa Café for light bites and (extra cost) fresh-squeezed juices. Runners should like the inclined exterior jogging track.

CELEBRITY EQUINOX
★★★★

THIS LARGE SHIP OFFERS CONTEMPORARY STYLE TO THOSE WHO LIKE TO TRAVEL WELL

Size:	Large Resort Ship	Passenger/Crew Ratio (lower beds):	2.3
Tonnage:	122,000	Cabins (total):	1,426
Cruise Line:	Celebrity Cruises	Size Range (sq ft/m):	182.9–1,668.4/17.0–155.0
Former Names:	none	Cabins (for one person):	0
Builder:	Meyer Werft (Germany)	Cabins with balcony:	1,216
Entered Service:	Aug 2009	Cabins (wheelchair accessible):	30
Length (ft/m):	1,033.4/315.0	Wheelchair accessibility:	Best
Propulsion/Propellers:	diesel (67,200kW)/2 azimuthing pods	Elevators:	12
		Casino (gaming tables):	Yes
Total Crew:	1,210	Self-Service Launderette:	No
Passengers (lower beds):	2,852	Onboard currency:	US$
Passenger Space Ratio (lower beds):	42.7		

THE SHIP. This is a sister ship to *Celebrity Eclipse, Celebrity Reflection, Celebrity Silhouette,* and *Celebrity Solstice.* The steeply sloping stern, with its mega-yacht-style ducktail platform above the propulsion pods, is attractive, and balances the ship's contemporary profile, while the bows are rounded to accommodate a helipad.

Between the two slim funnels (set one behind the other) is a grass outdoor area, the Lawn Club, with real grass that seems to like the salty air. The Lawn Club is open to all, so you can go putting, play croquet or bocce ball (like bowling or boules), or have a picnic on the grass.

There are several pool and water-play areas on Resort Deck: one in a solarium (with glass roof), a sports pool, a family pool, and a wet zone. However, the deck space around the two pools is not large enough for the number of passengers carried.

The interior decor is elegant, yet contemporary. Attractions include a Gastropub; a cocktail lounge with jazz; a bar with the look of an ocean-going yacht; Quasar, a bar with large screens that create a nightly light show synchronized to music; and an observation lounge with dance floor.

Celebrity's signature Martini Bar, with its frosted bar, includes a small alcove called Crush with an ice-filled table for caviar and vodka tastings.

Fortunes Casino has 16 gaming tables and 200 slot machines. There's a two-deck library, but the

BERLITZ'S RATINGS		
	Possible	Achieved
Ship	500	387
Accommodation	200	159
Food	400	258
Service	400	287
Entertainment	100	73
Cruise Experience	400	280

OVERALL SCORE 1444 points out of 2000

books on the upper shelves are impossible to reach. A Hot Glass Show, created in collaboration with Corning Museum of Glass, includes demonstrations and a narrated performance of glass-blowing, housed in an outdoor studio on the open deck as part of the Lawn Club.

Passenger niggles include poor drawer space in cabins; inadequate children's facilities and staff; congestion when you exit the showlounge; and noise in all areas of the lobby when the Martini Bar is busy.

Good points include the elevator call buttons, located in a floor-stand 'pod'; when an elevator arrives, a glass panel above it turns from blue to pink. Also, the ship has a good collection of designer chairs and sunloungers in various locations.

The ship sails year-round in the Caribbean. Gratuities are charged to your onboard account. A refurbishment in 2014 added more branded merchandise for shops, changed Cellar Masters into a Gastrobar featuring more than 40 craft beers and 'comfort food,' and online@Celebrity into the Celebrity iLounge (a computer room equipped with Apple Macs). The ship underwent a further refurbishment in 2019 (after this edition was completed) for an update and more enhancements, including The Retreat (a pay-extra, adults-only relaxation zone).

ACCOMMODATION. The accommodation is both practical and comfortable, with numerous price grades, depending on size and location. In non-suite-grade cabins there is little space between the bed and the wall, but all include twin beds convertible to queen- or king-size bed, with premium bedding, sitting area, and vanity desk with hairdryer, but little drawer space. Although closets have good hanging space, other storage space is limited. Bathrooms have a shower enclosure, toilet, and tiny washbasin. A charge for room service applies between 11pm and 6am.

Note that cabins 1551–1597 on the port side and 1556–1602 on the starboard side on Penthouse Deck (Deck 11) are directly beneath the overhanging Resort Deck, and have little exposure to sun or light, so sunbathing is out of the question. Many thick supporting struts ruin the view from these cabins, which are otherwise good.

Suites, of course, have much more space, plus larger balconies with good-quality sunloungers, and more personal amenities than those of lower grades.

DINING. Silhouette, the main dining room included in the cruise price, has ocean views on the port and starboard sides and two seating times; anyone choosing 'Celebrity Select Dining' is usually assigned to the upper level. It's contemporary, and, despite its size, very comfortable. A two-deck-high wine tower is a great focal point.

Suite occupants dine in Luminae, a restaurant with tableside preparation of signature dishes, and a selection of over 400 wines. Blu is a 128-seat specialty restaurant designated for occupants of Aqua-class cabins. The room has pleasing, but rather cool, blue decor.

Extra-cost eateries include Tuscan Grille for premium-quality steaks (it has beautifully curved archways – reminiscent of a high-tech winery, and great views from huge aft-view windows); QSine, a quirky fine-dining venue with iPad menus; Sushi on Five for sushi and cooked items, including noodle and hot pot dishes; and Café al Bacio & Gelateria coffee lounge for Lavazza Italian coffees (but it's small and lines form at peak times).

Oceanview Café and Grill is an expansive, tray-free, casual self-serve buffet. A number of food 'islands' help to prevent lines, and the flow is good; the signage is clear and concise. A wide variety of food items is available, and plates are available at each of the 'islands' and cooking stations (such as 'Eggs and More' for breakfast). However, it *is* challenging to get a warm plate for hot food items.

AquaSpa Café is for lighter options – low-salt dishes, including salad items and grilled meats and fish.

The Mast Bar Grill and Bar is an outside venue for fast-food items.

ENTERTAINMENT. The 1,115-seat Equinox Theater (showlounge) has a main level and two balconied sections set amphitheater-style around a stage with music lofts on either side.

Theme nights are held in the Sky Observation Lounge, where the daytime decor comes alive at night with mood lighting, while Celebrity Central hosts comedy, cooking demonstrations, enrichment lectures, and feature films. The Ensemble Lounge big-band-era cocktail lounge is for live jazz.

SPA/FITNESS. A two-deck Canyon Ranch Spa-Club at Sea has a fitness center with kinesis and cardio-vascular equipment. An extra-cost, unisex thermal suite has steam and shower mist rooms, and a glacial ice fountain, plus a calming relaxation area with heated tiled beds, and an acupuncture center.

CELEBRITY FLORA
NYR

THIS IS THE FIRST SHIP BUILT SPECIFICALLY FOR GALÁPAGOS CRUISING AND DISCOVERY

Size:	Boutique Ship	Passenger/Crew Ratio (lower beds):	2.0
Tonnage:	5,739	Cabins (total):	50
Cruise Line:	Celebrity Cruises	Size Range (sq ft/m):	333.6–1,291.7/31.0–120.0
Former Names:	none	Cabins (for one person):	50
Builder:	De Hoop (Netherlands)	Cabins with balcony:	29
Entered Service:	May 2019	Cabins (wheelchair accessible):	0
Length (ft/m):	333.0/101.5	Wheelchair accessibility:	None
Propulsion/Propellers:	diesel/2	Elevators:	1
Total Crew:	50	Casino (gaming tables):	No
Passengers (lower beds):	100	Self-Service Launderette:	No
Passenger Space Ratio (lower beds):	53.7	Onboard currency:	US$

THE SHIP. Small and smart, *Celebrity Flora* is designed specifically for cruising around the Galápagos islands in contemporary comfort (year-round). Four cost-extra private cabanas are located on deck outdoors.

The interior decor displays South American tastes in modern form, with earthy colors. The main public rooms include the Discovery Lounge, which acts as a lecture room; the Observatory – a lounge with wrap-around windows and a few bookshelves with Galápagos-related wildlife books and reference material. Because it's a boutique ship, the deck height is low.

The ship provides a good base for the rigorously programmed island-hopping wildlife experience, with small-group shore excursions in Zodiac inflatable led by Ecuadorian guides. Upon return, waiters greet you with refreshing drinks and towels. Included in the cruise price: excursions, gratuities to shipboard staff, house wine, Champagne, liquor, beer, and soda.

BERLITZ'S RATINGS		
	Possible	Achieved
Ship	500	NYR
Accommodation	200	NYR
Food	400	NYR
Service	400	NYR
Entertainment	100	NYR
Cruise Experience	400	NYR
OVERALL SCORE NYR points out of 2000		

ACCOMMODATION. There are numerous accommodation price grades. The price you pay depends on the size, location, and grade you choose. From the smallest cabin (all have outside views, and some have real or virtual balconies) to the largest Penthouse Suite, you simply pay more for more space.

DINING. The Seaside Restaurant seats everyone in a single open seating, but thick pillars impede the sight lines to the windows. It's bistro-style, so there are no tablecloths. While the cuisine is marginally international, it focuses mainly on the region, depending on the availability of local ingredients.

Outdoors is the Ocean Grill, for burgers, hot dogs, plus other fast food and salad items.

ENTERTAINMENT. The Galápagos is the entertainment (well, the wildlife is).

SPA/FITNESS. This consists of a massage room and small fitness room, with two hot tubs on an open deck.

CELEBRITY INFINITY
★★★+

THIS FAMILY-FRIENDLY, MODERN RESORT SHIP HAS PLENTY OF STYLE

Size:	Mid-size Ship
Tonnage:	90,940
Cruise Line:	Celebrity Cruises
Former Names:	Infinity
Builder:	Chantiers de l'Atlantique (France)
Entered Service:	Mar 2001
Length (ft/m):	964.5/294.0
Propulsion/Propellers:	gas turbine (39,000kW)/2 azimuthing pods
Total Crew:	999
Passengers (lower beds):	2,170
Passenger Space Ratio (lower beds):	41.9
Passenger/Crew Ratio (lower beds):	2.1
Cabins (total):	1,085
Size Range (sq ft/m):	165.1–2,530.0/15.34–235.0
Cabins (for one person):	0
Cabins with balcony:	606
Cabins (wheelchair accessible):	26 (17 with private balcony)
Wheelchair accessibility:	Best
Elevators:	12
Casino (gaming tables):	Yes
Self-Service Launderette:	No
Onboard currency:	US$

THE SHIP. Celebrity Infinity is a sister ship to Celebrity Constellation, Celebrity Millennium, and Celebrity Summit. Famous megayacht designer Jon Bannenberg created the exterior.

The atrium is the interior focal point; three decks high, it houses the reception desk, tour desk, and bank. Four glass-walled elevators travel through the ship's exterior (port) side, connecting the atrium with another seven decks, thus connecting 10 passenger decks, including the tender stations – a nice ride.

Michael's Club, which was a cigar smoker's haven when the ship was new, is now a pleasant, comfortable lounge for suite-grade occupants only.

Gaming sports include the ship's overly large Fortunes Casino, with blackjack, roulette, and slot machines, and lots of bright lights and action.

The ship provides a wide range of choices and possibilities. Travel in one of the suites and you will receive the highest level of personal service, while cruising in non-suite accommodation is much like in any ship. It all depends how much you are willing (and able) to pay. The two-seating dining and two nightly shows detract from an otherwise excellent product. A 15 percent gratuity is added to bar and wine accounts. Note that a charge of $3.95 for room service applies between 11pm and 6am.

ACCOMMODATION. There are many price grades from which to choose, depending on your prefer-

BERLITZ'S RATINGS	Possible	Achieved
Ship	500	355
Accommodation	200	148
Food	400	255
Service	400	279
Entertainment	100	71
Cruise Experience	400	262
OVERALL SCORE 1370 points out of 2000		

ence for size and location. These include Standard Interior (no view) and Outside View Cabins (with or without balcony) to spacious suite grades named Aqua, Concierge, Royal, Celebrity, and Penthouse. There are also wheelchair-accessible cabins (all with wheel-in showers), positioned close to elevators.

All accommodation grades are very comfortable, but suites, naturally, have more space. If you choose a balcony cabin on one of the upper decks, note that it could be shaded under the pool deck, which extends over the ship's side – and by many balconies (so, not good for private sunbathing).

DINING. The 1,170-seat Trellis Restaurant is the main dining room. It is two decks high; a grand staircase connects the two levels. A huge glass wall overlooks the sea at the stern (electrically operated shades provide several different backdrops), and a musicians' gallery on the upper level. There are two seatings for dinner (open seating for breakfast and lunch), at tables for two to 10. The dining room, like all large dining halls, can be extremely noisy. Menu variety is good, the food has taste, and it is attractively presented and served in an orchestrated fashion with European traditions and training. Full-service, in-cabin dining is also available for all meals, including dinner.

Suite occupants can dine in the exclusive setting of 'Luminae,' which features tableside preparation of signature dishes, an eclectic menu, and a selection of over 400 wines.

Blu, located on the port side of the upper level entrance of the Trellis dining room, is exclusively for the use of occupants of Aqua-class accommodation.

The former United States Restaurant, adjacent to the main lobby, is now the Tuscan Grille. The extra-cost, reservations-required venue features Kobe beef and premium-quality steaks, and includes a dine-in wine cellar and a demonstration galley.

Qsine is an extra-cost, reservations-required, tablecloth-free 'fun-food' restaurant, with digital food and wine menus that include cute foodie video snaps. It's all about quirky, multi-flavor, multi-color small-bite items that tease the taste buds. The 'show business' food is presented in unusual ways – even on sticks – rather like 'lollipop' cuisine.

Oceanview Café is a self-serve buffet-style eatery with around 750 seats, featuring various food stations and do-it-yourself options. Pizzas are made fresh on board and do not come ready-made for reheating, as with many cruise lines. There is also an outdoor grill, adjacent to the swimming pool, for fast-food items.

For Champagne and caviar lovers, not to mention Martinis, Carlisle's is the place to see and be seen.

Café al Bacio & Gelateria, on the uppermost (third) level of the atrium lobby, is for (extra-cost) coffees, pastries, cakes, and ice creams, while Sushi on Five features extra-cost sushi and cooked items including noodle and hot pot dishes.

ENTERTAINMENT. The 900-seat Celebrity Theater (showlounge) features production shows and major cabaret acts. Spanning three decks, it has seating on all three levels.

SPA/FITNESS. Canyon Ranch SpaClub facilities include a large thalassotherapy pool under a glass dome, with a 'health' bar for light breakfasts and lunches and freshly squeezed juices.

CELEBRITY MILLENNIUM
★★★+

THIS MID-SIZE, FAMILY-FRIENDLY SHIP HAS A TOUCH OF CLASS

Size:	Mid-size Ship	Passenger/Crew Ratio (lower beds):	2.1
Tonnage:	90,940	Cabins (total):	1,079
Cruise Line:	Celebrity Cruises	Size Range (sq ft/m):	170.0–2,350.0/15.7–235.0
Former Names:	Millennium	Cabins (for one person):	0
Builder:	Chantiers de l'Atlantique (France)	Cabins with balcony:	606
Entered Service:	Jun 2000	Cabins (wheelchair accessible):	26
Length (ft/m):	964.5/294.0	Wheelchair accessibility:	Best
Propulsion/Propellers:	gas turbine (39,000kW)/2 azimuthing pods	Elevators:	12
		Casino (gaming tables):	Yes
Total Crew:	999	Self-Service Launderette:	No
Passengers (lower beds):	2,158	Onboard currency:	US$
Passenger Space Ratio (lower beds):	42.1		

THE SHIP. *Celebrity Millennium* is a sister ship to *Celebrity Constellation, Celebrity Infinity,* and *Celebrity Summit.* Sadly, there is no walk-around wooden promenade deck outdoors. There are cushioned pads for poolside deck lounge chairs only, but not for chairs on other outside decks. Passenger participation activities are mostly amateurish.

The interiors exude understated elegance, with high-quality decor and materials (wood, glass, and marble) and a four-deck-high atrium. It hosts the reception desk, tour operator's desk, and bank. Four glass-walled elevators travel through 10 decks (including the tender stations).

Located directly in front of the main funnel, and with glass walls overlooking the ship's side, is a sports bar, Extreme; somehow, however, it just doesn't belong. Gaming sports include the overly large Fortunes Casino.

Aqua-class veranda cabins and Blu, a Mediterranean-themed specialty restaurant for Aqua-class passengers, were added when the ship was 'solsticized' in 2012. Also added were a Celebrity iLounge (for Apple products and computer classes); a Martini Bar with frosted bar top; Cellar-Masters wine bar; QSine, a quirky, extra-cost dining venue; and Bistro on Five crêperie. In 2019, the ship underwent a refurbishment, which refreshed all accommodation and dining venues. More suites/cabins were added, as was more seating in the main dining room. The

BERLITZ'S RATINGS

	Possible	Achieved
Ship	500	354
Accommodation	200	148
Food	400	255
Service	400	288
Entertainment	100	71
Cruise Experience	400	265

OVERALL SCORE 1381 points out of 2000

Wi-Fi is better (faster), and so is the more open layout of the self-serve Oceanview Café.

Celebrity Millennium delivers a well-defined North American cruise vacation at a relatively modest price, for the whole family.

ACCOMMODATION. Choose from either suite-grade or non-suite-grade accommodation, depending on your preference for the size and location. These include standard interior (no-view) and outside-view cabins (with or without balcony) to spacious suite grades (Aqua, Concierge, Royal, Celebrity, and Penthouse). There are also wheelchair-accessible cabins (all with wheel-in showers), close to elevators.

All accommodation grades are comfortable; suites, naturally, have more space. If you choose a balcony cabin on one of the upper decks, note that it could be shaded under the pool deck, which extends over the ship's side – and by many balconies (so, not good for private sunbathing). Some suites have extremely large balconies (always check the deck plan before choosing). Note that a charge for room service applies between 11pm and 6am.

DINING. The Metropolitan Restaurant is the main dining room with over 1,200 seats. Two decks high, it has a grand staircase connecting the two levels, and a huge glass wall aft overlooking the sea. There are two dinner seatings (open seating for breakfast and lunch), at tables for two to 10. Menu variety is good; the food is tasty and is attractively presented. Full-service, in-cabin dining is also available, with dinner menu items from the Metropolitan Restaurant.

Suite occupants dine in Luminae, with tableside preparation of some dishes, an eclectic menu, and a selection of over 400 wines.

Blu is exclusively for the use of Aqua-class occupants.

Celebrity Cruises created its first 'alternative' restaurant aboard this ship (it was the Olympic Restaurant, named after White Star Line's transatlantic ocean liner) but this has since been turned into the Tuscan Grill. There's also a dine-in wine cellar and a demonstration galley.

Oceanview Café is a self-serve buffet-style eatery with around 750 seats, featuring various food stations and do-it-yourself options. Pizzas are made on board and do not come ready-made for reheating, as with many cruise lines. There is also an outdoor grill, adjacent to the swimming pool, for fast-food items.

Café al Bacio & Gelateria, on the uppermost (third) level of the atrium lobby, is for (extra-cost) coffees, pastries, cakes, and ice creams, while Bistro on Five features extra-cost sushi, noodle and hot pot dishes.

ENTERTAINMENT. The 900-seat Celebrity Theater (showlounge) features production shows and major cabaret acts. Spanning three decks, it has seating on all three levels.

SPA/FITNESS. Canyon Ranch SpaClub facilities include a large thalassotherapy pool under a glass dome, a 'health' bar for light breakfast and lunch items and freshly squeezed juices.

CELEBRITY REFLECTION
★★★★

A PREMIUM-QUALITY SHIP FOR FAMILY-FRIENDLY CRUISING IN CONTEMPORARY STYLE

Size:	Large Resort Ship	Passenger/Crew Ratio (lower beds):	2.3
Tonnage:	125,366	Cabins (total):	1,523
Cruise Line:	Celebrity Cruises	Size Range (sq ft/m):	182.9–1,668.4/17.0–155.0
Former Names:	none	Cabins (for one person):	0
Builder:	Meyer Werft (Germany)	Cabins with balcony:	1,216
Entered Service:	Oct 2012	Cabins (wheelchair accessible):	30
Length (ft/m):	1,047.2/319.2	Wheelchair accessibility:	Best
Propulsion/Propellers:	diesel (70,500kW)/2 azimuthing pods	Elevators:	12
		Casino (gaming tables):	Yes
Total Crew:	1,271	Self-Service Launderette:	No
Passengers (lower beds):	3,046	Onboard currency:	US$
Passenger Space Ratio (lower beds):	41.1		

THE SHIP. *Celebrity Reflection* has a steeply sloping stern with a mega-yacht-style ducktail platform above the propulsion pods. It's attractive, and nicely balanced (the hull is 2ft (0.6m) wider, and has an additional deck, although the ship's superstructure is the same width, as *Celebrity Silhouette*).

Behind the funnels, the ship recreates the great outdoors with a Lawn Club, with real grass. You can go putting, play croquet or bocce ball (similar to boules), picnic on the grass, or walk barefoot. On the open deck, 'The Alcoves' are extra-cost 'private' Wi-Fi-equipped cabanas.

Celebrity Reflection has a larger number of passengers than *Celebrity Silhouette*, but the same number of elevators and an additional deck. The ship's name is positioned directly under the navigation bridge and not forward on the bows (for space reasons), and the rounded bows accommodate a helicopter winch pad.

Several pool and water-play areas are on Resort Deck: one under a glass-roofed solarium (with Aqua Café for light healthy bites). There's a sports pool, a family pool, and a wet zone. The open deck and sunning space around the main pool, however, isn't large enough for the number of passengers carried, although there are several other outdoor areas, including a music-free Solstice Deck high atop the ship – a nice space in which to relax.

The interior spaces are well designed, and the flow is good; most entertainment rooms are positioned forward, and dining venues are located aft.

BERLITZ'S RATINGS

	Possible	Achieved
Ship	500	390
Accommodation	200	160
Food	400	258
Service	400	285
Entertainment	100	73
Cruise Experience	400	282

OVERALL SCORE 1448 points out of 2000

Celebrity's signature Martini Bar has a frosted bar and carries over 100 varieties of vodka, as well as Martinis. It's lively (noisy) and can get congested, but it can be a lot of fun, as can the Molecular Bar, with its special mixologist concoctions.

Cellar Masters, which is hosted by a sommelier, provides a cozy space with list is extensive, and drinks are served in Riedel glasses.

A two-deck library is an open-ended space (operated on an 'honor' system – so you can check out a book 24/7), though books on the upper of 12 shelves are just for show.

Fortunes Casino is a gaming room with multiple tables for serious players and 235 slot machines. It is open sided, so anyone passing is subject to noise from the slot machines.

Elevator call buttons are in a floor-stand 'pod,' and, when an elevator arrives, a glass panel above it turns from blue to pink, which is fun. Also notable is a collection of designer chairs and sunloungers in various locations, although some are on the impractical side of comfort.

Public rooms include an Art Studio, for the budding artist in you (classes and projects are at extra cost). Have a look along the 'dining walkway,' where several specialty restaurants are located. Two pieces of art stand out: one is a delightful optical illusion, by Anthony James, featuring seemingly never-ending (kiln-dried) birch trees, set within glass-sided, mirrored boxes); the other is a fascinating video art piece that tells a story about a man, his flashlight, a forest, and things that happen – I won't tell you more – you'll simply have to experience it for yourself.

Passenger niggles include lack of usable drawer space in standard-grade cabins; congestion when exiting the showlounge after a show; and the noise level in all areas of the lobby (which has a marble dance floor), particularly when the Martini Bar on the deck above is busy. Gratuities are automatically charged to your onboard account.

ACCOMMODATION. The accommodation is both practical and comfortable. There are numerous price grades, depending on size and location. In non-suite-grades there is little space between the bed and the wall, but all include twin beds convertible to a queen- or king-size bed with premium bedding, sitting area, and vanity desk with hairdryer, but little drawer space. Although closets have good hanging space, other storage space is limited. Bathrooms have a shower enclosure, toilet, and tiny washbasin. A charge for room service now applies between 11pm and 6am.

Cabins 1551–1597 on the port side and 1556–1602 on the starboard side on Penthouse Deck (Deck 12) suffer from 'aircraft carrier' syndrome because they are directly under the overhanging Resort Deck. They have little exposure to sun or light, so sunbathing is out. Thick supporting struts ruin the view from these cabins, which are otherwise pleasant enough.

Other accommodation grades are: Veranda, Family Veranda, Concierge, Ocean View, and Interior cabins (no view). Suite-grade categories are: Aqua, Sky, Celebrity, Royal, and Penthouse. Suites have more space and larger balconies with good-quality sunloungers, and more personal amenities.

DINING. Meals in Opus, the expansive two-level, 1,454-seat main dining room, are included in the cruise price. It has ocean views on the port and starboard sides, and two seating times; anyone choosing 'Celebrity Select Dining' is usually assigned to the upper level. It's contemporary, and, despite its size, very comfortable. A two-deck-high wine tower is a great focal point.

The cuisine is creative, trendy, and slightly more health-oriented (i.e. less reliance on salt and food modifiers) than that of some competitors. If you like to eat in different venues instead of the main dining room, dining packages are available, so you can 'dine around.' These venues provide options for something different.

Suite occupants dine in Luminae, with tableside preparation of signature dishes, an eclectic menu, and a selection of over 400 wines.

Blu is a 128-seat restaurant for Aqua-class cabin occupants.

Murano is an extra-cost, 72-seat, reservations-required dinner venue (with tablecloths), offering high-quality cuisine with a French flair, fine table settings and Riedel wine glasses.

Tuscan Grille is an extra-cost, tablecloth-free venue, for Italian cuisine and premium steaks. It has nicely curved archways – like a high-tech winery. Large aft-facing windows offer a great view.

Qsine is a 90-seat 'fun-food' venue, with multi-flavored, multi-colored, small-bite items presented in a quirky fashion – even on sticks.

Sushi on Five offers extra-cost sushi, noodle and hot pot dishes. Close by is Café al Bacio & Gelateria, a coffee lounge for Lavazza Italian coffees.

Oceanview Café and Grill is a casual, tray-free self-serve buffet venue with a number of food islands and good signage.

AquaSpa Café provides light, healthier options, while the Mast Bar Grill and Bar is an outdoor fast-food venue.

For something different, try the Lawn Club Grill, a patio-style, glass-covered, outdoor lean-to-style venue that overlooks the lawn and reservable cabanas. It's *the* place to go for grilled steaks, lamb chops, and seafood dishes. You can even grill the food to your liking – with a chef at your side, of course.

Close by is The Porch (an enclosed venue), on the starboard side, for paninis and light bites throughout the day (including breakfast, with delightful fruit muffins and pastry items).

Oceanview Café and Grill is an expansive, tray-free, casual self-serve buffet. A number of food 'islands' help to prevent lines, and the flow is good; the signage is clear and concise. A wide variety of food items is available, and plates are available at each of the 'islands' and cooking stations (such as 'Eggs and More' for breakfast). However, it *is* challenging to get a warm plate for hot food items.

Try the Elegant Champagne High Tea in Murano. Presented once each cruise (usually on a sea day), it comes with a choice of teas and tisanes, a three-tier stand of finger sandwiches and pastry items, plus scones, clotted cream, and a glass of Perrier Jouet Champagne.

ENTERTAINMENT. The 1,160-seat Reflection Theater (showlounge) has a main level and two balconied sections set amphitheater-style around the stage, with good sightlines. Colorful nights are held in the Sky Observation Lounge, where the minimalist decor (relaxing by day) is transformed at night with mood lighting. Celebrity Central hosts adult-only stand-up comedy, cooking demonstrations, enrichment lectures, and feature films. Ensemble Lounge is a big-band-era-style cocktail lounge with live jazz.

SPA/FITNESS. The Canyon Ranch SpaClub at Sea is spread over two decks. A large fitness center includes kinesis equipment, plus all the familiar muscle-pumping machinery.

An extra-cost (free to occupants of AquaSpa-grade accommodation) unisex thermal suite contains several steam and shower mist rooms, and a glacial ice fountain, plus a calming relaxation area with heated tiled beds. Additionally, a small fitness 'suite' (for two) can be rented, so you can exercise in privacy.

CELEBRITY SILHOUETTE
★★★★

THIS PREMIUM LARGE SHIP HAS CONTEMPORARY DECOR AND IS QUITE STYLISH

Size:	Large Resort Ship	Passenger/Crew Ratio (lower beds):	2.3
Tonnage:	122,210	Cabins (total):	1,443
Cruise Line:	Celebrity Cruises	Size Range (sq ft/m):	182.9–1,668.4/17.0–155.0
Former Names:	none	Cabins (for one person):	0
Builder:	Meyer Werft (Germany)	Cabins with balcony:	1,216
Entered Service:	Jul 2011	Cabins (wheelchair accessible):	30
Length (ft/m):	1,047.2/319.2	Wheelchair accessibility:	Best
Propulsion/Propellers:	diesel (70,500kW)/2 azimuthing pods	Elevators:	12
		Casino (gaming tables):	Yes
Total Crew:	1,210	Self-Service Launderette:	No
Passengers (lower beds):	2,886	Onboard currency:	US$
Passenger Space Ratio (lower beds):	42.3		

THE SHIP. *Celebrity Silhouette* looks sleek, with its two slim funnels. Behind them is the great outdoors and Lawn Club, an area with real Bermudan grass. You can putt, play croquet or bocce ball (similar to boules), picnic on the grass, and enjoy walking around barefoot. Part of the Lawn Club is an interactive Lawn Club Grill, while The Porch is a 48-seat eatery overlooking the lawn, for complimentary breakfast and lunches, plus specialty coffees, wine, and beer (at extra cost).

Near the Lawn Club entrance is an Art Studio, for demonstrations and classes on various topics. Some are free, some cost extra.

Resort Deck has several water-play areas, one within a glass-roofed solarium. However, deck space around the two pools is small, considering the number of passengers carried. For open deck privacy, try 'The Alcoves'; these are garden cabanas for two to four persons, positioned on the lawn (naturally, they cost extra).

Michael's Club, an intimate lounge with classic English leather club chairs and a handsome fireplace, is for suite-grade occupants only.

Most entertainment rooms are positioned forward, with dining venues located aft. There's a wine bar; a jazz-age cocktail lounge; a bar with the look of an ocean-going yacht; Quasar, a bar with a nightly light show synchronized to music; and an observation lounge with a dance floor.

BERLITZ'S RATINGS		
	Possible	Achieved
Ship	500	387
Accommodation	200	159
Food	400	258
Service	400	286
Entertainment	100	73
Cruise Experience	400	280

OVERALL SCORE 1443 points out of 2000

The two-deck library is a delightful open-ended space. The card room – located in the center of the ship – has no ocean-view windows to distract players, but it attracts noise from adjacent areas, so it's almost useless as a serious card-playing room. Fortunes Casino (non-smoking) has gaming tables and slot machines.

Celebrity's signature Martini Bar carries over 100 varieties of vodka, as well as Martinis, of course. There's also a small alcove called Crush, with an ice-filled table where you can participate in caviar- and vodka-tasting, or host a private party. It's noisy and congested, but can be a lot of fun.

Passenger niggles include lack of usable drawer space in cabins; inadequate children's facilities and staff during school holidays; congestion when you exit the showlounge; and noise in all areas of the lobby when the Martini Bar is busy.

Gratuities are charged to your onboard account.

ACCOMMODATION. The accommodation is both practical and comfortable. There are numerous price grades, depending on size and location.

In non-suite-grade cabins there is little space between the bed and the wall, but all accommodation includes twin beds convertible to a queen- or king-size bed with premium bedding, a sitting area, and vanity desk with hairdryer, but little drawer space. Although closets have good hanging space, other storage space is limited. Bathrooms have a shower enclosure, toilet, and tiny washbasin. A charge for room service applies between 11pm and 6am.

Note that cabins 1551–1597 on the port side and 1556–1602 on the starboard side on Penthouse Deck (Deck 11) suffer from 'aircraft carrier' syndrome because they are directly under the overhanging Resort Deck. They have little exposure to sun or light, so sunbathing is out of the question. Many thick supporting struts ruin the view from these cabins, which are otherwise pleasant enough.

Other cabin accommodation grades are: Veranda; Family Veranda; Concierge; Ocean View; and Interior (no view). Suite-grade categories are: Aqua; Sky; Celebrity; Royal; and Penthouse. Suites have much more space, plus larger balconies with good-quality sunloungers, and more personal amenities than standard cabins.

DINING. Eating at Grand Cuvée, the ship's 1,430-seat main dining room, is included in the cruise price. It has ocean views on the port and starboard sides, and two seating times; anyone choosing 'Celebrity Select Dining' is usually assigned to the upper level. It's contemporary, and, despite its size, very comfortable. A two-deck-high wine tower is a great focal point.

Suite occupants dine in Luminae, with tableside preparation of signature dishes, an eclectic menu, and a selection of over 400 wines.

Blu is a 128-seat specialty restaurant, with tablecloths, exclusively for Aqua-class cabin occupants. It has pleasing but rather cool decor.

Murano is an extra-cost, 72-seat, reservations-required dinner venue (with tablecloths), offering high-quality traditional dining with a French flair, fine table settings and Riedel wine glasses. The food, its preparation and presentation, and the service are excellent.

Tuscan Grille is an extra-cost, tablecloth-free venue, for Italian cuisine, Kobe beef and premium-quality steaks. It has nicely curved archways – like a high-tech winery. Large aft-facing windows offer a great view.

Qsine is a 90-seat 'fun-food' venue, with multi-flavored, multi-colored, quirky small-bite items pre-sented in quirky fashion – even on sticks – sort of 'lollipop' cuisine.

Sushi on Five offers extra-cost sushi, noodle and hot pot dishes. Close by is Café al Bacio & Gelateria, a coffee lounge featuring Lavazza Italian coffee.

Oceanview Café and Grill is an expansive, tray-free, casual self-serve buffet. A number of food 'islands' help to prevent lines, and the flow is good; the signage is clear and concise. A wide variety of food items are on offer, and plates are available at each of the 'islands' and cooking stations (such as 'Eggs and More' for breakfast). However, it *is* challenging to get a warm plate for hot food items.

AquaSpa Café is for lighter options – low-salt dishes, including salad items – and grilled items like salmon and chicken.

The Mast Bar Grill and Bar is an outside fast-food venue.

ENTERTAINMENT. Celebrity Theater is a three-deck-high, 900-seat venue for production shows and major cabaret acts.

Theme nights are held in the Observation Lounge (whose daytime bland and minimalist decor comes alive at night), while 200-seat Celebrity Central hosts comedy, cooking demonstrations, lectures, and films.

The Entertainment Court showcases street performers, psychics, and caricaturists; it's in the center of the ship, linked to Quasar, a high-pulse, high-volume nightclub, while Ensemble Lounge is a big-band-era cocktail lounge with live music.

SPA/FITNESS. Canyon Ranch SpaClub at Sea includes a large thalassotherapy pool under a solarium glass dome, with a health bar for light food and fresh squeezed juices.

Facilities include 25 treatment rooms, including one for wheelchair-users. There's also an aerobics room, a gymnasium, large men's and women's saunas with a sizable ocean-view window, and a beauty salon.

An extra-cost (free to occupants of Aqua-grade accommodation) unisex thermal suite contains several steam and shower mist rooms and a glacial ice fountain, plus a calming relaxation area with heated tiled beds.

CELEBRITY SOLSTICE
★★★★

THIS SHIP HAS ELEGANT, UNDERSTATED DECOR IN A SEMI-PREMIUM SETTING

Size:	Large Resort Ship	Passenger/Crew Ratio (lower beds):	2.3
Tonnage:	121,878	Cabins (total):	1,426
Cruise Line:	Celebrity Cruises	Size Range (sq ft/m):	182.9–1,668.4/17.0–155.0
Former Names:	none	Cabins (for one person):	0
Builder:	Meyer Werft (Germany)	Cabins with balcony:	1,216
Entered Service:	Nov 2008	Cabins (wheelchair accessible):	30
Length (ft/m):	1,033.4/315.0	Wheelchair accessibility:	Best
Propulsion/Propellers:	diesel (67,200kW)/2 azimuthing pods	Elevators:	12
		Casino (gaming tables):	Yes
Total Crew:	1,210	Self-Service Launderette:	No
Passengers (lower beds):	2,852	Onboard currency:	US$
Passenger Space Ratio (lower beds):	42.7		

THE SHIP. *Celebrity Solstice* is a sleek-looking ship, with two slim funnels. The vessel has a steeply sloping stern; this includes a mega-yacht-style ducktail platform above the propulsion pods. The ship's name is positioned directly under the navigation bridge and not forward on the bows (for space reasons). A novel feature is an outdoor grass area (Lawn Club) that's open to all, so you can go putting, play croquet or bocce ball, or have a picnic on the grass, or walk barefoot.

Several pool and water-play areas are on Resort Deck; one within a glass-roofed solarium, sports pool, family pool, and fun wet zone. However, the space around the pools isn't large enough for the number of passengers carried.

The interior spaces are well designed; the decor is elegant yet contemporary. Most entertainment rooms are positioned forward, with dining venues mostly aft.

There's a wine bar with a sommelier; a pre-dinner cocktail lounge that reflects the jazz age of the 1930s; a bar with the look of an ocean-going yacht; Quasar, a retro bar with large screens that create a nightly light show synchronized to music; and an observation lounge with a dance floor.

Celebrity's signature Martini Bar has over 100 varieties of vodka, as well as Martinis. A small alcove (Crush) has an ice-filled table where you can participate in caviar- and vodka-tasting. It's noisy and congested, but fun.

BERLITZ'S RATINGS		
	Possible	Achieved
Ship	500	386
Accommodation	200	161
Food	400	258
Service	400	293
Entertainment	100	72
Cruise Experience	400	280

OVERALL SCORE 1450 points out of 2000

A two-deck library is a delightful open-ended space, though books on upper shelves are impossible to reach. The card room – located in the center of the ship, with no ocean-view windows to distract players – is open to noise from adjacent areas, so it's useless as a serious card playing room. Fortunes Casino (non-smoking) has gaming tables and 200 slot machines.

A Hot Glass Show, housed in an outdoor studio on the open deck as part of the Lawn Club and created in collaboration with Corning Museum of Glass, includes a novel glass-blowing show.

Public rooms include an Art Studio.

The Alcoves are extra-cost 'private' Wi-Fi-equipped cabanas on deck.

Niggles include cabin drawer space; limited children's facilities and staff during school holidays; congestion when you exit the showlounge; and noise in the lobby when the Martini Bar is busy. Gratuities are charged to your onboard account.

ACCOMMODATION. The accommodation is practical and comfortable. There are numerous price grades, depending on size and location.

In non-suite-grade cabins there is little space between the bed and the wall, but all cabins have twin beds convertible to a queen- or king-size bed with premium bedding, sitting area, and vanity desk with hairdryer, but little drawer space, although closets have good hanging space. Bathrooms have a shower enclosure, toilet, and tiny washbasin. A charge of $3.95 for room service applies between 11pm and 6am.

Note: cabins 1551–1597 (port side) and 1556–1602 (starboard side) on Penthouse Deck (Deck 11) are directly under the overhanging Resort Deck above. There's little exposure to sun or light, so sunbathing is out of the question. Many thick supporting struts ruin the view from these cabins, which are otherwise pleasant.

Other accommodation grades are: Veranda; Family Veranda; Concierge; Ocean View; and Interior cabins (no view). Suite-grade categories are: Aqua; Sky; Celebrity; Royal; and Penthouse. Suites have much more space, plus larger balconies with good-quality sunloungers, and more personal amenities than standard cabins.

DINING. Grand Epernay (main dining room), located aft, has ocean views on two sides, and a two-deck-high wine tower. The design is contemporary, but the almost-backless tub-style chairs are uncomfortable. The food is disappointing; the decreased quality all too obvious to Celebrity's repeat passengers.

Suite occupants dine in Luminae, with tableside preparation of signature dishes, an eclectic menu, and a selection of over 400 wines.

Blu is a 130-seat specialty restaurant for occupants of Aqua-class cabins. The room has pleasing (but rather cold) blue decor.

Tuscan Grille, an extra-cost, reservations-required venue, serves Kobe beef and high-quality steaks.

Qsine is a casual spot offering quirky small-bite, 'fun-food' cuisine.

The Lawn Club Grill, located on an open upper deck, is for cook-your-own steaks and seafood.

Bistro on Five has extra-cost sushi and cooked items, including noodles and hot pot dishes.

Café al Bacio & Gelateria, on one side of the main lobby, is a small coffeehouse for Lavazza Italian coffee; lines quickly form at peak times.

Oceanview Café and Grill is an expansive, tray-free, casual self-serve buffet. A number of food 'islands' help prevent lines, and the flow is good; the signage clear and concise. A wide variety of food items is available, with plates stacked at each 'island' and cooking station (such as 'Eggs and More' for breakfast). However, it *is* challenging to get a warm plate for hot food items.

AquaSpa Café is for lighter options – low-salt dishes, including salad items and grilled fish and meats.

ENTERTAINMENT. The 1,115-seat Solstice Theatre, stages custom-designed production shows, while colorful theme nights are put on in the Observation Lounge. Celebrity Central (200 seats) hosts comedy, cooking demos, enrichment lectures, and feature films while Quasar is a high-pulse, high-volume nightclub. The Ensemble Lounge is a big-band-era cocktail lounge with live jazz.

SPA/FITNESS. Canton Ranch SpaClub at Sea is spread over two decks. A large fitness center includes high-tech workout and muscle-pumping equipment. An extra-cost, unisex thermal suite has several steam and fragrant shower mist rooms, a glacial ice fountain, and calming relaxation area with heated tiled beds.

CELEBRITY SUMMIT
★★★+

A PREMIUM-QUALITY MID-SIZE SHIP THAT IS GOOD FOR FAMILY-FRIENDLY CRUISING

Size:	Mid-size Ship	Passenger/Crew Ratio (lower beds):	2.1
Tonnage:	90,940	Cabins (total):	1,079
Cruise Line:	Celebrity Cruises	Size Range (sq ft/m):	165.1–2,530.0/15.34–235.0
Former Names:	Summit	Cabins (for one person):	0
Builder:	Chantiers de l'Atlantique (France)	Cabins with balcony:	606
Entered Service:	Oct 2001	Cabins (wheelchair accessible):	26 (17 with private
Length (ft/m):	964.5/294.0		balcony)
Propulsion/Propellers:	gas turbine (39,000kW)/2 azimuthing pods	Wheelchair accessibility:	Best
		Elevators:	12
Total Crew:	999	Casino (gaming tables):	Yes
Passengers (lower beds):	2,158	Self-Service Launderette:	No
Passenger Space Ratio (lower beds):	42.1	Onboard currency:	US$

THE SHIP. *Celebrity Summit* is a sister ship to *Celebrity Constellation*, *Celebrity Infinity*, and *Celebrity Millennium*. Mega-yacht designer Jon Bannenberg was responsible for the exterior, with its royal blue-and-white hull. In early 2012, the ship underwent a 'Solsticizing' program, which meant more cabins, more facilities, and more dining options to match the newer ships in the fleet, but no extra elevators. In 2019 the ship underwent an extensive refurbishment, refreshing the interior decor and enhancing the overall onboard experience, although not the food. Sadly the two-deck library has gone.

Inside, the ship has a similar standard of decor and materials to other ships in this group, and public rooms that are user-friendly. An atrium spans three decks and houses the reception desk, tour operator's desk, and bank. Four glass-walled elevators travel through the ship's exterior (port) side, connecting the atrium with another seven decks, traveling through 10 decks, including the tender stations – a nice ride.

Facilities include a combination Conference Center, an expansive shopping arcade with oodles of retail store space (with designer labels such as Fendi, Fossil, Hugo Boss, and Versace), a lavish four-deck-high showlounge with high-tech sound and lighting, card room, music-listening room, and an observation lounge/discotheque with fine views.

The Retreat (formerly Michael's Club) is now a lounge for suite-grade occupants only; it has large

BERLITZ'S RATINGS		
	Possible	Achieved
Ship	500	354
Accommodation	200	148
Food	400	253
Service	400	279
Entertainment	100	70
Cruise Experience	400	265
OVERALL SCORE 1369 points out of 2000		

leather chairs and a fireplace. An Internet café hosts a few computers and extra-cost Internet connectivity.

Gaming sports include the ship's overly large Fortunes Casino, with lots of bright lights and action. Families with children will appreciate the Fun Factory (for younger children) and The Tower (for teenagers). Children's counselors and youth activities staff provide a wide range of supervised activities. Overall, the ship's interiors are attractive.

ACCOMMODATION. There are many price grades from which to choose, depending on your preference for the size and location – and your budget. These include standard interior cabins (no view) and outside-view cabins (with or without balcony) to spacious suite grades named Aqua, Concierge, Royal, Celebrity, and Penthouse. There are also wheelchair-accessible cabins (all with wheel-in showers), positioned close to elevators.

All accommodation grades are very comfortable, but the suites, naturally, have more space. If you choose a balcony cabin on one of the upper decks, note that it could be shaded under the pool deck, which extends over the ship's side – and by many balconies (not good for private sunbathing). Some suites have extremely large balconies – always check the deck plan before choosing. Note that a charge for room service applies between 11pm and 6am.

DINING. The Cosmopolitan Restaurant is a 1,170-seat main dining room. It is two decks high with a grand staircase connecting the two levels and a huge glass wall overlooking the sea aft (electrically operated shades provide several different backdrops). There are two seatings for dinner (open seating for breakfast and lunch), at tables for two to 10.

Suite occupants dine in Luminae, a restaurant featuring tableside preparation of signature dishes, an eclectic menu, and a selection of over 400 wines.

Blu, located on the port side of the upper level entrance to the Cosmopolitan dining room, is exclusively for occupants of Aqua-class accommodation.

Tuscan Grille, an extra-cost, reservations-required venue features Kobe beef and premium-quality steaks, with a dine-in wine cellar and a demonstration galley.

Oceanview Café is large, very casual, self-serve buffet-style eatery with various food stations and do-it-yourself options. Pizzas are made freshly on board (no ready-made pizzas to be seen, as is the case with many cruise lines). There is also an outdoor grill, adjacent to the swimming pool, for fast-food items.

Café al Bacio & Gelateria, on the uppermost level of the atrium lobby, serves (extra-cost) coffees, pastries, cakes, and ice creams, while Sushi on Five features (extra-cost) sushi, noodle and hot pot dishes.

ENTERTAINMENT. The 900-seat Celebrity Theater (showlounge) features production shows and major cabaret acts. Spanning three decks, it has seating on all three levels and good sightlines.

SPA/FITNESS. The Spa by Canyon Ranch includes a large thalassotherapy pool under a glass dome, with a 'health' bar for light breakfasts and lunches and freshly squeezed juice, a thermal room, body-treatment rooms, fitness center, aerobics studio, and hair salon. Note that body treatments are extremely pricey.

CELEBRITY XPEDITION
★★★+

A MODESTLY COMFORTABLE SHIP FOR EXPERIENCING THE GALÁPAGOS ISLANDS

Size:	Boutique Ship	Passenger/Crew Ratio (lower beds):		1.4
Tonnage:	2,842	Cabins (total):		45
Cruise Line:	Celebrity Cruises	Size Range (sq ft/m):	156.0–460.0/14.5–42.7	
Former Names:	Sun Bay	Cabins (for one person):		0
Builder:	Cassens-Werft (Germany)	Cabins with balcony:		8
Entered Service:	Jun 2001/Jun 2004	Cabins (wheelchair accessible):		0
Length (ft/m):	290.3/88.5	Wheelchair accessibility:		None
Propulsion/Propellers:	diesel (3,000kW)/2	Elevators:		0
Total Crew:	64	Casino (gaming tables):		No
Passengers (lower beds):	90	Self-Service Launderette:		No
Passenger Space Ratio (lower beds):	31.5	Onboard currency:		US$

THE SHIP. This was the first specialist boutique ship for Celebrity Cruises and it is like a small private club for Galápagos ecotourism. It will suit mature adults who want an intimate and casual cruise experience, and, of course, to see the famous Galápagos Islands.

There is a surprisingly good amount of open deck space – much of it with teakwood decking, as well as teak sunloungers and patio furniture. Although there is no swimming pool, there is a whirlpool tub. Stabilizers were installed in 2004.

All accommodation is located in the forward half, with the public rooms aft. The ambience is unhurried, yet subtly elegant. Except for the dining room, which can double as a conference room, there is only one public room: the main lounge, complete with bar, dance floor, and bandstand.

Shore excursions by Zodiac inflatable boats are in small groups led by Ecuadorian guides. On your return, waiters greet you with refreshing drinks and towels. Included in the fare: excursions, gratuities to shipboard staff, beverages including house wine, Champagne, liquor, beer, and soda.

ACCOMMODATION. There are four price categories in two cabin types: nine Suites measuring 247 sq ft (23 sq m); 34 Comfort Cabins, 172 sq ft (16 sq m); and three Comfort Cabins, 156 sq ft (14.5 sq m). All suites and cabins have twin beds (four comfort cabins have double beds), TV, sofa, drinks

BERLITZ'S RATINGS		
	Possible	Achieved
Ship	500	261
Accommodation	200	129
Food	400	221
Service	400	235
Entertainment	100	40
Cruise Experience	400	210

OVERALL SCORE 1096 points out of 2000

table, vanity desk with hairdryer, minibar/refrigerator, and personal safe. Bathrooms all have a good-size shower enclosure (there are no tubs) with soap/shampoo dispenser and white marble-clad walls.

The largest accommodation is in nine suites, each with a private balcony. One suite has forward-facing views and a sloping ceiling with character. Balcony partitions are almost private; the balcony deck is teak covered. Two of the suites can be joined together. One bedroom has two pull-down Murphy beds.

DINING. The Darwin Dining Room operates on an open-seating basis. A self-serve buffet offers salads, cold cuts, and cheeses. House wines and beer are included in the fare; a few premium wines can be purchased. The cuisine depends on local suppliers; fish seafood and fruits are good, but vegetables are inconsistent. The casual, self-serve Seagull Buffet is just behind the main lounge, with teak tables and chairs.

ENTERTAINMENT. After-dinner conversation with fellow passengers is the main entertainment.

SPA/FITNESS. There is a small fitness room, and adjacent unisex sauna located inside on the uppermost deck, while a small beauty salon is located on the lowest deck.

CELESTYAL CRISTAL
★★+

A CASUAL SHIP WITH FRIENDLY CREW FOR PORT-INTENSIVE CRUISES

Size:	Mid-size Ship	
Tonnage:	25,611	
Cruise Line:	Celestyal Cruises	
Former Names:	Louis Crystal, Silja Opera, SuperStar Taurus, Leeward, Sally Albatross, Viking Saga	
Builder:	Wartsila (Finland)	
Entered Service:	1980/Jul 2007	
Length (ft/m):	530.5/161.7	
Propulsion/Propellers:	diesel (19,120kW)/2	
Total Crew:	400	
Passengers (lower beds):	966	
Passenger Space Ratio (lower beds):	26.5	
Passenger/Crew Ratio (lower beds):	2.4	
Cabins (total):	483	
Size Range (sq ft/m):	107.6–462.8/10.0–43.0	
Cabins (for one person):	0	
Cabins with balcony:	53	
Cabins (wheelchair accessible):	6	
Wheelchair accessibility:	None	
Elevators:	4	
Casino (gaming tables):	Yes	
Self-Service Launderette:	No	
Onboard currency:	Euros	

THE SHIP. Celestyal Cristal has a wedge-shaped profile with a squared-off stern and short, stubby bows. It benefits from a decent walk-around teak promenade deck. The pool deck is very cramped, although the pool itself can be covered by a sliding glass dome. There is no forward-facing observation lounge. There is a reasonable array of public rooms, lounges, bars, including a casino with gaming tables and slot machines, a convenience store, an overly large duty-free shop, and an internet center (Wi-Fi costs extra).

Celestyal Cristal should appeal to anyone seeking to cruise the Greek Islands in a modicum of comfort, and at a very modest price. The dress code is casual throughout, with no formal nights. The ship operates 3-, 4- and 7-day cruises (many of them with themes, including history, wine, food, and health). Drinks packages are available. Note that gratuities are not included in the fare.

ACCOMMODATION. There are three suite categories (Imperial, Balcony, and Junior), and a mix of several outside-view cabins (some of which have balconies) and interior cabins in numerous price grades.

The top-grade suites have neatly angled private balconies and provide a decent amount of space for short cruises; bathrooms have a tub, separate shower, and good storage facilities for personal toi-

BERLITZ'S RATINGS	Possible	Achieved
Ship	500	257
Accommodation	200	107
Food	400	202
Service	400	216
Entertainment	100	50
Cruise Experience	400	213
OVERALL SCORE 1045 points out of 2000		

letries, but most standard cabins and bathrooms are dimensionally challenged, and in need of updating. Soundproofing is poor. Some cabins have views obstructed by safety equipment.

DINING. Olympus Restaurant is the main dining room, but there are a number of other dining spots and casual eateries. There are two seatings for dinner on most nights (open seating for the first night), and open seating for breakfast and lunch. Seating and table assignments for dinner are made during embarkation.

Celestyal Cruises (a sub-brand of Louis Cruises) specializes in Greek regional cuisine. All tables are laid with crisp white linen. Spa and vegetarian dishes are available on lunch and dinner menus.

Amalthia is an L-shaped self-serve buffet restaurant for casual meals and snacks, with some excellent views aft. Other casual eateries include Aura and Leda Casual Dining venues, both located aft of the swimming pool.

ENTERTAINMENT. The Muses Lounge is the ship's showlounge; it spans two decks and has decent sight lines.

SPA/FITNESS. Sana Beauty facilities include a beauty salon, fitness room, and men's and women's saunas and steam rooms. Wellness and beauty treatments are available.

CELESTYAL OLYMPIA
★★+

A MODERATELY COMFORTABLE, FAMILY-FRIENDLY SHIP FOR CASUAL GREEK ISLAND CRUISING

Size:	Mid-size Ship	Passenger/Crew Ratio (lower beds):	2.6
Tonnage:	37,773	Cabins (total):	725
Cruise Line:	Celestyal Cruises	Size Range (sq ft/m):	118.4–425.1/11.0–39.5
Former Names:	Louis Olympia, Thomson Destiny,	Cabins (for one person):	0
	Sunbird, Song of America	Cabins with balcony:	9
Builder:	Wartsila (Finland)	Cabins (wheelchair accessible):	0
Entered Service:	Dec 1982/May 2012	Wheelchair accessibility:	Fair
Length (ft/m):	705.0/214.8	Elevators:	7
Propulsion/Propellers:	diesel (16,480kW)/2	Casino (gaming tables):	Yes
Total Crew:	540	Self-Service Launderette:	No
Passengers (lower beds):	1,450	Onboard currency:	Euros
Passenger Space Ratio (lower beds):	26.0		

THE SHIP. Originally built for Royal Caribbean International, the all-white ship has nicely rounded lines, a sharply raked bow, and a single funnel with a cantilevered, wraparound lounge – with excellent views.

There's good open deck and sunbathing space, but it gets crowded when the ship is full, which is most of the time. There are some nicely polished wooden decks and rails and two pools (aft for children, forward for adults).

The interior decor is bright and breezy, but dated, and most of the public rooms have high ceilings. All are located one deck above the dining room and include the main showlounge, casino, and nightclub. There's also a small conference center for meetings, plus an Internet café with computer terminals.

There are no cushioned pads for the sunloungers. Standing in line for embarkation, disembarkation, shore tenders, and for self-serve buffet meals is an inevitable aspect of cruising aboard all large ships. Passenger niggles include the dated look of the ship's interiors.

Celestyal Olympia is best suited to adult couples, families and solo travelers taking a first or second cruise in the Greek Islands and Mediterranean.

Overall, Celestyal Cruises provides a consistent, well-packaged product, but the ship is really dated.

ACCOMMODATION. This is provided in several categories and price bands: interior cabins (paral-

BERLITZ'S RATINGS		
	Possible	Achieved
Ship	500	269
Accommodation	200	108
Food	400	204
Service	400	219
Entertainment	100	50
Cruise Experience	400	214

OVERALL SCORE 1064 points out of 2000

lel or L-shaped bed arrangement), outside-view cabins (parallel or L-shaped bed arrangement), deluxe cabins (with parallel twin beds that can convert to a queen-size bed), suites, and Grand Suites.

Most cabins are of a similar size – dimensionally challenged when compared to newer ships, and soundproofing is poor. The cabins have mediocre closets and little storage space, yet somehow everyone seems to manage (take only casual clothes). You can store shoes and luggage under the bed.

Most bathrooms host a washbasin, toilet, tiny shower enclosure, and little space for toiletries.

In some cabins, twin beds are fixed in a parallel mode – some are moveable and can convert to a queen-size bed (others may be in an L-shape). In almost all cabins there is a threshold of about 9ins (23cm) at the bathroom door to step over.

For more space, book one of the deluxe-grade cabins on Promenade Deck. These have twin beds convertible to a queen-size bed, set diagonally into a sleeping area adjacent to outside-view windows. The bathroom has a half-size tub and shower; bathrobes are provided (the largest of these is cabin 7000).

For more exclusivity, try one of nine suites, all located in a private area, with fine wood paneling and trim, more space, and better service. The bathroom is tiled and has a full-size enamel tub (rare in ships today) with shower, a pink granite-look washbasin, and ample storage space for toiletries.

Suite occupants also get a semi-private balcony – with a door that is heavy and hard to open, drinks table and two teak chairs. Book one of the two Grand Suites, and you'll get even more room – plus views over the front and a larger balcony (although these can be overlooked from the open deck above), more floor space, and a walk-in closet. Missing are a bedside telephone and a bathroom telephone. Note that the accommodation deck hallways are very narrow on some decks.

DINING. The large, two-seatings Seven Seas Restaurant consists of a central main section and two long, slim wings – the Magellan Room and Galileo Room – with large, ocean-view windows, but a low ceiling creates a high level of ambient noise. There are tables for two to eight (window tables are for two or six).

The menus are very standard, and deviation is difficult. Bottled water costs extra. There is an adequate wine list, and most drink prices (including the wine) are modest.

The Veranda Café is for casual, self-serve breakfasts and lunches, but the outdoor tables and seats outdoors are of metal and plastic, and the buffets are basic and old-fashioned. The low cruise fare dictates the use of plastic cups and plastic stirrers – teaspoons are unheard of. At night you can 'dine' under the steel-and-canvas canopy, which makes a pleasant, outdoors alternative to the dining room – and includes waiter service.

The excellent Italian illy coffee brand is available, plus a selection of fine teas, in several bars and lounges (at extra cost).

ENTERTAINMENT. The single-level Can Can Lounge, the entertainment venue, has a stage and hardwood dance floor. The revue-style shows are typical of the end-of-pier variety type, with an energetic, well-meaning cast of young people who act as cruise staff by day, together with some professional cabaret acts.

Another, smaller room, the Oklahoma Lounge, has a stage and dance floor, and may be used to present late-night comedy and other acts.

SPA/FITNESS. Although the Sana Spa facilities are not exactly generous, they include a gymnasium, sauna (no steam room), changing rooms, and a beauty salon. Sports facilities include basketball, badminton, and table tennis.

CLUB MED 2
★★★

THE SHIP'S FRENCH AMBIENCE AND STYLE PUTS WIND IN YOUR SAILS

Size:	Small Ship	Passenger/Crew Ratio (lower beds):	1.7
Tonnage:	14,983	Cabins (total):	186
Cruise Line:	Club Med Cruises	Size Range (sq ft/m):	193.8–322/18–30
Former Names:	none	Cabins (for one person):	0
Builder:	Ateliers et Chantiers du Havre	Cabins with balcony:	0
Entered Service:	Dec 1992	Cabins (wheelchair accessible):	0
Length (ft/m):	613.8/187.1	Wheelchair accessibility:	None
Propulsion/Propellers:	diesel (9,120kW)/2	Elevators:	2
Total Crew:	214	Casino (gaming tables):	No
Passengers (lower beds):	372	Self-Service Launderette:	No
Passenger Space Ratio (lower beds):	40.2	Onboard currency:	Euros

THE SHIP. *Club Med 2* is one of a pair of the world's largest high-tech sail-cruisers (the other is *Wind Surf*), part-cruise ship, part-yacht. Five huge masts rise 221ft (67.4m) above sea level; they carry seven triangular, self-furling Dacron sails with a total surface area of 26,881 sq ft (2,497 sq m). No human hands touch the sails, as everything is controlled by computer from the bridge. This also keeps the ship on an even keel via the movement of a hydraulic ballast system, so there is no rolling over 6°. The ship was refurbished in 2008, when 10 new cabins were added – but the ship is now dated.

An array of water-sports facilities is provided (all except scuba gear are included in the cruise fare), and equipment on the aft marina platform includes 12 windsurfers, three sailboats, two water-ski boats, several kayaks, 20 single scuba tanks, snorkels, and four motorized water-sports boats. There are two small saltwater swimming pools (really 'dip' pools).

Facilities include a main lounge, meeting room, and an extra-charge golf simulator, plus a fitness and beauty center, and piano bar. No gratuities are expected.

This ship appeals best to youthful French-speaking couples and solo travelers who want contemporary facilities and water sports in a casual but chic setting that's different from 'normal' cruise ships, with good food and service, and little or no entertainment.

BERLITZ'S RATINGS		
	Possible	Achieved
Ship	500	303
Accommodation	200	125
Food	400	218
Service	400	220
Entertainment	100	50
Cruise Experience	400	218

OVERALL SCORE 1134 points out of 2000

ACCOMMODATION. There are five suites and 192 standard cabins, all of equal size. All cabins are nicely equipped and very comfortable, and have an inviting decor that includes much blond wood cabinetry. They have a minibar/refrigerator, 24-hour room service (but you pay for food), a safe, television, plenty of storage space, bathrobes, and a hairdryer. There are six four-person cabins, and some 35 doubles are fitted with an extra Pullman berth.

DINING. The main dining room is Le Magellan, with tables for two to eight. There is open seating, so you can sit with whom you wish. Le Mediterranée Restaurant has a delightful open terrace for informal meals. Complimentary wines and beers are provided for lunch and dinner; there is also an à la carte (extra-cost) wine list. The cuisine provides French, Continental, and Japanese specialties, and the creativity and presentation are good.

ENTERTAINMENT. Apart from occasional cabaret acts, there is live music each evening.

SPA/FITNESS. The Health Spa (split over three different decks) includes a sauna, fitness room, beauty salon, and treatment rooms for massage, facials, and body wraps.

COLUMBUS
★★+

A DATED BUT VERY FRIENDLY SHIP FOR MATURE-AGE TRAVELERS

Size:	Mid-size Ship	Passenger/Crew Ratio (lower beds):	3.1
Tonnage:	63,786	Cabins (total):	775
Cruise Line:	Cruise and Maritime Voyages	Size Range (sq ft/m):	182.9–398.2/17.0–37.0
Former Names:	Pacific Pearl, Ocean Village, Arcadia, Star Princess, FairMajesty	Cabins (for one person):	150
		Cabins with balcony:	64
Builder:	Chantiers de l'Atlantique (France)	Cabins (wheelchair accessible):	8
Entered Service:	Mar 1989/Apr 2017	Wheelchair accessibility:	Good
Length (ft/m):	810.3/247.0	Elevators:	9
Propulsion/Propellers:	diesel-electric (42,000kW)/2	Casino (gaming tables):	Yes
Total Crew:	514	Self-Service Launderette:	Yes
Passengers (lower beds):	1,550	Onboard currency:	UK£
Passenger Space Ratio (lower beds):	41.1		

THE SHIP. Columbus (some UK cruisegoers may remember it as Ocean Village – one of her former names) is best suited to mature couples, and solo travelers who like to cruise in an older mid-size ship and are happy with food that offers quantity rather than quality, all at an attractive price. The ship's passenger capacity was reduced from the original, which means there's more space per person.

The ship was originally designed and built as Fair-Majesty for Sitmar Cruises, and was formerly operating in Australasian waters between 2010 and 2017.

Columbus is well proportioned, with decent open deck and sunbathing space. On the open leisure deck are two pools, one with sloping steps, the other with vertical steps (one has a sit-in 'splash' bar). An Oasis (quiet zone) with day beds and a hot tub is aft on Deck 8. There's no full walk-around promenade deck outdoors, but open port and starboard walking areas stretch partly along the sides. There is, however, a walking track on the uppermost open deck. The interiors are quite pleasant, with much attention paid to lighting. There are also a few items that have a link with the past, such as the Art Deco stainless-steel balustrades and soulless stainless-steel elevators.

The interior focal point is a three-deck-high atrium lobby and a multi-deck dual staircase. There are seven lounges and bars. Highlights include The Dome, an observation lounge, which sits atop the ship, for-

ward of the mast. It is a lounge for cocktails, but at night it turns into a night-spot, with a sunken, circular wooden dance floor. There's also a casino, card room, and a craft center. Most public rooms have ceilings higher than the average for modern-day cruise ships.

For retail therapy, several shops are clustered around the second and third levels of the atrium lobby.

ACCOMMODATION. There are four basic types: mini-suites; outsides with balcony; outside-view; and interior. They come in 20 different price grades, depending on location and size.

Most outside-view/interior cabins have twin beds that can, in most cases, be put together to form a queen-size bed. All have a good amount of storage, including wooden drawer units, plus some under-bed space for luggage, and a walk-in closet. Sound insulation between cabins could be better, though (TV sound late at night can be irritating). Decent-quality bed linen, duvets, and pillows are provided. Note that Cabins 8120–8157 and 9138–9149 have lifeboat and safety equipment-obstructed views.

The modular design bathrooms have good-size shower enclosures and a retractable clothesline. Only mini-suites have bathtubs (the ship was originally built for North American passengers, who tend to prefer showers). However, shower heads are fixed to the wall, denying you the ease of a flexible shower hose.

Mini-suites have a small private balcony, walk-in closet, masses of storage space, and wood-floored bathroom with bathtub and shower.

DINING. The Waterfront (main restaurant) seats 800-plus, with open seating. It has ocean-view windows, sit-down tablecloth dining, and tables for two to eight. It has a high ceiling, and seating sections help divide the room into comfortable spaces.

The food is straightforward, unfussy, and geared to British tastes, with little use of garnishes. For more intimate dining and (extra-cost) food cooked to order, try the Grill specialty venue, which has an open kitchen.

Plantation is a self-serve buffet venue, open for breakfast, lunch, and dinner. It's typically slow-going along straight buffet lines, so patience is needed. Tea and coffee are provided at the beverage stations.

The Café, for coffees, hot chocolate, and snacks, is adjacent to the forward swimming pool. Charlie's, a neat little coffee bistro, located on the lowest lobby level opposite the reception desk, is for extra-cost coffees, teas, pastries, and snacks. The pool has an ice cream bar.

ENTERTAINMENT. The Palladium Showlounge is a horseshoe-shaped showlounge with main and balcony levels, with a bar at the back on the main level. It has adequate sight lines from most of the banquette-style seating, but sight lines from the upper-level front-row seats are obstructed by a safety rail.

Although the ship isn't young and doesn't have the latest bells and whistles, the stage has a good LED lighting backdrop. Entertainment includes production shows and cabaret. There is also live music in several lounges and bars.

SPA/FITNESS. The Thermal spa facilities – located on the lowest deck – include a beauty salon, workout room, and a thermal/relax area that includes a unisex sauna, steam room, herbal showers, and two body-shaped tiled hot beds.

CORAL PRINCESS
★★★+

THIS IS A COMFORTABLE MID-SIZE SHIP FOR MATURE-AGE CRUISERS

Size: .... Mid-size Ship	Passenger/Crew Ratio (lower beds): 2.1
Tonnage: 91,627	Cabins (total): 987
Cruise Line: .... Princess Cruises	Size Range (sq ft/m): 156–470.0/14.4–43.6
Former Names: .... none	Cabins (for one person): 0
Builder: .... Chantiers de l'Atlantique (France)	Cabins with balcony: 727
Entered Service: .... Dec 2002	Cabins (wheelchair accessible): 20
Length (ft/m): 964.5/294.0	Wheelchair accessibility: .... Good
Propulsion/Propellers: .... gas turbine + diesel	Elevators: 14
(40,000kW)/2	Casino (gaming tables): .... Yes
Total Crew: 900	Self-Service Launderette: .... Yes
Passengers (lower beds): 1,974	Onboard currency: .... US$
Passenger Space Ratio (lower beds): 46.4	

THE SHIP. *Coral Princess* (sister to *Island Princess*) has an instantly recognizable funnel due to two jet engine-like pods high up on its structure, but these really are mainly for decoration. Four diesel engines provide the generating power.

The layout is quite user-friendly and less disjointed than on many ships of a similar size. The interior layout is similar to that of the *Grand*-class ships, but with two decks of public rooms, lounges, and bars instead of just one. Sensibly, it has three major stair towers. *Coral Princess* has a walk-around open promenade deck, a feature appreciated by many. An adults-only 'Sanctuary' area is available as an extra-cost quiet zone, with comfortable padded sunloungers. There's a large 'Movies Under the Stars' screen in a second pool area forward of the funnel.

The ship has a Wedding Chapel, from which a live web-cam can relay ceremonies via the Internet. The ship's captain can legally marry (American) couples, thanks to the ship's registry and a special dispensation – though this may depend on where you live – to be verified when in the planning stage. The Wedding Chapel can also host renewal of vows ceremonies, for a fee.

Also, at the forward end of decks 10 and 11, doors open onto an observation terrace.

Niggles: the forward elevators go between decks 15 and 7, so you need to change elevators to get down

BERLITZ'S RATINGS

	Possible	Achieved
Ship	500	326
Accommodation	200	128
Food	400	243
Service	400	263
Entertainment	100	70
Cruise Experience	400	264

OVERALL SCORE 1294 points out of 2000

to the dining rooms on Deck 5; the automated telephone system; the small cabin towels; paying extra for items such as ice cream; and coins needed for the washers/dryers in the self-service launderettes.

Overall, Princess Cruises delivers a consistently fine, comfortable, well-packaged product, always with a good degree of style, at a competitive price.

ACCOMMODATION. With many different price categories, there's a wide choice: suites with balcony; mini-suites with balcony; eight mini-suites without balcony; outside-view cabins with balcony; standard outside-view cabins; interior (no-view) cabins; and 20 wheelchair-accessible cabins. Almost all outside-view cabins have private balconies. Some cabins can accommodate a third, or third and fourth person, which is good for families with children. Some cabins on Emerald Deck (Deck 8) have a view obstructed by lifeboats.

Suites are located on either Deck 9 or Deck 10, but none has an aft view. There are also four Premium Suites, located sensibly in the ship's center, adjacent to a bank of six elevators. Six other suites, (Verandah Suites), are located further aft.

Nearly all accommodation is equipped with a refrigerator, personal safe, infotainment system, hairdryer, satellite-dial telephone, and twin beds convertible to a queen-size bed. Bathrooms have a shower enclosure and toilet. Suites and mini-suites have a bathtub, separate shower enclosure, and two TVs. Cabin attendants have many cabins to look after.

DINING. The two main dining rooms, Bordeaux and Provence, are located forward, on the two lowest passenger decks. Both are almost identical in design and layout. The ceilings are quite low and make the rooms appear confined. They have plenty of intimate alcoves, and tables are for two to eight. There are two seatings for dinner (or you can opt for 'Anytime Dining' in the Bordeaux Restaurant), while breakfast and lunch are on an open-seating basis. You may have to wait at peak times.

Although portions are generous, the food and its presentation are disappointing and standardized – it's mass catering, after all. Fish is often disguised with sauces or coatings, the choice of fresh green vegetables is limited, few garnishes are used, and cheese is either pre-sliced or diced. Pasta dishes are acceptable (though voluminous).

Horizon Court, a casual eatery open almost 24 hours, is in the forward section of Lido Deck, with ocean views. Several self-serve counters provide breakfast and lunch buffets, and bistro-style casual dinners in the evening. The venue is a bit short on seating, however.

There are two specialty dining rooms: Sabatini's and the Bayou Café (both cost extra). Sabatini's is an Italian eatery, with colorful tiled Mediterranean-style decor; it is named after Trattoria Sabatini, the historic institution in Florence. It has Italian-style pizzas and pastas – all served with flair. The food is both creative and tasty, with seriously sized portions. Sabatini's is by reservation only, and there's a cover charge.

Bayou Café (reservations required) opens for lunch and dinner and has a cover charge (this includes a Hurricane cocktail). It evokes the charm of New Orleans' French Quarter, with wrought-iron decoration, and features Cajun/Creole cuisine. The venue has a small stage with baby grand piano.

ENTERTAINMENT. The Princess Theater is two decks high and, unusually, has more seating in its upper level than on the main floor. Productions are colorful, glamorous affairs with well-designed costumes and good lighting.

A second entertainment room (Universe Lounge) is for cabaret-style shows. It also has two levels – a first for a Princess Cruises ship – and three separate stages, enabling non-stop entertainment without constant set-ups. The room, with a full kitchen set, is also used for cooking demonstrations and other life-enrichment participation activities.

SPA/FITNESS. Lotus Spa is located aft on an upper deck. It hosts men's and women's saunas, steam rooms, changing rooms, relaxation area, beauty salon, body-treatment rooms, and an aerobics exercise room and gymnasium with ocean views and high-tech muscle-pumping equipment.

Sports enthusiasts will find a nine-hole golf putting course, two computerized golf simulators, and a sports court.

COSTA ATLANTICA
★★★

A CONTEMPORARY SHIP FOR CHINESE PASSENGERS WITH ITALIAN STYLE AND HIGH VOLUME

Size:	Mid-size Ship	Passenger/Crew Ratio (lower beds):	2.4
Tonnage:	85,619	Cabins (total):	1,109
Cruise Line:	Carnival China Cruise Shipping (CSSC)	Size Range (sq ft/m):	161.4–387.5/15.0–36.0
Former Names:	none	Cabins (for one person):	0
Builder:	Kverner Masa-Yards (Finland)	Cabins with balcony:	742
Entered Service:	Jul 2000/Sept 2019	Cabins (wheelchair accessible):	8
Length (ft/m):	959.6/292.5	Wheelchair accessibility:	Good
Propulsion/Propellers:	diesel-electric (34,000kW)/2 azimuthing pods	Elevators:	12
		Casino (gaming tables):	Yes
Total Crew:	902	Self-Service Launderette:	No
Passengers (lower beds):	2,218	Onboard currency:	Euros
Passenger Space Ratio (lower beds):	38.6		

THE SHIP. *Costa Atlantica* (sister to *Costa Mediterranea*), has two central outdoor pools, one with a retractable glass dome cover (useful in poor weather). There's a small pool for children, and a winding waterslide spanning two decks.

Deck names are inspired by Federico Fellini; one deck is named after the Fellini movie, *Ginger and Fred*. The decor pays homage to Italy's great art and past masters of classical Italy, mixed with contemporary features, accented by splashes of red and gold – to suit Chinese tastes. There are several floor spaces for dancing, and bars and lounges for socializing, with a colorful lobby that spans eight decks – the social meeting place.

A winding shopping street has boutique stores, photo gallery, video games room, an observation balcony, casino, library, and card room (with striking red and gold decor).

Costa Atlantica is for young (and young-at-heart) couples and families with children. Now based year-round in China, the ship caters for Chinese preferences, particularly with cuisine. Announcements are in Mandarin, and signage is in Italian and Mandarin. Passengers are offered constant activity with an Italian ambience, and loud entertainment. Note; several pillars obstruct passenger flow and sight lines throughout the ship.

ACCOMMODATION. There are many different price categories, and 78 percent have an outside

BERLITZ'S RATINGS		
	Possible	Achieved
Ship	500	325
Accommodation	200	124
Food	400	196
Service	400	235
Entertainment	100	55
Cruise Experience	400	222

OVERALL SCORE 1157 points out of 2000

view. All cabins (decorated with bright red for Chinese tastes) have twin beds convertible to queen-size beds, air conditioning (but it can't be turned off), infotainment system, telephone, personal safe, and vanity desk with hairdryer (but you need to hold the on button continuously). Many cabins have lifeboat-obstructed views on Decks 4 and 5.

Some cabins have additional pull-down (Pullman-style) berths hidden in the ceiling by day. There is much use of fluorescent lighting, and soundproofing could be better. Bathrooms are simple, modular units with shower enclosures and soap dispensers. Some fixtures – bath and shower taps in particular – are frustrating to use.

Some of the most desirable suites and cabins have private balconies on five aft-facing decks (decks 4, 5, 6, 7, and 8). Many cabins with private balconies are not so private. However, balconies all have good views through glass and wood-topped railings, and a teak deck. The largest suites are really small when compared with suites aboard other ships of a similar size. However, they do at least offer more space to move around in, and a nicer bathroom.

DINING. The 1,320-seat, bi-level Tiziano Dining Room is aft; it has a spiral stairway. There are two seatings, with closely packed tables for two to eight (noisy). Also, artwork is placed at table height, making the room feel cramped. Some tables have an uncomfortable view of the harsh lighting of the escalators between galley and dining area. The cuisine is banquet-style food, modified for Chinese tastes.

An extra-cost, reservations-required 125-seat Ristorante Club Atlantica is a quieter venue, and the food, although nothing special, is cooked to order.

Botticelli Buffet, for casual self-serve buffet-style eats, has indoor and outdoor seating. Close by are a grill (for burgers and fast-food items), a pasta bar, and Napoli Pizzeria. Excellent (illy brand) cappuccino and espresso coffees are always available in various bars, served in proper china cups.

One place to see and be seen in is Caffè Florian – a replica of the famous indoor/outdoor café that opened in 1720 in Venice's St Mark's Square. It has four separate salons (Sala delle Stagioni, Sala del Senato, Sala Liberty, and Sala degli Uomini Illustri) and the same fascinating mosaic, marble and wood floors, opulent ceiling art, and special lampshades.

Even the espresso/cappuccino machine is a duplicate of the one found in the real thing, but the chairs are too small.

ENTERTAINMENT. A three-deck-high, 950-seat showlounge (Caruso Theater) is an imposing room, with spiral stairways at the back connecting all levels. Stage shows are best seen from the upper levels.

Directly underneath is the Coral Lounge (and bar). A resident troupe of singers and dancers performs colorful, high-energy shows. A number of bands and small musical units provide live music in many lounges and bars, and there is also Dante's Disco.

SPA/FITNESS. Ischia Spa spans two decks, and includes a solarium, eight treatment rooms, sauna and steam rooms for men and women, beauty parlor, gymnasium with ocean-view windows, and an aerobics room. There is an outdoor jogging track.

COSTA DELIZIOSA
★★★+

IT'S ITALY AFLOAT ABOARD THIS CASUAL, VERY BRIGHT CONTEMPORARY SHIP

Size:	Mid-size Ship	Passenger/Crew Ratio (lower beds):	2.1
Tonnage:	92,700	Cabins (total):	1,130
Cruise Line:	Costa Cruises	Size Range (sq ft/m):	134.5–534.0/12.5–49.6
Former Names:	none	Cabins (for one person):	0
Builder:	Fincantieri (Italy)	Cabins with balcony:	772
Entered Service:	Mar 2010	Cabins (wheelchair accessible):	12
Length (ft/m):	958.0/292.0	Wheelchair accessibility:	Good
Propulsion/Propellers:	diesel-electric (42,000kW)/2 azimuthing pods	Elevators:	12
		Casino (gaming tables):	Yes
Total Crew:	1,050	Self-Service Launderette:	No
Passengers (lower beds):	2,260	Onboard currency:	Euros
Passenger Space Ratio (lower beds):	41.0		

THE SHIP. *Costa Deliziosa* has a nicely balanced profile and a single large funnel in the Costa colors of yellow and blue. The ship, sister to *Costa Luminosa*, was named in Dubai, the first new cruise ship to be named in an Arab city (a bottle of fig juice, instead of Champagne, was used for the ceremony). A two-deck midships Lido area swimming pool can be covered with a sliding glass roof in poor weather. A large 194-sq-ft (18-sq-m) poolside movie screen plays feature films (and lots of Costa Cruises commercials).

The marble and gold interior decor pays tribute to the senses, although sensory overkill might be a better description; in any event, it's a lot of overdone bling, although amazingly the incredible mix of colors somehow manage to go together. The focal point (and always a good meeting place) is the atrium lobby.

Public rooms include 11 bars (one of the largest is Grand Bar Mirabilis), a large casino (Casino Gaius), many lounges, bars, entertainment venues and shops, including Cinema Etoiles – a 4D cinema highlights sound and lighting effects, with scent pumped in to heighten the experience.

Printed material – room service folio, menus, etc. – is typically in six languages. During peak European school holiday periods, particularly Christmas and Easter, expect to be cruising with a lot of children of all ages.

BERLITZ'S RATINGS		
	Possible	Achieved
Ship	500	372
Accommodation	200	135
Food	400	219
Service	400	249
Entertainment	100	62
Cruise Experience	400	241

OVERALL SCORE 1278 points out of 2000

Costa Deliziosa has a quasi-Italian style (most passengers are Italian, with a sprinkling of other nationalities), with bright surroundings accompanied by loud everything, with grainy and unflattering digital artwork on walls and panels, and inside elevators. You won't find many Italian crew members, although many senior officers are Italian. The dress code is 'casual sloppy,' except for 'white' nights. This ship is for those who like lively and brash. For some quiet, take earplugs – good ones, or choose a different ship. On European cruises, your fellow passengers will mostly speak Italian, Spanish, French, and German. Few staff members are on duty at the gangway when you embark so you will be merely pointed in the direction of your deck, or to the ship's elevators (no escort to your cabin). Gratuities are automatically added to your account. Overall, Costa provides a well-packaged cruise holiday for families.

Note that 'wallpaper' music is played 24 hours a day in all accommodation hallways and elevators, so you may well hear it if you are a light sleeper. Expect lots of announcements – especially for revenue activities such as art auctions, bingo, horse racing – and much hustling for drinks.

ACCOMMODATION. About 68 percent of all accommodation suites and cabins have an ocean view, and 772 cabins have balconies. Four suites and 52 Samsara Spa cabins are adjacent to (and considered part of) the wellness area, and occupants get unlimited access to the spa plus two treatments and fitness or meditation lessons as part of their package, and they can dine in one of the two Samsara restaurants.

A multi-choice pillow menu is available to suite-grade occupants, who also get bathrobes, better amenities, shaving mirror, and walk-in closets.

DINING. The 1,264-seat Albatros Restaurant is the main dining hall, located aft, and you eat at one of two seating times for dinner, at tables for two to eight, assigned according to your accommodation grade.

The cuisine is Continental European, with some regional Italian dishes and much emphasis on carbohydrate-rich food, with up to 50 pasta dishes. The presentation and quality are non-memorable, and the subject of many passenger comments – but this is banquet-style batch cooking. Green vegetables are hard to come by, and rice is used as a plate-filler. Breads and bakery items are not bad (but are made from frozen 'starter' dough); desserts are of supermarket quality and lack taste. There is heavy use of canned fruit, jellied desserts, and packets of jam and butter.

There are no sommeliers, so the waiters, who are young, serve the wine, which is also young. Note that table water is not provided – you are expected to purchase it. It's wise to buy a drinks package, which includes coffee and tea, bottled water and soft drinks, plus alcoholic beverages.

A reservations-required, 68-seat Samsara Restaurant is adjacent; it is a smaller, quieter, more intimate venue, and features healthier food with reduced calories, fat, and salt content. It is open for lunch and dinner to anyone in Samsara-grade accommodation, and to anyone else for dinner only at an extra daily or weekly charge.

The Restaurant Club Deliziosa is an extra-cost, reservations-required venue with 182 seats, and has

an open show kitchen. The food is cooked à la minute, and looks (and is) much more appetizing.

Buffet Muscadins is a large, self-serve casual eatery, but its disjointed layout invites congestion. While there appears to be a decent choice of food, it is extremely repetitive (particularly for breakfast), and after it closes in the afternoon, only basic pizza slices are available.

One event not to be missed is 'Elegant Teatime,' when rather nice cakes and sandwiches are served, together with a choice of teas or tisanes, in one of the lounges.

Extra-cost espresso coffees and cappuccinos (illy brand) are available in the Atrium Bar – a good place to sit and be seen/observe others.

ENTERTAINMENT. The Theater Duse, with over 800 seats, spans three decks (with seating on all three levels) and has the latest computer-controlled lighting and sound equipment. High-energy production shows are performed here by the ship's song and dance troupe.

SPA/FITNESS. Samsara Spa area is large: it spans two decks and includes a spacious fitness room, separate saunas, steam rooms, UVB solarium and changing rooms for men and women, and 10 private massage/body-treatment rooms. Two VIP treatment rooms, available to couples as a half-day rental, are on the upper level. Most fitness classes cost extra.

A day pass for the sauna/steam rooms, thermal suite, and relaxation area costs extra. There's also another free (no-charge) sauna for men and women, but to access it you must walk through an active fitness area.

For the sports-minded, a Grand Prix Formula One simulator is housed in a glass enclosure close to the spa. A golf simulator provides a choice of 37 18-hole courses.

COSTA DIADEMA
★★★+

THIS SPARKLY, FAMILY-FRIENDLY ITALIAN SHIP IS MORE WATER TAXI THAN CRUISE SHIP

Size:	Large Resort Ship	Passenger/Crew Ratio (lower beds):	2.9
Tonnage:	132,500	Cabins (total):	1,854
Cruise Line:	Costa Cruises	Size Range (sq ft/m):	125.9–554.3/11.7–51.5
Former Names:	none	Cabins (for one person):	0
Builder:	Fincantieri (Italy)	Cabins with balcony:	913
Entered Service:	Nov 2013	Cabins (wheelchair accessible):	8
Length (ft/m):	1,003.9/306.0	Wheelchair accessibility:	Good
Propulsion/Propellers:	diesel-electric (42,000kW)/2	Elevators:	19
Total Crew:	1,253	Casino (gaming tables):	Yes
Passengers (lower beds):	3,708	Self-Service Launderette:	No
Passenger Space Ratio (lower beds):	35.7	Onboard currency:	Euros

THE SHIP. *Costa Diadema* is one of the newest in the Costa Cruises fleet of family-friendly ships. Step aboard and you'll be greeted by a 4ft (1.2m) white humanoid robot named 'Pepper,' who is seaworthy and speaks English, German, and Italian, but he won't carry your carry-on luggage. You'll see more Pepper(s) around the ship, acting as information helpers.

The ship (its name means 'tiara') has a well-proportioned profile with a rounded front, bolt-upright Costa yellow funnel, and nicely tiered aft decks. The lifeboats are mounted lower down; this position gives a sense of balance to the ship's towering superstructure. *Costa Diadema* is equipped with a cold ironing facility, so it can access shore-side electric power, and all solid waste is collected for recycling. All exterior decks are covered in a rubberized material (no teak anywhere), but railings are made of hardwood. A nice feature is the outdoor 1,640-ft (500-m) walk-around promenade deck.

The interior decor is very bright and ultra-bold. The central focal point is an atrium lobby (Atrio Eliodoro), with four panoramic elevators. Look upwards and you'll see the inner part of the multi-deck atrium studded with diamonds – well, blue diamond-look lighting (you'll find it on the ceilings of other public areas, too). In fact, you'll see diamonds in the artwork throughout the ship. The reception and the shore-excursion desk (Costa Travel Office) are locat-

BERLITZ'S RATINGS		
	Possible	Achieved
Ship	500	374
Accommodation	200	135
Food	400	219
Service	400	249
Entertainment	100	62
Cruise Experience	400	242
OVERALL SCORE 1281 points out of 2000		

ed to one side, while comfortable seating is set around the lobby and adjacent areas.

There are seven restaurants and eateries (four of these cost extra) and 15 bars to enjoy, including the Birreria La Flamma (a pub with several draft beers/lagers).

A whole shopping street awaits in the form of the Portobello Market Piazza – filled with designer stores within its 11,840-sq-ft (1,100-sq-m) area. Other public rooms include a 4D racing-car experience, and a chapel – a Costa Cruises must-have.

Niggles include the fact that, in common with many large resort ships today, there is little open space on the upper decks, so be prepared to hunt for a sunbed around the main swimming pool. You'll need to take a towel from your cabin, as they are not provided at the pool. Note that passengers embark and disembark at each port of call, so a cruise is more like a water taxi; this means there is little communication between staff and passengers. This is also a high-density ship, with the lowest number of crew per passengers of all the ships in the Costa Cruises fleet. This is all about casual cruising for a youthful clientele who enjoy the Italian flair for life.

ACCOMMODATION. The accommodation configuration consists of Grand Suites, Suites, Mini-Suites, Balcony Cabins, Cove Balcony Cabins, Oceanview Cabins, and Interior (no-view) Cabins. The Grand

Suites are not true suites (there's no completely separate bedroom), and are small. Some suites/cabins are designated Samsara Spa-grade accommodation, whose occupants eat in the intimate Samsara Restaurant.

Suites have larger bathrooms (some with a tub/shower), while many cabins have a shower curtain, instead of a proper glazed door, and a shower head that is fixed (no flexible shower hose except in high-grade accommodation).

DINING. Restaurant Sissi is the cavernous main dining room; located aft, it is two decks high, with bright decor. Seating, allocated according to your accommodation grade and location, is at banquettes and individual chairs without armrests. A second dining room, the single-deck-height Scudo Rosso Restaurant, is located in the ship's center.

Don't expect Italian waiters, you'll likely be disappointed – although restaurant managers might be Italian. Few tables for two are available, most being for four to eight.

The cuisine is Continental European, with some regional Italian dishes and considerable emphasis on carbohydrate-rich food, with up to 50 pasta dishes (buffalo mozzarella cheese is made on board). The food is banquet-style batch cooking. The presentation and food quality are not memorable, and are the subject of many passenger comments. Green vegetables are hard to come by, and rice is used as a plate-filler. Breads and baked goods are decent enough (made from frozen 'starter' dough); desserts are of supermarket quality and lack taste. There is much use of canned fruit, jellied desserts, and packets of jam and butter.

There's a wine list, but no wine waiters (table waiters serve both food and wine). Almost all wines are young, and the glasses are small. Note that table water is not provided – you are expected to purchase it. It's wise to buy a drinks package, which includes coffee and tea, bottled water and soft drinks, plus alcoholic beverages).

Charges apply in the specialty restaurants.

A large self-serve lido buffet has basic items, but it is quite poor. The regular coffee is decent and quite strong, but the cost-extra (illy) coffee is better.

Samsara Restaurant is a smaller, more intimate venue for occupants of Samsara-grade accommodation. The cuisine focuses more on healthy items, with reduced calories and less fat and salt.

The self-serve Corona Blu Restaurant (a buffet on the Lido Deck) has tacky (AIDA-style), unhygienic cutlery stands on tables.

Costa has introduced some more ethnic-centric eating areas (some at extra cost), such as a Vinoteca, Prosecccheria (a Bavarian Bierkeller), a Japanese Tavola Teppanyaki Grill, an extra-cost pizzeria (it's in the Piazza, so it's called the Pizzeria in Piazza Pizza – a real mouthful!), and a Gelateria. Club Diadema restaurant is an extra-cost, reservations-required dining spot, and delivers more upscale cuisine. It's worth it if you are celebrating something special, or for something a little different to the noisy main dining room.

ENTERTAINMENT. The Emerald Theater – the ship's showlounge – is spread over three decks and has over 1,500 seats (with tables for drinks), many of which have upright backs, a large stage with proscenium arch, and the latest in LED lighting technology. Costa Cruises' revue-style shows – performed by a troupe of resident onboard singers/dancers – are all about color, lights, high-energy action, and volume.

A Country Rock Club is something new for Costa Cruises; it's an upbeat venue for listening to country-rock crossover music.

SPA/FITNESS. Samsara Spa is a large facility, spread over three decks. It includes a large gymnasium with the latest in muscle-training equipment, saunas, steam rooms, a thermal area, and several massage/body-treatment rooms. VIP treatment rooms are also available to couples for half-day rentals. You'll need to purchase a day pass in order to use the sauna/steam rooms, thermal suite, and relaxation area. Most fitness classes cost extra.

COSTA FASCINOSA
★★★+

UPBEAT ITALIAN DECOR AND STYLE, FOR TRENDY FAMILY CRUISING ABOARD THIS SHIP

Size:	Large Resort Ship	Passenger/Crew Ratio (lower beds):	2.7
Tonnage:	113,216	Cabins (total):	1,507
Cruise Line:	Costa Cruises	Size Range (sq ft/m):	179.7–482.2/16.7–44.8
Former Names:	none	Cabins (for one person):	0
Builder:	Fincantieri (Italy)	Cabins with balcony:	650
Entered Service:	May 2012	Cabins (wheelchair accessible):	12
Length (ft/m):	952.0/290.2	Wheelchair accessibility:	Good
Propulsion/Propellers:	diesel-electric (75,600kW)/2	Elevators:	14
Total Crew:	1,100	Casino (gaming tables):	Yes
Passengers (lower beds):	3,014	Self-Service Launderette:	No
Passenger Space Ratio (lower beds):	37.5	Onboard currency:	Euros

THE SHIP. *Costa Fascinosa* has an instantly recognizable single, large yellow funnel. On the open decks, two pool areas can be covered with retractable glass domes – useful for inclement weather conditions; one pool has a long waterslide, much liked by children; there is also a large poolside movie screen. However, the open deck space is pretty cramped when the ship is full, and plastic sunloungers are crammed together and lack cushioned pads.

With three decks packed with many bars and lounges, other public rooms and shops, there's a place for all tastes, but the interior decor is a little on the wild side. The focal social point is a three-deck-high atrium lobby (four glass panoramic elevators providing a neat view over its lobby bar), a good place for an espresso/cappuccino and people-watching.

Families like Costa Cruises for its perceived 'Italian' style, ambience and spirit, and most passengers will be Italian, with a sprinkling of other nationalities. However, most crew members, particularly the dining room and housekeeping staff, are from the Philippines and you won't find many Italian staff on board (although many of the officers are Italian). Note that during peak European school holiday periods, especially during Christmas and Easter, you can expect a lot of children and teens on board.

Announcements are made, and printed material is provided, in several languages. But, there is little information for passengers who want to be in-

BERLITZ'S RATINGS		
	Possible	Achieved
Ship	500	369
Accommodation	200	134
Food	400	219
Service	400	245
Entertainment	100	60
Cruise Experience	400	239

OVERALL SCORE 1266 points out of 2000

dependent in ports of call and not take the ship's organized excursions. There is extensive smoking (no-smoking zones and signs are often ignored, with ashtrays moved at whim, and many of the officers and crew also smoke).

However, Costa Cruises does a good job of providing families with children with a packaged vacation that mixes hints of sophistication with the noisy and utterly chaotic. Gratuities are automatically added to your account.

ACCOMMODATION. There are many accommodation price grades, from two-bed interior cabins to grand suites with private balcony, although in reality there are only three different sizes: suites with 'private' balcony – which are really not particularly large in comparison with some other large ships; two- or four-bed outside-view cabins; and two- or four-bed interior cabins. Fortunately, no cabins have lifeboat-obstructed views, and, in most cabins, twin beds can be changed to a double/queen-bed configuration.

Eight Grand Suites, in the ship's center on an uppermost deck, comprise the largest accommodation. Samsara Spa Suite occupants get unlimited spa access, two treatments, plus fitness or meditation lessons, and meals in one of two designated Samsara restaurants.

Suite-grade occupants get bathrobes and better amenities, including a shaving mirror, pillow menu, and walk-in closets (plastic hangers). Note that music is played 24/7 in accommodation hallways and elevators, so you may well hear it if you are a light sleeper.

DINING. There are two principal dining rooms (each with two seatings), Il Gattopardo and Otto e Mezzo. One is aft, the other in the ship's center. Tables for two (there are few) to eight are allocated according to your accommodation grade and location.

The cuisine is Continental European, banquet-style batch cooking, with some regional Italian dishes and considerable emphasis on carbohydrate-rich food, with up to 50 pasta dishes (buffalo mozzarella cheese is made on board). The presentation and food quality are unmemorable, and the subject of many passenger comments. Green vegetables are hard to come by, and rice is used as a plate-filler. Breads and bakery items are decent enough (but made from frozen 'starter' dough); desserts are of supermarket quality and lack taste. Canned fruit and jellied desserts feature heavily.

There's a wine list, but no wine waiters (table waiters serve both food and wine). Almost all wines are young, and glasses are small. Table water is not provided – you are expected to purchase it. It's wise to buy a drinks package, which includes coffee and tea, bottled water and soft drinks, plus alcoholic beverages.

For casual eats, a large self-serve lido buffet has basic items, but it is nothing special, and while the regular ship's coffee is decent and quite strong, the cost-extra (illy) coffee is much better.

Two Samsara restaurants – open for lunch and dinner to those in Samsara-grade suites and cabins, and to anyone (for dinner only) at an extra charge – have separate entrances. While the two main restaurants offer traditional cruise fare, these 'spa cuisine' spots feature healthier food – reduced calories, fat, and salt.

A reservations-required, cost-extra restaurant, Club Fascinosa, has decent table settings, leather-bound menus, and food prepared to order.

For really casual meals, the self-serve, buffet-style eatery, Tulipano Nero, is open for breakfast, lunch, afternoon pizzas, and coffee or tea at any time. A balcony level has more seating, but you'll need to carry your own plates because there are no trays. The food is repetitive, and a major source of complaint.

ENTERTAINMENT. The Fascinosa Showlounge seats over 800. It spans three decks and is for high-energy, high volume revue-style shows and cabaret acts, with a revolving stage, hydraulic orchestra pit, good sound, and seating on three levels.

SPA/FITNESS. Samsara Spa is a large facility that includes relaxation areas, spread over two decks. It has a large fitness room, separate saunas, steam rooms, UVB solarium, and changing rooms for men and women, and 10 rooms for body treatments. Two VIP treatment rooms, for couples (half-day rentals), are on the upper level.

The Spa/fitness facilities are staffed and operated by Steiner Leisure, a specialist spa/beauty concession. Some fitness classes are free, while some, such as Pathway to Yoga, Pathway to Pilates, and Pathway to Meditation, cost extra. It's wise to make appointments early, as time slots can go quickly.

You can buy a day pass in order to use the sauna/steam rooms, thermal suite and relaxation area. However, there's an additional no-charge sauna for men and women, but to access it you must walk through an active fitness area.

COSTA FAVOLOSA
★★★+

THIS SHIP HAS RATHER UPBEAT ITALIAN DECOR AND STYLE, FOR FAMILY CRUISING

Size:	Large Resort Ship
Tonnage:	113,216
Cruise Line:	Costa Cruises
Former Names:	none
Builder:	Fincantieri (Italy)
Entered Service:	Jul 2011
Length (ft/m):	952.0/290.2
Propulsion/Propellers:	diesel-electric (75,600kW)/2
Total Crew:	1,110
Passengers (lower beds):	3,014
Passenger Space Ratio (lower beds):	37.5
Passenger/Crew Ratio (lower beds):	2.7
Cabins (total):	1,507
Size Range (sq ft/m):	179.7–482.2/16.7–44.8
Cabins (for one person):	0
Cabins with balcony:	579
Cabins (wheelchair accessible):	12
Wheelchair accessibility:	Good
Elevators:	14
Casino (gaming tables):	Yes
Self-Service Launderette:	No
Onboard currency:	Euros

THE SHIP. Displaying a single, large funnel, *Costa Favolosa* is a close sister to *Costa Serena*. Two pool areas can be covered with retractable glass domes – useful in case of bad weather – and one has a long waterslide, which is great for kids. There is a large poolside movie screen and, on one of the upper decks, a Grand Prix simulator. However, the open deck space can be pretty cramped when the ship is full, so the sunloungers, which don't have cushioned pads, will be crammed together.

With three decks packed with many bars and lounges, other public rooms and shops, there's a place for all tastes, but the interior decor is a little on the wild side. The focal social point is a three-deck-high atrium lobby (four glass panoramic elevators providing a neat view over its lobby bar), a good place for an espresso/cappuccino and people-watching.

Families like Costa Cruises for its perceived 'Italian' style, ambience and spirit, and most passengers will be Italian, with a sprinkling of other nationalities. However, you won't find many Italian service staff on board (although many of the officers are Italian). Note that during peak European school holiday periods, especially during Christmas and Easter, you can expect to be cruising with a lot of children and teens.

Announcements are made and printed material is provided in several languages but, there is little information for passengers who want to be independent in ports of call and not take the ship's organized

BERLITZ'S RATINGS

	Possible	Achieved
Ship	500	369
Accommodation	200	134
Food	400	219
Service	400	245
Entertainment	100	60
Cruise Experience	400	239

OVERALL SCORE 1266 points out of 2000

excursions. There is extensive smoking (no-smoking zones and signs are often ignored, with ashtrays moved at whim.

However, Costa Cruises does a good job of providing families with children with a packaged vacation that mixes hints of sophistication with the noisy and utterly chaotic. Gratuities are automatically added to your account.

ACCOMMODATION. There are numerous accommodation price grades, from two-bed interior cabins (no view) to grand suites with private balcony, although in reality there are only three different sizes: suites with 'private' balcony – these are really not large in comparison with some other large ships; two- or four-bed outside-view cabins; and two- or four-bed interior cabins. Fortunately, no cabins have views obstructed by lifeboats or other safety equipment views, and, in most cabins, twin beds can be changed to a double/queen-bed configuration.

Two Grand Suites comprise the largest accommodation and include a large balcony with hot tub.

Twelve Samsara Spa Suites are located just aft of the spa itself, although 99 cabins, including these 12, are designated as Samsara-grade. Occupants get unlimited access to the spa plus two treatments and fitness or other lessons included, and can dine in one of two Samsara restaurants. All Samsara-designated accommodation grades have an Oriental decorative theme, and special Samsara bathroom personal amenities.

A pillow menu, with five choices, has been introduced in suite-grade accommodation. Only suite grades get bathrobes and better amenities, shaving mirror, and walk-in closets – although the hangers are still plastic.

DINING. There are two main dining rooms, Duke of Burgundy and Duke of Orleans. One is aft, the other is in the center. Tables for two to eight are allocated according to your accommodation grade and location, in one of two seating times. These dining rooms offer traditional cruise fare that is banquet-style, batch-cooked food.

Two 100-seat Samsara restaurants are for healthier food, with reduced calories, fat, and salt content (open for lunch and dinner to anyone in Samsara-grade accommodation, and to others for dinner only at an extra charge).

If you expect to be served by jovial Italian waiters, you'll be disappointed – although the restaurant managers might be Italian. Few tables for two are available, most being for four to eight.

The cuisine features some regional Italian dishes and much carbohydrate-rich food, with up to 50 pasta dishes. The presentation and quality are not memorable, and the subject of many comments. Green vegetables are hard to come by, and rice is used as a plate-filler. Breads and bakery items are quite decent (but made from frozen 'starter' dough), but desserts are of supermarket quality and lack taste. Expect much use of canned fruit and jellied desserts.

There is a wine list, but no wine waiters (table waiters serve both food and wine). The wines are young, and the glasses are small. Note that table water is not provided – you are expected to purchase it. It may be wise to buy a drinks package, which includes coffee and tea, bottled water and soft drinks, plus alcoholic beverages.

If you opt for one of the specialty restaurants, note that charges apply. The regular ship's coffee is decent enough and strong, but the extra-cost (illy) coffee is excellent.

The intimate Favolosa Club Restaurant sits under a huge glass dome and Murano-glass decorative elements. Fine table settings, china, silverware and leather-bound menus are provided. There's a cover charge and reservations are required.

The self-service Ca' d'Oro food court-style buffet restaurant is for breakfast, lunch, pizzas, and coffee and tea at any time. A balcony level provides additional seating, but you'll need to carry your own food plates (there are no trays). The food in this venue is very repetitive.

ENTERTAINMENT. The Teatro Hortensia showlounge, seating more than 800, has LED backdrop technology. Three decks high, the venue has Baroque-style decor, warm colors, and a Murano-glass chandelier. It is the venue for high-energy production shows and cabaret acts, and has a revolving stage, hydraulic orchestra pit, good sound, and seating on three levels – the upper levels are tiered.

SPA/FITNESS. Samsara Spa is a large two-deck facility. It includes a large fitness room, separate saunas, steam rooms, UVB solarium, changing rooms for men and women, and 10 rooms for body treatments. Two VIP treatment rooms, available to couples as a half-day rental, are located on the upper level.

Some fitness classes are free, but most cost extra. You can purchase a day pass in order to use the sauna/steam rooms, thermal suite, and relaxation area. There's an additional no-charge sauna for men and women, but to access it you must walk through an active fitness area, maybe with your bathrobe on, which some people might not be comfortable with.

COSTA FORTUNA
★★★+

A LARGE, COLORFUL FAMILY-FRIENDLY ITALIAN-STYLE FLOATING RESORT

Size:	Large Resort Ship	Passenger/Crew Ratio (lower beds):	2.5
Tonnage:	102,587	Cabins (total):	1,358
Cruise Line:	Costa Cruises	Size Range (sq ft/m):	179.7–482.2/16.7–44.8
Former Names:	none	Cabins (for one person):	0
Builder:	Cantieri Sestri Navale (Italy)	Cabins with balcony:	522
Entered Service:	Nov 2003	Cabins (wheelchair accessible):	8
Length (ft/m):	892.3/272.0	Wheelchair accessibility:	Good
Propulsion/Propellers:	diesel-electric (34,000kW)/2 azimuthing pods	Elevators:	14
		Casino (gaming tables):	Yes
Total Crew:	1,068	Self-Service Launderette:	No
Passengers (lower beds):	2,716	Onboard currency:	Euros
Passenger Space Ratio (lower beds):	37.7		

THE SHIP. The ship's name is an interesting one: in Greek mythology, Fortuna is the daughter of Poseidon (God of the sea). The name is also associated with the Temple Fortuna, located along one of Pompeii's conserved streets.

The aft decks are tiered, with cut-off quarters that make the stern look a little less square than it otherwise would. There are three pools, one of which can be covered by a sliding glass dome in case of inclement weather, while one pool (Barcelona Pool) features a long waterslide. There is not a lot of open deck space considering the number of passengers carried, so sunloungers tend to be crammed together (there's a lack of small tables for drinks – or for somewhere to place those small items you always take to the pool), and they lack cushioned pads.

The interior decor focuses on Italian passenger ships of yesteryear, replicating the Art Deco interiors fitted aboard ocean liners such as the *Conte de Savoia*, *Michelangelo*, *Rafaello*, *Rex*, etc., but in contemporary colors not associated with such ships, whose interiors were rather subdued.

The deck names are those of major cities in Europe and North and South America (Barcelona, Buenos Aires, Caracas, Lisbon, Genoa, Miami). The passenger flow is generally good, with few congestion points.

There are three decks full of lounges and bars to enjoy, and almost all have espresso coffee machines

BERLITZ'S RATINGS		
	Possible	Achieved
Ship	500	367
Accommodation	200	134
Food	400	219
Service	400	246
Entertainment	100	60
Cruise Experience	400	239

OVERALL SCORE 1265 points out of 2000

– a must for Italians – featuring the illy brand. The interior focal point is a nine-deck high, glass-domed atrium lobby: it houses a Costa Bar on the lower level, with three large sails. The lowest three decks connect the public rooms, the upper levels being mainly for accommodation (plus the pool deck).

For gamers, Neptunia 1932 Casino is the place to go (if you want to get from the center to the aft lounges you have to walk through it). There's also a chapel – standard aboard Costa ships – and a small library that's really a token gesture, an Internet center, card room, art gallery, and video games room.

Costa Fortuna – now over 10 years old, underwent a refurbishment in spring 2019 that modified several public areas following the ship's deployment in Asia, and several of the public rooms were refreshed. As aboard other Costa ships, note that for embarkation, few staff are on duty at the gangway when you arrive; they merely point you in the direction of your deck, or to the ship's elevators and do not escort you to your cabin. Also, note that 'wallpaper' music is played 24 hours a day in all accommodation hallways and elevators, so you may well hear it if you are a light sleeper. Other niggles include drinks packages and the numerous rules.

Costa Cruises is noted for its Italian style, ambience, and spirit, but there are few Italian crew members. Although many officers are Italian, most of the crew members, particularly the dining room and housekeeping staff, are from the Philippines. But the lifestyle on board is perceived to be Italian – lively, noisy, with lots of love for life and a love of all things casual, even on so-called formal nights.

All printed material – room service folio, menus, etc. – will typically be in six languages: Italian, English, French, German, Portuguese, and Spanish. During peak periods (European school holidays, particularly Christmas and Easter), you can expect to be cruising with a lot of children of all ages.

ACCOMMODATION. There are numerous price grades, from two-bed interior (no-view) cabins to grand suites with private balcony. In reality there are just three sizes: suites with balcony, two- or four-bed outside-view cabins (many have portholes rather than windows), and two- or four-bed interior cabins. There are also two cabins for solo travelers. In an example of good design, no cabins have lifeboat-obstructed views; this is something not easy to design in large ships such as this.

The largest accommodation can be found in eight Grand Suites, located in the center of the ship on one of the higher decks. They have a queen-size bed; bathrooms have two washbasins and a large enclosure with colored-light shower.

Note that 12 of the best (outside-view) wheelchair-accessible cabins are ludicrously located a long way from elevators; eight others are, however, located close to the elevators.

Dining. There are two dining rooms: the 1,046-seat Michelangelo 1965 Restaurant (aft), whose ceiling features frescoes by the Old Masters, and the 664-seat Rafaello 1965 Restaurant (midships); both are two decks high and each has two seatings for dinner, which is typically scheduled at 7pm and 9pm on European cruises. Few tables for two are available, most being for four to eight.

The cuisine is very average Continental European, with some regional Italian dishes and considerable emphasis on carbohydrate-rich food, with up to 50 different pasta dishes. Green vegetables are hard to come by, and rice is used as a plate-filler. Breads and bakery items are decent enough (but made from frozen 'starter' dough), but desserts are of supermarket quality and lack taste. There is heavy use of canned fruit, jellied desserts, and packets of jam and butter.

There's a wine list, but no wine waiters (table waiters serve both food and wine). Almost all the wines are young, and the glasses are small. Note that table water is not provided – you are expected to purchase it. It's wise to buy a drinks package, which includes coffee and tea, bottled water and soft drinks, plus alcoholic beverages).

If you opt for one of the specialty restaurants, note that charges apply. The regular coffee is decent and quite strong, but the extra-cost (illy) coffee is excellent.

Conte Grande 1927 Club is an intimate, upscale 94-seat venue under a large glass dome – if the lights were turned out, you might be able to see the stars. In its 'show' kitchen, chefs can be seen preparing the food. Fine table settings, china, silverware, and leather-bound menus are used. Reservations are required.

The Cristoforo Columbus 1954 Buffet Restaurant is a self-serve eatery. The food is repetitive, and a source of complaint. Pizzeria Pummid'Oro, on the pool deck, is for pizzas made with San Marzano tomatoes.

ENTERTAINMENT. The Rex 1932 Theater spans three decks in the ship's forward-most section. It is a stunning setting for all production shows and headline cabaret acts (seating on three levels – the upper levels being tiered through two decks).

SPA/FITNESS. Facilities in the two-deck high Saturnia Spa 1927 include a large solarium, private massage/ treatment rooms, sauna and steam rooms for men and women, and a beauty parlor. A gym has floor-to-ceiling windows on three sides, including forward-facing ocean views, and there's an aerobics section.

Some fitness classes are free; most cost extra. Make appointments early, as time slots can go quickly. If you like being near the spa, note that there are 18 two-bed cabins with ocean-view windows, located adjacent (just aft of it).

COSTA LUMINOSA
★★★+

THIS SHIP HAS BOLD DECOR AND BIG-SHIP FACILITIES THAT ARE GOOD FOR FAMILIES

Size:	Mid-size Ship	Passenger/Crew Ratio (lower beds):	2.1
Tonnage:	92,700	Cabins (total):	1,130
Cruise Line:	Costa Cruises	Size Range (sq ft/m):	134.5–534.0/12.5–49.6
Former Names:	none	Cabins (for one person):	0
Builder:	Fincantieri (Italy)	Cabins with balcony:	772
Entered Service:	Jun 2009	Cabins (wheelchair accessible):	12
Length (ft/m):	958.0/292.0	Wheelchair accessibility:	Good
Propulsion/Propellers:	diesel-electric (42,000kW)/2 azimuthing pods	Elevators:	12
		Casino (gaming tables):	Yes
Total Crew:	1,050	Self-Service Launderette:	No
Passengers (lower beds):	2,260	Onboard currency:	Euros
Passenger Space Ratio (lower beds):	41.0		

THE SHIP. *Costa Luminosa is a sister ship to Costa Deliziosa.* The ship's two-deck midships Lido area swimming pool can be covered with a sliding glass roof. There's also a large 194-sq-ft (18-sq-m) poolside movie screen.

The interior decor, which includes marble, wood, and mother of pearl, pays tribute to light and lighting – hence the name *Costa Luminosa* – so it feels like you are cruising in a stunning special-effects bubble, with reflections everywhere.

Public rooms include numerous bars, lounges, and entertainment venues, and a large Casino Vega (with gaming tables and slot machines). A 4D cinema highlights sound and lighting effects, with scent pumped in to heighten the experience. One thing you can't miss is a fascinating – and rather large, at 11ft long (3.4m) – *Reclining Woman 2004* bronze sculpture by Fernando Botero, in the Atria Supernova, the atrium lobby. Weighing 2,000lbs (907kg), the suntanned, rather voluminous woman is depicted staring into the atrium space, with her legs in a dynamic position of movement.

Although Costa Cruises is noted for its Italian style, ambience, and spirit, there are few Italian crew members on board (although many officers are Italian). But the lifestyle on board is perceived to be Italian – lively, noisy, with lots of love for life and a love of all things casual, even on so-called formal nights.

All printed material – room service folio, menus, etc. – is usually available in six languages: Italian,

BERLITZ'S RATINGS		
	Possible	Achieved
Ship	500	370
Accommodation	200	134
Food	400	218
Service	400	247
Entertainment	100	60
Cruise Experience	400	237

OVERALL SCORE 1266 points out of 2000

English, French, German, Portuguese, and Spanish. During the European school holidays, particularly Christmas and Easter, you can expect to be cruising with a lot of children of all ages.

As aboard other Costa ships, note that for embarkation, staff members merely point you in the direction of your deck, or to the ship's elevators and do not escort you to your cabin. Also, note that 'wallpaper' music is played 24 hours a day in all accommodation hallways and elevators – you may well hear it, if you are a light sleeper.

ACCOMMODATION. There are numerous price grades. About 68 percent of all accommodation suites and cabins have an ocean view. Four suites and 52 Samsara Spa cabins are located adjacent to (and considered part of) the designated wellness area. As part of their package, Samsara accommodation occupants get unlimited access to the spa plus two treatments and fitness or meditation lessons, Samsara bathroom amenities, and can dine in one of the two Samsara restaurants.

A pillow menu, with five choices, is available to suite-grade occupants, who also get bathrobes, better amenities than standard-grade cabin occupants, a shaving mirror, and walk-in closets – although the hangers are plastic.

All cabins have twin beds that can convert into a queen-size one, air conditioning, television, telephone, vanity desk with built-in hairdryer, infotainment system, personal safe, and one closet that has moveable shelves –providing useful space for storing luggage. Some cabins have views obstructed by lifeboats – on decks 4 and 5. Some cabins have pulldown Pullman berths that are fully hidden in the ceiling when not in use.

Some of the most desirable suites and cabins are on aft-facing decks 4, 5, 6, 7, and 8, with private balconies and views looking aft. In most other cabins with balconies are not as private – the partition between adjacent cabins is not full, so you may be able to hear your neighbors. However, these balcony occupants all have good views through glass and wood-topped railings, and the deck is teak.

Penthouse Suites are the largest type of accommodation, although they are small when compared with suites aboard other ships of a similar size.

DINING. The Taurus Restaurant is the large, main restaurant. It is located aft. There are two seatings, with assigned tables for two to eight, according to your accommodation grade. Some tables have an unwelcome view of the harsh lighting of the escalators between the galley and the two decks of the dining room. Also, a number of support pillars provide something of an obstacle course for the waiters. If you expect to be served by jovial Italian waiters, you'll be disappointed – although the restaurant managers might be Italian. Few tables for two are available, most being for four, six, or eight.

The cuisine is Continental European, with some regional Italian dishes and plenty of pasta dishes. However, it is banquet-style batch cooking and quite unmemorable. Green vegetables are hard to come by, and rice is used as a plate-filler. Breads and baked goods are decent enough (but made from frozen 'starter' dough), but the desserts are disappointing

There is a wine list, but no wine waiters (table waiters serve both food and wine). Almost all the wines are young, and the glasses are small. Note that table water is not provided – you are expected to purchase it. It may be wise to buy a drinks package, which includes coffee and tea, bottled water and soft drinks, plus alcoholic beverages.

If you opt for one of the specialty restaurants, note that charges apply.

The regular coffee is decent and quite strong, but the extra-cost (illy) coffee is excellent.

A Samsara Restaurant is for occupants of the Samsara-grade cabins, and is located adjacent to the Taurus Restaurant; because it's small, it provides a quieter environment in which to dine. Healthier food with reduced calories, fat, and salt content is featured.

The Club Restaurant is a reservations-only, intimate restaurant that features à la carte dining with a pristine show kitchen as part of the venue. The food is cooked to order and is therefore better than food in the main dining room. It's a good idea to go for a meal here, particularly to celebrate a special occasion.

The Andromeda Buffet is a self-serve casual food court-style eatery. While there appears to be a decent choice of food, it is extremely repetitive (particularly for breakfast), and is a major source of passenger complaints. Its layout invites congestion because of some narrow passageways between the indoor seating and the food dispensing areas.

ENTERTAINMENT. The Phoenix Theater (showlounge) with over 800 seats, spans three decks. It appears as if it is illuminated by a rainbow of effects using the latest computer-controlled lighting. Typical fare consists of revue-style shows performed by a small troupe of resident onboard singers/dancers, with fast-moving action and busy lighting and costume changes that all add up to a high-energy performance.

SPA/FITNESS. Samsara Spa facilities include a Venus beauty salon, saunas for men and women, several private treatment rooms, a fitness center, and a relaxation area.

Most fitness classes cost extra.

Close by, a Grand Prix Formula One simulator is housed in a glass enclosure. For tee-time, a golf simulator provides a choice of several 18-hole courses. Other sporting facilities include a roller-skating track.

COSTA MAGICA
★★★+

THIS IS A FAMILY-FRIENDLY LARGE SHIP WITH ULTRA-BRIGHT ITALIAN DECOR

Size:	Mid-size Ship
Tonnage:	102,587
Cruise Line:	Costa Cruises
Former Names:	none
Builder:	Fincantieri (Italy)
Entered Service:	Nov 2004
Length (ft/m):	893.3/272.3
Propulsion/Propellers:	diesel-electric (34,000kW)/2 azimuthing pods
Total Crew:	1,068
Passengers (lower beds):	2,718
Passenger Space Ratio (lower beds):	37.7
Passenger/Crew Ratio (lower beds):	2.5
Cabins (total):	1,359
Size Range (sq ft/m):	179.7–482.2/16.7–44.8
Cabins (for one person):	0
Cabins with balcony:	522
Cabins (wheelchair accessible):	8
Wheelchair accessibility:	Good
Elevators:	14
Casino (gaming tables):	Yes
Self-Service Launderette:	No
Onboard currency:	Euros

THE SHIP. *Costa Magica* (sister to *Costa Fortuna*) has a balanced all-white profile topped by a single large yellow funnel. The ship's aft decks are nicely tiered. There is not a lot of open deck space considering the number of passengers carried, so sunloungers on the open decks are crammed tightly together; unfortunately they don't have cushioned pads. An aft swimming pool has a retractable glass dome; another pool has a waterslide, which kids love.

BERLITZ'S RATINGS		
	Possible	Achieved
Ship	500	366
Accommodation	200	134
Food	400	218
Service	400	242
Entertainment	100	60
Cruise Experience	400	235

OVERALL SCORE 1255 points out of 2000

Decks are named after famous Italian artists. The decor is chic, and not overly glitzy. There are three decks of lounges and bars to choose from, including a very pleasant Piano Bar Capo Colonna. A nine-deck-high, glass-domed atrium lobby houses a bar on its lowest level (for cost-extra illy-brand coffees), and panoramic elevators. In the Sicilia Casino, some 65 sculptured soldier puppets adorn the venue and its gaming tables and slot machines. The ship is designed for upbeat and active families with children.

While a variety of nationalities are carried, most passengers are Italian, so the ship is lively and noisy, with lots of children running around, particularly during the European school holidays.

All printed material – room service folio, menus, etc. – is in six languages: Italian, English, French, German, Portuguese, and Spanish.

Note that for embarkation, staff members merely point you in the direction of your deck, or to the ship's elevators. Also, note that 'wallpaper'

music is played 24 hours a day in all accommodation hallways and elevators, so you may hear it if you are a light sleeper. Expect lots of announcements in several languages, especially for revenue activities such as art auctions, bingo, and horse racing – and much hustling for drinks. Gratuities are charged to your onboard account. Although Costa Cruises is noted for its Italian style, ambience, and spirit, there are few Italian crew members on board. Although many officers are Italian, most of the crew members, particularly the dining room and housekeeping staff, are from the Philippines.

ACCOMMODATION. There are numerous price grades, and accommodation ranges from two-bed interior cabins to grand suites with private balcony. There are also two solo-occupancy cabins. No cabins have lifeboat-obstructed views, due to the clever design.

There are eight Grand Suites, in the ship's center. These feature a queen-size bed; bathrooms have a tub, two washbasins, and ample storage space for personal toiletries. Note that some of the most desirable (outside-view) wheelchair-accessible cabins are located a long way from elevators – a design error.

DINING. The two main dining rooms are Costa Smeralda Restaurant (aft) and the Portofino Restaurant (midships); both span two decks and feature two seatings for dinner at assigned tables. If you expect to be served by jovial Italian waiters, you'll be disappointed – although the restaurant managers might be Italian. Few tables for two are available, most being for four to eight.

The cuisine is Continental European banquet-style batch cooking, with some regional Italian dishes and lots of pasta dishes. The presentation and food quality are not great, and the subject of many passenger comments. Green vegetables are hard to come by, and rice is used as a plate-filler. Breads and bakery items are decent enough (but made from frozen 'starter' dough), but desserts are tasteless. There is heavy use of canned fruit, jellied desserts, and packets of butter and preserves.

There is a wine list, but no wine waiters (table waiters serve both food and wine). Almost all the wines are young, and the glasses are small. Note that table water is not provided – you are expected to purchase it. It's wise to buy a drinks package, which includes coffee and tea, bottled water and soft drinks, plus alcoholic beverages).

If you opt for one of the specialty restaurants, note that charges apply. The regular coffee is decent and quite strong, but the cost extra (illy) coffee is much better.

Club Vincenza is an intimate dining venue with around 150 seats under a glass dome roof. There is a cover charge, and reservations are required, but it's worth it for food cooked to order and presented well, with classy china and silverware, and enough space around the tables for decent service.

The Bellagio Buffet Restaurant is a casual self-serve food court-style eatery for breakfast, lunch, afternoon pizzas, and beverages. The food is extremely repetitive, however.

ENTERTAINMENT. The Urbino Theater spans three decks in the forward-most section of the ship. It is the setting for all production shows and large-scale cabaret acts, is quite stunning, and has a revolving stage, hydraulic orchestra pit, good sound, and seating on three levels. In the ship's aft section is the Salon Capri – a dancing lounge and nightclub – always popular with Europeans.

SPA/FITNESS. Facilities in the two-deck high Saturnia Spa, with about 14,000 sq ft (1,300 sq m) of space, include a large solarium, eight treatment rooms, sauna and steam rooms for men and women, and a beauty parlor.

COSTA MEDITERRANEA
★★★

THIS SHIP HAS UPBEAT ITALIAN DECOR AND STYLE, FOR FAMILIES OF ANY AGE

Size:	Large Resort Ship
Tonnage:	85,700
Cruise Line:	Costa Cruises
Former Names:	none
Builder:	Kvaerner Masa-Yards (Finland)
Entered Service:	May 2003
Length (ft/m):	959.6/292.5
Propulsion/Propellers:	diesel-electric (34,000kW)/2 azimuthing pods
Total Crew:	920
Passengers (lower beds):	2,112
Passenger Space Ratio (lower beds):	40.5
Passenger/Crew Ratio (lower beds):	2.2
Cabins (total):	1,056
Size Range (sq ft/m):	161.4–387.5/15.0–36.0
Cabins (for one person):	0
Cabins with balcony:	742
Cabins (wheelchair accessible):	8
Wheelchair accessibility:	Good
Elevators:	12
Casino (gaming tables):	Yes
Self-Service Launderette:	No
Onboard currency:	Euros

THE SHIP. *Costa Mediterranea* has two centrally located swimming pools outdoors, one with a retractable glass dome – so it can be covered in poor weather conditions or when it's cold. Two hot tubs are adjacent. Another smaller pool is for children. There is a winding waterslide spanning two decks in height, starting on a platform bridge well aft of the funnel.

The interior design is bold and brash – a mix of Classical and contemporary Italy. There is good passenger flow, and a range of bars and lounges for socializing and dancing. The interior focal point is an eight-deck atrium lobby, with two grand stairways. It features a stunning wall decoration – two huge paintings and *Danza*, a 25-piece wall sculpture by Gigi Rigamonti. The squid-shaped wall-lighting sconces are neat, too.

The decor itself is inspired by many Italian palaces (some well-known, many less so) and by a love of art and architecture. It is extremely upbeat, bright, glitzy, and in your face.

With three decks packed with many bars and lounges, other public rooms and shops, the ship caters to all tastes, although the decor is wild.

Families like Costa Cruises for its perceived 'Italian' style, ambience and spirit, and most passengers will be Italian, with a sprinkling of other nationalities. However, you won't find many Italian service staff on board (although many of the officers are Italian). Most crew members, particularly the dining room

BERLITZ'S RATINGS

	Possible	Achieved
Ship	500	350
Accommodation	200	130
Food	400	212
Service	400	242
Entertainment	100	60
Cruise Experience	400	236

OVERALL SCORE 1230 points out of 2000

and housekeeping staff, are from the Philippines. During peak European school holiday periods, especially Christmas and Easter, there will be lots of children and teens.

However, Costa Cruises does a good job of providing families with children with a packaged vacation that mixes hints of sophistication with the noisy and utterly chaotic. Gratuities are automatically added to your account.

Announcements are made and printed material is provided in several languages, but there is little information for passengers who want to be independent in ports of call. There is extensive smoking (no-smoking zones and signs are often ignored). In 2020, the ship will be transferred to CSSC (Carnival China Cruise Shipping) to join former fleetmate Costa Atlantica for Chinese domestic market cruises.

ACCOMMODATION. There are several different price grades; this includes a healthy 78 percent proportion of outside-view to interior cabins. All cabins have twin beds that convert into a queen-size bed, individually controlled air conditioning, TV set, and telephone. Some cabins have views obstructed by lifeboats – on Deck 4 (Roma Deck), the lowest of the accommodation decks, as well as some cabins on Deck 5. Some cabins have pull-down Pullman berths that are fully hidden in the ceiling when not in use.

There is much use of fluorescent lighting in the suites and cabins, and soundproofing could be better. Some of the bathroom fixtures such as the bath and shower faucets can be frustrating to use at first.

Among the most desirable suites and cabins are those with private balconies on aft-facing decks 4, 5, 6, 7, and 8. Anyone in other cabins with 'private' balconies will find the balconies not so private – the partition between them is not a full partition, so you'll be able to hear your neighbors (and smell their smoke, if they are smokers).

However, these balcony occupants all have good views through glass and wood-topped railings, and teak decking. The cabins are well laid out, with twin beds that convert to queen-size, vanity desk (with built-in hairdryer), large television, personal safe, and one closet with moveable shelves – to provide more space for storing luggage. However, the lighting is fluorescent and harsh. The bedside control is for a master switch only – other lights cannot be controlled. Note: many cabins have lifeboat-obstructed views on decks 4 and 5.

The bathrooms are simple, modular units (bland and minimalist), with shower enclosures and soap dispensers; there is a good amount of storage space for personal toiletries.

The largest suites are Penthouse Suites, although they are small when compared with suites aboard other ships of a similar size. At least they do offer more space to move around in, and a slightly larger, better bathroom.

Samsara Spa cabin occupants get spa amenities and spa access. You pay a little extra for these cabins, but you get more, and it may be worth it if you want to focus on wellness.

DINING. The 1,320-seat Ristorante degli Argentieri (main dining room) is large. It is located in the aft section on two levels, connected by a spiral stairway. There are two seatings, with assigned tables for two to eight. Some tables have a less-than-comfortable view of harsh lighting of the escalators between the galley and the two restaurant decks. Also, a number of support pillars provide a bit of an obstacle course. If you expect to be served by jovial Italian waiters, you'll be disappointed – although restaurant managers might be Italian.

The cuisine is Continental European, with many regional Italian dishes and considerable emphasis on starchy food, particularly pasta: 50 pasta dishes per cruise (buffalo mozzarella cheese is made on board). The food is banquet-style catering. Except for the pasta dishes and cream sauces, the presentation and food quality are unmemorable, and the subject of negative passenger comments. Green vegetables are sparse, and rice is used as a plate-filler. Breads and bakery items are decent enough (but made from frozen 'starter' dough), but desserts are of supermarket quality and lack taste. There is heavy use of canned fruit and jellied desserts and packets of jam, butter, etc.

There's a wine list, but no wine waiters (table waiters serve both food and wine). Almost all the wines are young, and the glasses small. Table water is not provided – you are expected to purchase it – so it may be wise to buy a drinks package, which includes it.

If you opt for one of the specialty restaurants, charges apply. The regular coffee is decent and quite strong, but the extra-cost (illy) coffee is far better.

Club Medusa is a more upscale dining spot, spanning two of the uppermost decks under a large glass dome adjacent to the funnel. It seats around 125. An open kitchen provides a view into the cooking area, so you can watch the chefs preparing their masterpieces. Fine table settings, china, and silverware are used. Reservations are needed and there's a cover charge, although you may think it's worth it in order to have dinner in a setting that's quieter and more refined than the main dining room.

The Perla del Lago Buffet is a self-serve eatery forming the aft third of Deck 9, partly wrapped around the upper section of the multi-deck atrium. It includes a 24-hour Posillipo Pizzeria. Movement around the buffet area is slow. Venture outdoors and you'll find a grill for burgers and hot dogs, and a pasta bar, both conveniently located adjacent to the second of two swimming pools on the Lido Deck.

There is also the casual Oriental Café, with four separate 'salons' offering intimate spaces for drinks, conversation, and people-watching.

ENTERTAINMENT. The 949-seat Osiris Theater is for the production shows and cabaret acts. It spans three decks, with seating on all three levels. Sight lines to the stage are, however, a little better from the second and third levels. Curving stairways at the back of the showlounge connect all levels.

SPA/FITNESS. Located directly above the navigation bridge in the forward part of the ship (accessed by the forward stairway elevators), the expansive Ischia Spa spans two decks. Lower-level facilities: a solarium, eight private treatment rooms, sauna and steam rooms for men and women, and a beauty parlor. Upper level: a large gymnasium with floor-to-ceiling windows. Most exercise classes are at extra cost.

There's a jogging track outdoors, around the ship's mast and the forward third of the ship, as well as a multi-purpose court for basketball, volleyball, and deck tennis.

COSTA NEORIVIERA
★★★

THIS FAMILY-FRIENDLY, ULTRA-CASUAL SHIP IS REALLY RATHER DATED

Size:	Mid-size Ship	Passenger/Crew Ratio (lower beds):	2.0
Tonnage:	48,200	Cabins (total):	624
Cruise Line:	Costa neoCollection	Size Range (sq ft/m):	139.9–236.8/13.0–22.0
Former Names:	Grand Mistral, Mistral	Cabins (for one person):	0
Builder:	Chantiers de l'Atlantique (France)	Cabins with balcony:	90
Entered Service:	Jul 1999/Dec 2019	Cabins (wheelchair accessible):	2
Length (ft/m):	709.9/216.4	Wheelchair accessibility:	Fair
Propulsion/Propellers:	diesel-electric (31,680kW)/2	Elevators:	6
Total Crew:	600	Casino (gaming tables):	Yes
Passengers (lower beds):	1,248	Self-Service Launderette:	No
Passenger Space Ratio (lower beds):	38.6	Onboard currency:	Euros

THE SHIP. *Costa neoRiviera* (formerly *Grand Mistral*) is part of a new sub-brand of Costa Cruises, called Costa neoCollection – a strange name – for slower, longer cruises. The vessel's built-up stern makes it look bulky and less than handsome.

The lido deck surrounding the small outdoor pool has two whirlpool tubs and a large canvas-covered bandstand. There is no full walk-around outdoor promenade deck, only a partial walking deck on port and starboard sides under the lifeboats, and an oval jogging track atop ship.

The interior layout and passenger flow is decent, and the ship absorbs people quite well. It is light and cheerful without being too glitzy – not even a hint of colored neon – but much use of blond/cherry wood paneling and rich, textured soft furnishings.

Public rooms include several lounges and bars, while atop the ship is an observation lounge with a twist – it faces aft, and doubles as a disco. There's a video games room for teens, and a small children's center.

Although Costa Cruises is noted for its Italian style, ambience, and spirit, there are few Italian crew members on board. Most of the crew, particularly the dining room and housekeeping staff, is from the Philippines. But the lifestyle on board is perceived to be Italian – lively, noisy, with lots of gusto for life. Gratuities are charged to your onboard account. Note that,

BERLITZ'S RATINGS		
	Possible	Achieved
Ship	500	294
Accommodation	200	120
Food	400	207
Service	400	236
Entertainment	100	51
Cruise Experience	400	225
OVERALL SCORE 1133 points out of 2000		

in December 2019 this ship transfers to the AIDA Cruises brand to become *AIDAmira*.

ACCOMMODATION. There are three basic cabin types, in several different price grades. These include 'suites' (each with a private balcony and partial partitions), ocean-view standard cabins, and interior standard cabins. The price you pay will depend on grade, size, and location.

Cabins on Deck 10 are subject to noise from the Lido Deck above. Good design means that no outside-view cabins have lifeboat-obstructed views, but there are many interior (no-view) cabins. The cabin numbering system goes against maritime tradition, where even-numbered cabins are on the port side and odd-numbered cabins on the starboard; on this ship, the opposite is the case.

All cabins have twin beds that convert to a queen-size unit, colorful bedspreads, personal safe, flat-screen TV, and decent closet and drawer space. The bathrooms, although not large, have a good-size shower enclosure, plus storage space for toiletries.

The suites (they are really only larger cabins, as there is no separation of lounge and sleeping space) have more space, larger (walk-in) closets, more drawers and storage space, plus a two-person sofa, coffee table and additional armchair, vanity desk, floor-to-ceiling mirrors, and hairdryer; bathrooms have a tub/shower combination.

Six Grand Suites have a separate bedroom with flat-screen TV, bedside tables, vanity desk, floor-to-ceiling windows, and door to balcony; the lounge has an audio-visual center, sofa, dining table, plus a door to the balcony. A large bathroom has two washbasins, dark hardwood storage cabinets, Jacuzzi tub, separate shower enclosure (with hand-held shower), and bathrobes. Also, there are two interior wheelchair-accessible cabins.

DINING. There are two dining rooms (and two seatings for meals, with dinner at 6.30pm and 9pm) with ocean-view windows. The principal 612-seat Restaurant Cetara has round tables for two to eight, and a small podium with baby grand piano.

Restaurant Saint Tropez, seating 274 in chairs without armrests, is on a different deck. Smaller and more intimate, for passengers occupying Deck 10 accommodation; it has tables for two to six, and ocean-view windows. Note that table water is not provided – you are expected to purchase it.

The casual Vernazza Buffet (for alfresco self-serve breakfasts and lunches) has ocean-view windows, but the flow is awkward and cramped. There's an outdoor pizzeria and grilled food counter (for burgers and hot dogs). Also, there's a pleasant little coffee bar (Café Eze – for excellent illy coffees) on the upper level of the two-deck high lobby, but with lifeboat-restricted ocean views.

ENTERTAINMENT. The Teatro Ravello spans two decks, has a sloping floor, good sight lines from most seats (banquette seating), and a small balcony level at the back. Sadly, the designer forgot to include space for a live band (all shows are performed to pre-recorded backing tracks), and poor lighting. Entertainment is, without doubt, weak.

SPA/FITNESS. The Santai Spa located forward, includes a gymnasium with muscle-pump equipment (and ocean views), a thalassotherapy room, beauty salon, six rooms for body treatments, male and female saunas, and aerobics room.

COSTA NEOROMANTICA
★★★

THIS ELEGANT ITALIAN-STYLE SHIP IS FOR CRUISERS OF A MATURE AGE

Size:	Mid-size Ship	Passenger/Crew Ratio (lower beds):	2.3
Tonnage:	57,150	Cabins (total):	789
Cruise Line:	Costa neoCollection	Size Range (sq ft/m):	185.1–430.5/17.2–40.0
Former Names:	*Costa Romantica*	Cabins (for one person):	0
Builder:	Fincantieri (Italy)	Cabins with balcony:	74
Entered Service:	Nov 1993/Nov 1993	Cabins (wheelchair accessible):	6
Length (ft/m):	718.5/220.6	Wheelchair accessibility:	Good
Propulsion/Propellers:	diesel (22,800kW)/2	Elevators:	8
Total Crew:	662	Casino (gaming tables):	Yes
Passengers (lower beds):	1,578	Self-Service Launderette:	No
Passenger Space Ratio (lower beds):	36.2	Onboard currency:	Euros

THE SHIP. *Costa neoRomantica* (a play on the ship's original name of *Costa Romantica*) is now over 25 years old – the oldest ship in the fleet. Although not handsome, it is easily recognizable by its cluster of three upright yellow funnels. There is, however, no walk-around promenade deck outdoors, so contact with the sea is minimal, although there's some good open space on several of the upper decks.

In 2011–12, the ship was given an extensive €90 million renewal program that added more public rooms, two half-deck extensions, 111 new cabins, 120 suites and cabins with balcony, wine and cheese bar, a chocolate confectionary bar, new Pizzeria Capri (with its black-and-white tiled decor), a cabaret lounge and nightclub, and LED lighting. However, no additional elevators were installed for the increase in passenger numbers, the swimming pool remains very small, and the layout and flow are disjointed.

Facilities also include a Monte Carlo Lido indoor/outdoor bar; Vienna cabaret lounge; Piazza Italia Grand Bar (arguably the best place to see and be seen in); an atrium (with minimalist design features); the neoRomantica Club Restaurant; Casino Excelsior; and a Caffèteria that is part of the Via Condotti shopping area. Out on the pool deck (Lido Saint-Tropez) several 'private' cabanas, adjacent to the pool, can be rented.

Although Costa Cruises is noted for its Italian style, ambience, and spirit, there are few Italian crew

BERLITZ'S RATINGS	Possible	Achieved
Ship	500	323
Accommodation	200	126
Food	400	208
Service	400	244
Entertainment	100	54
Cruise Experience	400	224

OVERALL SCORE 1179 points out of 2000

members on board. But the lifestyle on board is perceived to be Italian – lively, noisy, with lots of love for life and a love of all things casual, even on so-called formal nights.

All printed material – room service folio, menus, etc. – will typically be in six languages: Italian, English, French, German, Portuguese, and Spanish. During peak European school holidays, particularly Christmas and Easter, you can expect to be cruising with a lot of children of all ages.

As aboard other Costa ships, few staff members are on duty at the gangway during embarkation; they merely point you in the direction of your deck, or to the ship's elevators and do not escort you to your cabin. Also, note that 'wallpaper' music is played 24 hours a day in accommodation hallways and elevators, so you may well hear it if you are a light sleeper. Gratuities are automatically charged to your onboard account.

ACCOMMODATION. There are several different price categories. These include 16 suites, 10 of which have a private semicircular balcony, while six suites command views over the ship's bows. The other cabins are fairly standard in size, shape, and facilities; the ones on the highest decks cost more.

There's a whole wedge of cabins with half-moon-shaped balconies, as well as normal balconies, in the mid-section of the ship.

Samsara Suites/Cabins. Occupants of these 6 suites and 50 cabins have access to Samsara Spa and its facilities, located forward. Samsara accommodation features organic cotton bed linen, a purifying shower filter, and a selection of Ayurvedic teas.

Suites/Mini-Suites. The suites (with floor-to-ceiling windows) and mini-suites are quite pleasant, except for the rounded balconies of the suites on Madrid Deck, where a solid steel half-wall blocks the view. A sliding door separates the bedroom from the living room, and bathrooms are of a decent size. Cherry wood walls and cabinetry help make these suites warm and attractive.

Six suites at the forward section of Monte Carlo Deck are the largest, with large glass windows with commanding forward views, but no balconies.

All other cabins are of a moderately generous size, and all have nicely finished cherry wood cabinetry and walls. However, the cabin bathrooms and shower enclosures are quite small. There are a number of triple and quad cabins, ideal for families with children. The company's in-cabin food service menu is extremely basic.

DINING. The 738-seat Botticelli Restaurant is of a fine design. There are tables for two to eight persons, and open-seating ('My Time') for all meals. Romantic candlelight dining is typically featured on 'formal' night. Traditional cruise fare is served, and best described as banquet-style food. Note that there are no sommeliers, so the waiters serve the wine. They also dance in the restaurant – an example of Costa Cruises' penchant for show business. Note that table water is not provided – you are expected to purchase it.

The 72-seat Samsara Restaurant is for occupants of Samsara-grade accommodation. The restaurant is located at the aft of the ship on the port side of Vienna Deck. The cuisine is more health-oriented, and the venue is quieter and more intimate than the main dining room.

The 90-seat Club neoRomantica Restaurant is an extra-cost, reservations-required, à la carte venue. While the banquette seating is unbecoming of 'fine' dining, this is still a rather pleasant and cozy spot for an intimate dinner, and it features contemporary French and Italian fare that is worth the extra cost.

For casual meals and snacks, the self-serve Giardino Buffet is a small, cramped buffet. The buffet food items are very much standard fare (repetitive breakfast items are a major source of passenger complaints), with the exception of some good commercial pasta dishes.

Pizzeria Capri has something unusual for any cruise ship – a real wood-burning oven – used for making proper Neapolitan-style pizzas (the venue makes 15 different ones).

Enoteco Verona is a wine and cheese bar that features more than 100 different wines, and 80 cheeses from around the world. Italian coffee machines are provided in all bars (coffees are at extra cost, however), so there's never a shortage of espressos and cappuccinos and the like.

ENTERTAINMENT. The Cabaret Vienna is the ship's main showlounge. It is an interesting amphitheater-like design that spans two decks, with seating on both levels. However, the seats are quite upright and uncomfortable, and 10 large pillars obstruct the sight lines from many seats. Typical fare consists of revue-style shows performed by a small troupe of resident singers/dancers, with fast-moving action and busy lighting and costume changes that all add up to a high-energy performance.

SPA/FITNESS. Samsara Spa spans two decks in the forward section of the ship. It contains a gymnasium with some high-tech muscle-pump machines, an aerobics exercise area, thalassotherapy pool, Turkish baths, health bar, sauna and steam rooms, a solarium, and a beauty salon. Occupants of the 56 adjacent Samsara Spa cabins also dine at the health-conscious, intimate Samsara Restaurant.

The spa/fitness facilities are staffed and operated by Steiner Leisure, a specialist spa/beauty concession. Some fitness classes are free, while some, such as Pathway to Yoga, Pathway to Pilates, and Pathway to Meditation, cost extra. It's wise to make appointments early, as time slots can go quickly.

COSTA PACIFICA
★★★+

THIS IS A COLORFUL, FAMILY-FRIENDLY ITALIAN-STYLE SHIP FOR CASUAL CRUSING

Size:	Large Resort Ship	Passenger/Crew Ratio (lower beds):	2.7
Tonnage:	114,500	Cabins (total):	1,506
Cruise Line:	Costa Cruises	Size Range (sq ft/m):	179.7–482.2/16.7–44.8
Former Names:	none	Cabins (for one person):	0
Builder:	Fincantieri (Italy)	Cabins with balcony:	579
Entered Service:	Apr 2009	Cabins (wheelchair accessible):	12
Length (ft/m):	952.0/290.0	Wheelchair accessibility:	Good
Propulsion/Propellers:	diesel-electric (34,000kW)/2 azimuthing pods	Elevators:	14
		Casino (gaming tables):	Yes
Total Crew:	1,110	Self-Service Launderette:	No
Passengers (lower beds):	3,012	Onboard currency:	Euros
Passenger Space Ratio (lower beds):	38.0		

THE SHIP. Sporting a single, large funnel, *Costa Pacifica* is sister to *Costa Serena*, which now operates short Asia cruises from its year-round base in Shanghai, China. Two pool areas can be covered with retractable glass domes – good in case of poor weather – and one of the pools has a waterslide that's great for kids. There is also a large screen for poolside movies.

However, the open deck space is cramped when the ship is full, so sunloungers tend to be crammed together, and lack cushioned pads.

The glass-domed atrium lobby is nine decks high, with great upward views from the lobby bar, as well as from its four glass panoramic elevators. The ship absorbs passengers reasonably well. The interior design theme is music's 'greatest hits' and the atrium lobby walls are covered in musical symbols and instruments.

In the large, glitzy Flamingo Casino; slot machines are in a separate area – better for serious gamers. There's also a tiny library, an Internet-connection center, a card room, an art gallery, and a video game room, plus several bars and lounges.

Costa Cruises are very good for families with children, who are divided into three age groups. Kids have their own swimming pool, playrooms and video games rooms.

Although Costa Cruises is noted for its Italian style, ambience and spirit, there are few Italian crew members on board its ships. Most of the crew

BERLITZ'S RATINGS		
	Possible	Achieved
Ship	500	367
Accommodation	200	134
Food	400	219
Service	400	246
Entertainment	100	60
Cruise Experience	400	236

OVERALL SCORE 1262 points out of 2000

– particularly the dining room and housekeeping staff – is from the Philippines. The lifestyle on board is, however, perceived to be Italian – lively, noisy, and embracing a casual lifestyle – even on so-called formal nights. Most passengers will be Italian, with a sprinkling of other European nationals.

Costa Pacifica has a quasi-Italian style and ambience with bright surroundings and everything loud, with grainy and unflattering digital artwork on walls and panels – even inside elevators. The dress code is very casual, except for 'white' nights. This is for those who like things lively. For quiet, take earplugs – good ones, or choose a different ship. On European cruises, your fellow passengers will mostly speak Italian, Spanish, French, and German. Few staff members are on duty at the gangway when you embark, but merely point you in the direction of your deck, or to the ship's elevators (no escort to your cabin). Gratuities are automatically added to your account. Overall, Costa provides a well-packaged cruise holiday, especially for families with kids, at a low price.

ACCOMMODATION. There are numerous price grades, from two-bed interior cabins to grand suites with private balcony, although in reality there are only three different sizes: suites with small 'private' balcony; two- or four-bed outside-view cabins; and two- or four-bed interior (no-view) cabins. No cabins have views obstructed by lifeboats or other safety equipment, and, in all cabins, twin beds can convert to a double/queen-bed.

Eight Grand Suites comprise the largest accommodation, in the center of the ship on one of the uppermost decks.

Some 12 Samsara Spa Suites are just aft of the spa – with 79 other cabins, designated as Samsara-grade (all with Oriental decorative theme, and special Samsara bathroom amenities). Occupants get unlimited access to the spa, with fitness or meditation lessons as part of a package, and dine in one of two Samsara restaurants.

A multi-choice pillow menu is available in suite accommodation grades, as are bathrobes and better amenities, shaving mirror, and walk-in closets (but the hangers are plastic).

DINING. There are two main dining rooms (the 1,036-seat New York, New York, and the 752-seat My Way), allocated according to your accommodation grade. There are two dinner seatings. If you expect to be served by jovial Italian waiters, you'll be disappointed – although the restaurant managers might be Italian. Few tables for two are available, most being for four to eight.

The cuisine is Continental European, with some regional Italian dishes and many pasta dishes. However, the presentation and overall food quality are unmemorable, and the subject of many passenger comments. Green vegetables are few, and rice is used as a plate-filler. Breads and bakery items are decent enough (but made from frozen 'starter' dough); desserts are bland. Canned fruit, jellied desserts, and packets of jam and butter feature heavily.

There's a wine list, but no wine waiters (table waiters serve both food and wine). Almost all the wines are young, and the glasses are small. Note that table water is not provided – you are expected to purchase it. It's wise to buy a drinks package, which includes coffee and tea, bottled water and soft drinks, plus alcoholic beverages.

If you opt for one of the specialty restaurants, note that charges apply. While the regular ship's coffee is decent and quite strong, the extra-cost (illy) coffee is the best.

Two Samsara restaurants have separate entrances to the My Way restaurant, and feature more health-conscious fare, with reduced calories and less fat and salt in the cooking. These dining venues are open for lunch and dinner for occupants of Samsara-grade suites and cabins, and to others (for dinner only) at extra cost.

Club Restaurant Blue Moon (reservations required) is an elegant, intimate venue, topped by a large glass dome. Fine table settings, china, silverware, and leather-bound menus are provided. A cover charge applies.

La Paloma Buffet Restaurant is a self-serve eatery with main room and balcony seating. You carry your own food plates – there are no trays, and the selection is really minimal

ENTERTAINMENT. The Stardust Theater seats more than 800, spans three decks, and is decorated in a Baroque style, with a Murano-glass chandelier. It is for all high-energy shows and large-scale cabaret acts, and has a revolving stage, hydraulic orchestra pit, superb sound, and seating on three levels.

SPA/FITNESS. Samsara Spa spans two decks. It includes a large fitness room, separate saunas, steam rooms, UVB solarium, changing rooms for men and women, and 10 treatment rooms. On the upper level, two VIP treatment rooms are available to couples for half-day rentals. Some fitness classes are free; others, such as Pathway to Yoga and Pathway to Pilates, cost extra.

A cost-extra day pass allows access to the sauna/steam rooms, thermal suite, and relaxation area. However, there's a small additional no-charge sauna for men and women.

COSTA SERENA
★★★+

THIS SHIP HAS REALLY FUNKY UPBEAT ITALIAN DECOR, FOR FAMILY CRUISING

Size:	Large Resort Ship
Tonnage:	114,147
Cruise Line:	Costa Cruises
Former Names:	none
Builder:	Fincantieri (Italy)
Entered Service:	May 2007
Length (ft/m):	952.0/290.2
Propulsion/Propellers:	diesel-electric (34,000kW)/2 azimuthing pods
Total Crew:	1,090
Passengers (lower beds):	3,000
Passenger Space Ratio (lower beds):	38.0
Passenger/Crew Ratio (lower beds):	2.7
Cabins (total):	1,500
Size Range (sq ft/m):	482.2–179.7/44.8–16.7
Cabins (for one person):	0
Cabins with balcony:	575
Cabins (wheelchair accessible):	12
Wheelchair accessibility:	Good
Elevators:	14
Casino (gaming tables):	Yes
Self-Service Launderette:	No
Onboard currency:	Euros

THE SHIP. *Costa Serena* absorbs passengers well and won't feel too crowded, except on open decks. The interior design is themed around the heavens and astrology. *Costa Serena* sails year-round from Shanghai, China, with mostly domestic Chinese passengers (and announcements in Mandarin).

There are three decks full of bars and lounges plus lots of other public rooms. This ship has a nine-deck-high glass-domed atrium lobby with four panoramic elevators providing great views. The Casino is large and glitzy, but always lively and entertaining. There's also a small library, Internet-connect center, card room, art gallery, and video game room, together with several other bars and lounges, plus a chapel.

Costa Cruises does a good job of providing first-time cruise passengers with a packaged holiday that is a mix of sophistication and basic fare. Gratuities are automatically charged to your onboard account.

ACCOMMODATION. There are numerous price grades, although in reality there are only three different sizes: suites with balcony, two- or four-bed outside-view cabins, and two- or four-bed interior cabins. Eight Grand Suites comprise the largest accommodation.

DINING. There are two main dining rooms: the 1,125-seat Ceres (aft), and the 775-seat Vesta (amid-

BERLITZ'S RATINGS

	Possible	Achieved
Ship	500	367
Accommodation	200	134
Food	400	218
Service	400	246
Entertainment	100	60
Cruise Experience	400	235

OVERALL SCORE 1260 points out of 2000

ships). Tables for two (there are very few) to eight are allocated according to your accommodation grade and location, in one of two seating times. If you expect to be served by jovial Italian waiters, you'll be disappointed – although the restaurant managers might be Italian.

The cuisine is Continental European, with some regional Italian dishes and much emphasis on carbohydrate-rich food, with up to 50 pasta dishes (buffalo mozzarella cheese is made on board). The food is banquet-style batch cooking. The presentation and food quality are unmemorable, and the subject of many passenger comments. Green vegetables are hard to come by, and rice is used as a plate-filler. Breads and bakery items are decent enough (but made from frozen 'starter' dough), but desserts are of supermarket quality and lack taste. There is heavy use of canned fruit, jellied desserts, and packets of jam, butter, etc.

There's a wine list, but no wine waiters (table waiters serve both food and wine), and wine glasses are small. Table water is not provided – you are expected to purchase it, so it may be wise to buy a drinks package, which includes coffee and tea, bottled water and soft drinks, plus alcoholic beverages.

If you opt for one of the specialty restaurants, charges will apply.

A large self-serve lido buffets with basic items. The regular coffee is decent and quite strong, but the extra-cost (illy) coffee is excellent.

Two Samsara Restaurants are for spa-style food, with reduced calories, fat, and salt. Menu creations are under the direction of dietary consultant and Michelin-starred chef Ettore Bocchia. This venue is open for lunch and dinner to those in Samsara-grade suites and cabins, and to anyone else for dinner only at an extra daily or weekly charge.

Other dining options. The 90-seat Bacco Club Restaurant is an upscale, intimate, extra-cost, reservations-required restaurant. The Promotea Buffet Restaurant is a self-serve eatery, with repetitive food (a source of complaints). The Caffeteria is the place to go for excellent (extra-cost) illy-brand Italian coffees and pastries.

ENTERTAINMENT. The three-deck-high 1,287-seat Giove Theater is the venue for all production shows and large-scale cabaret acts. Typically, it presents revue-style shows.

SPA/FITNESS. Samsara Spa spans two decks, with a fitness room, saunas, steam rooms, UVB solarium, changing rooms, and treatment rooms.

COSTA SMERALDA
NYR

THIS CASUAL, FAMILY-FRIENDLY SHIP HAS MANY CONTEMPORARY FEATURES AND ITALIAN STYLE

Size:	Large Resort Ship
Tonnage:	182,700
Cruise Line:	Costa Cruises
Former Names:	none
Builder:	Meyer Turku (Finland)
Entered Service:	Nov 2019
Length (ft/m):	1,105.6/337.0
Propulsion/Propellers:	LNG/diesel/2 azimuthing pods
Total Crew:	1,678
Passengers (lower beds):	5,224
Passenger Space Ratio (lower beds):	34.9
Passenger/Crew Ratio (lower beds):	3.1
Cabins (total):	2,612
Size Range (sq ft/m):	135.6–688.9/12.6–64.0
Cabins (for one person):	0
Cabins with balcony:	1,656
Cabins (wheelchair accessible):	33
Wheelchair accessibility:	Good
Elevators:	22
Casino (gaming tables):	Yes
Self-Service Launderette:	No
Onboard currency:	Euros

THE SHIP. *Costa Smeralda* is the company's first dual fuel-powered ship, and the largest ship in the fleet; it has a stark, almost upright, stubby bow, a single funnel, and lifeboats that overhang the hull. It certainly is a big ship – so there is more open deck space, an aqua (water) park, and more public bars, lounges, and eating venues (and more passengers) than competitor ships. A 'private,' extra-cost, two-deck retreat area is available if you seek a quieter outdoor space.

BERLITZ'S RATINGS		
	Possible	Achieved
Ship	500	NYR
Accommodation	200	NYR
Food	400	NYR
Service	400	NYR
Entertainment	100	NYR
Cruise Experience	400	NYR

OVERALL SCORE NYR points out of 2000

Step aboard and you'll be greeted by a 4ft (1.2m) white humanoid robot named 'Pepper,' who is seaworthy and speaks English, German, and Italian, but he won't take your carry-on luggage or walk you to your cabin. You'll see more Pepper(s) around the ship, acting as information helpers.

There are numerous restaurants and eateries, lounges, bars and drinking places, as well as a large fitness center and a casino, many of which are connected to The Colosseo (Coliseum) atrium lobby. Decks are named after Italian cities, with cabin art continuing the theme. Note: there is no deck 13 on Costa Cruises ships – good for superstitious travelers.

Costa Cruises loves families and children, who are catered for under several different age groups, and have their own swimming pool and outdoor water-park areas, playrooms, video-game rooms, programs, and activities.

Costa Cruises is noted for its 'Italian' style, ambience, and spirit, but there are few Italian crew members. Although many officers are Italian, most of the crew, particularly the dining room and housekeeping staff, are from the Philippines. But the lifestyle on board is perceived to be Italian – lively, noisy, with a love for life, even on so-called formal nights.

Because the ship is really large, taking time to do a little planning before you board will help you maximize your time and use of the facilities and eating places, and to budget accordingly.

ACCOMMODATION. There are many accommodation price grades, depending on size, location, and grade. From the smallest interior (no-view) cabin to the largest suite, the accommodation is designed with families in mind. A new category includes an over-the-sea balcony. The soft furnishings are of good quality and practical, with a muted color palette.

DINING. There are 11 restaurants, including several cost-extra venues and casual eateries. La Colombina, Il Meneghino and Il Rugantino are the three main (large) restaurants, and all are aft.

Costa's cuisine is Continental European, but includes some regional Italian dishes, although there is much emphasis on carbohydrate-rich food. It's all about banquet-style batch cooking. The presentation and food quality are unmemorable, green vegetables are hard to find, and rice is used as a plate-filler. Bread and bakery items are decent enough (made from frozen 'starter' dough), but the supermarket-quality desserts lack taste. There is heavy use of canned fruit, jellied desserts, and packets of jam, butter, etc., but one neat feature is the buffalo mozzarella cheese that's made on board.

Wine list – yes, wine waiters – no (table waiters serve food *and* wine). Almost all the wines are young, and the glasses are small. Table water is not provided, but is available for purchase. It may be wise to buy a drinks package, which includes coffee, tea, bottled water, and soft drinks, plus standard spirits.

Other dining venues and eateries (some at extra cost, reservations required) include L'Arlecchino, Ristorante Panorama, Ristorante Bellavista, Tutti a Tavola, Tep-panyaki Grill, La Spiaggia, Salty Beach Food, and a large Pizzeria Pummid'Oro.

A large self-serve buffet (Ristorante La Sagra dei Sapori) is a self-serve, food court-style eatery, with many different sections for specific food items.

ENTERTAINMENT. The Teatro San Remo show-lounge spans two decks, with seating on both levels. Colorful, high-energy production shows are the main attraction.

SPA/FITNESS. The two-deck Samsara Spa includes saunas, steam rooms, a hammam, a high-tech fitness center, a relaxation zone with hot tubs, and numerous treatment rooms.

COSTA VENEZIA
★★★+

THIS ITALIAN-STYLE SHIP FOR FAMILY CRUISING HAS A NOD TO ASIAN INFLUENCES

Size:	Large Resort Ship	Passenger/Crew Ratio (lower beds):	2.0
Tonnage:	135,500	Cabins (total):	2,116
Cruise Line:	Costa Cruises	Size Range (sq ft/m):	172.2–344.4/16.0–32.0
Former Names:	none	Cabins (for one person):	0
Builder:	Fincantieri (Italy)	Cabins with balcony:	1,047
Entered Service:	Mar 2019	Cabins (wheelchair accessible):	44
Length (ft/m):	1062.0/324.0	Wheelchair accessibility:	Good
Propulsion/Propellers:	diesel-electric (34,000kW)/2 azimuthing pods	Elevators:	16
		Casino (gaming tables):	Yes
Total Crew:	1,278	Self-Service Launderette:	No
Passengers (lower beds):	4,232	Onboard currency:	Yuan
Passenger Space Ratio (lower beds):	31.9		

THE SHIP. The large, resort-style *Costa Venezia* is dedicated to the Asian market and the growing number of Chinese domestic passengers. It is designed for families, with an outdoor Activity Deck water park and play area aft, featuring two long waterslides, rock climbing walls, and splash pools – popular with children. A midship pool has a retractable glass cover, and there are hot tubs, a mega-screen, and a walk-around promenade deck (lifeboats overhang the ship to provide more space). A separate, child-free area (Beach Club) is a cost-extra relaxation zone.

The central interior focal and meeting point is Piazza San Marco (St. Mark's Square – fortunately, minus the pigeons), with an interior design theme that is, as you might expect, all about Venice. There are also multiple bars and drinking places (including the entertaining Gondola Lounge), a large casino (Casino Dea Bandata) with gaming tables and few slot machines, and multiple shops.

Costa Cruises is noted for its 'Italian' style, ambience, and spirit, so expect the noise level to be high, because the ship is all about celebrating the famous Venice carnival. Be prepared to participate in parties donning Venetian masks, and displays of gold brashness. Some officers are Italian, but most hotel service crew are from the Philippines, with a high percentage of Chinese-speakers. Note: there is no deck 13 (considered unlucky for Ital-

BERLITZ'S RATINGS		
	Possible	Achieved
Ship	500	376
Accommodation	200	141
Food	400	217
Service	400	258
Entertainment	100	70
Cruise Experience	400	257

OVERALL SCORE 1319 points out of 2000

ians), but there is a deck 4 and deck 14 (considered unlucky for Chinese).

ACCOMMODATION. There are various accommodation price grades, depending on size, location, and grade, although many are actually are of a similar size (small). From the smallest interior (no-view) cabin (of which there are many) to the largest suite (it's still quite small), they all have decor associated with one of the port cities of Italy. All cabins have twin beds convertible to a double, but limited storage space, and a bathroom with small shower enclosure, washbasin, and toilet.

DINING. There are two main restaurants: Canal Grande Restaurant, located aft, spans two decks and has seating on both levels, and Marco Polo Restaurant, located forward, on one of the same decks. Waiters/waitresses serve food, as well as wines and other beverages, and are dressed in Venetian gondolier-style uniforms.

Overall, the cuisine is Italian fare, somewhat carbohydrate-rich, and includes many pasta dishes. It is standardized, banquet-style batch cooking, with little presentation or flair. Green vegetables are scarce, and white rice is generously used as a plate-filler. Bread and bakery items are made from frozen 'starter' dough, and supermarket-quality jellied desserts lack taste.

Extra-cost eateries include Casanova, La Fiorentina Steak House, Restaurant Frutti di Mare, Lu Hot Pot (good for noodle indulgence), and Yan Teppanyaki (for grilled show food – with lots of rice). These small venues are more intimate and have more items cooked to order (with better ingredients) than in the main dining rooms. A self-serve buffet eatery helps satisfy quick-bite seekers.

ENTERTAINMENT. Teatro Rossa spans two decks, with seating on both levels, and good sight lines from most seats. The razzle-dazzle shows are fast-paced, colorful, and geared to the ship's mostly Asian clientele.

SPA/FITNESS. Bellezza Spa includes a large ocean-view fitness room, beauty salon, and body-treatment rooms.

COSTA VICTORIA
★★★

THIS SHIP HAS DATED DECOR AND AN ITALIAN SETTING FOR CRUISES IN EUROPE

Size:	Mid-size Ship	
Tonnage:	75,166	
Cruise Line:	Costa Cruises	
Former Names:	none	
Builder:	Bremer Vulkan (Germany)	
Entered Service:	Jul 1996	
Length (ft/m):	823.0/251.0	
Propulsion/Propellers:	diesel (30,000kW)/2	
Total Crew:	800	
Passengers (lower beds):	1,928	
Passenger Space Ratio (lower beds):	38.9	
Passenger/Crew Ratio (lower beds):	2.4	
Cabins (total):	964	
Size Range (sq ft/m):	150.6–484.3/14.0–45.0	
Cabins (for one person):	0	
Cabins with balcony:	246	
Cabins (wheelchair accessible):	6	
Wheelchair accessibility:	Good	
Elevators:	12	
Casino (gaming tables):	Yes	
Self-Service Launderette:	Yes	
Onboard currency:	Euros	

THE SHIP. *Costa Victoria* – now well over 20 years old – has an outdoor walk-around promenade deck, although it tends to be full of sunloungers. Where this ship differs from many other ships is in its interior decor, with a decidedly Italian influence, and a cozy feeling.

A seven-deck-high 'planetarium' atrium is the focal point. The uppermost level has two outdoor swimming pools, plus a grill, and a gelateria. Also notable is a four-deck-high observation lounge with a glass elevator.

ACCOMMODATION. There are several different price categories. Six Panorama Suites (each with third/fourth Pullman berths in tiny compartments, like those on a train) and 14 mini-suites are the largest.

All cabins have wood cabinetry, mini-bar/refrigerator, and electric blackout window blinds, but storage space is very limited. The ocean-view cabins have large picture windows. Bathrooms are small but quite well appointed.

DINING. There are two main dining rooms: the 594-seat Sinfonia Restaurant and the 506-seat Fantasia Restaurant. Some tables have an uncomfortable

BERLITZ'S RATINGS		
	Possible	Achieved
Ship	500	297
Accommodation	200	126
Food	400	204
Service	400	237
Entertainment	100	53
Cruise Experience	400	220

OVERALL SCORE 1137 points out of 2000

view of harsh escalator lighting between the galley and the two decks of the restaurant. A number of support pillars provide an obstacle course for the waiters. Note that table water is not provided (you are expected to purchase it).

Ristorante Magnifico is an extra-cost, reservations-required venue with 158 seats and cooked-to-order food.

Buffet Bolero is a self-serve cafeteria for casual eats, although the food displays and variety are poor (and a constant source of complaints). Outdoors is a Pizzeria and Tavernetta, while extra-cost illy-brand coffees are available at various bars.

ENTERTAINMENT. The entertainment consists of revue-style shows performed by a small troupe of resident onboard singers/dancers in the Festival Theatre.

SPA/FITNESS. The congested spa/fitness area, on a lower deck, is small for the size of the ship. It has a beauty salon, tiny indoor swimming pool, treatment rooms, sauna, and steam room, but cramped changing areas. Sporting facilities include a covered walking/jogging track and a tennis court.

CROWN PRINCESS
★★★+

THIS SHIP HAS VERY COMFORTABLE, BUT SEDATE DECOR FOR MATURE-AGE CRUISERS

Size:	Large Resort Ship	Passenger/Crew Ratio (lower beds):	2.6
Tonnage:	116,000	Cabins (total):	1,557
Cruise Line:	Princess Cruises	Size Range (sq ft/m):	163–1,279/15.1–118.8
Former Names:	none	Cabins (for one person):	0
Builder:	Fincantieri (Italy)	Cabins with balcony:	881
Entered Service:	May 2006	Cabins (wheelchair accessible):	25
Length (ft/m):	951.4/290.0	Wheelchair accessibility:	Best
Propulsion/Propellers:	diesel-electric/2 azimuthing pods	Elevators:	14
		Casino (gaming tables):	Yes
Total Crew:	1,163	Self-Service Launderette:	Yes
Passengers (lower beds):	3,114	Onboard currency:	US$
Passenger Space Ratio (lower beds):	37.2		

THE SHIP. If you enjoy being with mature-age couples, families and fellow passengers who want a well-organized cruise experience with unpretentious cuisine, a good range of entertainment, and an excellent shore excursion program, *Crown Princess* is a good choice, although the interior decor is rather dated. The ship has a higher-than-average Passenger Space Ratio than some competitors, and service is friendly, not showy.

Outdoors, there is a sheltered teakwood strolling deck, which almost wraps around, and a walkway that leads to the enclosed bow of the ship. The outdoor pools have quasi-beach-like surroundings, while 'Movies Under the Skies' and major sporting events are shown on a poolside movie screen in front of the funnel (aft of the funnel is Skywalkers nightclub/disco). One useful feature is The Sanctuary, an extra-cost adults-only retreat located forward on the uppermost deck.

Inside, the decor is attractive, with lots of earth tones. Facilities include a decent library/computer room. Ship lovers should enjoy the wood-paneled Wheelhouse Bar, with memorabilia and ship models from parent company P&O's history. The large Gatsby's Casino has gaming tables and slot machines, while a Wedding Chapel with a live web-cam can relay ceremonies via the Internet (the ship's captain can legally marry American couples, thanks to the Bermuda registry). Gratuities are automatically

BERLITZ'S RATINGS		
	Possible	Achieved
Ship	500	357
Accommodation	200	139
Food	400	247
Service	400	289
Entertainment	100	74
Cruise Experience	400	268

OVERALL SCORE 1374 points out of 2000

charged to your onboard account (gratuities for children are at the same daily rate).

Passenger niggles include the user-unfriendly automated telephone system, the small cabin towels, several extra-cost items such as ice cream, and the charge (coins are needed) for the washers and dryers in self-service launderettes.

Overall, Princess Cruises delivers a consistently fine, comfortable, well-packaged product, always with a good degree of style, at a competitive price.

Note that lines can form at the reception desk, and for open-seating breakfast and lunch in the main dining rooms. You'll get turndown service and a pillow chocolate each night, and all cabins have a hairdryer, sensibly located in a vanity desk unit.

ACCOMMODATION. There are six principal types of cabins and configurations: grand suite; suite; mini-suite; outside-view double cabins with balcony; outside-view double cabins; and interior doubles, in a bewildering choice of over 30 different brochure price categories. All have 24-hour room service.

Cabin bath towels are small, and drawer space is limited. Cabin attendants have many cabins to look after (typically 20), which does not translate to fine personal service. All cabins receive toiletry kits and include a hairdryer.

Note that many outside-view cabins on Emerald Deck have lifeboat-obstructed views.

Some cabins can accommodate a third and fourth person in upper berths. However, in some cabins, the lower beds cannot then be pushed together to make a queen-size bed.

Most balcony suites and cabins can be overlooked both from the navigation bridge wing and from the port and starboard sections of the discotheque – above the ship aft. Note that eight balcony cabins forward on Emerald Deck may be the least desirable accommodation, as the balconies do not extend to the side of the ship and can be passed by walkers and gawkers on the adjacent walkway. There are 28 wheelchair-accessible cabins, but they lack full-length hanging space.

DINING. Of the three principal formal dining rooms (Botticelli, Da Vinci, and Michelangelo), one has traditional two-seating dining; the other two offer 'anytime dining.' All are divided into multi-tier sections in a non-symmetrical design to create more intimate sections. Six elevators go to Fiesta Deck, where two of the restaurants are located, but only four go to Plaza Deck 5, where the Michelangelo Restaurant is located – this can lengthen waits at peak times, particularly for those in wheelchairs.

Portions are generous, but the food and its presentation are non-memorable. Fish is often disguised with sauces or a coating, the choice of fresh green vegetables is limited, few garnishes are used, and cheese is either pre-sliced or diced. This is banquet catering, which means batch cooking and large quantities. Pasta dishes are voluminous, typically served by section headwaiters.

Extra-cost, reservations-required Sabatini's (for Italian-style pizzas and pastas) and Crown Grill (for premium steaks and grilled seafood) are both open on sea days.

Crown Grill is an extra cost 160-seat steakhouse serving premium-quality cooked to order steaks, grilled meat, and seafood.

Casual eateries include a poolside hamburger grill and pizzeria. Some items cost extra at the International Café coffee bar/patisserie in the atrium lobby.

Vines, in the atrium lobby, features sushi and cheese at no extra charge, and extra-cost wine. Other casual meals can be taken in the Horizon Court, open 24 hours a day, with ocean views.

For something different, try a private dinner on your balcony ('Ultimate Balcony Dinner') an all-inclusive evening or an 'Ultimate Balcony Breakfast.'

ENTERTAINMENT. The Princess Theater spans two decks and has comfortable seating on both levels. It has a nine-piece showband and a resident troupe of almost 20 singers and dancers.

Club Fusion, a second (aft) entertainment lounge, features cabaret at night, and lectures, bingo, and horse racing by day. Explorers, a third entertainment lounge, can also host cabaret acts and dance bands. Several other lounges and bars have live music, and several male dance hosts act as partners for sole female travelers.

SPA/FITNESS. The Lotus Spa, has separate saunas, steam rooms, and changing rooms for men and women, and a mixed-gender relaxation/ waiting zone, body-pampering treatment rooms, and a gymnasium with ocean views. Some fitness classes are free.

CRYSTAL ESPRIT
★★★★

THIS PREMIUM SHIP IS FOR DISCERNING MATURE-AGE SMALL GROUP TRAVELERS

Size:	Boutique Ship	Passenger/Crew Ratio (lower beds):	0.6
Tonnage:	3,300	Cabins (total):	31
Cruise Line:	Crystal Yacht Cruises	Size Range (sq ft/m):	226.0-516.6/21.0-48.0
Former Names:	MegaStar Aries, Aurora I, Lady Sarah	Cabins (for one person):	0
Builder:	Flender Werft (Germany)	Cabins with balcony:	0
Entered Service:	Feb 1992/Dec 2015	Cabins (wheelchair accessible):	0
Length (ft/m):	269.6/82.2	Wheelchair accessibility:	None
Propulsion/Propellers:	diesel/2	Elevators:	1
Total Crew:	91	Casino (gaming tables):	Yes
Passengers (lower beds):	62	Self-Service Launderette:	Yes
Passenger Space Ratio (lower beds):	53.2	Onboard currency:	US$

THE SHIP. *Crystal Esprit* has had several past lives (it was originally built for long-defunct Windsor Line but operated for many years by Star Cruises for private charters). Although it has a profile that is less than handsome, the interiors were tastefully refurbished in 2015, which help to turn it into a premium pocket-sized ship for well-educated travelers seeking a small village feel, rather than a big-city feel.

A small aft 'marina' includes water-sports equipment (kayaks, water skis, jet skis, wakeboard, scuba and snorkeling gear), fishing rods, and a two-person submersible (a 30-minute trip costs $600). Two Zodiac inflatable craft are for close-in trips, while several bicycles are carried for passenger use ashore.

Cove is a small main lounge at the ship's front, with comfortable seating for social gatherings. Other facilities include an outdoor Sunset Bar, pool deck grill (for fast-food items), a 'dip' pool, and a self-service laundry room.

Overall, *Crystal Esprit* is a very comfortable little 'yachtie'-style ship, but there's no elevator (stairs only). Almost everything is included – except a lot of space – and a submersible trip.

ACCOMMODATION. There are five accommodation price grades, and, although the company calls them 'suites,' they are definitely not – except for one Owner's Suite, measuring 516.6 sq ft (48 sq m). All other cabins measure either 226 or 279.8

BERLITZ'S RATINGS		
	Possible	Achieved
Ship	500	341
Accommodation	200	142
Food	400	290
Service	400	308
Entertainment	100	60
Cruise Experience	400	265

OVERALL SCORE 1406 points out of 2000

sq ft (21 or 26 sq m). The price you pay depends on the location, and grade you choose (none has a balcony, because the ship is too low to the waterline). Six cabins (Nos. 301–303, 203–306 and 205–207) have an interconnecting door. All accommodation is practical, and comes with lots of personal comfort items (cotton bathrobe, slippers, hairdryer, infotainment system, and ETRO personal toiletry items). But not even the Owner's Suite has a bathtub, although all have showers and two washbasins.

DINING. The Yacht Club (indoor) Restaurant is the main dining room; it's intimate, although the ceiling is low. The cuisine is based on specialties from the region the ship is in. Also, a Compass Room acts as a wine-tasting room, and can be booked for private parties.

The Patio Café is for casual bistro bites outside on deck.

ENTERTAINMENT. This is a pocket-size ship, so entertainment is minimal, although there is some live music.

SPA/FITNESS. Spa facilities consists only of a small beauty salon and body treatment area. A workout room (with exercise equipment), and two hot tubs are on a different deck.

CRYSTAL SERENITY
★★★★+

THIS ELEGANT, SPACIOUS SHIP HAS EXTREMELY GOOD FOOD, SERVICE, AND STYLE

Size:	Mid-size Ship	Passenger/Crew Ratio (lower beds):	1.7
Tonnage:	68,870	Cabins (total):	485
Cruise Line:	Crystal Cruises	Size Range (sq ft/m):	226–1,345.5/21–125
Former Names:	none	Cabins (for one person):	0
Builder:	Chantiers de l'Atlantique (France)	Cabins with balcony:	465
Entered Service:	Jun 2003	Cabins (wheelchair accessible):	8
Length (ft/m):	820.2/250.0	Wheelchair accessibility:	Best
Propulsion/Propellers:	diesel/2 azimuthing pods	Elevators:	8
Total Crew:	650	Casino (gaming tables):	Yes
Passengers (lower beds):	980	Self-Service Launderette:	Yes
Passenger Space Ratio (lower beds):	62.6	Onboard currency:	US$

THE SHIP. *Crystal Serenity* is the slightly larger, but still mid-size, close sister ship to *Crystal Symphony*, with a similar look and profile. There is an excellent amount of open deck, sunbathing space, and sports facilities. There is no sense of crowding anywhere, although the self-service buffet can get very busy. There is also a really wide walk-around teakwood deck for walking, and it's pleasingly uncluttered by sunloungers.

BERLITZ'S RATINGS		
	Possible	Achieved
Ship	500	424
Accommodation	200	164
Food	400	339
Service	400	337
Entertainment	100	83
Cruise Experience	400	340

OVERALL SCORE 1687 points out of 2000

Elegant public rooms include the Palm Court, evoking images of a Colonial-style grand hotel lounge; the Avenue Saloon, a favorite watering hole of late-nighters and a throwback to traditional gentlemen's clubs; the Connoisseur Club, for cigar and cognac enthusiasts; and the Stardust Club, a lounge/nightclub. There are shops, a private jewelry room, a computer-learning center with 24 terminals, and an Internet center. There's also the Vintage Room: a private dining room where 12 invited diners can enjoy exclusive vintages, paired with food, in special wine-tasting dinners. Another feature is a Yamaha keyboard-learning center for the excellent 'Passport to Music' program, which gives you a chance to learn how to play a keyboard instrument (and you get to take home a manual, so you can carry on learning); the program is free – great value indeed.

The 'inclusive' *Crystal Serenity* is best suited to sophisticated travelers, typically over 50, who seek contemporary ship surroundings, with fine-quality fittings and furnishings, a wide range of public rooms and facilities, and excellent food and service from a well-trained staff. This ship has just about everything for its target clientele (including a laid-back California lifestyle), plus an excellent array of guest lecturers.

ACCOMMODATION. This consists of cabins from large to smaller, but no matter what accommodation you choose, all have duvets, down pillows, a refrigerator and mini-bar, flat-screen infotainment system (close-captioned videos are available for the hearing-impaired), data laptop socket, satellite-linked telephone, and hairdryer. There's a range of Aveda toiletries (suite-grade occupants get personalized stationery on request, plus a larger list of 'inclusive' brands), a plush cotton bathrobe, and plenty of good-sized towels. A slight niggle is that the air conditioning in bathrooms and walk-in closets is quite noisy and cannot be turned off.

The accommodation includes: Crystal Penthouse suites with balcony; penthouse suites with balcony; Seabreeze penthouse suites with balcony; superior outside-view cabins with balcony; outside-view cabins with balcony; and outside-view cabins without balcony. Wheelchair-accessible accommodation is also available over several different grades and locations.

The best accommodation is on decks 11 and 10; all other accommodation is located on decks 7, 8, and 9. Each room has an electronic 'Do Not Disturb'/doorbell system. Butlers provide service in deck 10 and 11 suites, where room service arrives on silver trays. Afternoon-tea trolley service and evening hors d'oeuvres are delivered in butler-grade suites.

DINING. There is one main dining room – the open-seating Waterside Restaurant – and two specialty reservations-required venues. Waterside is quite elegant, with a crisp, clean style that includes plenty of space around each table. It is well laid-out and has a raised, circular central section. There are many tables for two, many positioned adjacent to ocean-view windows, and for four to eight.

Prego is for Italian food from a menu created by Piero Selvaggio; it offers Italian wines, and the service has flair.

Umi Uma by Nobu is for Asian-California fusion food, with a semi-separate sushi bar lined by counter stools, and chefs trained by Los Angeles-based Japanese super-chef Nobuyuki 'Nobu' Matsuhisa.

The Bistro, located on the upper level of the two-deck-high lobby, is a casual spot for coffees and pastries, with the atmosphere of a European street café.

For informal eats, the Marketplace has an extensive self-serve buffet area, with great views from its large picture windows.

For casual meals, Silk features regional cuisine and family-style service, and four vertical 'living walls' of greenery. There's also an ice cream/frozen yoghurt counter (no extra charge), and a Chinese street food zone (for steamed dumplings).

ENTERTAINMENT. The Galaxy Lounge (show-lounge) has a high ceiling, with a sloping floor for good sight lines from almost all seats (both banquette and individual seating is provided). The stage, lighting, and sound equipment are all first rate.

SPA/FITNESS. Crystal Spa is located aft on an uppermost deck. Facilities include men's and women's changing rooms with sauna (with a large porthole-shaped window), steam rooms, gymnasium with high-tech muscle-pumping equipment, an aerobics exercise area, and a reception/relaxation area.

CRYSTAL SYMPHONY
★★★★+

THIS HIGHLY COMFORTABLE SHIP HAS ELEGANT, REFINED DECOR AND STYLE

Size:	Mid-size Ship
Tonnage:	51,044
Cruise Line:	Crystal Cruises
Former Names:	none
Builder:	Masa-Yards (Finland)
Entered Service:	Mar 1995
Length (ft/m):	777.8/237.1
Propulsion/Propellers:	diesel-electric (33,880kW)/2
Total Crew:	545
Passengers (lower beds):	848
Passenger Space Ratio (lower beds):	53.1
Passenger/Crew Ratio (lower beds):	1.7
Cabins (total):	424
Size Range (sq ft/m):	201.2–981.7/18.7–91.2
Cabins (for one person):	0
Cabins with balcony:	276
Cabins (wheelchair accessible):	7
Wheelchair accessibility:	Best
Elevators:	8
Casino (gaming tables):	Yes
Self-Service Launderette:	Yes
Onboard currency:	US$

THE SHIP. *Crystal Symphony* has a nicely raked clipper bow and well-balanced lines. While some might not like the 'apartment-block' look of its exterior, it is the contemporary, fashionable look. This ship has an excellent amount of open deck, sunbathing space, and sports facilities, and a nice long swimming pool. There is no sense of crowding anywhere. It combines big-ship facilities with the intimacy of rooms found aboard many small vessels. There is a wide walk-around teakwood deck for strolling – pleasantly uncluttered by lounge chairs. The ship has, over the years, had a number of refurbishments that have brought it up to date.

The Palm Court, an observation lounge with forward-facing views over the ship's bows, is tranquil; one of the nicest rooms afloat, it is larger than its equivalent aboard *Crystal Serenity*.

There is an excellent library, combined with a business center. The cinema has high-definition video projection and headsets for hearing-impaired passengers. Useful self-service launderettes are provided on each deck.

Connoisseurs Club, adjacent to the Avenue Saloon, features fine premium brands of liquor, and cigars. The Computer Learning Center, with more than 20 stations, is popular; private lessons are available here, but they're expensive.

The ship achieves a high rating because of its fine facilities, space, service, and crew. It is the extra attention to detail that really counts. Crystal Cruises also provides impressive lecturers, and the 'Passport to Music' keyboard-learning center is excellent. The passenger mix is approximately 85 percent North American, and 15 percent other nationalities.

In March 2012, *Crystal Symphony* became an 'all-inclusive' (Crystal calls it 'All-Exclusive') ship, with gratuities to staff, wines for lunch and dinner, and bar drinks included – so, no signing for drinks, which makes for a more relaxed cruise experience. Except for the Connoisseur Lounge (cigar lounge), there's no smoking anywhere inside the ship.

Crystal Symphony is best suited to discerning adult travelers, typically over 50, who seek contemporary (but not brash) ship surroundings, with fine-quality fittings and furnishings, a wide range of public rooms and facilities, and excellent food and service. This is announcement-free cruising in a well-tuned, very well-run, service-oriented ship.

ACCOMMODATION. There are several categories, with the largest suites located on the highest accommodation deck (Deck 10). There are two Crystal Penthouses with large private balcony; Penthouse Suites with balcony; Seabreeze Penthouse Suites with balcony; cabins with balcony; and cabins without balcony. Some cabins have obstructed views. Except for the suites on Deck 10, most other cabin bathrooms are compact, but they are still comfortable.

BERLITZ'S RATINGS

	Possible	Achieved
Ship	500	419
Accommodation	200	163
Food	400	339
Service	400	337
Entertainment	100	83
Cruise Experience	400	337

OVERALL SCORE 1678 points out of 2000

Some have interconnecting doors, which is good for families with children.

Duvets and down pillows are provided for all occupants, as are many other niceties, including a data socket for computer connection, a refrigerator and minibar, infotainment system, satellite-linked telephone, hairdryer, a range of Aveda toiletries, a plush cotton bathrobe, and plenty of good-sized cotton towels. Suite-grades get a wider choice of drinks and personalized stationery on request. Excellent in-cabin infotainment programming is provided, including close-captioned videos for the use of hearing-impaired passengers.

Butlers provide the best in personal service in the top-grade suites on Deck 10. Afternoon tea and evening hors d'oeuvres are standard, and food arrives on silver trays.

DINING. The open-seating Waterside restaurant is quite elegant, with crisp design, plenty of space around each table, and many tables for two. The food, which is of a high standard, is always attractively presented and well served – it's a mix of plate service and silver service. European dishes are predominantly featured, but in an American style. The menus include a selection of meat, fish, and vegetarian dishes. Off-menu orders are also possible.

Kosher meals are also available (frozen when brought on board); Kosher pots, pans, and utensils are sterilized in saltwater, and all plates used during service are hand-washed.

Overall, the food is really good for the size of ship, and, with the choice of the two specialty dining spots, receives high praise. Dessert flambé specialties can be made at your table each day by the headwaiters.

Prego is a 75-seat restaurant, featuring fine Italian cuisine created by Piero Selvaggio, with good Italian wines, and service with flair.

Umi Uma by Nobu is for Asian fusion cuisine by Nobu Matsuhisa-trained chefs.

Afternoon tea in the Palm Court is a pleasant, civilized daily event, but do try the Mozart Teatime, for which the waiters all dress in period costume.

For informal eats, the Marketplace has great views from its windows and a good selection of items in several sections (it turns into a churrascaria by night). There is also Silk Kitchen (for pan-Asian eats), plus an ice cream/frozen yoghurt counter (no extra charge).

ENTERTAINMENT. The Galaxy Lounge has a high ceiling, but it's on one level with a tiered floor for good visibility. A few pillars obstruct sight lines from some seats. Both banquette and individual seating is provided. The stage, lighting, and sound equipment are all excellent.

The shows are elegant, with fantastic costuming and scenery, but they are too long, and too familiar to Crystal Cruises' many repeat passengers. On the plus side, the cabaret acts are of a good caliber, and constantly changing. The bands are also good, and there's plenty of music for social dancing. The ship also provides male dance hosts for solo female travelers.

SPA/FITNESS. Facilities include one room for yoga and Pilates, an aerobics/exercise room, plus sauna and steam rooms for men and women. There are seven treatment rooms and a beauty salon.

DEUTSCHLAND
★★★★

AN APPEALING SMALL SHIP WITH TRADITIONAL OCEAN LINER INTERIOR DECOR

Size:	Small Ship
Tonnage:	22,400
Cruise Line:	Semester at Sea
Former Names:	none
Builder:	Howaldswerke Deutsche Werft (Germany)
Entered Service:	May 1998/Apr 2015
Length (ft/m):	574.1/175.0
Propulsion/Propellers:	diesel (12,300kW)/2
Total Crew:	270
Passengers (lower beds):	552
Passenger Space Ratio (lower beds):	40.8
Passenger/Crew Ratio (lower beds):	2.0
Cabins (total):	294
Size Range (sq ft/m):	129.1–365.9/12.0–34.0
Cabins (for one person):	36
Cabins with balcony:	2
Cabins (wheelchair accessible):	1
Wheelchair accessibility:	Fair
Elevators:	3
Casino (gaming tables):	No
Self-Service Launderette:	No
Onboard currency:	Euros

THE SHIP. *Deutschland*, now over 25 years old but well maintained and in good condition, has an angular, low-in-the-water profile that is not particularly handsome, and a large, single, squat, traditional funnel.

Although there is no walk-around promenade deck outdoors as such – it's full of sunloungers around the swimming pool, you can walk along some of the open space. There are also port and starboard midship strolling decks under the inboard lifeboats. There is a decent amount of open deck and sunbathing space for a ship of this size, including three aft decks for open-air lovers (and some shaded areas), and teakwood deck chairs with thick cushioned pads.

The ship has a classic symmetrical layout, and the interior decor re-creates the atmosphere of 1920s ocean liners. It is finely decorated throughout (some might say overly so), with rich, dark woods and intricate brass and wrought-iron staircases that are reminiscent of old-style gentleman's clubs. There is much detail in the decorative work, especially in the ornate ceilings, and cleaning it all is labor-intensive. There are a number of statues, which don't fit well aboard a cruise ship, as well as many works of art on display.

There's a good range of public rooms and spaces, made possible only by making the cabins small, and eclectic decor from different periods.

There are two popular drinking places: Zum Alten Fritz (Old Fritz) Bar, with dark wood interior and

BERLITZ'S RATINGS		
	Possible	Achieved
Ship	500	450
Accommodation	200	122
Food	400	283
Service	400	274
Entertainment	100	55
Cruise Experience	400	246
OVERALL SCORE 1430 points out of 2000		

Belle Epoque ambience; and Lili Marleen Salon, with a mahogany channeled ceiling. Another nice room is the Lido Terrace, which nods to the winter gardens aboard the early transatlantic liners, and is a pleasant place to read or take afternoon tea.

The friendliness of the staff is good. Although the ship absorbs passengers well, the space ratio is poor. The onboard product is generally sound, with decent food and attentive service. While the interiors are attractive, the vessel does not come close to ships such as *Europa*, *Europa 2*, *Silver Shadow*, and *Silver Whisper*, with their much larger accommodation and open-seating dining. Just two suites have balconies.

Overall, *Deutschland* is a fine, traditional ship best suited to German-speaking couples and solo travelers of mature years looking for a very comfortable cruise ship with appealing itineraries and destinations, good food, and attentive service.

ACCOMMODATION. There are several price categories (the higher the deck, the higher the cost).

While most cabins are disappointingly small, all are furnished in fancy bird's-eye maple, and all ceilings are one-piece units, unlike the metal strip ceilings of most cruise ships, and they come with molded coving and ornamentation. The closet and drawer space is quite generous, and the attention to detail is good. All cabins have a TV set, direct-dial satellite telephone, minibar/refrigerator, and real cabin keys (not plastic cards). Many cabins have only one electrical outlet.

The bathrooms are nicely appointed, with pink marble washbasin, gold anodized fittings, gilt-edged mirrors, hairdryer, and ample space for personal toiletries. Both 110 and 230 volt power outlets are provided. Bathrobes are provided for all passengers.

Accommodation designated as suites (there are two grades) is more spacious than a standard cabin, and includes a living area with couch, coffee table, and two chairs; the bathroom has a full-size tub (all other cabins have showers only). The Executive Suites and Owner's Suites are located in the center of the ship; each has a small private balcony. There is one wheelchair-accessible cabin (8042).

DINING. Berlin, the 300-seat main restaurant, is a homely room. All the chairs have armrests, although space for serving at window-side tables is limited, and the hard chair backs are not really very comfortable.

There are tables for two, four, six, or eight, and two seatings for dinner. Two cold buffet bars for cold cuts of meat, cheese, and salad items – either your waiter can obtain the food for you or you can choose it yourself – are featured for breakfast and lunch. Overall, the cuisine is quite creative, with several courses, small portions of nouvelle cuisine, and a wide variety of choice and good taste. The place settings are extensive.

The Restaurant Vierjahreszeiten (Four Seasons), with 104 seats, is an intimate dining room, principally for suite occupants and à la carte dining (reservations required). There is much detailing in the decor, and the ornate ceiling lamps and indented coving create an elegant ambience. There are tables for two to six.

A small private dining room, the Chancellor Room has a large oval table seating 10 to 12 – for special occasions and celebrations.

An extensive wine list includes many wines from Germany and Austria (wine choices from other countries are limited).

The Lido Restaurant is for casual dining. It has large ocean-view windows on two sides and a multi-section self-serve buffet station. Additionally, there is a Lido Terrasse, aft, which has windows on three sides. It is on two slightly different levels, houses the ship's library, and has a garden conservatory-like setting, with a bar.

ENTERTAINMENT. The Kaisersaal (Emperor's Saloon) is the showlounge. It is a galleried period room with red velveteen chairs – more like a ballroom than a showlounge. Like a small opera house, it has a huge central chandelier. However, sight lines are obstructed from some seats on both levels by large marble-effect pillars.

SPA/FITNESS. The main spa area is on Deck 3. It includes a small indoor swimming pool with a statue of a female diver at one end, sauna, solarium, thalassotherapy baths, and body-therapy rooms; there is also a dialysis station. Deck 6 has a fitness/sport center with a few exercise machines, a sauna with sea view, and a steam room. A beauty salon is on a different deck.

DIAMOND PRINCESS
★★★+

THIS LARGE, COMFORTABLE RESORT SHIP IS GOOD FOR CRUISERS OF ANY AGE

Size:	Large Resort Ship	Passenger/Crew Ratio (lower beds):	2.4
Tonnage:	115,875	Cabins (total):	1,351
Cruise Line:	Princess Cruises	Size Range (sq ft/m):	168–1,329.3/15.6–123.5
Former Names:	none	Cabins (for one person):	0
Builder:	Mitsubishi Heavy Industries (Japan)	Cabins with balcony:	750
Entered Service:	Feb 2004	Cabins (wheelchair accessible):	28
Length (ft/m):	951.4/290.0	Wheelchair accessibility:	Good
Propulsion/Propellers:	diesel-electric (42,000kW)/2	Elevators:	14
Total Crew:	1,100	Casino (gaming tables):	Yes
Passengers (lower beds):	2,702	Self-Service Launderette:	Yes
Passenger Space Ratio (lower beds):	42.8	Onboard currency:	US$

THE SHIP. *Diamond Princess*, sister to *Sapphire Princess* (both built in Japan), has an instantly recognizable funnel due to two jet engine-like pods high up on its structure (these are mainly for decoration).

Four areas focus on swimming pools. One has a large poolside movie screen, and another is two decks high and is covered by a retractable glass dome, itself an extension of the funnel housing. One pool lies within The Sanctuary – an adults-only, extra-cost (it's worth it) relaxation area. There's also a children's pool. The passenger flow has been well thought-out aboard this ship, and works with little congestion. There is plenty of space inside the ship (but there are also plenty of passengers) and a wide array of public rooms, with many 'intimate' spaces and places to enjoy.

The decor is quietly attractive, with lots of earth tones. The interior focal point is a piazza-style atrium lobby, with Vines (wine bar), an International Café (for coffee, pastries, panini sandwiches, etc.) library/Internet-connect center, and Alfredo's sit-down pizzeria.

A Wedding Chapel has a web-cam that can relay ceremonies via the Internet. The ship's captain can legally marry American couples, due to the ship's Bermuda registry and a special dispensation (which should be verified when in the planning stage, according to where you reside). Princess Cruises of-

BERLITZ'S RATINGS		
	Possible	Achieved
Ship	500	357
Accommodation	200	139
Food	400	253
Service	400	283
Entertainment	100	77
Cruise Experience	400	280
OVERALL SCORE 1389 points out of 2000		

fers three wedding packages – Pearl, Emerald, Diamond; the fee includes registration and official marriage certificate. The Hearts & Minds chapel is useful for renewal of vows ceremonies.

The large Grand Casino has gaming tables, over 260 slot machines. Linked slot machines provide a combined payout.

Other facilities include a library/computer room and a card room. Ship lovers should enjoy the wood-paneled Wheelhouse Bar, housing memorabilia and ship models tracing part of parent company P&O's history. Aft of the International Dining Room is the Wake View Bar, with a spiral stairway leading down to a great viewing spot for watching the ship's wake; it is reached from the back of Club Fusion, on Promenade Deck. Skywalkers Nightclub is set around the base of the funnel structure and has a view overlooking the aft-facing cascading decks and children's pool.

There are many extra-charge items such as ice cream and freshly squeezed orange juice. There's an hourly charge for group babysitting services and a charge for use of the washers and dryers in the self-service launderettes.

In 2014 the ship underwent a $30 million refit that included the addition of 14 cabins, and the installation of the Izumi Japanese baths on Deck 15.

Diamond Princess operates cruises from Yokohama during the summer, with extra Japanese-speaking staff employed in key positions. The ship operates in Australasian waters during the Northern Hemisphere winter (Australia's summer).

Passenger niggles include the user-unfriendly automated telephone system, the small cabin towels, the extra cost for items such as ice cream, and the (coins-needed) charge for the washers and dryers in self-service launderettes.

Overall, Princess Cruises delivers a consistently fine, comfortable, well-packaged product, always with a good degree of style, at a competitive price.

ACCOMMODATION. All cabins receive turndown service and pillow chocolates each night, as well as bathrobes on request and toiletry kits (larger for suite/mini-suite occupants). A hairdryer is located at the vanity desk unit in the lounge area. The tiled bathrooms have a decent amount of open shelf storage space for toiletries.

Many outside cabins on Emerald Deck have lifeboat-obstructed views. Your name is typically placed outside your suite or cabin – making it simple for delivery service personnel, but limiting your privacy. There is 24-hour room service, but some room-service menu items are not available during early morning hours. Most balcony suites/cabins can be overlooked from the navigation bridge wing.

Note that the bath towels are small, and drawer space is limited. The top-grade suites are not really large in comparison to similar suites aboard some other ships of a similar size.

DINING. There are five principal dining rooms with themed decor and cuisine: International; Santa Fe; Savoy; Vivaldi; and Pacific Moon. These offer a mix of two seatings, assigned according to your cabin grade and location, and 'anytime dining,' where you choose when and with whom you want to eat ('anytime' is not available in the International Dining Room).

The main dining rooms are arranged in small sections, for a more intimate ambience and less noise. Specially designed dinnerware and good-quality linens and silverware include Dudson of England (dinnerware), Frette Egyptian cotton table linens, and Hepp silverware.

Although portions are generous, the food and its presentation are very standardized. Fish is often disguised by sauces or a coating, the choice of fresh green vegetables is limited, few garnishes are used, and cheese is either pre-sliced or diced. But, this is banquet catering, with its attendant 'batch' cooking. Pasta dishes are acceptable (though voluminous), typically served by section headwaiters, who may also make 'something special just for you.' If you like desserts, do try the sundaes.

Sabatini's (on Deck 7) is an informal Italian-style eatery (reservations needed) featuring Italian-style pizzas and pastas with a variety of sauces, and entrées (mains), all cooked to order and presented with flair by the waiters.

Next door is Kai Sushi – a 66-seat restaurant (added in 2014) with its own integral sushi bar. The venue features extra-cost, à la carte sushi (maki sushi, nigiri sushi, and sashimi), and matcha (green tea) ice cream, a noodle bar, regional tea tastings, and a special sake menu.

Sterling Steakhouse (on the starboard side aft of the Horizon Court on Deck 14) is an extra-cost (reservations-required) venue for prime steaks and grilled meats and seafood items, with everything cooked to order, but it's nothing special.

A poolside burger grill and a pizza bar (no additional charge) are eateries for casual bites, while extra charges will apply if you order items to eat at the Lobby bar/patisserie.

Other casual meals can be taken in the Horizon Court, open 24 hours a day, with large ocean-view on port and starboard sides and direct access to the two main swimming pools and Lido Deck. There is little presentation finesse, and oval-shaped plastic plates, not trays, are provided.

ENTERTAINMENT. The Princess Theater spans two decks and has comfortable seating on both main and balcony levels. Princess Cruises prides itself on its glamorous production shows, performed by its resident troupe of singers/dancers.

A second entertainment lounge, Club Fusion, presents cabaret acts at night, lectures, bingo, and other activities during the day. A third entertainment lounge can also host cabaret acts and dance bands. Many other lounges and bars have live music, and a number of male dance hosts act as partners for women traveling alone.

SPA/FITNESS. The Lotus Spa complex (on Deck 15 forward), with Japanese-style decor, surrounds a lap pool – you can have a massage or other spa treatment in an ocean-view treatment room. Facilities include a beauty salon, men's and women's saunas and changing rooms, an aerobics room and a gymnasium.

Izumi, a delightful 8,800-sq-ft (817.5-sq-m) onsen-style (with a daily charge) Japanese grand bath and garden area on Deck 15 aft, includes gender-separated indoor and outdoor cypress baths, stone baths with adjacent utase-yu hot water cascades, and saunas.

Activities such as yoga, group exercise bicycling, and kick-boxing classes cost extra. For exercise, there is a good sheltered faux teak promenade deck (it's actually painted steel), which almost wraps around the ship (three times around is one land mile).

DISNEY DREAM
★★★★

THIS IS THE ULTIMATE FAMILY-FRIENDLY FLOATING THEME PARK FOR ALL AGES

Size:	Mid-size Ship	Passenger/Crew Ratio (lower beds):	1.7
Tonnage:	129,690	Cabins (total):	1,250
Cruise Line:	Disney Cruise Line	Size Range (sq ft/m):	169–1,781/15.7–165.5
Former Names:	none	Cabins (for one person):	0
Builder:	Meyer Werft (Germany)	Cabins with balcony:	901
Entered Service:	Jan 2011	Cabins (wheelchair accessible):	37
Length (ft/m):	1,113.8/339.5	Wheelchair accessibility:	Good
Propulsion/Propellers:	diesel-electric (42,000kW)/2	Elevators:	14
Total Crew:	1,458	Casino (gaming tables):	No
Passengers (lower beds):	2,500	Self-Service Launderette:	No
Passenger Space Ratio (lower beds):	51.8	Onboard currency:	US$

THE SHIP. Made of pieces of steel and pixie dust, the ship's exterior is about 40 percent larger than the first two Disney ships, *Disney Magic* and *Disney Wonder*. It also has two extra decks, although the design is similar – a tribute to the grand ocean liners of the 1930s. As on all Disney ships, there are two large funnels. The bows have handsome gold scrollwork; the stern is reminiscent of one of those smooth Airstream trailers. The ship's exterior colors are also those of Mickey, in: red, white, yellow, and black. The lifeboats are yellow, and not the normal orange, by special dispensation.

The biggest outdoor 'wow' is the AquaDuck, a 765ft (233m) 'watercoaster' spanning four decks – two-and-a-half times the length of a football field. It's pure Disney splash-tastic.

Disney whimsy and Art Deco style are the hallmarks of the interior décor enhanced by original paintings, statues, and woodwork – all with Disney's noted attention to detail. In the three-deck-high lobby is a bronze statue of Admiral Donald (Duck).

Most public rooms have high ceilings, and the Art Deco theme of the old ocean liners or New York's Radio City Music Hall is tasteful. Have a look at the stainless-steel/pewter Disney detailing on the handrails and balustrades in the atrium lobby. Other facilities include a digital photo kiosk.

Grown-ups can inhabit their own area of the ship – away from kids. Known as The District, it includes

BERLITZ'S RATINGS		
	Possible	Achieved
Ship	500	387
Accommodation	200	151
Food	400	212
Service	400	269
Entertainment	100	88
Cruise Experience	400	312
OVERALL SCORE 1419 points out of 2000		

five different adults-only lounge venues. There's also a central Concierge Lounge and a private sundeck for occupants of Concierge Class accommodation on Deck 12.

There are several other lounges and bars (the best place for a quiet drink, however, is in the delightful Observation Bar) and several retail shops.

Disney Dream is ideal for families with children or grandchildren. Couples and solo travelers are also welcome, though there are few daytime activities for couples, and just enough entertainment at night. You will, however, need to be a real Disney fan, as everything revolves around Disney characters and the family theme. Gratuities are extra and 15 percent is added to all bar/drinks purchases. Disney Vacation Club members can exchange points for cruises.

ACCOMMODATION. There are nine types of suites and cabins, but many more price grades, depending on the size and location of the accommodation.

Interior cabins have a virtual porthole – you feel like you are in an outside-view cabin; it's done with high-definition cameras positioned on the outside decks with live video feed to each virtual porthole – you almost expect one or more Disney characters to pop by.

Bathrooms have round tubs with pull-down seat and hand-held shower hose –good for washing babies and small children. Bed frames are high so luggage can easily be stored underneath.

The largest accommodation is the Concierge Royal Suite (1,781 sq ft/165 sq m, including balcony), with hot tub. It can sleep five and has one master bedroom with a large walk-in closet, a lounge (with one additional pull-down wall double bed and one pull-down single bed), two bathrooms (one has two washbasins), dining room, media library, pantry, and wet bar, plus a large balcony. These suites are located in the best position in the ship, with great ocean views.

DINING. There are three main dining rooms, each with a different decor. You rotate through all three, together with your regular waiter (server in Disney-speak).

Expect to see the surfer-dude sea turtle from *Finding Nemo* swimming around Animator's Palate, making special appearances and interacting; the room transforms into a coral reef during dinner. It's all about 'foodertainment,' which Disney does well, but the noise level can be rather intense.

Royal Palace has decor inspired by classic Disney films *Cinderella*, *Snow White and the Seven Dwarfs*, *Beauty and the Beast*, and *Sleeping Beauty*.

The Enchanted Garden is a whimsical main dining room inspired by the gardens of Versailles, in France, and the lighting transforms from day to night (the central glass panel ceiling is almost covered in what can only be magical foliage).

Cabanas is open to all. At night, it becomes another venue where main restaurant menu meals are available in a very casual setting, but with waiter service.

For something different, Remy is an upscale French-style restaurant with menus created by Michelin-starred French chef Arnaud Lallement from L'Assiette Champenoise (close to Reims in France), and Scott Hunnel from Victoria & Albert's at Walt Disney World. An extra-cost, reservations-required venue, it offers leisurely dining – good for an evening out (without the kids, of course). The Ratatouille-inspired design sees rats everywhere – though not on your plate.

Palo is an Italian-cuisine themed adults-only restaurant, with items cooked to order. Afternoon High Tea is on sea days (a cover charge applies).

ENTERTAINMENT. Large-scale Disney shows are presented at the Walt Disney Theater, a 1,340-seat venue with a star-studded ceiling and arched proscenium stage.

The 399-seat Buena Vista Theater – not to be confused with the Walt Disney Theater – is the movie house.

There's live evening entertainment on deck including a Pirate Night with live fireworks. Everyone's favorite Disney characters are on board in different locations, so take your camera.

SPA/FITNESS. Senses Spa and Salon has 17 body-pamper rooms and private outdoor verandahs, while the Rainforest zone features steam heat, misty showers, and hydrotherapy. Teens can also have specially tailored spa treatments in their own chill-out zone.

DISNEY FANTASY
★★★★

THIS IS AN EXCELLENT FAMILY-FRIENDLY, VERY CASUAL, FLOATING THEME PARK

Size:	Mid-size Ship	Passenger/Crew Ratio (lower beds):	1.7
Tonnage:	129,690	Cabins (total):	1,250
Cruise Line:	Disney Cruise Line	Size Range (sq ft/m):	169–1,781/15.7–165.5
Former Names:	none	Cabins (for one person):	0
Builder:	Meyer Werft (Germany)	Cabins with balcony:	901
Entered Service:	Apr 2012	Cabins (wheelchair accessible):	37
Length (ft/m):	1,113.8/339.5	Wheelchair accessibility:	Good
Propulsion/Propellers:	diesel-electric (42,000kW)/2	Elevators:	14
Total Crew:	1,458	Casino (gaming tables):	No
Passengers (lower beds):	2,500	Self-Service Launderette:	No
Passenger Space Ratio (lower beds):	51.8	Onboard currency:	US$

THE SHIP. The ship's exterior is about 40 percent larger than the first two Disney ships, *Disney Magic* and *Disney Wonder*. It also has two extra decks, although the design is similar – a tribute to the grand ocean liners of the 1930s. As on all Disney ships, there are two large funnels. The bows have handsome gold scroll-work more typically seen adorning yesteryear's tall ships (the stern is reminiscent of one of those cool Airstream trailers). The ship's exterior colors (red, white, and black) are also those of Mickey himself – even the lifeboats are yellow, by special dispensation.

No doubt the outdoor 'wow' factor is AquaDuck, a 765ft (233m) AquaDuck 'watercoaster' that spans four decks – two-and-a-half times the length of a football field.

Disney whimsy and Art Deco style are the hallmarks of the stunning interior decor, too. In the main three-deck-high lobby stands a bronze statue of none other than Admiral Donald (Duck); a chandelier is its focal point. The Art Nouveau decor is enhanced by original paintings, statues, and woodwork, all with Disney attention to detail.

Most public rooms have high ceilings, and the Art Nouveau theme has been tastefully carried out. All the artwork in public areas comes from Disney films or animation features.

Grown-ups inhabit their own area of the ship, in The District, which includes five lounges. There's also a central Concierge Lounge, for occupants of

BERLITZ'S RATINGS		
	Possible	Achieved
Ship	500	387
Accommodation	200	151
Food	400	213
Service	400	269
Entertainment	100	88
Cruise Experience	400	315

OVERALL SCORE 1423 points out of 2000

Concierge Class accommodation, on Deck 12, with private sundeck.

Other venues include: Mickey's Mainsail, Sea Treasure, Whitecaps, and Whozits and Whatsits (retail shops); District Bar, Pink Champagne Bar, Skyline Bar, Waves Bar, Bon Voyage, Meridian Bar, 687 (sports bar), Currents Bar, and Arr-cade. There are several other lounges and bars (the best place for a quiet drink is in the Observation Bar) and retail shops.

Disney has its own private island, Castaway Cay, where the facilities are constantly being enhanced. At Port Canaveral, the Disney terminal was inspired by the original Ocean Terminal in Southampton, England, from which the famous ocean liners *Queen Elizabeth*, *Queen Mary*, and the ill-fated *Titanic* once sailed.

Disney Fantasy is ideal for families with children or grandchildren. Couples and solo travelers are also welcome, though there are few activities for couples in the daytime, and enough entertainment at night. Gratuities are extra, and 15 percent is added to all bar/drinks purchases. American Express cardholders get special perks.

ACCOMMODATION. There are nine types of suites and cabins, but many more price grades, depending on size and location.

Interior cabins have a virtual porthole, so you feel that you are in an outside cabin; it's done with high-definition cameras positioned on the outside decks with live video feed to each virtual porthole. You almost expect one or more Disney characters to pop by.

All bathrooms have round tubs with a pull-down seat and hand-held shower hose – excellent for bathing small children. Bed frames are high, so luggage can easily be stored underneath.

The largest accommodation is the Concierge Royal Suite (1,781 sq ft/165 sq m, including balcony with hot tub). It can sleep five and has one master bedroom with a large walk-in closet, a living room (with an additional pull-down wall double bed and a pull-down single bed), two bathrooms (one has two washbasins), dining room, pantry, and wet bar. It is in the best position, with great ocean views.

DINING. There are three main dining rooms, each with a different decor. Passengers rotate through all three, together with their regular waiter (server in Disney-speak).

Expect to see the surfer-dude sea turtle from *Finding Nemo* swimming around Animator's Palate, making special appearances; the room transforms into a coral reef during dinner. It's all about 'foodertainment,' which Disney does well, but the noise level can be really intense.

Royal Court has decor inspired by the classic Disney films *Cinderella*, *Snow White and the Seven Dwarfs*, *Beauty and the Beast*, and *Sleeping Beauty*.

The Enchanted Garden is a whimsical main dining room inspired by the gardens of Versailles, in France, and the lighting magically transforms from day to night (the central glass panel ceiling is almost covered in what can only be magical foliage).

Cabanas, which is open to all, is an alternative eatery (evening only). It's a more casual setting but has waiter service.

For a change from the big, lively dining rooms, try Remy, an upscale French-style restaurant with menus by Michelin-starred French chef Arnaud Lallement from L'Assiette Champenoise, close to Reims (France), and Scott Hunnel from Victoria & Albert's at Walt Disney World. An extra-cost, reservations-only venue, it offers leisurely dining – nice for an evening out without the kids. The design is rather ratty, too (think Disney's Ratatouille).

Palo is an Italian-cuisine themed adults-only restaurant, with items cooked to order. On days at sea, high tea is also served here, and there's a cover charge.

Guest chefs from Walt Disney World Resort prepare signature dishes each cruise, and also host cooking demonstrations.

Vegetarians and anyone seeking light, healthy cuisine will likely be underwhelmed by the lack of green vegetables.

ENTERTAINMENT. Live shows are presented at the Walt Disney Theater, the ship's 1,340-seat venue, which has a star-studded ceiling and proscenium arch stage.

The 399-seat Buena Vista Theater – which is not to be confused with the Walt Disney Theater – is a movie house.

There's live evening entertainment on deck including a Pirate Night, with live fireworks. Everyone's favorite Disney characters are on board in different locations (including some of the Star Wars characters as holographic models), so remember to take your camera.

SPA/FITNESS. Senses Spa and Salon has 17 treatment rooms and private outdoor verandahs. An area called Rainforest features steam heat, misty showers, and hydrotherapy for relaxation. Teens can also have specially tailored spa treatments in their own chill-out zone.

DISNEY MAGIC
★★★+

ULTRA FAMILY-FRIENDLY CRUISING IN A CASUAL THEME PARK SETTING

Size:	Mid-size Ship	Passenger/Crew Ratio (lower beds):	1.8
Tonnage:	83,338	Cabins (total):	875
Cruise Line:	Disney Cruise Line	Size Range (sq ft/m):	180.8–968.7/16.8–90.0
Former Names:	none	Cabins (for one person):	0
Builder:	Fincantieri (Italy)	Cabins with balcony:	388
Entered Service:	Jul 1998	Cabins (wheelchair accessible):	12
Length (ft/m):	964.5/294.0	Wheelchair accessibility:	Good
Propulsion/Propellers: diesel-electric (38,000kW)/2		Elevators:	12
Total Crew:	945	Casino (gaming tables):	No
Passengers (lower beds):	1,750	Self-Service Launderette:	Yes
Passenger Space Ratio (lower beds):	47.6	Onboard currency:	US$

THE SHIP. Disney Cruise Line's first ship's profile is sleek, and combines streamlining with tradition and nostalgia, a black hull, and two red-and-black funnels reminiscent of the ocean liners of yesteryear – *Disney Magic* was the first cruise ship built with two funnels since the 1950s. The forward funnel is a dummy containing various public spaces, including a teen center, Aloft.

There are two outdoor pools: one for adults only (in theory), and one for families (with a large poolside movie screen). In a 2013 makeover, a super-popular AquaDunk water-slide experience was added.

Inside, it's all pure Disney. Most public rooms have high ceilings, and the Art Deco theme of the old ocean liners or New York's Radio City Music Hall has been tastefully carried out. Check out the stainless-steel/pewter Disney detailing on the handrails and balustrades in the three-deck-high lobby – it provides a real photo opportunity, with a 6ft (1.8m) bronze statue of Mickey Mouse in the role of a ship's helmsman. There are several other lounges and bars (the best place for a quiet drink, however, is in the delightful Observation Bar) and retail shops.

A highlight for most is a day on Disney's private island, Castaway Cay in the Bahamas. It is an excellent private island, with its own pier for the ship to dock alongside. Water-sports equipment – floats, paddleboats, kayaks, hobie cats, aqua fins, aqua trikes, and snorkels – can be rented.

BERLITZ'S RATINGS		
	Possible	Achieved
Ship	500	368
Accommodation	200	143
Food	400	205
Service	400	265
Entertainment	100	86
Cruise Experience	400	305

OVERALL SCORE 1372 points out of 2000

Disney Magic is a seagoing Never-Never Land. In reality, it provides a highly programed, well-organized, and regimented onboard experience, with registrations and reservations needed for almost everything. Children of all ages (minimum 12 weeks old) should have a great time.

Take mainly casual clothing (although there are two 'formal' nights on seven-day cruises). Gratuities are extra, suggested at about $12 per person, per day, and 15 percent is added to all bar/beverage/wine and 18 percent for spa accounts.

ACCOMMODATION. There are six different cabin layouts, in several price grades, depending on the grade, size, and location chosen, and is linked to the resort accommodation for those taking a combined resort/cruise vacation. Spread over six decks, all types have been designed for practicality and have space-efficient layouts.

Most cabins have a neat vertical steamer trunk for clothes storage, illuminated closets, a hairdryer (located at a vanity desk or in the bathroom), and bathrobes for all. Many cabins have third and fourth pull-down berths that are hidden in the ceiling when not in use, but the standard interior and outside cabins, while acceptable for two, would be tight with three or four. Some cabins even accommodate a fifth person. Cabins with refrigerators can have them stocked, at extra cost, with one of several drinks/soft drinks packages.

Bathrooms, although compact due to the fact that the toilet is separate, are really functional units, designed with split-use facilities so that more than one person can use them at the same time – good for families. Many have bathtubs, which are really shower tubs.

Accommodation designated as suites offers much more space, and extra goodies including CD and DVD players, big-screen TVs, and extra beds (useful for larger families). Some suites are beneath the pool deck, teen lounge, or informal café, so there could be noise as the ceiling insulation is poor – although cabin-to-cabin insulation is good.

Wheelchair-users can choose from a variety of cabin sizes and configurations, including suites with a private balcony (although you can't get a wheelchair through the balcony's sliding door) and large bathrooms with good roll-in showers, and decent closet and drawer space. Almost the whole ship is accessible. For sight-impaired passengers, cabin numbers and elevator buttons are braille-encoded.

DINING. Three main dining rooms each have over 400 seats, two seating times, and unique themes. Deck 3: Lumiere's (Beauty and the Beast); Rapunzel's Restaurant; on Deck 4 aft, with ocean views, is Animator's Palate, the most visual of the three, with food and electronic art that changes the evening decor from black and white to color (the author's signature is on a hidden wall panel in this venue – done in the shipyard at Disney Cruise Line's invitation).

You eat in all three dining rooms in rotation – twice per seven-day cruise – and move with your assigned waiter and assistant waiter to each dining room in turn, thus providing the variety of different decor and different menus. It's a great concept – and unique in the cruise industry. As you will have the same waiter in each of the three restaurants, any gratuities go only to 'your' waiter. Parrot Cay and Lumiere's have open seating for breakfast and lunch, but the lunch menu is pitiful.

Palo is a 140-seat, reservations-required venue with a small cover/gratuity charge, for cooked to order Italian-style cuisine. It has a 270-degree view and is for adults only, and the wine list is good (but prices are high). Make reservations early or miss out on the ship's only decent food. Afternoon High Tea is on sea days (a cover charge applies).

Cabanas is a large self-serve, food-court-style buffet eatery (it's always busy for lunch). Other casual poolside spots include Eye Scream, Pete's Boiler Bites, Pinocchio's Pizzeria, and Daisy's De-Lites.

Vegetarians and anyone seeking light cuisine will likely be underwhelmed by the lack of green vegetables. Guest chefs from Walt Disney World Resort prepare signature dishes each cruise, and also host cooking demonstrations.

ENTERTAINMENT. Large-scale stage shows are presented in the stunning 977-seat showlounge, presenting original Disney musicals and the latest comedy productions. Sadly, there is no live orchestra, although the lighting, staging, and technical effects are excellent.

SPA/FITNESS. The Vista Spa measures 10,700 sq ft (994 sq m). The fitness/workout room (with high-tech muscle-toning equipment) has ocean-view windows overlooking the navigation bridge one deck below. There are 11 rooms for spa/beauty treatments – but note that the pounding from the basketball court on the sports deck above makes spa treatments less than relaxing.

DISNEY WONDER
★★★+

THIS IS GOOD, THEME-PARK, CASUAL CRUISING FOR THE WHOLE FAMILY

Size:	Mid-size Ship	Passenger/Crew Ratio (lower beds):	1.8
Tonnage:	85,000	Cabins (total):	875
Cruise Line:	Disney Cruise Line	Size Range (sq ft/m):	180.8–968.7/16.8–90.0
Former Names:	none	Cabins (for one person):	0
Builder:	Fincantieri (Italy)	Cabins with balcony:	388
Entered Service:	Aug 1999	Cabins (wheelchair accessible):	12
Length (ft/m):	964.5/294.0	Wheelchair accessibility:	Good
Propulsion/Propellers:	diesel-electric (38,000kW)/2	Elevators:	12
Total Crew:	945	Casino (gaming tables):	No
Passengers (lower beds):	1,750	Self-Service Launderette:	Yes
Passenger Space Ratio (lower beds):	48.5	Onboard currency:	US$

THE SHIP. *Disney Wonder* is the second of an identical pair of ships (the first was the 1998-built *Disney Magic*). The ship's profile is sleek, and combines streamlining with tradition and nostalgia, a black hull and two red-and-black funnels designed to remind you of the ocean liners of yesteryear – *Disney Magic* was the first cruise ship built with two funnels since the 1950s. One funnel is a dummy containing various public spaces, including a teen center.

There are three outdoor pools: one pool for adults only (in theory), one for families (with a large poolside movie screen), and one for children, with Mickey's face and ears painted into the bottom.

Inside, the ship is quite stunning. Most public rooms have high ceilings, and the Art Deco theme of the old ocean liners or New York's Radio City Music Hall has been tastefully carried out. Look at the stainless-steel/pewter Disney detailing on the handrails and balustrades in the three-deck-high lobby.

Apart from the ports of call, the highlight for most is a day spent on Disney's private island, Castaway Cay in the Bahamas. It is a good private island for families.

Disney Wonder is a seagoing Never-Never Land. In reality, the ship provides a highly programed, well-organized, strictly timed, regimented cruise experience, with registration and reservations necessary for almost everything. But for children of all ages (minimum 12 weeks old), it's hard to beat Disney's

BERLITZ'S RATINGS		
	Possible	Achieved
Ship	500	369
Accommodation	200	143
Food	400	205
Service	400	265
Entertainment	100	86
Cruise Experience	400	308

OVERALL SCORE 1376 points out of 2000

family entertainment. There's also an adults-only entertainment area ('After Hours') that includes a lounge/nightspot (Azure), the Cadillac Lounge piano bar with retro car design decor and seating, and a Crown and Fin pub.

Take just casual clothing. Gratuities are extra (suggested at $12 per person per day); 15 percent is added to all bar/beverage/wine and 18 percent for spa accounts.

In a 2016 refurbishment, Disney Wonder gained a new restaurant – Tiana's Place, a revamped British pub, a Twist and Spout waterslide, a Dory's Reef splash zone, and an Aqualab play area.

ACCOMMODATION. There are 12 grades, but just six different cabin layouts; the price will depend on the grade, size, and location chosen, and are linked to the resort accommodation for those taking a combined resort/cruise vacation. Spread over six decks, all suites and cabins have been designed for practicality and have space-efficient layouts.

Most cabins have a neat vertical steamer trunk for clothes storage, illuminated closets, a hairdryer (located at a vanity desk or in the bathroom), and bathrobes for all. Many cabins have third and fourth pull-down berths that are hidden in the ceiling when not in use, but the standard interior and outside cabins, while acceptable for two, are rather tight with three or four. Some cabins can also accommodate a fifth person. Cabins with refrigerators can have them stocked, at extra cost, with one of several drinks/soft drinks packages.

Bathrooms, although compact due to the fact that the toilet is separate, are really functional units, designed with split-use facilities so that more than one person can use them at the same time – good for families. Many have bathtubs, which are really shower tubs.

Suite occupants get more space, and extra goodies such as big-screen TVs, and extra beds (useful for larger families). Some suites are beneath the pool deck, teen lounge, or informal café, so there could be noisy as the ceiling insulation is poor – although cabin-to-cabin insulation is good.

Wheelchair-users can choose from a variety of cabin sizes and configurations, including suites with a private balcony (although you can't get a wheelchair through the balcony's sliding door) and large bathrooms with good roll-in showers, and decent closet and drawer space. Almost the whole ship is accessible. For sight-impaired passengers, cabin numbers and elevator buttons are braille-encoded.

The two largest suites, the Walter E. Disney Suite and the Roy O. Disney Suite, are located beside the central bank of elevators. These are luxurious living spaces, each with two bedrooms, and all the Disney trimmings you'd expect.

A 24-hour room service is available, and suites also get 'concierge service.' But the room service and cabin breakfast menu are limited. A 15 percent service charge applies to beverage deliveries, including tea and coffee.

DINING. There are has three main dining rooms, all non-smoking, each with over 400 seats, two seatings, and themed decor. Triton's (in the center), and Tiana's Place (with a New Orleans jazz-and-blues theme) on Deck 3. Animator's Palate (Deck 4 aft), is highly visual with electronic art that makes the evening decor change from black and white to color.

You eat in all three dining rooms in rotation – twice per seven-day cruise – and move with your assigned waiter and assistant waiter to each dining room in turn, to experience variety in decor and different menus. As you have the same waiter in each restaurant, any gratuities go only to 'your' waiter.

Palo is a 140-seat, reservations-required venue with a small cover/gratuity charge, for cooked-to-order, Italian-style cuisine. It has a 270-degree view and is for adults only; the wine list is good (but prices are high). Make reservations as soon as you board or miss out on the ship's only decent food. Afternoon High Tea is presented here, on sea days.

Cabanas is a large self-serve, food-court-style buffet eatery (it's always busy for lunch). Other casual poolside spots include Eye Scream, Pete's Boiler Bites, Pinocchio's Pizzeria, and Daisy's De-Lites.

Vegetarians and light cuisine seekers will probably be underwhelmed by the lack of green vegetables. Guest chefs from Walt Disney World Resort prepare signature dishes and host cooking demonstrations.

ENTERTAINMENT. The entertainment and activities programs for families and children are excellent. There are large-scale stage shows in the stunning 977-seat showlounge, presenting original Disney musicals and comedy productions, with a cast of Disney baddies from many Disney films. Sadly, there is no live orchestra, although the lighting, staging, and technical effects are excellent. There is also a Disney-themed Trivia Game Show.

SPA/FITNESS. The Senses Spa & Salon is a fitness/wellbeing complex measuring 10,700 sq ft (994 sq m). The fitness/workout room has high-tech Cybex muscle-toning equipment and ocean-view windows overlooking the navigation bridge. There are 13 rooms for spa/beauty treatments – but note that the pounding from the basketball court on the sports deck above makes spa treatments less than relaxing.

EMERALD PRINCESS
★★★+

THIS IS A CASUAL, VERY COMFORTABLE, FAMILY-ORIENTED LARGE RESORT SHIP

Size:	Large Resort Ship	Passenger/Crew Ratio (lower beds):	2.5
Tonnage:	113,561	Cabins (total):	1,557
Cruise Line:	Princess Cruises	Size Range (sq ft/m):	163–1,279/15.1–118.8
Former Names:	none	Cabins (for one person):	0
Builder:	Fincantieri (Italy)	Cabins with balcony:	881
Entered Service:	May 2007	Cabins (wheelchair accessible):	25
Length (ft/m):	951.4/290.0	Wheelchair accessibility:	Good
Propulsion/Propellers:	diesel-electric (42,000kW)/2	Elevators:	14
Total Crew:	1,200	Casino (gaming tables):	Yes
Passengers (lower beds):	3,114	Self-Service Launderette:	Yes
Passenger Space Ratio (lower beds):	36.2	Onboard currency:	US$

THE SHIP. *Emerald Princess* has the same profile as sister *Crown Princess* (similar to half-sisters *Diamond, Golden, Grand, Ruby, Sapphire,* and *Star Princess*). Although the ship takes over 500 more passengers than the half-sisters, outdoor deck space remains the same, as do the number of elevators, so waiting time increases at peak periods. The Passenger Space Ratio is also considerably reduced.

An extra-cost adults-only retreat (The Sanctuary), located forward on the uppermost deck, provides a 'private' place to relax and unwind. There are attendants to provide chilled face towels, and light bites are available; there are also two outdoor cabanas for massages.

The ship has a sheltered faux teak (actually painted steel) promenade deck, which almost wraps around (three times round equals 1 mile/1.6km) and a walkway that goes to the enclosed, protected bow of the ship. The outdoor pools have various beach-like surroundings. Movies Under the Skies and major sporting events are shown on a large movie screen at the pool in front of the large funnel structure.

Inside is a wide array of public rooms, with some 'intimate' (this being a relative term) spaces and places to play.

Aft of the funnel housing is a ship-wide glass-walled disco (Skywalkers), with fine views from port and starboard side windows (it would make a great penthouse).

BERLITZ'S RATINGS		
	Possible	Achieved
Ship	500	359
Accommodation	200	139
Food	400	248
Service	400	285
Entertainment	100	74
Cruise Experience	400	273

OVERALL SCORE 1378 points out of 2000

The interior decor is attractive, with lots of earth tones. An extensive collection of artworks complements the interior design and colors well. If you see something you like, you may be able to purchase it.

The ship also has a Hearts & Minds wedding chapel, with a live web-cam to relay ceremonies via the Internet. The captain can legally marry (American) couples, thanks to the ship's Bermuda registry. But getting married and taking close family members and entourage with you on your honeymoon may prove expensive.

Gamers should enjoy the large Gatsby's Casino, with more than 260 slot machines, and gaming tables.

Other features include a small library and a decent Internet-connect room. Ship lovers should enjoy the wood-paneled Wheelhouse Bar (a good place for cocktails and beer), finely decorated with memorabilia and ship models tracing part of parent company P&O's history. A sports bar has two billiard tables and several television screens.

The ship is a fine resort playground in which to roam when you are not ashore, and Princess Cruises consistently delivers a well-packaged cruise, always with a good degree of style, at an attractive, highly competitive price. With many choices and 'small' rooms to enjoy, the ship has been well designed, and you should have an enjoyable time.

As with any large resort ship it takes time to find your way around, despite the company's claim that it offers passengers a 'small ship feel, big ship choice.' There are several points of congestion, particularly outside the shops, when bazaar tables are set up outside on the upper level of the atrium lobby.

Passenger niggles include the automated telephone system, the small cabin towels, the extra cost for ice cream, and the (coins-needed) charge for the washers and dryers in self-service launderettes.

ACCOMMODATION. There are six main types of cabins and configurations: (a) grand suite, (b) suite, (c) mini-suite, (d) outside-view double cabins with balcony, (e) outside-view double cabins, and (f) interior double cabins. These come in many price categories (the choice is bewildering), depending on size and location. About 100 cabins have interconnecting doors (good for families).

DINING. Of the three main dining rooms – Botticelli, Da Vinci, and Michelangelo – one has two-seating dining and the other two have 'anytime dining' that allows you to choose when and with whom you want to eat. All three are split into multi-tier sections in a non-symmetrical design.

While four elevators go to the deck where two of the restaurants are located, only two go to Plaza Deck 5, where the Michelangelo Dining Room is located – this causes waiting problems at peak times, particularly for anyone in a wheelchair.

High-quality linens and silverware, Frette Egyptian cotton table linens, and Hepp silverware are provided in the main dining rooms. Note that 15 percent is added to all beverage bills, including wines.

Although portions are generous, the food and its presentation are disappointing, and standardized. Fish is often disguised by sauces or coatings, the choice of fresh green vegetables is limited, few garnishes are used, and cheese is either presliced or diced. This is banquet catering, with its attendant standardization and 'batch' cooking. Pasta dishes are acceptable (though voluminous),

typically served by section headwaiters. If you like desserts, order a sundae at dinner (most other items are just so-so).

There are two extra-cost, reservations-required venues. The first, SHARE by Curtis Stone, is located on a high deck aft of the funnel, and features a six-course degustation menu. The second, Crown Grill, located aft on Promenade Deck, features premium-quality American steaks and seafood.

Other eateries include a poolside burger grill and pizza bar (no additional charge). Extra charges apply if you order items to eat at the International Café (a coffee bar/patisserie) or in Vines seafood/wine bar in the atrium lobby. Other casual meals can be taken in the Horizon Court (open 24 hours a day). It has large ocean-view windows on port and starboard sides and direct access to the two principal swimming pools and Lido Deck. Although there is a wide variety of food, there is no presentation finesse, as plastic plates are provided.

ENTERTAINMENT. The 800-seat Princess Theater spans two decks, and has comfortable seating on both main and balcony levels. It has $3 million worth of sound and light equipment, plus a nine-piece band and a resident troupe of singers and dancers.

A second entertainment lounge, Club Fusion, is located aft, for cabaret acts and karaoke contests at night, and lectures, bingo, and horse racing during the day. Explorer's Lounge, a third entertainment lounge, can also host cabaret acts and live music.

A number of other lounges and bars feature live music, including a string quartet, and 'street performers' in the main atrium lobby.

SPA/FITNESS. The Lotus Spa, located forward on one of the uppermost decks (Sun Deck), has separate facilities for men and women, including a sauna, steam room, and changing rooms; common facilities include a relaxation/waiting zone, body-pampering treatment rooms, and a gymnasium packed with cardio-vascular equipment. Some fitness classes are free.

EMPRESS OF THE SEAS
★★+

THIS IS A DATED BUT FAMILY-FRIENDLY SHIP FOR ULTRA-CASUAL GETAWAYS

Size:	Mid-size Ship	Passenger/Crew Ratio (lower beds):	2.3
Tonnage:	48,563	Cabins (total):	800
Cruise Line:	Royal Caribbean International	Size Range (sq ft/m):	117.0–818/10.8–76
Former Names:	Empress, Empress of the Seas, Nordic Empress	Cabins (for one person):	0
		Cabins with balcony:	69
Builder:	Chantiers de l'Atlantique (France)	Cabins (wheelchair accessible):	4
Entered Service:	Jun 1990/Apr 2016	Wheelchair accessibility:	Fair
Length (ft/m):	692.2/211.0	Elevators:	7
Propulsion/Propellers:	diesel (16,200kW)/2	Casino (gaming tables):	Yes
Total Crew:	685	Self-Service Launderette:	No
Passengers (lower beds):	1,600	Onboard currency:	Euros
Passenger Space Ratio (lower beds):	30.2		

THE SHIP. Now over 25 years old (the oldest in the fleet), the all-white *Empress of the Seas* has a somewhat boxy profile. The swimming pool is tiny for the number of passengers carried (this is a very high-density ship), and there's little open deck space, so the unpadded sunloungers are crammed tight. There is, however, a walk-around outdoor promenade deck. Wrapped around the funnel, the Viking Crown Lounge is a nice place for drinks and good ocean views.

Inside, a nine-deck-high atrium is the social meeting place. Most public rooms are on two decks, including a Schooner Bar, shops, aft lounge, library, card room, plus facilities for children and teens at Adventure Ocean near the pool. A three-level Casino Royale has gaming tables and slot machines.

You'll be overwhelmed by the public spaces, but underwhelmed by the size of the cabins. However, for short cruises it's adequate if you pack lightly. The ship underwent a refurbishment in 2016, following a number of years being operated by Pullmantur Cruises. It is now back in the RCI fold.

ACCOMMODATION. From interior (no-view) cabins to larger suites; the price you pay depends on the location and size. All have twin beds that convert to a queen-size configuration, and tiny bathrooms.

DINING. The Dining Room is two decks high, but it really is a noisy room. There are two seatings, at tables for four to 10. The cuisine is typical of mass banquet catering, and pretty unmemorable.

Chops Grille is an extra-charge venue, with dishes available à la carte; reservations are required. Its intimacy makes it more inviting, with a number of tables for two.

For self-serve, food court-style casual meals, Windjammer Buffet provides an alternative to the Miramar Restaurant.

ENTERTAINMENT. The two-level Royal Theatre has poor sight lines in the upper lateral balconies, and the sight lines from the front rows of the balcony are ruined by railings. The entertainment throughout is upbeat – in fact, it is difficult to get away from music (it's everywhere – even in the elevators).

SPA/FITNESS. Vitality Spa facilities include saunas and a beauty salon. A fitness facility is in another location. For sports fans, there's an outdoor rock-climbing wall at the aft of the ship.

BERLITZ'S RATINGS		
	Possible	Achieved
Ship	500	264
Accommodation	200	107
Food	400	186
Service	400	214
Entertainment	100	48
Cruise Experience	400	208

OVERALL SCORE 1027 points out of 2000

ENCHANTMENT OF THE SEAS
★★★+

THIS COMFORTABLE SHIP HAS ELEGANT DECOR, FOR ACTIVE FAMILIES

Size:	Mid-size Ship	Passenger/Crew Ratio (lower beds):	2.6
Tonnage:	81,500	Cabins (total):	1,126
Cruise Line:	Royal Caribbean International	Size Range (sq ft/m):	158.2–1,267.0/14.7–117.7
Former Names:	none	Cabins (for one person):	0
Builder:	Kvaerner Masa-Yards (Finland)	Cabins with balcony:	248
Entered Service:	Jul 1997	Cabins (wheelchair accessible):	20
Length (ft/m):	990.1/301.8	Wheelchair accessibility:	Good
Propulsion/Propellers:	diesel-electric (50,400kW)/2	Elevators:	9
Total Crew:	840	Casino (gaming tables):	Yes
Passengers (lower beds):	2,252	Self-Service Launderette:	No
Passenger Space Ratio (lower beds):	36.1	Onboard currency:	US$

THE SHIP. *Enchantment of the Seas* (a *Vision*-class ship) has a fairly sleek profile, with a single funnel located well aft – almost a throwback to the designs of the 1950s, and a nicely rounded stern. There is a walk-around promenade deck outdoors, with sunloungers (but no cushioned pads).

A Viking Crown Lounge, a trademark lounge aboard some Royal Caribbean International ships, sits between the funnel and mast and overlooks the forward section of the pool deck.

In 2005, a $60 million 'chop-and-stretch' added a 72.8ft (22.2m) mid-section, stretching it to around 990ft (301m) and upping its gross tonnage. It added 151 passenger cabins, including two 'family' cabins that can sleep six. The pool deck was given more space plus soaring 'suspension' bridges. Special lifts were provided for the two pools, as was a new Splash Deck (kids love the 64 water jets).

Enchantment of the Seas is best suited to couples and families with children who don't need all the latest bells and whistles, but want to cruise with up-to-date facilities, and multiple dining choices. Finger-touch digital 'Wayfinder' direction screens make getting around easy.

The interior focal point (and the social hub of the ship) is a seven-deck-high Centrum (atrium lobby). On its various levels, it houses an R Bar (for some creative cocktails), passenger-service counters, an art gallery, and Café Latte-tudes (for coffee). Aerial entertainment

BERLITZ'S RATINGS	Possible	Achieved
Ship	500	344
Accommodation	200	133
Food	400	220
Service	400	260
Entertainment	100	75
Cruise Experience	400	262
OVERALL SCORE 1294 points out of 2000		

happens in the Centrum, too. Close by is the flashy Casino Royale (for table gaming and slot machines – and interesting exhibits under several glass floor panels), a Schooner Bar with nautical decor and maritime art, Boleros (for Latin sounds and dancing), Centrum shops, and a library.

There are several sculptures, principally by British artists; much of it is on the themes of classical music, ballet, and theater, and huge murals of opera scenes adorn several stairways. There are tropical plants to help counteract the plain, clinical pastel wall colors.

This company provides a well-organized but rather homogenous cruise experience, with the same decades-old passenger participation activities and events.

ACCOMMODATION. There are multiple price grades, but so many cabins are of the same or similar size. Room service offers only the most basic menu.

Most cabins have twin beds that convert to a queen-size one, just enough closet space for a week-long cruise, and good drawer space, although under-bed storage space is limited. Bathrooms have several mirrors. The plastic buckets, provided for Champagne/wine, are rather tacky.

DINING. The 1,365-seat My Fair Lady Dining Room spans two decks, connected by a sweeping stairway.

Choose one of two seatings, or 'My Time Dining' (eat when you want, during dining hours).

The cuisine is standardized banquet catering and batch cooking. Menu descriptions sound tempting, but the food, although prepared well enough, is just so-so. However, you can have cooked-to-order items such as lobster or filet mignon (steak) at an extra cost. Green vegetables are scarce, but salad items are plentiful, and desserts are pretty good. Rice is often used as a carbohydrate source. Breads and pastry items are so-so (they are baked from frozen 'starter' dough), and items such as croissants lack any hint of butter. Vegetarian and children's menus are also available. Note that there are no wine waiters.

The extra-cost, reservations-required Chops Grille Steakhouse serves prime steaks and veal chops. Aft is the Park Café: an indoor/outdoor deli for salads, sandwiches, soups, and pastries.

Casual, self-serve meals can be taken in the 790-seat casual Windjammer Marketplace, with its expanse of ocean-view glass windows. The decor is bright and cheerful, and buffet 'islands' contain food from around the world.

ENTERTAINMENT. The 875-seat Orpheum Theater (main showlounge) is a grand room in the forward section for large production shows and major cabaret.

A second showlounge, the 575-seat Carousel Lounge, is aft, for smaller shows and late-night adults-only comedy. Other lounges and bars have almost constant live music; in fact, there's no bar without music for a quiet drink. There's even background music in all corridors and elevators, and outdoors on the pool deck.

SPA/FITNESS. Vitality at Sea Spa is aft of the funnel and spans two decks. Facilities include a gymnasium, aerobics room, sauna and steam rooms, a beauty salon, and 13 private massage/body treatment rooms, including one for couples. Some fitness classes are free.

EURODAM
★★★+

A SPACIOUS AND PLEASANT MID-SIZED SHIP WITH DUTCH-STYLE INTERIOR DECOR

Size:	Mid-size Ship	Passenger/Crew Ratio (lower beds):	2.2
Tonnage:	86,273	Cabins (total):	1,052
Cruise Line:	Holland America Line	Size Range (sq ft/m):	170.0–1,318.6/15.7–122.5
Former Names:	none	Cabins (for one person):	0
Builder:	Fincantieri (Italy)	Cabins with balcony:	708
Entered Service:	Jul 2008	Cabins (wheelchair accessible):	30
Length (ft/m):	935.0/285.0	Wheelchair accessibility:	Good
Propulsion/Propellers:	diesel-electric (34,000kW)/2 azimuthing pods	Elevators:	14
		Casino (gaming tables):	Yes
Total Crew:	929	Self-Service Launderette:	No
Passengers (lower beds):	2,104	Onboard currency:	US$
Passenger Space Ratio (lower beds):	41.0		

THE SHIP. *Eurodam* has two funnels, one behind the other (not side by side). This design is the result of the machinery configuration, because the ship has, in effect, two engine rooms – one with three diesels, and one with two diesels, and a pod propulsion system.

On deck are 22 rentable cabanas, with goodies such as Champagne, chocolate strawberries, a music-loaded iPod, bathrobes, fresh fruit, and chilled towels. Designed for two adults and two children, they may not be 'quiet' spaces because they are on observation deck around the Lido Pool.

There is an exterior teak promenade deck, but it doesn't wrap-around the front section, and teak steamer-style sunloungers. There are two swimming pools outdoors, one with a retractable glass roof.

The ship has a bright interior decor designed for younger, multi-generational passengers, and a traditional artwork collection highlighting the line's connection with the former Dutch East Indies.

A small lobby spans three decks. Adjacent are interior and glass-walled elevators with ocean views through 11 decks. The information desk (on the lower level) is small and somewhat removed from the main passenger flow on the two decks above it.

There are two decks of public rooms, the most dramatic of which is the showlounge, spanning four decks. Other facilities include a winding shopping street with several boutique stores, card room, an art gallery, a photo gallery, several meeting rooms, and

BERLITZ'S RATINGS		
	Possible	Achieved
Ship	500	388
Accommodation	200	144
Food	400	220
Service	400	266
Entertainment	100	72
Cruise Experience	400	284
OVERALL SCORE 1374 points out of 2000		

a large casino with gaming tables and slot machines. One of the most popular public rooms is Explorations – a combination of a cost-extra coffee bar, lounge, library, and an Internet center in an attractive, open 'lifestyle' environment, adjacent to the Crow's Nest Lounge.

Other facilities include the Queen's Lounge, which doubles as a lecture room, a Culinary Arts Center (for cooking demonstrations), small screening room, and several bars.

Gratuities are automatically added to your account. Passenger niggles include noisy cabin air conditioning (it can't be turned off, the only regulation being for temperature control), and the many pillars that obstruct flow.

ACCOMMODATION. There are numerous price categories, with grades from interior (no-view) cabins to fairly spacious suites, including spa 'suites' adjacent to The Retreat, an extra-cost relaxation area.

All grades have plush Mariner's Dream beds, waffle/terry cloth robes, Egyptian cotton towels, flat-panel infotainment systems, make-up mirrors with halo lighting, massage shower heads, large hairdryers, and fruit baskets. Suites receive fresh flowers. Some cabins have interconnecting doors.

Cabins accommodating a third and fourth person have little closet space, and just one personal safe. Suite occupants have use of a Neptune Lounge and concierge service, priority embarkation and disembarkation, and other benefits. However, in many of the balcony suites/cabins the balconies can be overlooked from various public locations.

DINING. The Rembrandt Dining Room – a pleasant stunning bi-level room – is located aft. Choose open seating (you may have to wait for a table) or fixed (assigned tables) seating times.

With a few exceptions, the cuisine is unmemorable; it lacks passion and taste. There's a lack of green vegetables, but much use of rice, canned fruit, and ready-sliced and diced cheese. Still, you get friendly service from Indonesian and Filipino stewards, and the chinaware is nice.

'Lighter-option' meals are also available. HAL can also provide kosher meals (these are prepared ashore, frozen, and brought to your table sealed in their original containers).

The extra-cost, reservations-required 130-seat Pinnacle Grill is an intimate venue, with high-quality ingredients and good presentation. It fronts onto the second level of the atrium lobby; tables along its outer section are open to it and can suffer from Atrium Bar noise one deck below (but these tables are good for those who like to see and be seen). Pacific North-west food (premium-quality steaks and seafood) is featured. The wine list includes fine wines from around the world.

Tamarind is a pan-Asian (fusion cuisine) restaurant; there's no charge for lunch, but a cover charge applies for dinner.

For casual eats, there's the self-serve, food court-style Lido Market, with various counters and a salad bar. Movement along the buffet line can be slow. In the evenings, one section turns into the extra-cost Canaletto Restaurant – a quasi-Italian, informal, waiter-service eatery.

A poolside grill features multi-choice burgers (and special Dive-In sauce), hot dogs, and fries.

ENTERTAINMENT. The Mainstage showlounge presents colorful Vegas-style revues and cabaret. The sight lines are best from the two upper levels. Other venues for music and performance include Half Moon and Billboard Onboard.

SPA/FITNESS. Greenhouse Spa includes a thermal suite, hydropool, several private rooms for body treatments, and fitness center. Sports enthusiasts can enjoy a basketball court and a volleyball court.

EUROPA
★★★★★+

A SOPHISTICATED AND VERY SPACIOUS SHIP FOR ELEGANT, INFORMAL CRUISING

Size:	Small Ship	Passenger/Crew Ratio (lower beds):	1.4
Tonnage:	28,890	Cabins (total):	204
Cruise Line:	Hapag-Lloyd Cruises	Size Range (sq ft/m):	355.2-914.9/33.0-85.0
Former Names:	none	Cabins (for one person):	0
Builder:	Kvaerner Masa-Yards (Finland)	Cabins with balcony:	168
Entered Service:	Sep 1999	Cabins (wheelchair accessible):	2
Length (ft/m):	651.5/198.6	Wheelchair accessibility:	Best
Propulsion/Propellers:	diesel-electric (21,600kW)/2 azimuthing pods	Elevators:	4
		Casino (gaming tables):	No
Total Crew:	280	Self-Service Launderette:	No
Passengers (lower beds):	408	Onboard currency:	Euros
Passenger Space Ratio (lower beds):	70.4		

THE SHIP. This sleek-looking ship has a gracefully shaped stern topped by Hapag-Lloyd's signature orange-and-blue funnel. It is very stable at sea, with no vibration or noise – thanks to its pod propulsion and excellent build quality. Some 14 Zodiac landing craft for close-up coastal shore excursions and boot-washing areas are provided, as are over 20 bicycles free for use ashore, offloaded dockside in each port (where possible). A 2019 refurbishment saw the addition of two new dining venues (The Globe by Kevin Fehling, and Pearls); the introduction of a more informal/casual dress code and open seating dining; a refreshed atrium lobby; and more contemporary artwork.

There is an outdoor walking/jogging area with rubberized deck (plus a walk-around teak promenade deck), and sunloungers have thick cushioned pads.

A long, rectangular swimming pool is half indoors and half outdoors. While not the widest, it is longer than pools aboard many other cruise ships (measuring 56.7 x 16.8ft/17.3 x 5.12m). Movies can be screened poolside, and themed social events are held here on some evenings.

Most of *Europa's* hotel service crew understand the culture and can talk about German, Swiss, and Austrian life.

Europa, one of the world's most spacious purpose-built cruise ships, is now in informal cruising mode, with painstakingly accomplished service. The space

BERLITZ'S RATINGS		
	Possible	Achieved
Ship	500	471
Accommodation	200	183
Food	400	373
Service	400	360
Entertainment	100	91
Cruise Experience	400	374
OVERALL SCORE 1852 points out of 2000		

per person ratio is high, there is never a hint of a line, and both restaurant and showlounge can seat all passengers at once. Only the best-quality soft furnishings are used, blending traditional with modern designs. Most public rooms and hallways have high ceilings to further increase the sense of space and grandeur. The focal point is a seven-deck-high central atrium, with two glass-walled elevators (operated by 'piccolos' on embarkation day). The lower level features a white Steinway grand piano and Piano Bar, reception desk, concierge and shore-excursion desks. It's a cozy space for social gatherings.

Several public rooms are located along a curved 'street' leading aft from the atrium, and include Gatsby's – a speakeasy-style place to meet, chat, and be entertained, with superbly crafted vintage cocktails, half-moon-shaped bar, small stage, and wooden dance floor.

Highly comfortable, the sidewalk Havana Bar cigar lounge is a clubby room with cigar-colored armchairs and three large glass-fronted, conditioned humidor cabinets, and an extensive range of high-end, mostly Cuban, cigars. It also features a range of armagnacs, calvados, cognacs, and Cuban beer, while a wall-mounted digital jukebox has push-button songs and instrumental music. Do try an Irish coffee, correctly made (the glass is rotated while the sugar is blended with alcohol, then heated gently over a candle). Adjacent is a ship's jeweler/clothing boutique (Wempe).

On a higher deck, Club Belvedere is a lovely room, with a curved bar; afternoon tea takes place here (with cakes made fresh daily), as do intimate music recitals.

The library, home to an illuminated globe of the world and numerous bookcases, is open 24/7. Opposite is a small cinema/meeting/workshop room called the 'Studio.'

For wheelchair-users, a special ramp goes directly from the outdoor pool deck to the lifeboat; only three other ships have such a ramp (*Asuka II, Crystal Serenity*, and *Crystal Symphony*).

Europa is certainly a luxurious small cruise ship, mainly for German-speakers (the crew also speaks English). The tradition of indulgent cruising is taken to the highest level, with excellent food and culinary diversity, a wide range of creature comforts, and wonderful flower arrangements.

ACCOMMODATION. This consists of all-outside-view suites: two Penthouse Grand Suites (Hapag and Lloyd) and 10 Penthouse Deluxe Suites, suites with private balcony, standard-size suites, two suites (with private balcony) for limited-mobility passengers, and several suites with interconnecting doors.

Most have a balcony with wide teak deck and lighting, and a smoked glass screen topped by a teak rail. Twelve suites overlooking the stern are among the most sought-after accommodation, and include a balcony with canvas 'ceiling' for shade and privacy.

All have a wooden floor entryway, a sleeping area with twin beds convertible to queen-size (with duvets), bedside tables with lamps and two drawers, and a lounge area with curtain divider and bird's-eye maple wood cabinetry (with rounded edging). Also: Nespresso coffee machine, refrigerator/mini-bar (beer and soft drinks are included) writing/vanity desk, and couch with large table. An illuminated walk-in closet provides ample hanging space, six drawers, personal safe, umbrella, shoehorn, and clothes brush. Goodies include a practical shoulder travel bag and an insulated lunch bag for excursions. All suites have a 100 percent air-circulation system, and excellent soundproofing.

An infotainment system includes free 24/7 video and audio on-demand, a large flat-screen television, Internet connection via a wireless keyboard, and a data socket.

The marble-tiled bathrooms are well designed and include two good-size cabinets for toiletries. Each has a full bathtub, integral shower, retractable clothesline, and a separate glazed shower enclosure. Thick cotton bathrobes are provided, as are slippers and an array of personal amenities.

Deck 10 Suites. All have electronically adjustable beds, and Nespresso coffee machines. A teakwood entrance hall opens into a spacious living room with dining table and four chairs and a stocked drinks cabinet with refrigerator and complimentary bar set-up. Perks include laundry and ironing service, priority reservations, pre-dinner canapés daily, handmade chocolates, petit-fours, and other niceties. Balconies have teakwood decking and white canvas ceiling shades. For the ultimate in exclusivity, Penthouse Grand suites have very large bathrooms (with private sauna, angled bathtubs, and heated floor), and extensive forward views from their prime location, plus a large wrap-around balcony. Also: spacious walk-in closets (with a window), large infotainment screens, Robbe & Berking silver Champagne goblets, and Bulgari bathroom amenities. Well-trained butlers provide the highest level of unobtrusive service.

'Spa suites' have a large teak-decked balcony; twin or queen-size bed; walk-in closet; and dark wood cabinetry with a refrigerator stocked with fruit juices, mineral waters, and bar set-up. There's an infotainment system, ample storage space (including lockable jewelry drawer), writing/vanity desk, and floor-to-ceiling windows. A large window separates living/sleeping areas and Asian-decor bathroom, home to a Jacuzzi bath with underwater lighting, separate large shower enclosure with rain shower, toilet, gold, thick-glass washbasin, and hairdryer. Special teas and other services are provided by spa personnel.

Suites for limited-mobility passengers (Deck 7) have one electronically operated bed with hydraulic elevator, one regular bed, and a closet with drawers. Bathrooms have a roll-in shower, fittings at the right height, several grab handles, and an emergency call-for-help button. Wheelchair-accessible public toilets are provided on the main restaurant/entertainment deck.

DINING. The Europa Restaurant is a beautiful, high-ceilinged dining room, with open seating and tables for two to eight.

Table settings include Dibbern china, Robbe & Berking silverware, and Riedel wine glasses. The cuisine includes German favorites and regional dishes from around the world. Top-grade caviar is on the dinner menu at least once each week (and on request, at extra cost).

With a huge, diverse range of ingredients, the executive chef produces menus that don't repeat, even for around-the-world voyages. The cuisine is outstanding, and always full of surprises. Seasonal ingredients and totally fresh fish and seafood are standard. Plated presentation of food is provided for entrées, with silver service for additional vegetables. Portion size is sensible, and never overwhelming. The wine list is extensive.

On sea days, an additional Gourmet Breakfast menu includes items like beef tartare and smoked tuna carpaccio, while a Cuisine Légère menu features light, healthy and taste-filled spa cuisine.

The Globe by Kevin Fehling (the German chef is famed for his three-Michelin-starred restaurant 'The Table' in Hamburg) is a pocket-sized, intimate restaurant with multi-course menu. The restaurant – a haven for lovers of haute cuisine – is open for dinner nightly and for lunch on sea days, at no extra charge.

Venezia (completely refreshed and expanded slightly in 2019) is admired for its fine Italian cuisine, notably its range of olive oils and grappa, and its antipasti trolley. It is open for lunch and dinner, at no extra charge.

New indoor-outdoor casual eatery Pearls was added in 2019 and features caviar-based seafood and tapas.

A refreshed Lido Café is for casual self-serve breakfasts (with ship-made preserves), luncheons, and dinners, with indoor and outdoor seating (heated by lamps, when needed) and adjacent indoor/outdoor bar. Themed evening dining is also featured, with skilled waiter service. There is a wide variety of food, and many lunch buffets host popular themes and fresh local specialties.

Above the Lido Café is the popular indoor/outdoor, late-night hangout Sansibar (an outpost of the famed Sylt island restaurant), with great aft-facing views and excellent drinks.

Europa is also known for its real German sausages, available in Gatsby's and at a Bavarian Frühschoppen (featured each cruise in the Lido Café). Nautical tradition is maintained with bouillon on sea days, and other daily niceties include fresh waffles and ice cream poolside.

ENTERTAINMENT. The Studio (formerly Europa Lounge) is a traditional showlounge with a sloping floor, and raised stage – although several pillars obstruct sight lines. The intellectual entertainment program is tailored to the cruise theme – and includes a constant supply of high-quality classical and contemporary musical artistes, cabaret acts, and expert lecturers.

Small ensemble classical concerts and recitals take place in the Belvedere Lounge, with its dropped central circular wood floor.

SPA/FITNESS. Ocean Spa has a wide range of beauty services and treatments, and full-day spa packages. Facilities include a steam room and sauna (mixed), two shower enclosures and foot-washing stations, relaxation room, men's and women's changing/dressing rooms, and beauty salon. Treatment rooms have personal-choice music menus, while the gymnasium includes a 'miha bodytec' training machine and personal trainer.

An electronic golf simulator room complements a golf driving range; a PGA golf pro is carried on all cruises, and shuffleboard courts are on the open deck, as is a new fitness/exercise area.

EUROPA 2
★★★★★+

A STUNNING, SPACIOUS INFORMAL SHIP FOR STYLISH INTERNATIONAL TRAVELERS

Size:	Small Ship	Passenger/Crew Ratio (lower beds):	1.3
Tonnage:	42,830	Cabins (total):	258
Cruise Line:	Hapag-Lloyd Cruises	Size Range (sq ft/m):	376.7–1,227.1/35.0–114.0
Former Names:	none	Cabins (for one person):	0
Builder:	STX France	Cabins with balcony:	258
Entered Service:	May 2013	Cabins (wheelchair accessible):	2
Length (ft/m):	739.5/225.4	Wheelchair accessibility:	Best
Propulsion/Propellers:	diesel-electric (24,000kW)/2 azimuthing pods	Elevators:	4
		Casino (gaming tables):	No
Total Crew:	370	Self-Service Launderette:	No
Passengers (lower beds):	516	Onboard currency:	Euros
Passenger Space Ratio (lower beds):	83.0		

THE SHIP. *Europa 2* has a sleek profile and appearance, and Hapag-Lloyd's signature orange-and-blue funnel. Look down from an upper aft deck at its nicely tiered stern.

The whole ship is about relaxed luxury. Spaciousness, natural light, and contemporary style are evident everywhere. There is a complete walk-around deck – unusual for a ship of this size; teak decking is everywhere, with polished teak handrails on all balconies and outdoor stairways.

A two-level pool deck is a stunning space, with a 49-ft (15-m) rectangular heated pool, and a large sliding glass roof to cover the area as needed (when closed it's like a cozy winter garden). Balinese sleep beds inhabit the aft upper level (with more on the open aft deck), contemporary sun beds and drinks tables, bar and separate food bar (homemade waffles in the afternoon, ice cream, etc.), plus a removable movie screen.

A fleet of 12 Zodiacs – named after Hamburg suburbs – is carried for landings in small harbors and isolated bays, plus 20 bicycles for use at no charge.

Europa 2 is beautifully appointed, with high-quality fit and finish. The designers have created contemporary interiors together with some traditional Hapag-Lloyd touches from yesteryear, such as the indented handrails in the main stairways. It is different to the slightly more formal *Europa*. There's also an outstanding museum-quality art collection, including works by David Hockney and Damien Hirst. A light re-

BERLITZ'S RATINGS

	Possible	Achieved
Ship	500	477
Accommodation	200	185
Food	400	373
Service	400	362
Entertainment	100	92
Cruise Experience	400	375

OVERALL SCORE 1864 points out of 2000

fresh in 2018 has introduced some new public rooms and the ship is even better.

The atrium lobby has chic gray, black and chrome decor, boudoir-style seating, a long bar, and a specially commissioned gray Steinway grand piano. A high ceiling sets it off, together with what look like four large gray-and-black vase-like features, and a reception desk. A glass viewing wall on both sides provides multi-deck natural light connection with the sea. Adjacent is a Wempe boutique and jewelry store, and, along the walls, some superb pieces of art (including some by Gerhard Richter).

There are six restaurants, two lounges, and six bars – some with familiar names carried over from the tradition of *Europa*.

Collins has three large glass-fronted, temperature-controlled cigar cabinets and a bar with a wide range of spirits, all poured tableside, plus Cuban beer, and over 50 premium multi-country artisan gins, not to mention a turntable with vinyl records of several genres.

Sansibar is a sea-going outpost of the fashionable seafood/wine restaurant on Sylt (an island in northern Germany), with indoor-outdoor seating aft, a bar, a dance floor, and an à la carte menu, tapas-style nibbles, special wines, and a great club-like atmosphere. It's an 'in' place to be at night, but also offers a trendy 'late riser's' breakfast, and handmade artisanal coffees.

Other standout public rooms include Club 2, a trendy venue with dance floor, for live jazz, soul music, and other artistic presentations (at night it's like a speakeasy, with appropriate mood lighting).

There's also a Miele Culinary Arts School, and Belvedere, a 'lifestyle' and coffee/tea lounge with integral New England-style library, bar – for superb cakes, sandwiches and patisserie items, and a wide tea selection (including many Ayurvedic loose teas), served in elegant teapots.

There's no traditional captain's dinner, because it's an informal ship for anyone seeking the highest quality in a relaxed setting, although senior officers often dine with passengers in various venues. Details really matter, however, and examples include leather-covered tissue boxes and different-sized spoons for small or large coffees in your suite.

Considered the leader of the pack of high-end ships, it exudes discreet, bling-free quality at every turn, impressive culinary diversity, unobtrusive service with a smile, an outstanding wellness spa, flowers everywhere, and a caviar night once each cruise. Look out for the beer stein from an early 1900s ship, and the gorgeous blue Rosenthal teapot and vase from the 1981-built Europa, among other museum-quality pieces in glass display cabinets.

Europa 2 has a serious focus on cuisine, modern lifestyle, and wellness. It operates in English and German, and is aimed at youthful, sophisticated, cosmopolitan travelers and their families. Three areas are designed for kids and teens: a Knopf Club (a new 'Cap'n Knopf' bear was created specially by Steiff and is only available aboard Europa 2) for toddlers aged 2–3; a Kids' Club for 4- to 10-year-olds; and a Teens' Chill-out Room for 11 to 15s. Special (parent-free) shore excursions for children are also available. For something different, teens can indulge in a chocolate massage in the spa. Meanwhile, a kids' pool dinner party is really special.

ACCOMMODATION. There are several price categories and eight accommodation grades (sizes given include balcony). From the smallest (376.7 sq ft/34 sq m) to the largest two Owner's Suites (1,227 sq ft/114 sq m), they are extremely well designed and all have a balcony (even the smallest balcony is 75.3 sq ft/7 sq m), and all except seven Family suites (581 sq ft/54 sq m) have Jacuzzi bathtubs.

Two Owner's Suites are luxurious apartments (each is like a mini-villa, with hotel attached), double-width balconies, and Damien Hirst butterfly art. The standout feature is a large ocean-view wet room with steam sauna, 'rain' shower with chromotherapy lighting, separate hand-held shower hose, separate circular whirlpool tub large enough for four, window-side daybed, two large washbasins, and floor-to-ceiling windows. The spacious living area has an oversize walk-in closet, fully stocked refrigerator, large dining table and chair set, and an Eames lounge chair. There are multiple infotainment sets, including one integrated in a mirror adjacent to the wet room.

Two suites for the disabled each have a large bathroom with roll-in shower, three washbasins, and an integrated 'mirror' TV.

Facilities in even the smallest suite are excellent, with a layout that is well designed and practical. The overall decor is relaxing and includes custom-made deep-pile carpets. Beds have a torsion arrangement (variable from hard to soft, while both head and body/foot sections can be raised electrically. One neat feature is a push-button bedside lighting panel with different mood settings.

A wide choice of (full-size) daily newspapers is available (included for occupants of Penthouse Deck 10 suites, which also have multi-way electric beds). All suites have a Nespresso coffee machine and associated items, an anti-rattle 'butler's pantry'-like refrigerator/minibar cabinet (beer and soft drinks are included) with several 'quiet-close' storage trays for glasses, cups, and other bar amenities. There's also a writing/vanity desk, and couch with large table in a separate lounge area, and door-touch keycard holder. An integrated infotainment system includes 24/7 video and audio on-demand, and internet connection via a wireless keyboard or tablet, plus two USB sockets.

DINING. Europa 2 really is all about relaxed dining experiences and culinary adventures, including selections from Michael Hoffman's celebrated vegetarian and vegan dishes (with different choices in each restaurant). Open seating in all venues makes it easy for families with children to choose when to eat, and reservations are not needed anywhere for lunch. Dibbern china and Schott Zwiesel glassware are standard. Impressively (and unusually for a ship of this size), some 40 percent of all tables are for two – others are for four, six or eight. What makes most of the ship's double-deck height restaurants special is their detailed decor and individuality. Another knock-out feature is that the menus are constantly being refreshed, to meet the expectations of the ship's clientele – think the trend towards lighter, healthier cuisine and smaller portions, but always the highest quality possible.

Weltmeere (Worldwide): This 266-seat restaurant (with huge, whimsical, pink 'octopus' tentacle-like glass chandeliers) features international culinary favorites, and its contemporary chairs have armrests.

Tarragon: this chic, tile-floored 44-seat French-style bistro features tableside carving (the steak tartare – prepared tableside – is exceptional, and you choose the accompanying ingredients), regional/seasonal food, and a focus on fresh herbs. It is open for dinner (and on select days for lunch).

Serenissima: this 56-seat Italian restaurant has open seating for lunch and dinner. Large white columns add to the sense of grandeur, and the green glass chandeliers are stunning.

Elements is a 48-seat pan-Asian restaurant for lunch and dinner.

Sakura is a 58-seat sushi restaurant (part of the Yacht Club, for dinner), featuring Japanese cuisine and incorporating a sit-up sushi counter.

Yachtclub: this 276-seat (142 indoor and 134 outdoor seats) venue is open for breakfast, lunch, and dinner. It has multi-section, self-serve buffets (including an Ayurvedic 'bio-food' section), a rotisserie, two active cooking stations, and a superb manual Berkel meat-slicing machine for wafer-thin cold cuts. Outside on deck is a Pasta Bar (several types of pasta are made on board, as are six different sauces daily), and a separate Grill Bar (with several fish choices), and a canvas-like canopy incorporates heaters for cool-weather conditions.

Hapag-Lloyd Cruises has long been known for its culinary creativity and extremely high quality of food and service. This ship won't disappoint those seeking it.

Additionally, Sansibar is a trendy indoor-outdoor venue with special drinks, wines, and items from its namesake restaurant on the island of Sylt, Germany. It features special wines, has an à la carte late-riser's breakfast, and constantly changing tapas-style eats.

ENTERTAINMENT. The Theater is a two-level showlounge, with good sightlines from almost all seats, LED lighting for show backdrops, and a thrust stage. Edgy, multi-faceted entertainment is presented by the company's own production team, each designed to be highly visual to accommodate the bilingual and increasingly international travelers.

Club 2 is a standout for the cool stuff, along with wine tastings; its bar has a long drinks list. Meanwhile light classical and chamber concerts take place in various other venues.

SPA/FITNESS. The Ocean Spa is superb – a center of serenity and calm – and the largest wellness and spa zone for this size of ship, with indoor and outdoor areas of over 10,764 sq ft (1,000 sq m) that do justice to the trend for combining holidays and wellbeing.

Facilities include a beauty salon, eight massage/body-treatment rooms, a steam room and three dry saunas (Finnish, Herbal, and Bio) at different temperatures – two with glass walls looking aft; one has an illuminated interior wall of a Finnish forest. There are two relaxation rooms (one with hot tile beds); men's and women's changing/dressing rooms; showers, and a large outside relaxation deck. All are mixed gender, except for the changing rooms.

There are also two electronic golf simulators, a golf driving range and, unusually, a storage room for golf clubs.

EXPLORER DREAM
★★★★

THIS FAMILY-FRIENDLY SHIP IS FOR ULTRA-CASUAL CRUISING AND ENERGETIC ENTERTAINMENT

Size:	Mid-size Ship	Passenger/Crew Ratio (lower beds):	1.4
Tonnage:	75,338	Cabins (total):	935
Cruise Line:	Dream Cruises	Size Range (sq ft/m):	150.6–638.3/14.0–59.3
Former Names:	*SuperStar Virgo*	Cabins (for one person):	0
Builder:	Meyer Werft (Germany)	Cabins with balcony:	390
Entered Service:	Aug 1999/May 2019	Cabins (wheelchair accessible):	4
Length (ft/m):	879.2/268.0	Wheelchair accessibility:	Good
Propulsion/Propellers:	diesel/2	Elevators:	9
Total Crew:	1,225	Casino (gaming tables):	Yes
Passengers (lower beds):	1,870	Self-Service Launderette:	No
Passenger Space Ratio (lower beds):	41.7	Onboard currency:	

THE SHIP. *Explorer Dream* (formerly *SuperStar Virgo*) was transformed in March 2019 to cater to the needs of Asian and Australasian passengers. Its white hull is adorned with colorful, scroll-like artwork 'Waves of Dreams' by Chinese artist Kuri Huang; it depicts imaginative mythic creatures. There is a walk-around promenade deck outdoors – good for strolling. Inside are two boulevards and a large, two-deck-high central atrium lobby with three glass-walled elevators, shops, and cafés.

A Resorts World casino complex includes gaming tables and slot machines, and a smaller, members-only gaming club called Premium. Other facilities include the ESC Experience Lab for virtual-reality gaming. Lots of choices, dining options, and Asian hospitality all add up to an attractive package. The dress code is casual (no jacket and tie needed), and a no-tipping policy applies. While the initial cruise fare is reasonable, extra costs and charges can soon mount up when you indulge in more than the basics.

ACCOMMODATION. There are several types of accommodation, in a number of price categories. Three entire decks of cabins have private balconies, while two-thirds of all cabins have outside views. Both the standard outside-view and interior cabins really are very small, particularly since all cabins have extra berths for a third/fourth person. So, pack minimally, as there's little storage space for luggage. All cabins have a personal safe, cotton towels, and duvets. Bathrooms have a good-size shower enclosure, and personal toiletry items.

BERLITZ'S RATINGS		
	Possible	Achieved
Ship	500	379
Accommodation	200	138
Food	400	272
Service	400	258
Entertainment	100	74
Cruise Experience	400	284

OVERALL SCORE 1405 points out of 2000

An extensive 2019 refit added several new features, including The Palace, a 'ship-within-a-ship' private enclave, with 50 suites and butler service, together with its own Palace Restaurant, lounge, free Wi-Fi, pool, and private open deck space aft.

DINING. There's certainly no lack of choice, with a mix of East and West flavors. The main dining rooms, plus several other venues (some cost extra), include: Silk Road, Uma Uma, Blue Lagoon, Mozzarella Ristorante e Pizzeria (for Italian fare), Hot Pot (for noodle dishes), Seafood Grill by noted Australian chef Mark Best, and Blue Lagoon (sidewalk café for some excellent Asian street food). The Lido Café is a large self-serve buffet restaurant with indoor/outdoor seating for 400, adjacent to the main pool.

ENTERTAINMENT. The Zodiac Theatre (show-lounge) spans two decks, with main and balcony levels. The room has almost no support columns to obstruct the sight lines, and hosts a revolving stage for revues and other production shows, with recorded show music.

Bands and small musical units provide plenty of live music for dancing and listening in the various lounges.

SPA/FITNESS. Crystal Life Spa has a gymnasium full of high-tech equipment, an aerobics room, a hair and beauty salon, saunas and steam rooms (extra charge), changing rooms for men and women, several body treatment rooms, and aqua-swim pools with counter-flow jets.

EXPLORER OF THE SEAS
★★★+

THIS LARGE RESORT SHIP WILL ENTERTAIN THE WHOLE FAMILY IN COMFORT

Size:	Large Resort Ship	Passenger/Crew Ratio (lower beds):	2.6
Tonnage:	137,308	Cabins (total):	1,557
Cruise Line:	Royal Caribbean International	Size Range (sq ft/m):	151.0–1,358.0/14.0–126.1
Former Names:	none	Cabins (for one person):	0
Builder:	Kvaerner Masa-Yards (Finland)	Cabins with balcony:	757
Entered Service:	Oct 2000	Cabins (wheelchair accessible):	26
Length (ft/m):	1,020.6/311.1	Wheelchair accessibility:	Best
Propulsion/Propellers:	diesel-electric (75,600kW)/3 pods (2 azimuthing, 1 fixed)	Elevators:	14
		Casino (gaming tables):	Yes
Total Crew:	1,181	Self-Service Launderette:	No
Passengers (lower beds):	3,114	Onboard currency:	US$
Passenger Space Ratio (lower beds):	44.0		

THE SHIP. *Explorer of the Seas* (a Voyager-class ship) is a large, floating leisure resort with a whole host of facilities yet offers a healthy amount of space per passenger, and excellent entertainment for the whole family. Outdoor decks are full of fun water park features, and a rock-climbing wall, so there's little room left to just sit and relax or sunbathe. This is consistent, but homogeneous mainstream cruising for young-minded cruisers of all ages who enjoy mingling in a large ship with plenty of life and constant activity. One neat feature is an outdoors observation deck at the very front (good for photos, if you face aft, with most of the ship behind you).

A four-deck-high Royal Promenade, 394ft (120m) long, is the main interior focal point (entertaining street parades take place here). Two American football fields long, it has two internal lobbies that rise through 11 decks. Eateries, bars and shops line the street, and interior 'with-view' cabins look into it. Look up: you'll see a large moving, asteroid-like sculpture (constantly growing and contracting).

Arched across the promenade is a captain's balcony, while a central stairway connects with the deck below and the Schooner Bar (a piano lounge common to all RCI ships) and a large, flashy Casino Royale.

Other standouts include a regulation-size ice-skating rink (Studio B), with real ice, with 'bleacher' seating for up to 900 and broadcast facilities.

BERLITZ'S RATINGS

	Possible	Achieved
Ship	500	353
Accommodation	200	131
Food	400	222
Service	400	266
Entertainment	100	74
Cruise Experience	400	257

OVERALL SCORE 1303 points out of 2000

Overall, this is a fine all-round ship for all age groups but be aware of the extra cost for many optional items (including drinks, drink packages, and excursions).

In 2015, the ship underwent an extensive refurbishment, adding a number of dining options, a Flowrider surf simulator, 'virtual' balconies for interior cabins, and a 3D cinema.

Facilities for children and teenagers are extensive and include Adventure Beach, a family area, with swimming pools, a waterslide, and outdoor game areas.

Expect lines for the reception desk, shore excursions, shore tenders, and at the self-serve buffet stations. Do budget extra for additional cost items and expect to be subjected to flyers and advertising promotions.

Niggles include intrusive photographers, few quiet places to sit and read – almost everywhere there is intrusive rap-rich 'background' music (particularly on the pool deck), no cushioned pads for deck sunloungers, small cabin 'bath' towels, noisy (vacuum) toilets, and frosted drinks in 'souvenir' glasses pushed to the hilt. Service personnel are friendly, however, and the digital 'Wayfarer' system is informative, but the speaking 'elevator going up/going down' becomes boring.

ACCOMMODATION. There is a wide range of cabin price grades, including: interior (no-view) cabins, balcony cabins, and suites (the largest is the Royal Suite). Many cabins are of a similar size, which is good for incentives and large groups, and 300 have interconnecting doors (good for families).

Some 138 interior cabins have bay windows views into the interior Royal Promenade horizontal atrium – a cruise industry first when the ship originally debuted. Occupy a cabin with a connecting door to another cabin and you may be able to hear your neighbors.

DINING. The huge Sapphire Dining Room has three levels, all with the same menu. Place settings, china, and cutlery are of good quality. Choose one of two seating timings, or My Time Dining (eat when you want during dining room hours).

Main dining room cuisine is all about standardized banquet catering and batch cooking. Menu descriptions sound tempting, but the food, although prepared well enough, is just so-so. Items like lobster or premium steaks come at extra cost, but they will be cooked individually to your liking. Green vegetables are scarce – provided basically for decoration – but salad items are plentiful, and desserts are pretty good. Rice is often used as a filler. Bread and pastry items are so-so (these are thawed and then baked from frozen 'starter' dough), and croissants lack any hint of butter. Vegetarian and children's menus are also available. Note that there are no wine waiters.

Other dining venues (most at an extra cost) include: Chops Grille (open for lunch and dinner, for prime steaks, other meats, and grilled seafood items); Giovanni's Table (for lunch and dinner; Italian classics served family-style); Izumi Asian Cuisine (for lunch and dinner; includes a sushi bar and sizzling hot-rock cooked items); Chef's Table (this 'private' experience is co-hosted by the executive chef and sommelier and features a multi-course dinner with wine pairing); and Park Café (for breakfast, lunch and dinner, this indoor/outdoor deli is for salads, sandwiches, soups, and pastries).

Johnny Rockets, a retro 1950s all-day, diner-style eatery, has hamburgers, malt shakes (at extra cost), and jukebox hits, with both indoor and outdoor seating.

Promenade Café: for Continental breakfasts, all-day pizzas, and specialty coffees (in paper cups).

Sprinkles, located on the Royal Promenade, is for round-the-clock ice cream and yogurt, pastries, and coffee.

For casual, self-serve meals, a cavernous Windjammer Cafe has several sections. It is open almost round-the-clock.

ENTERTAINMENT. The stunning 1,350-seat Palace showlounge spans five decks, with only a few slim pillars and almost no disruption of sight lines – an example of fine design and shipbuilding.

Strong cabaret acts perform in the main showlounge, while others perform in Maharaja's Lounge, also the venue for adult-only late-night comedy. The best shows are the Ice Spectaculars.

SPA/FITNESS. The Vitality at Seas Spa includes an aerobics room, workout center, treatment rooms, and men's and women's sauna/steam rooms. Another 10,000 sq ft (930 sq m) of space features a Solarium (with sliding glass-dome roof) to relax in after you've exercised.

Aft of the funnel is a 33ft (10m) rock-climbing wall, with five climbing tracks. Other sports facilities include a roller-blading track, a dive-and-snorkel shop (equipment rentals available), a full-size basketball court, and a nine-hole, par-26 golf 'course.'

FIFTY YEARS OF VICTORY
★★★★

NUCLEAR-POWERED, THIS IS THE ULTIMATE NORTH POLE AND ARCTIC EXPEDITION SHIP

Size:	Boutique Ship	Passenger/Crew Ratio (lower beds):	0.9
Tonnage:	23,439	Cabins (total):	66
Cruise Line:	Various expedition operators	Size Range (sq ft/m):	148.5–367.0/13.8–34.1
Former Names:	Ural	Cabins (for one person):	0
Builder:	Baltic Works, St Petersburg (Russia)	Cabins with balcony:	0
Entered Service:	Mar 2007	Cabins (wheelchair accessible):	0
Length (ft/m):	523.6/159.6	Wheelchair accessibility:	None
Propulsion/Propellers:	nuclear reactors (2)/3	Elevators:	1
	propulsion motors (75,000 hp)	Casino (gaming tables):	No
Total Crew:	140	Self-Service Launderette:	Yes
Passengers (lower beds):	132	Onboard currency:	US$
Passenger Space Ratio (lower beds):	177.5		

THE SHIP. An advanced vessel of the *Arktika*-class of icebreaking ships, *Fifty Years of Victory* is an outstanding polar expedition ship that carries adventurous, hardy outdoors types of mature years. It is powered by two nuclear reactors (it can only operate in cold water conditions so that the water can cool the pressurized water reactors) providing 75,000hp, and carries enough fuel to power it for five years.

This dramatic, incredibly impressive vessel (50 *Let Pobedy* in Russian) is the world's largest and most powerful icebreaker, capable of breaking through ice up to 8ft (2.4m) thick. While the noise created by the ice-crushing capability of this marine machine is intense, it is all part of the great adventure.

There are more crew members than passengers, giving a most impressive passenger/space ratio. The ship is comfortable, and it carries a fleet of Zodiac inflatable landing craft, as well as two helicopters for passenger use, expedition leaders, and experienced, highly specialized lecturers. The crew is experienced in challenging conditions.

Fifty Years of Victory typically leaves from its northern Russian base city of Murmansk before heading north. Approaching the North Pole – 90° north and 1,000 miles (1,600km) from the closest tree – aboard a Russian icebreaker is the ultimate prize of a true Arctic Expedition voyage, and the most spectacular voyage by ship.

A library is stocked with books about polar exploration, nature, and wildlife. Because there are so few voyages to the North Pole, places sell out quickly.

BERLITZ'S RATINGS		
	Possible	Achieved
Ship	500	359
Accommodation	200	143
Food	400	260
Service	400	273
Entertainment	100	80
Cruise Experience	400	302

OVERALL SCORE 1417 points out of 2000

Parkas and rubber boots are provided, but you should take waterproof trousers and thermal wear. Gratuities to the crew are at your discretion.

ACCOMMODATION. There are two 'suite' grades and three cabin grades. The suites have a spacious bedroom and separate lounge room, while the bathroom has a tub. Suites also have a coffee-making machine, and fresh fruit is replenished daily. All suites/cabins have windows that open. Each has private bathroom facilities (with shower, except the suites with bathtub), TV/DVD player, and a decent amount of storage space. Only two cabins (46 and 48) have obstructed views.

DINING. The dining room operates in a single open seating, so you sit with whomever you wish. Expect the food to be carbohydrate-rich, hearty fare that will provide the energy you need for the adventures ahead.

ENTERTAINMENT. There isn't any as such: conversation among all participants is the main event each day, as well as evening recaps, and, of course, wildlife spotting.

SPA/FITNESS. Facilities include a sauna, fitness center, basketball, and an indoor volleyball court. There is a small 'dip' pool at the stern, underneath the helicopter deck.

FRAM
★★★

THIS IS EXPEDITION-STYLE CRUISING IN A MODERN, BUT MINIMALIST SHIP

Size:	Small Ship	Passenger/Crew Ratio (lower beds):	3.3
Tonnage:	11,647	Cabins (total):	127
Cruise Line:	Hurtigruten	Size Range (sq ft/m):	113.0–415.5/10.5–38.6
Former Names:	none	Cabins (for one person):	0
Builder:	Fincantieri (Italy)	Cabins with balcony:	6
Entered Service:	Apr 2007	Cabins (wheelchair accessible):	2
Length (ft/m):	374.0/114.0	Wheelchair accessibility:	Fair
Propulsion/Propellers:	diesel (4.6MW)/2	Elevators:	2
Total Crew:	75	Casino (gaming tables):	No
Passengers (lower beds):	254	Self-Service Launderette:	No
Passenger Space Ratio (lower beds):	45.8	Onboard currency:	Norwegian krona

THE SHIP. Designed to operate in polar waters, *Fram's* itineraries include expedition-style cruises to Antarctica in the winter. It suits mature adults who like exploring independently. The ship underwent refurbishment in 2019; this included updated, more environmentally friendly engines and technical equipment.

The ship's design reflects Norwegian and Greenlandic culture, using a mix of wool, leather, oak, and Inuit interiors. The few public rooms include the Explorer Lounge, an Internet café, a science boardroom, and a small shop. There is no walk-around promenade deck. Hurtigruten doesn't have a great culture of hospitality and service, so many passengers feel they are traveling with a transportation company rather than a cruise line. The crew to passenger ratio is really low, and service training is minimal, so there's little attention to detail.

In Antarctica, the ship is a modestly capable (but oversized) expedition vessel, but it can still get stuck in heavy pack-ice. An Expedition Leader organizes everything to do with a specific voyage. Expedition specialists provide daily lectures. Boots are provided; they come in European sizes – so it helps to know yours before you go.

Life on board is very relaxed (no formal attire). Smoking is allowed only on the open deck – and never when *Fram* is in port. The ship operates in Norwegian and English. There are no safety deposit boxes. Hurtigruten operates a no-tipping-required policy. All in all, the ship should provide an expedition-style experience in a modicum of comfort, although it feels cramped

BERLITZ'S RATINGS		
	Possible	Achieved
Ship	500	303
Accommodation	200	111
Food	400	207
Service	400	222
Entertainment	100	51
Cruise Experience	400	225
OVERALL SCORE 1119 points out of 2000		

due to low ceiling heights. In 2020 the ship is due for a total refurbishment, which may result in a more comfortable experience.

ACCOMMODATION. There are many price categories, according to size and location (fortunately, no cabins have obstructed views). The largest accommodation is one Owner's Suite, with a bedroom, living room, and bathroom with Jacuzzi tub. Six aft cabins overlooking the ship's wake have a shared balcony. Most cabins have one bed and a sofa that converts to a fold-down bed, or two pull-down sofa beds; there's little room and only a few shelves; these cabins, although refreshed in 2019, are not very practical for expedition-style voyages.

DINING. The main dining room, Imaq, is aft and connects to the main lobby via an arcade. Local cuisine and recipes, including bison meat and fresh fish, are featured. However, several meals are of the self-help buffet variety only. An extra-charge bistro and self-serve buffet is available for snacks. Dessert items are particularly good. Alcohol prices are very high.

ENTERTAINMENT. There isn't any. Guides and lecturers organize talks and informative briefings based on the cruise area.

SPA/FITNESS. Saunas are one deck above the exercise area; there's also a small but well-equipped exercise room.

FREEDOM OF THE SEAS
★★★+

THIS IS A LARGE FLOATING THEME PARK – GOOD FOR THE WHOLE FAMILY

Size:	Large Resort Ship	Passenger/Crew Ratio (lower beds):	2.6
Tonnage:	154,407	Cabins (total):	1,817
Cruise Line:	Royal Caribbean International	Size Range (sq ft/m):	153.0–2,025.0/14.2–188.1
Former Names:	none	Cabins (for one person):	0
Builder:	Kvaerner Masa-Yards (Finland)	Cabins with balcony:	842
Entered Service:	Jun 2006	Cabins (wheelchair accessible):	32
Length (ft/m):	1,112.2/339.0	Wheelchair accessibility:	Best
Propulsion/Propellers: diesel-electric (75,600kW)/3 pods (2 azimuthing, 1 fixed) (42,000kW)		Elevators:	14
		Casino (gaming tables):	Yes
Total Crew:	1,360	Self-Service Launderette:	No
Passengers (lower beds):	3,634	Onboard currency:	US$
Passenger Space Ratio (lower beds):	42.4		

THE SHIP. *Freedom of the Seas* (with sisters *Independence of the Seas* and *Liberty of the Seas*) is an extension of the popular *Voyager*-class of ships, introduced in 1999. For this ship, the length and beam were extended, enabling an increase in cabins and passenger capacity, and a combined pool area 43 percent larger than the *Voyager*-class – but with 500 more passengers (and, after a 2015 refit, even more passengers), yet the same number of elevators. The ship is the length of 37 London double-decker buses.

The open upper deck is full of water park features (H20 Zone), including water cannons, spray fountains, water jets, ground gushers and a Flowrider body/board surfing zone aft (which creates a wall of water, at 35,000 gallons per minute). Twin central pools consist of a main and a sports pool, with grandstand-style seating and competitive games.

There are multiple bars and lounges, a whole street full of shops, and munching and drinking spots along its four-decks-high, indoor mall-like environment called the Royal Promenade (some interior-facing cabins have great views into it).

The forward section leads into a large nightclub – Star Lounge –for late-night adult-only comedy. One deck down is Casino Royale (gaming tables and slot machines) and more bars and lounges.

A lively large resort ship, with tasteful decor, *Freedom of the Seas* is a good ship for young, active families with children, as long as you don't mind lines when signing up for popular activities (the Flowrider surf area, rock-climbing wall, and full-size boxing ring, for example).

ACCOMMODATION. There is a wide range of suites and cabins in several categories and price grades, from a Presidential Family Suite that can sleep up to 14 to twin-bed, two-person interior cabins without a view, and interior cabins with bay windows that look into the Royal Promenade. The price you pay depends on the size, grade, and location. There are many family-friendly cabins, good for reunions, but no solo-occupancy cabins. All outside-view cabins have even numbers; all interior cabins have odd numbers.

DINING. The large main dining room is set on three levels, each with a theme and different name – Leonardo, Isaac, and Galileo – all have the same menus and food. A dramatic staircase connects the three levels, but huge support pillars obstruct the sight lines from many seats.

Choose one of two seatings, or My Time Dining (eat when you want during dining-room hours). The cuisine is all about standardized, batch-cooked banquet catering. Menu descriptions sound tempting, but the food, although prepared well enough, is just so-so. However, you can have items such as lobster or filet mignon (steak) cooked to order at an

BERLITZ'S RATINGS

	Possible	Achieved
Ship	500	353
Accommodation	200	132
Food	400	222
Service	400	280
Entertainment	100	70
Cruise Experience	400	250

OVERALL SCORE 1307 points out of 2000

extra cost. Green vegetables are used primarily for decoration, but salad items are plentiful and desserts are pretty good. Rice is often used as a source of carbohydrates. Breads and pastry items are adequate (these are thawed and then baked from frozen 'starter' dough), and items such as croissants lack any hint of butter. Vegetarian and children's menus are also available. Note that there are no wine waiters.

Other dining venues and eateries (some of which cost extra, but the food is mostly cooked to order) include favorites such as Chops Grille Steakhouse for premium veal chops, steaks, and seafood; Giovanni's Table for Italian-American cuisine; Sabor for 'authentic' Mexican specialty cuisine; and Johnny Rockets, a retro, 1950s diner-style eatery for burgers, hot dogs, malt shakes, and sodas. Reservations are required (make them through the digital system – and as early as possible to avoid disappointment); note that the menu is the same each day.

No reservations are needed for Promenade Café (Continental breakfast, sandwiches, and coffees); Cupcake Cupboard (for fairy cakes); Sorrento's (pizzas and Italian cakes); Sprinkles Ice Cream Parlor (for round-the-clock ice cream and yoghurt, pastries, and coffee); and Windjammer Café, a large, sprawling venue for casual buffet-style, self-serve meals – part of this, Jade 'Restaurant,' does Asian-themed food.

ENTERTAINMENT. The 1,350-seat Arcadia Theater spans three decks (five if you count the orchestra pit and scenery storage space). It is a well-designed showlounge, with only a small number of pillars disrupting the sight lines to the stage.

SPA/FITNESS. A large Vitality at Sea Spa and Fitness Center includes a spacious aerobics room, fitness center, several treatment rooms, men's and women's sauna/steam rooms, and relaxation areas. Most exercise classes cost extra.

GENTING DREAM
★★★★+

THIS FAMILY-FRIENDLY SHIP IS FOR ASIA CRUISING IN HIGH-TECH SURROUNDINGS

Size:	Large Resort Ship	Passenger/Crew Ratio (lower beds):	1.6/1
Tonnage:	151,300	Cabins (total):	1,680
Cruise Line:	Dream Cruises	Size Range (sq ft/m):	139.9–2,411.1/13.0–224.0
Former Names:	none	Cabins (for one person):	0
Builder:	Meyer Werft (Germany)	Cabins with balcony:	1,188
Entered Service:	Nov 2016	Cabins (wheelchair accessible):	32
Length (ft/m):	1,100.0/335.3	Wheelchair accessibility:	Good
Propulsion/Propellers:	diesel-electric/2 azimuthing pods	Elevators:	16
		Casino (gaming tables):	Yes
Total Crew:	2,030	Self-Service Launderette:	No
Passengers (lower beds):	3,360	Onboard currency:	CNY (RMB)
Passenger Space Ratio (lower beds):	45.0		

THE SHIP. This is the first stunning large resort ship for Dream Cruises (a 'premium' brand created in 2015, owned by Genting Hong Kong, of Crystal Cruises and Star Cruises). *Genting Dream* has really extensive facilities and entertainment features for the whole family. Its smooth lines and profile are similar to those of Norwegian Cruise Line's Norwegian Escape, in terms of exterior design and styling (but with the lifeboats hanging out from the ship's side). The attention-getting hull, conceived by Chinese Pop artist Jacky Tsai, features a story involving a mermaid and an astronaut, painted in flamboyant red and gold. The superstructure glows with LED lighting at night.

There is a complete walk-around outside promenade deck (with indoor-outdoor seaside eateries), multiple pools (including a private, extra-cost, adults-only pool and relaxation area), and, in the ship's center (adjacent to the main pool), the Wet 'n' Wild Water Park, with six waterslides. Zouk Beach and bar, music lounge, and a sports bar are located aft of the funnel.

Inside, the decor is ultra-upbeat, with a clutch of bright colors. There are numerous bars, lounges, karaoke and Mahjong rooms, as well as a large Genting Casino with gaming tables and slot machines (and private gaming rooms), Resorts World Casino, Resorts World Premium Club, and Maxim's – for card games. Also, there is a street night 'market' with hawker stalls featuring Asian delicacies. Two standout drinking places

BERLITZ'S RATINGS		
	Possible	Achieved
Ship	500	416
Accommodation	200	153
Food	400	313
Service	400	290
Entertainment	100	86
Cruise Experience	400	311

OVERALL SCORE 1569 points out of 2000

include a dedicated Johnnie Walker bar, and a Penfolds Wine Vault (with some lovely vintage wines).

Genting Dream has three home ports: Guangzhou (Nansha Port), Hong Kong, and Sanya, which means that there really is no beginning or end to a cruise, just a rotating itinerary, although Singapore is the home port. Overall, this ship has all the right ingredients for Asia cruises for Asians, served mostly by Asians, who understand the cultures of the region better than the western cruise lines.

ACCOMMODATION. There are many accommodation grades. From the smallest interior (no-view) cabin (measuring 150 sq ft/14 sq m) to the largest suite (142 Dream Suites), which measures 1,970 sq ft/183 sq m and spread over two decks, the price you pay depends on the size, location, and grade you choose.

The more you pay, the more you get – for occupants of the Dream Palace (with 25,000 gross tons assigned to it), a private-access VIP area located in a section at the front of the ship above the navigation bridge (similar to but more expansive than MSC Cruises' 'Yacht Club' and Norwegian Cruise Line's 'The Haven'). Dream Suite occupants have free Wi-Fi and access to a private outdoor pool, hot tubs, gym, relaxation area, and cabanas, Horizons Lounge (observation lounge), and a private club for gaming (so there's no need to go downstairs to the busier Resorts World and other casino areas).

Over 100 family-friendly cabins have interconnecting doors, so parents can take their young ones and feel comfortable.

DINING. With an abundance of dining, eatery and drinking options, the ship can cater to just about any taste and dietary and ethnic persuasion. Main dining venues include a large bi-level Windows, located aft, with ocean views from its huge dining hall windows (a window table is definitely one to have). A second 'main' dining room is Genting Palace.

The culinary emphasis is, naturally, on the Asia-Pacific region, including Chinese lunchtime favorite – dim-sum (whose meaning, literally, is 'to touch the heart'); Halal cuisine is also available from a dedicated Halal section in the World Buffet. Noted Australian chef Mark Best has his first restaurant at sea; his 'Bistro' menu's focuses on small producer Australian beef, lamb, river fish and the freshest seafood.

Other venues (indoor and outdoor) include:

Silk Road, for à la carte Chinese regional and provincial cuisine in a tablecloth setting.

Blue Lagoon, the venue for tuck-in Chinese street (finger) food and clay pot cuisine.

Umi-Uma, a Japanese restaurant with Teppanyaki grills, and sushi bar.

Positano, an Italian eatery reminiscent of the Amalfi Coast.

Genting Palace, another venue featuring Chinese (Cantonese) dishes.

Makan Makan, for South-East Asian cuisine, including Chinese and Malaysian specialties.

World Buffet, an international food court-style area with self-serve food from various display counters and active cooking stations, while adjacent and outside is a pool bar and grill.

Bread Box and Tiffin Café, a 'see and be seen in' venue for coffees/teas and light bites.

Drinking places include a Red Lion Pub, Johnnie Walker bar (with a wall full of decorative bottles of JW and a special Dream Cruises JW whisky), a Martini bar, Bar City, Boba Cha, Bar 360, and several other bars.

ENTERTAINMENT. The multi-deck 1,000-seat Zodiac Theater is the main showlounge. It features glamorous production shows (including acrobatics) and major cabaret acts.

Silk Road is an extra-cost, bordello-look nightclub with topless Burlesque show. Adjacent are several (bookable, extra-cost) Karaoke rooms.

SPA/FITNESS. Crystal Life Spa has two sections (East, and Aeris West), one for Asians (for whom ambience and 'flow-through' are more important than the range of treatments offered), and one for Westerners. The spa – the largest at sea – has its own eatery (Aeris Spa Café), for 'healthy' food and drinks (some of which are at extra cost). Genting Dream also has an MRI scanner (it was the first cruise ship to carry one). Sports facilities in various locations include a bowling alley, basketball court, a climbing wall, and an extensive Dreamcatcher rope-climbing course.

GOLDEN PRINCESS
★★★+

THIS IS A COMFORTABLE, INFORMAL, FAMILY-FRIENDLY LARGE RESORT SHIP

Size:	Large Resort Ship	Passenger/Crew Ratio (lower beds):	2.1
Tonnage:	108,865	Cabins (total):	1,312
Cruise Line:	P&O Australia	Size Range (sq ft/m):	161.4–764.2/15.0–71.0
Former Names:	none	Cabins (for one person):	0
Builder:	Fincantieri (Italy)	Cabins with balcony:	720
Entered Service:	May 2001/Oct 2020	Cabins (wheelchair accessible):	28
Length (ft/m):	951.4/290.0	Wheelchair accessibility:	Best
Propulsion/Propellers:	diesel-electric (42,000kW)/2	Elevators:	14
Total Crew:	1,100	Casino (gaming tables):	Yes
Passengers (lower beds):	2,624	Self-Service Launderette:	Yes
Passenger Space Ratio (lower beds):	41.4	Onboard currency:	US$

THE SHIP. *Golden Princess*, sister to *Grand Princess* and *Star Princess*, has a racy 'spoiler' at the stern that is an observation lounge with aft-facing views by day (good for book-reading), and a discotheque by night. The ship has a rather flared snub-nosed bow and a galleon-like transom stern.

There is a good sheltered faux teak promenade deck – it's actually painted steel – which almost wraps around (three times round is equal to 1 mile/1.6km) and a walkway that goes to the enclosed bow. The outdoor pools have various beach-like surroundings, plus a large poolside movie screen. One lap pool has a pumped 'current' to swim against. The Sanctuary is an area for adults only; it has plush padded lounge chairs, two private massage cabanas, and Serenity Stewards.

There is plenty of space inside the ship and a wide array of public rooms. The passenger flow is good, with minimal congestion. The decor is mildly attractive, and includes many earth tones.

The main lobby, La Piazza, has live entertainment; the International Café for extra-cost coffees, cookies, pastries, panini, and tapas; and Vines, a wine bar.

There is a Wedding Chapel, with a web-cam to relay ceremonies via the Internet. The ship's captain can legally marry (American) couples, thanks to the ship's Bermuda registry (this should, however, be verified when in the planning stage – it may vary according to where you reside).

BERLITZ'S RATINGS	Possible	Achieved
Ship	500	320
Accommodation	200	121
Food	400	242
Service	400	260
Entertainment	100	71
Cruise Experience	400	261
OVERALL SCORE 1275 points out of 2000		

A large casino, on Deck 7, has gaming tables and slot machines, while the wood-paneled Wheelhouse Bar is decorated with memorabilia and ship models tracing part of parent company P&O's history.

Passenger niggles include the user-unfriendly automated telephone system, the small cabin towels, the extra cost for items such as ice cream, and the (coins-needed) charge for the washers and dryers in self-service launderettes.

Overall, however, Princess Cruises delivers a consistently fine, comfortable, well-packaged product, always with a good degree of style, at a competitive price.

Note that in October 2020 the ship will undergo refurbishment prior to joining the P&O Australia fleet as the renamed *Pacific Adventure*.

ACCOMMODATION. There are six main cabin types, from small interior (no-view) cabins to the largest suite (the Grand Suite – B748), at the stern, but a bewildering number of price categories. The price depends on grade, size, and location.

Note that some of the most expensive accommodation has balconies that can be overlooked, so there is no privacy (suites C401, 402, 409, 410, 414, 415, 420, 421, 422, 423, 424, and 425 on Caribe Deck in particular). Also, the extremely large suites D105 and D106 (Dolphin Deck) have balconies that can be seen from above.

Standard interior and outside-view cabins (the outside ones come either with or without private balcony) are of a functional, practical design, although almost no drawers are provided. They are attractive, with warm, pleasing decor and decent soft furnishings.

Two family suites consist of two suites with an interconnecting door, plus a large balcony. These can sleep up to 10 (if at least four are children), or up to eight adults.

Note that the views from most outside cabins on Emerald Deck are obstructed by lifeboats. Some cabins can accommodate a third and fourth person in upper berths, but the lower beds are fixed and cannot then be pushed together

Cabins with balconies on Dolphin, Caribe, and Baja decks are overlooked by passengers on balconies on the deck above; they are, therefore, not at all private. However, perhaps the least desirable balcony cabins are the eight located forward on Emerald Deck, as the balconies don't extend to the side of the ship and can be passed by walkers and gawkers on an adjacent walkway (so occupants need to keep their curtains closed most of the time). Cabin attendants have many cabins to look after (typically 20), which cannot translate to fine personal service. Other niggles include the limited drawer space.

DINING. For 'formal' meals there are three principal dining rooms (Bernini, Canaletto, and Donatello). There are two seatings in one restaurant, and the others have 'anytime dining,' where you choose your time and companions. The dining rooms are split into multi-tier sections in a non-symmetrical design that breaks what are large spaces into many smaller sections. Each dining room has its own galley. While four elevators go to Fiesta Deck for Canaletto and Donatello, only two go to Plaza Deck 5 for Bernini, which can mean long wait problems at peak times, particularly for anyone in a wheelchair. Note that 15 percent is added to all beverage bills, including wines, coffees, etc.

Although portions are generous, the food and its presentation are standardized. Fish is often disguised by sauces or coatings, green vegetable choice is limited, few garnishes are used, and cheese is either pre-sliced or diced. This is banquet catering (batch cooking). Pasta dishes are acceptable (though voluminous), typically served by section headwaiters. If you like desserts, order a sundae at dinner (most other desserts are just so-so).

Two extra-cost, reservations-required dining venues are: Sabatini's and Crown Grill. Sabatini's for Italian-style pizzas and pastas, with a variety of sauces. Sabatini's is open for lunch or dinner on sea days only. Crown Grill has a viewable galley, and features premium-quality steaks and grilled seafood items. It's worth it for food cooked to order.

Poolside burger grill and pizza bars offer casual bites. Other casual meals can be taken in the 24-hour Horizon Court, with large ocean-view windows and direct access to the two main swimming pools and Lido Deck, and outdoor seating. Plastic plates are provided instead of trays.

ENTERTAINMENT. The 748-seat Princess Theater spans two decks and has comfortable seating on both levels. Princess Cruises prides itself on its glamorous, all-American production shows, always with live music.

Vista Lounge is a second entertainment venue and multi-function room. It presents cabaret acts at night, and lectures, bingo, and horse racing during the day.

Explorers is a third entertainment lounge for cabaret acts and live bands; it has a decent-sized dance floor.

Many other lounges and bars have live music, and there are male dance hosts as partners for women traveling alone.

SPA/FITNESS. Lotus Spa is a complex that surrounds one of the swimming pools at the forward end of the ship. It comprises a large fitness room with all the high-tech workout machinery, an aerobics room, sauna and steam rooms, beauty salon, treatment rooms, and a relaxation area.

GRAND CELEBRATION
★★+

THIS FAMILY-FRIENDLY SHIP IS FOR LOW-COST PARTY CRUISES TO THE BAHAMAS

Size:	Mid-size Ship	Passenger/Crew Ratio (lower beds):	2.4
Tonnage:	47,262	Cabins (total):	751
Cruise Line:	Bahamas Paradise Cruise Line	Size Range (sq ft/m):	184.0/17.1
Former Names:	*Grand Celebration, Celebration*	Cabins (for one person):	0
Builder:	Kockums (Sweden)	Cabins with balcony:	10
Entered Service:	Mar 1987/Jun 2008	Cabins (wheelchair accessible):	14
Length (ft/m):	732.6/223.3	Wheelchair accessibility:	Fair
Propulsion/Propellers:	diesel (23,520kW)/2	Elevators:	8
Total Crew:	620	Casino (gaming tables):	Yes
Passengers (lower beds):	1,502	Self-Service Launderette:	Yes
Passenger Space Ratio (lower beds):	31.4	Onboard currency:	US$

THE SHIP. *Grand Celebration*, now 30 years old, is really a large water-taxi to the Bahamas. It also has extremely short bows and a swept-back, wing-tipped blue funnel just aft of the ship's center. The swimming pools are very small, and the open deck space is extremely limited, which makes it feel crowded.

It has a double-width indoor promenade and a good selection of public rooms, including a large (Paradice – cute spelling!) casino, and several lounges and bars. There is no walk-around open promenade deck.

ACCOMMODATION. There are several accommodation grades, and several price categories: suite with balcony; junior suite with balcony; outside-view; and interior cabins. The cabins are quite standard, are of fairly generous proportions, except for the interior cabins, which are very small. A 24-hour room service menu is provided. The best living spaces are in 10 suites, each of which has much more space than a standard cabin, plus its own private balcony, a larger bathroom and more closet, drawer, and storage space.

DINING. There are two dining rooms: the 550 seat Restaurant Vistahermosa and the 450-seat Res-

BERLITZ'S RATINGS		
	Possible	Achieved
Ship	500	262
Accommodation	200	108
Food	400	171
Service	400	215
Entertainment	100	52
Cruise Experience	400	203

OVERALL SCORE 1011 points out of 2000

taurant Riazor. They are cramped when full, and extremely noisy. There are tables for four, six, or eight, but none for two. The decor is bright and extremely colorful. Dining is in two seatings. Meals for vegetarians and special children's menus are available.

Food presentation is simple, and few garnishes are used. Some meat and fowl dishes are disguised with gravies and sauces. There is much use of canned fruit and jellied desserts. This is strictly banquet catering, with all its standardization and production cooking. For casual meals, there's the 280-seat, self-serve Buffet Triana.

ENTERTAINMENT. Gran Teatro Mirasierra is the venue for high energy, high volume shows. Almost every lounge/bar onboard has live bands and musical units, so there's always plenty of live music in the evening.

SPA/FITNESS. The Indulgence Spa is located on the ship's uppermost deck. It has a gymnasium with muscle-pumping equipment, men's and women's changing rooms, and saunas. The beauty salon is elsewhere. Massages, facials, pedicures, and beauty treatments cost extra.

GRAND CLASSICA
★★+

THIS OLD-STYLE SHIP IS GOOD FOR ACTIVE, SUN-LOVING PARTYGOERS

Size:	Mid-size Ship	Passenger/Crew Ratio (lower beds):	2.0
Tonnage:	52,950	Cabins (total):	658
Cruise Line:	Bahamas Paradise Cruise Line	Size Range (sq ft/m):	185.1–430.5/17.2–40.0
Former Names:	Costa neoClassica, Costa Classica	Cabins (for one person):	0
Builder:	Fincantieri (Italy)	Cabins with balcony:	10
Entered Service:	Jan 1992/Apr 2018	Cabins (wheelchair accessible):	6 (interior)
Length (ft/m):	718.5/220.6	Wheelchair accessibility:	Good
Propulsion/Propellers:	diesel (22,800kW)/2	Elevators:	8
Total Crew:	650	Casino (gaming tables):	Yes
Passengers (lower beds):	1,316	Self-Service Launderette:	No
Passenger Space Ratio (lower beds):	40.2	Onboard currency:	US$

THE SHIP. *Grand Classica* (formerly *Costa Classica*), an all-white ship, now over 25 years old, has an unflattering slab-sided profile, topped by a trio of funnels, with lifeboats positioned high.

There is a good range of public rooms, lounges, and bars, although the interior decor needs work – there are large portholes instead of windows in cabins on lower decks, in the dining room, self-serve buffet area, coffee bar, and discotheque, for example. The social center is a multi-level atrium that is stark and angular, but the marble-covered staircases look good, while the Sports Bar (observation lounge) sits atop ship like a lump of cheese.

The ship is for casually dressed, young-at-heart party-goers who enjoy city life, with constant activity, lots of bustle, and a relaxed vibe.

Note that rap-rich music is played 24 hours a day in accommodation hallways and elevators, so there's no escape. Niggles include the lack of a walk-around promenade deck outdoors. Note that the open deck space is very limited, and the dining room air-conditioning system is noisy.

ACCOMMODATION. There are several categories, including 10 suites (for more space). Cabins on the higher decks cost more, but they are all similar in size, shape, and facilities. All have twin lower beds, infotainment system and telephone, cherry wood veneered cabinetry, and vanity desk unit with a mirror.

BERLITZ'S RATINGS

	Possible	Achieved
Ship	500	302
Accommodation	200	119
Food	400	177
Service	400	223
Entertainment	100	54
Cruise Experience	400	204

OVERALL SCORE 1079 points out of 2000

Sliding doors access the bathroom and closets; overall cabin soundproofing is poor, however. Some cabins have one or two extra pulldown (Pullman-style) berths – good for families with small children.

Suites. These include a private rounded balcony, marble-clad bathroom with Jacuzzi tub, and separate shower enclosure. There is plenty of space in the living and sleeping areas, and for luggage.

DINING. The Yellow Elder Dining Room (named after the national flower of The Bahamas) has an indented white ceiling. Open seating is the norm for all meals. The cuisine is banquet-style food. Note that there are no sommeliers, so waiters serve the wine – all of which are young.

For casual outdoor eating, Alfresco Café has teak decking and a canvas sailcloth awning. Breakfast and luncheon buffets are repetitious and uncreative. Interactive hot-rock cooking (of steaks) is available at extra cost, while extra cost coffees are available in various bars.

ENTERTAINMENT. The Theater (showlounge) has an amphitheater-like design, but the seats are bolt upright and uncomfortable.

SPA/FITNESS. The Spa has a gymnasium with forward-facing views, muscle-pumping machines, an aerobics exercise area, hot tubs, health bar, saunas, steam rooms, and beauty salon.

GRANDEUR OF THE SEAS
★★★

A FAMILY-FRIENDLY, CASUAL MID-SIZE SHIP WITH MULTIPLE-CHOICE DINING

Size:	Mid-size Ship	Passenger/Crew Ratio (lower beds):	2.5
Tonnage:	73,817	Cabins (total):	975
Cruise Line:	Royal Caribbean International	Size Range (sq ft/m):	158.2–1,267.0/14.7–117.7
Former Names:	none	Cabins (for one person):	0
Builder:	Kvaerner Masa-Yards (Finland)	Cabins with balcony:	212
Entered Service:	Dec 1996	Cabins (wheelchair accessible):	14
Length (ft/m):	916.0/279.6	Wheelchair accessibility:	Good
Propulsion/Propellers:	diesel-electric (50,400kW)/2	Elevators:	9
Total Crew:	760	Casino (gaming tables):	Yes
Passengers (lower beds):	1,950	Self-Service Launderette:	No
Passenger Space Ratio (lower beds):	37.8	Onboard currency:	US$

THE SHIP. *Grandeur of the Seas* (a *Vision*-class ship) has an attractive shape, with a single funnel located well aft – almost a throwback to some ship designs used in the 1950s – and a nicely rounded stern. A Viking Crown Lounge, a trademark of former Royal Caribbean International (RCI) ships, sits between the funnel and mast at the top of the atrium lobby, and overlooks the forward section of the swimming pool deck, with access provided from stairway off the central atrium. This, together with the forward mast, provides three distinct focal points of the ship's exterior profile. There is a walk-around promenade deck outdoors, but there are no cushioned pads for the plastic sunloungers.

Grandeur of the Seas is best suited to couples and families with children that want to have multiple dining choices for more convenience.

The ship features a varied collection of artworks, including several sculptures, principally by British artists, with classical music, ballet, and theater themes. Huge murals of opera scenes adorn several stairways.

A seven-deck-high atrium lobby, called the Centrum, is the social focal point within the ship. On its various levels it houses an R Bar (for some creative cocktails), several passenger-service counters, an art gallery, Casino Royale (for table gaming and slot machines – and viewing the the-

BERLITZ'S RATINGS		
	Possible	Achieved
Ship	500	333
Accommodation	200	129
Food	400	218
Service	400	234
Entertainment	100	70
Cruise Experience	400	250

OVERALL SCORE 1234 points out of 2000

atrical glass-covered underfloor exhibits), the popular Schooner Bar, with its nautical-theme decor and maritime art, Café Lattetudes (for coffee), and a library. Aerial entertainment happens in the Centrum, too.

There is a good use of tropical plants throughout the public rooms, which helps counteract the otherwise rather plain and clinical pastel wall colors.

Niggles include charges for shuttle buses in many ports of call; the high cost of bottled water; and receipts that provide an extra line 'for additional gratuity,' when a gratuity has already been added.

ACCOMMODATION. There are numerous price grades, including several grades of suites, the largest of which is the Royal Suite. Many cabins are of the same, or similar, size, well appointed, and with pleasing decor, best described as Scandinavian Modern, with wood and color accenting. There are, however, a huge number of interior cabins (no view).

All cabins have twin beds that convert to a queen-size one, decent closet space for a week-long cruise, and a good amount of drawer space, although under-bed storage space is not good for large suitcases. Bathrooms have multiple mirrors. Plastic buckets are provided for Champagne or wine; a hairdryer is also provided.

Room service offers only a basic menu, and no hot items for breakfast.

DINING. The 1,171-seat Great Gatsby Dining Room is spread over two decks, with both levels connected by a grand, sweeping staircase. When you book, choose one of the two seatings for dinner or 'My Time Dining' – so you can eat when you want, during dining-room hours. A neat Champagne terrace bar sits forward of the lower level of the two-deck-high dining room.

Main dining room cuisine is all about standardized banquet catering and batch cooking. Menu descriptions sound tempting, but the food, although prepared well enough, is just average. However, you can have items such as lobster or filet mignon (steak) at an extra cost – and at least they will be cooked individually for you. Green vegetables are difficult to come by – they're provided basically for decoration – but salad items are plentiful, and desserts are pretty good. Rice is often used as a filler. Breads and pastry items are also disappointing (these are thawed and then baked from frozen 'starter' dough), and items such as croissants lack any hint of butter. Vegetarian and children's menus are available. Note that there are no wine waiters.

The large (790-seat), glass-walled Windjammer Café is a casual eatery for self-serve breakfast, lunch and dinner buffet items. Note that there are no cups and saucers for tea – only paper cups or plastic mugs, and only plastic plates are provided (so hot food doesn't stay hot long).

For decent (extra-cost) Seattle's Best espressos/cappuccinos, head for Cafe Latte-tudes on Deck 6.

Other eateries (some at extra cost) include: Giovanni's Table, an Italian trattoria (a service charge applies); Izumi (located in a delightful spot just forward of the funnel) for pan-Asian cuisine including hot-rock cooking (service charge and à la carte menu pricing apply); Park Café outdoor market; Chops Grille steakhouse; and Chef's Table, an exclusive hosted event (it is located on the starboard side aft, within the dining room) with a five-course, wine-paired menu (worth it for celebrating a birthday or special event, perhaps).

ENTERTAINMENT. The 875-seat Palladium Theater is the main showlounge. Located at the forward part of the ship, it is used for big production shows. It has excellent sight lines from 98 percent of the seats.

Another showlounge, the 575-seat South Pacific Lounge, is used for smaller shows and cabaret acts, including smutty late-night adult-only comedy.

SPA/FITNESS. Vitality at Sea spa is aft of the funnel and spans two decks. Facilities include a gymnasium with all the latest muscle-pumping exercise machines, an aerobics exercise room, sauna and steam rooms, a beauty salon, and a clutch of private massage/body treatment rooms. The spa is staffed and operated by specialist Steiner Leisure.

There's also a rock-climbing wall with several separate climbing tracks located outdoors at the aft end of the funnel, just behind the spa. A jogging track (outside on Deck 10) takes you around most of the ship.

GRAND PRINCESS
★★★+

A MULTI-CHOICE LARGE RESORT SHIP FOR INFORMAL FAMILY CRUISING

Size:	Large Resort Ship	Passenger/Crew Ratio (lower beds):	2.3
Tonnage:	108,806	Cabins (total):	1,300
Cruise Line:	Princess Cruises	Size Range (sq ft/m):	161.4–764.2/15.0–71.0
Former Names:	none	Cabins (for one person):	0
Builder:	Fincantieri (Italy)	Cabins with balcony:	710
Entered Service:	May 1998	Cabins (wheelchair accessible):	28
Length (ft/m):	951.4/290.0	Wheelchair accessibility:	Best
Propulsion/Propellers:	diesel-electric (42,000kW)/2	Elevators:	14
Total Crew:	1,100	Casino (gaming tables):	Yes
Passengers (lower beds):	2,600	Self-Service Launderette:	Yes
Passenger Space Ratio (lower beds):	41.8	Onboard currency:	US$

THE SHIP. *Grand Princess* was first in a series of *Grand*-class ships, whose interior design and configuration evolved with each new ship in the series. Now looking quite tired in places (it's almost 20 years old), it has a flared dolphin-like bow and a galleon-like transom stern. There is a sheltered faux teak promenade deck – it's actually painted steel – which almost wraps around, and a walkway that goes to the enclosed, protected bow.

Unlike the outside decks, there is plenty of space inside the ship and a decent array of public rooms, with some 'intimate' (this being a relative word) spaces. The decor is attractive, with lots of earth tones.

Four areas center on swimming pools, which have various beach-like surroundings; one 'lap' pool has a pumped 'current' to swim against. One pool is two decks high and can be covered by a retractable glass dome.

Facilities include a Piazza Atrium (a good place to sit, watch, and meet others), with an integral International Café, Vines wine bar (including tapas and sushi items and wines for purchase); and Leaves Tea Lounge and A motion-based 'virtual reality' room has enclosed motion-based rides. There is a library/computer room, and a separate card room. Youngsters have a two-deck-high playroom, teen room, and trained counselors. Gamers should enjoy the large casino, with gaming tables and over 260 slot machines. The wood-paneled Wheelhouse Bar is

BERLITZ'S RATINGS		
	Possible	Achieved
Ship	500	320
Accommodation	200	122
Food	400	240
Service	400	260
Entertainment	100	71
Cruise Experience	400	262

OVERALL SCORE 1275 points out of 2000

decorated with memorabilia and ship models tracing part of the history of sister company P&O.

Gratuities are automatically charged to your account, and tips for children are at the same rate. If you want to pay less than the automatic rate, go to the reception desk.

Passenger niggles include the user-unfriendly automated telephone system, the small cabin towels, the extra cost for items such as ice cream, and the (coins-needed) charge for the washers and dryers in self-service launderettes.

Overall, however, Princess Cruises delivers a consistently fine, comfortable, well-packaged product, always with a good degree of style, at a competitive price.

ACCOMMODATION. There are six types of cabins and configurations, from the smallest interior (no-view) cabin to the largest (the Grand Suite), in a bewildering choice of price categories. Many balcony cabins overhang the ship's lower hull section.

There are two family suites, consisting of two suites with an interconnecting door, plus a large balcony. They can sleep up to 10 (if at least four are children), or up to eight adults.

Some outside cabins on Emerald Deck have views obstructed by lifeboats. Sadly, there are no cabins for solo travelers. Your name is placed outside your suite or cabin – making it simple for delivery service personnel but compromising privacy. Many cabins can accommodate a third and fourth person in upper berths – but in such cabins, the lower beds cannot then be pushed together to make a queen-size one.

Perhaps the least desirable balcony cabins are eight located forward on Emerald Deck (E101–121), whose balconies do not extend to the side of the ship and can be passed by walkers and gawkers on the adjacent Upper Promenade walkway. Cabin attendants have many cabins to look after, which unfortunately does not translate to fine personal service.

DINING. There are three main dining rooms, each with its own galley: Botticelli (504 seats), Da Vinci (486), and Michelangelo (486). There are two seatings in one restaurant; the others have 'Anytime Dining' where you choose when, and with whom, you want to eat. All three split into multi-tier sections in a non-symmetrical design. Four elevators go to Fiesta Deck for the Botticelli and Da Vinci restaurants, but only two go to Plaza Deck 5 for Michelangelo – this can cause long waits at peak times, especially for wheelchair-users.

Although portions are generous, the food and its presentation are disappointing, and standardized. Fish often has crumb or batter coating, fresh green vegetable choice is limited, and few garnishes are used. This is big-ship banquet catering, with all its attendant standardization and 'batch' cooking. Pasta dishes are acceptable (though voluminous), typically served by section headwaiters, who may also make 'something special just for you' – in search of favorable comments. If you like desserts, try a sundae at dinner (most other items are just so-so). Other, extra-cost, reservations-required dining venues include Sabatini's, an Italian eatery with colorful tiled Mediterranean-style, for Italian-style pizzas and pasta.

Crown Grill steakhouse – for premium American steaks and seafood, with plenty of space around diners' tables.

A poolside burger grill and a pizza bar (no charge) for casual bites. Extra charges apply if you order items to eat at the coffee bar/patisserie, or the caviar/ Champagne bar.

Other casual eats can be taken in the self-serve Horizon Court buffet – open almost around the clock. Note that plastic plates are used (there are no trays).

ENTERTAINMENT. The 748-seat Princess Theater spans two decks and has comfortable seating on both main and balcony levels. Princess Cruises has long been known and liked for its traditional colorful Hollywood-style (rather than Vegas-style) production shows.

The Vista Lounge, a second entertainment lounge, presents cabaret acts by night, and lectures by day. Explorers, a third lounge, can also host cabaret acts and dance bands. Just aft of the funnel is the One5 nightclub.

SPA/FITNESS. Lotus Spa complex surrounds one of the swimming pools at the forward end. It comprises a large gymnasium with all the usual equipment, an aerobics room, sauna and steam rooms, salon, ocean-view treatment rooms, and a relaxation area. It is operated by Steiner Leisure.

HAMBURG
★★★

THIS SMALL SHIP IS FOR PORT-INTENSIVE CRUISING FOR GERMAN SPEAKERS

Size:	Small Ship
Tonnage:	14,903
Cruise Line:	Plantours Cruises
Former Names:	*Columbus*
Builder:	MTW Schiffswerft (Germany)
Entered Service:	Jul 1997/Jun 2012
Length (ft/m):	472.8/144.1
Propulsion/Propellers:	diesel (10,560kW)/2
Total Crew:	170
Passengers (lower beds):	408
Passenger Space Ratio (lower beds):	36.5
Passenger/Crew Ratio (lower beds):	2.4
Cabins (total):	205
Size Range (sq ft/m):	139.9–339.0/13.0–31.5
Cabins (for one person):	2
Cabins with balcony:	2
Cabins (wheelchair accessible):	2
Wheelchair accessibility:	Fair
Elevators:	2
Casino (gaming tables):	No
Self-Service Launderette:	No
Onboard currency:	Euros

THE SHIP. *Hamburg* has an ice-strengthened hull, useful for cold-weather cruise areas. While it's a comfortable ship, the swimming pool is small – it's really a 'plunge' pool – as is the open deck space, and there is no walk-around promenade deck outdoors.

Palm Garden doubles as an observation lounge. Shipwide, cost-extra Wi-Fi is available. The fit and finish of the interiors is a little utilitarian.

This ship will appeal to German-speaking couples and solo travelers seeking good value for money on a first cruise, aboard a ship with contemporary, comfortable, and unpretentious surroundings, and good itineraries, at a very modest price.

ACCOMMODATION. The standard cabins are really small. All but 10 cabins have lower berths. Except for two forward-facing suites, there are only two balcony cabins, and no room service except for accommodation designated as suites. There are several single-occupancy cabins. Note that 16 cabins on Deck 4 have lifeboat-obstructed views. The cabin decor is bright and upbeat, and there's a good amount of closet and shelf space. All cabins have a minibar/refrigerator, flat-screen TV, personal safe, and hairdryer.

There are eight suites, each at least double the size of a standard cabin, with a curtained partition

BERLITZ'S RATINGS	Possible	Achieved
Ship	500	289
Accommodation	200	121
Food	400	203
Service	400	230
Entertainment	100	47
Cruise Experience	400	219

OVERALL SCORE 1109 points out of 2000

between lounge and sleeping areas. Two suites at the bows each have a narrow private balcony and an excellent amount of storage space.

DINING. Restaurant Alsterblick, aft, has large, ocean-view windows on three sides. All passengers can be seated in a single seating, at assigned tables (breakfast is open seating). There are just two tables for two, but others can accommodate up to 16. The unstuffy cuisine is good, though the choice is limited. Breakfast and lunch can also be taken in the bright but casual setting of the self-serve Palm Garden, which doubles as a comfortable observation lounge. Light dinners can also be taken there; a small dance floor adds another dimension.

ENTERTAINMENT. The Hamburg Lounge is a single-level H-shaped room, with banquette and individual seating in tub chairs, and a bar located at the back of the room. Because the small apron stage is in the center of the room, the sight lines from many seats are poor.

SPA/FITNESS. A fitness room is located on the uppermost deck of the ship, while a sauna is on the lowest passenger deck, next to the beauty salon.

HANSEATIC INSPIRATION
NYR

A NEW, SPECIALIZED SHIP WITH A RELAXED AMBIENCE FOR IN-DEPTH EXPEDITIONS AND DISCOVERIES

Size:	Boutique Ship	Passenger/Crew Ratio (lower beds):	1.4
Tonnage:	16,100	Cabins (total):	120
Cruise Line:	Hapag-Lloyd Expedition Cruises	Size Range (sq ft/m):	226.0–764.2/21–71.0
Former Names:	none	Cabins (for one person):	0
Builder:	Vard Holdings (Norway)	Cabins with balcony:	102
Entered Service:	Oct 2019	Cabins (wheelchair accessible):	1
Length (ft/m):	452.7/138.0	Wheelchair accessibility:	Good
Propulsion/Propellers:	diesel-electric/2 azimuthing pods	Elevators:	2
		Casino (gaming tables):	No
Total Crew:	170	Self-Service Launderette:	No
Passengers (lower beds):	230	Onboard currency:	Euros
Passenger Space Ratio (lower beds):	67.0		

THE SHIP. With its blue and white hull, new expedition ship *HANSEATIC inspiration* (sister to *HANSEATIC nature*) has been well thought out and is sensibly proportioned. The navigation bridge wings can be folded, designed for cruising in the Great Lakes (sister *HANSEATIC nature* doesn't have them) or other narrow passages, an ice-hardened hull with the highest passenger vessel ice classification (Polar Code 6), and so much open deck space. It is built to a size that can even reach Iquitos (Peru) on Amazon sailings – a destination inaccessible for anything larger.

You can almost touch the ice from the forward outdoor observation deck, while the aft Marina Deck allows for easy access to Zodiacs and kayaks. The ship carries 17 environmentally friendly regular and electric Zodiacs for up-close-and-personal wildlife viewing in natural habitats, and wet landings. Rubber boots, parkas, boot-washing stations, and storage rooms are provided.

Inside, you'll find high-quality, tasteful luxury fittings and soft furnishings, with an interior design focusing on marine life and animals.

Public rooms include the Alaska Lounge (a multi-purpose, multi-function room), Club Lounge, Ocean Academy (a technology-rich interactive center for discovery) and even a smokers' lounge.

Safety is paramount, particularly in Antarctica, and this is where the company excels – with professionalism, pride, and well-established and skilled

BERLITZ'S RATINGS		
	Possible	Achieved
Ship	500	NYR
Accommodation	200	NYR
Food	400	NYR
Service	400	NYR
Entertainment	100	NYR
Cruise Experience	400	NYR
OVERALL SCORE NYR points out of 2000		

seamanship. Most of each day will be spent ashore, and evenings consist mainly of dinner and daily re-caps. Lectures, briefings, and the information provided about the itinerary, ports of call, and expedition landings are of the highest quality. Well-qualified lecturers and naturalists accompany each cruise, and a discreet crew and service staff are the hallmarks of this ship. A relaxed ambience and informal dress code prevail.

The ship is for international participants, though staff members speak several languages between them. All port taxes, insurance, staff gratuities, and Zodiac trips are included.

Hapag-Lloyd publishes its own excellent handbooks (in both English and German) on expedition regions such as the Arctic, Antarctica, Amazonia, and the South Sea Islands, as well as exclusive maps.

The company provides destination-intensive nature cruises and expeditions in elegant but unstuffy surroundings, at a suitably handsome price that includes good food and service. It really is all about seeing and experiencing nature comfortably and safely. The ship is at its best in the Arctic and Antarctic, but you should be wary of the difficult conditions for shore landings in these areas and must be fully mobile.

ACCOMMODATION. The voyage price depends on the size, location, and grade you choose. From the smallest to the largest (two Grand Suites with an interconnecting door to create a fine double suite), there is something for all wallets. Among the most popular are those at the stern, with an aft view from the balcony. There's also one accessible suite. All bathrooms have a heated wall (for towels and wet parkas). Two suites have really stunning and innovative glass-floor balconies that extend over the ship's side. All grades have a coffee machine and stocked minibar (both complimentary), binoculars, Nordic walking poles, and a rain shower and heated wall in the bathroom (for wet parkas and towels). The decor is 'polar practical,' and both European and US two-pin electrical sockets and USB charge points are provided.

DINING. There are three dining venues (none cost extra), including a main restaurant with many win-dow-side tables for two or four. There's also a speciality venue for Cape Cod-style cuisine (think: seafood), with indoor-outdoor seating, plus a bistro for casual self-serve meals.

First-rate cuisine and relaxed service are the hallmarks of Hapag-Lloyd Expedition Cruises. Only the highest-quality ingredients are provided, with many items bought fresh (and sourced locally) when possible. In some ports, you can go shopping with the chef to source regional ingredients and fresh fish.

ENTERTAINMENT. Evening recaps and after-dinner conversation provide plenty of entertainment and shared experiences with like-minded participants.

SPA/FITNESS. The Spa includes several body-pampering treatment rooms, plus sea-view (co-ed) saunas, steam rooms, and a techno-gym.

HANSEATIC NATURE
★★★★★

THIS IS TRULY THE BENCHMARK FOR ALL SPECIALIZED EXPEDITION SHIPS

Size:	Boutique Ship
Tonnage:	16,100
Cruise Line:	Hapag-Lloyd Expedition Cruises
Former Names:	none
Builder:	Vard Holdings (Norway)
Entered Service:	May 2019
Length (ft/m):	452.7/138.0
Propulsion/Propellers:	diesel-electric/2 azimuthing pods
Total Crew:	170
Passengers (lower beds):	230
Passenger Space Ratio (lower beds):	67.0
Passenger/Crew Ratio (lower beds):	1.4
Cabins (total):	120
Size Range (sq ft/m):	226.0–764.2/21–71.0
Cabins (for one person):	0
Cabins with balcony:	102
Cabins (wheelchair accessible):	1
Wheelchair accessibility:	Good
Elevators:	2
Casino (gaming tables):	No
Self-Service Launderette:	No
Onboard currency:	Euros

THE SHIP. *HANSEATIC nature* lives up to its name – the theme of the whole ship is nature. Looking like a smaller version of *Europa 2*, but with a blue and white hull, this stunning new expedition ship is a replacement for the now-withdrawn *Hanseatic*) has been extremely well thought out and is sensibly proportioned. It has a bridge with open bridge wings and an ice-hardened hull with the highest passenger vessel ice classification (Polar Code 6). It is also built to a size that can even reach Iquitos (Peru) on specialized Amazon sailings – a destination impossible for anything larger.

You can almost touch the ice from the forward outdoor observation deck; in fact, you can go out on the bow to the very front of the ship for wildlife watching on the Nature Walk, which can accommodate up to 70 participants. An aft Marina Deck allows easy access to Zodiacs and kayaks – there are also two loading platforms on each side of the ship. There's also an outstanding boot-storage room and motorized boot-washing and disinfection station. The ship carries 17 environmentally friendly regular and electric Zodiacs for up-close-and-personal wildlife viewing in natural habitats. Rubber boots, parkas, and storage rooms are provided. This ship is about going to the less-populated regions of the world and exploring them, but in supremely comfortable surroundings, with huge swathes of glass that connect you with sea and sky.

BERLITZ'S RATINGS

	Possible	Achieved
Ship	500	466
Accommodation	200	178
Food	400	353
Service	400	356
Entertainment	100	88
Cruise Experience	400	350

OVERALL SCORE 1791 points out of 2000

Inside, very wide hallways and high-ceilinged public rooms give a feeling of spaciousness that other expedition ships can only dream of, and the lighting in all areas is a model of outstanding design and execution. There are fine-quality luxury fittings and soft furnishings, with an interior design that is focused on marine life, animals, and, of course, nature, with earthy colors and natural materials such as wood and stone. In one corner of the pool is a colorful penguin made of recycled plastic sandals from Africa (there's almost no other plastic on board, except for the toilet seats, and one whimsical wall decoration of empty plastic bottles).

A teak pool deck can be completely covered with a moveable ceiling canopy, and what is really stunning is the 'over-the-sea' walk that extends over both side of the ship – an engineering marvel.

The public rooms are really enticing and include the multi-purpose, multi-function HanseAtrium Lounge (with bar, juke box, dance floor, and overhead LED display ceiling); an Observation Lounge with bar, an integral library, a fireplace, and an interactive, illuminated world globe; the immersive Ocean Academy, a science- and technology-rich interactive center for discovery and education; and even an Invisible Lounge (for smokers).

With safety paramount – particularly in Antarctica – the company excels with professionalism, pride, and well-established, skilled seamanship. Most of each day is taken up with being ashore, and evenings consist mainly of dinner and daily recaps. Lectures, briefings, and the information provided about the itinerary, ports of call, and expedition landings are of the highest quality. Highly qualified lecturers and naturalists accompany each cruise, while a discreet crew and unobtrusive service staff are the hallmarks of this ship. A relaxed ambience and very informal dress code prevail.

The ship is for German-speaking participants, though many staff members are at least bi-lingual. All port taxes, insurance, staff gratuities, and Zodiac trips are included.

Hapag-Lloyd publishes its own excellent handbooks (in both English and German) on expedition regions such as the Arctic, Antarctica, Amazonia, and the South Sea Islands, as well as exclusive maps.

Hapag-Lloyd Expedition Cruises provides destination-intensive expeditions in elegant but relaxed surroundings at a suitably handsome price that includes outstanding cuisine and service. It really is all about seeing and experiencing nature in high comfort. The ship really is at its best in the Arctic and Antarctic, but you should be wary of the difficult conditions for shore landings in these areas – it's physically very challenging and most suited to fully mobile passengers. This is expedition cruising done right – In fact, it simply can't get any better than this.

ACCOMMODATION. The price depends on size, location, and grade. From the smallest to the largest (two Grand Suites), there is something for all wal-lets. Most have a private balcony, but two suites have really stunning and innovative solid glass-floor balconies that extend over the ship's side. Among the most popular are those with aft views from large balconies. There's also one accessible suite. All bathrooms have a heated wall (for towels and for drying wet parkas). All grades have a coffee machine and a stocked minibar (both free), superb binoculars, Nordic walking poles, a heated wall in the bathroom (for wet parkas and towels), and rain showers. Both European and US two-pin electrical sockets, and USB charge points, are provided.

DINING. There are three dining venues (all are included): Hauptrestaurant, the main restaurant, which has many window-side tables for two or four; The Hamptons, a specialty dining venue; and The Bistro – a casual self-serve eatery with indoor-outdoor seating (it includes an outdoor barbecue grill).

Expect first-rate cuisine made with only the highest-quality ingredients, with many items bought fresh (and sourced locally) when available. In some ports, you can go shopping with the chef to source local, regional ingredients and fresh fish.

ENTERTAINMENT. Evening recaps of the day's events and after-dinner conversation provide plenty of entertainment and shared experiences with like-minded participants and specialists.

SPA/FITNESS. The large spa includes several body-pampering treatment rooms, plus (co-ed) sea-view saunas, steam rooms, and a fine techno-gym.

HARMONY OF THE SEAS
★★★★

THIS ULTRA-LARGE RESORT SHIP IS AN IDEAL PLAYGROUND FOR HIGH-ENERGY FAMILIES

Size:	Large Resort Ship	Passenger/Crew Ratio (lower beds):	2.2
Tonnage:	226,693	Cabins (total):	2,747
Cruise Line:	Royal Caribbean International	Size Range (sq ft/m):	96.8–2,389.6/9.0–222.0
Former Names:	none	Cabins (for one person):	15
Builder:	STX France (France)	Cabins with balcony:	2,000
Entered Service:	May 2016	Cabins (wheelchair accessible):	46
Length (ft/m):	1,187.9/362.1	Wheelchair accessibility:	Best
Propulsion/Propellers:	diesel-electric/3 pods (2 azimuthing, 1 fixed)	Elevators:	24
Total Crew:	2,394	Casino (gaming tables):	Yes
Passengers (lower beds):	5,479	Self-Service Launderette:	No
Passenger Space Ratio (lower beds):	41.4	Onboard currency:	US$

THE SHIP. Longer by 7ft (2.1m) than the first two *Oasis*-class ships (*Allure of the Seas* and *Oasis of the Seas*, which, when built, were the largest cruise ships in the world), *Harmony of the Seas* is absolutely stunning for families with children. It is a benchmark for self-contained resorts that move – and 20 percent more efficient than its two sister ships, with 38 more cabins. No matter what your entertainment and activity interests are, this ship delivers – and then some. Neat fact: there are four bow thrusters, each with more power than seven Ferraris.

This is a stunning ship and a credit to its design team. There is a lot of outdoor and indoor/outdoor space for aqua-bathing and sports, but little actual relaxation and sunbathing space (unless you have suite-grade accommodation, so you can use the pay-extra adults-only Suite Sundeck, located forward), because much of it is taken up by Splashaway Bay – a water park with mind-numbing 'Perfect Storm' waterslides (called The Abyss – a ride through 10 decks that you won't easily forget), fountains, water cannons, and sports activities. Sadly, there's not a hint of teak decking or wood-topped railings (railings have plastic tops). An adults-only open-air solarium and rentable cabanas are part of the outdoor scene.

As aboard each *Oasis*-class ship, the inner 'city' is divided into seven neighborhoods: The Royal Promenade, with a Bionic Bar staffed by non-speaking robot bartenders (you'll still have to tip) and a fun 90s street

BERLITZ'S RATINGS		
	Possible	Achieved
Ship	500	403
Accommodation	200	140
Food	400	226
Service	400	281
Entertainment	100	87
Cruise Experience	400	286

OVERALL SCORE 1423 points out of 2000

party (look out for a rather large 'head'); Central Park, with numerous real trees, scores of plants, and a Rising Tide Bar; The Boardwalk, with shops, eateries, and a superb children's carousel; the Pool and Sports Zone; Entertainment Place; Youth Zone; and Vitality at Sea Spa and Fitness Center.

In all, there are around three dozen bars/lounges, and more than 20 restaurants, cafés, and other eateries, although some are exclusive to Pinnacle members, certain suite accommodation grades, and SeaPass gold card holders. It's part of the 'pay more, get more' system of class distinction, like anywhere else. There's also a large Casino Royale, with gaming tables (plus a players club and poker room) and slot machines.

Plan wisely to get the most out of your cruise vacation. Almost everything requires you to make reservations/sign up in advance. Do budget extra for additional cost items and promotions.

Niggles include lines for the reception desk, for shore tenders, excursions, and the self-serve buffet; intrusive photographers; few quiet places to sit and read; no cushioned pads for sunloungers; and unwelcome announcements for revenue activities. Also: small cabin 'bath' towels, noisy (vacuum) toilets, fiberglass – not wood – railings, expensive ice-laden frosted drinks in 'souvenir' glasses, the speaking 'elevator going up/going down', rap-rich music everywhere (even in elevators, hallways, and saunas), and loud live music. Plus, if you have an interconnecting door cabin, you may hear your next-door neighbors.

Super-high-speed Internet enables video streaming, Skyping, and social-media sharing (at a hefty price).

The 'wow' factor comes in the entertainment (particularly the big theater and ice shows), and not just the waterslides and sports facilities, rather than the food.

Service personnel are friendly, however, and the digital 'Wayfarer' system is informative. Do budget extra for additional-cost items and expect flyers and advertising promotions. Overall, this is a fine all-round ship for all age groups, but be aware of the extra cost for many optional items (including drinks, drink packages, and excursions).

ACCOMMODATION. From the smallest cabin (for solo occupancy) to the largest (Presidential Suite), there is a wide range of cabins and larger suites to suit all tastes, including Royal Family Suites, Loft Suites, and family cabins. Choosing the right one for your needs is not easy. Some 15 Studio category cabins are for solo occupancy, while over 690 have a third/fourth bed – good for families with small children. Some 76 Interior cabins have virtual balconies (this feature can be turned off). All cabins have a minibar.

However, the cabin-numbering system is confusing. Also, cabin doors open outwards (towards you), as in many European hotels. In many lower grade rooms, closet access is awkward (most are dimensionally challenged), but just manageable for a week.

All suite-class accommodation and balcony cabins have floor-to-ceiling sliding glass doors, and different (better) amenities, and the six most expensive suite grades can access a private sun deck and eat in the Coastal Kitchen restaurant.

CUISINE. The cavernous main restaurant, spans decks 3 to 5 and is in three sections: Silk, The Grande, and American Icon Grill. It operates in two seating times (early or late) for dinner (or you can choose 'My Time Dining' and eat at your preferred time). There are tables of all sizes, including some for family reunions.

The cuisine is standardized banquet catering and batch cooking. Menu descriptions may sound tempting, but the food isn't. However, cooked-to-order (extra-cost) lobster or filet mignon (steak) is available on request. Green vegetables are scarce but salads are plentiful, and desserts are decent. Rice is often used as a filler. Bread and pastry items are average. Vegetarian and children's menus are also available. Note that there are no wine waiters.

Other free dining/eating venue options include:

Central Park Café for deli-style sandwiches, salad items, paninis, crêpes, and hearty soups.

Windjammer Marketplace is an extremely large self-serve, casual food court/buffet-style eatery, with several different sections featuring different food types, salad bar, etc. It can be extremely crowded due to the number of passengers carried, but the layout of the various food islands and sections is good.

Other snacking spots include: Boardwalk Dog House, Sabor Taqueria, Starbucks, Solarium Bistro, and Vitality Café.

The following restaurants are at extra cost:

150 Central Park for the best, most exclusive, cooked-to-order cuisine.

Chops Grille, a 'signature' steakhouse featuring large, premium-quality steaks and other grilled food items (open for dinner, reservations required).

Izumi Hibachi and Sushi for Japanese-style dishes.

Jamie's Italian, a tablecloth-free, Euro-Italian, bistro-style trattoria with rustic decor; open for lunch and dinner (reservations are required, and there's a cover charge for dinner).

Johnny Rockets, diner-style, for burgers and ice cream shakes.

Sabor Taqueria for Mexican-style eats.

Vintages, a nice, sociable wine bar with cheese and tapas (at à la carte prices).

Wonderland, a funky two-deck-high venue (with decor and seating inspired by Alice in Wonderland) for quirky small-portion molecular cuisine (fussy, but lacking substance).

ENTERTAINMENT. The 1,380-seat Royal Theater (main showlounge) spans three decks. Reservations for shows can be made up to three months ahead (there is no charge). The hit musical Grease is the star, together with Columbus, The Musical (an RCI original).

The Ice Skating Rink (on Deck 4) has seats for about 900, and the shows are dazzlingly top-notch.

Adult-only (smutty) comedy is featured in 'The Attic Comedy Club.'

A 750-seat Aqua Theater, located outside at the ship's stern with a 6,000-sq-ft (557-sq-m) stage, is a stunning combination show theatre, sound stage, and events space (some great viewing places can be found high in the aft wings of the ship on both sides). The stern has some 'overhang,' to accommodate the venue.

There's also a delightful, intimate venue called Jazz on 4 (because it's on Deck 4) for (relatively) quiet evenings with live jazz ensembles.

SPA/FITNESS. Set low down forward on decks 5 and 6, Vitality at Sea Spa includes a large fitness center (with cardio and resistance equipment) and beauty salon, while an extra-cost Thermal Suite pass allows you access to men's and women's saunas, steam rooms, and heated, tiled relaxation loungers; there's also a 60-seat Vitality Café for extra-cost 'health' drinks and snacks.

Other highlights include two Flowriders for body surfing, a zipline that careers over The Boardwalk (and its inner balcony cabins), and three waterslides that career over Central Park. There's also a Sports Pool, Harmony Dunes (mini-golf), a Sports Court, two rock-climbing walls (aft), and an ice-skating rink.

HEBRIDEAN PRINCESS
★★★★

THIS IS A REALLY CHARMING AND VERY TRADITIONAL SCOTTISH COUNTRY INN AFLOAT

Size:	Boutique Ship
Tonnage:	2,112
Cruise Line:	Hebridean Island Cruises
Former Names:	Columba
Builder:	Hall Russell (Scotland)
Entered Service:	1964/May 1989
Length (ft/m):	235.0/71.6
Propulsion/Propellers:	diesel (1,790kW)/2
Total Crew:	38
Passengers (lower beds):	50
Passenger Space Ratio (lower beds):	42.2

Passenger/Crew Ratio (lower beds):	1.3
Cabins (total):	30
Size Range (sq ft/m):	144.0–340.0/13.4–31.6
Cabins (for one person):	10
Cabins with balcony:	4
Cabins (wheelchair accessible):	0
Wheelchair accessibility:	None
Elevators:	0
Casino (gaming tables):	No
Self-Service Launderette:	No
Onboard currency:	UK£

THE SHIP. Small and old can be chic and comfortable. *Hebridean Princess*, originally one of three Scottish ferries built for David Mac-Brayne Ltd – although actually then owned by the British government – was skillfully converted into a real gem of a cruise ship in order to operate island-hopping itineraries in Scotland, together with the occasional jaunt to Norway and an occasional sailing around the UK coast. It was renamed in 1989 by the Duchess of York, and underwent a facelift in 2015.

This little ship has a warm, totally cosseted and traditional Scottish (think: tartan) country house ambience and stately home service that's unobtrusive but always at hand when you need it. It best suits mature-age adult couples and solo travelers who enjoy learning about the natural sciences, geography, history, gardening, art, architecture, and enjoy a very small ship with almost no entertainment.

There is an outdoors deck for occasional relaxation and alfresco meals, and a bar for occasional formal cocktail parties (when weather conditions are right). There is no walk-around promenade deck, although there is an open deck atop ship. The ship carries two Zodiac inflatable runabouts (*Calgary* and *Kiloran*) and two shore tenders (*Sanda* and *Shona*).

Use of the ship's small boats, speedboat, a dozen or so bicycles, and fishing gear are included in the price, as are entrance fees to gardens, castles, other attractions, and the occasional coach tour, depending

BERLITZ'S RATINGS

	Possible	Achieved
Ship	500	346
Accommodation	200	151
Food	400	317
Service	400	307
Entertainment	100	60
Cruise Experience	400	291

OVERALL SCORE 1472 points out of 2000

on the itinerary. The destination-intensive cruises have very creative itineraries, and there's plenty to do, despite the lack of big-ship features. Specialist guides, who give daily talks about the destinations to be visited, accompany all cruises.

What passengers appreciate is the fact that the ship does not have photographers or some of the trappings found aboard larger ships. They also love the fact that there is no bingo, art auctions, or parlor games.

The principal public room inside the ship is the charming Tiree Lounge, which has a real brick-walled inglenook fireplace, plus a very cozy bar with a wide variety of whiskies – the selection of single malts is excellent – and cognacs for connoisseurs. Naturally, the ship specializes in Scottish spirits.

Agatha Christie's Inspector Hercule Poirot would be right at home here, particularly in the Tiree Lounge. Who needs floating theme parks when you can take a retro-cruise aboard this little gem?

Hebridean Princess has UK officers and service staff; all are discreet and provide unobtrusive service. This little ship remains one of the world's best-kept travel secrets. Queen Elizabeth II chartered it for a family-only celebration of her 80th birthday in 2006, and again for a family holiday in 2010, which raised its profile.

It is also popular with solo travelers. Children under nine are not accepted. Despite the shortcomings of the ship itself, it's the food that rates highly.

If you cruise from Oban, you can be met at Glasgow station (or airport) and taken to/from the ship by private motor coach. Passengers are piped aboard at embarkation by a Scottish bagpiper – a neat touch. All drinks (except premium brands, which incur a small charge), soft drinks, and bottled Scottish mineral water are included in the fare, as are gratuities – the company requests that no additional gratuities be given.

Although this vessel is strong, it does have structural limitations and noisy engines that cause some vibration. However, the engines do not run at night because the ship anchors before bedtime, providing soul-renewing tranquility – except for the sound of a single generator. The ship doesn't have an elevator, so anyone with walking disabilities may find it challenging – and there may be several tender ports on each itinerary. It is often cold and very wet in the Scottish highlands and islands, so take plenty of warm clothing for layering.

ACCOMMODATION. All cabins have different names – there are no numbers, and, refreshingly, no door keys, although cabins can be locked from the inside. The older cabins feature delightfully eclectic curtains, sweeping drapes over the beds, and lots of cushions. One third of the cabins were refurbished for 2017, using smart woollen plaid fabric from Mulberry as a base fabric to create what the line calls a 'comfortable contemporary twist,' although the traditional look is still maintained. They come in a wide range of configurations (some with single, some with double, some with twin beds), including four with a private balcony – a private and self-indulgent bonus.

All cabins have a private bathroom with bath or shower. All have a refrigerator, ironing board with iron, trouser press, brass clock, and tea/coffee-making set – there's something magical about getting up in the morning, making fresh tea in your cabin using mineral water and organic teas, and sitting outside on a protected balcony watching Scotland's islands come and go. All seems right with the world.

Cabins have Victorian-style bathroom fittings, many of which are gold-plated, and some have brass cabin portholes or windows that actually open. Three of the newest cabins are outfitted in real Scottish Baronial style. All towels and bathrobes are 100 percent cotton, as is the bed linen. Some cabins in the front of the ship are subject to noise from the anchor being weighed each morning.

Each cabin has Villeroy & Boch china, fairtrade coffee, organic teas, and fresh milk – not the irradiated long-life milk or chemical milk found aboard many ships these days.

DINING. The Columba Restaurant has ocean-view windows and tables laid with crisp white linen and classic white Schönwald china. There is a single seating at assigned tables. Some chairs have armrests, while some do not. While days are casual, dinner means jackets and ties, and formal attire typically twice per cruise.

Menus offer just one meat choice and one fish dish (a different fish each day), plus an alternative, casual option. Fresh ingredients are sourced and purchased locally, supporting Scottish suppliers – a welcome change from the mass catering of most ships. Although there are no flambé items – the galley has electric, not gas, ranges – what is created is beautifully presented and of the highest standard. Just remember to save space for the desserts.

The breakfast menu is standard each day, although you can always ask for any favorites, and each day there's a specialty item, plus a help-yourself buffet table. Try the porridge and a 'wee dram' (Scotch whisky – single malt, of course) – it's lovely on a cold morning, and it sets you up for the whole day.

Not to be missed is the exclusive theatrical treat 'a tasting o' haggis wi' bashed neeps an champit tatties,' (haggis with mashed swede and potatoes), accompanied by bagpipe music and an 'address to the haggis' ceremony, traditionally given by the captain. Although there is waiter service for most things, there is also a good buffet table display during breakfast and luncheon. Wines are provided at lunch and dinner, although an additional connoisseur's list is available for those seeking fine vintage wines. Highly personal and attentive service from an attentive staff completes the picture.

ENTERTAINMENT. The Tiree Lounge is the equivalent of a main lounge aboard this very small ship. Dinner is the entertainment of the evening. Occasionally, there might be after-dinner drinks, poetry readings, and an occasional storyteller, but little else (passengers neither expect nor need it).

SPA/FITNESS. There is no spa, as the ship is too small. The only concessions to fitness are an exercycle and treadmill.

HEBRIDEAN SKY
★★★★

FOR LIFE ENRICHMENT CRUISES IN A HIGHLY COMFORTABLE SMALL-SHIP ENVIRONMENT

Size:	Boutique Ship
Tonnage:	4,280
Cruise Line:	Noble Caledonia
Former Names:	*Sea Explorer, Corinthian II, Island Sun, Sun, Renaissance VII, Regina Renaissance, Renaissance VII*
Builder:	Nuovi Cantieri Appaunia (Italy)
Entered Service:	Dec 1991/May 2016
Length (ft/m):	297.2/90.6
Propulsion/Propellers:	diesel (5,000kW)/2
Total Crew:	66
Passengers (lower beds):	115
Passenger Space Ratio (lower beds):	37.5
Passenger/Crew Ratio (lower beds):	1.6
Cabins (total):	55
Size Range (sq ft/m):	234.6–353.0/21.8–32.8
Cabins (for one person):	0
Cabins with balcony:	4
Cabins (wheelchair accessible):	0
Wheelchair accessibility:	None
Elevators:	1
Casino (gaming tables):	No
Self-Service Launderette:	No
Onboard currency:	UK£

THE SHIP. *Hebridean Sky* has a smart profile and handsome styling, with twin flared funnels and a 'ducktail' (or sponson) stern to provide fairly decent stability and seagoing comfort. Purchased by Noble Caledonia in 2014, it has a narrow teak walk-around promenade deck outdoors, and a decent amount of open deck space.

The interior design is elegant, with polished wood-finish paneling throughout. There is also a very small book and video library. Although *Hebridean Sky* is not up to the standard of a Seabourn or Silversea ship, it will provide a good cruise experience at a moderate cost. Gratuities are appreciated but not required.

This intimate little ship is very comfortable and inviting, and operates in regions devoid of large cruise ships. It suits mature adults who like to discover small ports in a relaxed lifestyle combined with good food and service, and itineraries that enable you to get away from it all, but in comfort.

ACCOMMODATION. The cabins are quite spacious and combine highly polished imitation rosewood paneling with lots of mirrors and hand-crafted Italian furniture, lighted walk-in closets, and vanity mirrors. In fact, there are a lot of mirrored surfaces in the decor, as well as just about everything you need, including a TV set and DVD player, a refrigerator, and

BERLITZ'S RATINGS		
	Possible	Achieved
Ship	500	341
Accommodation	200	151
Food	400	303
Service	400	287
Entertainment	100	60
Cruise Experience	400	271

OVERALL SCORE 1413 points out of 2000

free soft drinks and bottled water. The beds are fixed, so there's no under-bed storage space.

The bathrooms are extremely compact; they have real teakwood floors and marble vanities, and shower enclosures. None have tubs, not even the Owner's Suite. Cabins with balconies have glass panels topped with a polished wood railing.

DINING. The dining room operates in an open-seating arrangement, so you sit where you like, with whom you like, and at what time you like. It is small but quite smart, with tables for two, four, six, and eight. The meals are self-service, buffet-style cold foods for breakfast and lunch, with hot foods chosen from a table menu and served properly, and sit-down service for dinner. The food quality, choice, and presentation are all very good.

ENTERTAINMENT. There is no formal entertainment in the main lounge, the venue for all social activities. However, six pillars obstruct the sight lines to the small stage area, so it's not easy to see the speaker/lecturer.

SPA/FITNESS. Sports-related facilities include an aft platform, and Zodiacs for close-in coastal visits.

HORIZON
★★★

THIS IS A FAMILY-FRIENDLY AND CASUAL SHIP SPECIFICALLY FOR SPANISH-SPEAKERS

Size:	Mid-size Ship	Passenger/Crew Ratio (lower beds):	2.0
Tonnage:	47,427	Cabins (total):	721
Cruise Line:	Pullmantur Cruises	Size Range (sq ft/m):	172.2–500.5/16–46.5
Former Names:	*Pacific Dream, Island Star, Horizon*	Cabins (for one person):	0
Builder:	Meyer Werft (Germany)	Cabins with balcony:	68
Entered Service:	May 1990/Mar 2017	Cabins (wheelchair accessible):	4
Length (ft/m):	682.4/208.0	Wheelchair accessibility:	Good
Propulsion/Propellers:	diesel (19,960kW)/2	Elevators:	7
Total Crew:	620	Casino (gaming tables):	Yes
Passengers (lower beds):	1,442	Self-Service Launderette:	No
Passenger Space Ratio (lower beds):	32.8	Onboard currency:	Euros

THE SHIP. *Horizon* was originally built for and owned and operated by Celebrity Cruises. Although now around 25 years old, it still has a fairly contemporary, but angular, profile that looks powerful thanks to its blue hull (designed by mega-yacht designer Jon Bannenberg).

The exterior pool deck has two pools (one for children, one for adults), plus hot tubs shower enclosures, and sunloungers (but no cushioned pads).

Inside, there is a similar interior layout to its sister ship *Zenith*, with restrained decor, interesting artwork, and high-quality soft furnishings, and its elegant, Art Deco-style bi-level lobby is reminiscent of Miami Beach hotels.

Many of the public entertainment rooms are on a deck with a double-wide indoor promenade – good for strolling and people-watching. Other facilities include the Rendezvous Lounge, Le Piano Bar; Café Moka; an Internet center, a This ship is well suited to young (and young-at-heart) couples and families.

Passenger niggles include lines for self-serve buffet meals, and heavy public restroom doors.

ACCOMMODATION. There are several price grades, from interior (no-view) cabins to two Royal Suites midships on Deck 10, and forward on Deck 11. Note that many outside-view cabins on the safety equipment deck have lifeboat-obstructed views. The standard maritime cabin numbering system (even numbers port side, odd numbers starboard side) is reversed on this ship.

BERLITZ'S RATINGS		
	Possible	Achieved
Ship	500	295
Accommodation	200	117
Food	400	203
Service	400	229
Entertainment	100	58
Cruise Experience	400	222

OVERALL SCORE 1124 points out of 2000

DINING. Le Splendide, the main dining room, has two seating times for dinner and open seating for breakfast and lunch. It has a raised central section, tables for two to 10, and chairs devoid of armrests. The cuisine, its presentation, and service are passable, but uninspiring.

For informal meals, Marché Gourmand has an old-style, single-line, self-service buffet for breakfast and lunch, and includes a pasta station, rotisserie, and pizza ovens. At peak times, it is simply too small, too crowded, and noisy. It is also open (as Bistro Gourmand) for casual dinner each evening.

The Terrace and Grill, outdoors adjacent to the Bistro, serves typical fast-food items (burgers and hot dogs), while Café Moka is for cost-extra coffees in a plaza-like setting.

ENTERTAINMENT. The bi-level Broadway Theater, with main and balcony levels, has good sight lines from almost all seats, but the front of balcony level railing impedes sight lines.

Shows are geared to the family audience carried on most cruises. There is also a Saphir Dance Club (disco). Participation activities are amateurish.

SPA/FITNESS. The Salle de Fitness (just aft of the funnel) includes a small gymnasium with ocean-view windows and muscle-pumping equipment, an exercise area, several therapy rooms including a Rasul (Arabian mud treatment) room, and men's/women's saunas.

INDEPENDENCE OF THE SEAS
★★★+

THIS SHIP HAS EXCELLENT FAMILY-FRIENDLY FACILITIES AND PLENTY OF ENTERTAINMENT

Size:	Large Resort Ship
Tonnage:	154,407
Cruise Line:	Royal Caribbean International
Former Names:	none
Builder:	Kvaerner Masa-Yards (Finland)
Entered Service:	May 2008
Length (ft/m):	1,112.2/339.0
Propulsion/Propellers:	diesel-electric (75,600kW)/3 pods (2 azimuthing, 1 fixed)
Total Crew:	1,397
Passengers (lower beds):	3,634
Passenger Space Ratio (lower beds):	42.0
Passenger/Crew Ratio (lower beds):	2.6
Cabins (total):	1,817
Size Range (sq ft/m):	149.0–2,025.0/13.8–188.1
Cabins (for one person):	0
Cabins with balcony:	842
Cabins (wheelchair accessible):	32
Wheelchair accessibility:	Good
Elevators:	14
Casino (gaming tables):	Yes
Self-Service Launderette:	No
Onboard currency:	US$

THE SHIP. This *Freedom*-class ship is essentially split into three separate areas, rather like Disney's cruise ships: adults-only, family, and main. A 2019 refurbishment added new venues and eateries and relocated some facilities.

The ship's 'wow' factor (particularly for children) is its connection with water in the design of a dramatic sports park, with The Perfect Storm dual water slides, Sky Climber, rock-climbing wall, and FlowRider surf simulator (added in 2019). There are numerous bars and lounges to enjoy, plus a whole street of shops and food/ drink spots along an indoor mall-like environment called the Royal Promenade – it is four decks high, and some cabins have great views into it.

Some Royal Caribbean favorites include the large Casino Royale, Schooner Bar (piano bar), Boleros Lounge (a Latin hangout), a photo gallery and shop, and a large library/internet center.

A regulation-size ice-skating rink (Studio B) has real ice, with 'bleachers'-style seating, and broadcast facilities. Outstanding Ice Follies shows take place here but note that a number of slim pillars obstruct the view.

On an upper deck is RCI's trademark Viking Crown Lounge, plus the Escape Room and Olive or Twist jazz lounge.

After the extensive refit, the flow throughout the public areas is better, and new features and facilities (and around 70 new cabins in various grades)

BERLITZ'S RATINGS		
	Possible	Achieved
Ship	500	352
Accommodation	200	132
Food	400	231
Service	400	284
Entertainment	100	71
Cruise Experience	400	250
OVERALL SCORE 1320 points out of 2000		

have made a big difference to the overall experience. Independence of the Seas is a really good all-round ship for all age groups (and a favorite for many British families), but be aware of the many extra costs for optional items (including drinks/ drink packages, excursions, and alternative dining venues).

ACCOMMODATION. There is a wide range of suites and cabins in several categories and different price grades, from a two-bedroom villa to twin-bed two-person interior (no-view) cabins, and interior cabins with bay windows that look into an interior shopping/strolling atrium promenade. The price you pay depends on the size, grade, and location you choose. There are no solo-occupancy cabins. All outside-view cabins have even numbers; all interior cabins have odd numbers.

DINING. In 'The Dining Room', a dramatic staircase connects three decks, but large support pillars obstruct many sight lines. When you book, choose one of two seatings, or 'My Time Dining' (eat when you want, during dining-room hours). Tables are for four to 12 persons, and have good-quality place settings, china, and cutlery.

The cuisine is standardized banquet catering with very average dishes, no matter how tempting the description may sound. However, you can have items such as lobster or filet mignon (steak) at an extra cost, cooked to order. Green vegetables are limited, but salad items are plentiful, and desserts are pretty good. Bread and pastry items are pretty average, and croissants lack any hint of butter. Vegetarian and children's menus are available, but there are no wine waiters.

Other eating venues include:

Promenade Café for Continental breakfast, and Sorrento's for all-day pizzas, sandwiches, and coffee.

Giovanni's Table is a Euro-Italian venue, open for dinner only. Reservations are required; there's a cover charge, and a set menu.

Izumi for Japanese-style eats, including sushi.

Chops Grille, an intimate restaurant for steaks and seafood. There's a cover charge (worth it for freshly cooked items) and reservations are required.

Johnny Rockets, a retro 1950s diner-style eatery – within the kids' area – for burgers, hot dogs, and other fast food items, plus malt shakes.

Windjammer Cafe is a large, sprawling venue for casual buffet-style, self-serve breakfast (the busiest time of the day), lunch, and light dinners; it can be difficult to find a table and by the time you do, your food could be cold. The venue bears the brunt of many passenger complaints regarding lukewarm food and complacent staff.

ENTERTAINMENT. The 1,350-seat Royal Theater – a stunning showlounge – is located forward. It spans five decks in height, with a few slim pillars and almost no disruption of sight lines. The venue has a hydraulic orchestra pit and huge stage area, together with sonic-boom sound.

SPA/FITNESS. Independence Day Spa includes an aerobics room, a workout room, several rooms for body treatments, men's and women's sauna/steam rooms, and relaxation areas. Some exercise classes are free, but most cost extra.

INSIGNIA
★★★+

THIS COMPACT, CONTEMPORARY SHIP IS GOOD FOR WORLDWIDE CRUISING

Size:	Small Ship	Passenger/Crew Ratio (lower beds):	1.7
Tonnage:	30,277	Cabins (total):	342
Cruise Line:	Oceania Cruises	Size Range (sq ft/m):	145.3–968.7/13.5–90.0
Former Names:	Columbus 2, Insignia, R One	Cabins (for one person):	0
Builder:	Chantiers de l'Atlantique	Cabins with balcony:	232
Entered Service:	Jul 1998/Apr 2014	Cabins (wheelchair accessible):	3
Length (ft/m):	593.7/181.0	Wheelchair accessibility:	Good
Propulsion/Propellers:	diesel (18,600kW)/2	Elevators:	4
Total Crew:	386	Casino (gaming tables):	Yes
Passengers (lower beds):	684	Self-Service Launderette:	Yes
Passenger Space Ratio (lower beds):	44.2	Onboard currency:	US$

THE SHIP. *Insignia* started life as one of a series of almost identical ships built for the now-defunct Renaissance Cruises. The all-white ship has a large, square funnel, and a pleasant lido and pool deck outdoors, with teak overlaid decking and high-quality lounge chairs. In 2019, the ship underwent a refurbishment that made the interiors seem lighter and more open (like the look and feel of the newer, larger Marina and Riviera). Suites had bathtubs replaced by glazed-in showers. There is, however, no walk-around promenade deck outdoors.

The decor is a stroll through the ocean liners of the 1920s. It's all in fine taste, though a bit fake in places, with detailed ceiling cornices, both real and faux wrought-iron staircase balustrades, leather-paneled walls, trompe l'oeil ceilings, and rich carpeting in the hallways.

Public rooms are spread over three decks. The reception hall has a scaled-down version of *Titanic's* First-class staircase. Horizon Lounge is located high atop ship, featuring a bar with ocean views and abundant seating, and a dance floor.

There are several bars, including one in each restaurant entrance (except Toscana). Perhaps the nicest is Martinis, a lovely room with an inviting marble fireplace, sofas, individual armchairs, and a dance floor.

There may not be marble bathroom fittings, but the value for money is good. Note that a whopping 18

BERLITZ'S RATINGS

	Possible	Achieved
Ship	500	354
Accommodation	200	126
Food	400	291
Service	400	282
Entertainment	100	67
Cruise Experience	400	262

OVERALL SCORE 1382 points out of 2000

percent gratuity is added to bar purchases. The dress code is informal.

Overall, this ship is suitable for couples who like good food and style, but want informality, and interesting itineraries at a price well below what the luxury ships charge, in an informal setting that approaches elegant, and with almost no announcements.

ACCOMMODATION. There are several cabin categories and price grades. The standard interior and outside-view cabins (the lowest four grades) are compact – tight for two persons, particularly for longer cruises. They have twin beds or a queen-size bed (with LED treading lights and bedside USB sockets), with good under-bed storage areas, personal safe, vanity desk with large mirror, good closet and drawer space, dark wood furniture, cotton bathrobe and towels, slippers, clothes brush, and shoehorn.

Suite occupants get Bulgari bathroom amenities, complimentary shoeshine, cashmere throw blanket, bottle of Champagne on arrival, hand-held hairdryer, and priority restaurant reservations. The most desirable are the spacious Owner's Suites. These are fine living spaces located aft on decks 6, 7, and 8, with a bed that faces the sea through floor-to-ceiling windows and sliding glass door.

DINING. Flexibility and choice are what the dining is about. There are four restaurants:

Grand Dining Room (about 320 seats) has open seating and a raised central section. There are large ocean-view windows on three sides, with prime tables overlooking the stern. The chairs are comfortable and have armrests.

Toscana is an Italian restaurant with almost 100 seats, windows along two sides, and a set menu (reservations required); it was nicely refreshed in 2019.

Also with around 100 seats, Polo Grill has windows along two sides; it features prime steaks and seafood (reservations required).

The Terrace Café self-serve buffet has indoor and outdoor seating, and is open for breakfast, lunch, and casual dinners (including Tapas on the Terrace). It also has a small pizzeria.

There is also a Poolside Grill outdoors. On sea days, afternoon teatime is presented in the Horizon Lounge, with formally dressed staff, cake display trolleys, and a selection of different teas.

ENTERTAINMENT. The Insignia Lounge hosts entertainment, cabaret, lectures, and some social events. There is also live music in several bars and lounges.

SPA/FITNESS. Lido Deck has a swimming pool and good sunbathing space, plus a thalassotherapy tub. A jogging track encircles the swimming pool deck (one deck above). The uppermost outdoors deck includes a golf driving net and shuffleboard court. Canyon Ranch SpaClub consists of a beauty salon, three treatment rooms, men's and women's changing rooms, steam room (but no sauna), and a good range of body treatments. An 18 percent gratuity is added for spa and beauty treatments and services.

IONA
NYR

THIS LARGE RESORT SHIP OOZES MODERN AND CLASSIC STYLES FOR BRITISH PASSENGERS

Size:	Large Resort Ship	Passenger/Crew Ratio (lower beds):	2.8
Tonnage:	183,900	Cabins (total):	2,500
Cruise Line:	P&O Cruises	Size Range (sq ft/m):	
Former Names:	none	Cabins (for one person):	
Builder:	Fincantieri (Italy)	Cabins with balcony:	
Entered Service:	May 2020	Cabins (wheelchair accessible):	
Length (ft/m):	1,105.6/337.0	Wheelchair accessibility:	Best
Propulsion/Propellers: LNG/diesel/2 azimuthing pods		Elevators:	22
Total Crew:	1,800	Casino (gaming tables):	Yes
Passengers (lower beds):	5,200	Self-Service Launderette:	Yes
Passenger Space Ratio (lower beds):	35.5	Onboard currency:	UK£

THE SHIP. *Iona* is the largest ship in the P&O Cruises fleet, and is named after an island of the same name in Scotland's Inner Hebrides. The ship features a host of new innovations, including the SkyDome – a two-deck-high swimming pool and bar, topped by a spectacular glass dome; it's an all-weather venue that changes from day to night mode for entertainment and casual dining. Also, with an LNG power plant, Iona is now the most environmentally efficient ship in the company's history.

An uninterrupted half-mile promenade around Deck 8 provides access to alfresco eateries at several restaurants, plus relaxation areas under shaded pavilion awnings. Glass walls spanning three decks let light into the ship's atrium.

The interior focal and social meeting point is a three-deck-high Grand Atrium (lobby), with glass walls and a sweeping stairway. Choice and flexibility are integral to the ship's interior design, with inventive use of space, and an extensive range of dining, entertainment, and relaxation zones (but shared with over 5,000 fellow passengers). There are 17 places to eat (including seven specialty restaurants and eateries), 12 places to have a drink and view the sea, multiple entertainment venues, 16 hot tubs, three outdoor swimming pools and one indoors (in the SkyDome), nine breakfast places, five afternoon tea spots, and seven coffee hangouts.

Many of the most popular P&O ocean bars and lounges are on board, such as Anderson's, Brodie's, Crow's Nest, Headliners Theatre, Limelight Club, plus

BERLITZ'S RATINGS		
	Possible	Achieved
Ship	500	NYR
Accommodation	200	NYR
Food	400	NYR
Service	400	NYR
Entertainment	100	NYR
Cruise Experience	400	NYR
OVERALL SCORE NYR points out of 2000		

eateries like The Glass House, Sindhu, and The Epicurean.

Iona is limited in its choice of ports, because any tender operation is going to prove tedious and frustrating for many. However, Iona makes a good choice for families with children, and many facilities will be familiar to P&O's many repeaters.

Because this really is a large resort ship, it will be wise to plan your time (depending on the itinerary), particularly if you want to eat in any of the restaurants as an alternative to the main dining rooms, or watch a show in the evening.

ACCOMMODATION. There are numerous accommodation price grades, depending on deck, location, and size – from the smallest interior (no-view) cabin to the largest suite (three-room Sky Suite). All except the top suite grades have shower-only bathrooms. Some balcony cabins have folding floor-to-ceiling windows opening to a 'sun balcony' (an idea first introduced aboard the European riverships). Some cabins have extra berths, and some interior cabins are for solo occupancy.

DINING. There are two large dining rooms (Coral and Pearl – one above the other, both with aft views), connected by an interior stairway, and two smaller dining rooms, Aqua and Opal. Marco Pierre White's menu choices for gala evenings are destination-driven.

Other dining venues and eateries (some for food-to-go), include some P&O favorites and some new ones (some at extra cost):

The Epicurean, adjacent to the Crow's Nest (observation lounge), features 'fine dining' in a quieter atmosphere; it also hosts a 'Chef's Table' for private parties and special celebrations.

Sindhu is for Indian-style cuisine, popular with British passengers.

Olive Grove features Mediterranean-style plates (think lighter fare).

Boardwalk Diner is for American-style fast-food items such as burgers and hot dogs.

The Glass House is for wine choices by Olly Smith, and dinners with aerial entertainment.

For casual eats, Horizon is an expansive self-serve, food court-style venue (it includes The Beach House for evening meals). For the sweet of tooth, Eric Lanlard's cost-extra patisserie items are available in Vistas Café Bar in the Grand Atrium.

ENTERTAINMENT. Headliners Theatre, the main showlounge, spans two decks and has amphitheatre-style seating, and hosts colorful, large-scale production shows.

SkyDome is another main entertainment location; it comes alive with aerial performances, dome roof light projections, and immersive shows, while Ocean Studios is a 'premium' (extra-cost) surround-sound cinema.

SPA/FITNESS. Oasis Spa is on two of the lower decks and includes a gym with muscle-training equipment, changing rooms, body treatment rooms, and a cost-extra thermal suite. It's actually rather small for the number of passengers carried, but functional.

ISLAND PRINCESS
★★★+

THIS IS A COMFORTABLE CONTEMPORARY SHIP FOR MATURE-AGE CRUISERS

Size:	Mid-size Ship	Passenger/Crew Ratio (lower beds):	2.1
Tonnage:	91,627	Cabins (total):	987
Cruise Line:	Princess Cruises	Size Range (sq ft/m):	156–470.0/14.4–43.6
Former Names:	none	Cabins (for one person):	0
Builder:	Chantiers de l'Atlantique (France)	Cabins with balcony:	727
Entered Service:	Jun 2003	Cabins (wheelchair accessible):	20
Length (ft/m):	964.5/294.0	Wheelchair accessibility:	Good
Propulsion/Propellers:	gas turbine + diesel	Elevators:	14
	(40,000kW)/2	Casino (gaming tables):	Yes
Total Crew:	900	Self-Service Launderette:	Yes
Passengers (lower beds):	1,974	Onboard currency:	US$
Passenger Space Ratio (lower beds):	46.4		

THE SHIP. *Island Princess* has an instantly recognizable funnel due to two jet engine-like pods that sit high up on its structure, but these are mainly for decoration.

There are two decks full of public rooms, lounges, and bars instead of just one. Sensibly, there are three major stair towers for passengers, with plenty of elevators for easy access. There is a full walk-around exterior promenade deck.

A large 'Movies Under the Stars' screen is located in the second of two pool areas on the open deck. Adults using the cost-extra 'Sanctuary' area have their own splash pool.

Facilities include a flower shop where you can order flowers and Godiva chocolates for cabin delivery – nice for a birthday or anniversary – plus a cigar and cognac lounge (Churchill Lounge), and a Martini bar (Crooners). The casino has a London theme, and both gaming tables and slot machines.

An AOL Internet Café is conveniently located on the top level of the four-deck-high lobby. Adjacent is the Wedding Chapel, with a live web-cam to relay ceremonies via the Internet. The captain can legally marry American couples, thanks to the ship's registry and a special dispensation. The Wedding Chapel can host renewal of vows ceremonies, for a fee.

This ship has lots of nooks and crannies – so you can hide away and just read a book if you want to. Also, at the forward end of decks 10 and 11, doors

BERLITZ'S RATINGS		
	Possible	Achieved
Ship	500	326
Accommodation	200	128
Food	400	243
Service	400	263
Entertainment	100	70
Cruise Experience	400	264
OVERALL SCORE 1294 points out of 2000		

open onto an observation terrace. There are also several self-service launderettes.

Niggles include the fact that the forward elevators go between decks 15 and 7, but you need to change elevators to get down to the dining rooms on Deck 5 (strangely, the 'panoramic' elevators go only between decks 5 and 8; passengers find this a trifle confusing, but it's all about the way the layout has to work – from a designer's point of view, that is). Also: the user-unfriendly automated telephone system, the small cabin towels, extra cost for ice cream, and the (coins-needed) charge for the washers and dryers in self-service launderettes.

Overall, Princess Cruises delivers a consistently fine, comfortable, well-packaged product, always with a good degree of style, at a competitive price.

ACCOMMODATION. There are numerous price categories, in six types: suites with balcony; mini-suites with balcony; mini-suites without balcony; outside-view cabins with balcony; standard outside-view cabins; interior (no-view) cabins. Wheelchair-accessible cabins measure 217–374 sq ft/20.2–34.7 sq m. Some cabins have an extra bed for a third person, and all have a minibar, personal safe, info-tainment system, hairdryer, satellite-link telephone, twin or queen-sized beds (with premium-quality bedding), and pillow chocolates each night. All have a bathroom with shower enclosure and toilet (suites have a bathtub and separate shower enclosure). Note that most ocean-view cabins on Emerald Deck 8 have lifeboat-obstructed views.

DINING. The two, almost-identical, main dining rooms, Bordeaux and Provence, are in the forward section of the ship, on the two lowest passenger decks. They have quite low ceilings, plenty of intimate alcoves and cozy dining spots, and tables for two to eight and two seatings for dinner (or you can opt for 'Anytime' Dining in the Bordeaux Restaurant).

Although portions are generous, the food and its presentation are standardized. Fish often has a crumb or batter coating, the choice of fresh green vegetables is limited, few garnishes are used, and cheese is pre-sliced and diced. But, this is banquet-style catering and batch cooking. Pasta dishes are acceptable (though voluminous), typically served by section headwaiters, who may also make 'something special just for you.'

There are two extra-charge, reservations-required restaurants: Sabatini's (for Italian-style fare) and the Bayou Café (for Cajun/Creole-style cuisine).

Horizon Court is a casual, most of the day self-serve buffet eatery, in the forward section of Lido Deck. Sadly, there's just not enough seating for the number of people using the facility.

Other casual spots include La Pâtisserie, in the lobby, a coffee, cakes, and pastries spot and good for informal meetings. There's also a pizzeria, burger grill, and an ice cream bar (extra charge for the ice cream).

ENTERTAINMENT. The Princess Theater is two decks high, and, unusually, there is more seating on the upper level than on the main floor. Princess Cruises prides itself on its colorful Hollywood-style production shows.

A second entertainment venue, the Universe Lounge, is more for cabaret-style features, using three separate stages, enabling non-stop entertainment to be provided without constant set-ups. It is also used for cooking demonstrations (it has a full kitchen set-up) and other participation activities.

Princess Cruises provides plenty of live music in bars and lounges, with a wide mix of light classical, jazz, and dance music, from solo entertaining pianists to showbands, and volume is normally kept to an acceptable level.

SPA/FITNESS. Lotus Spa is located aft on one of the ship's uppermost decks. It contains men's and women's saunas, steam rooms, changing rooms, relaxation area, beauty salon, an aerobics exercise room, and a gymnasium with aft-facing ocean views. There are several large rooms for individual treatments.

Sports enthusiasts will find a nine-hole golf putting course, two computerized golf simulators, and a sports court.

ISLAND SKY
★★★★

A DELIGHTFUL VERY COMFORTABLE SHIP FOR LIFE-ENRICHMENT CRUISES

Size:	Boutique Ship	Passenger/Crew Ratio (lower beds):	1.7
Tonnage:	4,280	Cabins (total):	59
Cruise Line:	Noble Caledonia	Size Range (sq ft/m):	234.6–353.0/21.8–32.8
Former Names:	Sky, Renai II, Renaissance VIII	Cabins (for one person):	0
Builder:	Nuovi Cantieri Appaunia (Italy)	Cabins with balcony:	4
Entered Service:	Dec 1991/May 2004	Cabins (wheelchair accessible):	0
Length (ft/m):	297.2/90.6	Wheelchair accessibility:	None
Propulsion/Propellers:	diesel (5000kW)/2	Elevators:	1
Total Crew:	66	Casino (gaming tables):	No
Passengers (lower beds):	122	Self-Service Launderette:	No
Passenger Space Ratio (lower beds):	35.0	Onboard currency:	UK£

THE SHIP. *Island Sky* has contemporary mega-yacht looks and handsome styling, with twin flared funnels that give it a smart profile, and a 'ducktail' (sponson) stern that provides stability and seagoing comfort. This ship was originally built as one of a series of eight similar ships for the now-defunct Renaissance Cruises.

There is a narrow teak walk-around promenade deck outdoors, and a reasonable amount of open deck and sunbathing space. The ship has a fleet of Zodiac inflatables for shore landings.

Inside, the interior design is elegant, with polished wood-finish paneling throughout. There is a very small library with two Internet-connect workstations. Gratuities are included, as are house wine, beer, and soft drinks during lunch and dinner.

This comfortable, intimate ship operates in areas devoid of large cruise ships. Although not quite matching the standard of Seabourn or Silversea ships, it provides a fine cruise experience at a moderate cost. It suits seasoned travelers who like a relaxed lifestyle, good food and service, and an itinerary that promises to get away from it all, but in comfort.

ACCOMMODATION. The spacious cabins combine highly polished imitation rosewood paneling

BERLITZ'S RATINGS

	Possible	Achieved
Ship	500	340
Accommodation	200	151
Food	400	317
Service	400	307
Entertainment	100	60
Cruise Experience	400	291

OVERALL SCORE 1466 points out of 2000

with many mirrors and hand-crafted furniture, illuminated walk-in closets, three-sided vanity mirrors – in fact, there are a lot of mirrored surfaces in the decor – and just about everything you need, including a mini-fridge, an infotainment system, and Wi-Fi access. The bathrooms are extremely compact, but have real teakwood floors and marble vanities, and shower enclosures, but none have tubs, not even the Owner's Suite.

DINING. The dining room operates with open seating for all meals. Small, but quite smart, it has tables for two, four, six, and eight. You sit where you like, with whom you like, and at what time you like. The meals are self-service, buffet-style foods for breakfast and lunch, with hot foods chosen from a table menu and served properly. The dining room operation works well. The food quality, choice, and presentation are all very decent.

ENTERTAINMENT. There is no formal entertainment in the main lounge, the venue for all social activities. Six pillars obstruct sight lines to the small stage area.

SPA/FITNESS. Facilities include an aft platform, and Zodiac inflatable craft.

JEWEL OF THE SEAS
★★★+

THIS MID-SIZED SHIP IS A GOOD CHOICE FOR FAMILY-FRIENDLY CASUAL CRUISING

Size:	Mid-size Ship	Passenger/Crew Ratio (lower beds):	2.4
Tonnage:	90,090	Cabins (total):	1,055
Cruise Line:	Royal Caribbean International	Size Range (sq ft/m):	165.8–1,216.3/15.4–113.0
Former Names:	none	Cabins (for one person):	0
Builder:	Meyer Werft (Germany)	Cabins with balcony:	577
Entered Service:	Jun 2004	Cabins (wheelchair accessible):	14
Length (ft/m):	961.9/293.2	Wheelchair accessibility:	Good
Propulsion/Propellers:	gas turbine (39,000kW)/2 azimuthing pods	Elevators:	9
		Casino (gaming tables):	Yes
Total Crew:	858	Self-Service Launderette:	No
Passengers (lower beds):	2,110	Onboard currency:	US$
Passenger Space Ratio (lower beds):	42.9		

THE SHIP. *Jewel of the Seas* (a *Radiance*-class ship) is contemporary, with a two-deck-high Viking Crown Lounge in the forward section of the funnel; it functions as an observation lounge during the daytime, with views of the pool. In the evening, the space morphs into a nightclub.

The ship's gently rounded stern has nicely tiered decks, giving it a balanced look. In the front of the ship is a helipad/viewing platform.

Inside, the decor is modern, elegant, bright, and cheerful. The artwork is eclectic and provides a spectrum of color works. The focal point is a nine-deck-high atrium lobby with glass-walled elevators, providing a link with the ocean. The Centrum (atrium) has several public rooms connected to it, and a glass dome sits over it.

Facilities include a Schooner Bar with maritime art, a large, colorful Casino Royale (with gaming tables and slot machines), a small dedicated screening room for movies (with space for two wheelchairs), a small business center.

This ship is best suited to young-minded adult couples, solo travelers, and families with children of all ages, who like to mingle in a mid-sized ship setting with some city-like life and high-energy entertainment. The food is acceptable, stressing quantity rather than quality, unless you pay extra to dine in the specialty restaurant.

Niggles? The lack of cushioned pads for sunloungers, and small deck towels. It is virtually impossible

BERLITZ'S RATINGS

	Possible	Achieved
Ship	500	343
Accommodation	200	132
Food	400	228
Service	400	278
Entertainment	100	71
Cruise Experience	400	250

OVERALL SCORE 1302 points out of 2000

to escape background music (it's even played in the hallway outside your cabin).

ACCOMMODATION. There's a range of suites and standard outside-view and interior cabins to suit different tastes, requirements, and depth of wallet, in several different categories and numerous price groups, plus 14 wheelchair-accessible cabins, (eight have a balcony).

Apart from six Owner's Suites, which have king-size beds, almost all other cabins have twin beds that convert to a queen-size bed. All cabins have rich but faux wood cabinetry, including a vanity desk with hairdryer, faux wood drawers that close silently (hooray), television, personal safe, and three-sided mirrors. Some cabins have ceiling-recessed, pull-down third and fourth berths, although closet and drawer space would be extremely tight. Some cabins have interconnecting doors, allowing families with children to cruise together in adjacent cabins. Data ports are provided in all cabins.

Many 'private' balcony cabins aren't so private – they can be overlooked by anyone standing in the port and starboard wings of the Solarium, and from other locations.

Most bathrooms have a (rather small) half-moon shaped shower enclosure. There is little space to stow toiletries for two or more.

Suite occupants can use a private Concierge Lounge.

DINING. Tides (main dining room) spans two decks; the upper deck level has floor-to-ceiling windows, while the lower deck level has picture windows. It is a noisy dining hall and eight huge, thick pillars obstruct the sight lines. It seats over 1,200 and there's a cascading water theme. There are tables for two to 10, in two seating timings for dinner. Two small private dining rooms (Illusions and Mirage) are located off the main dining room.

Menu descriptions make the food sound better than it is, and the selection of breads, rolls, fruit, and cheese is poor. Overall, meals are rather hit and miss – in fact it's unmemorable. Additionally, if you want lobster or a decent filet mignon (steak), you will be asked to pay extra.

Extra-cost venues include Giovanni's Table, with 112 seats (for Italian-style fare), and Chops Grille Steakhouse, with 95 seats (for premium quality steaks and chops). Both have food that is of a better quality than in the main dining room. They are typically open 6–11pm. There is a cover charge, and reservations are required.

Casual breakfasts, lunches, and dinners can be taken in the self-serve, buffet-style Windjammer Café, which can be accessed directly from the pool deck. It has about 400 seats, 'islands' for specific food types, and indoor and outdoor seating. Additionally, there is Seaview Café, open for lunch and dinner. You can choose from the self-serve buffet, or from the menu for casual, fast-food seafood items, including fish 'n' chips, plus burgers and hot dogs.

ENTERTAINMENT. The three-level Coral Theater (showlounge) has 874 seats, and there are good sight lines from most seats. A second entertainment venue is the Safari Club, for cabaret. All the ship's entertainment is upbeat and loud, so it's virtually impossible to get away from noise pollution.

SPA/FITNESS. The Day Spa health and fitness facilities have themed decor and include a large solarium with counter current swimming under a retractable glass roof, a gymnasium, an aerobics room, sauna and steam rooms, and massage/body treatment rooms.

There are sports activities galore – including a 30-ft (9-m-) high rock-climbing wall – a nine-hole miniature golf course, golf simulator, jogging track, and basketball court. Want to play pool? You can, thanks to two special tables whose gyroscopic technology adjusts to the ship's movement.

KAPITAN KHLEBNIKOV
★★★

THIS RUGGED SHIP IS BUILT FOR POLAR EXPLORATION IN BASIC COMFORT

Size:	Boutique Ship	Passenger/Crew Ratio (lower beds):	1.4
Tonnage:	12,228	Cabins (total):	51
Cruise Line:	Quark Expeditions	Size Range (sq ft/m):	150.6-269.1/14.0-25.0
Former Names:	none	Cabins (for one person):	0
Builder:	Wartsila (Finland)	Cabins with balcony:	0
Entered Service:	1981	Cabins (wheelchair accessible):	0
Length (ft/m):	401.9/122.5	Wheelchair accessibility:	None
Propulsion/Propellers:	diesel-electric/2	Elevators:	1
Total Crew:	70	Casino (gaming tables):	No
Passengers (lower beds):	102	Self-Service Launderette:	No
Passenger Space Ratio (lower beds):	120.4	Onboard currency:	US$

THE SHIP. *Kapitan Khlebnikov* is a true polar-class icebreaker that was designed and built to take the rigors of northern Siberia. Now renowned in the realm of adventure travel and discovery, it is extremely reliable and well equipped for Arctic expedition voyages (particularly the notorious Northwest Passage). The ship has an extremely thick hull, its diesel-electric powerplant delivers 24,000 hp, and the bow looks like an inverted whale head. It really is a tough vessel that can plough through ice several feet thick. In 1997 it became the first passenger ship to circumnavigate Antarctica. There's plenty of open deck space for viewing, and the vessel has an open bridge policy.

The interior decor is spartan, but then this is a real, classic working icebreaker with an ice-experienced crew. Communal facilities include a lecture room that seats all participants. There is always a team of expert naturalists and lecturers, because the voyages are all about nature, wildlife, and other specialisms.

ACCOMMODATION. The 51 cruise cabins are spread over four decks. The price depends on the

BERLITZ'S RATINGS		
	Possible	Achieved
Ship	500	279
Accommodation	200	118
Food	400	219
Service	400	253
Entertainment	100	50
Cruise Experience	400	234

OVERALL SCORE 1153 points out of 2000

size, location, and grade you choose. From largest to smallest, they are basic but comfortable, each with two lower beds (one is a fixed bed, the other a convertible sofa bed, either in a twin or L-shaped format), large closets, storage for outerwear and boots, and portholes that can be opened. The bathrooms are practical units, but storage space for personal amenities items is tight. Four suites simply have a little more space.

DINING. The open seating dining room is plain and unpretentious, but quite comfortable. The food is hearty fare, with an emphasis on fish and potatoes. Fruits, vegetables, and international cheeses tend to be in limited supply. Quark Expeditions has its own catering team on board.

ENTERTAINMENT. This consists of recaps and after-dinner conversation with fellow travelers.

SPA/FITNESS. There is a workout room with some fairly basic equipment; there's also a tiny (heated) pool, and a sauna.

KONINGSDAM
★★★★

FAMILY-FRIENDLY SHIP WITH A GOOD MIX OF MODERN AND DUTCH TRADITIONAL DECOR

Size:	Large Resort Ship	Passenger/Crew Ratio (lower beds):	2.5
Tonnage:	99,500	Cabins (total):	1,331
Cruise Line:	Holland America Line	Size Range (sq ft/m): 127.0–1,291.1/11.7–120.0	
Former Names:	none	Cabins (for one person):	12
Builder:	Fincantieri (Italy)	Cabins with balcony:	912
Entered Service:	May 2016	Cabins (wheelchair accessible):	27
Length (ft/m):	983.5/299.8	Wheelchair accessibility:	Good
Propulsion/Propellers:	diesel/2 azimuthing pods	Elevators:	12
Total Crew:	1,025	Casino (gaming tables):	Yes
Passengers (lower beds):	2,650	Self-Service Launderette:	No
Passenger Space Ratio (lower beds):	37.7	Onboard currency:	US$

THE SHIP. The first of Holland America Line's *Pinnacle*-class ships, *Koningsdam* includes some contemporary features while maintaining the company's Dutch heritage.

The exterior profile (black hull and white upper part) is not exactly handsome, due to extra decks added forward and above the navigation bridge, but the single large funnel somehow balances the upper structure. Its name honors the first Dutch king in more than a century – King Willem-Alexander. It's the company's largest ship to date, although it is really an extension of the Vista class of ships – for example, the company's previous new build, *Nieuw Amsterdam*.

There is a complete walk-around exterior teak promenade deck, with hardwood steamer-style sun-loungers, and a jogging track is located in the forward third of the ship around its mast. Exterior glass elevators, mounted midships on both port and starboard sides, provide ocean views from any one of 10 decks. One of two central swimming pools outdoors can be used in inclement weather thanks to a retractable sliding glass roof. Two hot tubs, adjacent to the pools, are bridged by a bar. There's also a small pool for children.

The interior focus is the three-deck-high atrium lobby. Decks are named after famous composers, including Beethoven and Gershwin.

Facilities (spread over two decks) include the Queen's Lounge (it's also a lecture and demonstra-

BERLITZ'S RATINGS		
	Possible	Achieved
Ship	500	396
Accommodation	200	151
Food	400	225
Service	400	288
Entertainment	100	71
Cruise Experience	400	281
OVERALL SCORE 1412 points out of 2000		

tion room); a Culinary Arts Center (for cooking demonstrations); a large casino with gaming tables and slot machines; and the Crow's Nest – an observation lounge that includes a library and Explorations Café (extra cost).

Other facilities include a shopping street, card room, an art gallery, a photo gallery, and several small meeting rooms. The ship doesn't have rock-climbing walls, rope walks, and other gimmicky features. Holland America Line is known for its slower, more relaxed pace of living, and delivers a decent onboard experience, although the dining experience just doesn't cut it.

ACCOMMODATION. There are many price categories for the various accommodation grades, from small cabins for solo travelers to the largest (Grand Pinnacle) suites, including solo-occupancy and family-together cabins.

DINING. The Dining Room is on two levels, with two seatings (dining at set times). The decor is pure Americana, in white and cream – like a throwback to the steamboat era. The focal point is a bi-level wine tower, but the large restaurant is not helped by many slim, straight, and curved pillars (although this could be part of its decorative 'charm').

With a few exceptions, the cuisine is unmemorable, because it's all about batch cooking. There's a distinct lack of variety of green vegetables, and too much use of rice, canned fruit, and ready-prepared cheese. Still, you get friendly service from smiling Indonesian and Filipino stewards, and the plates are nice.

HAL can provide Kosher meals (if requested when you book), although these are prepared ashore, then frozen, and brought to your table sealed in their original containers.

Extra-cost (reservations-required) venues include:

Pinnacle Grill, for premium steaks and grilled seafood items – part of the line's focus on 'Pacific Northwest' cuisine.

Tamarind, for Asian 'fusion' cuisine (it includes a sushi bar).

Sel de Mer, a French-style seafood brasserie.

Culinary Arts Center – open for dinner; the venue is more bistro than restaurant, but it does grow microgreens in a glass-enclosed growing area.

For pastries and coffee, try the Grand Dutch Café.

For casual eating, there is the extensive Lido Market, a self-serve, buffet-style eatery that wraps around the funnel, with indoor-outdoor seating and ocean views. It includes several sections, including a salad bar, an Asian stir-fry and sushi section, deli sandwiches, and a separate dessert buffet, although lines can form for made-to-order items such as omelets for breakfast and pasta for lunch. Each evening, Canaletto (within the Lido Market) features quasi-Italian cuisine.

ENTERTAINMENT. Spanning two decks is the 'circular' World Stage main showlounge, which features a 270-degree LED screen that acts as a surround stage backdrop; it's a sort of 'theater in the round' within the showlounge. Music plays a big part in Lincoln Center Stage and Billboard Onboard.

SPA/FITNESS. The Greenhouse Spa is a good-sized, two-decks-high facility, located above the navigation bridge. It includes a solarium, hydrotherapy pool, and unisex thermal suite (with steam rooms and aromatic steam rooms), a beauty salon, private massage/body-treatment rooms (including one for couples), and a large fitness room with floor-to-ceiling windows and ocean views, and muscle-toning equipment.

L'AUSTRAL
★★★★

A CONTEMPORARY SHIP WITH STYLE TO SUIT FRENCH SPEAKERS

Size:	Small Ship	Passenger/Crew Ratio (lower beds):	1.5
Tonnage:	10,944	Cabins (total):	132
Cruise Line:	Ponant	Size Range (sq ft/m):	226.0–581.2/21.0–54.0
Former Names:	none	Cabins (for one person):	0
Builder:	Fincantieri (Italy)	Cabins with balcony:	125
Entered Service:	May 2011	Cabins (wheelchair accessible):	3
Length (ft/m):	465.8/142.0	Wheelchair accessibility:	Fair
Propulsion/Propellers:	diesel-electric (4,600kW)/2	Elevators:	3
Total Crew:	140	Casino (gaming tables):	No
Passengers (lower beds):	264	Self-Service Launderette:	No
Passenger Space Ratio (lower beds):	41.4	Onboard currency:	Euros

THE SHIP. One of four almost identical sister ships (the others are Le Boréal, Le Lyrial, and Le Soléal) catering to French speakers, L'Austral (South Wind) is a gem of contemporary, uncluttered design and chic details. With a dark gray hull and sleek white superstructure, it looks like a large private yacht rather than a traditional cruise ship. The passenger/space ratio, a healthy 53.5, decreases if the 40 deluxe cabins that convert into 20 larger suites are all occupied by two persons.

L'Austral has a smart 'sponson' skirt built-in at the stern for operational stability, and carries a fleet of 12 Zodiac landing craft for soft expedition voyages. For Antarctic voyages, passenger numbers are kept to a maximum of 199. The ship does not, however, have boot storage lockers.

There is some sunbathing space outdoors forward of the funnel and around the small pool – aft of the casual eatery one deck below – together with one shower enclosure. Aft of the funnel is an outdoor bar (Copernico) and grill, but seating is limited.

Almost all public rooms are aft, with accommodation located forward; the elevators go to all decks except the uppermost one (Deck 7). The decor is minimalist and super-yacht chic – relaxing and pleasant, with lots of browns and creams and a splash of red here and there. Glitz is entirely absent, although there are many reflective surfaces, and the overall feeling of the decor is cool rather than warm.

BERLITZ'S RATINGS

	Possible	Achieved
Ship	500	388
Accommodation	200	149
Food	400	288
Service	400	289
Entertainment	100	71
Cruise Experience	400	292

OVERALL SCORE 1477 points out of 2000

The focal point is the main lobby, with a central, circular seating and tiled floor surround; its small central section spans two decks. The other flooring is wood, which can be noisy. The lower decks of the main stairway are made of faux gray wood, while the upper decks are carpeted – a strange combination that somehow works.

L'Austral is well suited to couples and solo travelers who enjoy sophisticated facilities in a relaxed but chic, premium, yacht-like environment that's different from most cruise ships, with good food and decent service.

This is all-inclusive cruising – except for spa treatments – with drinks, table wine for lunch and dinner, bottled mineral water, port charges, and Zodiac excursions on expedition-style cruises included in the fare. The crew is English- and French-speaking, with many hotel service staff from Asia. How delightful – cruise tickets are provided in a proper document pouch and sent to you, and ship-wide Wi-Fi is free. One thing that's missing – fresh flowers.

Passenger niggles? There's no outside walking or jogging deck. The interior stairways are a quite steep and have short steps. The restaurant is noisy. The entertainment system is not user-friendly, and Internet connection is slow. Overall, it's difficult for French-speaking and non-French-speaking passengers to mix.

ACCOMMODATION. Of the 132 suites/cabins, there are three Prestige Suites with 301 sq ft plus a 54-sq-ft balcony (28 plus 5 sq m). Forty of the 94 deluxe cabins – 200 sq ft plus a 43-sq-ft balcony (18.6 plus 4 sq m) – can be combined into 20 larger suites, each with two bathrooms, and separate living area and bedroom. All cabinetry is made in elegant dark woods. A real plus is that there are no interior (no-view) cabins – all cabins have a view of the outside – and cabin insulation is good.

Each deluxe and standard cabin has a large ocean-view window, two beds that convert to a queen-size bed, and a long vanity desk with good lighting. Facilities include a TV set, DVD player, refrigerator, and personal safe. The marble-appointed bathrooms have large, rather heavy hand-held shower hoses. Amenities include a minibar, hairdryer, bathrobe, and French bathroom products. All other cabins have good-size beds, although the corners of the bed frames are square, so, be careful when passing between the bed and the storage units – these are quite large, with two deep drawers. Other facilities include wall mirror, good-size wardrobe-style closet (armoire) with personal safe, and a vanity desk with drawer and a small shelf.

The small cabin bathrooms (the entrance door is only 20.5ins/52cm wide) also have a sliding partition window that enables you to see through the cabin to the ocean, and a deep, half-size tub/shower combination. The lip between floor and bathroom is just over 6ins (15cm) high. L'Occitane products are provided.

There are no shelves for toiletries, but there are two drawers under the washbasin – although they are not very practical. A separate cubicle houses the vacuum toilet. Balconies have faux wood decking and a fine (real) wood handrail, although solid paneling obstructs views when seated and makes the cabin seem dark – glass panels would have been nicer; the balconies are also narrow. The closet space is quite good, although the doors, with excellent white leather handles, are wide – at 31ins (79cm), they are wider than the cabin door, and can't be opened with-out first closing the bathroom and toilet doors that are directly opposite.

Good-quality bed linen, overlays, and cushions are provided, although there is no choice of pillows.

DINING. The main restaurant is chic but not pretentious. It accommodates all passengers in an open-seating arrangement and has two integral wine display cabinets (not temperature-controlled). The chairs are square and have thin armrests and low backs – but they look good. And the food? While appetizers and entrées (mains) are reasonably good, but certainly nothing special, the cakes and desserts are delightful.

A casual indoor/outdoor Grill (although there is no actual grill) has seating for up to 130, with self-serve buffet set-up for breakfast and lunch, and a 'fast grill' dinner in an alfresco setting. But the layout is disjointed, and the port and starboard sides are separated by two elevators. There are two main buffet display units (one for cold food, one for hot), a separate table set-up for bread, and an active cooking station (eggs for breakfast, pasta dishes at lunchtime).

Veuve Clicquot is the Champagne chosen by Ponant, a perfect example of French *savoir-faire*, and premium selections include Brut Carte Jaune, Rosé, and La Grande Dame varieties.

ENTERTAINMENT. French Line, the showlounge/lecture hall, has amphitheater-style seating for 260, and a raised stage suited to concerts and cabaret. The production shows are weak, repetitive, and loud. The venue is also used for expert specialist lecturers, and expedition-style recaps. Two large pillars obstruct the sight lines from several seats.

SPA/FITNESS. The Yacht Spa facilities include a fitness room with starboard-side ocean views, an adjacent kinetic wall, and a steam room, but there's no changing room. A wide range of massage and other body treatments are provided by Carita of Paris, which staffs and oversees the facility.

LE BOREAL
★★★★

THIS SMALL SHIP EXUDES FRENCH AMBIENCE AND CHIC YACHT-LIKE STYLE

Size:	Small Ship	Passenger/Crew Ratio (lower beds):	1.5
Tonnage:	10,700	Cabins (total):	132
Cruise Line:	Ponant	Size Range (sq ft/m):	226.0–581.2/21.0–54.0
Former Names:	none	Cabins (for one person):	0
Builder:	Fincantieri (Italy)	Cabins with balcony:	124
Entered Service:	May 2010	Cabins (wheelchair accessible):	3
Length (ft/m):	465.8/142.0	Wheelchair accessibility:	Fair
Propulsion/Propellers:	diesel-electric (4,600kW)/2	Elevators:	3
Total Crew:	140	Casino (gaming tables):	No
Passengers (lower beds):	264	Self-Service Launderette:	No
Passenger Space Ratio (lower beds):	41.4	Onboard currency:	Euros

THE SHIP. One of four almost identical new ships catering to French speakers, *Le Boréal* (North Wind) is a gem of contemporary design – chic and uncluttered. The ship has a smart 'sponson' skirt built-in at the stern for operational stability, and carries a fleet of 12 Zodiac landing craft for soft expedition voyages.

There is some sunbathing space outdoors forward of the funnel and around the small pool – aft of the casual eatery one deck below – together with one shower enclosure. Aft of the funnel is an outdoor bar/grill, but not much seating.

Almost all public rooms are aft, with accommodation located forward; the elevators go to all decks except the uppermost one (Deck 7). The decor is minimalist and super-yacht chic – relaxing and pleasant, with lots of browns and creams and a splash of red here and there. Glitz is entirely absent, although there are many reflective surfaces, and the overall feeling of the decor is cool rather than warm.

The focal point is the main lobby, with a central, circular seating and tiled floor surround; its small central section spans two decks. The other flooring is wood, which can be noisy. The lower decks of the main stairway are made of faux gray wood, while the upper decks are carpeted – a strange combination that somehow works.

Le Boréal is best suited to young-minded couples and solo travelers who want some contemporary,

BERLITZ'S RATINGS

	Possible	Achieved
Ship	500	388
Accommodation	200	149
Food	400	288
Service	400	291
Entertainment	100	71
Cruise Experience	400	291

OVERALL SCORE 1478 points out of 2000

sophisticated facilities and a chic yet relaxed yacht-like environment quite different to most cruise ships, with very good food and decent service. The ship is often chartered or part-chartered by 'premium' travel organizers, such as Abercrombie & Kent, Gohagan, and Tauck, who prefer smaller ships.

This is inclusive cruising – except for spa treatments – with drinks, table wine for lunch and dinner, bottled mineral water, port charges, and Zodiac excursions on expedition-style cruises all included in the fare. The crew is English- and French-speaking, with many hotel service staff from Asia. It's refreshing to note that cruise tickets and documents are provided in a proper ticket pouch and sent to you – so, there's no digital frustration, but much anticipation, and ship-wide Wi-Fi is included.

Passenger niggles? There's no outside walking or jogging deck. The interior stairways are a quite steep and have short steps. The restaurant is noisy, the entertainment system is not user-friendly, internet connection is slow, and there are no fresh flowers. Overall, it's difficult for French-speaking and non-French-speaking passengers to mix.

ACCOMMODATION. Of the 132 suites/cabins, there are three Prestige Suites, while 40 of 94 deluxe cabins can be combined into 20 larger suites, with his and hers bathrooms, separate living area and bedroom. All cabinetry is made in elegant dark woods. There are no interior (no-view) cabins – every cabin has an outside view, and the insulation is good. Amenities include French bathroom products.

Each deluxe and standard cabin has a large ocean-view window, two beds convertible to queen-size, and a long vanity desk with good lighting. Facilities include an infotainment system, a minibar, hairdryer, and personal safe. The marble-appointed bathrooms have heavy hand-held shower hoses.

All other cabins have good-size beds, although the bed frame corners are square, so you need to be careful when passing between the bed and adjacent storage units – these are quite large, with two deep drawers. Other facilities include a refrigerator, television, wall mirror, good-size wardrobe-style closet (armoire) with personal safe, and a vanity desk with drawer and a small shelf.

The small cabin bathrooms (the entrance door is only 20.5ins/52cm wide) also have a sliding partition window for a view through the cabin to the ocean, and a deep, half-size tub/shower combination. The lip between floor and bathroom is just over 6ins (15cm) high.

There are no shelves for toiletries, but there are two drawers under the washbasin – although they are not really practical. A separate cubicle houses the (vacuum) toilet. The narrow balconies have faux wood decking and a real wood handrail, but solid paneling obstructs views when seated and makes the cabin seem dark – glass panels would be nicer. The closet space is quite good, although the doors, with white leather handles, are wide – at 31ins (79cm), they are wider than the cabin door, and can't be opened without first closing the bathroom and toilet doors, which are directly opposite. Good-quality bed linen, overlays,

and cushions are provided, although there is no choice of pillows.

DINING. The main restaurant, La Licorne, is chic but unfussy; it accommodates all passengers in an open seating and has two integral wine display cabinets (not temperature-controlled). The chairs are rather square and have thin armrests and low backs – but they look good. And the food? While appetizers and entrées (mains) are reasonably good but nothing special, the cakes and desserts are delightful.

La Boussole, an indoor/outdoor Grill (there's no actual grill), has casual seating for up to 130, with a self-serve buffet for breakfast and lunch, and a 'fast grill' dinner in an alfresco setting. However, the layout is quite disjointed, and the port and starboard sides are separated by two elevators. There are two main display units – one for cold food, one for hot – a separate table for bread, and an active cooking station (eggs for breakfast, pasta at lunchtime).

ENTERTAINMENT. French Line, the show lounge/lecture hall, has amphitheater-style seating for 260, and a raised stage suited to concerts and cabaret presentations. The production shows are weak, repetitive, and loud. The venue is also used for expert specialist lecturers and expedition-style recaps. Two large pillars obstruct the sight lines from several seats, however.

SPA/FITNESS. The Yacht Spa facilities include a fitness room with starboard-side ocean views, an adjacent kinetic wall, and a steam room, but no changing room. A wide range of massage and body treatments are provided by Carita of Paris, which staffs and operates the facility.

LE BOUGAINVILLE
★★★★

THIS SHIP IS FOR DISCOVERING DESTINATIONS IN A STYLISH AND VERY FRENCH CONTEMPORARY SETTING

Size:	Boutique Ship	Passenger/Crew Ratio (lower beds):	1.6
Tonnage:	10,000	Cabins (total):	92
Cruise Line:	Ponant	Size Range (sq ft/m):	247.5–807.3/23.0–75.0
Former Names:	none	Cabins (for one person):	4
Builder:	Vard (Norway)	Cabins with balcony:	92
Entered Service:	Jun 2019	Cabins (wheelchair accessible):	0
Length (ft/m):	431.1/131.4	Wheelchair accessibility:	Fair
Propulsion/Propellers:	Diesel-electric/2 azimuthing pods	Elevators:	3
		Casino (gaming tables):	No
Total Crew:	110	Self-Service Launderette:	No
Passengers (lower beds):	180	Onboard currency:	Euros
Passenger Space Ratio (lower beds):	55.5		

THE SHIP. *Le Bougainville* (sister to *Le Champlain* and *Le Laperouse*) is designed to take you to some of the more remote areas of the planet in comfort. The shape is similar to the larger general-purpose 'yacht'-style Ponant ships, but with an open (trawler) stern that provides access to the marine equipment and doubles as a landing platform.

This expedition-style ship has some premium contemporary touches in its interiors. What's really impressive – and different – is seating under the sea. It's in an underwater lounge called the 'Blue Eye.'

The interior design is quite practical, but feels a little closed-in due to the low ceiling height. Public rooms include the Panorama Lounge, Main Lounge, a Theatre/Lecture Room, and the aforementioned 'Blue Eye' lounge (with an underwater camera).

This is all-inclusive cruising with free ship-wide Wi-Fi, drinks, table wine for lunch and dinner, bottled mineral water, port charges, and Zodiac excursions on 'expedition-style' cruises all included in the fare. Note, however, that the cruise line chooses the drinks and wine – not you. The crew is English- and French-speaking, with many hotel service staff from Asia. However, there's no outside walking or jogging deck. The interior stairways are a little steep and have short steps.

If you are looking for sophisticated facilities in a relaxed but chic, French, yacht-like environment – quite different to most large cruise ships – with decent food, and friendly, informal service, then *Le Bougainville* should fit the bill. The ship can also be chartered or

BERLITZ'S RATINGS		
	Possible	Achieved
Ship	500	403
Accommodation	200	155
Food	400	289
Service	400	289
Entertainment	100	71
Cruise Experience	400	298

OVERALL SCORE 1505 points out of 2000

part-chartered by 'premium' travel organizers who prefer smaller ships. There are many French products such as superb Boudier butter, Ladurée macarons and Veuve Clicquot champagne on gala nights, but it doesn't quite reach the Berlitz five-star level, due in part to the non-carpeted stairways, the bistro-style design of the restaurant, and the lack of fresh flower displays.

ACCOMMODATION. There are several accommodation price grades. The price you pay depends on the size, location, and grade you choose. From the smallest cabin (247 sq ft/23 sq m) to the largest suite (807 sq ft/75 sq m), all are really comfortable, and many have balconies. French bathroom cosmetics are provided.

DINING. The main restaurant, located aft, is chic but not at all pretentious. It accommodates all passengers in an open-seating arrangement and has an integral wine display cabinet.

ENTERTAINMENT. The show lounge/lecture hall has amphitheater-style seating for all passengers, and a raised stage suited to mini-concerts, other shows, and cabaret presentations. It's also used for specialist lecturers and expedition-style recaps.

SPA/FITNESS. The Yacht Spa facilities include a fitness room with ocean views, a kinetic wall, and a steam room with shower, but no changing room. A range of massage and body treatments are available.

LE CHAMPLAIN
★★★★

THIS SHIP HAS FRENCH CHIC AND STYLE FOR EXPLORING THE MORE REMOTE REGIONS

Size:	Boutique Ship
Tonnage:	10,000
Cruise Line:	Ponant
Former Names:	none
Builder:	Vard (Norway)
Entered Service:	Sept 2018
Length (ft/m):	419.9/128.0
Propulsion/Propellers:	diesel-electric/2 azimuthing pods
Total Crew:	110
Passengers (lower beds):	180
Passenger Space Ratio (lower beds):	55.5
Passenger/Crew Ratio (lower beds):	1.6
Cabins (total):	92
Size Range (sq ft/m):	247.5–807.3/23.0–75.0
Cabins (for one person):	4
Cabins with balcony:	92
Cabins (wheelchair accessible):	0
Wheelchair accessibility:	Fair
Elevators:	3
Casino (gaming tables):	No
Self-Service Launderette:	No
Onboard currency:	Euros

THE SHIP. *Le Champlain* is named after the French explorer Samuel de Champlain. It is designed primarily to take you to some of the more remote areas of the planet in contemporary comfort. The shape is similar to the larger general-purpose yacht-style Ponant cruise ships, but with an open (trawler) stern that provides access to the marine equipment and acts as a landing platform.

This expedition-style ship has some premium contemporary touches in its interiors. What's really impressive – and different – is seating under the sea, in an underwater lounge called the 'Blue Eye.'

The interior design itself is functional, but the ship feels a little closed-in, due to low ceiling heights. Public rooms include a Panoramic Lounge, Main Lounge (which seats all passengers at once), a Theatre/Lecture Room, and the aforementioned 'Blue Eye' lounge.

This ship is really for anyone looking for sophisticated contemporary facilities in a relaxed but chic, French, yacht-like environment – quite different to most large cruise ships – with decent food, and friendly, casual service from a French- and English-speaking crew. Also, there is free ship-wide Wi-Fi. There are many good things about the ship, such as several excellent French

BERLITZ'S RATINGS		
	Possible	Achieved
Ship	500	403
Accommodation	200	155
Food	400	289
Service	400	289
Entertainment	100	71
Cruise Experience	400	297

OVERALL SCORE 1504 points out of 2000

products, including its butter, Ladurée macaroons, and Veuve Clicquot champagne on gala evenings, although it doesn't quite reach the Berlitz five-star level, due in part to the non-carpeted (noisy) stairways, the bistro-style design of the restaurant, and the lack of live flower displays.

ACCOMMODATION. There are numerous accommodation price grades, and the price you pay depends on the size, location, and grade you choose. From the smallest interior (no-view) cabin to the largest suite, all are comfortable, and many have balconies. French bathroom cosmetics are provided.

DINING. The Restaurant, located aft, is cheerful, and has both indoor and outdoor seating.

ENTERTAINMENT. Movies are shown in the Theater/showlounge.

SPA/FITNESS. The Yacht Spa facilities include a fitness room with starboard-side ocean views, a kinetic wall, and a steam room with shower, but no changing room. A range of massage and body treatments are provided by Sothys, whose staff operates the facility.

LE DUMONT D'URVILLE
★★★★

A CHIC FRENCH SHIP FOR EXPLORING THE MORE REMOTE REGIONS IN STYLE

Size:	Boutique Ship	Passenger/Crew Ratio (lower beds):	1.6
Tonnage:	10,000	Cabins (total):	92
Cruise Line:	Ponant	Size Range (sq ft/m):	247.5–807.3/23.0–75.0
Former Names:	none	Cabins (for one person):	4
Builder:	Vard (Norway)	Cabins with balcony:	92
Entered Service:	Sep 2019	Cabins (wheelchair accessible):	0
Length (ft/m):	419.9/128.0	Wheelchair accessibility:	Fair
Propulsion/Propellers:	diesel-electric/2 azimuthing pods	Elevators:	3
		Casino (gaming tables):	No
Total Crew:	110	Self-Service Launderette:	No
Passengers (lower beds):	180	Onboard currency:	Euros
Passenger Space Ratio (lower beds):	55.5		

THE SHIP. *Le Dumont d'Urville* (sister ship to *Le Bougainville*, *Le Champlain*, and *Le Lapérouse*) is named after the French explorer, naval officer, and rear admiral Jules Sébastien César Dumont d'Urville. The ship is designed primarily to take passengers to some of the more remote areas of the planet in contemporary comfort. The ship has an open (trawler) stern that provides access to the marine equipment and acts as a landing platform.

This exploration-style ship has some premium contemporary touches in its interiors – a standout is its underwater lounge: the 'Blue Eye' (reached by a dedicated elevator).

The interior design itself is functional, but the ship does feel a little closed-in, due to the low ceilings. Other public rooms include the Panoramic Lounge, Main Lounge (which can seat all passengers at once), Theatre/Lecture Room, a reception lobby, and the 'Blue Eye' lounge.

Le Durmont d'Urville is good for anyone looking for sophisticated facilities in a relaxed but very chic, French, yacht-like environment that also doubles as an expedition-style ship – quite different to most large cruise ships. You can expect decent food and friendly, casual service.

BERLITZ'S RATINGS

	Possible	Achieved
Ship	500	403
Accommodation	200	155
Food	400	289
Service	400	289
Entertainment	100	71
Cruise Experience	400	298

OVERALL SCORE 1505 points out of 2000

ACCOMMODATION. There are numerous accommodation grades, and the price depends on the size, location, and grade. From the smallest interior (no-view) cabin to the largest suite, all are practically designed and very comfortable, and many have balconies.

DINING. The restaurant, aft, is cheerful, and has indoor and (some) outdoor seating, but inside is extremely noisy, due to the constant opening and closing of the galley doors during service, the low ceiling height, and noisy waiter stations. Dining is open seating, with tablecloths for dinner, but not for breakfast or lunch. Some Alain Ducasse-designed special menu items add sparkle. The cheese selection is really good, as are desserts, pastries, and cakes. The outdoor Grill eatery is an extension of the lounge, and features almost the same food, including buffet items, but in the afternoon, look for those delicious Ladurée macarons.

ENTERTAINMENT. Movies shown in the theater.

SPA/FITNESS. Yacht Spa facilities include a fitness room with ocean views, a kinetic wall, and a steam room with shower, but no changing room. A range of massage and body treatments are available.

LE LAPÉROUSE
★★★★

THIS SHIP HAS FRENCH CHIC FOR DISCOVERING DESTINATIONS IN STYLISH COMFORT

Size:	Boutique Ship	Passenger/Crew Ratio (lower beds):	1.6
Tonnage:	10,000	Cabins (total):	92
Cruise Line:	Ponant	Size Range (sq ft/m):	247.5–807.3/23.0–75.0
Former Names:	none	Cabins (for one person):	4
Builder:	Vard (Norway)	Cabins with balcony:	92
Entered Service:	Jul 2018	Cabins (wheelchair accessible):	0
Length (ft/m):	419.9/128.0	Wheelchair accessibility:	Fair
Propulsion/Propellers:	diesel-electric/2 azimuthing pods	Elevators:	3
		Casino (gaming tables):	No
Total Crew:	110	Self-Service Launderette:	No
Passengers (lower beds):	180	Onboard currency:	Euros
Passenger Space Ratio (lower beds):	55.5		

THE SHIP. Le Lapérouse (sister to Le Champlain) is designed to take you to some the more remote areas in comfort. The ship's profile is similar to the larger-capacity, general-purpose, 'yacht'-style Ponant ships (but slightly shorter), but with an open (trawler) stern that provides access – via a cleverly designed hydraulic foldout platform – to the marine equipment and acts as a landing platform for its fleet of 15 Zodiac landing craft, which are also used for close-up excursions, while two lifeboats can act as fast tender boats. There is no walkaround exterior deck, and all decks are covered with wood-look Bolidt (a sort of rubberized deck covering).

This 'soft' expedition-style ship has some premium contemporary touches in its interiors, and there is no glitz or bling. What's really impressive is seating under the sea, in an underwater lounge called the 'Blue Eye.' Other public rooms include the Observatory Lounge, Main Lounge, and a Theatre/Lecture Room.

Ponant prides its association with French products such as Ladurée macarons and Veuve Clicquot champagne (gala nights only), and Hermes bathroom products. The crew is English- and French-speaking, and ship-wide Wi-Fi is included. There are many good things about the ship, but it doesn't quite reach the Berlitz five-star level, due in part to its non-carpeted stairways, the bistro-style design, layout, and noise of the restaurant, and lack of fresh flower displays.

Refreshingly, documents are provided in a proper ticket pouch and sent to you, so there's no digital frustration.

BERLITZ'S RATINGS		
	Possible	Achieved
Ship	500	402
Accommodation	200	155
Food	400	289
Service	400	289
Entertainment	100	71
Cruise Experience	400	297
OVERALL SCORE 1503 points out of 2000		

ACCOMMODATION. Grades depend on size and location. From the smallest interior cabin (no view) to the largest suite, all are very comfortable, with wood-look decor and white cabinetry. Many have narrow balconies, with slide-open glass doors. Bathrooms are small, but practical, although shower enclosures are a decent size. Air conditioning cannot be turned off.

DINING. The restaurant, located aft, is cheerful, and has indoor and (some) outdoor seating, but inside is extremely noisy, due to the constant opening and closing of the galley doors during service, the low ceiling height, and noisy waiter stations. Dining is open seating (tablecloths for dinner, but not for breakfast or lunch). Some Alain Ducasse-designed special menu items add sparkle. The cheese selection is very good, and the desserts, pastries, and cakes are outstanding. The service, while friendly, could be more professional. An outdoor Grill eatery features almost the same food, which tend to be repetitive for breakfast and lunch.

ENTERTAINMENT. Small stage shows, concerts, lectures (most are in French), and other presentations take place in the tiered-seating theatre.

SPA/FITNESS. The Yacht Spa facilities include a small fitness room with ocean views, a sauna with a large ocean-view window, but no changing room (you go there in a bathrobe). A range of massage and body treatments are provided by Sothys.

LE LYRIAL
★★★★

THIS IS A SMALL, CHIC, AND CONTEMPORARY FRENCH YACHT-LIKE SHIP

Size:	Boutique Ship	Passenger/Crew Ratio (lower beds):	1.5
Tonnage:	10,944	Cabins (total):	122
Cruise Line:	Ponant	Size Range (sq ft/m):	226.0–710.4/21.0–66.0
Former Names:	none	Cabins (for one person):	0
Builder:	Fincantieri (Italy)	Cabins with balcony:	122
Entered Service:	Apr 2015	Cabins (wheelchair accessible):	3
Length (ft/m):	465.8/142.0	Wheelchair accessibility:	Fair
Propulsion/Propellers:	diesel-electric/2	Elevators:	3
Total Crew:	140	Casino (gaming tables):	No
Passengers (lower beds):	244	Self-Service Launderette:	No
Passenger Space Ratio (lower beds):	44.8	Onboard currency:	Euros

THE SHIP. *Le Lyrial* (its name refers to the Lyra constellation in the northern hemisphere) has a smart 'sponson' skirt built-in at the stern for operational stability, and a fleet of 12 Zodiac landing craft is carried for shore landings and viewing excursions during soft expedition and nature cruises. The hull is the color of gray slate.

There is some sunbathing space outdoors forward of the funnel and around the small pool – aft of the casual eatery on the deck below – together with a shower enclosure. Aft of the funnel is an outdoor bar/grill, but there's really not enough seating if the ship operates in warm-weather areas.

It's trendy and uncluttered, with contemporary super-yacht-chic interiors; relaxing and pleasant, with lots of blue and white. Glitz is absent, although there are many reflective surfaces, and the overall 'feel' of the decor is cool rather than warm.

Although it carries slightly fewer passengers, it's the same size as sister ships *L'Austral*, *Le Boréal*, and *Le Soleil*. So, it is classed as a Boutique ship, and not a small ship. Almost all public rooms are aft, with accommodation located forward; the elevators go to all decks except the uppermost one (Deck 7).

The focal point is a two-deck-high main lobby, which has a central, circular seating area, although its design is not exactly warm.

This is inclusive cruising with drinks, table wine for lunch and dinner, bottled mineral water, ship-

BERLITZ'S RATINGS		
	Possible	Achieved
Ship	500	396
Accommodation	200	153
Food	400	288
Service	400	296
Entertainment	100	72
Cruise Experience	400	293
OVERALL SCORE 1498 points out of 2000		

wide Wi-Fi, port charges, and Zodiac excursions on 'discovery-style' cruises all included in the fare; spa treatments cost extra, however. Note that the cruise line chooses the drinks and wine – not you.

It is refreshing (and retro) to see that cruise tickets and documents are provided in a proper ticket pouch and sent to you, so, there's no digital frustration – just anticipation.

The crew is English- and French-speaking, with many hotel service staff from Asia. However, there's no outside walking or jogging deck. The interior stairways are a quite steep and have short steps.

Le Lyrial is best suited to young-minded couples and solo travelers who are looking for sophisticated facilities in a relaxed but chic French yacht-like environment that is different to large cruise ships, with decent food, and informal service, although fresh flowers are sadly missing.

ACCOMMODATION. There are 122 suites/cabins (10 fewer than the earlier sister ships).

The largest accommodation includes: eight suites of 484.3 sq ft (45 sq m), one larger Owner's Suite measuring 721.2 sq ft (67 sq m), and a Grand Deluxe Suite of 581.2 sq ft (54 sq m).

The cabin cabinetry is crafted in elegant woods. A real plus is that there are no interior (no-view) cabins – each cabin has an outside view, plus good-quality bed linen, overlays, cushions, refrigerator, personal safe, television, wall mirror, L'Occitane bathroom products, and good sound-proofing. However, note that the step into the bathroom is high, at 6.5ins (16.5 cm).

CUISINE. The Restaurant Gastronomique is chic but not overly pretentious. It accommodates all passengers in an open seating and has an integral wine display cabinet. The chairs are square and have thin armrests and low backs – but they look good.

An indoor/outdoor Grill (though there's no grill) has casual seating for up to 130, with a self-serve buffet setup for breakfast and lunch, and a 'fast grill' dinner in an alfresco setting. However, the layout is rather disjointed, and the port and starboard sides are separated by two elevators. There are two main buffet display units – one for cold food, one for hot – a separate table for bread and an active cooking station (eggs for breakfast, pasta at lunchtime).

ENTERTAINMENT. Le Theatre (showlounge/lecture room) has amphitheater-style seating for all passengers, and a raised stage suited to mini-concerts, other shows, and cabaret presentations. It's also used for specialist lecturers and recaps. Two large pillars obstruct the sight lines from several seats, however.

SPA/FITNESS. The Yacht Spa facilities include a fitness room with port-side ocean views, an adjacent kinetic wall, and a steam room with shower (there's no separate shower aboard L'Austral, Le Boreal, or Le Soleil), although isn't a changing room. A range of massage and body treatments are provided by Sothys, which staffs and oversees the facility.

LE PONANT
★★★+

CHIC DECOR AND RELAXED YACHT-STYLE CRUISING FOR FRENCH-SPEAKERS

Size:	Boutique Ship	Passenger/Crew Ratio (lower beds):	2.1
Tonnage:	1,489	Cabins (total):	32
Cruise Line:	Ponant	Size Range (sq ft/m):	145.3–164.6/13.5–15.3
Former Names:	none	Cabins (for one person):	0
Builder:	SFCN (France)	Cabins with balcony:	0
Entered Service:	Jun 2009	Cabins (wheelchair accessible):	0
Length (ft/m):	288.7/88.0	Wheelchair accessibility:	None
Propulsion/Propellers:	diesel/sail power/1	Elevators:	0
Total Crew:	32	Casino (gaming tables):	No
Passengers (lower beds):	64	Self-Service Launderette:	No
Passenger Space Ratio (lower beds):	23.2	Onboard currency:	Euros

THE SHIP. Ultra sleek, and very efficiently designed, this contemporary sail-cruise ship has three masts that rise 54.7ft (16.7m) above the water line, and electronic winches that assist in the furling and unfurling of the sails. The total sail area measures approximately 16,140 sq ft (1,500 sq m). This captivating ship has plenty of room on its open decks for sunbathing. Although they have padded cushions, the off-white plastic sun-loungers are still not at all elegant.

The interior design is clean, stylish, functional, and high-tech. Three public lounges have pastel decor, soft colors, and great flair. One price fits all. The ship is marketed mainly to young, sophisticated French-speaking passengers who love yachting and the sea. The company has a fleet of super-yacht cruise ships.

Gratuities are 'not required', but they are expected. It's refreshing to find that cruise tickets and documents are provided in a proper ticket pouch and sent to you (so, there's no digital frustration – just anticipation).

ACCOMMODATION. There are five cabins on Antigua Deck (the open deck) and 27 on Marie-Galante Deck (the lowest one). Crisp, clean blond woods and pristine white cabins have twin beds that convert to a double. There's a minibar, personal safe, and a bathroom. All cabins have port-

BERLITZ'S RATINGS		
	Possible	Achieved
Ship	500	340
Accommodation	200	148
Food	400	267
Service	400	282
Entertainment	100	70
Cruise Experience	400	217

OVERALL SCORE 1324 points out of 2000

holes, artwork, and a refrigerator. There is limited storage, however, and few drawers – they are also very small. The cabin bathrooms are quite small, but efficient.

DINING. The lovely Karukéra dining room has an open-seating policy. There is fresh fish daily, when available, and dinner is always treated as a true gastronomic affair. Free wines are included for lunch and dinner, and the cuisine is, naturally, classic French. That Gallic inclination also means the selection of cheeses, breads, and breakfast croissants is good. There are free cappuccinos and espressos. For casual breakfasts and luncheons, there is a charming outdoor café under a canvas sailcloth awning.

ENTERTAINMENT. There is no professional entertainment as such, although occasionally the crew may put on a little soirée. Dinner is the main event each evening, and, being a French product, dinner can provide several hours of entertainment in itself.

SPA/FITNESS. There is no spa, fitness room, sauna, or steam room. However, for recreation, there are water-sports facilities, and these include an aft marina platform from which you can swim. There is also windsurfing, water-ski boating, and scuba and snorkel equipment. Scuba diving costs extra, charged per dive.

LE SOLEAL
★★★★

FRENCH AMBIENCE AND SMALL MEGA-YACHT PREMIUM CHIC ABOARD THIS SHIP

Size:	Small Ship	Passenger/Crew Ratio (lower beds):	1.5
Tonnage:	10,944	Cabins (total):	132
Cruise Line:	Ponant	Size Range (sq ft/m):	226.0–581.2/21.0–54.0
Former Names:	none	Cabins (for one person):	0
Builder:	Fincantieri (Italy)	Cabins with balcony:	125
Entered Service:	Jul 2013	Cabins (wheelchair accessible):	3
Length (ft/m):	465.8/142.0	Wheelchair accessibility:	Fair
Propulsion/Propellers:	diesel-electric (4,600kW)/2	Elevators:	3
Total Crew:	140	Casino (gaming tables):	No
Passengers (lower beds):	264	Self-Service Launderette:	No
Passenger Space Ratio (lower beds):	41.4	Onboard currency:	Euros

THE SHIP. One of four almost identical sister ships catering mainly to French speakers, *Le Soléal* is contemporary, chic, and uncluttered. With a dark gray hull and sleek white superstructure, the ship looks more like a large private yacht than a traditional cruise ship.

The ship has a smart 'sponson' skirt built in at the stern – this is for operational stability – and carries a fleet of 12 Zodiac landing craft for exploring shore landings. There is some sunbathing space outdoors forward of the funnel and around the small pool – aft of a casual eatery located one deck below – together with a shower enclosure.

Almost all public rooms are located in the aft section, with accommodation forward; the elevators go to all decks except the uppermost one (Deck 7). The decor is minimalist and super-yacht chic – relaxing and pleasant, with lots of browns and creams and a splash of red here and there. However, there are many reflective surfaces, and the overall feeling of the decor is cool rather than warm and cosseting.

The focal point of the interior is the main lobby, with a central, circular seating and tiled floor surround; its small central section spans two decks. The other flooring is wood, which can be noisy. The lower decks of the main stairway are made of faux gray wood, while the upper decks are carpeted – a strange combination that somehow works.

Le Soléal is geared to young-minded couples and solo travelers who want semi-sophisticated

BERLITZ'S RATINGS		
	Possible	Achieved
Ship	500	388
Accommodation	200	151
Food	400	288
Service	400	293
Entertainment	100	72
Cruise Experience	400	291
OVERALL SCORE 1483 points out of 2000		

facilities in a relaxed but stylish yacht-like environment that's different from most cruise ships, and are happy with reasonably good food and service. Missing are fresh flower displays.

This is all-inclusive cruising (and that includes ship-wide Wi-Fi) – except for spa treatments – with drinks, table wine for lunch and dinner, bottled mineral water, port charges, and Zodiac excursions on expedition-style cruises included in the fare. The crew is English- and French-speaking, with many hotel service staff from Asia. Refreshingly, cruise tickets and documents are provided in a proper ticket pouch and sent to you.

Passenger niggles? There's no outside walking or jogging deck. The interior stairways are a quite steep and have short steps. The restaurant is noisy. The entertainment system is not user-friendly, and the Internet connection is slow and expensive. Overall, it's difficult for French-speaking and non-French-speaking passengers to mix.

ACCOMMODATION. Of the 132 suites/cabins, there are three Prestige Suites measuring 355 sq ft (33 sq m). Forty of the 94 deluxe cabins can be combined into 20 larger suites, each with two bathrooms (his and hers), and separate living area and bedroom. All cabinetry is made in elegant dark woods. A real plus is that there are no interior cabins, which means that every cabin has an outside view. Cabin insulation is also good, so you shouldn't hear your neighbor.

The deluxe and standard cabins have a large ocean-view window, two beds that convert to a queen-size one, and a long vanity desk with good lighting. Facilities include an infotainment system, a DVD player, refrigerator, and personal safe. The bathrooms are marble-appointed, but have very heavy hand-held shower hoses. Amenities include a minibar, hairdryer, bathrobe, and French (L'Occitane) bathroom products.

All other cabins have good-size beds, although the corners of the bed frames are square, so be careful when passing between bed and an adjacent storage unit – it's quite large, with two deep drawers. Other facilities include a refrigerator, television, wall mirror, good-size wardrobe-style closet (armoire) with personal safe, and a vanity desk with drawer and a small shelf.

The small cabin bathrooms (the entrance door is only 20.5ins/52cm wide) also have a sliding partition window that enables you to see through the cabin to the ocean, and a deep, half-size tub/shower combination. The lip between floor and bathroom is just over 6ins (15cm) high.

There are no shelves for toiletries, but there are two drawers under the washbasin – although they are not very practical. A separate cubicle houses the vacuum toilet. Balconies have faux wood decking and a fine (real) wood handrail, although solid paneling obstructs views when seated and makes the cabin seem dark – glass panels would have been nicer; the balconies are also narrow. The closet space is decent enough, although the doors, with nice white leather handles, are wide – at 31ins (79cm), they are wider than the cabin door, and can't be opened without first closing the bathroom and toilet doors that are directly opposite.

Good-quality bed linen, overlays, and cushions are provided, although there is no choice of pillows.

DINING. Restaurant Gastronomique is chic but not pretentious – or even warm. It accommodates all passengers in an open-seating arrangement and has two integral wine-display cabinets. The chairs are rather square and have very thin armrests and low backs – but they look good. And the food? While the appetizers and entrées (mains) are reasonably good but nothing special, the cakes and desserts are delightful.

An indoor/outdoor Grill has casual seating for up to 130, with a self-serve buffet for breakfast and lunch, and a 'fast grill' dinner in an alfresco setting. The layout is disjointed, and port and starboard sides are separated by two elevators. There are two main buffet display units – one for cold food, one for hot, plus a separate table set-up for bread and an active cooking station (eggs for breakfast, pasta at lunchtime, for example).

ENTERTAINMENT. The showlounge, which doubles as a lecture hall, has amphitheater-style seating for 260, and a raised stage for concerts and cabaret-style entertainment. The 'production' shows are weak, repetitive, and loud, but they do have a sort of French flair. The venue is also used for expedition-style recaps and lectures, but two large pillars obstruct sight lines from several seats.

SPA/FITNESS. The Yacht Spa facilities include a fitness room with starboard-side ocean views, an adjacent kinetic wall, and a steam room, but there is no changing room. A wide range of massage and body treatments are provided by Carita of Paris, which staffs and oversees the facility.

LIBERTY OF THE SEAS
★★★+

A LARGE RESORT SHIP FOR CASUAL, BUT ACTIVE CRUISING FOR THE WHOLE FAMILY

Size:	Large Resort Ship	Passenger/Crew Ratio (lower beds):	2.5
Tonnage:	154,407	Cabins (total):	1,815
Cruise Line:	Royal Caribbean International	Size Range (sq ft/m):	149.0–2,025.0/13.8–188.1
Former Names:	none	Cabins (for one person):	0
Builder:	Kvaerner Masa-Yards (Finland)	Cabins with balcony:	842
Entered Service:	May 2007	Cabins (wheelchair accessible):	32
Length (ft/m):	1,112.2/339.0	Wheelchair accessibility:	Best
Propulsion/Propellers:	diesel-electric (75,600kW)/3 pods (2 azimuthing, 1 fixed)	Elevators:	14
		Casino (gaming tables):	Yes
Total Crew:	1,397	Self-Service Launderette:	No
Passengers (lower beds):	3,630	Onboard currency:	US$
Passenger Space Ratio (lower beds):	42.5		

THE SHIP. *Liberty of the Seas* (a *Freedom*-class ship) – a large resort at sea – is a really good choice for families with children. The ship's 'pod' propulsion system virtually eliminates vibration. The outer decks are full of water features for the whole family. Splashaway Bay is a water-themed play area for families, with water cannons, geysers, and more (above it is a large movie screen).

The water and sports facilities are good for adults, too. Aft is a boomerang-style water slide, called Tidal Wave, and two great racer slides (Cyclone and Typhoon) adjacent to a Flowrider surf simulator. Two 16-person hot tubs are cantilevered 12ft (3.7m) over the ship's sides in an adults-only Solarium area.

There are 16 bars and lounges to enjoy, plus a series of shops, munching and drinking spots along the Royal Promenade. One deck down from the Royal Promenade is the large Casino Royale, The Catacombs disco, Schooner Bar, Boleros Lounge, and a photo gallery and shop, while the forward section leads into the three-deck-high Platinum Theater.

A regulation-size ice-skating rink (Studio B) has real ice, with bleachers seating. Outstanding Ice Follies shows are presented here, but note that a number of slim pillars obstruct clear-view arena stage sight lines. Adjacent is the On Air broadcast studio.

Almost at the top of the ship is the company's trademark Viking Crown Lounge, the Olive or

BERLITZ'S RATINGS		
	Possible	Achieved
Ship	500	354
Accommodation	200	132
Food	400	218
Service	400	283
Entertainment	100	71
Cruise Experience	400	250

OVERALL SCORE 1308 points out of 2000

Twist jazz lounge, and a Wedding Chapel. Other facilities include a cigar-smoker's lounge, conference center, a concierge lounge (for suite occupants only), and a comfortable 3,600-book library.

Liberty of the Seas is an exciting and very comfortable ship, with contemporary decor. However, there are only four banks of elevators (two forward and two aft) totaling 14, so if you have a cabin in the center of the ship, you'll need to walk in order to travel vertically between decks; there are also only two major passenger stairways – one forward, one aft. More cabins were added in a 2015 refit, but no extra elevators.

Niggles include the high cost for internet connectivity, the constant push to sell you ice-laden drinks, lines for the security check when re-boarding in ports, the poor quality of food at the Windjammer Buffet, the lack of green vegetables in main dining room food, and poor cheese and fruit choices.

Accommodation. There is a wide range of cabins to choose from. These go from a rather compact Interior (no-view) Cabin (there are many) for two (some rooms accommodate three or four) and measure just 152 sq ft (14.1 sq m) to a superb Presidential Family Suite with balcony: it sleeps up to 14 (at a pinch) and measures 1,215 sq ft (112.9 sq m) plus balcony: 810 sq ft (75.3 sq m).

All cabins have a private bathroom (with tub and shower, or shower only), vanity desk with hairdryer, minibar, safe, flat-screen infotainment system, iPod dock, radio, and satellite telephone. A room service menu is provided. Suite occupants have access to a Concierge Lounge, for personal service – it saves standing in line at the reception desk.

DINING. The main dining room is large and is set on three levels, each with a different name: Botticelli, Michelangelo, and Rembrandt. A dramatic staircase connects all three, but huge support pillars obstruct the sight lines. When you book, choose one of two seatings, or 'My Time Dining' (be prepared to wait for a table at peak times). Tables are for four to 12. The place settings, porcelain, and cutlery are of good quality.

The main dining room cuisine is standardized banquet catering so the food, although prepared well enough, is not amazing. However, you can have items such as lobster or filet mignon (steak) at an extra cost – and at least they will be cooked to order. Green vegetables are scarce – they're provided basically for decoration – but there are plenty of salad choices, and desserts are pretty good. Rice is heavily used as a filler. Breads and pastry items are average (these are thawed and then baked from frozen), and items such as croissants lack any hint of butter. Vegetarian and children's menus are available. Note that there are no wine waiters, and wine glasses are small.

Other eateries include: Sabor (for modern tastes of Mexico); Giovanni's Table (open for lunch and dinner, a trattoria featuring Italian classics served family-style); Izumi Asian Cuisine (open for lunch and dinner, includes a sushi bar and sizzling hot-rock cooked items); Chef's Table (open for dinner only, this 'private' experience features a wine pairing dinner); and Park Café (open for all meals, this indoor/outdoor deli is for salads, sandwiches, soups, and pastries). All except Park Café incur a cover charge.

There's also:

Café Promenade for Continental breakfast, all-day pizzas (Sorrento's), sandwiches, and coffees (in paper cups).

Windjammer Café, a really large, sprawling venue for casual buffet-style, self-help breakfast (this tends to be the busiest time of the day), lunch, and light dinners; it's often difficult to find a table and by the time you do, your food could be cold.

Chops Grille, an intimate restaurant for steaks and seafood; a cover charge applies.

Johnny Rockets, a retro 1950s all-day, all-night diner-style eatery for burgers, hot dogs, other fast-food items, and malt shakes; there is both indoor and outdoor seating (indoor tables have a mini-jukebox). There's a cover charge.

Sprinkles for round-the-clock ice cream and yoghurt, pastries, and coffee.

ENTERTAINMENT. The Platinum Theater is a well-designed showlounge located forward, with only a few slim pillars and almost no disruption of sight lines. It has a hydraulic orchestra pit and huge stage areas, as well as superb lighting equipment.

A performance not to be missed is the Greatest Show at Sea Parade – a 15-minute extravaganza that bumbles along the Royal Promenade; it replicates the parade of stars and animals at a circus of yesteryear. This is when it's really good to have one of those interior-view atrium cabins. Otherwise, get a position early along the Royal Promenade.

SPA/FITNESS. The Steiner-operated Day Spa is large. It includes a large aerobics room, fitness center, treatment rooms, and sauna/steam rooms and relaxation areas. Some basic exercise classes are free, but others cost extra. Active types can go body-boarding, boxing in the full-size boxing ring, go rock-climbing, in-line skating, jog, putt, swim, surf, play in the golf simulators or on the mini-golf course (Liberty Dunes).

MAASDAM
★★★

THIS SHIP FEATURES TRADITIONAL DUTCH-STYLE DECOR FOR MATURE-AGE TRAVELERS

Size:	Mid-size Ship
Tonnage:	55,451
Cruise Line:	Holland America Line
Former Names:	none
Builder:	Fincantieri (Italy)
Entered Service:	Dec 1993/Dec 1993
Length (ft/m):	719.3/219.3
Propulsion/Propellers:	diesel-electric (34,560kW)/2
Total Crew:	557
Passengers (lower beds):	1,266
Passenger Space Ratio (lower beds):	43.8
Passenger/Crew Ratio (lower beds):	2.2
Cabins (total):	632
Size Range (sq ft/m):	186.2–1,124.8/17.3–104.5
Cabins (for one person):	0
Cabins with balcony:	150
Cabins (wheelchair accessible):	6
Wheelchair accessibility:	Good
Elevators:	8
Casino (gaming tables):	Yes
Self-Service Launderette:	Yes
Onboard currency:	US$

THE SHIP. *Maasdam* (now over 25 years old and tired) is one of four almost identical ships, along with *Ryndam* (now *Vasco da Gama*) *Statendam* (now *Pacific Aria*), and *Veendam*. Although the exterior styling is angular (some say boxy – the funnel is), it is balanced by its black hull. There is a full walk-around teak promenade deck outdoors – excellent for strolling. The wooden sunloungers on the exterior promenade deck have comfortable cushioned pads; those at the swimming pool on Lido Deck are plastic. A hydraulic glass roof covers the reasonably sized swimming pool/hot tubs and central Lido area, whose focal point is a large dolphin sculpture.

There is good passenger flow throughout the public areas, with an asymmetrical layout that helps reduce congestion. Most public rooms are on the Promenade Deck and Upper Promenade Deck. In general, the decor is restrained, with contemporary materials combined with traditional woods and ceramics. There is, thankfully, little glitz anywhere.

Some $2 million worth of artwork is peppered throughout the ship, including several oil paintings of the line's former ships by Stephen Card (a former ship's captain) adorning stairway landings. Also noticeable are the flower arrangements in the public areas. Atop the ship, with ocean views, is the Crow's Nest Lounge. By day, a pleasant observation lounge, with ocean-view windows, it turns into a nightclub with extremely variable lighting in the evenings.

BERLITZ'S RATINGS		
	Possible	Achieved
Ship	500	295
Accommodation	200	125
Food	400	218
Service	400	251
Entertainment	100	60
Cruise Experience	400	238
OVERALL SCORE 1187 points out of 2000		

The atrium foyer is three decks high, although its light-catching green glass sculpted centerpiece (*Totem* by Luciano Vistosi, composed of almost 2,000 pieces of glass) makes it feel cramped. This ship has a relaxing library, card room, the Explorer's Lounge (for afternoon tea and after-dinner coffee), Piano Bar, and a casino with gaming tables and slot machines. However, note that part of the casino is open, and passers-by can be subject to cigarette smoke (yes, smoking is still permitted),

HAL's many repeat passengers seem to enjoy the fact that social dancing is always on the menu. HAL continues its strong maritime traditions and keeps its vessels clean and tidy, but the food and service components let the rest of the cruise experience down.

Other niggles? A pointless escalator travels between two of the lower decks, one of which was originally planned for embarkation. The charge to use the washing machines and dryers in the self-service launderette is petty. The men's public restroom urinals are unusually high. The ship is now looking decidedly tired and past its sell-by date.

ACCOMMODATION. The accommodation ranges from small interior (no-view) cabins to a Penthouse Suite, in multiple price categories. Interior and outside standard cabins have twin beds convertible to a queen-size bed, with sofa and coffee table. Drawer space is generally good, but closet space is very tight, particularly for long cruises, although adequate for a seven-night cruise. Bathrobes are provided for all, as are hairdryers and a small range of toiletries. The bathrooms are quite well laid out, but the bathtubs are really just shower tubs.

DINING. The Rotterdam Dining Room spans two decks, aft. It has a grand staircase, panoramic views on three sides, and a music balcony. Either open seating or assigned seating is available, while breakfast and lunch are only open seating (you'll be taken to your table by restaurant staff as you enter). The waiter stations are noisy for anyone seated near them.

With a few exceptions, the cuisine is unmemorable, and there's a lack of green vegetables, a heavy use of rice, canned fruit, and already sliced and diced cheese. Still, you get friendly service from the Indonesian and Filipino stewards.

A 66-seat, extra-cost Pinnacle Grill is located just forward of the balcony level of the main dining room on the starboard side. It features Pacific Northwest cuisine (prime steaks and seafood), and reservations are needed. A Bulgari show plate, Rosenthal china, Riedel wine glasses, and Frette table linen are provided. It's a better, more relaxed dining experience than the main dining room and worth the extra cost, if your budget allows.

The Lido Market is open for casual dinners on all except the last night of each cruise. It's open seating, and the tables are set with crisp linens, flatware, and stemware. It is also open for breakfasts and lunches. The beverage station, which is similar to those found in family outlets in the United States, is poor. Additionally, the poolside 'Dive-In at the Terrace Grill' features burgers, hot dogs, and fries.

Passengers have to use the Lido Buffet on days when the dining room is closed for lunch, depending on the itinerary.

ENTERTAINMENT. The Showroom at Sea (forward) spans two decks, with banquette seating on both levels. The ceiling is low, and the sight lines from the balcony level are quite poor. Meanwhile, music features heavily in the Half Moon venue.

SPA/FITNESS. The Ocean Spa is one deck below the navigation bridge. It has ocean views and includes a gymnasium with muscle-pumping exercise machines, a beauty salon with port-side ocean-views, several treatment rooms, and men's and women's sauna, steam room, and changing areas.

MAGELLAN
★★★+

THIS IS AN INFORMAL, COLORFUL, ADULTS-ONLY SHIP FOR BRITISH CRUISERS

Size:	Mid-size Ship	Passenger/Crew Ratio (lower beds):	2.2
Tonnage:	46,052	Cabins (total):	726
Cruise Line:	Cruise and Maritime Voyages	Size Range (sq ft/m):	189.2–420.0/17.0–39.0
Former Names:	*Grand Holiday, Holiday*	Cabins (for one person):	0
Builder:	Aalborg Vaerft (Denmark)	Cabins with balcony:	10
Entered Service:	Jul 1985/Jun 2015	Cabins (wheelchair accessible):	15
Length (ft/m):	726.0/221.3	Wheelchair accessibility:	None
Propulsion/Propellers:	diesel (22,360kW)/2	Elevators:	8
Total Crew:	660	Casino (gaming tables):	Yes
Passengers (lower beds):	1,452	Self-Service Launderette:	No
Passenger Space Ratio (lower beds):	31.7	Onboard currency:	Euros

THE SHIP. *Magellan* (formerly *Grand Holiday*) is a rather boxy-looking, all-white vessel, although CMV has managed to soften its looks with a bow-to-stern stripe. It does, however, have a distinctive swept-back, wing-tipped funnel.

The salt-water swimming pools are quite small, as are the hot tubs, but the open deck and sunning space atop ship is decent. There is an exterior walking area, although it doesn't wrap around the front of the ship. There are numerous public rooms (with British names such as Hampton's, Kensington, etc.) on two main entertainment decks, and these flow from a wide indoor promenade. Unusually, the Neptune Observation Bar is aft. Still, you can see where you've been!

This ship is best suited to British mature-age adults seeking a low-cost cruise experience. The good: the staff escort to your cabin when you embark; the staff is friendly; and the decor is appealingly non-glitzy. The not-so-good: there is no walk-around promenade deck outdoors, although the outdoor space itself is reasonably good; a lot of chairs in the two restaurants have no armrests; many of the low-back tub chairs have no back support. The cabin walls are paper-thin, so you can almost hear your neighbor brushing their hair. Also, the air conditioning tends to be overly cold throughout the ship.

ACCOMMODATION. There are just four cabin categories: Suite with balcony; Junior Suite with balcony; exterior cabins; and interior (no-view) cabins, in 15 different price grades. The standard outside and interior cabins are plain but functional units and they provide

BERLITZ'S RATINGS		
	Possible	Achieved
Ship	500	250
Accommodation	200	104
Food	400	192
Service	400	207
Entertainment	100	51
Cruise Experience	400	197
OVERALL SCORE 1001 points out of 2000		

all the basics, including a small vanity/writing desk. TV sets are typically placed high in one corner and are not easy to see. The bathrooms are practical, with decent-size shower enclosures.

DINING. There are two main restaurants: Kensington (in the center) and Waldorf (aft – with some nice ocean-view tables at the back). Both are large, have low ceilings and raised center sections, and feel cramped. Remember that this really is banquet-style catering, so standardization and cooking on a large scale is the norm. Several traditional British favorite dishes are part of the offerings. Also, the wine list is very limited, and there are no wine waiters.

Raffles Bistro is a self-serve buffet area that provides all the basics (except service and enough seats), although its layout is old in style, which makes the venue seem more like a canteen than a bistro. Still, it's adequate for a quick meal.

ENTERTAINMENT. The Magellan Show Lounge is the venue for colorful, low-cost production shows and cabaret acts, but note that pillars obstruct the views from several seats. Most lounges and bars also have live music.

SPA/FITNESS. The Jade Wellness Center is located on an upper deck, but the fitness room is on a different deck. Some fitness classes are free, while some may cost extra. Book early for massages, facials, or other beauty treatments, because time slots go quickly.

MAGELLAN EXPLORER
NYR

THIS BOUTIQUE SHIP IS CUSTOM-BUILT FOR NO-FRILLS FLY-CRUISES TO ANTARCTICA

Size:	Boutique Ship
Tonnage:	4,900
Cruise Line:	Antarctica21
Former Names:	none
Builder:	Asenav (Chile)
Entered Service:	Dec 2019
Length (ft/m):	298.0/90.7
Propulsion/Propellers:	diesel/2
Total Crew:	60
Passengers (lower beds):	69
Passenger Space Ratio (lower beds):	49.0

Passenger/Crew Ratio (lower beds):	1.1
Cabins (total):	35
Size Range (sq ft/m):	215.2–430.5/20.0–40.0
Cabins (for one person):	0
Cabins with balcony:	42
Cabins (wheelchair accessible):	0
Wheelchair accessibility:	None
Elevators:	0
Casino (gaming tables):	No
Self-Service Launderette:	No
Onboard currency:	US$

THE SHIP. Owned by Germany-based Minke Shipping Company, and chartered to Antarctica21 (the world's first air-cruise operator to Antarctica), *Magellan Explorer* may be a reasonable choice for anyone wanting a no-frills expedition-style experience and up-close-and-personal nature encounters. The dark hull, however, has an unhandsome paint job, with several white letter As (for Antarctica 21) adorning it. The ship carries 10 Zodiac landing craft, and several items for cost-extra activities, such as kayaking, hiking, and snow-shoeing. You will need to purchase your own parka (Antarctica jacket). The ship is based at King George Island in Antarctica, and the company flies you here in a chartered BAE 146 aircraft (landing, however, depends on weather conditions), which takes two hours, rather than the two days to cross the Drake Passage by ship, from Punta Arenas, Chile.

Public rooms include one lounge/briefing room (with bookshelves and regional and wildlife refer-

BERLITZ'S RATINGS		
	Possible	Achieved
Ship	500	NYR
Accommodation	200	NYR
Food	400	NYR
Service	400	NYR
Entertainment	100	NYR
Cruise Experience	400	NYR

OVERALL SCORE NYR points out of 2000

ence books), one dining room, an outdoor observation area, and a small boutique.

ACCOMMODATION. The price depends on the size, location, and grade. From the smallest interior (no-view) cabin to the largest, the 50 cabins are small, with limited storage space and compact bathrooms with small shower enclosure. Some have windows, and some have portholes; the walls are plain, as is the lighting.

DINING. The (tablecloth-less) dining room hosts all participants and expedition staff; it's a little rustic.

ENTERTAINMENT. After-dinner talk, or choose one of the reference books in the library.

SPA/FITNESS. There is a small fitness room and a sauna.

MAJESTY OF THE SEAS
★★★+

THIS OLDER BUT REVITALIZED FAMILY-FRIENDLY SHIP IS ADEQUATE FOR A FIRST CRUISE

Size:	Mid-size Ship	Passenger/Crew Ratio (lower beds):	2.8
Tonnage:	73,941	Cabins (total):	1,190
Cruise Line:	Royal Caribbean International	Size Range (sq ft/m):	118.4–670.0/11.0–62.2
Former Names:	none	Cabins (for one person):	0
Builder:	Chantiers de l'Atlantique (France)	Cabins with balcony:	63
Entered Service:	Apr 1992	Cabins (wheelchair accessible):	4
Length (ft/m):	879.9/268.2	Wheelchair accessibility:	Fair
Propulsion/Propellers:	diesel/2	Elevators:	11
Total Crew:	827	Casino (gaming tables):	Yes
Passengers (lower beds):	2,380	Self-Service Launderette:	No
Passenger Space Ratio (lower beds):	30.8	Onboard currency:	US$

THE SHIP. *Majesty of the Seas* looks a bit tired, although a 2016 refresh helped lift it a little. The open deck space is cramped when full, although there appears to be plenty of it; in the refit three waterslides (Cyclone, Supercell, and Typhoon), plus water cannons and a tipping bucket, were added to an outdoor AquaPark.

The interior layout is a little awkward, because it was designed (cleverly, actually) in a vertical stack, with most public rooms located aft, and accommodation forward. There's a decent array of public rooms (although the decor is from the Ikea school of interior design), including shops with lots of tacky merchandise, a library, Boleros (Latin) Lounge, Schooner Bar (a nautical-themed hangout), and a casino (with gaming tables and slot machines). There's a decent range of children's and teens' programs (teens have their own chill-out room – adults not allowed) and youth counselors.

There is often a long wait for elevators, particularly at peak times after dinner, shows, and talks (at least the restrooms are quite welcoming).

The dress code is casual, and the crew is friendly and attentive. Overall, you will be overwhelmed by the public spaces and underwhelmed by the size of the cabins. Note that there is constant background music in the corridors, elevators, and on the lido (pool) deck.

BERLITZ'S RATINGS

	Possible	Achieved
Ship	500	253
Accommodation	200	88
Food	400	194
Service	400	221
Entertainment	100	52
Cruise Experience	400	209

OVERALL SCORE 1017 points out of 2000

ACCOMMODATION. There are numerous accommodation price grades. From the smallest interior (no-view) cabin to the largest suite, the price you pay depends on the size, location, and grade you choose.

The majority of outside-view and interior (no-view) cabins are extremely small, although an arched window treatment and colorful soft furnishings give the illusion of more space. Almost all have twin beds convertible to queen-size, with moveable bedside tables, and flat-screen TVs. There is little closet and drawer space – you will need some luggage engineering to stow your cases. So, pack only minimal clothing – just what you really need for a short cruise. All cabins have a bathroom with ultra-compact shower enclosure, toilet, and washbasin. Suite-grade occupants get more space, a queen-sized bed, and larger bathroom.

DINING. There are two main dining rooms: Moonlight, on the lowest atrium (Centrum) level lobby, and Starlight, one deck above. When you book, choose early or late seating, or 'My Time Dining' (eat when you want, during dining-room hours), at tables for two to eight. The food operation is well orchestrated, with emphasis on highly programmed, extremely hurried service that many find insensitive.

For casual self-serve breakfasts and lunches, Windjammer Marketplace is split into various areas, including American, Asian, Latin, and Mediterranean fare. Compass Deli is where you can 'build' your own sandwich.

Themed specialty (extra-cost) dining spots include: Giovanni's Table (for Italian trattoria-style favorites); Izumi (for Japanese-style bites) and Sabor (for a taste of Mexico).

Johnny Rockets is a 1950s retro diner for fast foods (burgers, hot dogs, sodas, and shakes), located on an upper deck section of the Windjammer Marketplace (a cover charge applies).

At no extra cost, try Sorrento's for American-Italian pizzas.

Café Latte-tudes, in the lobby, features Starbucks cost-extra coffees in paper cups, free desserts and pastries. And for ice cream lovers, there's Freeze Ice Cream.

ENTERTAINMENT. The Chorus Line (show-lounge) has 1,027 seats on two levels; it has banquette seating, but many pillars prevent good sight lines from many side seats on the lower level.

SPA/FITNESS. Spa del Mar has a workout room with aft views, an aerobics studio, a beauty salon, a sauna, and body-pampering treatment rooms. For active types, there is a rock-climbing wall with several separate climbing tracks. It is located outdoors aft of the funnel, as is a basketball court – and shuffleboard.

MAJESTIC PRINCESS
★★★★

THIS MULTI-CHOICE, FAMILY-FRIENDLY RESORT SHIP HAS CONTEMPORARY ASIAN STYLING

Size:	Large Resort Ship
Tonnage:	144,216
Cruise Line:	Princess Cruises
Former Names:	none
Builder:	Fincantieri (Italy)
Entered Service:	Apr 2017
Length (ft/m):	1,082.6/330.0
Propulsion/Propellers:	diesel-electric/2
Total Crew:	1,346
Passengers (lower beds):	3,560
Passenger Space Ratio (lower beds):	40.5
Passenger/Crew Ratio (lower beds):	2.6/1
Cabins (total):	1,780
Size Range (sq ft/m):	163–1,279/15.1–118.8
Cabins (for one person):	0
Cabins with balcony:	1,438
Cabins (wheelchair accessible):	36
Wheelchair accessibility:	Best
Elevators:	14
Casino (gaming tables):	Yes
Self-Service Launderette:	Yes
Onboard currency:	US$

THE SHIP. Although large, the ship's profile, which is tailored somewhat for the Asian/Chinese market has a decent balance. In terms of practical design, the lifeboats are located outside the main public room areas, so they don't impair the view from balcony cabins. There is a complete walk-around promenade deck.

The over-the-water SeaWalk, an open deck glass-bottomed enclosed walkway (introduced in 2013 aboard *Royal Princess*) on the starboard side extends almost 30ft (9.2m) and forms part of a lounge/bar venue. It's the place to view the sea 128ft (39m) below, so you *can* 'walk' on water (well, over it).

There are two principal stair towers and elevator banks, plus four panoramic-view elevators in a third, central bank (these elevators do not go between decks 7 and 16 – stairways are only at the forward and aft elevator banks).

The interior decor includes an abundance of bright colors to suit Chinese tastes. This ship features a large amount of space dedicated to gaming, including VIP and private gaming rooms (for high rollers).

The Piazza Atrium is the ship's multi-faceted, multi-level social and dining hub, with a horseshoe-shaped flowing stairway and four panoramic elevators. The base level includes the Harmony Chinese Restaurant and large International Café.

Princess Cruises delivers a consistent, well-packaged cruise vacation, with a range of entertainment

BERLITZ'S RATINGS

	Possible	Achieved
Ship	500	394
Accommodation	200	139
Food	400	268
Service	400	294
Entertainment	100	82
Cruise Experience	400	298

OVERALL SCORE 1475 points out of 2000

options, at an attractive price, for families. One downside (and a serious design flaw) is the lack of a central stairway above two of the main restaurants, which leads to severe crowding of the adjacent elevators.

ACCOMMODATION. There are six accommodation types and numerous price grades: (a) Grand Suite; (b) suites with balcony; (c) mini-suites with balcony; (d) deluxe outside-view balcony cabins; (e) outside-view cabins with balcony; and (f) interior cabins (no view). Pricing depends on two things: size and location. Outside-view cabins account for about 81 percent of all accommodation, and all have a small balcony; those located aft are the quietest and most sought-after. Some of the most sought-after suites are located aft, occupying the corner (port and starboard) positions.

All accommodation grades share energy-efficient key card-controlled lighting. All cabins have beds with upholstered headboards, wall-mounted flat-screen TV sets, 220v electrical socket, turn-down service, bathrobes (on request, unless you are in suite-grade accommodation), and toiletries. A hairdryer is provided, sensibly located at the vanity desk unit. Bathrooms have good shelf storage space for toiletries, and all have hand-held, flexi-hose showers, and decent shower enclosures.

DINING. There are three 'formal' main dining rooms (Allegro, Concerto, and Symphony), assigned according to your accommodation grade. The Harmony Chinese Restaurant, located off The Piazza (atrium) features Cantonese cuisine with menus designed by Richard Chen. Other restaurants and eateries clustered around various levels of The Piazza include La Mer features French bistro-style cuisine, with menus by three-Michelin-star chef Emmanuel Renaut; Alfredo's Pizzeria (named for Princess Cruises' executive chef Alfredo Marzi); the International Café (for extra-cost coffees and teas); and Vines Wine Bar (for wines and tapas).

Elsewhere, there's the Crown Grill, serving extra-cost steaks and seafood. For casual meals, there's a large self-serve buffet venue, World Fresh Marketplace, which offers food by theme and features active cooking stations.

ENTERTAINMENT. The Princess Theater (showlounge) is a two-deck-high venue for the colourful large-scale production shows that Princess Cruises is renowned for. There's also a 'Princess Live' auditorium for and other small-audience entertainment features.

SPA/FITNESS. Lotus Spa is located forward on the lower atrium level. Separate facilities for men and women include a sauna, steam room, and changing rooms; common facilities include a relaxation/waiting zone, body-pampering treatment rooms, and a gymnasium with the latest high-tech, muscle-pumping cardio-vascular equipment. Some fitness classes are free, while others cost extra. Children and teens have their own fitness rooms adjacent to their age-related facilities.

You can make online reservations for any spa treatments before your cruise, which could be a great time-saver, as long as you can plan ahead.

MARCO POLO
★★

A FAIRLY COMFORTABLE, CLASSIC, MODEST SHIP FOR FRUGAL CRUISERS

Size:	Mid-size Ship	Passenger/Crew Ratio (lower beds):	2.3
Tonnage:	22,080	Cabins (total):	425
Cruise Line:	Cruise and Maritime Voyages	Size Range (sq ft/m):	93.0–484.0/8.6–44.9
Former Names:	*Aleksandr Pushkin*	Cabins (for one person):	0
Builder:	VEB Mathias Thesen Werft (Germany)	Cabins with balcony:	0
Entered Service:	Apr 1966/Apr 2008	Cabins (wheelchair accessible):	2
Length (ft/m):	578.4/176.2	Wheelchair accessibility:	Fair
Propulsion/Propellers:	diesel(14,444kW)/2	Elevators:	4
Total Crew:	356	Casino (gaming tables):	No
Passengers (lower beds):	848	Self-Service Launderette:	No
Passenger Space Ratio (lower beds):	26.0	Onboard currency:	UK£

THE SHIP. Growing old gracefully, *Marco Polo* was built as one of five sister ships for the Russian/Ukrainian cruise fleet. Originally designed in 1966 to re-open the Leningrad to Montréal transatlantic route (inoperative since 1949), it has a 'real ship' profile, an extremely strong ice-strengthened hull, huge storage spaces for long voyages, thick, polished exterior wood railings, and, with a deep draft, it rides well in unkind sea conditions.

It passed to Norwegian Cruise Line in 1998, and in 2007 to Greek owners. In 2008, it operated under charter to Transocean Tours, who sub-chartered it to the UK's Cruise & Maritime Voyages. It received a £3 million refurbishment in 2009. It operates adults-only cruises from the UK (although during school vacation periods anyone 16 and over becomes an eligible passenger), with Tilbury (London International Cruise Terminal) as its home port.

Marco Polo has modern navigational aids and a biological waste treatment center, and carries 10 Zodiac landing craft for in-depth shore trips in eco-sensitive areas. There are two large, forward-facing open-deck viewing areas. The teakwood-decked aft swimming pool/Lido Deck area is kept in good condition. Joggers and walkers can circle around the ship – not on the promenade deck, but one deck above, although this goes past vast, noisy air intakes, and the walkway is narrow.

When you walk aboard, you feel a warm, homely ambience. There is a wide range of public rooms,

BERLITZ'S RATINGS		
	Possible	Achieved
Ship	500	229
Accommodation	200	101
Food	400	188
Service	400	207
Entertainment	100	48
Cruise Experience	400	193

OVERALL SCORE 966 points out of 2000

most of which are arranged on one deck, and a sense of spaciousness pervades, as most rooms have high ceilings. The interior decor is quite tasteful, with careful use of mirrored surfaces and colors that do not clash but aren't boring. Subdued lighting helps maintain an air of calmness.

Now over 50 years old, the ship is still in decent shape, and the interiors are constantly being refurbished and refreshed. It operates well-planned, destination-intensive cruises (mostly taken up by couples and solo travelers of mature years) and offers really good value for money in very comfortable, unpretentious but tasteful surroundings, while an accommodating crew helps to make a cruise a pleasant, no-hassle experience. Gratuities are automatically applied to your onboard account.

Niggles? There is no observation lounge with forward-facing views over the bows. There are many raised thresholds, so you need to be on your guard when walking through the ship – particularly when negotiating the exterior stairways.

ACCOMMODATION. The cabins, which come in various price grades, depending on location and size, are a profusion of different sizes and configurations. All are pleasingly decorated, practical units with good, solid, rich wood cabinetry, wood and mirror-fronted closets, adequate drawer and storage space, TV, thin cotton bathrobe (upper grades only), and bathroom-mounted hairdryer and non-vacuum, non-noisy toilets. Carpets, curtains, and bedspreads are all nicely color-coordinated. Weak points include extremely poor sound insulation between cabins – you can probably hear your neighbors brushing their hair – and the fact that the bathrooms are quite small.

The largest accommodation is found in two suites: Dynasty and Mandarin, on Columbus Deck. These have a separate living room, and marble bathroom with tub/shower, walk-in closet, refrigerator, TV and DVD player. Slightly smaller are two Junior Suites on Pacific Deck. All suites have superior locations with forward-facing views over the ship's bow.

Also, quite comfortable are the superior deluxe ocean-view cabins, with two lower beds (some convertible to a queen-size bed), marble bathroom with tub/shower, and refrigerator.

Some cabins have lifeboat-obstructed views. Avoid cabins 310/312; these are located close to the engine room doorway, with considerable noise. No cabins have a balcony – the ship was built for long-distance ocean/sea crossings before they became popular.

DINING. The Waldorf, in the ship's center, is nicely decorated in soft pastel colors. It functions well, but has a low ceiling, is noisy, and tables are close together. There are two seatings for dinner, with tables for two to 10, and good place settings/china. The food itself is of a modest standard, and lacks presentation, quality, and taste. The (mostly young) wines and prices are reasonable.

Marco's Restaurant is for informal self-serve breakfasts and lunches – there is seating inside as well as outdoors around the ship's single, aft swimming pool. On most evenings, it also becomes an alternative dining spot for about 75 people.

ENTERTAINMENT. The Marco Polo Lounge is the venue for shows and lectures. A single-level room, it has banquette seating and fairly decent sight lines, although several pillars obstruct the view from some seats. Entertainment is low-key and low-budget. There's live music (and some dancing) in several bars and cocktail lounges.

SPA/FITNESS. Built when spa and wellbeing facilities were not really standard features, a Health Spa was added in a refit. It is located aft on Upper Deck, with a small gymnasium, a beauty salon, a sauna, changing facilities, and body treatment rooms.

MARELLA CELEBRATION
★★★

A DATED, 'INCLUSIVE' FAMILY-FRIENDLY SHIP FOR A LOW-BUDGET FIRST CRUISE

Size:	Mid-size Ship
Tonnage:	33,930
Cruise Line:	Marella Cruises
Former Names:	*Celebration, Noordam*
Builder:	Chantiers de l'Atlantique (France)
Entered Service:	Apr 1984/May 2005
Length (ft/m):	704.2/214.6
Propulsion/Propellers:	diesel (21,600kW)/2
Total Crew:	520
Passengers (lower beds):	1,254
Passenger Space Ratio (lower beds):	27.0
Passenger/Crew Ratio (lower beds):	2.4/1
Cabins (total):	627
Size Range (sq ft/m):	140.0–430.0/13.0–40.0
Cabins (for one person):	0
Cabins with balcony:	26
Cabins (wheelchair accessible):	4
Wheelchair accessibility:	Fair
Elevators:	7
Casino (gaming tables):	Yes
Self-Service Launderette:	Yes
Onboard currency:	UK£

THE SHIP. This ship suits couples and solo travelers taking their first or second cruise, seeking a fairly modern but not glitzy ship. It is exclusively chartered by Marella Cruises (formerly Thomson Cruises), so most passengers will be British, typically over 55.

Marella Celebration has a good amount of open deck space, and traditional teakwood decks outdoors, which include a walk-around promenade deck. The ship, however, is dated and can suffer from vibration. It has a spacious interior design and layout. Public lounges include an Explorers' Lounge, Niggles include charges for shuttle buses in some ports, minimum linen changes, and the high cost of bottled water. Overall, it's a very pleasant ship (particularly for families with children) who don't need the bells and whistles of the really big ships but want a choice of dining venues, with (selected) drinks and gratuities included.

ACCOMMODATION. There are four accommodation grades: suite-grade, deluxe, outside, and interior (no view). Four cabins with great forward-facing views are designated for the passengers with disabilities. You can pre-book your preferred cabin for an extra fee. Cabins are adequately appointed and practically laid out. There is good counter but limited storage space, a large mirror, and a small bathroom. Some cabins have bathtubs; others have shower enclosures only. Some cabins have additional upper berths for a third/fourth person (useful for families with small children). Room service is provided 24/7, at extra cost. Note that cabin insulation

is poor. Some cabins on Mariner and Bridge decks have lifeboat-obstructed views.

DINING. The 600-seat Meridian Restaurant has warm decor, and operates in an open-seating arrangement. Although there are a few tables for two, most are for four to eight. Dinners typically include a choice of four mains. Children have their own menu. Dessert and pastry items will usually be of good quality, made for British tastes.

A small à la carte restaurant, Mistral's, is an intimate dining spot; reservations are required, and there's a per-person cover charge. It has superior food and service plus a more refined atmosphere. The Kora La restaurant features Asian cuisine.

The casual self-serve Lido Restaurant is active 24 hours a day. Each week a themed buffet may be offered. However, self-serve buffets are quite repetitive. On Lido Deck, the outdoor Terrace Grill provides fast-food grilled items, pasta at lunchtime, and pizza.

ENTERTAINMENT. The Broadway Show Lounge, located mid-ship, is a 600-seat venue for production shows. It is two decks high, and several pillars obstruct sight lines. Liberties is a multi-functional room for quizzes, dancing, karaoke, and a late-night disco. Bands and musical units provide live music in several lounges and bars.

SPA/FITNESS. Oceans Health Club has good ocean views. Facilities include an exercise room, a gym, men's and women's saunas, and body-treatment rooms.

MARELLA DISCOVERY
★★★+

TRY THIS LIVELY MID-SIZED SHIP FOR BRITISH FAMILY-FRIENDLY CRUISING

Size:	Mid-size Ship	Passenger/Crew Ratio (lower beds):	2.5
Tonnage:	69,492	Cabins (total):	915
Cruise Line:	Marella Cruises	Size Range (sq ft/m):	137.7–1,147.4/12.8–106.6
Former Names:	TUI Discovery, Splendour of the Seas	Cabins (for one person):	0
Builder:	Chantiers de l'Atlantique (France)	Cabins with balcony:	357
Entered Service:	Mar 1996/Jun 2016	Cabins (wheelchair accessible):	17
Length (ft/m):	867.0/264.2	Wheelchair accessibility:	Good
Propulsion/Propellers:	diesel (40,200kW)/2	Elevators:	11
Total Crew:	720	Casino (gaming tables):	Yes
Passengers (lower beds):	1,830	Self-Service Launderette:	No
Passenger Space Ratio (lower beds):	37.9	Onboard currency:	UK£

THE SHIP. *Marella Discovery,* now over 20 years old, has a fairly smart profile with a wavy blue-and-white hull paint job and nicely raked bow. Transferred to Marella Cruises from Royal Caribbean International in 2016 it was modified for British family cruising. The pool deck amidships overhangs the hull. Thanks to amidships engines, there's little noise and little vibration.

Finger-touch digital screens help you find your way around. Natural light is brought inside in many places, with lots of glass to connect you with the sea. A sliding glass roof over one of two pools provides a multi-activity, all-weather indoor/outdoor area (the Glass House). Two public room decks host many of the lounges, bars, and shops (children's facilities are separate), while a seven-deck-high atrium lobby is the focal point and *the* social meeting place.

Niggles include intrusive music, and the high cost of bottled water. Overall, it's a very pleasant ship – particularly for families with children who don't need the bells and whistles of larger ships but want a choice of (extra-cost) dining venues, with selected drinks (premium brands are at extra cost) and gratuities included.

ACCOMMODATION. There are numerous cabin price grades, depending on size and location. All cabins have an infotainment system, sitting area, twin beds convertible to double configuration, and ample closet and drawer space, although there's little room around the bed, and the shower enclosure is cramped.

Some cabins have a larger wheelchair access door in addition to the cabins for mobility-limited passengers,

BERLITZ'S RATINGS		
	Possible	Achieved
Ship	500	324
Accommodation	200	123
Food	400	242
Service	400	254
Entertainment	100	64
Cruise Experience	400	254
OVERALL SCORE 1261 points out of 2000		

and the ship is mostly accessible, with good ramped areas and sloping decks. Cabin 8500 (the largest), is a fine, well-deigned living space. It has a baby grand piano and whirlpool bathtub. Most cabins, however, are pretty small.

DINING. 47o (main dining room) has two-deck-high glass side walls with ocean views. The food is similar to what you'd get in a decent family restaurant, but with better presentation, table settings, friendly service, and sauces and soups made from scratch. Part of the balcony level (Galleries 47o) becomes an Italian-style venue, with carbohydrate-rich Italian fare. Extra-cost, reservations-required venues include Surf 'n' Turf (for steaks and grilled seafood), Kora La (for pan-Asian-style cuisine), and a Sushi Bar. For casual eats, a large Islands self-serve buffet with indoor-outdoor seating can be cramped when busy. Outside on deck is Snack Shack, while deli-style eats can be had from the Glass House (solarium).

ENTERTAINMENT. The 802-seat Broadway Show Lounge has tiered seating and good sightlines from most seats. An orchestra pit can be raised or lowered as required. Some cabaret acts are featured in the 338-seat Live Lounge.

SPA/FITNESS. The small Oceans Spa, aft, has a fitness center, an exercise area, beauty salon, sauna, and several body treatment rooms. Sports facilities include a rock-climbing wall on the aft wall of the funnel, and an 18-hole mini-golf course and shuffleboard.

MARELLA DISCOVERY 2
★★★+

A SHIP WITH EUROPEAN DECOR FOR FAMILY-FRIENDLY BRITISH CRUISERS

Size:	Mid-size Ship
Tonnage:	69,472
Cruise Line:	Royal Caribbean International
Former Names:	*Legend of the Seas*
Builder:	Chantiers de l'Atlantique (France)
Entered Service:	May 1995
Length (ft/m):	867.0/264.2
Propulsion/Propellers:	Diesel/2
Total Crew:	726
Passengers (lower beds):	1,804
Passenger Space Ratio (lower beds):	38.4

Passenger/Crew Ratio (lower beds):	2.4
Cabins (total):	902
Size Range (sq ft/m):	137.7–1,147.4/12.8–106.6
Cabins (for one person):	0
Cabins with balcony:	231
Cabins (wheelchair accessible):	17
Wheelchair accessibility:	Good
Elevators:	11
Casino (gaming tables):	Yes
Self-Service Launderette:	NO
Onboard currency:	UK£

THE SHIP. *Marella Discovery 2* has a fairly modern profile and tiered stern, although its 'duck-tail' stern, fitted to aid stability, is unhandsome. The pool deck amidships overhangs the hull to provide an extremely wide deck, while still allowing the ship to navigate the Panama Canal. With engines placed midships, there is little noise, no noticeable vibration, and a fast operating speed.

The outside light is brought inside in many places. There's a single-level sliding glass roof over the more formal setting of one of two swimming pools, providing an all-weather indoor-outdoor area (Solarium). Inside, two full entertainment decks sit between five cabin decks, so there are plenty of public rooms to lounge and drink in. A seven-deck-high Atrium (lobby) is the main focal point (it's *the* social meeting place), and connects with various lounges, bars, service counters, and a casino (with table gaming and slot machines). Set around the base of the funnel is a Sky Lounge, bar and an extra-cost à la carte restaurant.

Overall, *Marella Discovery 2* should provide a very pleasant cruise experience if you don't need the bells and whistles of the latest ships, but like several dining options, and contemporary bars and lounges. However, the ship is showing its age in some areas.

ACCOMMODATION. There are many different cabin price grades. Some cabins on Deck 8 have

BERLITZ'S RATINGS

	Possible	Achieved
Ship	500	355
Accommodation	200	128
Food	400	238
Service	400	259
Entertainment	100	70
Cruise Experience	400	261

OVERALL SCORE 1311 points out of 2000

a larger door for wheelchair access, and there are other cabins that are suitable for less-mobile passengers; the ship's open layout makes it easy to get around.

All cabins have a sitting area and a queen-sized bed, and there is ample closet and drawer space. Generally, there is very little space around the bed, though, and the showers could have been better designed (bathrooms are mostly really small, too).

The largest accommodation is the Royal Suite, which is well designed and nicely decorated, and even has a baby grand piano.

Dining. The 1,050-seat Main Restaurant has dramatic two-deck-high glass side walls. Part of the upper level is an Italian restaurant, Gallery 47o, for carbohydrate-rich cuisine.

Other eateries include an extra-cost, reservations-required, à la carte restaurant (part of the Sky Lounge – with great views high atop the ship).

Islands is a large self-serve eatery – like a food court – with good ocean views on three sides. However, there are mainly large tables, so table sharing is part of the experience; the food selection is adequate, nothing more.

Overall, it's a comfortable ship.

ENTERTAINMENT. The single-level Broadway Show Lounge seats 802, with tiered seating levels and good sight lines from almost all seats. A second entertainment lounge, the Lounge, is for cabaret acts, including late-night adult comedy.

Entertainment throughout is upbeat – in fact, it is difficult to get away from music and noise. There is even background music in corridors and elevators, and on the pool deck. If you want a quiet relaxing holiday, choose another ship.

SPA/FITNESS. Champneys Spa and Fitness Center has a small workout room, aft of the funnel, with a small selection of muscle-pump equipment. There is also an aerobics studio, a beauty salon, saunas for men and women, and rooms for body-pampering treatments. While the facilities are quite small compared with those aboard the company's newer ships, they are adequate.

MARELLA DREAM
★★★

THIS NOW QUITE DATED MID-SIZE SHIP IS FOR FRUGAL, FAMILY-FRIENDLY CRUISES

Size:	Mid-size Ship	Passenger/Crew Ratio (lower beds):	2.5/1
Tonnage:	54,763	Cabins (total):	753
Cruise Line:	Marella Cruises	Size Range (sq ft/m):	129.1–425.1/12.0–39.5
Former Names:	... Costa Europa, Westerdam, Homeric	Cabins (for one person):	18
Builder:	Meyer Werft (Germany)	Cabins with balcony:	0
Entered Service:	May 1986/Dec 2010	Cabins (wheelchair accessible):	4
Length (ft/m):	797.9/243.2	Wheelchair accessibility:	Fair
Propulsion/Propellers:	diesel (23,830kW)/2	Elevators:	7
Total Crew:	600	Casino (gaming tables):	Yes
Passengers (lower beds):	1,506	Self-Service Launderette:	Yes
Passenger Space Ratio (lower beds):	36.3	Onboard currency:	UK£

THE SHIP. *Marella Dream* is good for families with children of all ages. Originally *Homeric* for the long-defunct Home Lines, the ship was acquired by Marella Cruises (formerly Thomson Cruises) in 2009 and extensively refurbished to cater to the company's mainly British clientele.

There is good exterior teak decking, and a walk-around promenade deck, plus decent space for sunbathing. There is also a (very small) pool. There are several bars and lounges, shops, plus lots of nooks and crannies to relax in, including a library/Internet lounge, and card room.

Marella Dream has a decent amount of space for children's facilities.

Passenger niggles include poor exterior area maintenance, not enough elevators, irritating announcements, expensive shore excursions, lack of an observation lounge, and the high cost of bottled water. Overall, it's a very pleasant ship (particularly for families with children) who don't need the bells and whistles of the really big ships but want a choice of dining venues, with (selected) drinks and gratuities included.

ACCOMMODATION. Suites, mini-suites, outside-view cabins, and interior (no-view) cabins are priced according to grade, size, and location. You can pre-book your preference for a per-cabin fee. Except for suite categories, each with king-size beds, separate lounge area, and bathroom with full-size tub, almost all other cabins are of a similar size. Some larger cabins have a sofa that turns into a bed.

BERLITZ'S RATINGS	Possible	Achieved
Ship	500	297
Accommodation	200	122
Food	400	223
Service	400	247
Entertainment	100	66
Cruise Experience	400	239
OVERALL SCORE 1194 points out of 2000		

Soundproofing is poor, however. Most cabins have twin beds, but some have berths (useful for families with small children). There are four cabins for passengers with disabilities; these are located on higher decks, close to the elevators.

DINING. The Orion Restaurant is a traditional dining venue with port and starboard-side portholes illuminated at night. Open seating is normal but tables are close together, and the noise level can be high. The cuisine is British-Continental, and there's plenty of it. However, it's all provided at a low price point; in other words, you get what you pay for.

The Grill is an extra-cost, reservations-required, à la carte steak and seafood restaurant, with tablecloths and candlelight dining. Andromeda Restaurant and Sirens Restaurant provide meals in a self-serve buffet setting, while a poolside Terrace Grill is for fast food (barbeque items, pizzas, pasta, and salads).

ENTERTAINMENT. Facilities include the Atlante Theatre, a two-deck-high showlounge. Pillars obstruct sight lines from some seats. A resident troupe present colorful, high-energy production shows and cabaret acts. A number of bands and small musical units provide live music in many lounges and bars, so there's always plenty of music to dance or listen to.

SPA/FITNESS. Oceans Spa, in an interior location, includes a gymnasium, saunas, and massage rooms. The facility is really small for the number of passengers carried.

MARELLA EXPLORER
★★★+

THIS SHIP HAS CONTEMPORARY STYLE FOR CASUAL, FAMILY-FRIENDLY CRUISING

Size:	Mid-size Ship	Passenger/Crew Ratio (lower beds):	2.4
Tonnage:	77,713	Cabins (total):	962
Cruise Line:	Marella Cruises	Size Range (sq ft/m):	127.2-1,054/16.0-98.0
Former Names:	Galaxy	Cabins (for one person):	0
Builder:	Meyer Werft (Germany)	Cabins with balcony:	430
Entered Service:	Dec 1996	Cabins (wheelchair accessible):	8
Length (ft/m):	865.8/263.9	Wheelchair accessibility:	Good
Propulsion/Propellers:	Diesel/2	Elevators:	10
Total Crew:	780	Casino (gaming tables):	Yes
Passengers (lower beds):	1,924	Self-Service Launderette:	No
Passenger Space Ratio (lower beds):	40.3	Onboard currency:	Euros

THE SHIP. *Marella Explorer* (originally built for Celebrity Cruises), was transferred in 2009 to then-newcomer TUI Cruises (part of the TUI Group – Europe's largest tour operator) but joined Marella Cruises in May 2018.

This mid-size ship has just about all you need for an enjoyable and rewarding family cruise experience; with 10 bars, four restaurants, six bistros, and good family facilities, it provides good value for money.

Although there are more than 4.5 acres (1.8 hectares) of space on the open decks, it can be cramped when the ship is full. Nice touches include two-person cabanas on an upper, outside deck; they have ocean views and are insulated from the life that goes on around the ship.

Inside, a four-deck-high main foyer houses the reception desk and shore-excursion station. There are a number of lounges, bars, shops, and facilities for children and teens.

Niggles include charges for shuttle buses in some ports, minimum linen changes, and the high cost of bottled water. Overall, it's a very pleasant ship for those (particularly for families with children) who don't need the bells and whistles of the really big ships but want a choice of dining venues, with (selected) drinks and gratuities included. The ship has a contemporary environment, good itineraries and food, and British-style service from a hotel crew that delivers good value.

ACCOMMODATION. There are several price grades, depending on the size and location of your liv-

BERLITZ'S RATINGS

	Possible	Achieved
Ship	500	328
Accommodation	200	124
Food	400	244
Service	400	267
Entertainment	100	64
Cruise Experience	400	256

OVERALL SCORE 1283 points out of 2000

ing space, but the accommodation is comfortable. Every cabin has its own Nespresso machine, with two free coffee pods.

The standard outside-view/interior (no-view) cabins are of a decent size and are nicely furnished, with twin beds convertible to a queen-size bed. Bathrooms have generous-size showers, hairdryers, and space for personal toiletries. Baby-monitoring telephones are provided. There are several cabins for solo travelers.

Most Deck 10 suites/cabins are of generous proportions and have balconies with full floor-to-ceiling partitions and large flat-screen infotainment screens.

Two Penthouse Suites amidships are the largest accommodation. Each has a butler's pantry, and an interconnecting door for linking to the adjacent suite.

Most suites with balconies have floor-to-ceiling windows and sliding balcony doors, while a few have outward opening doors. Suite occupants get special cards to open their doors, plus several extra perks and access to a private 100-seat concierge lounge/bar and social venue atop the ship, with ocean views.

DINING. Restaurants and bistros range from self-serve buffet style to service. There is no pre-defined seating, so you can dine when you want, and with whomever you want – good for multigenerational families. The emphasis is on healthy food, including power food, brain food, soul food, and even erotic food.

The Atlantik Restaurant is a two-level dining hall – reminiscent of the dining halls aboard 1930s ocean liners – with a grand stairway that flows between both levels and perimeter alcoves with intimate dining spaces. Tables are for two to 10.

Other dining venues/eateries include:

The Dining Club, an extra cost reservations-only venue, with a calming, restful wood-laden interior, where high-quality dining and service are featured.

Surf 'n' Turf Steakhouse is an extra-cost, reservations-required venue featuring premium steaks and grilled seafood.

Umi Sushi (for nigiri rolls, sushi, and sashimi); Kora La (for Asian-style curries and noodle dishes); and Coffee Port (lounge) set around the atrium lobby (for specialty coffees and pastries).

For casual breakfasts and lunches, head to the two-level, self-serve Marketplace Buffet, which has several serving counters and 'active' food islands, wood-accented decor, and eight bay windows.

Aft of the buffet is The Mediterranean, home to Mediterranean Tapas & Hot Stone eatery, and the Mediterranean Italian eatery.

ENTERTAINMENT. The 927-seat Broadway Show Lounge spans two decks, with seating on both main and (cantilevered) balcony levels; there are good sight lines from all seats. It has a revolving stage, 'hard' curtain, and large fly tower.

SPA/FITNESS. Champneys Spa includes a large fitness/exercise area with the latest machines and exercise bikes, a beauty salon, thalassotherapy pool, body treatment rooms, and a Rasul room (for mud and gentle steam bathing). Ocean-view private 'spa suites' can be rented.

MARELLA EXPLORER 2
★★★+

THIS STYLISH MID-SIZE SHIP IS FOR ADULTS-ONLY CRUISING IN COMFORTABLE SURROUNDINGS

Size:	Mid-size Ship	Passenger/Crew Ratio (lower beds):	2.0
Tonnage:	71,545	Cabins (total):	907
Cruise Line:	Marella Cruises	Size Range (sq ft/m):	168.9–1,514.5/15.7–140.7
Former Names:	*Century*	Cabins (for one person):	0
Builder:	Meyer Werft (Germany)	Cabins with balcony:	386
Entered Service:	Dec 1995	Cabins (wheelchair accessible):	8
Length (ft/m):	807.1/246.0	Wheelchair accessibility:	Good
Propulsion/Propellers:	Diesel/2	Elevators:	9
Total Crew:	858	Casino (gaming tables):	Yes
Passengers (lower beds):	1,814	Self-Service Launderette:	No
Passenger Space Ratio (lower beds):	39.4	Onboard currency:	Euros

THE SHIP. *Marella Explorer 2*, originally built as *Mercury* for Celebrity Cruises but recently operating in the Chinese domestic cruise market, is being extensively refurbished and started operations for the UK's Marella Cruises in May 2019 as an all-inclusive, adults-only ship.

The exterior profile is quite well balanced, despite its squared-off stern (back). With a decent passenger/space ratio, there is no sense of crowding. There is a good amount of open deck space, a pool with a sliding glass roof (Magrodome), a bi-level teakwood promenade deck, and a jogging track atop the ship. A premium (extra-cost) sunbathing space – The Verandah – is also available, with (extra-cost) 'exclusive' cabanas.

Inside, the focal point is an atrium lobby that is three decks high; it is calm, relaxing, and elegant, and not at all glitzy. In fact, many public rooms have ceilings that are quite high, providing a sense of space. An observation lounge (Indigo) has great views, but there are several other lounges and bars, plus a casino with gaming tables and slot machines.

What is it like? Adults-only ships are increasing in popularity as cruise audiences mature and now like to have a child-free environment to cruise with, preferably in a smaller ship rather than the really large family-friendly ships (also, many people have downsized from the large resort ships). However, the cost of add-ons (sparkling wine at embarkation, Verandah Cabanas, Champagne Breakfast, upgrading your accommodation deck etc.) can quickly add up.

BERLITZ'S RATINGS		
	Possible	Achieved
Ship	500	334
Accommodation	200	126
Food	400	245
Service	400	257
Entertainment	100	66
Cruise Experience	400	259

OVERALL SCORE 1287 points out of 2000

ACCOMMODATION. There are numerous grades, with many different configurations. All cabins have well-made wood cabinetry, personal safe, minibar/refrigerator, and interactive infotainment systems; beds have duvets. Suites have balconies have floor-to-ceiling windows and sliding doors, although a few cabins have outward-opening doors.

DINING. A grand staircase connects the upper and lower levels of the bi-level Latitude 53 restaurant; huge windows look aft, and several support pillars obstruct sight lines. The food is almost totally geared to British tastes (with a nod to Mediterranean fare), and tables are for two to 10.

Casual self-serve eats can be taken in The Marketplace and The Mediterranean (these are different names for what is essentially the same venue).

Extra-cost reservations-required dining venues include: The Dining Club (a fine-dining venue); Surf 'n' Turf Steakhouse (for premium steaks and grilled seafood); and Kora La (for Asian-style cuisine).

ENTERTAINMENT. The Broadway Show Lounge is a well-designed, two-level, 1,000-seat showlounge, with balcony alcoves on both sides. It has a large stage and a split orchestra pit (hydraulic).

SPA/FITNESS. Champneys Spa has a good amount of space dedicated to wellbeing and body treatments. It includes a large fitness/exercise area, with high-tech muscle-pumping exercise equipment, a thalassotherapy pool, Rasul chamber, and several treatment rooms.

MARINA
★★★★+

THIS SHIP PROVIDES PREMIUM COUNTRY CLUB STYLE FOR MATURE-AGE CRUISERS

Size:	Mid-size Ship	Passenger/Crew Ratio (lower beds):	1.5
Tonnage:	66,084	Cabins (total):	629
Cruise Line:	Oceania Cruises	Size Range (sq ft/m):	172.2–2,000/16.0–185.0
Former Names:	none	Cabins (for one person):	0
Builder:	Fincantieri (Italy)	Cabins with balcony:	593
Entered Service:	Jan 2011	Cabins (wheelchair accessible):	6
Length (ft/m):	776.5/236.7	Wheelchair accessibility:	Good
Propulsion/Propellers:	diesel-electric/2	Elevators:	6
Total Crew:	800	Casino (gaming tables):	Yes
Passengers (lower beds):	1,258	Self-Service Launderette:	Yes
Passenger Space Ratio (lower beds):	52.5	Onboard currency:	US$

THE SHIP. *Marina* is the first new-build for this growing small cruise line. Its profile is quite handsome, with a nicely rounded front and a swept-back funnel. It can cruise at a speed 25 percent faster than the smaller ships.

Oceania Cruises has been successful in keeping the warm and tasteful 'country house' decor style for which it has become known, together with an uncomplicated layout.

The interior focal point is the stunning wrought-iron and Lalique glass horseshoe-shaped staircase in the main lobby. Public rooms include nine bars and lounges, including a 2,000-book library on the port side of the funnel housing, while the Monte Carlo Casino has its own soft lavender-colored Casino Bar.

The Culinary Center, a cooking demonstration kitchen with 24 workstations run in conjunction with the US-based *Bon Appétit* magazine, incurs a fee for each of several cookery classes, but you get to eat your creations. The Artist's Loft hosts constantly changing artists – bring your own paintbrushes. If you like art, look for the genuine Picassos on board; there are 16 of them, including six in the casino.

The dress code is country club – no pajamas or track suits, but no ties, either. Note that a gratuity of 18 percent is added to bar and spa accounts.

Marina is really comfortable, although you will need to walk a little more than on many cruise ships. It will suit mature-age adults who appreciate qual-

BERLITZ'S RATINGS		
	Possible	Achieved
Ship	500	420
Accommodation	200	169
Food	400	309
Service	400	307
Entertainment	100	77
Cruise Experience	400	312

OVERALL SCORE 1594 points out of 2000

ity and style, with plenty of space, plus excellent cuisine and service, in an informal setting with realistic pricing.

In 2012, some of the modifications made when building its close sister *Riviera* were incorporated in its first drydocking; these include better lighting and deeper drawers in suites/cabins, teak decking, plus hand-held shower hoses in suites with bathtubs, and chandeliers in public rooms. Overall, a cruise aboard Marina is a very pleasant experience.

ACCOMMODATION. There are several price categories, including four suite grades: Owner's Suite; Oceania Suite; Vista Suite; and Penthouse Suite. There are four cabin grades: concierge-level veranda cabin; veranda cabin; deluxe ocean-view cabin; and interior cabin. Price depends on size and location, but all have one thing in common – a good-size bathroom with tub, and separate (but small) shower enclosure, plus two toiletry cabinets.

Around 96 percent of all accommodation has teak-decked balconies. The decor includes browns, creams, and white – earthy colors that don't jar the senses. All suites and cabins have dark wood cabinetry with rounded edges.

Standard veranda cabins measure 282 sq ft (26 sq m). Veranda and Concierge-level cabins have a sitting area and teak balcony with faux wicker furniture. Concierge-level grades receive L'Occitane toiletries.

Penthouse Suites measure 420 sq ft (39 sq m) with living/dining room separate from the sleeping area, walk-in closet, and bathroom with a double vanity.

Oceania Suites measure about 1,030 sq ft (96 sq m).

Vista Suites range from 1,200 to 1,500 sq ft (111–139 sq m).

At more than 2,000 sq ft (186 sq m), the Owner's Suite spans the ship's entire beam. It is decked out in furniture, fabrics, lighting, and bedding from the Ralph Lauren Home collection, with design by New York-based Tocar, Inc. It is outfitted with a Yamaha baby grand piano, private fitness room, laptop computers, Bose audio system, and a teak-decked balcony with Jacuzzi tub.

Suite-category occupants get Champagne on arrival, 1,000-thread-count bed linen, large plasma TV sets, Hermès and Clarins bath products, butler service, en-suite delivery from any of the restaurants, and priority check-in, early embarkation, and priority luggage delivery. Amenities include Tranquility beds, Wi-Fi laptop computer, refrigerated minibar with unlimited free soft drinks and bottled water replenished daily, personal safe, writing desk, cotton bathrobes, slippers, and marble and granite bathroom.

Occupants of Owner's, Vista, Oceania, and Penthouse suites can enjoy in-suite course-by-course dining from any restaurant menu, making private dining possible as a change to being in the restaurants.

Some grades get access to an Executive Lounge or Concierge Lounge. These are great little hideaways, with sofas, Internet-connect computers, Continental breakfast items, soft drinks, and magazines. Self-service launderettes are on each accommodation deck, which is useful for long voyages.

DINING. Six open-seating dining venues provide choice, enough even for long cruises, although banquette seating in some venues does not evoke the image of premium dining as much as individual seating. Also, it would be hard to describe some of the specialty dining venues as intimate. This is, however, a foodie's ship, with really high-quality ingredients and effectively fancy presentation. Particularly notable are the delicious breads, rolls, croissants, and brioches – all made on board from French flour and Isigny butter. The Grand Dining Room has 566 seats, and a delightful domed, or raised, central ceiling. Versace bone china, Christofle silver, and fine linens are used. Canyon Ranch Spa dishes are available at all meals.

French celebrity chef Jacques Pépin, Oceania's executive culinary director, has his first sea-going restaurant, Jacques, with 124 seats, antique oak flooring, antique flatware, and Lalique glassware. It offers fine dining in an elegant but informal setting, with roast free-range meats, classic French dessert items, and a choice of AOC cheeses.

Polo Grill, with 134 seats, features steaks and seafood, including Oceania's signature 32oz (900g) bone-in King's Cut prime rib. The setting is classic traditional steakhouse, with dark wood paneling and white tablecloths, although tables are a little close together.

Toscana, with 124 seats, features Italian-style cuisine, served on Versace china.

Privée, with seating for up to 10 in a private setting, invites exclusivity for its seven-course dégustation menu.

La Réserve offers a choice of two multi-course small-portion dégustation menus paired with wines. With just 24 seats, it's really intimate.

Terrace Café is the casual self-serve buffet-style venue (but with a low ceiling height, the noise level can be high); outdoors, as an extension of the café, is Tapas on the Terrace – good for light bites.

Red Ginger features 'classic and contemporary' Asian cuisine; the setting is visually refined, with ebony and dark wood finishes, but the banquette-style seating lets it down. Your waiter will ask you to choose your chopsticks from a lacquered presentation box.

The poolside Waves Grill, shaded from the sun, serves Angus beef burgers, fishburgers, veggie burgers, seafood, and other fast food, cooked to order.

Baristas coffee bar overlooks the pool deck and has excellent (and free) illy coffee. However, in the bars the tonic mixed with gin and vodka is of poor quality.

ENTERTAINMENT. The Marina Lounge spans two decks, with tiered amphitheater-style seating for 600. It's more cabaret-style entertainment than big production shows, in keeping with the cruise line's traditions, which suits the passenger clientele just fine.

SPA/FITNESS. Canyon Ranch SpaClub provides wellness and personal spa treatments. It includes a fitness center, beauty salon, several treatment rooms, thalassotherapy pool, sauna and steam rooms. A jogging track is located aft of the funnel, above two of the restaurants.

MARINER OF THE SEAS
★★★+

THIS LARGE RESORT SHIP IS FOR ENERGETIC FAMILY-FRIENDLY, ULTRA-CASUAL CRUISING

Size:	Large Resort Ship	Passenger/Crew Ratio (lower beds):	2.6
Tonnage:	137,276	Cabins (total):	1,557
Cruise Line:	Royal Caribbean International	Size Range (sq ft/m):	151.0–1,358.0/14.0–126.1
Former Names:	none	Cabins (for one person):	0
Builder:	Kvaerner Masa-Yards (Finland)	Cabins with balcony:	765
Entered Service:	Nov 2004	Cabins (wheelchair accessible):	26
Length (ft/m):	1,020.6/311.1	Wheelchair accessibility:	Best
Propulsion/Propellers:	diesel-electric (75,600kW)/3 pods (2 azimuthing, 1 fixed)	Elevators:	14
		Casino (gaming tables):	Yes
Total Crew:	1,185	Self-Service Launderette:	No
Passengers (lower beds):	3,114	Onboard currency:	US$
Passenger Space Ratio (lower beds):	44.0		

THE SHIP. *Mariner of the Seas* (a *Voyager*-class ship) is a large, floating leisure resort. It has a healthy passenger/space ratio and extensive facilities such as a regulation-size ice-skating rink.

In 2018, Sky Pad, a virtual reality trampoline, was added, as was The Perfect Storm (dual waterslides) and a FlowRide surfing simulator.

A stunning four-deck-high Royal Promenade is the main interior focal point; it's a fun place to hang out or meet friends. Imagine the length of two American football fields, with two 11-deck-high internal lobbies. Cafés, shops, and entertainment locations line this 'street,' and interior-view cabins look into it (an imaginative design). Arched across the promenade is a captain's balcony, while a central stairway connects with the deck below and the Schooner Bar (a piano lounge common to all RCI ships) and a large, flashy Casino Royale.

Other standouts include a regulation-size ice-skating rink (Studio B), with real ice, with 'bleacher' seating for up to 900 and broadcast facilities.

Expect lines for the reception desk, shore excursions, shore tenders, and in the self-serve buffet stations. Niggles include intrusive photographers, few quiet places to sit and read, no cushioned pads for deck sunloungers, small cabin 'bath' towels, noisy (vacuum) toilets, and frosted drinks in 'souvenir' glasses pushed to the hilt.

Service personnel are friendly, however, and the digital 'Wayfarer' system is informative, but the

BERLITZ'S RATINGS

	Possible	Achieved
Ship	500	343
Accommodation	200	132
Food	400	221
Service	400	278
Entertainment	100	71
Cruise Experience	400	250

OVERALL SCORE 1295 points out of 2000

speaking 'elevator going up/going down' becomes boring. Also, if you have a cabin with an interconnecting door to another cabin, be aware that you'll be able to hear your next-door neighbors.

Overall, this is a fine all-round ship for all age groups but be aware of the extra cost for many optional items (including drinks, drink packages, and excursions). Do budget extra for additional cost items and expect to be subjected to flyers and advertising promotions.

ACCOMMODATION. There is a wide range of cabin price grades, in four major groupings. Premium ocean-view suites and cabins, interior (atrium-view) cabins, ocean-view cabins, and interior cabins. Many cabins are of a similar size, and 300 have interconnecting doors (for families).

The standard outside-view and interior (no-view) cabin are of an adequate size (it's best not to bring many clothes), with just enough facilities to make them functional, but, overall, they're cramped.

Some grades have a refrigerator/minibar, crammed with 'take-and-pay' items.

Cabins with 'private balconies' aren't so private. The balcony decking is rubberized – not wood, though the balcony rail is wood. Cabin bath towels are small and skimpy. Room service offers a very basic menu.

Some 138 interior cabins have bay windows that look into the Royal Promenade. However, you need to keep the curtains closed in the bay windows, because you can be seen easily from adjacent bay windows.

Suites: Royal Suite, measuring 1,146 sq ft (106 sq m) is the largest private living space; Royal Family Suites (two aft on Deck 9, two aft on Deck 8), each measure around 574 sq ft (53 sq m); Owner's Suites are around 468 sq ft (43 sq m).

DINING. The main dining room, with a seating capacity of 1,900, is set on three levels: Rhapsody in Blue, Top Hat and Tails, and Sound of Music, all with the same menus and food. A dramatic staircase connects all three levels, but huge, fat support pillars obstruct sight lines from many seats. When you book, choose one of two timed seatings, or 'My Time Dining'. Tables are for 4 to 12 people. The place settings, chinaware, and cutlery are of good quality.

Main dining room cuisine is all about standardized banquet catering and batch cooking. Menu descriptions sound tempting, but the food, although prepared well enough, is just average. However, items such as lobster or filet mignon (steak) can be cooked to order at an extra cost. Green vegetables are scarce, but salad items are plentiful and desserts are pretty good. Rice features heavily. Breads and pastry items are not fantastic – the croissants lack any hint of butter. Vegetarian and children's menus are available. There are no wine waiters.

Dining options for casual and informal meals include: Promenade Café: for Continental breakfast, all-day pizzas, and specialty coffees (paper cups only). Windjammer Café, a large, sprawling venue for casual buffet-style, self-serve breakfast, lunch, and light dinners (but not on the last night of the cruise).

Also, Jamie's Italian (for bistro-style Italian fare), Chop's Grille (for premium steaks and seafood items), and Izumi Hibachi and Sushi (for Japanese-style eats) are extra-cost, reservations-required venues. Johnny Rockets, a retro 1950s eatery, has burgers, malt shakes, and jukebox hits, with indoor/outdoor seating. Sprinkles, located on the Royal Promenade, offers round-the-clock ice cream and yogurt, pastries, and (extra-cost) Starbucks coffee.

ENTERTAINMENT. The 1,350-seat Savoy Show-lounge is a stunning room, with a hydraulic orchestra pit, a huge stage, and excellent lighting. The company's entertainment is always upbeat.

SPA/FITNESS. Vitality at Sea Spa is reasonably large. It has an aerobics room, fitness center, treatment rooms, and sauna/steam rooms. There's also a Solarium (with sliding glass-dome roof) to relax in.

On the funnel's back is a 32.8ft (10m) rock-climbing wall, with five climbing tracks – it's a great buzz being 200ft (60m) above the ocean while the ship is moving. Other facilities include a roller-blading track, a full-size basketball court, and a nine-hole, par 26 golf course. A dive-and-snorkel shop provides equipment for rental, and dive classes.

MEIN SCHIFF 1
★★★★+

ÜBER-CASUAL, PREMIUM MULTI-CHOICE PLAYGROUND FOR GERMAN-SPEAKING FAMILIES

Size:	Large Resort Ship	Passenger/Crew Ratio (lower beds):	2.8
Tonnage:	111,500	Cabins (total):	1,447
Cruise Line:	TUI Cruises	Size Range (sq ft/m):	172.2-828.0/8.0-77.0
Former Names:	None	Cabins (for one person):	0
Builder:	Meyer Turku (Finland)	Cabins with balcony:	1,046
Entered Service:	May 2018	Cabins (wheelchair accessible):	12
Length (ft/m):	1,033.4/315.0	Wheelchair accessibility:	Good
Propulsion/Propellers:	diesel-electric/2	Elevators:	10
Total Crew:	1,000	Casino (gaming tables):	Yes
Passengers (lower beds):	2,894	Self-Service Launderette:	No
Passenger Space Ratio (lower beds):	38.5	Onboard currency:	Euros

THE SHIP. Building on the success, layout, and interior design of other ships in the fleet, *Mein Schiff 1* is slightly larger, longer, wider, and has more open deck space and more space for public rooms (plus a few extra passengers).

The propulsion system is extremely quiet, with no vibration anywhere, due to a pod propulsion system. It has an excellent spa, and younger cruisers will have an enthusiastic team of children's activity hosts to look after and entertain them (kids should keep a lookout for Captain Sharky). Standout facilities include a 25-meter swimming pool (half an Olympic-sized pool).

With 12 restaurants and bistros, 15 bars and lounges, and excellent entertainment facilities, there really is something for all members of the family. Included are favorites for passengers on the other ships (for example a fine Studio auditorium designed to a high acoustic specification – for classical concerts and cultural presentations), a shore-excursion information and booking lounge, an array of shops selling upscale items, plus a multitude of dining and eatery choices.

This is really a very comfortable, laid-back ship, with almost no sense of crowding anywhere – except perhaps for the pool deck on a sunny day. It has a number of proven passenger-friendly features, including water-dispenser units on each accommodation deck.

BERLITZ'S RATINGS	Possible	Achieved
Ship	500	435
Accommodation	200	162
Food	400	316
Service	400	328
Entertainment	100	83
Cruise Experience	400	311

OVERALL SCORE 1636 points out of 2000

ACCOMMODATION. There are numerous accommodation price grades. The price depends on the size, location, and grade you choose. From the smallest interior (no-view) cabin to the largest suite, there's something for all needs, including three types of family-friendly suites that can sleep up to six. All grades have a Nespresso coffee machine, hairdryer, and personal bathroom amenities. Also, note that all cabin doors open outwards, not inwards, and even-numbered cabins are on the starboard side – contrary to nautical tradition, with even-numbered lifeboats on the port side.

DINING. With a total of 12 dining venues and eateries (some at extra cost), there is plenty of choice for the whole family. Atlantik, the main restaurant, is included in the cruise fare. It is divided into three sections, each with a different menu: Classic (for dishes such as steak with roasted shallots and a chili-chocolate reduction); Mediterranean (for choices including homemade pasta); and Brasserie (French-style grilled fish and lamb with Provençal herbs, etc.).

The restaurant Gosch Sylt features fresh fish and well-prepared seafood dishes, with daily specials (including fresh oysters from the German island of Sylt, and lobster) listed on a blackboard.

Surf 'n' Turf Steakhouse features a large glass-enclosed cabinet for dry-aging meat (particularly for steaks. You choose your steak knife from a boxed selection of six.

Hanami (it means flower-watching – particularly cherry blossom) is an extra-cost Japanese restaurant (try the shabu-shabu beef), which incorporates a sushi bar.

The Day & Night Bistro provides regional and international snacks, including Currywurst, around the clock, while in the coffee lounge at the stern, baristas brew superb international coffees and present *Mein Schiff*'s own hand-crafted pralines and chocolates.

For something different, try one of three private barbecue stations (each seats up to six – excellent for a family, or for two or three couples); these are located outdoors on a small section of an aft deck (exclusive to *Mein Schiff 4*). They come with a superb selection of seafood and meat items, cooked right in front of you by a private chef (it's exclusive and great value).

A real bakery, an adjunct of the self-serve buffet restaurant Anckelmannsplatz, features freshly baked bread, rolls, paninis, cakes, and pastry items (including gluten-free selections). You can also buy artisan bread – specially baked and packaged on the last day of the cruise – to take home.

ENTERTAINMENT. The showlounge is quite stunning and spans three decks, with seating on all levels, and features colorful, on-trend production shows and major cabaret acts.

SPA/FITNESS. Spa and Meer wellness and fitness facilities are extensive and include a large (mixed-gender) sauna, steam rooms, and numerous body-pampering treatment rooms (including a private (rentable) spa room for couples, with integral sauna, massage tables, shower, and relaxation areas), a double-sided vertical wall of living plants, and juice/tea bar. The fitness room, with high-tech muscle-pump equipment, overlooks the main pool.

MEIN SCHIFF 2
★★★★+

THIS IS SUPER-COMFORTABLE CRUISING IN STYLE FOR GERMAN-SPEAKING FAMILIES

Size:	Large Resort Ship	Passenger/Crew Ratio (lower beds):	2.8
Tonnage:	111,500	Cabins (total):	1,447
Cruise Line:	TUI Cruises	Size Range (sq ft/m):	182.9-581.2/17.0-54.0
Former Names:	none	Cabins (for one person):	0
Builder:	Meyer Turku (Finland)	Cabins with balcony:	1,162
Entered Service:	Feb 2019	Cabins (wheelchair accessible):	12
Length (ft/m):	1,033.4/315.0	Wheelchair accessibility:	Good
Propulsion/Propellers:	diesel-electric/2	Elevators:	10
Total Crew:	1,000	Casino (gaming tables):	Yes
Passengers (lower beds):	2,897	Self-Service Launderette:	No
Passenger Space Ratio (lower beds):	38.5	Onboard currency:	Euros

THE SHIP. *Mein Schiff 2* is a sister ship to *Mein Schiff 1* and *Mein Schiff 7* (to debut in 2022), and has state-of-the-art environmental equipment, including catalytic convertors (also, the hotel department uses only GOTS certified organic cotton for its bed linen, bathrobes, and towels). This premium ship features a wide choice of dining venues, has an excellent spa, and, for younger cruisers, there's an enthusiastic team of children's activity hosts (kids should lookout for Captain Sharky).

Outdoors is a lap pool (at 82ft/25m it's long by cruise ship standards and half the length of an Olympic-sized pool) and adjacent hot tubs, plus a second, indoor-outdoor pool.

This ship has arguably the most restful interior decor and colors of all the ships in the fleet. It is instantly welcoming, and cossets you in contemporary comfort. With 12 restaurants and bistros, 15 bars and lounges, and excellent entertainment facilities, there really is something for all the family, including some extensive facilities and playrooms for children of all ages. Also included are favorites for passengers on the other ships (for example, a fine Studio auditorium designed to a high acoustic specification – for classical concerts and cultural presentations), a shore-excursion information and booking lounge, an array of shops selling upscale items, plus a multitude of dining and eatery choices.

BERLITZ'S RATINGS		
	Possible	Achieved
Ship	500	435
Accommodation	200	162
Food	400	316
Service	400	328
Entertainment	100	84
Cruise Experience	400	313
OVERALL SCORE 1638 points out of 2000		

This really is an easy-going, very comfortable ship, with almost no sense of crowding anywhere – although the pool deck is busy on sunny days. Perhaps the 'diamond in the crown' is a two-deck-high glass enclosure, with different restaurants and fine views aft. What makes a cruise aboard *Mein Schiff 2* really user-friendly for families is the inclusive pricing (but excluding spa treatments and excursions).

ACCOMMODATION. The cabins are well designed and practically laid out, with an excellent interactive infotainment system, a Nespresso coffee machine, hairdryer, several personal amenities, and a good amount of storage space (and much more in the larger categories and suites). There are numerous accommodation price grades. The price pay depends on the size, location, and grade you choose, from the smallest interior (no-view) cabin to the largest 'loft' suite with large terrace. A number of water-dispenser units are on each accommodation deck. A USB charge point is only on the back of the infotainment system.

Suite-grade accommodation occupants can access the X-Lounge, a combination lounge (with indoor/outdoor seating) and eatery (for self-serve breakfasts and lunches, and waiter served dinners). While one deck above is a grill area, bar, and an array of sunbeds.

DINING. Atlantic 'Classic' (for classic French and international cuisine) and Atlantic 'Brasserie' (with more emphasis on Mediterranean cuisine) are the two main dining rooms, in an open-seating format. There are 'speciality' restaurants and casual eateries, with many items included, and some at extra cost, although, from my experience, they provide excellent value, with high-quality ingredients.

The reservations-required Surf & Turf Restaurant has a large dry-aging meat cabinet within it. Smartphone-equipped waiters take orders, which are then digitally sent to the galley (kitchen), so the waiter stays at his station for you.

Manufaktur Kreativ-Küche is part cooking school and eatery, where you can choose ingredients, create something (under a chef's direction, of course), and then eat what you created; it's very entertaining. Adjacent is an Italian eatery, with some very tasty food.

Day & Night is a very popular bistro for around-the-clock regional and international snacks, including Currywurst and other home-comfort food items.

Ganz Schön Gesund ('Very Healthy') Bistro serves creative, mostly plant-based 'feel good food.'

Anckelmannsplatz is a self-serve buffet restaurant with a real bakery (Backstube), features freshly baked bread, rolls, paninis, cakes, and pastry items (including gluten-free selections). You can also buy artisan bread – specially baked and packaged on the last day of the cruise – to take home.

Fish Market is a fish and seafood venue, aft of Anckelmannsplatz, with an integral sushi bar.

Bosporus, outside on deck, is the place for donor kebabs and other Turkish favorites created to order, while Osteria is for hand-made pizzas, pasta, and other Italian culinary classics.

ENTERTAINMENT. The Theater seats around 1,000 in comfortable seats, for trendy production shows, with multiple LED backdrop screens and surround sound.

Something special is The Studio, a stunning small concert hall developed in conjunction with renowned acoustics experts. It provides an outstanding setting for live classical and jazz concerts, theatrical readings, lectures, and surround-sound movies. Also, there are live bands and musical units in various lounges.

SPA/FITNESS. Spa and Meer wellness and fitness facilities are extensive and include large (mixed-gender) saunas, steam rooms, and numerous body-pampering treatment rooms (including one for couples), relaxation area, and a large fitness room (with high-tech muscle-pump equipment).

MEIN SCHIFF 3
★★★★+

THIS STYLISH SHIP HAS IT ALL FOR YOUTHFUL GERMAN-SPEAKING FAMILIES

Size:	Large Resort Ship
Tonnage:	99,300
Cruise Line:	TUI Cruises
Former Names:	none
Builder:	STX Europe (Finland)
Entered Service:	May 2014
Length (ft/m):	967.8/295.0
Propulsion/Propellers:	diesel-electric (28,000kW)/2
Total Crew:	1,000
Passengers (lower beds):	2,506
Passenger Space Ratio (lower beds):	39.7
Passenger/Crew Ratio (lower beds):	2.5
Cabins (total):	1,250
Size Range (sq ft/m):	182.9–581.2/17.0–54.0
Cabins (for one person):	0
Cabins with balcony:	1,033
Cabins (wheelchair accessible):	10
Wheelchair accessibility:	Good
Elevators:	10
Casino (gaming tables):	Yes
Self-Service Launderette:	No
Onboard currency:	Euros

THE SHIP. Mein Schiff 3 is aimed at German-speaking families. Larger than Mein Schiff 1 and Mein Schiff 2, this ship incorporates the best of the previous two ships, and has added more facilities and tailored the design to its passengers' needs. Its new-generation propulsion system is stunningly quiet in operation, with absolutely no vibration anywhere.

A superb 82ft (25m) lap pool (long by cruise ship standards and half the length of an Olympic-sized pool) is featured outdoors, together with a large-scale movie screen and a spacious sports area for basketball and volleyball, while a second, indoor pool and adjacent hot tubs provide plenty of choice for families with children.

High up on Deck 14 is what's known as the Blue Balcony, a 118.4-sq-ft (11-sq-m) glass-floored platform some 121.3ft (37m) above the sea, which gives the sensation of floating over the ocean.

Public rooms are plentiful, and include a superb music academy-style concert hall (auditorium), which has been designed to the highest acoustic specifications.

What makes a cruise aboard Mein Schiff 3 really user-friendly for families is the inclusive pricing, though this excludes spa treatments, excursions, and the extra-cost restaurants: Richards Feines Essen, Blaue Welt Sushi Bar, Gosch Sylt, and a Surf 'n' Turf Steakhouse, among others. The dress code is smart-casual. But the real diamond in the crown is

BERLITZ'S RATINGS		
	Possible	Achieved
Ship	500	427
Accommodation	200	160
Food	400	313
Service	400	326
Entertainment	100	82
Cruise Experience	400	306
OVERALL SCORE 1614 points out of 2000		

the two-deck-high glass enclosure, which houses two restaurants – with great views over the ship's stern – and an outstanding barista-style coffee lounge.

Mein Schiff 3 has a really comforting feel, and boasts a number of outstanding passenger-friendly features, including: a half-Olympic sized swimming pool; water-dispenser units on each accommodation deck (special quartz crystals are provided for negative ion purification); vertical walls of living plants; a large meat-aging (proving) cabinet adjacent to the Surf 'n' Turf Restaurant; smartphone food ordering for waiters (sent electronically to the kitchen, so the waiter is always at his/her station to attend to passengers); a Nespresso coffee machine in every cabin; large spa and wellness facilities; a wide range of (included and extra-cost) dining venues and eateries; and a completely enclosed shore-excursion information and booking lounge. Plus, there's Captain Sharky to appeal to the kids.

ACCOMMODATION. A high percentage of all cabins have private balconies, and each one features a hammock. Likewise, every cabin comes with a Nespresso coffee machine.

Combination balcony cabins allow for interconnecting balconies, and a 'holiday home' package provides a Mein Schiff 3 chef to prepare a barbecue on the balcony grill.

Spa accommodation is located near the spa and part of a package that includes a massage for two in one of the most extensive wellness spa environments at sea.

A Captain's Suite, at 581.2 sq ft (54 sq m), is the largest suite aboard; appropriately, it's located near the navigation bridge. Meanwhile, each of the spacious Sea & Sky Suites has its own large roof terrace and private sunbathing and shaded areas, including a large hammock and upscale sunbeds. Premium veranda cabins offer large, diagonal terraces. Family-friendly suites sleep up to six (they come in three different types). All suites/cabins have Xbox game consoles.

DINING. With a choice of 11 dining venues, there really is plenty of choice. The Atlantik Restaurant is the ship's main restaurant. It is divided into three sections, and focuses on three styles of food: Classic, Mediterranean, and Eurasian. Five-course menus include antipasti, homemade pasta, grilled fish, and Asian dishes, and are part of the inclusive offering.

Aft is a 1,798-sq-ft (167-sq-m) multifaceted glass structure, nicknamed the 'diamond' and spanning two decks. Inside it are two restaurants: Richards Feines Essen for fine dining and the Surf 'n' Turf Steakhouse, which features a superb glass-enclosed meat dry-aging cabinet.

Hanami (it means flower-watching – particularly cherry blossom) is an extra-cost Japanese restaurant (try the shabu-shabu beef), which incorporates a sushi bar.

A real bakery, an adjunct of the self-serve buffet restaurant Anckelmannsplatz, features freshly baked crispy rolls, paninis, and cakes all day long. Already appearing aboard *Mein Schiff 1* and *Mein Schiff 2*, the popular informal Gosch Sylt now has about 130 seats aboard *Mein Schiff 3* (versus 88 seats aboard *Mein Schiff 1* and *Mein Schiff 2*), and offers fresh fish and well-prepared seafood dishes, with daily specials listed on a blackboard.

Day & Night Bistro provides regional and international snacks, including Currywurst, around the clock, while in a modern coffee lounge a barista brews international coffees and presents *Mein Schiff's* own hand-crafted pralines and chocolates.

ENTERTAINMENT. The Theater is the ship's showlounge. It is a three-deck venue with 949 seats, and features colorful, razzle-dazzle production shows and major cabaret acts.

What is really innovative, however, is a stunning concert hall/movie theater called Klanghaus, which was developed in conjunction with renowned acoustics experts from leading opera houses and concert halls. It provides a really fine setting for live classical and jazz concerts, theatrical readings, lectures, and movies with surround sound.

Numerous bands, small musical units, and solo musical entertainers provide live music in several of the lounge venues throughout the ship.

SPA/FITNESS. Spa and Meer wellness and fitness facilities are really extensive, and include a large (mixed-gender) sauna, steam rooms, and several body-pampering treatment rooms. They also include a private (rentable) spa room for couples, with integral sauna, massage tables, shower, and relaxation areas. Sports facilities include a large arena in the aft section of the ship for volleyball, basketball, and football.

MEIN SCHIFF 4
★★★★+

THIS IS LAID-BACK CRUISING IN STYLE FOR GERMAN-SPEAKING FAMILIES

Size:	Large Resort Ship	Passenger/Crew Ratio (lower beds):	2.5
Tonnage:	99,300	Cabins (total):	1,250
Cruise Line:	TUI Cruises	Size Range (sq ft/m):	182.9–581.2/17.0–54.0
Former Names:	none	Cabins (for one person):	0
Builder:	Meyer Turku (Finland)	Cabins with balcony:	1,033
Entered Service:	May 2015	Cabins (wheelchair accessible):	10
Length (ft/m):	967.8/295.0	Wheelchair accessibility:	Good
Propulsion/Propellers:	diesel-electric/2	Elevators:	10
Total Crew:	1,000	Casino (gaming tables):	Yes
Passengers (lower beds):	2,506	Self-Service Launderette:	No
Passenger Space Ratio (lower beds):	39.7	Onboard currency:	Euros

THE SHIP. *Mein Schiff 4*, the sister ship to *Mein Schiff 3*, is for youthful German-speaking families. Its latest-generation propulsion system is extremely quiet in operation, with no vibration anywhere. The premium ship features a wide choice of dining venues, has an excellent spa, and, for younger cruisers, there's an enthusiastic team of children's activity hosts (kids should keep a lookout for Captain Sharky).

BERLITZ'S RATINGS		
	Possible	Achieved
Ship	500	427
Accommodation	200	160
Food	400	313
Service	400	326
Entertainment	100	82
Cruise Experience	400	306
OVERALL SCORE 1614 points out of 2000		

A fine 82ft (25m) lap pool (long by cruise ship standards and half the length of an Olympic-sized pool) is outdoors (check out the meerkats), and a second, indoor, pool and adjacent hot tubs provide plenty of choice for families with children.

High on Deck 14 is 'Blue Balcony,' a 118-sq-ft (11-sq-m) glass-floored platform 121ft (37m) above the sea, giving the sensation of floating over the ocean.

There are numerous public rooms; these include a superb music academy-style concert hall (auditorium), designed to the highest acoustic specifications.

What makes a cruise aboard *Mein Schiff 4* really user-friendly for families is the all-inclusive pricing, though this excludes spa treatments, excursions, and the extra-cost restaurants: Richards Feines Essen, Blaue Welt Sushi Bar, Gosch Sylt, and a Surf 'n' Turf Steakhouse, among others. The dress code is smart casual. But the diamond in the crown, and with fine views over the ship's stern, is the two-deck high glass enclosure, which houses two different restaurants and a fine barista coffee lounge.

Mein Schiff 4, in keeping with sister *Mein Schiff 3*, feels comfortable and spacious. Its features include: the joint-longest swimming pool of any cruise ship; water-dispenser units on each accommodation deck (special quartz crystals are provided to add to the water pitcher for negative ion purification); vertical walls of living plants; a large meat-aging (proving) cabinet adjacent to the Surf 'n' Turf Steakhouse; and a Nespresso coffee machine in every cabin. The spa and wellness facilities are large and well run. With its included (and extra-cost) dining venues and eatery choices, this ship really delivers laid-back cruising with style.

ACCOMMODATION. The cabins are well designed, practically laid out, and the interactive infotainment system is excellent. Also, each comes with a Nespresso coffee machine, hairdryer, several personal amenities, and a decent amount of storage space (and much more in the larger categories and suites).

Combination balcony cabins allow for interconnecting units, and a 'holiday home' package provides a chef to prepare a barbecue on the balcony grill.

Spa accommodation is located adjacent to the spa and is available as part of a package that includes a massage for two in what is one of the most extensive wellness spa environments at sea.

A Captain's Suite, at 581 sq ft (54 sq m), is the largest suite; it is located near the navigation bridge.

Meanwhile, each of the spacious Sea & Sky Suites has its own large 312 sq ft (29 sq m) roof terrace and private sunbathing (including a large hammock, up-scale sunbeds, and shaded areas). Premium veranda cabins offer large, diagonal terraces, and there are three suite categories. Family-friendly suites sleep up to six (they come in three different types). One example measures about 452 sq ft (42 sq m), but there's also a huge balcony measuring 506 sq ft (47 sq m). The total adds up to a very large 958 sq ft (89 sq m). All come with Xbox game consoles.

DINING. With 11 dining venues (some at extra cost), there really is abundant choice. The largest is the Atlantik Restaurant, which is included in the cruise fare. It is divided into three sections, each with a slightly different menu: Classic – for dishes such as steak with roasted shallots and a chili-chocolate reduction; Mediterranean – for choices including homemade pasta; and Brasserie – for French-style grilled fish and meat dishes and herbs from Provence. Some dining venues have both indoor and outdoor seating – slightly different from *Mein Schiff 3*. Smartphones are provided to waiters for orders (digitally sent to the kitchen, so the waiter is always at his station to attend to you).

Aft is a 1,798-sq-ft (167-sq-m) multifaceted glass structure (the 'diamond'), spanning two decks. In-side is a spacious coffee and chocolate lounge and two restaurants: Richards Feines Essen for haute cuisine, and the Surf 'n' Turf Steakhouse, which fea-tures a large glass-enclosed meat dry-aging cabinet.

Hanami (it means flower-watching – particularly cherry blossom) is an extra-cost Japanese restau-rant (try the shabu-shabu beef), which incorporates a sushi bar.

A real bakery, an adjunct of the self-serve buf-fet restaurant Anckelmannsplatz, features freshly baked bread, rolls, paninis, cakes, and pastry items (including gluten-free selections). You can also buy specially packaged artisan bread to take home.

Gosch Sylt has about 130 seats and features fresh fish and well-prepared seafood dishes, with daily specials, such as supremely tasty oysters from the German island of Sylt itself, and lobster, all listed on a blackboard.

The Day & Night Bistro provides regional and in-ternational snacks, including Currywurst, around the clock, while in the coffee lounge at the stern, baristas brew superb international coffees and present *Mein Schiff*'s own hand-crafted pralines and chocolates, which are made in front of you.

For something different, book one of the three pri-vate barbecue stations (each seats up to six – excel-lent for a family, or for two or three couples); these are located outdoors on a small section of an aft deck (exclusive to *Mein Schiff 4*). They come with a superb selection of seafood and meat items, cooked right in front of you by a private chef (it's exclusive and great value).

ENTERTAINMENT. The Theater is the ship's showlounge. A three-deck venue with 949 seats, it features colorful, razzle-dazzle production shows and major cabaret acts.

What is really innovative, however, is the Klang-haus, a stunning small concert hall/movie theater developed in conjunction with renowned acoustics experts. It provides a really fine setting for live clas-sical and jazz concerts, theatrical readings, lectures, and movies with surround sound.

Numerous bands, small musical units, and solo musical entertainers provide live music in several of the lounge venues throughout the ship.

SPA/FITNESS. Spa and Meer wellness and fit-ness facilities are extensive, and include a large (mixed-gender) sauna, steam rooms, and several body-pampering treatment rooms. They also in-clude a private (rentable) spa room for couples, with integral sauna, massage tables, shower, and relaxation areas.

Sports facilities include a large arena in the aft section of the ship for volleyball, basketball, football, and stadium-style seating (look out for the big sun-glasses). Sport bikes are also carried for excursions.

MEIN SCHIFF 5
★★★★+

THIS FAMILY-FRIENDLY SHIP HAS SOME FINE FACILITIES AND A BUCKETFUL OF STYLE

Size:	Large Resort Ship	Passenger/Crew Ratio (lower beds):	2.5
Tonnage:	99,980	Cabins (total):	1,276
Cruise Line:	TUI Cruises	Size Range (sq ft/m):	182.9–581.2/17.0–54.0
Former Names:	none	Cabins (for one person):	0
Builder:	Meyer Turku (Finland)	Cabins with balcony:	1,033
Entered Service:	Jun 2016	Cabins (wheelchair accessible):	10
Length (ft/m):	967.8/295.0	Wheelchair accessibility:	Good
Propulsion/Propellers:	diesel-electric/2	Elevators:	10
Total Crew:	1,000	Casino (gaming tables):	Yes
Passengers (lower beds):	2,552	Self-Service Launderette:	No
Passenger Space Ratio (lower beds):	39.1	Onboard currency:	Euros

THE SHIP. *Mein Schiff 5* is a close sister ship to *Mein Schiff 3* and *Mein Schiff 4*, but with 16 more cabins. It is recommended for youthful German-speaking families. There is a wide choice of dining venues, has an excellent spa, and, for younger cruisers, there's an enthusiastic team of children's activity hosts (kids should keep a lookout for Captain Sharky). Also, the propulsion system is extremely quiet, with no vibration anywhere.

An outstanding 82ft (25m) lap pool (long by cruise ship standards and half the length of an 'Olympic'-sized pool) is outdoors – together with a large movie screen and sports area for basketball and volleyball.

High on Deck 14 (aft) is 'Blue Balcony,' a 118-sq-ft (11-sq-m) glass-floored platform 121ft (37m) above the sea, giving a sensation of 'floating' over the water.

There are numerous public rooms (in a slightly different arrangement to *Mein Schiff 3* and *Mein Schiff 4*); these include a superb Studio auditorium, designed to a high acoustic specification, a shore-excursion information and booking lounge, and shops selling upscale items.

What makes a cruise aboard *Mein Schiff 5* really user-friendly for families is the inclusive nature of the pricing, though this excludes spa treatments, excursions, and the extra-cost restaurants: Hanami Restaurant and Sushi Bar, Gosch Sylt, Surf 'n' Turf Steakhouse, and Schmankerl Osteria (for Austrian cuisine). The diamond in the crown is a two-deck-

BERLITZ'S RATINGS	Possible	Achieved
Ship	500	432
Accommodation	200	161
Food	400	314
Service	400	327
Entertainment	100	82
Cruise Experience	400	309
OVERALL SCORE 1625 points out of 2000		

high glass enclosure, which houses three different restaurants – with fine views over the ship's stern.

This is a very comfortable ship, with a laid-back feel, and little sense of crowding anywhere, except the pool deck on a sunny day. It boasts a number of outstanding passenger-friendly features, including water-dispenser units on each accommodation deck (special quartz crystals are provided in each cabin to add to the water pitcher for negative ion purification); a large dry-aging meat (proving) cabinet adjacent to the Surf 'n' Turf Restaurant; and smartphone food ordering for waiters – sent electronically to the galley (kitchen), so the waiter stays at his station to attend to you. The dress code is smart-casual.

ACCOMMODATION. There are numerous accommodation price grades; the price depends on the size, location, and grade you choose. Strangely, even-numbered cabins are on the starboard side – contrary to nautical tradition, with even-numbered lifeboats on the port side.

All accommodation grades have a Nespresso coffee machine, hairdryer, and personal bathroom amenities. Also, note that all doors open outwards, not inwards.

From the smallest to the largest, there's something for all needs, including three types of family-friendly suites that can sleep up to six. One example measures about 452 sq ft (42 sq m), plus an extensive balcony of 506 sq ft (47 sq m), totaling 958 sq ft (89 sq m).

Premium veranda cabins offer large, diagonal terraces, and there are three suite categories. Each of the spacious Sea & Sky Suites has its own large 312 sq ft (29 sq m) roof terrace, and private lounging/sunbathing space (including a large hammock, upscale sunbeds, and shaded areas). A Captain's Suite, at 581 sq ft (54 sq m), is the largest; it is located near the navigation bridge.

DINING. With a total of 12 dining venues (some at extra cost), there is plenty of choice. Atlantik, the main restaurant, is included in the cruise fare. It is divided into two, each with a different menu: Classic (for dishes such as steak with roasted shallots and a chili-chocolate reduction) and Mediterranean (for choices including homemade pasta).

Aft, a 1,798-sq-ft (167-sq-m) multifaceted glass structure (nicknamed the 'diamond') spans two decks. It contains three restaurants: Schmankerl (for Austrian regional specialties); Hanami, which means flower-watching (particularly cherry blossom), for pan-Asian cuisine and incorporating a sushi bar with sit-up stools; and Surf 'n' Turf Steakhouse, which features a large glass-enclosed meat dry-aging display cabinet with various cuts of beef, and an open-view kitchen.

Gosch Sylt has about 130 seats and features fresh fish and all kinds of well-prepared seafood dishes, plus daily specials (including fresh oysters from the German island of Sylt, and lobster), which are listed on a blackboard.

Day & Night Bistro provides regional and international snacks, including around-the-clock Currywurst, while in a coffee lounge baristas brew an array of superb international specialist coffees and also the ship's own hand-crafted pralines and truffle chocolates.

Osteria is for hand-made pizzas, pasta, and other Italian culinary favorites.

A real bakery, an adjunct of the self-serve, food court-style buffet restaurant Anckelmannsplatz, features freshly baked bread, rolls, paninis, cakes, and pastry items (including gluten-free selections). You can also buy artisan bread – specially baked and packaged on the last day of the cruise – to take home).

ENTERTAINMENT. The Theater is a three-deck-high showlounge with approximately 950 seats. It's used for colorful, trendy production shows and major cabaret acts.

What is really innovative is the Klanghaus concert hall/movie theater, developed in conjunction with renowned acoustics experts. It provides an outstanding setting for live classical and jazz concerts, theatrical readings, lectures, and movies with surround sound.

Numerous bands, small musical units, and solo musical entertainers provide live music in several of the lounges.

SPA/FITNESS. The Spa and Meer wellness and fitness facilities are extensive, and include a large (mixed-gender) sauna, steam rooms, and numerous body-pampering treatment rooms (including a private (rentable) spa room for couples, with integral sauna, massage tables, shower, and relaxation areas), a double-sided vertical wall of living plants, and juice/tea bar.

Sports facilities include a large arena in the aft section of the ship for volleyball, basketball, and football. Sport bikes are also carried.

MEIN SCHIFF 6
★★★★+

THIS FAMILY-FRIENDLY SHIP EXUDES CONTEMPORARY STYLE AND EXCELLENT DINING VENUES

Size:	Large Resort Ship	Passenger/Crew Ratio (lower beds):	2.5/1
Tonnage:	99,800	Cabins (total):	1,276
Cruise Line:	TUI Cruises	Size Range (sq ft/m):	182.9–581.2/17.0–54.0
Former Names:	none	Cabins (for one person):	0
Builder:	Meyer Turku (Finland)	Cabins with balcony:	1,033
Entered Service:	Winter 2017	Cabins (wheelchair accessible):	10
Length (ft/m):	967.8/295.0	Wheelchair accessibility:	Good
Propulsion/Propellers:	diesel-electric/2	Elevators:	10
Total Crew:	1,000	Casino (gaming tables):	Yes
Passengers (lower beds):	2,552	Self-Service Launderette:	No
Passenger Space Ratio (lower beds):	39.1	Onboard currency:	Euros

THE SHIP. *Mein Schiff 6*, sister to *Mein Schiff 5*, is for youthful German-speaking families. The propulsion system is extremely quiet, with no vibration anywhere. It has choice of dining venues, an excellent spa, and younger cruisers will have an enthusiastic team of children's activity hosts to look after and entertain them (kids should keep a lookout for Captain Sharky).

An outstanding 82ft (25m) outdoor lap pool (long by cruise ship standards and half the length of an Olympic-sized pool), together with a large movie screen and sports area for basketball and volleyball, while a second, indoor pool and adjacent hot tubs provide ample choice.

Outside on Deck 14 aft is 'Blue Balcony,' a 118-sq-ft (11-sq-m) glass-floored platform 121ft (37m) above the sea, for that floating over the water feeling.

There are numerous public rooms; these include a fine Studio auditorium designed to a high acoustic specification (for classical concerts and cultural presentations), a shore-excursion information and booking lounge, and an array of shops selling upscale items.

What makes a cruise aboard *Mein Schiff 6* really user-friendly for families is the inclusive pricing, though this excludes spa treatments, excursions, and the extra-cost restaurants: Hanami Restaurant and Sushi Bar, Gosch Sylt, Surf 'n' Turf Steakhouse, and Schmankerl Osteria (for Austrian cuisine). But the diamond in the crown is a two-

BERLITZ'S RATINGS		
	Possible	Achieved
Ship	500	432
Accommodation	200	161
Food	400	314
Service	400	327
Entertainment	100	82
Cruise Experience	400	310
OVERALL SCORE 1626 points out of 2000		

deck-high glass enclosure, which houses three different restaurants and has fine views over the ship's stern.

This is a very comfortable, laid-back ship, with almost no sense of crowding anywhere – except perhaps for the pool deck on a sunny day. It has a number of proven passenger-friendly features, including water-dispenser units on each accommodation deck (special quartz crystals are provided in each cabin to add to the water pitcher for negative ion purification); a large dry-aging meat (proving) cabinet adjacent to the Surf 'n' Turf Restaurant; and smartphone food ordering for waiters – sent electronically to the galley (kitchen), so the waiter stays at his station to attend to you.

ACCOMMODATION. There are numerous accommodation price grades, with the price dependent on the size, location, and grade you choose. Strangely, even-numbered cabins are on the starboard side – contrary to nautical tradition, with even-numbered lifeboats on the port side. All accommodation grades have a Nespresso coffee machine, hairdryer, and personal bathroom amenities. Also, note that all doors open outwards, not inwards.

From the smallest to the largest, there's something for all needs, including three types of family-friendly suites that can sleep up to six. One example measures about 452 sq ft (42 sq m), plus an extensive balcony of 506 sq ft (47 sq m), totaling 958 sq ft (89 sq m).

Premium veranda cabins offer large, diagonal terraces, and there are three suite categories. Each of the spacious Sea & Sky Suites has its own large 312 sq ft (29 sq m) roof terrace, and private lounging/sunbathing space (including a large hammock, upscale sunbeds, and shaded areas).

DINING. With a total of 12 dining venues and eateries (some at extra cost), there is plenty of choice. Atlantik, the main restaurant, is included in the cruise fare. It is divided into three sections, each with a different menu: Classic (for dishes such as steak with roasted shallots and a chili-chocolate reduction); Mediterranean (for choices including homemade pasta); and Brasserie (French-style grilled fish and lamb with Provençal herbs, etc.).

Aft, a 1,798-sq-ft (167-sq-m) multifaceted glass structure (nicknamed the 'diamond') spans two decks. Within it are three restaurants: Schmankerl (for authentic Austrian regional specialties in the setting of a real Austrian tavern); Hanami – it means flower-watching – particularly cherry blossom (for pan-Asian cuisine – do try the beef shabu-shabu); and Surf 'n' Turf Steakhouse, which features a large glass-enclosed meat dry-aging display cabinet various steak cuts, an open-view kitchen, and a choice of several different steak knives.

The casual restaurant Gosch Sylt has about 130 seats, and features fresh fish and well-prepared seafood dishes, with daily specials (including fresh oysters from the German island of Sylt, and lobster) listed on a blackboard.

Osteria is for hand-made pizzas, pasta, and other Italian culinary favorites.

A real bakery, an adjunct of the self-serve buffet restaurant Anckelmannsplatz, features freshly baked bread, rolls, paninis, cakes, and pastry items (including gluten-free selections). You can also buy artisan bread – specially baked and packaged on the last day of the cruise – to take home).

The Day & Night Bistro provides regional and international snacks, including Currywurst, around the clock, while in a delightful coffee lounge baristas brew an array of fine international specialist coffees, and chocolatiers also create the ship's own hand-crafted pralines and truffle chocolates.

ENTERTAINMENT. The Theater is the showlounge. It's a three-deck-high venue with approximately 950 seats, and features colorful, very trendy production shows and major cabaret acts.

What is really innovative is the Klanghaus concert hall/movie theater, developed in conjunction with renowned acoustics experts. It provides an outstanding setting for live classical and jazz concerts, theatrical readings, lectures, and movies with surround sound.

Numerous bands, small musical units, and solo musical entertainers provide live music in several of the lounges.

SPA/FITNESS. Spa and Meer wellness and fitness facilities are extensive and include a large (mixed-gender) sauna, steam rooms, and numerous body-pampering treatment rooms (including a private rentable spa room for couples, with integral sauna, massage tables, shower, and relaxation areas), a double-sided vertical wall of living plants, and juice/tea bar.

Sports facilities include a large arena in the aft of the ship for volleyball, basketball, and football. Sport bikes are also carried.

MEIN SCHIFF HERZ
★★★+

A STYLISH PREMIUM MID-SIZE SHIP THAT IS GOOD FOR THE WHOLE FAMILY

Size:	Mid-size Ship	Passenger/Crew Ratio (lower beds):	2.4
Tonnage:	77,713	Cabins (total):	956
Cruise Line:	Marella Cruises	Size Range (sq ft/m):	172.2–1,054.0/16.0–98.0
Former Names:	*Celebrity Mercury, Mercury*	Cabins (for one person):	0
Builder:	Meyer Werft (Germany)	Cabins with balcony:	220
Entered Service:	Nov 1997/May 2011	Cabins (wheelchair accessible):	8
Length (ft/m):	865.8/263.9	Wheelchair accessibility:	Good
Propulsion/Propellers:	diesel (31,500kW)/2	Elevators:	10
Total Crew:	780	Casino (gaming tables):	Yes
Passengers (lower beds):	1,912	Self-Service Launderette:	No
Passenger Space Ratio (lower beds):	40.6	Onboard currency:	Euros

THE SHIP. *Mein Schiff Herz*, formerly *Mein Schiff 2*, was renamed in 2019. This inclusive mid-size ship has just about all that's needed for an enjoyable cruise experience for German-speaking families, with numerous bars, four restaurants, six bistros, and good children's facilities.

Although there are more than 4.5 acres (1.8 hectares) of space on the open decks, it can, however, become crowded when the ship is full. Two-person cabanas can be rented on an upper, outside deck, with great ocean views, insulated from shipboard life.

Inside, a four-deck-high main foyer houses the reception desk and shore excursion station. There's a small cinema which doubles as a conference and meeting center, a large shopping area, including ultra-smart shops such as Swarovski, and a private club-like cigar lounge and bar.

The interior decor is contemporary in style, but nothing is garish – except, perhaps, for the starkly contrasting wall-covering of blood-red capillaries in the Blue World Bar.

The ship has 'Meditation Islands' installed on the open deck: the ship's rail is fitted with mini-balconies, equipped with special blinds, and created as spaces for private relaxation.

This is for German-speaking families with children (who should look out for Captain Sharky), who want to cruise aboard a ship with a contemporary environment, good itineraries, great food, and Eu-

BERLITZ'S RATINGS		
	Possible	Achieved
Ship	500	342
Accommodation	200	137
Food	400	265
Service	400	281
Entertainment	100	66
Cruise Experience	400	270
OVERALL SCORE 1361 points out of 2000		

ropean-style service from a well-trained crew. What makes it even more family-friendly is the inclusive pricing, though this excludes spa treatments, excursions, and some cost-extra restaurants. The dress code is smart-casual. When you are on board, see if you can find 'Wine poured upon the sea' (hint: it's on a curved interior wall).

ACCOMMODATION. There are several price grades, depending on size and location, but the accommodation is comfortable. Each cabin has a Nespresso coffee machine, which comes with two free coffee pods (any additional packets cost €1 each, although they are free in suites). All accommodation grades are no-smoking.

Standard outside-view/interior (no-view) cabins are of a decent size and have twin beds that are convertible to a queen-size bed. The bathrooms are spacious and have generous-size showers, hairdryers, and space for toiletries. A box containing three crystal-mineral stones provides special filtration for the ship's own water.

Two Penthouse Suites, located amidships, are the largest. Each has its own butler's pantry, and an interconnecting door to link it to the next-door suite.

DINING. Restaurants and bistros range from self-serve buffet style to service, with no pre-defined seating. The emphasis is on healthy food, including power food, brain food, soul food, erotic food, and fresh fish. The Atlantik Klassik Restaurant is a lovely, two-level Art Deco grand dining hall with a grand staircase and tables for two to 10.

Also included in the cruise fare: three eateries and a bar, in an area covered by a retractable glass dome aft: Bistro La Vela for specialist Italian cuisine, including an 'active' pasta-cooking station; Gosch Sylt for fresh fish and seafood, with daily specials (it's hugely popular, so make reservations early); and Cliff 24, a 24-hour poolside grill.

For informal breakfasts and lunches, the two-level self-serve, food-court-style Anckelmannsplatz Buffet is the place, with multiple serving counters and 'active' food islands, plus a bakery with many gluten-free items.

Cost-extra, reservations-required venues include: La Spezia, for Italian fare; Surf 'n' Turf Steakhouse, for premium steaks and grilled seafood, with aged beef, displayed in a 'proving' or maturing cabinet (when installed it was a cruise industry first); Blaue Welt (Blue World) Sushi Bar, on the upper level of the atrium. Also: Vino, a wine-tasting bar specializing in Austrian and German wines; and TUI Bar lounge around the atrium lobby for specialty coffees and pastries, with a praline chocolate counter.

ENTERTAINMENT. The Theater is a bi-level, 927-seat showlounge, with seating on both main and cantilevered balcony levels, and good sight lines from all seats. The large-scale production shows are excellent.

SPA/FITNESS. The Spa and More, at the front of the ship above the navigation bridge, has 18,299 sq ft (1,700 sq m) of space; it includes a large gym, a beauty salon, thalassotherapy pool, 15 treatment rooms, a Rasul chamber for mud and steam bathing, and a sauna.

Private 'spa suites,' bookable for an hour or two, or a half- or full-day, are extremely large, and include a steam/shower cabinet, thalassotherapy bath, two hydraulic massage/relaxation tables, relaxation seating, and great floor-to-ceiling windows. A balcony adjacent to the sauna is designated as an 'FKK' (Freikörperkultur) deck for nude sunbathing.

MONARCH
★★

A MID-SIZED FAMILY-FRIENDLY SHIP, FOR SPANISH SPEAKERS

Size:	Mid-size Ship	Passenger/Crew Ratio (lower beds):	2.8
Tonnage:	73,937	Cabins (total):	1,192
Cruise Line:	Pullmantur Cruises	Size Range (sq ft/m):	118.4–670.0/11.0–62.2
Former Names:	Monarch of the Seas	Cabins (for one person):	0
Builder:	Chantiers de l'Atlantique (France)	Cabins with balcony:	62
Entered Service:	Nov 1991/Apr 2013	Cabins (wheelchair accessible):	4
Length (ft/m):	879.9/268.2	Wheelchair accessibility:	Fair
Propulsion/Propellers:	diesel (21,844kW)/2	Elevators:	11
Total Crew:	858	Casino (gaming tables):	Yes
Passengers (lower beds):	2,384	Self-Service Launderette:	No
Passenger Space Ratio (lower beds):	31.0	Onboard currency:	Euros

THE SHIP. *Monarch* (an ex-Royal Caribbean International ship) has a deep blue hull, and a lounge and bar wrapped around the funnel and a bird's-eye view – a nice place to sit and enjoy a decent coffee. The open deck space itself is cramped when the ship is full.

The interior layout is designed vertically, with most public rooms located aft, and accommodation forward.

There's a good array of spacious, contemporary public rooms, although the decor brings to mind the IKEA school of interior design. A five-deck-high Centrum lobby has cascading stairways and two glass-walled elevators. You will be overwhelmed by the public spaces but underwhelmed by the size of the cabins.

Children and teens are well catered for, and there's a whole team of youth activity staff. The dress code is ultra-casual. All gratuities and port taxes are included in the cruise fare. Lively music (and noise) is everywhere. For a quiet relaxing holiday, choose another ship.

Although Pullmantur Cruises markets this ship in Europe, it focuses more on Latin America, and provides a visa-free alternative for several nationalities and a chance for South Americans to cruise the Caribbean in their winter. This ship provides the basics for a somewhat impersonal, short cruise experience for Spanish-speaking families.

ACCOMMODATION. There are numerous categories, priced by grade, size, and location: from the cramped interior (no-view) cabins to balcony cabins and the largest suite (the Royal Suite).

BERLITZ'S RATINGS

	Possible	Achieved
Ship	500	244
Accommodation	200	88
Food	400	187
Service	400	216
Entertainment	100	48
Cruise Experience	400	195

OVERALL SCORE 978 points out of 2000

Most outside-view and interior cabins are very small, but most have twin beds that convert to a queen-size or double bed. However, when in a queen-bed configuration, the bed is flush against the wall, with access only from one side, and little closet and drawer space.

DINING. Two main dining rooms, Auster and Boreas, have tables for four to eight, (none for two), and two seating times. The cuisine is based on mass banquet catering, comparable to family-style eateries ashore. While menu descriptions are tempting, the actual food may be unmemorable. A selection of light meals is also provided, and a vegetarian choice is also available.

For casual self-serve food, Buffet Panorama is the place to go, although there are often long lines at peak times.

ENTERTAINMENT. Entertainment across the ship is upbeat. Broadway is the showlounge, on two levels and banquette seating, but sight lines from many balcony seats are poor. A second, smaller venue is the Salon Broadway Lounge, while Cyan Nightclub provides ear-splitting sounds for frenetic youth.

SPA/FITNESS. Spa del Mar is small, but has a fitness center, an aerobics studio, a beauty salon, and a sauna, plus small body treatment rooms. For sports there is a basketball court, a rock-climbing wall, and jogging track.

MSC ARMONIA
★★★+

THIS IS A COMFORTABLE MID-SIZED SHIP FOR PAN-EUROPEAN CRUISERS

Size:	Mid-size Ship	Passenger/Crew Ratio (lower beds):	2.7
Tonnage:	65,542	Cabins (total):	976
Cruise Line:	MSC Cruises	Size Range (sq ft/m):	139.9–236.8/13.0–22.0
Former Names:	*European Vision*	Cabins (for one person):	0
Builder:	Chantiers de l'Atlantique (France)	Cabins with balcony:	224
Entered Service:	Jun 2001/May 2004	Cabins (wheelchair accessible):	2
Length (ft/m):	902.2/275.0	Wheelchair accessibility:	Good
Propulsion/Propellers:	diesel-electric (31,680kW)/2 azimuthing pods	Elevators:	9
		Casino (gaming tables):	Yes
Total Crew:	721	Self-Service Launderette:	No
Passengers (lower beds):	1,952	Onboard currency:	Euros
Passenger Space Ratio (lower beds):	33.5		

THE SHIP. As *European Vision*, the ship began its working life auspiciously, having been used to accommodate the leaders and staff of the G8 summit in 2001. When its owner, Festival Cruises, ceased operations in 2004, it was bought by MSC Cruises (a Swiss-based company with Italian roots) and renamed *MSC Armonia*. The exterior deck space is barely adequate for the number of passengers carried. The Lido Deck surrounding the outdoor swimming pool also has whirlpool tubs, and a large bandstand is set in raised canvas-covered pods. All sunloungers have cushioned pads.

In August 2014 a 'chop-and-stretch' operation added an 82ft (25m) mid-section, almost 200 additional cabins, more public rooms, entertainment facilities and shops (but no additional elevators), a greater amount of exterior deck space, and a large waterpark for children. Families with children will also find special kids' areas equipped with Chicco® and LEGO® products, and an energetic multilingual youth activity team.

Inside, the layout and passenger flow became slightly disjointed after the 'stretch.' The decor is modern European and includes crisp, clean lines and minimalist furniture. The interior colors are good; nothing jars the senses, but rather calms them.

Facilities include Amadeus, a nightclub; Ambassador, a cigar-smoking room; and the Red Bar, a piano lounge. There is an extensive Internet café, and

BERLITZ'S RATINGS		
	Possible	Achieved
Ship	500	364
Accommodation	200	148
Food	400	238
Service	400	288
Entertainment	100	60
Cruise Experience	400	267

OVERALL SCORE 1365 points out of 2000

an English pub, the White Lion. The Lido Casino has gaming tables plus an array of slot machines.

Wheelchair-users should note that there is no access to the uppermost forward and aft decks, but access throughout most of the interior is good. The passenger hallways are a little narrow on some accommodation decks to pass when housekeeping carts are in place.

MSC Armonia will suit those keen to travel with an international mix of passengers. It is best for adult couples and solo travelers, and families with children, who enjoy constant activity accompanied by lots of noise, late nights, and loud entertainment.

ACCOMMODATION. There are numerous categories, with the price depending on the grade, size, and location you choose. These include 132 'suites' with private balcony (whose partitions are partial and not full), outside-view cabins, and interior (no-view) cabins.

Suite-grade accommodation – not true suites, as there's no separate bedroom and lounge – has more room than standard cabins, a larger lounge area, walk-in closet, wall-to-wall vanity counter, a bathroom with combination tub and shower, toilet, and private balcony with light. Bathrobes are provided. However, except in accommodation of the highest category, the bathrooms are plain, with white plastic washbasins and white walls, small shower enclosures, and mirrors that steam up.

Even the smallest interior cabins are acceptable, however, with enough space between two lower beds. All grades of accommodation have a TV, mini-bar/refrigerator, personal safe cleverly positioned behind a vanity desk mirror, hairdryer, and bathroom with shower and toilet. But standard grade cabins, at a modest 140 sq ft (13 sq m), are really small when compared to those in many other ships.

DINING. The main dining room, the 610-seat Marco Polo Restaurant, has two sittings for dinner, and an open seating (so you can arrive for dinner when you like, during dining hours) for breakfast and lunch. During open seating, you may well be seated with others with whom you may not necessarily be able to communicate very easily, given the wide mix of nationalities and languages on board.

MSC Cruises highlights regional Italian cuisine and wines, with dining room menus that feature food from throughout Italy. Always-available items include spaghetti (with a tomato sauce freshly made each day), chicken breast, salmon fillet, and vegetables of the day. All pizza dough is made on board, and risotto is a daily signature item, as is fresh pasta. Several varieties of Italian breads such as bruschetta, focaccia, and panettone are provided. Light 'always available' meals and vegetarian dishes are also provided.

The wine list has quite a wide variety of wines at fairly reasonable prices, although most of the wines are very young.

La Pergola, the most formal restaurant, features stylish Italian cuisine. It is assigned to occupying suite-grade occupants, although others can dine in it too, on a reservations-only basis.

Il Girasole, on the starboard side aft, adjacent to the ship's funnel, is a grill area for fast food. La Brasserie is a casual, self-serve buffet eatery, and includes a sit-down, casual dinner each evening with waiter service. Café San Marco, on the upper, second level of the main lobby, serves extra-cost coffees, and pastry items.

ENTERTAINMENT. Teatro La Fenice spans two decks and is the venue for production shows, cabaret acts, and other theatrical presentations. It is well designed, except that there's no space for a live showband – productions are performed to pre-recorded backing tracks. The sight lines from most seats are good, and four entrances allow easy access and exit.

SPA/FITNESS. The Atlantica Spa has numerous body-pampering treatments, a gymnasium with ocean views, and high-tech equipment. A thermal suite has several steam rooms with aromatherapy infusions, and a Rasul (mud) chamber. The spa offers a wide range of wellbeing treatments.

For the active there is a climbing wall, volleyball/basketball court, and mini-golf.

MSC BELLISSIMA
★★★★+

THIS SHIP IS REALLY A STUNNING FLOATING BEACH FOR FAMILY-IMMERSIVE RESORT CRUISING

Size:	Large Resort Ship	Passenger/Crew Ratio (lower beds):	2.9
Tonnage:	171,598	Cabins (total):	2,244
Cruise Line:	MSC Cruises	Size Range (sq ft/m):	172.2-699.6/16.0-65.0
Former Names:	none	Cabins (for one person):	0
Builder:	STX (France)	Cabins with balcony:	1,401
Entered Service:	Mar 2019	Cabins (wheelchair accessible):	47
Length (ft/m):	1,033.4/315.0	Wheelchair accessibility:	Good
Propulsion/Propellers:	Diesel-electric/2 azimuthing pods	Elevators:	16
		Casino (gaming tables):	Yes
Total Crew:	1,536	Self-Service Launderette:	No
Passengers (lower beds):	4,488	Onboard currency:	Euros
Passenger Space Ratio (lower beds):	38.2		

THE SHIP. *MSC Bellissima* (meaning 'beautiful' in Italian) is really quite a handsome vessel, with a sleek, streamlined, and contemporary funnel that is, unusually, almost in the center of the ship. It has been specifically tailored for total family-immersive cruising, with Zoe – a voice-activated digital assistant supporting NFC (near-field communication) in a joint venture with Samsung.

One of several pools can be covered by a retractable glass dome for inclement weather, and there is a lot of open deck and sunbathing space.

Atop and aft of the funnel, an Aqua Park play area (aft) is full of spray cannons, water-stream jets, tipping bucket, three waterslides, and a scary 'Himalayan Bridge' walking (ropes) course.

Indoors, the focal and social meeting point is the stunning Galleria Bellissima, an indoor promenade with an impressive 80m (260ft)-long LED dome displaying a constant stream of digital scenes and themes. The area – part of the 96m (315ft)-long Mediterranean Promenade – is home to a parade of shops (slightly more than aboard sister ship MSC Meraviglia), restaurants, and bars, with decks named after other ships in the MSC Cruises fleet.

The layout makes it reasonably easy to find your way around, and, with its 'open-flow' design, public areas merge seamlessly into each other. Almost all public rooms, bars, and lounges (including a casino with gaming tables and an array of slot machines),

BERLITZ'S RATINGS		
	Possible	Achieved
Ship	500	422
Accommodation	200	161
Food	400	275
Service	400	308
Entertainment	100	78
Cruise Experience	400	311

OVERALL SCORE 1555 points out of 2000

plus hangouts for coffee, chocolates, and crêpes, a 4D cinema, and a shopping center (with some well-known designer brands) are located on decks 5, 6, and 7, with accommodation on the decks above. Standouts include the six Swarovski stairways (each step has 640 Swarovski crystals). Facilities for children and teens are excellent, and MSC Cruises has a team of enthusiastic counselors and many programs to entertain its younger passengers.

An exclusive key-card access area (MSC Yacht Club) is like a 'ship within a ship' of 'suite-grade' accommodation, with large bathrooms, and even duplex suites. Exclusive facilities include a large indoor-outdoor observation/lifestyle lounge (with good ocean views and small dance floor) and a sunbathing deck with dip pool, hot tubs, bar, open deck eatery, and relaxation zones; it has its own dedicated restaurant and concierge services. In 2020, *MSC Bellissima* homeports in Shanghai, China, for Asia-Pacific cruises.

Niggles include the many reflective surfaces and the number of extra-cost items.

ACCOMMODATION. There are many accommodation price grades; the price depends on the size, location, and grade you choose. From the smallest to the largest, they are comfortable, well laid out (the upper grades have ample closet and drawer space, but the lower grade accommodation lacks drawer space). All bathrooms have glazed shower enclosures, shelves for personal toiletries, and towels of a decent size. Some family cabins are set in a cluster, so three can be interlinked – good for large families.

All Yacht Club accommodation grades have an espresso coffee machine, and a choice of four additional pillow types. The bed linen is gorgeous, as are the premium mattresses.

Contrary to maritime tradition, even-numbered cabins are on the starboard (right, facing forward) side (they should be on the port side – left when looking forward, as are the lifeboats); it's strange for a maritime ship-owning family.

DINING. The Posidonia and smaller Il Ciliegio and Le Cerisier restaurants have many tables for two to eight persons. MSC Cruises has upped its attention to its cuisine, adapting it to various markets.

Mediterranean cuisine is the focus, including regional Italian dishes. All pizza dough is made on board, and risotto is a daily signature item, as is fresh pasta. Light 'always-available' items (chicken, salmon, and pasta) and vegetarian selections are also available.

Yacht Club Restaurant is exclusively for Yacht Club accommodation occupants; at the front of the ship, it has good views, and stairway access from the expansive Yacht Club lounge below. The Gala Dinner menu was devised by the French two-Michelin-star superchef Raymond Blanc.

Extra-cost eateries include Butcher's Cut (for premium-quality, dry-aged steaks and grilled food items cooked to order); Kaito (for Japanese cuisine) sushi bar and teppanyaki grill room; L'Atelier Bistro & 'Hola' tapas eatery, both by Michelin-starred chef Ramón Freixa; and Crêpes & Gelato and Chocolate Bar (watch the speciality chocolates being made by hand), both by Jean-Philippe Maury.

The Marketplace Buffet Bar is a large self-serve, food-court style eatery. At night, it becomes a casual eatery (with the same menus as in the main dining rooms).

Extra-cost Segafredo (Italian) coffees are available in most bars and lounges – all served in proper china cups.

ENTERTAINMENT. The stunning two-deck-high, amphitheatre-style London Theatre (showlounge) has very comfortable seating and excellent sight lines.

Carousel Lounge, aft, specially built to host (extra-cost) Cirque du Soleil shows, seats 400.

SPA/FITNESS. The Aurea Spa is extensive (it includes an outdoor section). Facilities include a large workout room (with Technogym cardiovascular equipment), saunas, steam and relaxation rooms for men and women, a large beauty salon, and several body-pampering treatment rooms. Sports facilities include a tennis/basketball court, and a bowling alley.

MSC DIVINA
★★★★

A HIGHLY COMFORTABLE, LARGE FAMILY-FRIENDLY, MULTI-CHOICE RESORT SHIP

Size:	Large Resort Ship	Passenger/Crew Ratio (lower beds):	2.5
Tonnage:	139,400	Cabins (total):	1,751
Cruise Line:	MSC Cruises	Size Range (sq ft/m):	148.5–568.3/13.8–52.8
Former Names:	none	Cabins (for one person):	0
Builder:	STX France	Cabins with balcony:	1,125
Entered Service:	Jun 2012	Cabins (wheelchair accessible):	45
Length (ft/m):	1,093.5/333.3	Wheelchair accessibility:	Good
Propulsion/Propellers:	diesel-electric (40,000kW)/2	Elevators:	17
Total Crew:	1,388	Casino (gaming tables):	Yes
Passengers (lower beds):	3,502	Self-Service Launderette:	No
Passenger Space Ratio (lower beds):	39.8	Onboard currency:	US$

THE SHIP. *MSC Divina* is sister to *MSC Preziosa*, and features green-technology engines. Its exclusive area, the MSC Yacht Club, includes a large Top-Sail Lounge (an observation/lifestyle lounge and social meeting place), private sunbathing deck with integral dip pool, two hot tubs, concierge services, and bar/snack bar. Yacht Club-grade occupants are escorted to their cabins by their butlers on embarkation. Housekeeping staff point passengers in the right direction but no longer escort them to their cabins.

The interior decor is quite stunning. There are basically two decks full of public lounges, bars, and eateries, including a large two-deck-high theater-style showlounge, a nightclub/disco, library, card room, an Internet center, a virtual-reality center, shopping gallery, and large casino. Drinking places include a large number of lounges and bars, most with live music. One lounge in the aft section is for adults only, as is an aft swimming pool and relaxation deck. The Golden Jazz Bar is a must (the walls are 'stoned'). Additionally, there are conference and small group meeting facilities.

The ship's interior focal point is a gorgeous three-decks-high atrium lobby with shimmering Swarovski crystal stairways and elegant, Art Deco-influenced decor. Reception and financial-services desks are located on the lower level, which also has a stage and seating in oversized armchairs.

BERLITZ'S RATINGS		
	Possible	Achieved
Ship	500	419
Accommodation	200	160
Food	400	273
Service	400	308
Entertainment	100	78
Cruise Experience	400	301

OVERALL SCORE 1539 points out of 2000

You can drive an F1 Ferrari racing car in a simulator, and experience seat-of-your-pants rides in a 4D theater.

This large, elegantly attired resort ship has a trendy infinity pool and 'beach' zone, and will appeal to young adult couples, solo travelers, and families with children and teens.

Niggles include the fact that all the lounges 'flow' into each other, and music from each one bleeds into the adjacent room. Men should note that the public restrooms have cubicles (there are no urinals).

ACCOMMODATION. There are nine types of accommodation, in numerous cabin price grades. Included are two Royal Suites, three Executive/Family Suites, and a mix of outside-view (with or without balconies) and interior cabins. The price you pay depends on the grade, size, and location you choose. Contrary to maritime tradition (and even more strange given it is a maritime family), even-numbered cabins are on the starboard (right, facing forward) side. Nautical tradition aboard ocean-going ships dictates that even-numbered cabins should be on the port side (left when looking forward; the same as the lifeboats).

The 'Yacht Club' exclusive (ship-within-a-ship) accommodation consists of 67 'suites,' in a key-operated access-only area of the ship. It comes with butler service, interactive TV, minibar, personal safe, hairdryer, and satellite-link telephone. Number 16007 is the Sophia Loren Suite, in rich reds, specially designed lamps, and stunning photos of her great movie roles, together with a replica of the dressing table that Ms Loren uses in her home.

DINING. There are two main restaurants. The two-level Black Crab has 626 seats on one level and 529 on the other, and assigned tables and seating for dinner. The second is the 766-seat Villa Rossa Restaurant.

MSC Cruises highlights regional Italian cuisine and wines, with dining room menus that feature food from Calabria, Piedmont, Lazio, Puglia, and Sicily. Items that are always available include spaghetti (with a tomato sauce freshly made each day), chicken breast, salmon fillet, and vegetables of the day. However, the company has tailored its cuisine to North American tastes, and included some down-home favorites, produced with Italian flair.

All pizza dough is made on board, and risotto is a daily signature item, as is fresh pasta. Several varieties of Italian breads such as bruschetta, focaccia, and panettone are provided.

Occupants of Yacht Club accommodation grades eat in Le Muse, a private, quite intimate restaurant that overlooks an aft infinity pool area. The service here is less hurried and much more personalized.

Other options include the bistro-style, extra-cost Eataly, which is a sea-going version of a chain of the same name. It has ultra-clean white decor. The portions (especially the steaks) are impressively large, and everything is cooked to order.

Lido-style, self-serve buffet cafeterias (Calumet and Manitou – named after peace pipes and spirits of Native Americans; each has about 400 seats) are for breakfasts and lunches, and served, casual dinners. The buffets are open for up to 20 hours daily, so there's always something to eat whenever you're hungry.

Additional foodie-type places include La Cantina di Bacco (a wine bar and pizzeria), Piazza del Doge (for Italian pastries, coffees, and huge selection of gelato), Italia Bar for coffees (Lavazza is featured, always served in proper china cups) and pastries. Also, Galaxy, an à la carte eatery located as part of the disco, which overlooks the entire mid-ship pool deck, and is good for a late-riser's brunch (featuring several trendy tapas-style dishes, steaks, and seafood).

The Sports and Bowling Diner features a classic American food experience (including sandwiches and burgers).

ENTERTAINMENT. The 1,603-seat Pantheon Theater is spread over two decks. Because passengers really are multinational, the entertainment shows are highly visual, including dancing and acrobatics, and are performed to recorded music. A number of bands and small musical groups provide live music for dancing or listening in most lounges and bars.

SPA/FITNESS. The large Aurea Spa and Wellbeing Center houses a beauty salon, numerous body-treatment rooms (with Balinese therapists and 21 types of massage), a bar (for fruit drinks and smoothies), relaxation room, solarium, and a gymnasium with great ocean views. A thermal suite contains two steam rooms and four saunas combined with herbal aromatherapy infusions. This is the first cruise ship to have a halotherapy (Himalayan salt crystal) bed for body detoxing. There's also a Shu Uemura Art of Hair Cabin. Gratuities to spa staff are at your discretion.

Sports facilities include basketball, tennis court, volleyball, a power-walking track, bowling, and shuffleboard.

MSC FANTASIA
★★★★

THIS SHIP HAS COMFORT, SPACE, AND A MEDITERRANEAN LIFESTYLE FOR FAMILIES

Size:	Large Resort Ship	Passenger/Crew Ratio (lower beds):	2.3
Tonnage:	137,936	Cabins (total):	1,637
Cruise Line:	MSC Cruises	Size Range (sq ft/m):	161.4–699.6/15–65
Former Names:	none	Cabins (for one person):	0
Builder:	STX Europe (France)	Cabins with balcony:	1,260
Entered Service:	Dec 2008	Cabins (wheelchair accessible):	43
Length (ft/m):	1,093.5/333.3	Wheelchair accessibility:	Best
Propulsion/Propellers:	diesel-electric (40,000kW)/2	Elevators:	14
Total Crew:	1,370	Casino (gaming tables):	Yes
Passengers (lower beds):	3,274	Self-Service Launderette:	No
Passenger Space Ratio (lower beds):	42.1	Onboard currency:	Euros

THE SHIP. Built in 67 blocks, some more than 600 tons, *MSC Fantasia* is one of the largest ships built for a European cruise company. It is about 33ft (10m) longer than the Eiffel Tower is high, and the propulsion power is the equivalent of 120 Ferraris. There are four swimming pools, one of which can be covered by a glass dome.

The interior design is an enlargement and extension of MSC's smaller *Musica-* and *Orchestra-*class ships, but with the addition of an exclusive area called the MSC Yacht Club for occupants of the 99 suites. This 'club' includes a Top-Sail Lounge, private sunbathing with integral dip pool, two hot tubs, and concierge services such as making dining reservations, and booking excursions and spa treatments.

If your wallet allows, it's worth paying extra to stay in one of the 'suites' in the Yacht Club accommodation. You'll get silver-tray room service by a team of well-trained butlers, a reserved (quieter) section of the Il Cerchio d'Oro restaurant, plus keycard access to a members-only sundeck sanctuary area that includes its own bar and food counters, a small dip pool, two hot tubs, and expansive open but sheltered lounging deck. It's a world away from the hustle and bustle of the main pool decks and solarium on the decks below.

The interior decor is quite stunning. There are basically two decks full of public lounges, bars, and eateries, including a large two-deck-high theater-style showlounge, a nightclub/disco, library, card room, an

BERLITZ'S RATINGS		
	Possible	Achieved
Ship	500	413
Accommodation	200	160
Food	400	271
Service	400	306
Entertainment	100	77
Cruise Experience	400	305

OVERALL SCORE 1532 points out of 2000

Internet center, virtual-reality center, shopping gallery, and large casino (inhabited by many people who can smoke at the bar). There's a big city-like environment in the shopping areas. The Monte Carlo Casino features blackjack, poker, and roulette games, plus an array of slot machines.

Drinking places include a pub-like venue and several comfortable lounges with live music. Note that 15 percent is added to all drinks/beverage orders. A neat mini-golf course is on the port side of the funnel, and a walking and jogging track encircles the two swimming pools.

This ship appeals to young adult couples, solo travelers, and families with children and teens – anyone who enjoys big ships, a big-city lifestyle, and a mix of nationalities, mostly European. You can drive an F1 Ferrari racing car in a simulator, and experience hair-raising, seat-of-your pants rides in a 4D theater. Note that only Yacht Club-grade occupants are escorted to their cabins by their butlers. Housekeeping staff point passengers in the right direction, but no longer escort them to their cabins.

Niggles include the fact that all the lounges flow into each other, and music from each one bleeds into any adjacent room.

ACCOMMODATION. Eighty percent of cabins have an outside view, and 95 percent of these have a balcony – a standard balcony cabin will measure almost 172 sq ft (16 sq m), plus bathroom and balcony. There are 72 suites in a MSC Yacht Club VIP section; each comes with butler service. The price you pay depends on the grade, size, and location. Contrary to maritime tradition (even stranger is that the family company that owns the ships is a maritime family), even-numbered cabins are on the starboard (right, facing forward) side. Nautical tradition aboard ocean-going ships dictates that even-numbered cabins should be on the port side (left when looking forward; the same as the lifeboats).

In a 2011 refit, 28 Aurea Suites were created with direct access to the Aurea Spa. The spa suites come with amenities and 'extras,' including a non-alcoholic cocktail at the Aurea Spa Bar, unlimited access to the Thermal Suite (sauna and steam room) and a private consultation with the spa doctor. Also included in the price are a Balinese massage, a facial relax treatment using skin-firming cream, and a solarium session for full-body tanning.

A black marble floor leads to a magnificent Swarovski glass staircase that connects the concierge facilities between decks 15 and 16 under a glass-domed ceiling.

DINING. There are four dining venues. The two-deck-high Red Velvet, the main restaurant, is aft. It has a ship-wide balcony level, with a stairway connecting both levels.

MSC Cruises highlights regional Italian cuisine and wines, featuring food from Calabria, Piedmont, Lazio, Puglia, and Sicily. Always-available items include spaghetti (with a tomato sauce freshly made each day), chicken breast, salmon fillet, and vegetables of the day. All pizza dough is made on board, and risotto is a daily item, as is fresh pasta. Several varieties of Italian breads such as bruschetta, focaccia, and panettone are provided. Light 'always available' and vegetarian dishes are also provided.

Il Cerchio d'Oro is a single-level specialty restaurant, with a different menu each evening devoted to a different region of Italy. The Murano chandeliers are quite lovely, and definitely worth admiring.

L'Etoile is a classic French restaurant, with decor reminiscent of the Belle Epoque era. Menus focus either on the sea, the countryside, or the kitchen garden, and change seasonally. There's also an extra-charge Butcher's Cut, for excellent large cooked-to-order, premium-quality steaks.

Casual breakfasts, lunches, and sit-down, served, but casual, dinners can be taken in the large self-serve L'Africana Café, a self-serve, buffet-style eatery that is open 20 hours daily.

A casual spot that's good for people-watching is the Il Cappuccino coffee bar. Located two decks above the main reception area, featuring Lavazza and Segafredo coffee, as well as fine chocolate delicacies.

La Cantina Toscana is a neat wine bar that pairs wines with food from several regions of Italy, in a setting that includes alcove seating.

The Sports and Bowling Diner features a classic American food experience (including sandwiches and burgers).

ENTERTAINMENT. L'Avanguardia, the main showlounge, has 1,603 seats, and facilities that rival almost any to be found on land. Shows are highly visual, due to the multi-national passenger make-up. Additionally, live music is performed in most lounges by small musical groups and solo musicians.

SPA/FITNESS. The Aurea Spa has a beauty salon, several treatment rooms, and a gymnasium with great ocean views. A thermal suite contains different kinds of steam rooms combined with herbal aromatherapy infusions, in a calming Asia-themed environment. The spa is operated by OceanView, a specialist spa provider. Gratuities are not included, but left to your discretion.

Sports facilities include deck quoits, shuffleboard courts, a large tennis/basketball court, mini-golf, and a jogging track.

MSC GRANDIOSA
NYR

THIS IS A FAMILY-FRIENDLY, LIVELY, AND ULTRA-STYLISH SHIP WITH MANY 'WOW' FEATURES

Size:	Large Resort Ship	Passenger/Crew Ratio (lower beds):	2.8
Tonnage:	181,000	Cabins (total):	2,421
Cruise Line:	MSC Cruises	Size Range (sq ft/m):	172.2–699.6/16.0–65.0
Former Names:	none	Cabins (for one person):	0
Builder:	STX (France)	Cabins with balcony:	1,651
Entered Service:	Nov 2019	Cabins (wheelchair accessible):	47
Length (ft/m):	1,087.2/331.4	Wheelchair accessibility:	Good
Propulsion/Propellers:	diesel-electric/2 azimuthing pods	Elevators:	26
Total Crew:	1,703	Casino (gaming tables):	Yes
Passengers (lower beds):	4.842	Self-Service Launderette:	No
Passenger Space Ratio (lower beds):	37.0	Onboard currency:	Euros

THE SHIP. *MSC Grandiosa* (close sister to *MSC Bellissima* and *MSC Meraviglia*) is a really stunning ship that will appeal to young-at-heart couples, solo travelers, and families with children who enjoy an urban lifestyle, with a mix of mostly European nationalities.

Standout features include real Cirque du Soleil shows (custom-designed for MSC Cruises), an Aqua Park aft and atop ship with five waterslides, and an 'Adventure Trail' ropes course with bridges, towers, and climb-through spaces.

Inside, a superb, two-deck-high Grandiosa Promenade has an impressive 98.5m-long domed LED projection ceiling that streams thematic digital scenes. The indoor area, which leads off from an expansive multi-deck atrium, is home to a parade of shops, restaurants, and bars (just like a village). The Champagne Bar features a wide variety of Champagnes and sparkling wines, plus caviar, oysters, and crab; there's also an English pub.

There are five clubs, many children's and teens' facilities, numerous bars and lounges, and a casino with gaming tables and slot machines.

A key card-access area called the MSC Yacht Club is like a 'ship within a ship' of 'suite-grade' accommodation, with larger bathrooms and duplex suites. Exclusive facilities include a large observation/lifestyle lounge with forward views, restaurant, private sunbathing with dip pool, hot tubs, and concierge services for making dining

BERLITZ'S RATINGS		
	Possible	Achieved
Ship	500	NYR
Accommodation	200	NYR
Food	400	NYR
Service	400	NYR
Entertainment	100	NYR
Cruise Experience	400	NYR
OVERALL SCORE NYR points out of 2000		

reservations, booking excursions and spa treatments, and arranging private parties.

ACCOMMODATION. There are numerous accommodation price grades and name designations (such as Fantastica Cabins), which come with different inclusions (such as discounts on fitness classes, 24-hour room service, etc.). Price depends on size, location, and grade. From the smallest to the largest, all have two lower beds (convertible to a twin or double format), safe, and minibar/fridge. Some cabins have interconnecting doors to make larger family cabins; some are Duplex Suites (with upper and lower sections). Contrary to maritime tradition, even-numbered cabins are on the starboard side (even stranger considering the company that owns the ship is a maritime family).

DINING. The Restaurant (there are two, on two different decks) has both 'fixed time' (same waiter for the whole cruise) and 'flexi time' (different waiter each day) dining options.

MSC Cruises highlights regional Italian cuisine and wines. Always-available items include spaghetti (with a tomato sauce freshly made each day), chicken breast, and salmon fillet. Pizza dough is made on board, and risotto is a daily signature item, as is fresh pasta. Several varieties of Italian breads such as bruschetta, focaccia, and panettone are provided. Light 'always available' and vegetarian dishes are also provided.

Some special dishes were developed for Gala, Christmas and New Year menus by Michelin-starred Italian celebrity chef Carlo Cracco, who also developed a cooking experience for the DoRe-Mi kids' club.

A large, self-serve Buffet Restaurant is open 20 hours a day for casual breakfasts and lunches, and waiter-served dinners in a relaxed setting. A bakery corner provides freshly baked breads and rolls.

Butcher's Cut is an all-American steakhouse for extra-cost steaks and grilled seafood. Michelin-starred Chef Ramón Freixa's HOLA! Tapas Bar offers premium quality light bites.

Award-winning French chocolatier Jean-Philippe Maury is behind the onboard Chocolat & Café, while extra-cost proper Italian coffees are available in several locations.

ENTERTAINMENT. A Cirque du Soleil-designed multi-level showlounge hosts stunning, colorful acrobatic shows by a real Cirque du Soleil troupe, featuring a dinner-and-show package.

The Lounge has a stage (mainly for cabaret-style shows) and a dance floor; it is adjacent to a 5D cinema. Most bars and 'small' lounges have live music. Atop ship is an observation lounge (Piano Lounge), with great views.

SPA/FITNESS. The large Aurea Spa includes many body-treatment rooms, saunas and steam rooms for men and women, a relaxation area, a workout room with Technogym equipment, a beauty salon and hairdressers.

MSC LIRICA
★★★+

THIS IS A STRETCHED, EURO-STYLE, INFORMAL, FAMILY-FRIENDLY SHIP

Size:	Mid-size Ship	Passenger/Crew Ratio (lower beds):	2.7
Tonnage:	65,875	Cabins (total):	988
Cruise Line:	MSC Cruises	Size Range (sq ft/m):	139.9–302.0/13.0–28.0
Former Names:	none	Cabins (for one person):	0
Builder:	Chantiers de l'Atlantique (France)	Cabins with balcony:	224
Entered Service:	Mar 2003	Cabins (wheelchair accessible):	4
Length (ft/m):	902.2/275.0	Wheelchair accessibility:	Good
Propulsion/Propellers:	diesel (31,680kW)/2 azimuthing pods	Elevators:	9
Total Crew:	721	Casino (gaming tables):	Yes
Passengers (lower beds):	1,976	Self-Service Launderette:	No
Passenger Space Ratio (lower beds):	33.3	Onboard currency:	Euros

THE SHIP. *MSC Lirica*, sister to *MSC Opera*, was the first of a pair of new-builds for Mediterranean Shipping Cruises (MSC Cruises), a Swiss-based company with Italian roots. The ship's deep blue funnel is quite sleek; it has a swept-back design. The ship is fitted with an azimuthing pod propulsion system.

In 2015 the ship underwent a 'chop-and-stretch' operation, which added an 82ft (25m) mid-section, almost 200 additional cabins, more public rooms, entertainment facilities, new shops (but no additional elevators), a greater amount of exterior deck space, plus a large waterpark for children. Families with children will find kids' areas equipped with Chicco® and LEGO® products, and an energetic multilingual youth activity team.

Inside, the layout and passenger flow are quite good, with the exception of some congestion points – typically when first-seating passengers exit the dining room and second-seating passengers are waiting to enter.

An abundance of real woods and marble are used extensively in the interiors, and the standard of the fit and finish reflects MSC's commitment to high quality.

Facilities include a large main showlounge, a nightclub/disco, multiple lounges and bars, an Internet center, a virtual-reality center, a children's club, and a shopping gallery named Rodeo Drive with stores that have an integrated bar and entertainment area, where you can conveniently shop,

BERLITZ'S RATINGS		
	Possible	Achieved
Ship	500	373
Accommodation	200	150
Food	400	237
Service	400	299
Entertainment	100	60
Cruise Experience	400	270

OVERALL SCORE 1389 points out of 2000

drink, and be entertained all in one place. The Las Vegas Casino offers blackjack, poker, and roulette games, together with an array of slot machines. There is also a card room, but the integral library is small and disappointing, and there are no hardback books.

The ship is designed to accommodate families with children, who have their own play center, youth counselors, and activity programs. Wheelchair-users should note that there is no access to the uppermost forward and aft decks, although access throughout most of the interior is very good and there are also several wheelchair-accessible public restrooms. But passenger hallways are a little narrow on some decks, when housekeeping carts are in place.

MSC Lirica is best suited to young adult couples, solo travelers, and families with children who enjoy big-ship surroundings and facilities, and passengers of different nationalities and languages (mostly European). The decor has many Italian influences, including clean lines, minimalism in furniture design, and an eclectic collection of colors and soft furnishings that somehow work well together without any hint of garishness.

Some things that passengers find irritating: the ship's photographers always seem to be in your face; the telephone numbering system to reach such places as the information bureau (2224) and hospital (2360) are not easy to remember – single digit numbers would be better. Gratuities are extra, even though bar drinks already includes a 15 percent service charge added to all drinks/beverage orders.

ACCOMMODATION. There are several different price levels for accommodation, depending on grade and location: one suite category including 132 'suites' with private balcony, five outside-view cabin grades, and five interior cabin grades.

All cabins have a minibar and personal safe, satellite-linked television, several audio channels, and 24-hour room service. While tea and coffee are complimentary, snacks from room service incur a delivery charge.

Accommodation designated as suites (they are not true suites, as there is no separate bedroom and lounge) offers more room, a larger lounge area, walk-in closet, wall-to-wall vanity counter, a bathroom with combination tub and shower, toilet, and semi-private balcony with a light but partitions that are partial, not full. The bathrobes are 100 percent cotton. However, the suite bathrooms are very plain, with white plastic washbasins and white walls, and mirrors that steam up.

Some cabins on Scarlatti Deck have views obstructed by lifeboats, while those on Deck 10 aft (10105–10159) can be subject to late-night noise from the disco on the deck above.

DINING. There are two dining rooms: La Bussola Restaurant, and the smaller L'Ippocampo Restaurant, located one deck above. Both have ocean-view picture windows at the aft end of the ship, with tables for two to eight.

La Pergola is the most formal restaurant, offering stylish Italian cuisine. It is assigned to passengers in accommodation designated as suites, although other passengers can dine in it, too, on a reservations-only basis. The food and service are superior to that in the main dining rooms.

Casual, self-serve buffets for breakfast and lunch can be taken in Le Bistrot Buffet. For fast foods, there is also the La Pergola grill and pizzeria, adjacent to the swimming pool and funnel.

Coffee Corner, located on the upper, second level of the main lobby, is for extra-cost Lavazza coffees, and pastry items – and for people-watching. Although there are windows, the view is not of the ocean, but of the stowed gangways and associated equipment.

ENTERTAINMENT. The Broadway Theater (showlounge), is located forward. It has tiered seating, a sloping floor, and sight lines are good from most seats. There is no separate bandstand, so shows have recorded backing tracks,

The Lirica Lounge, one deck above the showlounge, is for social dancing, with live music. For the lively set, there is The Blue Club, the ship's throbbing, ear-melting nightclub.

SPA/FITNESS. The Lirica Health Center is located one deck above the navigation bridge at the forward end of the ship. The complex has a beauty salon, several private massage/body treatment rooms, plus a fitness center with ocean views and muscle-pumping equipment. There's also a cost-extra thermal suite, with aromatherapy-infused steam rooms.

The spa is operated by the Italian company Ocean-View, with European hairstylists and Balinese massage and body-treatment staff.

MSC MAGNIFICA
★★★★

THIS LARGE, FAMILY-FRIENDLY SHIP HAS STYLISH, BRIGHT INTERIOR DECOR

Size:	Large Resort Ship	Passenger/Crew Ratio (lower beds):	2.4
Tonnage:	95,128	Cabins (total):	1,259
Cruise Line:	MSC Cruises	Size Range (sq ft/m):	150.6–301.3/14.0–28.0
Former Names:	none	Cabins (for one person):	0
Builder:	Aker Yards (France)	Cabins with balcony:	827
Entered Service:	Mar 2010	Cabins (wheelchair accessible):	17
Length (ft/m):	963.9/293.8	Wheelchair accessibility:	Good
Propulsion/Propellers:	diesel (31,680kW)/2	Elevators:	13
Total Crew:	1,038	Casino (gaming tables):	Yes
Passengers (lower beds):	2,518	Self-Service Launderette:	No
Passenger Space Ratio (lower beds):	37.7	Onboard currency:	Euros

THE SHIP. *MSC Magnifica* is one of a quartet of the same class, the others: *MSC Musica*, *MSC Poesia*, and *MSC Orchestra*. The ship sports a dark blue funnel, which has a swept-back design that balances its large-ship profile. The hull has large circular, porthole-style windows instead of square or rectangular ones.

This large resort ship is designed for families with children, who have their own play center, video games room, youth counselors, and activity programs. The interior layout and passenger flow are quite good, with decks named after Mediterranean destinations such as Capri, Positano, Portovenere, and Ischia. The focal point is a main three-deck-high lobby, with a water-feature backdrop and a crystal (glass) piano on a small stage that appears to float on a pond.

The decor has an abundance of Italian and general Mediterranean influences, clean lines, minimalism in furniture design, and a collection of soft furnishings and fabrics that work well together. Real wood and marble have been used extensively, and the quality reflects the commitment MSC Cruises (a Swiss-based company with Italian roots) has in cruising. Some artwork is quite whimsical, which suits the ship's contemporary design.

Facilities include a large main showlounge (Royal Theater), a nightclub, Atlantic City Casino, a disco with two bowling lanes, numerous lounges and bars, a library, card room, an internet center, a 4D virtual-real-

BERLITZ'S RATINGS		
	Possible	Achieved
Ship	500	402
Accommodation	200	151
Food	400	242
Service	400	298
Entertainment	100	62
Cruise Experience	400	291

OVERALL SCORE 1446 points out of 2000

ity center, and a cigar lounge (Cuba Lounge) with a selection of cigars.

A standout is the Tiger Lounge/Bar, with animal-themed décor, sumptuous chairs, and long curvy bar. A shopping area is well integrated with bars and lounges.

Drinking places include a pub-like venue as well as several comfortable lounges with live music. Although access throughout most of the interior is very good, wheelchair-users should note that accommodation hallways are narrow on some decks for passing housekeeping carts. Sadly, there is no walk-around open promenade deck.

ACCOMMODATION. There are numerous different price levels, depending on grade and location. Included are 'suites' with private balcony, mini-suites, outside-view cabins, and interior cabins. Contrary to nautical convention, the cabin numbering system has even-numbered cabins on the starboard side and odd-numbered cabins on the port side.

All cabins have high-quality Italian bed linen, minibar, safe, satellite flat-screen TV, several audio channels, and 24-hour room service. Continental breakfast is complimentary in cabins from 7.30 to 10am, and snacks are available from room service at extra cost at any other time.

Accommodation designated as 'suites' (they are not true suites, as there is no separate bedroom and lounge) also has more space, although less suites on some other major cruise lines. Each has a larger lounge area, walk-in closet, vanity desk with drawer-mounted hairdryer, bathroom with tub/ shower combination, toilet, and semi-private balcony with light. Partitions between each balcony are of the partial, not full, type. The bathrobes and towels are cotton, and a pillow menu with a choice of five pillows is available.

Views from many cabins on Camogli Deck are obstructed by lifeboats. The sought-after options are those in the aft section of the ship, with views over the stern from the balcony cabins. The 17 cabins for disabled passengers are spacious and well equipped.

DINING. Two main dining rooms: L'Edera and Quattro Venti are located aft, on different decks, with large ocean-view picture windows. There are two seatings at assigned tables for two to eight. Seating is both banquette-style and in individual chairs, although the chairs are slim and lack armrests.

MSC Cruises highlights regional Italian cuisine and wines, with menus featuring food from Calabria, Piedmont, Lazio, Puglia, and Sicily. Always-available items include spaghetti (with a tomato sauce freshly made each day), chicken breast, and salmon fillet. All pizza dough is made on board, and risotto is a daily signature item, as is fresh pasta. Several varieties of Italian breads such as bruschetta, focaccia, and panettone are provided. Light and vegetarian dishes are also provided.

Casual, self-serve buffets for breakfast and lunch are provided in the food court-style Sahara Cafeteria, with sit-down dinner service each evening. There's also a pool deck fast-food eatery for burgers.

Enclosed in the ship's center, Shanghai is a Chinese extra-cost, reservations-required restaurant with high-temperature wok cooking, dim sum, and other Chinese and Asian specialties available à la carte. The food embraces Beijing, Cantonese, Shanghai, and Szechuan cuisines.

L'Oesi is a reservation-required, extra-charge, à la carte dining spot that, by day, forms the aft section of the Sahara Cafeteria, complete with Moroccan-style decor. Dinners are cooked to order from the adjacent galley.

A Sports Bar is for cost-extra, light-bite snacks.

Silver trays full of late-night snacks are taken throughout the ship by waiters, and, on some days, special late-night desserts, such as flambé items, are showcased in various lounges. Ice cream is made on board.

ENTERTAINMENT. The Royal Theater is the main showlounge, and tiered seating spans three decks, with good sight lines from most of the plush, comfortable seats. The room also serves as a venue for large groups or social functions. All the large-scale production shows are performed to recorded backing tracks (there is no stage for a live band).

L'Amethista Lounge is for social dancing and functions, including cooking demonstrations. For the lively crowd, there's an ear-blasting T32 disco; with floor-to-ceiling windows, it is a quiet, pleasant place to relax and read during sea days.

Additionally, big-screen movies are shown on a mega-screen above the forward pool, just behind the ship's mast. Live music is provided in most bars and lounges.

SPA/FITNESS. Aurea Spa has a beauty salon, several rooms for body-pampering treatments, and a gymnasium with forward ocean views. There's also a cost-extra Middle East-themed thermal suite, containing steam rooms and saunas with aromatherapy infusions, and a relaxation/hot tub room; there's an extra charge for using these facilities.

Sports facilities include table tennis, a tennis court, mini-golf course, golf practice net, two shuffleboard courts, and jogging track.

MSC MERAVIGLIA
★★★★+

THIS STUNNING, FAMILY-FRIENDLY, ULTRA-STYLISH SHIP HAS SERIOUS WOW FACTOR

Size:	Large Resort Ship	Passenger/Crew Ratio (lower beds):	2.9/1
Tonnage:	167,900	Cabins (total):	2,244
Cruise Line:	MSC Cruises	Size Range (sq ft/m):	172.2–699.6/16.0–65.0
Former Names:	none	Cabins (for one person):	0
Builder:	STX (France)	Cabins with balcony:	1,401
Entered Service:	Jun 2017	Cabins (wheelchair accessible):	47
Length (ft/m):	1,033.4/315.0	Wheelchair accessibility:	Good
Propulsion/Propellers:	diesel-electric/2 azimuthing pods	Elevators:	16
Total Crew:	1,540	Casino (gaming tables):	Yes
Passengers (lower beds):	4,488	Self-Service Launderette:	No
Passenger Space Ratio (lower beds):	37.3	Onboard currency:	Euros

THE SHIP. *MSC Meraviglia* is an absolutely stunning ship, with a large indoor atrium, and outdoor sports and water-park facilities. This ship will appeal to young-at-heart adult couples, solo travelers, and families with children and teens enjoying an urban lifestyle, with a mix of mostly European nationalities and style.

Standout features include real Cirque du Soleil shows (custom-designed for MSC Cruises) and an Aqua Park aft and atop ship with five slides and a lot of water entertainment features for children. Above it all is an 'Adventure Trail' ropes course with bridges, towers, climb-through spaces – all subject to water attacks from below. There are many excellent facilities and features on board for children and teens, including five clubs for different age groups, with a whole team of youth specialists to take care of them.

Indoors, a two-deck-high Promenade 'Village' has an impressive LED-screen domed ceiling showing constantly changing digital scenes. The indoor area, which leads off from an expansive multi-deck atrium, is home to a parade of shops, restaurants, and bars. One bar (Champagne Bar) features a wide variety of Champagnes and sparkling wine, plus caviar, oysters, and crab; there's also a good English pub. Other facilities include numerous bars and lounges, and a casino (with gaming tables and slot machines). An exclusive key-card access area called the MSC Yacht Club is like a 'ship within a ship' of 'suite-grade' accommodation, with

BERLITZ'S RATINGS		
	Possible	Achieved
Ship	500	418
Accommodation	200	161
Food	400	276
Service	400	308
Entertainment	100	78
Cruise Experience	400	310
OVERALL SCORE 1551 points out of 2000		

large bathrooms and duplex suites. Exclusive facilities include a large indoor-outdoor observation/lifestyle lounge (with great views) with its own dedicated Yacht Club Restaurant, plus concierge services for making dining and spa reservations.

Overall, this ship is a mighty impressive playground for multigenerational families, and should provide a memorable vacation.

ACCOMMODATION. There are numerous accommodation price grades and name designations (such as Fantastica Cabins), which come with different inclusions (such as discounts on fitness classes, 24-hour room service, etc.). The price you pay depends on the size, location, and grade you choose. From the smallest to the largest, all have two lower beds (convertible to a twin or double format) personal safe, and minibar/fridge. Some cabins have interconnecting doors to make larger family cabins. Some are Duplex Suites (with upper and lower sections). Contrary to maritime tradition (even though the family company that owns the ships is a maritime family), even-numbered cabins are on the starboard (right, facing forward) side, whereas nautical tradition aboard ocean-going ships dictates that even-numbered cabins should be on the port side (left when looking forward; the same as the lifeboats).

All Yacht Club-grade accommodation has a Nespresso coffee machine and larger bathroom with bathtub, and its occupants eat in a dedicated restaurant.

DINING. There are two main dining rooms, Waves and Panorama, one on each of two different decks) with both 'Fixed Time' (you have the same waiter for the whole cruise) and 'Flexi Time' (you have a different waiter each day) dining options.

MSC Cruises highlights regional Italian cuisine and wines, with dining-room menus that feature food from Calabria, Piedmont, Lazio, Puglia, and Sicily. Items that are always available include spaghetti (with a tomato sauce freshly made each day), chicken breast, salmon fillet, and vegetables of the day. All pizza dough is made on board, and risotto is a daily signature item, as is fresh pasta. Several varieties of Italian breads such as bruschetta, focaccia, and panettone are provided. Light 'always available' and vegetarian dishes are also provided.

Michelin-starred Italian celebrity chef Carlo Cracco developed special dishes for Gala, Christmas and New Year menus, and developed a cooking experience for the DoReMi kids club.

For casual eats, the self-serve, food court-style Marketplace Buffet is large. It is open 20 hours a day for breakfasts and lunches, and for waiter-served dinners in a relaxed evening setting. A bakery corner provides freshly baked breads and rolls throughout the day.

Extra-cost venues include Butcher's Cut – MSC's answer to the all-American steakhouse experience, with premium-quality king-sized steaks cooked to order); Kaito Teppanyaki (for Japanese-style sushi and assorted dishes, plus Teppanyaki grills for show food); Ristorante Italiana is for extra-special tastes of Italy – the 'slow-food' way, while HOLA! Tapas Bar is for high-quality light bites by famed Michelin-starred Spanish chef Ramón Freixa.

Also, award-winning French chocolatier Jean-Philippe Maury is behind Chocolat & Café, which features an open chocolate atelier. Meanwhile, extra-cost Segafredo coffees are available in several locations.

ENTERTAINMENT. A Cirque du Soleil-designed multi-level showlounge (it cost a whopping €20 million) has excellent sight lines from almost all seats in its amphitheater-style setting. The colorful acrobatic shows are provided by a real Cirque du Soleil troupe as part of a joint venture with MSC Cruises, featuring a dinner-and-show package.

A second entertainment venue, called The Lounge, has a stage (mainly for cabaret-style shows and other presentations), and a dance floor; it is adjacent to a small 5D cinema.

Atop ship is an observation lounge called Piano Lounge, with great views.

SPA/FITNESS. The Aurea Spa is large. Facilities include several body-treatment rooms, saunas, steam rooms and changing rooms for men and women, a large workout room full of high-tech Technogym cardiovascular equipment, and a beauty salon.

MSC MUSICA
★★★★

THIS SHIP EXUDES LIVELY ITALIAN DECOR AND GOOD STYLE FOR FAMILY CRUISING

Size:	Large Resort Ship	Passenger/Crew Ratio (lower beds):	2.5
Tonnage:	92,409	Cabins (total):	1,275
Cruise Line:	MSC Cruises	Size Range (sq ft/m):	150.6–301.3/14.0–28.0
Former Names:	none	Cabins (for one person):	0
Builder:	Aker Yards (France)	Cabins with balcony:	827
Entered Service:	Jul 2006	Cabins (wheelchair accessible):	17
Length (ft/m):	963.9/293.8	Wheelchair accessibility:	Good
Propulsion/Propellers:	diesel (31,680kW)/2	Elevators:	13
Total Crew:	1,014	Casino (gaming tables):	Yes
Passengers (lower beds):	2,550	Self-Service Launderette:	No
Passenger Space Ratio (lower beds):	36.2	Onboard currency:	Euros

THE SHIP. *MSC Musica* suits couples, solo travelers, and families with children of all ages who enjoy big-ship surroundings and a big-city lifestyle, with different multi-lingual (mostly European) nationalities. Youngsters have their own multi-room play center, youth counselors, and activity programs.

The sleek, deep blue funnel features a swept-back design with the MSC logo in gold. The overall profile is quite well balanced. The hull has large circular porthole-style windows instead of square or rectangular ones. Unfortunately, there is no walk-around open promenade deck.

Real wood and marble are used extensively in the interiors, reflecting the commitment that MSC Cruises (a Swiss-based company with Italian roots) has in cruising.

The interior focal point is a main three-deck-high lobby, with a water-feature backdrop and a crystal (glass) piano on a small stage that appears to float on a pond. Other principal facilities include a large main show lounge, a nightclub, disco, numerous lounges and bars (including a wine bar), library, card room, an Internet center, virtual-reality center, children's club, and cigar lounge with a selection of cigars (including Cuban).

A shopping gallery has an integrated bar and entertainment area flowing through the main lobby, while close by is the expansive San Remo Casino.

Drinking places include a pub-like venue as well as several comfortable lounges with live music.

BERLITZ'S RATINGS		
	Possible	Achieved
Ship	500	396
Accommodation	200	150
Food	400	242
Service	400	298
Entertainment	100	61
Cruise Experience	400	289
OVERALL SCORE 1436 points out of 2000		

Some of the artwork is whimsical, but fishermen will appreciate the stuffed head from a blue marlin caught by Pierfrancesco Vago, chairman of MSC Cruises, in 2004; it weighs 588lbs (267kg) and stands at the Blue Marlin Bar on the pool deck. And do check out the 'restroom with a view' – the cubicles have a great ocean view (if you leave the door open).

Although access throughout most of the interior of the ship is good, wheelchair-users should note that passenger hallways are narrow on some decks. Although the interior layout (and passenger flow) is good, congestion occurs when first-seating passengers exit the two main dining rooms, as diners on the second seating are waiting to enter.

ACCOMMODATION. There are several price levels, depending on grade and location. There are suites with private balcony, mini-suites, outside-view cabins, and interior (no-view) cabins. Contrary to nautical convention, the cabin-numbering system has even-numbered cabins on the starboard side, and odd-numbered cabins on the port side.

All cabins have a minibar and personal safe, satellite flat-screen TV with audio channels, and 24-hour room service. Continental breakfast is complimentary from 7.30 to 10am, but room service costs extra at any other time.

Accommodation designated as 'suites' – they are not true suites, as there is no separate bedroom and lounge – is more roomy than standard accommodation, although suites are small compared to those on some other cruise lines. They have a larger lounge area, walk-in closet, vanity desk with drawer-mounted hairdryer, and a bathroom with combination tub and shower. There is a semi-private balcony with light, but the partitions between each balcony are partial, not full. Suite bathrooms are plain, with plastic washbasins, white walls, and mirrors that steam up.

Many cabins on Forte Deck have views obstructed by lifeboats. Cabins on Cantata Deck are subject to the noise of sunloungers being dragged across the deck above when it is set up early in the morning. Some of the most popular cabins are those with aft views from the balcony cabins (on Virtuoso, Adagio, Intermezzo, and Forte decks). The cabins for disabled passengers are spacious and well equipped.

DINING. There are two main dining rooms, L'Oleandro and Le Maxim's, both aft, with large ocean-view picture windows and tables for two to eight. Seating is both banquette-style and in individual chairs; the chairs are slim and lack armrests.

MSC Cruises highlights regional Italian cuisine and wines, with dining-room menus that feature food from Calabria, Piedmont, Lazio, Puglia, and Sicily. Items that are always available include spaghetti (with a tomato sauce freshly made each day), chicken breast, salmon fillet. All pizza dough is made on board, and risotto is a daily signature item, as is fresh pasta. Several varieties of Italian breads such as bruschetta, focaccia, and panettone are provided. Light 'always available' and vegetarian dishes are also provided.

Passengers occupying suite- and deluxe-grade accommodation are typically assigned the best tables in the quietest sections of Le Maxim's restaurant, which is quieter than L'Oleandro.

Gli Archi Cafeteria (a section of which forms the reservations-only Il Giardino) is for casual, self-serve breakfast and lunch buffets and for sit-down, served, but casual dinners with waiter service each evening. It's actually open for 20 hours daily, so there's always something available. There's also a pool deck fast-food eatery for burgers and other grilled food items. Several bars adjacent to the midships atrium lobby,

serve extra-cost Segafredo Italian coffees, and tea and pastries.

Il Giardino is an extra-cost, à la carte dining venue, and requires reservations.

Kaito is a Japanese sushi bar with counter and table seating and a menu that has a fine array of extra-cost, à la carte sashimi pieces, nigiri and temaki sushi and maki rolls, tempura and teriyaki items, and a choice of several types of cold or hot sake, and Japanese beer. Reservations are needed.

Enoteca Wine Bar, a creative wine bar, provides a selection of famous regional Italian cheeses, hams, honey, and wines in a relaxing bistro-style setting.

Silver trays full of late-night snacks are taken throughout the ship by waiters, and, on some days, special late-night desserts, such as flambé items may be showcased in various lounges. The ship also makes its own ice cream.

ENTERTAINMENT. Teatro La Scala, the principal showlounge, is in the ship's forward section. It has tiered seating on two levels, and sight lines are good from most of the plush, comfortable seats. The room also serves as a venue for large groups or social functions. MSC Cruises focuses on visual, rather than vocal, production shows, all with pre-recorded backing tracks because there is no space for a bandstand.

Il Tucano Lounge and Crystal Lounge both function as large social spots with dance floor and live music, while G32 is an ear-splitting nightclub, which, by day, with its floor-to-ceiling windows, is a quiet, pleasant place to relax and read.

Big-screen movies are shown on a poolside screen.

SPA/FITNESS. The Aloha Beauty Farm is located above the navigation bridge at the forward end of the ship. The complex has a beauty salon, several body-treatment rooms, and a gymnasium with forward ocean views and an array of high-tech, muscle-toning, and strengthening equipment. An extra-cost, Middle East-themed thermal suite has steam rooms, saunas, and a relaxation/hot tub room.

Sports facilities include table tennis, a tennis court, mini-golf course, golf practice net, two shuffleboard courts, and a walking/jogging track.

MSC OPERA
★★★+

THIS MID-SIZED FAMILY-FRIENDLY SHIP HAS GREAT EUROPEAN STYLE AND FLAIR

Size:	Mid-size Ship
Tonnage:	65,875
Cruise Line:	MSC Cruises
Former Names:	none
Builder:	Chantiers de l'Atlantique (France)
Entered Service:	Mar 2004
Length (ft/m):	902.2/275.0
Propulsion/Propellers:	diesel (31,680kW)/2 azimuthing pods
Total Crew:	721
Passengers (lower beds):	2,142
Passenger Space Ratio (lower beds):	30.7
Passenger/Crew Ratio (lower beds):	2.9
Cabins (total):	1,071
Size Range (sq ft/m):	139.9–302.0/13.0–28.0
Cabins (for one person):	0
Cabins with balcony:	232
Cabins (wheelchair accessible):	4
Wheelchair accessibility:	Good
Elevators:	9
Casino (gaming tables):	Yes
Self-Service Launderette:	No
Onboard currency:	Euros

THE SHIP. *MSC Opera* is best for couples, solo travelers, and families who enjoy big-ship surroundings and a big-city lifestyle.

The ship's deep blue funnel is sleek, with a swept-back design featuring the MSC logo.

In 2015 the ship underwent a 'chop-and-stretch' operation, which added an 82ft (25m) mid-section, almost 200 additional cabins, more public rooms, entertainment facilities and new shops (but no additional elevators), and more exterior deck space, which houses a large waterpark for children. All decks are named after well-known operas. The interior layout and passenger flow are quite good, except for a couple of points of congestion, typically when the first seating exits the dining room and passengers on second seating are waiting to enter. The decor has many Italian and other Mediterranean influences, including clean lines, minimalist furniture, and a collection of colors, soft furnishings, and fabrics that work well together, and without any hint of garishness. Real wood and marble have been used extensively in the interiors, and the fit and finish are good.

Facilities include the ship's main showlounge, a nightclub/disco, several lounges and bars, an Internet center with 10 terminals, a virtual-reality center, a children's club, and the Via Condotti shopping gallery with shops, integrated bar, and entertainment area – so that you can shop, drink, and be entertained conveniently all in the one place. The Monte

BERLITZ'S RATINGS

	Possible	Achieved
Ship	500	378
Accommodation	200	151
Food	400	239
Service	400	295
Entertainment	100	60
Cruise Experience	400	276

OVERALL SCORE 1399 points out of 2000

Carlo Casino provides blackjack, poker, and roulette games, together with an array of slot machines. There is also a card room, but the integral library is small, uncared for, and disappointing, and there are no hardback books.

Drinking places include the Sotto Vento Pub (under the showlounge) and the La Cabala lounge. A 15 percent gratuity is added to all drinks/beverage orders.

Wheelchair-users should note that there is no access to the uppermost forward and aft decks, although access throughout most of the interior of the ship is very good, and there are several wheelchair-accessible public restrooms. In passenger hallways it can be a squeeze to get past housekeeping carts at certain hours.

Families with children will find special kids' areas equipped with Chicco® and LEGO® products, and an energetic multilingual youth activity team.

Minor niggles include: the in-your-face photographers; constant music in every lounge; and standing in line for embarkation, disembarkation, shore tenders, self-serve buffet meals. Sadly, there is no forward observation lounge.

ACCOMMODATION. There are several different price levels, depending on grade and location: one suite category including 'suites' with private balcony, five outside-view cabin grades, and five interior cabin grades. The cabin-numbering system has even-numbered cabins on the starboard side, and odd-numbered cabins on the port side – contrary to nautical convention.

All cabins have minibar and personal safe, satellite TV, several audio channels, and 24-hour room service. Tea and coffee are complimentary, but snacks delivered by room service cost extra.

Although the 'suites' are not true suites (there is no separate bedroom and lounge), they do have more room, a larger lounge area, walk-in closet, wall-to-wall vanity counter, bathroom with combination tub/shower combination, and semi-private balcony with a light. Cotton bathrobes are provided. The suite bathrooms are plain, with white plastic washbasins and walls, and mirrors that steam up.

Some cabins on Othello Deck and Rigoletto Deck have lifeboat-obstructed views, while those on Turandot Deck aft (10192–10241) may be subject to late-night and early-morning noise from the cafeteria above. Cabins on the uppermost accommodation deck are subject to deck chairs and tables being dragged across the deck, when it is set up or cleaned early in the morning.

DINING. There is one principal dining room, La Caravella Restaurant, with ocean-view picture windows in the aft section, and tables are for two to eight.

MSC Cruises highlights regional Italian cuisine and wines, with menus that feature food from Calabria, Piedmont, Lazio, Puglia, and Sicily. Items that are always available include spaghetti (with a tomato sauce freshly made each day), chicken breast, salmon fillet, and vegetables. All pizza dough is made on board, and risotto is a daily signature item, as is fresh pasta fresh. Several varieties of Italian breads such as bruschetta, focaccia, and panettone are provided. Light 'always available' and vegetarian dishes are also provided.

L'Approdo Restaurant is assigned to all passengers occupying accommodation designated as suites, although other passengers can dine in it, too, on a reservations-only basis. As you might expect, the food and service are superior to that in the main dining room.

Casual, self-serve buffets for breakfast and lunch can be taken in Le Vele Cafeteria, although the serving lines on both port and starboard sides are quite cramped, and the food is quite basic, or at the pool deck outside the fast-food eatery, with grill and pizzeria. Le Vele is also open for sit-down, served, but casual, dinners – it's actually open 20 hours a day. Extra-cost Segafredo coffees and pastries are featured in the Aroma Café, on the upper level of the two-deck-high atrium lobby, but annoying videos constantly play on TV sets in the forward section.

ENTERTAINMENT. The 713-seat Teatro dell'Opera (the main showlounge) has tiered seating, a sloping floor, and good sight lines from most seats, which are plush. The venue is also used for large social functions. There is no bandstand, so the production shows use pre-recorded backing tracks.

The Opera Lounge, one deck above the showlounge, is for social dancing, and features a live band. Meanwhile, for the young and lively set, there is the Byblos Discotheque. A number of bands and musical groups provide live music in the various bars and lounges.

SPA/FITNESS. The Opera Health Center has a beauty salon, several treatment rooms for body-pampering treatments, a gymnasium with ocean views, and an extra-cost thermal suite, with various steam rooms and sauna.

The health center is operated by the excellent Italian company OceanView, with European hairstylists and Balinese massage and body-treatment staff. Gratuities are not included, and are at your discretion.

Outside on deck, sports fans will appreciate a neat eight-hole mini-golf course that wraps around the funnel, while a walking/jogging track encircles the two swimming pools in the center of the ship.

MSC ORCHESTRA
★★★★

THIS LARGE, COMFORTABLE, FAMILY-FRIENDLY SHIP HAS ELEGANT DECOR AND STYLE

Size:	Large Resort Ship	Passenger/Crew Ratio (lower beds):	2.4
Tonnage:	92,409	Cabins (total):	1,275
Cruise Line:	MSC Cruises	Size Range (sq ft/m):	150.6–301.3/14.0–28.0
Former Names:	none	Cabins (for one person):	0
Builder:	Aker Yards (France)	Cabins with balcony:	827
Entered Service:	May 2007	Cabins (wheelchair accessible):	17
Length (ft/m):	963.9/293.8	Wheelchair accessibility:	Good
Propulsion/Propellers:	diesel-electric (40,4000kW)/2	Elevators:	13
Total Crew:	1,054	Casino (gaming tables):	Yes
Passengers (lower beds):	2,550	Self-Service Launderette:	No
Passenger Space Ratio (lower beds):	36.2	Onboard currency:	Euros

THE SHIP. *MSC Orchestra* is sister to *MSC Musica* and *MSC Poesia*. It has a sleek deep blue funnel and a swept-back design with the MSC logo in gold lettering. The overall profile is quite well balanced. The hull has large circular porthole-style windows, rather than square or rectangular windows.

Among the numerous lounges and bars, the Out of Africa Savannah Lounge is stunning. A delightful four-piece classical ensemble regularly performs in the atrium lobby. Much real wood and marble are used in the interiors, and the high quality reflects the commitment that MSC Cruises (a Swiss-based company with Italian roots) has in the vessel's future.

The focal point is a three-deck-high lobby, with a water-feature backdrop and a crystal piano on a small stage that appears to float on a pond. Other facilities include a large main show lounge, a nightclub, disco, numerous lounges and bars (including a wine bar), library, card room, an Internet center, a virtual-reality center, children's club, and cigar lounge with specialized smoke extraction.

A shopping gallery has an integrated bar and entertainment area that flows through the main lobby.

Drinking places include a pub-like venue as well as several comfortable lounges with live music. Some of the artwork is whimsical. And, speaking of whimsical, check out the 'restrooms with a view' – the men's/ladies' toilet cubicles adjacent to the

BERLITZ'S RATINGS		
	Possible	Achieved
Ship	500	396
Accommodation	200	151
Food	400	241
Service	400	298
Entertainment	100	62
Cruise Experience	400	291
OVERALL SCORE 1439 points out of 2000		

forward pool deck bar have a great ocean view, and you can even watch the passing scenery while sitting on the toilet – if you leave the door open.

The decor has many Italian influences. There are clean lines and minimalist furniture, combined with a wide range of colors, soft furnishings, and fabrics that work well together, although it's a little more garish than one would expect.

Wheelchair-users should note that the accommodation hallways are narrow on some decks. Note that there is no walk-around open promenade deck.

Although the interior layout and passenger flow are good, congestion occurs when first seating exits the two main dining rooms and second-seating passengers are waiting to enter.

The MSC Cruises crew does its best to provide good service to a multi-national clientele, and the ship exudes a noticeable feel-good factor.

ACCOMMODATION. There are several price levels, depending on grade and location. There are suites with private balcony, mini-suites, outside-view cabins, and interior (no-view) cabins. Contrary to nautical convention, the cabin-numbering system has even-numbered cabins on the starboard side, and odd-numbered cabins on the port side.

All cabins have a minibar, personal safe, flat-screen TV with audio channels, and 24-hour room service. Continental breakfast is complimentary from 7.30 to 10am, but snacks from room service cost extra at any other time.

Accommodation designated as 'suites' are not true suites (the bedroom and lounge are not separate), but simply larger cabins, and have a lounge area, walk-in closet, vanity desk with drawer-mount hairdryer, a bathroom with tub/shower combination, and a semi-private balcony with light. The suite bathrooms are plain, with plastic washbasins and white walls, and the mirrors steam up.

Many cabins on Forte Deck have views obstructed by lifeboats. Cabins on the uppermost accommodation deck may get noise from sunloungers being dragged across the deck above when it is set up or cleaned. Perhaps the most popular cabins are aft, with views over the ship's stern from the balcony cabins (Virtuoso, Adagio, Intermezzo, and Forte decks). The 17 cabins for disabled passengers are spacious and well equipped.

DINING. There are two main dining rooms, Villa Borghese Restaurant and L'Ibiscus, located aft, with large ocean-view windows. There are two seatings for dinner (open seating for breakfast and lunch), with tables for two to eight, plus alcove banquette-style seats.

MSC Cruises highlights regional Italian cuisine and wines, with menus that feature food from Calabria, Piedmont, Lazio, Puglia, and Sicily. Items that are always available include spaghetti (with tomato sauce made fresh daily), chicken breast, salmon fillet, and vegetables of the day. All pizza dough is made on board, as is fresh pasta. Several varieties of Italian breads such as bruschetta, focaccia, and panettone are provided. Light 'always available' meals and vegetarian dishes are also provided.

Shanghai Chinese Restaurant makes a change from the main restaurants. This was the first real Chinese restaurant aboard any cruise ship – mainly because of the challenge to provide high-temperature woks and deep fryers. Beijing, Cantonese, Shanghai, and Szechuan cuisines are featured.

The Four Seasons Restaurant features extra-cost Italian cuisine in a garden-style setting with fine china; regional and seasonal cuisine is cooked to order. Reservations are required.

La Piazzetta Café is open 20 hours a day for casual, self-serve, buffet-style breakfasts and for sit-down, served dinners in a relaxed environment.

ENTERTAINMENT. Covent Garden is a stunning large showlounge. The Opera Lounge, one deck above, is the place for social dancing, with live music. The G32 nightclub is for the more energetic, while a poolside screen provides movies and sports events.

SPA/FITNESS. The Orchestra Health Center, operated by the Italian company OceanView, includes a beauty salon, several treatment rooms offering massage and other body-pampering treatments, and a fitness center with ocean views and high-tech muscle-toning equipment.

There's also a thermal suite, containing different kinds of steam rooms combined with aromatherapy infusions, at extra cost. There's a neat juice and smoothie bar opposite the reception desk. Gratuities are at your discretion.

Additional sports facilities include deck quoits, shuffleboard courts, tennis and basketball courts, mini-golf, and a jogging track.

MSC POESIA
★★★★

THIS IS AN ELEGANT LARGE, INFORMAL, AND COMFORTABLE FAMILY-FRIENDLY SHIP

Size:	Large Resort Ship	Passenger/Crew Ratio (lower beds):	2.4
Tonnage:	92,627	Cabins (total):	1,275
Cruise Line:	MSC Cruises	Size Range (sq ft/m):	150.6–301.3/14.0–28.0
Former Names:	none	Cabins (for one person):	0
Builder:	Fincantieri (Italy)	Cabins with balcony:	827
Entered Service:	Oct 2008	Cabins (wheelchair accessible):	17
Length (ft/m):	963.9/293.8	Wheelchair accessibility:	Good
Propulsion/Propellers:	diesel (58,000kW)/2	Elevators:	13
Total Crew:	1,039	Casino (gaming tables):	Yes
Passengers (lower beds):	2,550	Self-Service Launderette:	No
Passenger Space Ratio (lower beds):	36.3	Onboard currency:	Euros

THE SHIP. *MSC Poesia* is sister to *MSC Musica* and *MSC Orchestra*; it has a sleek, deep blue funnel and swept-back design with the MSC logo. The hull has large circular porthole-style windows instead of square or rectangular windows.

The interior focal point is a main three-deck-high lobby, which has a grand water-feature backdrop and a crystal (glass) piano on a small stage that appears to float on a pond. Other facilities include a large showlounge, nightclub, disco, numerous lounges and bars, a library, card room, Internet center, virtual-reality center, children's club, and cigar lounge.

The musically themed decor has many Italian influences, including clean lines, minimalism in furniture design, and a collection of colors, soft furnishings, and fabrics that work well together, although it's a little more garish than one would expect.

Real wood and marble have been used extensively in the interiors, and the high quality reflects the commitment that Switzerland-based MSC Cruises has in the vessel's future.

The interior layout and passenger flow are good – with the exception of a couple of points of congestion, typically when the first seating exits the two main dining rooms, and passengers on the second seating are waiting to enter.

An integrated bar and entertainment area, plus shops, flows through the main lobby; close by is the expansive Casino Royale.

BERLITZ'S RATINGS		
	Possible	Achieved
Ship	500	395
Accommodation	200	151
Food	400	241
Service	400	298
Entertainment	100	62
Cruise Experience	400	292

OVERALL SCORE 1439 points out of 2000

Some of the artwork is quite whimsical and photogenic. Do check out the 'restroom with a view' – the men's/ladies' toilet cubicles adjacent to the pool deck bar – they have a great ocean view, and you can even watch the passing scenery while sitting on the toilet, if you leave the door open.

Although access throughout most of the ship is good, wheelchair-users should note that the passenger hallways are a little narrow on some decks for you to pass when housekeeping carts are in place. There is no walk-around open promenade deck.

ACCOMMODATION. There are several price levels, depending on grade and location. Included are 18 'suites' with private balcony, mini-suites, outside-view cabins, and interior cabins. Contrary to nautical convention, the cabin-numbering system has even-numbered cabins on the starboard side, and odd-numbered cabins on the port side.

All cabins have a minibar, personal safe, flat-screen TV with audio channels, and 24-hour room service (Continental breakfast is complimentary from 7.30 to 10am; snacks from room service cost extra at any other time).

Accommodation designated as 'suites' are simply larger cabins with lounge area, walk-in closet, vanity desk with drawer-mounted hairdryer, and a bathroom with combination tub and shower (but plain washbasins).

Many cabins on Forte Deck have views obstructed by lifeboats. Cabins on the uppermost accommodation deck may be subject to noise from sunloungers being dragged across the deck above when it is set up or cleaned. Some of the most popular cabins are those aft, with views over the ship's stern from the balcony cabins on four of the aft decks. The accessible cabins are spacious and well equipped.

DINING. There are two principal dining rooms (Le Fontane and Il Palladio), both located aft on different decks, with large, ocean-view picture windows. There are two seatings for meals, and tables are for two to eight; seating is both banquette-style and in individual armless chairs.

MSC Cruises highlights regional Italian cuisine and wines, with menus featuring food from Calabria, Piedmont, Lazio, Puglia, and Sicily. All pizza dough is made on board, and risotto is a daily signature item, as is fresh pasta. Several Italian breads such as bruschetta, focaccia, and panettone are provided. Light 'always available' meals and vegetarian dishes are also provided.

Kaito is a delightful, extra-cost Japanese restaurant, with a sushi bar and an extensive menu; reservations are required.

The Tex-Mex Restaurant is an extra-cost, à la carte dining spot, for which reservations are necessary.

The Wine Bar (Enoteca) provides a selection of famous regional cheeses, hams, and a variety of wines in a bistro-style setting that is relaxing and entertaining.

The Villa Pompeiana Cafeteria is for casual, food court-style, self-serve buffets for breakfast and lunch and for sit-down, served (but casual) dinners (it's actually open for 20 hours a day). Burgers and other grilled fast-food items are available poolside. Extra-cost Segafredo Italian coffees, together with a variety of teas and pastry items, are also served in several bars adjacent to the atrium midships lobby.

Silver trays full of late-night snacks are taken throughout the ship by waiters, and, on some days, special late-night desserts, such as flambé items, are showcased in various lounges.

ENTERTAINMENT. Teatro Carlo Felice, the showlounge, has tiered seating on two levels, and sight lines are good from most of the plush seats. There is no showband – all shows are performed to pre-recorded music.

Another large lounge (Zebra Bar), aft of the showlounge, is for social dancing and cooking demonstrations.

Big-screen movies are shown on a large poolside screen.

SPA/FITNESS. The Poesia Health Center features a beauty salon, several body-pampering treatment rooms, and a gymnasium with forward ocean views and muscle-toning equipment. There's also a cost-extra thermal suite, containing steam rooms and saunas with aromatherapy infusions, and a relaxation/hot tub room.

Sports facilities include table tennis, a tennis court, mini-golf course, golf practice net, two shuffleboard courts, and a jogging track. A mini-golf course is on the port side of the funnel, while a walking/jogging track encircles an upper level above the two swimming pools.

MSC PREZIOSA
★★★★

THIS FINE, LARGE, FAMILY-FRIENDLY SHIP IS DESIGNED WITH EUROPEANS IN MIND

Size:	Large Resort Ship	Passenger/Crew Ratio (lower beds):	2.5
Tonnage:	139,400	Cabins (total):	1,751
Cruise Line:	MSC Cruises	Size Range (sq ft/m):	148.5–568.3/13.8–52.8
Former Names:	none	Cabins (for one person):	0
Builder:	STX France	Cabins with balcony:	1,125
Entered Service:	Mar 2013	Cabins (wheelchair accessible):	45
Length (ft/m):	1,093.5/333.3	Wheelchair accessibility:	Good
Propulsion/Propellers:	diesel-electric (40,000kW)/2	Elevators:	16
Total Crew:	1,370	Casino (gaming tables):	Yes
Passengers (lower beds):	3,502	Self-Service Launderette:	No
Passenger Space Ratio (lower beds):	39.8	Onboard currency:	Euros

THE SHIP. This large resort ship, a close sister to *MSC Divina*, *MSC Fantasia*, and *MSC Splendida*, will appeal to young-at-heart adult couples, solo travelers, and families with children and teens enjoying an urban lifestyle, with a mix of mostly European nationalities and style.

MSC Preziosa was originally ordered by the Libyan government-owned shipping company GNMTC (the contract was signed by Captain Hannibal Muammar Gaddafi – fifth-eldest son of Colonel Gaddafi) before Switzerland-based cruise line MSC Cruises acquired the hull and configured the ship as the fourth in its *Fantasia*-class. It has the latest in green-technology engines.

Outside on the expansive main pool deck, there is a main swimming pool, together with an Aqua Park with hot tubs and numerous water features. Slightly forward of the pool deck is a family swimming pool; it's open well into the late evening, and can be covered by a sliding glass dome in inclement weather.

Facilities include a three-deck-high, theater-style showlounge, a nightclub, library, card room, an Internet center, a small 4D virtual-reality center, multi-deck shopping gallery, a large Millennium Star Casino with gaming tables and slot machines and a nicely-shaped stairway. In the aft section, an 'infinity' pool overlooks the stern and 'beach club' area. Drinking places include numerous lounges and bars (including a trendy 'Green Sax' jazz lounge/bar), most with live music. One lounge in the aft section of the ship is for adults only.

BERLITZ'S RATINGS		
	Possible	Achieved
Ship	500	416
Accommodation	200	157
Food	400	273
Service	400	308
Entertainment	100	77
Cruise Experience	400	301

OVERALL SCORE 1532 points out of 2000

An area called the MSC Yacht Club – an exclusive community of 'suite'-grade accommodation – includes a large observation/lifestyle lounge (the private club-like Top-Sail Lounge); private sunbathing space with integral dip pool; hot tubs; and concierge services for making dining reservations, booking excursions and spa treatments, and arranging private parties. A marble floor leads to a shiny Swarovski glass staircase that connects the concierge facilities between decks 15 and 16 under a glass-domed ceiling.

Overall, this is a very comfortable ship, with elegant decor and fine furnishings, special multi-room areas for children of all ages, and a friendly crew that enjoys helping you to enjoy life at sea.

ACCOMMODATION. If the budget allows, it's worth paying extra to stay in one of the Yacht Club 'suites'. You'll get silver-tray room service by a team of impressive, well-trained butlers. The suites have a minibar, interactive TV, personal safe, hairdryer, and satellite-link telephone.

Contrary to maritime tradition (strangely, the family that owns the ships has a maritime background), even-numbered cabins are on the starboard (right, facing forward) side. Nautical tradition aboard ocean-going ships dictates that even-numbered cabins should be on the port side (left when looking forward; the same as the lifeboats).

DINING. There are two main restaurants: the bi-level Golden Lobster and L'Arabesque, with two seatings for dinner, and open seating for breakfast and lunch. Tables are for two to eight, and include cozy alcoves with banquette seating (although it's challenging for waiters to serve these tables properly). Both restaurants feature Mediterranean cuisine, with an abundance of Italian-style favorites.

Yacht Club accommodation occupants have their own intimate La Palmeraie Restaurant, with North African decor, Moroccan-style arches, and hanging brass lamps. Dining is in an open-seating arrangement.

Ristorante Italiana provides a taste of Italy – the 'slow food' way; expect an emphasis on local artisanal producers, and sustainable sourcing. The cost-extra, reservations-required venue provides a change from the main dining rooms, and the cuisine is good.

There's also a popular Butcher's Cut (a cost-extra steakhouse) for premium quality steaks cooked to order). Galaxy Restaurant is an extra-charge venue above the main pool, with great views. It has a trendy vibe (it forms part of the disco), and the food – Mediterranean fusion cuisine (including meats and seafood items) – is good.

Casual serve-yourself, buffet-style meals can be taken in the large food court-style Inca and Maya Buffet (open almost around the clock) for breakfasts and lunches, and for waiter-served dinners in a relaxed atmosphere in the evening. A bakery corner provides freshly baked breads and rolls throughout the day.

The Sports and Bowling Diner features sandwiches and burgers. Meanwhile, Italian (extra-cost) coffees are available in several locations.

ENTERTAINMENT. The 1,600-seat Platinum Theater is a large showlounge – it's really more like a concert theatre and auditorium. It is spread over three decks, and there are good sight lines from almost all seats except for a few rows at the back on port and starboard sides. It is a well-designed room, except for the fact that no space is allocated for a live showband.

The shows concentrate more on visual entertainment such as mime, magic, dancing, and acrobatics, because the clientele is so multinational. Productions are performed with recorded music (known as a 'click-track'), and introductions are done at breakneck speed by the multilingual cruise director.

There is live music in almost all the other lounge/bar venues.

SPA/FITNESS. Aurea Wellbeing Center is large and houses a beauty salon, body-pampering treatment rooms, and a gymnasium with great ocean views. A thermal suite contains different kinds of steam rooms combined with herbal aromatherapy infusions, in a calming Asia-themed environment. Features include a Shu Uemura Art of Hair cabin, a vintage barbershop, and a Himalayan salt crystal 'bed.' The spa is operated by OceanView, a specialist spa provider, and most of the therapists are from Bali.

Sports facilities include deck quoits, shuffleboard courts, large tennis/basketball court, mini-golf, and a jogging track.

MSC SEASIDE
★★★★+

THIS REALLY IS MIAMI BEACH AT SEA FOR STYLISH FAMILY-IMMERSIVE RESORT CRUISING

Size:	Large Resort Ship	Passenger/Crew Ratio (lower beds):	2.9
Tonnage:	153,516	Cabins (total):	2,067
Cruise Line:	MSC Cruises	Size Range (sq ft/m):	129.1–968.7/12.0–90.0
Former Names:	none	Cabins (for one person):	0
Builder:	Fincantieri (Italy)	Cabins with balcony:	1,519
Entered Service:	Nov 2017	Cabins (wheelchair accessible):	54
Length (ft/m):	1,059.7/323.0	Wheelchair accessibility:	Good
Propulsion/Propellers:	diesel-electric/2	Elevators:	18
Total Crew:	1,413	Casino (gaming tables):	Yes
Passengers (lower beds):	4,134	Self-Service Launderette:	No
Passenger Space Ratio (lower beds):	37.1	Onboard currency:	US$

THE SHIP. *MSC Seaside* is really quite a handsome vessel, with a refreshing beach-resort look aft. It has a sleek, streamlined, and contemporary funnel that, unusually, is almost in the center of the ship. It has been specifically tailored for total family-immersive cruising.

The outstanding design has created a really intelligent use of the aft of the ship, giving it a combination of an upscale Miami Beach apartment and beach club look; included are panoramic glass elevators that connect the promenade deck with the upper deck Aqua Park non-stop. A 360-degree, walk-round outdoor promenade deck (with two over the sea glass floors) has a number of indoor/outdoor eateries and is destined to be the 'strolling to be seen' area. One of several pools can be covered by a retractable glass dome for inclement weather, and there is a lot of open deck and sunbathing space.

Atop ship and aft of the funnel, an Aqua Park play area is full of spray cannons, water-stream jets, and tipping buckets. There are five large waterslides (between 367 and 525ft long (112–160m), including two for side by side races down Duelling High-Speed Aqua Tubes, with a challenge for riders to match colored strobe lights along the route. There's also a 'Himalayan Bridge' walking (ropes) course.

Inside, the layout makes it easy to find your way around, and, because of the ship's 'open-flow' design, most public rooms flow seamlessly from one to

BERLITZ'S RATINGS		
	Possible	Achieved
Ship	500	422
Accommodation	200	162
Food	400	277
Service	400	308
Entertainment	100	78
Cruise Experience	400	307

OVERALL SCORE 1554 points out of 2000

another (however, there are several unexpected dead ends, and accessing the family buffet venue on Deck 16 can be challenging). Almost all the public rooms, bars and lounges for socializing (including a casino with gaming tables and an array of slot machines), plus hangouts for coffee and chocolate, a 5D cinema, and a shopping arcade (with some very well-known luxury designer brands) are located on decks 5, 6, 7, and 8, with accommodation decks above. Multiroom facilities for children and teens are good, and the ship has enthusiastic counselors and many programs for entertaining its younger passengers.

Niggles include the fact that the interior design has many reflective surfaces; there are also a number of extra-cost items, and no proper library (but there is a paperback exchange). Also, the showlounge is too small for the number of passengers, and there are several dead ends in passenger hallways that are confusing.

MSC Seaside is based year-round in Miami, for follow-the-sun Caribbean cruises, and the onboard currency is the US dollar.

ACCOMMODATION. The accommodation price grades depend on size and location. From the smallest to the largest, they are comfortable, well laid out (the upper grades have ample closet and drawer space, but the lower grade accommodation lacks drawer space). All bathrooms have glazed shower enclosures, shelves for personal toiletries, and decent-sized towels.

Yacht Club ('ship-within-a-ship') accommodation occupants have access to an exclusive observation lounge, and concierge service desk. All Yacht Club accommodation grades have a DeLonghi coffee machine, and occupants dine in a dedicated restaurant on a balcony level of the observation lounge, which incorporates a small dance floor and light-bite food bar. The bed linen is gorgeous, as are the premium mattresses, and a choice of four additional pillow types is available.

Contrary to maritime tradition, even-numbered cabins are on the starboard (right, facing forward) side (they should be on the port side – left when looking forward; the same as the lifeboats); a strange decision for a maritime ship-owning family.

DINING. The two main restaurants (Seaside and Ipanema) have many tables for two, and for four to eight persons. MSC Cruises has certainly been paying more attention to its cuisine recently, in an effort to appeal to a more international clientele. Michelin-starred Italian celebrity chef Carlo Cracco has developed special dishes for the Gala, Christmas, and New Year menus for the company, and introduced a cooking experience for the DoRe-Mi kids club.

MSC Cruises highlights popular North American cuisine, together with some regional Italian favorites, while the wine list contains many popular American wines. Items that are always available include chicken, salmon, and pasta dishes. All pizza dough is made on board, and risotto is a daily signature item, as is fresh pasta. Light 'always available' and vegetarian selections are also available.

Several extra-cost restaurants are positioned close to Yacht Club accommodation (forward) in an area called Chef's Court. These include Butcher's Cut (a steakhouse for premium quality steaks and grilled food items cooked to order), Ocean Cay (a good-value fish/seafood restaurant), Asian Market Kitchen by Roy Yamaguchi (for à la carte pan-Asian cuisine, with two large Teppanyaki grills and an adjacent sushi bar) – all in a cluster on Deck 16.

Biscayne Bay, a large self-serve, food-court style buffet area, is located low and aft. At night, this becomes a casual eatery (with the same menus as in the main dining rooms – but in a quieter environment). It is conveniently accessible to the aft 'beach' and outdoor promenade area on Deck 8, which includes a French-style crêperie and an ice cream parlor (both by the famous chocolatier and pastry chef Jean-Philippe Maury). A smaller 'family' buffet is on an upper deck (but it's only accessible from the aft stairway).

Extra-cost Segafredo (Italian) coffees are available in several bars and lounges, and all are served in proper china cups. Also, don't miss the Venchi Chocolaterie (founded by Silvano Venchi, from the Piedmont area of Italy) to see some delightful chocolates being made by hand.

ENTERTAINMENT. The stunning two-deck-high Metropolitan Theatre is a 934-seat amphitheatre-style showlounge, with very comfortable seating and excellent sight lines. Some shows cost extra.

A Comedy Club, located in the ship's center near the atrium lobby, is the venue for improv comedy.

SPA/FITNESS. Located on a lower deck, the Aurea Spa is extensive (it includes an outdoor section). Facilities include a large workout room (with Technogym cardiovascular equipment), saunas, steam and relaxation rooms for men and women, large beauty salon, and several body-pampering treatment rooms. Sports facilities include a tennis/basketball court, and a bowling alley.

MSC SEAVIEW
★★★★+

THIS FAMILY-IMMERSIVE RESORT PROVIDES A STUNNING WAY TO CRUISE IN HIGH STYLE SURROUNDINGS

Size:	Large Resort Ship	Passenger/Crew Ratio (lower beds):	2.9
Tonnage:	153,519	Cabins (total):	2,067
Cruise Line:	MSC Cruises	Size Range (sq ft/m):	129.1–968.7/12.0–90.0
Former Names:	None	Cabins (for one person):	0
Builder:	Fincantieri (Italy)	Cabins with balcony:	1,519
Entered Service:	May 2018	Cabins (wheelchair accessible):	54
Length (ft/m):	1,059/323.0	Wheelchair accessibility:	Good
Propulsion/Propellers:	Diesel-electric/2	Elevators:	18
Total Crew:	1,413	Casino (gaming tables):	Yes
Passengers (lower beds):	4,134	Self-Service Launderette:	No
Passenger Space Ratio (lower beds):	37.1	Onboard currency:	Euros

THE SHIP. *MSC Seaview* really is a handsome being, and has a refreshing, sporting look for a large resort ship, with a sleek, streamlined, centrally located funnel. The ship is tailored totally to family-immersive cruising, with water parks, sports activities, and multigenerational entertainment. One of several pools can be covered by a retractable glass dome for inclement or cool weather conditions.

The design is extremely good (it's like an enhancement of the *Oasis of the Seas* class of ships but with more open access); it has created an intelligent use of the aft of the ship, giving it a combination of St Tropez apartment and upscale beach club look, while panoramic elevators connect the promenade deck with the Aqua Park deck non-stop. A 360-degree, walk-around outdoor promenade deck has a number of indoor/outdoor restaurants and eateries, and is a 'strolling to be seen' area.

The outdoor Aqua Park play area is full of spray cannons, water stream jets, tipping buckets, and more, located high and aft of the funnel. It also has five large waterslides (between 112 and 160m/367 and 525ft long), including two for side-by-side races – with internal game controllers and players challenged to match colored strobe lights along the route, plus a 'Himalayan Bridge' walking (ropes) course.

Inside, the layout makes it fairly easy to find your way around, and, because of the ship's 'open

BERLITZ'S RATINGS		
	Possible	Achieved
Ship	500	423
Accommodation	200	162
Food	400	277
Service	400	308
Entertainment	100	78
Cruise Experience	400	310

OVERALL SCORE 1558 points out of 2000

flow' design, public rooms flow seamlessly from one to another (although there are a few dead ends). Almost all the public rooms, bars and lounges for socializing (including a casino with gaming tables and slot machines), and 'see and be seen in' hangouts for coffee and chocolate, plus a 5D cinema and shopping arcade (with well-known 'luxury' designer brands) are located on decks 5, 6, 7, and 8, with accommodation decks above. Facilities for children and teens are also excellent, and MSC Cruises has excellent counselors and busy programs to keep them busy.

An exclusive key-card access area called the MSC Yacht Club is like a 'ship within a ship' of 'suite'-grade accommodation, with large bathrooms and duplex suites. Exclusive facilities include a large indoor-outdoor observation/lifestyle lounge (great views), with its own dedicated Yacht Club Restaurant, plus concierge services for making dining reservations, booking excursions and spa treatments. This connects to a large outdoor, private club-like setting: a sunbathing deck with dip pool, hot tubs, bar and open deck eatery.

Overall, the ship has an elegant interior with fine furnishings and fabrics – a welcoming vacation environment. However, there are a few dead ends in the layout (these cause confusion for first-timers), and the showlounge is simply too small for the number of passengers carried.

ACCOMMODATION. The different accommodation price grades depend on the size and location you choose. From the smallest to the largest, they are comfortable, well laid out, with ample closet and drawer space. All bathrooms have glazed shower enclosures, shelves for personal toiletries, and good-sized towels.

Yacht Club accommodation occupants have a delightful, exclusive observation lounge, reception area, concierge desk and a small library area. All Yacht Club accommodation grades have a Nespresso coffee machine, and all dine in a dedicated restaurant, located directly above the Yacht Club (observation) lounge, which also incorporates a small dance floor and food area.

DINING. The two main restaurants Golden Sand (922 seats) and Silver Dolphin (806 seats) are both comfortable and well laid out; there are many tables for two, as well as tables for four to eight. MSC Cruises has concentrated a lot of effort into its cuisine recently, and producing high-quality meals is a priority, but presentation could be better.

Two-Michelin-star Italian chef Carlo Cracco developed special dishes for the Gala, Christmas, and New Year menus for the company, and developed a cooking experience for the DoReMi kids club (very popular).

Three extra-cost restaurants are positioned in the same area, close to Yacht Club accommodation (forward). These include a Mediterranean Steakhouse (for steaks and grilled food items), a fish/seafood and an Asian Fusion restaurant, two Teppanyaki grills, and an adjacent sushi bar – all on deck 16.

A large self-serve, food court-style buffet area is located low and aft and is conveniently accessible to the 'beach' and outdoor promenade area on Deck 8; it includes a crêperie and a 'gourmet' ice cream parlor (both are outposts of famous chocolatier and pastry chef Jean-Philippe Maury).

ENTERTAINMENT. The two-deck-high Odeon theatre is an amphitheatre-style showlounge, with comfortable seating and excellent sight lines. The production shows (performed three times an evening due to the venue's low capacity) are more visual than vocal, and include comedic sketches and high-energy dancing and aerial displays. Recorded backing tracks are used because there is no space for a bandstand (unless the band is at the back of the stage for a featured vocalist).

A dedicated Comedy Club, located in the ship's center near the atrium lobby, provides an entertainment alternative.

SPA/FITNESS. Located on a lower deck, the Aurea Spa is extensive (it also includes an outdoor section). Facilities include a large workout room (full of Technogym cardio-vascular equipment), saunas, steam and relaxation rooms for men and women, a large beauty salon, and several body pampering treatment rooms. Sports facilities include a tennis/basketball court, and a bowling alley.

MSC SINFONIA
★★★+

THIS IS A COMFORTABLE EURO-STYLE, INFORMAL, FAMILY-FRIENDLY MID-SIZED SHIP

Size:	Mid-size Ship	Passenger/Crew Ratio (lower beds):	2.7
Tonnage:	65,542	Cabins (total):	876
Cruise Line:	MSC Cruises	Size Range (sq ft/m):	139.9–236.8/13–22
Former Names:	*European Stars*	Cabins (for one person):	0
Builder:	Chantiers de l'Atlantique (France)	Cabins with balcony:	224
Entered Service:	Apr 2002/Mar 2005	Cabins (wheelchair accessible):	2
Length (ft/m):	902.0/275.0	Wheelchair accessibility:	Good
Propulsion/Propellers:	diesel (31,680kW)/2 azimuthing pods	Elevators:	9
		Casino (gaming tables):	Yes
Total Crew:	721	Self-Service Launderette:	No
Passengers (lower beds):	1,952	Onboard currency:	Euros
Passenger Space Ratio (lower beds):	33.5		

THE SHIP. *MSC Sinfonia* (sister to *MSC Armonia*), is best for adult couples and solo travelers, and families with children, who enjoy lots of activity, accompanied by lots of noise, in a setting exuding Mediterranean family values. The international mix of passengers adds to the overall ambience of the cruise experience.

The exterior deck space is barely adequate for the number of passengers carried. The Lido Deck surrounding the outdoor swimming pool also has whirlpool tubs and a bandstand, and all sunloungers have cushioned pads.

In 2015, the ship had a 'chop-and-stretch' operation, which added an 82ft (25m) mid-section, almost 200 additional cabins, more public rooms, entertainment facilities and new shops (but no additional elevators), and more exterior deck space, which houses a large waterpark for children.

The interior decor is modern European, with clean lines and minimalist furniture design – including some chairs that look interesting but are totally impractical.

Niggles include lines for embarkation, disembarkation, shore tenders, and self-serve buffet meals – an inevitable aspect of cruising aboard ships of this size.

Wheelchair-users should note that there is no access to the uppermost forward and aft decks, although most of the interior access is good. Also,

BERLITZ'S RATINGS

	Possible	Achieved
Ship	500	366
Accommodation	200	148
Food	400	238
Service	400	289
Entertainment	100	55
Cruise Experience	400	267

OVERALL SCORE 1363 points out of 2000

accommodation hallways are a little narrow on some decks, making it difficult to pass housekeeping carts.

The company keeps prices low by providing air transportation that may be at inconvenient times, or that involves long journeys by bus. In other words, be prepared for a little discomfort in getting to and from your cruise in exchange for low cruise rates.

Families with children are well catered to, and have dedicated rooms for kids, some equipped with Chicco® and LEGO® products, and an energetic multilingual youth activity team.

Overall, the ship is pleasant enough, but the cruise experience is marred by too many announcements (in multiple languages), and dining-room food that lacks flair and presentation.

ACCOMMODATION. There are numerous categories, with the price depending on the grade, size, and location you choose. These include 'suites' with private balcony (with partial partitions only, not full ones), outside-view cabins, and interior (no-view) cabins.

DINING. There are two main dining rooms, Il Galeone and Il Covo; both have two seating times and the same menu. The cuisine is reasonably sound, and, with varied menus and good presentation, should prove a highlight for most passengers. The wine list has a wide variety of wines at fairly reasonable prices, although almost all are very young.

MSC Cruises highlights regional Italian cuisine and wines, with menus that feature food from Italy. Always-available items include spaghetti (with a tomato sauce freshly made each day), chicken breast, and salmon fillet. All pizza dough is made on board, and risotto is a daily signature item, as is fresh pasta. Italian breads such as bruschetta, focaccia, and panettone are provided. Light 'always available' meals and vegetarian dishes are also provided.

La Terrazza is a casual, self-serve, food court-style buffet eatery open 20 hours a day, including sit-down, waiter-served dinners in a relaxed setting. The selections are standardized, and lack inspiration. Café del Mare, on the pool deck, is a grill station for burgers and other fast-food items.

Extra-cost Italian coffees and pastries are available in Le Baroque Café, set around the upper level of the two-deck-high atrium lobby. It's a good location for people-watching, but annoying music videos are constantly played on TV monitors in the forward sections.

ENTERTAINMENT. The two-deck-high Teatro San Carlo (showlounge) features colorful shows that are mainly visual, due to the international multilingual passenger mix. There is bandstand, so pre-recorded backing tracks are provided.

SPA/FITNESS. The Aurea Spa features a gymnasium with ocean views, and high-tech, muscle-toning equipment. A thermal suite has multiple steam rooms with aromatherapy infusions such as chamomile and eucalyptus, and a Rasul (mud) chamber. The spa offers a wide range of body-pampering wellbeing treatments.

For the active there's a simulated climbing wall outdoors aft of the funnel, as well as a volleyball/basketball court, and mini-golf.

MSC SPLENDIDA
★★★★

THIS LARGE, FAMILY-FRIENDLY SHIP HAS TASTEFUL, ELEGANT DECOR AND STYLE

Size:	Large Resort Ship	Passenger/Crew Ratio (lower beds):	2.3
Tonnage:	137,936	Cabins (total):	1,637
Cruise Line:	MSC Cruises	Size Range (sq ft/m):	161.4–699.6/15–65
Former Names:	none	Cabins (for one person):	0
Builder:	Aker Yards (France)	Cabins with balcony:	1,260
Entered Service:	Jul 2009	Cabins (wheelchair accessible):	43
Length (ft/m):	1,093.5/333.3	Wheelchair accessibility:	Good
Propulsion/Propellers:	diesel (40,000kW)/2	Elevators:	14
Total Crew:	1,370	Casino (gaming tables):	Yes
Passengers (lower beds):	3,274	Self-Service Launderette:	No
Passenger Space Ratio (lower beds):	42.1	Onboard currency:	Euros

THE SHIP. *MSC Splendida* will appeal to young adult couples, solo travelers, and families with children and teens who enjoy big ships with a mix of nationalities, mostly European. Children appreciate Virtual World's five white-knuckle 4D rides in a 10-seat thrill room. It all feels rather like a European city center, and is full of large and small rooms, nooks and crannies, and places to play in.

BERLITZ'S RATINGS		
	Possible	Achieved
Ship	500	410
Accommodation	200	156
Food	400	275
Service	400	307
Entertainment	100	77
Cruise Experience	400	301
OVERALL SCORE 1526 points out of 2000		

A sister ship to *MSC Fantasia*, *MSC Splendida* is a stunning ship, and one of the largest ships built for a European cruise company. It is about 33ft (10m) longer than the Eiffel Tower is high, and the propulsion power is the equivalent of 120 Ferraris. There are four swimming pools, one of which can be covered by a glass dome.

The interior includes an exclusive area called the MSC Yacht Club for the occupants of some 99 suites. This 'club' includes a Top-Sail Lounge (with butler service, canapés, and bite-sized food items); private sunbathing with an integral dip pool; two hot tubs; and concierge services for making dining reservations, and booking excursions and spa treatments.

If your budget allows, it's worth paying extra to stay in Yacht Club accommodation. You'll get silver-tray room service from a butler, a reserved (quieter) section of the Villa Verde Restaurant, and keycard access to the members-only sundeck sanctuary area. It's a world away from the hustle and bustle of the main pool decks and solarium on the decks below.

The ship's interior decor is stunning. There are basically two decks full of public lounges and bars (most with live music), and eateries, including a large two-deck-high, theater-style showlounge (The Strand), a nightclub/disco (The Aft Lounge), library, card room, an Internet center, a virtual-reality center, an extensive shopping gallery (that has the feel of a city), and a large casino (inhabited by many who can smoke at the bar). The Royal Palm Casino features gaming tables plus an array of slot machines.

The ship is well designed to accommodate families with children. A 15 percent gratuity is added to all drinks/beverage orders.

Niggles include the fact that all the lounges flow into each other, and so the music from each one bleeds into the adjacent room. Note that only Yacht Club-grade occupants are escorted to their cabins by butlers. Men should note that the public restrooms have cubicles (there are no urinals).

ACCOMMODATION. Eighty percent of the cabins are outsides, and 95 percent of these have a balcony – the standard balcony cabin is almost 172 sq ft (16 sq m), plus bathroom and balcony. If the budget allows, it's worth paying extra to stay in one of the 72 'suites' (each 312 sq ft/29 sq m) in the Yacht Club area at the top, front end of the ship.

Spa Suites include unlimited access to the sauna and steam room, a private consultation with the spa doctor, a Balinese massage, a facial relax treatment, and a solarium session.

The Yacht Club has its own serene concierge lounge, small library, and reception desk. A Swarovski glass stairway leads to the Yacht Club suites, and private elevator accesses the Aurea Spa, located one deck below. The lounge has its own galley and dedicated chef.

DINING. La Reggia, the main restaurant, spans two decks, has two seatings for dinner (open seating for breakfast and lunch) and tables are for two to eight. A second restaurant, the single-level Villa Verde, is for suite-grade accommodation occupants and has panoramic windows aft.

MSC Cruises highlights regional Italian cuisine and wines, with menus that feature food from Calabria, Piedmont, Lazio, Puglia, and Sicily. All pizza dough is made on board, and risotto is a daily signature item, as is fresh pasta. Several varieties of Italian breads such as bruschetta, focaccia, and panettone are provided. Light 'always available' and vegetarian dishes are also available.

L'Olivo is an Italian/Mediterranean extra-cost, reservations-required venue, located in a smaller, intimate setting aft, overlooking a small pool and relaxation area. Food is cooked to order, and dining here is a pleasant experience.

Buffet Bora Bora/Pago Pago are casual self-serve eateries for breakfast and lunch, and for sit-down, casual, waiter-served evening dinners.

Other (cost-extra) venues include Butcher's Cut (steaks and grilled seafood), Sea Pavilion (fish and seafood), and a Dim Sum Bar, while extra-cost Lavazza coffees are available in several locations.

ENTERTAINMENT. The Strand Theater has plush seating in tiers for up to 1,700, and good sight lines. The shows concentrate on visual entertainment such as mime, magic, dancing, and acrobatics, performed with recorded music (there is no orchestra pit). Live music for dancing and listening to is provided by a number of bands and soloists throughout the ship.

SPA/FITNESS. The Aurea Spa (16,000 sq ft/1,485 sq m) has a beauty salon, well-equipped treatment rooms, and a large gymnasium with ocean views. Included is a large thermal suite, and saunas. The decor is welcoming and restful. The spa is run by OceanView. Gratuities to spa staff are at your own discretion. Sports facilities include deck quoits, large tennis/basketball court, mini-golf, and a jogging track.

NATIONAL GEOGRAPHIC ENDURANCE
NYR

THIS EXPEDITION SHIP IS BUILT FOR IN-CLOSE AND PERSONAL POLAR CRUISING

Size:	Boutique Ship	Passenger/Crew Ratio (lower beds):	1.1
Tonnage:	12,300	Cabins (total):	69
Cruise Line:	Lindblad Expeditions	Size Range (sq ft/m):	139.9–204.5/13.0–19.0
Former Names:	none	Cabins (for one person):	12
Builder:	Ulstein Verft (Norway)	Cabins with balcony:	53
Entered Service:	Feb 2020	Cabins (wheelchair accessible):	0
Length (ft/m):	408.1/124.4	Wheelchair accessibility:	Poor
Propulsion/Propellers:	diesel-electric/2 azimuthing pods	Elevators:	2
		Casino (gaming tables):	No
Total Crew:	112	Self-Service Launderette:	No
Passengers (lower beds):	126	Onboard currency:	US$
Passenger Space Ratio (lower beds):	28.2		

THE SHIP. *National Geographic Endurance* (Polar Class 5) has a sloping, patented, smooth 'X-Bow' front, designed to help the ship smooth out any unkind sea conditions.

The public rooms consist of an observation lounge with forward views, and a lounge with electronic ship's position charts. Sadly, there are many pillars throughout the public rooms, which intrude on sight lines.

ACCOMMODATION. There are 69 cabins (all with Wi-Fi), including 12 solo cabins; 53 have a small balcony. While they are not luxurious in their appointments, they are practical. Bathrooms have glazed shower enclosures.

BERLITZ'S RATINGS		
	Possible	Achieved
Ship	500	NYR
Accommodation	200	NYR
Food	400	NYR
Service	400	NYR
Entertainment	100	NYR
Cruise Experience	400	NYR

OVERALL SCORE NYR points out of 2000

DINING. The main restaurant seats all participants in one open seating, so you can sit with whomever you wish. Expedition team members will also eat with you. The meals consist of hearty fare. Lighter meals can be taken in a second, smaller area of the observation lounge.

ENTERTAINMENT. Daily recaps, general expedition talks, and discussions are all that's needed.

SPA/FITNESS. There are two (different temperature) saunas, two treatment rooms, a yoga studio and, on a separate deck, a fitness center. There is also an 'infinity' pool aft.

NATIONAL GEOGRAPHIC EXPLORER

★★+

A STURDY LITTLE SHIP FOR UP-CLOSE NATURE AND WILDLIFE CRUISES

Size:	Boutique ship	Passenger/Crew Ratio (lower beds):	2.1
Tonnage:	6,471	Cabins (total):	81
Cruise Line:	Lindblad Expeditions	Size Range (sq ft/m):	n/a
Former Names:	Lyngen, Midnatsol II, Midnatsol	Cabins (for one person):	10
Builder:	Ulstein Hatlo (Norway)	Cabins with balcony:	13
Entered Service:	1982/Jun 2008	Cabins (wheelchair accessible):	1
Length (ft/m):	367.4/112.0	Wheelchair accessibility:	None
Propulsion/Propellers:	diesel/2	Elevators:	1
Total Crew:	70	Casino (gaming tables):	No
Passengers (lower beds):	152	Self-Service Launderette:	No
Passenger Space Ratio (lower beds):	42.5	Onboard currency:	US$

THE SHIP. Originally built as *Midnatsol* for Hurtigruten in 1982, it was purchased by Lindblad Expeditions in 2007 and extensively refitted for expedition-style cruising, with some good facilities and expedition equipment.

The ship has an ice-strengthened hull and has stabilizers, so movement is minimized. Twin funnel uptakes are unusually located at the very back. There is little outdoor deck space, but it's not needed in cold-weather areas.

The main facilities include a lecture room, bistro bar with espresso machine adjacent to the restaurant, and boot-washing stations. This ship best suits adventurous types who enjoy being with nature and wildlife in some of the most extraordinary places on earth, cosseted aboard a small, minimally comfortable ship.

The dress code is completely casual; layered clothing and sturdy outerwear is recommended. Gratuities to staff are not included in the price.

ACCOMMODATION. Price depends on size and location. The cabins are small, as are the bathrooms, although they are nicely designed, practical units. Some have queen-size beds, others have twin beds (some can be pushed together, some are

BERLITZ'S RATINGS		
	Possible	Achieved
Ship	500	257
Accommodation	200	109
Food	400	194
Service	400	232
Entertainment	100	60
Cruise Experience	400	215
OVERALL SCORE 1067 points out of 2000		

fixed). There are several cabins for solo occupancy. Tiled bathrooms have shower enclosures and small shelves for toiletries. Suites have two washbasins, premium bedding, and fluffy duvets.

There is a decent supply of electrical outlets and an ethernet connection for laptops. Closet doors slide open, to minimize noise and banging when the ship is in tough weather conditions. Naturally, a National Geographic Atlas is provided.

DINING. There is one main dining room, as well as areas for self-serve buffet-style food. The food is hearty and fairly healthy, although you should not expect to find fresh greens in some of the more out-of-the-way areas.

ENTERTAINMENT. Lectures, briefings, and recaps, plus after-dinner conversation with fellow participants, are the main entertainment – if you're not too tired after exhausting days of landings and other adventures.

SPA/FITNESS. There are two body-treatment rooms – with skylights, for wildlife-inspired wellness, facials, and massage, including a special 'ice-bear massage,' as well as a fitness/workout room.

NATIONAL GEOGRAPHIC ORION
★★★★

MATURE TRAVELERS SHOULD ENJOY THIS COZY 'SOFT' ADVENTURE SHIP

Size:	Boutique Ship	Passenger/Crew Ratio (lower beds):	1.4
Tonnage:	4,050	Cabins (total):	53
Cruise Line:	Lindblad Expeditions	Size Range (sq ft/m):	175.0–345.0/16.3–32.1
Former Names:	*Orion*	Cabins (for one person):	4
Builder:	Cassens-Werft (Germany)	Cabins with balcony:	9
Entered Service:	Nov 2003/Mar 2014	Cabins (wheelchair accessible):	0
Length (ft/m):	337.0/102.7	Wheelchair accessibility:	None
Propulsion/Propellers:	diesel/1	Elevators:	1
Total Crew:	75	Casino (gaming tables):	No
Passengers (lower beds):	102	Self-Service Launderette:	No
Passenger Space Ratio (lower beds):	38.2	Onboard currency:	Australian $

THE SHIP. This pocket-sized ship with its dark blue hull topped by a yellow/gold line is enjoyed by mature couples and solo travelers for discovering destinations that large cruise ships can't visit.

The former *Orion* (Orion Expedition Cruises) was acquired in 2013 by Lindblad Expeditions, renamed *National Geographic Orion*, and transferred to the new operator in March 2014, when it became part of Lindblad Expeditions/National Geographic. Snorkeling and diving gear for 24 dive participants was added, together with kayaks and an ROV (remote-operated vehicle) able to descend to 1,000ft (305m).

National Geographic Orion (according to one myth, Neptune was Orion's father, while Queen Euryale of the Amazon – sister of Medusa – was his mother) features nature- and wildlife-rich, expedition-style cruises in high-quality surroundings. It has all the comforts of home, plus specialist equipment for expedition cruising. Although small, it has stabilizers and bow and stern thrusters for maximum maneuverability, a fleet of 14 heavy-duty Zodiac inflatable landing craft, a fishing boat, BeeKay, and an aft marina platform for swimming off.

There is no swimming pool, but a hot tub is set amid an open deck, together with a bar and a small rock garden/water feature. All outdoor tables, chairs, and steamer-style sunloungers are made of tropical hardwood.

The interior decor is inviting, providing a cozy yet contemporary environment. Public rooms include

BERLITZ'S RATINGS		
	Possible	Achieved
Ship	500	379
Accommodation	200	154
Food	400	274
Service	400	294
Entertainment	100	73
Cruise Experience	400	293
OVERALL SCORE 1467 points out of 2000		

an observation lounge and library (plus a nautical chart table and a self-serve beverage station), opening to a walk-around open promenade deck; it also connects with the small Health Spa.

Other public rooms include a main lounge, an observation lounge, a boutique, and a dedicated theater with surround-sound system for lectures/movies. National Geographic provides stunning photographic images of the oceans as artwork.

Some rooms are clustered around a glass-walled atrium and the single elevator. A 'mud room,' with boot-washing stations, is adjacent to a portside Zodiac/tender loading platform.

This is about as far away from big cruise ships as you can get, with well-planned itineraries.

ACCOMMODATION. There are four suite grades, and two cabin grades; the facilities in all of them are very good. All have twin beds that convert to a queen-size bed, a TV infotainment system, a mini-refrigerator, ample closet space, a good-sized vanity desk, and a small personal safe.

The marble-clad bathroom (with glazed shower enclosure) has a small toiletries cabinet, single washbasin, and a large shower enclosure, with a retractable clothesline. The cabinetry was custom-made, and bathrooms fitted individually – rare in today's modular-fit world.

There are several suites, some with a small 'French' balcony (you can open the door, but cannot step outside). These have more space, and some share a narrow communal balcony (meaning there is no partition between them), a sofa, glass drinks table, and good-size vanity desk. Four Owner's Suites have a bathtub; all other suites/cabins have large shower enclosures.

DINING. The Restaurant has ocean-view picture windows, artwork based on the astrological signs, and operates one open seating. Its low ceiling, however, makes it rather noisy.

The cuisine is modestly good, and the wine selection is adequate. While portions are not large, they are colorful and creative.

The Outdoor Café, an open deck aft of the Leda Lounge, serves as an alfresco dining spot for casual breakfasts, lunches, and occasional barbeque dinners.

Continental breakfast and afternoon tea are also available in the Galaxy Lounge. Espressos and cappuccinos are available in two lounges/bars and restaurant.

ENTERTAINMENT. Each evening, lecturers provide daily recaps.

SPA/FITNESS. There's a workout center, sauna, shower enclosure, and private treatment room (for massages). A beauty salon is located two decks below.

NAUTICA
★★★+

THIS PREMIUM SHIP HAS TRADITIONAL DECOR, FOR MATURE-AGE CRUISERS

Size:	Small Ship	Passenger/Crew Ratio (lower beds):	1.7
Tonnage:	30,277	Cabins (total):	342
Cruise Line:	Oceania Cruises	Size Range (sq ft/m):	145.3–968.7/13.5–90.0
Former Names:	R Five	Cabins (for one person):	0
Builder:	Chantiers de l'Atlantique	Cabins with balcony:	232
Entered Service:	Dec 1998/Nov 2005	Cabins (wheelchair accessible):	3
Length (ft/m):	593.7/181.0	Wheelchair accessibility:	Good
Propulsion/Propellers:	diesel (18,600kW)/2	Elevators:	4
Total Crew:	386	Casino (gaming tables):	Yes
Passengers (lower beds):	684	Self-Service Launderette:	Yes
Passenger Space Ratio (lower beds):	44.2	Onboard currency:	US$

THE SHIP. *Nautica*, almost identical to *Insignia* and *Regatta*, is all-white, with a large square funnel and a pleasant Lido and Pool Deck outdoors, with teak overlaid decking and high-quality sunloungers. It is best suited to couples who like good food and style, with informality and interesting itineraries.

In 2014, a refurbishment program included the addition of Barista's coffee bar (for illy coffees), new bathrooms for Owner's Suites and Vista Suites, and refreshed decor in all other cabins. The interior decor is a throwback to the ocean liners of the 1920s and 1930s, with dark woods and warm colors, all in good taste, if a little fake in places. It includes detailed ceiling cornices, both real and faux, wrought-iron staircase railings, leather-paneled walls, trompe l'oeil ceilings, and rich carpeting in hallways with an Oriental rug-look center section.

Public rooms are spread over three decks, while a large observation lounge, the Horizon Bar, is high atop ship.

There are plenty of bars, including one in each restaurant entrance. Perhaps the nicest is the casino bar/lounge, a rectangular-shaped room that includes a Martini bar. It has an inviting marble fireplace, comfortable sofas, and individual chairs.

The Gratuities are automatically added to your onboard account. Accommodation designated as suites pay more, for the butler. An 18 percent gratuity is added to bar and spa accounts.

BERLITZ'S RATINGS		
	Possible	Achieved
Ship	500	356
Accommodation	200	126
Food	400	291
Service	400	282
Entertainment	100	67
Cruise Experience	400	262

OVERALL SCORE 1384 points out of 2000

ACCOMMODATION. There are many price grades, depending on size and location. These range from standard interior (no-view) and outside-view cabins (with or without balcony) to spacious suite grades.

All standard interior and outside-view cabins are really compact, with twin beds or a queen-size bed, personal safe, vanity desk with large mirror, good closet and drawer space in rich, dark woods, cotton bathrobe and towels, slippers, clothes brush, and shoehorn. Note that the underbed space is small so it's difficult to store your luggage.

About 100 cabins qualify as 'Concierge Level' accommodation, and occupants get extra goodies such as better bathroom amenities, complimentary shoeshine, tote bag, cashmere throw blanket, bottle of Champagne on arrival, hairdryer, priority restaurant reservations, priority embarkation, and dedicated check-in desks.

Owner's Suites. These measure 962 sq ft (89.4 sq m); they are fine, large living spaces located aft on decks 6, 7, and 8, but are subject to movement and vibration.

Vista Suites. These measure around 786 sq ft (73 sq m), located forward on decks 5 and 6.

Penthouse Suites. These are not suites, but large cabins (the bedrooms aren't separate from the living areas), and measure around 323 sq ft (30 sq m).

Cabins with private balconies (around 216 sq ft/20 sq m) have partial, not full, balcony partitions and sliding glass doors, and 14 cabins on Deck 6 have lifeboat-obstructed views and no balcony.

Outside-view and interior cabins measure around 160–165 sq ft (14.9–15.3 sq m).

DINING. There are four different restaurants:

The Grand Dining Room, with around 340 seats, has a raised central section, but the noise level is very high when the dining room is full, due to the low ceiling. Being located aft, it has large ocean-view windows on three sides – prime tables overlook the stern. The chairs are comfortable and have armrests. The menus change daily for lunch and dinner.

Toscana Italian Restaurant has 96 seats, windows along two sides, and a set menu plus daily chef's specials (reservations required).

Polo Grill has 98 seats, windows along two sides, and a set menu including prime steaks and seafood (reservations required).

The Terrace Café has indoor and outdoor seating. It is open for breakfast, lunch, and casual dinners, with tapas (Tapas on the Terrace) and other Mediterranean food items, and it incorporates a small pizzeria. There are basic salads, a meat-carving station, and a reasonable selection of cheeses.

All restaurants have open seating, so you can dine when you want, with whom you wish. Reservations are needed in Toscana Restaurant and Polo Grill, but there's no extra charge; tables are mainly for four or six, with few for two. There is also a Poolside Grill Bar. All cappuccino and espresso coffees cost extra.

The food and service staff is provided by a respected maritime catering company with an interest in Oceania Cruises. This is a foodie's ship, with high-quality ingredients. Particularly notable are the breads, rolls, croissants, and brioches – made on board from French flour and d'Isigny butter.

On sea days, an elegant tea is presented in the Horizon Lounge, with formally dressed staff, cake trolleys, and an array of cakes and scones. Sadly, teabags – not loose tea – prevail.

ENTERTAINMENT. The Nautica Lounge has entertainment, lectures, and some social events. There is little entertainment because of the intensive nature of the itineraries. However, there is live music in several bars and lounges.

SPA/FITNESS. The Lido Deck has a swimming pool and good sunbathing space, plus a thalassotherapy tub. A jogging track circles the swimming pool deck, but one deck above. The uppermost outdoors deck includes a golf driving net and shuffleboard court. The Canyon Ranch SpaClub features a beauty salon, three treatment rooms, men's and women's changing rooms, and steam room (but no sauna). An 18 percent gratuity applies to massages and treatments.

NAVIGATOR OF THE SEAS
★★★+

THIS IS A COLORFUL, ADVENTURE-FILLED LARGE RESORT SHIP FOR FAMILY CRUISING

Size:	Large Resort Ship
Tonnage:	137,276
Cruise Line:	Royal Caribbean International
Former Names:	none
Builder:	Kvaerner Masa-Yards (Finland)
Entered Service:	Dec 2002
Length (ft/m):	1,020.6/311.1
Propulsion/Propellers:	diesel-electric (75,600kW)/3 pods (2 azimuthing, 1 fixed)
Total Crew:	1,185
Passengers (lower beds):	3,286
Passenger Space Ratio (lower beds):	44.0
Passenger/Crew Ratio (lower beds):	2.6
Cabins (total):	1,643
Size Range (sq ft/m):	151.0–1,358.0/14.0–126.1
Cabins (for one person):	0
Cabins with balcony:	779
Cabins (wheelchair accessible):	26
Wheelchair accessibility:	Best
Elevators:	14
Casino (gaming tables):	Yes
Self-Service Launderette:	No
Onboard currency:	US$

THE SHIP. *Navigator of the Seas* (a Voyager-class ship) is a large, floating leisure resort with a whole host of facilities, yet offers a healthy amount of space per passenger, and excellent entertainment for the whole family. Following an extensive refurbishment, the outdoor decks are now full of fun waterpark features, including an adrenaline-pumping, two-person raft and the super-Aquacoaster – a 243m/800ft-long ride called 'The Blaster' and its counterpart 'Riptide.'

A stunning four-deck-high Royal Promenade is the standout interior focal point; it's a fun place to hang out or meet friends (entertaining street parades take place here). The length of two American football fields, with two 11-deck-high internal lobbies, the promenade is lined by cafés, shops, and entertainment venues – all overlooked by interior cabins from above. Arched across the promenade is a captain's balcony, while a central stairway connects with the deck below and the Schooner Bar (a piano lounge common to all RCI ships) and the large, flashy Casino Royale.

Other standouts include a regulation-size ice-skating rink (Studio B), with real ice, with 'bleacher' seating for up to 900 and broadcast facilities.

You'll need to plan what you want to do wisely – almost everything requires you to make reservations/sign up in advance. There is no escape from recorded rap-rich background music everywhere –

BERLITZ'S RATINGS

	Possible	Achieved
Ship	500	354
Accommodation	200	137
Food	400	220
Service	400	257
Entertainment	100	73
Cruise Experience	400	259

OVERALL SCORE 1300 points out of 2000

even in elevators, passenger hallways, and saunas. Live music is on the volume-heavy side, and there are unwelcome (and unnecessary) announcements for revenue-generating activities, such as art auctions and bingo.

Expect lines for the reception desk, shore excursions, shore tenders, and in the self-serve buffet stations. Niggles include intrusive photographers, few quiet places to sit and read, no cushioned pads for deck sunloungers, small cabin 'bath' towels, noisy (vacuum) toilets, and frosted drinks in 'souvenir' glasses pushed to the hilt. Do budget extra for additional cost items and expect to be subjected to flyers and advertising promotions.

Service personnel are friendly, however, and the digital 'Wayfarer' system is informative, but the speaking 'elevator going up/going down' is annoying. Also, if you have a cabin with an interconnecting door to another cabin, be aware that you'll be able to hear your next-door neighbors.

This is consistent, homogeneous mainstream cruising for young-minded cruisers of all ages who enjoy mingling in a large ship with plenty of life and constant activity. Overall, this is a fine all-round ship for all age groups but beware of so many extra costs for optional items (drinks, drink packages, and excursions).

ACCOMMODATION. There is a wide range of cabin price grades, in four major groupings: premium ocean-view suites and cabins; interior (atrium-view) cabins; ocean-view cabins; and interior cabins (which now have 'virtual balconies' projected on a formerly blank wall – a really great feature). Many cabins are of a similar size (good for incentives and large groups), and 300 have interconnecting doors (good for families). Some 138 interior cabins have bay windows that look into the Royal Promenade.

This was the first ship in the fleet to receive 'virtual balconies' for all interior (no-view) cabins – a neat feature installed during a 2013/14 revitalization, which also added 81 cabins, but no extra elevators.

Regardless of which cabin grade you choose, all except for the Royal Suite and Owner's Suite have twin beds that convert to a queen-size unit, an infotainment system, a radio and telephone, personal safe, vanity unit, hairdryer, and bathroom. However, you'll need to keep the curtains closed in the bay windows if you are scantily clad, as you can be seen easily from adjacent bay windows.

Standard outside-view and interior cabins are of a reasonably adequate size, with just enough facilities to make them comfortable and functional, but, overall, they're rather cramped.

DINING. The Sapphire (main dining room) has capacity for 1,889 across three levels (a dramatic stairway connects them), but the menu is the same. Huge, fat support pillars obstruct sight lines from a number of seats.

Choose one of two seating timings, or 'My Time Dining' (eat when you want during dining room hours). Tables are for four to 12. Place settings, china, and cutlery are of good quality. Two small private wings serve small groups: La Cetra and La Notte, each with 58 seats.

Main dining-room cuisine is standardized banquet catering, and the food is just average. However, you can have extra-cost items such as lobster or filet mignon (steak) cooked to order. Green vegetables are scarce but salad items are plentiful, and desserts are good. Rice features heavily, while breads and pastry items are rather mediocre. Vegetarian and children's menus are also available. Note that there are no wine waiters.

Other dining spots (some cost extra and reservations may be required, but the food is mostly made to order) include favorites such as Chops Grille Steakhouse (for premium veal chops, steaks, and seafood items), Giovanni's Table (an Italian family-style eatery), Izumi (for Asian-style cuisine), Jamie's Italian (for contemporary Italian light bistro-style cuisine), Sabor (for extra-cost Mexican-style cuisine), Hooked Seafood (crab claws and other seafood items), and Starbucks (for cost-extra paper cup coffees).

Johnny Rockets, a retro 1950s all-day, all-night diner-style eatery for fast food and malt shakes, with indoor and outdoor seating, plus a small pop-up version (Johnny Rockets Express) for poolside bites.

Windjammer Café is an expansive, sprawling venue for casual buffet-style, self-serve (always busy) meals. Note that it's often difficult to find a table. Island Grill (a section of the Windjammer Café) is for casual dinners (no reservations needed), and has an open kitchen.

Promenade Café is for Continental breakfast and all-day pizzas, while Starbucks is for extra-cost, on-the-go coffees.

ENTERTAINMENT. The 1,350-seat Metropolis Theater is a stunning showlounge, located forward. It has Art Nouveau-themed decor and spans three decks, with only a few slim pillars, and good sight lines from most seats. Production shows are presented by a large cast and a live band.

SPA/FITNESS. The ShipShape health spa is reasonably large, and measures 15,000 sq ft (1,400 sq m). It includes an aerobics room, a fitness center (with stairmasters, treadmills, exercise bikes, weight machines, and free weights), treatment rooms, and men's and women's sauna/steam rooms. Another 10,000 sq ft (930 sq m) of space is devoted to a Solarium (with sliding glass-dome roof).

NIEUW AMSTERDAM
★★★+

THIS SHIP FEATURES DUTCH DECOR, TRADITIONS, AND COMFORT FOR ENTIRE FAMILIES

Size:	Mid-size Ship	Passenger/Crew Ratio (lower beds):	2.2
Tonnage:	86,700	Cabins (total):	1,053
Cruise Line:	Holland America Line	Size Range (sq ft/m):	170.0–1,318.6/15.7–122.5
Former Names:	none	Cabins (for one person):	0
Builder:	Fincantieri (Italy)	Cabins with balcony:	708
Entered Service:	Jul 2010	Cabins (wheelchair accessible):	30
Length (ft/m):	935.0/285.0	Wheelchair accessibility:	Good
Propulsion/Propellers:	diesel-electric (34,000kW)/2 azimuthing pods	Elevators:	14
Total Crew:	929	Casino (gaming tables):	Yes
Passengers (lower beds):	2,106	Self-Service Launderette:	No
Passenger Space Ratio (lower beds):	41.1	Onboard currency:	US$

THE SHIP. *Nieuw Amsterdam* is close sister to *Eurodam, Noordam, Oosterdam, Westerdam,* and *Zuiderdam,* and is named for the Dutch name for New York City. Its interior design also reflects the great metropolis. It has two upright 'dustbin lid' funnels in a close-knit configuration; the twin working funnels are the result of the machinery configuration. Thus, the ship has, in effect, two engine rooms, and a pod propulsion system, so there's no vibration.

There is a complete walk-around exterior teak promenade deck, with teak steamer-style sunloungers. A jogging track outdoors is located around the mast and the forward section of the ship. Exterior glass elevators, mounted midships on both the port and starboard sides, provide ocean views from any of 10 decks. One of two centrally located swimming pools outdoors can be used in inclement weather (it has a retractable glass roof). Two hot tubs, adjacent to the pools, are abridged by a bar. There's also a small swimming pool for children.

There are two entertainment/public room decks, the most dramatic space being a showlounge spanning four decks in the forward section. Other facilities include a winding shopping street with boutique stores and logo shops, a card room, an art gallery, a photo gallery, and several small meeting rooms. The large casino is equipped with an array of gaming tables and slot machines, and you have to walk through it to get from the restaurant to the showlounge.

Explorations – perhaps the most popular public room – is a combination coffee bar (for cost-extra coffees and other drinks), lounge, an extensive library, and Internet-connect center in an attractive, open 'lifestyle' environment. It's popular for relaxation and reading, although noise from the coffee machine is intrusive.

On other, lower decks, you'll find the Queen's Lounge (part lecture room and part Culinary Arts Center – for culinary demonstrations and cooking classes). There are several other bars and lounges, including the Explorer's Lounge, with live string and piano music for evening cocktails and warm hors d'oeuvres. There is also a small movie-screening room.

The information desk in the lobby is small and somewhat removed from the main passenger flow on the two decks above it. Many pillars obstruct the passenger flow and lines of sight throughout the ship. There are no self-service launderettes – something that families with children tend to miss, although special laundry packages are available.

Gratuities are automatically added to your onboard account. Passenger niggles include noisy cabin air conditioning (the flow can't be regulated or turned off).

ACCOMMODATION. There are many price categories for the various accommodation grades, from small cabins for solo travelers to the largest (Grand Pinnacle) suites. Note that some cabins on the lowest accommodation deck have lifeboat-obstructed views.

Some cabins that can accommodate a third and fourth person have little closet space and only one personal safe. Some cabins have interconnecting doors. Suite occupants have exclusive use of a concierge lounge and service, priority embarkation and disembarkation, and other benefits. Note: many suites and cabins with private balconies – the balconies can be overlooked from above.

DINING. The 1,045-seat Manhattan Dining Room spans two decks, with seating at tables of two to eight, with friendly service from smiling Indonesian and Filipino stewards. Both open seating and assigned seating are available for dinner; breakfast and lunch are open seating (you'll be seated by restaurant staff as you enter).

HAL can provide Kosher meals (if requested when you book), although these are prepared ashore, then frozen, and brought to your table sealed in their original containers.

The extra-cost, reservations-required 148-seat Pinnacle Grill is an intimate venue, with high-quality ingredients and very good presentation. It fronts onto the second level of the atrium lobby; tables along its outer section are open to it and can suffer from Atrium Bar noise (one deck below), although these tables are good for those who like to see and be seen. Pacific Northwest food (think: premium-quality steaks and seafood) is featured, as are fine wines from around the world. Another (extra-cost, reservations-required) option is Tamarind, for Southeast Asian cuisine.

For casual eating, there is the large, self-serve Lido Market, an eatery that wraps around the funnel, with indoor-outdoor seating and ocean views. It includes several sections for various food types, including a large salad bar, although lines can form for made-to-order items such as omelets (breakfast) and pasta (lunch).

The poolside 'Dive-In at the Terrace Grill' features multi-choice signature burgers (with special Dive-In sauce), hot dogs, and fries. On certain days, barbecues and other eats are available poolside.

ENTERTAINMENT. The 867-seat Mainstage Lounge hosts Vegas-style revues and major cabaret shows. The main floor level includes a bar in its aft section, and spiral stairways connect all levels. Shows are best seen from the upper levels (better sight lines). Other entertainment venues include Lincoln Center Stage, Half Moon (piano lounge), B.B. King's Blues Club, and Billboard Onboard.

SPA/FITNESS. Greenhouse Spa is a two-deck-high facility, located forward. It includes a solarium, hydrotherapy pool, and a unisex thermal suite – incorporating a laconium (gentle sauna), hammam (mild steam), and chamomile grotto (small aromatic steam room).

There is a beauty salon, several private massage/treatment rooms (including one for couples), and a large gymnasium with floor-to-ceiling windows on three sides and forward-facing ocean views, and the latest high-tech muscle-toning equipment. There's also a basketball court, volleyball court, and a golf simulator.

NIEUW STATENDAM
★★★★

THIS SHIP MIXES DUTCH TRADITIONAL HERITAGE WITH CONTEMPORARY STYLE WELL

Size:	Mid-size Ship
Tonnage:	86,700
Cruise Line:	Holland America Line
Former Names:	none
Builder:	Fincantieri (Italy)
Entered Service:	Jul 2010
Length (ft/m):	935.0/285.0
Propulsion/Propellers:	diesel-electric (34,000kW)/2 azimuthing pods
Total Crew:	929
Passengers (lower beds):	2,106
Passenger Space Ratio (lower beds):	41.1
Passenger/Crew Ratio (lower beds):	2.2
Cabins (total):	1,053
Size Range (sq ft/m):	170.0–1,318.6/15.7–122.5
Cabins (for one person):	0
Cabins with balcony:	708
Cabins (wheelchair accessible):	30
Wheelchair accessibility:	Good
Elevators:	14
Casino (gaming tables):	Yes
Self-Service Launderette:	No
Onboard currency:	US$

THE SHIP. The sister to Koningsdam (but with nine more cabins), this *'Pinnacle'*-class ship includes up-to-date features while marketing and maintaining the company's essentially Dutch heritage. The exterior profile (black hull and white upper part) is not particularly handsome, due to extra decks added forward and above the navigation bridge, but the single large funnel does somewhat balance the upper structure.

There is a complete walk-around exterior teak promenade deck, with sunloungers, and a jogging track is located in the forward third of the ship and around the mast. Exterior amidships glass elevators on both the port and starboard sides, provide ocean views from any one of 10 decks. One of the two centrally located swimming pools outdoors has a retractable sliding glass roof. Two hot tubs, adjacent to the pools, are bridged by a bar. There's also a small pool for children.

The interior focus is the three-deck-high atrium lobby. Decks are named after famous composers, including Beethoven and Gershwin. Facilities (spread over two decks) include the Queen's Lounge (it also acts as a lecture and demonstration room); Club Orange (for cooking demonstrations and classes), a large casino with gaming tables and slot machines; Crow's Nest observation lounge with a library, and Explorations Café (with extra-cost coffees).

BERLITZ'S RATINGS

	Possible	Achieved
Ship	500	396
Accommodation	200	151
Food	400	225
Service	400	288
Entertainment	100	75
Cruise Experience	400	281

OVERALL SCORE 1416 points out of 2000

Other facilities include a shopping street, card room, an art gallery, a photo gallery, and four small meeting rooms. Overall, Nieuw Statendam is a very comfortable ship, and, no, it doesn't have rock climbing walls, rope walks, and other gimmicky features. Holland America Line is known for its slower, more relaxed pace of living, and delivers a decent onboard experience.

ACCOMMODATION. There are a large number of different price categories for the various accommodation grades, from small cabins for solo travelers to family-together cabins to grand suites. Of note are 12 very small solo-occupancy cabins (127–172 sq ft/11.8–16 sq m), forward on the lowest deck. Suite-occupants have access to the Neptune Lounge (for concierge services, snacks and drinks, and the Club Orange restaurant) and dine in The Retreat.

DINING. The Dining Room is on two levels, with two seating times. The decor is pure Americana, in white and cream – like a throwback to the steamboat era. The room's focal point is a wine tower spanning two decks, but the venue is not helped by many straight and curved pillars.

The food in the main dining room is rather underwhelming. It's pre-cooked in batches and re-heated, so it's acceptable at best. There is a lack of dark green vegetables, and desserts are disappointing. If you like good, cooked-to-order food, go for one of the cost-extra dining venues. HAL can provide Kosher meals (request when you book), although these are prepared ashore, then frozen, and brought to your table sealed in their original containers.

Themed restaurants and eateries:

Pinnacle Grill, for premium steaks and grilled seafood items – the line features uncomplicated 'Pacific Northwest' cuisine (plus a novel pop-up Sel de Mer French seafood brasserie, which is good); Tamarind is for great Asian fusion cuisine, and includes a sushi bar. Club Orange, open for dinner, is more bistro than restaurant, but it includes a glass-enclosed, microgreens-sprouting area. For pastries and coffee, try the Grand Dutch Café, on the third level of the atrium.

For casual eating, Lido Market is a self-serve, buffet-style eating hall. It has several sections, although lines form for made-to-order items such as omelets for breakfast and pasta for lunch. Each evening, Canaletto (within the venue) is for quasi-Italian cuisine. Poolside outlets feature burgers, hot dogs, pizzas, and gelato.

ENTERTAINMENT. Spanning two decks is the circular World Stage showlounge, with a 270-degree LED screen that acts as a surround-stage backdrop.

The ship has several music venues: Lincoln Center Stage, B.B. King's Blues Club, Half Moon, Rolling Stone Rock Room. For quieter music (where you are able to carry on a conversation) try Billboard piano bar.

SPA/FITNESS. The Greenhouse Spa is a good-sized, two-deck-high facility, located above the navigation bridge. It includes a solarium, hydrotherapy pool, and unisex thermal suite (with steam rooms and aromatic steam rooms), a beauty salon, private massage/body-treatment rooms (including one for couples), and a large gymnasium with floor-to-ceiling windows and ocean views.

NIPPON MARU
★★★★

THIS SHIP FEATURES MODERN, COMFORTABLE STYLING FOR JAPANESE-SPEAKING CRUISERS

Size:	Small Ship	Passenger/Crew Ratio (lower beds):	2.5
Tonnage:	22,472	Cabins (total):	204
Cruise Line:	Mitsui OSK Passenger Line	Size Range (sq ft/m):	150.6–430.5/14.0–40.0
Former Names:	none	Cabins (for one person):	6
Builder:	Mitsubishi Heavy Industries	Cabins with balcony:	27
Entered Service:	Sep 1990	Cabins (wheelchair accessible):	2
Length (ft/m):	546.7/166.6	Wheelchair accessibility:	Fair
Propulsion/Propellers:	diesel (15,740kW)/2	Elevators:	5
Total Crew:	230	Casino (gaming tables):	Yes
Passengers (lower beds):	408	Self-Service Launderette:	Yes
Passenger Space Ratio (lower beds):	55.0	Onboard currency:	Japanese Yen

THE SHIP. *Nippon Maru* is really for Japanese-speaking couples and solo travelers who want very comfortable surroundings combined with decent food and good service, all at a reasonable cost.

The interior's focal point is an atrium lobby that spans six decks. Public rooms include a show-lounge, piano lounge, a 54-seat screening room/lecture room (Mermaid Theater), a gaming corner with giveaways rather than cash prizes, and a Chashitsu tatami room within the Horizon Lounge. The Neptune Bar has probably the most extensive assortment of Scotch whiskies (including many rare single malts) at sea.

ACCOMMODATION. The newer suites, on Deck 6, are large and have separate sleeping and living areas. A sofa, two chairs, and coffee table occupy one section of the lounge; there is also a writing desk with Nespresso machine and tea-making facilities. The two beds can be pushed together. The bathroom includes a 'washlet,' (a toilet with a built-in water spray for washing – very popular in Japan), but the step into the bathroom is high, at 8ins (20cm). Slippers and bathrobes are provided. Nine suites include two with huge balconies. Suites and deluxe-grade cabins are nicely decorated, and the living area has a table and two chairs, and two beds; there's also a personal computer.

BERLITZ'S RATINGS		
	Possible	Achieved
Ship	500	369
Accommodation	200	147
Food	400	305
Service	400	301
Entertainment	100	78
Cruise Experience	400	285
OVERALL SCORE 1485 points out of 2000		

All standard cabins have blond wood cabinetry and good drawer space. Many have a third (or third and fourth) pull-down upper Pullman berth. Tea-making sets are provided, as is a good range of personal toiletry items.

DINING. The Mizuho dining room, which seats around 320, serves both traditional Japanese cuisine and Western dishes. There is one open seating. The ship is known for its high-quality food. A premium dining room, Kasuga, is for suite- and deluxe-grade occupants only; adjacent is the excellent Shiosai sushi bar – always with some very high-quality sashimi and sushi and a good selection of sakés.

ENTERTAINMENT. The two-deck-high Dolphin Hall has a proscenium-arched stage, wooden dance floor, and seating on both the main and balcony levels. There's social dancing, with gentlemen hosts available as partners, and a rich program of lecturers and musicians.

SPA/FITNESS. The Terraké Spa includes beauty and nail-treatment rooms, three body-treatment rooms, and a small fitness room. There's a traditional Japanese Grand Bath (one for women, one for men, open until 1am), with washing stations and a sauna. Adjacent is a sports-massage room.

NOORDAM
★★★+

THIS FAMILY-FRIENDLY SHIP HAS AN ABUNDANCE OF DUTCH EAST INDIES ARTWORK

Size:	Mid-size Ship
Tonnage:	82,318
Cruise Line:	Holland America Line
Former Names:	none
Builder:	Fincantieri (Italy)
Entered Service:	Feb 2006
Length (ft/m):	935.0/285.0
Propulsion/Propellers:	diesel-electric (34,000kW)/2 azimuthing pods
Total Crew:	820
Passengers (lower beds):	1,924
Passenger Space Ratio (lower beds):	42.7
Passenger/Crew Ratio (lower beds):	2.3
Cabins (total):	959
Size Range (sq ft/m):	170.0–1,318.6/15.7–122.5
Cabins (for one person):	0
Cabins with balcony:	641
Cabins (wheelchair accessible):	28
Wheelchair accessibility:	Good
Elevators:	14
Casino (gaming tables):	Yes
Self-Service Launderette:	No
Onboard currency:	US$

THE SHIP. *Noordam* is a *Vista*-class ship, designed to appeal to multi-generational families. The twin working funnels are the result of the slightly unusual machinery configuration; the ship has, in effect, two engine rooms. A pod propulsion system is provided, so there's no vibration.

There is a complete walk-around exterior teak promenade deck, with teak steamer-style sunloungers. A jogging track outdoors is located around the mast and the forward third of the ship. Exterior glass elevators provide fine ocean views from any one of 10 decks. One of two swimming pools outdoors has a retractable sliding glass roof. Two hot tubs, adjacent to the swimming pools, are abridged by a bar. There's also a small swimming pool for children.

The intimate lobby – the ship's central spot – spans three decks, and is topped by a rotating Waterford Crystal globe of the world. Adjacent are interior and glass-walled elevators with exterior views. The information desk (on the lobby's lowest level) is small and somewhat removed from the main passenger flow on the two decks above it.

The interior decor is bright in many areas, and the ceilings are particularly noticeable. A collection of artwork is a standard feature, and the pieces reflect the history of the former Dutch East Indies.

There are two whole entertainment/public room decks, the most dramatic space being a showlounge spanning four decks in the forward

BERLITZ'S RATINGS		
	Possible	Achieved
Ship	500	368
Accommodation	200	142
Food	400	220
Service	400	273
Entertainment	100	69
Cruise Experience	400	276
OVERALL SCORE 1348 points out of 2000		

section. Other facilities include a winding shopping street with several boutique stores and logo shops, card room, an art gallery, a photo gallery, and several small meeting rooms. The large casino has gaming tables and slot machines – you have to walk through it to get from the restaurant to the showlounge.

Explorations is a combination of a coffee bar (where coffees and other drinks cost extra), lounge, an extensive library, and Internet center – it's a popular area for relaxation and reading, although noise from the coffee machine can interrupt concentration.

On other decks (lower down), you'll find the Queen's Lounge and bar, which acts as a lecture room and Culinary Arts Center, where cooking demonstrations and cooking classes are held.

Gratuities are automatically added to your onboard account. Passenger niggles? Noisy cabin air conditioning – the flow can't be regulated or turned off, the only regulation being for temperature control. Also, several pillars obstruct flow and lines of sight throughout the ship. There are no self-service launderettes, although special laundry packages are available.

ACCOMMODATION. There are many price categories for the various accommodation grades, from small cabins for solo travelers to the largest (Grand Pinnacle) suites. Note that some cabins on the lowest accommodation deck have a life-boat-obstructed view.

Some cabins that can accommodate a third and fourth person have little closet space and only one personal safe. Some cabins have interconnecting doors. Occupants of suites have exclusive use of a concierge lounge and service, priority embarkation and disembarkation, and other benefits. In many suites and cabins with private balconies, the balconies aren't really private (many can be overlooked from above).

DINING. Located aft, the 1,045-seat Vista Dining Room spans two decks, with seating at tables for two to eight on both levels. It provides a traditional HAL dining experience, with friendly service from Indonesian and Filipino stewards. Both open seating and assigned seating are available for dinner, while breakfast and lunch are open seating – you'll be taken to a table by restaurant staff when you enter.

With a few exceptions, the cuisine is reasonable, but non-memorable, and is missing passion and taste, because it's all about mass catering (batch cooking). There's a distinct lack of variety of green vegetables, much use of rice, canned fruit, and pre-sliced and diced cheese. Still, you get friendly service, and the plates are nice.

Kosher meals are also available (if requested when you book), although these are prepared ashore, then frozen, and brought to your table sealed in their original containers.

The extra-cost, reservations-required Pinnacle Grill is an intimate venue, with high-quality ingredients and very good presentation. It fronts onto the second level of the atrium lobby; tables along its outer section are open to it and can suffer from Atrium Bar noise (one deck below), although these tables are good for those who like to see and be seen. Pacific Northwest cuisine (think: premium-quality steaks and seafood) is featured. The wine list includes fine wines from around the world. Another (extra-cost, reservations-required) option is Tamarind, for Southeast Asian cuisine.

The Lido Café is a casual self-serve eatery that wraps around the funnel, with indoor-outdoor seating. Several sections include a salad bar, stir-fry and sushi section, deli sandwiches, and a dessert buffet, although lines can form for made-to-order items. Also, the poolside 'Dive-In at the Terrace Grill' features multi-choice burgers (with special Dive-In sauce), hot dogs, and fries.

ENTERTAINMENT. The 867-seat Mainstage hosts Las Vegas-style revues and major cabaret shows. The main floor level has a bar, and spiral stairways at the back connect all levels. Shows are best seen from the upper levels, from where the sight lines are decent. Additionally, there's Lincoln Center Stage, B.B. King's Blues Club, Billboard Onboard, and Half Moon (piano lounge).

SPA/FITNESS. The Greenhouse Spa, a two-decks-high facility, is located directly above the navigation bridge. It includes a solarium, hydrotherapy pool, thermal suite – a unisex area incorporating sauna and steam rooms – plus a beauty salon, several private massage/therapy rooms (including one for couples), and a large gym with ocean views and high-tech muscle-toning equipment. More sports facilities include a basketball court, volleyball court, and a golf simulator.

NORWEGIAN BLISS
★★★★

AN ÜBER-CASUAL ENTERTAINMENT-FILLED PLAYGROUND FOR THE ENTIRE FAMILY

Size:	Large Resort Ship	Passenger/Crew Ratio (lower beds):	2.3
Tonnage:	168,028	Cabins (total):	2,043
Cruise Line:	Norwegian Cruise Line	Size Range (sq ft/m):	96.8–1,087.1/9.0–101.0
Former Names:	none	Cabins (for one person):	82
Builder:	Meyer Werft (Germany)	Cabins with balcony:	1,571
Entered Service:	Jun 2018	Cabins (wheelchair accessible):	38
Length (ft/m):	1,066.2/325.0	Wheelchair accessibility:	Good
Propulsion/Propellers:	diesel-electric/2 azimuthing pods	Elevators:	16
		Casino (gaming tables):	Yes
Total Crew:	1,730	Self-Service Launderette:	No
Passengers (lower beds):	4,004	Onboard currency:	US$
Passenger Space Ratio (lower beds):	41.9		

THE SHIP. *Norwegian Bliss* is a large resort ship for urbanites – for families, single parents, and solo travelers, with a mountain of entertainment choices, in an environment that is a pure playground for active cruising. The ship, a close sister to *Norwegian Getaway* has hull artwork designed by marine life artist Robert Wyland, featuring cruising with whales.

Norwegian Bliss is cool, with a nod towards Alaska. It has some really good outdoor features for active types (including a superb jungle-like rope trek high above the aft decks). There are extensive pool deck facilities, including an Aqua Park with multiple waterslides and a rock-climbing wall and rope walk (more for adult kids). Aft is a large movie screen with amphitheater-style seating. Despite the ship's size, open deck space for sunbathing is minimal, because of the exclusive Haven area in the forward section, where suite occupants have their own sunbathing space, bar, pool, hot tubs, and beach club-like area. The rest of the ship shares multiple pools and water-fun exterior decks, designed for families and children.

Most of the public rooms, shops, entertainment spots, the casino, and a number of bars, themed dining venues and eateries with indoor and outdoor (on the 'Waterfront' deck) seating are on decks 6, 7, and 8 – a three-deck, indoor-outdoor complex called 678 Ocean Place. However, the flow is somewhat disjointed and invites congestion. A forward-facing observa-

BERLITZ'S RATINGS	Possible	Achieved
Ship	500	402
Accommodation	200	144
Food	400	244
Service	400	277
Entertainment	100	77
Cruise Experience	400	290

OVERALL SCORE 1434 points out of 2000

tion lounge/bar is a nice addition to Deck 15 (it's not on close sisters Norwegian Escape or Norwegian Joy due to an additional deck).

Planning and time management will help make the most of all this ship has to offer, which sort of negates the freestyle aspect of a large resort ship cruise. You'll be sharing the ship with about 4,000-plus others, so there's no doubt it will be a lively travel experience.

Gratuities are automatically charged to your onboard account, or you can pre-pay online. Overall, unless you are happy to settle for basic food, you'll need to pay extra to eat in one or more restaurants and eateries not included. It's all the extras that make a cruise aboard *Norwegian Bliss* rather expensive (but still a good value) vacation. Note that some public room and eatery names were not available at the time of going to press.

ACCOMMODATION. There is an almost endless variety of accommodation grades and suite/cabin types, shapes, and sleeping capacities, from small interior (no-view) cabins to two-bedroom Villa suites.

The more exclusive accommodation is located in a two-deck-high section (The Haven), really a 'ship within a ship,' with suites, a private restaurant, cocktail bar, and concierge desk (for dining, entertainment, and spa reservations), a pool, changing areas, hot tubs, gym, saunas, massage rooms, and sun deck with bar. Occupants get private access to the spa and fitness center, butler service, and in-suite, white-tablecloth dining service. Suite occupants get a platinum key card, which attracts better recognition in the rest of the ship – who said the class system was dead?

Other accommodation includes Spa mini-suite rooms and Spa balcony cabins, all with easy access to the adjacent spa and its facilities. While most outside-view cabins have a balcony, some have only windows, but all have flat-screen televisions, satellite-linked telephone, and private bathroom. There are also many Family 'suites' with ocean views, and many cabins with interconnecting doors.

Balcony suites/cabins have rich wood-look paneling with warm tones. Each has a queen-size bed (or twins), with a pillow-top mattress, a lighted recess above the bed for books or other items. Each has a sofa bed with additional storage. A flat-screen television is mounted on the wall and tilts for viewing from the sofa or the bed. A built-in vanity area has shelving and decent storage space. There's also a full-size closet with sliding doors. The cabins are energy-efficient, with key-card access to control lighting in the room.

The balcony bathroom features clean design and is spacious. An enclosed under-washbasin vanity hides the trash bin. A private shower with a shaving bar for women completes the picture. Mini-suite bathrooms get a rain shower plus a hand-held shower hose.

There are 59 studio (solo-occupancy) interior-only small cabins; these are colorful, trendy, and minimal, with little closet space. Still this is a neat way to cruise solo – just don't bring many clothes. Many interior cabins also have one or two additional upper berths, while the lower twin beds convertible to a queen-size bed – good for families with young children.

Note that cabin doors open *outwards* (towards you) rather than inwards. Also, when music is being played late at night in the lobby, cabins located above it may suffer from volume levels that are quite intrusive, despite some generally good soundproofing. Room service incurs a 'convenience' per order charge (free for occupants of The Haven).

DINING. Freestyle Dining means no assigned dining rooms, tables, or seats, so you can choose which restaurant to eat in, at what time, and with whom. In practice, the wealth of choices means making reservations, which takes a little planning and waiting. To see a show in the evening, your dining time will be dictated by the time of the show, which rather limits your choice.

There are three main dining rooms. Other venues include Cagney's Steakhouse (an open-kitchen classic American steakhouse; excellent for meat-eaters) and Moderno Churrascaria (a Brazilian-style steakhouse with tableside carved meat service by passadores, plus a salad bar); these are located one deck above, with a view into the Tropicana Room.

The Waterfront is a boardwalk-style outdoor area with bars and eateries. These include La Cucina (Italian family food with a focus on Tuscany), or, for alfresco eating; Maltings, and an à la carte Tapas Bar; Le Bistro, for classic French-style cuisine; a Teppanyaki restaurant with 12 flat-top grills (think show and noise); a Supper Club (for set dinner and show); Bayamo by Jose Garces (for Mexican cuisine); and an Asian fusion restaurant (including a sushi bar). All cost extra, and reservations are required.

Casual eateries: O'Sheehan's Neighborhood Bar & Grill (a free, always-open fast-food joint, with a screen for sporting events, bowling lanes, and interactive games), and Atrium Café and Bar (for extra-cost Lavazza brand coffees and pastries). Perhaps in a tribute to Man v. Food (the US food reality television show), the Dolce Gelato Bar signature item is extra-cost sundaes, with multiple scoops of ice cream in up to three flavors topped with 'everything under the sun.'

Garden Café is an extremely large, self-serve buffet, with indoor and outdoor seating. It's open round the clock. Different counters provide themed and ethnic food varieties, and there's a special section for kids.

ENTERTAINMENT. The two-deck-high Escape Theater, located at the front, is a stunning showlounge for the line's production shows, with smaller shows presented in the Manhattan Room, and the Supper Club.

SPA/FITNESS. The Mandara Spa and fitness center, spread over two decks, houses a large gymnasium, with high-tech cardiovascular exercise equipment. The complex includes an extra-cost thermal suite (herbal rain showers, a snow grotto, saunas and steam rooms, and relaxation area with hot-tile beds), a beauty salon, and multiple body-treatment rooms, including massage rooms for couples. The fitness room has Technogym fitness and cardio equipment, linked to Apple devices.

A Sports Complex includes Aqua Park's multiple thrilling waterslides, a multi-elevated rope course (with over than 40 elements), The Plank (a platform extending over the ship's side), a rock-climbing wall, a spider-web-like enclosed spiral climbing cage, a bungee trampoline, and a bocce ball court.

NORWEGIAN BREAKAWAY
★★★★

ÜBER-CASUAL, MULTI-CHOICE FLOATING PLAYGROUND FOR THE WHOLE FAMILY

Size:	Large Resort Ship
Tonnage:	144,017
Cruise Line:	Norwegian Cruise Line
Former Names:	none
Builder:	Meyer Werft (Germany)
Entered Service:	Apr 2013
Length (ft/m):	1,066.2/325.0
Propulsion/Propellers:	diesel-electric (79,800kW)/2 azimuthing pods
Total Crew:	1,657
Passengers (lower beds):	3,963
Passenger Space Ratio (lower beds):	36.3
Passenger/Crew Ratio (lower beds):	2.3
Cabins (total):	1,994
Size Range (sq ft/m):	96.8–1,022.6/9.0–95.0
Cabins (for one person):	59
Cabins with balcony:	1,252
Cabins (wheelchair accessible):	40
Wheelchair accessibility:	Good
Elevators:	16
Casino (gaming tables):	Yes
Self-Service Launderette:	No
Onboard currency:	US$

THE SHIP. *Norwegian Breakaway* is for young, trendy urbanites. It provides families with children, single parents, couples, and solos with numerous entertainment choices, in an environment that is a pure playground for an active multi-dining choice cruise vacation.

It has a more streamlined and balanced profile than slightly larger *Norwegian Epic*, with signature hull artwork depicting New York City – created by American-based illustrator and graphic artist Peter Max.

Families with kids love the pool-deck facilities and Aqua Park – with five waterslides, a large rock-climbing and rappelling wall, and a rope walking course with a small section extending over the ship's side. Aft is a movie screen with amphitheater-style seating in an adults-only area (Spice H2O).

Despite the ship's size, however, open deck space for sunbathing is limited, made smaller by an exclusive 'Haven' area forward, whose suites-only occupants are given enough sunbathing space in a beach-club-like setting.

Inside, the decor is upbeat and jazzy. Most of the public rooms, shops, entertainment spots, the casino, and a number of bars, themed dining venues and eateries with indoor and outdoor (on the 'Waterfront' deck) seating – a three-deck indoor-outdoor complex called 678 Ocean Place that includes a large casino area. However, the flow is somewhat disjointed and invites congestion.

BERLITZ'S RATINGS	Possible	Achieved
Ship	500	395
Accommodation	200	144
Food	400	245
Service	400	275
Entertainment	100	86
Cruise Experience	400	284
OVERALL SCORE 1429 points out of 2000		

Planning will help make the most of all this ship has to offer. You'll be sharing the ship with about 4,000 others, so it will be a lively travel experience.

A non-changeable, per-person service charge is automatically added to your account daily for staff gratuities; a service charge applies to bar and spa charges.

ACCOMMODATION. The 'standard' cabins have a traditional, practical bathroom layout, with ample storage space and a clean design, with compact, but comfortable sleeping and living areas.

More exclusive accommodation can be found in a two-deck-high section called The Haven – a 'ship within a ship,' with 42 suites, a restaurant, bar, relaxation zone, concierge desk, private pool, changing areas, hot tubs, gym, saunas, massage rooms, and sun deck with bar. Occupants get 'butler' service, and in-suite, tablecloth dining, and priority reservations for restaurants, spa, and entertainment venues.

The cabins are energy-efficient, with key card-controlled lighting. Bathrooms feature a clean design, with rich-wood shelves.

There are 59 small, trendy, capsule-hotel style solo-occupancy cabins (Studios), with minimalist design and closet space. Still, this is a neat way to cruise on your own – just don't bring too much luggage.

Many interior cabins also have one or two additional upper berths, while the lower beds are twins that convert to a queen-size bed – good for families with young children.

Room service (other than coffee/tea and Continental breakfast) incurs a per order 'convenience' charge (except for occupants of The Haven).

DINING. There are many restaurants (including the largest venues, Savor and Taste), dining venues, and casual eateries from which to choose. Food in the main dining rooms is mediocre (with few vegetables and garnishes, and an overuse of rice).

'Freestyle Dining' lets you try different types of cuisine, when you want, although you need to make reservations – sometimes frustrating. It takes planning and – often – waiting. Wall-based, touch-screen reservations systems let you see instantly how long you need to wait if your chosen restaurant is fully booked.

The Manhattan Room (included in the fare) is both dinner and entertainment; it is large, with a dance floor and big ocean-view windows. Other dining venues (Cagney's Steakhouse and Moderno Churrascaria) are one deck above, with views into the Manhattan Room.

Because the lifeboats hang over the side of the ship's hull, and not inboard as is usual, the promenade deck is an oceanfront extension of the eateries *inside*, creating a New York sidewalk-style experience, called The Waterfront.

Inside, 678 Ocean Place connects with several interior extra-cost dining spots and the Breakaway Casino, cigar-smoking room, and some entertainment venues. These include Moderno Churrascaria, a Brazilian-style steakhouse with salad bar, and tableside carved-meat service by 'passadores'; Cagney's Steakhouse, a classic American steakhouse, with open kitchen; La Cucina, for Tuscan-style Italian family food, with inside seating; for alfresco eating on The Waterfront, Maltings (bar) and Ocean Blu by

Geoffrey Zakarian – an à la carte seafood and raw bar/eatery, designed and overseen by the Food Network chef.

Other venues: Le Bistro, for classic French-style cuisine; a 96-seat Teppanyaki restaurant with 12 flat-top grills and a lot of show, a Japanese rock garden with bamboo plants and bonsai trees; and Cirque Dreams and Dinner (supper club).

Casual eateries (no extra cost) include O'Sheehan's Neighborhood Bar & Grill, a sports bar and fast-food joint; the Atrium Café and Bar (for coffees and pastries); and Shanghai's Noodle Bar (for Chinese-style noodle dishes). The Ice Cream Bar has sundaes (try the Breakaway Sundae or Getaway Sundae), with nine scoops of ice cream in up to three flavors and toppings.

Garden Café is a large, self-serve buffet, with indoor/outdoor seating, with different counters providing themed food varieties; there's a special section for kids, too.

ENTERTAINMENT. Breakaway Theater is a two-deck-high showlounge, for those large-scale, razzle-dazzle production shows and cabaret acts.

Spiegel Tent is a two-deck-high domed Cirque-like space, combining an extra-cost supper club show (think in-your-face street theater, acrobatics, and Berlin-style 'foodertainment').

Fat Cats Jazz & Blues Club is an intimate room that's often standing room only (when live jazz is on), while Howl at the Moon features a piano duel.

SPA/FITNESS. Mandara Spa center spans two decks and hosts a warehouse-size gymnasium. It includes an extra-cost thermal suite (herbal rain showers, saunas and steam rooms, and relaxation area with hot-tile beds), a salt room, a beauty salon, and multiple body-treatment rooms, including massage rooms for couples.

NORWEGIAN DAWN
★★★+

THIS CASUAL MID-SIZE SHIP IS FOR LIVELY, FAMILY-FRIENDLY CRUISING

Size:	Mid-size Ship	Passenger/Crew Ratio (lower beds):	2.2
Tonnage:	92,250	Cabins (total):	1,238
Cruise Line:	Norwegian Cruise Line	Size Range (sq ft/m):	142.0–5,350.0/13.2–497.0
Former Names:	*SuperStar Scorpio*	Cabins (for one person):	0
Builder:	Meyer Werft (Germany)	Cabins with balcony:	511
Entered Service:	Oct 2002	Cabins (wheelchair accessible):	20
Length (ft/m):	964.9/294.1	Wheelchair accessibility:	Best
Propulsion/Propellers:	diesel-electric/2 azimuthing pods	Elevators:	12
		Casino (gaming tables):	Yes
Total Crew:	1,032	Self-Service Launderette:	No
Passengers (lower beds):	2,340	Onboard currency:	US$
Passenger Space Ratio (lower beds):	39.4		

THE SHIP. *Norwegian Dawn*, sister to *Norwegian Star*, was built in 64 sections and has a pod propulsion system, so there's no vibration. In 2011, some 58 additional suites/cabins were added, making the ship more crowded.

Facilities include a large Dawn Club Casino gaming area, a library, a 1,150-seat showlounge, and a retail shopping area.

Plenty of choices, including many dining options, add up to an attractive vacation package suitable for families with children – in a contemporary floating leisure center that provides ample facilities for you to have an enjoyable time. Despite the company's name, Norwegian Cruise Line (NCL), there's almost nothing Norwegian about it.

A non-changeable, per-person service charge is automatically added to your account daily for staff gratuities; a service charge also applies to bar and spa charges.

ACCOMMODATION. Although the suites and junior suites are quite spacious, the standard interior and outside-view cabins are compact. The bathrooms are of a decent size, and have large shower enclosures. There are many different price grades. All accommodation was refreshed during a 2016 refurbishment. Many cabins have third- and fourth-person pull-down berths or trundle beds.

A small room service menu is available; non-food items cost extra, and a per-order service charge is added to your account. Bottled water is placed in each cabin, but it's chargeable if opened.

The largest accommodation: two Garden Villas (Horizon and Vista) provide the largest living spaces atop the ship in a pod overlooking the pool/recreation deck. Each measure 5,350 sq ft (497 sq m), has three bedrooms and bathrooms, and is combinable to create a double-size 'house,' with butler service, and a private elevator.

DINING. With Freestyle Dining, you can choose which restaurant to eat in, at what time, and with whom (no assigned dining rooms, tables, or seats). While this is fine in theory, in practice it means making reservations for a specific time.

There are three main dining rooms, plus several themed eateries, giving a wide choice (some cost extra and require reservations). Two decks incorporate 10 restaurants and eateries. NCL's dress code states that 'jeans, T-shirts, tank tops, and bare feet are not permitted in restaurants.'

Venetian: the first main dining room (seats 472) offers traditional dining. It is aft, with good views over the stern (at least in the daytime), although 14 pillars means obstructed views from some seats. The room has a baby grand piano. Quieter tables are in the two wings in the forward section near the entrance/steps. Aqua: the second main dining room seats 344.

BERLITZ'S RATINGS

	Possible	Achieved
Ship	500	356
Accommodation	200	138
Food	400	235
Service	400	268
Entertainment	100	67
Cruise Experience	400	270

OVERALL SCORE 1334 points out of 2000

Other (extra-cost) reservations-required venues include:

Bamboo (a Taste of Asia), a Japanese/Thai/Chinese restaurant, with 140 seats, a conveyor-belt sushi bar, sake bar, show galley, and a Teppanyaki grill room.

Le Bistro, for French-style cuisine; it's very good and worth the extra cost.

Cagney's Steak House has a show kitchen and serves excellent (large) US prime steaks and seafood.

Moderno Churrascaria is for Argentine-style meats presented at your table by attendants in gaucho uniforms.

Garden Café is an indoor/outdoor, self-serve (no-cost) buffet. It includes 'action stations' with made-to-order omelets, waffles, fruit, soups, ethnic specialties, and pasta.

Other casual spots include O'Sheehan's (sports eatery and bar); Java, an atrium lobby café and bar (hot and frozen coffees, teas, and pastries); a Beer Garden (for grilled foods); a Gelato Bar (ice cream); and a Gym and Spa Bar (health food snacks and drinks).

ENTERTAINMENT. The 1,037-seat Stardust Theater is the venue for colorful, Vegas-style production shows and major cabaret acts. Designed in the style of an opera house, spans three decks, it has a steeply tiered main floor and port and starboard balconies. High-energy, razzle-dazzle shows feature extensive use of pyrotechnics, lasers, and other fancy lighting.

SPA/FITNESS. For wellness devotees the two-deck-high Mandara Spa complex is located at the stern, with ocean-view windows on three sides. There are many facilities and services, almost all at extra cost, including Thai massage in the spa, outdoors on deck, in your cabin, or on your balcony.

NORWEGIAN ENCORE
NYR

THIS IS AN ENTERTAINMENT-FILLED CASUAL SHIP FOR THE ENTIRE FAMILY

Size:	Large Resort Ship	Passenger/Crew Ratio (lower beds):	2.3
Tonnage:	167,600	Cabins (total):	2,043
Cruise Line:	Norwegian Cruise Line	Size Range (sq ft/m):	96.8–1,087.1/9.0–101.0
Former Names:	none	Cabins (for one person):	82
Builder:	Meyer Werft (Germany)	Cabins with balcony:	1,571
Entered Service:	Oct 2019	Cabins (wheelchair accessible):	38
Length (ft/m):	1,066.2/325.0	Wheelchair accessibility:	Good
Propulsion/Propellers:	diesel-electric/2 azimuthing pods	Elevators:	16
Total Crew:	1,730	Casino (gaming tables):	Yes
Passengers (lower beds):	4,004	Self-Service Launderette:	No
Passenger Space Ratio (lower beds):	41.9	Onboard currency:	US$

THE SHIP. *Norwegian Encore* is a large resort ship for urbanites – for families, single parents, and solo travelers, with a mountain of entertainment choices. It is a close sister to *Norwegian Bliss* and has splashy, colorful artwork on the hull.

The ship is a playground for active types, including a jungle-like rope trek high above the aft decks and an Aqua Park with multiple waterslides and a rock-climbing wall. There's also a poolside movie screen with amphitheater-style seating. However, the open deck sunbathing space is minimal, due to an exclusive Haven area in the forward section for suite occupants (the rest of the ship shares multiple pools and water-fun exterior decks, designed for families and children).

Multiple public rooms, shops, entertainment spots, bars, and themed dining venues are spread across a three-deck, indoor-outdoor complex (678 Ocean Place) that includes a large casino; however, the flow is disjointed and invites congestion.

Planning is the best way to make the most of all this ship has to offer, as you'll be sharing the ship with about 4,000 others.

Gratuities are automatically charged to your account (or you can pre-pay online). Overall, unless you are happy to settle for basic food, you'll need to pay extra to eat in additional-cost restaurants.

ACCOMMODATION. There is a wide variety of accommodation grades and suite/cabin types, from

BERLITZ'S RATINGS		
	Possible	Achieved
Ship	500	NYR
Accommodation	200	NYR
Food	400	NYR
Service	400	NYR
Entertainment	100	NYR
Cruise Experience	400	NYR
OVERALL SCORE NYR points out of 2000		

small interior (no-view) cabins to two-bedroom Villa suites.

The more exclusive accommodation is located in The Haven, a two-deck-high 'ship within a ship', with suites, restaurant, cocktail bar, concierge desk (for dining, entertainment, and spa reservations), pool, hot tubs, gym, saunas, massage rooms, and sun deck with bar. Occupants get butler service and a platinum key card that attracts better recognition in the rest of the ship.

Other accommodation includes Spa mini-suite rooms and Spa balcony cabins – all with easy spa access. While most outside-view cabins have a balcony, some have only windows; all have flat-screen televisions and private bathroom. There are also many Family 'suites' with ocean views, and many cabins with interconnecting doors.

Balcony suites/cabins have a queen-size bed (or twins), with a pillow-top mattress, sofa bed, flat-screen television, vanity area, and full-size closet (lots of storage space). The cabins are energy-efficient, with key-card access to control lighting. Spacious bathrooms feature a shower. Mini-suite bathrooms get a rainshower, plus hand-held shower hose.

Colorful studio, interior-only cabins are small with little closet space (pack minimal clothing), but provide a neat way to cruise solo. Many interior cabins also have one or two additional upper berths, while the lower twin beds convertible to a queen-size bed – good for families with young children.

Note that cabin doors open *outwards* (towards you) rather than inwards, and late-night lobby music can be intrusive, despite good soundproofing. Room service incurs a 'convenience' per order charge (free for The Haven occupants).

DINING. Freestyle Dining means you can choose which restaurant to eat in, at what time, and with whom; although, in practice, the wealth of choices means making reservations. To see a show in the evening, your dining time will be dictated by the time of the show, which rather limits your choice.

Restaurants/eateries include: Savor; Taste; Manhattan; Q Texas Smokehouse; Cagney's Steakhouse; Le Bistro (for French-style cuisine); Ocean Blue (seafood); Onda by Scarpetta (a sea-going version of the Scarpetta-brand restaurant in the UK and USA); Le Bistro (classic French-style cuisine); Teppanyaki (with multiple flat-top grills for lively food and conversation); The District Brew House (a free, always-open fast-food eatery), Atrium Café and Bar (for extra-cost Lavazza coffees and pastries); and Garden Café (large, self-serve, food court-style buffet, open 24/7.

ENTERTAINMENT. The two-deck-high Encore Theater is a stunning showlounge for super-colorful, razzle-dazzle production shows, while smaller song and dance shows are presented in the Manhattan Room.

SPA/FITNESS. The two-deck Mandara Spa and fitness center houses a large gymnasium, an extra-cost thermal suite (herbal rainshowers, a snow grotto, saunas and steam rooms, and relaxation area with hot-tile beds), a beauty salon, and multiple treatment rooms (including couples' massage rooms).

A Sports Complex includes an Aqua Park, a multi-elevated rope course (with over than 40 elements), The Plank (a platform extending over the ship's side), a rock-climbing wall, a spider web-like spiral climbing cage, a bungee trampoline, and a bocce ball court.

NORWEGIAN EPIC
★★★+

THIS IS AN EPIC-SIZED, FAMILY-FRIENDLY, MULTIPLE-CHOICE RESORT SHIP

Size:	Large Resort Ship	Passenger/Crew Ratio (lower beds):	2.33
Tonnage:	155,873	Cabins (total):	2,100
Cruise Line:	Norwegian Cruise Line	Size Range (sq ft/m):	96.8–100.1/9.0–79.0
Former Names:	none	Cabins (for one person):	128
Builder:	STX Europe (France)	Cabins with balcony:	1,415
Entered Service:	Jun 2010	Cabins (wheelchair accessible):	42
Length (ft/m):	1,080.7/329.4	Wheelchair accessibility:	Good
Propulsion/Propellers:	diesel-electric (79,800kW)/2 azimuthing pods	Elevators:	16
		Casino (gaming tables):	Yes
Total Crew:	1,724	Self-Service Launderette:	No
Passengers (lower beds):	4,100	Onboard currency:	US$
Passenger Space Ratio (lower beds):	38.0		

THE SHIP. *Norwegian Epic* is a blast for youthful families and solo travelers. It's all about lifestyle – bistro eateries, lots of dining choices, color and noise, the perceived über-chic South Beach nightlife at sea, stuffed with entertainment. It is 'all-exclusive' cruising – a throwback to the days when First Class, Cabin Class, and Tourist Class meant passengers could not access certain areas of the ship (the 'pay more, get more' principle). The profile is ungainly because several decks above the navigation bridge make it look top-heavy, like a lump of cheese.

Major family attractions include an Aqua Park, with three large waterslides – one involves inner tubes that give you a spin before spitting you out into a big bowl.

Aft is a large movie screen with amphitheater-style seating, and a nightclub within Spice H2O and a sun deck. However, despite the ship's size, the open deck space for sunbathing is extremely small – diminished by the 'exclusive' Courtyard block in the forward section, whose occupants do have enough sunbathing space.

Inside, decks 6, 7, and 8 house the main entertainment venues, restaurants and other eateries, show lounges, and an expansive casino, but the overall flow is disjointed and invites congestion. Check out the dramatic three-deck-high chandelier in the lobby – it could be the largest at sea.

BERLITZ'S RATINGS		
	Possible	Achieved
Ship	500	378
Accommodation	200	141
Food	400	240
Service	400	273
Entertainment	100	85
Cruise Experience	400	278
OVERALL SCORE 1395 points out of 2000		

Two escalators do nothing to reduce congestion – and even encourage gridlock.

Novel features include an Ice Bar, a chill-out hangout inspired by the original Scandinavian ice bars and ice hotels. In this frozen vodka chamber, the centerpiece is a giant ice cube that glows and changes color. You'll be given fur coats, gloves, and hats to wear while in here because the temperature stays below –8°C (around 17°F); the cover charge includes two drinks.

It's a big ship, but elevators are only forward and aft (none in the middle), which is challenging for mobility-limited passengers. Yet *Norwegian Epic* has more elevators than the larger *Oasis of the Seas*.

A 'ship-within-a-ship', two-deck complex provides a private courtyard/pool area, men's and women's steam rooms, concierge lounge, and private dining rooms and lounge for those willing to pay more for exclusivity.

Niggles include cigarette smokers in the casino, a walk-through area.

A non-changeable per person service charge is automatically added to your account daily.

ACCOMMODATION. There are many different accommodation price levels and accommodation grades. In true nautical tradition, even-numbered cabins are on the port side (red carpet), with odd-numbered cabins on the starboard side (blue carpet).

Outside-view suites/cabins have a 'private' balcony, 'wave' shape curved walls, LED lighting, backlit domed ceiling, sofa seating (except standard cabins), vanity desk, and minibar. See-through (no-privacy) bathrooms have a separate toilet; tub or tub/shower combination, and separate vanity washbasin (few people like the see-through toilet).

There's an efficient use of space, achieved by separating the toilet and shower to either side of the entryway, and by curving the bulkheads and furniture to give the cabins a more open, wavy, and contemporary feel. However, space at the foot of the bed is poor. Also, you need to take a towel before stepping into the shower, because they are in a different location.

Standouts include Courtyard Suites (decks 16 and 17), located in the 'cheese block' forward (The Haven). There are six Courtyard 'Villas' – although none has a balcony. Occupants have access to gated-community facilities, with Concierge Lounge, courtyard and pool, steam rooms, and sunbathing areas – so there's no need to go to the rest of the ship under you, except to disembark or go out to the entertainment decks to play, or escape.

There are 128 studio cabins for solo travelers (many interconnect), like a capsule hotel. A small window looks into the interior passageway. Although priced for solo occupancy, they can accommodate two as there is a double bed. They are extremely small but you have access to a common lounge with hostess, and free espressos/cappuccinos. In interior (no-view) cabins and studio categories, the bed faces the cabin door (no privacy).

DINING. Norwegian Cruise Line features 'Freestyle Dining' – so you can try different types of cuisine, in different settings. In practice, it means making reservations. This takes planning and can be frustrating. Generally, the cuisine is poor to average (with few vegetables and garnishes, and an overuse of rice as a carbohydrate source), but it can be much better in the extra-cost venues.

Several different food outlets have been created in numerous locations – many are included in the cruise fare; others require a per-person cover or à la carte charge. Because gratuities are automatically added to your account, if you change dining venues, there's no need to think about tips.

Cagney's Steakhouse & Churrascaria (think: skewered meats presented by tableside 'gauchos') has 276 seats and a central self-help salad bar.

Taste, on Deck 5 is touted as a European retro-chic restaurant. The menu includes traditional and contemporary cuisine for breakfast, lunch, and dinner.

The Manhattan Room, aft, is two decks high and like an elegant Art Deco supper club, with dance floor and live Celebrity Look-Alike shows. It has a spectacular glass window wall aft.

La Cucina is a Tuscan-style eatery, with great ocean views.

The 124-seat Le Bistro features French cuisine (there has been a Le Bistro aboard all NCL ships since the first one aboard the now-scrapped *Norway*).

Asian-themed venues include Shanghai's for Chinese dishes and noodle bar specialties, with open kitchen; the 20-seat Wasabi for sushi and sakes; and a showy, food-chopping Teppanyaki Gril.

The Epic Club and Courtyard Grill, in the Courtyard Villas complex, is for suite/villa occupants and split between a private club-style restaurant with a large wine display and a casual outdoor area for breakfast and lunch.

O'Sheehan's neighborhood-style sports bar and grill is open 24 hours (no extra charge). It is adjacent to a bowling alley though, which disturbs the ambience.

Café Jardin (Garden Café) is a large self-serve buffet, with 728 seats; it is like an English country garden conservatory (but with a French name and ocean views). It includes 'action' stations, where chefs prepare pasta and other items. An outdoor seating area (the Great Outdoors) overlooks the Aqua Park. One section, Kids Café, has low-height tables and seats.

ENTERTAINMENT. The two-deck-high Epic Theater presents hit show Priscilla Queen of the Desert, plus mainline cabaret acts. Another entertainment venue, the Bliss Ultra Lounge, is a decadent venue mainly for late-night comedy.

Spiegel Tent is a two-deck-high, Cirque-like space, combining a show (a cover charge applies) with dinner (like the Teatro ZinZanni dinner theater in San Francisco and Seattle). It's in-your-face street theater, acrobatics, and Berlin-style 'foodertainment,' with interactive clowning and satire during the two-hour show.

The Cavern Club (named after the club where The Beatles started) is home ground for rock 'n' roll lovers, and as part of a Check In, Rock Out program, guitar enthusiasts can (for a daily fee) rent a Gibson guitar and headphones for cabin use.

SPA/FITNESS. The Smile Spa and Pulse Fitness Center complex is in the center so some of the 24 treatment rooms have no view.

Sports facilities include bowling lanes in several venues a full-size basketball court, volleyball, soccer, dodge ball, a batting cage, bungee trampoline, a 24-ft (7.3-m) -high climbing cage (the Spider Web), an abseiling wall, and a walking track.

NORWEGIAN ESCAPE
★★★★

A MULTI-CHOICE, ÜBER-CASUAL PLAYGROUND THAT WORKS FOR THE ENTIRE FAMILY

Size:	Large Resort Ship	Passenger/Crew Ratio (lower beds):	2.4
Tonnage:	165,157	Cabins (total):	2,174
Cruise Line:	Norwegian Cruise Line	Size Range (sq ft/m):	96.8–1,090.0/9.0–101.0
Former Names:	none	Cabins (for one person):	82
Builder:	Meyer Werft (Germany)	Cabins with balcony:	1,571
Entered Service:	Oct 2015	Cabins (wheelchair accessible):	47
Length (ft/m):	1,068.5/325.7	Wheelchair accessibility:	Good
Propulsion/Propellers:	diesel-electric/2 azimuthing pods	Elevators:	16
		Casino (gaming tables):	Yes
Total Crew:	1,7333	Self-Service Launderette:	No
Passengers (lower beds):	4,266	Onboard currency:	US$
Passenger Space Ratio (lower beds):	38.7		

THE SHIP. *Norwegian Escape* is a large resort ship for young and trendy urbanites – and perhaps the best ship in the fleet. Families with children, single parents, couples, and solo travelers have a mountain of entertainment choices, in an environment that is a pure playground for an active, feature-filled cruise.

Norwegian Escape has a more streamlined, balanced profile than its slightly larger sibling ship, *Norwegian Epic*, with a less boxy look to its forward section, and a small, squat funnel, plus a better Passenger Space Ratio (more space per passenger). The hull artwork is designed by marine wildlife artist and champion of ocean conservation, Guy Harvey, featuring an underwater scene of marine wildlife.

The ship is cool, but the ambience is Miami's South Beach in heat, with all the hype and volume to prove it. It has some really good outdoor features for the active. Families with children can enjoy an extensive Aqua Park, with multiple waterslides, rock-climbing wall and rope walk (more for adult kids). Aft is a large movie screen with amphitheater-style seating. Despite the ship's size, the open deck space for sunbathing is tight, reduced by the exclusive Haven area forward, whose suites-only occupants have sunbathing space in a beach club-like setting. Still, the pool deck is where all the mainstream family action takes place, especially on sea days.

Most public rooms, shops, entertainment spots, the casino, and a number of bars, themed dining ven-

BERLITZ'S RATINGS		
	Possible	Achieved
Ship	500	396
Accommodation	200	144
Food	400	245
Service	400	282
Entertainment	100	86
Cruise Experience	400	289

OVERALL SCORE 1442 points out of 2000

ues and eateries with indoor and outdoor (on the 'Waterfront' deck) seating are on a three-deck, indoor-outdoor complex (678 Ocean Place) that includes a large casino area. However, the flow is somewhat disjointed and invites congestion. It includes Tobacco Road, after the Miami icon that closed in 2014 after 102 years. Elements of the former include the original iconic neon sign, memorabilia, and photographs of Miami's history over the past century.

Planning will help make the most of all this ship has to offer. You'll be sharing the ship with about 4,000 others, so you can expect a lively travel experience.

Gratuities are automatically charged to your onboard account, or you can pre-pay online. Overall, unless you are happy with basic food, it may be wise to pay extra to eat in one or more venues not included in the cruise fare.

ACCOMMODATION. There are many accommodation grades and suite/cabin types, shapes, and sleeping capacities, from small interior (no-view) cabins to two-bedroom Villa suites.

The most exclusive accommodation is in a two-deck-high section called The Haven – really a 'ship within a ship' with 42 suites, a restaurant, bar, and concierge lounge. The Haven occupants have private spa access, butler service, in-suite, white-tablecloth dining service, and a platinum key card, which gives better recognition in the rest of the ship – who said the 'class system' was dead?

Balcony suites/cabins have rich wood-look paneling with warm tones. Each has a queen-size bed (or twins), with a pillow-top mattress. Each has a sofa bed with additional storage space. The wall-mounted infotainment system tilts for viewing from the sofa or bed. A built-in vanity area has shelving and decent storage space, while closets have sliding doors. Energy-efficient accommodation has key card access for lighting control. Bathrooms are contemporary, with generous space, while an enclosed under-washbasin vanity hides the trash bin; a shower with a leg-shaving bar completes the picture.

There are 59 studio (single-occupancy) interior-only cabins. They are colorful, trendy, and minimalist – especially the closet space, but they are good for solo cruisers (just don't bring many clothes).

Many interior cabins also have one or two additional upper berths, while lower beds are twins that convert to a queen-size bed – good for families with young children.

Note that cabin doors open *outwards* (towards you) rather than inwards, as is traditional. Also, when music is being played late at night in the lobby, cabins located above it may suffer from intrusive volume levels, despite good soundproofing.

DINING. Freestyle Dining means no assigned dining rooms, tables or seats, so you choose which restaurant to eat in, at what time, and with whom. In practice, you'll need to make reservations wherever you choose to eat, so be prepared for a bit of waiting – just like you would ashore. If you want to see a show in the evening, then your dining time will be dictated by the time of the show, which rather limits choice. Wall-based, touch-screen reservation systems work well, so you can see instantly how long you may have to wait if your chosen restaurant is fully booked.

'Freestyle Dining' is good in that you can try different types of cuisine, in different settings. In practice, however, it means you need to make reservations, which can prove frustrating. Food in the main dining rooms is poor to average (with few vegetables and garnishes, and an overuse of rice.

There are three main dining rooms: Savor, Taste, and Tropicana Room. Other dining venues include Cagney's Steakhouse (an open-kitchen classic American steakhouse) and Moderno Churrascaria (Brazilian-style steakhouse with table-side carved meat service by passadores, plus salad bar), on the deck above, with a view into the Tropicana Room.

The Waterfront is a boardwalk-style outdoor area with bars and eateries include La Cucina (Italian family food with a focus on Tuscany), and, for alfresco eating, there's Maltings, and Pinchos Tapas Bar (à la carte).

Other venues include Le Bistro (classic French-style cuisine); a 96-seat Teppanyaki restaurant with 12 flat-top grills, plus show and noise; the Supper Club (for set dinner and show); Bayamo by Jose Garces (for Mexican cuisine); and Food Republic, for Asian fusion cuisine (including a sushi bar). All cost extra, and reservations are required.

Casual eateries (no extra cost) include O'Sheehan's Neighborhood Bar & Grill, an always-open fast-food joint for sports fans, with two bowling lanes and interactive games; Margaritaville – a Jimmy Buffet-themed outdoor eatery; and the Atrium Café and Bar, for extra-cost (Lavazza) coffees, and pastries. Perhaps in a tribute to Man v. Food (the US reality television show), the Dolce Gelato Bar signature item is a ship-specific, extra-cost sundae (Breakaway Sundae or Getaway Sundae), with multiple scoops of ice cream in up to three flavors topped with 'everything under the sun.'

Garden Café is a large, self-serve buffet, with indoor and outdoor seating. It's open round the clock, with different counters for themed and ethnic food varieties, with a special section for kids.

ENTERTAINMENT. A two-deck-high Escape Theater, located at the front of the ship, is a stunning showlounge, for colorful, high-energy, razzle-dazzle production shows.

SPA/FITNESS. Mandara Spa and fitness center spans two decks, has a large gymnasium, with high-tech muscle-pump equipment, an extra-cost thermal suite (herbal rainshowers, snow grotto, saunas and steam rooms, and relaxation area with hot-tile beds), a beauty salon, and multiple body treatment rooms, including couples' massage rooms.

A Sports Complex includes Aqua Park's multiple thrilling waterslides, a multi-elevated rope course (with over 40 elements), The Plank (a platform extending over the ship's side), a rock-climbing wall, a spider-web-like enclosed climbing cage, bungee trampoline, and a bocce ball court.

NORWEGIAN GEM
★★★+

A FAMILY-FRIENDLY, MID-SIZE SHIP WITH MULTIPLE EATING VENUE CHOICES

Size:	Mid-size Ship	Passenger/Crew Ratio (lower beds):	2.2
Tonnage:	93,530	Cabins (total):	1,197
Cruise Line:	Norwegian Cruise Line	Size Range (sq ft/m):	142.0–4,390.0/13.2–407.8
Former Names:	none	Cabins (for one person):	0
Builder:	Meyer Werft (Germany)	Cabins with balcony:	540
Entered Service:	Oct 2007	Cabins (wheelchair accessible):	27
Length (ft/m):	964.8/294.1	Wheelchair accessibility:	Good
Propulsion/Propellers:	diesel-electric/2 azimuthing pods	Elevators:	12
		Casino (gaming tables):	Yes
Total Crew:	1,070	Self-Service Launderette:	Yes
Passengers (lower beds):	2,394	Onboard currency:	US$
Passenger Space Ratio (lower beds):	39.0		

THE SHIP. A multitude of choices, including many dining options, add up to a very attractive vacation package, highly suitable for families with children, in a floating leisure center that provides ample facilities for enjoyment.

The design and layout of *Norwegian Gem* is similar to that of *Norwegian Pearl*, and there is a pod propulsion system for vibration-free cruising. The white hull has a colorful string of gems along its sides as a design. There are plenty of deck lounge chairs – more than the total of passengers. Waterslides are included for the adult swimming pools. Children have their own pools at the ship's stern.

Inside the ship is an entertaining mix of bright, warm colors and decor that you probably wouldn't have in your home, and yet somehow they all work well.

The dress code is ultra-casual: no jacket and tie needed. Service levels and finesse may be inconsistent, but the hospitality factor is good. There's plenty of lively music, constant activity, entertainment, and food that is mainstream and acceptable but nothing more – even when you pay extra to eat in the specialty dining spots.

There are many lounges and bars to explore, most connected to the atrium lobby. The lobby hosts a Java Bar, plus a two-deck-high movie screen. One standout room is the Bliss Ultra Lounge & Night Club (aft); it houses a V-shaped sports bar and lounge complex, including a bowling alley with four

BERLITZ'S RATINGS

	Possible	Achieved
Ship	500	350
Accommodation	200	141
Food	400	234
Service	400	269
Entertainment	100	66
Cruise Experience	400	268

OVERALL SCORE 1328 points out of 2000

real bowling lanes (limited to six persons per lane). The lounge has few seats, but it does have a couple of decadent beds.

There are many revenue centers designed to help you part with even more money than you paid for your cruise ticket. Expect to be subjected to flyers advertising art auctions, 'designer' watches, gold and silver chain by the inch, and other promotions – and the cruise director's long program announcements three times a day.

A non-changeable, per-person daily 'service charge' is automatically added to your account.

ACCOMMODATION. There are many, many different price grades, from small interior cabins to lavish suites in a private courtyard setting.

Although they are nicely furnished and quite well equipped, the standard outside-view and interior (no-view) cabins are small, particularly when occupied by three or four people. A small room service menu is available – all non-food items cost extra, and a service charge is automatically added to your account. Bottled water is placed in each cabin, but you will be charged if you open the bottle.

The following suites (from largest to smallest), part of The Haven, are also available:

Two Courtyard Villas/Garden Villas, each measuring 4,390 sq ft (408 sq m), and 10 Courtyard Villas share a private courtyard with a small pool, hot tub, small fitness room, and butler service. It's rather like living in a gated community – where others cannot live unless they pay the asking price.

Deluxe Owner's Suites. Black Pearl and Golden Pearl suites have stunning ocean views, and have a master bedroom, a dining/lounge area, a decent-size balcony, and access to a private courtyard.

Penthouse Suites. Located at the front of the ship, they have a partly private balcony under the navigation bridge.

DINING. The main dining rooms are the 304-seat Grand Pacific, with minimalist decor; and the 558-seat Magenta Restaurant. There are several other themed eating spots, giving a wide range of choice; some cost extra, and require advance reservations, particularly for dinner. There are no assigned dining rooms, tables, or seats, so you'll need to plan your meals and times accordingly.

With multiple video screens throughout the ship, you can check how busy each dining venue is. The system generally works well, with colored bars to indicate whether a restaurant is 'full,' 'moderately busy,' or 'empty,' which minimizes frustration. Note that NCL's dress code states that 'jeans, T-shirts, tank tops, and bare feet are not permitted in restaurants.'

Additional dining venues, some of which cost extra, include Cagney's Steak House (for steaks from 5oz to 48oz, and grilled seafood); Blue Lagoon (for trendy fast-food street snacks); Moderno Churrascaria (for Argentinian-style grilled meats); Le Bistro for classic French cuisine; Orchid Garden (an Asian-style eatery with sushi bar and Teppanyaki grill, where showman cooks put on a display in front of you); La Cucina Italian Restaurant; O'Sheehan's Neighborhood Bar & Grill; Garden Café, a large self-serve, food court-style buffet restaurant, for casual meals; Kids' Café; and Java Café, for extra-cost Lavazza coffee, in the lobby.

ENTERTAINMENT. The 1,042-seat Stardust Theater hosts colorful, Las Vegas-style production shows and major cabaret acts. Designed in the style of an opera house, it spans three decks, and has a steeply tiered main floor and port and starboard balconies.

SPA/FITNESS. The Yin-Yang Health Spa complex spans two decks, and is located in the front of the ship, with large ocean-view windows on three sides. There are many facilities and services to pamper you, and multiple treatment rooms. There's also a 37ft (11m) indoor lap pool, hydrotherapy pool, two sit-in deep tubs, aromatherapy and wellness centers, and a mud-treatment room.

Body Waves fitness and exercise rooms are within the spa and have Cybex muscle-pumping equipment. Most classes cost extra.

Recreational sports facilities include a jogging track, golf driving range, and basketball and volleyball courts, as well as several levels of sunbathing decks, plus four bowling lanes, and a funnel-mounted rock-climbing wall.

NORWEGIAN GETAWAY
★★★★

THIS IS A MULTI-CHOICE, SUPER-CASUAL FLOATING PLAYGROUND FOR THE FAMILY

Size:	Large Resort Ship	Passenger/Crew Ratio (lower beds):	2.3
Tonnage:	145,655	Cabins (total):	1,994
Cruise Line:	Norwegian Cruise Line	Size Range (sq ft/m):	96.8–1,022.6/9.0–95.0
Former Names:	none	Cabins (for one person):	59
Builder:	Meyer Werft (Germany)	Cabins with balcony:	1,252
Entered Service:	Feb 2014	Cabins (wheelchair accessible):	40
Length (ft/m):	1,066.2/325.0	Wheelchair accessibility:	Good
Propulsion/Propellers:	diesel-electric (79,800MW)/2 (2 azimuthing pods)	Elevators:	16
		Casino (gaming tables):	Yes
Total Crew:	1,646	Self-Service Launderette:	No
Passengers (lower beds):	3,929	Onboard currency:	US$
Passenger Space Ratio (lower beds):	36.7		

THE SHIP. *Norwegian Getaway* (sister to *Norwegian Breakaway*) has a more streamlined, balanced profile than its slightly larger close-sister ship, *Norwegian Epic*, with a less boxy look to its forward section. Miami artist and muralist David 'Lebo' Le Batard provided the artwork on the hull depicting a whimsical mermaid holding the sun above the waves.

The ship is cool, but the ambience is pure South Beach in heat, with all the hype and volume to prove it. Families have extensive pool deck facilities, including an Aqua Park, with multiple water slides, rock-climbing wall and rope walk (good for adult kids). Aft is a large movie screen with amphitheater-style seating. But, despite the ship's size, the open deck space for sunbathing is tight, made smaller by an exclusive The Haven area in the forward section, whose suites-only occupants have their own sunbathing space, bar, pool, and hot tubs. The rest of the ship shares multiple pools and water-fun exterior decks, designed for families and children, who will love it. Lower down, on an outdoor promenade deck, a 'Waterfront' boardwalk-style outdoor area with bar and eateries brings you closer to the sea. It forms part of the outdoor experience, away from the hubbub of the family-friendly sun/sports action deck atop the ship.

Inside, the decor is decidedly more traditional and provides a relaxed feel and ambience, although this is all relative and still rather upbeat.

Most public rooms, shops, entertainment spots, casino, and bars, themed dining venues and eateries with

BERLITZ'S RATINGS

	Possible	Achieved
Ship	500	397
Accommodation	200	144
Food	400	244
Service	400	272
Entertainment	100	86
Cruise Experience	400	288

OVERALL SCORE 1431 points out of 2000

indoor and outdoor (on the 'Waterfront' deck) seating are on decks 6, 7, and 8 – part of an indoor-outdoor complex called 678 Ocean Place. However, the flow is somewhat disjointed and invites congestion.

Planning and time management will help make the most of all this ship has to offer, which sort of negates its freestyle aspect. You'll be sharing the ship with about 4,000 others, so it will be a lively travel experience.

Norwegian Getaway really is a ship for youthful urbanites and provides families with children, single parents, couples, and solo travelers with a mountain of entertainment.

ACCOMMODATION. There is a huge variety of accommodation grades and suite/cabin types, shapes, and sleeping capacities, so you'll need to decide what you are looking for.

The cabin doors open *outwards* (towards you) rather than inwards, as is more traditional. Also, note that when music is being played late at night in the lobby, cabins located above it can suffer from intrusive volume levels, despite the generally good soundproofing.

Many interior (no-view) cabins have one or two additional upper berths, while the lower beds are twins that convert to queen-size unit – useful for families with young children. Room service incurs a per-order 'convenience' charge.

There are 59 studio (solo-occupancy) interior-only cabins (none has a sea view). They are colorful, trendy, and small, with a minimalist design – especially the closet space. Still this is a neat way to cruise on your own – just don't overpack.

Balcony suites/cabins have rich wood-look paneling with warm tones. Each has twin or queen-size bed with a tufted leather headboard to make sitting up in bed and reading more comfortable. There's a lighted recess above the bed for books, etc. Each room has a sofa bed with additional storage. A built-in flat-screen television is wall-mounted and tilts for viewing from either sofa or bed. A built-in vanity area has shelving and decent storage space. There's also a full-size closet with sliding doors. The cabins are energy-efficient, using key card access to control lighting in the room.

Bathrooms feature a contemporary, clean design. An enclosed vanity unit underneath the (generously sized) washbasin hides the trash bin. A private shower with a shaving bar for women completes the picture. Mini-suite bathrooms have a rain shower plus a hand-held shower hose.

More exclusive accommodation is in a two-deck-high section called The Haven – a 'ship within a ship,' and includes a private restaurant, cocktail bar, and concierge desk for making dining, entertainment, and spa reservations. There is a pool, changing areas, two hot tubs, gym, saunas, two massage rooms, and sun deck with bar. The Haven occupants get butler service, and in-suite, white-tablecloth dining service. Occupants also get a different key card for better recognition in the rest of the ship – who said the 'class system' was dead?

Two Deluxe Owner's Suites in The Haven, with a contemporary apartment look, include an elegant living/dining room with wet bar, and two bathrooms. Deluxe Owner's Suites can be joined to the Owner's Suites to create a grand suite that sleeps up to eight. There are several other categories within The Haven complex.

DINING. Freestyle Dining means no assigned dining rooms, tables or seats, so you can choose which restaurant to eat in, at what time, and with whom. In practice, however, it means you need to make reservations, which can prove frustrating at times. This takes a little planning and, often, waiting. Food in the main dining rooms is poor to average (with few vegetables and garnishes, and an over use of rice as a carbohydrate source), but is much better in the extra cost venues.

The Tropicana Room is a large restaurant (included in the fare), with an integral dance floor (for shows and dancing during dinner) and large ocean-view windows aft. Other dining venues (Cagney's Steakhouse and Moderno Churrascaria – a Brazilian-style steakhouse with meat carved at your table by 'passadores,' and with a salad bar) are located one deck above, with views into the Tropicana Room.

The Waterfront is a boardwalk-style outdoor area with bar and eateries, while Geoffrey Zakarian's 678 Ocean Place (meaning decks 6, 7, and 8) connects it with several interior extra-cost dining venues as well as the extensive Getaway Casino, a cigar-smoking room, and several

entertainment and dining venues. These include: Moderno Churrascaria; La Cucina, for Italian family food with a focus on Tuscany, with inside seating; or, for alfresco eating on The Waterfront, Ocean Blu (designed and overseen by US TV's Food Network's Geoffrey Zakarian). The celebrity chef uses fresh-as-possible ingredients and techniques employed in his land-based establishments.

Other venues include Le Bistro, for classic French-style cuisine; a 96-seat Teppanyaki restaurant with 12 flat-top grills and a knife and noise show, and The Illusionarium – a combination magic show with dinner.

Casual eateries (no extra cost) include O'Sheehan's Neighborhood Bar & Grill, a sports bar and popular always-open fast-food joint, with a big screen for sporting events, miniature bowling alley, pool and air hockey tables, and interactive games; Starbucks for coffees, pastries, and music; and Shanghai's Noodle Bar, for Chinese-style noodle dishes. There's also Wasabi (à la carte sushi).

The Garden Café is an extremely large, self-serve buffet, with indoor and outdoor seating. It's open almost round the clock. Many different counters provide themed and ethnic food varieties, and there's a special section for kids

ENTERTAINMENT. The two-deck-high Getaway Theater, located at the front, is a stunning showlounge for major production shows and cabaret acts. A specially produced version of seven-time Tony-award nominated *Legally Blonde* is a highlight, while *Burn the Floor* is an excellent, fast-paced and exciting Latin dance show (it is presented in the Tropicana Room).

Really cool: The Illusionarium and its Grand Master Magic Show with Dinner. It's presented in a circular room with a large dome (think South Beach meets handcuffs and magic wand). The show is the result of collaboration between NCL's entertainment department and Broadway director/choreographer Patricia Wilcox, Tony Award-winning scenic designer David Gallo, and veteran magician Jeff Hobson. Its design is inspired by the science fiction of Jules Verne, the artistry of legendary magicians such as Houdini, and by the supernatural. Whether you can get your water changed into wine remains to be seen. Grammy Experience at Sea is a small venue featuring headline-name musical artists.

SPA/FITNESS. The spa and fitness center, spread over two decks, houses a warehouse-size gymnasium. The complex includes an extra-cost thermal suite (herbal rain showers, saunas and steam rooms, relaxation area with hot-tile beds), a beauty salon, and multiple body-treatment rooms, including massage rooms for couples.

The Sports Complex includes Aqua Park's five thrilling waterslides, a multi-elevated rope course (with over 40 elements), The Plank (a platform extending over the ship's side), rock-climbing wall, a spider-web-like enclosed spiral climbing cage, bungee trampoline, and a nine-hole miniature golf course.

NORWEGIAN JADE
★★★+

GOOD ENTERTAINMENT AND A CASUAL LIFESTYLE FOR THE WHOLE FAMILY

Size:	Mid-size Ship
Tonnage:	93,558
Cruise Line:	Norwegian Cruise Line
Former Names:	Pride of Hawaii
Builder:	Meyer Werft (Germany)
Entered Service:	May 2006/Mar 2008
Length (ft/m):	964.8/294.1
Propulsion/Propellers:	diesel-electric (40,000kW)/2 azimuthing pods
Total Crew:	1,037
Passengers (lower beds):	2,402
Passenger Space Ratio (lower beds):	37.9

Passenger/Crew Ratio (lower beds):	2.3
Cabins (total):	1,233
Size Range (sq ft/m):	142.0–4,390.0/13.2–407.8
Cabins (for one person):	0
Cabins with balcony:	763
Cabins (wheelchair accessible):	27
Wheelchair accessibility:	Good
Elevators:	12
Casino (gaming tables):	Yes
Self-Service Launderette:	No
Onboard currency:	US$

THE SHIP. Built from 67 blocks, this is a sister ship to *Norwegian Jewel*. After service as *Pride of Hawaii* and a small transformation, it gained a casino, and became *Norwegian Jade* for European and Caribbean cruises – with some interior decor elements from the ship's former Hawaiian life remain. It has a pod propulsion system, so it's quiet, with minimal vibration.

The ship's interior focal gathering place is Bar Central, with three specialty bars that are connected but have distinct personalities. They are on the deck above the reception lobby. There are about a dozen bars and lounges. Other facilities include a casino, three meeting rooms, a chapel, card room, bridge viewing room, and the SS *United States* The dress code is ultra-casual, but there are many revenue centers designed to help part with your money. You can expect to be subjected to flyers advertising daily art auctions, 'designer' watches, and 'inch of gold' sales outlets.

A non-negotiable, per-person 'service charge' is automatically added to your account daily.

Norwegian Jade best suits youthful adult couples, solo travelers, and families with children/teenagers who enjoy upbeat surroundings, good facilities, a wide range of entertainment lounges and bars – all in a neat, highly programmed and well-packaged cruise. Although the initial fare seems very reasonable, extra costs and charges can soon add up.

BERLITZ'S RATINGS		
	Possible	Achieved
Ship	500	349
Accommodation	200	141
Food	400	234
Service	400	269
Entertainment	100	66
Cruise Experience	400	267
OVERALL SCORE 1326 points out of 2000		

Passenger niggles include waiting to use the interactive dining reservation screens in public areas; and lines for breakfast in main dining spots, particularly before the shore excursions start.

ACCOMMODATION. There are many different price grades, determined by size and location. Although they are nicely furnished and quite well equipped, the standard outside-view and interior cabins are quite small, particularly when occupied by three or four people.

A small room service menu is available; all non-food items cost extra. Bottled water is placed in each cabin, but it's chargeable if you open the bottle.

Garden Villas. Two multi-room villas have great views over the pool deck and ocean. Each has a roof terrace and private garden, with open-air dining, hot tub, and private sunning and relaxation areas. Each measures approximately 4,390 sq ft (408 sq m), the ultimate in living space, exclusivity and privacy.

Courtyard Villas (up to 660 sq ft/61 sq m) share a private courtyard, small pool, hot tub, massage bed, and fitness room – all in a distinctly Asian setting. Owner's Suites. These five units measure approximately 1,195 sq ft (111 sq m). Penthouse Suites. These measure up to 600 sq ft (56 sq m). All villas and suites have a private balcony, walk-in closet, rich cherry wood cabinetry, tea/coffee/espresso/cappuccino makers, plus butler and concierge service.

DINING. Freestyle Dining has no assigned dining rooms, tables, or seats, so you can choose which restaurant to eat in, at what time, and with whom. In reality, this means you have to make reservations for a specific time, so 'freestyle dining' turns out to be programmed dining. Ten restaurants and eateries are spread over two entire decks. Some are included in the cruise fare, others cost extra.

The two main restaurants, included in the cruise fare, are Alizar (310 seats) and Grand Pacific (486 seats). Specialty dining venues include Cagney's Steak House, Blue Lagoon (a casual eatery serving American food), Le Bistro (a classic French restaurant (check out the beautiful, genuine, Van Gogh painting), the neighborhood 24-hour O'Sheehans Bar and Grill (for pub-style eats), and Pit Stop (for poolside American diner fare).

Others eateries include a Moderno Churrascaria (a Brazilian style steakhouse with adjacent self-help salad bar), Jasmine Garden (with sushi counter, sake bar, and Teppanyaki Grill for grilled food and knife show), La Cucina (for Italian fare). Self-serve buffet-style meals can be taken in the ultra-casual Garden Café and its outdoor section, while extra-cost Lavazza coffees can be found in the Aloha Café.

You can make reservations via the Freestyle Dining information system; plasma screens showing waiting times for the various venues are located in high-traffic areas.

ENTERTAINMENT. The 1,042-seat Stardust Theater hosts colorful, Las Vegas-style production shows and major cabaret acts. It is designed in the style of an opera house, spans three decks, and has a steeply tiered main floor and port and starboard balconies.

Bands and solo entertaining musicians provide live music for listening and dancing to in several lounges and bars. Throughout the ship, loud music prevails. In Spinnakers Lounge, a nightclub located high atop the ship with great ocean views on three sides, a Pachanga Party (a Miami South Beach rave) is held during each cruise.

SPA/FITNESS. The two-deck-high Yin and Yang health spa complex is at the stern, with ocean-view windows on three sides. There are many facilities and services, almost all costing extra. In addition, there is a 37ft (11m) indoor lap pool, hydrotherapy pool, two sit-in deep tubs, aroma-therapy and wellness centers, and mud-treatment rooms, including one for couples.

The fitness and exercise rooms are located not within the spa, but at the top of the glass-domed atrium lobby. Included is a room for exercycle classes.

Recreational sports facilities include a jogging track, two golf driving nets (there's a golf pro shop, too), basketball and volleyball courts, paddle tennis, mini-golf, oversize chess, and several sunbathing decks.

NORWEGIAN JEWEL
★★★+

A CASUAL MID-SIZE SHIP FOR LIVELY, FAMILY-FRIENDLY CRUISING AND ENTERTAINMENT

Size:	Mid-size Ship	Passenger/Crew Ratio (lower beds):	2.2
Tonnage:	93,502	Cabins (total):	1,188
Cruise Line:	Norwegian Cruise Line	Size Range (sq ft/m):	142.0–4,390.0/13.2–407.8
Former Names:	none	Cabins (for one person):	0
Builder:	Meyer Werft (Germany)	Cabins with balcony:	540
Entered Service:	Aug 2005	Cabins (wheelchair accessible):	27
Length (ft/m):	964.8/294.1	Wheelchair accessibility:	Good
Propulsion/Propellers:	diesel-electric (40,000kw)/2 azimuthing pods	Elevators:	12
Total Crew:	1,069	Casino (gaming tables):	Yes
Passengers (lower beds):	2,376	Self-Service Launderette:	No
Passenger Space Ratio (lower beds):	39.3	Onboard currency:	US$

THE SHIP. *Norwegian Jewel*, assembled from 67 blocks, has a basic design and layout similar to that of *Norwegian Gem* and *Norwegian Pearl*, and a pod propulsion system. The white hull has a colorful, funky design on its sides featuring sparkling jewels. There are plenty of sunloungers – in fact, more than the number of passengers carried. Waterslides are included for the adult swimming pools. Children have their own pools at the stern, out of sight of adult areas.

Inside the ship, you'll be met by an eclectic mix of colors and decor that you probably wouldn't have in your home, and yet somehow it works extremely well in this mid-size ship designed to attract the young and active.

There are over a dozen bars and lounges to enjoy.

Despite the company's name, there's little that's Norwegian about this product, except for a few senior officers. There's plenty of lively music, constant activities, entertainment, and food that is mainstream and acceptable but no more, unless you pay extra to eat in the specialty dining spots. All this is delivered by a smiling, friendly and willing service staff that lacks polish.

A multitude of choices, including many dining options, add up to an attractive vacation package, highly suitable for families with children, in a floating leisure center with ample facilities. However, the ship is full of revenue centers designed to

BERLITZ'S RATINGS		
	Possible	Achieved
Ship	500	347
Accommodation	200	141
Food	400	234
Service	400	269
Entertainment	100	66
Cruise Experience	400	267
OVERALL SCORE 1324 points out of 2000		

part you from your cash. Expect to be subjected to flyers advertising daily art auctions and 'designer' watches. The initial cruise fare is reasonable, but extra costs can mount up and there is a mandatory per-person 'service charge'.

ACCOMMODATION. There are numerous price grades, and something for all tastes, from small interior cabins to lavish Penthouse Suites in a private courtyard setting – part of the exclusive two-deck Haven complex. Although they are nicely furnished and quite well equipped, the standard outside-view and interior cabins are quite small, particularly when occupied by three or four people.

A small room service menu is available, and a 'service charge' is added to your account. Bottled water is placed in each cabin, but you will be charged if you open the bottle.

The largest: two Garden Villas – duplex apartments, with a spiral stairway between upper and lower quarters. Each measures 4,390 sq ft/408 sq m), and 10 Courtyard Villas share a private courtyard with a small pool, hot tub, massage bed, and fitness room, a private concierge lounge with the two largest villas, and butler and concierge service. These units enjoy exclusivity – rather like accommodation in a gated community.

DINING. There are two large dining rooms: the 552-seat Tsar's Palace, which looks like the interior of Catherine the Great's St Petersburg palace in Russia, and the 310-seat Azura. Freestyle Dining means no assigned dining rooms, tables, or seats, so you can choose which restaurant to eat in, at what time, and with whom. In reality, this means you have to make reservations for a specific time, so it's not as 'freestyle' as all that. The restaurants and eateries are spread over two decks. Some are included in the cruise fare, others cost extra (and reservations are required).

Computer screens around the ship enable you to check how long you'll have to wait for a table in each dining spot. The system works well, although on formal nights when you may want to see a show, congestion can occur. Note: Norwegian Cruise Line's dress code states: 'jeans, T-shirts, tank tops, and bare feet are not permitted in restaurants.'

Established favorites include: Cagney's Steakhouse (for fine steaks and seafood); Moderno Churrascaria (a Brazilian-style steakhouse for meat and seafood dishes); and Le Bistro (for fine classic French cuisine). In a 2014 refit, O'Sheehan's Neighborhood Bar and Grill was added, for homey pub food and beer. Chin Chin is an Asian eatery with a Teppanyaki Grill and sushi counter adjacent. La Cucina Italian Restaurant has a long wooden table running through the room to create the ambience of a Tuscan farmhouse.

Garden Café is a large self-serve buffet-style eatery, and incorporates an ice cream bar, and Kid's Café, with its own kid-height counter, located opposite the children's play areas. For coffee, head to the Atrium Café in the lobby, and taste some of Buddy Valasco's cupcakes in Carlo's Bakery, adjacent.

ENTERTAINMENT. The 1,037-seat Stardust Theater features colorful large-scale production shows and cabaret acts. Designed in the style of an opera house, it spans three decks, and has a steeply tiered main floor and port and starboard balconies. Spinnakers Lounge is a late-night club.

SPA/FITNESS. Tthe two-deck-high Bora Bora health spa complex is located in the front, with large ocean-view windows on three sides. There are a number of facilities and services to pamper you, almost all at extra charge.

In addition, there is a 37ft (11m) indoor lap pool, hydrotherapy pool, two sit-in deep tubs, aromatherapy and wellness centers, and mud-treatment rooms. There are 15 treatment rooms in all, including one specifically for couples, and heated tile loungers in a relaxation area.

Recreational sports facilities include a jogging track, golf driving range, basketball and volleyball courts, as well as four levels of sunbathing decks.

NORWEGIAN JOY
★★★★

THIS FAMILY-FRIENDLY UBER-CASUAL SHIP IS TOTALLY DEDICATED TO AMERICAN TASTES

Size:	Large Resort Ship	Passenger/Crew Ratio (lower beds):	2.1
Tonnage:	167,725	Cabins (total):	1,925
Cruise Line:	Norwegian Cruise Line	Size Range (sq ft/m):	96.8–1,087.1/9.0–101.0
Former Names:	none	Cabins (for one person):	0
Builder:	Meyer Werft (Germany)	Cabins with balcony:	1,252
Entered Service:	Jun 2017	Cabins (wheelchair accessible):	47
Length (ft/m):	1,068.5/325.7	Wheelchair accessibility:	Good
Propulsion/Propellers:	diesel-electric/2 azimuthing pods	Elevators:	16
		Casino (gaming tables):	Yes
Total Crew:	1,821	Self-Service Launderette:	No
Passengers (lower beds):	3,883	Onboard currency:	US$
Passenger Space Ratio (lower beds):	43.1		

THE SHIP. *Norwegian Joy* is a large floating resort for youthful urbanites. There is a wide range of dining, sports, and entertainment choices, in an environment that is a pure playground for an active, feature-filled cruise experience.

The novel artwork on the ship's hull is provided by renowned Chinese artist Tan Ping; its theme is the mythical bird, the phoenix. Also, in a cruise industry first, in partnership with Scuderia Ferrari watches there's a real open-air track for go karting, where you can reach speeds of up to 20mph (32kph), just forward of the ship's low-slung funnels. Meanwhile, an activity-driven Aqua Park has multiple thrilling waterslides, a multi-elevation rope course, and many other sports-related activity centers.

Despite the ship's size, the open deck space is actually quite small because ofthe exclusive Haven area in the forward section, whose suites-only occupants (pay more, get more) have private sunbathing space, bar, pool, hot tubs, and beach-club-like setting.

Most public rooms, shops, entertainment spots, the casino, and a number of the bars and themed dining venues are located on decks 6, 7, and 8 – a three-deck indoor-outdoor complex. Here, the 'Waterfront' boardwalk-style outdoor areas with bars and eateries bring you more in contact with the sea. They form part of the outdoor experience and take you away from the hubbub of the family-friendly sun/sports action deck atop the ship.

BERLITZ'S RATINGS		
	Possible	Achieved
Ship	500	396
Accommodation	200	143
Food	400	258
Service	400	277
Entertainment	100	77
Cruise Experience	400	284

OVERALL SCORE 1435 points out of 2000

One neat area is the Galaxy Pavilion, with its hang-gliding simulator, racing-car simulator, and other virtual-reality experiences, including hovercraft bumper cars.

Some planning and time management will be needed to make the most of all this ship has to offer, which sort of negates the freestyle aspect of a large resort ship. You'll be sharing the ship with almost 4,000 others, so be prepared for a really lively cruise experience.

ACCOMMODATION. There is an almost endless variety of accommodation grades and suite/cabin types, shapes, and sleeping capacities, from small interior (no-view) cabins to two bedroom Villa suites. The price you pay depends on the size, location, and grade you choose.

Note that the cabin doors open outwards (towards you) rather than inwards, as is more traditional. Also, when music is being played late at night in the lobby, cabins located above it may suffer from volume levels that are quite intrusive, despite the generally good soundproofing. Room service breakfasts incur a per-order 'convenience' charge (free for occupants of The Haven accommodation).

Instead of solo-occupancy Studio cabins, this ship has two-bedroom interior (no-view) 'suites' with a virtual balcony. Occupants have access to a dedicated concierge for making dining, entertainment and spa reservations.

The Haven accommodation is in a two-deck-high section and consists of large suites, a private pool, changing areas, hot tubs, gym, saunas, private massage rooms, and sun deck with bar. Occupants have private access to the spa and fitness center, butler service, in-suite, white-tablecloth dining service, and access to a private VIP (high stakes) gambling room. There are has four Deluxe Owner's Suites, including an extra-spacious wrap-around private balcony. Deluxe Owner's Suites can be joined to Owner's Suites, creating a grand suite that can sleep up to eight. Two-bedroom Family Villas have two bathrooms and two bedrooms. On other (non-Haven) decks throughout the ship are eight aft-facing penthouses and 10 forward-facing penthouses, plus Courtyard Penthouses. Concierge-grade suites (located above The Haven in a separate complex) are something new for the cruise line with larger balconies and a private lounge/bar.

DINING. Freestyle Dining means no assigned dining rooms, tables or seats, so you can choose which restaurant to eat in, at what time, and with whom you want. In reality, the wealth of choices means that you'll need to make reservations in whichever venue you want to eat, so be prepared for a bit of planning and waiting – just like you would ashore.

There are multiple dining venues and eateries (nine are complimentary), including the Large Savor, and Taste, and some fleet-wide favorites: Cagney's Steakhouse (for premium-grade steaks), La Cucina (for Italian fare), Le Bistro (for French cuisine), and Manhattan Room (a large two-deck-high dining spot with Chinese and Western cuisine with entertainment). Extra-cost venues include a Supper Club (dinner and show), Neptune's (for premium seafood), Grand Tea Room (for traditional, elegant teatime), and a Noodle Bar.

ENTERTAINMENT. The two-deck-high Joy Theater, located at the front, is a stunning showlounge, for the line's signature productions. ;

SPA/FITNESS. The Spa and Fitness Center spans two decks and hosts a large gymnasium, an extra-cost thermal suite (herbal rainshowers, snow grotto, saunas, steam rooms, and relaxation area with hot-tile beds), beauty salon, and multiple body-treatment rooms, including some for couples.

NORWEGIAN PEARL
★★★+

A CASUAL, FAMILY-FRIENDLY SHIP WITH MULTI-CHOICE DINING OPTIONS

Size: .... Mid-size Ship	Passenger/Crew Ratio (lower beds): 2.2
Tonnage: 93,530	Cabins (total): 1,197
Cruise Line: .... Norwegian Cruise Line	Size Range (sq ft/m): 142.0–4,390.0/13.2–407.8
Former Names: .... none	Cabins (for one person): 0
Builder: .... Meyer Werft (Germany)	Cabins with balcony: 540
Entered Service: .... Dec 2006	Cabins (wheelchair accessible): 27
Length (ft/m): 964.8/294.1	Wheelchair accessibility: .... Good
Propulsion/Propellers: diesel-electric (39,000kW)/2	Elevators: 12
azimuthing pods	Casino (gaming tables): .... Yes
Total Crew: 1,072	Self-Service Launderette: .... No
Passengers (lower beds): 2,394	Onboard currency: .... US$
Passenger Space Ratio (lower beds): 39.0	

THE SHIP. The ship's white hull has a colorful, funky design on its sides featuring sparkling jewels. There are plenty of sunloungers – in fact, more than the number of passengers carried. Waterslides are included for the adult swimming pools. Children have their own pools at the stern, out of sight of adult areas.

Inside, you'll be met by an eclectic mix of colors and decor that you probably wouldn't have in your home, and yet somehow it works extremely well in this mid-sized ship designed for the young and active.

There are 13 bars and lounges to choose from. Standouts include Shakers Martini and Cocktail Bar (a 1960s-inspired lounge); Magnum's Champagne and Wine Bar recalls Paris of the 1920s and the liner *Normandie*; and Maltings Beer and Whiskey Pub, a contemporary bar with artwork themed around whiskey and beer production.

Despite the company's name, there's little that's Norwegian, except for a sprinkling of senior officers. There's plenty of lively music, constant activity, entertainment, and food that is mainstream and acceptable but nothing more, unless you pay extra to eat in the specialty dining spots. All this is delivered by a smiling, friendly service staff that lacks polish but is willing.

Plenty of choices, including many dining options, add up to an attractive vacation package that is highly suitable for families with children, in a floating lei-

BERLITZ'S RATINGS		
	Possible	Achieved
Ship	500	347
Accommodation	200	138
Food	400	235
Service	400	269
Entertainment	100	66
Cruise Experience	400	269
OVERALL SCORE 1324 points out of 2000		

sure center that provides ample facilities for enjoyment. The ship is, however, full of revenue centers designed to part you from your cash. Expect to be subjected to a flyers advertising art auctions, 'designer' watches, and 'inch of gold/silver.'

The initial cruise fare is reasonable, but extra costs soon mount up if you want more than the basics. A mandatory per-person 'service charge' is added to your account daily.

ACCOMMODATION. There are numerous accommodation price grades, so there's something for all tastes, from small interior (no-view) cabins to lavish Penthouse Suites in a private courtyard setting – part of 'The Haven' complex. Although they are nicely furnished and quite well equipped, the standard outside-view and interior cabins are quite small, particularly when occupied by three or four people.

A small room-service menu is available, and a service charge is added to your account. Bottled water is placed in each cabin, but you will be charged if you open the bottle.

Two Garden Villas (each measures 4,390 sq ft/408 sq m), and 10 Courtyard Villas share a private courtyard with a small pool, hot tub, massage bed, and fitness room. They also share a private concierge lounge with the two largest villas, as well as butler service. These units are like accommodation in a gated community – where others cannot live unless they pay the asking price. The two largest are duplex apartments, with a spiral stairway between the upper and lower quarters.

Two deluxe Owner's Suites have stunning ocean views, a master bedroom with king-size bed, a dining/lounge area, a decent-size balcony, and access to a private courtyard.

DINING. Freestyle Dining has no assigned dining rooms, tables or seats, so you can choose which restaurant to eat in, at what time, and with whom. In reality, this means you have to make reservations for a specific time, so 'freestyle dining' turns out to be programmed dining. Some restaurants and eateries are included in the cruise fare, others cost extra.

The two largest dining rooms are the 304-seat Indigo, with its minimalist decor, and the 558-seat Summer Palace, plus several other themed eating spots. Various video screens display waiting times for a table at each dining venue. Norwegian Cruise Line's dress code states: 'jeans, T-shirts, tank tops, and bare feet are not permitted in restaurants.'

Other dining options (some cost extra) include Cagney's Steakhouse (for premium steaks and seafood); Moderno Churrascaria (for Argentinian-style meats and seafood); Le Bistro (for fine French-style cuisine); Mambo's (for tapas/Latin fare); Lotus Garden (an Asian eatery featuring a Teppanyaki Grill and sushi counter); O'Sheehan's Neighborhood Bar & Grill (for pub-style eats); while La Cucina Italian Restaurant has a long wooden table running through the room to create the ambience of a Tuscan farmhouse.

For casual (self-serve) buffet-style eating, there's the Great Outdoors, while the Garden Café incorporates an ice cream bar, and Kid's Café, with its own kid-height counter (located opposite the children's play areas). Java Café, in the lobby is for extra-cost coffees.

ENTERTAINMENT. The 1,037-seat Stardust Theater hosts colorful production shows and major cabaret acts. It is designed in the style of an opera house, spans three decks, and has a steeply tiered main floor and port and starboard balconies.

A number of bands and solo entertaining musicians provide live music for listening and dancing in lounges and bars.

SPA/FITNESS. Bodywaves is located in the front of the ship with large ocean-view windows on three sides. There are numerous facilities and services to pamper you, almost all at extra charge.

In addition, there is a 37ft (11m) indoor lap pool, hydrotherapy pool, two sit-in deep tubs, aromatherapy and wellness centers, mud-treatment rooms, and 15 private massage/body-treatment rooms including one for couples.

The fitness and exercise rooms, with high-tech equipment, are located not in the spa, but at the top of the glass-domed atrium lobby. Included is a room for exercycle classes. Some classes cost extra.

Additional facilities include a jogging track, golf driving range, basketball and volleyball courts, as well as four levels of sunbathing decks.

NORWEGIAN SKY
★★★+

A MULTI-CHOICE SHIP GEARED TO CASUAL, UPBEAT, FAMILY-FRIENDLY CRUISING

Size:	Mid-size Ship
Tonnage:	77,104
Cruise Line:	Norwegian Cruise Line
Former Names:	*Pride of Aloha, Norwegian Sky*
Builder:	Lloyd Werft (Germany)
Entered Service:	Aug 1999/Jun 2008
Length (ft/m):	853.0/260.0
Propulsion/Propellers:	diesel-electric (50,000kW)/2
Total Crew:	899
Passengers (lower beds):	2,004
Passenger Space Ratio (lower beds):	38.4
Passenger/Crew Ratio (lower beds):	2.1
Cabins (total):	1,001
Size Range (sq ft/m):	120.5–488.6/11.2–45.4
Cabins (for one person):	0
Cabins with balcony:	252
Cabins (wheelchair accessible):	6
Wheelchair accessibility:	Good
Elevators:	12
Casino (gaming tables):	Yes
Self-Service Launderette:	No
Onboard currency:	US$

THE SHIP. In 2004 *Norwegian Sky* morphed into *Pride of Aloha* for Norwegian Cruise Line's (NCL) Hawaii cruise operation; however, it was withdrawn from that market in 2008 and transferred to NCL.

Norwegian Sky, a comfortable resort, caters well to a multi-generational clientele, with many choices for dining and entertainment. The interior focal point is an eight-deck-high atrium lobby, with spiral sculptures and rainbow-colored sails. The ship underwent a refurbishment in 2019, which added new dining venues.

There are many bars and lounges, a large casino, and multiple dining and snacking options. But the ship is full of revenue centers, designed to help you part from your money. You can expect to be subjected to a stream of flyers advertising daily art auctions, 'designer' watches, and other promotions, with 'artworks' for auction everywhere.

Niggles? Many announcements – particularly annoying are those already stated in the daily program – and plain accommodation hallways.

A mandatory per-person 'service charge' is added to your account daily.

ACCOMMODATION. There are numerous price categories, from the smallest interior (no-view) cabins to four largest Owner's Suites, which have a hot tub on the balcony. The price you pay depends on size, grade, and location.

BERLITZ'S RATINGS		
	Possible	Achieved
Ship	500	347
Accommodation	200	138
Food	400	234
Service	400	265
Entertainment	100	74
Cruise Experience	400	267

OVERALL SCORE 1325 points out of 2000

Most cabins have two lower beds that convert to a queen-size bed, a small sitting area with sofa and table, and a decent amount of closet space, but little drawer space. Over 200 outside-view cabins have a private balcony. Bottled water is placed in each cabin – but your account will be charged if you open it.

DINING. Freestyle Dining means no assigned dining rooms, tables or seats, so you can choose which restaurant to eat in, at what time, and with whom. This means you have to make reservations for a specific time, so 'freestyle dining' turns out to be programmed dining.

The largest dining rooms – Palace Restaurant, and Crossings Restaurant, both seating over 500 – have tables for four to eight and open seating. The cuisine in both includes regional specialties. However, it's best to have dinner in one of the other restaurants, as the food in these two dining rooms is just so-so.

The 83-seat Plantation Club Restaurant is an à la carte, light-eating option, for 'healthy' spa dishes and tapas. It has half-moon-shaped alcoves and several tables for two. The wine list is quite decent and well arranged, with moderate prices, although you won't find many good vintage wines. The cutlery is quite ordinary, and there are no fish knives.

For classic and nouvelle French cuisine, the 102-seat Bistro has decor inspired by royal and aristocratic gardens. For premium steaks and lamb chops, there's Cagney's Restaurant, with intimate seating alcoves, and good food at extra cost. Adjacent is Pinnacle Lounge and Sushi Bar (for Asian fusion cuisine); while La Cucina is for classic Italian favorites.

Other eateries include The Local Bar & Grill (for 'pub' food); Topsiders Bar & Grill; and Pacific Heights, a casual Pacific Rim/Asian Fusion eatery for steaks and seafood. Self-serve, buffet-style meals (for breakfast, lunch, and dinner) can be taken in the Garden Café (indoors) and The Great Outdoors; Starbucks is for those essential cost-extra coffees.

ENTERTAINMENT. The 1,000-seat, two-deck-high (main and balcony levels) Stardust Theater stages production shows and cabaret, although sight lines are poor from some seats. Bands and solo entertaining musicians provide live music for listening and dancing in various lounges.

SPA/FITNESS. Body Waves includes an exercise studio, a fitness room, and several treatment rooms. A sizeable gratuity is automatically added to your account for any spa treatments.

Sports facilities include a large basketball/volleyball court, baseball-batting cage, golf-driving net, platform tennis, shuffleboard, and table tennis. A sports bar, with baseball and surfing themes, has live satellite television coverage of sports events, while joggers can hit a walk-around indoor/outdoor track.

NORWEGIAN SPIRIT
★★★+

THIS IS A MID-SIZED SHIP THAT PROVIDES A CASUAL, LIVELY, ACTIVE VACATION

Size:	Mid-size Ship
Tonnage:	75,904
Cruise Line:	Norwegian Cruise Line
Former Names:	*SuperStar Leo*
Builder:	Meyer Werft (Germany)
Entered Service:	Oct 1998/May 2004
Length (ft/m):	879.2/268.0
Propulsion/Propellers:	2 diesels (50,400kW)/2
Total Crew:	912
Passengers (lower beds):	2,018
Passenger Space Ratio (lower beds):	38.1

Passenger/Crew Ratio (lower beds):	2.2
Cabins (total):	988
Size Range (sq ft/m):	150.6–638.3/14.0–59.3
Cabins (for one person):	0
Cabins with balcony:	374
Cabins (wheelchair accessible):	4
Wheelchair accessibility:	Good
Elevators:	9
Casino (gaming tables):	Yes
Self-Service Launderette:	No
Onboard currency:	US$

THE SHIP. A full walk-around promenade deck outdoors is good for strolling and has lots of space, including an area devoted to children's outdoor activities and pool. Inside, there are two indoor boulevards and a two-deck-high central atrium lobby, which has three glass-walled lifts and ample space to sample the shops and cafés. The lobby itself is modeled after the lobby of Hong Kong's Hyatt Hotel, with little clutter from the usual run of desks found aboard other cruise ships.

The interior design theme revolves around art, architecture, history, and literature. The ship has a mix of Eastern and Western design and decor details. Three stairways are each carpeted in a different color, which helps new passengers find their way around.

A 450-seat room atop the ship functions as an observation lounge by day and a nightclub at night. From it, a spiral stairway takes you down to a navigation bridge viewing area, where you can see the captain and bridge officers at work. There is a business and conference center, and a cigar smoking room. A shopping concourse is set around the second level of the lobby.

The casino complex is at the forward end of the atrium boulevard (not between showlounge and restaurant as in most Western ships). This is Maharajah's, with gaming tables and slot machines.

The dress code is very casual. With many dining choices, some of which cost extra, to accommodate

BERLITZ'S RATINGS		
	Possible	Achieved
Ship	500	348
Accommodation	200	138
Food	400	234
Service	400	269
Entertainment	100	66
Cruise Experience	400	267
OVERALL SCORE 1322 points out of 2000		

different tastes and styles, your cruise and dining experience will largely depend on how much you are prepared to spend.

Norwegian Spirit features a wide choice of dining venues. Delivering a consistently good product depends, however, on the quality of the service staff. Watch out for the many extra-cost items in addition to the extra-charge dining spots.

A non-changeable, per-person service charge is added to your account daily; 15 percent is also added for bar charges, and a hefty 18 percent for spa treatments.

ACCOMMODATION. Three whole cabin decks have balconies, while two-thirds of all cabins have an outside view. Both the standard outside-view and interior cabins really are very small – particularly given that all cabins have extra berths for a third/fourth person – although the bathrooms have a good-size shower enclosure. So, take only the least amount of clothing you can manage with. All cabins have a personal safe, cotton towels, and cotton duvets. In cabins with balconies, the balconies are extremely narrow, and the cabins themselves are very small – the ship was originally constructed for three- and four-day cruises.

Choose one of the six largest Executive Suites (named Hong Kong, Malaysia, Shanghai, Singapore, Thailand, and Tokyo) and you get an excellent amount of private living space, with separate lounge and bedroom with a large en-suite bathroom with mosaic tiled floors, kidney bean-shaped jet tubs, dual washbasins, separate shower enclosures with floor-to-ceiling ocean-view windows, and separate toilets with glass doors. The Singapore and Hong Kong suites and the Malaysia and Thailand suites can be combined to form a double suite – useful for families with children. Butler service and a concierge come with the territory.

A small room-service menu is available; all non-food items cost extra, and a service charge and a gratuity are added to your account.

DINING. There are eight places to eat, two at extra cost, so you need to plan where you want to eat well in advance or you may be disappointed.

Waiter stations are tucked neatly away in side wings, which helps keep down noise levels.

'Freestyle' dining means you choose when and where you want to eat (some are included, some cost extra). Windows Restaurant is the largest dining room, with 632 seats. Others include:

The Garden Room Restaurant, with 268 seats.

Raffles Terrace Café, a large, self-serve buffet restaurant with indoor/outdoor seating for 400 and Raffles Hotel-like decor, with rattan chairs, overhead fans, etc.

Moderno Churrascaria: a Brazilian steakhouse with 'passadores' serving skewered meats tableside. Reservations are required, and there's a cover charge.

Taipan: a Chinese Restaurant, with Hong Kong-themed decor and dim sum made from fresh, not frozen, ingredients. Cover charge applicable; reservations required.

Shogun Asian Restaurant: a Japanese-style restaurant and sushi bar. A section can be closed off to make the Samurai Room, with 22 seats, while a traditional Tatami Room has seats for eight, plus a Teppanyaki grill, with 10 seats, where the chef cooks in front of you and displays his knife-juggling skills.

Maxim's: a small à la carte restaurant with ocean-view windows; fine cuisine in the classic French style. Cover charge applicable, reservations necessary.

Blue Lagoon Café: a small, casual café for cooked-to-order savory fast food.

In addition, The Café, in the atrium lobby, is a cost-extra patisserie and coffee shop.

ENTERTAINMENT. The Stardust Theater (show-lounge), with just under 1,000 seats, spans two decks and has a revolving stage for the high-energy, razzle-dazzle production shows. There are almost no support columns to obstruct the sight lines. It is also used as a large-screen cinema, with excellent surround sound.

SPA/FITNESS. The Roman Spa and Fitness Center is on an upper deck, just forward of the Tivoli Pool. It has a gymnasium with muscle-toning equipment, an aerobics exercise room, a hair and beauty salon, saunas, steam rooms, and changing rooms for men and women, plus several treatment rooms, and aqua-swim pools with counter-flow jets for swimming against the current.

The fitness and exercise rooms, with Cybex muscle-pumping equipment, are located not within the spa, but at the top of the glass-domed atrium lobby. Included is a room for exercycle classes. Sports facilities include a jogging track, golf driving range, basketball and tennis courts, and there are four levels of sunbathing decks.

NORWEGIAN STAR
★★★+

THIS IS A FINE FAMILY-FRIENDLY, MULTI-CHOICE SHIP FOR ACTIVE TYPES

Size:	Mid-size Ship	Passenger/Crew Ratio (lower beds):	2.2
Tonnage:	91,740	Cabins (total):	1,174
Cruise Line:	Norwegian Cruise Line	Size Range (sq ft/m):	142.0–5,350.0/13.2–497.0
Former Names:	SuperStar Libra	Cabins (for one person):	0
Builder:	Meyer Werft (Germany)	Cabins with balcony:	410
Entered Service:	Dec 2001	Cabins (wheelchair accessible):	20
Length (ft/m):	964.9/294.1	Wheelchair accessibility:	Best
Propulsion/Propellers:	diesel-electric (39,000kW)/2 azimuthing pods	Elevators:	12
		Casino (gaming tables):	Yes
Total Crew:	1,031	Self-Service Launderette:	No
Passengers (lower beds):	2,348	Onboard currency:	US$
Passenger Space Ratio (lower beds):	39		

THE SHIP. *Norwegian Star*, sister to *Norwegian Dawn*, has a pod propulsion system, and the hull is adorned with a decal consisting of a burst of colorful stars and streamers.

There is a main pool deck for families, and an adults-only area called Spice H2O is aft.

Facilities include an Internet café, a showlounge with main level plus two balcony levels, 3,000-book library, card room, writing and study room, business center, karaoke lounge, conference and meeting rooms, a large retail shopping complex, and a casino.

With many dining choices, some cost extra. The dress code is ultra-casual, although you are welcome to dress up if you wish. Although service levels and finesse are sometimes inconsistent, the level of hospitality is very good. But the hustling for passengers to attend art auctions is aggressive and annoying. Reaching room service tends to be an exercise in frustration.

A mandatory per-person service charge is added to your account daily, and a gratuity is added for beverage charges.

ACCOMMODATION. With many price grades, there is something for everyone. There are 36 suites, including two of the largest aboard any cruise ship, balcony-class standard cabins, outside-view cabins (no balcony), interior cabins, and 20 wheelchair-accessible cabins. Suites and cabins with private

BERLITZ'S RATINGS		
	Possible	Achieved
Ship	500	356
Accommodation	200	138
Food	400	235
Service	400	266
Entertainment	100	67
Cruise Experience	400	268

OVERALL SCORE 1330 points out of 2000

balconies have easy-to-use sliding glass doors.

All have a hairdryer, tea- and coffee-making sets, and rich cherry wood cabinetry, and a bathroom with a sliding door and a separate toilet, and shower enclosure and washbasin compartments. There is plenty of wood accenting in all accommodation, including wood frames surrounding balcony doors. Some cabins have interconnecting doors – good for families with children – and many cabins have third- and fourth-person pull-down berths or trundle beds.

A small room-service menu is available (a service charge is added to your account). Bottled water is placed in each cabin, but you'll be charged for it if you open it.

The largest accommodation: two huge Garden Villas (Vista and Horizon), in a pod forward of the funnel, overlooking the main pool. Each measure 5,350 sq ft (497 sq m) and can be combined to create a huge, double-size 'house.' They have glass walls and landscaped private roof gardens (with Japanese- or Thai-style garden) for outdoor dining, and huge private sunbathing areas. Each has a large living room with Yamaha baby grand piano, glass dining table, eight chairs, plus private elevator and stairway access.

There are many suites (the smallest measures 290 sq ft/27 sq m) in different configurations. Some overlook the aft, while others are in the forward section.

All are well furnished, although closet space in some of the smaller ones is tight.

DINING. Norwegian Cruise Line's 'Freestyle Dining' is good in that you can try different types of cuisine, in different settings, when you want, although you need to make reservations. This takes a little planning and, often, involves waiting. Food in the main dining rooms is poor to average (with few vegetables and garnishes, and an overuse of rice as a carbohydrate source), but it is better in the extra-cost venues.

Versailles, a large (375-seat), ornate dining room, is aft; it offers traditional multi-course dining, and windows that span two decks.

Aqua is a second, large (374-seat), contemporary-styled dining venue, for lighter fare. It has an open galley, where you can view the preparation of pastries and desserts.

Cagney's Steakhouse: for (cost-extra, but worth it) prime USDA steaks and grilled seafood items.

Moderno Churrascaria: a Brazilian-style steakhouse for meat and seafood dishes.

Ginza Restaurant and sushi bar (with moving sushi belt), Japanese Hot Rock Ishiyaki cuisine, and an adjacent Teppanyaki Grill (for lots of show and go), and a Noodle bar for Chinese noodles, wok-fried dishes, and dim sum.

Le Bistro: a French restaurant, with 66 seats, serving nouvelle cuisine and six courses.

Market Café: a large, indoor/outdoor, self-serve buffet eatery, with almost 400ft (122m) of counter space – and a food-court style. 'Action Stations' have made-to-order omelets, waffles, fruit, soups, ethnic specialties, and pasta dishes. Outside is Topsiders Grill, for burgers and hot dogs.

O'Sheehans Neighborhood Bar and Grill: for down-home comfort food and drinks.

La Cucina: for casual, family-style Italian cuisine.

Other spots include the Atrium Café (a lobby bar-café for hot and frozen coffees, teas, and pastries); Bier Garten, a beer garden for grilled foods; and Sprinkles ice cream bar.

ENTERTAINMENT. The 1,037-seat Stardust Theater is for colorful, Las Vegas-style production shows and major cabaret acts.

SPA/FITNESS. The two-deck-high Barong health spa complex, is aft, with large ocean-view windows. Facilities include an indoor lap pool, a hydrotherapy pool, aromatherapy and wellness centers, several treatment rooms, and a juice bar.

The fitness and exercise rooms, with the latest equipment, are at the top of the atrium lobby. Recreational sports facilities include a jogging track, golf driving range, basketball and volleyball courts, as well as four levels of sunbathing decks.

NORWEGIAN SUN
★★★+

THIS IS ULTRA-CASUAL CRUISING IN A FAMILY-FRIENDLY, MID-SIZE SHIP

Size:	Mid-size Ship	Passenger/Crew Ratio (lower beds):	2.1
Tonnage:	78,309	Cabins (total):	968
Cruise Line:	Norwegian Cruise Line	Size Range (sq ft/m):	120.5–488.6/11.2–45.4
Former Names:	none	Cabins (for one person):	0
Builder:	Lloyd Werft (Germany)	Cabins with balcony:	252
Entered Service:	Nov 2001	Cabins (wheelchair accessible):	6
Length (ft/m):	853.0/260.0	Wheelchair accessibility:	Good
Propulsion/Propellers:	diesel-electric (50,000kW)/2	Elevators:	12
Total Crew:	906	Casino (gaming tables):	Yes
Passengers (lower beds):	1,936	Self-Service Launderette:	No
Passenger Space Ratio (lower beds):	40.4	Onboard currency:	US$

THE SHIP. *Norwegian Sun* is a close sister ship to *Norwegian Sky*, but with an additional deck of balcony cabins and accommodation for the extra 200 crew. The outdoor space is decent, especially with its wide pool deck, two pools, four hot tubs, and plenty of sunloungers arranged in camping-style rows. Cruises now have all-inclusive pricing.

There are many bars and lounges, a large casino, and multiple dining and snacking options, but the ship is full of revenue centers, designed to help part you from your money. You can expect to be subjected to flyers advertising daily art auctions, 'designer' watches, and other promotions, while 'artworks' for auction are all over. A mandatory per-person service charge is added to your account daily.

ACCOMMODATION. There are many different price categories, depending on size and location. Standard interior (no-view) and outside-view cabins are small when compared to those of other major cruise lines, but all have common facilities, such as two lower beds that convert to a queen-size, a small sitting area with sofa and table, and a decent amount of closet and drawer space, although the cabins themselves are disappointingly small. Over 200 outside-view cabins have a private balcony. All cabins have tea-/coffee-making sets, a safe, satellite-linked telephone, and bathroom with bath or shower. The

BERLITZ'S RATINGS		
	Possible	Achieved
Ship	500	355
Accommodation	200	138
Food	400	234
Service	400	265
Entertainment	100	74
Cruise Experience	400	268
OVERALL SCORE 1334 points out of 2000		

largest accommodation can be found in the two Owner's Suites.

DINING. Freestyle Dining lets you choose which restaurant you would like to eat in, at what time, and with whom. Except for two large dining rooms, there are a number of other themed eating establishments – although it is wise to plan in advance, particularly for dinner. Some incur an extra charge. The dress code states that: 'jeans, T-shirts, tank tops, and bare feet are not permitted in restaurants.'

The two main dining rooms – the Four Seasons Dining Room and the Seven Seas Dining Room – have tables for two to eight. Sandwiched between the two (rather like a train carriage) is an 84-seat Italian restaurant, Il Adagio, for extra-charge, reservations-required dining, with tables for two or four by the windows.

Overall, the food is decent, but lacks quality in terms of presentation, although the menus make the dishes sound good. There's a decent selection of breads, rolls, cheeses, and fruits. The wine list is quite good and moderately priced, though the glasses are small.

Most dining venues are located on an uppermost deck, with great views from large picture windows, including:

Le Bistro: a 90-seat dining spot for French-style meals, including tableside cooking. Reservations required.

Las Ramblas: a Spanish/Mexican style eatery for tapas (light snack items).

Ginza: a Japanese restaurant, with sushi bar and Teppanyaki grill (show cooking in a U-shaped setting where you sit around the chef). Reservations required.

East Meets West: a Pacific Rim fusion restaurant, featuring California/Hawaii/Asian cuisine à la carte. Reservations are necessary for dinner.

Moderno Churrascaria: Brazilian steakhouse and salad bar, with tableside meat carving. Reservations required.

Garden Café: a busy, indoor/outdoor, buffet-style eatery for self-serve fast foods and salads; open 24 hours a day.

There is no formal afternoon tea; you can make your own at beverage stations (but it's difficult to get fresh milk, as non-dairy creamers are typically supplied).

ENTERTAINMENT. The Stardust Theater is a two-level showlounge with over 1,000 seats and a large proscenium arch-topped stage for large-scale, high-energy production shows. However, the sight lines are obstructed in a number of seats by several slim pillars.

The ship carries a number of bands and solo entertaining musicians. These provide live music for listening and dancing in several of the lounges and bars, including the loud Dazzles, home to musical groups.

SPA/FITNESS. Bodywaves, at the top of the atrium, is a large health/fitness spa (including an aerobics room and separate gymnasium), several treatment rooms, and men's and women's saunas/steam rooms and changing rooms.

Sports facilities include a large basketball/volleyball court, baseball-batting cage, golf-driving net, platform tennis, shuffleboard, and table tennis. A sports bar has live satellite television coverage of sports events, while joggers can circuit the indoor/outdoor track.

OASIS OF THE SEAS
★★★★

THIS HUGE FLOATING RESORT HAS ACTIVITIES GALORE FOR FAMILIES WITH BOUNDLESS ENERGY

Size:	Large Resort Ship	Passenger/Crew Ratio (lower beds):	2.4
Tonnage:	225,282	Cabins (total):	2,704
Cruise Line:	Royal Caribbean International	Size Range (sq ft/m):	150.6–1,523.1/14.0–141.5
Former Names:	none	Cabins (for one person):	0
Builder:	Aker Yards (Finland)	Cabins with balcony:	1,956
Entered Service:	Dec 2009	Cabins (wheelchair accessible):	46
Length (ft/m):	1,181.1/360.0	Wheelchair accessibility:	Good
Propulsion/Propellers:	diesel-electric/3 pods (2 azimuthing, 1 fixed)	Elevators:	24
		Casino (gaming tables):	Yes
Total Crew:	2,164	Self-Service Launderette:	No
Passengers (lower beds):	5,408	Onboard currency:	US$
Passenger Space Ratio (lower beds):	41.6		

THE SHIP. Oasis of the Seas (the world's first cruise ship measuring over 200,000 tons) is now 10 years old. It is a huge, stunning leisure resort afloat with a whole host of facilities and some really excellent entertainment for the whole family – including slightly scaled-down versions of a well-known Broadway show. This is a real 'Moveable Resort Vacation' (MRV) for families, and a credit to the company's design team, packed with innovative elements. The outdoor decks are full of fun water-park and sports features, including the obligatory rock-climbing wall, so there's little room to sit and relax. Sunloungers are so tightly packed together that there's little space to put your belongings. But this is consistent, if homogeneous, mainstream cruising for young-minded cruisers of all ages who enjoy mingling in a large ship with plenty of life and constant activity. An adults-only, open-air solarium and rentable cabanas are part of the outdoor scene.

There are many bars and places to eat/snack, so public spaces are arranged as seven 'neighborhoods': Central Park, the Coney Island-style Boardwalk, the Royal Promenade, the Pool and Sports Zone, Vitality at Sea Spa/Fitness Center, Entertainment Place, and Youth Zone.

The huge Royal Promenade is the main focal point and social center; it is a shopping mall, with casual eateries (including Starbucks), shops, video screens, changing color lights at every step, and parades. Interior-view cabins have balconies with Central Park views. A hydraulic, oval-shaped Rising Tide Bar moves slowly

BERLITZ'S RATINGS	Possible	Achieved
Ship	500	397
Accommodation	200	140
Food	400	220
Service	400	281
Entertainment	100	87
Cruise Experience	400	284

OVERALL SCORE 1409 points out of 2000

through three decks to link the Royal Promenade with Central Park.

The Boardwalk (Coney Island) has shops, several eateries, and a superb carousel. Central Park has real vegetation (trees, and a living plant wall).

It's best to plan what you want to do to get the most out of your cruise, and almost everything requires you to make reservations/sign up in advance. Do budget extra for additional-cost items and promotions.

Niggles include lines at the reception desk, for shore tenders and excursions, self-serve buffet stations, intrusive photographers, few quiet places to sit and read, no cushioned pads for the sunloungers, small cabin 'bath' towels, noisy (vacuum) toilets, unwelcome announcements for revenue activities, fiberglass – not wood – railings, expensive ice-laden frosted drinks in 'souvenir' glasses, speaking 'elevator going up/going down, loud recorded 'music' everywhere (in elevators, hallways, and saunas), and deafening live music. Also, if you have an interconnecting door cabin, you may be able to hear your next-door neighbors.

Service personnel are friendly, however, and the digital 'Wayfarer' system is informative. Do budget extra for additional-cost items, and expect flyers and advertising promotions.

Overall, this is a fine all-round ship for all age groups, but be aware of the extra cost for many optional items (including drinks, drink packages, and excursions).

In 2019, the ship underwent an extensive refurbishment, improving the open deck waterplay areas and introducing Splashaway Bay for kids, plus a trio of slides, including The Ultimate Abyss (the tallest waterslide at sea). Other additions include Music Hall, a new karaoke venue, and several new eateries such as Portside BBQ.

ACCOMMODATION. There are numerous accommodation price grades, reflecting the choice of location and size. Suite occupants get concierge lounge access and associated services. There are many family-friendly cabins, but none for solo occupancy. The numbering system is confusing. Note that cabin doors open outwards (towards you), as in many European hotels. In many of the lower accommodation grades, closet access is awkward. Most cabins are extremely small, given the size of the ship, and electrical sockets are located below the vanity desk unit in a user-unfriendly position; it's difficult to watch television from the bed, and washbasins in many cabins are tiny and low, at just 30.5ins (77.5cm) above floor level. Be careful – it's easy to hit your head on the mirror above. Small soap bars are provided; shampoo is in a dispenser in the shower enclosure, and the shower is fixed (no flexible hose). Although there is no soap dish or indentation in the washbasin surround for soap, useful touches include a blue ceiling bathroom nightlight.

Boardwalk cabins are exposed to noise and events, including rehearsals and sports activities in the Aqua Theater aft, bells from the carousel, plus screaming zipliners during the day, loud music from poolside bands, and exceedingly loud announcements by the cruise director repeating what's already printed in the daily program.

Loft Suites. Although a few ships, such as the now-withdrawn QE2, *Saga Rose,* and *Saga Ruby,* had upstairs/downstairs suites, RCI introduced its version ('loft' suites) to the *Oasis*-class ships. One Crown Accessible Loft Suite includes an elevator to aid mobility-challenged passengers.

DINING. Spanning three decks, the main dining room is cavernous. It has two seating times (early or late) for dinner, or you can choose 'My Time Dining' and eat at your preferred time. There are tables of all sizes, including some for family reunions.

The cuisine is standardized banquet catering and batch cooking. Menu descriptions may sound tempting, but the food is less so. However, items such as lobster or filet mignon (steak) can be made to order (at an extra cost). Green vegetables are scarce but salad items are plentiful, and desserts are pretty good. Rice is overused. Breads and pastry items are just okay. Vegetarian and children's menus are available. There are no wine waiters.

Other dining venues and eateries (some cost extra, but have cooked-to-order food) include Chops Grille Steakhouse (for premium veal chops, steaks and seafood items) and Portofino (for Italian-American cuisine). Reservations (make them through the digital system) are required; note that menus do not change.

Others eateries include: 150 Central Park, the ship's most exclusive restaurant, combines cutting-edge cuisine with interesting design. An observation window into the kitchen allows passers-by to watch the chefs in action, preparing the multi-course tasting menu (open for dinner only).

Chef's Table (Concierge Lounge, upper level) offers a multi-course meal with wine, hosted by the executive chef, with just 14 seats.

Giovanni's Table, a casual Italian dining spot with a rustic feel.

Izumi Hibachi & Sushi, with pseudo-Japanese cuisine, including a Teppanyaki menu (a show grill featuring cooks with acrobatic knives).

Sabor Taqueria & Tequila Bar is for modern tastes of Mexico.

Vintage is a wine bar with a robust selection of wines, accompanied by cheese and tapas (per-item charge).

Other snacking spots include: Central Park Café, a casual indoor/outdoor deli-style eatery; Boardwalk Dog House; Sorrento's Pizzeria; Park Café (for salads and light bites); Wipe Out Café; Donut Shop; Ice Cream Shoppe, and a 1940s-style Cupcake Shop. For more health-conscious fare, there's a self-serve section in the Solarium Bistro.

Windjammer Café is the (free) casual, self-serve eatery common to all RCI ships. No trays are provided – just oval plates; because they're plastic, it's impossible to have a hot plate. If you are disabled or have mobility difficulties, do ask for help. Unfortunately, it is simply too small to handle the number of peak time invaders (try some of the other eateries to avoid the overcrowding). The food varies from quite acceptable to less so – fresh fruit tends to be hard and unripe. It's best to arrive early, when the food has just been cooked and displayed. Although there's a decent enough variety, the quality of some of the meat is poor, and the food often overcooked.

Weak coffee is free in many venues, but espressos and cappuccinos (in paper cups) in Starbucks cost extra.

ENTERTAINMENT. The 1,380-seat main showlounge (Opal Theater), spread over three decks, stages an excellent, 90-minute-long production of a Broadway show, while *Frozen in Time* is a stunning, must-see ice show at the ice-skating rink.

The large Aqua Theater, located aft on The Boardwalk, has a 6,000-sq-ft (557-sq-m) stage; it is an excellent combination show theatre and sound stage (some great viewing places can be found high in the aft wings of the ship on both sides). The ship's aft has some 'overhang,' to accommodate the venue.

SPA/FITNESS. Vitality at Sea Spa sits alongside Vitality Café, for extra-cost health drinks and snacks. Its fitness center has cardio and resistance machines. An extra-cost thermal suite includes saunas, steam rooms, and heated, tiled loungers. You can't just take a sauna without paying for a one-day pass, however.

OCEANA
★★★+

THIS SHIP IS FOR FAMILY-FRIENDLY CRUISING IN A COMFORTABLE ENVIRONMENT

Size:	Mid-size Ship	Passenger/Crew Ratio (lower beds):	2.2
Tonnage:	77,499	Cabins (total):	975
Cruise Line:	P&O Cruises	Size Range (sq ft/m):	158.2–610.3/14.7–56.7
Former Names:	Ocean Princess	Cabins (for one person):	0
Builder:	Fincantieri (Italy)	Cabins with balcony:	410
Entered Service:	Feb 2000/Nov 2002	Cabins (wheelchair accessible):	19
Length (ft/m):	857.2/261.3	Wheelchair accessibility:	Good
Propulsion/Propellers:	diesel-electric (28,000kW)/2	Elevators:	11
Total Crew:	850	Casino (gaming tables):	Yes
Passengers (lower beds):	1,950	Self-Service Launderette:	Yes
Passenger Space Ratio (lower beds):	39.7	Onboard currency:	UK£

THE SHIP. *Oceana* is all about British-ness and will be comfortingly familiar for families with children who want to travel and take their British traditions and food with them. It is suited to adults of all ages and families with children of all ages, and offers good value for money.

The all-white *Oceana* has a pleasing profile and is well balanced by its large funnel, which contains a deck tennis/basketball/volleyball court in its sheltered aft base. There is a decent amount of open deck space and a wide, teakwood walk-around promenade deck. The pool deck, however, is cluttered with white plastic chairs with no cushioned pads.

There is a range of public rooms, lounges, and bars, and the social meeting point is a four-deck-high atrium lobby (the Captain's cocktail party is held here) with winding, double stairways and two panoramic glass-walled lifts. Other public areas include the Monte Carlo Club Casino (while large, it's out of the main passenger flow) and the Yacht and Compass Bar, decorated in the style of a turn-of-the-century, wood-paneled gentlemen's club.

In the quest for increased onboard revenue, even birthday cakes are an extra-cost item, as are espressos and cappuccinos (unauthentic ones, made from instant coffee, are available in the dining rooms), ice cream and bottled water – items that can add up to a considerable amount. Expect to be subjected to flyers advertising daily art auctions, 'designer' watches, and other promotions.

BERLITZ'S RATINGS

	Possible	Achieved
Ship	500	330
Accommodation	200	127
Food	400	235
Service	400	270
Entertainment	100	68
Cruise Experience	400	254

OVERALL SCORE 1284 points out of 2000

ACCOMMODATION. There are many different cabin grades, from suites with private balcony to interior (no-view) cabins. Although the standard cabins are small, they are well designed and functional, and decorated in earth tones accentuated by colorful bedspreads.

Many outside-view cabins have private (narrow) balconies, although the balcony partition is not of the floor-to-ceiling type, so you can hear your neighbors clearly. Balconies have no lights. Many cabins have third- and fourth-person upper bunk beds – good for families with children – and all cabins have useful tea- and coffee-making facilities.

There is a reasonable amount of closet and abundant drawer and other storage space in all cabins. A refrigerator is also provided, and each night a chocolate will appear on your pillow. Bathrooms are small but practical. Fortunately, there is a good-sized shower enclosure, plus a small amount of shelving for toiletries, and a hairdryer.

Also standard in all cabins: Slumberland sprung mattresses, duvets, cotton towels, and tea-/coffee-making facilities with specialty teas and long-life milk.

The largest accommodation is in six suites, two on each of three decks at the aft of the ship, with a private balcony giving great aft views. Each – Orcades, Orion, Orissa, Orontes, Oronsay, and Orsova (all P&O ships of yesteryear) – has a large balcony, marble-clad bathrooms, Jacuzzi tub, and separate shower enclosure. The bedroom has wood accenting, indented ceiling, and TV screens in sleeping and lounge areas, plus a dining room table and four chairs.

DINING. There are two principal asymmetrically designed dining rooms, Adriatic and Ligurian (each with about 500 seats) just off the two lower levels of the atrium lobby. One is for open seating, the other for two seatings. Each has its own galley, and is split into multi-tier sections, creating a feeling of intimacy, although there is much noise from waiter stations. Open-seating breakfast and lunch are provided; dinner is in two seatings.

The cuisine is decidedly British – seldom adventurous, but always with curry dishes and other standard British comfort-food dishes. Don't expect exquisite dining – this is unpretentious British hotel catering that is attractive and tasty, with good gravies and sauces, and decent desserts. A statement in the onboard cruise folder states that P&O Cruises does not knowingly purchase genetically modified foods, but forgets to mention all the commercial American GM cereals provided. The wine list is average, but good value, although both red and white wine glasses are small.

The Plaza self-serve buffet above the navigation bridge morphs at night into an informal dinner setting with sit-down waiter service.

Outdoors on deck, Horizon Grill has fast-food items for sunbathers.

For other informal eats, there is Café Jardin, with a Frankie's Bar & Grill-style menu, on the uppermost level of the atrium lobby.

Explorer's is for extra-cost 'premium' coffees, teas, and pastries; Magnums is a Champagne/caviar bar.

ENTERTAINMENT. Footlights (located forward) is a 550-seat showlounge, for production shows, drama presentations, and movies. Starlights (located aft) is a 480-seat cabaret-style lounge with bar.

SPA/FITNESS. The Ocean Spa facilities are contained in a glass-walled complex on a high aft deck, with gymnasium, an exercise room, a sauna, steam room, and several treatment rooms.

One swimming pool is 'suspended' aft between two decks and forms part of the spa complex. Two other (small) pools are located in the ship's center. Sports facilities include basketball, volleyball, badminton, paddle tennis, and an electronic golf simulator (no need to bring your own clubs).

OOSTERDAM
★★★+

THIS IS A CONTEMPORARY, FAMILY-FRIENDLY SHIP WITH TRENDY DUTCH DECOR

Size:	Mid-sized Ship
Tonnage:	82,305
Cruise Line:	Holland America Line
Former Names:	none
Builder:	Fincantieri (Italy)
Entered Service:	Aug 2003
Length (ft/m):	935.0/285.0
Propulsion/Propellers:	diesel-electric (35,240kW)/2 azimuthing pods
Total Crew:	800
Passengers (lower beds):	1,918
Passenger Space Ratio (lower beds):	42.9
Passenger/Crew Ratio (lower beds):	2.3
Cabins (total):	924
Size Range (sq ft/m):	185.0–1,318.6/17.1–122.5
Cabins (for one person):	0
Cabins with balcony:	623
Cabins (wheelchair accessible):	28
Wheelchair accessibility:	Good
Elevators:	14
Casino (gaming tables):	Yes
Self-Service Launderette:	No
Onboard currency:	US$

THE SHIP. *Oosterdam* is one of a series of ships designed for younger, vibrant, multi-generational, family-oriented cruisers. It has twin working funnels – the result of two engine rooms.

The ship has a complete walk-around exterior teak promenade deck, with teak steamer-style sun-loungers, while an outdoor jogging track is laid around the mast. Exterior midships glass elevators, on both port and starboard sides, provide ocean views. There are two centrally located swimming pools outdoors; one can be used in poor weather thanks to its retractable sliding glass roof. Two whirlpool tubs, adjacent, are abridged by a bar. A small pool is available for children.

The ship offers a range of public rooms with a comfortable, almost intimate atmosphere, and in true Holland America Line tradition, a collection of Dutch artworks and artifacts.

The small lobby spans just three decks, with a beautiful, rotating Waterford crystal globe of the world. The interior decor is bright, yet comfortable. Public room ceilings are particularly noticeable, as are the cast-aluminum elevator doors – the design inspired by the Art Deco designs from New York's Chrysler Building.

There are two decks of entertainment/public rooms. A winding shopping street has several boutiques, and includes an Internet center, a library, card room, an art gallery, a photo gallery, and sev-

BERLITZ'S RATINGS		
	Possible	Achieved
Ship	500	356
Accommodation	200	144
Food	400	220
Service	400	254
Entertainment	100	67
Cruise Experience	400	261
OVERALL SCORE 1302 points out of 2000		

eral small meetings rooms. A casino (with gaming tables and slot machines) is large, and you have to walk through it to get from the restaurant to the showlounge.

On other decks, you'll find the Queen's Lounge – a combination lecture room and Culinary Arts Center, plus bars and lounges, including the Explorer's Lounge (lifestyle/coffee lounge) and a small movie-screening room.

Many pillars obstruct passenger flow and lines of sight throughout the ship. There are no self-service launderettes – something that families with children will miss, although special laundry packages are available.

ACCOMMODATION. There are many price categories for the various accommodation grades, from small cabins for solo travelers to the largest (Grand Pinnacle) suites. Some cabins can accommodate a third and fourth person but have little closet space, and only one personal safe. Suite occupants get access to the Neptune Lounge and concierge, priority embarkation and disembarkation, and other benefits. In many of the suites/cabins with private balconies the balconies are not so private and can be overlooked from various public locations.

Niggles include noisy air conditioning – the flow in cabins and bathrooms can't be turned off, and the only regulation is for temperature control.

DINING. The 1,045-seat Vista Dining Room is aft. It spans two decks and is a stunning room, with seating on both levels. Both open and fixed seating are available for dinner, while breakfast and lunch are open seating (restaurant staff seat you when you enter). There are tables for two to eight. The waiter stations can be noisy for anyone seated adjacent to them.

With a few exceptions, the cuisine is unmemorable, because it's all about batch cooking for large numbers. There's a distinct lack of variety of green vegetables, too much use of rice, canned fruit, and already sliced and diced cheese. Still, you get friendly service from smiling Indonesian and Filipino stewards, and the plates are nice.

'Lighter option' meals are always available for the nutrition- and weight-conscious. Kosher meals are also available; these are prepared ashore, frozen, and brought to your table sealed in their original containers.

The Pinnacle Grill has high quality ingredients and good presentation. Pacific Northwest cuisine is featured. There are fine table settings, china, and silverware. A wine bar offers mostly American wines. Reservations are required, and there's a cover charge.

For casual eating, Lido Market is a self-serve, buffet-style eatery that wraps around the funnel housing and extends aft, with fine views over the multi-deck atrium. Movement through the buffet can be slow at peak times. Each evening, one side is turned into the extra-cost, 72-seat Canaletto Restaurant – a quasi-Italian informal eatery with waiter service.

Also, the poolside 'Dive-In at the Terrace Grill' features multi-choice signature burgers (with Dive-In sauce), hot dogs, and fries.

An extra-cost Windsurf Café in the atrium lobby (open most of the day) has coffee, pastries, snack foods, deli sandwiches, and, in the evenings, liqueur coffees.

ENTERTAINMENT. The 867-seat Main Stage (showlounge) features Vegas-style revues and cabaret shows. The main-floor level includes a bar and spiral stairways. Shows are best seen from the upper levels, which have good sight lines.

Other entertainment/music-centric venues include Lincoln Center Stage, Half Moon, and Billboard Onboard.

SPA/FITNESS. The Greenhouse Spa spans two decks, located above the navigation bridge. It includes a solarium, a hydrotherapy pool, and a unisex thermal suite, incorporating a laconium, hammam, and chamomile grotto. There is also a salon, several private massage/body-treatment rooms, including one for couples, and a fitness room with floor-to-ceiling windows. Sports enthusiasts can enjoy a basketball court, volleyball court, and golf simulator.

OVATION OF THE SEAS
★★★★

A HIGH-TECH, HIGH-ENERGY, BLING-FILLED CRUISE SHIP FOR THE WHOLE FAMILY

Size:	Large Resort Ship	Passenger/Crew Ratio (lower beds):	3.2
Tonnage:	168,666	Cabins (total):	2,090
Cruise Line:	Royal Caribbean International	Size Range (sq ft/m):	101.1–799.7/9.4–74.3
Former Names:	none	Cabins (for one person):	34
Builder:	Meyer Werft (Germany)	Cabins with balcony:	1,571
Entered Service:	May 2016	Cabins (wheelchair accessible):	34
Length (ft/m):	1112.2/339.0	Wheelchair accessibility:	Good
Propulsion/Propellers:	diesel-electric/2 azimuthing pods	Elevators:	16
Total Crew:	1,300	Casino (gaming tables):	Yes
Passengers (lower beds):	4,180	Self-Service Launderette:	No
Passenger Space Ratio (lower beds):	40.3	Onboard currency:	US$

THE SHIP. *Ovation of the Seas* is a sister ship to *Anthem of the Seas*, *Quantum of the Seas*, and *Spectrum of the Seas* – innovative ships designed with 'wow' factor for families with children and technology fans.

Novel attractions include North Star; it's a 14-person (including the operator) glass pod that lifts you from ship's uppermost deck for a moving, bird's-eye view below, like a giant 'cherry picker' (it's quite a ride). It's just behind the mast, is complimentary (and wheelchair-accessible), and operates only on sea days.

Also neat is RipCord by iFly – a simulated skydiving experience in a vertical wind tunnel that lets you experience the thrill of skydiving in a controlled environment; it accommodates 13 for each class, including two 'hovering in the air' experiences, instruction, and gear. Both attractions are bookable at interactive digital kiosks (adjacent to elevators) and tablets in public areas.

Facilities include a SeaPlex complex, under the North Star, that features bumper-car rides, and alternates as a roller-skating rink and basketball court; a rock-climbing wall, and a FlowRider surfing simulator. Outside, perched atop the SeaPlex is Mama and Baby (a giant art installation of a panda and its baby).

Two70º is an innovative multi-level venue at the stern that provides a casual living area by day and at night becomes a foot-stomping, high-energy en-

BERLITZ'S RATINGS		
	Possible	Achieved
Ship	500	404
Accommodation	200	137
Food	400	289
Service	400	272
Entertainment	100	88
Cruise Experience	400	277
OVERALL SCORE 1467 points out of 2000		

tertainment venue, with multiple dynamic robotic screens.

The decor is contemporary and glitzy. There are some delightful Asian touches throughout (about $3.1 million was spent on art), including some interesting East-meets-West pieces – look for 'the 'gold finger' at Wonderland, and some eclectic white keyhole chairs. The multi-deck-high, silk-effect, sashaying 'tapestry' that adorns the Royal Esplanade (indoor promenade – the focal point and social meeting 'street') is a delight, as is the kinetic ceiling sculpture called Sky Wave.

The Royal Esplanade includes bars (including a Bionic Bar), Music Hall (a two-deck-high entertainment venue), several brand-name shops and the large Casino Royale – with gaming tables (including Chinese table games) and slot machines. A separate, super-exclusive room (by invitation only) is for high-stake players.

Ovation of the Seas provides an active cruise experience for the whole family (young ones absolutely love the facilities and programs aboard this ship), but it's important to make reservations for the various restaurants and eateries if you want to be sure not to miss out. High-speed Wi-Fi is expensive, but at least all cabins come equipped with one or more USB sockets for charging digital items. As on most large resort ships, if you stay in suite-grade accommodation, you receive more privileges and perks. If you don't, you'll be just one of the crowd.

ACCOMMODATION. There are many different price grades and categories, from interior (no view or 'virtual view') to family suite, Loft Suites, and solo-occupancy Studio cabins. What you pay depends on the size and location you choose. Fortunately, every cabin aboard this ship has a view – whether real or virtual. 'Virtual' balconies were first introduced aboard *Navigator of the Seas* (in 2013) and are a neat feature of interior (no-view) cabins; they can provide real-time ocean views, but you *can* turn them off, if you wish. Costing more than standard interior cabins, they're worth it.

Even the smallest bathroom is well designed, with thoughtful touches such as a night light, and shower and vanity hooks, while cabins have bedside power outlets, and ample storage space.

On the negative side, tablet-based infotainment systems don't answer questions.

DINING. There are 18 restaurant and eatery choices (there's no single main dining room as such). Suite occupants can eat in Coastal Kitchen (a private section of the Windjammer Marketplace).

Main dining room cuisine is all about standardized banquet catering and batch cooking. Menu descriptions can sound tempting, but the food is less so. Green vegetables don't feature much but salad items are plentiful, and desserts are pretty good. Rice is offered with everything. Breads and pastry items are also average. Vegetarian and children's menus are available. Note that there are no wine waiters.

Some extra-cost restaurants require reservations. Note that the menus are the same each night in most extra-cost restaurants, and service can be slow (there are no assistant waiters). Dining 'packages' are available for purchase – these include costs for 3, 4, or 5 nights.

The following are complimentary (with tablecloths for dinner):

The Grande: with around 430 seats, the elegant Southern mansion-style hospitality restaurant features classic dishes reminiscent of the days of the grand ocean liners of yesteryear.

Chic: this 434-seat restaurant serves 'contemporary' cuisine and sauces made from scratch.

Silk: this restaurant features pan-Asian cuisine with a touch of spice.

American Icon Grill: this 430-seat restaurant does many of America's favorite 'comfort-food' dishes.'

Extra-cost venues, with either a cover charge or à la carte pricing, include:

Wonderland: based on the (real and imagined) elements of Fire, Ice, Water, Earth, and Dreams, this surreal 62-seat Alice in Wonderland-inspired venue features food with a quirky touch, using ingredients such as Japanese bonito flakes.

Jamie's Italian: it's a 132-seat, tablecloth-free, Euro-Italian bistro – British celebrity chef Jamie Oliver's second restaurant at sea. Reservations are required.

Chops Grille: for premium-quality steaks and grilled seafood (but an additional cost for dry-aged steaks and lobster, on top of the cover charge).

Chef's Table: this exclusive 16-seat venue (located within Chops Grille) can be booked for private parties, with wine-and-food pairing the specialty.

Izumi: a 44-seat Japanese-Asian fusion cuisine venue, including hot-rock tableside cooking, sashimi, sushi, and sake.

Kung Fu Panda's Noodle Bar (located on the pool deck): this is the venue for some bold flavors, and traditional Chinese desserts. Look out for Po!

For casual meals at no extra cost, the 860-seat Windjammer Marketplace is a self-serve, buffet-style eatery. Other casual (included) spots include: The Café at Two70º; SeaPlex Dog House; Sorrento's – for pizza slices and calzones; and Café Promenade.

ENTERTAINMENT. The Royal Theater spans three decks and seats 1,299. It is the showlounge for large-scale production shows and cabaret by a resident troupe of singers and dancers (reservations advised).

Music Hall is a two-deck-high venue (with pool tables on the lower deck) for live shows that feature tribute acts from the rock scene.

SPA/FITNESS. The Vitality at Sea Spa facilities include: a thermal suite (extra cost), beauty salon, barber shop, and gymnasium with Technogym equipment. Massage and other body-pampering treatments take place in 19 treatment rooms, including one for acupuncture and two bookable, private treatment rooms for couples.

PACIFIC ARIA
★★★+

THIS FAMILY-FRIENDLY SHIP HAS TRENDY DECOR AND FOOD FOR AUSTRALASIANS

Size:	Mid-size Ship	Passenger/Crew Ratio (lower beds):	2.2
Tonnage:	55,820	Cabins (total):	630
Cruise Line:	P&O Cruises (Australia)	Size Range (sq ft/m):	186.2–1,124.8/17.3–104.5
Former Names:	Ryndam	Cabins (for one person):	0
Builder:	Fincantieri (Italy)	Cabins with balcony:	150
Entered Service:	Jan 1993/Nov 2015	Cabins (wheelchair accessible):	6
Length (ft/m):	719.4/219.3	Wheelchair accessibility:	Good
Propulsion/Propellers:	diesel-electric (34,560kW)/2	Elevators:	8
Total Crew:	560	Casino (gaming tables):	Yes
Passengers (lower beds):	1,260	Self-Service Launderette:	Yes
Passenger Space Ratio (lower beds):	44.3	Onboard currency:	Australian $

THE SHIP. This ship formerly sailed for Holland America Line and was refurbished and 'Aussified' for its new role. Those in the know may find it strange to see P&O on a white funnel, and might notice the dark hull leftover from the vessel's HAL days.

The exterior styling is quite angular, but there is a full walk-around teakwood Promenade Deck outdoors – excellent for strolling and watching the sea. A hydraulic glass roof covers the swimming pool, whirlpools, and central Lido area. Aft is The Oasis, a quiet area for (adult-only) relaxation, with its own small (dip) pool.

Inside, an asymmetrical layout hosts most public rooms, spread across two decks, and this creates a spacious feel. Atop the ship, with forward-facing views that wrap around the sides, is The Dome, an observation lounge with ocean-view windows; by night it's a trendy nightspot.

The ship has a large, relaxing library and Internet-connect center, a room for card games, a Mix Lounge for relaxing in and afternoon tea, an intimate Piano Bar, an indoor cinema, and a casino with gaming tables and slots.

ACCOMMODATION. There are a number of different cabin price grades (a lot for this size of ship), but not many have a balcony. The accommodation ranges from small interior cabins (with little storage space) to cabins with balcony, to a large Penthouse Suite.

BERLITZ'S RATINGS	Possible	Achieved
Ship	500	313
Accommodation	200	127
Food	400	239
Service	400	264
Entertainment	100	64
Cruise Experience	400	249

OVERALL SCORE 1256 points out of 2000

Occupants of suite-grade accommodation also get use of a Nespresso coffee machine and an iPod docking station pre-loaded with music, plus priority reservations for specialty dining venues, spa treatment bookings, and shore excursions.

DINING. The Waterfront restaurant, located aft, has open seating, with tables for two to 10, but the waiter stations are noisy for anyone seated near them. The food is large-scale catering, but it's decent enough.

Other dining spots include: Angelo's, for Italian cuisine; Dragon Lady for Asian fusion cuisine. For more casual eating, head to The Pantry, an array of self-serve, food court-style outlets, or Shell & Bones for good seafood.

ENTERTAINMENT. The Marquee Theatre is the showlounge; it spans two decks, with banquette-style seating. It is basically a well-designed room, but sight lines from the balcony level are poor. Colorful, razzle-dazzle production shows are presented in the evening.

SPA/FITNESS. The Spa includes a gym with high-tech exercise machines, an aerobics area, a beauty salon, treatment rooms, and men's and women's sauna, steam room, and changing areas.

PACIFIC DAWN
★★★+

THIS OLDER MID-SIZE SHIP IS A GOOD CHOICE FOR FAMILY-FRIENDLY CRUISING

Size:	Mid-size Ship	Passenger/Crew Ratio (lower beds): 2.2
Tonnage:	70,285	Cabins (total): 773
Cruise Line:	P&O Cruises (Australia)	Size Range (sq ft/m): 193.7–592.0/18.0–55.0
Former Names:	*Regal Princess*	Cabins (for one person): 0
Builder:	Fincantieri Navali (Italy)	Cabins with balcony: 148
Entered Service:	Aug 1991/Nov 2007	Cabins (wheelchair accessible): 13
Length (ft/m):	811.0/247.2	Wheelchair accessibility: Fair
Propulsion/Propellers:	diesel (24,000kW)/2	Elevators: 9
Total Crew:	725	Casino (gaming tables): Yes
Passengers (lower beds):	1,546	Self-Service Launderette: Yes
Passenger Space Ratio (lower beds):	44.0	Onboard currency: Australian $

THE SHIP. *Pacific Dawn* has all the right facilities to provide a pleasant cruise in comfortable, but somewhat dated, surroundings. A new waterpark was added in a 2017 refit, so sunbathing space is a bit tight when the ship is full.

There is no walk-around promenade deck outdoors – the only walking space being along the sides of the ship. Inside, the understated decor of soft pastel shades is highlighted by colorful artwork. A striking, elegant, three-deck-high atrium has a grand staircase with fountain sculpture. The Dome, an observation dome set high atop the ship, houses a multi-purpose lounge/comedy club with live music.

ACCOMMODATION. There are numerous different price grades, ranked by location and size. In a recent refit, some 282 cabins had upper berths fitted to accommodate two adults and two children. In general, the cabins are well designed, with large bathrooms and good soundproofing. All cabins have walk-in closets, refrigerator, personal safe, and TV. Twin beds convert to queen-size beds in standard cabins. Lifeboats obstruct the view from the outside-view cabins for disabled passengers.

BERLITZ'S RATINGS

	Possible	Achieved
Ship	500	315
Accommodation	200	134
Food	400	239
Service	400	265
Entertainment	100	68
Cruise Experience	400	256

OVERALL SCORE 1277 points out of 2000

The 14 most expensive suites, each with a private balcony, are well equipped, and storage space is generous, adequate even for long cruises.

DINING. The Waterfront Restaurant has open seating for all meals. The food tastes good thanks to the use of fresh produce. An 'always-available' selection is combined with multiple daily additions; vegetable and potato side orders are always provided.

Alternative eateries, with food prepared to order, include the poolside Salt Grill by Australian chef Luke Mangan; Shell and Bones for extra-cost grilled seafood and steaks; The Pantry, a self-serve, food court-style buffet venue; and The Café for barista coffees and light bites.

ENTERTAINMENT. The Marquee Showlounge spans two decks. There's plenty of live music for the bars and lounges, with a wide mix of classical, jazz, and dance, from solo pianists to showbands. Several times each cruise, a stunning laser light and sound show is presented in the atrium.

SPA/FITNESS. The Aqua Spa and fitness center has a gymnasium, exercise room, steam room, and sauna.

PACIFIC EXPLORER
★★★+

THIS MID-SIZE SHIP HAS STYLISH DECOR FOR AUSTRALASIAN FAMILIES

Size:	Mid-size Ship	Passenger/Crew Ratio (lower beds):	2.1
Tonnage:	77,441	Cabins (total):	999
Cruise Line:	P&O Cruises Australia	Size Range (sq ft/m):	135.0–635.0/12.5–59.0
Former Names:	*Dawn Princess*	Cabins (for one person):	0
Builder:	Fincantieri (Italy)	Cabins with balcony:	446
Entered Service:	May 1997/Jun 2017	Cabins (wheelchair accessible):	19
Length (ft/m):	857.2/261.3	Wheelchair accessibility:	Good
Propulsion/Propellers:	diesel-electric/2	Elevators:	11
Total Crew:	924	Casino (gaming tables):	Yes
Passengers (lower beds):	1,998	Self-Service Launderette:	Yes
Passenger Space Ratio (lower beds):	39.7	Onboard currency:	Australian $

THE SHIP. *Pacific Explorer* has a fairly stylish profile and a large funnel. There is a wide, teak walk-around outdoor promenade deck and 93,000 sq ft (8,640 sq m) of space, plus two waterslides in a mega-waterpark (great for kids – but watch out for the 'flying fox'), a large poolside movie screen, an adults-only (extra-cost) Sanctuary relaxation area, and an outdoor barefoot lawn bowling green (added in 2018).

The interiors have attractive decor and appealing colors. There are a number of dead ends in the interior layout, so it's not as user-friendly as a ship this size should be. The interior focal point is a four-deck-high atrium lobby with winding, double stairways, two panoramic glass-walled elevators, and a dance floor.

There are numerous public rooms, bars and lounges, including a library, casino (with gaming tables and slot machines), an Internet-connect center, shops (Atrium Boutiques), a photo gallery, café, and an art gallery. One bar is decorated in the style of a late 19th-century gentleman's club, with dance floor and comfortable seating. The focal point is a large ship model, *Kenya*, from the P&O collection archives.

Niggles include the fact that cruising aboard ships like this has become increasingly about extra onboard revenue; also, the swimming pools are small, given the number of passengers. As aboard most ships, if you live in the top suites, you'll be well cared for; if not, you'll just be one of a crowd.

BERLITZ'S RATINGS		
	Possible	Achieved
Ship	500	351
Accommodation	200	145
Food	400	239
Service	400	275
Entertainment	100	68
Cruise Experience	400	268
OVERALL SCORE 1346 points out of 2000		

ACCOMMODATION. There are many, many different cabin price grades. Although the standard interior (no-view) and outside-view cabins are small, they are well designed and functional in layout; they are decorated in earth tones, accentuated by splashes of color from the bedspreads. Proportionately, there are a lot of interior (no-view) cabins. Many outside-view cabins are quite well soundproofed. Note that the balcony partition on cabins with private balconies is not the floor-to-ceiling type, so you can hear your neighbors clearly, or smell their smoke (if they smoke). The balconies are very narrow, only just large enough for two small chairs, and there is no outdoor light fitting. All cabins have reasonable closet and abundant drawer and shelf space, and a refrigerator. The bathrooms are really tight spaces, only appropriate for one person at a time. However, they do have a decent shower enclosure, a small amount of shelving for toiletries, a hairdryer, and a bathrobe.

The largest accommodation comes in the form of six suites, two on each of three decks located aft. There are also wheelchair-accessible cabins, measuring 213–305 sq ft (19.7–28.2 sq m) in seven outside-view and 12 interior (no-view) cabins.

DINING. Waterfront Restaurant is the main dining room. Breakfast and lunch are provided in an open-seating arrangement, while dinner is in two seatings. There are no wine waiters.

Other dining spots include: Angelo's (for Italian cuisine); Dragon Lady (for Asian fusion cuisine); and the popular Salt Grill by Luke Mangan in a great location overlooking the pool area (open for lunch, dinner, and High Tea).

The Black Circus is an extra-cost, reservations-required supper club, with entertainment.

The Pantry is a casual self-serve, food court-style eatery (it includes Nic and Toni's for Mediterranean specialties), while poolside there's a lobster and burger bar.

ENTERTAINMENT. There are two showlounges, both theatre and cabaret style. The main one, Marquee Theater, has a sloping floor, with aisle-style seating (as found in shoreside movie theaters) that is well tiered, and with good sight lines to the raised stage from most of the 500 seats.

A second showlounge, Vista Lounge, located aft is for cabaret, lectures, and other presentations.

SPA/FITNESS. A glass-walled health spa complex, located high atop the ship, includes a gymnasium with the latest high-tech machines. One swimming pool is 'suspended' aft between two decks. There are two other pools, although they are not large for the size of the ship.

Sports facilities are located in an open-air sports deck positioned inside the funnel and adaptable for basketball, volleyball, badminton, or paddle tennis. Joggers can exercise on the walk-around open Promenade Deck.

PACIFIC PRINCESS
★★★+

THIS SHIP HAS ENGLISH COUNTRY-HOUSE DECOR AND STYLE FOR MATURE-AGE CRUISERS

Size:	Small Ship	Passenger/Crew Ratio (lower beds):	1.8
Tonnage:	30,277	Cabins (total):	344
Cruise Line:	Princess Cruises	Size Range (sq ft/m):	145.3–968.7/13.5–90.0
Former Names:	R Three	Cabins (for one person):	0
Builder:	Chantiers de l'Atlantique (France)	Cabins with balcony:	232
Entered Service:	Aug 1999/Nov 2002	Cabins (wheelchair accessible):	3
Length (ft/m):	593.7/181.0	Wheelchair accessibility:	Good
Propulsion/Propellers:	diesel-electric (18,600kW)/2	Elevators:	4
Total Crew:	373	Casino (gaming tables):	Yes
Passengers (lower beds):	688	Self-Service Launderette:	Yes
Passenger Space Ratio (lower beds):	44.1	Onboard currency:	US$

THE SHIP. *Pacific Princess* is a decent choice for mature adults who seek value for money aboard a comfortable small ship with plenty of dining choices and limited entertainment.

The ship (the smallest in the fleet) has an all-white hull, which makes it appear larger than it is – and a large, square-ish funnel. The Lido Deck has a swimming pool and good sunbathing space, while one of the aft decks has a thalassotherapy pool. A jogging track circles the swimming pool deck, but one deck above. The uppermost outdoors deck includes a golf driving net and shuffleboard court.

Although there is no walk-around promenade deck outdoors, there is a small jogging track around the upper perimeter of the swimming pool, and on port and starboard side decks by the lifeboats. Instead of wooden decks outdoors, these are covered by Bolidt, a sand-colored, rubberized material. Room service is extremely limited. Stairways, although carpeted, are tinny. In order to keep the prices low, often the air routing to get to/from your ship is not the most direct.

The interior decor is quite stunning and elegant, a throwback to ship decor of the ocean liners of the 1920s and '30s, executed in fine taste. This includes detailed ceiling cornices, both real and faux wrought-iron staircase railings, leather- and cherry wood-paneled walls, trompe l'oeil ceilings, and rich carpeting in hallways with an Oriental rug-look center section. The overall feel echoes that of an old-world country

BERLITZ'S RATINGS		
	Possible	Achieved
Ship	500	341
Accommodation	200	141
Food	400	242
Service	400	287
Entertainment	100	71
Cruise Experience	400	271

OVERALL SCORE 1353 points out of 2000

club. The staircase in the main, two-deck-high foyer recalls the staircase in the 1997 movie *Titanic*.

The public rooms are spread over three decks. The reception hall has a staircase with intricate wrought-iron railings. The Nightclub, with forward-facing views, sits high in the ship and has some Polynesian-inspired decor and furniture.

There are plenty of bars – including one in the entrance to each restaurant. Perhaps the nicest of all bars and lounges are in the casino bar/lounge that is a beautiful room reminiscent of London's grand hotels and understated gaming clubs. It has an inviting marble fireplace – in fact, there are three such fireplaces aboard – and comfortable sofas and individual chairs. There is also a large Card Room, which incorporates an Internet center with eight stations.

The As with all Princess Cruises ships, most drink prices are moderate, but beer prices are high. A standard gratuity is automatically added to onboard accounts – to reduce the amount, you'll need to go to the reception desk.

There is a charge – tokens must be obtained from the reception desk – for using the machines in the self-service launderette. A change machine in the launderette itself would be more user-friendly.

ACCOMMODATION. There is a variety of different cabin types to choose from, with prices linked to grade, location, and size.

All of the standard interior cabins (no view) and outside-view cabins are extremely compact, with twin or queen-size beds, with good under-bed storage areas. Bathrooms have tiled floors and plain walls, are compact, with a shower enclosure and strong hand-held shower unit, small hairdryer, cotton towels, storage shelves for toiletries, and retractable clothesline.

Note that the suites/cabins that have private balconies have partial, not full, balcony partitions, and sliding glass doors. Thanks to good design and layout, only 14 cabins on Deck 6 have lifeboat-obstructed views. The balcony floor is covered in thick plastic matting – teak would be nicer.

Accommodation designated as mini-suites are just larger cabins than standard, as sleeping and lounge areas are not divided. While not overly large, the bathrooms have a good-size tub and ample space for storing toiletries. The living area has a refrigerated minibar, lounge area with breakfast table, and a balcony with two plastic chairs and a table.

The most spacious accommodation is the 10 Owner's Suites. These are fine, large living spaces located forward and aft. Particularly nice are those that overlook the stern, on decks 6, 7, and 8. They have bigger balconies that really are private and cannot be overlooked by anyone. They host an entrance foyer, lounge, bedroom, bathroom with jet tub, and small guest bathroom. The bed faces the sea, which can be seen through the floor-to-ceiling windows and sliding glass door.

Note that suites/cabins located at the stern may suffer from vibration and noise, particularly when the ship is proceeding at or close to full speed, or maneuvering in port.

DINING. There are four different dining spots – three restaurants and one casual self-serve buffet:

The Club Restaurant has around 340 seats, all with armrests. There are large ocean-view windows on three sides, and some prime tables that overlook the stern, as well as a small bandstand for occasional live dinner music. However, the noise level can be high because of the single-deck-height ceiling.

Although portions are generous, the food and its presentation are not really memorable. Fish is often disguised by a crumb or batter coating, the choice of fresh green vegetables is limited, few garnishes are used, and cheese is already sliced and diced. This is banquet-style catering, which means standardization and cooking in batches. Pasta dishes are acceptable (though voluminous), typically served by section headwaiters, who may also make 'something special just for you' – in search of favorable comments.

Extra-cost, reservations-required Sabatini's Trattoria has 96 seats (all with armrests), windows along two sides, and a set 'Bellissima' dégustation menu.

Sterling Steakhouse is an 'American steak house' (extra cost, reservations required), with a good selection of prime steaks and other meats and seafood. It has 98 comfortable seats (with armrests), and windows along two sides. It has a set menu, together with added daily chef's specials.

The serve-yourself Lido Café buffet is open for breakfast, lunch, and casual dinners. In addition, there is a Poolside Grill and Bar for fast food.

ENTERTAINMENT. The 345-seat Cabaret Lounge, in the forward part of the ship on Deck 5, is for entertainment and some social functions. The single-level room has a stage, and circular hardwood dance floor with banquette and individual tub chair seating and raised sections on both sides. It is for mini-revue style shows with colorful costumes, presented by a troupe of resident singer/dancers.

SPA/FITNESS. Facilities, which are located in the forward part of the ship on a high deck, include a workout room with ocean-view windows, muscle-toning equipment, and treadmills. There are steam rooms but no sauna, changing areas for men and women, and a windowed beauty salon.

Some fitness classes are free, while most cost extra.

PACIFIC VENUS
★★★

THIS SHIP HAS COMFORTABLE DECOR AND DECENT STYLE FOR JAPANESE CRUISERS

Size:	Small Ship
Tonnage:	26,518
Cruise Line:	Venus Cruise
Former Names:	none
Builder:	Ishikawajima Heavy Industries (Japan)
Entered Service:	Apr 1998
Length (ft/m):	601.7/183.4
Propulsion/Propellers:	diesel (13,636kW)/2
Total Crew:	220
Passengers (lower beds):	476
Passenger Space Ratio (lower beds):	55.7
Passenger/Crew Ratio (lower beds):	2.1
Cabins (total):	238
Size Range (sq ft/m):	164.6–699.6/15.3–65.0
Cabins (for one person):	0
Cabins with balcony:	20
Cabins (wheelchair accessible):	1
Wheelchair accessibility:	Fair
Elevators:	4
Casino (gaming tables):	Yes
Self-Service Launderette:	Yes
Onboard currency:	Japanese yen

THE SHIP. The company Venus Cruise is part of Japan Cruise Line, which is itself part of SHK Line Group, a joint venture between the Shin Nihonkai, Hankyu, and Kampu ferry companies, which operate more than 20 ferries. There is a decent amount of open deck space aft of the funnel – good for deck sports – while protected sunbathing space is provided around a small swimming pool. All sunloungers have cushioned pads. The open walking promenade decks are rubber-coated steel – hardwood would be more desirable.

The base of the funnel is the site of a day/night lounge, which overlooks the pool; this is slightly reminiscent of Royal Caribbean International's funnel-wrapped Viking Crown lounges aboard its earlier ships. There is plenty of space per passenger. The decor is clean and fresh, with much use of pastel colors and blond woods, giving the interiors a feeling of warmth.

The dining rooms are located off Deck 7, which has a double-width indoor promenade, with high ceiling height. A three-deck-high atrium has a crystal chandelier as its focal point, and a white baby grand piano sits on its lower level, close to the Reception Desk.

There are special rooms for meetings and conference organizers, for use when the ship is chartered. A piano salon has colorful low-back chairs, and a large main hall has a finely sculptured high ceiling and over 700 moveable seats. There's a

BERLITZ'S RATINGS		
	Possible	Achieved
Ship	500	316
Accommodation	200	128
Food	400	256
Service	400	251
Entertainment	100	54
Cruise Experience	400	241
OVERALL SCORE 1246 points out of 2000		

350-seat main lounge for cabaret shows and ballroom dancing, a small movie theater, and a library/writing room and card room. A casino gaming area is located as part of the Top Lounge set at the front of the funnel. Winners receive prizes instead of cash, under Japanese law. There's also a smoking room, Chashitsu (tatami mat) room, karaoke room (for rent), card room/ Mahjong room, free self-service launderettes on each accommodation deck, and two (credit card/ coin) public telephone booths.

Overall, this company provides a well-packaged cruise in a ship that has a comfortable, serene environment. The dress code is relaxed, and no tipping is allowed.

The ship has two classes: Salon Class and Standard Class. Salon Class passengers pay more, but get suite-grade accommodation, eat in a private dining room, and are given extra perks and services, including a welcome embarkation basket, more toiletries, and priority tickets for shows and shore tenders.

Pacific Venus is best suited to Japanese-speaking couples and solo travelers of mature years who appreciate very comfortable surroundings and good food and service, all at a relatively moderate cost. The ship is often operated under charter to travel organizations, so drinks aren't always included in the fare; when operated by Venus Cruise, alcoholic drinks are not included.

ACCOMMODATION. There are five types: Royal Suites, suites, deluxe cabins, state cabins (in four price grades), and standard cabins. All are located from the uppermost to lowermost decks, respectively. All suites and cabins have an outside view, but few cabins have a private balcony.

The four Royal Suites (Archaic, Elegant, Modern, and Noble) are decorated in two different styles – one contemporary, one in a more traditional Japanese style. Each has a private balcony (with a drinks table and two chairs) with sliding door, an expansive lounge with large sofa and plush armchairs, coffee table, window-side chairs and drinks table, floor-to-ceiling windows, and a large flat-screen TV set, with separate DVD unit. The bedroom has twin beds or a queen-size one, vanity/writing desk, and a large walk-in closet with personal safe. Also provided are high-quality binoculars, camera tripod, humidifier, tea/coffee-making set, and free minibar set-up. The large bathroom has ocean-view windows, Jacuzzi tub, a separate shower enclosure, and his/her washbasins.

Sixteen other suites have private balconies (with teak table and two chairs), a good-size living area with vanity/writing desk, dining table, chair and curved sofa, separate sleeping area, and bathroom with deep tub slightly larger than the Royal Suites, and single large washbasin. There is ample illuminated closet and drawer space (two locking drawers instead of a personal safe), and a DVD unit.

Some 20 deluxe cabins have large picture windows fronted by a large, curtained arch, a sleeping area with twin or queen beds, plus a daytime sofa that converts into a third bed.

So-called 'state' cabins, many with upper berths for third passengers, are in three price levels, and have decor that is best described as basic, with reasonable closet space but very little drawer space.

Standard cabins, however, are really plain, but can accommodate three persons – useful for families – although the drawer and storage space is a bit tight.

All accommodation grades have a tea set with electric kettle, TV set, telephone, and stocked minibar/refrigerator – all items included in the cruise price. Bathrooms have a hairdryer and lots of Shiseido toiletries, particularly in the suites. All room-service menu items cost extra – this is typical of all Japanese cruise ships – except for Salon Class suite-grade accommodation. All passengers receive a yukata (a Japanese-style light cotton robe). Suite occupants also get a plush bathrobe, and all accommodation grades have electric, automatic toilets (washlets) with heated seats.

DINING. The Primavera Restaurant is located aft, with ocean views on three sides, and a high ceiling. Passengers dine in one seating, at tables for six, 10, or 12. The food consists of both Japanese and Western items; the menu is varied, and the food is attractively presented. For breakfast and lunch it includes a self-serve buffet, while dinner is typically a fully served set meal.

A separate, intimate 42-seat restaurant, Grand Siècle, is reserved for occupants of suite-grade (Salon Class) accommodation; it is tastefully decorated in Regency style, with fine wood-paneling and a detailed, indented ceiling. It has mostly tables for two (with plenty of space for correct service), better-quality chopsticks, nori seaweed, and better-quality fine china. Cold and hot towels are provided.

ENTERTAINMENT. Le Pacific Main Lounge is the venue for all shipboard entertainment and also functions as a lecture and activities room during the day. It is a single-level room with seating clustered around a thrust stage, so that entertainers are in the very midst of their audience.

On most cruises, special featured entertainers such as singers, instrumentalists, storytellers, and dance champions are brought on board from ashore.

SPA/FITNESS. Spa facilities comprise men's and women's Grand Baths, which include two bathing pools and health/cleansing stations. There are ocean-view windows, a steam room, a gymnasium with ocean-view windows (in a different location just aft of the funnel), and a sauna.

Japanese massage is available, as are hairdressing and barber services in the small salon, located on the lowest passenger-accessible deck of the ship.

PAUL GAUGUIN
★★★+

AN ELEGANT, COOL SHIP FOR CHIC, WARM-WEATHER ISLAND CRUISING

Size:	Small Ship	Passenger/Crew Ratio (lower beds):	1.5
Tonnage:	19,200	Cabins (total):	166
Cruise Line:	Paul Gauguin Cruises	Size Range (sq ft/m):	200.0-588.0/18.5-54.6
Former Names:	none	Cabins (for one person):	0
Builder:	Chantiers de l'Atlantique (France)	Cabins with balcony:	89
Entered Service:	Jan1998	Cabins (wheelchair accessible):	1
Length (ft/m):	513.4/156.5	Wheelchair accessibility:	Fair
Propulsion/Propellers:	Diesel-electric/2	Elevators:	4
Total Crew:	215	Casino (gaming tables):	Yes
Passengers (lower beds):	332	Self-Service Launderette:	No
Passenger Space Ratio (lower beds):	57.8	Onboard currency:	US$

THE SHIP. Built by a French company specifically to operate in shallow waters, *Paul Gauguin* is under long-term charter to Pacific Beachcombers of Tahiti, owners of the Intercontinental Tahiti, Intercontinental Bora Bora Le Moana, Intercontinental Bora Bora, and Intercontinental Moorea. The ship cruises around French Polynesia and the South Pacific, and, while it could carry many more passengers in terms of its size, it is forbidden to do so by French law. It has a well-balanced, all-white profile, and a single funnel.

Paul Gauguin is suited to couples and solo travelers seeking out-of-the-ordinary itineraries, good regional cuisine and service, and scuba and snorkeling opportunities. It suits those who are happy with almost no entertainment. Where the ship really shines is in its variety of water-sports equipment, and its shallow draft that allows it to navigate and anchor in places that larger ships couldn't possibly reach.

The ship has a retractable aft marina platform and carries water-skiing boats and inflatable craft, windsurfers, paddleboard, kayaks, and scuba and snorkeling gear, all included in the cruise fare (except scuba gear). Its shallow draft means there could be some movement, as the ship is a little high-sided for its size.

Inside, there is a decent array of public rooms; artwork and decor have a French Polynesia look. The colors are restful, if bland, but the direction signage

BERLITZ'S RATINGS		
	Possible	Achieved
Ship	500	351
Accommodation	200	139
Food	400	270
Service	400	287
Entertainment	100	60
Cruise Experience	400	252

OVERALL SCORE 1359 points out of 2000

is good (note that the tub chairs in some of the public rooms are uncomfortable).

A Fare (pronounced *foray*) Tahiti Gallery features books, film, and other materials on the unique art, history, and culture of the islands, and original Gauguin sketches are displayed.

The dress code is relaxed, but evening attire is like country club wear. The standard itinerary means the ship docks only in Papeete, and shore tenders are used in other ports. The crew-to-passenger ratio translates to a good level of personalized service.

Wi-Fi spots are provided, but Internet charges are high. Le Casino has blackjack and roulette tables, plus 13 machines.

A *Paul Gauguin* cruise is immersive French Polynesia, and the ship carries lecturers to inform you about the life, history, and sea life of the region. There are no children's facilities.

All in all, the ship will provide a delightful, intimate cruise. Note that if you fly out to Tahiti a day or so before the cruise and stay in a hotel, bugs (insects) are a problem encountered by many travelers, so it is wise to take some insect repellent.

ACCOMMODATION. There are several suite/cabin grades, priced according to location and size. Most cabins are nicely equipped, and most have large windows (except those on the lowest accommodation deck, which have portholes). Each has twin-size beds convertible to a queen, and wood-accented cabinetry with rounded edges; soundproofing could be better. A minibar/refrigerator stocked with complimentary beer and soft drinks (replenished daily), personal safe, hairdryer, and umbrellas are standard. L'Occitane toiletries are provided.

The marble-look bathrooms are quite large and have a tub/shower. All passengers are provided with cotton bathrobes and slippers. The two largest suites have a private balcony at the front and side. Although there's a decent amount of in-cabin space, with a long vanity unit and plenty of drawer space, the bathrooms are disappointingly small and modular. Butler service is provided in suite-grade accommodation.

DINING. L'Etoile, the main (open seating) dining room, is open for dinner only, and chairs have armrests. La Veranda and Le Grill are alternatives eateries. Select wines and drinks are included in the fare, with a limited selection of premium wines at extra cost.

La Veranda Restaurant, one deck above L'Etoile, has indoor/outdoor seating and is the self-serve buffet venue. Breakfast buffets are repetitive (especially the boxed cereals), and lunch buffets are underwhelming. At night, the venue features more creative fare in pleasant surroundings (reservations are required, but there's no extra charge, and capacity is limited to 75 persons). La Veranda provides dinner by reservation, with alternating French and Italian menus; the French menus are provided by Jean-Pierre Vigato, chef of the Michelin-starred Apicius, in Paris.

Le Grill (outdoors) provides informal fare on deck aft of the pool, with up 100 seats. Each evening it becomes Pacific Grill and features Polynesian cuisine; and there is no extra charge.

ENTERTAINMENT. Le Grand Salon is the venue for small shows and cabaret acts. It is a single-level room, with banquettes and individual tub chair seating. Sight lines are decent from most seats, although there are some obstructions. The main entertainment consists of local Polynesian shows brought on board from ashore, plus the odd cabaret act. There's also a piano lounge.

SPA/FITNESS. The Deep Nature Spa, on Deck 6 in the ship's center, includes a fitness center (it's a windowless room), a steam room (no charge), several treatment rooms, tiny changing area, and beauty salon (there is no sauna).

PEARL MIST
★★★+

THIS SMALL SHIP SPECIALIZES IN US COASTAL AREA CRUISES

Size:	Boutique Ship	Passenger/Crew Ratio (lower beds):	3.4
Tonnage:	5,600	Cabins (total):	108
Cruise Line:	Pearl Seas Cruises	Size Range (sq ft/m):	302.0–580.0/28.0–53.8
Former Names:	none	Cabins (for one person):	10
Builder:	Irving Shipbuilding (Canada)	Cabins with balcony:	108
Entered Service:	Jun 2014	Cabins (wheelchair accessible):	4
Length (ft/m):	335.0/102.1	Wheelchair accessibility:	Fair
Propulsion/Propellers:	diesel (4,700kW)/2	Elevators:	1
Total Crew:	60	Casino (gaming tables):	No
Passengers (lower beds):	206	Self-Service Launderette:	No
Passenger Space Ratio (lower beds):	27.1	Onboard currency:	US$

THE SHIP. Pearl Seas Cruises is an offshore outgrowth of the all-American company, American Cruise Lines, based in Connecticut. But don't confuse the US's Pearl Seas Cruises with Australia's Pearl Sea Cruises.

Pearl Mist is designed to be a much more comfortable and upscale ship than the smaller *American Glory*, *American Spirit*, and *American Star*. It has greater speed, the latest navigational technology and propulsion equipment, and better onboard facilities and service. It is meant to appeal to passengers who enjoy discovering ports in the company of likeminded people, away from the hunting grounds of crowded large resort ships.

Public rooms include two principal lounges, the Pacific Lounge, and the Atlantic Lounge; one is above, and the other is below the navigation bridge. Other public rooms include a small Coral Lounge, located just behind the mast; a library; and two small midship lounges – one named Caribbean Lounge. A single elevator goes to all decks, including the outdoor sun deck. Shipwide Wi-Fi is complimentary, but Internet access is patchy.

The ship cruises in the east coast waters of the US and Canada during the summer season and in the Caribbean during the winter season. Gratuities are not included. Niggles: there is no laundry; some cabins (particularly aft) are noisy; and there are no personal safes.

BERLITZ'S RATINGS	Possible	Achieved
Ship	500	361
Accommodation	200	140
Food	400	264
Service	400	274
Entertainment	100	57
Cruise Experience	400	251
OVERALL SCORE 1347 points out of 2000		

Pearl Mist is best suited to couples and solo travelers of mature years who want to cruise in an all-American environment aboard a very small ship where the destinations are a more important consideration than food, service, or entertainment.

ACCOMMODATION. There are seven cabin price grades, but all accommodation grades offer outside-view suites/cabins with private balcony (although the balcony is quite slender). All cabins feature twin beds that convert to a king-sized bed, and have high-quality bed linens; bathrooms have a walk-in shower. Some cabins can be interconnected, so a couple (partners or friends traveling together, for example) can have a bathroom each.

DINING. The single dining room, which is aft, accommodates all passengers at a set time in an open seating, so you can sit where and with whom you want. Complimentary cocktails and hors d'oeuvres are offered before dinner in the lounges.

ENTERTAINMENT. The Main Lounge is the venue for evening entertainment, lectures, and recaps, plus any entertainment that is brought on board from ashore in the various ports of call. However, it doesn't accommodate all passengers at once.

SPA/FITNESS. The small spa has a beauty salon. There is also one hot tub on deck.

PRIDE OF AMERICA
★★★

A FAMILY-FRIENDLY RESORT SHIP TO CRUISE AROUND THE HAWAIIAN ISLANDS

Size:	Mid-size Ship	Passenger Space Ratio (lower beds):	36.7
Tonnage:	80,439	Passenger/Crew Ratio (lower beds):	2.3
Cruise Line:	Norwegian Cruise Line	Cabins (total):	1,171
Former Names:	none	Size Range (sq ft/m):	129.1–1,377.8/12.0–128.0
Builder:	Ingalls Shipbuilding (USA)/Lloyd Werft	Cabins (for one person):	4
	(Germany)	Cabins with balcony:	785
Entered Service:	Jul 2005	Cabins (wheelchair accessible):	21
Length (ft/m):	920.3/280.5	Wheelchair accessibility:	Good
Propulsion/Propellers:	diesel-electric (32,000kW)/2	Elevators:	10
	azimuthing pods	Casino (gaming tables):	No
Total Crew:	927	Self-Service Launderette:	No
Passengers (lower beds):	2,186	Onboard currency:	US$

THE SHIP. *Pride of America* sails on inter-island cruises, focusing on Hawaii's islands. The expansive open-deck space includes a sunbathing/pool deck with beach-like decor.

The interior is modeled after a 'Best of America' theme, with public rooms named after famous Americans. Facilities include the Capitol Atrium, an eight-deck-high lobby said to be inspired by the Capitol Building and White House; a large casino with gaming tables and slot machines; a conservatory with tropical landscaped gardens; SoHo Art Gallery, for displaying 'art' and holding auctions; Washington A non-changeable, daily service charge (as distinct from a gratuity) is added to your onboard account and pooled for all crew and provides payment when they are on vacation. In addition, a 15 percent gratuity plus Hawaii's sales tax (because of the ship's US registry) is added to all bar (and 18 percent for spa treatment) accounts.

Although the islands are pleasant, a cruise aboard this ship might well test your patience, since most of the all-American crew simply don't cut it. That said, the ship is popular with couples, solo travelers, and families with children who enjoy upbeat surroundings in a well-packaged cruise, with plenty of entertainment.

ACCOMMODATION. About 75 percent of all cabins have ocean views. Outside-view cabins have

BERLITZ'S RATINGS		
	Possible	Achieved
Ship	500	346
Accommodation	200	139
Food	400	211
Service	400	209
Entertainment	100	68
Cruise Experience	400	242
OVERALL SCORE 1215 points out of 2000		

either a window or porthole, depending on location, twin beds convertible into a queen-size bed.

There are also family-friendly interconnecting cabins (some can sleep up to six), and many cabins have third/fourth upper berths. Some suites have king-size beds but most cabins have twin beds convertible to a queen-size bed. 'Butler' and concierge service is provided for suite-grade occupants, who also get Lavazza espresso makers. A number of cabins are wheelchair-accessible; some are equipped for hearing-impaired passengers.

DINING. Freestyle Cruising means you get a choice of several restaurants and casual eateries. There are two main dining rooms, plus à la carte and casual venues (some cost extra).

Main restaurants include the Skyline Restaurant – with decor inspired by the skyscrapers of the 1930s – and the Liberty Dining Room, with two seatings.

The extra-cost Lazy J Texas Steak House is a contemporary steakhouse with Texas decor – artwork includes Houston Space Center, Texas Rangers, and the Dallas Cowboys.

East Meets West is an intimate, 32-seat Pacific Rim/Asian Fusion restaurant with sushi/sashimi bar and a grill room with two Teppanyaki tables. Jefferson's Bistro, seating 104, has an à la carte menu of classic and French nouvelle cuisine. The decor is inspired by Thomas Jefferson's home in Monticello (Jefferson was the US ambassador to France from 1785 to 1789, before becoming America's third president).

Cadillac Diner has indoor and outdoor seating, quirky Cadillac-shaped seats, and a video jukebox; it is open for fast food: burgers and hot dogs, fish and chips, and pot pies.

Moderno Churrascaria is a Brazilian steakhouse, for meat delivered on a skewer by 'gaucho' costumed staff.

Cagney's Steak House is for prime American steaks and grilled seafood. A cover charge applies to both venues and reservations are required.

Aloha Café/Kids Café is an indoor/outdoor, self-serve, buffet-style eatery with a Hawaiian theme. A section for children has counter tops at just the right height, as well as chairs and tables shrunk to a child-friendly size. Other eateries include La Cucina (for Italian-style eats), Gold Rush Saloon (pub with karaoke and darts board), plus a Cigar Bar (inspired by Hawaii's Pink Palace Hotel on Waikiki Beach). Outdoor eateries and drinking places include the Key West Bar and Grill.

ENTERTAINMENT. The Hollywood Theater seats 840 and stages large-scale production and local Hawaiian shows. A 590-seat Mardi Gras cabaret lounge, located above the showlounge, has features cabaret and late-night (low-brow) comedy.

SPA/FITNESS. Mandara Spa is decorated with artefacts from New Mexico. Some fitness classes are free, others cost extra.

QUANTUM OF THE SEAS
★★★★

A HIGH-ENERGY, STATE-OF-THE-ART, GIZMO-FILLED FAMILY-FRIENDLY FLOATING RESORT

Size:	Large Resort Ship	Passenger/Crew Ratio (lower beds):	3.2
Tonnage:	168,666	Cabins (total):	2,090
Cruise Line:	Royal Caribbean International	Size Range (sq ft/m):	101.1–799.7/9.4–74.3
Former Names:	none	Cabins (for one person):	34
Builder:	Meyer Werft (Germany)	Cabins with balcony:	1,571
Entered Service:	Oct 2014	Cabins (wheelchair accessible):	34
Length (ft/m):	1,145.0/348.0	Wheelchair accessibility:	Good
Propulsion/Propellers:	diesel-electric (41,000kW)/2 azimuthing pods	Elevators:	16
		Casino (gaming tables):	Yes
Total Crew:	1,300	Self-Service Launderette:	No
Passengers (lower beds):	4,180	Onboard currency:	US$
Passenger Space Ratio (lower beds):	40.3		

THE SHIP. *Quantum of the Seas* has a slender profile. It is based in Tianjin (the port for Beijing), China, and the whole family will love it because it incorporates the latest tech-intensive and creative features. You can even go flying! It's a lot of Royal Caribbean wow in an all-weather environment.

The ship employs the latest in hydrodynamics, hull shape, low emissions, and, importantly, low fuel consumption. The stern (back of the ship) slopes nicely – it looks like it could be the front. It contains Two70° – an innovative multi-level venue that is a casual living area by day and a stunning, high-energy entertainment venue by night, with dynamic robotic screens complementing its huge video wall.

Several fun features include North Star – quite the engineering marvel – a 13-person (plus operator) glass capsule that lifts you from the ship's uppermost deck to provides a bird's-eye view of all below you as it moves. It's like a posh giant 'cherry picker' with attitude – and, lifting you almost 300ft (91m) above sea level (with an outreach of almost 135ft (41m), is quite a ride. Located just behind the mast, it is complimentary (and wheelchair-accessible), but only operates at sea.

The second stunner is RipCord by iFly – an extra-cost simulated skydiving experience in a two-storey high vertical wind tunnel that lets you experience the thrill of skydiving. It uses a powerful air flow to keep you up in the air and free-flying

BERLITZ'S RATINGS		
	Possible	Achieved
Ship	500	408
Accommodation	200	136
Food	400	292
Service	400	273
Entertainment	100	85
Cruise Experience	400	282

OVERALL SCORE 1476 points out of 2000

– like a giant hairdryer. It is aft of the funnel and accommodates 13 persons for each class, including 'hovering in the air' experiences, instruction, and gear. You can book both attractions with interactive digital kiosks (adjacent to elevators) and tablets in public areas. Look out for Felicia, the magenta-colored bear located outside on the starboard side of Deck 15 aft.

Meanwhile, a SeaPlex complex – located just underneath the North Star offers a circus 'school' and adrenalin-boosting bumper-car rides, and acts as a roller-skating rink and basketball court. It's an active interactive sporting venue. Other features include a rock-climbing wall, and a FlowRider surfing simulator.

The decor is extremely colorful, contemporary, and jazzy. The interior focal point is a three-storey-high Royal Esplanade (the main indoor focal point and social center) is a shopping mall, with casual eateries, a Bionic Bar and other bars, and several shops. This is where the action is day and night – note that it can be noisy. The ship operates from China and Singapore for part of each year.

ACCOMMODATION. There are many different price grades and categories, from interior (no view or 'virtual view') to family suite, Loft Suites, and solo-occupancy Studio cabins. What you pay depends on the size and location you choose. Fortunately, every cabin aboard this ship has a view – whether real or virtual. 'Virtual' balconies were first introduced aboard *Navigator of the Seas* (in 2013) and are a neat feature of interior (no-view) cabins; they can provide real-time ocean views, but you *can* turn them off, if you wish. Costing more than standard interior cabins, they're worth it.

Even the smallest bathroom is well designed, with thoughtful touches such as a night light, and shower and vanity hooks, while cabins have bedside power outlets, and ample storage space.

On the negative side, tablet-based infotainment systems don't answer questions.

DINING. There are 18 restaurant and eatery choices (there's no designated main dining room as such), part of what the line calls Dynamic Dining. So you will need to make reservations in some venues – a concept first introduced by Star Cruises.

The following are complimentary:

The 432-seat Grande: an elegant restaurant (think Southern mansion hospitality), featuring classic dishes reminiscent of the days of the yesteryear's grand ocean liners.

Chic: this 434-seat restaurant features 'contemporary' cuisine and sauces made from scratch.

Silk: this 434-seat restaurant features pan-Asian cuisine.

American Icon Grille: this 430-seat restaurant features America's favorite 'comfort-food' dishes, including New England clam chowder, Southern buttermilk fried chicken, and New Orleans gumbo.

Extra-cost dining venues include:

Wonderland: based on the (real and imagined) elements Fire, Ice, Water, Earth, and Dreams, this surreal 62-seat Alice in Wonderland-inspired venue offers food with a quirky touch (such as the oddly shaped 'hoodie' chairs), I can just imagine a Mad Hatter's Tea Party here.

Jamie's Italian: a 132-seat, tablecloth-free, Euro-Italian eatery – British celebrity chef Jamie Oliver's first restaurant at sea. Reservations are required.

Chops Grille: for premium-quality steaks and grilled seafood (plus an integral Chef's Table).

Chef's Table: an exclusive 16-seat venue for private parties, with wine-and-food pairing.

Izumi: a 44-seat Japanese-Asian fusion cuisine venue with hot-rock tableside cooking, sashimi, sushi, and sake. The lantern lights fit perfectly into the decor.

Johnny Rockets: a retro 1950s all-day, all-night diner-style eatery (near the main pool) for hamburgers, malt shakes, and jukebox hits (the tables feature a mini-jukebox). À la carte pricing applies.

For casual eats at no extra cost, the 860-seat Windjammer Marketplace is a self-serve, buffet-style eatery. Other casual spots include: The Café @ Two70°; SeaPlex Dog House; Sorrento's – for pizza slices and calzones; and Café Promenade.

ENTERTAINMENT. The Royal Theater spans three decks and is the showlounge for 'booked' shows and large-scale production shows by a resident troupe of singers and dancers.

Two70° is a multi-level, glass-walled 'living' room almost three decks high. It has a food-court-style marketplace and sit-down eateries, including The Café @ Two70°. By night, the big venue morphs into an entertainment house, with Robo-screens and Bionic Bar with high-tech wizardry.

Music Hall is a two-deck-high rock-'n'-roll joint, outfitted with all the right paraphernalia, and features DJs and theme nights.

SPA/FITNESS. The Vitality at Sea Spa facilities include a thermal suite (extra cost), beauty salon, barber shop, and gymnasium with Technogym equipment. Massage and other body-pampering treatments take place in 19 treatment rooms.

QUEEN ELIZABETH
★★★★+

THIS SHIP HAS DELIGHTFUL INTERIOR DECOR THAT REPRESENTS TASTEFUL BRITISH HERITAGE

Size:	Mid-size Ship	Passenger/Crew Ratio (lower beds):	2.0
Tonnage:	90,900	Cabins (total):	1,046
Cruise Line:	Cunard Line	Size Range (sq ft/m):	152.0–1,493 sq.ft/14.0–138.5
Former Names:	none	Cabins (for one person):	9
Builder:	Fincantieri (Italy)	Cabins with balcony:	820
Entered Service:	Oct 2010	Cabins (wheelchair accessible):	20
Length (ft/m):	964.5/294.0	Wheelchair accessibility:	Good
Propulsion/Propellers:	diesel-electric (64,000kW)/2 azimuthing pods	Elevators:	12
		Casino (gaming tables):	Yes
Total Crew:	1,005	Self-Service Launderette:	Yes
Passengers (lower beds):	2,101	Onboard currency:	US$
Passenger Space Ratio (lower beds):	43.2		

THE SHIP. *Queen Elizabeth*, a cruise ship that longs to be an ocean liner, suits mature adults and solo travelers, and families with children. It's pitched at traditionalists who like to dress nicely for dinner, and sail with a sense of timeless style.

The ship, named in the company's 170th year (the company began operations in 1840), is the second-largest Cunarder ordered in that long history. Although Cunard purports to offer a resolutely British experience, the marketing hype is undermined by the use of US dollars as the onboard currency, and trying to find British service staff is challenging. The Cunard red funnel is instantly recognizable.

Once inside, the ship feels instantly comfortable. Although still classic and timeless, it has brighter decor than *Queen Victoria*, with few glitzy brass or chrome surfaces, and more of an ocean-liner look, including some fine carpeting.

Features include a three-deck-high Grand Lobby with sweeping staircase, sculpted balconies, elegant decorative touches, and the adjacent Cunarders' Galleria, where floating memorabilia is displayed in glass cabinets. The Royal Arcade is a cluster of shops, selling goods connected with traditional and modern-day British goods.

The Gratuities – called a Hotel and Dining charge (depending on your accommodation grade) – are added to your onboard account daily.

BERLITZ'S RATINGS

	Possible	Achieved
Ship	500	415
Accommodation	200	144
Food	400	299
Service	400	315
Entertainment	100	81
Cruise Experience	400	308

OVERALL SCORE 1562 points out of 2000

Queen Elizabeth provides an elegant setting for a traditional-style cruise experience, with a wide choice of public rooms, bars, and lounges, and a mostly attentive staff. But, in the final analysis, the finesse is missing, and the ship's Princess Cruises-style cabins are below the standard expected.

ACCOMMODATION. There are four accommodation class categories: Queens Grill; Princess Grill; and Britannia Club and Britannia Restaurant grade – think location, location, location, but however much you pay, all passengers embark and disembark via the same gangway. Note that the air conditioning cannot be turned off in cabins or bathrooms.

All accommodation grades (nicely refreshed in 2018) have both British three-pin (240-volt) sockets and American (110-volt) and European-style two-pin (220-volt) sockets. Penhaligon's toiletries are in bathrooms, and a hairdryer is stored in the vanity desk units. Some cabins have nicely indented ceilings with suffused lighting.

Most cabins are small, but functional, although the cabinetry is austere. There's a lack of drawer space in a cabin supposedly designed for two persons; additional drawers are located under the bed, but these can be difficult for some to use. The premium mattresses are extremely good, and European duvets are standard. The bathrooms are rather bland, like those aboard the ships of Princess Cruises, with small washbasins, and little storage space for toiletries.

The largest accommodation is in four Grand Suites: 1,918–2,131 sq ft (178–197 sq m), named Bisset, Charles, Illingworth, and Rostron (all former Cunard captains). These are aft, with great ocean views from private wrap-around balconies. In-suite dining from Queens Grill menus is available.

DINING. The 878-seat Britannia Restaurant – the name is taken from a former Cunard ship of 1914–50 – is aft. It spans two decks, with seating on both stairways' linked levels, and two seatings for dinner. An adjacent restaurant is for Britannia Club passengers, with single-seat dining.

The Queens Grill (on the starboard side), with single-seating dining, is for those in suites and the top accommodation grades and provides the best cuisine and service. The Cunard Grill experience includes alfresco dining in The Courtyard (in a wind-protected terrace), and access for Grill Class passengers to an exclusive lounge and bar and upper terrace deck.

The Princess Grill (on the port side), with single seating, is for passengers in middle-class accommodation grades.

The Steakhouse at The Verandah Restaurant is a reservations-only venue featuring premium-grade steaks and seafood. It carries on the tradition of extra-tariff restaurants first seen aboard the original Queen Mary and Queen Elizabeth, with its classic ocean-liner decor. It is available to all passengers, and is on the second level of the three-deck high lobby.

The Lido Café (on Deck 9) has panoramic views, indoor/outdoor seating for approximately 470, and operates a standard multi-line self-serve buffet arrangement. It's a bit downmarket for what is supposed to be a stylish ship. At night, the venue is transformed into three distinct flavor districts: Asado (South American Grill); Aztec (Mexican cuisine); and Jasmine (Asian cuisine), each with a small cover charge.

For good Italian coffees there's Café Carinthia, one deck above the purser's desk and adjacent to the popular Veuve Clicquot Champagne bar.

For traditional British comfort food, the Golden Lion Pub offers fish and chips, steak and mushroom pie, a ploughman's lunch, and, of course, bangers (sausages) and mash, plus, there's a wide range of draft beers and lagers.

ENTERTAINMENT. The 830-seat, three-deck-high Royal Court Theatre is designed in the style of a classic opera house, with 20 private reservable boxes for special nights. A package includes Champagne, chocolates, and a ticket printed with name and box number – in the tradition of a real London West End theatre. There's a lounge for pre-show drinks.

SPA/FITNESS. The Canyon Ranch Spa includes a beauty salon, a gymnasium with muscle-pumping equipment and ocean views, an aerobics area, a Rasul chamber for private hammam-style bathing, and a Mareel Hydro pool and wellness area. There are male and female changing rooms, each with an ocean-view sauna, several treatment rooms, a relaxation area, and sauna and steam rooms (extra-cost day or multi-use passes are available). A gratuity is added to all spa treatments.

QUEEN MARY 2
★★★★+

THIS STURDY OCEAN LINER IS BUILT SPECIFICALLY FOR TRANSATLANTIC CROSSINGS

Size:	Large Resort Ship	Passenger/Crew Ratio (lower beds):	2.1
Tonnage:	151,400	Cabins (total):	1,360
Cruise Line:	Cunard Line	Size Range (sq ft/m):	194.0–2,249.7/18.0–209
Former Names:	none	Cabins (for one person):	0
Builder:	Chantiers de l'Atlantique (France)	Cabins with balcony:	953
Entered Service:	Jan 2004	Cabins (wheelchair accessible):	30
Length (ft/m):	1,131.8/345.0	Wheelchair accessibility:	Best
Propulsion/Propellers:	gas turbine + diesel-electric	Elevators:	22
	(103,000kW)/4 pods (2 azimuthing, 2 fixed)	Casino (gaming tables):	Yes
Total Crew:	1,250	Self-Service Launderette:	Yes
Passengers (lower beds):	2,705	Onboard currency:	US$
Passenger Space Ratio (lower beds):	55.9		

THE SHIP. RMS *Queen Mary 2*, designated a Royal Mail Ship by the British Post Office, is the largest ocean liner ever built in terms of gross tonnage, length, and beam, though not the number of passengers. A powerful propulsion system allows it to go backwards faster than many cruise ships can go forwards. It was the first new ship to be built for Cunard since 1969. In addition to its scheduled transatlantic crossings, *QM2* also operates an annual round-the-world cruise, and other, shorter cruises.

Almost everything about the liner says British style (even the four tender stations have London names: Belgravia, Chelsea, Kensington, and Knightsbridge), but it does have some American decor input and accents. There is a wide walk-around promenade deck outdoors (the forward section is under cover from the weather) – three times around is about 1.2 miles (1.9km). Teak 'steamer' chairs adorn the walk-around deck, with ample room for walkers to pass, but plastic sunloungers are provided on some other open decks.

Some standout public rooms include Illuminations (and integral planetarium), the Royal Court Theatre, G32 nightclub, Carinthia Lounge, and the Illuminations, the first and only full-scale planetarium at sea, is a stunning multi-purpose showlounge that also functions as a 473-seat grand cinema and broadcast studio. As a planetarium, it has tiered seating rows in a special area with 150 reclining seats, under a dome, which is 38ft (11.5m) in diameter and almost 20ft (6m) deep – the

BERLITZ'S RATINGS		
	Possible	Achieved
Ship	500	430
Accommodation	200	174
Food	400	319
Service	400	335
Entertainment	100	86
Cruise Experience	400	337
OVERALL SCORE 1681 points out of 2000		

setting for the night sky. It's worth reserving a seat for at least one of the seven outstanding 20-minute programs (with narration by Hollywood stars, including Harrison Ford, Sigourney Weaver, and Tom Hanks). The venue also screens 3D movies.

The ship's *Queen Mary 2* (*QM2*) offers the pleasures of crossing the North Atlantic comfortably on a regular schedule. It is really suited to couples and solo travelers who enjoy the cosmopolitan setting of a floating city with an unequaled maritime heritage. It's also for anyone who can't contemplate sailing without their dog or cat – it's the only liner with kennels. (Note that if you want to take your cat, you need to reserve two kennels – one is for the litter box.) Note that the ship operates in U.S. dollars.

Scores given are averaged for all accommodation grades.

ACCOMMODATION. Although there are four separate categories – Queens Grill, Princess Grill, Britannia Club, and Britannia – *QM2* really operates as a two-class ship (Grill Class and Britannia Class); the restaurant to which you are assigned depends on your accommodation grade. You even get a different cabin breakfast menu in all accommodation grades, plus a tea-/coffee-making set.

All grades have a flat-screen infotainment system, European duvets, a mini-fridge, safe, and hand-held hairdryer. All bathrooms have Penhaligon's toiletries. Other features include digital video on demand (English-, French-, and German-language movies are available), music on demand with 3,000 titles, and audiobooks on demand. One channel covers Cunard's eventful history since 1840.

Beware of cabins on deck 6 located under the Kings Court – they can be subject to noise from the casual eatery on the deck above, with its almost constant trolley movement.

From the smallest to the largest, they are as follows:

Standard outside-view/interior cabins.

Atrium-view cabins with views into the six-deck-high atrium lobby.

Deluxe/premium balcony cabins.

Junior Suites (Grade P1/P2).

Suites (Grade Q5/Q6).

Penthouse Suites (Grade Q4).

Queen Anne/Queen Victoria Suites (Grade Q3), with outstanding views over the ship's long bows.

Queen Elizabeth/Queen Mary Suites (Grade Q2), located just under the navigation bridge, with good views over the ship's long bows. Each has the convenience of private elevator access.

Duplex apartments (Grade Q2); Buckingham, Windsor, and Holyrood.

Balmoral/Sandringham Duplexes (Grade Q1). The largest stand-alone accommodation, these have excellent views along the ship's exterior length.

Wheelchair-accessible cabins come in various prices and size categories. All have pull-down rails in the closet, an above-bed emergency pull-cord, and large, well-equipped bathrooms with roll-in showers and handrails. Braille signs and tactile room signs are provided. Eight wheelchair-accessible elevators service the dining areas. Also, some cabins accommodate deaf or hearing-impaired passengers.

DINING. There are 10 dining rooms and eateries (and seven galleys to service them), and all dining venues have ocean-view windows. The wines and Champagnes have been selected by Michael Broadbent, one of the world's top wine experts.

Britannia Restaurant. This main dining room seats 1,347 and spans the ship's beam. Almost three decks high, it has two grand sweeping staircases, so you can make your entry in style. Breakfast and lunch are open seating, while dinner is in two seatings, all with crisp linen and fine china. Vegetarian options are included on all lunch and dinner menus. One downside of open seating for breakfast or lunch is that each time you'll probably have a different waiter, who won't know your preferences. Also, if you are seated on the lower level underneath the balcony formed along the sides of the upper level, you may feel enclosed in an inferior space. It's better to get a table in the central well or on the upper level.

Queens Grill/Princess Grill. There are two Grill dining salons: the 200-seat Queens Grill and the 178-seat Princess Grill. Which you dine in depends on your accommodation grade and fare. Both are located aft and have, in theory, fine ocean-view windows – although walkers passing by on the exterior promenade deck can be distracting in the daytime. Canyon Ranch SpaClub recommendations and vegetarian options are provided on all lunch and dinner menus.

The Steakhouse at The Verandah Restaurant is a reservations-only venue featuring premium-grade steaks and seafood. It carries on the tradition of extra-tariff restaurants first seen aboard the original Queen Mary and Queen Elizabeth. The room has intimate detailing and overlooks the Pool Terrace, for alfresco dining.

Kings Court. This revamped, informal, open-plan eatery offers self-serve breakfast and lunch. Breakfasts are repetitive, but include British traditional standards such as eggs, bacon, kippers, and fried tomatoes. Lunch menus change daily, and include several popular British-Indian dishes. At night, decorated screens transform sections into extra-cost dining areas.

Comfort foods are available in the outdoors Boardwalk Café, weather permitting, while pub lovers can find traditional British fare in the popular Golden Lion Pub. The multi-use Carinthia Lounge is for extra-cost coffees and light items for breakfast and lunch; it includes a patisserie, and is a good venue for socializing, with some evening entertainment.

Note: You can also order from the restaurant menus and have breakfast, lunch, and dinner served in your own suite or cabin.

ENTERTAINMENT. The Royal Court Theatre, a lovely, cozy venue, has tiered seating for 1,094, though some sight lines are less than ideal. It stages West End-style productions and hosts headline entertainers and cabaret acts. The Royal Academy of Dramatic Art (RADA) supplies actors to give Shakespearean performances, lead acting workshops, and take part in street-theater performances. Movie stars and notable celebrities who have sailed aboard the Cunard 'Queens' can be seen together with famous former Cunard ocean liners, in a superb display (you can see everything on a self-guided tour called Maritime Quest).

SPA/FITNESS. Health Spa and Beauty Services are provided in a 20,000-sq-ft (1,858-sq-m) Canyon Ranch SpaClub, arranged on two decks. There's a thalassotherapy pool, whirlpool, and thermal suite (at extra cost, but waived if you buy a treatment). There are 20 treatment rooms. Sports facilities include an electronic golf simulator, giant chess board, and a paddle-tennis court.

QUEEN VICTORIA
★★★★+

A PRETEND OCEAN LINER THAT REALLY SUITS TRADITIONAL BRITISH TASTES

Size:	Mid-size Ship	Passenger/Crew Ratio (lower beds):	2.2
Tonnage:	90,049	Cabins (total):	1,046
Cruise Line:	Cunard Line	Size Range (sq ft/m):	143.0–2,131.3/13.2–198.0
Former Names:	none	Cabins (for one person):	9
Builder:	Fincantieri (Italy)	Cabins with balcony:	718
Entered Service:	Dec 2007	Cabins (wheelchair accessible):	20
Length (ft/m):	964.5/294.0	Wheelchair accessibility:	Good
Propulsion/Propellers:	diesel-electric (64,00kW)/2 azimuthing pods	Elevators:	12
		Casino (gaming tables):	Yes
Total Crew:	1,001	Self-Service Launderette:	Yes
Passengers (lower beds):	2,083	Onboard currency:	US$
Passenger Space Ratio (lower beds):	44.5		

THE SHIP. *Queen Victoria*, which underwent a $40-million refit in 2017, will appeal to any Anglophile, because Cunard is still a British experience. (To some extent, this is marketing hype, since British members of staff are rather thin on the ground nowadays.)

Basically a stretched, modified platform and layout as the *Vista* series of ships (examples include: *Arcadia*, *Carnival Legend*, *Costa Atlantica*, and *Oosterdam*), the Cunard version has an additional passenger deck, a specially strengthened hull lengthened by 36ft (11m). It also has a more traditional interior layout reminiscent of yesteryear's ocean liners.

The interior decor is 'traditional' in Cunard-speak, with many public rooms finely decorated in Edwardian/Victorian styles, with wrought-iron balustrades on staircases and in some bars. A three-deck-high Grand Lobby has a sweeping staircase and sculpted balconies. The Cunardia museum's glass cabinets display models of former Cunard ships, old menus, and daily programs.

The Royal Arcade houses a cluster of shops in an arcade-like environment.

Other public areas worth mentioning include the following:

The Golden Lion Pub is a favorite aboard a 'Cunarder,' and is a good gathering place for karaoke, singalong, and quiz enthusiasts, plus it provides tasty pub food.

BERLITZ'S RATINGS		
	Possible	Achieved
Ship	500	412
Accommodation	200	144
Food	400	299
Service	400	313
Entertainment	100	81
Cruise Experience	400	309
OVERALL SCORE 1558 points out of 2000		

The Commodore Club is a large observation lounge; adjacent on the starboard side is a small Churchill's Cigar Lounge.

Chart Room Bar has Cunard memorabilia displays, while the adjacent Hemispheres overlooks the wood-decked Pavilion Pool; this is the high-volume disco and themed nightclub. There's also a casino on the lower level of the Royal Court.

The grand conservatory-style Winter Gardens has a moveable glass wall to an open-air swimming pool. Rattan furniture and ceiling fans help to conjure up the area's colonial theme.

Queen Victoria, a very comfortable, likeable cruise ship posing as an ocean liner, is best suited to a couples and solo travelers who enjoy traditional British ocean liner-style decor, and dressing for dinner. Gratuities ('Hotel and Dining' charge) are automatically added to your account daily. The onboard currency is the US dollar – a reason to take the Britishness claims with a pinch of salt.

Sadly, there's no help with hand luggage at embarkation. Quality has decreased in little things such as toilet paper and facial tissues – do they think no one notices? The variety of cheese is limited now (even in Grill Class venues). Other niggles include many staff touting for extra gratuities, lack of attention to detail, dispensers in the Lido buffet for condiments such as mustard, ketchup, and mayonnaise.

ACCOMMODATION. There are numerous price grades and different types of accommodation, ranging from ample but basic to opulent. Nine cabins for solo-occupancy were added in 2015, and in 2017 43 Britannia Club-grade cabins were added.

All accommodation grades have both British three-pin (240-volt) sockets and American (110-volt) and European-style two-pin (220-volt) sockets. Penhaligon's toiletries are supplied to all passengers, and a hairdryer is in the vanity desk. Some cabins have nicely indented ceilings with suffused lighting.

The regular cabins (Grades C/D) are small, but functional, although completely lacking in 'wow' factor. The cabinetry is a bit austere and lacking in character. There is a distinct lack of drawer space in a cabin supposedly designed for two; it's noticeable on long voyages, and additional drawers located under the bed have proved challenging to use. The premium mattresses are excellent, as is the bed linen, with duvets as standard. Bathrooms are stunningly bland, with small washbasins, little storage space for toiletries, cold, tiled floors, and wall-mounted showerheads.

DINING. Cunard is respected for its cuisine and service, with a variety of well-prepared and presented dishes. The Britannia Restaurant – the name is taken from a former Cunard ocean liner of 1914–50 (not P&O Cruises' *Britannia*) – is located in the aft section. It is two decks high, with seating on both levels (two seatings for dinner, but open seating for breakfast and lunch). A horseshoe-shaped stairway links both levels. While lower-level diners have a good sea view through large picture windows, balcony diners get a promenade view. Waterford Wedgwood china is used, and there's a wide range of wines (and prices).

Queens Grill and Princess Grill, two Grill Class-only restaurants, with an open-seating arrangement, provide more exclusive dining. On the port side, the Queens Grill is for passengers in suite and top-category accommodation occupants, and provides the best cuisine and service aboard. On the starboard side, the Princess Grill is for passengers in middle-class accommodation grades.

The Grills also includes alfresco dining in a seldom-used courtyard terrace (The Courtyard), protected from the wind, and with exclusive access to an upper terrace deck, with dedicated staff, as well as the Grills' lounge and bar.

A Britannia Club Restaurant was added in a 2017 refit, for Britannia Club-class accommodation occupants.

The Steakhouse at The Verandah Restaurant is a reservations-only venue featuring premium-grade steaks and seafood. It carries on the tradition of extra-tariff restaurants first seen aboard the original Queen Mary and Queen Elizabeth, with its classic ocean-liner decor. It is available to all passengers, and is on the second level of the three-deck-high lobby.

Lido Restaurant, on Deck 11, has panoramic views, indoor/outdoor seating for 468, and offers a somewhat standard multi-line, self-serve buffet arrangement.

For traditional British pub food, the Golden Lion Pub features fish and chips, steak and mushroom pie, ploughman's lunch, and bangers (sausages) and mash; all are particularly good at lunchtime – with a nice draft pint of bitter, naturally.

Excellent extra-cost *illy* coffee and Godiva chocolates are available on the second level of the lobby.

ENTERTAINMENT. The 830-seat, three-deck-high Royal Court Theatre is designed in the style of a classic opera house, complete with royal boxes.

SPA/FITNESS. The Canyon Ranch Spa includes a beauty salon, large gymnasium, several body-treatment rooms, and changing rooms for men and women, each with its own ocean-view sauna; a Thermal Area with sauna and steam rooms (extra-cost day passes) are available.

RADIANCE OF THE SEAS
★★★+

THIS MID-SIZE, FAMILY-FRIENDLY SHIP IS FOR CASUAL CRUISING

Size:	Mid-size Ship	Passenger/Crew Ratio (lower beds):	2.5
Tonnage:	90,090	Cabins (total):	1,072
Cruise Line:	Royal Caribbean International	Size Range (sq ft/m):	165.8–1,216.3/15.4–113.0
Former Names:	none	Cabins (for one person):	0
Builder:	Meyer Werft (Germany)	Cabins with balcony:	578
Entered Service:	Apr 2001	Cabins (wheelchair accessible):	14
Length (ft/m):	961.9/293.2	Wheelchair accessibility:	Good
Propulsion/Propellers:	Gas turbine (40,000kW)/2 azimuthing pods	Elevators:	9
		Casino (gaming tables):	Yes
Total Crew:	858	Self-Service Launderette:	No
Passengers (lower beds):	2,146	Onboard currency:	US$
Passenger Space Ratio (lower beds):	42.0		

THE SHIP. *Radiance of the Seas* was the first RCI ship to use gas and steam turbine power instead of the more conventional diesel or diesel-electric combination. Pod propulsion is provided. At the front is a helipad, which also acts as a viewing platform for passengers.

This is a modern-looking ship, with a two-deck-high walk-around structure forward of the funnel. Along the ship's starboard side, a central glass wall protrudes, giving great views – cabins with balconies occupy the space directly opposite on the port side. The rounded aft has nicely tiered decks. One of two swimming pools can be covered by a glass dome for use as an indoor/outdoor pool.

Inside, the decor is contemporary, yet elegant, bright, and cheerful. A nine-deck-high atrium lobby has glass-walled elevators that travel through 12 decks, face the sea, and provide a link with nature and the ocean, while a finger-touch digital 'way-finder' system helps you find your way around. The Centrum (city center), as the atrium is called, is the social hub of the ship. It is nine decks high, and most public rooms and service desks are connected to it. Standouts include Schooner Bar (the nautical-themed bar has maritime art), and the flashy Casino Royale (for casino gamers and slot machine fans; it has a French Art Nouveau decorative theme with 11 crystal chandeliers). The Viking Crown Lounge is set around the base of the funnel functions as an ob-

BERLITZ'S RATINGS

	Possible	Achieved
Ship	500	335
Accommodation	200	134
Food	400	230
Service	400	278
Entertainment	100	70
Cruise Experience	400	250

OVERALL SCORE 1297 points out of 2000

servation lounge by day, with views forward over the swimming pool.

Shipwide Wi-Fi is available for a fee, and Internet-access terminals are located in Books 'n' Coffee, a bookshop with coffee and pastries, located in an area of shops.

The artwork is eclectic, with a spectrum of color, ranging from Jenny M. Hansen's *A Vulnerable Moment* glass sculpture to David Buckland's *Industrial and Russian Constructionism 1920s* to a huge, multi-deck-high, contemporary bicycle-cum-paddle-wheel sculpture suspended in the atrium.

Radiance of the Seas has comfortable public areas. Sadly, 'background' music pervades all corridors, elevators, and on the pool deck.

In 2020 the ship will undergo a multimillion make-over.

ACCOMMODATION. There is a wide range of suites and standard outside-view and interior (no-view) cabins in various categories and price groups.

Except for the largest suites (Owner's Suites), which have king-size beds, most all other cabins have convertible twin/queen beds. All have rich (but faux) wood cabinetry, including a vanity desk with silent-close drawers, flat-screen television, personal safe, three-sided mirrors, and hairdryer. Some cabins have ceiling-recessed, pull-down berths for third and fourth persons, although closet and drawer space would be extremely tight for four, even if two were small children; some have interconnecting doors, so families with children can cruise together in separate but adjacent cabins.

Many bathrooms have a terrazzo-style tiled floor, and a half-moon-shaped small shower enclosure, cotton towels, toiletries cabinet, and a shelf, but there is little space to stow toiletries for two (or more).

The largest accommodation consists of a family suite with two bedrooms. One bedroom has twin beds that convert to queen-size bed; a second has two lower beds and two upper Pullman berths, a combination that can sleep up to eight. Note: many of the 'private' balcony cabins aren't very private, as they can be overlooked.

DINING. Cascades, the main dining room spans two decks. The upper level has floor-to-ceiling windows; the lower deck level has picture windows. It is a pleasant, but noisy, dining hall, although eight thick pillars obstruct sight lines. It seats around 1,100 and has cascading water-themed decor, and a large glass mural on one wall. Tables are for two to 10. A small private dining room (Tides, with 30 seats) is adjacent. When you book, choose one of two seatings, or 'My Time Dining,' so you can eat when you want, during dining room hours.

The cuisine is standard batch cooking. Menu descriptions may sound appealing but the food is just so-so. However, extra-cost items such as lobster or filet mignon (steak) can be cooked to order. Green vegetables are sparse, but there are plenty of salads, and desserts are pretty good. Rice is over-used. Baked goods are also pretty average. Vegetarian and children's menus are available. Note that there are no wine waiters.

Optional dining/eateries (some at extra cost) include:

Boardwalk Dog House, for hot dogs and toppings (open for lunch and dinner).

Reservations-required Giovanni's Table is a trattoria with Italian classics served family-style (open for lunch and dinner).

Reservations-required Izumi, a sushi bar with hot-rock cooking (open for lunch and dinner).

Park Café, an indoor/outdoor market for salads, sandwiches, soups, and pastries (open for breakfast, lunch and dinner; no added cost, but reservations are required).

Rita's Cantina, a casual (reservations-required) indoor/outdoor Mexican eatery caters to families by day, and adults by night.

Chef's Table, a private experience co-hosted by the executive chef and sommelier for a multi-course wine-pairing dinner. Reservations are required.

Samba Grill, a Brazilian churrascaria (steakhouse), features meats, chicken, and seafood brought to the table, ready to slice and serve on request (open for dinner only, and reservations are required).

For casual eats, the expansive Windjammer Café is a food court-style, self-serve venue.

ENTERTAINMENT. The three-level Aurora Theater has 874 seats (including 24 wheelchair stations) and good sight lines from most seats; it's the venue for large-scale shows and cabaret acts. The Colony Club hosts casual cabaret shows, including late-night adult comedy, and has live music for dancing. The entertainment throughout is lively and upbeat.

SPA/FITNESS. The Day Spa fitness and spa facilities have themed decor, and include a gymnasium with numerous cardiovascular machines, a large exercise room, sauna and steam rooms, and body-pampering treatment rooms. All are located on two of the uppermost decks, forward of the mast, with access from the forward stairway.

A climate-controlled 10,176-sq-ft (945-sq-m) indoor/outdoor Solarium has a sliding glass roof that can be closed in inclement weather.

Sports facilities include a 30ft (9m) rock-climbing wall with five separate climbing tracks, an exterior jogging track, a nine-hole miniature golf course with novel 17th-century decorative ornaments, and an indoor/outdoor country club with golf simulator, a jogging track, basketball court, plus two specially stabilized pool tables (within the Bombay Billiard Club).

REGAL PRINCESS
★★★★

THIS LARGE, MULTI-CHOICE FAMILY-FRIENDLY RESORT SHIP HAS STYLE

Size:	Large Resort Ship	Passenger/Crew Ratio (lower beds):	2.6
Tonnage:	142,229	Cabins (total):	1,780
Cruise Line:	Princess Cruises	Size Range (sq ft/m):	161.4–554.3/15–51.5
Former Names:	none	Cabins (for one person):	0
Builder:	Fincantieri (Italy)	Cabins with balcony:	1,438
Entered Service:	May 2014	Cabins (wheelchair accessible):	36
Length (ft/m):	1,082.6/330.0	Wheelchair accessibility:	Best
Propulsion/Propellers:	diesel-electric (52,000kW)/2	Elevators:	14
Total Crew:	1,346	Casino (gaming tables):	Yes
Passengers (lower beds):	3,560	Self-Service Launderette:	Yes
Passenger Space Ratio (lower beds):	39.9	Onboard currency:	US$

THE SHIP. *Regal Princess* is sister to *Royal Princess*, which debuted in 2013. The ship's profile is quite well balanced – an enhancement of the older *Grand*-class ships. For practicality, lifeboats are located outside the main public room areas, so they don't impair the view from balcony cabins. It has an almost complete walk-around promenade deck.

The over-the-water SeaWalk, an open deck glass-bottomed enclosed walkway (first introduced in 2013 aboard sister ship *Royal Princess*), on the starboard side extends almost 30ft (9.1m) beyond the vessel's edge and forms part of a lounge/bar venue. This is the place to go for dramatic (downward) views, including to the sea 128ft (39m) below, so you *can* 'walk' on water (or, at least, over it). On the port side is a SeaView bar.

There are two main stair towers and elevator banks, plus some panoramic-view elevators in a third, central bank (these elevators do not go between decks 7 and 16 – a serious design omission because stairs are only at the forward and aft elevators). The interior decor is warm and attractive, with many earth tones. One hallmark venue, the Piazza Atrium, was significantly expanded, compared to the older ships in the fleet. This is the ship's multi-faceted social hub and combines a specialty dining venue, snack-food items, pastries, beverages, entertainment, shopping, and guest services. It has a horseshoe-shaped flowing stairway and good mood-lighting effects.

BERLITZ'S RATINGS

	Possible	Achieved
Ship	500	393
Accommodation	200	139
Food	400	267
Service	400	294
Entertainment	100	82
Cruise Experience	400	295

OVERALL SCORE 1470 points out of 2000

The base level includes an International Café, for coffees, teas, panini, and pastries (and to see and be seen); Sabatini's, a Tuscan specialty extra-cost restaurant (located just off the atrium), and a gift shop. Upstairs, level two hosts Alfredo's Pizzeria, Bellini's (a bar for Bellini drinks), a photo gallery, reception and shore excursion desks. On the third level, Crooners Bar features entertaining pianists. The Piazza Atrium is all about food, entertainment, and passenger services.

Niggles include the user-unfriendly automated telephone system, the small cabin towels, extra cost for items like ice cream, and the charge (coins needed) for the washers and dryers in the self-service launderettes.

Overall, however, Princess Cruises delivers a consistently fine, comfortable, well-packaged product, always with a good degree of style, at a competitive price.

ACCOMMODATION. There are six main types of accommodation in many price grades: (a) Grand Suite; (b) suites with balcony; (c) mini-suites with balcony; (d) deluxe outside-view balcony cabins; (e) outside-view cabins with balcony; and (f) interior cabins. Pricing depends on two things: size and location. Suites and balcony cabins, aft, are the quietest and most sought-after. Each accommodation deck houses a self-service launderette.

All accommodation grades have energy-efficient lighting and key card readers, beds with upholstered headboards, wall-mounted TV screen, additional 220v electrical socket, turndown service and heart-shaped chocolates on pillows each night, bathrobes (on request, unless you are in suite-grade accommodation), and hairdryer. Bathrooms have decent open-shelf storage space for toiletries, and all bathrooms have hand-held, flexi-hose showers, and large shower enclosures.

Suite and mini-suite grade occupants have a concierge lounge for making dining, spa, and shore-excursion reservations. They also get more amenities, larger infotainment screens, and dual washbasin bathrooms.

Note that the balconies of cabins on Marina Deck 15 can be seen by anyone on the overhanging Skywalk on the deck above, so choose your cabin wisely.

DINING. Allegro, Concerto, and Symphony are the main dining rooms. You can choose either traditional two seating times, or 'anytime dining,' so you can choose when and with whom you want to eat.

Although portions are generous, the food and its presentation are standardized. Fish is often disguised by a crumb or batter coating, the choice of fresh green vegetables is limited, few garnishes are used, and cheese is pre-sliced and diced. This is big-ship banquet catering. Pasta dishes are acceptable (though voluminous), typically served by section headwaiters, who may also make 'something special just for you' – in search of favorable comments and gratuities. If you like desserts, order a sundae at dinner (most other items are just so-so).

Extra-cost, reservations-required Sabatini's is an Italian restaurant with Tuscan decor. It's named after Trattoria Sabatini, in Florence, with both a table-d'hôte and an à la carte menu. The venue also hosts Italian wine tastings.

Ocean Terrace, on the atrium's second level is seafood bar. International Café, on the atrium's lowest level is for extra-cost coffees, pastries, panini, and more. Vines Wine Bar, adjacent to Sabatini's, is for a glass of extra-cost wine, and for tapas. This is a pleasant area to while away a late afternoon, trying out new wines.

Crown Grill is an extra-cost, à la carte dining venue, adjacent to the Wheelhouse Bar, and is for steaks and seafood.

For casual eats the self-serve buffet venue (Horizon Court) seats 900 indoors and 350 outdoors. There are multiple 'active' cooking stations and themed sections, including a deli section. Certain nights feature special themes and foods, with rotiseries, carvings, hibachi grill, and other active cooking stations. The Horizon Bistro Pastry Shop offers freshly baked bread, croissants, pastries, and waffles.

ENTERTAINMENT. The Princess Theater (showlounge) spans two decks, and is the venue for the large-scale production shows for which Princess Cruises is renowned. There's also a 'Princess Live' auditorium for stand-up comedy and other small-audience entertainment features. Aft on the same deck is a Vista Lounge; it has a large dance floor. The ship carries several gentlemen dance hosts on each cruise for female passengers without partners.

SPA/FITNESS. The Lotus Spa is on the lower level of the atrium, so it doesn't take away outdoor-view real estate space. Separate facilities for men and women include a sauna, steam room, and changing rooms; common facilities include a relaxation/waiting zone, body-pampering treatment rooms, and a fitness room. Some fitness classes are free. Children and teens have their own fitness rooms adjacent to their age-related facilities.

REGATTA
★★★+

THIS IS AN INFORMAL SHIP WITH COUNTRY CLUB DECOR THAT SUITS MATURE-AGE CRUISERS

Size:	Small Ship	Passenger/Crew Ratio (lower beds):	1.7
Tonnage:	30,277	Cabins (total):	342
Cruise Line:	Oceania Cruises	Size Range (sq ft/m):	145.3–968.7/13.5–90.0
Former Names:	R Two	Cabins (for one person):	0
Builder:	Chantiers de l'Atlantique	Cabins with balcony:	232
Entered Service:	Dec 1998/Dec 2003	Cabins (wheelchair accessible):	3
Length (ft/m):	593.7/181.0	Wheelchair accessibility:	Good
Propulsion/Propellers:	diesel (18,600kW)/2	Elevators:	4
Total Crew:	386	Casino (gaming tables):	Yes
Passengers (lower beds):	684	Self-Service Launderette:	Yes
Passenger Space Ratio (lower beds):	44.2	Onboard currency:	US$

THE SHIP. *Regatta* was originally one of eight almost identical ships built for long-defunct Renaissance Cruises. The uniform color (all white) of the exterior and large, square funnel help to balance the ship's high sides. Teak overlaid decking and high-quality lounge chairs help create a very comfortable Lido and Pool Deck.

A 2014 refurbishment added Barista's coffee bar (for illy coffees), and installed new bathrooms for Owner's and Vista suites. Also added were a miniature golf course, shuffleboard courts, and other deck games.

There is no walk-around promenade deck outdoors, but there is a small jogging/walking track, above the swimming pool.

The elegant interior decor is a throwback to the ocean liners of the 1920s and 1930s, with dark woods and warm colors, all carried out in fine taste – if a bit faux in places. It feels like an old-world country club.

Public rooms are spread over three decks. The reception hall has a staircase with intricate wrought-iron railings. A large observation lounge, the Horizon Bar, is located high atop ship. There are plenty of bars, including one in each restaurant entrance. Perhaps the nicest is the casino bar/lounge, a beautiful room reminiscent of London's grand hotels. It has an inviting marble fireplace, sofas, and chairs.

The dress code is 'smart casual.' Gratuities are added to your account daily. A rather large 18 percent is added to bar and spa accounts.

BERLITZ'S RATINGS		
	Possible	Achieved
Ship	500	360
Accommodation	200	132
Food	400	291
Service	400	282
Entertainment	100	67
Cruise Experience	400	262

OVERALL SCORE 1394 points out of 2000

Oceania Cruises is a company that aims to provide a high level of food and service in an informal setting that's elegant yet comfortable. *Regatta* suits couples who like really good food and style, but want informality and not formal nights on board, as well as interesting itineraries, all at a reasonable price.

Passenger niggles include inventive extra charges that can be incurred. What's refreshing is the fact that there are almost no intrusive announcements.

ACCOMMODATION. The accommodation price grades depend on size and location. All standard interior and outside-view cabins (the lowest four grades) are extremely tight for two people, particularly for cruises longer than five days. They have twin beds or a queen-size bed, with good under-bed storage areas, personal safe, vanity desk with large mirror, good closet and drawer space in rich, dark woods, 100 percent cotton bathrobe and towels, slippers, clothes brush, and shoehorn.

Certain cabin categories (about 100 of them) qualify as Concierge Level accommodation, and occupants get extra goodies such as enhanced bathroom amenities, complimentary shoeshine, tote bag, cashmere throw blanket, bottle of Champagne on arrival, a hand-held hairdryer, priority restaurant reservations, and priority embarkation.

Outside-view and interior (no-view) cabins have twin beds convertible to queen-size, and a bathroom with a shower enclosure with removable hand-held showerhead, hairdryer, storage shelves for toiletries, retractable clothesline, washbasin, and toilet. Although not large, they are quite comfortable, with a decent amount of storage space.

Cabins with balcony comprise about two-thirds of all cabins (14 cabins on Deck 6 have lifeboat-obstructed views).

Penthouse Suites are actually large cabins rather than suites, as the bedrooms aren't separate from the living areas.

Vista Suites have beds that face the sea, which is also visible through the floor-to-ceiling windows and a sliding glass door.

Owner's Suites are fine living spaces. Located aft, they are subject to more movement and some vibration. Beds face the sea, also viewable through floor-to-ceiling windows and a sliding glass door.

DINING. Flexibility and choice are what Oceania Cruises ships are all about. There are four restaurants, all open seating.

The Grand Dining Room has around 340 seats, and a raised central section, but the problem is the noise level – because of the low ceiling height – it's awful when the dining room is full. Located aft, there are large ocean-view windows on three sides, and the prime tables overlook the stern. The chairs are comfortable, with armrests. Menus change daily for lunch and dinner.

Toscana Italian Restaurant has 96 seats, windows along two sides, and a set menu plus daily chef's specials.

The cozy Polo Grill has 98 seats, windows along two sides and a set menu including prime steaks and seafood.

The Terrace Café has both indoor and outdoor seating. It is open for breakfast, lunch, and casual dinners, with some fine tapas and other Mediterranean dishes, and it incorporates a small pizzeria and grill.

A poolside Waves Grill serves fish burgers, veggie burgers, and sandwiches, plus Angus beef burgers and hot dogs.

Reservations are needed in the Toscana Restaurant and Polo Grill (but there's no extra charge), where there are mostly tables for four or six, and few tables for two.

The food and service staff are provided by a respected maritime catering company. This is a foodie's ship, with high-quality ingredients. Particularly notable are the delicious breads, rolls, croissants, and brioches – all made on board from French flour and d'Isigny butter.

On sea days, afternoon tea is presented in the Horizon Lounge, with formally dressed staff, cake trolleys, and an array of cake and scones.

ENTERTAINMENT. The Regatta Lounge has entertainment, lectures, some social events, and a mix of production shows and cabaret acts.

SPA/FITNESS. A Lido Deck has a swimming pool, and good sunbathing space, plus a thalassotherapy tub. The uppermost outdoors deck includes a golf driving net and shuffleboard court. Canyon Ranch SpaClub consists of a beauty salon, three treatment rooms, changing rooms, and steam room (but no sauna).

RCGS RESOLUTE
★★★★

A DELIGHTFUL, SMALL EXPEDITION SHIP FOR DISCOVERY CRUISE

Size:	Boutique Ship	Passenger/Crew Ratio (lower beds):	1.4
Tonnage:	8,378	Cabins (total):	73
Cruise Line:	One Ocean Expeditions	Size Range (sq ft/m):	231.4–470.3/21.5–43.7
Former Names:	Hanseatic, Society Adventurer	Cabins (for one person):	0
Builder:	Rauma Yards (Finland)	Cabins with balcony:	0
Entered Service:	Mar 1993/Nov 2018	Cabins (wheelchair accessible):	2
Length (ft/m):	402.9/122.8	Wheelchair accessibility:	None
Propulsion/Propellers:	diesel (5,880kW)/2	Elevators:	2
Total Crew:	100	Casino (gaming tables):	No
Passengers (lower beds):	146	Self-Service Launderette:	No
Passenger Space Ratio (lower beds):	57.3	Onboard currency:	Euros

THE SHIP. The all-white *RCGS Resolute* (formerly *Hanseatic*, operated for many years by Hapag-Lloyd Expedition Cruises) was designed for worldwide expedition and discovery-style cruises (in contemporary surroundings (it was the first non-Russian ship to sail through the Northwest Passage). Although it looks chunky from the front, it has a fully enclosed bridge, an ice-strengthened hull with a high ice classification, a helicopter pad, high-tech navigation equipment, and a science laboratory. A fleet of 14 Zodiac inflatable craft (each named for a famous explorer) is used for shore landings and up-close wildlife viewing. Rubber boots, parkas, boot-washing stations, and storage rooms are provided.

Inside, the ship is equipped with high-quality fittings and soft furnishings, and exudes a microclimate of good taste. Most public rooms are aft, with accommodation forward. All are well furnished and have high ceilings, helping to make the ship feel larger than it is. A comfortable library/observation lounge hosts geographical, travel, and wildlife books, and has a sunken bar. A lecture hall, with excellent audio-visual facilities, on a lower deck, can accommodate all passengers.

Well-qualified lecturers and naturalists accompany each cruise. Overall, *Resolute* provides destination-intensive cruises and expeditions in unstuffy surroundings at a price that includes modestly good food and service.

ACCOMMODATION. There are no bad cabins, and accommodation is priced in various grades. The all-outside cabins, located in the forward section,

BERLITZ'S RATINGS		
	Possible	Achieved
Ship	500	373
Accommodation	200	153
Food	400	306
Service	400	306
Entertainment	100	72
Cruise Experience	400	298

OVERALL SCORE 1504 points out of 2000

are large and well equipped, and include a separate lounge next to a large picture window (with blackout blind and curtains). There is a divider between bed and lounge areas. Each cabin has a minibar, infotainment system, three-channel radio, locking drawers, alarm clock, good closet and drawer space, and two separate cupboards and hooks for all-weather outerwear. One useful feature of all cabins is a blue night/safety light. Bathrooms have a large shower enclosure with curved glass wall, toiletries cabinets, hairdryer, and bathrobe. There are only two types of cabins; 34 have double beds, others have twins. Laundry, dry cleaning, and pressing services are available.

DINING. The 186-seat Marco Polo restaurant is welcoming, with large picture windows on two sides and aft, one seating for dinner, and open seating for breakfast and lunch. The meals are nicely presented, with a decent selection of breads, cheeses, desserts, and pastry items. In the Arctic or Antarctic, table setups are often minimal, due to possible ship movement. An alternative dining spot is the Bistro Lemaire, with 74 seats indoors, and ample seating at outdoor tables.

ENTERTAINMENT. After-dinner recaps and conversation is all that's needed.

SPA/FITNESS. There is a decent-size gymnasium (with muscle-toning equipment, treadmills, and exercycles), sauna, solarium and hot tub. Massage is available in a rather clinical room in the medical facility.

RHAPSODY OF THE SEAS
★★★+

THIS MODERN SHIP IS GOOD FOR CASUAL, FAMILY-FRIENDLY VACATIONS

Size:	Mid-size Ship	Passenger/Crew Ratio (lower beds):	2.6
Tonnage:	78,491	Cabins (total):	1,000
Cruise Line:	Royal Caribbean International	Size Range (sq ft/m):	135.0–1,270.1/12.5–118.0
Former Names:	none	Cabins (for one person):	0
Builder:	Chantiers de l'Atlantique (France)	Cabins with balcony:	229
Entered Service:	May 1997	Cabins (wheelchair accessible):	14
Length (ft/m):	915.3/279.0	Wheelchair accessibility:	Good
Propulsion/Propellers:	diesel-electric (50,400kW)/2	Elevators:	9
Total Crew:	765	Casino (gaming tables):	Yes
Passengers (lower beds):	2,000	Self-Service Launderette:	No
Passenger Space Ratio (lower beds):	39.2	Onboard currency:	US$

THE SHIP. This all-white (*Vision*-class) ship has a nicely rounded stern and a single, slim funnel aft. There is a reasonable amount of outdoor walking space, although this tends to be cluttered with sunloungers.

The ship shares design features that make many, but not all, Royal Caribbean International (RCI) ships identifiable, including a domed Viking Crown Lounge, above the atrium lobby. The artwork is upbeat and colorful, with a musical theme. There's a wide range of interesting public rooms, lounges, and bars, and the interiors have been cleverly designed to avoid congestion and aid flow into revenue areas.

The seven-deck high atrium lobby – called the Centrum – is the interior focal and social hub of the ship. It hosts bars, lounges, service counters, an art gallery, and a café. Close by is the flashy Casino Royale (with gaming tables and slot machines), and Schooner Bar, with nautical-theme decor.

Ship-wide (chargeable) Wi-Fi is available , as is a digital direction-finding system, electronic mustering, and an outdoor poolside movie screen. Ship enthusiasts will like the chair fabric in the Shall We Dance Lounge, with its large aft-facing windows, and the glass case-enclosed mechanical sculptures.

ACCOMMODATION. There are numerous accommodation grades, priced by size and location. The standard interior and exterior-view cabins are very small but

BERLITZ'S RATINGS		
	Possible	Achieved
Ship	500	337
Accommodation	200	126
Food	400	220
Service	400	260
Entertainment	100	63
Cruise Experience	400	258
OVERALL SCORE 1264 points out of 2000		

have just enough functional facilities for a one-week cruise (longer might prove confining). The decor is bright and cheerful, although ceilings are plain, like a modern Scandinavian hotel. Twin beds are convertible to queen-size, and there is decent closet and drawer space, but little room to maneuver between bed and desk/infotainment unit .

Bathrooms are small but functional. The shower units are small, there is no cabinet for toiletries, and towels are thin. In the passageways, upbeat artwork depicts musical themes.

Suite-grade accommodation gives you more space and larger bathrooms (some with bathtubs). For the best accommodation, choose the Royal Suite, which comes with a white baby grand piano.

DINING. The two-level Edelweiss Dining Room is attractive and works well as a large restaurant, although the noise level can be high. When you book, choose one of two seatings (fixed for dinner) for dinner or My Time Dining (eat when you want, during dining room hours).

Expect standard batch catering in the main dining room, with extra-cost lobster or filet mignon (steak) cooked to order. While salads are plentiful, green vegetables are not, but desserts are pretty good. Rice is over used. Breads and pastry items are average (these are baked from frozen). Vegetarian and children's menus are available. Note that there are no wine waiters.

Other dining venues and eateries are as follows. Some cost extra, but food is mostly cooked to order. Reservations (make them through the digital system) are required; note that menus do not change.

Chops Grille Steakhouse features premium veal chops and steaks and seafood items. Giovanni's Table is for Italian trattoria-style cuisine. Izumi Asian Cuisine includes a sushi bar and features hot-rock cooking; it is open for lunch and dinner. A la carte menu pricing applies to all three venues.

Chef's Table is a private experience co-hosted by the executive chef and sommelier for a multi-course wine-pairing dinner.

Park Café is a casual no-charge market-style eatery for salads, sandwiches, soups, and pastries, while Windjammer Café – located at the front of the ship with commanding ocean views – is a large food-court-style, self-serve buffet venue.

ENTERTAINMENT. The Broadway Melodies Theater is the showlounge. It is a large, but well-designed room with main and balcony levels, and good sight lines from most of the banquette seats.

Cabaret and late-night comedy acts are presented in the Shall We Dance Lounge, aft.

The entertainment, for which RCI gets abundant praise, is upbeat and colorful. However, it's difficult to escape from background music everywhere else – even in the passenger hallways and elevators, and outdoors on the pool deck.

SPA/FITNESS. The Vitality at Sea Spa and Fitness Center is on one of the aft uppermost decks. Egypt is the decor theme, with pharaohs lining an indoor/outdoor solarium pool. It is staffed by a specialist concession.

Other facilities include a rock-climbing wall aft of the funnel, with several climbing tracks.

RITZ-CARLTON AZORA
NYR

THIS SMALL UPSCALE SHIP IS THE FIRST FOR RITZ-CARLTON BRAND DEVOTEES

Size:	Small Ship	Passenger/Crew Ratio (lower beds):	1.0
Tonnage:	26,500	Cabins (total):	149
Cruise Line:	Ritz-Carlton Yacht Collection	Size Range (sq ft/m):	376.7–1,689.9/35.0–157.0
Former Names:	none	Cabins (for one person):	0
Builder:	Astilleros Barreras HJB (Spain)	Cabins with balcony:	149
Entered Service:	Feb 2020	Cabins (wheelchair accessible):	3
Length (ft/m):	623.3/190.0	Wheelchair accessibility:	Good
Propulsion/Propellers:	diesel-electric/2 azimuthing pods	Elevators:	3
		Casino (gaming tables):	No
Total Crew:	298	Self-Service Launderette:	No
Passengers (lower beds):	298	Onboard currency:	US$
Passenger Space Ratio (lower beds):	88.9		

THE SHIP. Small and designed to appeal to the well-traveled set that likes Ritz-Carlton hotels. Although marketed as a 'yacht,' at 24,000 tons, this is a small ship. However, it is sleek, with a deep blue hull and nicely raked bows; it looks a little like an oligarch's mega-yacht – with sunglasses on! In other words, it's a hybrid, because it has a capacity for 292 oligarchs (for comparison, about the same as Silversea Cruises' *Silver Shadow* and *Silver Whisper*).

The social gathering place is the Living Room, with its integral library and café. Others include an observation lounge, cigar lounge, marina lounge, meeting rooms, and a small kids' club. Wi-Fi and gratuities are included (as they should be at this price level), as are drinks (but the line chooses the drinks, which translates to a more limited choice of brands). Whether *Ritz-Carlton Azora* can challenge Hapag-Lloyd's famed top-rated *Europa 2* remains to be seen.

ACCOMMODATION. There are six accommodation grades and sizes. The size, location, and grade defines the price. From the smallest outside-view cabin to the largest (Owner's Suite), all have a bal-

BERLITZ'S RATINGS		
	Possible	Achieved
Ship	500	NYR
Accommodation	200	NYR
Food	400	NYR
Service	400	NYR
Entertainment	100	NYR
Cruise Experience	400	NYR
OVERALL SCORE NYR points out of 2000		

cony ('terrace' in Ritz-Carlton-speak), espresso coffee machine, walk-in closet, refrigerator, and high-grade beds and bed linen. Bathrooms all have dual washbasins and glazed shower enclosures (three grades have bathtubs).

DINING. The L-shaped Main Dining Experience is the 'see-and-be-seen-in' principal restaurant, but it includes many smaller, alcove-style sections.

Aqua has menus overseen by chef Sven Elverfeld of the three Michelin-starred restaurant at the Ritz-Carlton Hotel in Wolfsburg, Germany (think: modern interpretation of classic German cuisine). An Asian-Fusion eatery is adjacent, while an outdoor grill/bar is for steaks and seafood.

ENTERTAINMENT. This is strictly low-key, because of the size of the ship, but will include live jazz and classical music.

SPA/FITNESS. The Ritz-Carlton Spa includes men's/women's changing rooms, barber, beauty salon, saunas, steam rooms, and a fitness center.

RIVIERA
★★★★+

A HOMEY, VERY COMFORTABLE, MID-SIZE SHIP WITH A COUNTRY-CLUB FEEL

Size:	Mid-size Ship	Passenger/Crew Ratio (lower beds):	1.5
Tonnage:	66,084	Cabins (total):	629
Cruise Line:	Oceania Cruises	Size Range (sq ft/m):	172.2–2,000/16.0–185.0
Former Names:	none	Cabins (for one person):	0
Builder:	Fincantieri (Italy)	Cabins with balcony:	593
Entered Service:	Jul 2012	Cabins (wheelchair accessible):	6
Length (ft/m):	776.5/236.7	Wheelchair accessibility:	Good
Propulsion/Propellers:	diesel-electric/2	Elevators:	6
Total Crew:	800	Casino (gaming tables):	Yes
Passengers (lower beds):	1,258	Self-Service Launderette:	Yes
Passenger Space Ratio (lower beds):	52.5	Onboard currency:	US$

THE SHIP. *Riviera* is the second newbuild (close sister to *Marina*) for this small premium cruise line. Its profile is quite handsome; it has a nicely rounded front, and is topped by a swept-back funnel.

The ship suits mature-age adults who appreciate quality and style, plenty of space and comfort (no lines), and high-level cuisine and service, in a semi-casual country house setting with realistic pricing.

The interior layout is uncomplicated, and the focal point is a stunning wrought-iron and Lalique glass horseshoe-shaped staircase in the main lobby. Differences from *Marina* – there are reportedly 727 of them – include better steps on the lobby staircase, a higher ceiling on one public deck, changes to drawer depth in cabins, a hand-held shower in suites with bathtub, and faster Internet speed.

There are nine bars and lounges. There is a 2,000-book library, set on the port side of the funnel housing, which also contains a staffed computer center, and Barista's coffee bar/lounge (serving illy coffee). The ship also showcases a collection of fine Latin artwork by some renowned artists from Cuba's Vanguard Movement in the second quarter of the 20th century.

Monte Carlo Casino is located between two bars – the Grand Bar and Martinis, with its own soft lavender-colored Casino Bar. Martinis houses a beautiful special-edition Steinway baby grand piano. There are also three boutiques and several dining venues.

BERLITZ'S RATINGS		
	Possible	Achieved
Ship	500	423
Accommodation	200	170
Food	400	309
Service	400	307
Entertainment	100	77
Cruise Experience	400	313

OVERALL SCORE 1599 points out of 2000

There aren't that many different lounges as such, because most are drinking venues.

A Culinary Center includes a cooking-demonstration kitchen and 24 workstations, with various classes run in conjunction with US-based *Bon Appétit* magazine – there's a charge for these, but you get to eat your creations.

You can bring your paintbrushes to an Artist's Loft that has constantly changing artists. Other classes may include photography, needlepoint, scrap-booking, drawing, and quilting.

The dress code is 'elegant country club attire' – no pajamas or track suits, but no ties either. A gratuity of 18 percent is added to all bar and spa accounts.

ACCOMMODATION. There are four suite grades and four cabin grades. Price depends on size and location, but all have one thing in common – a good-sized bathroom with tub and separate shower enclosure, plus his 'n' hers toiletry cabinets. All suites/cabins have dark wood cabinetry with rounded edges. The decor includes chocolate brown, cream, and white – earthy colors that don't jar the senses. Around 96 percent of all accommodation has teak-decked balconies.

Standard veranda cabins. These measure 282 sq ft (26 sq m).

Penthouse Suites. These measure 420 sq ft (39 sq m).

Oceania Suites. These measure about 1,030 sq ft (96 sq m).

Vista Suites. These range from 1,200 to 1,500 sq ft (111–139 sq m).

Owner's Suite. At more than 2,000 sq ft (186 sq m), this spans the entire beam of the ship (about 105ft/32m). It is decked out in furniture, fabrics, lighting, and bedding from the Ralph Lauren Home collection with interior design by New York-based Tocar Inc. It is outfitted with a Yamaha baby grand piano, private fitness room, laptop computers, Bose audio system, and a teak-decked balcony with Jacuzzi tub.

Suite-category occupants get niceties such as Champagne on arrival, 1,000-thread-count bed linen, large plasma TVs, Hermès and Clarins bath amenities, butler service, and en-suite delivery from any of the ship's restaurants. Amenities include Tranquillity beds, Wi-Fi laptop computer, refrigerated minibar with unlimited free soft drinks and bottled water replenished daily, personal safe, writing desk, cotton bathrobes, slippers, and marble and granite bathroom. Priority check-in and early embarkation and priority luggage delivery are perks.

Some grades get access to an Executive or Concierge Lounge, with sofas, Internet-connect computers, breakfast items, soft drinks, magazines, and more. Self-service launderettes are on each accommodation deck – useful for long voyages.

DINING. This ship uses good-quality ingredients and has a number of dining venues, providing plenty of choice, even for long cruises. Particularly good are the breads, rolls, croissants, and brioches – made on board from French flour and d'Isigny butter.

The Grand Dining Room is elegant. It has 566 seats, and a domed central ceiling. Versace bone china, Christofle silver, and fine linens are provided, while Canyon Ranch Spa dishes are available for all meals.

However, banquette seating in some venues does not evoke the image of premium dining as much as individual seating does.

Other dining/eatery options include: Jacques, with 124 seats – the second seagoing restaurant for French celebrity chef Jacques Pépin, Oceania's executive culinary director. With antique oak flooring, antique flatware, and Lalique glassware, it provides fine dining in an elegant but informal setting,

with roast free-range meats, classic French dessert items, and a choice of AOC cheeses.

Polo Grill, with about 130 seats, serves steaks and seafood, including Oceania's signature 32oz (907g) bone-in King's Cut prime rib. The setting is traditional steakhouse, with dark wood paneling and classic white tablecloths, although the tables are close together.

Toscana is a 124-seat venue for Italian-style cuisine (including some tasty desserts), and Versace china.

Privée, with seating for up to 10 in a private setting, invites exclusivity for its seven-course dégustation menu.

La Réserve is an intimate, 24-seat venue for wine and food with small-portion, wine-paired dégustation menus.

The Terrace Café is the casual self-serve buffet-style venue. Outdoors, as an extension of the café, is Tapas on the Terrace, good for light bites – although the ceiling is low and tables are close together, so it can be noisy.

Red Ginger offers 'classic and contemporary' Asian cuisine. The setting is refined, but the banquette-style seating lets the venue down. You'll be asked by the waiter to choose your chopsticks from a lacquered presentation box.

Waves Grill, located poolside and shaded from the sun, is for burgers (including fishburgers and veggie burgers), seafood, and other fast food, cooked to order. Baristas coffee bar overlooks the pool deck and has excellent, free *illy* Italian coffee – though, sadly, it's served in paper cups.

ENTERTAINMENT. The 600-seat Marina Lounge spans two decks, with tiered amphitheater-style seating. It's more cabaret-style entertainment than big production shows. Overall, the entertainment is, at best, adequate.

SPA/FITNESS. The Canyon Ranch SpaClub provides wellness and personal spa treatments (at high prices). The facility includes a fitness center, beauty salon, several treatment rooms (including a couples room), sauna and steam rooms, and a large thalassotherapy pool. Treatments incur an automatic 18 percent gratuity. A jogging track is located aft of the funnel.

ROALD AMUNDSEN
★★★+

THIS SHIP IS FOR HARDY OUTDOOR TYPES WHO DON'T MIND FAIRLY BASIC FACILITIES

Size:	Small Ship
Tonnage:	20,889
Cruise Line:	Hurtigruten
Former Names:	*none*
Builder:	Kleven Verft (Norway)
Entered Service:	Jul 2019
Length (ft/m):	459.3/140.0
Propulsion/Propellers:	diesel-electric/2 azimuthing pods
Total Crew:	120
Passengers (lower beds):	530
Passenger Space Ratio (lower beds):	39.4
Passenger/Crew Ratio (lower beds):	4.4
Cabins (total):	265
Size Range (sq ft/m):	161.4–398.2/15.0–37.0
Cabins (for one person):	0
Cabins with balcony:	139
Cabins (wheelchair accessible):	0
Wheelchair accessibility:	Poor
Elevators:	2
Casino (gaming tables):	No
Self-Service Launderette:	No
Onboard currency:	Norwegian Krona

THE SHIP. Based somewhat on the company's *Fram*, this new expedition-style ship is larger, more up to date, with almost upright bows, a tender-loading platform, and hybrid engines for propulsion. Outdoors, a half-ship walking deck encircles the front of the ship. Public areas include an observation lounge and outdoor viewing area, 'infinity' pool (it's the first Hurtigruten ship to have a real pool) a lecture hall, shop, Internet corner, lobby with reception and shore-excursion counters, and a video games room. The interior design is Scandinavian, and minimalist, but includes artwork depicting the polar Arctic and Antarctic regions. However, several pillars obstruct sightlines in the observation lounge.

Note that when on expedition voyages, many things cost extra (such as kayaking in Antarctica).

ACCOMMODATION. There are numerous accommodation price grades (15, actually) in three categories (Polar outside cabin, Arctic Superior cabin, and Expedition suites). The price you pay

BERLITZ'S RATINGS		
	Possible	Achieved
Ship	500	361
Accommodation	200	126
Food	400	232
Service	400	254
Entertainment	100	52
Cruise Experience	400	244

OVERALL SCORE 1269 points out of 2000

depends on the size, location, and grade you choose. From the smallest cabin to the largest suite (sleeping up to four), appointments are rather sparing, although all have an espresso machine and kettle, and sea-facing beds. Contrary to maritime tradition, even-numbered cabins are on the starboard side, with odd-numbered cabins on the port side.

DINING. The T. Auno Restaurant is the main dining room, with open seating, including window-side seats, and a Nordic-style self-serve buffet section in the center. Most meals are buffet-style, although some dinners have waiter service.

Lindstrom Restaurant is an extra-cost venue, with better, cooked-to-order food. There's also Fredheim Restaurant, for casual international bites.

ENTERTAINMENT. Lectures are held on board for all voyages.

SPA/FITNESS. Facilities include a fitness room, two saunas (on an outdoor pool deck), and hot tubs.

ROTTERDAM
★★★+

DUTCH HERITAGE AND DECOR ABOUND FOR CRUISERS OF AN UPPER-AGE

Size:	Mid-size Ship	Passenger/Crew Ratio (lower beds):	2.2
Tonnage:	59,855	Cabins (total):	702
Cruise Line:	Holland America Line	Size Range (sq ft/m):	184.0–1,124.8/17.1–104.5
Former Names:	none	Cabins (for one person):	0
Builder:	Fincantieri (Italy)	Cabins with balcony:	192
Entered Service:	Dec 1997	Cabins (wheelchair accessible):	25
Length (ft/m):	777.5/237.0	Wheelchair accessibility:	Best
Propulsion/Propellers:	diesel-electric (37,500kW)/2	Elevators:	12
Total Crew:	620	Casino (gaming tables):	Yes
Passengers (lower beds):	1,404	Self-Service Launderette:	Yes
Passenger Space Ratio (lower beds):	42.6	Onboard currency:	US$

THE SHIP. Now 20 years old, *Rotterdam* is the sixth HAL ship to bear the same name. It has a nicely raked bow and a more rounded exterior. Also retained are the familiar interior flow and design style, and twin-funnel.

Promenade Deck and Upper Promenade Deck host most public rooms; these are sandwiched between several accommodation decks. The layout is uncomplicated, and signage is good.

The interior decor is restrained, with much wood accenting, and lots of the traditional ocean liner detailing so loved by HAL's frequent passengers. A three-deck-high oval shaped atrium's focal point is a huge custom-made clock, based on an antique Flemish original that includes an astrolabe, an astrological clock, and 14 other clocks.

One room has a glass ceiling similar to that aboard a former *Statendam*, while the Ambassador's Lounge has an unusual brass dance floor, similar to the dance floor that adorned the Ritz-Carlton room aboard the previous *Rotterdam*.

There are three main stairways – good for safety and accessibility. A pool, on the Lido Deck (between the mast and the ship's twin funnels), is covered by a glass dome.

Popcorn is available at the Wajang Theatre for moviegoers, while adjacent is the popular Java Café. The casino, located in the middle of a major passenger flow, has gaming tables and slot machines.

BERLITZ'S RATINGS		
	Possible	Achieved
Ship	500	374
Accommodation	200	142
Food	400	220
Service	400	268
Entertainment	100	73
Cruise Experience	400	276

OVERALL SCORE 1353 points out of 2000

HAL has a long legacy in Dutch maritime history. The $2 million worth of artwork includes a collection of 17th-century Dutch and Japanese artifacts, plus contemporary works created for the ship.

'Mix' is a pleasant open area with comfortable sofa and armchair seating in a small alcove-like setting adjacent to a shopping area. The trendy space combines three specialty theme bars: Champagne, Martinis, and Spirits & Ales (a sports bar).

With one whole deck of suites – and a dedicated Concierge Lounge – the ship is a two-class environment. Passenger niggles include poor room service and staff communication, and the charge to use the washing machines and dryers in the self-service launderette.

Overall, this fairly contemporary ship has light, bright decor; it is extremely comfortable, with elegant decorative features. But these plus points are marred by poor dining room food and service, and a lack of understanding of what it takes to make the 'luxury' cruise experience touted in the company's brochures.

ACCOMMODATION. There are several categories, priced by grade, size, and location. Note that some cabins have full or partially obstructed views. No cabin is more than 144ft (44m) from a stairway, which makes it easy to get from cabins to public rooms. All cabin doors have a bird's-eye maple look, and hallways have framed fabric panels to make them less clinical.

All standard inside and outside cabins are tastefully furnished, with twin beds that convert to a queen-size one, though space is tight for walking between beds and vanity unit. There is a decent amount of closet and drawer space, but this will prove tight for longer voyages.

The tiled bathrooms are disappointingly small, particularly for long cruises, and have small shower tubs, utilitarian toiletries cupboards, and exposed under-sink plumbing.

Disabled passengers have a choice of 20 cabins, including two of the Penthouse Suites that include concierge services. However, there are different cabin configurations, and it is wise to check with your booking agent.

DINING. The ship's La Fontaine Dining Room seats 747, spans two decks, and has tables for four to eight, but few tables for two. Both open seating and assigned seating are available, while breakfast and lunch are open seating (you'll be taken to your table by restaurant staff as you enter). Fine Rosenthal china and good cutlery are provided (but there are no fish knives).

With a few exceptions, the cuisine is unmemorable, because it's all about mass batch catering. There's a lack of variety of green vegetables, and much use of rice, canned fruit, and already sliced and diced cheese. Still, you get friendly service from Indonesian and Filipino stewards, and the plates are nice.

Pinnacle Grill is an extra-cost (reservations-required) 88-seat restaurant that is more upscale and more intimate than the main dining room. It also features higher-quality ingredients and better presentation than the main dining room. It is on Promenade Deck and fronts onto the second level of the atrium lobby. Pacific Northwest cuisine is featured, including an array of premium-quality steaks. There are good table settings, china, and silverware, and leather-bound menus. The wine list consists mostly of American wines.

For casual meals, the Lido Restaurant is a self-serve buffet venue. A section of this restaurant turns into the Canaletto Restaurant by night, when Italian dishes are featured (reservations are required and a cover charge applies).

Also, a Lido Deck poolside 'Dive-In at the Terrace Grill' features signature burgers, hot dogs, and fries; on certain days, barbeques and other culinary treats may be featured.

ENTERTAINMENT. The 577-seat Showroom at Sea is the venue for production shows, cabaret acts, and other entertainment. It spans two decks, with seating on both levels. The decor includes umbrella-shaped gold ceiling lamps made from Murano glass (from Venice), and the stage has hydraulic lifts and three video screens, as well as a closed-loop system for the hearing-impaired.

SPA/FITNESS. Ocean Spa is one deck above the navigation bridge. It includes a gymnasium with muscle-pumping exercise machines, plus an abundance of treadmills, with forward views over the ship's bows. There's an aerobics exercise area, beauty salon with port-side ocean-views, several treatment rooms, and men's and women's sauna, steam room, and changing areas.

ROYAL CLIPPER
★★★★

THIS FINE SAIL-CRUISE SHIP EXUDES ABUNDANT CHARACTER AND CHARM

Size:	Boutique Ship	Passenger/Crew Ratio (lower beds):	2.1
Tonnage:	5,061	Cabins (total):	114
Cruise Line:	Star Clippers	Size Range (sq ft/m):	100.0–320.0/9.3–29.7
Former Names:	none	Cabins (for one person):	0
Builder:	De Merwede (Holland)	Cabins with balcony:	14
Entered Service:	Oct 2000	Cabins (wheelchair accessible):	0
Length (ft/m):	439.6/134.0	Wheelchair accessibility:	None
Propulsion/Propellers:	diesel (3,700kW)/1	Elevators:	0
Total Crew:	106	Casino (gaming tables):	No
Passengers (lower beds):	228	Self-Service Launderette:	No
Passenger Space Ratio (lower beds):	22.1	Onboard currency:	Euros

THE SHIP. The culmination of an owner's childhood dream, *Royal Clipper* is a stunning sight under sail. It's the world's largest fully rigged sailing ship and has five masts, whereas the company's two other, smaller ships (*Star Clipper* and *Star Flyer*) have just four. The vessel best suits couples and solo travelers who would probably never consider a 'normal' cruise ship, but who enjoy sailing and the thrill of ocean and wind. It's ideal for those who want a package that includes accommodation, food, like-minded companions, and interesting destinations, without the bother of owning or chartering their own yacht. This is the bee's knees.

Royal Clipper's design is based on the only other five-masted sailing ship ever to be built, the 1902-built German tall ship *Preussen*. It has approximately the same dimensions, albeit 46ft (14m) shorter.

The construction time for this ship was remarkably short, because its hull had almost been completed (at Gdansk shipyard, Poland) for another owner, before becoming available to Star Clippers. It is instantly recognizable due to its geometric blue-and-white hull markings. Power winches, as well as hand winches, are employed in deck fittings, as well as a mix of horizontal furling for the square sails and hydraulic power assist to roll the square sails along the yardarm. The sail-handling system, designed by the owner Mikael Krafft, is such that the vessel can

BERLITZ'S RATINGS		
	Possible	Achieved
Ship	500	401
Accommodation	200	138
Food	400	288
Service	400	296
Entertainment	100	80
Cruise Experience	400	309

OVERALL SCORE 1512 points out of 2000

quickly be converted from a full rigger to a schooner.

The masts reach 197ft (60m) above the waterline, and the top 19ft (5.8m) can be hinged over 90 degrees to clear bridges, cable lines, and other port-based obstacles. Watching the sailors manipulate ropes, rigging, and sails is like watching ballet – the precision and cohesion of a group of people, who make it all look so simple.

Passengers may be allowed to climb to special lookout points aloft, and on the bridge at any time – but they cannot go in the galley or engine room.

The ship has a large amount of open deck space and sunning space – something most tall ships lack – although, naturally, this is laid with rigging ropes. An aft marina platform can be lowered, so that passengers can use surfboards, sailing dinghies, take a ride on the banana boat, or go waterskiing or swimming. Snorkeling gear is available free, but there is a charge for scuba gear. You will be asked to sign a waiver if you use the water-sports equipment.

Inside, a small midships atrium, three decks high, sits under one of the ship's three swimming pools, and sunlight streams down through a piano lounge on the uppermost level inside the ship and into the lower level dining room. A forward observation lounge is a real plus – it's connected to the piano lounge via a central corridor. An Edwardian library/card room includes a Belle Epoque fireplace. The Captain Nemo Club lets you observe fish and marine life when the ship is at anchor, through thick glass portholes; it's floodlit from underneath at night to attract the fish.

The ship operates cruises in the Grenadines and Lower Windward Islands of the Caribbean in winter and Mediterranean cruises in summer. Officers navigate using both traditional (sextant) and contemporary methods (advanced electronic positioning system).

This being a tall ship with true sailing traditions, there is, naturally, a parrot (it is sometimes kept in a gilded cage, but it may be seen around the ship on someone's shoulder); it's considered to be part of the crew. The ambience is extremely relaxed, friendly, and unpretentious. The dress code is always casual (shorts and casual tops are the order of the day – yachting wear), with no ties needed ever.

The suites and cabins are, in general, smaller than aboard *Sea Cloud* and *Sea Cloud II*. I do not include the Windstar Cruises ships (*Wind Spirit*, *Wind Star*, *Wind Surf*), because they are not tall ships. *Royal Clipper*, however, is exactly that – a real, working, wind-and-sails-in-your-face tall ship.

This vessel is not suitable for disabled passengers, or for children. The steps of the internal stairs are steep, as in most sailing vessels. Any gratuities you give are pooled and divided among all crew members. What gives the ship a little extra in the scoring department is the fact that many water sports are included in the price.

ACCOMMODATION. There are several accommodation grades, priced according to size, type, and location: Owner's Suites (2), Deluxe Suites (14), and categories 1–6. All have polished wood-trimmed cabinetry and wall-to-wall carpeting, personal safe, full-length mirror, small TV set with audio channels and 24-hour text-based news, and private bathroom. All have twin beds (86 of which convert into a queen-size bed, while 28 are fixed queen-size beds), hairdryer, and satellite-linked telephone. The six interior cabins and a handful of other cabins have a permanently fixed double bed.

Most cabins have a privacy curtain, so that you can't be seen from the hallway when the cabin attendant opens the door – useful if you're undressed. Additionally, 27 cabins can sleep three.

Two Owner's Suites, located aft, provide the most lavish accommodation, and have one queen-size bed and one double bed, a living area with semicircular sofa, vanity desk, mini-bar/refrigerator, marble-clad bathroom with whirlpool bathtub, plus one guest bathroom, and butler service. They have an interconnecting door, so a combined super-suite can sleep eight.

The 'Deck Suites' have interesting names, including Ariel, Cutty Sark, Doriana, Eagle Wing, Flying Cloud, France, Gloria, Golden Gate, Great Republic, Passat, Pommern, Preussen, and Thermopylae.

However, they are not actually suites, as the sleeping area can't be separated from the lounge – they are simply larger cabins with a nicer interior, more storage space, and a larger bathroom. Each has two lower beds convertible to a queen-size one, small lounge area, mini-bar/refrigerator, writing desk, small private balcony, and marble-clad bathroom with combination whirlpool tub/shower, washbasin, and toilet. The door to the balcony can be opened, so that fresh air floods the room; note that there is a 12ins (30cm) threshold to step over. There are no curtains, only roll-down shades for the windows and balcony door. The balcony itself typically has two white chairs and a drinks table. The balconies are not particularly private, and most have ship's tenders or Zodiacs overhanging them, or some rigging obscuring the views.

Two other named cabins (Lord Nelson and Marco Polo) are located aft. Their facilities are similar to those of the Deck Suites, but they lack private balconies.

The interior cabins and the lowest grades of outside-view cabins are extremely small and tight, with little room to move around the beds. So take only the minimum amount of clothing and luggage. When in cabins where beds are linked together to form a double bed, you need to clamber up over the front of the bed, as both sides have built-in storm barriers (this applies in inclement weather conditions only).

There is a small room service menu (all items cost extra).

DINING. The Dining Room is on several connecting levels (getting used to the steps is not easy), and seats all passengers at one seating under a three-deck-high atrium dome. You can sit with whom you wish at tables for four to 10. However, it is noisy, due to the numerous waiter stations. Some tables are badly positioned, so that correct waiter service is impossible; much reaching over has to be done in order to serve everyone.

One corner can be closed off for private parties. Breakfasts and lunches are self-serve buffets, while dinner is a sit-down affair with table service; the ambience is always friendly and lighthearted. The wine list consists of young wines, and prices are high. The cuisine, although perfectly acceptable, is nothing to write home about.

ENTERTAINMENT. There are no shows, nor are any expected by passengers aboard a tall ship such as this, where sailing is the main purpose. There is, however, live music, provided by a single lounge pianist/singer.

SPA/FITNESS. The Royal Spa is located on the lowest passenger deck and, although not large, incorporates a beauty salon, an extra-charge Moroccan steam room, and a small gymnasium.

ROYAL PRINCESS
★★★★

THIS IS A LARGE, FAMILY-FRIENDLY, MULTI-CHOICE CONTEMPORARY RESORT-STYLE SHIP

Size:	Large Resort Ship	Passenger/Crew Ratio (lower beds):	2.6
Tonnage:	142,229	Cabins (total):	1,780
Cruise Line:	Princess Cruises	Size Range (sq ft/m):	161.4–554.3/15–51.5
Former Names:	none	Cabins (for one person):	0
Builder:	Fincantieri (Italy)	Cabins with balcony:	1,438
Entered Service:	Jun 2013	Cabins (wheelchair accessible):	36
Length (ft/m):	1,082.6/330.0	Wheelchair accessibility:	Best
Propulsion/Propellers:	diesel-electric (52,000kW)/2	Elevators:	14
Total Crew:	1,346	Casino (gaming tables):	Yes
Passengers (lower beds):	3,560	Self-Service Launderette:	Yes
Passenger Space Ratio (lower beds):	39.9	Onboard currency:	US$

THE SHIP. *Royal Princess* has an almost streamlined look. Sadly, there is no complete walk-around promenade deck. An aft-deck swimming pool was added in a retro-fit. Although this reduced some open deck space, it is much-appreciated. Lifeboats are located outside the main public room areas, so they don't impair the view from balcony cabins.

Two 'over-the-water' SeaWalks, top-deck glass-floor enclosed walkways on both sides, extend almost 30ft (9.1m) beyond the edge. Go there for dramatic views of the sea – some 128ft (39m) below.

For real escapees, an extra-cost, adults-only retreat (The Sanctuary) is larger than aboard the Grand-class ships and has more amenities. It includes four rentable cabanas and two extra-cost Lotus Spa-operated 'couples' cabanas, and has its own retreat pool and relaxation areas (in both sunny and shaded positions). The adjacent Retreat area has grown in size, and so other passengers have less open deck space.

The Piazza Atrium is the multi-faceted social hub, and combines specialty eateries, for light meals, snacks, pastries, beverages, entertainment, shopping, and passenger services all in one area, with multi-level horseshoe-shaped stairways, mood lighting, and a small dance floor.

The atrium's base level includes an International Café, for coffees, teas, panini, and pastries; Sabatini's

BERLITZ'S RATINGS		
	Possible	Achieved
Ship	500	393
Accommodation	200	139
Food	400	268
Service	400	293
Entertainment	100	82
Cruise Experience	400	295

OVERALL SCORE 1470 points out of 2000

(adjacent to the atrium), a Tuscan specialty extra-cost restaurant, has both regular and à la carte menus; and a gift shop. Upstairs, level two includes Alfredo's Pizzeria (pizzas are free), Bellini's (featuring Bellini drinks), a photo gallery, and the reception and shore-excursion counters. On the third level is Crooners Bar, with solo pianist entertainers, and a small Seafood Bar.

One design fault is the complete lack of a central stairway above the two main restaurants (between decks 7 and 16 – a design fault because stairs are only at the forward and aft elevator banks); this leads to severe crowding of the forward and aft elevators, and the Berlitz Rating score reflects this omission.

Passenger niggles include the user-unfriendly automated telephone system, the small cabin towels, the extra cost for items such as ice cream, and the (coins-needed) charge for the washers and dryers in self-service launderettes.

Overall, however, Princess Cruises delivers a consistently fine, comfortable, well-packaged product, always with a good degree of style, at a competitive price, so passengers keep returning.

ACCOMMODATION. There are five main types of accommodation and a bewildering number of different price grades: (a) Grand Suites; (b) suites with balcony; (c) mini-suites with balcony; (d) deluxe outside-view balcony cabins; (e) outside-view cabins with balcony; and (f) interior (no-view) cabins. Pricing depends on two things: size and location. Outside-view cabins account for about 81 percent of all accommodation, and have a balcony; those located aft are the quietest. Some 68 cabins have lifeboat-obstructed views, and many cabins on Deck 8 above the show-lounge are subject to noise pollution from the shows until late in the evening.

All grades have energy-efficient lighting and key card readers that automatically turn off lights when occupants leave. All cabins have beds, upholstered headboards, wall-mounted TV sets, 220v electrical sockets, turndown service and heart-shaped chocolates on pillows nightly, bathrobes (on request unless you are in suite-grade accommodation), and toiletries. A hairdryer is sensibly located at the vanity desk unit in the living area. Bathrooms generally have a good amount of open shelf storage space for toiletries.

Suite- and mini-suite-grade occupants have access to their own Concierge Lounge, more amenities, larger TV sets, larger towels, and two washbasins.

Some of the most sought-after suites are located aft, occupying the corner (port and starboard) positions. Be aware that the balconies of cabins on Marina Deck 15 can be seen by anyone on the overhanging Skywalk on the deck above (so pick your cabin wisely).

DINING. There are three 'formal' main dining rooms: Allegro, Concerto, and Symphony. Choose either traditional two-seating dining (typically 6pm and 8.15pm for dinner), or 'anytime dining' – where you choose when and with whom you want to eat. However, if you want to see an evening show, your dining time will be dictated by the time of the show, limiting your choice.

A 12-seat circular table is located within the Wine Cellar of the Allegro and Symphony dining rooms. This extra-cost, reservations-required venue is for private functions. Also available is a private Chef's Table Lumière; it's within the Concerto dining room, and has a custom-made glass dining table and fine-dining utensils.

Although portions are generous, the food and its presentation are standardized and non-memorable. Fish is often disguised by a crumb or batter coating, the choice of fresh green vegetables is limited, few garnishes are used, and cheese is already sliced and diced. This is big-ship banquet catering, with 'batch' cooking. Pasta dishes are acceptable (though voluminous), typically served by section headwaiters. If you like desserts, order a sundae at dinner (most other items are just so-so).

Extra-cost, reservations-required Sabatini's just off the lower atrium level, has Italian-style food and

Tuscan decor; it is named after Trattoria Sabatini, the historic institution in Florence. This venue also hosts Italian wine tasting.

Alfredo's is a sit-down pizzeria named after Alfredo Marzi, corporate chef for Princess Cruises; the venue specializes in 'authentic,' family-friendly-size pizzas.

Ocean Terrace, located on the upper level of the atrium lobby, is a seafood bar. International Café, on the lowest level of the Piazza Atrium, is the place for extra-cost coffees, pastries, paninis, and more.

Vines Wine Bar is close to Sabatini's and provides an escape from the noise and hubbub – for a glass of extra-cost wine and tapas. It's a pleasant area in which to while away a late afternoon, trying out new wines.

Crown Grill is an extra-cost, reservations-required venue, serving premium-quality steaks and grilled seafood, and is adjacent to the Wheelhouse Bar, which can be noisy at times.

For casual meals, the self-serve buffet Horizon Court (it seats 900 indoors and 350 outdoors) has multiple 'active' cooking stations, but few beverage stations. Sections highlight specific themes, such as Mediterranean, Asian, and Italian cuisine, plus a deli section. At night, the aft section becomes the Horizon Bistro, for casual dinners. Some evenings feature themes, such as British pub food or as a Brazilian churrascaria (for carved meat dishes). A hibachi grill and other active cooking stations (for regional specialties) are part of the scenario. It's a flexible large-scale eatery – but useful as a change to the main dining rooms. Additionally, Horizon Court has its own bakery.

Outside, the poolside Trident Grill (for burgers, hot dogs, and other fast-food grilled items during the day) becomes a smokehouse barbeque in the evenings. Meanwhile, Mexican-style eats can be obtained from the Outrigger Bar.

ENTERTAINMENT. The 1,000-seat Princess Theater is the showlounge. Two decks high, it is designed for the large-scale production shows, and has good views from all seats – no pillars to spoil the view – an outstanding achievement in such a large room.

SPA/FITNESS. The large Lotus Spa is forward of the atrium's lower level, so it doesn't take away premium outdoor-view real estate space. Separate facilities for men and women include a sauna, steam room, and changing rooms; common facilities include a relaxation/waiting zone and body-pampering treatment rooms. A gymnasium packed with high-tech equipment is located aft on a higher deck.

RUBY PRINCESS
★★★+

THIS FAMILY-FRIENDLY RESORT SHIP HAS PLEASANT DECOR AND DINING OPTIONS

Size:	Large Resort Ship	Passenger/Crew Ratio (lower beds):	2.5
Tonnage:	113,561	Cabins (total):	1,557
Cruise Line:	Princess Cruises	Size Range (sq ft/m):	163–1,279/15.1–118.8
Former Names:	none	Cabins (for one person):	0
Builder:	Fincantieri (Italy)	Cabins with balcony:	881
Entered Service:	Sep 2008	Cabins (wheelchair accessible):	25
Length (ft/m):	951.4/290.0	Wheelchair accessibility:	Good
Propulsion/Propellers:	diesel-electric (42,000kW)/2	Elevators:	14
Total Crew:	1,200	Casino (gaming tables):	Yes
Passengers (lower beds):	3,114	Self-Service Launderette:	Yes
Passenger Space Ratio (lower beds):	36.4	Onboard currency:	US$

THE SHIP. *Ruby Princess* has the same profile, interior layout, and public rooms as sister ships *Crown Princess* (2006) and *Emerald Princess* (2007). The ship accommodates over 500 more passengers than earlier half-sisters (such as *Diamond Princess*), but with the same outdoor deck space and number of elevators.

The Sanctuary, an extra-cost adults-only retreat, is worth paying extra for in warm-weather areas. Forward on the uppermost deck, it is a 'private' place to relax and unwind.

There's a good sheltered faux wood promenade strolling deck – it's actually painted steel – which almost wraps around the front and aft of the ship; three times round is equal to 1 mile (1.6km). Movies Under the Skies and major sporting events are shown on a 300-sq-ft (28-sq-m) screen located at the pool forward of the large funnel structure.

The main public bars and lounges are located off a double-width promenade deck. The main lobby is the focal meeting point. Called The Plaza, it's like a town square, and includes an International Café (patisserie/deli with cakes and pastries), and Vines, a combination wine/cheese and sushi/tapas counter.

A library is in the corner adjacent to the wood-paneled Wheelhouse Bar. There are several bars and lounges to enjoy, including Crooners, an intimate New York-style piano bar, with around 70 seats on the upper level of the lobby, but perhaps the nicest is Adagio's.

BERLITZ'S RATINGS

	Possible	Achieved
Ship	500	348
Accommodation	200	122
Food	400	247
Service	400	282
Entertainment	100	74
Cruise Experience	400	268

OVERALL SCORE 1341 points out of 2000

The casino, Gatsby's, has over 260 slot machines and tables for gamers.

Passenger niggles include the user-unfriendly automated telephone system, the small cabin towels, the extra cost for items such as ice cream, and the (coins-needed) charge for the washers and dryers in self-service launderettes.

Overall, however, Princess Cruises delivers a consistently fine, comfortable, well-packaged product, always with a good degree of style, at a competitive price.

ACCOMMODATION. There are six types of cabins and configurations: (a) Grand Suite, (b) suite, (c) mini-suite, (d) outside-view double cabins with balcony, (e) outside-view double cabins, and (f) interior (no-view) double cabins. These come in a multitude of different brochure price categories, depending on size and location. Two family suites have an interconnecting door, plus a large balcony; these can sleep up to 10, if at least four are children, or up to eight adults.

By comparison, the largest suite is slightly smaller, and the smallest interior cabin is slightly larger than the equivalent suites/cabins aboard *Golden*, *Grand*, and *Star Princess*. Almost all balcony suites and cabins can be overlooked both from the navigation bridge wing, and from the port and starboard sections of Skywalkers, high and aft. Suites C401, 402, 404, 406, 408, 410, 412, 401, 405, 411, 415, and

417 on Riviera Deck 14, and D105 and D106 (Dolphin Deck 9) have only semi-private balconies that can be seen from above, so there is little privacy. Also, most outside-view cabins on Emerald Deck have views obstructed by lifeboats.

Some cabins can accommodate a third and fourth person in upper berths, but, in these, the lower beds can't be pushed together to make a queen-size bed.

Cabin bath towels are small, and drawer space is tight. Suite occupants get better service, personal amenities, and other perks.

The largest accommodation is a Grand Suite (A750); it is located aft. It has a large bedroom with queen-size bed, huge walk-in closets, two bathrooms, a lounge with fireplace, sofa bed, wet bar, refrigerator, and a large private balcony on the port side, with a hot tub accessible from both balcony and bedroom.

Wheelchair-accessible cabins measure 250–385 sq ft (23–35.8 sq m), but there's no mirror for dressing, and no full-length hanging space.

DINING. There are several dining options, including three main dining rooms, plus a Crown Grill and SHARE by Curtis Stone.

The three dining rooms are Botticelli, Da Vinci, and Michelangelo. Botticelli Dining Room has traditional two-seating dining for dinner, while 'Anytime Dining' – where you choose when and with whom you want to eat – is offered in Da Vinci and Michelangelo. Each is split into various sections in a non-symmetrical design that presents smaller sections, and each has its own galley.

Portions are generous, but the food and its presentation are standardized. Fish is often disguised by a crumb or batter coating, but green vegetable choice is limited; few garnishes are used; and cheese

is already sliced and diced. This is big-ship banquet catering (think batch cooking). Pasta dishes are acceptable (though large), served by section headwaiters, who may also make 'something special just for you' – in search of gratuities.

The extra-cost SHARE by Curtis Stone and Crown Grill both require reservations. The former is located on a high deck aft of the funnel, and features a degustation menu. The latter is a 138-seat restaurant serving premium steaks, chops, and grilled seafood items (everything is cooked to order); it is located off the main indoor Deck 7 promenade. Seating is mainly in semi-private alcoves, and there's a show kitchen, so you can watch the action.

Horizon Court has indoor-outdoor seating, is open almost 24 hours a day for casual meals (on plastic plates), and has ocean-view windows on two sides.

Other casual eateries include a poolside burger grill and pizza bar.

There's also the International Café, on Deck 5 in The Plaza – for coffees and pastries, light lunches, and yummy afternoon cakes, most at no extra cost.

ENTERTAINMENT. The Princess Theater spans two decks and has comfortable seating on both levels. A live orchestra backs the colorful production shows and major cabaret acts. The ship has a resident troupe of singers and dancers, plus an army of audio-visual support staff.

SPA/FITNESS. The Lotus Spa is located forward on Sun Deck. Separate facilities for men and women include a sauna, steam room, and changing rooms; common facilities include a relaxation/waiting zone, body-pampering treatment rooms, and a gymnasium with muscle-pumping equipment and great ocean views. Some fitness classes are free.

SAGA SAPPHIRE
★★★+

A SMALL, ELEGANT SHIP FOR BRITISH CRUISERS OF A CERTAIN AGE

Size:	Small Ship	Passenger/Crew Ratio (lower beds):	1.7
Tonnage:	37,301	Cabins (total):	374
Cruise Line:	Saga Cruises	Size Range (sq ft/m):	161.4–678.1/15.0–63.0
Former Names:	Bleu de France, Holiday Dream,	Cabins (for one person):	56
	SuperStar Aries, SuperStar Europe, Europa	Cabins with balcony:	19
Builder:	Bremer Vulkan (Germany)	Cabins (wheelchair accessible):	2
Entered Service:	Jan 1982/Mar 2012	Wheelchair accessibility:	Good
Length (ft/m):	654.9/199.6	Elevators:	4
Propulsion/Propellers:	diesel (21,270kW)/2	Casino (gaming tables):	No
Total Crew:	415	Self-Service Launderette:	Yes
Passengers (lower beds):	706	Onboard currency:	UK£
Passenger Space Ratio (lower beds):	49.6		

THE SHIP. *Saga Sapphire* was originally built as the fifth incarnation of *Europa* for Hapag-Lloyd Cruises, and was for many years the pride of the German cruise industry. It was originally to have twin side-by-side funnels, but the idea was dropped in favor of a single funnel. The ship is in good shape, despite the fact that it is now over 35 years old. Saga Cruises tailored the ship to British tastes when it took delivery in April 2012.

BERLITZ'S RATINGS		
	Possible	Achieved
Ship	500	366
Accommodation	200	141
Food	400	259
Service	400	278
Entertainment	100	64
Cruise Experience	400	266

OVERALL SCORE 1374 points out of 2000

It has a deep blue hull and white upper structure, and a sponson stern – a kind of 'skirt' added in order to comply with the latest stability regulations. But it still maintains its moderately handsome, balanced profile. There is an excellent amount of open outdoor deck space. The ship has both outdoor and outdoor/indoor pools. While there is no walk-around outdoors promenade deck, there are half-length teak port and starboard promenades.

The interior focal point is a three-deck high lobby, with a 'floating' fish sculpture. (I counted over 1,000 of them, including one red herring!) There is a good range of public rooms, most with high ceilings, and wide interior stairways create a feeling of spaciousness on a grand scale. Subtle, hidden lighting is used throughout, particularly on the stairways. Public rooms are positioned aft in a 'cake-layer' stacking, with accommodation located forward.

Facilities include a delightful observation lounge (The Drawing Room), and an integral, extensive library plus Internet-connected computer stations (iPads can also be provided); light entertainment is presented here in the evenings, and excellent Lavazza coffees are available, with delightful cakes in mid-morning (free). Quirky table lamps are made from old clarinets and fishing rods.

For a enjoyable hideaway, head to Cooper's, named after the British comedian and magician Tommy Cooper. There are numerous black-and-white photos on the wall of some of the UK's best-known comedians of yesteryear and today, including Spike 'Milligna' – the well-known typing error. The table lamps are topped by Tommy Cooper's trademark fez. Then there's Aviators – a cute little pre-dining room bar with Spitfire aircraft model (from World War II), with, of course, Spitfire draft beer.

The ship, with its amusing and quirky artwork, provides an informal, relaxed, yet elegant setting, and many public rooms have a high ceiling. Saga Cruises includes many things other UK-based operators charge extra for – that's why its cruises may appear to cost more – such as private car transfers to the ship (check brochure for details), all gratuities, shuttle buses in ports of call where possible, and newspapers in the library in each port of call, when available. Saga also provides excellent user-friendly port and shore-excursion information booklets.

Saga Sapphire is best suited to couples and solo travelers, almost all of whom tend to be British, seeking a holiday afloat in spacious, classy surroundings. It provides decent accommodation, good food, and friendly service, plus interesting itineraries and destinations. Passengers must be over 50, but spouses and partners can be as young as 45. Note that Saga Sapphire will leave the fleet in August 2020 when Spirit of Adventure debuts.

ACCOMMODATION. There is a wide range of suites and cabins (including many for solo travelers), in a multitude of price grades. All of the original cabins are quite spacious, and have illuminated closets, dark wood cabinetry with rounded edges, full-length mirrors, mini-bar/refrigerator, personal safe, hairdryer, and good cabin insulation. Some suites/cabins have table lamps made from old cameras such as the Kodak Brownie and similar 'box' cameras - delightfully quirky!

Most bathrooms (163 to be precise) have deep tubs (cabins without a bathtub have large shower enclosures), two deep washbasins (not all cabins), toiletries cabinet, and handsome toiletries - Citrus, created exclusively for Saga Cruises by Clarity, an organization that provides employment for blind persons.

Even the standard, lower-priced cabins are very comfortable, the ship having been designed for long voyages.

DINING. Pole to Pole, the main restaurant, seats 620 and has ocean-view windows on two sides, yet still manages to have a clubby feel thanks to different areas styled to the theme of four continents: Africa, the Americas, Asia, and Europe. Both self-serve buffet and full-service meals are provided. There is open seating, so you can dine wherever you choose. For dinner, a number of tables can be reserved for fixed dining times when you book.

The Grill and Verandah, an indoor/outdoor venue, provides lighter, healthier grilled meals, with food cooked to order in a show kitchen. It's open for breakfast, lunch, and relaxed dinner. The 'spider's web' alcove seating partitions are novel - I haven't found any big spiders yet! One neat feature is a slicing machine to produce cold cuts of meat, so you know it's fresh.

Asian-fusion cuisine (Indian, Sri Lankan, and Thai) is featured in the intimate 64-seat East to West restaurant; the decor includes traditional wood carvings, reflecting the mood of the East. Adjacent is The Grill - for steaks and seafood, in a room with an open kitchen.

The Beach, adjacent to the indoor/outdoor pool, provides fish and chips and other light British fare, traditional desserts, and ice cream (the machine is inside a blue-and-white-striped beach hut, and there are jars of boiled sweets in a second beach hut - all very British and a throwback to yesteryear).

ENTERTAINMENT. The Britannia Lounge is for major social events and shows. The sight lines are mostly good, although some thin pillars present problems from some seats - the room was originally built more for use as a single-level concert salon than a room for shows - but the setting is elegant. The productions are performed by a small troupe of dancers, plus cabaret acts. There is live music for listening or dancing to in various bars and lounges. Male dance hosts are aboard for the many solo women passengers.

SPA/FITNESS. An area of about 8,611 sq ft (800 sq m) is host to a rather homey indoor wellness center. It includes an indoor swimming pool (few ships have them today). Adjacent facilities include a sauna and steam room, a fitness/exercise area, several treatment rooms, and a beauty salon. Sporting facilities include St. Andrews, a crazy-golf course located outdoors.

SAPPHIRE PRINCESS
★★★+

THIS IS A MULTI-CHOICE LARGE SHIP FOR INFORMAL FAMILY-FRIENDLY CRUISING

Size:	Large Resort Ship	Passenger/Crew Ratio (lower beds):	2.1
Tonnage:	115,875	Cabins (total):	1,337
Cruise Line:	Princess Cruises	Size Range (sq ft/m):	168–1,329.3/15.6–123.5
Former Names:	none	Cabins (for one person):	0
Builder:	Mitsubishi Heavy Industries (Japan)	Cabins with balcony:	750
Entered Service:	May 2004	Cabins (wheelchair accessible):	28
Length (ft/m):	951.4/290.0	Wheelchair accessibility:	Good
Propulsion/Propellers:	diesel-electric (42,000kW)/2	Elevators:	14
Total Crew:	1,238	Casino (gaming tables):	Yes
Passengers (lower beds):	2,674	Self-Service Launderette:	Yes
Passenger Space Ratio (lower beds):	43.3	Onboard currency:	US$

THE SHIP. *Sapphire Princess* is quite a grand playground in which to roam and play when you're not ashore. Princess Cruises delivers a fine, well-packaged holiday product, with some sense of style, at an attractive, highly competitive price, and this ship will appeal to those who really enjoy big-city life with all the trimmings.

The ship has an instantly recognizable funnel due to two jet engine-like pods that sit high up on its structure, but really they are mainly for decoration.

Several areas focus on swimming pools. One has a large poolside movie screen, one is two decks high and is covered by a retractable glass dome, itself an extension of the funnel housing, and one pool lies within The Sanctuary – an adults-only, extra-cost relaxation area.

The interiors were overseen and outfitted by the Okura Group, whose Okura Hotel is one of Tokyo's best. Fit and finish quality is superior to that of the Italian-built *Golden Princess*, *Grand Princess*, and *Star Princess*. Unlike the outside decks, there is plenty of space inside the ship – but there are also plenty of passengers – and a wide array of public rooms, with many 'intimate' (this being a relative term) spaces and places to enjoy. The passenger flow is good, and there's little congestion.

The interior focal point is a piazza-style atrium lobby, with Vines (wine bar), an International Café (for cost-extra coffee, pastries, panini, etc.), library/

BERLITZ'S RATINGS		
	Possible	Achieved
Ship	500	348
Accommodation	200	139
Food	400	247
Service	400	289
Entertainment	100	76
Cruise Experience	400	282

OVERALL SCORE 1381 points out of 2000

Internet-connect center, and Alfredo's sit-down pizzeria.

A Wedding Chapel has a live web-cam to relay ceremonies via the Internet. The ship's captain can legally marry American couples, due to the ship's Bermuda registry and a dispensation that should be verified in advance according to where you reside. Princess Cruises offers three wedding packages – Pearl, Emerald, and Diamond.

The Grand Casino has gaming tables and over 260 slot machines (some are linked and may provide a combined payout). The wood-paneled Wheelhouse Bar is finely decorated with memorabilia and ship models tracing part of the history of sister company P&O. The Wake View Bar has a spiral stairway leading down to a great viewing spot for watching the ship's wake.

The ship is full of revenue centers. Expect to be subjected to flyers advertising daily art auctions, designer watches, and the like.

The dress code is formal or smart casual – interpreted by many as jeans and trainers. Gratuities to staff are auto-added to your account, with gratuities for children charged at the same rate (these charges can be adjusted at the reception desk).

Lines form for many things aboard large ships, but particularly so for the information office, and for open-seating breakfast and lunch in the four main dining rooms. Long lines for shore excursions and shore tenders are also a fact of life, as is waiting for elevators at peak times, and embarkation and dis-embarkation.

The many extra-charge items include ice cream and freshly squeezed orange juice (and most exercise classes cost extra). There's an hourly rate for group babysitting services, and a charge for using washers and dryers in the self-service launderettes.

ACCOMMODATION. Everyone receives turndown service and nightly chocolates on pillows, bathrobes on request, and toiletries. A hairdryer is provided in all cabins. All bathrooms are tiled and have a decent amount of open shelf storage space for toiletries.

Most outside cabins on Emerald Deck have views obstructed by the lifeboats. Your name is typically placed outside your suite or cabin – handy for delivery service personnel but eroding your privacy. Most balcony suites and cabins can be overlooked from the navigation bridge wing. There is 24-hour room service, though some menu items aren't available during early morning hours.

Cabin bath towels are small, and drawer space is limited. There are no butlers, even for the top-grade suites – which aren't really large in comparison to similar suites aboard some other ships.

DINING. All dining rooms are located on one of two decks in the ship's center. There are five dining rooms with themed decor and cuisine: Sterling Steakhouse for steak and grilled meats; Vivaldi for Italian fare; Santa Fe for cuisine from the US Southwest; Pacific Moon for Asian cuisine; and International, the largest, located aft, with two seatings and 'traditional' cuisine. These offer a mix of two seatings and 'Anytime Dining,' where you choose when and with whom you want to eat. All dining rooms are split into sections in a non-symmetrical design that breaks what are quite large spaces into many smaller sections, for better ambience and less noise pollution.

Specially designed dinnerware and good-quality linens and silverware are used. Note that 15 percent is added to all beverage bills, including wines.

Although portions are generous, the food and its presentation are quite standardized. Fish is often disguised by coatings, the choice of fresh green vegetables is limited, few garnishes are used, and cheese is already sliced and diced. But, this is big-ship banquet catering, with all its attendant standardization and batch cooking. Pasta dishes are decent, but large, typically served by section headwaiters, who may make 'something special just for you' – in search of favorable comments and gratuities. If you like desserts, order a sundae at dinner (most other items are just so-so).

Sabatini's is an informal Italian-style eatery (reservations required and a cover charge applies). The cuisine is prepared with good-quality ingredients and attention to presentation and taste.

A poolside hamburger grill and a pizza bar (no additional charge) are additional casual eateries. Other casual eats can be taken in the Horizon Court, open almost 24 hours a day, with ocean views on two sides.

ENTERTAINMENT. The Princess Theater spans two decks and has comfortable seating on both levels.

Princess Cruises has glamorous, colourful, all-American production shows and a live showband.

A second entertainment lounge, Club Fusion, hosts cabaret acts at night, and lectures, bingo, and horse racing during the day. Most lounges have live music, and a number of male dance hosts act as partners for women traveling alone. Skywalkers is the late-night spot, just aft of the funnel.

SPA/FITNESS. The Lotus Spa (forward on Sun Deck) has separate facilities for men and women, including sauna, steam room, and changing rooms; common facilities include a relaxation/waiting zone, body-pampering rooms, a gymnasium with muscle-pumping equipment, and great views. Some fitness classes are free but most cost extra.

SCARLET LADY
NYR

THIS LARGE RESORT SHIP IS A FLOATING ADULT PLAYGROUND WITH EDGY FOOD AND ENTERTAINMENT GALORE

Size:	Mid-size ship	Passenger/Crew Ratio (lower beds):	2.4
Tonnage:	110,000	Cabins (total):	1,430
Cruise Line:	Virgin Voyages	Size Range (sq ft/m):	355.2–2,152.8/33.0–200.0
Former Names:	none	Cabins (for one person):	0
Builder:	Fincantieri (Italy)	Cabins with balcony:	0
Entered Service:	Jan 2020	Cabins (wheelchair accessible):	n/a
Length (ft/m):	912.0/278.0	Wheelchair accessibility:	Best
Propulsion/Propellers: diesel-electric/2 azimuthing		Elevators:	n/a
	pods	Casino (gaming tables):	Yes
Total Crew:	1,150	Self-Service Launderette:	No
Passengers (lower beds):	2,860	Onboard currency:	US$
Passenger Space Ratio (lower beds):	38.4		

THE SHIP. *Scarlet Lady* is the first of four large resort ships for Virgin Voyages, with a swanky, stream-lined look (reminiscent of Japanese Shinkansen 'bullet' trains), not-exactly handsome rounded bows, and a red Virgin mermaid logo on the hull. The exterior includes a chic promenade, similar in design to that of *MSC Seaside*. Zero vibration 'pod' propulsion is provided for comfort. However, the ship lacks a long, resort-style swimming pool.

The ship has lots of bling for urban adults with a focus on 'young-at-heart' travelers (minimum age 18), particularly millennials – all called 'sailors'.

Virgin Voyages promised it would be radically different from anything else – but in fact, the interior layout is similar to other large resort ships, but with re-imagined spaces that have an ultra-contemporary, edgy feel (you'll need to like the Virgin scarlet color). The interior design centers on seven neighborhoods, and, naturally, everything is utterly casual. Tattoos are available in the Squid Ink tattoo parlor (the ink is actually vegan, despite the name), as well as body piercing. One thing that really is different is a record store, selling vinyl records of all genres and associated sounds.

ACCOMMODATION. There are numerous accommodation price grades. The price depends on size, location, and grade; about 86 percent have balconies ('sea terraces,' in Virgin-speak). From the smallest interior

BERLITZ'S RATINGS

	Possible	Achieved
Ship	500	NYR
Accommodation	200	NYR
Food	400	NYR
Service	400	NYR
Entertainment	100	NYR
Cruise Experience	400	NYR

OVERALL SCORE NYR points out of 2000

(no-view) cabin to the largest suite, all are designed with young adults in mind, although the white-plank ceilings are boringly plain. Most balcony cabins have one hammock (cozy).

The suites have neat names like Fab Suite, Posh Suite, Gorgeous Suite, Rebellious Suite, Rock Star Suite, and Massive Suite. Occupants have access to a private lounge (like Celebrity's X Lounge). The most outrageous are two 'Massive Suites' above the navigation bridge, each with a second bedroom that includes guitars and amplifiers. Occupants have access to 'Richard's Rooftop' (private enclave 'club').

Natural filtered water stations are scattered throughout each accommodation deck (also free in any bar).

Overall, this floating adult playground should provide you with a very entertaining relief from life on land, with edgy food and entertainment thrown in. Finally, if you want to get to the ship in style, private jet transport can be yours – at a price, of course.

DINING. There are around 20 restaurants and eateries – all included in the cruise price (which does make it different to other large resort ships). There is no assigned dining or seating (think: free-for-all), and no fine dining – only urban food, including vegetarian and vegan eats.

There are bars and drinks everywhere, and cocktail commandos to mix a 'dizzle' or two for you. Indeed, the whole ship invites you to consume alcohol – and lots of it.

Notable venues: The aft-located Wake is the most glam venue, based on London's classic The Wolseley (which is nothing special), for steaks and seafood; it has an elegant staircase, and aft views.

Then there's Pink Agave (for Mexican shared-plate fare); Extra Virgin (for Italian food); Razzle Dazzle (take sunglasses) for some vegetarian-style eats; and The Dock – for small-plate eats by day, and skewers of flamed meat at night.

The closest thing to a buffet is the food court-like The Galley, with eight 'stores' and food carts for grab 'n' munch fare. Elsewhere, there's a pizzeria with individual orders (no pre-cooked slices); Geonbae, a Korean-style barbeque featuring soju drinking games at each table; and a diner-style Test Kitchen with fun, ingredient-based cooking-stations.

ENTERTAINMENT. The bi-level Manor Ballroom is for dancing, socializing, and cabaret, while there are drag shows in various locations (including eateries). Think edgy, upbeat (loud), razzle-dazzle shows for adults.

SPA/FITNESS. Redemption Spa is designed like an underwater cave, and includes mud and salt rooms, a hydrotherapy pool, cold pool, thermal suite, and body treatment rooms, but at night it turns into a dancing area (just don't fall into the hot tubs).

The Athletics Club includes a boxing ring, strength-training and gym equipment, and, of course, a scarlet jogging track. One neat item is the fishing net-like lounge area, not to mention a rather neat bar for a gym and tonic.

SCENIC ECLIPSE
NYR

THIS SHIP IS DESIGNED SPECIFICALLY FOR IN-DEPTH 'SOFT' EXPEDITION ADVENTURES

Size:	Boutique Ship	Passenger/Crew Ratio (lower beds):	1.2/1
Tonnage:	22,498	Cabins (total):	114
Cruise Line:	Scenic	Size Range (sq ft/m):	344.4-2,099.0/32.0-195.0
Former Names:	none	Cabins (for one person):	0
Builder:	Uljanik Group (Croatia)	Cabins with balcony:	114
Entered Service:	Aug 2019	Cabins (wheelchair accessible):	0
Length (ft/m):	551.1/168.0	Wheelchair accessibility:	Fair
Propulsion/Propellers:	diesel-electric/2 azimuthing pods	Elevators:	1
		Casino (gaming tables):	No
Total Crew:	176	Self-Service Launderette:	Yes
Passengers (lower beds):	228	Onboard currency:	Euros
Passenger Space Ratio (lower beds):	72.3		

THE SHIP. This ultra-smart-looking specialist expedition ship – designed from the ground up to operate in the Polar regions – and marketed by Scenic as 'the world's first discovery yacht' – is powered by Azipods, marine propulsion units that provide operational flexibility.

The ship carries a 6-person submarine, ROV submersible (remotely operated vehicle with camera), and a 6-seat helicopter. It also has a fleet of 12 rigid inflatable Zodiacs, plus kayaks, jet-skis, e-bikes, plus snow-shoeing, scuba-diving and snorkeling equipment. The six-passenger U-Boat Worx Cruise Submarine has a pressurized cabin and can dive to a depth of 100ft (30m); two passenger pods have seats than can swivel 180 degrees. Two Airbus H130 helicopters (one of the most environmentally sound) can carry the pilot and up to six passengers, and have excellent visibility and five cameras (mounted inside and outside) to record each flight.

Public rooms include an observation lounge, library, and lecture theater.

ACCOMMODATION. There are numerous accommodation price grades, but all are designated as

BERLITZ'S RATINGS		
	Possible	Achieved
Ship	500	NYR
Accommodation	200	NYR
Food	400	NYR
Service	400	NYR
Entertainment	100	NYR
Cruise Experience	400	NYR

OVERALL SCORE NYR points out of 2000

suites (all with butler service). The price you pay depends on the size, location, and grade you choose. From the largest owner's suite to the smallest suite, they all feature contemporary design and fittings. However, for expedition-style cruises, you won't be in your cabin much, because of the destination-immersive nature of the voyages.

DINING. There are several dining options (all at no extra cost), which include Elements (main dining room); Lumiere (for French cuisine), an Italian/Steak restaurant; Koko's (an Asian-fusion cuisine venue including an 8–10 seat sushi bar), and a Teppanyaki grill. Also, there's a Yacht Club self-serve buffet and grill. Epicure is a fully equipped culinary studio for cost-extra Epicure cooking classes.

ENTERTAINMENT. The Theatre is the venue for expedition lectures, and even small revue shows.

SPA/FITNESS. Spa Sanctuary has wellness facilities, a gym, exercise studio for yoga and Pilates, and indoor and outdoor pools.

SEA CLOUD
★★★★★

THIS IS QUITE SIMPLY THE MOST BEAUTIFUL SAIL-CRUISE SHIP IN THE WORLD

Size:	Boutique Ship	
Tonnage:	2,532	
Cruise Line:	Sea Cloud Cruises	
Former Names:	Sea Cloud of Grand Cayman, IX-99,	
	Antama, Patria, Angelita, Sea Cloud, Hussar	
Builder:	Krupp Werft (Germany)	
Entered Service:	1931/1979	
Length (ft/m):	359.2/109.5	
Propulsion/Propellers:	sail power + diesel	
	(4,476kW)/2	
Total Crew:	60	
Passengers (lower beds):	64	
Passenger Space Ratio (lower beds):	39.5	
Passenger/Crew Ratio (lower beds):	1.1	
Cabins (total):	32	
Size Range (sq ft/m):	102.2–409.0/9.5–38.0	
Cabins (for one person):	0	
Cabins with balcony:	0	
Cabins (wheelchair accessible):	0	
Wheelchair accessibility:	None	
Elevators:	0	
Casino (gaming tables):	No	
Self-Service Launderette:	No	
Onboard currency:	Euros	

THE SHIP. *Sea Cloud* is a completely authentic 1930s barque whose 85th birthday was in 2016. It is the largest private yacht ever built – three times the size of Captain Cook's *Endeavour* – and a stunningly beautiful ship when under sail in both the Caribbean and European/Mediterranean waters. Its four masts are almost as high as a 20-story building, the main one being 178ft (54m) above the Main Deck, and, with its full complement of 30 sails (measuring some 32,292 sq ft (3,000 sq m) billowing in the wind, it really is a sight to behold.

This was the largest private yacht ever built when completed in 1931 by Edward F. Hutton for his wife, Marjorie Merriweather Post, the American cereal heiress. Originally constructed for $1 million as *Hussar* in the Germany's Krupp shipyard in Kiel, the steel-hulled vessel saw action during World War II as a weather-observation ship, under the code name IX-99.

There is plenty of deck space (but lots of ropes on deck, and other nautical equipment), even under the vast expanse of white sail, and the Promenade Deck outdoors still has wonderful varnished sea chests. The decks themselves are made of mahogany and teak, and wooden steamer-style sunloungers are provided.

One of the most delightful aspects of sailing aboard this ship is its 'Blue Lagoon,' located at the stern. Weather permitting, you can lie down on the

BERLITZ'S RATINGS

	Possible	Achieved
Ship	500	432
Accommodation	200	174
Food	400	336
Service	400	336
Entertainment	100	91
Cruise Experience	400	333

OVERALL SCORE 1702 points out of 2000

thick blue padding and gaze up at the stars and night sky – it's glorious, particularly when the ship is under sail, with engines turned off.

The original engine room, with diesel engines, is still in operation for the rare occasions when sail power can't be used. An open-bridge policy is the norm, except during poor weather or navigational maneuvers. Passengers are not, however, allowed to climb the rigging. This is because the mast rigging on this vintage sailing ship is of a very different type to more modern sailing vessels such as *Royal Clipper*, *Star Clipper*, *Star Flyer*, and *Sea Cloud II*.

In addition to the retained and refurbished original suites and cabins, some newer, smaller cabins were added in 1979 when a consortium of German yachtsmen and businessmen bought the ship and spent $7.5 million refurbishing it. The interiors exude warmth and are finely hand-crafted. There is much antique mahogany furniture, fine original oil paintings, gorgeous carved oak paneling, parquet flooring, and burnished brass everywhere, as well as some finely detailed ceilings. Marjorie Merriweather Post had been accustomed to the very finest things in life.

A cruise aboard the intimate *Sea Cloud* is really exhilarating. A kind of stately home afloat, it remains one of the world's best travel experiences. The activities are few, and so relaxation is the key, in a setting that provides fine service and style, but in an unpretentious way. The only dress-up nights are the Welcome Aboard, and Farewell dinners, but otherwise, smart casual clothing is all that is needed.

Bear in mind that a big sailing vessel such as this can heel to one side occasionally, so flat shoes are preferable to high heels. Note that shorter skirts are not the most practical garments for climbing some of the ship's steep staircases.

White and red wines and beer are included for lunch and dinner, and soft drinks, espresso and cappuccino coffees are included at any time. Shore excursions are an optional extra, as are gratuities, which can be charged to your onboard account.

Although now aged 85 years – I doubt if any modern cruise ship will last this long – Sea Cloud is so lovingly maintained and operated that anyone who sails aboard it cannot fail to be impressed. The food and service are good, as is the interaction between passengers and mixed-nationality crew, many of whom have worked aboard the ship for many, many years. Once a cruise, a sailors' choir (made up of officers and crew members) sings seafaring songs. One bonus is the fact that the doctor on board is available at no charge for medical emergencies or seasickness medication.

Sea Cloud is the most romantic sailing ship afloat. It is best suited to couples and solo travelers (not children) who would probably never consider a 'normal' cruise ship, but who enjoy sailing aboard a real tall ship that is packaged to include accommodation, good food, like-minded companions, and interesting destinations. It operates under charter to various travel companies for much of the year, as well for individual bookings.

Hamburg-based Sea Cloud Cruises also operates companion sailing ship, Sea Cloud II, with 23 sails.

ACCOMMODATION. Because Sea Cloud was built as a private yacht, there is a wide variation in cabin sizes and configurations. Some cabins have double beds, while some have twins (side by side or in an L-shaped configuration) that are fixed and cannot be placed together. Many of the original cabins have a fireplace, now with an electric fire.

All the cabins are very comfortable, but those on Main Deck (cabins 1–8) were part of the original accommodation. Of these, the two Owner's Suites (cabins 1 and 2) are really opulent, and have original Chippendale furniture, fine gilt detailing, a real fireplace, French canopy bed, and large Italian Carrara marble bathrooms with gold fittings.

Owner's Cabin Number 1 is decorated in white throughout, and has a French double bed, a marble fireplace, and Louis Philippe chairs; the bathroom is appointed in Carrara marble, with cut-glass mirrors, and faucets (taps) in the shape of swans. Owner's Cabin Number 2, completely paneled in rich woods, retains the mahogany secretary used 60 years ago by Edward F. Hutton, with its dark wood decor reminiscent of the 1930s.

Other cabins – both the original ones, and some newer additions – are beautifully furnished. All were refurbished in 1993 and are surprisingly large for the size of the ship. There is a good amount of closet and drawer space, and all cabins have a personal safe and telephone. The cabin bathrooms, too, are quite luxurious, and equipped with everything you might need, including bathrobes and hairdryer, and an assortment of toiletries. There is a 110-volt AC shaver socket in each bathroom, and toilets are of the 'quiet flush' type. The 'new' cabins are rather small for two persons, so it's best to take minimal luggage.

There is no cabin food or beverage service. Also, if you occupy one of the original cabins on Main Deck, you may be subjected to some noise when the motorized capstans are used to raise and lower or trim the sails. On one day each cruise, an 'open-house' cocktail party is held on the Main Deck, with cabins available for passengers to see.

DINING. The exquisitely elegant dining room, created from the original owner's living room/saloon, is in the center of the vessel, and also houses the ship's library. It has beautiful wood-paneled walls and a wood beam ceiling.

There is ample space at each table for open-seating meals. German chefs are in charge, and the high-quality cuisine is very international, with a good balance of nouvelle cuisine and regional dishes, although there is little choice, due to the size of the galley. There is always excellent seafood and fish, which are purchased locally, when available, as are most other ingredients.

For breakfast and lunch, there are self-serve buffets. Wines accompany lunch and dinner. Soft drinks and bottled water are included in the fare, while alcoholic drinks cost extra.

ENTERTAINMENT. A keyboard player/singer is available for the occasional soirée, but after-dinner conversation constitutes the main entertainment each evening.

SPA/FITNESS. There are no spa or fitness facilities. However, for recreation (particularly at night), there is the Blue Lagoon, an area of seating with blue cushioned pads at the very aft of the ship, where you can lie down and watch the heavens.

SEA CLOUD II
★★★★★

THIS FINE SHIP PROVIDES EXCLUSIVE, RELAXING SAIL-CRUISES FOR COUPLES

Size:	Boutique Ship	
Tonnage:	3,849	
Cruise Line:	Sea Cloud Cruises	
Former Names:	none	
Builder:	Astilleros Gondan, Figueras (Spain)	
Entered Service:	Feb 2001	
Length (ft/m):	383.8/117.0	
Propulsion/Propellers:	sail power + diesel (2,500kW)/2	
Total Crew:	60	
Passengers (lower beds):	94	
Passenger Space Ratio (lower beds):	40.9	

Passenger/Crew Ratio (lower beds):	1.6
Cabins (total):	47
Size Range (sq ft/m):	215.2–322.9/20.0–30.0
Cabins (for one person):	0
Cabins with balcony:	0
Cabins (wheelchair accessible):	0
Wheelchair accessibility:	None
Elevators:	0
Casino (gaming tables):	No
Self-Service Launderette:	No
Onboard currency:	Euros

THE SHIP. This three-mast tall ship (called a barque) is slightly longer and beamier than the original *Sea Cloud*, and has the look, ambience, and feel of a 1930s sailing vessel (think polished woods, brass elements, gold fittings, and marble fireplaces), while benefiting from the latest high-tech navigational aids. It complements the company's original, 1931-built *Sea Cloud* in almost every way, including its external appearance – except for a very rounded stern in place of the counter stern of the original ship.

The interior designers have managed to replicate the same beautiful traditional look and special decorative touches, so anyone who has sailed aboard *Sea Cloud* will feel instantly at home. Whether the modern materials used in this ship (which entered service in 2001) will stand up to 85 years of use like those of the original remains to be seen, but it's certainly quality. The main lounge is truly elegant, with sofa and large individual tub chair seating around oval drinks tables. The ceiling is ornate, with an abundance of wood detailing, and an oval centerpiece is set around skylights to the open deck above. A bar is set into the aft port side of the room, which has audio-visual aids built in for lectures and presentations.

A treasured aspect of sailing aboard this ship is its 'Blue Lagoon,' at the very stern – part of the Lido outdoor bar and casual dining area. Weather permitting, you can lie on thick blue padding and gaze up at

BERLITZ'S RATINGS		
	Possible	Achieved
Ship	500	432
Accommodation	200	173
Food	400	339
Service	400	335
Entertainment	100	90
Cruise Experience	400	332

OVERALL SCORE 1701 points out of 2000

the stars and warm night sky – it's a huge pleasure, particularly when the ship is under sail, with engines off.

In terms of interior design, degree of luxury in appointments, the passenger flow, fabrics, food, service, the ceiling height of public rooms, larger cabins, great open deck space, and excellent passenger/space ratio and crew per passenger ratio, there is none better than *Sea Cloud II*. I have sailed aboard both this and its sister vessel, and I can promise you a memorable sail-cruise experience.

A small water-sports platform is built into the aft quarter of the starboard side (with adjacent shower), and the ship carries four inflatable craft for close-in shore landings, as well as snorkeling equipment.

There are three masts and 30 sails, measuring a billowing 32,292 sq ft (3,000 sq m). There are: Bowsprit, flying jib, fore topgallant staysail, outer jib, inner jib; fore topmast staysail, fore mast, fore royal, fore topgallant, fore upper topsail, fore lower topsail, fore course; main royal staysail, main topgallant staysail, main mast, sky sail, main royal, main topgallant, main upper topsail, main lower topsail, main course, mizzen topgallant staysail, mizzen topmast staysail; mizzen mast, upper spanker, lower spanker, mizzen spanker boom, middle gaff, and upper gaff.

This is just about as exclusive as it gets – sailing in the lap of luxury aboard one of the world's finest true sailing ships – although your experience will depend on which company is operating the ship (it may be under charter) when you sail, and what is included in the package.

ACCOMMODATION. The decor in the cabins is very tasteful 1920s retro, with lots of bird's-eye maple wood paneling, brass accenting, and beautiful molded white ceilings. All cabins have a vanity desk, hairdryer, refrigerator (typically stocked with soft drinks and bottled water), and a combination TV/DVD unit. Comparisons are bound to be made between this and its sister ship, and if you have sailed aboard the original *Sea Cloud*, you may be disappointed with the smaller space and decoration of the equivalent cabins aboard this ship.

All cabins have a private bathroom with shower enclosure (or tub/shower combination), and plenty of storage space for products. Toilets are of the quiet, gentle flush type. The cabin current is 220 volts, although bathrooms also include a 110-volt socket for shavers.

There are two suites. Naturally, these have more space – but not as much space as the two Owner's Suites aboard *Sea Cloud*. They comprise a completely separate bedroom, with four-poster bed, and living room, while the marble-clad bathroom has a full-size tub.

There are 16 Junior Suites. These provide a living area and sleeping area with twin beds that convert to a queen-size bed. The marble-clad bathroom is quite opulent, and has a small tub/shower combination, with lots of cubbyholes to store toiletries.

DINING. The one-sitting dining room is open seating, so you can dine with whom you wish. It is decorated in a light, modern maritime style, with wood and carpeted flooring, comfortable chairs with armrests, and circular light fixtures. The gold-rimmed plates used for the captain's dinner – typically a candlelit affair – have the ship's crest embedded in the white porcelain; they are extremely elegant and highly collectible (purchase on board is available). The place settings for dinner, also often by candlelight, are green and white.

There is always excellent seafood and fish, purchased fresh, locally, when available, as are many other ingredients. For breakfast and lunch, there are self-serve buffets. These are really good, and beautifully presented – usually indoors for breakfast, and outdoors on the Promenade Deck for lunch. Meal times are announced by the ringing of a bell.

European wines typically accompany lunch and dinner – mostly young vintages. Soft drinks and bottled water are included in the fare, while alcoholic drinks cost extra.

ENTERTAINMENT. There is a keyboard player/singer for the occasional soirée, but nothing else – nothing else is needed since the thrill of sailing is the entertainment. Dinner and after-dinner conversation with fellow passengers really becomes the main evening activity. So, if you are feeling anti-social and don't want to talk to your fellow passengers, take a good book or two.

SPA/FITNESS. There is a health/fitness area, with a small gymnasium, and sauna. Massage and facials are available.

SEA PRINCESS
★★★+

THIS FAMILY-FRIENDLY MID-SIZE SHIP IS A COMFORTABLE FIT FOR GENERAL CRUISING

Size:	Mid-size Ship	Passenger/Crew Ratio (lower beds):	2.2
Tonnage:	77,690	Cabins (total):	1,008
Cruise Line:	Princess Cruises	Size Range (sq ft/m):	158.2–610.3/14.7–56.7
Former Names:	*Adonia, Sea Princess*	Cabins (for one person):	0
Builder:	Fincantieri (Italy)	Cabins with balcony:	411
Entered Service:	Dec 1998/Apr 2005	Cabins (wheelchair accessible):	19
Length (ft/m):	857.2/261.3	Wheelchair accessibility:	Good
Propulsion/Propellers:	diesel-electric (46,080kW)/2	Elevators:	11
Total Crew:	850	Casino (gaming tables):	Yes
Passengers (lower beds):	2,016	Self-Service Launderette:	Yes
Passenger Space Ratio (lower beds):	39.3	Onboard currency:	US$

THE SHIP. *Sea Princess* (now over 20 years old), like sister *Sun Princess,* cruises in Australasian and South Pacific waters.

The all-white ship has a profile balanced by a large, swept-back funnel, with a deck-tennis/basketball/volleyball court in its sheltered base. It has a wide, teak walk-around outdoor promenade deck, and ample outdoor space. An extra cost adults-only sunbathing and pool retreat, The Sanctuary, provides 'me' space away from kids.

The interiors are attractive and welcoming with pastel colors and decor that includes countless wall murals and other artworks. *Sea Princess* absorbs passengers well and some areas have an intimate feel. There is a wide range of public rooms, bars, and lounges. The interior focal and social meeting point is a four-deck-high atrium lobby, with winding double stairways and two panoramic glass-walled elevators.

A Grand Casino is slightly out of the main passenger flow and so doesn't generate the 'walk-through and gawk' factor found aboard so many ships.

Perhaps the most popular drinking venue is the Wheelhouse Bar, with decor that is a pleasing mix of traditional and modern, a bandstand and dance floor; it's like a gentlemen's club, with wood paneling and comfortable seating. For families with kids, plenty of space is provided in The Fun Zone children's center.

Niggles include the disjointed layout and number of dead ends. Also, the cabin-numbering system is

BERLITZ'S RATINGS		
	Possible	Achieved
Ship	500	329
Accommodation	200	126
Food	400	242
Service	400	266
Entertainment	100	68
Cruise Experience	400	265

OVERALL SCORE 1296 points out of 2000

illogical, the accommodation hallways are plain, the automated telephone system is user-unfriendly, the cabin towels are small, as are the swimming pools, and the pool deck is cluttered with white plastic sunloungers (no cushioned pads). Extra-cost items include ice creams, except in the restaurant, and bottled water; these can add up to a considerable amount on a long cruise. Overall, however, Princess Cruises delivers a consistently decent, comfortable, well-packaged product, always with a decent degree of style, at a competitive price.

ACCOMMODATION. There are numerous accommodation price grades, designated as suites with private balcony, mini-suites with private balcony, outside-view twin-bedded cabins with balcony, outside-view twin-bedded cabins, and interior twin-bedded cabins. Standard outside-view and interior cabins are a little small, but they are functional. Proportionately, there are quite a lot of interior (no-view) cabins. The cabin-numbering system is illogical, and the room service menu is poor.

Many outside-view cabins have narrow private balconies, and lack an outside light. Some cabins have third- and fourth-person upper bunk beds – good for families.

Storage space is adequate for a seven-night cruise (challenging for longer). Also provided is a refrigerator, and each night a chocolate will appear on your pillow. Bathrooms are practical units, but they really are tight spaces. Fortunately, they have a decent shower enclosure, real glasses, a hairdryer, and a small shelf for toiletries.

DINING. Rigoletto and Traviata are the two main, asymmetrically designed, dining rooms (each with about 500 seats), on the two lower levels of the atrium lobby (your cabin location determines which you are assigned to). Each has its own galley and is split into multi-tier sections that help create a feeling of intimacy. Breakfast and lunch are open seating, and dinner is in two seatings.

Portions are generous, but the food and its presentation are standardized and uninspiring. Fish is often disguised by a crumb or batter coating, fresh green vegetable choice is limited, few garnishes are used, and cheese is already sliced and diced. But this is banquet catering, with all its attendant standardization. Pasta dishes are acceptable (though voluminous), typically served by section headwaiters, who may make 'something special just for you' – in search of favorable gratuities.

Horizon Court is an almost 24-hour casual, self-serve buffet. At night, one section becomes the Steakhouse, with cooked-to-order premium steaks.

Outdoors, with a sheltered view over the Riviera Pool, the Terrace Grill has fast-food items for sunbathers. In the evening, the grill offers steaks, seafood, and a 'white sisters' mixed grill (a cover charge applies for dining under the stars).

Café Corniche, on the upper atrium level, is for extra-cost Italian classic dishes, and premium coffees.

ENTERTAINMENT. The Princess Theater, forward, is a 550-seat showlounge, for production shows and movies. A second venue, Vista Lounge, located aft, is a 480-seat lounge and bar for cabaret and lectures.

SPA/FITNESS. The Lotus Spa has facilities contained in a glass-walled complex located on Lido Deck aft. It includes an ocean-view fitness room with muscle-pumping equipment, an exercise room, sauna and steam room, and several body-treatment rooms.

Forming part of the outside complex, one swimming pool is 'suspended' aft between two decks. Two other pools are located in another area in the ship's center, although they are small. Joggers can use the wraparound open Promenade Deck.

SEABOURN ENCORE
★★★★+

THIS IS A SMALL, ELEGANT SHIP FOR WELL-TRAVELED, HIGH-COMFORT SEEKERS

Size:	Small Ship	Passenger/Crew Ratio (lower beds):	1.3
Tonnage:	40,350	Cabins (total):	302
Cruise Line:	Seabourn	Size Range (sq ft/m):	295.0–438.1/27.5–133.6
Former Names:	none	Cabins (for one person):	0
Builder:	Mariotti (Italy)	Cabins with balcony:	199
Entered Service:	Dec 2016	Cabins (wheelchair accessible):	7
Length (ft/m):	650.0/198.1	Wheelchair accessibility:	Good
Propulsion/Propellers:	diesel-electric/2	Elevators:	3
Total Crew:	450	Casino (gaming tables):	Yes
Passengers (lower beds):	604	Self-Service Launderette:	Yes
Passenger Space Ratio (lower beds):	67.2	Onboard currency:	US$

THE SHIP. *Seabourn Encore* has two outdoor pools, midships and aft; the aft ('dip' only) pool is in a delightful area, although there's little open sunbathing space. For stargazing, the hot tub located by the ship's bows is a delight; it's dimly lit and peaceful. By day it's a great place to sit and chill out when the ship is underway, just in front of the navigation bridge. The top deck Retreat has 15 extra-cost cabanas for rent in the most peaceful part of the ship, shielded from the sun (but there's no sea view).

The front of the ship houses the accommodation section, with public rooms located aft, in a vertical stacking that is not so user-friendly.

Seabourn Square is the focal social gathering point, and has a relaxed, club-like ambience. It includes a library, shops, eight computers (Internet use is chargeable – at high cost – a major source of passenger complaints), an outdoor terrace, and a coffee bar. Its 'concierges' can provide in-port shopping tips, set up shore excursions, and make dinner reservations in ports of call, etc. There's a private diamond showroom, called The Collection. Drinks, wines with meals, and all gratuities are included, though premium brands and high-quality wines cost extra.

While real teak is used in most outdoor areas, faux teak (called Flexteak) is used in some others. Cabin doors are narrow, and other doors inside the cabins are of varying heights and sizes, and feel utilitarian. Most public rooms are of a single deck height, so

BERLITZ'S RATINGS		
	Possible	Achieved
Ship	500	428
Accommodation	200	178
Food	400	310
Service	400	328
Entertainment	100	76
Cruise Experience	400	308

OVERALL SCORE 1628 points out of 2000

there's not such a good feeling of spaciousness, and support pillars are everywhere.

ACCOMMODATION. Seabourn markets all accommodation as suites, but the smaller ones are really large cabins, not suites. However, there are six grades spread over seven decks, and all have a 'private' balcony. The price you pay depends on the size, location, and grade you choose. From the smallest (Verandah suite) to the largest (Wintergarden suite), all are comfortable. Note that the Wintergarden suite's balcony is tiny. For a larger balcony, try a Signature suite.

The suites are contemporary, homey living spaces, although the walls are plain and the decor is unimaginative. The beds are high enough off the floor to enable even the largest suitcases to be stowed underneath, and all drawers are fitted with soft gel for quiet closing.

DINING. The Restaurant has open-seating dining at tables for two to eight. It has white-on-white decor (think weddings) and a double-height ceiling in its central section; the port and starboard sides sections have windows, but the ceiling height is low, making it feel cramped.

The Grill by Thomas Keller (reservations required) is a classic American steak and seafood house, with 50 seats on Deck 8. The decor is designed as a tribute to the Big Band era. There's also a venue for sushi on the same deck, with sushi counter and table seating (and bento boxes at lunchtime).

The casual self-serve Colonnade eatery, located aft, has indoor/outdoor seating, although its free-flow design is quite poor, because there's too little outdoor seating for the demand in warm-weather cruise areas.

Patio Grill is in a casual poolside setting outdoors – it's enjoyable on a balmy evening, as a change to the air-conditioned interior venues.

Also, a 24-hour, in-suite menu offers the à la carte items served in the main dining room during dinner hours. Extra-cost Silver or Gold 'connoisseur' wine packages provide a choice of red and white vintage wines for a set amount – perhaps a good idea for longer cruises.

ENTERTAINMENT. The Grand Salon is the venue for shows, cabaret performances, social dancing, and for use as a cinema. It has a gently sloping main and tiered balcony banquette seating.

Small production shows (remember this is a small ship) and a live six-piece band complete the picture.

Another venue, The Club, is a large, cool, trendy, but high-volume nightclub/disco with a wooden dance floor, large bar, and minimalist design. Located beneath the Grand salon, it incorporates a small casino, plus 15 slot machines.

SPA/FITNESS. The Spa at Seabourn, operated by Elemis (Steiner Leisure), occupies the aft section of two decks, and is quite large, at 11,500 sq ft (1,068 sq m). It offers full services in a pleasant setting that includes a two-deck-high waterfall at the entrance and seven indoor/outdoor treatment rooms, a Kneipp 'walk-in-the-water' experience, an extra-cost thermal suite, and salon facilities, with a hot tub and relaxation area on the deck above accessible by a spiral staircase. Separate saunas and steam rooms for men and women are provided, but they are really small. In the gymnasium, personal-training sessions, yoga classes, mat Pilates, and body-composition analysis are available at extra cost, but some basic exercise programs are free.

SEABOURN ODYSSEY
★★★★+

THIS SMALL SHIP HAS CONTEMPORARY DECOR FOR THE STYLISH AND WELL-TRAVELED

Size:	Small Ship	Passenger/Crew Ratio (lower beds):	1.3
Tonnage:	32,000	Cabins (total):	225
Cruise Line:	Seabourn	Size Range (sq ft/m):	295.0–438.1/27.5–133.6
Former Names:	none	Cabins (for one person):	0
Builder:	Mariotti (Italy)	Cabins with balcony:	199
Entered Service:	Jun 2009	Cabins (wheelchair accessible):	7
Length (ft/m):	650.0/198.1	Wheelchair accessibility:	Good
Propulsion/Propellers: diesel-electric (23,040kwW)/2		Elevators:	3
Total Crew:	330	Casino (gaming tables):	Yes
Passengers (lower beds):	450	Self-Service Launderette:	Yes
Passenger Space Ratio (lower beds):	71.1	Onboard currency:	US$

THE SHIP. *Seabourn Odyssey*, the first of a new series of ships for Seabourn, looks like an up-sized version of its three former (smaller) vessels. However, this and sister Seabourn ships *Encore, Ovation, Quest,* and *Sojourn* have very high passenger/space ratios – so there's no crowded feeling anywhere.

There are two outdoor pools, midships and aft; the aft pool is in a more secluded area, although there's not much sunbathing space, and the steel-mesh sunloungers are uncomfortable. One pleasant outdoor area is the Sky Bar, and for stargazing, a hot tub located by the ship's bow is a delight. While real teak decking is used in most outdoor areas, faux teak is used in some locations.

Accommodation areas are forward, with most public rooms aft, so the accommodation is quiet, but you'll need to pass through several decks to get to some public rooms. An Observation Lounge, which has ocean views, is a well-laid-out, very comfortable room. A Marina, at the stern, has a staging area from which water sports are organized. The interior decor uses light woods, tame colors, and rich soft furnishings to create a contemporary, restrained, relaxing environment, which is good considering the low ceiling height in most public rooms.

Seabourn Square is a relaxed, club-like area designed for sociability, with a library, computer terminals, an outdoor terrace, and a coffee bar – good for

BERLITZ'S RATINGS

	Possible	Achieved
Ship	500	426
Accommodation	200	178
Food	400	309
Service	400	328
Entertainment	100	76
Cruise Experience	400	307

OVERALL SCORE 1624 points out of 2000

late-riser coffees and pastries. Wi-Fi is available throughout.

Drinks, wines with meals, and all gratuities are included, though premium brands and high-quality wines do cost extra.

This is a ship with a yacht-like ambience. Strong points include the staff, decent service levels, some attention to detail, and the wellness facilities. Passenger niggles include the high charge for Internet-connectivity and spa use. The ship's 'vertical stacking' layout is not very user-friendly. The cabin doors are rather narrow; doors within cabins are of varying heights and sizes, and feel utilitarian. Most public rooms are of a single deck height, making them feel somewhat cramped. There are support pillars everywhere, and many fire doors protrude outside bulkheads instead of being integral to them.

ACCOMMODATION. There are several different grades of suites in many price categories, although the smaller 'suites' are simply large cabins. There are many balcony cabins (about 90 percent, in fact), giving you plenty of personal privacy. Even the smallest cabin measures a comfortable 269 sq ft (25 sq m). All cabins have a separate tub and shower enclosure in a granite bathroom setting, twin beds convertible to a queen-size bed, flat-screen infotainment system, mini-bar, vanity desk with hairdryer, world atlas, personalized stationery, and large walk-in closet with personal safe.

The interior designers have crafted homey, contemporary living spaces in the suites and cabins, although walls and ceilings are bland. The beds are high enough off the floor to accommodate large suitcases to be stowed underneath. All drawers are fitted with soft gel, so they are quiet – no more slamming contests with your next-door neighbor.

The cabinetry has many seams and strips covering joints, which suggest that the ship's outfitters would benefit from a joinery course. One neat, very creative feature is a leather-clad vanity stool/table that converts into a backgammon table.

Seabourn Suites and Veranda Suites are quite narrow, and feel cramped, with little space between the bed and the opposite wall. However, the bathrooms are generously proportioned, and have gray/chocolate-brown decor, two washbasins, a bathtub, and a separate shower enclosure.

Some size examples (excluding balcony): Grand Suites 1,135 sq ft (105 sq m), including two-bedrooms; Signature Suites 819 sq ft (76 sq m); Wintergarden Suites 914 sq ft (85 sq m) – rather neat suites within a glass-enclosed solarium, set in front of the funnel, with a side balcony; Owner's Suites 611–675 sq ft (57–63 sq m); Penthouse Suites 436–611 sq ft (41–57 sq m); Veranda Suites 269–298 sq ft (25–28 sq m); and Seabourn Suites, measuring 295 sq ft (27 sq m).

Four Penthouse Spa Suites were added in a 2013 refit. These are located above the spa (and connect to it via a spiral stairway), and measure between 688 sq ft (64 sq m) and 710 sq ft (66 sq m), including a balcony, plus free access to the spa's Serene Area.

DINING. There are three dining venues plus a poolside grill: The Restaurant has open-seating dining at tables for two to eight. It is a large venue that feels more clinical than classical, with white-on-white decor and double-height ceiling in its central section. The most-sought-after seats are located in the center, rather than along the port and starboard sides, which have a window but low ceilings. Extra-cost Silver or Gold 'connoisseur' wine packages provide a choice of red and white vintage wines for a set amount – perhaps a good idea for longer cruises.

As an alternative, The Grill by Thomas Keller has 44 seats; it is a classic American steak and seafood house, adjacent to The Colonnade. The food is cooked to order, and the extra cost may be worth it, because of higher-quality ingredients. However, the ceiling height is rather low, which makes it feel rather cramped. Reservations are required.

The casual self-serve Colonnade eatery, located aft, has indoor/outdoor seating and is nicely decorated, although its free-flow design could be better; there's too little outdoor seating for the demand in warm-weather areas, when many passengers like to eat outdoors. During dinner on designated formal nights, passengers who are dressed accordingly have to share the space with those who are casually dressed.

The Patio Grill is located in a casual poolside setting outdoors – and is most enjoyable on balmy evenings, as a change to the air-conditioned interior dining venues.

In addition, a 24-hour, in-suite menu offers the à la carte items served in the main dining room during dinner hours.

ENTERTAINMENT. The Grand Salon (refreshed in 2018 with an LED screen backdrop) is for shows, cabaret, social dancing, and movies. The stage is small – large enough for a band, but performers must use the dance floor area. Nine thick pillars make it awkward to see anything at all, although the floor is gently sloped. In the central section is an unattractive black, 'decorative,' steel ceiling grating. There's banquette seating in the front and mid-section, and, strangely, sofa-style leather seating along the side walls to the rear, which means you actually sit with your back to the stage – a strange arrangement!

Another venue, The Club, is a large, cool, trendy but high-volume nightclub/disco with a wooden dance floor, large bar, and minimalist design. Located beneath the Grand Salon, it incorporates a comfortable casino.

SPA/FITNESS. The Spa at Seabourn, operated by Elemis, occupies the aft section of two decks. At 11,500 sq ft (1,068 sq m), it is quite large, and offers full services in a very pleasant setting that includes a two-deck-high waterfall at the entrance. Facilities include seven indoor/outdoor treatment rooms, a Kneipp 'walk-in-the-water' experience, a thermal suite (for which a pass costs extra), salon facilities, and gymnasium, with a hot tub and relaxation area on the deck above, accessed by a spiral staircase. Small, separate saunas and steam rooms for men and women are provided. Some basic exercise programs are free, but most cost extra.

SEABOURN OVATION
★★★★+

A HIGHLY COMFORTABLE SMALL SHIP WITH PREMIUM STYLE FOR MATURE TRAVELERS

Size:	Small Ship	Passenger/Crew Ratio (lower beds):	1.3
Tonnage:	40,350	Cabins (total):	225
Cruise Line:	Seabourn	Size Range (sq ft/m):	295.0–438.1/27.5–133.6
Former Names:	none	Cabins (for one person):	0
Builder:	Mariotti (Italy)	Cabins with balcony:	199
Entered Service:	May 2018	Cabins (wheelchair accessible):	7
Length (ft/m):	688.9/210.00	Wheelchair accessibility:	Good
Propulsion/Propellers:	diesel-electric/2	Elevators:	3
Total Crew:	330	Casino (gaming tables):	Yes
Passengers (lower beds):	604	Self-Service Launderette:	Yes
Passenger Space Ratio (lower beds):	67.2	Onboard currency:	US$

THE SHIP. *Seabourn Ovation* is the fifth ship of the similar size and layout for Seabourn (a division of Holland America Line). The outside decks house two small outdoor pools, midships, and aft; the aft ('dip' only) pool is in a pleasant area, but there's little space for sunbathing. For stargazing, a hot tub located near the ship's bows is really pleasant, being peaceful and dimly lit. By day it's good for sitting and chilling out when the ship is underway, located as it is just in front of the navigation bridge. On the top deck, The Retreat has 15 cabanas for rent in the most peaceful part of the ship, shielded from the sun and elements (but lacking a sea view); they are rather expensive.

The front section houses the accommodation section, with public rooms located aft, in a vertical stacking that is not so much user-friendly as elevator-friendly.

Inside, the social gathering point – with its relaxed, club-like ambience – is called Seabourn Square. It includes a library, several shops (including a private diamond showroom called The Collection – do people really go to ships to buy diamonds?), computer terminals (Internet use is chargeable), an outdoor terrace, and a coffee bar. 'Concierges' can provide in-port shopping tips, set up shore excursions, and make dinner reservations in ports of call, etc. Alcoholic drinks, wines with meals, and all gratuities are included, though premium brands and high-quality wines cost extra.

BERLITZ'S RATINGS		
	Possible	Achieved
Ship	500	428
Accommodation	200	178
Food	400	309
Service	400	328
Entertainment	100	76
Cruise Experience	400	309

OVERALL SCORE 1628 points out of 2000

Overall impressions: Although some outdoor deck areas have teak wood, faux teak (called Flexteak) is used for most. Narrow doors and other doors inside the cabins are of different heights and sizes and feel utilitarian. Most public rooms are of a single deck height, so there's no feeling of spaciousness, and there are many support pillars, and the showlounge is poorly designed.

ACCOMMODATION. Although the company markets all accommodation as suites, the smaller ones are simply large cabins, although all of them do have a 'private' balcony. Six category grades are spread over seven decks. The price depends on the size, location, and grade you choose. From the smallest to the largest grade, all are very comfortable.

The larger suites are contemporary, homey living spaces, but with walls that are quite plain. The beds are high off the floor, so even the largest suitcases can be stowed underneath. All drawers are fitted with soft gel for quiet closing.

DINING. There is one main dining room, plus a few alternatives. The Restaurant (main dining room) has open-seating dining at tables for two to eight. It feels clinical with its white-on-white decor and double-height ceiling in its central section; the port and starboard sides sections have windows, but the ceiling height of those areas is low, so it feels rather cramped.

The Grill by Thomas Keller (reservations needed) is a 'classic' American steak and seafood venue, with comfortable, contemporary decor, and less than 100 seats – including several in an al fresco area. Adjacent to The Colonnade, it has a low ceiling height, and feels somewhat cramped.

Other dining options include a second specialty restaurant, plus a sushi venue, with counters and table seating, and bento boxes at lunchtime, while the casual, self-serve Colonnade eatery has indoor/outdoor seating. Its free-flow design could be better, and there is too little outdoor seating for the demand in warm-weather cruising areas.

Patio Grill, in a casual poolside setting, is enjoyable on a balmy evening, as a change to the air-conditioned interior venues.

A 24-hour, in-suite menu offers the à la carte items served in the main dining room during dinner hours. Extra-cost Silver or Gold 'connoisseur' wine packages provide a choice of red and white vintage wines for a set amount – perhaps a good idea for longer cruises.

ENTERTAINMENT. The Grand Salon (it's not grand at all) is for shows, cabaret performances, social dancing, and movies. The stage is small – enough for a live band – but performers must use the dance floor. Sadly, nine thick pillars make it awkward to see anything at all, although the floor is gently sloped. There's banquette seating at the front and in the mid-section, and, strangely, sofa-style leather seating along the side walls to the rear, which means you actually sit with your back to the stage – a poor arrangement.

Small production shows (remember this is a small ship) are performed to pre-recorded background, and the audio equipment and sound dispersion are good.

Another venue, The Club, is a large, high-volume nightclub/disco with a wooden dance floor, large bar, and minimalist design. Located beneath the Grand Salon, it incorporates a small casino with gaming tables and slot machines.

SPA/FITNESS. The Spa at Seabourn is aft on two decks. The entrance has a pleasing two-deck-high waterfall. Facilities include seven indoor/outdoor treatment rooms, an extra-cost thermal suite, beauty salon facilities, plus a hot tub and relaxation area one deck above, accessed by a spiral stairway. There are separate, small saunas and steam rooms for men and women. Most fitness classes and personal-training sessions cost extra.

SEABOURN QUEST
★★★★

AN ELEGANT, INCLUSIVE SMALL SHIP CONVERTED FOR DISCOVERY-STYLE CRUISES

Size:	Small Ship	Passenger/Crew Ratio (lower beds):	1.3
Tonnage:	32,346	Cabins (total):	225
Cruise Line:	Seabourn	Size Range (sq ft/m):	295.0–438.1/27.5–133.6
Former Names:	none	Cabins (for one person):	0
Builder:	Mariotti (Italy)	Cabins with balcony:	199
Entered Service:	Jun 2011	Cabins (wheelchair accessible):	7
Length (ft/m):	650.0/198.1	Wheelchair accessibility:	Good
Propulsion/Propellers:	diesel-electric (23,040kW)/2	Elevators:	3
Total Crew:	330	Casino (gaming tables):	Yes
Passengers (lower beds):	450	Self-Service Launderette:	Yes
Passenger Space Ratio (lower beds):	71.8	Onboard currency:	US$

THE SHIP. *Seabourn Quest's* attractions are its staff, good service levels, and wellness facilities. Like sister ships, *Seabourn Odyssey* and *Seabourn Sojourn*, it has a high passenger space ratio, so there's no crowding anywhere.

It has two small outdoor pools, midships and aft; the aft pool is in a pleasant area, but there's little sunbathing space, and the pool is just a 'dip' pool. A popular outdoor area is the Sky Bar, good for balmy evenings. For stargazing, the hot tub by the ship's bow is pleasant (dimly lit and peaceful); by day it's for sitting and chilling out. The Marina, aft, has a staging area for expedition equipment, Zodiac shore-landing craft, a boot-washing station, and storage area.

All accommodation areas are in the forward section, with most public rooms located aft, so the accommodation areas are quiet; however, you'll need to walk through several decks to get to some public rooms.

Seabourn Square, the focal social gathering point and 'concierge lounge,' has a relaxed, club-like ambience. The area includes a library, shops (including a private diamond room), eight computers (Internet use is chargeable – at high cost – a source of complaints), a coffee bar, and an outdoor terrace. While drinks, wines with meals, and all gratuities are included, premium brands and premium wines cost extra.

The 'vertical stacking' layout is not user-friendly. While real teak is used in most outdoor areas, faux

BERLITZ'S RATINGS		
	Possible	Achieved
Ship	500	412
Accommodation	200	169
Food	400	292
Service	400	308
Entertainment	100	61
Cruise Experience	400	287

OVERALL SCORE 1529 points out of 2000

teak is used in others. Cabin doors are narrow, and doors within the cabins are of varying heights and sizes, and feel utilitarian. Most public rooms are of a single deck height, so there's not a feeling of spaciousness, and support pillars are everywhere. It's a pretend expedition-style ship with upscale surroundings.

ACCOMMODATION. There are 13 accommodation grades in many price categories, although the smaller 'suites' are really just large cabins. However, there are many balcony cabins – good for personal privacy.

All cabins have a separate tub and shower enclosure in a granite bathroom setting, twin beds convertible to a queen-size, infotainment system, mini-bar, vanity desk with hairdryer, world atlas, personalized stationery, and walk-in closet with personal safe. They are homey, contemporary living spaces, although the walls are rather plain and unimaginative. The beds are high enough off the floor for even the largest suitcases to be stowed. All drawers are of the soft-close (quiet) variety.

The cabinetry has many seams and strips covering joints, which suggest that the ship's outfitters need joinery lessons. One neat feature is a leather-clad vanity stool/table that converts to a backgammon table. Also, a 'cube table' can be inserted under a glass-topped table when not being used as a footrest – a smart idea.

Note that Seabourn and Veranda Suites are narrow, and confining, with little space between the bed and the wall opposite. However, the bathrooms are generously proportioned, with gray/chocolate-brown decor, two washbasins, bathtub, and separate shower enclosure.

DINING. There are three venues, plus a Poolside Grill. The Restaurant has open-seating dining at tables for two, four, six, or eight. It is a large venue that feels more clinical than classical with its white-on-white decor and double-height ceiling in the center (the most sought-after for seating)

The Grill by Thomas Keller is for classic American steaks and seafood, aft on Deck 8. The food is cooked to order, so the extra cost may be worth it, with higher-quality ingredients. The wine list consists of around 90 selections. However, the ceiling height is low, so it can feel cramped.

The casual Colonnade self-serve eatery, aft, has indoor/outdoor seating and pleasant decor, but its free-flow design is poor, and there is too little outdoor seating.

The Patio Grill is a poolside setting – enjoyable on a balmy evening, as a change to the air-conditioned interior dining venues.

In addition, a 24-hour, in-suite menu offers the à la carte items from the main dining room during opening hours.

Extra-cost Silver or Gold 'connoisseur' wine packages provide a choice of red and white vintage wines for a set amount – perhaps useful on a longer cruise.

ENTERTAINMENT. The Grand Salon is for shows, cabaret acts, social dancing, and as a cinema. However, the stage is small – large enough for a live band, but performers need to use the dance floor area – and the room has nine thick pillars that make it very awkward to see anything at all, even though the room has a gentle slope. On the ceiling of the central section there is a black, cold, unappealing decorative steel grating. There is banquette seating in the front and mid-section, and, strangely, sofa-style leather seating along the side walls to the rear, which means you sit with your back to the stage – an unhelpful arrangement. Shows are performed well to pre-recorded tracks.

Another venue, The Club, is a large, trendy, but high-volume nightclub/disco with a wood dance floor, bar and minimalist design. Located under the Grand salon, it incorporates a casino.

SPA/FITNESS. The Spa at Seabourn is aft on two decks; it is quite large and has a pleasant setting, including a two-deck-high waterfall at the entrance. There are several indoor/outdoor body treatment rooms, plus a Kneipp 'walk-in-the-water' experience, a thermal suite (a pass costs extra), and salon, with a hot tub and relaxation area on the deck above, accessed by a spiral staircase. The separate saunas and steam rooms for men and women are tiny. Some basic exercise programs are free, but most others cost extra.

SEABOURN SOJOURN
★★★★+

THIS IS AN UPSCALE, ELEGANT SMALL SHIP FOR THE WELL-TRAVELED

Size:	Small Ship	Passenger/Crew Ratio (lower beds):	1.3
Tonnage:	32,346	Cabins (total):	225
Cruise Line:	Seabourn	Size Range (sq ft/m):	295.0–438.1/27.5–133.6
Former Names:	none	Cabins (for one person):	0
Builder:	Mariotti (Italy)	Cabins with balcony:	199
Entered Service:	Jun 2010	Cabins (wheelchair accessible):	7
Length (ft/m):	650.0/198.1	Wheelchair accessibility:	Good
Propulsion/Propellers:	diesel-electric (23,040kW)/2	Elevators:	3
Total Crew:	330	Casino (gaming tables):	Yes
Passengers (lower beds):	450	Self-Service Launderette:	Yes
Passenger Space Ratio (lower beds):	71.8	Onboard currency:	US$

THE SHIP. *Seabourn Sojourn*, the second of Seabourn's three larger ships (the three former boutique-sized Seabourn ships were sold to Windstar Cruises in 2014), has two small outdoor swimming pools, midships and aft; the aft pool is in a delightful area, although there's not a lot of sunbathing space. One of the most pleasing outdoor areas is the Sky Bar, and, for stargazing, the hot tub located on the ship's foredeck is a peaceful delight.

All the accommodation areas are in the forward section, with most public rooms located aft, but you'll need to traverse through several decks to get to some of the public rooms. The Marina, at the stern, has a staging area from which water sports are organized.

Seabourn Square, the focal social gathering point, is a 'concierge lounge,' with a relaxed, club-like ambience. The area includes a library, shops, eight computers (Internet connection is charge-able), an outdoor terrace, and a coffee bar. Its 'concierges' can provide in-port shopping tips, set up shore excursions, and make dinner reservations in ports of call, etc. There's a private diamond showroom, called The Collection. Drinks, wines with meals, and all gratuities are included, though premium brands and high-quality wines cost extra. Wi-Fi is available throughout the ship.

There's plenty of space per passenger, so there is no hint of it being crowded. Minus points? The

BERLITZ'S RATINGS		
	Possible	Achieved
Ship	500	424
Accommodation	200	178
Food	400	306
Service	400	328
Entertainment	100	76
Cruise Experience	400	306

OVERALL SCORE 1618 points out of 2000

'vertical stacking' layout is not really user-friendly. While real teak is used in most outdoor areas, faux teak is used in other areas. The cabin doors are rather narrow, and doors within the cabins vary in height and size, and feel utilitarian. The canapés provided each evening need to be improved.

Most public rooms are of a single deck height, so there's not such a good feeling of spaciousness, and support pillars are everywhere – Mariotti, the ship-builder, should look at *Europa* to see that it's not necessary to have so many pillars.

ACCOMMODATION. There are several grades of suites in multiple price categories. The smaller 'suites' are really large cabins, and not true suites. However, there are many balcony cabins, for personal privacy (about 90 percent of all suites/cabins have them).

All cabins have a separate tub and shower enclosure in a granite bathroom setting, twin beds convertible to a queen-size bed, flat-screen TV plus CD and DVD player, mini-bar, vanity desk with hairdryer, world atlas, personalized stationery, and large walk-in closet with personal safe.

The interior designers have created very cozy, contemporary living spaces in the suites and cabins, although the walls are rather plain and unimaginative. It's good to see that the beds are high enough off the floor to enable even the largest suitcases to be stowed underneath. All drawers are fitted with soft gel, which means they are quiet – no more slamming contests with your next-door neighbor.

The cabins are bathed in soft earthy tones, although a splash of color wouldn't go amiss. The cabinetry has many seams and strips covering joints, which suggest that the ship's outfitters would benefit from a joinery course. It's also strange that several internal doors are of different sizes, widths, and heights. One neat, very creative feature is a leather-clad vanity stool/table that converts into a backgammon table. The design of a 'cube table' that can be inserted under a glass-topped table, when not being used as a footrest, is a smart idea for making more space.

Seabourn Suites and Veranda Suites are quite narrow, and feel cramped, with little space between the bed and the opposite wall. However, the bathrooms are generously proportioned, with gray and chocolate-brown decor; there are two washbasins, a bathtub, and a separate shower enclosure.

Some size examples (excluding balcony): Grand Suites 1,135 sq ft (105 sq m), including two-bedrooms; Signature Suites 819 sq ft (76 sq m); Wintergarden Suites 914 sq ft (85 sq m) – rather neat suites within a glass-enclosed solarium, set in front of the funnel, with a side balcony; Owner's Suites 611–675 sq ft (57–63 sq m); Penthouse Suites 436–611 sq ft (41–57 sq m); Veranda Suites 269–298 sq ft (25–28 sq m); and Seabourn Suites, measuring 295 sq ft (27 sq m).

Four Spa Suites were added in a 2013 refit. These are located directly above the spa itself (connected to it via a spiral stairway), and measure between 688 sq ft (64 sq m) and 710 sq ft (66 sq m), including a balcony. The suites have a living and dining area with seating for four, a separate bedroom, walk-in closet, a bathroom with tub and shower, and balcony. Occupants get free use of the 'Serene' relaxation area of the spa.

DINING. There are three venues, plus a poolside grill. The Restaurant has open-seating dining at tables for two, four, six, or eight, with menus designed by American celebrity chef Charlie Palmer. It is a large venue that actually feels more clinical than classical with its white-on-white decor and double-height ceiling in its central section. The most-sought-after seats are in the center rather than along the port and starboard sides, which have a window, but low ceiling height.

The Grill by Thomas Keller has 44 seats and is a ship's classic American steak and seafood house, adjacent to The Colonnade. The food is cooked to order, and the extra cost is worth it, because of higher-quality ingredients. However, the ceiling height is rather low, which makes it feel cramped.

The self-serve Colonnade eatery, located aft, has indoor/outdoor seating and is nicely decorated, although its free-flow design could be better; there's too little outdoor seating for the demand in warm-weather areas, when many passengers like to eat outdoors. During dinner on designated formal nights passengers who are dressed accordingly have to share the space with those who are more casually dressed. The venue is also adjacent to one of the fine dining restaurants.

The Patio Grill is located in a casual poolside setting outdoors; it is at its most enjoyable on balmy evenings, as a change to the air-conditioned interior dining venues.

In addition, a 24-hour, in-suite menu offers the à la carte items served in the main dining room during dinner hours.

Extra-cost Silver or Gold 'connoisseur' wine packages provide a choice of red and white vintage wines for a set amount – perhaps a good idea for a longer cruise.

ENTERTAINMENT. The Grand Salon (with an LED screen backdrop, added in 2019) is for shows, cabaret performances, social dancing, and movies. However, the stage is small so performers need to use the dance floor area – and the room has nine thick pillars that make it awkward to see anything at all, although the floor has a gentle slope. On the ceiling of the central section a black 'decorative' steel grating is cold-looking, and unappealing. The room has banquette seating in the front and mid-section, and, strangely, sofa-style leather seating along the side walls to the rear, which means you actually sit with your back to the stage – a rather unhelpful arrangement.

Small production shows (remember this is a small ship) are performed well to pre-recorded tracks, and the audio equipment and sound dispersion are extremely good. Just don't expect big ship entertainment, though.

Another venue, The Club, is a large, cool, trendy, but high-volume nightclub/disco with a wooden dance floor, large bar, and minimalist design. Located beneath the Grand salon, it incorporates a comfortable casino.

SPA/FITNESS. The Spa at Seabourn, operated by Elemis, occupies the aft section of two decks, and is quite large, at 11,500 sq ft (1,068 sq m). It offers full services in a relaxing setting, with a two-deck-high waterfall at the entrance and seven indoor/outdoor treatment rooms, as well as a thalassotherapy wave pool; there's also a cost-extra thermal suite, and complete salon facilities, while a hot tub and relaxation area on the deck above are accessed by a spiral staircase. Separate saunas and steam rooms for men and women are provided, but they are extremely small. Some basic exercise programs are free, but most cost extra.

SEADREAM I
★★★★+

THIS IS ABOUT ULTRA-STYLISH CRUISING ON AN INFORMAL, POCKET-SIZED SHIP

Size:	Boutique Ship	Passenger/Crew Ratio (lower beds):	1.1
Tonnage:	4,253	Cabins (total):	56
Cruise Line:	SeaDream Yacht Club	Size Range (sq ft/m):	195.0–446.7/18.1–41.4
Former Names:	Seabourn Goddess I, Sea Goddess I	Cabins (for one person):	0
Builder:	Wartsila (Finland)	Cabins with balcony:	0
Entered Service:	Apr 1984/May 2002	Cabins (wheelchair accessible):	0
Length (ft/m):	343.8/104.8	Wheelchair accessibility:	None
Propulsion/Propellers:	diesel (3,540kW)/2	Elevators:	1
Total Crew:	95	Casino (gaming tables):	Yes
Passengers (lower beds):	112	Self-Service Launderette:	No
Passenger Space Ratio (lower beds):	37.9	Onboard currency:	US$

THE SHIP. *SeaDream I* is a motor yacht for the well-traveled. Rejecting today's huge standard resort cruise ships, its clientele is looking for a small ship with excellent food approaching gourmet standards, and fine European-style service in surroundings that border on the elegant and refined, while remaining informal.

SeaDream I (and sister ship *SeaDream II*) were originally funded by about 800 investors, and operated under the Norske Cruise banner, and named *Sea Goddess I* and *Sea Goddess II*. They have a sleek profile, deep blue hull and white superstructure, and the ambience of a private club. Purchased by SeaDream Yacht Club in 2001, they were completely refurbished, with many changes to public rooms and outdoor areas. Some new features were added to create contemporary, chic, and desirable, if aging, vessels.

A 'Top of the Yacht' bar, crafted in warm wood, was added to both ships. So were eight special alcoves set to the port and starboard sides of the funnel, equipped with two-person sunloungers with thick pads (and two equipped for one person); however, there is quite a bit of noise from the adjacent funnel. You are encouraged to sleep under the stars, if you wish, and cotton sleep suits are provided.

At the front part of the deck there are more sunloungers and a couple of large hammocks, as well as a golf simulator with a choice of 30 courses.

BERLITZ'S RATINGS		
	Possible	Achieved
Ship	500	415
Accommodation	200	162
Food	400	336
Service	400	357
Entertainment	100	80
Cruise Experience	400	329
OVERALL SCORE 1679 points out of 2000		

Inside, there is a feeling of unabashed but discreet sophistication. Elegant public rooms have flowers and potpourri everywhere. The main social gathering places are the lounge, a delightful library/living room with a selection of about 1,000 books, a piano bar – which can be more like a karaoke bar at times – and a small casino with two blackjack tables and five slot machines.

All drinks (including good-quality Champagne, but not premium drink brands and connoisseur wines), farmed caviar, and gratuities are included, but port charges and insurance are not.

ACCOMMODATION. There are four types – in six price categories (depending on location, size, and grade). From the smallest to the largest these are: Yacht Club (standard) Cabin; Commodore Club Suite; Admiral Suite; and Owner's Suite.

Incorrectly called 'suites' in the brochure, Yacht Club Cabins are, more accurately, fully equipped mini-suites with an outside view through windows or portholes, depending on deck and price category. Each measure 195 sq ft (18 sq m), which is small by today's cruise ship standards; however, it is large compared to cabins aboard many private motor yachts, and extremely large when compared to oceangoing racing yachts. The sleeping area has twin beds that can be put together to form a queen-size bed, positioned next to the window or porthole, so you can entertain in the living area without going past the sleeping area, as you must aboard the slightly larger Seabourn or Silversea ships. A curtain separates the sleeping and lounge areas. All cabinetry and furniture is of thick blond wood, with nicely rounded edges.

In the lounge area, a long desk has six drawers, plus a vertical cupboard unit that houses a sensible safe, refrigerator, and drinks cabinet stocked with your choice of drinks. There is also a 20-ins (51-cm) flat-screen television, CD and DVD player, and an MP3 audio player with more than 100 selections. The beds have the finest linens, including thick cotton duvets, and hypoallergenic pillows are also available. There's little room under the beds for luggage, although this can be taken away and stored.

One drawback is the fact that the insulation between cabins is not particularly good, although rarely does this present a problem, as most passengers are generally quiet, considerate types, who are allergic to noise.

For larger accommodation, choose one of 16 Commodore Club Suites. These consist of two standard cabins with an interconnecting door, thus providing you with a healthy 380 sq ft (35 sq m) of living space. One cabin is made into a lounge and dining room, with table and up to four chairs, the other becomes your sleeping area. The advantage is that you get two bathrooms.

The largest living space is in the Owner's Suite, which measures 490 sq ft (46 sq m). It has a bathroom with a full-size tub; there's also a separate shower enclosure and lots of space for toiletries.

Added in 2008–9, the Admiral Suite occupies space previously devoted to the ship's boutique, adjacent to the piano bar/library. It's a little smaller than the Owner's Suite, but is well laid out and extremely comfortable, and also has a bathroom with bathrub and separate glazed shower enclosure.

When the ships became *SeaDream I* and *II*, all the bathrooms were totally refurbished. The cheerful decor is chic, with soft colors and large (beige) marble tiles. The former tiny sit-in bathtubs were taken out – missed by some passengers – and replaced by a multi-jet power, glazed shower enclosure. A washbasin set in a marble-look surround and two glass shelves make up the facilities, and an under-sink cupboard provides further space for larger toiletries.

However, the bathrooms really are small, particularly for anyone of larger-than-average build. Also, the bathroom door opens inwards, so space inside is at a premium. The toilet is located in an awkward position, and, unless you close the door, you can see yourself in the mirror of the closets opposite the bathroom door.

DINING. The Restaurant is elegant and inviting, and has bird's-eye maple wood-paneled walls and alcoves showcasing beautiful handmade glass creations. It is cozy, yet with plenty of space around each table for fine service, and the ship provides a culinary celebration in an open-seating arrangement, so you can dine whenever, and with whomever, you want. Course-by-course meals can also be served on the open deck.

Tables can be configured for two, four, six, or eight. They are laid with a classic setting of a real glass base (show) plate, Porsgrund china, pristine white monogrammed table linen, and fresh flowers.

Candlelit dinners and leather-bound menus are part of the inviting setting. There's even a box of spare spectacles for reading the menu, should you forget your own.

The SeaDream Yacht Club experience really is all about good food, with the freshest, high-quality ingredients used. Fine, unhurried European service is provided. Additionally, good-quality Champagne is available whenever you want it, and so is caviar. The ice cream, which is made on board, is very good.

Everything is prepared individually to order for dinner, and the cuisine is extremely creative, including a wide range of plant-based food. Special orders are possible. You can also dine course by course in your suite for any meal, at any time during meal hours. The dining room isn't open for lunch, which disappoints those who don't want to eat outside, particularly in hot climates.

Decent quality table wines are included in the cruise fare for lunch and dinner. Wine connoisseurs, however, will appreciate the availability of an extra wine list, with vintage and premier crus at extra cost. For something different, you can also dine on the open (but covered) deck, overlooking the swimming pool – a rather romantic setting.

Topside Restaurant is an informal, open-air eatery with roll-down sides (in case of inclement weather), open for breakfast, lunch, and sometimes for dinner. Teak tables and chairs add a touch of class.

ENTERTAINMENT. There is no evening entertainment as such (it's not needed), other than a duo or solo musician to provide music for listening and dancing to in the lounge. Dinner is the main event; DVDs are available.

SPA/FITNESS. The holistic approach to wellbeing plays a big part in relaxation and body pampering aboard *SeaDream I*. The Asian Spa/Wellness Centre has three massage rooms, a small sauna, and steam shower enclosure.

SEADREAM II
★★★★+

IT'S LIKE HAVING YOUR OWN MEGA-YACHT FOR STYLISH, RELAXING CRUISES

Size:	Boutique Ship
Tonnage:	4,333
Cruise Line:	SeaDream Yacht Club
Former Names:	Seabourn Goddess II, Sea Goddess II
Builder:	Wartsila (Finland)
Entered Service:	May 1985/Jan 2002
Length (ft/m):	343.8/104.8
Propulsion/Propellers:	diesel (3,540kW)/2
Total Crew:	95
Passengers (lower beds):	112
Passenger Space Ratio (lower beds):	37.9
Passenger/Crew Ratio (lower beds):	1.1
Cabins (total):	56
Size Range (sq ft/m):	195.0–446.7/18.1–41.5
Cabins (for one person):	0
Cabins with balcony:	0
Cabins (wheelchair accessible):	0
Wheelchair accessibility:	None
Elevators:	1
Casino (gaming tables):	Yes
Self-Service Launderette:	No
Onboard currency:	US$

THE SHIP. SeaDream II is best suited to sophisticated and well-traveled couples who are typically over 40 – in fact, anyone looking for a small ship with excellent food approaching gourmet standards, and fine European-style service in surroundings that border on the elegant and refined while remaining trendy.

SeaDream II (sister to SeaDream I) was operated under the Norske Cruise banner as Sea Goddess I and Sea Goddess II. It has a deep blue hull and white superstructure, and the ambience of a private club. It was completely refurbished in 2001, with many changes to public rooms and outdoor areas, and several new features added to create what is a contemporary, chic, and desirable motor yacht.

A 'Top of the Yacht' bar, crafted in warm wood, was added, as were eight special alcoves set to the port and starboard sides of the funnel, equipped with two-person sunloungers with thick pads (and two equipped for solo travelers); however, there is quite a bit of noise from the adjacent funnel. You can sleep under the stars if you wish (cotton sleep suits are provided).

Inside, there is unabashed but discreet sophistication, and the public rooms have flowers everywhere. The main social gathering places are the lounge, a delightful library/living room with a selection of about 1,000 books, a piano bar (more like a karaoke bar at times), and a small casino with blackjack tables and slot machines.

BERLITZ'S RATINGS

	Possible	Achieved
Ship	500	415
Accommodation	200	162
Food	400	336
Service	400	357
Entertainment	100	80
Cruise Experience	400	329

OVERALL SCORE 1679 points out of 2000

SeaDream II really is like having your own private yacht, in which hospitality, anticipation, and personal recognition are art forms practiced to a high level. The staff is delightful and accommodating, and the dress code is resort casual. Fine-quality furnishings and fabrics are used throughout, with warming marble and blond wood accents.

SeaDream II could be a good choice if you don't like the idea of large resort cruise ships, with glitzy lounges and a platoon of people running around, or dressing up – no tuxedos or gowns are allowed, and ties aren't needed. It's all about personal indulgence and refined, unstructured living at sea, in a casual setting akin to that on a private mega-yacht. One delightful feature of each cruise in warm-weather areas is a 'caviar in the surf' beach barbecue.

SeaDream I and II were the first of the mega-yacht-style ships when built, and none of the cabins has a private balcony – but anyway, yachts don't have balconies. Embarkation never starts before 3pm, in case you are eager to get aboard.

ACCOMMODATION. There are four types – in six price categories (depending on location, size, and grade) – which, from the largest to the smallest, are: Owner's Suite; Admiral Suite; Commodore Club Suite; and Yacht Club (standard) Cabin.

For the largest living space, go for the Owner's Suite. This measures 490 sq ft (46 sq m). It has a bathroom with a full-size tub, a separate shower enclosure, and lots of space for toiletries.

An Admiral Suite is adjacent to the piano bar/library. It's a little smaller than the Owner's Suite, but is well laid out, extremely comfortable, and has a large bathroom with bathtub and separate glazed shower enclosure.

For accommodation larger than standard, choose one of the 16 Commodore Club Suites. These consist of two standard cabins with an interconnecting door, thus providing you with a healthy 380 sq ft (35 sq m) of living space. One cabin is made into a lounge and dining room, with table and up to four chairs, while the other becomes your sleeping area. The advantage is that you get two bathrooms. One disadvantage is that the soundproofing between cabins could be better.

Incorrectly called 'suites' in the brochure, Yacht Club Cabins are, more accurately, fully equipped mini-suites with an outside view through windows or portholes, depending on deck and price category. Each measures 195 sq ft (18 sq m) . The sleeping area has twin beds that can be put together to form a queen-size configuration; a curtain separates the sleeping and lounge areas.

In the lounge area, a vertical cupboard unit houses a safe, refrigerator, and drinks cabinet, flat-screen television, CD and DVD player, and an MP3 audio player. The beds have fine linens, including thick cotton duvets; hypoallergenic pillows are also available. There's little room under the beds for luggage, although this can be taken away and stored. Note that the insulation between cabins is not particularly good, although this rarely presents a problem.

When the ships became *SeaDream I* and *II*, all bathrooms were totally refurbished. The cheerful decor is nicer than before, with soft colors and large marble tiles. The former tiny sit-in bathtubs were taken out and replaced by multi-jet power glassed-in shower enclosures. Bulgari toiletries are provided, as are gorgeously plush cotton SeaDream-logo bathrobes and towels. However, despite their having been completely rebuilt, the bathrooms are small, particularly for those of larger-than-average build. Also, the bathroom door opens inward, so space inside is at a premium.

DINING. The Restaurant, is elegant and inviting. It is cozy, yet has enough space around each table for fine service, and an open-seating arrangement means you can dine whenever, and with whomever, you want. Course-by-course meals can also be served out on deck. Tables can be configured for two to eight.

There's even a box of spare spectacles for reading the menu, in case you forget your own. You get leather-bound menus, and close-to-impeccable personalized European service.

The SeaDream Yacht Club experience really is all about dining, and culinary excellence prevails, using the freshest and finest-quality ingredients. Additionally, good-quality Champagne is available whenever you want it, as is caviar. The ice cream, which is made on board, is excellent. In addition to the regular menus, an extensive array of plant-based menu selections is provided.

You can also dine course by course in your suite for any meal, at any time during meal hours. The dining room isn't open for lunch, which disappoints those who don't want to eat outside, particularly in hot climates.

Good-quality table wines are included in the cruise fare for lunch and dinner. Wine connoisseurs, however, will appreciate the availability of an extra wine list, full of special vintages and premier crus at extra cost. If you want to do something different with a loved one, you can also arrange to dine one evening on the open (but covered) deck.

The Topside Restaurant is an informal open-air eatery, with roll-down sides (in case of inclement weather), and is open for breakfast, lunch, and sometimes dinner.

ENTERTAINMENT. There is no evening entertainment as such (it's not needed), other than a duo or solo musician to provide music for listening and dancing to in the lounge. Dinner is the main event, and DVDs are available to take to your cabin.

SPA/FITNESS. The holistic approach to wellbeing plays a big part in relaxation and body pampering aboard *SeaDream II*. There are three massage rooms, a small sauna, and steam shower enclosure. The Spa, located in a private area, is operated as a concession by Universal Maritime Services. Massage on the beach is available when the ship stages its famous beach party.

For golfers, there's an electronic golf simulator, and choice of several golf courses to play. There is a small, retractable water sports platform at the stern. Equipment carried includes a water-ski boat, sailboat, wave runners (jet skis), kayaks, wake boards, snorkeling equipment, and two Zodiacs – all included in the price of a cruise. Ten mountain bikes are also carried; these can be used on shore visits.

SERENADE OF THE SEAS
★★★+

THIS MID-SIZE SHIP IS GOOD FOR CASUAL, FAMILY-FRIENDLY CRUISING

Size:	Mid-size Ship	Passenger/Crew Ratio (lower beds):	2.4
Tonnage:	90,090	Cabins (total):	1,050
Cruise Line:	Royal Caribbean International	Size Range (sq ft/m):	165.8–1,216.3/15.4–113.0
Former Names:	none	Cabins (for one person):	3
Builder:	Meyer Werft (Germany)	Cabins with balcony:	577
Entered Service:	Aug 2003	Cabins (wheelchair accessible):	14
Length (ft/m):	961.9/293.2	Wheelchair accessibility:	Best
Propulsion/Propellers:	gas turbine (40,000kW)/2 azimuthing pods	Elevators:	9
		Casino (gaming tables):	Yes
Total Crew:	858	Self-Service Launderette:	No
Passengers (lower beds):	2,097	Onboard currency:	US$
Passenger Space Ratio (lower beds):	42.9		

THE SHIP. *Serenade of the Seas* uses gas and steam turbine power, as do sister ships *Brilliance of the Seas, Jewel of the Seas,* and *Radiance of the Seas,* instead of the conventional diesel or diesel-electric combination.

As aboard all Royal Caribbean International (RCI) vessels, the navigation bridge is fully enclosed. In the very front of the ship is a helipad, which also acts as a viewing platform for passengers (it makes for a good photo opportunity). One of two swimming pools can be covered by a glass dome, and there's a large poolside screen for screening movies in the open air.

A contemporary ship, it has a two-deck-high walk-around structure forward of the funnel. Along the starboard side, is a protruding central glass wall, with great views; cabins with balconies occupy the space opposite on the port side. The gently rounded stern has nicely tiered decks, which gives the ship a well-balanced look.

The interior focal point is the Centrum (city center), a nine-deck-high atrium lobby with glass-walled elevators (on the port side only) that travel through 12 decks, face the sea, and provide a link with nature and the ocean. Centrum is *the* social meeting place. It houses several lounges, bars, food outlets, and an art gallery. Close by is Casino Royale (for gamers and slot-machine lovers), and the Schooner Bar, with its nautical-themed decor and maritime art.

Other facilities include a delightful, but small, library. There's also a little screening room for mov-

BERLITZ'S RATINGS

	Possible	Achieved
Ship	500	344
Accommodation	200	131
Food	400	221
Service	400	259
Entertainment	100	73
Cruise Experience	400	255

OVERALL SCORE 1283 points out of 2000

ies, as well as a 194-seat conference center and a business center.

A Viking Crown Lounge, an RCI trademark, is set around the base of the funnel. It is an observation lounge by day, with views forward over the pool deck. In the evening, it morphs into a dance club.

This is a ship for the whole family. There are no cushioned pads for sunloungers, and the deck towels provided are small and thin. It is virtually impossible to escape background music.

ACCOMMODATION. There is a wide range of suites and standard outside-view and interior cabins, in many different categories.

Apart from the six Owner's Suites, which have king-size beds, almost all other cabins have twin beds that convert to a queen. All cabins have rich (faux) wood cabinetry, including a vanity desk with hairdryer, silent-close drawers, an infotainment system, personal safe, and three-sided mirrors. Some cabins have ceiling-recessed, pull-down berths for third and fourth persons, although closet and drawer space is very tight for four people, even if two are children.

Most cabin bathrooms have tiled accenting and a terrazzo-style tiled floor, a rather small shower enclosure in a half-moon shape, 100 percent Egyptian cotton towels, a small cabinet for toiletries, and a small shelf. In reality, there is little space to stow toiletries for two or more people.

The largest accommodation consists of a family suite with two bedrooms. One bedroom has twin beds convertible to a queen, while a second has two lower beds and two upper Pullman berths, a combination that can sleep up to eight people – this would suit large families.

Suite occupants have access to a Concierge Lounge, where priority dining reservations, shore-excursion bookings, and beauty salon/spa appointments can be made.

Note that many 'private' balcony cabins aren't private, as they can be overlooked by anyone from the port and starboard wings of the Solarium, and other locations.

DINING. Reflections, the main dining room, seats 1,096 at tables for two to 10. With a water-themed decor, it spans two decks; the upper deck level has floor-to-ceiling windows; the lower level has windows. It is a pleasant but inevitably noisy dining hall, reminiscent of those aboard the ocean liners of yesteryear, although eight thick pillars obstruct sight lines. Two small private dining rooms – Illusions with 94 seats and Mirage with 30 seats – are adjacent. You can choose one of two seatings, or My Time Dining (to eat when you want during dining room hours).

Meals are average – this is standardized batch cooking after all. However, you can have items such as lobster or filet mignon (steak) at an extra cost, cooked to order. Greens are scarce but salad items are plentiful, and desserts are pretty good. Rice is over used as a filler. Breads and pastry items are also just okay – croissants for example lack any hint of butter. Vegetarian and children's menus are available. Note that there are no wine waiters.

Other dining venues and eateries (some cost extra, but the food is mostly cooked to order) include Chops Grille Steakhouse (for premium veal chops, steaks, and seafood items), Portofino (for Italian-American cuisine), and Giovanni's Table (for Italian trattoria-style dishes). Reservations (make them through the digital system) are required, and the menus for each venue do not change.

Windjammer Marketplace is a cavernous, casual self-serve buffet eatery, but note that plastic plates for hot items become mildly warm, at best. Breakfast buffet items and lunchtime salad items are repetitive. Beverage stations have just the basics. Burgers and hot dogs in self-serve buffet locations are displayed in steam dishes. If you are disabled or have mobility difficulties, do ask for help.

Izumi: an extra-cost Asian-style eatery with a sushi bar and hot-rocks cooking (open for lunch and dinner, with a small cover charge plus à la carte menu pricing).

Extra-cost Chef's Table: for a private experience, typically co-hosted by the executive chef and sommelier for a multi-course wine-pairing dinner.

Park Café is a casual, no-charge market-style eatery for salads, sandwiches, soups, and pastries.

ENTERTAINMENT. Facilities include the three-level, 874-seat Tropical Theater, which also has 24 wheelchair stations, and good sight lines from most seats.

A second venue is Safari Club, for cabaret shows and late-night adult comedy. Entertainment is always upbeat – in fact, it is almost impossible to get away from music and noise. There is even background music in all corridors and elevators, and constant music on the pool deck. If you want a quiet vacation, choose another cruise line.

SPA/FITNESS. The Vitality Spa and Fitness center has themed decor. It includes a 10,176-sq-ft (945-sq-m) solarium, a gym, aerobics room, saunas, steam rooms, and therapy treatment rooms. The climate-controlled, Balinese-themed indoor/outdoor solarium has a sliding glass dome roof that can be closed in cool or inclement weather conditions and includes a whirlpool and counter-current swimming.

For active types, there is activity galore – including a 30ft (9m) rock-climbing wall with five separate climbing tracks. It is at the aft end of the funnel. Other facilities include a nine-hole miniature golf course, and an indoor/outdoor country club with golf simulator, a jogging track, and basketball court.

SERENISSIMA
★★+

DATED BUT TOUGH, THIS CASUAL LITTLE SHIP IS GOOD FOR COASTAL CRUISING

Size:	Boutique Ship	Passenger/Crew Ratio (lower beds):	2.1
Tonnage:	2,632	Cabins (total):	59
Cruise Line:	Premier Cruises	Size Range (sq ft/m):	66.0-236.8/6.1-22.0
Former Names:	*Andrea, Harald Jarl*	Cabins (for one person):	0
Builder:	Trondheims Mek (Norway)	Cabins with balcony:	4
Entered Service:	Jun 1960/Dec 2012	Cabins (wheelchair accessible):	0
Length (ft/m):	286.7/87.4	Wheelchair accessibility:	None
Propulsion/Propellers:	diesel/2	Elevators:	1
Total Crew:	55	Casino (gaming tables):	No
Passengers (lower beds):	107	Self-Service Launderette:	No
Passenger Space Ratio (lower beds):	24.5	Onboard currency:	Euros

THE SHIP. This intimate ship is best for cruising in coastal regions. It is suited to couples and solo travelers of mature years who enjoy nature and wildlife at close range, and who would not dream of cruising in the mainstream sense aboard ships with large numbers of people. This is for the hardy, adventurous types who don't need constant entertainment or parlor games.

The 107-passenger *Serenissima* began her career as *Harald Jarl*, cruising the Norwegian coastline and fjords. Extensively renovated in 2003, she began her career as a classic cruise ship. In spring 2012 the ship was purchased by the owner of the Russian riverership *Volga Dream*, and renamed *Serenissima*. After a thorough renovation, this charming ship commenced cruise operations in April 2013. With her small size she is able to dock close to the heart of Europe's historic centers and is able to navigate into smaller, remote ports inaccessible to large resort ships.

Serenissima has a good amount of outdoors space (including a forward-viewing and observation platform), and the rather nice semi-covered aft area of the Boat Deck. The ship also now has stabilizers to counteract her well-known rolling motion.

ACCOMMODATION. Several different grades of cabins are arranged over five decks, and, with the exception of the five interior cabins, all have either windows or portholes. Because of the nature of this

BERLITZ'S RATINGS		
	Possible	Achieved
Ship	500	221
Accommodation	200	98
Food	400	199
Service	400	241
Entertainment	100	42
Cruise Experience	400	184

OVERALL SCORE 985 points out of 2000

eclectic ship, the cabins do vary in shape and size, giving the ship more character: from dimensionally challenged interior cabins of approximately 108 sq ft (10 sq m), to 'executive suites' of 273 sq ft (25.4 sq m) with small balconies, minibar, and other amenities. Two Owner's Suites are located at the front, directly under the navigation bridge, with forward-facing views; they measure 244 sq ft (22.7 sq m). Dedicated standard single-occupancy cabins range in size from 107 to 137 sq ft (9.9 to 12.7 sq m). The cabins are very nicely furnished.

Cabin 407 is designated for limited-mobility passengers (an adjacent elevator serves decks 3 to 6).

DINING. There is a cozy, one-seating Venice Restaurant, but the chairs do not have armrests, so lingering over a meal is not as comfortable as it could be. The food is tasty and well presented, and there is a good variety. Casual eats can be taken in the aft-facing open-deck Café.

ENTERTAINMENT. With this kind of ship, it's the after-dinner conversation that creates most of the evening's entertainment, although there is usually a solo pianist or other musical unit.

SPA/FITNESS. A small fitness center has only a limited amount of equipment (treadmills, bicycles, and free weights), plus an adjacent massage room.

SEVEN SEAS EXPLORER
★★★★+

AN ELEGANT AND EXTREMELY SPACIOUS SHIP WITH CONTEMPORARY STYLE

Size:	Small Ship	Passenger/Crew Ratio (lower beds):	1.3
Tonnage:	56,000	Cabins (total):	375
Cruise Line:	Regent Seven Seas Cruises	Size Range (sq ft/m):	301.3–3,875.1/3,875.1–360.0
Former Names:	none	Cabins (for one person):	0
Builder:	Fincantieri (Italy)	Cabins with balcony:	375
Entered Service:	Jul 2016	Cabins (wheelchair accessible):	3
Length (ft/m):	731.6/223.0	Wheelchair accessibility:	Best
Propulsion/Propellers:	diesel-electric/2	Elevators:	6
Total Crew:	552	Casino (gaming tables):	Yes
Passengers (lower beds):	750	Self-Service Launderette:	Yes
Passenger Space Ratio (lower beds):	74.6	Onboard currency:	US$

THE SHIP. This all-suite, all-balcony ship is the flagship of Regent Seven Seas Cruises, although its exterior design is not particularly handsome. It is most suited to couples and solo travelers who appreciate space, creature comforts, and stylish surroundings.

Incorporating many of the design features for which the company is known, *Seven Seas Explorer* is another example of the evolution of spacious, small-capacity ships. Sadly, there's no wrap-around outdoor promenade deck (although there is a jogging track atop ship), nor is there an exterior deck with forward-facing views (always nice to use when going through scenic areas).

Inside, the main focal point is a two-deck high atrium lobby, with a lovely, sweeping grand stairway. Facilities include an Observation Lounge (with retro decor reminiscent of a 1920s speakeasy), Connoisseur Club (for cigar enthusiasts – cigars cost extra), a very nice library, card room, business center, and coffee bar (for illy Italian coffees).

So, is it the 'most luxurious ship ever built,' as claimed by this cruise line? Not really, although some aspects are certainly in keeping with the word luxury; it is, however, an extremely comfortable ship. It's not just the hardware, but the software (crew, hospitality, training, service finesse, and communication skills) that are important in the overall picture of perceived luxury.

BERLITZ'S RATINGS		
	Possible	Achieved
Ship	500	427
Accommodation	200	171
Food	400	299
Service	400	323
Entertainment	100	78
Cruise Experience	400	320

OVERALL SCORE 1618 points out of 2000

ACCOMMODATION. The accommodation price grades depend on size and location. Some suites have interconnecting doors – good for an extended family cruising together. All suites have a mini-bar replenished daily, walk-in closet, personal safe, hairdryer, marble-clad bathroom with bathtub or shower enclosure (or both), L'Occitane products, bathrobe and slippers, 24-hour room service, and balconies with teak decking. You can also order meals in your suite if you wish.

The smallest accommodation units are Verandah Suites (approximately 215.2 sq ft/20 sq m without balcony, and 307 sq ft/29 sq m for those with a balcony).

The most expansive is an opulent 3,875 sq ft (360 sq m) – or 4,443 sq ft (412.7 sq m) if you add a second adjoining bedroom – Regent Suite, which spans the whole beam of the front of the ship on the uppermost deck. It has an in-built spa (with sauna, steam shower, two heated relaxation loungers – and unlimited private spa treatments), plus an Arabesque baby grand Steinway piano (and a Savoir bed). However, unless you are considering a longer cruise and don't plan to go ashore much (if you do, a private car and driver will be available in each port), it may not be worth it.

DINING. Compass Rose Restaurant is the main dining room; its focal point is a cascading aqua-blue chandelier. It has over 30 tables for two while others seat four or eight. The wine selection is very good, the beer selection is not.

To book a meal in one of the alternative venues (or make changes to reservations), a single reservation desk is a big help.

Restaurant Chartreuse is a stylish, romantic venue for French cuisine, cooked to order and placed on fine Bernardaud china. Seating is in small, intimate moon-shaped alcoves and at tables for two or four, plus some banquette seating.

Richly decorated Prime 7 (reservations required) is a premium-quality steakhouse, with banquette and individual seating, plus intimate alcoves.

Pacific Rim features pan-Asian cuisine (and a Tibetan-style prayer wheel outside).

The decor of La Verandah relives the 1960s glamour of the Italian Riviera, with mahogany detailing, terrazzo flooring, and brass accents. It's open for self-serve breakfast and lunch, and transforms into a modestly elegant restaurant, Sette Mari La Veranda for dinner.

The casual Pool Grill, for burgers, fresh grilled seafood, sandwiches, and fresh salads, has open-air and glass-enclosed seating. Milk shakes, malts, and ice-cream desserts are also available.

ENTERTAINMENT. The 694-seat Constellation Theater (showlounge) spans two decks, with seating on both levels (some sightlines are obstructed by pillars). It is an amphitheatre-style showlounge with a thrust stage, and music is provided by a live showband. During the day, it doubles as a cooking school (extra cost), with 18 workstations.

SPA/FITNESS. The Canyon Ranch Spa Club occupies space partly along the starboard side and at the aft of the ship – an open-air relaxation zone with its own dip pool. Facilities include seven body-treatment rooms plus one for couples. A circular stairway leads to the fitness studio on the deck above. Sports facilities include a bocce court, shuffleboard, paddle tennis, a putting green, and a jogging track.

SEVEN SEAS MARINER
★★★★

THIS ALL-INCLUSIVE, VERY SPACIOUS PREMIUM SHIP IS FOR SENIOR-AGE TRAVELERS

Size:	Small Ship	Passenger/Crew Ratio (lower beds):	1.6
Tonnage:	48,075	Cabins (total):	354
Cruise Line:	Regent Seven Seas Cruises	Size Range (sq ft/m):	301.3–2,002.0/28.0–186.0
Former Names:	none	Cabins (for one person):	0
Builder:	Chantiers de l'Atlantique (France)	Cabins with balcony:	354
Entered Service:	Mar 2001	Cabins (wheelchair accessible):	6
Length (ft/m):	713.0/217.3	Wheelchair accessibility:	Best
Propulsion/Propellers:	diesel-electric (16,000kW)/2 azimuthing pods	Elevators:	6
		Casino (gaming tables):	Yes
Total Crew:	445	Self-Service Launderette:	Yes
Passengers (lower beds):	708	Onboard currency:	US$
Passenger Space Ratio (lower beds):	67.9		

THE SHIP. *Seven Seas Mariner* is best suited to well-traveled couples and solo travelers, typically over 50, who seek excellent itineraries, fine food, and good service, with some entertainment, wrapped up in a contemporary, elegant ship. Its passenger/space ratio is among the highest in the cruise industry.

This was the first ship in the fleet to have a pod propulsion system, replacing the traditional shaft and rudder. The ship was extensively refurbished in 2014.

There is a wide range of public rooms, almost all of which are under the accommodation decks. With three sets of stairways (forward, center, and aft) it is easy to find your way around. An atrium lobby spans nine decks, with the lowest level opening directly onto the tender landing stage.

Facilities include a comfortable observation lounge, a small casino (with gaming tables and slot machines), a shopping concourse with 'open market' area, a garden lounge/promenade arcade, a large library (incorporating several computer workstations) and adjacent room with Internet-connect computers, coffee lounge, card player's room, conference room, cigar-smoking lounge (Connoisseur Club), and a Park West art gallery.

Basic gratuities are included, as are all alcoholic and non-alcoholic beverages and table wines for lunch and dinner. Premium and connoisseur selections are available at extra cost, and Internet-connection charges are high. Shore excursions

BERLITZ'S RATINGS	Possible	Achieved
Ship	500	397
Accommodation	200	164
Food	400	296
Service	400	308
Entertainment	100	77
Cruise Experience	400	303

OVERALL SCORE 1545 points out of 2000

and pre- or post-cruise hotel stays are also included, depending on the itinerary.

ACCOMMODATION. There are several accommodation categories. *Seven Seas Mariner* was the cruise industry's first all-suite, all-balconies ship – though that's not technically correct, as not all accommodation has sleeping areas completely separated from living areas.

Most grades have private, marble-clad bathrooms with tub or half-tub, and suite entrances are neatly recessed away from the passenger hallways to provide quiet (refreshingly, there's no music in the hallways, although there is some in the elevators).

In terms of sizing, accommodation is as follows:

Concierge Suites and Deluxe Suites: 301 sq ft (28 sq m).

Penthouse Suites: 449 sq ft (41.7 sq m).

Horizon Suites: 627 sq ft (58 sq m). There are 12 of these; they overlook the stern and have very large balconies.

Seven Seas Suites: 600–697 sq ft (56–65 sq m). They also overlook the ship's stern.

Grand Suites: 707 sq ft (66 sq m).

Mariner Suites: 739 sq ft (69 sq m).

Master Suites: 1,580 sq ft (147 sq m).

Six wheelchair-accessible suites are located as close to an elevator as one could possibly get, and provide ample living space, together with a large roll-in shower and all bathroom fittings located at the correct height.

DINING. Four dining venues all operate on an open-seating basis, so you can dine when and with whomever you choose. Reservations are required in two of the four venues. In general, the cuisine is good to very good, with creative presentation and a wide variety of food choices (Kosher meals can be provided).

The main dining room, the 570-seat Compass Rose Restaurant, has a light, fresh decor, and seating at tables for two, four, six, or eight – although tables for six or eight predominate. With a one-and-a-half deck height, the restaurant has an open feel to it, and there's enough space around most tables for good service.

The 80-seat Prime 7 Steakhouse is the smallest of the specialty dining venues. It features USDA prime, dry-aged steaks, chops, oven-roasted half chicken, Alaskan king crab legs, and Maine lobster. It's the most intimate dining spot – but again, the single-deck ceiling height makes it feel busy – and it can become noisy. Seating is for two to six, and reservations are required.

Chartreuse is a 120-seat venue with ocean views along the port side. It is directed and staffed by chefs wearing the white toque and blue riband of Le Cordon Bleu, the prestigious culinary society for classic French cuisine. Doors open onto a covered area outdoors, with small stage and dance floor. Seating is at tables of two to six, and reservations are required. However, the single-deck ceiling height robs the room of the grandeur that suits fine classic French cuisine best.

For more casual meals, La Veranda is a large self-serve indoor/outdoor café with seats for 450 and fresh, light decor. This eatery has several food islands and substantial counter display space. At night, it is transformed into Sette Mari – an Italian eatery with some excellent pasta-based dishes.

The outdoor Pool Grill and ice-cream bar, adjacent to the swimming pool, is a popular eatery. It features a creative list of burgers (a choice of 11, to be exact), including Black Angus beefburger, Philly beefburger, southwestern beefburger, pesto beefburger, Portobello and feta cheese burger, Asian salmon burger, tofu veggie burger, roasted garlic teriyaki mushroom turkey burger – and others – as well as various sandwiches.

ENTERTAINMENT. The Constellation Theater spans two decks and is delightful, with good sight lines from almost all seats. The proscenium arch stage also has a front thrust stage – useful for presenting more intimate cabaret acts – and an LED backdrop for dramatic show scenery images.

The Horizon Lounge, located aft, is a combination day lounge with bar, and the venue for afternoon tea and daily quizzes. A number of bands, small musical units, and solo pianists provide live music in lounges and bars.

There is also Stars nightclub, with an oval-shaped dance floor, and a stairway connecting it to the casino on the deck above.

SPA/FITNESS. Canyon Ranch Spa facilities include an extensive health spa with gymnasium and aerobics room, beauty parlor, and separate changing, sauna, and steam rooms for men and women.

Sports devotees can play on the paddle-tennis court and in the golf driving and practice cages.

SEVEN SEAS NAVIGATOR
★★★+

A MOSTLY PREMIUM, ALL-INCLUSIVE SHIP FOR MATURE-AGE CRUISERS

Size:	Small Ship	Passenger/Crew Ratio (lower beds):	1.5
Tonnage:	28,550	Cabins (total):	245
Cruise Line:	Regent Seven Seas Cruises	Size Range (sq ft/m):	301.3–1,173.3/28.0–109.0
Former Names:	none	Cabins (for one person):	0
Builder:	T. Mariotti (Italy)	Cabins with balcony:	196
Entered Service:	Aug 1999	Cabins (wheelchair accessible):	4
Length (ft/m):	559.7/170.6	Wheelchair accessibility:	Good
Propulsion/Propellers:	diesel (13,000kW)/2	Elevators:	5
Total Crew:	325	Casino (gaming tables):	Yes
Passengers (lower beds):	490	Self-Service Launderette:	Yes
Passenger Space Ratio (lower beds):	58.2	Onboard currency:	US$

THE SHIP. *Seven Seas Navigator* was built using a hull already constructed in St. Petersburg, Russia, as the research vessel *Akademik Nikolay Pilyugin*. The superstructure was incorporated into the hull in an Italian shipyard – the result being that, in effect, a new ship was delivered in record time. The result is less than handsome – particularly at the stern – but it's large enough to be stable over long stretches of water, and there is an excellent amount of space per passenger. In 2009, a 'ducktail' stern was added to aid stability and buoyancy.

The interiors (refreshed in a 2016 makeover) have a mix of classical and modern Italian styling and decor, with warm, soft colors and fine-quality soft furnishings and fabrics. The Galileo Lounge features a Steinway piano, and has good views over the stern. A Navigator's Lounge has warm mahogany and cherry wood paneling and large, comfortable, mid-back tub chairs. Next door, cigars and cognac can be taken in the Connoisseur's Club. An extensive library, with a faux fireplace, also has several computers with Internet access.

There is no walk-around promenade deck outdoors, although there's a jogging track high atop the aft section around the funnel housing. Two of the upper, outer decks are laid with green Astroturf, which cheapens the look of the ship – they would be better in teak. The ceilings in several public rooms, including the main restaurant, are quite low, which makes

BERLITZ'S RATINGS		
	Possible	Achieved
Ship	500	325
Accommodation	200	155
Food	400	275
Service	400	287
Entertainment	100	68
Cruise Experience	400	282

OVERALL SCORE 1392 points out of 2000

the ship feel smaller and more closed-in than it is. It still suffers from a considerable amount of vibration, which detracts from the comfort level when compared with other vessels of the same size.

The ship is best suited to well-traveled couples and solo travelers, typically over 50, who seek excellent itineraries, fine food, and good service, with some entertainment, all wrapped up in a contemporary ship that's elegant and comfortable. Designed for worldwide cruise itineraries, this is one of the upscale ships in the diverse Regent Seven Seas Cruises fleet.

Basic gratuities are included in the fare, as are alcoholic and non-alcoholic beverages, plus table wines for lunch and dinner (premium wines are available at extra cost). Shore excursions and any pre- or post-cruise hotel stays are also included.

ACCOMMODATION. There are several different price grades, and the company markets this as an 'all-suites' ship. Even the smallest suite is quite large, and all have outside views (all were refreshed in the 2016 revamp). Almost 90 percent of all suites have a private balcony, with floor-to-ceiling sliding glass doors, while 10 suites are interconnecting, and 38 have an extra bed for a third occupant. By comparison, even the smallest suite is more than twice the size of the smallest cabin aboard the world's largest cruise ships, Royal Caribbean International's *Oasis*-class ships.

All accommodation grades have a walk-in closet, European king-size bed or twin beds, wooden cabinetry with nicely rounded edges, plenty of drawer space, mini-bar/refrigerator stocked with complimentary soft drinks and bar set-up on embarkation, infotainment system, and personal safe. The marble-appointed bathroom has a full-size tub, as well as a separate shower enclosure, cotton bathrobe and towels, and hairdryer. Balconies benefit from real teak decking.

The largest living spaces are in four Grand and Master Suites. Then there are Navigator Suites, which are located in the ship's center, directly underneath the pool deck, although this means that they are subject to early morning noise attacks – when deck cleaning is carried out, and chairs are dragged across the deck. Despite this, they are delightful living spaces.

Four suites aimed at passengers with physical disabilities have private balconies, and are ideally located adjacent to the elevators. However, while they are generally very practical, it is almost impossible to access the balcony because of the high threshold at the bottom of the sliding glass door.

DINING. The 384-seat Compass Rose Dining Room has large ocean-view picture windows and open-seating dining, which means that you can choose your companions. There are a few tables for two, but most are for four, six, or eight persons. With a low ceiling height and noisy waiter stations, the overall feeling is cramped and unbecoming in terms of the lack of space and grace. Complimentary wines are served during dinner, and a connoisseur wine list is available at extra cost. The company also promotes 'heart healthy' cuisine.

La Veranda is the casual self-serve eatery for breakfast and lunch. Each evening, it is transformed into Sette Mari, for informal dining, and serves dinners with an emphasis on Italian cuisine (reservations required for dinner). Alfresco dining is also available.

The 70-seat Prime 7 is the place for steaks and seafood, and is in an elegant setting, for dinner only (reservations required). For fast food, there is a small outdoor Grill one deck above.

You can also dine in your cabin. There is a 24-hour room service menu and, during regular dinner hours, you can choose from the full dining room menu. For coffee lovers, there's Coffee Connection (for illy coffees), close to the Navigator Lounge.

ENTERTAINMENT. The Seven Seas Lounge, a two-deck-high showlounge, has reasonable sight lines from most seats on both main and balcony levels, although pillars obstruct views from some side balcony seats. *Seven Seas Navigator* puts on both production shows and cabaret acts. Bands, small musical units, and solo pianist entertainers provide live music in the lounges and bars.

SPA/FITNESS. The spa, fitness center, and beauty salon are in the most forward part of the top deck. Canyon Ranch SpaClub operates the spa and beauty services as a concession, provides the staff, and sells its own beauty products. An 18 percent gratuity is included in treatment and beauty salon services prices.

SEVEN SEAS VOYAGER
★★★★+

A PREMIUM ALL-INCLUSIVE CRUISE SHIP WITH OODLES OF SPACE AND STYLE

Size:	Small Ship
Tonnage:	42,363
Cruise Line:	Regent Seven Seas Cruises
Former Names:	none
Builder:	T. Mariotti (Italy)
Entered Service:	Mar 2003
Length (ft/m):	669.2/204.0
Propulsion/Propellers:	diesel-electric (16,000kW)/2 azimuthing pods
Total Crew:	445
Passengers (lower beds):	708
Passenger Space Ratio (lower beds):	59.8
Passenger/Crew Ratio (lower beds):	1.6
Cabins (total):	354
Size Range (sq ft/m):	356.0–1,399.3/33.0–130.0
Cabins (for one person):	0
Cabins with balcony:	354
Cabins (wheelchair accessible):	4
Wheelchair accessibility:	Best
Elevators:	6
Casino (gaming tables):	Yes
Self-Service Launderette:	Yes
Onboard currency:	US$

THE SHIP. *Seven Seas Voyager* was built in 32 blocks, with the same basic hull design as *Seven Seas Mariner*, with a few modifications. Following a 2016 multi-million dollar makeover, the ship has been refreshed and has a more elegant feel. There is a complete outdoor teak walk-around deck, and a keyhole-shaped pool with two adjacent hot tubs.

Inside, there is a good array of public rooms, almost all located below the accommodation decks. Three sets of stairways mean it is easy to find your way around. An atrium lobby spans eight decks, with the lowest level opening directly onto the tender landing stage.

Facilities include five bars, a showlounge that spans two decks, an observation lounge (with heavy, but very comfortable white chairs), the Horizon Lounge (strangely, at the back of the ship), a small casino (with gaming tables and slot machines), a shopping concourse, large library, Internet-connect center (Club.com), business center (Coffee.com), card room, and small conference room. There is also a nightclub, Voyager, with an oval-shaped dance floor, the Connoisseur Club for cigars and cognacs, and an 'art' gallery.

Seven Seas Voyager is ideally suited to well-travelled couples and solo travelers, typically over 50, seeking excellent itineraries, good food and service, with some entertainment, in a contemporary ship that's elegant and very comfortable. (Only several

BERLITZ'S RATINGS		
	Possible	Achieved
Ship	500	403
Accommodation	200	169
Food	400	298
Service	400	312
Entertainment	100	77
Cruise Experience	400	309

OVERALL SCORE 1568 points out of 2000

pillars and low ceilings in public rooms mar the feeling of spaciousness.) It's an 'all-inclusive' ship, although the company chooses the drink brands, not you.

ACCOMMODATION. There are about a dozen different accommodation price grades. As the ship was built with a central hallway design, it allowed for larger suites and bathrooms than aboard sibling *Seven Seas Mariner*. Regent Seven Seas Cruises says it's an 'all-suites, all-balconies' ship – although that's incorrect, as not all sleeping areas are completely separated from living areas. Electrical outlets are both US and European-style.

All accommodation grades have private, marble-clad bathrooms, and walk-in closet with personal safe, and most suite entrances are recessed away from passenger hallways to provide extra quiet. All have a small private balcony. Partitions are mostly of the partial type. From the smallest to the largest, there is something for all wallets.

Deluxe Suites are the smallest; they have twin beds convertible to a queen-size bed, but the sleeping area is separated from the living area only by partial room dividers, and therefore they are cabins – albeit good-size ones – not suites.

Two Master Suites (1100 and 1001) are the largest of the accommodation.

Four wheelchair-accessible suites (761, 762, 859, and 860) are all close to an elevator, and provide ample living space, together with a large roll-in shower and all bathroom fittings at the correct height.

DINING. The 570-seat Compass Rose Restaurant is the main dining room. It has tables for two to 10, and dining is on an open seating basis, so you can dine with whomever you like, when you choose. In general, the cuisine is very good, and there's plenty of choice, although it lacks the wow factor you might expect. It is a shame, too, to find packets of sugar and jams on an elegant ship.

Chartreuse is an intimate, stylish venue for experiencing some classic French cuisine, cooked to order and presented on fine Bernardaud china.

Prime 7 Steakhouse is the smallest of the specialty dining venues, with 80 seats. It features a range of USDA prime, dry-aged steaks as well as chops, oven-roasted half chicken, Alaskan king crab legs, and Maine lobster. It's the most intimate dining spot – although the single-deck ceiling height makes it feel busy – and it can get noisy. There is seating for two, four, or six, and reservations are required.

Signatures 'supper club' seats 120, and has ocean views along the room's port side. It is directed and staffed by chefs wearing the white toque and blue riband of Le Cordon Bleu, the prestigious culinary society for classic French cuisine. Seating is at tables of two, four, or six, and reservations are required.

For more casual meals, La Veranda is a large self-serve, indoor/outdoor café with seats for 450, and fresh, light decor. This eatery has several food islands and substantial counter display space. At night, it morphs into Sette Mari – an Italian-style eatery featuring pasta-based dishes.

The outdoor Pool Grill and ice-cream bar, adjacent to the swimming pool, is a popular eatery. It features a creative list of burgers and various sandwiches.

ENTERTAINMENT. The Constellation Showlounge spans two decks, and sight lines are very good from almost all of the (mostly banquette) seats. A troupe of singers/dancers provides colorful (mini) Vegas-style revues and production shows. Cabaret acts provide stand-alone evening shows. The ship carries a main showband, several small musical groups, and soloists.

SPA/FITNESS. Canyon Ranch SpaClub facilities include an extensive health spa with gymnasium and aerobics room, beauty parlor, and separate changing, sauna, and steam rooms for men and women.

An 18 percent gratuity is included in the price of treatments and beauty salon services.

SILVER CLOUD
★★★+

AN INCLUSIVE, UPMARKET BUT QUITE DATED SMALL SHIP FOR DISCOVERY-STYLE CRUISING

Size:	Small Ship	Passenger/Crew Ratio (lower beds):	1.2
Tonnage:	16,927	Cabins (total):	130
Cruise Line:	Silversea Cruises	Size Range (sq ft/m):	240.0–1,314.0/22.2–122.0
Former Names:	none	Cabins (for one person):	0
Builder:	Visentini/Mariotti (Italy)	Cabins with balcony:	110
Entered Service:	Apr 1994/2014	Cabins (wheelchair accessible):	2
Length (ft/m):	514.4/155.8	Wheelchair accessibility:	Fair
Propulsion/Propellers:	diesel (11,700kW)/2	Elevators:	4
Total Crew:	208	Casino (gaming tables):	Yes
Passengers (lower beds):	260	Self-Service Launderette:	Yes
Passenger Space Ratio (lower beds):	64.6	Onboard currency:	US$

THE SHIP. *Silver Cloud*, now well over 20 years old, has a fairly decent profile, with a sloping stern reminiscent of an Airstream trailer. Following a 2017 conversion to make it more like an expedition-style ship, *Silver Cloud* carries 18 Zodiac landing craft, and has a deep blue hull. The ship has an ice-class hull modification for sailing in the polar regions and carries a maximum of 260 passengers (200 on Antarctic voyages). But it's not a real expedition ship (it was definitely not designed or built for rough waters like the Drake Passage), but a conversion (it lacks properly designed 'mud' rooms, boot-washing areas, and equipment storage rooms).

The vertical cake-layer stacking of public rooms aft and the location of accommodation forward ensures quiet cabins. There is a synthetic turf-covered (this doesn't equate with luxury) walk-around promenade deck outdoors.

The spacious interior has bland decor, but fine-quality soft furnishings accented by the gentle use of brass fittings, fine woods, and creative ceilings.

An excellent amount of space per passenger means there is no hint of a line anywhere in this unhurried environment.

All drinks, gratuities, and port taxes are included, and no further tipping is necessary – though it is not prohibited.

Niggles? Some vibration is evident when bow thrusters or the anchors are used, particularly in

BERLITZ'S RATINGS		
	Possible	Achieved
Ship	500	326
Accommodation	200	140
Food	400	283
Service	400	278
Entertainment	100	66
Cruise Experience	400	273

OVERALL SCORE 1366 points out of 2000

the forward-most cabins. The self-service launderette is not large enough for longer cruises. Crew facilities are minimal, leading to a high crew turnover, which undermines service.

ACCOMMODATION. There are several price grades in this 'all-suites' ship. The all-outside-view suites, three-quarters of which have fine private teakwood balconies, have convertible queen-to-twin beds, and are beautifully fitted out. They have large floor-to-ceiling windows, large walk-in closets, dressing table, writing desk, stocked minibar/refrigerator (no charge), and fresh flowers.

Marble-floored bathrooms have a tub, fixed showerhead, single washbasin, and plenty of high-quality towels.

The walk-in closets don't provide much hanging space, particularly for such items as full-length dresses, and it would be better for the door to open outward instead of inward. The drawers themselves are poorly positioned, but several other drawers and storage areas are provided in the living area.

Although the cabin insulation above and below is good, between cabins it is not, and a privacy curtain between entry door and sleeping area would be useful. Light from the passageway leaks into the cabin, so it's hard to achieve a dark room.

Top-grade suites have teak balcony furniture (others do not), but all balconies have teak floors. Suites with balconies on the lowest deck suffer from sticky salt spray when the ship is moving, so balconies always need cleaning. Each evening, the stewardesses bring plates of canapés to your suite – just right for a light bite with cocktails. In Grand, Royal, Rossellini, or Owner's suites, you get butler service.

DINING. The Restaurant provides open-seating dining in somewhat elegant surroundings. It has an attractive arched gazebo center and a wavy ceiling design as its focal point, and is set with fine Eschenbach china and Christofle silverware. Meals are in an open seating, which means you can eat with whom you like.

Standard table wines are included for lunch and dinner – with premium wines at extra charge.

La Saletta, adjacent to the main dining room, is an intimate 24-seat specialty dining salon. Dégustation menus include dishes designed by chefs from Relais & Châteaux and paired with selected wines. Reservations are required, and there's a cover charge.

La Terrazza is for self-serve breakfast and lunch buffets. Both indoor and outdoor seating is at teakwood tables and chairs.

In-cabin dining is also available, but the balcony tables in the standard suites are too low for outdoor dining.

ENTERTAINMENT. The Showlounge hosts entertainment events and some social functions. The tiered-floor room spans two decks; banquette and individual seating is provided, and sight lines are good.

Silversea Cruises places more emphasis on food than entertainment, so what is provided is tasteful, not overbearing. A band provides live music in the evenings.

SPA/FITNESS. The Spa at Silversea is compact. Facilities include a separate sauna for men and women, body treatment rooms, a beauty salon, and a separate gymnasium (in another location).

SILVER DISCOVERER
★★★★

A SMALL EXPEDITION-STYLE SHIP THAT IS BUILT FOR DISCOVERY CRUISES

Size:	Boutique Ship	Passenger/Crew Ratio (lower beds):	1.2
Tonnage:	5,218	Cabins (total):	62
Cruise Line:	Silversea Cruises	Size Range (sq ft/m):	182.9–258.3/17–24
Former Names:	*Clipper Odyssey, Oceanic Odyssey,*	Cabins (for one person):	0
	Oceanic Grace	Cabins with balcony:	8
Builder:	NKK Tsu Shipyard (Japan)	Cabins (wheelchair accessible):	1
Entered Service:	Apr 1989/May 2014	Wheelchair accessibility:	Fair
Length (ft/m):	337.9/103.0	Elevators:	1
Propulsion/Propellers:	diesel (5,192kW)/2	Casino (gaming tables):	No
Total Crew:	96	Self-Service Launderette:	No
Passengers (lower beds):	124	Onboard currency:	US$
Passenger Space Ratio (lower beds):	42.0		

THE SHIP. *Silver Discoverer* is liked by couples and solo travelers who seek nature and wildlife up close and personal, but in highly comfortable surroundings, and who wouldn't dream of cruising aboard anything larger.

The ship has quite a smart, chic, mega-yacht-like profile, with a flared bow, square stern, and twin funnels that sweep up from each of the ship's sides. Designed in Holland and built in Japan, it tried to copy the *SeaDream* small ship/ultra-yacht concept, originally for the Japanese market. Operated by Japan's Showa Line, it wasn't suited to Japan's often choppy seas, so, after 10 years, it was sold to Clipper Cruise Line. In 2013 it was purchased by Silversea Cruises and renamed following a substantial refit and refurbishment program.

There are expansive areas outdoors for its size, and these are excellent for viewing nature and wildlife. A small swimming pool is just a 'dip' pool, but there is a wide teakwood outdoor jogging track. Snorkeling equipment is available, as is a fleet of 12 Zodiacs for shore landings, and a glass-bottom boat for marine-life exploration.

Inside, nothing jars the senses, as the interior design concept is balanced. The ambience is warm and intimate. There are, however, several pillars throughout the public areas, which spoil the decor and sight lines. The ship concentrates on exploring regions such as Australia's Kimberley, the

BERLITZ'S RATINGS		
	Possible	Achieved
Ship	500	324
Accommodation	200	135
Food	400	295
Service	400	313
Entertainment	100	59
Cruise Experience	400	295
OVERALL SCORE 1421 points out of 2000		

Russian Far East, and the Bering Sea area.

ACCOMMODATION. There are several cabin categories, and the all-outside cabins are tastefully furnished with blond wood cabinetry, twin- or queen-size beds, living area with sofa, personal safe, minibar/refrigerator, TV and three-sided mirror. Some cabins have private balconies; but these are very small, with awkward door handles. All bathrooms have shower enclosures; note that the toilet seats are extremely high.

There is one suite, which is the size of two cabins. It provides more room, of course, than a standard cabin, with a lounge area, and more storage space.

DINING. The dining room has large ocean-view picture windows. It is quite warm and inviting, and all passengers eat in a single seating. The cuisine includes fresh foods from local ports where possible.

ENTERTAINMENT. There is no entertainment as such, although evening recaps, dinner and after-dinner conversation with fellow passengers in the ship's lounge/bar really is the entertainment.

SPA/FITNESS. There is a tiny beauty salon, and an adjacent massage/body-treatment room. A small fitness room is located on a different deck.

SILVER EXPLORER
★★★★

THIS SMALL 'SOFT' EXPEDITION SHIP HAS SOME PREMIUM CHARACTERISTICS

Size: ....Boutique Ship	Passenger Space Ratio (lower beds): 42.1
Tonnage: 6,072	Passenger/Crew Ratio (lower beds):........................ 1.2
Cruise Line: ....Silversea Cruises	Cabins (total): 72
Former Names: .... *Prince Albert II, World*	Size Range (sq ft/m): 172.2–785.7/16.0–73.0
Discoverer, Dream 21, Baltic Clipper, Sally Clipper, Delfin	Cabins (for one person):... 0
Star, Delfin Clipper, World Adventurer, Delfin Clipper	Cabins with balcony:.............. 6 + 14 French balconies
Builder: .... Rauma-Repola (Finland)	Cabins (wheelchair accessible): 0
Entered Service: .... Jul 1989/Jun 2008	Wheelchair accessibility: ....None
Length (ft/m): 354.3/108.0	Elevators:.. 2
Propulsion/Propellers: .... diesel (4,500kW)/2	Casino (gaming tables): .... No
Total Crew: 117	Self-Service Launderette:...................................... No
Passengers (lower beds): 144	Onboard currency: .... US$

THE SHIP. Twin swept-back outboard funnels highlight the semi-smart exterior design of this small specialist expedition cruise ship. It has a dark ice-hardened hull, carries a fleet of eight Zodiac inflatable landing craft for shore landings and exploration, and has one boot-washing station, the Mud Room, with six bays. There is no walk-around promenade deck outdoors.

The accommodation is located forward, with all public rooms aft except for an observation lounge, an arrangement that helps keep noise to a minimum in the accommodation areas. The interior has many European design elements, including warm color combinations. Public rooms include an observation lounge, which, following a 2017 refurbishment, now incorporates reference books that were in the former library, plus a panorama lounge (a strange name for a room at the back of the ship), large lecture room/cinema with bar, and boutique.

Silver Explorer has many of the creature comforts of much larger vessels and will provide a very comfortable expedition-style cruise experience in tasteful and elegant surroundings. All passengers receive a pre-cruise amenities package that typically includes a field guide, backpack, carry-on travel bag, and luggage tags.

The ship is best suited to adventurous couples and solo travelers of mature years who enjoy seeing nature at close range, but want an extremely comfortable setting, plus good food and service.

BERLITZ'S RATINGS		
	Possible	Achieved
Ship	500	354
Accommodation	200	144
Food	400	286
Service	400	322
Entertainment	100	58
Cruise Experience	400	289
OVERALL SCORE 1453 points out of 2000		

ACCOMMODATION. There is a range of accommodation and price grades. The cabins, which are quite large for such a small ship, are outfitted to a good standard, with ample closet and drawer space. All have outside views and twin beds that convert to a queen-size bed, flat-screen TV, telephone, hairdryer, refrigerator, and lockable drawer. The bathrooms have rainshowers.

Although only six suites have a large private balcony (they're really not needed in cold-weather regions), several 'suites' have glass doors that open onto a few inches of space outdoors. The Owner's Suites have two rooms, linked by an interconnecting door, to provide a separate lounge, bedroom, and two bathrooms.

DINING. The spacious dining room, with pastel-colored decor, accommodates all passengers in one seating. Casual alfresco bites can be had at the outdoor grill.

ENTERTAINMENT. Daily recaps and after-dinner conversation make up the onboard entertainment.

SPA/FITNESS. Facilities include a small gymnasium, sauna, and treatment room for massage.

SILVER GALAPAGOS
★★★+

A FINE SHIP TO USE AS A FLOATING BASE IN THE GALÁPAGOS

Size:	Boutique Ship
Tonnage:	4,203
Cruise Line:	Silversea Cruises
Former Names:	Renaissance Three, Galapagos Explorer II
Builder:	Cantieri Navale Ferrari (Italy)
Entered Service:	Aug 1990/Sep 2013
Length (ft/m):	293.1/89.3
Propulsion/Propellers:	diesel (3,514kW)/2
Total Crew:	75
Passengers (lower beds):	100
Passenger Space Ratio (lower beds):	42.0

Passenger/Crew Ratio (lower beds):	1.3
Cabins (total):	50
Size Range (sq ft/m):	231.4–282.0/21.5–26.2
Cabins (for one person):	0
Cabins with balcony:	24
Cabins (wheelchair accessible):	0
Wheelchair accessibility:	None
Elevators:	1
Casino (gaming tables):	No
Self-Service Launderette:	No
Onboard currency:	US$

THE SHIP. *Silver Galapagos* operates two specific Galápagos cruise itineraries year-round from Baltra, Ecuador. It suits couples and solo travelers who want to cruise around the islands in comfortable, stylish surroundings.

It is an inviting ship, built as one of a series of eight similar small ships for the defunct Renaissance Cruises. While the vessel is in good condition, maintenance could be better. Its looks are quite contemporary in the style of a mega-yacht, and there is a wooden promenade deck outdoors. The limited number of public rooms have smart and restful, non-glitzy decor. The main lounge doubles as a lecture room, but perhaps it is the piano bar that provides the best place to relax after dinner in the evening. A doctor is carried at all times.

This ship (first operated by Silversea Cruises in 2013) provides a destination-intensive, refined, quiet, and relaxed cruise for those who don't like crowds or dressing up. Trained naturalist guides lead the shore excursions (included in the fare); the ship carries two glass-bottom boats, plus wetsuits and snorkeling equipment.

All drinks, bottled water, and soft drinks are included in the fare. Also included are guided visits to the islands.

BERLITZ'S RATINGS		
	Possible	Achieved
Ship	500	338
Accommodation	200	150
Food	400	259
Service	400	292
Entertainment	100	50
Cruise Experience	400	267
OVERALL SCORE 1356 points out of 2000		

There is little sunbathing space. The service lacks finesse, but the crew is willing. The small library is attractive, but the book selection is limited. In summer 2020, this ship will be replaced by Silver Origin.

ACCOMMODATION. This is located forward, with public rooms aft. Pleasant, all-outside suites have a large picture window, hand-crafted Italian furniture, and wet bar. All cabins have a queen-size bed, a sitting area, a minibar/refrigerator, TV, DVD player, and hairdryer. The small bathrooms have showers with a fold-down seat, real teakwood floors, and marble vanities.

DINING. The small, elegant, intimate dining room has open seating and tables for two, four, six, and eight. The meals at dinner are à la carte, while lunch is buffet-style (sometimes on the open deck), with local Ecuadorian delicacies and meat.

ENTERTAINMENT. After-dinner conversation with fellow passengers forms the entertainment each evening.

SPA/FITNESS. There is a small sauna. Snorkel gear is also available.

SILVER MUSE
★★★★+

THIS SHIP IS WELL-SUITED TO SOPHISTICATED INTERNATIONAL TRAVELERS

Size:	Small Ship	Passenger/Crew Ratio (lower beds):	1.4
Tonnage:	40,700	Cabins (total):	298
Cruise Line:	Silversea Cruises	Size Range (sq ft/m):	387.5–1,969.8/36.0–183.0
Former Names:	none	Cabins (for one person):	0
Builder:	Fincantieri (Italy)	Cabins with balcony:	298
Entered Service:	Apr 2017	Cabins (wheelchair accessible):	4
Length (ft/m):	698.8/213.0	Wheelchair accessibility:	Best
Propulsion/Propellers:	diesel/2	Elevators:	6
Total Crew:	411	Casino (gaming tables):	Yes
Passengers (lower beds):	596	Self-Service Launderette:	Yes
Passenger Space Ratio (lower beds):	78.8	Onboard currency:	US$

THE SHIP. An evolution of the smaller *Silver Spirit*, *Silver Muse* has more space, more dining options, larger public rooms, and more passengers. It has nicely tiered aft decks, and there is a good amount of open deck space. Inside, public rooms include an observation lounge (named Tor's – after Torstein Hagen, chairman of Viking Cruises and a longtime friend of Silversea Cruises' chairman), panorama lounge, Connoisseur's Corner (for cigar-smokers), Dolce Vita (a main lounge and social gathering place, with a tiny bar), an Arts Café, a library, and children's center.

A high degree of comfort and style, together with 'Italian flair' go hand in hand with good culinary offerings for a cosmopolitan clientele. Silversea Cruises has 'all-inclusive' pricing (although it doesn't include things such as shore excursions or spa treatments), except for premium drink brands and really good vintage wines.

Overall, it's the largest ship in the fleet (and carries more passengers), but the interior design, colors, and furnishings are far superior to those on all the other Silversea ships. There are more dining and food choices, and the suites (particularly the smallest ones) are better designed.

ACCOMMODATION. There are numerous accommodation price grades, with the price dependent on the size, location, and grade you choose.

BERLITZ'S RATINGS		
	Possible	Achieved
Ship	500	417
Accommodation	200	179
Food	400	320
Service	400	338
Entertainment	100	84
Cruise Experience	400	322

OVERALL SCORE 1660 points out of 2000

From the smallest to the largest (Owner's Suites – four of them, one of which – Balsorano – displays photos of the founding family of Silversea Cruises), this all-suite ship has some delightfully spacious accommodation. Note that balconies have faux teak decking.

DINING. There is no single main restaurant. Instead, Atlantide (for seafood and grilled food) and Indochine (for Indian, Thai, Vietnamese, etc.) are the two largest dining venues. This is all about open-seating dining, in attractive surroundings, with unhurried, unobtrusive service, and seating with whomever you wish. The restaurants are open for breakfast, lunch, and dinner; tables are set with fine china, silverware, and Riedel wine glasses.

Other restaurants and eateries include: La Dame by Relais & Châteaux, an extra-cost, reservations-required finer-dining venue; Silver Note, a dinner/dancing venue, for tapas-style bites in an elegant, jazzy setting (with music based on jazz and swing); Kaiseki, an extra-cost, reservations-required Japanese-style venue for lunch and dinner; and a Teppanyaki grill (with seating) in the evening. La Terrazza is an indoor/outdoor, self-serve casual eatery for breakfast and lunch. The casual Spaccanapoli is the venue for pizzas, while the tablecloth-free Hot Rocks is an outdoor 'under-the-stars' venue for steaks and grilled sea-food items.

In case you want to be private, you can eat, course-by-course, in the privacy of your suite, which may occasionally be very welcome.

ENTERTAINMENT. The showlounge, which is used for shows and social functions, has a classic thrust stage. It spans two decks and has a sloping floor and tiered seating levels. Colorful, small-cast song-and-dance shows and cabaret acts are featured.

SPA/FITNESS. Zagara Spa, operated by Steiner Leisure, has saunas and steam rooms for men and women, a thermal suite (day passes are at extra cost), nine rooms for body treatments, an out-door relaxation area (with hot tub and relaxation loungers), and a fitness center with cardiovascular equipment.

SILVER SHADOW
★★★★+

THIS ALL-INCLUSIVE PREMIUM SHIP IS A GOOD CHOICE FOR MATURE-AGE CRUISERS

Size:	Small Ship	Passenger/Crew Ratio (lower beds):	1.4
Tonnage:	28,258	Cabins (total):	194
Cruise Line:	Silversea Cruises	Size Range (sq ft/m):	287.0–1,435.0/26.6–133.3
Former Names:	none	Cabins (for one person):	0
Builder:	Visentini/Mariotti (Italy)	Cabins with balcony:	166
Entered Service:	Sep 2000	Cabins (wheelchair accessible):	2
Length (ft/m):	610.2/186.0	Wheelchair accessibility:	Good
Propulsion/Propellers:	diesel/2	Elevators:	5
Total Crew:	302	Casino (gaming tables):	Yes
Passengers (lower beds):	388	Self-Service Launderette:	Yes
Passenger Space Ratio (lower beds):	72.8	Onboard currency:	US$

THE SHIP. This ship is best suited to discerning, well-traveled couples, typically over 50, who seek a small ship with excellent food that approaches gourmet standards, and fine service in surroundings bordering on the elegant and luxurious.

Silver Shadow is one of the second generation of ships in the Silversea Cruises fleet, and slightly larger than *Silver Cloud* and *Silver Wind*, with a more streamlined forward profile and large, sleek single funnel. However, the ship's stern is not particularly handsome. There is a generous amount of open deck and sunbathing space, and aluminum/teak deck furniture is provided.

The company's many international passengers react well to the ambience, food, service, and the helpful staff. The cruise line has 'all-inclusive' fares, including gratuities and many things that cost extra aboard many rivals' ships, but the fares don't include vintage wines, massage, or other personal services.

Although the ship shows signs of wear, the onboard product is very good, particularly the cuisine and its presentation. Shuttle buses are provided in most ports of call, and all the little extras that passengers receive make this an extremely pleasant experience, in surroundings that are comfortable and contemporary without being extravagant, with open-seating dining and drinks included, cold canapés and hot hors d'oeuvres served in the bars

BERLITZ'S RATINGS		
	Possible	Achieved
Ship	500	400
Accommodation	200	177
Food	400	311
Service	400	318
Entertainment	100	78
Cruise Experience	400	313

OVERALL SCORE 1597 points out of 2000

in the pre-dinner cocktail hour, a captain's welcome aboard, and farewell cocktail party.

The swimming pool is surprisingly small, as is the fitness room, although it was expanded in 2007. The Humidor by Davidoff (a cigar lounge) has 25 seats and is in the style of an English smoking club. There is a Champagne bar and a four-terminal computer center (Wi-Fi costs extra).

In December 2019, *Silver Shadow* will undergo a ship-wide refurbishment, with a location change for the casino. The spa will be revitalized (to be named Zagara Beauty Spa and Fitness Center), and the former Observation Lounge will morph into the Observation Accommodation. There are eight price grades in this all-suites ship. Each suite has a double vanity, tub, and separate shower enclosure in its marble-floored bathroom. All grades receive Silversea-monogrammed Frette bed linen, an eight-pillow menu (from soft down to memory foam), 100 percent cotton bathrobes, a range of Acqua di Parma bathroom products, and personalized stationery. Stay in the Grand, Royal, Rossellini, or Owner's suites and you also receive unobtrusive service from butlers certified by London's Guild of Professional Butlers.

The Vista Suites measure 287 sq ft (27 sq m); they don't have a private balcony.

Verandah Suites (really Vista Suites plus a veranda) measure 345 sq ft (32 sq m).

Silver Suites are 701 sq ft (65 sq m).
Owner's Suites measure 1,208 sq ft (112 sq m).
Royal Suites are either 1,312 sq ft (122 sq m) or 1,352 sq ft (126 sq m).

There are two Grand Suites, one measuring 1,286 sq ft (119 sq m), and the other (including an adjoining suite with interconnecting door) 1,435 sq ft (133 sq m).

There are also two Disabled Suites (535 and 537), both adjacent to an elevator and next to each other; these measure a generous 398 sq ft (37 sq m). They are well equipped with an accessible hanging rail, and roll-in bathroom with roll-in shower unit.

DINING. The main dining room, The Restaurant, has open seating in elegant surroundings. Three grand chandeliers provide an upward focal point. Meals can also be served, course-by-course, in your suite, although the balcony tables are rather low for dining outdoors. The cuisine is very good, with a choice of formal and informal areas. Standard table wines are included for lunch and dinner, with an extra-cost 'connoisseur list' of premium wines. Once each cruise, there's a Galley Brunch when the galley is transformed into a large 'chef's kitchen.'

For something special, Le Champagne is a more intimate extra-cost venue that allows diners to sample highly specialized dégustation menus marrying international cuisine with vintage wines selected by Relais & Châteaux sommeliers. Reservations are needed, and the wines also cost extra.

For more informal meals, La Terrazza provides self-serve breakfast and lunch buffets; outdoor seating is at teakwood tables and chairs. The buffet design and set-up presents flow problems during breakfast, and 'active' stations for cooking eggs or pasta to order would help.

Adjacent to La Terazza is a wine bar and a cigar-smoking room. A poolside grill provides a casual alternative daytime bistro-style eatery, for grilled and fast-food items, and becomes The Grill for evening dining, with food cooked on hot stones.

ENTERTAINMENT. The Showlounge, the venue for entertainment and some social functions, spans two decks and has a sloping floor; both banquette and individual seating are provided, with good sight lines from almost all seats.

Although Silversea Cruises places more emphasis on food than entertainment, what is provided is quite tasteful. A decent array of cabaret acts does the Silversea circuit, and small, colorful production shows have been reintroduced. More emphasis is placed on classical music ensembles. There is a band and several small musical units for live music in the evenings in The Bar and the Panorama Lounge.

SPA/FITNESS. The Spa at Silversea health/fitness facility, just behind the Observation Lounge, high atop the ship, had a complete makeover in 2007. It includes a gymnasium, beauty salon, and separate saunas and steam rooms for men and women, plus several treatment rooms.

SILVER SPIRIT
★★★★+

A STYLISH UPPER-CLASS SHIP FOR SOPHISTICATED CRUISING AND GOOD FOOD

Size:	Small Ship	Passenger/Crew Ratio (lower beds):	1.5
Tonnage:	39,519	Cabins (total):	304
Cruise Line:	Silversea Cruises	Size Range (sq ft/m):	312.1–1,614.6/29–150
Former Names:	none	Cabins (for one person):	0
Builder:	Fincantieri (Italy)	Cabins with balcony:	258
Entered Service:	Dec 2009	Cabins (wheelchair accessible):	4
Length (ft/m):	691.3/210.7	Wheelchair accessibility:	Best
Propulsion/Propellers:	diesel-electric (26,100kW)/2	Elevators:	6
Total Crew:	412	Casino (gaming tables):	Yes
Passengers (lower beds):	608	Self-Service Launderette:	Yes
Passenger Space Ratio (lower beds):	64.9	Onboard currency:	US$

THE SHIP. *Silver Spirit* is an 'all-inclusive' ship – although 'all-inclusive' doesn't include the specialty dining venues. Sharing its name with a famous Rolls-Royce car, *Silver Spirit* was 'stretched' in 2018, when a new 15m (49ft) mid-section was added, as were new speciality dining spots and eateries, and more suites.

Although there's a main pool and hot tub deck, there's little shade, and no hot tubs on any other deck. The ship also lacks a walk-around outdoor promenade deck.

The interior layout has a cake-layer stacking of almost all the public rooms in the aft section, and the accommodation located forward, so there is minimal noise in passenger accommodation, although it means there are more stairs and no flow-through horizontal deck where passengers can parade. But regular Silversea Cruises passengers are used to this arrangement, and it's good exercise. The decor is elegant and understated, with muted colors; style-wise, it's a mix of Art Deco and modern, but not contemporary.

The Observation Lounge, at the front of the ship with access from a central passageway, has fine ocean views, and is a very comfortable place in which to relax and read. The Panorama Lounge, at the stern, is a comfortable multi-function room. Non-smokers should note that smoking is allowed on the port side. A cigar lounge, with doors that open in to the casino, has a pleasing list of cigars. The casino has five blackjack tables, an American Roulette table, and 52 slot machines.

BERLITZ'S RATINGS

	Possible	Achieved
Ship	500	413
Accommodation	200	177
Food	400	316
Service	400	328
Entertainment	100	83
Cruise Experience	400	316

OVERALL SCORE 1633 points out of 2000

The company's 'all-inclusive' fares include gratuities, drinks with meals, and many things that cost extra on competitor ships. Vintage wines, massage, and other personal services do cost extra, though. Passengers appreciate open-seating dining, cold canapés and hot hors d'oeuvres served at the bars in the pre-dinner cocktail hour, a captain's welcome aboard, and a farewell cocktail party. Shuttle buses are provided in most ports of call.

The passenger mix includes many nationalities, which makes for a more interesting experience, although most passengers are North American. Children are sometimes seen aboard, but they are not really welcomed by most people.

The ship suits discerning, well-traveled couples and solo travelers, typically over 50, who are looking for a smaller ship with fine food and European-style service in surroundings bordering on the elegant and luxurious without being extravagant. All the little extras passengers receive make a cruise an extremely pleasant experience.

Passenger niggles include the lack of electrical sockets in cabins; there are almost no shaded outdoor areas; and the butler service is sometimes poor, not least because each butler has about 15 cabins to look after.

ACCOMMODATION. *Silver Spirit*, like other Silversea Cruises ships, has 'all-suites' accommodation.

Some can accommodate a third person, and some have interconnecting doors, so families and friends can be adjacent.

Accommodation (from largest to smallest) consists of Owner's Suites; Grand Suites; Royal Suites; Silver Suites; Midship Veranda Suites; Veranda Suites; and Vista Suites. Owner's, Grand, and Royal suites all have interconnecting doors for an available second bedroom.

All accommodation comes with personalized stationery, an eight pillow choice menu (from soft down to memory foam), bathrobes, and an array of Bulgari bathroom amenities. All have walk-in closets with personal safe, infotainment system, DVD unit, and vanity desk with hairdryer. The bathrooms are marble-clad, with marble and wood floors, toilet, one or two washbasins, a full-size tub, and a shower enclosure with a fixed 'rain shower' and a separate handheld shower. Occupants of Owner's Suites or Grand Suites receive unobtrusive service from butlers certified by London's Guild of Professional Butlers.

The suites have recessed lighting in the ceiling – a nice touch that allows a little diffused mood lighting when needed. Balconies have sliding doors that can move if not securely locked when not in use. Nonsmokers should be aware that Silversea Cruises allows smoking in cabins.

DINING. While Silversea's cuisine has, in the past been very good, many passengers have noticed a decrease in the quality and in the variety of the dishes provided lately, and service has become more hurried.

There is no main dining room as such, but the dining area is split into three separate venues: Atlantide is a light, airy venue with open seatng and an integral dance floor, but the ceiling height is disappointingly low. It has moderately elegant surroundings, with unhurried, unobtrusive service. Tables are set with fine china, silverware, and Riedel wine glasses. For complete privacy, meals can also be served, course-by-course, in your suite.

Adjacent venues include: Indochine, an Asian-fusion venue; and Seishin, with just 24 seats (featuring Kobe beef, sushi, and Asian seafood).

On the deck above, Silver Note is a dinner/dancing venue, for tapas-style bites in an elegant, jazzy setting (with music based on jazz and swing).

La Terrazza is for self-serve buffet-style items for breakfast and lunch. Each evening, it turns into an Italian-themed dining spot, with waiter service and regional Italian cuisine cooked to order. Reservations are required for dinner (not open for lunch).

Stars Supper Club, with a dance floor, is designed in the manner of an English supper club of the 1920s to provide an intimate, club-like ambience and all-night (volume-intrusive) entertainment. Reservations are required for dinner (not open for lunch).

The Pool Grill is a casual outside eatery serving steaks, seafood, and pizza. Meals are served on hot stones that act as plates, so you can't touch them. Additionally, a lobby bar serves Lavazza Italian coffees, wines, spirits, and pastries.

ENTERTAINMENT. The Showlounge, in the aft section, has a main stage and two side stages. It seats about 320 passengers, and there are good sight lines from all seats but no beverage service. It's a lovely room, and seating consists of two-person love seats, and each has a small table for personal items. Production shows have been re-introduced, and these, together with cabaret acts, provide a balanced entertainment program.

SPA/FITNESS. The Zagara Spa at Silversea is quite large for this size of ship, and includes a sanctuary for total relaxation and detox. Located at the stern of the ship, one deck below La Terrazza, it is a haven for me-time and personal treatments.

SILVER WHISPER
★★★★+

'INCLUSIVE' CRUISING WITH SPACE, STYLE, SOME GOOD FOOD, AND COMFORT

Size:	Small Ship	Passenger/Crew Ratio (lower beds):	1.4/1
Tonnage:	28,258	Cabins (total):	194
Cruise Line:	Silversea Cruises	Size Range (sq ft/m):	287.0–1,435.0/26.6–133.3
Former Names:	none	Cabins (for one person):	0
Builder:	Visentini/Mariotti (Italy)	Cabins with balcony:	166
Entered Service:	Jul 2001	Cabins (wheelchair accessible):	2
Length (ft/m):	610.2/186.0	Wheelchair accessibility:	Good
Propulsion/Propellers:	diesel/2	Elevators:	5
Total Crew:	302	Casino (gaming tables):	Yes
Passengers (lower beds):	388	Self-Service Launderette:	Yes
Passenger Space Ratio (lower beds):	72.8	Onboard currency:	US$

THE SHIP. *Silver Whisper*, which Russian President Vladimir Putin chartered in 2003 to host guests for the three-day celebrations of St. Petersburg's 300th anniversary, is the second generation of vessels in the Silversea Cruises fleet. It is sister to *Silver Shadow*, and is slightly larger than the line's first two ships, *Silver Cloud* and *Silver Wind*, but with a more streamlined profile and a large, sleek single funnel.

BERLITZ'S RATINGS		
	Possible	Achieved
Ship	500	399
Accommodation	200	178
Food	400	311
Service	400	318
Entertainment	100	78
Cruise Experience	400	313
OVERALL SCORE 1597 points out of 2000		

The ship has 'all-inclusive' fares, including gratuities (although additional tips are not expected, they are not prohibited). The fares do not include vintage wines, or massage, or other personal services, but they do include many things that are extra-cost items compared with ships of some other cruise lines. Shuttle buses are provided in most ports of call.

The passenger mix includes many nationalities, although the majority of passengers are North American. Children are sometimes seen aboard, but not really welcomed by most passengers.

Silversea Cruises' emphasis on quality has earned it a good reputation, particularly for cuisine, and all the little extras that passengers receive make sailing on this ship an extremely pleasant experience. The surroundings are very comfortable and contemporary without being extravagant. There is open-seating dining with drinks included; cold canapés and hot hors d'oeuvres are served in the bars in the pre-dinner cocktail hour; and there are captain's welcome aboard and farewell cocktail parties.

Aluminum/teak deck furniture is placed by the swimming pool, but the pool itself is quite small. The Humidor, by Davidoff, a 25-seat cigar-smoking lounge, has been styled like an English smoking club. There's a wine bar and computer-learning center.

This ship suits discerning, well-traveled couples who like a small ship, good food, and European-style service in elegant, highly comfortable surroundings. Silversea Cruises promotes its Italian Heritage theme, and its many international passengers respond well to the ambience, food, and the staff, most of whom go out of their way to please.

ACCOMMODATION. This 'all-suites' ship has several price categories. All grades have double vanities in the marble-floored bathrooms, plus tub and separate shower enclosure. Premium Italian bed linen is provided in all grades, as is an eight-pillow menu from soft down to memory foam, 100 percent cotton bathrobes, a fine array of Acqua di Parma bathroom amenities, and personalized stationery. In the Grand, Royal, Rossellini (named after the Italian actress), or Owner's suites, you get unobtrusive service from butlers certified by London's Guild of Professional Butlers.

Vista Suites measure 287 sq ft (27 sq m) and don't have a private balcony. Veranda Suites (really Vista Suites plus a veranda) measure 345 sq ft (32 sq m).

Silver Suites measure 701 sq ft (65 sq m). Owner's Suites each measure 1,208 sq ft (112 sq m). Royal

Suites measure 1,312 sq ft (122 sq m) or 1,352 sq ft (126 sq m). Grand Suites: one measures 1,286 sq ft (119 sq m); the other, including an adjoining suite with interconnecting door, 1,435 sq ft (133 sq m).

There are two adjacent suites for passengers with disabilities (535 and 537), both beside an elevator. They measure a generous 398 sq ft (37 sq m) and are well equipped with an accessible hanging rail, and roll-in bathroom with roll-in shower unit.

DINING. The Restaurant (the main dining room) has open-seating dining in elegant surroundings. Three grand chandeliers provide an upward focal point. Meals can also be served, course-by-course, in your suite, although the balcony tables are rather low for dining outdoors. The cuisine is good throughout the ship, with a choice of formal and informal areas, and Cristofle silverware is provided. 'Standard' table wines are included for lunch and dinner, and there is an extra-cost 'connoisseur list' of premium wines.

As an alternative, the extra-cost Le Champagne offers a more intimate, reservation-only dining spot. Here, passengers can enjoy highly specialized dégustation menus marrying international cuisine with vintage wines selected by Relais & Châteaux sommeliers.

La Terrazza is for self-serve breakfast and lunch buffets. The buffet design and set-up presents flow problems during breakfast, however, and 'active' stations for cooking eggs or pasta to order would help. In the evening, this room serves regional Italian cuisine, and has softer lighting to create a more intimate atmosphere.

Adjacent to the café is a wine bar and a cigar-smoking room. A poolside grill provides a casual alternative daytime dining spot; in the evening it turns into The Grill, with food cooked using the Black Rock (hot stone) method.

ENTERTAINMENT. The Showlounge spans two decks and has a sloping floor; both banquette and individual seating are provided, with good sight lines from almost all seats.

A decent array of cabaret acts does the Silversea circuit, most providing intelligent entertainment; colourful productions are also featured. Musically, more emphasis is placed on classical music ensembles. A band and small groups/ensembles perform in the evenings in The Bar and the Panorama Lounge.

SPA/FITNESS. The Spa at Silversea health/fitness facility, just behind the Observation Lounge, includes a gymnasium, beauty salon, separate saunas and steam rooms for men and women, plus several treatment rooms. A range of body-pampering services is offered to men and women. Massage and other treatments, facials, pedicures, and beauty treatments cost extra.

SILVER WIND
★★★★

AN INCLUSIVE, BUT DATED SMALL SHIP FOR THE SOPHISTICATED AND WELL-TRAVELED

Size:	Small Ship	Passenger/Crew Ratio (lower beds):	1.3
Tonnage:	17,400	Cabins (total):	151
Cruise Line:	Silversea Cruises	Size Range (sq ft/m):	240.0–1,314.0/22.2–122.0
Former Names:	none	Cabins (for one person):	0
Builder:	Visentini/Mariotti (Italy)	Cabins with balcony:	123
Entered Service:	Jan 1995	Cabins (wheelchair accessible):	2
Length (ft/m):	514.4/155.8	Wheelchair accessibility:	Fair
Propulsion/Propellers:	diesel (11,700kW)/2	Elevators:	4
Total Crew:	222	Casino (gaming tables):	Yes
Passengers (lower beds):	302	Self-Service Launderette:	Yes
Passenger Space Ratio (lower beds):	57.6	Onboard currency:	US$

THE SHIP. This ship is best suited to discerning couples, typically over 50, who seek a small ship with fine cuisine, European-style service, and surroundings that border on the elegant. An announcement-free ambience prevails, and there is no pressure or hype, and an enthusiastic staff knows how to pamper you.

Silver Wind has a sloping stern reminiscent of an Airstream trailer. The size is just about ideal for personalized cruising in an upscale environment (refreshed in 2018). The vertical cake-layer stacking of public rooms aft and the location of accommodation units forward ensures quiet cabins. There is a synthetic, turf-covered (not quite equating with luxury) walk-around promenade deck outdoors – which should be upgraded to teak or Bolidt – and a fairly spacious swimming pool and sunbathing deck with teak/aluminum deck furniture. Little touches such as cold towels, water sprays, and fresh fruit provide poolside pampering on hot days.

The ship has had several makeovers, but more modification in 2020 to add some ice-classification possibilities means the ship can travel further into cold-weather areas (although it is by no means an ice-breaker – nor is it suitable for Antarctic sailings). The spacious interior has elegant, non-glitzy decor and fine-quality soft furnishings, accented by brass fittings, fine woods, and creative ceilings. There is an excellent amount of space per passenger, and no hint of a line anywhere. There is a useful

BERLITZ'S RATINGS	Possible	Achieved
Ship	500	343
Accommodation	200	158
Food	400	293
Service	400	301
Entertainment	100	67
Cruise Experience	400	307

OVERALL SCORE 1469 points out of 2000

Internet center, a 24-hour library, and a cigar lounge.

Before your cruise, good documentation is provided in a high-quality document wallet and presentation box. Insurance, once included in the fare, now costs extra. All drinks, gratuities, and port taxes are included, and no further tipping is necessary (although not prohibited). Not included, however, are vintage wines, spa treatments, or other personal services. It would be hard not to have a good cruise aboard this ship, albeit at a fairly high price. The company's many international passengers like the ambience, food, service, and the staff, who generally go out of their way to please.

Shuttle buses are provided in most ports of call, and all the little extras that passengers receive aboard this ship makes it an extremely pleasant experience, in surroundings that are comfortable and contemporary without being extravagant, with open seating dining, cold canapés and hot hors d'oeuvres served in the bars in the pre-dinner cocktail hour, a captain's welcome aboard, and a farewell cocktail party.

Silversea Cruises has a defined product based on an Italian Heritage theme.

The passenger mix includes many nationalities, although most passengers are North American. Children are occasionally seen aboard.

Passenger niggles include the fact that vibration is evident when bow thrusters or the anchors are used, particularly in the forward-most suites. The self-service launderette is poor and too small for longer cruises, when passengers like to wash their own small items. Crew facilities are minimal, so turnover is quite high, making it difficult to maintain consistency.

ACCOMMODATION. There are several price grades. The all-outside suites, 75 percent with fine private teakwood-floor balconies, have convertible queen-to-twin beds. They include large floor-to-ceiling windows, large walk-in closets, dressing table, writing desk, stocked minibar/refrigerator (no charge), and fresh flowers. Marble floored bathrooms have a tub, fixed showerhead, single washbasin, and plenty of high-quality towels. An eight-pillow menu, bathrobes, and an array of Acqua di Parma bathroom amenities are provided.

In the Grand, Royal, Rossellini or Owner's suites, you get unobtrusive service from butlers certified by London's Guild of Professional Butlers.

All suites have infotainment systems. However, walk-in closets provide little hanging space, particularly for such items like full-length dresses; it would be better for the door to open outward instead of inward. Drawers are poorly positioned, although several other drawers and storage areas are provided in the living area. Although the cabin insulation above and below each suite is good, insulation between them is not – a privacy curtain installed between entry door and sleeping area would be useful – and light from the passageway leaks into the suite, making it hard to achieve a dark room.

The top suite grades have teak balcony furniture, while others don't – but all balconies have teak floors. Suites with balconies on the lowest deck can suffer from sticky salt spray when the ship is moving, so the balconies need lots of cleaning. Each evening, the stewardesses bring canapés to your suite – just right for a light bite with cocktails.

DINING. The main dining room, The Restaurant, provides open-seating dining in elegant surroundings. It has a wood floor, an attractive arched gazebo center, and a wavy ceiling design as its focal point, and is set with fine Limoges china and well-balanced Christofle silverware. Meals are served in an open seating, which means you can eat when you like within the given dining room opening times, and with whom you like.

The cuisine/dining experience is good, with a choice of three dining salons. Standard table wines are included for lunch and dinner, but there is also a 'connoisseur list' of premium wines at extra charge. All meals are prepared as à la carte items, with almost none of the pre-preparation that used to exist. Special orders are also possible.

A specialty dining salon, the intimate 24-seat La Saletta, adjacent to the main dining room, has dégustation menus that include dishes designed for Silversea Cruises by chefs from Relais & Châteaux Gourmands (the cuisine-oriented division of Relais & Châteaux); these are paired with selected wines. Reservations are required, and there's a cover charge.

For more casual dining, La Terrazza offers self-serve breakfast and lunch buffets. In the evening it serves Italian regional dishes and has softer lighting, with both indoors and outdoors seating at teakwood tables and chairs.

There is a 24-hour in-cabin dining service; full course-by-course dinners are available, although the balcony tables in the standard suites are rather low for dining outdoors.

ENTERTAINMENT. The Showlounge is the venue for all entertainment events and some social functions. The room spans two decks and has a sloping floor; both banquette and individual seating are provided, with good sight lines from almost all seats.

Although Silversea Cruises places more emphasis on food than entertainment, what is provided is quite tasteful and not overbearing, as aboard some larger ships. A decent array of cabaret acts does the Silversea circuit. Most of the cabaret acts provide intelligent entertainment.

Also, more emphasis is now placed on classical music ensembles. There is also a band, as well as several small musical units for live music in the evenings in The Bar and the Panorama Lounge.

SPA/FITNESS. Although The Spa at Silversea facility isn't large, it underwent a sea change in 2007 with redesigned, more welcoming, decor, and an updated range of treatments and spa packages for both men and women. Massage and other body-pampering treatments, facials, pedicures, and beauty treatments cost extra.

Facilities include a mixed sauna for men and women, several treatment rooms, and a beauty salon. A separate gymnasium, formerly an observation lounge, located atop the ship, provides sea views.

SIRENA
★★★+

THIS INFORMAL SMALLER SHIP IS GOOD FOR THOSE OF A MATURE AGE

Size:	Small Ship	Passenger/Crew Ratio (lower beds):	1.8
Tonnage:	30,277	Cabins (total):	344
Cruise Line:	Princess Cruises	Size Range (sq ft/m):	145.3–968.7/13.5–90.0
Former Names:	Tahitian Princess, R Four	Cabins (for one person):	0
Builder:	Chantiers de l'Atlantique (France)	Cabins with balcony:	232
Entered Service:	Nov 1999/Apr 2016	Cabins (wheelchair accessible):	3
Length (ft/m):	593.7/181.0	Wheelchair accessibility:	Good
Propulsion/Propellers:	diesel-electric (18,600kW)/2	Elevators:	4
Total Crew:	373	Casino (gaming tables):	Yes
Passengers (lower beds):	688	Self-Service Launderette:	Yes
Passenger Space Ratio (lower beds):	44.1	Onboard currency:	US$

THE SHIP. *Sirena* (refurbished in 2016) is best suited to mature-age couples and older solo travelers who like a small ship setting with pleasing, elegant surroundings and are happy with small-stage entertainment, and fine food and service, all at an affordable price.

Formerly *Ocean Princess* (known as *Tahitian Princess* until 2009), *Sirena* is an ideal size for smaller ports. The value for money is good, and gives you a chance to cruise in comfort aboard a small ship with some attractive dining choices.

The interior decor is easy on the eye, with the traditional touches of a grand hotel, and a throwback to ocean liner decor of the 1920s and '30s. This includes detailed ceiling cornices, both real and faux wrought-iron staircase railings, leather- and cherry wood-paneled walls, trompe l'oeil ceilings, rich carpeting in hallways with an Oriental rug-look center section, and many other interesting and expensive-looking decorative touches. The staircase in the main, two-deck-high foyer may remind you of the one in the movie *Titanic*.

The public rooms are spread over three decks. The reception hall has a staircase with intricate wrought-iron railings.

There are plenty of bars – including one in the entrance to each restaurant. Perhaps the nicest can be found in the casino bar/lounge, a beautiful room reminiscent of London's grand hotels and understated gaming clubs. It has an inviting marble fireplace,

BERLITZ'S RATINGS		
	Possible	Achieved
Ship	500	360
Accommodation	200	127
Food	400	291
Service	400	282
Entertainment	100	67
Cruise Experience	400	262

OVERALL SCORE 1389 points out of 2000

comfortable sofas, and individual chairs. There is also a large card room, which incorporates an Internet center, with eight stations.

There is no walk-around promenade deck outdoors, though there's a small jogging track around the perimeter of the swimming pool, and port and starboard side decks. There are no wooden decks outdoors; instead, they are covered by a rubberized material (striped to look like wood). There is no sauna. Stairways, although carpeted, are tinny. To keep prices low, the air routing to get to and from your ship is often not the most direct. There is a charge for using machines in the self-service launderette, and you have to obtain tokens from the reception desk – a change machine in the launderette itself would be better. Drinks prices are extremely high.

ACCOMMODATION. There are several different cabin types. The standard interior and outside-view cabins are extremely tight for two persons, particularly for cruises longer than seven days. Cabins have twin beds (convertible to a queen-size one), with good under-bed storage, infotainment system, personal safe, vanity desk with large mirror, good closet and drawer space in rich, dark woods, and a bathrobe. The bathrooms, which have tiled floors and plain walls, are compact, and have a shower enclosure with a removable, strong hand-held shower unit, hairdryer, cotton towels, storage shelves for toiletries, and a retractable clothesline. Note that the underbed space is small so it's difficult to store your luggage.

The suites/cabins with private balconies have partial, and not full, balcony partitions, and sliding glass doors. Due to good design and layout, only 14 cabins on Deck 6 have lifeboat-obstructed views.

Mini-Suites are simply larger cabins than the standard cabins, because sleeping and lounge areas aren't divided. While not overly large, the bathrooms have ample space for personal toiletries. The living area has a mini-fridge/ mini-bar, lounge area with breakfast table, and a balcony with two plastic chairs and a table.

There are 10 Owner's Suites; these large living spaces are located in the forward-most and aft-most sections; particularly nice are those that overlook the stern, on decks 6, 7, and 8. They have more extensive balconies that can't be overlooked by anyone from the decks above. There is an entrance foyer, living room, bedroom, bathroom with Jacuzzi tub, and a small guest bathroom. The bed faces the sea, which can be seen through the floor-to-ceiling windows and sliding glass door.

Accommodation at the stern may suffer from vibration and noise, particularly when the ship is close to full speed, or maneuvering in port.

DINING. Flexibility and choice are what this mid-size ship's dining facilities are all about. There is a choice of four different dining spots, including a self-serve buffet:

The (open-seating) Grand Dining Room has 338 seats (all with armrests), and a large raised central section. There are large windows on three sides, and several prime tables overlooking the stern. The noise level can be high, due to its single deck height ceiling.

Red Ginger is a Pan-Asian restaurant, with windows along two sides.

The Tuscan Steak Restaurant combines an American-style steak house and a rustic Tuscan eatery, complete with hardwood floor (but contemporary platinum/silver decor). The 98 seats all have armrests, and there are windows along two sides, but few tables for two.

The Terrace Café has both indoor and outdoor seating. It is open for breakfast, lunch, and casual dinners, with some fine tapas and other Mediterranean dishes. It incorporates a small pizzeria and grill.

All restaurants have open-seating dining, so you can dine when you want, with whom you wish. Reservations are needed in the Toscana Steakhouse and Red Ginger (but there's no extra charge).

ENTERTAINMENT. The 345-seat Cabaret Lounge has a stage, and circular hardwood dance floor with banquette and individual tub chair seating, and raised sections on port and starboard sides. It is not large (not designed for production shows), so cabaret acts are the norm, plus mini-revue style shows presented by a troupe of resident singer/dancers.

A band, small musical units, and solo entertaining pianists provide live music for shows and dancing in the various lounges and bars before and after dinner.

SPA/FITNESS. A gymnasium has ocean-view windows, high-tech muscle-toning equipment and treadmills, steam rooms (no sauna), changing areas for men and women, and a beauty salon with ocean views. The spa is operated by Canyon Ranch. A lido deck has a swimming pool and good sunbathing space, while an aft deck has a thalassotherapy pool. A jogging track circles the pool deck, but one deck above. The uppermost outdoors deck includes a golf driving net and shuffleboard court.

SKY PRINCESS
NYR

THIS IS MULTI-CHOICE, PREMIUM LARGE RESORT SHIP THAT'S GOOD FOR THE WHOLE FAMILY

Size:	Large resort ship	Passenger/Crew Ratio (lower beds):	2.6
Tonnage:	142,229	Cabins (total):	1,780
Cruise Line:	Princess Cruises	Size Range (sq ft/m):	161.4–554.3/15–51.5
Former Names:	none	Cabins (for one person):	0
Builder:	Fincantieri (Italy)	Cabins with balcony:	1,438
Entered Service:	Oct 2019	Cabins (wheelchair accessible):	36
Length (ft/m):	1,082.6/330.0	Wheelchair accessibility:	Best
Propulsion/Propellers:	diesel-electric/2	Elevators:	14
Total Crew:	1,346	Casino (gaming tables):	Yes
Passengers (lower beds):	3,560	Self-Service Launderette:	Yes
Passenger Space Ratio (lower beds):	39.9	Onboard currency:	US$

THE SHIP. Although large, the ship's profile is quite well balanced. As for practical design, the lifeboats are located outside the main public room areas, so they don't impair the view from balcony cabins. Yes, you *can* walk on water (well, over it) on the open deck SeaWalk, a glass-bottomed, enclosed walkway first introduced aboard *Royal Princess* in 2012. It extends almost 30ft (9.2m) beyond the edge as part of a lounge/bar venue. A lower deck hosts a complete walk-around promenade deck.

There are two main stair towers and elevator banks, plus four panoramic-view elevators in a third, central bank (they don't go between decks 7 and 16, and stairways are only at the forward and aft elevator banks). The interior decor is tasteful, and there's little in the way of glitz.

Piazza Atrium is the multi-faceted, multi-level social and dining hub, with a horseshoe-shaped flowing stairway and four panoramic elevators.

Princess Cruises delivers a comfortable, consistent, well-packaged cruise vacation, with a whole range of entertainment and dining options, at an attractive price. Niggles include the lack of a central stairway above two of the main restaurants, severe crowding by the adjacent elevators, the frustrating automated telephone system, and additional charges for things like ice cream.

ACCOMMODATION. There are many types of accommodation and price grades, from interior

BERLITZ'S RATINGS

	Possible	Achieved
Ship	500	NYR
Accommodation	200	NYR
Food	400	NYR
Service	400	NYR
Entertainment	100	NYR
Cruise Experience	400	NYR

OVERALL SCORE NYR points out of 2000

(no-view) cabins, to expansive Sky suites. Pricing depends on two things: size and location. Outside-view cabins account for about 80 percent of all accommodation. Some of the most sought-after suites are located aft, occupying the corner (port and starboard) positions, but the two largest suites (Sky Suites) also have extremely large balconies (1,012 sq ft/95 sq m starboard side; 947 sq ft/88 sq m port side); unfortunately, an aft section is open to sounds from the pool deck below.

All accommodation comes with energy-efficient controlled lighting, beds with upholstered headboards, a wall-mounted flat-screen infotainment system, 220v electrical socket, turndown service, hairdryer, bathrobes (on request, unless you are in suite-grade accommodation), and personal bathroom amenities. Bathrooms have decent storage space for toiletries, and all have hand-held, flexi-hose showers, and practical shower enclosures.

DINING. One of three 'formal' main dining rooms (Allegro – with two seating times, Concerto and Symphony – both for 'Anytime Dining') is assigned to you, according to your accommodation grade. Portions are generous, but this is banquet catering, with all its attendant standardization and batch cooking. If you like desserts, order a sundae at dinner (most other items are just so-so).

Smaller restaurants and eateries clustered around various levels of the Piazza include Sabatini's (for Italian fare with flair); La Mer features French bistro-style cuisine, with menus by three-Michelin-star chef Emmanuel Renaut; Alfredo's Pizzeria (named for Princess Cruises' executive chef Alfredo Marzi); Ocean Terrace Seafood Bar; International Café (for extra-cost coffees and teas), and Vines Wine Bar (for wines and tapas).

Elsewhere, there's Crown Grill for extra-cost steaks and seafood, or World Fresh Marketplace for casual, buffet-style meals.

ENTERTAINMENT. The Princess Theater (show-lounge) spans two decks, with seating on both levels. Colorful, large-scale production shows are what Princess Cruises is renowned for. There's also a 'Princess Live' auditorium for other small-audience entertainment, and entertainment in several other lounge venues.

SPA/FITNESS. The Lotus Spa is located on the lower atrium level, with separate saunas, steam rooms, and changing rooms for men and women. Common facilities include a relaxation/waiting zone, body-pampering treatment rooms, and a gymnasium with the latest high-tech equipment. Most fitness classes cost extra. Children and teens have their own fitness rooms, adjacent to their age-related facilities. Make online reservations for spa treatments before your cruise if you want to plan ahead and save time.

SOVEREIGN
★★+

THIS DATED MID-SIZE SHIP IS GOOD FOR SPANISH-SPEAKING FAMILY CRUISING

Size:	Mid-size Ship	Passenger/Crew Ratio (lower beds):	2.8
Tonnage:	73,192	Cabins (total):	1,153
Cruise Line:	Pullmantur Cruises	Size Range (sq ft/m):	118.4–670.0/11.0–62.2
Former Names:	*Sovereign of the Seas*	Cabins (for one person):	0
Builder:	Chantiers de l'Atlantique (France)	Cabins with balcony:	62
Entered Service:	Jan 1988/Mar 2009	Cabins (wheelchair accessible):	6
Length (ft/m):	879.9/268.2	Wheelchair accessibility:	Fair
Propulsion/Propellers:	diesel (21,844kW)/2	Elevators:	13
Total Crew:	820	Casino (gaming tables):	Yes
Passengers (lower beds):	2,306	Self-Service Launderette:	No
Passenger Space Ratio (lower beds):	31.7	Onboard currency:	Euros

THE SHIP. This ship is best suited to Spanish-speaking families, young couples, and solo travelers seeking a first cruise at an all-inclusive price that even covers drinks. The high-density ship is well run and highly programmed, and is geared to families with children.

Sovereign has a smart profile and nicely rounded lines. The ship has a lounge and bar that is wrapped around the blue funnel and provides a stunning view. Open deck space isn't generous, but there's a wide walk-around polished wood promenade deck. The interior layout is unusual in that most of the public rooms are located aft in a stack, like layers on a cake, with the accommodation situated forward.

There's an array of spacious public rooms, including a library, and card players' room, plus a Monte Carlo Casino. Children and teens are well catered for, and there's a whole team of youth-activity staff, together with a range of rooms for children and teens. The dress code is very casual. All gratuities and port taxes are included in the cruise fare.

ACCOMMODATION. There are several cabin price grades. The price depends on size, grade and location. Some cabins have interconnecting doors, which is useful for families. Thirteen suites on Bridge Deck, the largest of which is the Royal Suite, are reasonably large and nicely furnished, with separate living and sleeping spaces.

BERLITZ'S RATINGS		
	Possible	Achieved
Ship	500	260
Accommodation	200	86
Food	400	195
Service	400	228
Entertainment	100	56
Cruise Experience	400	221

OVERALL SCORE 1046 points out of 2000

The standard outside-view and interior cabins are very small, although arched windows and colorful soft furnishings give the illusion of more space. Almost all cabins have twin beds that convert to a queen-size or double-bed configuration. There is little closet and drawer space. All cabins have a private bathroom, with shower, toilet, and washbasin.

DINING. El Guardiana and El Duero, two dining rooms off the Centrum (lobby), have tables for four, six, or eight persons but none for two. Both have two seatings, with table wines included in the fare. An additional restaurant offers better menus (à la carte) at an extra cost. For casual meals and snacks, the two-level Buffet Panorama is open almost 24 hours a day, although it is usually congested at peak times.

ENTERTAINMENT. The Broadway Showlounge has both main and balcony levels, with banquette seating. A smaller venue for late-night dancing or chilling out is the Disco Zoom.

SPA/FITNESS. In the Spa del Mar, you'll find a gym with fine ocean views, full of cardiovascular equipment. There's also an aerobics studio, a salon, and sauna, as well as 11 treatment rooms, including one for couples' massages. An outdoor rock-climbing wall, located on the aft of the ship's blue funnel, has several climbing tracks.

SPECTRUM OF THE SEAS
★★★★

THIS IS A HIGH-TECH, HIGH-ENERGY, GIZMO-FILLED FLOATING RESORT FOR ASIAN FAMILIES

Size:	Large Resort Ship	Passenger/Crew Ratio (lower beds):	3.2
Tonnage:	168,800	Cabins (total):	2,090
Cruise Line:	Royal Caribbean International	Size Range (sq ft/m):	101.1–799.7/9.4–74.3
Former Names:	none	Cabins (for one person):	18
Builder:	Meyer Werft (Germany)	Cabins with balcony:	1,570
Entered Service:	Apr 2019	Cabins (wheelchair accessible):	34
Length (ft/m):	1,145.0/348.0	Wheelchair accessibility:	Good
Propulsion/Propellers:	diesel-electric/2 azimuthing pods	Elevators:	16
Total Crew:	1,300	Casino (gaming tables):	Yes
Passengers (lower beds):	4,180	Self-Service Launderette:	No
Passenger Space Ratio (lower beds):	40.3	Onboard currency:	US$

THE SHIP. *Spectrum of the Seas* is sister to *Anthem of the Seas* (2015), *Ovation of the Seas* (2016), and *Quantum of the Seas* (2014), and incorporates the latest tech-intensive bling and entertainment features. The ship's exterior design employs the latest in hydrodynamics, hull shape, low emissions, and, importantly, low fuel consumption and technology. The stern slopes nicely – it looks like it could be the front.

Novel attractions include the RipCord by iFly simulated skydiving experience and North Star, a 13-person glass pod that rises above the ship's uppermost deck for a moving, bird's-eye view.

You can book both attractions with interactive digital kiosks (adjacent to elevators) and tablets in public areas.

Other facilities include a SeaPlex complex, which features bumper-car rides, and alternates as a roller-skating rink and basketball court; a rock-climbing wall; FlowRider surfing simulator; and SkyvPad (virtual-reality bungee jumping, located aft).

Inside the ship, the decor is contemporary, rainbow-colorful, and high-vibe jazzy. The interior focal point is a three-storey Royal Esplanade, filled with multiple shops, restaurants, eateries, bars, and lounges.

This ship provides a fine cruise experience for the whole family, but, be warned: you'll need forward

BERLITZ'S RATINGS		
	Possible	Achieved
Ship	500	404
Accommodation	200	137
Food	400	289
Service	400	272
Entertainment	100	88
Cruise Experience	400	277

OVERALL SCORE 1467 points out of 2000

planning and to make reservations for the best cruise experience.

What this fine resort ship does superbly well is entertainment, because of the excellent range of activities, entertainment, and good dining. Niggles include the high cost for fast Wi-Fi connectivity.

ACCOMMODATION. There are many different accommodation price grades and categories, depending on size (from interior no-view cabins to the largest family suites) and location. Each cabin has a real or virtual view. 'Virtual' balconies – first introduced aboard *Navigator of the Seas* in 2013 – are neat for the interior cabins and provide real-time ocean views (you *can* turn them off). Optional wristbands (with RFID technology) provide cabin access and act as a charge card (you have to take them off in order to give them to the bartender). Most cabins are larger than those aboard the Oasis-class ships.

Even the smallest bathroom is well designed, with a night light, shower, and vanity hooks, while cabins have bedside power outlets, ample storage space, and a USB socket. Note that the tablet-based infotainment systems don't answer questions. Suite-grade accommodation occupants can take all their meals in the exclusive Coastal Kitchen.

Interconnecting family cabins located aft, are practical for multi-generational groups, and consist of a junior suite, balcony cabin, and interior studio (total: three bedrooms, three bathrooms, and balcony). Some 34 'studio' cabins are for solo occupancy.

This is the first Royal Caribbean ship to feature a 'ship within a ship' area for the top suite occupants, with a private elevator and key-card access, plus a dedicated restaurant and lounge, and an outdoor zone.

DINING. The cavernous main dining room (included in the cruise price) spans two decks and features both Chinese and international cuisine, with daily menu changes, while the smaller Silver Dining and Golden Dining restaurants are for suite occupants only (but the chairs lack armrests).

Other venues and eateries (some cost extra) include: Wonderland (a quirky *Alice in Wonderland*-inspired venue); Jamie's Italian (a tablecloth-free, Euro-Italian bistro); Chops Grille (for premium-quality steaks and seafood); Izumi (for Japanese-Asian fusion cuisine, including hot-rock tableside cooking);

Teppanyaki Grill; Sichuan Red (for Chinese specialty dishes from Sichuan province); Sorrento's (for Italian fare); Chef's Table (a 14-seat venue for exclusive dinners); and a Noodle Bar.

For self-serve (no extra cost) eats, Windjammer Marketplace is a large food court-style, buffet eatery.

ENTERTAINMENT. The three-deck-high Royal Theater features colorful, large-scale production shows by a resident troupe of singers and dancers. There's also entertainment in the Music Hall and Two70, a multi-level venue that transforms from casual daytime lounge to high-energy entertainment venue by night.

SPA/FITNESS. Vitality at Sea Spa facilities include a cost-extra thermal suite, a beauty salon, barber shop, gymnasium with Technogym equipment, and 19 treatment rooms.

SPIRIT OF DISCOVERY
NYR

THIS MID-SIZE SHIP IS QUINTESSENTIALLY BRITISH AND COMES WITH ALL THE SAGA TRIMMINGS

Size:	Mid-size Ship	Passenger/Crew Ratio (lower beds):	1.8
Tonnage:	58,250	Cabins (total):	540
Cruise Line:	SAGA Cruises	Size Range (sq ft/m):	232.5–755.7/21.6–79.5
Former Names:	None	Cabins (for one person):	81
Builder:	Meyer Werft (Germany)	Cabins with balcony:	540
Entered Service:	Jul 2019	Cabins (wheelchair accessible):	10
Length (ft/m):	767.7/234.0	Wheelchair accessibility:	Best
Propulsion/Propellers:	diesel-electric/2	Elevators:	6
Total Crew:	530	Casino (gaming tables):	No
Passengers (lower beds):	999	Self-Service Launderette:	Yes
Passenger Space Ratio (lower beds):	58.3	Onboard currency:	UK£

THE SHIP. *Spirit of Discovery* (the first brand new ship for Saga Cruises) is distinctly British – in style, public rooms, and ambiance. The interior design and layout are similar to the spacious ships *Saga Rose* and *Saga Ruby* previously operated by Saga, combined with decor that is attractive, modestly elegant, and immediately comfortable, and not at all brash or glitzy. Standout public rooms include The Living Room – the social gathering spot and a cozy multi-purpose lounge and bar, and the Britannia Lounge, a double deck-high observation lounge – a fine hangout for pre-dinner cocktails and after-dinner dancing (although spoiled by several slim pillars).

Spirit of Discovery is best suited to couples and solo travelers, almost all of whom tend to be British, seeking a holiday afloat in spacious, classy surroundings. It provides decent accommodation, good food, and friendly service, plus interesting itineraries and destinations. Passengers must be over 50, but spouses and partners can be as young as 45.

Saga Cruises includes many things other UK-based operators charge extra for – that's why its cruises may appear to cost more – such as private car transfers to the ship (check brochure for details), all gratuities, shuttle buses in ports of call where possible, and newspapers in the library in each port of call, when available.

ACCOMMODATION. Price grades depend on cabin size and location. From the smallest interior (no view)

BERLITZ'S RATINGS		
	Possible	Achieved
Ship	500	NYR
Accommodation	200	NYR
Food	400	NYR
Service	400	NYR
Entertainment	100	NYR
Cruise Experience	400	NYR
OVERALL SCORE NYR points out of 2000		

cabin to the largest suite, all offer a high degree of comfort. Contrary to maritime tradition, both even- and odd-numbered cabins are on both sides of the ship, whereas nautical tradition aboard ocean-going ships dictates that even-numbered cabins should be on the port side (left when looking forward; the same as the lifeboats), and most companies follow this rule.

DINING. The single-seating, two-deck high Grand Dining Room (another tribute to *Saga Rose* and *Saga Ruby*) is a truly delightful, traditional, grand hotel-style restaurant (with chandeliers, tablecloths, and proper service). Afternoon tea (think: scones and real clotted cream) is also provided here.

Other dining spots include The Grill (for steaks, other grilled meats, and seafood), with indoor-outdoor seating; Coast to Coast (a specialty seafood venue); and East to West (a pan-Asian bistro-style eatery). Reservations are required, but there's no additional cost.

ENTERTAINMENT. The Playhouse has 430 tiered seats and an adjacent foyer bar. Saga's onboard troupe of dancers and singers provide the shows, and cabaret acts change regularly. Male dance hosts will be aboard each cruise for the many solo women passengers.

SPA/FITNESS. A comforting space, The Spa has an indoor aqua-pool, fitness center, steam room, infra-red sauna, and several body treatment rooms.

STAR BREEZE
★★★★

THIS IS A CONTEMPORARY, HANDY-SIZED SHIP FOR MATURE-AGE CRUISERS

Size:	Boutique Ship
Tonnage:	9,975
Cruise Line:	Windstar Cruises
Former Names:	Seabourn Spirit
Builder:	Seebeckwerft (Germany)
Entered Service:	Nov 1989/Apr 2015
Length (ft/m):	439.9/134.1
Propulsion/Propellers:	diesel (5,355kW)/2
Total Crew:	124
Passengers (lower beds):	212
Passenger Space Ratio (lower beds):	47.0
Passenger/Crew Ratio (lower beds):	1.7
Cabins (total):	106
Size Range (sq ft/m):	279.8–570.5/26.0–53.0
Cabins (for one person):	0
Cabins with balcony:	6
Cabins (wheelchair accessible):	4
Wheelchair accessibility:	None
Elevators:	3
Casino (gaming tables):	Yes
Self-Service Launderette:	Yes
Onboard currency:	US$

THE SHIP. Star Breeze will undergo a 'chop-and-stretch' operation in October 2019 that will add an 83.9ft (25.6m) mid-section, 50 more suites/cabins, and two new venues. The ship's engines will be replaced; many other technical items will be upgraded or renewed. A new midship elevator will be added, and the spa will be extended and improved. The new configuration means passenger capacity increases from 212 to 312, so the ship moves into the Small Ship category (250–750 passengers). Star Legend and Star Pride will undergo the same changes, due for completion by November 2020. It is best suited to sophisticated and well-traveled couples.

The ship's sleek yacht-like exterior styling, and handsome profile will remain. It is an identical twin to Star Pride. An aft water-sports platform and marina can be used in suitably calm warm-water areas (typically only once per cruise). Water-sports facilities include a small, enclosed 'dip' pool, sea kayaks, snorkel equipment, windsurfers, and water-ski boat (their use is complimentary).

Inside, a wide central passageway divides port and starboard accommodation. The inviting public rooms have quiet, non-jarring colors and fine fixtures. They include a main lounge (The Lounge), a nightclub (Compass Rose), a Yacht Club (observation lounge) with bar, a library, card room, shop, computer room, and a mini-casino with gaming tables and a few slot machines.

BERLITZ'S RATINGS		
	Possible	Achieved
Ship	500	368
Accommodation	200	167
Food	400	270
Service	400	292
Entertainment	100	71
Cruise Experience	400	295

OVERALL SCORE 1463 points out of 2000

Star Breeze provides friendly personal service and a relaxed cruise experience. Open-seating dining and use of equipment for water sports are included, as are soft drinks and bottled water (alcoholic drinks cost extra). Other cost-extra items: gratuities, port charges, insurance, and internet use.

Passenger niggles: there is no walk-around promenade deck outdoors; there is only one dryer in the self-service launderette; and the beverage service staff in the dining room are lacking in training. Overall, this is a premium (not luxury) ship that provides a pleasant, relaxing experience, but the food is underwhelming, and there are fewer crew members than when the ship was operated by previous owner Seabourn.

ACCOMMODATION. This is spread over three decks, with nine price categories. The all-outside cabins (called suites in brochure-speak) are comfortably large and nicely equipped with everything one could reasonably need. Electric blackout blinds are provided for the large windows, in addition to curtains. Cabinetry is made of blond woods, with softly rounded edges, and cabin doors are neatly angled away from the passageway.

All suites have a sleeping area, with duvets and fine linens. A separate lounge area has a Bose Wave audio unit, DVD player and flat-screen TV, vanity desk with hairdryer, world atlas, minibar/refrigerator, and 110/220-volt power outlets. A large walk-in closet illuminates automatically when you open the door. Other items include wooden hangers, personal safe, umbrella, and wall-mounted clock and barometer.

Marble-clad bathrooms have one or two washbasins, depending on the accommodation grade, a decent but small bathtub (four suites have a shower enclosure only – no tub), plenty of storage areas, thick cotton towels, terrycloth bathrobe, designer soaps, and L'Occitane personal amenities.

Suites on two out of three accommodation decks have French balconies. These are not balconies in the true sense of the word, but have two doors that open onto a tiny teakwood balcony that is just 10.6ins (27cm) wide. The balconies allow you to have fresh sea air (and salt spray).

Course-by-course in-cabin dining is available during dinner hours, and the cocktail table can be raised to form a dining table. There is 24-hour room service. Four Owner's Suites (King Haakon/King Magnus, each measuring 530 sq ft (49 sq m), and Amundsen/ Nansen, each 575 sq ft (53 sq m), and two Classic Suites (King Harald/King Olav), each 400 sq ft (37 sq m), offer fine living spaces.

DINING. The 'AmphorA' Restaurant is a part-marble, part-carpeted dining room with portholes and restful decor. Open-seating dining means that you can dine when you want, with whom you wish. The lighting, however, is far too bright, and the chairs are not very comfortable.

The menus are decent enough, and feature some regional specialties. Overall, the meals are nothing special, and could really do with some improvement. Kosher meals can be provided, if ordered in advance. There is now only a limited selection of fruits and cheeses. The wine list is sound, with prices ranging from moderate to high.

Breakfasts and lunch buffets (plus some à la carte items) are provided at Candles (offering indoor seating at just eight tables) or the adjacent outdoor Veranda Café. At night the indoor/outdoor venue becomes Candles Grill, a reservations-required steakhouse.

The Star Bar provides an above-poolside setting for candlelit dining. It specializes in sizzling steaks and seafood.

ENTERTAINMENT. The Lounge has a sloping floor that provides good sight lines from almost all seats. The shows are of limited scope, as dinner is usually the main event. The Club (above the showlounge) is the gathering place for the late-night set. All entertainment and activities are geared towards North American tastes, despite the increasingly international passenger mix.

SPA/FITNESS. The Spa is a small but wellequipped health center. It has sauna and steam rooms (separate facilities for men and women), an equipment-packed gymnasium – but the ceiling height is low – and a beauty salon.

The spa is staffed and operated by concession Elemis by Steiner. Treatment prices equal those in an expensive land-based spa. The beauty salon has hair-beautifying treatments and conditioning.

STAR CLIPPER
★★★+

THIS SHIP OFFERS A REAL TALL-SHIP EXPERIENCE THAT PUTS WIND IN YOUR SAILS

Size:	Boutique Ship	Passenger/Crew Ratio (lower beds):	2.3/1
Tonnage:	2,298	Cabins (total):	85
Cruise Line:	Star Clippers	Size Range (sq ft/m):	95.0–225.0/8.8–21.0
Former Names:	none	Cabins (for one person):	0
Builder: Scheepswerven van Langerbrugge (Belgium)		Cabins with balcony:	0
Entered Service:	May 1992	Cabins (wheelchair accessible):	0
Length (ft/m):	378.9/115.5	Wheelchair accessibility:	None
Propulsion/Propellers:	sail power + diesel (1,030kW)/1	Elevators:	0
		Casino (gaming tables):	No
Total Crew:	72	Self-Service Launderette:	No
Passengers (lower beds):	170	Onboard currency:	Euros
Passenger Space Ratio (lower beds):	13.5		

THE SHIP. This tall sail-cruise ship suits couples and solo travelers who would probably never even consider a 'normal' cruise ship, but who enjoy sailing and the thrill of ocean and wind, with everything packaged to include accommodation, decent food, like-minded companions, interesting destinations, and an almost unstructured lifestyle.

Star Clipper is one of a pair of almost-identical sailing ships; it's the sister ship to *Star Flyer*, the first clipper sailing ship to be built for 140 years and the first commercial sailing vessel to cross the North Atlantic in 90 years. It is, first and foremost, a sailing vessel with cruise accommodation that evokes memories of the 19th-century clipper sailing ships. This is an accurate four-mast, barquentine-rigged schooner with graceful lines, a finely shaped hull, and masts that are 206ft (63m) tall. Some amenities found aboard large cruise vessels are provided, such as air conditioning, cashless cruising, occasional live music, a small shop, and two pools to 'dip' in.

Breathtaking when under full sail, the ship displays excellent sea manners – heeling is kept to a very comfortable 6 degrees. This working sailing ship relies on the wind about 80 percent of the time. During a typical cruise, you may be able to climb the main mast to a platform 75ft (23m) above the sea and help with the ropes and sails at appropriate times – this could be an unnerving experience, if you're not used to heights, but it is exhilarating when the ship is moving under

BERLITZ'S RATINGS

	Possible	Achieved
Ship	500	346
Accommodation	200	131
Food	400	235
Service	400	264
Entertainment	100	66
Cruise Experience	400	257

OVERALL SCORE 1299 points out of 2000

sail. One really neat chill-out pleasure is to lie in the netting at the front of the ship's bows, watching the bow wake as it streams along the ship's sides.

A diesel engine provides the propulsion when the ship is not under sail (in poor wind conditions), and two generators supply electrical power and help desalinate 40 or so tons of seawater each day for shipboard needs. The crew performs almost every task, including hoisting, trimming, winching, and repairing the sails, helped by electric winches. Watersports facilities include a water-ski boat, sunfish, scuba and snorkel equipment, and eight Zodiac inflatables. Sports directors provide basic dive instruction for a fee.

Inside the vessel, classic Edwardian nautical decor throughout is clean, warm, intimate, and inviting. The paneled library has a fireplace and comfortable chairs. There are no lines and no hassle. Sailing a Square Rigger and other nautical classes are a part of every cruise, as is stargazing at night.

Depending on the itinerary and region, passengers may gather for 'captain's storytime,' normally held on an open deck area adjacent to the bridge, or in the bar – which, incidentally, has a collection of single malt whiskies. The captain may explain sailing maneuvers when changing the rigging or directing the ship as it sails into port, and note the important events of the day.

The sail-ship promotes total informality and provides a carefree sailing experience in an unstructured and relaxed setting at a fair price. Take minimal clothing: short-sleeved shirts and shorts for men, shorts and tops for women are the order of the day (smart-casual at night). No jackets, ties, high-heeled shoes, cocktail dresses, or formal wear are needed. Take flat shoes because there are lots of ropes and sailing rig to negotiate on deck, not to mention the high thresholds to climb over and steps to negotiate – this is, after all a tall ship, not a cruise ship. The deck crew consists of real sailors, brought up with yachts and tall ships – most wouldn't set foot aboard a 'normal' cruise ship.

The steps of the internal stairways are short and steep, as in all sailing vessels, and so this ship cannot be recommended for anyone with walking disabilities. Also, there is no doctor on board, although there is a nurse.

For yachting enthusiasts, sailing aboard *Star Clipper* is like finding themselves in heaven, as there is plenty of sailing during a typical one-week cruise. The whole experience evokes the feeling of sailing aboard some famous private yacht, and even the most jaded traveler should enjoy the feel of the wind and sea close at hand. Just don't expect fine food to go with what is decidedly a fine sailing experience – which is what *Star Clipper* is all about. Note that a 12.5 percent gratuity is added to all beverage purchases.

For the nautically minded, the sailing rig consists of 16 manually furled sails, measuring a billowing 36,221 sq ft (3,365 sq m). These include: fore staysail, inner jib, outer jib, flying jib, fore course, lower topsail, upper topsail, lower topgallant, upper topgallant, main staysail, upper main staysail, mizzen staysail, main fisherman, jigger staysail, mizzen fisherman, and spanker. The square sails are furled electronically by custom-made winches.

ACCOMMODATION. There are six cabin price grades, plus one Owner's Suite. Generally, the higher the deck, the more expensive a cabin. The cabins are quite well equipped and comfortable, with rosewood-trimmed cabinetry and wall-to-wall carpeting, two-channel audio, color TV and DVD player, personal safe, and full-length mirrors. The bathrooms are very compact but practical units, and have gray marble tiling, glazed rosewood toiletries cabinet and paneling, some under-shelf storage space, washbasin, shower stall, and toilet. There is no 'lip' to prevent water from the shower from moving over the bathroom floor.

The cabins in the lowest price grade are interior cabins with upper and lower berths, and not two lower beds – so someone will need to be agile to climb a ladder to the upper berth. A handful of cabins have a third, upper Pullman-style berth – good for families with children, but closet and drawer space will be at a premium with three persons in a cabin. Larger luggage can be stored under the bed.

There is no cabin food or beverage service.

The deluxe cabins (called 'deck cabins') are larger, with additional features including a full-size Jacuzzi tub or corner tub, flat-screen television and DVD player, and minibar/refrigerator. However, these cabins are subject to noise pollution from the same-deck Tropical Bar's music at night (typically until midnight), from the electric winches during sail maneuvers, and from noisy walkabout exercisers in the early morning.

DINING. The dining room is cozy and quite attractive. There are self-serve buffet breakfasts and lunches, together with a mix of buffet and à la carte dinners, generally with a choice of three entrées (mains), in an open-seating environment.

The seating, mostly at tables of six, adjacent to a porthole or inboard, makes it difficult for waiters to serve properly – food is passed along the tables that occupy a porthole position. However, you can dine with whomever you wish, and this is supposed to be a casual experience, after all.

While cuisine aboard the ship is perhaps less than the advertised 'gourmet' excellence as far as presentation and choice are concerned, it is fairly creative – and there's plenty of it. Also, one has to take into account the small galley. Passenger niggles include repetitive breakfasts and lunchtime salad items, because lack of space prevents more choices. But most passengers are happy with the dinners, which tend to be good, although there is a lack of green vegetables. There's a good choice of bread rolls, pastry items, and fruit.

Tea and coffee is available 24 hours a day in the lounge – mugs, tea cups, and saucers are provided. There is no cabin food service.

ENTERTAINMENT. There are no shows as such, except for an occasional local folklore show from ashore, nor are any expected by passengers aboard a tall ship such as this. Live music is typically provided by a solo lounge pianist/singer. Otherwise, dinner is the main evening event, as well as 'captain's storytime,' recapping the day's events, and conversation with fellow passengers.

During the day, when the ship is sailing, passengers can learn about the sails and their repair, and the captain or chief officer will give briefings as the sails are being furled and unfurled. The closest this tall ship comes to any kind of 'show' is perhaps one provided by members of the crew, plus a few traditional sea shanties.

SPA/FITNESS. There are no fitness facilities, or beauty salon, although a masseuse provides Oriental massage. For recreation, the ship does have a program for water sports. Facilities include kayaks, a water-ski boat, sunfish, scuba and snorkel equipment, and eight Zodiac inflatable craft. The use of scuba equipment costs extra.

STAR FLYER
★★★+

THIS PROPER SAILING SHIP PROVIDES AN ANTIDOTE TO 'NORMAL' CRUISE SHIPS

Size:	Boutique Ship	Passenger/Crew Ratio (lower beds):	2.3/1
Tonnage:	2,298	Cabins (total):	85
Cruise Line:	Star Clippers	Size Range (sq ft/m):	95.0–225.9/8.8–21.0
Former Names:	none	Cabins (for one person):	0
Builder: Sheepswerven van Langerbrugge (Belgium)		Cabins with balcony:	0
Entered Service:	Jul 1991	Cabins (wheelchair accessible):	0
Length (ft/m):	378.9/115.5	Wheelchair accessibility:	None
Propulsion/Propellers:	sail power + diesel (1,030kW)/1	Elevators:	0
		Casino (gaming tables):	No
Total Crew:	72	Self-Service Launderette:	No
Passengers (lower beds):	170	Onboard currency:	Euros
Passenger Space Ratio (lower beds):	13.5		

THE SHIP. The first clipper sailing ship to be built for 140 years, *Star Flyer* became the first commercial sailing vessel in more than 90 years to cross the North Atlantic. It suits those who would never consider a 'normal' cruise ship.

Star Flyer is one of a pair of almost identical tall ships – its sister ship is *Star Clipper*. It is, first and foremost, a sailing vessel with cruise accommodation that evokes memories of the 19th-century clipper sailing ships. This is an accurate four-mast, barquentine-rigged schooner with graceful lines, a finely shaped hull, masts that are 206ft (63m) tall, and 16 manually furled sails totaling 36,221 sq ft (3,364 sq m). Some amenities found aboard large cruise vessels are provided, such as air conditioning, cashless cruising, live music, a small shop, and two pools to 'dip' in.

Breathtaking when under full sail, the ship displays excellent sea manners and relies on the wind about 80 percent of the time, and heeling is kept to a very comfortable 6 degrees.

During the cruise, you'll be able to climb the main mast to a platform 75ft (23m) above the sea and help with the ropes and sails at appropriate times. One really neat chill-out pleasure is to lie in the netting at the front of the ship's bows.

A diesel engine provides propulsion when the ship is not under sail (in poor wind conditions), and two generators supply electrical power and help desalinate 40 or so tons of seawater each day for shipboard

BERLITZ'S RATINGS		
	Possible	Achieved
Ship	500	347
Accommodation	200	131
Food	400	235
Service	400	263
Entertainment	100	66
Cruise Experience	400	261

OVERALL SCORE 1303 points out of 2000

needs. Engine-room visits may be offered for anyone interested. Water-sports facilities include a water-ski boat, sunfish, scuba and snorkel equipment, and eight Zodiac inflatables. Sports directors provide basic dive instruction for a fee.

Inside, classic Edwardian nautical decor throughout is clean, warm, intimate, and inviting. The paneled library has a fireplace and comfortable chairs. There are no lines and no hassle. Sailing a Square Rigger and other nautical classes are a part of every cruise, as is stargazing at night.

Depending on the itinerary and region, passengers may gather for 'captain's storytime,' normally held on an open deck area adjacent to the bridge, or in the bar – which, incidentally, has a collection of single malt whiskies. The captain may explain sailing maneuvers when changing the rigging or directing the ship as it sails into port, and notes the important events of the day.

The sail-ship promotes total informality and provides a carefree sailing experience in a totally unstructured and relaxed setting at a reasonable price. Take minimal clothing: short-sleeved shirts and shorts for men, shorts and tops for women are the order of the day (smart-casual at night). No jackets, ties, high-heeled shoes, cocktail dresses, or formal wear are needed. Take flat shoes because there are lots of ropes and sailing rig to negotiate on deck, not to mention the high thresholds to climb over and steps to negotiate – this is, after all, a tall ship, not a cruise ship.

The steps of the internal stairways are short and steep, as in all sailing vessels, and so this ship cannot be recommended for anyone with walking disabilities. Also, there is no doctor on board, although there is a nurse.

For yachting enthusiasts, sailing aboard *Star Flyer* is like finding themselves in heaven, as there is plenty of sailing during a typical one-week cruise. The whole experience evokes the feeling of sailing aboard some famous private yacht, and even the most jaded passenger should enjoy the feel of the wind and sea close at hand. Just don't expect fine food to go with what is decidedly a fine sailing experience – which is what *Star Flyer* is all about. Note that a 12.5 percent gratuity is added to all beverage purchases.

For the nautically minded, the sailing rig consists of 16 manually furled sails: fore staysail, inner jib, outer jib, flying jib, fore course, lower topsail, upper topsail, lower topgallant, upper topgallant, main staysail, upper main staysail, mizzen staysail, main fisherman, jigger staysail, mizzen fisherman, and spanker. The square sails are furled electronically by custom-made winches.

ACCOMMODATION. There are six cabin price grades, plus one Owner's Suite. Generally, the higher the deck, the more expensive a cabin. The cabins are quite well equipped and comfortable; they have rosewood-trimmed cabinetry and wall-to-wall carpeting, two-channel audio, color TV and DVD player, personal safe, and full-length mirrors. The bathrooms are very compact but practical units, and have gray marble tiling, glazed rosewood toiletries cabinet and paneling, some under-shelf storage space, washbasin, shower stall, and toilet. There is no 'lip' to prevent water from the shower from moving over the bathroom floor.

Individual European 100 percent individual cotton duvets are provided. There is no cabin food or beverage service.

The deluxe cabins (called 'deck cabins') are larger, and additional features include a full-size Jacuzzi tub or corner tub, flat-screen television and DVD player, and minibar/refrigerator. However, these cabins are subject to noise pollution from the same-deck Tropical Bar's music at night (typically until midnight), from the electric winches during sail maneuvers, and from noisy walkabout exercisers in the early morning.

The cabins in the lowest price grade are interior cabins with upper and lower berths, and not two lower beds – so someone will need to be agile to climb a ladder to the upper berth. A handful of cabins have a third, upper Pullman-style berth, which is good for families with children, although closet and drawer space will be at a premium with three people in a cabin.

DINING. The dining room is quite attractive, and has lots of wood and brass accenting and nautical decor. There are self-serve buffet breakfasts and lunches, together with a mix of buffet meals and dining à la carte, generally with a choice of three entrées (mains), in an open-seating environment.

The seating is mostly at tables of six, and either adjacent to a porthole or inboard; it makes it difficult for waiters to serve properly – so the food is passed along the tables that occupy a porthole position. However, you can dine with whomever you wish, and this is supposed to be a casual experience, after all.

While cuisine aboard the ship is perhaps less than the advertised 'gourmet' excellence as far as presentation and choice are concerned, it is fairly creative – and there's plenty of it. Also, one has to take into account the small galley. Passenger niggles include repetitive breakfasts and lunchtime salad items, because lack of space prevents more choices. But most passengers are happy with the dinners, which tend to be good, although there is a lack of green vegetables. There's a good choice of bread rolls, pastry items, and fruit.

Tea and coffee is available 24 hours a day in the lounge – mugs, tea cups, and saucers are provided. There is no cabin food service.

ENTERTAINMENT. There are no shows as such, except for an occasional local folklore show from ashore, nor are any expected by passengers aboard a tall ship such as this. Live music is typically provided by a solo lounge pianist/singer. Otherwise, dinner is the main evening event, as well as 'captain's story-time,' recapping the day's events, and conversation with fellow passengers.

During the day, when the ship is sailing, passengers can learn about the sails and their repair, and the captain or chief officer will give briefings, as the sails are being furled and unfurled. The closest this tall ship comes to any kind of 'show' is perhaps one provided by members of the crew, plus a few traditional sea shanties.

SPA/FITNESS. There are no fitness facilities, or beauty salon, although a masseuse provides Oriental massage. For recreation, the ship has a water-sports program. Facilities include kayaks, a water-ski boat, scuba and snorkel equipment, and eight Zodiac inflatable craft. The use of scuba equipment costs extra.

STAR LEGEND
★★★★

A POCKET-SIZED, COZY, AND ELEGANT SHIP FOR MATURE-AGE CRUISERS

Size:	Boutique Ship	Passenger/Crew Ratio (lower beds):	1.7
Tonnage:	9,961	Cabins (total):	106
Cruise Line:	Windstar Cruises	Size Range (sq ft/m):	279.8–570.5/26.0–53.0
Former Names:	Seabourn Legend, Queen Odyssey, Royal Viking Queen	Cabins (for one person):	0
		Cabins with balcony:	6
Builder:	Schichau Seebeckwerft (Germany)	Cabins (wheelchair accessible):	4
Entered Service:	Mar 1992/May 2015	Wheelchair accessibility:	None
Length (ft/m):	442.9/135.0	Elevators:	3
Propulsion/Propellers:	diesel (7,280kW)/2	Casino (gaming tables):	Yes
Total Crew:	124	Self-Service Launderette:	Yes
Passengers (lower beds):	212	Onboard currency:	US$
Passenger Space Ratio (lower beds):	46.9		

THE SHIP. *Star Legend* can cruise to places where large cruise ships can't, thanks to its ocean-yacht size. For a grand, boutique-size ship vacation in premium surroundings, with just over 100 other couples as neighbors, it's hard to beat. It is best suited to sophisticated, well-travelled couples who want to relax.

Star Legend is a contemporary ship with a handsome profile, almost identical in looks and size to sisters *Star Breeze* and *Star Pride*, but younger and built to a higher standard, with streamline 'decorator' bars made by Mercedes-Benz located along the side of the upper superstructure and a slightly different swept-over funnel design.

An aft water-sports platform and marina can be used in suitably calm warm-water areas. Water-sports facilities include a small, enclosed 'dip' pool, sea kayaks, snorkel equipment, windsurfers, and water-ski boat (use of water-sports equipment is complimentary).

Inside, a wide central passageway divides port and starboard side accommodation. High-quality interior fixtures, fittings, and fabrics are combined in its sumptuous public areas, including a main lounge, observation lounge, nightclub, screening room, library, reception desk, shop and mini-casino (with tables and a few slot machines). There is no glitz anywhere, and the dress code is always relaxed.

Passenger gripes: There is no walk-around promenade deck, gratuities are not included, and Internet

BERLITZ'S RATINGS		
	Possible	Achieved
Ship	500	374
Accommodation	200	169
Food	400	270
Service	400	292
Entertainment	100	71
Cruise Experience	400	297

OVERALL SCORE 1473 points out of 2000

use costs extra. Almost all entertainment and activities are geared towards American tastes. Overall, this is a premium ship that provides a relaxing experience, but don't expect any 'wow' factor from the food – it's disappointing and lacks flair. Also, there are fewer crew members than when operated by the previous owner.

Star Legend will undergo a 'chop-and-stretch' operation in 2020 that will add a 83.9ft (25.6m) mid-section, 50 more suites/cabins, and two new venues. The ship's engines will be replaced; many other technical items will be upgraded or renewed. A new mid-ship elevator will be added, and the spa will be extended and improved. The new configuration means passenger capacity increases from 212 to 312, so the ship moves into the Small Ship category (250–750 passengers). Star Pride will undergo the same changes, to be completed by November 2020 (Star Breeze undergoes the same operation in October 2019).

ACCOMMODATION. This is spread over three decks, and there are several price categories. All suites are comfortably sized and comprehensively equipped. They are, for example, larger than those aboard the smaller *SeaDream I* and *SeaDream II*, but then the ship is also larger, with almost twice as many passengers. All suites have a sleeping area with premium bedding, duvets and high-quality linens, a large walk-in closet that illuminates automatically when you open the door, digital safe, umbrella, wall-mounted clock and barometer, and 110/220-volt power outlets.

Marble-clad bathrooms have one or two washbasins, depending on accommodation grade, a decent but not full-size tub (four suites have a shower enclosure only – no bathtub), plenty of storage areas, thick cotton towels, plush terrycloth bathrobe, and designer soaps.

In 2001, 36 French balconies were added to suites on two out of three accommodation decks. These have two doors that open wide onto a tiny teakwood 'balcony' that is just 10.6ins (27cm) deep – just enough for your toes. The balconies do allow you to have fresh sea air, however, together with some salt spray.

The largest accommodation are four Owner's Suites (Ibsen/Grieg, each 530 sq ft/49 sq m, and Eriksson/Heyerdahl, each 575 sq ft/53 sq m), and two Classic Suites (Queen Maud/Queen Sonja, each 400 sq ft/37 sq m) – these are superb, private living spaces. There is a fully secluded, forward- or side-facing balcony, with sun lounge chairs and wooden drinks table (Ibsen and Grieg don't have balconies).

DINING. 'AmphorA' Restaurant is a part-marble, part-carpeted dining room that has portholes and elegant decor. Open-seating dining means that you can dine when you want, with whom you wish.

The menus are creative and quite well balanced, with a decent selection of dishes, including some regional specialties. The food is nicely presented, with some items cooked to order, but it's not life-changing. The selection of fruit and cheese is small. The wine list is quite sound, with prices ranging from moderate to high. Overall, while the accommodation is good, the meals are disappointing, and experienced staff members are lacking.

Breakfasts and lunch buffets (plus some à la carte items) are provided in Candles (which has indoor seating at just eight tables) or the adjacent outdoor Veranda Café. At night the indoor/outdoor venue becomes Candles Grill, a reservations-required steakhouse.

Additionally, the Star Bar provides an above-poolside setting for candlelit dining (steaks and seafood).

ENTERTAINMENT. The Lounge is the venue for small-scale shows, cabaret acts, lectures, and most social functions. It has a sloping floor with good sight lines.

SPA/FITNESS. The Spa is a small but well-equipped health spa/fitness center, located just aft of the navigation bridge. It provides sauna and steam rooms with separate facilities for men and women, an integral changing room, and a beauty salon.

STAR PRIDE
★★★★

AN INTIMATE, INCLUSIVE SHIP FOR STYLISH, INFORMAL CRUISING

Size:	Boutique Ship	Passenger/Crew Ratio (lower beds):	1.7
Tonnage:	9,975	Cabins (total):	106
Cruise Line:	Windstar Cruises	Size Range (sq ft/m):	279.8-570.5/26.0-53.0
Former Names:	Seabourn Pride	Cabins (for one person):	0
Builder:	Seebeckwerft (Germany)	Cabins with balcony:	6
Entered Service:	Dec 1988/May 2014	Cabins (wheelchair accessible):	4
Length (ft/m):	439.9/134.1	Wheelchair accessibility:	None
Propulsion/Propellers:	diesel (5,355kW)/2	Elevators:	3
Total Crew:	124	Casino (gaming tables):	Yes
Passengers (lower beds):	212	Self-Service Launderette:	Yes
Passenger Space Ratio (lower beds):	47.0	Onboard currency:	US$

THE SHIP. *Star Pride* is best for sophisticated, well-traveled couples seeking an informal small ship experience. The ship's big advantage is being able to cruise where larger ships can't, thanks to its handy ocean-yacht size. You sail with only 210 others, creating a sense of intimate camaraderie.

Pleasantly appointed, the ship has sleek exterior styling, a handsome profile with swept-back, rounded lines, and is an identical twin to *Star Breeze*. It has two fine mahogany water taxis for use as shore tenders. An aft water-sports platform and marina can be used in suitably calm warm-water areas. Water-sports facilities include a small, enclosed 'dip' pool, sea kayaks, snorkel equipment, windsurfers, water-ski boat, and Zodiac inflatable boats.

A wide central passageway divides the port and starboard accommodation. Inviting, warm public areas have high-quality interior fixtures and fittings. For a small ship, there's a wide range of public rooms, all updated by Windstar Cruises. These include a main lounge (for shows), a nightclub, and The Yacht Club (observation slash-lifestyle lounge and coffee bar). There is a library, shop, small screening room, and a mini-casino with roulette and blackjack tables and a few slot machines.

The ship was acquired by Xanterra Parks & Resorts, parent company of Windstar Cruises, in May 2014. Two sister ships *Star Breeze* and *Star Legend* joined the fleet in 2015.

BERLITZ'S RATINGS		
	Possible	Achieved
Ship	500	369
Accommodation	200	167
Food	400	270
Service	400	292
Entertainment	100	71
Cruise Experience	400	295

OVERALL SCORE 1464 points out of 2000

Passenger niggles? There is no outdoor walk-around deck, gratuities are not included, and internet use costs extra. Overall, this is a premium (not luxury) ship that provides a relaxing environment – just don't expect great food. There are also far fewer crew members than when operated by the previous owner, and maintenance is poor.

Star Pride will undergo a 'chop-and-stretch' operation in 2020 that will add a 83.9ft (25.6m) mid-section, 50 more suites/cabins, and two new venues. The ship's engines will be replaced; many other technical items will be upgraded or renewed. A new mid-ship elevator will be added, and the spa will be extended and improved. The new configuration means passenger capacity increases from 212 to 312, so the ship moves into the Small Ship category (250–750 passengers). The changes will be completed by November 2020 (*Star Breeze* undergoes the same operation in October 2019, and *Star Legend* in 2020).

ACCOMMODATION. This is spread over three decks, with several different price categories. The all-outside cabins (called suites in brochure-speak) are comfortably large and beautifully equipped with everything one could reasonably need. Electric blackout blinds are provided for the large windows in addition to curtains, and beds have premium bedding, duvets, and fine drapes. The cabinetry is made of blond woods and has softly rounded edges, and cabin doors are neatly angled away from the passageway.

A large walk-in closet is illuminated automatically when you open the door; wooden hangers, personal safe, umbrella, wall-mounted clock and barometer, and 110/220-volt power outlets are also provided. The decor is contemporary, but warm, in blues and beiges.

Marble-clad bathrooms have one or two wash-basins, depending on the accommodation grade, a decent, but not full-size, bathtub (four suites have a shower enclosure only – no tub), plenty of storage areas, cotton towels, bathrobe, and personal amenities.

On two out of three accommodation decks, some 36 suites have French balconies. These are not balconies in the true sense of the word, but they do have two doors that open wide onto a tiny teakwood balcony that is 10.6ins (27cm) wide (just enough for your feet). The balconies allow you to have fresh sea air, and salt spray.

Four Owner's Suites, each measuring between 530 sq ft (49 sq m) and 575 sq ft (53 sq m), and two Classic Suites, each 400 sq ft (37 sq m), offer superb, private living spaces. Each is named after a Windstar destination (Bora-Bora Suite, for example). Each has a walk-in closet, second closet, full bathroom plus a guest toilet with washbasin. There is a fully secluded forward- or side-facing balcony, with sunloungers and drinks table.

DINING. 'AmphorA' Restaurant, the main dining room, has portholes and restful decor. Open-seating dining means that you can dine when you want, with whom you wish.

The menus sound appealing, with a selection of contemporary cuisine and regional foods, but there's little taste and a lack of green vegetables – overall, it's underwhelming. Fruit and cheese selections are poor, as are salads. The wine list is fairly decent, with prices ranging from moderate to high.

Alternative dining can be found at Candles (indoor seating at just eight tables) or the adjacent outdoor Veranda Café. At night the indoor/outdoor venue becomes Candles Grill, a reservations-required steakhouse.

The Star Bar provides an above-poolside setting for candlelit dining. It specializes in sizzling steaks and seafood.

ENTERTAINMENT. The Lounge has a sloping floor that provides good sight lines from almost all seats. Small-scale shows, and the occasional cabaret act, are presented here. Non-American passengers should note that almost all entertainment and activities are geared towards North American tastes.

SPA/FITNESS. The Spa is a small but well-equipped health spa, with a small fitness room. It has sauna and steam rooms (separate facilities for men and women), an equipment-packed gymnasium (with a low ceiling) and a beauty salon.

The spa is staffed and operated by concession Elemis by Steiner. Treatment prices equal those in an expensive land-based spa. The beauty salon has hair-beautifying treatments and conditioning. In the gymnasium, personal training sessions and some classes may be at extra cost.

STAR PRINCESS
★★★+

THIS LARGE, MULTIPLE-CHOICE, RESORT SHIP IS GOOD FOR THE WHOLE FAMILY

Size:	Large Resort Ship	Passenger/Crew Ratio (lower beds):	2.3/1
Tonnage:	108,977	Cabins (total):	1,301
Cruise Line:	Princess Cruises	Size Range (sq ft/m):	161.4–1,314.0/15.0–122.0
Former Names:	none	Cabins (for one person):	0
Builder:	Fincantieri (Italy)	Cabins with balcony:	711
Entered Service:	Feb 2002	Cabins (wheelchair accessible):	28
Length (ft/m):	951.4/290.0	Wheelchair accessibility:	Best
Propulsion/Propellers:	diesel-electric (42,000kW)/2	Elevators:	14
Total Crew:	1,200	Casino (gaming tables):	Yes
Passengers (lower beds):	2,602	Self-Service Launderette:	Yes
Passenger Space Ratio (lower beds):	41.8	Onboard currency:	US$

THE SHIP. *Star Princess* is a well-designed grand resort, with many choices and 'small' rooms to enjoy. The odds are that you'll have a fine time, in a controlled, well-packaged way.

This large resort ship (close sister to *Golden Princess* and *Grand Princess*, and slightly larger half-sister *Caribbean Princess*) has a bold, forthright profile, with a racy 'spoiler' at its galleon-like transom stern (the 'spoiler' acts as a stern observation lounge by day, and disco by night).

There is a good sheltered faux teak promenade deck – it's actually painted steel – which almost wraps around (three times round is equal to 1 mile/2km) and a walkway that goes to the enclosed bow. The outdoor pools have beach-like surroundings. One lap pool has a pumped 'current' to swim against.

Unlike on the outside decks, there is plenty of space inside the ship – but there are also plenty of passengers – and a wide array of public rooms, with many smaller spaces and places to enjoy. The passenger flow works quite well. The decor is attractive, with lots of muted earth tones.

Four areas center on swimming pools, one of which is two decks high and is covered by a glass dome, itself an extension of the funnel housing.

The Grand Casino has gaming tables and more than 260 slot machines, including specially linked slot machines that provide a combined payout.

BERLITZ'S RATINGS		
	Possible	Achieved
Ship	500	344
Accommodation	200	139
Food	400	247
Service	400	279
Entertainment	100	75
Cruise Experience	400	278

OVERALL SCORE 1362 points out of 2000

Other facilities include a library/computer room, and separate card room. Ship lovers should enjoy the wood-paneled Wheelhouse Bar, with memorabilia and ship models tracing part of the history of sister company P&O (this ship highlights the 1950-built cargo ship *Ganges*). A sports bar, Shooters, has two billiard tables, and several television screens.

The dress code is formal or 'smart-casual,' the latter interpreted by many as jeans and trainers. Daily per-person gratuities are automatically added to your account, for both adults and children.

Niggles include the user-unfriendly automated telephone system, the small cabin towels, and extra-cost items such as ice cream; also, the charge (coins needed) for the washers and dryers in self-service launderettes.

Overall, however, Princess Cruises delivers a consistently fine, comfortable, well-packaged product, always with a good degree of style, at a competitive price. At the end of 2021, Star Princess will be transferred to the P&O Australia fleet.

ACCOMMODATION. There are six principal types of cabins: (a) grand suite, (b) suite, (c) mini-suite, (d) outside-view double cabin with balcony, (e) outside-view double cabin, and (f) interior double cabin; these come in many price categories. Most interior (no-view) cabins and standard ocean-view cabins are extremely small. Some cabins can accommodate a third and fourth person in upper berths, although the lower beds cannot then be pushed together to make a queen-size bed.

All accommodation has morning and evening turndown service (with chocolates on pillows each night), bathrobes on request, and toiletry kits (larger for suite/mini-suite occupants). A hairdryer is provided, sensibly located at the vanity desk unit in the lounge area. All bathrooms have tiled floors, and there is a decent amount of open shelf storage space for toiletries, although the plain beige decor is basic. Princess Cruises typically carries CNN, CNBC, ESPN, and TNT, when available, on the in-cabin television system.

Lifeboats obstruct most outside-view cabins on Emerald Deck. Your name is placed outside your suite or cabin in a document-holder – making it simple for delivery service personnel but privacy-insensitive. There is 24-hour room service, though some items on the menu are not available during early morning hours.

Most balcony suites and cabins can be overlooked both from the navigation bridge wing, as well as from the port and starboard sections of the ship's disco – located high above the ship at the stern. Cabins with balconies on Dolphin, Caribe, and Baja decks are also overlooked by passengers on balconies on the deck above. However, perhaps the least-desirable balcony cabins are eight ones located forward on Emerald Deck – the balconies don't extend to the side of the ship and can be passed by walkers and gawkers on the adjacent Upper Promenade walkway, so occupants need to keep their curtains closed most of the time. Also, passengers in some the suites with balconies aft may experience vibration during certain ship maneuvers.

DINING. For formal meals there are three main restaurants: Amalfi, Capri, and Portofino. Seating is assigned according to your cabin location. There are two seatings in Amalfi, while Capri and Portofino offer 'Anytime Dining' (you choose when and with whom you want to eat). All three are split into multi-tier sections in a non-symmetrical design to break them into small sections. Each dining room has its own galley.

Four elevators go to Fiesta Deck, where the Amalfi and Portofino restaurants are located, but only two elevators go to Plaza Deck 5, where the Capri Restaurant is located; this causes long wait problems at peak times, particularly for anyone in a wheelchair.

Dinnerware by Dudson of England, Frette Egyptian cotton table linens, and Hepp of Germany sil-

verware are used in the main dining rooms. Note that 15 percent is automatically added to all beverage bills, including wines.

Although portions are generous, the food and its presentation are disappointing, and standardized. Fish is often disguised by a crumb or batter coating, the choice of fresh green vegetables is limited, few garnishes are used, and cheese is already sliced and diced. This is big-ship mass catering, with all its attendant standardization. Pasta dishes are acceptable (though voluminous), typically served by section headwaiters, who may make 'something special just for you' – in search of favorable comments.

There are two extra-charge restaurants: Sabatini's and Tequila's, both open for lunch and dinner on days at sea. Sabatini's (think colorful, tiled Mediterranean-style décor) serves Italian-style dishes, pizzas and pastas, provided with flair by the waiters. Reservations are required.

Tequila's features food from the American Southwest (a cover charge applies for lunch or dinner) on sea days only. The restaurant is spread over the ship's entire beam and two walkways intersect it, which means that it's an open area, with people walking by as you eat – not a comfortable dining experience. Reservations are needed.

A poolside hamburger grill and a pizza bar are casual eateries. Note that it costs extra to eat at the coffee bar/patisserie, or the caviar/Champagne bar.

Other casual meals can be taken in the Horizon Court, open almost 24 hours a day, with large ocean-view windows on two sides. There is no real finesse in presentation because plastic plates (no trays) are provided.

ENTERTAINMENT. The Princess Theater (showlounge) spans two decks and has comfortable seating on both levels. Colorful production shows for which Princess Cruises is well known are accompanied by a live showband.

Vista Lounge, a second entertainment venue, features cabaret acts at night, and lectures, bingo, and horse racing during the day. Explorers, a third lounge, also hosts cabaret acts and dance bands. Various other lounges and bars have live music, and the ship has a number of male dance hosts as partners for women traveling alone.

SPA/FITNESS. The Lotus Spa has Japanese-style decor, and surrounds one of the swimming pools. You can have a massage or other spa treatment in an ocean-view treatment room. Some of the massage-treatment rooms are located directly under the jogging track.

SUN PRINCESS
★★★+

THIS LARGE, FAMILY-FRIENDLY RESORT SHIP HAS FAIRLY MODERN DECOR

Size:	Mid-size Ship	Passenger/Crew Ratio (lower beds):	2.0
Tonnage:	77,499	Cabins (total):	975
Cruise Line:	Princess Cruises	Size Range (sq ft/m):	134.5–753.4/12.5–70.0
Former Names:	none	Cabins (for one person):	0
Builder:	Fincantieri (Italy)	Cabins with balcony:	410
Entered Service:	Dec 1995	Cabins (wheelchair accessible):	19
Length (ft/m):	857.2/261.3	Wheelchair accessibility:	Good
Propulsion/Propellers:	diesel-electric (28,000kW)/2	Elevators:	11
Total Crew:	900	Casino (gaming tables):	Yes
Passengers (lower beds):	1,950	Self-Service Launderette:	Yes
Passenger Space Ratio (lower beds):	39.7	Onboard currency:	Australian $

THE SHIP. This all-white ship, which is now over 20 years old (it's the oldest in the fleet), has a decent profile that is balanced by its large funnel (this contains a deck tennis/basketball/volleyball court in its sheltered aft base). There is a wide, teakwood walk-around promenade deck outdoors, some real teak steamer-style deck chairs with royal blue cushioned pads, and 93,000 sq ft (8,640 sq m) of space outdoors. An extensive glass area on the upper decks provides plenty of light and connection with the outside world.

Sun Princess absorbs passengers well, and has a quasi-intimate feel, with warm, welcoming decor. A wide array of public rooms includes several intimate rooms and spaces, so that you don't feel overwhelmed by large spaces. The interior focal point (and always a good place to arrange to meet others) is a pleasant four-deck-high atrium lobby with winding, double staircases, and two panoramic glass-walled elevators.

The main entertainment rooms are located under three decks of cabins. There is plenty of space, the flow is good, and the ship absorbs people well. There are two showlounges, one at each end of the ship; one is a pleasant theater-style space, where movies are also shown, and the other is a cabaret-style lounge, complete with bar.

The library is a warm, welcoming room with ocean-view windows. There is a conference center for up to 300, as well as a business center. The col-

BERLITZ'S RATINGS		
	Possible	Achieved
Ship	500	325
Accommodation	200	128
Food	400	242
Service	400	266
Entertainment	100	68
Cruise Experience	400	265

OVERALL SCORE 1294 points out of 2000

lection of artwork, particularly on the stairways, helps make the ship feel smaller than it is, although in places it isn't coordinated.

The most traditional room (a standard on all Princess ships) is the Wheelhouse Lounge/Bar, decorated like a late 19th-century gentlemen's club, with wood paneling and comfortable seating. Its focal point is a large ship model from the P&O archives.

Niggles include the layout: there are a number of dead ends in the interior, so it's not as user-friendly as a ship this size should be. The cabin-numbering system is extremely illogical, with numbers going through several hundred series on the same deck. The walls of the passenger accommodation decks are very plain. The swimming pools are small for the number of passengers carried, and the pool deck is cluttered with white plastic sunloungers that lack cushioned pads.

ACCOMMODATION. There are many different cabin grades. Although the standard outside-view and interior cabins are small, they are well designed, functional, have abundant drawer space and a mini-fridge, although the closet space is small. Many outside-view cabins have private balconies, and all are well soundproofed, although the balcony partition is not floor-to-ceiling type, so you can hear your neighbors clearly. The balconies are very narrow, just large enough for two small chairs.

Cabin bathrooms are practical, although they really are tight, one-person-at-a-time spaces. They have a decent shower enclosure, real glasses, a hair-dryer and bathrobe, and a small amount of shelving for toiletries.

The largest accommodation is in six suites, two on each of three aft decks, with large private balcony (536–754 sq ft/50–70 sq m, including balcony). Some are 19 wheelchair-accessible cabins, which measure 213–305 sq ft (20–28 sq m), in a mix of seven outside-view and 12 interior cabins.

DINING. There are two main dining rooms of asymmetrical design – Marquis and Regency – located adjacent to the two lower levels of the four-deck-high atrium lobby. Each seat around 500, has its own galley, and is split into multi-tier sections that help create a feeling of intimacy, although there is a lot of noise from the waiter stations adjacent to many tables. Breakfast and lunch are provided in an open-seating arrangement, while dinner is in two seatings.

The wine list is reasonable, but there are no wine waiters. A 15 percent is automatically added to all beverage bills, including for wines.

Although portions are generous, the food and its presentation are non-memorable and standardized. Fish is often disguised by a crumb or batter coating, the choice of fresh green vegetables is limited, few garnishes are used, and cheese is already sliced and diced. This is big-ship banquet catering, which means cooking in large batches. Pasta dishes are acceptable (though voluminous), typically served by section headwaiters, who may also make 'something special just for you' – in search of favorable comments and gratuities. If you like desserts, order a sundae at dinner (most other items are just so-so).

'SHARE' by Curtis Stone, located on the upper level of the atrium lobby, features a multi-course 'degustation' menu.

For premium meats, consider the extra-cost Sterling Steakhouse; with four different cuts of Angus beef – Filet Mignon, New York Strip, Porterhouse, and Rib-Eye, first presented on a silver tray. This is available as an alternative to the dining rooms, but, instead of being a separate, intimate room, it is located in a section of the Horizon Buffet, with its own portable bar and some decorative touches to set it apart from the regular buffet area.

The Horizon Buffet itself is open almost around the clock, and, at night, has an informal dinner setting with sit-down waiter service. The buffet displays are, for the most part, fairly repetitious. There is no real finesse in presentation, however (plastic plates are provided, instead of trays).

There is also a patisserie (for extra-cost coffees and pastries), a wine/caviar bar, and a pizzeria (complete with cobblestone floors and wrought-iron decorative features), and a choice of pizzas.

ENTERTAINMENT. There are two showlounges. Princess Theater has a sloping floor, with aisle-style seating that is well tiered, and with good sight lines to the raised stage from most of the 500 seats.

The 480-seat Vista Lounge, at aft, features cabaret and acts as a daytime lecture and presentation room. Princess Cruises has a good stable of regular cabaret acts to draw from, so there should be something for most tastes.

SPA/FITNESS. A glass-walled Lotus Spa is located in an aft area of Riviera deck, and includes a gymnasium with high-tech machines, several massage/body-treatment rooms, and a beauty salon. The facility is staffed and operated by a specialist spa concession.

Sports facilities are located in an open-air sports deck inside the funnel and adaptable for basketball, volleyball, badminton, or paddle tennis. Joggers can exercise on the walk-around open Promenade Deck.

SUPERSTAR AQUARIUS
★★★

THIS FAMILY-FRIENDLY CASUAL CRUISER SHIP IS GOOD FOR CASINO GAMERS

Size:	Mid-size Ship
Tonnage:	50,764
Cruise Line:	Star Cruises
Former Names:	*Norwegian Wind, Windward*
Builder:	Chantiers de l'Atlantique (France)
Entered Service:	Jun 1993/May 2007
Length (ft/m):	754.0/229.8
Propulsion/Propellers:	diesel (18,480kW)/2
Total Crew:	889
Passengers (lower beds):	1,529
Passenger Space Ratio (lower beds):	33.1
Passenger/Crew Ratio (lower beds):	1.7/1
Cabins (total):	765
Size Range (sq ft/m):	139.9–349.8/13.0–32.5
Cabins (for one person):	0
Cabins with balcony:	74
Cabins (wheelchair accessible):	11
Wheelchair accessibility:	Fair
Elevators:	10
Casino (gaming tables):	Yes
Self-Service Launderette:	No
Onboard currency:	Hong Kong $

THE SHIP. *SuperStar Aquarius* was transferred from Norwegian Cruise Line to the Star Cruises fleet in 2007 to operate overnight and short cruises from Hong Kong. The dress code is strictly casual. Several cabins are specially equipped for hearing-impaired passengers. All gratuities for staff are included.

The exterior design emphasizes a clever use of large windows that helps to create a sense of open space, but there are many smaller public rooms. There is no big atrium lobby, and the ceiling height is low.

Public rooms include bars and lounges, such as Skyline Karaoke, which has five private karaoke rooms. There's a Mahjong/card room, childcare center, video arcade, Genting Club for invited gaming guests, business meeting rooms, an Internet-connect center/library, a cigar lounge, and a small boutique. There is a blue rubber-covered, walk-around promenade deck outdoors. Outdoor stairways are numerous and confusing, while the carpeted steel interior stairwell steps are tinny.

ACCOMMODATION. There are several different cabin price grades. No cabin includes the number '4,' as this signifies 'death' in China. Most cabins have outside views and wood-trimmed cabinetry and warm decor, but there's almost no drawer space (although the closets have open shelves), so be minimalist when packing. All cabins have a sitting area. The bathrooms are small but practical.

BERLITZ'S RATINGS

	Possible	Achieved
Ship	500	275
Accommodation	200	119
Food	400	237
Service	400	247
Entertainment	100	60
Cruise Experience	400	232

OVERALL SCORE 1170 points out of 2000

There are 18 suites (12 with a private entrance and a small, private balcony), each with separate living room and bedroom, and plenty of closet and drawer space. Occupants of suites receive 'concierge' service. In addition, 16 suites and 70 cabins have interconnecting doors.

DINING. Freestyle Dining venues include the 280-seat Dynasty Restaurant, for Chinese family-style food. It has some prime tables at ocean-view window seats in a section that extends from the ship's port and starboard sides in half-moon shapes. There's also Spices Restaurant, an Asian specialty buffet venue with 180 seats; Oceana Barbecue, an outdoor buffet venue; Blue Lagoon, a 24-hour bistro, with 80 seats; and Mariner's Buffet, an international self-service buffet.

ENTERTAINMENT. The 700-seat Stardust Lounge is two decks high, but the banquette and individual tub chair seating is only on the main level. There is no live showband, only recorded music. High-volume razzle-dazzle shows are presented to a pre-recorded track, as well as special individual cabaret acts.

SPA/FITNESS. A gymnasium has high-tech muscle-toning equipment, reflexology lounge, and Oscar Hair and Beauty Salon. There's a ping-pong table, basketball/volleyball court, golf driving range, and a jogging track.

SUPERSTAR GEMINI
★★★

THIS CASUAL, FAMILY-FRIENDLY SHIP IS POPULAR WITH ASIAN CRUISERS

Size:	Mid-size Ship
Tonnage:	50,764
Cruise Line:	Star Cruises
Former Names:	*Norwegian Dream, Dreamward*
Builder:	Chantiers de l'Atlantique (France)
Entered Service:	Dec 1992/Jan 2013
Length (ft/m):	754.0/229.8
Propulsion/Propellers:	diesel (18,480kW)/2
Total Crew:	889
Passengers (lower beds):	1,529
Passenger Space Ratio (lower beds):	33.1

Passenger/Crew Ratio (lower beds):	1.7/1
Cabins (total):	765
Size Range (sq ft/m):	139.9–349.8/13.0–32.5
Cabins (for one person):	0
Cabins with balcony:	74
Cabins (wheelchair accessible):	10
Wheelchair accessibility:	Fair
Elevators:	10
Casino (gaming tables):	Yes
Self-Service Launderette:	No
Onboard currency:	Hong Kong $

THE SHIP. *SuperStar Gemini* is a mid-sized ship that is popular with Asian families and couples looking for a general cruise experience in modernish surroundings.

The ship has a profile that is balanced (a 'chop-and-stretch' operation in 1998 added a 131ft (40m) mid-section).

The tiered pool deck aft is neat, as are the multi-deck aft sun terraces and the fore and aft connecting exterior stairways. The overall exterior design emphasizes a clever and extensive use of large windows that create a sense of open space. There is no big atrium lobby, as one might expect.

Public rooms include a Mahjong room, an activity center, several shops (including a duty-free store, a tea corner for premium teas, and a jewelry store), an Observatory Lounge (Karaoke Lounge), Genting Club, and the Star Club casino with gaming tables and slot machines.

ACCOMMODATION. There are several grades of cabins (the price you pay will depend on the grade, size, and location you choose). Most cabins have outside views, wood-trimmed cabinetry, with warm decor and multicolored soft furnishings, but there is

BERLITZ'S RATINGS

	Possible	Achieved
Ship	500	283
Accommodation	200	113
Food	400	237
Service	400	247
Entertainment	100	60
Cruise Experience	400	233

OVERALL SCORE 1173 points out of 2000

little drawer space (the closets have open shelves). All cabins benefit from a sitting area, but this takes away space, making movement pretty tight. The bathrooms are small but practical.

DINING. There are plenty of choices. The main full-service dining room is Bella Vista (the nicest, with prime tables and ocean-view window seats); Dynasty (a self-serve Chinese buffet); Mariners Restaurant (a self-serve buffet); Oceana Barbecue (outdoors, for grilled specialties and buffet-style eats); and Blue Lagoon (à la carte and open 24-hours). The cuisine is Asian, and adequate.

ENTERTAINMENT. The Stardust Lounge is the showlounge. Two decks high, it is located in the ship's center, with cabins in front of it, and other public rooms and dining spots behind it.

SPA/FITNESS. Spa/fitness facilities are located just aft of the observation lounge, and include a gymnasium with muscle-toning equipment, a beauty salon, several massage and associated treatment rooms, and men's and women's saunas and changing rooms.

SYMPHONY OF THE SEAS
★★★★

THIS EXTREME FLOATING THEME PARK PROVIDES MANY, MANY CHOICES FOR THE WHOLE FAMILY

Size:	Large Resort Ship
Tonnage:	228,081
Cruise Line:	Royal Caribbean International
Former Names:	none
Builder:	STX France
Entered Service:	Apr 2018
Length (ft/m):	1,187.9/362.1
Propulsion/Propellers:	Diesel-electric/3 pods (2azimuthing, 1 fixed)
Total Crew:	2,200
Passengers (lower beds):	5,503
Passenger Space Ratio (lower beds):	41.3
Passenger/Crew Ratio (lower beds):	2.5
Cabins (total):	2,759
Size Range (sq ft/m):	172.2–2,389.6/16.0–222
Cabins (for one person):	15
Cabins with balcony:	2,000
Cabins (wheelchair accessible):	46
Wheelchair accessibility:	Best
Elevators:	24
Casino (gaming tables):	Yes
Self-Service Launderette:	No
Onboard currency:	US$

THE SHIP. *Symphony of the Seas* – officially the world's largest resort cruise ship – is absolutely stunning for families with children, with bling and ultra-buzz everywhere. It is a benchmark for self-contained resorts (it's slightly larger and more efficient than its three sister ships, with almost 40 more cabins). No matter what your entertainment and activity interests are, this ship should really turn you on – as long as you plan ahead. Neat fact: there are four bow thrusters, and each has more power than seven Ferraris.

This ship is quite stunning – and a real credit to its design team. There is little quiet actual relaxation and sunbathing space outdoors (unless you have suite-grade accommodation and can use the more exclusive adults-only Suite Sundeck), because much of it is taken up by an extensive water park. This includes mind-numbing 'Perfect Storm' waterslides (try The Abyss at the aft of the ship – a ride through 10 decks that you won't forget in a hurry), fountains, water cannons, and sports features – including the obligatory rock-climbing wall and body surfing 'Flowriders'. Sunloungers are tightly packed so there's little space to put your belongings. Sadly, there's not a hint of teak decking or wood-topped railings anywhere (railings have plastic tops).

The inner 'city' is divided into seven neighborhoods: Central Park (including numerous real trees and scores of plants) and a Rising Tide Bar; The

BERLITZ'S RATINGS

	Possible	Achieved
Ship	500	404
Accommodation	200	140
Food	400	226
Service	400	281
Entertainment	100	87
Cruise Experience	400	287

OVERALL SCORE 1425 points out of 2000

Boardwalk (Coney Island-style, with a fine children's carousel); the Royal Promenade; the Pool and Sports Zone; Entertainment Place; Youth Zone; and Vitality at Sea Spa and Fitness Center. The 'see and be seen' strolling areas are the Boardwalk, with its new sports bar; Central Park, a delightful open park-like space (both open to the air); and the indoor Royal Promenade – look for a huge, 12,000-piece stainless steel sculpture called 'Paradox Void.'

In all, there are around three-dozen bars/lounges, and over 20 restaurants, cafés, and eateries to experience (some are exclusive to certain suite accommodation grades). It's part of the 'pay more, get more' system of class distinction, like anywhere else. There's also a very large Casino Royale, with gaming tables (plus a player's club and poker room) and slot machines.

The wow factor aboard this ship come in the entertainment (particularly the big theater shows), and not just the waterslides and sports facilities – rather than the food. Super-high-speed Internet enables video streaming, Skyping, and social-media sharing (at a hefty price).

Niggles include lines for shore tenders and excursions, self-serve buffet and burger stations, intrusive photographers, few quiet places to sit and read, no cushioned pads for sunloungers, small cabin 'bath' towels, unwelcome announcements for revenue activities, fiberglass (not wood) railings, expensive ice-laden frosted drinks in 'souvenir' glasses, the speaking 'elevator going up/going down, and rap-rich 'music' everywhere (even in elevators, hallways and saunas).

Overall, this is a good all-round ship for all age groups, but be aware of the many extra costs for the various dining venues, optional items (including drinks and drink packages), and excursions. Do budget extra for additional-cost items and expect flyers and advertising promotions.

ACCOMMODATION. There's a big choice of accommodation sizes, locations and price grades, from the smallest interior (no-view) cabin (measuring 172 sq ft/16 sq m) to the largest suite (with baby grand piano, measuring 2,390 sq ft/222 sq m). The huge upstairs/downstairs Family Suite is a mini-apartment Suite (like a seagoing play pen).

The cabin numbering system is awkward, however. Also, cabin doors open outwards (towards you), as in many European hotels. In many lower grade rooms, closet access is awkward, as most are dimensionally challenged and quite tight – but just manageable for a week.

Many cabins have 'infinite' balconies, whereby it is incorporated, with fresh air from large openable windows (copied from European riverships). Many interior (no-view) cabins have virtual balconies (this feature can be turned off), and all accommodation grades have a minibar.

DINING. Quantum, the cavernous main restaurant, spans decks 3 to 5; it is in three sections: The Chic, The Grande, and American Icon Grill. It operates early or late seating times for dinner (or you can choose 'My Time Dining' and eat at your preferred time – maybe). There are tables of all sizes, including some for family reunions.

Other free dining/eating venue options include:

Central Park Café for deli-style sandwiches, salad items, paninis, crêpes, and hearty soups.

Windjammer Marketplace is an extremely large, self-serve buffet, casual food-court eatery, with several different sections featuring different food types, salad bar, etc. The venue can be extremely crowded due to the number of passengers carried, but the layout of the various food islands and sections is good.

Other snacking spots include: Boardwalk Dog House, Rita's Cantina, Donut Shop, Starbucks, Solarium Bistro, Vitality Café, and Ice Cream Parlor.

These restaurants/eateries cost extra:

150 Central Park, for the best cooked-to-order cuisine.

Chops Grille, a 'signature' steakhouse featuring large, premium-quality steaks and other grilled food items (open for dinner, reservations required).

El Loco Mexican for Mexican-style eats.

Hooked, a seafood brasserie located inside the three-deck high Solarium.

Izumi Hibachi and Sushi for Japanese-style dishes.

Jamie's Italian, a tablecloth-free, Euro-Italian, bistro-style trattoria with rustic decor; open for lunch and dinner (reservations required and there's a cover charge for dinner).

Johnny Rockets, diner-style – for burgers and ice cream shakes.

Wonderland, a funky, two-deck-high venue for quirky small-portion molecular show cuisine (fussy, but lacking substance); decor and seating are inspired by Alice in Wonderland.

Vintages, a pleasant wine bar with cheese and tapas (at à-la-carte prices).

ENTERTAINMENT. The 1,380-seat Royal Theater (main showlounge) spans three decks. Reservations for shows can be made ahead (no charge), and the hit musical *Hair* is the star show. The Ice Skating Rink (on Deck 4) has seats for about 900, and the shows are dazzlingly top-notch.

A 750-seat Aqua Theater, located outside on The Boardwalk, aft, has a 6,000 sq ft (557 sq m) stage and an aqua pool (the aquatic/acrobatic show is stunning). 'The Attic Comedy Club' is for adults-only (smutty) comedy.

SPA/FITNESS. Vitality at Sea Spa has a large fitness center (cardio and resistance equipment) and beauty salon. An extra-cost Thermal Suite pass allows you access to men's and women's saunas, steam rooms, and heated tiled relaxation loungers, plus a Vitality Café for extra-cost 'health' drinks and snacks.

Sports features include two Flowriders for body surfing, a zipline that careers over The Boardwalk (and its inner balcony cabins), and three waterslides that career over Central Park. There's a Sports Pool, Harmony Dunes (mini-golf), a Sports Court, two rock climbing walls (aft), and the Abyss waterslide.

VASCO DA GAMA
★★+

THIS DECENT MID-SIZE SHIP IS GOOD FOR BUDGET-MINDED, MATURE-AGE TRAVELERS

Size:	Mid-size Ship	Passenger/Crew Ratio (lower beds):	2.2
Tonnage:	55,819	Cabins (total):	630
Cruise Line:	Transocean Cruises/CMV	Size Range (sq ft/m):	186.2–1,124.8/17.3–104.5
Former Names:	*Pacific Eden, Statendam*	Cabins (for one person):	0
Builder:	Fincantieri (Italy)	Cabins with balcony:	150
Entered Service:	Nov 1994/Apr 2019	Cabins (wheelchair accessible):	6
Length (ft/m):	719.3/219.3	Wheelchair accessibility:	Fair
Propulsion/Propellers:	diesel-electric/2	Elevators:	8
Total Crew:	560	Casino (gaming tables):	Yes
Passengers (lower beds):	1,260	Self-Service Launderette:	Yes
Passenger Space Ratio (lower beds):	44.3	Onboard currency:	UK£

THE SHIP. Formerly cruising in Australasia under the P&O Cruises banner, *Vasco da Gama* was sold to CMV in 2019 and operates under its Transocean Cruises brand, mainly for the budget German-speaking market. The ship's exterior styling is pretty boxy, but there is a full walk-around teakwood Promenade Deck outdoors, while aft is a quiet adults-only relaxation area, with its own small dip pool. The main lido pool area was nicely refurbished and updated in the 2019 refit.

Inside, an asymmetrical layout helps reduce bottlenecks, and most public rooms are mostly on two decks, creating a feeling of spaciousness. Atop the ship is an observation lounge with ocean-view windows by day; by night it's a trendy nightspot. The atrium foyer is three decks high, although a sculptured centerpiece, *Fountain of the Sirens*, invades the space.

There is a good array of lounges and bars, plus a decent-sized library/internet center, card games room, an intimate Piano Bar, indoor cinema, and a casino with gaming tables and slots.

ACCOMMODATION. There are many cabin price grades; just under a quarter of all cabins have a

BERLITZ'S RATINGS

	Possible	Achieved
Ship	500	287
Accommodation	200	110
Food	400	185
Service	400	222
Entertainment	100	47
Cruise Experience	400	202

OVERALL SCORE 1053 points out of 2000

balcony. Cabins range from small interior cabins (with little storage space) to a seriously large Penthouse Suite. Occupants of suite-grade accommodation also get a Nespresso coffee machine. .

DINING. There are three 'main' restaurants, all with open seating: Waterfront (aft, with a high ceiling). One deck above, Waterfront Eurasia (for Asian-style cuisine) and Waterfront Mediterranean (for Mediterranean fare). There's also The Grill (for premium-quality steaks and seafood), and a Chef's Table for special dinners. For more casual eats, it's Club Bistro, for casual, self-serve outlets (similar to a food court).

ENTERTAINMENT. The Hollywood Showlounge spans two decks, and has banquette-style seating. It is basically a well-designed, multi-function room, but sight lines from the balcony level are not good. Colorful production shows are presented in the evening.

SPA/FITNESS. The JadeSpa includes a workout room with ocean views, high-tech equipment, an aerobics area, a beauty salon, treatment rooms, saunas, steam rooms, and changing areas.

VEENDAM
★★★

A MID-SIZE SHIP WITH DUTCH HERITAGE AND DECOR FOR MATURE-AGE TRAVELERS

Size:	Mid-size Ship	Passenger/Crew Ratio (lower beds):	2.2
Tonnage:	57,092	Cabins (total):	674
Cruise Line:	Holland America Line	Size Range (sq ft/m):	186.2–1,124.8/17.3–104.5
Former Names:	none	Cabins (for one person):	0
Builder:	Fincantieri (Italy)	Cabins with balcony:	182
Entered Service:	May 1996	Cabins (wheelchair accessible):	8
Length (ft/m):	719.3/219.3	Wheelchair accessibility:	Fair
Propulsion/Propellers:	diesel-electric (34,560kW)/2	Elevators:	8
Total Crew:	561	Casino (gaming tables):	Yes
Passengers (lower beds):	1,348	Self-Service Launderette:	Yes
Passenger Space Ratio (lower beds):	42.4	Onboard currency:	US$

THE SHIP. *Veendam* is one of four almost identical ships, the others being *Maasdam*, *Pacific Aria* (formerly *Ryndam*), and *Pacific Eden* (formerly *Statendam*). Although the exterior styling is angular (some say boxy – the funnel certainly is), it is balanced somewhat by its black hull. A ducktail sponson stern was added in 2009 for better stability and ride. There is a full walk-around teakwood promenade deck outdoors, which is good for strolling.

The Retreat includes a hot tub, Slices pizzeria, a bar, sunloungers within a wading pool, and a large movie screen.

Most public rooms are concentrated on two decks, Promenade Deck, and Upper Promenade Deck, which creates a decent, spacious feel. In general, the approach to interior styling is restrained, using a mix of contemporary materials combined with traditional woods and ceramics. There's little glitz anywhere.

The artwork showcases HAL's Dutch heritage. Also noticeable are live flower arrangements for brightening up the otherwise dull decor.

Atop the ship is the Crow's Nest Lounge, an observation lounge with ocean-view windows by day; in the evening it's a nightclub with variable lighting.

A three-deck-high atrium foyer is a good meeting place, although its sculpted centerpiece makes it feels crowded, leaving little room in front of reception. A hydraulic glass dome covers the swimming pool/whirlpools and central Lido area, for all-

BERLITZ'S RATINGS		
	Possible	Achieved
Ship	500	297
Accommodation	200	125
Food	400	218
Service	400	251
Entertainment	100	60
Cruise Experience	400	237

OVERALL SCORE 1188 points out of 2000

weather use, with a large dolphin sculpture.

There is a relaxing reference library within the lifestyle area, with three theme bars in one central area (Champagne, Martinis, and Spirits & Ales). Touchscreen technology is available for playing checkers and chess, air hockey, and other games.

The company continues its maritime traditions, although maintenance and the food and service components still let down the rest of the cruise experience. The service staff is Indonesian; although they are mostly quite charming, communication can prove frustrating, and service is inconsistent.

An escalator travels between two of the lower decks (one was originally planned to be the embarkation point). The charge to use the washing machines and dryers in the self-service launderette is petty. The men's public restroom urinals are unusually high.

ACCOMMODATION. The accommodation ranges from small interior cabins to a large Penthouse Suite, in many different price categories.

The interior and outside-view standard cabins have twin beds convertible to a queen-size bed, and there is a separate living space with sofa and coffee table. Drawer space is generally good, but closet space is tight, particularly for long cruises. The tiled bathrooms are compact but practical.

Bathrobes, hairdryers, and a small number of toiletries are provided for all suites/cabins, but the bathtubs are simply shower tubs. Some cabins have interconnecting doors.

On Navigation Deck, suites can accommodate four persons, with in-suite dining as an alternative to dining in public. They are spacious, tastefully decorated, and well laid-out, with a separate living room, bedroom with two lower beds that convert to a king-size bed, a good-size living area, dressing room, plenty of closet and drawer space, and marble bathroom with Jacuzzi tub.

The largest accommodation is a Penthouse Suite, on the starboard side of Navigation Deck at the forward staircase.

DINING. The Rotterdam Dining Room spans two decks aft, with two grand staircases connecting each level, and panoramic views on three sides. Both open seating and assigned-table seating are available, although breakfast and lunch are just open seating (you'll be taken to a free table by restaurant staff when you enter). There are tables for two to eight, Rosenthal china, and good-quality cutlery, but the waiter stations are noisy for anyone seated near them.

With just a few exceptions, the cuisine is unmemorable; it lacks passion and taste, because it's all about production (batch) cooking. There's a distinct lack of variety of green vegetables, and a heavy use of rice, canned fruit, and ready-sliced and diced cheese. Still, you get friendly service from Indonesian and Filipino stewards, and the plates are nice.

A more intimate, extra-cost, reservations-required Pinnacle Grill is located just forward of the balcony level of the main dining room on the starboard side. The 66-seat venue features premium steaks and seafood. A Bulgari show plate, Rosenthal china, Riedel wine glasses, and Frette table linen are used.

For more casual evening eating, the self-serve Lido Buffet is open for dinners on all except the last night of each cruise, in an open-seating arrangement. Tables are set with crisp linens, flatware, and stemware. A set menu is featured, with a choice of entreés (mains). This is also the place for casual breakfasts and lunches. Each evening, a section transforms into Canaletto (reservations required) for casual Italian meals.

You may need to eat in the Lido Buffet on days when the dining room is closed for lunch – typically once or twice per cruise, depending on the itinerary.

Also, a Lido Deck poolside 'Dive-In at the Terrace Grill' features burgers, hot dogs, fries, and, occasionally, barbecue items.

ENTERTAINMENT. The Showroom at Sea, forward, spans two decks, has banquette seating on both levels. The ceiling is low, and sight lines from the balcony level are limited.

SPA/FITNESS. The Ocean Spa is underneath the navigation bridge. It includes a gymnasium with muscle-pumping machines, plus an abundance of treadmills. It has ocean views, a large beauty salon with ocean-view windows to the port side, several treatment rooms, a sauna, steam room, and changing areas.

VENTURA
★★★+

THIS LARGE, FAMILY-FRIENDLY SHIP IS AIMED AT THOSE WITH BRITISH TASTES

Size:	Large Resort Ship	Passenger/Crew Ratio (lower beds):	2.4/1
Tonnage:	116,017	Cabins (total):	1,546
Cruise Line:	P&O Cruises	Size Range (sq ft/m):	134.5–534.0/12.5–49.6
Former Names:	none	Cabins (for one person):	18
Builder:	Fincantieri (Italy)	Cabins with balcony:	880
Entered Service:	Apr 2008	Cabins (wheelchair accessible):	25
Length (ft/m):	951.4/290.0	Wheelchair accessibility:	Good
Propulsion/Propellers:	diesel-electric (42,000kW)/2	Elevators:	12
Total Crew:	1,239	Casino (gaming tables):	Yes
Passengers (lower beds):	3,074	Self-Service Launderette:	Yes
Passenger Space Ratio (lower beds):	37.7	Onboard currency:	UK£

THE SHIP. *Ventura* (now over 10 years old) suits British passengers looking for a big-ship environment with comfortable but unstuffy surroundings and plenty of options. This is the P&O version of Princess Cruises' *Grand*-class ships, along with close sister *Azura*.

There are promenade walking decks to port and starboard sides, underneath the lifeboats; you can't walk completely around unless you use some steps at the front (which are often closed). There are three pools: two on the main pool deck, one coverable by a glass-roof, and one aft. There's little outdoor deck space – unless you pay extra for a covered, adults-only, quiet zone called The Retreat (located above the spa), with private cabanas and steward service.

Inside, a three-deck atrium is the focal social meeting point. Designed like a town centre, central to which are four towering black granite archways sourced from India, it's the place to see and be seen. The upper-deck public room layout is challenging, because you can't go from one end of the ship to the other without first going down, along, and up – poor for anyone with mobility problems.

Public rooms include several shops, a small library, a Cruise Sales Centre, a (small) Fortunes Casino, and several bars, including The Exchange (an 'urban warehouse' bar), The Beach House (outside with aft and ship's sides views – over everyone's balcony), and Red bar.

BERLITZ'S RATINGS		
	Possible	Achieved
Ship	500	367
Accommodation	200	142
Food	400	246
Service	400	283
Entertainment	100	68
Cruise Experience	400	261

OVERALL SCORE 1367 points out of 2000

Passenger niggles include the push for on-board revenue, low passenger/space ratio, lack of a dedicated card room, mediocre self-service buffet food, and charge for shuttle buses in some ports.

It's possible to get married on board, with the captain officiating.

ACCOMMODATION. There are many different accommodation price grades, according to location chosen, from suites with balcony to outside-view twin/queen (no balcony) and interior no-view cabins.

Over one-third of the accommodation is comprised of interior (no-view) cabins. Some cabins have extra berths that fold down from the ceiling. While suites are quite spacious, they are small when compared to those aboard many other cruise lines. There are 18 solo-occupancy cabins (12 outside and six interior), as aboard *Azura*.

Standard in all cabins: bed runners, Slumberland sprung mattresses, and Egyptian cotton towels. Basic tea-/coffee-making facilities and packets of UHT milk, not fresh milk, are provided. Bathrobes are available only for passengers occupying grades A, B, and D accommodation. Three-pin UK and US-style 110-volt sockets are provided for electrical devices.

Cabins have open closets (no doors = no money wasted), providing easy access. Some balcony cabins have teak patio furniture, and an outside light.

Wheelchair-accessible cabins have a shower enclosure, except R415, which has a bathtub with integral shower. To take breakfast in the self-serve Waterside casual eatery, wheelchair-users (mostly accommodated in the ship's forward section) must go across the decks containing the Beachcomber and Laguna pools and past many deck chairs – not easy. Alternatively, room service breakfast – typically cold items only – can be ordered. Note that there is no room service breakfast on disembarkation day.

DINING. P&O's marketing blurb claims there are 10 restaurants. There really aren't. There are five genuine restaurants (Bay Tree, Cinnamon, Saffron, The Epicurian, and Sindhu); the others are casual eateries.

The three main dining rooms, Bay Tree, Cinnamon, and Saffron, have standard menus. Bay Tree has fixed seating (Club) dining, with assigned tables and seating times. Cinnamon and Saffron have open seating, so you can eat when you want, with whom you want, during meal times (Freedom Dining), but there can be long wait times for a table.

The cuisine is straightforward, no-nonsense British food, presented on Wedgwood china. It's rather bland and uninspiring, but typical of mass-banquet catering, comparable to that found in a family hotel in a classic English seaside town.

Special themed dinners are provided in the main dining rooms, including a 'Chaîne des Rôtisseurs' event. The wine list is 'ho-hum' average, but good value, although the wine glasses are small.

Specialty (extra-cost, reservation-required) dining venues include: The Epicurian, above the children's play area, with a quarter of the tables on an adjacent open deck. Modern European, cooked-to-order dishes are served in an intimate, unstuffy environment. Indian-themed Sindhu is overseen by Michelin-starred chef Atul Kochhar (think British-Indian fusion cuisine).

The Waterside is a large, self-serve, 'seaside chic' buffet with indoor-outdoor seating. Unfortunately, the cramped seating is poorly designed, and the food selection is limited (better for lunch than for breakfast or dinner). The Beach House (a closed off section of The Waterside) is a cost-extra casual evening dining venue.

Adjacent to the forward pool, are Frankie's Grill and Frankie's Pizzeria. Tazzine, a coffee lounge by day, turns into a cocktail bar in the evening.

Marco's roof-side café offers pizzas, grills, and ice-cream flavors such as chocolate truffle and prune and Armagnac. Children's cutlery, bibs, and beakers are available.

ENTERTAINMENT. The 785-seat Arena Theatre, at the front, spans two decks. Havana, the main nightclub (movies are sometimes shown here), is an activities room by day and a sultry Cuba-inspired club by night, but the sight lines are really poor from many seats.

A cool wall in Metropolis screens real-time footage of seven world famous city skylines – Hong Kong, Las Vegas, London, New York, Paris, Rio de Janeiro, and Sydney.

SPA/FITNESS. The Oasis Spa is located forward, almost atop the ship. It includes a gymnasium, aerobics room, beauty salon, men's and women's saunas and steam rooms, and 11 body treatments rooms. An internal stairway connects to the deck below, and an extra-charge Thermal Suite. Treatments include special packages for couples, and the SilverSpa Generation.

VIKING JUPITER

THIS SHIP IS FOR MATURE-AGE TRAVELERS WHO WANT TO EXPLORE NEW DESTINATIONS IN COMFORT

Size:	Mid-size Ship
Tonnage:	47,800
Cruise Line:	Viking Ocean Cruises
Former Names:	none
Builder:	Fincantieri (Italy)
Entered Service:	Mar 2019
Length (ft/m):	754.5/230.0
Propulsion/Propellers:	Diesel-electric/2
Total Crew:	545
Passengers (lower beds):	928
Passenger Space Ratio (lower beds):	51.5
Passenger/Crew Ratio (lower beds):	1.7
Cabins (total):	465
Size Range (sq ft/m):	270.0–1,163.0/25.0–108.0
Cabins (for one person):	0
Cabins with balcony:	464
Cabins (wheelchair accessible):	7
Wheelchair accessibility:	Good
Elevators:	8
Casino (gaming tables):	No
Self-Service Launderette:	Yes
Onboard currency:	US$

THE SHIP. *Viking Jupiter* (sixth in a series of eight identical ships) is well proportioned, with a host of Scandinavian design elements. Step aboard, and it immediately feels like you're in a Nordic home: comfortable, practical, and entirely lacking in 'bling.' There are plenty of public areas and dining options, plus an abundance of glass walls that help connect you with the sea on all levels.

BERLITZ'S RATINGS		
	Possible	Achieved
Ship	500	459
Accommodation	200	171
Food	400	338
Service	400	325
Entertainment	100	76
Cruise Experience	400	322

OVERALL SCORE 1691 points out of 2000

The ship is powered by energy-efficient hybrid engines, solar panels, and has equipment for minimizing air pollution. The company focuses on enhancing the destination experience (rather than the ship being your only destination) and provides interactive touchscreen stations that provide a wealth of destination information. This ship provides an excellent base for the various destinations covered on Viking's itineraries. The interior design is tasteful, and leaves an uncluttered impression, so you won't find overly opulent surroundings – it's more Hyatt (premium) than Four Seasons (luxe).

A walk-around promenade deck is on a lower deck, and fairly well sheltered from any wind – good for strolling and people-watching. Meanwhile, on the largest upper open deck, a sliding glass dome covers the main pool deck on the deck below, just forward of the main pool; aft of the pool is a spacious Wintergarden, with wood cladding around its support pillars, plus a large screen for poolside movies. A second pool (and an adjacent hot tub) on the same deck, but aft, is the 'infinity' pool (modern jargon for a pool with one glass wall) that forms part of the Aquavit Terrace, an alfresco casual eatery. The sunloungers have retractable footrests; square drinks tables have a thick wood top and are very practical.

Inside, the main focal point is an elegant, rectangular-shaped, three-decks-high atrium lobby; it has light woods and abundant glass that lets in plenty of natural light, and all levels have seating.

The very comfortable Explorer's Lounge spans two decks. It is an observation lounge and incorporates a library and a Viking Café deli-counter; the upper level has glass cabinets displaying items of exploration and discovery.

The company concentrates on destination-rich and immersive itineraries, and a program of shore excursions focused on cultural experiences.

Viking Jupiter fares include ship-wide Wi-Fi, one shore excursion in each port of call, overnight stays in embarkation or disembarkation ports, and complimentary beer and wine with lunch and dinner.

ACCOMMODATION. There are five accommodation categories, but many different prices, according to deck and location. All are comfortable and practical – not frivolous – and typical of the efficient Scandinavian approach to design. All cabins/suites have a private balcony (Viking calls them 'verandas'), a *king*-size bed, and a generous shower enclosure (the suites have bathtubs), and all bathrooms have heated floors – a nice touch. If you like more space, it's worth considering one of the Explorer Suites located forward and aft – most with a wrap-around balcony.

A superb Owner's Suite is conveniently positioned adjacent to the Explorer's Lounge. It includes a master bedroom, lounge, dining area, walk-in closet, wet room, and private sauna.

DINING. There are several restaurants and eateries, and all operate on an open-seating basis, so you can dine when and with whom you like. All are included in the cruise price. Most venues also have an alfresco option (Viking emphasises fresh-air dining).

The Dining Room (an easy name to remember) has a sliding glass wall that opens onto the wraparound promenade deck aft, with a few tables for alfresco dining.

The cuisine is decidedly international and unfussy and includes 'always available' comfort classics. The focus is on regional and sustainably sourced ingredients.

Other dining options:

Manfredi's Italian Restaurant features Italian food with a focus on Tuscany; its decoration includes real accordions (the national instrument of Italy).

The Chef's Table is for a food-and-wine-paired specialty dining experience. The Kitchen Table is an intimate venue for chef's selections by night; by day the venue can be used for cooking classes and for 'Shopping with the Chef' preparations.

Mamsen's, a sort of Norwegian deli, is on the lower level of the Explorer's Lounge. World Café is a casual self-serve Lido Café – with open kitchen, and moveable glass doors that open onto an outdoor area called the Aquavit Terrace (a term borrowed from the sister company's riverships), adjacent to the infinity pool and hot tub.

Complimentary specialty coffees and teas are available, as is 24-hour room service, while an afternoon High Tea is featured in The Wintergarden.

ENTERTAINMENT. The 250-seat Theater is a single-deck-height showlounge, designed more for cabaret acts, recitals, and lectures than production shows because most of the experience involves destinations (including overnight visits in some), so there's little need for much entertainment.

SPA/FITNESS. The Spa is expansive and beautifully designed. On the lowest passenger deck, it includes a beauty salon, workout center, 'snow' room, and a salt-water thermal pool (with swim-against-the-flow feature), in a relaxing backdrop with glass-fronted fireplaces. Separate areas for men and women include a sauna, plunge bath, changing area, clothing cupboards, and relaxation space. The whole spa area is Nordic – spacious and elegant, with well-trained staff who don't push to sell bodycare products.

VIKING ORION
★★★★+

THIS SHIP IS FULL OF DOWN-HOME CREATURE COMFORTS AND HAS A DELIGHTFUL SPA

Size:	Mid-size Ship
Tonnage:	47,800
Cruise Line:	Viking Ocean Cruises
Former Names:	none
Builder:	Fincantieri (Italy)
Entered Service:	Jun 2018
Length (ft/m):	754.5/230.0
Propulsion/Propellers:	Diesel-electric/2
Total Crew:	545
Passengers (lower beds):	928
Passenger Space Ratio (lower beds):	51.5
Passenger/Crew Ratio (lower beds):	1.7
Cabins (total):	465
Size Range (sq ft/m):	270.0–1,163.0/25.0–108.0
Cabins (for one person):	0
Cabins with balcony:	464
Cabins (wheelchair accessible):	7
Wheelchair accessibility:	Good
Elevators:	8
Casino (gaming tables):	No
Self-Service Launderette:	Yes
Onboard currency:	US$

THE SHIP. *Viking Orion* (fifth in a series of eight identical ships) is a well-proportioned contemporary ship with a host of Scandinavian design elements. Step aboard, and it immediately feels homey – like a highly comfortable moving hotel. There are plenty of public areas and dining options, plus an abundance of glass walls that help connect you with the sea on every level.

The ship is powered by energy-efficient hybrid engines, and there are solar panels, and equipment for minimizing air pollution. The company focuses on enhancing the destination experience (rather than the ship being your only destination) and provides interactive touchscreen stations that provide a wealth of destination information. This ship is an excellent base, and its tasteful interior design leaves an uncluttered impression, so you won't find overly opulent surroundings – it's more Hyatt (premium) than Four Seasons (luxe).

A walk-around promenade deck is on a lower deck, so it's fairly well sheltered from wind, and good for strolling. Meanwhile, on the largest upper open deck, a sliding glass dome covers the main pool deck on the deck below, just forward of the main pool; aft of the pool is a spacious Wintergarden, with wood cladding around its support pillars, plus a large screen for poolside movies. A second pool (and adjacent hot tub) on the same deck, but aft, is the infinity pool that forms part of the Aquavit Terrace, an alfresco casual eatery. The sunloungers have retract-

BERLITZ'S RATINGS

	Possible	Achieved
Ship	500	458
Accommodation	200	171
Food	400	338
Service	400	325
Entertainment	100	76
Cruise Experience	400	322

OVERALL SCORE 1690 points out of 2000

able footrests; square drinks tables have a thick wood top (smart).

Inside, the main focal point is an elegant, rectangular-shaped atrium lobby three decks high; it features light woods and abundant glass that lets in plenty of natural light, and all levels have seating.

The very comfortable Explorer's Lounge spans two decks. It is an observation lounge with great views and incorporates a library and a Viking Café deli-counter; the upper level features glass cabinets displaying items of exploration and discovery.

Viking Ocean Cruises is expert at concentrating on destination-rich and immersive itineraries, and a program of shore excursions focused on cultural experiences.

Viking Orion is almost all-inclusive; the fare includes ship-wide Wi-Fi, one shore excursion in each port of call, overnight stays in embarkation or disembarkation ports, and complimentary beer and wine with lunch and dinner.

ACCOMMODATION. There are five accommodation categories, but many different price grades, according to deck and location. It is comfortable and practical – perhaps a little too minimalist and not sumptuous enough for some – and typical of the efficient Scandinavian approach to design. All cabins/suites have a private balcony (Viking calls them 'verandas'), a *king*-size bed, and a spacious shower enclosure (the suites have bathtubs), and all bathrooms have heated floors, which is a nice touch. If you like more space, it's worth considering one of the Explorer Suites located at the very front or back of the ship – most have a wrap-around balcony.

A superb Owner's Suite is conveniently positioned adjacent to the Explorer's Lounge. It includes a master bedroom, lounge, dining area, walk-in closet, wet room, and private sauna.

DINING. There are several restaurants and eateries, and all operate on an open-seating basis, so you can dine when and with whom you like. All are included in the cruise price. Most venues also have an alfresco option (Viking emphasises fresh-air dining).

The Dining Room (an easy name to remember) has a sliding glass wall that opens onto the wrap-around promenade deck aft, with a few tables for alfresco dining.

The cuisine is decidedly international and unfussy and includes 'always available' comfort classics. The focus is on regional and sustainably sourced ingredients.

Other dining options:

Manfredi's Italian Restaurant features Italian food with a focus on Tuscany; its decoration includes real accordions (the national instrument of Italy).

The Chef's Table is for a food-and-wine-paired specialty dining experience. The Kitchen Table is an intimate venue for chef's selections by night; by day the venue can be used for cooking classes and for 'Shopping with the Chef' preparations.

Mamsen's (a sort of Norwegian deli) is on the lower level of the Explorer's Lounge. World Café is a casual self-serve Lido Café – with open kitchen, and moveable glass doors that open onto an outdoor area called the Aquavit Terrace (a term borrowed from the sister company's riverships), adjacent to the infinity pool and hot tub.

Complimentary specialty coffees and teas are available, as is 24-hour room service, while an afternoon High Tea is featured in The Wintergarden.

ENTERTAINMENT. The 250-seat Theater is a single-deck-height showlounge, designed more for cabaret acts, recitals, and lectures than production shows because most of the experience involves destinations (including overnight visits in some), so there's little need for much entertainment.

SPA/FITNESS. The Spa is expansive and beautifully designed. Located on the lowest passenger deck, it includes a beauty salon, workout center, 'snow' room, and a salt-water thermal pool (with swim-against-the-flow feature), in a delightfully relaxing backdrop with glass-fronted fireplaces. Separate areas for men and women include a sauna, plunge bath, changing area, clothing cupboards, and relaxation space. The whole spa area is Nordic, elegant, and has well-trained staff who don't push to sell bodycare products.

VIKING SEA
★★★★+

A SMART-LOOKING PREMIUM SHIP FOR THE EXPERIENCED TRAVELER

Size:	Mid-size Ship	Passenger/Crew Ratio (lower beds):	1.7/1
Tonnage:	47,800	Cabins (total):	465
Cruise Line:	Viking Ocean Cruises	Size Range (sq ft/m):	312.1–1,668.4/29.0–155.0
Former Names:	none	Cabins (for one person):	0
Builder:	Fincantieri (Italy)	Cabins with balcony:	465
Entered Service:	May 2016	Cabins (wheelchair accessible):	2
Length (ft/m):	745.4/227.2	Wheelchair accessibility:	Good
Propulsion/Propellers:	diesel-electric / 2	Elevators:	6
Total Crew:	545	Casino (gaming tables):	No
Passengers (lower beds):	930	Self-Service Launderette:	Yes
Passenger Space Ratio (lower beds):	51.5	Onboard currency:	US$

THE SHIP. *Viking Sea* (third in a series of eight identical ships) is a handsome contemporary ship with Nordic attitude – excellent for grown-ups who want to experience destinations in comfort. There are numerous public areas and dining options for its size, plus an abundance of glass walls that help connect you with the sea on every level. Hybrid energy-efficient engines help minimize air pollution.

The company focuses on enhancing the destination experience (rather than the ship being your only destination).

A walk-around promenade deck is on a lower deck, and fairly well sheltered from wind – good for strolling. On the largest upper open deck, a sliding glass dome covers the main pool deck; aft is a spacious Wintergarden, with wood cladding around its support pillars. There's also a large screen for poolside movies. A second pool (and adjacent hot tub) on the same deck, but at the aft of the ship, is the infinity pool that forms part of an alfresco casual eatery with fine ocean views – the Aquavit Terrace. Sunloungers have retractable footrests, and square drinks tables with a thick wood top.

The interior design is uncluttered; there are no opulent surroundings – it's more Hyatt (premium) than Four Seasons (luxe). The main focal point is an elegant rectangular atrium lobby three decks high; it features light woods and clean Scandina-

BERLITZ'S RATINGS		
	Possible	Achieved
Ship	500	457
Accommodation	200	171
Food	400	338
Service	400	325
Entertainment	100	76
Cruise Experience	400	322

OVERALL SCORE 1689 points out of 2000

vian design that lets in plenty of natural light, and there is seating on all levels.

The Explorer's Lounge spans two decks. It is a fine, comfortable observation lounge with great views, and incorporates a library, practical seating, and a deli-counter called Viking Café – rather like an all-in-one living space, or lifestyle lounge. The upper level is reminiscent of the Polaris Lounge aboard the ships of the former Royal Viking Line, and has glass cabinets displaying items connected with exploration and discovery, plus historic ship models.

Together with extremely good value pricing, these are all included: ship-wide Wi-Fi; a shore excursion in each port; overnight stays in embarkation or disembarkation ports; complimentary self-service laundry; specialty coffees and teas; no extra charges for any restaurant or eatery; 24-hour room service; stocked minibar (in most accommodation grades); and beer and wine with lunch and dinner. Viking Ocean Cruises straddles the line between premium-plus and luxury and is perhaps the best value in cruising today.

ACCOMMODATION. There are just five accommodation categories, but with many different price grades, according to deck and location.

The interior decor is simple – typical of efficient Scandinavian design and a philosophy that works well for the company's river cruise division. It is comfortable and practical, but perhaps a little minimalist for some. All cabins feature a private balcony (Viking calls them 'verandas') and a *king*-size bed, and even the smallest cabin has a shower enclosure spacious enough to bathe in (only suites have bathtubs). If you like more space, the Explorer Suites, located at the very front or back of the ship, are the ones to go for; most of these have a wrap-around balcony.

The largest accommodation is a superb Owner's Suite, adjacent to the Explorer's Lounge. It has a master bedroom, lounge, dining area, walk-in closet, wet room, and private sauna.

DINING. There are several restaurants and eateries to choose from, all of which operate on an open-seating basis, so you can dine with whom you like, when you like, and all of which are included in the cruise price. Most venues also have an alfresco option (there is a great emphasis on dining in the fresh air).

The Dining Room (main) has a sliding glass wall that can open onto the wrap-around promenade deck aft, with a few tables for alfresco dining, weather permitting.

The cuisine is international, with some 'always-available' comfort classics. The focus is on regional and sustainably sourced ingredients.

Manfredi's Italian Restaurant features Italian food with a focus on Tuscany; its decoration includes real accordions (the national instrument of Italy).

The Chef's Table is for food-and-wine-paired specialty dining experience. The Kitchen Table is an intimate venue for chef's selections by night; by day the venue is used for cooking classes and 'Shopping with the Chef' preparations.

Viking Café is part of the Explorer's Lounge, World Café (Lido Café) has an outdoor area known as the Aquavit Terrace (a term borrowed from the sister company's riverships).

Complimentary specialty coffees and teas are available around-the-clock, as is 24-hour room service, while an afternoon 'High Tea' can be experienced in the Wintergarden.

ENTERTAINMENT. The 250-seat Star Theater is a single-deck-height showlounge, designed more for cabaret acts, recitals, and lectures than for large production shows because most of the cruise experience is about the destinations (including overnight visits in some), so there's little need for entertainment.

SPA/FITNESS. The Spa is expansive and beautifully designed. It includes a beauty salon, workout center, 'snow' room, and a salt-water thermal pool (with swim-against-the-flow feature), in a relaxing backdrop with glass-fronted fireplaces. Separate men's and women's areas include a sauna, plunge bath, changing rooms, cupboards for clothes, and a relaxation space. It's Nordic, elegant, and has well-trained staff, who refreshingly don't push for sales of expensive bodycare items.

VIKING SKY
★★★★+

A WELL-PROPORTIONED SHIP WITH PREMIUM STYLE FOR EXPERIENCED TRAVELERS

Size:	Mid-size Ship	Passenger/Crew Ratio (lower beds):	1.7/1
Tonnage:	47,800	Cabins (total):	465
Cruise Line:	Viking Ocean Cruises	Size Range (sq ft/m):	312.1–1,668.4.0/29.0–155.0
Former Names:	none	Cabins (for one person):	0
Builder:	Fincantieri (Italy)	Cabins with balcony:	464
Entered Service:	Feb 2017	Cabins (wheelchair accessible):	7
Length (ft/m):	754.5/230.0	Wheelchair accessibility:	Good
Propulsion/Propellers:	diesel-electric/2	Elevators:	8
Total Crew:	545	Casino (gaming tables):	No
Passengers (lower beds):	930	Self-Service Launderette:	Yes
Passenger Space Ratio (lower beds):	51.5	Onboard currency:	US$

THE SHIP. *Viking Sky* is a very smart-looking contemporary ship (fourth in a series of eight ships and reminiscent of the former Royal Viking Line's *Royal Viking Sky*). It exudes style and is aimed squarely at adults who want comfort and some elements of luxe, without glitz. It has a lot of public areas and dining options for its size, plus abundant glass walls that connect you with the sea on every level, providing the feeling that you are cruising in a floating residence.

The sleek, uncluttered design of this ship – powered by hybrid energy-efficient engines, solar panels, and equipment for minimizing air pollution – is focused on destination experiences (rather than the ship being the destination), so you'll find interactive stations that provide a wealth of destination information. What you won't find is overly opulent surroundings – the result of design elements that are more Hyatt (premium) than Four Seasons (luxe), and approaching *Europa 2*'s beautiful interior design.

On a lower deck (Deck 2), there's a walk-around promenade deck that is fairly well sheltered from any wind, which is good for a stroll. On the largest upper open deck, a sliding glass dome covers the main pool deck (and adjacent rectangular hot tub with its fine geometric-design tile surround) on the deck below, just forward of the main pool; aft of the pool is a large screen for poolside movies. Another pool on the same deck, but at the aft of the ship, is the infinity pool (with adjacent tiled hot tub), which is cantile-

BERLITZ'S RATINGS		
	Possible	Achieved
Ship	500	457
Accommodation	200	170
Food	400	338
Service	400	325
Entertainment	100	76
Cruise Experience	400	323
OVERALL SCORE 1689 points out of 2000		

vered off the ship's stern; it is part of the Aquavit Terrace, an alfresco casual eatery with fine ocean views. Sunloungers include retractable footrests, while square drinks tables have thick wooden tops, which is both smart and practical.

Viking uses the interior space well, which provides a restrained wow factor. The main focal point is an elegant rectangular atrium lobby, called The Living Room. Three decks high, its clean Scandinavian design, with light woods, lets in plenty of natural light. There is excellent, inviting seating on all levels, while a coffee bar, large lounge chairs, sofas, and low tables add to the comfortable and spacious living-room ambience. A grand stairway, located forward, is wide, with a large LED backdrop screen projecting constantly changing images of Norway; underneath it is a lichen garden.

The two-deck, split-level Explorer's Lounge is an extremely comfortable observation lounge with fine views; the soft furnishings include an abundance of cushions. The room incorporates library books, and Mamsen's deli-counter for Nordic treats, including Norwegian waffles and fresh berries for a breakfast snack – the teacups and coffee mugs here are the same as those used in the family home of Torstein Hagen, Viking's CEO. The Explorer Lounge's upper level is reminiscent of the Polaris Lounge (the observation lounge) aboard the ships of the former Royal Viking Line; it has glass cabinets displaying items connected with exploration and discovery by Norwegians Roald Amundsen, Leif Erikson, and Thor Heyerdahl, and models of historic ships, and is a delightful spot to chill-out and relax.

Viking Ocean Cruises is the first new start-up cruise line to build new ships since 1998, when Disney Cruise Line built two. It's the sister company of the well-established and highly experienced Viking River Cruises. The company has concentrated on devising itineraries that really are destination-rich and immersive, so the program of shore excursions is focused much more on the cultural experience than most, and on really learning about the destinations.

Despite an initial impression of Scandinavian minimalism, the interior designers have created a beautiful, cozy and warm, homey environment. There are lots of delightful, quirky details – in fact, to find them all, you'll need to take another cruise. You may not find flowers, but you will see bonsai, arrangements of moss, bark, lichen, and other tactile items, including some beautiful fabrics and touchy-feely surfaces.

Together with extremely good-value pricing, the following are all included: ship-wide Wi-Fi; a shore excursion in each port; overnight stays in embarkation or disembarkation ports; complimentary self-service laundry; specialty coffees and teas; no extra charges for any restaurant or eatery; 24-hour room service; stocked minibar (in most accommodation grades); and beer and wine with lunch and dinner. Viking Ocean Cruises straddles the line between premium-plus and luxury and is perhaps the best value in cruising today.

ACCOMMODATION. There are just five accommodation categories, but with many different price grades, according to deck and location.

The decor is simple – a philosophy that has worked well for its river cruise division. It is comfortable and practical (perhaps a little minimalist for some), but typical of the Scandinavian design efficiency approach. All cabins and suites have a private balcony (Viking calls them verandas) and a *king*-size bed, and even the smallest cabin has a spacious shower enclosure (only suites have bathtubs). If you like more space, the Explorer Suites, located at the very front or back of the ship, are the ones to go for; most of these have a wrap-around balcony.

The largest accommodation is a superb Owner's Suite, which is conveniently positioned adjacent to the Explorer's Lounge, and includes a master bedroom, lounge, dining area, walk-in closet, wet room, and private sauna.

DINING. There are several restaurants and eateries from which to choose. All operate on an open-seating basis, so you can dine with whom you like, when you like. All are included in the cruise price, and most

also have an alfresco option (in fact, there is a great emphasis on dining in fresh air).

The principal dining venue is called, quite simply, The Dining Room, with tablecloths for all meals, fine plates, and cutlery that is of an ideal weight. It has a sliding glass wall that can open onto the wraparound promenade deck aft, with some tables for alfresco dining.

The cuisine is decidedly international, but with some 'always-available' comfort classics. The focus is on regional and sustainably sourced ingredients, with everything cooked from scratch (no pre-mixed sauces, soups, or bread purchased from outside sources).

There are other dining options, three of which are located on the deck below the Dining Room. Manfredi's Italian Restaurant features Italian food with a focus on Tuscany; its decoration includes real accordions (the national instrument of Italy).

The Chef's Table is for a food-and-wine-paired specialty dining experience. The Kitchen Table is an intimate venue for chef's selections by night; by day the venue can be used for cooking classes and for 'Shopping with the Chef' preparations.

You'll find Mamsen's (a sort of Norwegian deli) as part of the lower level of the Explorer's Lounge. World Café is a casual self-serve Lido Café – with open kitchen, and moveable glass doors that open onto an outdoor area called the Aquavit Terrace (a term borrowed from the sister company's riverships), adjacent to the infinity pool and hot tub.

Additionally, complimentary specialty coffees and loose-leaf teas are available around-the-clock, as is 24-hour room service, while an afternoon High Tea can be taken in the Wintergarden. Do try one of the superb armagnacs, with vintages starting in 1935 – you'll find them in a hide-away bar called Torshavn.

ENTERTAINMENT. The 250-seat Star Theater is the ship's single-deck-height showlounge, designed more for cabaret acts, recitals, and lectures than for large production shows. This is because most of the experience aboard this ship involves the destinations (including overnight visits in some), so there's little need for entertainment on a grand scale.

SPA/FITNESS. The Spa is expansive and beautifully designed. Located indoors on the lowest passenger deck, it includes a beauty salon, workout center, 'snow' room, and a salt-water thermal pool (with swim-against-the-flow feature), in a delightfully relaxing backdrop that includes glass-fronted fireplaces. Separate men's and women's areas include a sauna, plunge bath, changing area, cupboards for clothes, and a relaxation area. Operated by LivNordic, the whole spa area is precisely that – Nordic – and elegant, with well-trained staff, who refreshingly don't push for sales of expensive bodycare products.

VIKING STAR
★★★★+

THIS HANDSOME-LOOKING PREMIUM SHIP IS FOR THE WELL-TRAVELED

Size:	Mid-size Ship	Passenger/Crew Ratio (lower beds):	1.7/1
Tonnage:	47,800	Cabins (total):	465
Cruise Line:	Viking Ocean Cruises	Size Range (sq ft/m):	312.1–1,668.4/29.0–155.0
Former Names:	none	Cabins (for one person):	0
Builder:	Fincantieri (Italy)	Cabins with balcony:	465
Entered Service:	Apr 2015	Cabins (wheelchair accessible):	2
Length (ft/m):	745.4/227.2	Wheelchair accessibility:	Good
Propulsion/Propellers:	diesel-electric / 2	Elevators:	6
Total Crew:	545	Casino (gaming tables):	No
Passengers (lower beds):	930	Self-Service Launderette:	Yes
Passenger Space Ratio (lower beds):	51.5	Onboard currency:	US$

THE SHIP. *Viking Star* is a very smart-looking contemporary ship (delightfully reminiscent of the former Royal Viking Line's *Royal Viking Star*), exuding style. It is aimed squarely at adults who want comfort and some elements of luxe, but no glitz. It has a lot of public areas and dining options for its size, plus an abundance of glass walls that help connect you with the sea on every level, creating the feeling that you are cruising in a floating residence.

The sleek, uncluttered design of this ship – powered by hybrid energy-efficient engines, solar panels, and equipment for minimizing air pollution – is focused on enhancing the destination experience (rather than the ship being your only destination), so throughout the ship you'll find interactive stations that provide a wealth of destination information. It is uncluttered and extremely comfortable.

A walk-around promenade deck is on a lower deck (Deck 2) and is fairly well sheltered from any wind, which is good for a stroll (and very popular). On the largest upper open deck, a sliding glass dome covers the main pool deck (and adjacent rectangular hot tub with its fine geometric-design tile surround) on the deck below, just forward of the main pool; aft of the pool is a large screen for poolside movies. Another pool on the same deck, but at the aft of the ship, is the infinity pool (and adjacent tiled hot tub) that is cantilevered off the ship's stern; it is part of the Aquavit Terrace, an alfresco casual eatery with

BERLITZ'S RATINGS		
	Possible	Achieved
Ship	500	457
Accommodation	200	171
Food	400	338
Service	400	325
Entertainment	100	76
Cruise Experience	400	321

OVERALL SCORE 1688 points out of 2000

fine ocean views. The sunloungers include a retractable footrest, while square drinks tables have a thick wood top – smart – and practical.

Inside, it is clear that Viking uses space efficiently, and provides a restrained 'wow' factor. The main focal point is a stunning, elegant, rectangular atrium lobby called The Living Room. It is three decks high and features clean Scandinavian design, with light woods, that lets in plenty of natural light. There is an abundance of inviting seating on all levels, while a coffee bar, large lounge chairs, sofas, and low tables really do provide a spacious living room ambiance.

At two decks high, the split-level Explorer's Lounge is a supremely comfortable observation lounge with fine views (and tactile seat decoration, including furry animal pelts thrown over chairs and sofas, and an abundance of cushions). It incorporates a library, and Mamsen's – a deli-counter featuring Nordic treats – including Norwegian waffles and fresh berries for a breakfast snack (the teacups and coffee mugs are the same as used in the family home of the Viking chairman, Torstein Hagen). The upper level is reminiscent of the Polaris Lounge (the observation lounge) aboard the ships of the former Royal Viking Line; it includes glass cabinets displaying items connected with exploration and discovery by Norwegians Roald Amundsen, Leif Erikson, and Thor Heyerdahl, and models of historic ships, and is a delightful spot to relax in.

Viking Ocean Cruises is the first new start-up cruise line to build new ships since 1998, when Disney Cruise Line built two. It's the sister company of the well-established and highly experienced Viking River Cruises. Viking has concentrated on devising itineraries that really are destination-rich and immersive, so the shore-excursion program is focused much more on the cultural experience than most, and really learning about the destinations.

Despite an initial impression of Scandinavian minimalism, the interior designers have created a beautiful, cozy and warm home-like environment. There are lots of delightful, quirky details, including bonsai, some beautiful fabrics and touchy-feely surfaces.

Together with extremely good value pricing, these are all included: ship-wide Wi-Fi; a shore excursion in each port; overnight stays in embarkation or disembarkation ports; complimentary self-service laundry; specialty coffees and teas; no extra charges for any restaurant or eatery; 24-hour room service; stocked minibar (in most accommodation grades); and beer and wine with lunch and dinner. Viking Ocean Cruises straddles the line between premium-plus and luxury and is perhaps the best value in cruising today.

ACCOMMODATION. There are just five accommodation categories, plus a superb Owner's Suite that is conveniently positioned adjacent to the Explorer's Lounge – it includes a master bedroom, lounge, dining area, walk-in closet, wet room, and private sauna. There are many different prices, according to deck and location. All accommodation has a private balcony ('veranda').

Viking likes to keep things like interior decor simple – a philosophy that has worked very well for its river cruise division. It is comfortable and practical, but perhaps a little minimalist for some, which is typical of the Scandinavian design approach.

All accommodation grades feature a *king*-size bed, and even the smallest cabin has a shower enclosure spacious enough to bathe in (only suites have bathtubs). If you like more space, the Explorer Suites, located at the very front or back of the ship, are the ones to go for; most of these have a wrap-around balcony.

DINING. There are several restaurants and eateries to choose from, all of which operate on an open-seating basis, so you can dine with whom you like, when you like, and all of which are included in the cruise price. Most also have an alfresco option (in fact, there is a great emphasis on dining in the fresh air).

The principal dining venue is called, quite simply, The Dining Room, with tablecloths for all meals, and fine plates and cutlery that is of an ideal weight. It has a sliding glass wall that can open onto the wrap-around promenade deck aft, with some tables for alfresco dining, weather permitting.

The cuisine is decidedly international, but with some 'always-available' comfort classics. The focus is on regional and sustainably sourced ingredients, with everything cooked from scratch (no pre-mixed sauces, soups, or bread purchased from outside sources).

In terms of other dining venues, three of these are located on the deck below the main dining room. Manfredi's Italian Restaurant features Italian food with a focus on Tuscany; its decoration includes real accordions (the national instrument of Italy), and photographs of Italian film stars.

The Chef's Table is for a specialty dining experience, for food and wine pairing. The Kitchen Table is an intimate venue for chef's selections at night; during the daytime it can be used for cooking classes. Mamsen's (a sort of Norwegian deli) is part of the lower level of the Explorer's Lounge. World Café is the ship's casual self-serve Lido Café – with open kitchen, and moveable glass doors that can open onto an outdoor area called the Aquavit Terrace that is adjacent to the infinity pool and hot tub.

Additionally, complimentary specialty coffees and loose-leaf teas are available around-the-clock, as is 24-hour room service, while an afternoon High Tea can be taken in The Wintergarden. Do try one of the superb armagnacs, with vintages starting in 1935 – you'll find them in a hideaway bar called Torshavn.

ENTERTAINMENT. The 250-seat Star Theater is the ship's single-deck-height showlounge, designed more for cabaret acts, recitals, and lectures rather than large production shows. This is because most of the experience aboard this ship involves the destinations (including overnight visits in some), so there's little need for entertainment on a grand scale.

SPA/FITNESS. The Spa is expansive and beautifully designed. It includes a beauty salon, fitness center, 'snow' room, and a salt-water thermal pool (with swim-against-the-flow feature), in a delightfully relaxing backdrop that includes glass-fronted fireplaces. Separate men's and women's areas include a sauna, plunge bath, changing rooms, cupboards for clothes, and a relaxation space. Operated by LivNordic, the whole spa is precisely that – Nordic – and elegant, with well-trained staff, who refreshingly don't push for sales of expensive bodycare items. However, body-pampering treatments are on the pricey side.

VIKING SUN
★★★★+

A WELL-DESIGNED PREMIUM SHIP THAT IS RECOMMENDED FOR STYLISH TRAVELERS

Size:	Mid-size Ship	Passenger/Crew Ratio (lower beds):	1.7/1
Tonnage:	47,800	Cabins (total):	465
Cruise Line:	Viking Ocean Cruises	Size Range (sq ft/m):	270.0–1,163.0/25.0–108.0
Former Names:	none	Cabins (for one person):	0
Builder:	Fincantieri (Italy)	Cabins with balcony:	464
Entered Service:	Oct-17	Cabins (wheelchair accessible):	7
Length (ft/m):	754.5/230.0	Wheelchair accessibility:	Good
Propulsion/Propellers:	diesel-electric/2	Elevators:	8
Total Crew:	545	Casino (gaming tables):	No
Passengers (lower beds):	928	Self-Service Launderette:	Yes
Passenger Space Ratio (lower beds):	51.5	Onboard currency:	US$

THE SHIP. *Viking Sun* is a very well-proportioned contemporary ship with a host of clean Scandinavian design elements. Step aboard, and it immediately feels homey – like a highly comfortable moving hotel. There are plenty of public areas and dining options, plus an abundance of glass walls that help connect you with the sea on every level.

The ship is powered by energy-efficient hybrid engines, and there are solar panels, and equipment for minimizing air pollution. Viking Ocean Cruises focuses on enhancing the destination experience (rather than the ship being your only destination) and provides interactive touch-screen stations that provide a wealth of destination information. This ship provides an excellent base for the various destinations covered on Viking's itineraries. The interior design is tasteful, and leaves an uncluttered impression, so you won't find overly opulent surroundings – it's more Hyatt (premium) than Four Seasons (luxe).

A walk-around promenade deck is on a lower deck (Deck 2), so it's fairly well sheltered from any wind, and good for a stroll. Meanwhile, on the largest upper open deck, a sliding glass dome covers the main pool deck on the deck below, just forward of the main pool; aft of the pool is a spacious Wintergarden, with wood cladding around its support pillars. There's also a large screen for poolside movies. A second pool (and adjacent hot tub) on the same deck, but

BERLITZ'S RATINGS		
	Possible	Achieved
Ship	500	457
Accommodation	200	171
Food	400	338
Service	400	325
Entertainment	100	76
Cruise Experience	400	322

OVERALL SCORE 1689 points out of 2000

at the aft of the ship, is the infinity pool that forms part of the Aquavit Terrace, an alfresco casual eatery with fine ocean views. Sunloungers have a retractable footrest, while the drinks tables are square with a thick wood top – both smart and practical.

Inside, the main focal point is a delightful, elegant, rectangular atrium lobby that is three decks high and features light woods and abundant glass that lets in plenty of natural light. There is an abundance of seating on all levels.

An Explorer's Lounge spans two decks. It is a very comfortable observation lounge with great views, and incorporates a library, practical seating, and a deli counter called Viking Café. The upper level is reminiscent of the popular Polaris (observation) Lounge aboard the former Royal Viking Line ships; it features glass cabinets displaying items connected with exploration and discovery, and historic ship models.

Viking Ocean Cruises concentrates on destination-rich and immersive itineraries, and a program of shore excursions focused on cultural experiences. Together with extremely good-value pricing, these are all included: ship-wide Wi-Fi; a shore excursion in each port; overnight stays in embarkation or disembarkation ports; complimentary self-service laundry; specialty coffees and teas; no extra charges for any restaurant or eatery; 24-hour room service; stocked minibar (in most accommodation grades); and beer and wine with lunch and dinner. Viking

Ocean Cruises straddles the line between premium-plus and luxury and is perhaps the best value in cruising today.

ACCOMMODATION. The accommodation price grades depend on size and location. It is comfortable and practical – perhaps a little too minimalist and not sumptuous enough for some – and typical of the efficient Scandinavian approach to design. All cabins/suites have a private balcony (Viking calls them 'verandas'), a *king*-size bed, and a spacious shower enclosure (the suites have bathtubs), and all bathrooms have heated floors, which is a nice touch. If you like more space, it's worth considering one of the Explorer Suites located at the very front or back of the ship – most have a wrap-around balcony.

The largest accommodation is a superb Owner's Suite, which is conveniently positioned adjacent to the Explorer's Lounge. It includes a master bedroom, lounge, dining area, walk-in closet, wet room, and private sauna.

DINING. There are several restaurants and eateries, all of which operate on an open-seating basis, so you can dine with whom you like, when you like, and all of which are included in the cruise price. Most venues also have an alfresco option (there is a great emphasis on dining in the fresh air).

The Dining Room (an easy name to remember) has a sliding glass wall that can open onto the wrap-around promenade deck aft, with a few tables for alfresco dining, weather permitting.

The cuisine is decidedly international and unfussy, and it includes 'always-available' comfort classics. The focus is on regional and sustainably sourced ingredients.

Other dining options include three restaurants located on the deck below the Dining Room. Manfredi's Italian Restaurant features Italian food with a focus on Tuscany; its decoration includes real accordions (the national instrument of Italy).

The Chef's Table is for a food-and-wine-paired specialty dining experience. The Kitchen Table is an intimate venue for chef's selections by night; by day the venue can be used for cooking classes and for 'Shopping with the Chef' preparations.

You'll find Mamsen's (a sort of Norwegian deli) as part of the lower level of the Explorer's Lounge. World Café is a casual self-serve Lido Café – with open kitchen, and moveable glass doors that open onto an outdoor area called the Aquavit Terrace (a term borrowed from the sister company's river-ships), adjacent to the infinity pool and hot tub.

Viking Café is part of the Explorer's Lounge, on its lower level. World Café (Lido Café) also has an outdoor area known as the Aquavit Terrace (a term borrowed from the sister company's riverships).

Additionally, complimentary specialty coffees and teas are available around-the-clock, as is 24-hour room service, while an afternoon High Tea can be taken in The Wintergarden.

ENTERTAINMENT. The 250-seat Sun Theater is a single-deck-height showlounge, designed more for cabaret acts, recitals, and lectures than production shows. This is because most of the experience aboard this ship involves the destinations (including overnight visits in some), so there's little need for entertainment on a grand scale.

SPA/FITNESS. The Spa is expansive and beautifully designed. Located on the lowest passenger deck, it includes a beauty salon, workout center, 'snow' room, and a salt-water thermal pool (with swim-against-the-flow feature), in a delightfully relaxing backdrop that includes glass-fronted fireplaces. Separate areas for men and women include a sauna, plunge bath, changing area, cupboards for clothes, and relaxation space. Operated by LivNordic, the whole spa area is precisely that – Nordic – and elegant, with well-trained staff, who refreshingly don't push for sales of expensive bodycare products.

VISION OF THE SEAS
★★★+

THIS GOOD-LOOKING SHIP HAS SLEEK LINES AND IS VERY COMFORTABLE

Size: .... Mid-size Ship	Passenger/Crew Ratio (lower beds): 2.7
Tonnage: 78,491	Cabins (total): 1,000
Cruise Line: .... Royal Caribbean International	Size Range (sq ft/m): 135.0–1,270.1/12.5–118.0
Former Names: .... none	Cabins (for one person): 0
Builder: .... Chantiers de l'Atlantique (France)	Cabins with balcony: 229
Entered Service: .... May 1998	Cabins (wheelchair accessible): 14
Length (ft/m): 915.3/279.0	Wheelchair accessibility: .... Good
Propulsion/Propellers: diesel-electric (50,400kW)/2	Elevators: 9
Total Crew: 735	Casino (gaming tables): .... Yes
Passengers (lower beds): 2,000	Self-Service Launderette: .... No
Passenger Space Ratio (lower beds): 39.2	Onboard currency: .... US$

THE SHIP. *Vision of the Seas* (a *Radiance*-class ship), with its slim funnel placed at the very aft, is for the whole family to enjoy, and offers a good choice of restaurants and eateries. The ship shares the design features that make all Royal Caribbean International (RCI) ships identifiable. The ship's stern is beautifully rounded.

There are two swimming pools; the main pool, which also has a large movie screen, and an aft pool, which is within a Solarium indoor/outdoor area (with a retractable dome). There's a decent amount of open-air walking space, although this is cluttered with sunloungers that lack cushioned pads. While not as large as the newer ships in the fleet, the ship is perhaps more suited to couples and families with children that don't need all those bells and whistles, but want to cruise with up-to-date facilities and have multiple dining choices for more convenience.

A multi-level atrium lobby called the Centrum is the focal interior point and *the* social meeting place. On its various levels it houses an R Bar (for some creative cocktails), several passenger service counters, an art gallery, and Café Latte-tudes (for coffee). Close by are the flashy Casino Royale, Schooner Bar, with nautical-theme decor and maritime art, and the Centrum shops.

Other public rooms include the Take time to look at some of the $6 million worth of artwork throughout the ship's interior – it's both colorful and creative.

BERLITZ'S RATINGS		
	Possible	Achieved
Ship	500	348
Accommodation	200	137
Food	400	222
Service	400	258
Entertainment	100	73
Cruise Experience	400	256

OVERALL SCORE 1294 points out of 2000

ACCOMMODATION. There's a range of suites and cabin types to choose from, and the price you pay depends on the size, grade, and location. All cabins/suites have a flat-screen infotainment system.

The many standard cabins are of an adequate size and have enough functional facilities to make them comfortable. Twin lower beds convert to a queen-size one, and there is a reasonable amount of closet and drawer space, but little room between the bed and desk. Bathrooms are small but functional, the shower units are very small, and there is no cabinet for personal toiletries.

For the ultimate accommodation, choose the Royal Suite (think Palm Beach apartment), which includes a white baby grand piano.

DINING. The expansive Aquarius Dining Room spans two levels, with large ocean-view windows on two sides and a connecting stairway. Choose either one of two seating times (with fixed times for dinner), or My Time Dining, where you can eat when you want, during dining-room hours.

Food in the Main dining room is unfortunately standardized banquet catering. Extra-cost, made-to-order items such as lobster or filet mignon (steak) are available, though. Green vegetables are difficult to come by but salad items are plentiful, and desserts are pretty good. Rice is heavily used. Breads and pastry items are average. Vegetarian and children's menus are also available. Note that there are no wine waiters.

Other eateries include:

The extra-cost Chops Grille, opposite the Schooner Bar, for large-size, premium-quality steaks and seafood items (reservations are required).

The extra-cost Giovanni's Table, adjacent to Chops Grille, for Italian cuisine in a rustic setting (reservations are required).

Izumi, an extra-cost Asian-style eatery with a sushi bar and hot-rocks cooking; it's open for lunch and dinner (reservations required).

The extra-cost, reservations-required Chef's Table is located in one corner of the lower level of the Aquarius main dining room. This is a private experience, typically co-hosted by the executive chef and sommelier for a multi-course wine-pairing dinner. It's expensive, but worth it for a special occasion.

Park Café is a casual, no-charge, market-style eatery for salads, sandwiches, soups, pastries, and wraps.

A drinks package is also available at all bars, in the form of cards or stickers. This enables you to pre-pay for a selection of standard soft and alcoholic drinks, but the packages are not exactly easy to understand.

Windjammer Café is the casual dining spot for self-serve buffets (open for all meals and late-night snacks). It is quite large, and, because it's positioned at the front of the ship, has fine ocean views.

ENTERTAINMENT. The Masquerade Theater, the showlounge, is located forward and presents production shows and major cabaret performances. It is a large, but well-designed, room with main and balcony levels, and good sight lines from most of the banquette seating.

Some Enchanted Evening Lounge, aft, is for cabaret, (low brow) late-night comedy, and live music for dancing.

The entertainment is upbeat, and it's difficult to get away from it. There's even background music in all corridors and elevators, and constant music outdoors on the pool deck.

SPA/FITNESS. The Vitality at Sea Spa and Fitness Center has a solarium, an indoor/outdoor dome-covered pool, Inca- and Mayan-theme decor, sauna/steam rooms, and a gymnasium. Other facilities include a rock-climbing wall with several separate climbing tracks, located outdoors aft of the funnel.

VOLENDAM
★★★

DATED SHIP WITH DUTCH DECOR AND ABUNDANT HERITAGE FOR MATURE-AGE CRUISERS

Size:	Mid-size Ship	Passenger/Crew Ratio (lower beds):	2.2
Tonnage:	61,214	Cabins (total):	717
Cruise Line:	Holland America Line	Size Range (sq ft/m):	113.0–1,126.0/10.5–104.6
Former Names:	none	Cabins (for one person):	0
Builder:	Fincantieri (Italy)	Cabins with balcony:	197
Entered Service:	Nov 1999	Cabins (wheelchair accessible):	23
Length (ft/m):	781.0/238.00	Wheelchair accessibility:	Good
Propulsion/Propellers:	diesel-electric (37,500kW)/2	Elevators:	12
Total Crew:	650	Casino (gaming tables):	Yes
Passengers (lower beds):	1,432	Self-Service Launderette:	Yes
Passenger Space Ratio (lower beds):	42.5	Onboard currency:	US$

THE SHIP. *Volendam* has the flow, artwork, and comfortable feeling that repeat passengers will recognize from other Holland America Line ships. The name is taken from a fishing village north of Amsterdam. The hull is dark blue, in keeping with all HAL ships. A glass-dome-covered pool on the Lido Deck, between the mast and the funnel, is located one deck higher than on earlier *Statendam*-class ships, with the positive result that there is direct access between the aft and midships pools.

The interior design theme is flowers, and the interior focal point is a huge crystal sculpture, *Caleido*, in the three-deck-high atrium, by one of Italy's leading contemporary glass artists, Luciano Vistosi.

In the casino bar, which is also known as the sports bar, a cinematic theme gives visions of Hollywood, and includes a collection of costumes, props, photos, and posters of movies and the actors who starred in them. The ship looks somewhat tired.

ACCOMMODATION. This ranges from interior (no-view) cabins to a Penthouse Suite. The interior and outside cabins are tastefully furnished, and have twin beds that convert to a queen-size bed, but space is tight. The fully tiled bathrooms are small, and have small shower tubs, utilitarian toiletries cupboards, and exposed under-sink plumbing.

Suite occupants share a private Concierge Lounge. Strangely, there are no butlers. Suite passengers re-

BERLITZ'S RATINGS		
	Possible	Achieved
Ship	500	297
Accommodation	200	125
Food	400	218
Service	400	251
Entertainment	100	60
Cruise Experience	400	237

OVERALL SCORE 1188 points out of 2000

ceive complimentary laundry and ironing services, cocktail-hour hors d'oeuvres and other goodies, as well as priority embarkation and disembarkation, but the bathrooms (except for the Penthouse Suite) are really small. For the ultimate in accommodation choose the Penthouse Suite. It has a bedroom, separate living room with baby grand piano, and a dining room, dressing room, walk-in closet, butler's pantry, and private balcony – though the balcony is still small. Other facilities include an audio-visual center, a wet bar, large bathroom with Jacuzzi, and guest bathroom.

All outside-view suites and cabin bathrooms have a tub/shower, while interior cabins have a shower only. The 23 cabins for passengers with limited mobility have a roll-in shower enclosure for wheelchairs – none has bathtubs, no matter the category.

There is a charge to use the washing machines and dryers in the self-service launderette, although it really should be included for the occupants of high-priced suites. Although room service is adequate, it remains a weak point.

DINING. The Rotterdam Dining Room (with 747 seats) is a traditional, grand room spread over two decks. Both open seating and fixed seating with assigned tables and times are available, while breakfast and lunch are open seating. Rosenthal porcelain and good-quality cutlery are provided. Tables are for two, four, six, or eight.

With a few exceptions, the cuisine is rather unmemorable, and is missing passion and taste, because it's all about batch cooking. There's a distinct lack of variety of green vegetables, and too much rice, canned fruit, and already sliced and diced cheese. Still, you get friendly service from Indonesian and Filipino stewards, and the plates are decent ones.

Pinnacle Grill is an extra-cost (reservations-required) venue featuring Pacific Northwest cuisine, including premium steaks and seafood (suite occupants get priority reservations).

Lido Market is a self-serve café for casual breakfasts and luncheons; it is also open for dinner in an open-seating arrangement. Canaletto (a section of the Lido Buffet) is set aside and features Italian-style cuisine. Reservations are required. The Lido Deck poolside Dive-In at the Terrace Grill does burgers, hot dogs, and fries, and on some days, barbecues.

ENTERTAINMENT. The Frans Hals Showlounge spans two decks and is a fairly well-designed room, although sight lines from the balcony level are poor. Music is the main feature in the Lincoln Center Stage venue.

SPA/FITNESS. The Ocean Spa facilities are decent, and include a gym, separate saunas and steam rooms, and several treatment rooms. There are practice tennis courts outdoors, as well as shuffleboard courts, a jogging track, and a full walk-around teakwood promenade deck.

VOYAGER OF THE SEAS
★★★+

THIS LARGE, FAMILY-FRIENDLY SHIP OFFERS LOTS OF CHOICE FOR DINING DAY AND NIGHT

Size:	Large Resort Ship
Tonnage:	137,280
Cruise Line:	Royal Caribbean International
Former Names:	none
Builder:	Kvaerner Masa-Yards (Finland)
Entered Service:	Nov 1999
Length (ft/m):	1,020.6/311.1
Propulsion/Propellers:	diesel-electric (28,000kW)/ 2 azimuthing pods
Total Crew:	1,176
Passengers (lower beds):	3,114
Passenger Space Ratio (lower beds):	44.0
Passenger/Crew Ratio (lower beds):	2.6
Cabins (total):	1,557
Size Range (sq ft/m):	151.0–1,358.0/14.0–126.1
Cabins (for one person):	0
Cabins with balcony:	757
Cabins (wheelchair accessible):	26
Wheelchair accessibility:	Best
Elevators:	14
Casino (gaming tables):	Yes
Self-Service Launderette:	No
Onboard currency:	US$

THE SHIP. *Voyager of the Seas* is a large, floating leisure resort with a host of facilities for the whole family. It's spacious, too, and provides excellent entertainment for the whole family. Outdoor decks are full of fun water-park features, including the obligatory rock-climbing wall, so there's little room left to just sit and relax or sunbathe. This is consistent, homogeneous, mainstream cruising for young-minded cruisers of all ages who enjoy mingling in a large, lively ship with constant activity.

Standout features include a four-deck-high Royal Promenade in the style of London's chic Burlington Arcade. It is the main interior social and focal point (entertaining street parades take place here), and the company's chairman donated his own treasured Morgan sports car to grace it. The length of two American football fields, it rises through 11 decks at both ends, and has cafés, shops, bars, and interior 'promenade view' bay window cabins that look into it. Comedy art is part of the scene. Arched across the promenade is a captain's balcony, while a central stairway connects with the deck below and the Schooner Bar (a piano lounge common to all RCI ships) and a large, flashy Casino Royale.

Other standouts include a regulation-size ice-skating rink (Studio B), with real ice, with 'bleacher' seating for up to 900 and broadcast facilities.

Although the ship is large, cabin hallways have a warm and attractive feel, with artwork cabinets

BERLITZ'S RATINGS

	Possible	Achieved
Ship	500	342
Accommodation	200	131
Food	400	220
Service	400	258
Entertainment	100	73
Cruise Experience	400	253

OVERALL SCORE 1277 points out of 2000

and wavy lines that lead the way and break up the monotony. The theme-park, banquet-style regimentation is well organized. You will, however, need to plan, otherwise you'll miss out on some of the things that you might like to include in your vacation.

Because the cruise fare is quite low, there's always a push for extra-revenue items, drinks packages, and extra-cost dining options, etc. In the end, however, you should have a decent cruise trip. Facilities for children and teenagers (in four age groupings) are quite extensive and include Adventure Beach – with swimming pools, a waterslide, splash, and game areas.

ACCOMMODATION. The cabin price grades are in four major groupings: premium ocean-view suites and cabins; interior (atrium-view) cabins; ocean-view cabins; and interior cabins. Many cabins are of a similar size – good for incentives and large groups – and 300 have interconnecting doors (good for families).

Standard outside-view and interior (no-view) cabins are of a reasonably adequate size, with just enough facilities to make them comfortable and functional. Twin lower beds convert to queen-size beds, and there is decent closet and drawer space, but the bed(s) take up most of the space. Bathrooms are small but functional, with dimensionally challenged shower enclosures, and no cabinet for personal toiletries. Overall, they're cramped.

Some 138 'interior' cabins have bay windows that look into an interior horizontal atrium – a cruise industry first when the ship debuted (you'll need to keep the curtains closed in the bay windows if you are scantily clad, because you can be seen from adjacent bay windows). Regardless of which cabin grade you choose, all except for the Royal Suite and Owner's Suite have twin beds that convert to a queen-size unit, TV, radio and telephone, personal safe, vanity unit, hairdryer, and private bathroom.

Some accommodation grades have a refrigerator/minibar, full of 'take-and-pay' items. If you take anything from it on the day of embarkation in Miami, Florida, sales tax is added to your bill.

Note that cabins with 'private' balconies aren't so private. The balcony decking is a sort of rubberized sand – though the balcony rail is wood. If you have a cabin with a connecting door to another cabin, note that you may hear your next-door neighbors. The bathroom vacuum toilets are explosively noisy. Cabin bath towels are small and skimpy. The menus from room service are basic.

DINING. Sapphire, the main dining room, is very large and is on three levels, each is operatically themed: Carmen, La Bohème, and Magic Flute. A stunning staircase connects the three levels, but fat support pillars obstruct sight lines from many seats. All three have the same menus and food. Choose one of two seatings, or My Time Dining, which allows you to eat when you want during dining-room hours. Tables are for four to 12, and the place settings, china, and cutlery are good.

The main dining room cuisine is standard banquet fare, mass-produced and lacking passion. You can order items such as lobster or filet mignon (steak) at an extra cost and they will be cooked fresh for you. Green vegetables are hard to come by, but salad items are plentiful, and the desserts are pretty good. Rice is a little over-used. Breads and pastry items are average. Vegetarian and children's menus are available. Note that there are no wine waiters.

Other dining venues and eateries (some cost extra, but the food is mostly cooked to order) include favorites such as Chops Grille Steakhouse (for pre-mium veal chops, steaks, and seafood items), Portofino (for Italian-American cuisine), and Giovanni's Table (for Italian trattoria-style dishes). Reservations (make them through the digital system) are required; note that menus do not change.

Windjammer Marketplace is a cavernous, casual, self-serve buffet eatery, but the plastic plates for hot items are mildly warm, at best. Breakfast buffet items and lunchtime salad items are pretty repetitive. Beverage stations have just the basics. Burgers and hot dogs in self-serve buffet locations are displayed in steam dishes. If you are disabled or have mobility difficulties, do ask for help.

Johnny Rockets is a retro 1950s all-day, all-night diner-style eatery for burgers and malt shakes. All indoor tables have a mini-jukebox with dimes provided to make your selection of vintage records. There's a cover charge, whether you eat in or take out.

Café Promenade is for Continental breakfast, all-day pizzas, sandwiches, and coffees in paper cups; Sprinkles has round-the-clock ice cream and yogurt, pastries, and coffee.

ENTERTAINMENT. The 1,347-seat La Scala Theater, a fine showlounge, is located at the front and spans five decks, with a few slim pillars and almost no disruption of sight lines. The room has a hydraulic orchestra pit and huge stage areas, together with rather loud sound, and superb lighting equipment.

In addition, the ship has an array of cabaret acts. There is also late-night, adults-only comedy. Arguably, however, the best shows are the Ice Spectaculars.

SPA/FITNESS. The Voyager Day Spa and Fitness Center is reasonably large, and has a main and an upper level, and includes an aerobics room, fitness center, several private body-treatment rooms, and men's and women's sauna/steam rooms. More space is provided for a Solarium (with sliding glass-dome roof) to relax in after you've exercised.

Aft is a 32.8ft (10m) rock-climbing wall, with five climbing tracks. Other sports facilities include a roller-blading track, a dive-and-snorkel shop (for equipment rental and dive lessons), a full-size basketball court, and a nine-hole, par 26 golf 'course.'

WESTERDAM
★★★+

THIS MID-SIZED SHIP FEATURES MANY TRADITIONAL DUTCH DECOR AND ARTEFACTS

Size:	Mid-size Ship
Tonnage:	82,348
Cruise Line:	Holland America Line
Former Names:	none
Builder:	Fincantieri (Italy)
Entered Service:	Apr 2004
Length (ft/m):	935.0/285.0
Propulsion/Propellers:	diesel-electric (35,240kW)/2 azimuthing pods
Total Crew:	817
Passengers (lower beds):	1,916
Passenger Space Ratio (lower beds):	41.9
Passenger/Crew Ratio (lower beds):	2.3
Cabins (total):	958
Size Range (sq ft/m):	170.0–1,318.6/15.7–122.5
Cabins (for one person):	0
Cabins with balcony:	641
Cabins (wheelchair accessible):	28
Wheelchair accessibility:	Good
Elevators:	14
Casino (gaming tables):	Yes
Self-Service Launderette:	No
Onboard currency:	US$

THE SHIP. *Westerdam* is designed to appeal to younger, active vacationers. It has two funnels, placed close together, one in front of the other, the result of the configuration of the machinery. The ship has, in effect, two engine rooms – one with three diesels, and one with two diesels and a gas turbine. Pod propulsion is provided, powered by a diesel-electric system (so there's almost no vibration), and a small gas turbine in the funnel helps reduce emissions.

There's a complete walk-around exterior teak promenade deck, with teak steamer-style sun-loungers, and a jogging track that goes around the forward third of the ship. Exterior glass elevators, midships on both sides, provide ocean views. There are two centrally located swimming pools outdoors (one can be used in poor weather thanks to a retractable glass roof). Another smaller pool is for children.

An adults-only 'Retreat' is available at extra cost; it has 14 cabanas (at a further additional cost per day).

The main lobby spans three decks, topped by a lovely rotating Waterford crystal globe of the world. There are two entertainment/public room decks. The most dramatic room is the showlounge, which spans three decks in the forward part of the ship. Other facilities include a winding shopping street with boutique stores and logo shops, an Internet center, a decent library, card room, an art gallery, photo gallery, and several small meeting rooms. The casino

BERLITZ'S RATINGS		
	Possible	Achieved
Ship	500	358
Accommodation	200	142
Food	400	234
Service	400	254
Entertainment	100	67
Cruise Experience	400	262

OVERALL SCORE 1317 points out of 2000

is large – one has to walk through it to get from the restaurant to the showlounge on one of the entertainments decks.

On lower decks are a Queen's Lounge, a combination lecture room, and a Culinary Arts Center. There are also several other bars and lounges, and a small 40-seat movie-screening room.

Niggles include several pillars that obstruct sight lines throughout the ship; there are no self-service launderettes, although special laundry packages are available; and the air conditioning cannot be turned off in cabins or bathrooms.

ACCOMMODATION. There are many price categories. From the smallest interior (no-view) cabins (at 183 sq ft/17 sq m) to the largest Penthouse Verandah Suites (1,318 sq ft/122 sq m) including balcony, there's something for all tastes. Note that some cabins on the lowest accommodation deck have a lifeboat-obstructed view.

Some cabins that can accommodate a third and fourth person have little closet space and only one personal safe. Some cabins have interconnecting doors. Suite occupants have exclusive use of a concierge lounge and service, priority embarkation and disembarkation, and other benefits. In many suites and cabins with private balconies the balconies aren't really private (many can be overlooked from above). An improved room-service menu provides more choice.

DINING. Options range from full-service meals in the main dining room and à la carte restaurant to casual, self-serve, buffet-style meals and fast-food outlets. The 1,045-seat Vista Dining Room, aft, is two decks high, with seating on both levels. Either open seating or assigned seating is available; breakfast and lunch are open seating (you'll be taken to a table by restaurant staff when you enter).

There are tables for two to eight. The waiter stations can be noisy for anyone seated adjacent to them. Rosenthal porcelain and decent cutlery are provided, but there are no fish knives. Lighter-option meals are available for the nutrition-conscious, and Kosher meals can be provided, although these are prepared ashore, frozen, and brought to the table sealed in their original containers.

With a few exceptions, the cuisine is unmemorable, missing passion and taste, because it's all about batch cooking. There's a lack of variety of green vegetables, heavy use of rice, canned fruit, and already sliced and diced cheese, but you do get friendly service from Indonesian and Filipino stewards, and the plates are nice.

The extra-cost, reservations-required Pinnacle Grill is an intimate venue, with high-quality ingredients and good presentation. It fronts onto the second level of the atrium lobby; tables along its outer section are open to it and can suffer from Atrium Bar noise (one deck below), although these tables are good for those who like to see and be seen. Pacific Northwest food (think: premium-quality steaks and seafood) is featured. The wine list includes fine wines from around the world. Another (extra-cost, reservations-required) option is Tamarind, for Southeast Asian cuisine.

An extensive self-serve Lido Café (buffet) wraps around the funnel housing and extends aft. It includes a pizzeria counter, a salad bar, Asian stir-fry counter, deli sandwiches, and a dessert section. Movement around it can be slow, particularly at peak times. In the evenings, one side of this venue is turned into an extra-cost, 72-seat Canaletto Restaurant – a quasi-Italian informal eatery with waiter service.

Also, the poolside Dive-In at the Terrace Grill features several signature burgers (with special Dive-In sauce), hot dogs, and fries, and, on certain days, barbecues.

Meanwhile, the Windsurf Café in the atrium lobby is open for extra-cost coffees, pastries, snack foods, deli sandwiches, and, in the evening, liqueur coffees.

ENTERTAINMENT. The 846-seat Vista Lounge features revue shows and major cabaret; it spans three decks in the forward section. The main floor level has a bar in its starboard aft section. Spiral stairways at the back of the lounge connect all levels. The upper levels have better sight lines. Music is the feature in Half Moon and Billboard Onboard.

SPA/FITNESS. The large, two-deck-high Greenhouse Spa is located above the navigation bridge. Facilities include a solarium, hydrotherapy pool, and a unisex thermal suite – an area incorporating saunas and steam rooms. There's also a beauty salon, several massage/therapy rooms (including one for couples), and a gym with ocean views and high-tech equipment.

Sports facilities include a basketball court, volleyball court, and golf simulator.

WIND SPIRIT
★★★+

THIS MODERN SAIL-CRUISE SHIP HAS CHIC, CONTEMPORARY STYLE

Size:	Boutique Ship	Passenger/Crew Ratio (lower beds):	1.6
Tonnage:	5,350	Cabins (total):	74
Cruise Line:	Windstar Cruises	Size Range (sq ft/m):	185.0–220.0/17.0–22.5
Former Names:	none	Cabins (for one person):	0
Builder:	Ateliers et Chantiers du Havre	Cabins with balcony:	0
Entered Service:	Apr 1988	Cabins (wheelchair accessible):	0
Length (ft/m):	439.6/134.0	Wheelchair accessibility:	None
Propulsion/Propellers:	(a) diesel-electric (1,400kW)/1; (b) sails	Elevators:	0
		Casino (gaming tables):	Yes
Total Crew:	88	Self-Service Launderette:	No
Passengers (lower beds):	148	Onboard currency:	US$
Passenger Space Ratio (lower beds):	36.1		

THE SHIP. *Wind Spirit*, an identical twin to *Wind Star*, is a sleek-looking craft that is part-yacht, part-cruise ship, with four masts that tower 170ft (52m) above the deck, and with computer-controlled sails. The masts, sails, and rigging cost $5 million, when the ship was built. A computer keeps the ship on an even keel via the movement of a water hydraulic ballast system of 142,653 US gallons (540,000 liters), so there is no rolling over 6 degrees. You may be under sail for less than 40 percent of the time, depending on the conditions and cruise area winds prevailing.

Because of the amount of complex sail machinery, there is little open deck space. At the stern is a small water-sports platform for use when at anchor, but only in really calm sea conditions. Water-sports toys include a banana boat, kayaks, sunfish sailboats, windsurf boards, water-ski boat, scuba and snorkel equipment, and four Zodiacs. You will need to sign a waiver if you wish to use the water-sports equipment.

The ship has a finely crafted interior with pleasing blond woods, and soft, complementary colors and decor that is chic, even elegant, but a little cold. Note that the main lounge aboard this ship is of a slightly different design from that aboard *Wind Star*.

No scheduled activities help to make this a really relaxing, unregimented 'escape-it-all' vacation. It's about an unstructured environment.

BERLITZ'S RATINGS		
	Possible	Achieved
Ship	500	324
Accommodation	200	139
Food	400	240
Service	400	260
Entertainment	100	67
Cruise Experience	400	256

OVERALL SCORE 1286 points out of 2000

Niggles? The swimming pool is just a tiny 'dip' pool. Be prepared for the whine of the generators, which are needed to run the air conditioning and lighting systems 24 hours a day. Beverage prices are a little high. The library is small and needs more hardback fiction. Members of staff, though friendly, are generally casual and a little sloppy at times in the finer points of service.

This sail-cruise ship is ideally suited to youthful couples and solo travelers seeking contemporary facilities and some water sports in a relaxed but chic setting that's different from 'normal' cruise ships.

The dress code is low-key (casual), with no jackets and ties, even for dinner. Gratuities are added to your account daily, and 15 percent is added to bar and wine accounts.

ACCOMMODATION. All cabins are nicely equipped, have a minibar/refrigerator (stocked when you embark, but all drinks cost extra), 24-hour room service, personal safe, and plenty of storage space. The TV rotates so that it is viewable from both bed and bathroom. All cabins have two outside-view portholes, and deadlights (steel covers that can be closed in poor weather conditions). The decor is a pleasant mix of rich woods, natural fabrics and colorful soft furnishings, and hi-tech yacht-style amenities. A basket of fruit is replenished daily.

The bathrooms are compact units, designed in a figure of eight, with a teakwood floor in the central section. There is decent storage space for toiletries in two cabinets, as well as under-sink cupboard space. A wall-mounted hairdryer is also provided. The shower enclosure (no cabins have bathtubs) is circular and has both a hand-held as well as a fixed shower. L'Occitane bathroom products are provided, as are a vanity kit and shower cap.

The lighting is not strong enough for make-up application – for this it's better to use the vanity desk in the cabin, which has more powerful overhead (halogen) lighting. Bathrobes and towels are 100 percent cotton.

DINING. The elegant 'AmphorA' Restaurant has ocean views from large, picture windows, a lovely wood ceiling, and wood-paneled walls. California-style nouvelle cuisine is served, with attractively presented dishes. Also, signature dishes created by master chefs Joachim Splichal and Jeanne Jones are featured. It's open seating, so you can dine when you want and with whomever you wish.

The service staff are mostly Indonesians and Filipinos, who struggle sometimes at communicating, although their service is friendly. The selection of breads, cheeses, and fruits could be better. There is a big push to sell wines, but prices are high, as they are for most alcoholic drinks – and even for bottled water.

There is often casual dinner on the open deck under the stars, with grilled seafood and steaks. At the bars, hot and cold hors d'oeuvres appear at cocktail times.

Fancy something quiet and romantic? At no extra charge, a 'Cuisine de l'Amour' romantic dinner for two can be served to you in your cabin, complete with candle.

ENTERTAINMENT. There is no showlounge, shows, or cabaret. However, these are not needed, because a cruise aboard this high-tech sailing ship provides an opportunity to get away from all that noise and 'entertainment.' The main lounge, a corner of which houses a small casino, has a small dance floor, and, typically, a trio plays there.

The main lounge is also used for social functions. Otherwise, it's down to more personal entertainment, such as a DVD in your cabin late at night – or, much more romantic, after-dinner hours spent outside strolling or simply lounging on deck.

SPA/FITNESS. A gymnasium (with a modicum of muscle-toning equipment, treadmills, and exercycles) and sauna are located aft, adjacent to the water-sports platform. Extra-cost spa packages can be pre-booked before you arrive at the ship.

WIND STAR
★★★+

A CONTEMPORARY SAIL-CRUISE SHIP FOR SMART CASUAL CRUISING

Size:	....	Boutique Ship
Tonnage:	....	5,350
Cruise Line:	....	Windstar Cruises
Former Names:	....	none
Builder:	....	Ateliers et Chantiers du Havre
Entered Service:	....	Dec 1986
Length (ft/m):	....	439.6/134.0
Propulsion/Propellers:	....	(a) diesel-electric (1,400kW)/1; (b) sails
Total Crew:	....	88
Passengers (lower beds):	....	148
Passenger Space Ratio (lower beds):	....	36.1
Passenger/Crew Ratio (lower beds):	....	1.6
Cabins (total):	....	74
Size Range (sq ft/m):	....	185.0–220.0/17.0–22.5
Cabins (for one person):	....	0
Cabins with balcony:	....	0
Cabins (wheelchair accessible):	....	0
Wheelchair accessibility:	....	None
Elevators:	....	0
Casino (gaming tables):	....	Yes
Self-Service Launderette:	....	No
Onboard currency:	....	US$

THE SHIP. *Wind Star* is a long, sleek-looking craft that is part-yacht, part-cruise ship, with four masts towering 170ft (52m) above the deck, and with computer-controlled sails. The computer keeps the ship on an even keel via the movement of a water hydraulic ballast system of 142,653 US gallons (540,000 liters), so there is no rolling over 6 degrees. You may be under sail for less than 40 percent of the time, depending on the conditions and cruise area winds. Because of the amount of sail machinery, there is little open deck space when the ship is full. A small, aft water-sports platform can be used when at anchor. Water-sports facilities include a banana boat, kayaks, sunfish sailboats, windsurf boards, water-ski boat, scuba and snorkel equipment, and four Zodiacs.

The ship has a nicely crafted interior with blond woods, together with soft, complementary colors and decor that is chic, but a little cold. This ship had a complete makeover in 2012.

No scheduled activities help to make this a relaxing, unregimented 'escape-it-all' vacation. Windstar ships offer cruising in very comfortable surroundings bordering on the luxurious, in an unstructured environment.

The dress code is very low-key (casual), with no jackets and ties. Gratuities are charged to your onboard account, and 15 percent is added to bar, wine, and spa accounts.

BERLITZ'S RATINGS		
	Possible	Achieved
Ship	500	324
Accommodation	200	139
Food	400	240
Service	400	260
Entertainment	100	66
Cruise Experience	400	256

OVERALL SCORE 1285 points out of 2000

Niggles? The swimming pool is really only a tiny 'dip' pool. Be prepared for the whine of the vessel's generators. You'll hear it at night in your cabin; it takes some passengers a day or two to get used to. Beverage prices are quite steep. The library is small. The staff, though friendly, is a little sloppy at times in the finer points of service.

Overall, Wind Star is suited to youthful couples and solo travelers who want contemporary facilities and some water sports in a relaxed but chic setting.

ACCOMMODATION. The cabins are nicely equipped, have crisp, inviting decor and a minibar/refrigerator (stocked when you embark, but all drinks cost extra), 24-hour room service, personal safe, and plenty of storage space. The TV rotates so that it is viewable from the bed and the bathroom. All cabins all have two portholes. The bathrooms are compact, but have a teakwood floor. There is a good amount of storage space for toiletries in two cabinets, as well as under-sink cupboard space. A wall-mounted hairdryer is also provided. The shower enclosure (no cabins have bathtubs) is circular and has both a hand-held as well as a fixed shower unit. L'Occitane toiletries are provided.

DINING. The main dining room, the 'AmphorA' Restaurant is chic, and has ocean views. California-style cuisine is served, with attractively presented dishes.

Additionally, signature dishes created by master chefs Joachim Splichal and Jeanne Jones are offered. Open seating means you dine when and with whom you want to.

The service staff members are mostly Indonesians and Filipinos, who struggle sometimes at communicating, although their service is pleasant. The selection of breads, cheeses, and fruits could be better. There is a big push to sell wines, although the prices are extremely high, as they are for most drinks – even bottled water is the highest in the industry, at $7 per liter bottle.

There is often casual dinner on the open deck under the stars, with grilled seafood and steaks. At the bars, hot and cold hors d'oeuvres appear at cocktail times. For something quiet and romantic, a 'Cuisine de l'Amour' romantic dinner for two can be served to you in your cabin. The menu offers a choice of appetizer, a set soup, choice of salad, and two entrée (main) options, and a set dessert to finish.

ENTERTAINMENT. There is no showlounge, so no shows, or cabaret. The main lounge, a corner of which houses a small casino, has a small dance floor, and, typically, a trio plays there. Otherwise, it's down to more personal entertainment, such as a movie in your cabin late at night – or, much more romantic, after-dinner hours spent outside strolling or simply lounging on deck.

SPA/FITNESS. A fitness room and sauna are located aft. The spa is operated by a specialist concession. Special spa packages can be pre-booked.

WIND SURF
★★★+

ELEGANT DECOR FOR CASUAL SAIL-CRUISING IN RELAXED, LOW-KEY COMFORT

Size:	Small Ship	Passenger/Crew Ratio (lower beds):	1.9
Tonnage:	14,745	Cabins (total):	156
Cruise Line:	Windstar Cruises	Size Range (sq ft/m):	188.0–500.5/17.5–46.5
Former Names:	Club Med I	Cabins (for one person):	0
Builder:	Ateliers et Chantiers du Havre	Cabins with balcony:	0
Entered Service:	Feb 1990/May 1998	Cabins (wheelchair accessible):	0
Length (ft/m):	613.5/187.0	Wheelchair accessibility:	None
Propulsion/Propellers:	(a) diesel-electric (1,400kW)/1; (b) sails	Elevators:	2
		Casino (gaming tables):	Yes
Total Crew:	163	Self-Service Launderette:	No
Passengers (lower beds):	312	Onboard currency:	US$
Passenger Space Ratio (lower beds):	47.2		

THE SHIP. This sail-cruise ship is a good choice for couples seeking informality (no jackets or ties), but who don't want the inconvenience of the workings of a real tall ship. It cruises in the Caribbean (Nov–Mar) and in the Mediterranean (May–Oct).

Wind Surf, one of a pair of the world's largest sail-cruisers, is part-cruise ship, part-yacht – its sister ship operates as *Club Med II*. This is a larger, grander sister to the original three Windstar Cruises vessels. Five huge masts of 164ft (50m), rising 221ft (67m) above sea level, carry seven triangular, self-furling Dacron sails, with a total surface area of 26,881 sq ft (2,497 sq m).

No human hands touch the sails – instead, everything is handled electronically by computer control from the bridge, which some might think is a little boring. Also, because European sailings take place at night, with days spent in port, there seems little point to having the sails, as you won't get to experience them.

A computer keeps the ship on an even keel via the movement of a water hydraulic ballast system of 266,800 US gallons (1 million liters), so there is no heeling over 6 degrees. When the ship isn't using the sails, four diesel-electric motors propel it at up to approximately 12 knots. The ship is very quiet when moving.

Swimming from the aft water-sports platform isn't allowed. But extensive water-sports facilities include

BERLITZ'S RATINGS		
	Possible	Achieved
Ship	500	343
Accommodation	200	144
Food	400	259
Service	400	268
Entertainment	100	68
Cruise Experience	400	282
OVERALL SCORE 1364 points out of 2000		

windsurfers, sailboats, water-ski boats, scuba tanks, snorkels, fins, masks, and inflatable Zodiac motorized boats for water-skiing – all at no extra charge, except for the scuba tanks.

There are two salt-water swimming pools – little more than 'dip' pools. One is amidships on the uppermost deck; the other is aft, together with two hot tubs, and an adjacent bar. There are no showers at either of the pools, so passengers get into the pools or hot tubs while covered in oil or lotion, an unhygienic arrangement.

A meeting room can accommodate 30–60 people. The casino/main lounge has four blackjack tables, one roulette table, and 21 slot machines. It has an unusually high ceiling for the size of the ship.

A Yacht Club includes books and DVDs for in-cabin use and provides comfortable seating for relaxation or listening to music loaded for you on iPods available from reception. An espresso bar offers extra-cost Lavazza coffee, plus other drinks and deli sandwiches. Eight computers have Internet access, and there's Wi-Fi access.

Hotel service is provided mostly by Filipino and Indonesian staff. Gratuities are charged to your onboard account, and 15 percent is added to bar and wine accounts, and to all spa treatments and services. The quality of food and its presentation is a definite plus, as is the policy of no music in passenger hallways or elevators.

ACCOMMODATION. There are just three price categories. Unusually, the cabin numbers (port side: even numbers; starboard side: odd numbers) are sequenced with lower numbers aft, while higher numbers are forward. All cabins are very nicely equipped, with crisp, inviting decor. They have a minibar/refrigerator (stocked when you embark, but all drinks are at extra cost), 24-hour room service, personal safe, a flat-screen TV set viewable from the bed or sofa, depending on cabin configuration, plenty of storage space, and two portholes. There are six four-person cabins; 35 doubles are fitted with an extra Pullman berth, and several cabins have an interconnecting door – good for families. Spa Suite packages are available at extra cost. All cabins have Wi-Fi access, at extra cost.

The bathrooms are compact, designed in a figure of eight, with a teakwood floor in the central section. There is a good amount of storage space for toiletries in two cabinets, as well as under-basin storage space, and a wall-mounted hairdryer. The circular shower enclosure has both a hand-held and a fixed shower. The lighting is not strong enough for applying make-up – this is better applied at the cabin's vanity desk.

Almost all suites have two bathrooms, a separate living/dining area, a sleeping area that can be curtained off, two vanity/writing desks, and four portholes instead of two. There are two TV sets (one in the lounge, one in the sleeping area), video player and CD player, and Bose SoundDock for iPods. Popcorn for movie viewing is available from room service. Bathrooms have granite countertops, open shelving, toiletries cabinets, and magnifying mirror.

A further two Bridge Deck suites (around 495 sq ft/46 sq m) would be delightful for a honeymoon; each has a bedroom, separate living/dining room, and marble bathroom with Jacuzzi tub, two washbasins, separate toilet, and a walk-in closet.

Spa Suite packages, introduced in 2010, also include a queen-size bed with microfiber bed linen, bathrobes, an orchid flower arrangement, two bathrooms, a flat-screen TV with DVD player, and Bose SoundDock speakers for iPods. A pillow menu provides several choices, including a 'snore-no-more' hypoallergenic pillow.

Tea collections include wellbeing, herbal, or exotic teas. Brewing service includes contemporary porcelain tea-ware and is available from room service 24 hours a day. Berlitz tip: ask for it to be made with mineral water, not the standard chlorinated ship's water.

DINING. The 'AmphorA' Restaurant seats 272 and has tables for two, four, or six. It has open seating with no pre-assigned tables, and is open only for dinner, typically 7.30–9.30pm. California-style nouvelle cuisine is served, with dishes attractively presented.

The 124-seat Degrees Bistro, a specialty dining venue, features Mediterranean cuisine. Located atop the ship, on Star Deck, it has picture windows on port and starboard sides, an open kitchen, and tables for two to six. Reservations are required for dinner, although there's no extra charge.

The Veranda, amidships on Star Deck, has an open terrace for informal, self-serve breakfast and lunch buffets. It is pleasant to be outside, eating an informal breakfast or lunch. Do try the bread pudding, available daily at lunch – the ship is famous for it, and each day has a variation on the theme.

The Compass Rose, an indoor/outdoor casual eatery, provides deli-style snack items plus some pastries and coffee for breakfast, lunch, and afternoon tea. At night, it turns into Candles for alfresco dining around the aft pool. A permanent outdoor barbecue offers fresh grilled items.

Windstar Cruises food is generally good and geared toward American tastes. Europeans and other nationals should note that items such as bacon may be overcooked, and the choice of cheeses and teas is limited. Service in the dining room is also quite fast – geared towards those who haven't yet learned to unwind.

A nice feature is a 'Cuisine de l'Amour' romantic candlelight dinner for two, served in your cabin at no extra charge. The menu, with seductive-sounding selections, offers a choice of appetizer, a set soup, choice of salad, two entrée (main) options, and a set dessert to finish.

Finally, there's quite an extensive room service menu.

ENTERTAINMENT. There is no showlounge as such (this is a yachting-style experience, after all), although the main lounge (with a wooden dance floor), which incorporates a small casino, serves as an occasional cabaret room, and is also used for cocktail parties and other social functions.

SPA/FITNESS. The Health Spa has a unisex sauna (bathing suits required), beauty salon, and several treatment rooms for massage, facials, and body wraps. There is a decent gymnasium – on a separate deck, with ocean views – and an aerobics workout room. Unfortunately, the spa facilities are split over three separate decks, making them rather disjointed. Special spa packages can be pre-booked through your travel agent.

WORLD DREAM
★★★★+

THIS FAMILY-FRIENDLY SHIP IS FOR PREMIUM ASIA CRUISING IN HIGH-TECH SURROUNDINGS

Size:	Large Resort Ship	Passenger/Crew Ratio (lower beds):	1.6/1
Tonnage:	151,300	Cabins (total):	1,680
Cruise Line:	Dream Cruises	Size Range (sq ft/m):	139.9–2,411.1/13.0–224.0
Former Names:	none	Cabins (for one person):	0
Builder:	Meyer Werft (Germany)	Cabins with balcony:	1,188
Entered Service:	Nov 2017	Cabins (wheelchair accessible):	32
Length (ft/m):	1,100.0/335.3	Wheelchair accessibility:	Good
Propulsion/Propellers:	diesel-electric/2 azimuthing pods	Elevators:	16
		Casino (gaming tables):	Yes
Total Crew:	2,030	Self-Service Launderette:	No
Passengers (lower beds):	3,360	Onboard currency:	CNY (RMB)
Passenger Space Ratio (lower beds):	45		

THE SHIP. *World Dream* is the second of two stunning large resort ships for Dream Cruises – the 'premium' brand created in 2015, owned by Genting Hong Kong, operator of Star Cruises. The attention-grabbing hull is painted in flamboyant red and gold (it was conceived by Chinese Pop artist Jacky Tsai, and features a story involving a mermaid and an astronaut); the ship's exterior comes to life with LED lighting at night.

This large, family-friendly resort ship has upper exterior decks filled with sports and active waterpark attractions that are good for all ages. There is a complete, 2,000-ft- (610-m-) long walk-around outside promenade deck (with indoor-outdoor seaside eateries), multiple pools (including a private extracost, adults-only pool and relaxation area), and the Wet 'n' Wild Water Park, in the ship's center (adjacent to the main pool), with six waterslides for children and teens. Zouk Beach and bar, music lounge, and a sports bar are located aft of the funnel.

Inside, the decor is decidedly upbeat, with an abundance of colors. There are numerous bars, lounges, karaoke and mahjong rooms, a large duty-free shopping street, entertainment facilities including large showlounges (for lavish shows), as well as a large Genting Casino filled with gaming tables and slot machines (plus private gaming rooms), Resorts World Casino, Resorts World Premium Club, and Maxim's – for card games. Other facilities in-

BERLITZ'S RATINGS		
	Possible	Achieved
Ship	500	417
Accommodation	200	153
Food	400	313
Service	400	290
Entertainment	100	86
Cruise Experience	400	310
OVERALL SCORE 1569 points out of 2000		

clude a business center and meeting rooms. A special night street 'market' has hawker stalls featuring Asian delicacies. Two standout drinking places are the Johnnie Walker bar and Penfolds Wine Vault (with some lovely vintage wines).

Travelers on shorter cruises (particularly those under seven days' duration) may be overwhelmed by the variety of restaurants on offer – there are so many to choose from.

ACCOMMODATION. There are numerous accommodation grades, from the smallest interior (no-view) cabin (measuring 150 sq ft/14 sq m) to the largest Dream Suite, measuring 1,970 sq ft/183 sq m and spread over two decks. The price you pay depends on the size, location, and grade you choose.

Occupants of Dream Palace (with 25,000 gross tons assigned to it), have a private area located in a touch-card-access section above the navigation bridge (similar to, but more expansive than, MSC Cruises' 'Yacht Club' and Norwegian Cruise Line's 'The Haven'), with access to a private outdoor pool, hot tubs, gym, relaxation area, and cabanas, Horizons Lounge (observation lounge), free Wi-Fi, and private gaming club (so there's no need to go downstairs to the busier – and noisier – Resorts World and other casino areas).

Over 100 family-friendly cabins have interconnecting doors, so parents can take their young ones and feel comfortable that they'll be well looked after (actually, they won't want to leave the ship after the cruise).

DINING. With an abundance of dining, eatery, and drinking options, the ship is able to cater to almost any dietary and ethnic persuasion and taste. The largest dining venues include Windows, a bi-level dining hall, located aft, with ocean views from huge windows (a window table is definitely one to have). Another large restaurant is Genting Palace. The culinary emphasis throughout the ship is, naturally, on the Asia-Pacific region; this includes the Chinese lunchtime favorite – dimsum (whose meaning, literally, is: to touch the heart). During the summer, specialties from Okinawa (such as goya/bitter gourd and pumpkins, and Sheikwasha (flat lemon) juice and brown sugar) are featured.

Noted Australian chef Mark Best has a 'Bistro' venue (his second at sea), with a menu that focuses on small-producer Australian beef, lamb, river fish, and the freshest seafood.

Other indoor and outdoor venues (some are extra cost):

Silk Road for à la carte Chinese regional and provincial cuisine (with tablecloths).

Blue Lagoon for tuck-in Chinese street (finger) food and clay pot cuisine.

Umi-Uma, a Japanese venue with Teppanyaki grills and a sushi bar.

Positano, an Italian eatery with lots of pasta dishes, which may remind you of the Amalfi Coast.

Genting Palace, featuring traditional Cantonese-style Chinese dishes.

Makan Makan for South-East Asian cuisine, including Chinese and Malaysian specialties.

World Buffet, an ultra-casual, international food court-style area with serve-yourself food from various display counters and active cooking stations, while adjacent and outside on deck is a pool bar and grill.

Bread Box and Tiffin Café, two 'see-and-be-seen-in' venues for coffees/teas and light bites.

Drinking places include a Red Lion Pub, Johnnie Walker bar (with a wall full of decorative bottles of JW and a special-edition Dream Cruises JW whisky), a Martini bar, Bar City, Boba Cha, and Bar 360, among others. The ship also features a Penfolds (the celebrated Australian winery) Wine Vault.

ENTERTAINMENT. The multi-deck, 1,000-seat Zodiac Theater is the principal showlounge. It features glamorous production shows, including aerial acrobatics and major cabaret acts.

Silk Road is an extra-cost supper club/nightclub featuring a colorful Burlesque show; adjacent are several bookable karaoke rooms.

SPA/FITNESS. Crystal Life Spa has two sections – one for Asians (for whom the 'flow-through' is much more important than the range of treatments offered), and one is for Westerners. The spa (the largest at sea) has its own spa café for 'healthy' food and drinks (some at extra cost). World Dream is only the second cruise ship with an MRI scanner (the first being sister ship Genting Dream). Sports facilities in various locations include a bowling alley, basketball court, a climbing wall, and an extensive Dreamcatcher rope-climbing course – great for kids and adults alike.

WORLD EXPLORER
NYR

THIS SMALL SHIP IS FOR EXPLORING OUT-OF-THE-WAY DESTINATIONS IN COMFORT

Size:..Boutique Ship	Passenger/Crew Ratio (lower beds):........................ 1.4
Tonnage: 9,431	Cabins (total): 88
Cruise Line: .... Mystic Cruises	Size Range (sq ft/m): 182.9–441.3/17.0–41.0
Former Names: .... none	Cabins (for one person):... 0
Builder: .... WestSea Shipyard (Portugal)	Cabins with balcony:.. 62
Entered Service: .... Jul 2019	Cabins (wheelchair accessible): 2
Length (ft/m): 413.3/126.0	Wheelchair accessibility: .... Poor
Propulsion/Propellers: diesel-electric/2	Elevators: 2
Total Crew: 125	Casino (gaming tables): .... No
Passengers (lower beds): 176	Self-Service Launderette:.. No
Passenger Space Ratio (lower beds): 53.5	Onboard currency: .... US$

THE SHIP. One of a series of four 'soft' expedition ships built in Portugal, *World Explorer* (owned by Mystic Invest, parent company of Mystic Cruises) is presently shared by two companies: Quark Expeditions (for Arctic and Antarctic expedition cruises), and Nicko Cruises (for Mediterranean, Northern Europe, Greenland Iceland, and South America cruises). It has a sharply raked bow and carries a fleet of 16 Zodiac rigid inflatable rubber craft for up-close shore landings, and has a mud room (for boot washing), adjacent to the loading area.

The main public rooms include an Explorer's Lounge – a glass-domed Observation Lounge (several support pillars are intrusive) with access to a forward outdoor deck and Lecture Hall (lecturers about the region, wildlife, etc., are on board for every sailing). Medevac insurance is included when the ship is operated by Quark Expeditions (very useful). Some activities (for example, kayaking) are at extra cost.

Overall, this is a comfortable, nicely equipped ship in which to cruise to the remote areas of the world.

BERLITZ'S RATINGS		
	Possible	Achieved
Ship	500	NYR
Accommodation	200	NYR
Food	400	NYR
Service	400	NYR
Entertainment	100	NYR
Cruise Experience	400	NYR
OVERALL SCORE NYR points out of 2000		

ACCOMMODATION. The price you pay depends on the size, location, and grade (there are six), from the smallest window-only cabin (measuring about 183 sq ft/17 sq m) to the largest Balcony Suite (there are two, measuring about 473 sq ft/44 sq m). Except for the lowest deck of cabins, all others have either a sit-outside or French (open-air) balcony. They have contemporary, but relaxing, colors. Note that cabin electric supply is 220 volts.

DINING. The Dining Room is located aft and has both indoor and outdoor seating. There's also a small Lido café on deck.

ENTERTAINMENT. After-dinner recaps and social conversation are de rigueur.

SPA/FITNESS. A small (very small) spa area, with fitness room, changing rooms, and sauna, is located around the funnel housing on the uppermost deck.

ZAANDAM
★★★

THIS SHIP FEATURES DUTCH-STYLE DECOR FOR THOSE OF A CERTAIN AGE

Size:	Mid-size Ship
Tonnage:	61,396
Cruise Line:	Holland America Line
Former Names:	none
Builder:	Fincantieri (Italy)
Entered Service:	May 2000
Length (ft/m):	777.5/237.0
Propulsion/Propellers:	diesel-electric (37,500kW)/2
Total Crew:	650
Passengers (lower beds):	1,432
Passenger Space Ratio (lower beds):	42.6
Passenger/Crew Ratio (lower beds):	2.2
Cabins (total):	716
Size Range (sq ft/m):	113.0–1,126.3/10.5–104.6
Cabins (for one person):	0
Cabins with balcony:	197
Cabins (wheelchair accessible):	23
Wheelchair accessibility:	Good
Elevators:	12
Casino (gaming tables):	Yes
Self-Service Launderette:	Yes
Onboard currency:	US$

THE SHIP. *Zaandam*'s hull is dark blue, in keeping with all HAL ships, with a large, single funnel. A glass-covered pool is located on the Lido Deck between mast and funnel for all-weather use. As on *Volendam*, the Lido Deck swimming pool is located one deck higher than on the *Statendam*-class ships, so that you can have direct access between the aft and midships pools (not so aboard the S-class ships). This has created more space for extra cabins on the Navigation Deck below.

There are three principal passenger stairways (better than two for safety, accessibility, and flow). The interior decor is restrained, with traditional ocean liner detailing and wood accenting – but what's special is the design theme of music.

Memorabilia on show was mostly acquired from the 'Pop and Guitars' auction at Christie's in London in 1997, and includes a Fender Squire Telecaster guitar signed by Mick Jagger, Keith Richards, Charlie Watts, Ronnie Wood, and Bill Wyman of The Rolling Stones; a Conn saxophone signed on the mouthpiece by former US president Bill Clinton; an Ariana acoustic guitar signed by David Bowie and Iggy Pop; a Fender Stratocaster guitar signed in silver ink by the members of Queen; a Bently Les Paul-style guitar signed by artists including Carlos Santana, Eric Clapton, B.B. King, Robert Cray, Keith Richards, and Les Paul. Perhaps the ship should be renamed *Rockerdam*.

BERLITZ'S RATINGS		
	Possible	Achieved
Ship	500	308
Accommodation	200	127
Food	400	218
Service	400	267
Entertainment	100	63
Cruise Experience	400	246
OVERALL SCORE 1229 points out of 2000		

The focal point is a three-deck-high atrium, with the reception desk, shore-excursions desk, photo shop, and photo gallery grouped around it. It also houses a real showpiece – a fancy 22ft (6.7m) -high pipe organ with puppets that move with the music. One of the largest such Dutch band organs ever built, it was custom-made for the ship in Hilversum in the Netherlands.

Explorations is a combination café, Internet connection center, and library. There are limited children's and teens' play areas. Popcorn is provided for moviegoers, and there's a kitchen for HAL's Culinary Arts program, for interactive cooking demonstrations. The casino has gaming tables and slot machines.

With one whole deck of suites and a private concierge lounge (with key-card access), this clearly a two-class ship.

Niggles include the irritating charge to use the washing machines and dryers in the self-service launderette; communication in English with many staff (particularly in the dining room and buffet areas) can be frustrating; and room service needs help.

ACCOMMODATION. The range is comparable to that found aboard the similarly sized *Rotterdam*, with many different price categories. There is one Penthouse Suite, suites, and mini-suites, with the rest a mixture of outside-view and interior (no-view) cabins. The hallways showcase pleasant artwork.

The cabins are tastefully furnished, with twin beds convertible to a queen-size bed (but space is tight between the beds and vanity unit). There is a decent amount of closet and drawer space. The tiled bathrooms are disappointingly small and have small shower tubs, utilitarian toiletries cupboards, and exposed under-sink plumbing. Occupants in Verandah and Penthouse Suite share a private concierge lounge (Neptune Lounge, accessible by private key card). Each suite has a separate bedroom, dressing, and living area, but no butlers.

Except in the Penthouse Suite (forward on the starboard side), the bathrooms in all other suites and mini-suites are disappointingly small and lack character, as one might expect. All outside-view suites and cabin bathrooms have a tub/shower, while interior cabins have only a shower. Some 23 cabins for limited-mobility passengers are, however, quite spacious and have a large roll-in shower enclosure (some also have a bathtub), and ramped access to a balcony.

DINING. The Rotterdam Dining Room, a large, traditional room, spans two aft decks, with ocean views and an imposing staircase connecting both levels. Open or assigned seating is available, while breakfast and lunch are open seating. You'll be taken to a table by restaurant staff when you enter. Tables are for two to eight.

With a few exceptions, the cuisine is unmemorable, missing passion and taste, because it's mass catering. There's a lack of variety of green vegetables, too much use of rice, canned fruit, and pre-diced cheese. Still, you get friendly service from the Indonesian and Filipino stewards, and the Rosenthal plates are good. Lighter-option meals are available for the nutrition- and weight-conscious, as are Kosher (pre-prepared) meals.

Pinnacle Grill is more intimate and features Pacific Northwest cuisine. There's a cover charge, and reservations are required (suite-grade occupants get priority reservations).

The Lido Market is a casual, self-serve canteen for breakfasts and luncheons. Canaletto (open in the evening) is in a section of the Buffet and features Italian dishes. Waiter service is provided (reservations are required).

Also, the Lido Deck poolside 'Dive-In at the Terrace Grill' features signature burgers, hot dogs, and fries, and, on certain days, barbecues and other culinary treats may be featured.

ENTERTAINMENT. The Mondriaan Show Lounge, located forward, spans two decks; it has banquette seating on both the main and upper levels. It is basically a well-designed room, but the ceiling is low, and balcony-level sight lines are poor. Good music is the feature in Lincoln Center Stage.

SPA/FITNESS. The Greenhouse Spa facilities are decent and include a gymnasium with muscle-toning equipment, separate saunas and steam rooms for men and women, and several treatment rooms, each with a shower and toilet. Outdoor facilities include basketball and shuffleboard courts, a jogging track, and a full walk-around teakwood promenade deck for strolling.

ZENITH
★★★

THIS FAMILY-FRIENDLY, CASUAL SHIP IS FOR SPANISH SPEAKING CRUISERS

Size: .... Mid-size Ship	Passenger/Crew Ratio (lower beds): 2.0
Tonnage: 52,090	Cabins (total): 670
Cruise Line: .... Pullmantur Cruises	Size Range (sq ft/m): 172.2–500.5/16–46.5
Former Names: .... *Le Zenith, Zenith*	Cabins (for one person): 0
Builder: .... Meyer Werft (Germany)	Cabins with balcony: 110
Entered Service: .... Apr 1992/Mar 2017	Cabins (wheelchair accessible): 4
Length (ft/m): 682.4/208.0	Wheelchair accessibility: .... Good
Propulsion/Propellers: .... diesel (19,960kW)/2	Elevators: 7
Total Crew: 670	Casino (gaming tables): .... Yes
Passengers (lower beds): 1,340	Self-Service Launderette: .... No
Passenger Space Ratio (lower beds): 37.3	Onboard currency: .... Euros

THE SHIP. *Zenith* was originally operated by Celebrity Cruises (as Zenith). Although now 20-plus years old, it still has a contemporary, though angular, profile that gives the impression of power and speed.

Inside there is elegant and restrained decor. Soothing, pastel colors and high-quality soft furnishings are used throughout the interiors. The Art Deco-style, hotel-like lobby, reminiscent of hotels in Miami Beach, has a spacious feel and is home to the reception desk.

The principal deck, containing many of the public entertainment rooms, has a double-width indoor promenade. There is a good-size library. Other facilities include a cigar-smoking lounge, complete with fireplace and leather-bound volumes on the shelves; an Internet-connect center; and the Plaza Café for coffee and (loud) chat. A large, elegantly appointed casino (with gaming tables and slot machines) has its own bar.

The hospitality and the range and variety of food have been tailored to its French-speaking family clientele. You will usually find a lot of smokers aboard.

Passenger niggles? Standing in line is inevitable; public restroom doors are rather heavy; there are no cushioned pads for poolside sunloungers.

ACCOMMODATION. There are several price grades, from interior (no-view) cabins to two Royal Suites midships on Deck 10, and forward on Deck 11. Note that many outside-view cabins on the safety equipment

BERLITZ'S RATINGS		
	Possible	Achieved
Ship	500	299
Accommodation	200	117
Food	400	203
Service	400	229
Entertainment	100	58
Cruise Experience	400	223

OVERALL SCORE 1129 points out of 2000

deck have lifeboat-obstructed views. The standard maritime cabin numbering system (even numbers port side, odd numbers starboard side) is reversed on this ship.

DINING. The Caravelle Dining Room has several tables for two to eight. There are two seating times for dinner, and open seating for breakfast and lunch, at tables for two, four, six, eight, or 10. The cuisine, its presentation, and service are more about quantity rather than quality, and green vegetables are hard to come by.

For informal meals, the Windsurf Buffet has a traditional, single-line, self-service buffet for breakfast and lunch and includes a pasta station, rotisserie, and pizza ovens. At peak times, the buffet is simply too small, too crowded, and very noisy. The Grill, located outdoors adjacent to the Windsurf Buffet, serves fast food such as pizzas.

ENTERTAINMENT. The two-level Showlounge, with main and balcony levels, has good sight lines from most seats, although a railing at the front of the balcony level impedes the view. Cabaret acts are the main feature and are geared to a family audience.

SPA/FITNESS. The Spa is aft of the funnel. It has a gym with ocean-view windows and high-tech equipment, an exercise area, several therapy treatment rooms including a Rasul chamber, and men's/women's saunas.

ZUIDERDAM
★★★+

THERE IS DUTCH HERITAGE AND DECOR ABOARD THIS FAMILY-FRIENDLY CRUISE SHIP

Size:	Mid-size Ship	Passenger/Crew Ratio (lower beds):	2.3
Tonnage:	82,305	Cabins (total):	924
Cruise Line:	Holland America Line	Size Range (sq ft/m):	185.0–1,318.6/17.1–122.5
Former Names:	none	Cabins (for one person):	0
Builder:	Fincantieri (Italy)	Cabins with balcony:	623
Entered Service:	Dec 2002	Cabins (wheelchair accessible):	28
Length (ft/m):	935.0/285.0	Wheelchair accessibility:	Good
Propulsion/Propellers: diesel-electric (35,240kW)/2 azimuthing pods		Elevators:	14
		Casino (gaming tables):	Yes
Total Crew:	800	Self-Service Launderette:	No
Passengers (lower beds):	1,848	Onboard currency:	US$
Passenger Space Ratio (lower beds):	44.5		

THE SHIP. *Zuiderdam* has two funnels, placed close together, one in front of the other, and not side by side, as aboard the smaller *Amsterdam* and *Rotterdam*. This placement is because the ship has two engine rooms – one with three diesels, and one with two diesels and a gas turbine. Pod propulsion is provided, powered by a diesel-electric system, so there's almost no discernible vibration.

Several glass elevators provide ocean views. There are two centrally located swimming pools outdoors, and one of the pools can be used in inclement weather conditions due to its retractable, glass-domed cover. Two whirlpool tubs, adjacent to the swimming pools, are abridged by a bar, while another (smaller) pool is provided for children.

The lobby space is small and spans just three decks. It has a stairway, and the lobby's focal point is a 10ft (3m)-high transparent Waterford crystal 'seahorse.' The decor is extremely bright for a Holland America Line ship, with an eclectic color and pattern mix that assails you from all directions.

There are two entertainment/public room decks, the upper of which has an exterior promenade deck – something new for this traditional cruise line. Although it doesn't go around the whole ship, it's long enough for walking. There is also a jogging track outdoors.

The most dramatic public room is the Vista Lounge, which spans three decks in the forward section of the

BERLITZ'S RATINGS		
	Possible	Achieved
Ship	500	352
Accommodation	200	139
Food	400	218
Service	400	255
Entertainment	100	67
Cruise Experience	400	268

OVERALL SCORE 1299 points out of 2000

ship. The casino is equipped with all the gaming paraphernalia and slot machines you can think of, and it is so large that you have to walk through it to get from the restaurant to the showlounge.

The Crow's Nest is a multi-function 'lifestyle' area, encompassing the ship's library, a lounge area with fine ocean views, and the Explorations Café.

The ship is designed to appeal to young, vibrant, family-oriented passengers, with a good array of public rooms, bars, and lounges.

Niggles include the fact that many of the 'private' balconies aren't so private and can be overlooked from various public locations. Also, some pillars obstruct the passenger flow and lines of sight on the main public decks. It can sometimes be difficult to escape from smokers, and from those walking around in unsuitable clothing.

ACCOMMODATION. There are numerous accommodation price grades. The price you pay depends on the size, location, and grade you choose. From largest to smallest: Penthouse Verandah Suites (1,318 sq ft/122 sq m, including balcony); Deluxe Verandah Suites (563 sq ft/52 sq m); Verandah Suites (284 sq ft/26 sq m); outside-view cabins (197 sq ft/18 sq m); and interior (no-view) cabins, which are slightly smaller, at 183 sq ft (17 sq m).

A number of cabins on Main Deck have views obstructed by lifeboats. Some cabins that can accommodate a third and fourth person have very little closet space, and only one personal safe. Audio channels are provided on the in-cabin TV system.

Each morning, an eight-page edition of *The New York Times* (Times Fax) is provided for each cabin. Fresh fruit is available on request. Shoe-shine service and evening turndown service are also provided, as is a small range of toiletries.

DINING. The 1,045-seat Vista Dining Room is aft. Spanning two decks, it is a pleasant room, with seating on the main and balcony levels. Both open seating (you may have to wait a considerable time for a table), and fixed seating (assigned tables and times) are available; you'll be taken to a table by restaurant staff when you enter. With a few exceptions, the cuisine is best described as uneventful and unmemorable, and is missing passion and taste, because it's all about mass catering. There's a distinct lack of variety of green vegetables, and an overuse of rice, canned fruit and already sliced and diced cheese. Still, you get friendly service from smiling Indonesian and Filipino stewards, and the plates are nice.

Breakfast and lunch are open seating, so you'll be seated by restaurant staff. Tables are for two to eight. The waiter stations can be noisy if you are seated adjacent to them. Live music is provided for dinner. Lighter-option meals are always available for the nutrition- and weight-conscious, as are Kosher meals, although these are prepared ashore, frozen, and brought to your table sealed in their original containers.

The 130-seat Pinnacle Grill is an upscale dining spot with higher-quality ingredients cooked to order. Located on Lower Promenade Deck, it fronts onto the second level of the atrium lobby. The cuisine is Pacific Northwest, plus premium-quality steaks from hand-selected cuts of beef. Reservations are needed, and there's a cover charge, but the steaks are worth it.

For casual eating, there's an extensive Lido Market, which includes a pizzeria/Italian specialties counter, salad bar, Asian stir-fry counter, deli sandwiches, and a separate dessert buffet. Movement through the buffet area can be very slow, particularly at peak times. In the evenings, one side of this venue is turned into an extra-cost, 72-seat Canaletto Restaurant – a quasi-Italian informal eatery with waiter service.

Also, the poolside 'Dive-In at the Terrace Grill' features multi-choice signature burgers (with special Dive-In sauce), hot dogs, fries, and, on certain days, barbecues and other culinary treats.

The Windsurf Café in the atrium lobby (open 20 hours a day) serves extra-cost coffees, pastries, snack foods, deli sandwiches, and, in the evenings, liqueur coffees.

ENTERTAINMENT. The 867-seat Vista Lounge is the venue for Las Vegas-style revue shows and major cabaret presentations. It spans three decks in the forward section, and the main floor level has a bar in its starboard aft section. Spiral stairways at the back of the lounge connect all levels. Stage shows are best seen from the upper levels, from where the sight lines are quite good.

SPA/FITNESS. The Greenhouse Spa spans two decks, above the navigation bridge. Facilities include a solarium, and an extra-cost thermal suite – a unisex area incorporating a Laconium, Hammam, and Chamomile Grotto, plus a swim-against-the-current Hydropool. There's also a beauty salon and several private treatment rooms, including one for couples. A large gymnasium with floor-to-ceiling windows has the latest equipment.

SHIPS RATED BY SCORE

Ship	Score	Rating	Ship	Score	Rating
Europa 2	★★★★★+	1864	MSC Splendida	★★★★	1526
Europa	★★★★★+	1852	Celebrity Edge	★★★★	1512
HANSEATIC nature	★★★★★	1791	Royal Clipper	★★★★	1512
Sea Cloud	★★★★★	1702	Le Bougainville	★★★★	1505
Sea Cloud II	★★★★★	1701	Le Dumont d'Urville	★★★★	1505
Viking Jupiter	★★★★+	1691	Le Champlain	★★★★	1504
Viking Orion	★★★★+	1690	RCGS Resolute	★★★★	1504
Viking Sea	★★★★+	1689	Le Lapérouse	★★★★	1503
Viking Sky	★★★★+	1689	Le Lyrial	★★★★	1498
Viking Sun	★★★★+	1689	Anthem of the Seas	★★★★	1494
Viking Star	★★★★+	1688	Amadea	★★★★	1486
Crystal Serenity	★★★★+	1687	Nippon Maru	★★★★	1485
Queen Mary 2	★★★★+	1681	Azamara Pursuit	★★★★	1483
SeaDream I	★★★★+	1679	Le Soleal	★★★★	1483
Crystal Symphony	★★★★+	1678	Le Boreal	★★★★	1478
SeaDream II	★★★★+	1675	L'Austral	★★★★	1477
Silver Muse	★★★★+	1660	Quantum of the Seas	★★★★	1476
Mein Schiff 1	★★★★+	1654	Majestic Princess	★★★★	1475
Mein Schiff 2	★★★★+	1654	Star Legend	★★★★	1473
Silver Spirit	★★★★+	1633	Hebridean Princess	★★★★	1472
Seabourn Encore	★★★★+	1628	Azamara Quest	★★★★	1471
Seabourn Ovation	★★★★+	1628	Regal Princess	★★★★	1470
Mein Schiff 6	★★★★+	1626	Royal Princess	★★★★	1470
Mein Schiff 5	★★★★+	1625	Azamara Journey	★★★★	1469
Seabourn Odyssey	★★★★+	1624	Silver Wind	★★★★	1469
Seabourn Sojourn	★★★★+	1618	Caledonian Sky	★★★★	1468
Seven Seas Explorer	★★★★+	1618	National Geographic Orion	★★★★	1467
Mein Schiff 3	★★★★+	1614	Ovation of the Seas	★★★★	1467
Mein Schiff 4	★★★★+	1614	Spectrum of the Seas	★★★★	1467
Riviera	★★★★+	1599	Island Sky	★★★★	1466
Silver Shadow	★★★★+	1597	Star Pride	★★★★	1464
Silver Whisper	★★★★+	1597	Star Breeze	★★★★	1463
Marina	★★★★+	1594	Silver Explorer	★★★★	1453
Asuka II	★★★★+	1586	Celebrity Solstice	★★★★	1450
Genting Dream	★★★★+	1569	Britannia	★★★★	1448
World Dream	★★★★+	1569	Celebrity Reflection	★★★★	1448
Seven Seas Voyager	★★★★+	1568	MSC Magnifica	★★★★	1446
Queen Elizabeth	★★★★+	1562	Celebrity Equinox	★★★★	1444
MSC Seaview	★★★★+	1558	Celebrity Eclipse	★★★★	1443
Queen Victoria	★★★★+	1558	Celebrity Silhouette	★★★★	1443
MSC Bellissima	★★★★★+	1555	Norwegian Escape	★★★★	1442
MSC Seaside	★★★★★+	1554	MSC Orchestra	★★★★	1439
MSC Meraviglia	★★★★★+	1551	MSC Poesia	★★★★	1439
Seven Seas Mariner	★★★★	1545	MSC Musica	★★★★	1436
MSC Divina	★★★★	1539	Norwegian Joy	★★★★	1435
MSC Fantasia	★★★★	1532	Norwegian Bliss	★★★★	1434
MSC Preziosa	★★★★	1532	Artania	★★★★	1431
Seabourn Quest	★★★★	1529	Norwegian Getaway	★★★★	1431

Ship	Score	Rating	Ship	Score	Rating
Deutschland	★★★★	1430	Nieuw Amsterdam	★★★+	1348
Norwegian Breakaway	★★★★	1429	Noordam	★★★+	1348
Symphony of the Seas	★★★★	1425	Pearl Mist	★★★+	1347
Disney Fantasy	★★★★	1423	Pacific Explorer	★★★+	1346
Harmony of the Seas	★★★★	1423	Balmoral	★★★+	1342
Silver Discoverer	★★★★	1421	Ruby Princess	★★★+	1341
Disney Dream	★★★★	1419	Caribbean Princess	★★★+	1339
Fifty Years of Victory	★★★★	1417	Norwegian Dawn	★★★+	1334
AIDAperla	★★★★	1416	Norwegian Sun	★★★+	1334
Bremen	★★★★	1416	Norwegian Star	★★★+	1330
Allure of the Seas	★★★★	1414	Norwegian Gem	★★★+	1328
Hebridean Sky	★★★★	1413	Norwegian Jade	★★★+	1326
AIDAprima	★★★★	1412	Norwegian Sky	★★★+	1325
Koningsdam	★★★★	1412	Le Ponant	★★★+	1324
Oasis of the Seas	★★★★	1409	Norwegian Jewel	★★★+	1324
Crystal Esprit	★★★★	1406	Norwegian Pearl	★★★+	1324
Explorer Dream	★★★★	1405	Norwegian Spirit	★★★+	1322
MSC Opera	★★★+	1399	Independence of the Seas	★★★+	1320
Norwegian Encore	★★★+	1395	Costa Venezia	★★★+	1319
Regatta	★★★+	1394	AIDAblu	★★★+	1318
Seven Seas Navigator	★★★+	1392	AIDAbella	★★★+	1317
Azura	★★★+	1390	Westerdam	★★★+	1317
Diamond Princess	★★★+	1389	AIDAstella	★★★+	1311
MSC Lirica	★★★+	1389	Marella Discovery 2	★★★+	1311
Sirena	★★★+	1389	AIDAluna	★★★+	1309
Nautica	★★★+	1384	AIDAsol	★★★+	1309
Insignia	★★★+	1382	Liberty of the Seas	★★★+	1308
Celebrity Millennium	★★★+	1381	AIDAmar	★★★+	1307
Sapphire Princess	★★★+	1381	Freedom of the Seas	★★★+	1307
Emerald Princess	★★★+	1378	Serenade of the Seas	★★★+	1305
Disney Wonder	★★★+	1376	AIDAdiva	★★★+	1304
Crown Princess	★★★+	1374	Explorer of the Seas	★★★+	1303
Eurodam	★★★+	1374	Star Flyer	★★★+	1303
Saga Sapphire	★★★+	1374	Arcadia	★★★+	1302
Disney Magic	★★★+	1372	Carnival Panorama	★★★+	1302
Celebrity Infinity	★★★+	1370	Jewel of the Seas	★★★+	1302
Celebrity Summit	★★★+	1369	Oosterdam	★★★+	1302
Celebrity Constellation	★★★+	1368	Navigator of the Seas	★★★+	1300
Ventura	★★★+	1367	Star Clipper	★★★+	1299
Silver Cloud	★★★+	1366	Zuiderdam	★★★+	1299
MSC Armonia	★★★+	1365	Zuiderdam	★★★+	1299
Wind Surf	★★★+	1364	Radiance of the Seas	★★★+	1297
MSC Sinfonia	★★★+	1363	Carnival Horizon	★★★+	1296
Amera	★★★+	1362	Sea Princess	★★★+	1296
Star Princess	★★★+	1362	Mariner of the Seas	★★★+	1295
Mein Schiff Herz	★★★+	1361	Coral Princess	★★★+	1294
Paul Gauguin	★★★+	1359	Enchantment of the Seas	★★★+	1294
Amsterdam	★★★+	1356	Island Princess	★★★+	1294
Silver Galapagos	★★★+	1356	Sun Princess	★★★+	1294
Pacific Princess	★★★+	1353	Vision of the Seas	★★★+	1294
Rotterdam	★★★+	1353	Aurora	★★★+	1290

Ship	Score	Rating	Ship	Score	Rating
Brilliance of the Seas	★★★+	1288	Veendam	★★★	1188
Marella Explorer 2	★★★+	1287	Volendam	★★★	1188
Wind Spirit	★★★+	1286	Maasdam	★★★	1187
Wind Star	★★★+	1285	AIDAcara	★★★	1182
Carnival Vista	★★★+	1284	Albatros	★★★	1179
Oceana	★★★+	1284	Costa neoRomantica	★★★	1179
Marella Explorer	★★★+	1283	Braemar	★★★	1175
Costa Diadema	★★★+	1281	SuperStar Gemini	★★★	1173
AIDAAura	★★★+	1278	SuperStar Aquarius	★★★	1170
Costa Deliziosa	★★★+	1278	Carnival Inspiration	★★★	1163
Pacific Dawn	★★★+	1277	Carnival Elation	★★★	1162
Voyager of the Seas	★★★+	1277	Carnival Fascination	★★★	1161
Adventure of the Seas	★★★+	1275	Carnival Paradise	★★★	1160
Golden Princess	★★★+	1275	Marella Celebration	★★★	1159
Grand Princess	★★★+	1275	Carnival Imagination	★★★	1158
AIDAvita	★★★+	1274	Carnival Ecstasy	★★★	1157
Roald Amundsen	★★★+	1269	Costa Atlantica	★★★	1157
Costa Fascinosa	★★★+	1266	Carnival Fantasy	★★★	1154
Costa Favolosa	★★★+	1266	Kapitan Khlebnikov	★★★	1153
Costa Luminosa	★★★+	1266	Carnival Sensation	★★★	1152
Costa Fortuna	★★★+	1265	Costa Victoria	★★★	1137
Rhapsody of the Seas	★★★+	1264	Club Med 2	★★★	1134
Costa Pacifica	★★★+	1262	Costa neoRiviera	★★★	1133
Marella Discovery	★★★+	1261	Aegean Odyssey	★★★	1131
Costa Serena	★★★+	1260	Zenith	★★★	1129
Pacific Aria	★★★+	1256	Horizon	★★★	1124
Costa Magica	★★★+	1255	Fram	★★★	1119
Carnival Breeze	★★★+	1252	Astor	★★★	1117
Pacific Venus	★★★	1246	Hamburg	★★★	1109
Carnival Dream	★★★	1236	Celebrity Xpedition	★★+	1096
Grandeur of the Seas	★★★	1234	Astoria	★★+	1080
Carnival Freedom	★★★	1230	Grand Classica	★★+	1079
Costa Mediterranea	★★★	1230	Columbus	★★+	1075
Zaandam	★★★	1229	National Geographic Explorer	★★+	1067
Boudicca	★★★	1221	Celestyal Olympia	★★+	1064
Carnival Conquest	★★★	1220	Vasco da Gama	★★+	1053
Carnival Glory	★★★	1217	Sovereign	★★+	1046
Black Watch	★★★	1216	Celestyal Cristal	★★+	1045
Pride of America	★★★	1215	Berlin	★★+	1034
Carnival Magic	★★★	1214	Empress of the Seas	★★+	1027
Carnival Splendor	★★★	1213	Majesty of the Seas	★★+	1017
Carnival Spirit	★★★	1210	Grand Celebration	★★+	1011
Carnival Miracle	★★★	1205	Magellan	★★+	1001
Carnival Sunshine	★★★	1205	Serenissima	★★	985
Carnival Legend	★★★	1204	Monarch	★★	978
Carnival Liberty	★★★	1203	Marco Polo	★★	966
Carnival Sunrise	★★★	1201	Celebrity Flora	NYR	NYR
Carnival Pride	★★★	1200	Costa Smeralda	NYR	NYR
Carnival Valor	★★★	1198	HANSEATIC inspiration	NYR	NYR
Carnival Victory	★★★	1195	Iona	NYR	NYR
Marella Dream	★★★	1194	Magellan Explorer	NYR	NYR

Ship	Score	Rating
MSC Grandiosa	NYR	NYR
National Geographic Endurance	NYR	NYR
Norwegian Epic	NYR	NYR
Ritz-Carlton Azora	NYR	NYR
Scarlet Lady	NYR	NYR
Sky Princess	NYR	NYR
AIDAnova	NYR	NYR
Nieuw Statendam	NYR	NYR
Scenic Eclipse	NYR	NYR
Sky Princess	NYR	NYR
Spirit of Discovery	NYR	NYR
World Explorer	NYR	NYR

Credits

Photo Credits

AIDA 132/133, 194, 196, 198, 200, 202, 204, 206
All Leisure Holidays 71, 88, 152
Antarctica 21 465
Ayako Ward 11, 72, 155, 162, 172
Azamara Club Cruises 146, 232, 234
Bahamas Paradise Cruise Line 417
Carnival Cruises 19, 29, 61, 135, 258, 260, 262, 264, 266, 268, 270, 272, 274, 276, 278, 280, 282, 284, 286, 288, 290, 292, 294, 296, 298, 300, 302, 304, 306, 308, 310
Carnival/Andy Newman 24, 136
Celebrity Cruises 1, 10, 41, 107, 108, 164, 316, 320
Celebrity/Michel Verdure 106, 137
Celebrity/Quentin Bacon 126
Celebrity/Steve Beaudet 138
Celestyal Cruises 101, 334, 335
Costa Cruises 139, 342, 344, 346, 348, 350, 352, 354, 356, 358, 362, 364, 366, 368, 370, 372, 378
Cruise & Maritime Voyages 227, 338, 709
Crystal Cruises 148
Crystal Yacht Cruises 375
Cunard 17, 66, 96, 149, 179, 603, 605, 607
Cunard/Indusfoto 170
Dennis Jarvis 598
Didier Descouens 242
Disney Cruise Line 32, 59, 114, 127, 150, 384, 386, 388, 390
Douglas Ward 9, 12, 23, 28, 30, 31, 46, 48, 50, 51, 73, 74, 77, 78, 80, 86, 90, 92, 96/97, 103, 105, 113, 119, 129, 144, 153, 159, 166, 167, 168, 171, 174, 186, 188, 190, 192, 208, 210, 225, 228, 249, 376, 399, 408, 422, 429, 432, 449, 464, 472, 499, 515, 541, 545, 546, 613, 651, 653, 657, 674/675, 681, 730
Dream Cruises 405, 412, 740
Ester Kokmeijer 409

Fred Olsen Cruise Lines 240, 243, 245, 247
Getty Images 6/7, 18, 26, 68, 109, 124
Hapag-Lloyd Cruises 13, 25, 55, 79, 95, 99, 128, 151, 178, 181, 182, 402, 423, 424/425
Holland America Line 140, 218, 397, 445, 462, 543, 584, 622, 710, 728, 732, 743, 746
Hurtigruten 621
Hurtigruten/Ørjan Bertelsen 87
iStock 102
Jesse Chandler 594
Lindblad Expeditions 532/533, 534, 535
Lindblad/Sisse Brimberg & Cotton Coulson 49
Michael S. Nolan/Linblad 83
Michel Verdure/Royal Caribbean 176
Ming Tang-Evans/Apa Publications 98
MSC Cruises 56, 67, 69, 141, 501, 503, 505, 507, 508/509, 511, 513, 517, 519, 521, 523, 525, 527, 529, 531
NCL 21, 38, 44, 57, 64, 75, 116, 118, 122, 125, 142, 548, 550, 552, 554, 556, 558, 560, 562, 564, 566, 568, 570, 572, 574, 576, 578, 599
NCL/Susan Seubert 120
nicko cruises 742
Noble Caledonia 255, 431, 441
Norbert Nagel 416
Oceania Cruises 435, 480, 537, 619, 683
One Ocean Expeditions 615
P&O Cruises Australia 588, 589, 590
P&O Cruises 94, 222, 230, 238, 253, 437, 582, 712
Paul Gauguin Cruises 8, 157, 596
Phoenix Reisen 212, 215, 217, 224, 380
Piergiuliano Chesi 360
Pjotr Mahhonin 337, 470, 659
Ponant 447, 451, 452, 453, 454, 455, 457, 458

Princess Cruises 36, 62, 143, 256, 340, 373, 382, 392, 414, 420, 439, 468, 592, 611, 626, 628, 632, 641, 701, 703
Public domain 394
Pullmantur Cruises 498, 687, 745
Quark Expeditions 444
Ralph Lee Hopkins/Lindblad Expeditions 85
Regent Seven Sea Cruises 52, 130, 156, 660, 662, 664, 666
Regent Seven Seas Cruises/Michel Verdure 20
Ritz-Carlton Yacht Collection 618
Royal Caribbean 3MR, 4/5, 16, 33, 34/35, 42, 43, 45, 47, 60, 65, 70, 104, 110, 115, 145, 183, 213, 220, 236, 251, 312, 314, 318, 321, 323, 325, 327, 329, 331, 333, 395, 406, 410, 418, 427, 433, 442, 460, 466, 482, 538/539, 580, 586, 601, 609, 616, 688, 707, 726
Saga 630, 685, 690
Scenic 636
Sea Cloud Cruises 91, 637, 639
Seabourn 158, 643, 645, 647, 649
SeaDream Yacht Club 123, 655
Shutterstock 27, 163, 169, 177, 718
Silversea Cruises 160, 668, 670, 671, 672, 673, 677, 679
Star Clippers 624, 693
Star Cruises 705, 706
Steve Dunlop Photographer/P&O Cruises 154
Thomson Cruises 476
TUI Group 472/473, 474, 477, 479, 484, 486, 488, 490, 492, 494, 496
Viking Cruises 37, 161, 180, 714, 716, 720, 722, 724
Virgin Voyages 634
Voyages to Antiquity 185
Windstar Cruises 690/691, 695, 697, 699, 734, 736, 738

Cover Credits

Front cover: Cruise Ship in Cook's Bay, Moorea *Reinhard Schmid/4Corners Images*
Back cover: CocoCay *Royal Caribbean*; Pride of America Library *NCL*; Pooldeck of the Europa *Hapag-Lloyd Cruises*; Douglas Ward *Ayako Ward*

Berlitz/Insight Guide Credits

Distribution
UK, Ireland and Europe
Apa Publications (UK) Ltd
sales@insightguides.com

United States and Canada
Ingram Publisher Services
ips@ingramcontent.com

Australia and New Zealand
Woodslane
info@woodslane.com.au

Southeast Asia
Apa Publications (SN) Pte
singaporeoffice@insightguides.com

Worldwide
Apa Publications (UK) Ltd
sales@insightguides.com

Special Sales, Content Licensing
and CoPublishing

Insight Guides can be purchased in bulk quantities at discounted prices. We can create special editions, personalised jackets and corporate imprints tailored to your needs. sales@insightguides.com; www.insightguides.biz

Printed in China by CTPS

Berlitz Trademark Reg. U.S. Patent Office and other countries. Marca Registrada. Used under licence from the Berlitz Investment Corporation

First Edition 1985
Twenty-Eighth Edition 2020

www.berlitzpublishing.com

Author
Douglas Ward

Managing Editor
Rachel Lawrence

Copyeditor
Joanna Reeves

Picture Editor
Tom Smyth

Head of DTP and Pre-Press
Rebeka Davies

Layout
Aga Bylica

TELL US YOUR THOUGHTS

Dear Cruiser,

I hope you have found this edition of Berlitz Cruising and Cruise Ships both enjoyable and useful. If you have any comments or queries, or experiences of cruising that you would like to pass on, or perhaps some ideas for subjects that could be included in the future, I would be delighted to read them. With your help, I can improve and expand the guide in future editions.

The world of cruising is evolving fast and certain facts and figures may have changed since this guide went to print, so if you have found any outdated information in these pages, please do let me know and I will make sure it is corrected as soon as possible.

You can write to me by email at:
shipratings@hotmail.com

Or by post to:
APA Publications
PO Box 7910
London SE1 1WE
United Kingdom

Thank you,
Douglas Ward

Index